A Review of the Events of 1981

The 1982 World Book Year Book

The Annual Supplement to The World Book Encyclopedia

World Book, Inc.
a Scott Fetzer company

Chicago London Sydney Toronto

Staff

Editorial Director
William H. Nault

Editorial Staff
Editor
A. Richard Harmet

Executive Editor
Wayne Wille

Associate Editor
Sara Dreyfuss

Copy Editors
Robert J. Hemsing
Daniel A. Rogers

Senior Editors
Marsha F. Goldsmith
Barbara A. Mayes
Beverly Merz
Jay Myers

Staff Editors
William T. Graham
Sandra Streilein

Research Editor
Irene B. Kelier

Cartographic Editor
H. George Stoll

Index Editor
Claire Bolton

Statistical Editor
Katherine Norgel

Editorial Assistant
Lettie Zinnamon

Art Staff
Executive Art Director
William Hammond

Art Director
Roberta Dimmer

Senior Artist
Nikki Conner

Artists
Rosa Cabrera
Alice F. Dole
Margot McMahon

Photography Director
John S. Marshall

Photographs Editors
Jo Anne M. Martinkus
Sandra M. Ozanick

Research and Services
Director of Editorial Services
Susan C. Kilburg

Head, Editorial Research
Mary Norton

Researcher
Robert Hamm

Product Production
Executive Director
Peter Mollman

Director of Manufacturing
Joseph C. LaCount

Director of Pre-Press
J. J. Stack

Production Control Managers
Sandra Grebenar
Barbara Podczerwinski

Assistant Product Manager
Madelyn Krzak

Film Separations Manager
Alfred J. Mozdzen

Film Separations Assistant Manager
Barbara J. McDonald

Manager, Research and Development
Henry Koval

Printed in the United States of America
ISBN 0-7166-0482-5
ISSN 0084-1439
Library of Congress Catalog Card Number: 62-4818

Preface

During 1981, nations throughout the world observed the International Year of Disabled Persons (IYDP). The United Nations proclaimed the IYDP to direct attention to the needs of the world's millions of physically or mentally disabled persons. It was fitting, then, that the TALKING WORLD BOOK – the world's first recorded encyclopedia – went into distribution to schools and libraries during 1981.

The TALKING WORLD BOOK is a revolutionary advance for students and adults who are blind or partially sighted, and for those who have sight but prefer to receive information by ear. Three components make up this unique encyclopedia. The first is a 19-volume WORLD BOOK index in braille and large type. Inside the covers of these volumes is the second component – 219 four-track tape cassettes. Each cassette contains six hours of recorded WORLD BOOK articles. Finally, there is the third component, the key to the success of the encyclopedia – a fast-forward, quick-access cassette player. The user determines from the index which cassette holds the desired information. Then, he or she puts the cassette into the player, dials the index information into it, and pushes a button. In less than a minute – about as long as it would take a sighted person to find the same information – the recorded information is being played.

The American Printing House for the Blind developed the TALKING WORLD BOOK in cooperation with World Book, Inc., and distributes it on a not-for-profit basis. We at WORLD BOOK are proud to be a part of this important project. WAYNE WILLE

After locating the information she wants in the TALKING WORLD BOOK's index, a student inserts a cassette into the special tape player.

Contents

8   **Chronology**
A month-by-month listing highlights some of the significant
events of 1981.

22   **The Year in Focus**
THE YEAR BOOK Board of Editors discuss the meaning of some of the
important events and trends of 1981.
Harrison Brown, Director, the East-West Resource Systems Institute,
the East-West Center, Honolulu, Hawaii.
Lawrence A. Cremin, President, Teachers College, Columbia University.
James J. Kilpatrick, Columnist for the Universal Press Syndicate.
Sylvia Porter, Columnist for the Universal Press Syndicate.
Carl T. Rowan, Columnist for the Field Newspaper Syndicate.

52   **Special Reports**
Six articles give special treatment to wide-ranging subjects of current
interest and importance.

54   **Leader for These Times,** an interview with President
Ronald Reagan, conducted by Hugh Sidey
Reagan talks about his first year as President — why he wanted the
job, what he likes most about it, what he likes least, and what
prepared him for it.

74   **The Plight of the Panda** by Nancy Nash
Efforts to ensure the survival of one of the world's most
endearing — but endangered — animals are going into high gear.

92   **The Threats to Our Water Supply** by Peter Gwynne
The United States faces a drier future if industry, government,
agriculture, and the public fail to deal with a host of problems.

108   **Shuttle Opens New Space Era** by Marsha F. Goldsmith
The flawless maiden flight of the space shuttle *Columbia* excites the
hopes of scientific and commercial pioneers.

122   **The Airport's Unseen City** by Mark Perlberg
A major airport is actually a city of thousands of people and hundreds
of facilities, all working to make air travel possible.

138   **A Robot in Your Future?** by William J. Cromie
Nobody expects robots to become smarter than people and take over
all our jobs, but many people are doing work that robots could do.

154   **A Year in Perspective**
       THE YEAR BOOK casts a glance back at the events and the personalities
       that made the year 1881 what it was.

170   **The Year on File**
       YEAR BOOK contributors report the major events of 1981 in
       alphabetically arranged articles, from "Advertising" to "Zoos and
       Aquariums."

521   **Census Supplement**
       This section lists official population figures for states, counties,
       metropolitan areas, and cities from the 1980 United States census.

558   **World Book Supplement**
       Six new or revised articles are reprinted from the 1982 edition of THE
       WORLD BOOK ENCYCLOPEDIA: "Elephant," "Vanuatu," "Malaysia," "Kuala
       Lumpur," "Inflation," and "Mental Illness."

581   **Dictionary Supplement**
       Here is a listing of important words and definitions that will be
       included in the 1982 edition of THE WORLD BOOK DICTIONARY.

585   **Index**
       A 17-page cumulative index covers the contents of the 1980, 1981,
       and 1982 editions of THE YEAR BOOK.

A tear-out page of cross-reference tabs for insertion in THE WORLD
BOOK ENCYCLOPEDIA appears after page 16.

Contributors

Contributors not listed on these pages are members of THE WORLD BOOK YEAR BOOK editorial staff.

Adachi, Ken, M.A.; Literary Critic, *The Toronto Star.* [LITERATURE, CANADIAN]

Alexiou, Arthur G., B.A., M.S.; Associate Director, Office of Sea Grant. [OCEAN]

Alridge, Ron, B.A.; Television and Radio Critic, *Chicago Tribune.* [RADIO; TELEVISION]

Anderson, Virginia E., B.A., M.S.W.; Free-Lance Writer. [COMMUNITY ORGANIZATIONS; HANDICAPPED; NATIONAL PTA (NATIONAL CONGRESS OF PARENTS AND TEACHERS); SOCIAL SECURITY; WELFARE; YOUTH ORGANIZATIONS]

Barber, Margaret, B.A., M.L.S.; Director, Public Information Office, American Library Association. [AMERICAN LIBRARY ASSOCIATION]

Beckwith, David C., A.B., M.S., J.D.; National Economics Correspondent, *Time* Magazine. [COURTS AND LAWS; CRIME; PRISON; SUPREME COURT]

Bennett, Joyce, Editor, *Crafts* Magazine. [HOBBIES]

Benson, Barbara N., A.B., M.S., Ph.D.; Associate Professor, Biology, Cedar Crest College. [BOTANY; ZOOLOGY]

Berger, Philip A., M.D.; Assistant Professor of Psychiatry, Stanford University School of Medicine. [WORLD BOOK SUPPLEMENT: MENTAL ILLNESS]

Berkwitt, George J., B.S.J.; Chief Editor, *Industrial Distribution Magazine.* [MANUFACTURING]

Boyum, Joy Gould, B.A., M.A., Ph.D.; Professor of English, New York University; Film Critic, *The Wall Street Journal.* [MOTION PICTURES]

Bradsher, Henry S., A.B., B.J.; Foreign Affairs Analyst. [ASIA and Asian Country Articles]

Brown, Kenneth, Editor, *United Kingdom Press Gazette.* [EUROPE and European Country Articles]

Brown, Merrill, B.A.; Financial Reporter, *Washington Post.* [COMMUNICATIONS]

Bushinsky, Jay, B.A., M.S.Ed., M.S.J.; Special Correspondent, *Chicago Sun-Times.* [MIDDLE EAST (Close-Up)]

Cain, Charles C., III, A.B.; former Automotive Editor, Associated Press. [AUTOMOBILE]

Camper, John, B.A.; Editorial Writer, *Chicago Sun-Times.* [CHICAGO; CITY]

Campion, Owen, B.A.; Editor, Tennessee Register. [ROMAN CATHOLIC CHURCH]

Carlson, Eric D., Ph.D.; Senior Astronomer, Adler Planetarium. [ASTRONOMY]

Chandler, David P., B.A., M.A., Ph.D.; Research Director, Center of Southeast Asian Studies, Monash University, Clayton, Australia. [WORLD BOOK SUPPLEMENT: KUALA LUMPUR; MALAYSIA]

Clancy, Katherine L., Ph.D.; Nutrition Consultant. [FOOD]

Clark, Phil, B.A.; Free-Lance Garden and Botanical Writer. [GARDENING]

Cromie, William J., B.S.; Executive Director, Council for the Advancement of Science Writing. [BUILDING AND CONSTRUCTION; HOUSING; SPACE EXPLORATION; Special Report: A ROBOT IN YOUR FUTURE?]

Cuscaden, Rob, Editor, *Home Improvement Contractor* Magazine. [ARCHITECTURE]

Cviic, Chris, B.A., B.Sc.; Leader Writer and Correspondent on East Europe, *The Economist.* [Eastern European Country Articles]

Datre, Donna M., B.A.; Public Information Manager, Toy Manufacturers of America, Inc. [GAMES AND TOYS]

Deffeyes, Kenneth S., M.S.E., Ph.D.; Professor of Geology, Princeton University. [GEOLOGY]

DeFrank, Thomas J., B.A., M.A.; White House Correspondent, *Newsweek* Magazine. [ARMED FORCES]

Dent, Thomas H., Executive Manager, The Cat Fanciers' Association, Inc. [CAT]

Dewey, Russell A., B.A., Ph.D.; Assistant Professor of Psychology, Georgia Southern College. [PSYCHOLOGY]

Dixon, Gloria Ricks, A.B.J.; Vice-President for Public Affairs and Education, Magazine Publishers Association. [MAGAZINE]

Dunson, Lynn R., former Reporter, *Washington Star.* [WASHINGTON, D.C.]

Eaton, William J., B.S.J., M.S.J.; Washington Correspondent, *Los Angeles Times.* [U.S. Political Articles]

Esseks, J. Dixon, Ph.D.; Associate Professor, Department of Political Science, Northern Illinois University. [AFRICA and African Country Articles]

Farr, David M. L., D.Phil.; Professor of History and Director, Paterson Centre for International Programs, Carleton University, Ottawa. [CANADA; Canadian Province Articles; SCHREYER, EDWARD RICHARD; TRUDEAU, PIERRE ELLIOTT]

Feather, Leonard, Author, Broadcaster, Composer. [MUSIC, POPULAR; RECORDINGS]

Fireman, Ken, B.A.J.; City Hall Bureau Chief, *Detroit Free Press.* [DETROIT]

Fisher, Robert W., B.A., M.A.; Economist, U.S. Bureau of Labor Statistics. [LABOR]

Francis, Henry G., B.S.; Executive Editor, *Contract Bridge Bulletin,* American Contract Bridge League. [BRIDGE, CONTRACT]

French, Charles E., B.S., A.M., Ph.D.; Agricultural Programs Coordinator, Agency for International Development. [FARM AND FARMING]

Goldner, Nancy, B.A.; Dance Critic, *Christian Science Monitor, Soho News.* [DANCING]

Goldstein, Jane, B.A.; Publicity Director, Santa Anita Park. [HORSE RACING]

Graham, Jarlath J., B.A.; Vice-President, Director of Editorial Development, Crain Communications, Inc. [ADVERTISING]

Griffin, Alice, B.A., M.A., Ph.D.; Professor of English, Special Assistant for the Lehman College Center for Performing Arts, Lehman College, City University of New York. [THEATER]

Gwynne, Peter, B.A., M.A.; Free-Lance Science Writer. [Special Report: THE THREATS TO OUR WATER SUPPLY]

Hales, Dianne, B.A., M.S.; Writer, Hales Medical. [DRUGS; HEALTH AND DISEASE; HOSPITAL; MEDICINE; MENTAL HEALTH; PUBLIC HEALTH]

Haverstock, Nathan A., A.B.; Director, The Latin American Service. [LATIN AMERICA and Latin American Country Articles]

Hechinger, Fred M., B.A.; President, *The New York Times* Company Foundation, Inc. [EDUCATION]

Huenergard, Celeste, B.A., M.A.; Midwest Editor, *Editor & Publisher* Magazine. [NEWSPAPER; PUBLISHING]

Jacobi, Peter P., B.S.J., M.S.J.; former Professor, Medill School of Journalism, Northwestern University. [MUSIC, CLASSICAL]

Johanson, Donald C., B.A., M.A., Ph.D.; Director, The International Institute for the Study of Human Origins. [ANTHROPOLOGY]

Joseph, Lou, B.A.; News and Information Chief, American Dental Association. [DENTISTRY]

Kaiman, Arnold G., M.A., D.D.; Rabbi, Congregation Kol Ami. [JEWS AND JUDAISM]

Karr, Albert R., M.S.; Reporter, *The Wall Street Journal.* [TRANSPORTATION and Transportation Articles]

Kind, Joshua B., B.A., Ph.D.; Associate Professor of Art History, Northern Illinois University. [VISUAL ARTS]

Kisor, Henry, B.A., M.S.J.; Book Editor, *Chicago Sun-Times.* [LITERATURE]

Kitchen, Paul, B.A., B.L.S.; Executive Director, Canadian Library Association. [CANADIAN LIBRARY ASSOCIATION]

Knapp, Elaine, B.A.; Senior Editor, Council of State Governments. [STATE GOVERNMENT]

Koenig, Louis W., B.A., M.A., Ph.D., L.H.D.; Professor of Government, New York University. [CIVIL RIGHTS]

Langdon, Robert, Executive Officer, Pacific Manuscripts Bureau, Australian National University. [PACIFIC ISLANDS; WORLD BOOK SUPPLEMENT: VANUATU]

Larsen, Paul A., P.E., B.S., Ch.E.; Member: American Philatelic Society; Collectors Club of Chicago; Royal Philatelic Society, London. Past President, British Caribbean Philatelic Study Group. [STAMP COLLECTING]

Lawrence, Richard, B.E.E.; Reporter, International Economic Affairs, *The Journal of Commerce.* [INTERNATIONAL TRADE AND FINANCE]

Levy, Emanuel, B.A.; Editor and Publisher, *Insurance Advocate.* [INSURANCE]

Litsky, Frank, B.S.; Assistant Sports Editor, *The New York Times.* [DEATHS OF NOTABLE PERSONS (Close-Up); Sports Articles]

Maki, John M., B.A., M.A., Ph.D.; Professor Emeritus, University of Massachusetts. [JAPAN]

Maloiy, G. M. O., B.Sc., Ph.D.; Professor of Physiology, University of Nairobi, Kenya. [WORLD BOOK SUPPLEMENT: ELEPHANT]

Martin, Lee, Director of Advertising and Associate Editor, Behn Miller Publications. [COIN COLLECTING]

Marty, Martin E., Ph.D.; Fairfax M. Cone Distinguished Service Professor, University of Chicago. [PROTESTANTISM; RELIGION]

Mather, Ian, B.A., M.A.; Defense Correspondent and Diplomatic Staff, *The Observer.* [GREAT BRITAIN; GREAT BRITAIN (Close-Up); IRELAND; NORTHERN IRELAND]

McNair, Sylvia, A.B.; Travel Writer and Editor. [TRAVEL]

Merina, Victor, B.A., M.S.; Staff Writer, *Los Angeles Times.* [LOS ANGELES]

Mielke, Arthur E., B.S.; Information Specialist, U.S. Bureau of the Census. [CENSUS]

Miller, J. D. B., M.Ec., M.A.; Professor of International Relations, Australian National University. [AUSTRALIA]

Miller, Julie Ann, M.A.J., Ph.D.; Life Sciences Editor, *Science News.* [BIOCHEMISTRY; BIOLOGY]

Moritz, Owen, B.A.; Urban Affairs Editor, *New York Daily News.* [NEW YORK CITY]

Morris, Bernadine, B.A., M.A.; Chief Fashion Writer, *The New York Times.* [FASHION]

Morrison, Rodney J., B.A., M.A., M.S., Ph.D.; Professor of Economics, Wellesley College. [WORLD BOOK SUPPLEMENT: INFLATION]

Mullen, Frances A., Ph.D.; Secretary General Emeritus, International Council of Psychologists. [CHILD WELFARE]

Murray, G. E., B.A., M.A.; Poetry Columnist, *Chicago Sun-Times.* [POETRY]

Nash, Edward G., B.A.; Senior Editor, Operations, Crain Communications. [ARMED FORCES (Close-Up); Biographies]

Nash, Nancy, Free-Lance Journalist. [Special Report: THE PLIGHT OF THE PANDA]

Newman, Andrew L., A.B., M.A.; Senior Information Officer, U.S. Department of the Interior. [CONSERVATION; ENVIRONMENT; FISHING; FISHING INDUSTRY; FOREST AND FOREST PRODUCTS; HUNTING; INDIAN, AMERICAN; WATER]

Oatis, William N., United Nations Correspondent, The Associated Press. [UNITED NATIONS]

Perlberg, Mark, B.A.; Manager, Communications Department, Rotary International. [Special Report: THE AIRPORT'S UNSEEN CITY]

Poli, Kenneth, Editor, *Popular Photography.* [PHOTOGRAPHY]

Price, Frederick C., B.S., Ch.E.; Free-Lance Writer. [CHEMICAL INDUSTRY]

Prochaska, Peter, B.A.; Associate Director, U.S. Chess Federation. [CHESS]

Rabb, George B., B.S., M.A., Ph.D.; Director, Chicago Zoological Park. [ZOOS AND AQUARIUMS]

Reed, Pat, Assistant Metro Editor, *Houston Chronicle.* [HOUSTON]

Rowse, Arthur E., I.A., M.B.A.; President, Consumer News, Inc. [CONSUMER AFFAIRS; SAFETY]

Schaffer, Jan, B.S.J., M.S.J.; Staff Reporter, *Philadelphia Inquirer.* [PHILADELPHIA]

Schmemann, Alexander, S.T.D., D.D., LL.D., Th.D.; Dean, St. Vladimir's Orthodox Theological Seminary, New York. [EASTERN ORTHODOX CHURCHES]

Shand, David A., B.C.A., B.Com.; Director of Research, Parliament of Victoria. [NEW ZEALAND]

Shaw, Robert J., B.S., B.A.; former Editor, *Library Technology Reports,* American Library Association. [LIBRARY]

Shearer, Warren W., Ph.D., J.D.; former Chairman, Department of Economics, Wabash College. [ECONOMICS]

Sidey, Hugh, B.S.; Contributing Editor, *Time* Magazine. [Special Report: LEADER FOR THESE TIMES]

Spencer, William, A.B., A.M., Ph.D.; Professor of History Emeritus, Florida State University. [MIDDLE EAST; Middle Eastern Country Articles; North Africa Country Articles]

Starr, Kenneth, B.A., M.A., Ph.D.; Director, Milwaukee Public Museum. [MUSEUM]

Swanton, Donald, B.S., M.S., Ph.D., M.B.A.; Chairman, Department of Finance, Roosevelt University. [Finance Articles]

Thompson, Carol L., M.A.; Editor, *Current History* Magazine. [U.S. Government Articles]

Thompson, Ida, Ph.D.; Research Associate, Center for Coastal and Environmental Studies, Rutgers University. [PALEONTOLOGY]

Tiegel, Eliot, B.A.; Managing Editor, *Billboard Magazine.* [MUSIC, POPULAR; RECORDINGS]

Tullier, Paul C., B.Sp., B.A.; Free-Lance Writer. [POPULATION]

Verbit, Lawrence, Ph.D.; Professor of Chemistry, State University of New York at Binghamton. [CHEMISTRY]

Vesley, Roberta, A.B., M.L.S.; Library Director, American Kennel Club. [DOG]

Walker, Gerald M., A.B.; Editorial Director, *Broadcast Management/Engineering.* [ELECTRONICS]

Weininger, Jean, A.B., M.S., Ph.D.; Research Fellow, Department of Nutritional Sciences, University of California at Berkeley. [NUTRITION]

White, Thomas O., B.S., Ph.D.; University Lecturer and Fellow of King's College, University of Cambridge, Cambridge, England. [PHYSICS]

Windeyer, Kendal, Transport Editor, *The Gazette,* Montreal. [MONTREAL]

Woods, Michael, B.S.; Science Editor, *The Toledo Blade.* [COAL; ENERGY; MINES AND MINING; PETROLEUM AND GAS; STEEL]

Zimansky, Paul E., Ph.D.; Adjunct Assistant Professor, Department of History, State University of New York at Stony Brook. [ARCHAEOLOGY]

Chronology

1976
1977
1978
1979
1980
1981

A month-by-month listing presents highlights
of some of the significant events of 1981.

See October 6, page 19.

Jan. 20   Jan. 20

January

				1	2	3
4	5	6	7	8	9	10
11	12	13	14	15	16	17
18	19	20	21	22	23	24
25	26	27	28	29	30	31

1   **Greece joins** the European Community (Common Market) as its 10th member.
Senegal's Prime Minister Abdou Diouf replaces President Leopold Sedar Senghor, who resigned one day earlier.

9   **Australia announces** a 3.7 per cent national wage increase.
Representative Raymond F. Lederer (D., Pa.) is convicted of charges stemming from the Federal Bureau of Investigation's (FBI) Abscam probe of political corruption.

14   **United Nations conference** on Namibia ends in Geneva, Switzerland, without a cease-fire agreement.

15   **President Jimmy Carter** submits a budget that calls for an 11.5 per cent spending increase during fiscal 1982.

16   **The United States is "stronger,** wealthier, more compassionate, and freer than it was four years ago," Carter says in his final State of the Union message.

19   **New York City declares** a drought emergency.
Philippines' President Ferdinand E. Marcos

relinquishes legislative powers to the National Assembly but retains the right to issue decrees.
Canada announces a three-year program of industrial development and unemployment benefits.

20   **Ronald Reagan takes oath** as 40th President of the United States.
Iran frees 52 United States hostages after 444 days in captivity.

23   **Consumer Price Index** rose 12.4 per cent in 1980, U.S. Department of Labor reports.
Russia releases statistics showing that it fell short of most of its economic goals for the five years ending in 1980.

24   **South Korea ends martial law** imposed in October 1979.

25   **Chiang Ching** (Jiang Qing), widow of China's former Communist Party Chairman Mao Tse-tung (Mao Zedong), receives a death sentence, suspended for two years, after Gang of Four trial in Peking (Beijing).
Oakland Raiders win Super Bowl XV, defeating the Philadelphia Eagles, 27-10.

26   **Great Britain approves** a two-year, $2.38-billion aid package for BL Limited, the state-owned automaker.

27   **Indonesian passenger ship** sinks, with about 500 persons feared drowned.

28   **President Reagan lifts** most oil price controls.
Fighting breaks out near disputed border between Ecuador and Peru.

29   **Reagan orders** a 60-day freeze on pending government regulations.

31   **Poland agrees** in principle to a five-day workweek after successful boycotts of Saturday labor on January 10 and 24.

Feb. 4

Feb. 23

Feb. 23

February

1	2	3	4	5	6	7
8	9	10	11	12	13	14
15	16	17	18	19	20	21
22	23	24	25	26	27	28

2   **General Motors Corporation** announces that it lost money in 1980, for its first full-year loss since 1921.

4   **Gro Harlem Brundtland** becomes Norway's first woman prime minister.

5   **Reagan warns** in first televised address that America faces "an economic calamity of tremendous proportions."
Marine Robert R. Garwood is convicted of collaborating with the enemy while a prisoner of war in Vietnam.

6   **Canada and Ontario** agree to guarantee a stock issue by Massey-Ferguson Limited, the financially troubled farm-machinery firm.

9   **Wojciech Jaruzelski** replaces Jozef Pinkowski as chairman of Poland's Council of Ministers.
Argentina's banking system is shaken when Sasetru, the country's largest conglomerate, goes broke, leaving a $1.2-billion debt.

10   **Leopoldo Calvo Sotelo y Bustelo** becomes Spain's prime minister, replacing Adolfo Suarez Gonzalez, who resigned in January.
China announces that it has put the first Chinese-made nuclear reactor into operation.
Fire kills eight persons and injures 200 at the Las Vegas (Nevada) Hilton Hotel.

13   **The Times** of London is bought by Australian newspaper magnate Rupert Murdoch.
Pullout of foreign troops from Afghanistan and Cambodia is called for by nonaligned nations' foreign ministers.

17   **Chrysler Corporation** loan guarantees of $150-million are "reluctantly" agreed to by Canada.

18   **President Reagan** calls for budget cuts of $41.4 billion and a tax reduction in his State of the Union message.
Independent Student Association in Poland is registered as Eastern Europe's only student group that is not directly under Communist Party control.
Reagan Administration affirms that it will follow the terms of the Carter Administration's agreement with Iran on the freeing of the hostages.

19   **Ford Motor Company reports** its first yearly loss since 1946, says it totaled $1.54 billion.

23   **Military plot** against Spain's government fails.
Summit conference with President Reagan is suggested by Russia's Supreme Soviet Presidium Chairman Leonid Ilich Brezhnev at opening of 26th Congress of the Communist Party.

24   **Headmistress Jean S. Harris** is convicted of murdering cardiologist Herman Tarnower, author of *The Complete Scarsdale Diet.*
Prince Charles's engagement to Lady Diana Spencer is announced in Great Britain.

March 30

March 5

March

1	2	3	4	5	6	7
8	9	10	11	12	13	14
15	16	17	18	19	20	21
22	23	24	25	26	27	28
29	30	31				

2　**U.S. grants** El Salvador $25 million in military aid and sends 20 additional military advisers to help combat left wing guerrillas.

3　**President Chun Doo Hwan** of South Korea is sworn into office after winning February 11 election. He seized power in 1979.

5　**Scott Hamilton** of the United States and Switzerland's Denise Biellmann, shown above, win world figure-skating championships in Hartford, Conn.

6　**Ecuador and Peru** announce a border peace agreement.

9　**Francisco Pinto Balsemao** takes oath as Portugal's prime minister, succeeding Francisco Sa Carneiro, who died in a December 1980 airplane crash.

10　**U.S. Postal Service announces** a hike in first-class postage from 15 to 18 cents.
President Reagan submits a budget for fiscal 1982 that is $48.6 billion smaller than the Carter budget.

14　**Three Pakistani aircraft hijackers** surrender in Syria after they exchange 100 passengers and crewmen for 54 Pakistani prisoners. The hijackers seized the plane on March 2.

16　**Los Angeles Board of Education** votes to end mandatory school busing.

17　**U.S. housing starts** dropped 24.6 per cent in February, the sharpest decline since March 1960, the U.S. Commerce Department reports.

19　**Australia's largest corporate loss** ever is reported by its leading automotive firm. General Motors Holden's Limited lost $152 million in 1980.

22　**Italy devalues the lira** 6 per cent against the other currencies in the European Monetary System.

26　**Social Democratic Party** is formed in Great Britain by defectors from the Labour Party.

27　**Millions of Polish workers** strike for four hours to protest beatings of union activists.
Actress Carol Burnett wins $1.6 million in damages in libel suit against *National Enquirer* magazine. Damages are reduced to $800,000 in May.

29　**General Roberto Eduardo Viola** becomes president of Argentina, succeeding Jorge Rafael Videla, who retired.

30　**President Reagan is shot** in the chest outside the Washington Hilton Hotel. Presidential Press Secretary James S. Brady and two security officers are also wounded. The alleged assailant, John W. Hinckley, Jr., is seized at the scene.
Indiana University wins the national championship of college basketball.

31　***Ordinary People,*** a film about a troubled family, wins Oscar as the best picture. Best actress and actor awards go to Sissy Spacek and Robert De Niro.

April 13

April 11-12

April 12-14

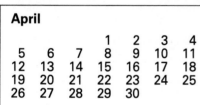

April						
			1	2	3	4
5	6	7	8	9	10	11
12	13	14	15	16	17	18
19	20	21	22	23	24	25
26	27	28	29	30		

1-3   **Coup attempt** by military officers fails in Thailand.

2   **Lebanese Christian militiamen** clash with Syrian troops in the heaviest fighting in Lebanon since the 1976 civil war.
Philadelphia transit workers end 19-day strike.

4   **San Antonio voters** elect Henry G. Cisneros, the first Mexican American mayor of a major U.S. city.

6   **Mark Eyskens replaces** Wilfried Martens as Belgium's prime minister.

8   **Russia's Brezhnev declares** that Poland "will be able, one should believe," to solve its political problems.
Omar N. Bradley, 88, the last U.S. five-star general, dies of a heart attack.

9   **Japanese freighter sinks** after colliding with a U.S. nuclear submarine.

10   **Poland's *Sejm*** (parliament) suspends for two months the right to strike.

11   **President Reagan returns** to the White House and a limited work schedule after 11 days in a hospital recuperating from an attempted assassination on March 30.

11-12   **Riots injure** more than 100 policemen in south London's Brixton neighborhood.

12   **Joe Louis,** 66, heavyweight boxing great, dies of a heart attack.

12-14   **U.S. space shuttle *Columbia*,** the first reusable spacecraft, is launched, orbits earth 36 times, then lands with astronauts John W. Young and Robert L. Crippen aboard.

13   **Parti Québécois wins** its second consecutive five-year term as Quebec's governing party, led by Premier René Lévesque.

17   **Poland officially recognizes** Rural Solidarity, a union of private farmers.

24   **President Reagan lifts** the 15-month-old grain embargo against Russia.

27   **Maryland court rules** that Spiro T. Agnew took bribes when he was governor of Maryland and Vice-President of the United States and orders him to repay the state $248,735.

28   **Israel intervenes** in fighting between Syria and Lebanese Christians, shoots down two Syrian helicopters. Israel says it has commitments not to allow the Christians to be annihilated.

29   **Peter Sutcliffe,** a 35-year-old British truckdriver, confesses to killing 13 women in the "Yorkshire Ripper" case.

29-30   **Syria installs** Russian-made surface-to-air missiles (SAM's) in Lebanon.

30   **Laetrile is ineffective** as a cancer drug, the National Cancer Institute announces after a $500,000 study.

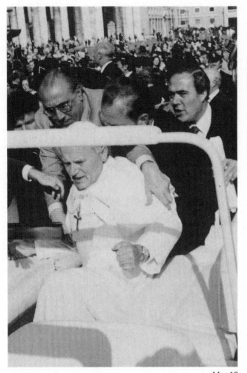

May 7

May 10

May 13

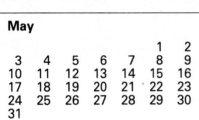

May

					1	2
3	4	5	6	7	8	9
10	11	12	13	14	15	16
17	18	19	20	21	22	23
24	25	26	27	28	29	30
31						

1   **Japan announces** that it will voluntarily limit automobile exports to the United States for two years.
Senator Harrison A. Williams, Jr., (D., N.J.), is convicted of crimes stemming from the Abscam investigation.

4   **Massachusetts Governor** Edward J. King signs a bill that aids Boston's bankrupt school system.

6   **U.S. orders Libya** to close its embassy in Washington, D.C., because of "a general pattern of unacceptable conduct."

7   **Robert Sands,** an imprisoned member of the Irish Republican Army (IRA), is buried after dying May 5 on the 66th day of a hunger strike. Riots erupt in Northern Ireland following his death.

10   **François Mitterrand** is elected the first Socialist president of France since the Fifth Republic was founded in 1958.

13   **Pope John Paul II is shot** in St. Peter's Square in Rome. Police arrest gunman Mehmet Ali Agca, an escaped Turkish killer.

14   **Boston Celtics win** the National Basketball Association championship, defeating Houston, four games to two.

20   **United States reverses** a decision that had cut the influx of Indochinese refugees.

20-21   **U.S. Congress ratifies** a compromise budget resolution projecting a $37.65-billion deficit for fiscal 1982.

21   **Pierre Mauroy,** mayor of Lille, is named prime minister of France.
Israel demands that Syria remove missiles from Lebanon and pull its troops back from Syrian territory bordering Lebanon.
New York Islanders win professional hockey's Stanley Cup, defeating Minnesota, four games to one.

24   **Ecuador's President** Jaime Roldos Aguilera dies in an airplane crash.

26   **Italy's government falls** after revelation that powerful officials belong to an illegal secret Masonic lodge.
Oil-price freeze and production cuts are announced by 12 of the 13 members of the Organization of Petroleum Exporting Countries (OPEC). Saudi Arabia is the lone holdout.
U.S. Marine Corps jet aircraft crashes on the aircraft carrier *Nimitz,* killing 14 persons and injuring 48.

28   **Stefan Cardinal Wyszyński,** 79, the Roman Catholic primate of Poland, dies.

30   **Bangladesh President** Ziaur Rahman is shot to death in a military coup attempt. Vice-President Abdus Sattar becomes acting president.

June 30

June

	1	2	3	4	5	6
7	8	9	10	11	12	13
14	15	16	17	18	19	20
21	22	23	24	25	26	27
28	29	30				

June 12

2   **Lindsay Thompson is named premier** of Australia's state of Victoria, replacing Rupert Hamer, who resigned.

6   **U.S. coal miners** end 72-day strike by ratifying a 40-month contract.

7-8   **Israeli warplanes bomb** a partially built nuclear reactor near Baghdad, Iraq. The United States and many other nations condemn the strike, but Israel claims that Iraq planned to use the reactor to make atomic bombs for possible use against Israel.

12   **Major-league baseball players** strike because of a dispute with owners over free-agent compensation.

15   **U.S. agrees** to provide Pakistan with $3 billion in military and economic aid from October 1982 to October 1987.

16   **U.S. reverses** its position against arms sales to China.

19   **European Space Agency's *Ariane*** rocket puts two satellites into orbit.

19-25   ***Superman II*** sets 10 motion-picture box-office records in its opening week.

21   **French Socialists win** a majority of seats in the National Assembly in nationwide elections on June 14 and 21.
Wayne B. Williams, a free-lance photographer, is charged with killing one of the 28 young blacks slain in the Atlanta area over a two-year period. On July 17, he is charged with a second murder.

22   **Iran's President** Abol Hasan Bani-Sadr is dismissed by Ayatollah Ruhollah Khomeini after the *Majlis* (parliament) declares him unfit to hold office. Bani-Sadr is thought to have fled Iran.

23   **Great Britain announces** its highest rate of unemployment since the 1930s — 11.1 per cent.
Communists are named to four of 44 French Cabinet posts.

25   **Excluding women** from military draft registration is constitutional, the Supreme Court of the United States rules.

28   **Bomb explodes** in an Iran political office, killing 72 persons, including Chief Justice Ayatollah Mohammed Beheshti.
Giovanni Spadolini, leader of Italy's small Republican Party, becomes prime minister, heading a five-party coalition government.

29-30   **China's Communist Party** condemns Mao Tse-tung's policies during the Cultural Revolution of 1966-1976, names Hu Yao-pang (Hu Yaobang) party chairman, succeeding Hua Kuo-feng (Hua Guofeng).

30   **Israel's Likud Party,** led by Prime Minister Menachem Begin, shown above, narrowly wins parliamentary elections.
Ireland's *Dáil Éireann* (House of Deputies) elects Garret FitzGerald, leader of the Fine Gael party, prime minister after June 11 elections give no party a majority.

July 29

July

			1	2	3	4
5	6	7	8	9	10	11
12	13	14	15	16	17	18
19	20	21	22	23	24	25
26	27	28	29	30	31	

3   **European Community nations** ratify a plan to end subsidies to steel companies.

3-4   **Chris Evert Lloyd** and John McEnroe win Wimbledon tennis titles.

3-13   **Youth riots** break out in London and Liverpool, spread to more than 30 British cities and towns.

7   **Reagan nominates** Sandra Day O'Connor as the first woman justice of the Supreme Court of the United States.

10   **California Governor** Edmund G. Brown, Jr., orders large-scale aerial spraying of the pesticide malathion in an effort to wipe out the Mediterranean fruit fly, or Medfly.

11   **Writers Guild of America** ends a 13-week strike against film and television producers.

12-20   **Floods in China's** Szechwan (Sichuan) and Hupeh (Hubei) provinces kill 768 persons and injure more than 28,000.

14-20   **Poland's Communist Party** holds an emergency congress. Delegates elect their leaders by secret ballot, the first such vote in any Communist country.

17   **Two aerial walkways** collapse in the Hyatt Regency Hotel in Kansas City, Mo., killing 113 persons.

19-21   **Economic summit meeting** in Ottawa, Canada, is attended by leaders of Canada, France, Great Britain, Italy, Japan, the United States, and West Germany.

22   **Chrysler Corporation reports** that it earned $11.6 million in the second quarter, its first profit since 1978.

23   **Poland announces** sharp hikes in food prices.

24   **Iranians elect** Mohammad Ali Rajai president.
Israel and the Palestine Liberation Organization (PLO) endorse cease-fire agreements, virtually ending combat along the Israel-Lebanon border.

25   **Rugby fans clash** with demonstrators in Hamilton, New Zealand, preventing a match with South Africa's Springboks team. New Zealand's police commissioner calls the riot the worst in the country's history.

27   **A $1-billion emergency plan** to curb youth unemployment is proposed by Great Britain's Prime Minister Margaret Thatcher.

28   **Canada's dollar plunges** to a value of 81.5 U.S. cents, a 48-year low.

29   **Prince Charles** and Lady Diana Spencer are married at St. Paul's Cathedral in London before a worldwide television audience of about 700 million persons.
France grants political asylum to Abol Hasan Bani-Sadr, who was ousted as president of Iran on June 22.

31   **Major-league baseball players** end strike after 49 days.

Here are your
1982 YEAR BOOK
Cross-Reference Tabs

For insertion in your WORLD BOOK

Each year, THE WORLD BOOK YEAR BOOK adds a valuable dimension to your WORLD BOOK set. The Cross-Reference Tab System is designed especially to help youngsters and parents alike *link* THE YEAR BOOK's new and revised WORLD BOOK articles, its Special Reports, and its Close-Ups to the related WORLD BOOK articles they update.

How to Use These Tabs

First, remove this page from THE YEAR BOOK.
Begin with the first Tab, "AIRPORT."

Then, turn to the *A Volume* of your WORLD BOOK set and find the page of the "AIRPORT" article. Moisten the gummed Tab and affix it to that page.

There is no "VANUATU" article in your WORLD BOOK. So for the New Article on "VANUATU," mount the Tab in the *U-V Volume* where it should appear in its alphabetical sequence.

Special Report
AIRPORT
1982 Year Book, p. 122

Year Book Close-Up
BRADLEY, OMAR NELSON
1982 Year on File (Armed Forces)

Special Section
CENSUS
1982 Year Book, p. 521

Year Book Close-Up
CHARLES, PRINCE
1982 Year on File (Great Britain)

New Article
ELEPHANT
1982 Year Book, p. 560

Year Book Close-Up
HANDICAPPED
1982 Year on File (United Nations)

New Article
INFLATION
1982 Year Book, p. 572

Year Book Close-Up
IRAN
1982 Year on File (Iran)

New Article
KUALA LUMPUR
1982 Year Book, p. 572

Year Book Close-Up
LOUIS, JOE
1982 Year on File (Deaths)

New Article
MALAYSIA
1982 Year Book, p. 568

New Article
MENTAL ILLNESS
1982 Year Book, p. 575

Special Report
PANDA
1982 Year Book, p. 74

Special Report
PRESIDENT OF THE U.S.
1982 Year Book, p. 54

Special Report
ROBOT
1982 Year Book, p. 138

Year Book Close-Up
SADAT, ANWAR AL-
1982 Year on File (Middle East)

Special Report
SPACE TRAVEL
1982 Year Book, p. 108

Year Book Close-Up
SUPREME COURT OF THE U.S.
1982 Year on File (Supreme Court)

New Article
VANUATU
1982 Year Book, p. 567

Special Report
WATER
1982 Year Book, p. 92

Aug. 13

Aug. 5

Aug. 25

Aug. 3

August

						1
2	3	4	5	6	7	8
9	10	11	12	13	14	15
16	17	18	19	20	21	22
23	24	25	26	27	28	29
30	31					

1   **Airplane crash** kills Panama's strongman leader, National Guard Commander Omar Torrijos Herrera.

3   **U.S. air traffic controllers** strike. A federal judge finds their union, the Professional Air Traffic Controllers Organization, in contempt of court. Two days later, the government begins to fire strikers as airlines cut service to 75 per cent of capacity.

  Egypt and Israel sign an agreement that sets up an international force to patrol the Sinai Peninsula after Israeli troops withdraw.

3-8   **Rebel officers** force Bolivia's President Luis Garcia Meza Tejada to resign, and win concessions from the military junta that succeeds him.

4   **Battle for control** of Conoco, Incorporated, is won by E. I. du Pont de Nemours & Company against Seagram Company and Mobil Oil Corporation. Du Pont pays $7.54 billion for the oil firm in the costliest take-over in U.S. history.

5   **Truck and bus drivers** end a 50-hour street blockade in Warsaw, Poland, in a protest against food shortages.

  Israel's Knesset (parliament) approves Prime Minister Menachem Begin's coalition government, made up of his Likud Party and three religious parties.

10   **U.S. announces** that it will assemble neutron warheads.

  Canadian postal workers end 43-day strike.

11   **Street protests** against food shortages "could lead to the greatest national tragedy," warns Poland's Communist Party First Secretary Stanislaw Kania.

  Italy announces a $70-billion energy plan to reduce the risk that the country "will drop out of the group of industrialized nations forever."

13   **President Reagan signs** bills that cut taxes and drastically reduce the budget.

17   **U.S. ends 10-week suspension** of delivery of military aircraft to Israel.

19   **U.S. fighter aircraft** down two Libyan jets over the Mediterranean Sea about 60 miles (100 kilometers) from Libya's coast.

24   **South Africa sends** two armored columns 80 miles (130 kilometers) into Angola.

25   **Voyager 2 spacecraft** passes within 63,000 miles (101,000 kilometers) of Saturn, revealing that the planet has thousands of rings, as shown in the artificially colored photograph above.

30   **Bomb blast kills** Iran's President Mohammad Ali Rajai and Prime Minister Mohammad Jad Bahonar. Minister of the Interior Ayatollah Mohammad Riza Mahdavi-Kani becomes provisional prime minister two days later.

SOLIDARITY DAY
SEPTEMBER 19TH • WASHINGTON, D.C.
AFL - CIO

Sept. 19

Sept. 16

September

		1	2	3	4	5
6	7	8	9	10	11	12
13	14	15	16	17	18	19
20	21	22	23	24	25	26
27	28	29	30			

1   **Canada's federal government** and the oil-rich province of Alberta reach agreement on the pricing of petroleum products.

1-2   **President David Dacko** of the Central African Republic is toppled from power by Andre Kolingba, the armed forces' chief of staff, who declares himself president.

2   **Portugal's Prime Minister** Francisco Pinto Balsemao forms a new government after resigning on August 11.

3-4   **Egypt arrests** more than 1,500 opponents of the government, including religious activists, artists, journalists, and politicians.

4-12   **About 100,000 Russian troops** hold war games on the Polish border.

5   **Solidarity,** Poland's independent trade union, begins its first national congress.

9   **Nicaragua declares** a state of economic emergency and bans strikes.

13   **"Hill Street Blues,"** a television series about police, wins a record eight Emmy awards.
U.S. Secretary of State Alexander M. Haig says the United States has "physical

evidence" that Russia and its allies used poisonous biological weapons in Laos, Cambodia, and Afghanistan.

13-14   **Norway's ruling Labor Party** loses parliamentary elections.

14   **Sweden devalues** its currency and freezes prices.

15   **Pope John Paul II** issues his third encyclical, *On Human Work.*
Egypt expels Russia's ambassador.

16   **Boxer "Sugar Ray" Leonard** defeats Thomas Hearns in the richest sports event in history. It grossed about $35 million.
Canadian grain handlers end a 15-day strike at Thunder Bay, Ont., the country's largest grain port.

19   **Protesting cuts** in federal social and safety programs, 260,000 members of labor organizations and other groups march in Washington, D.C.
Brazil's President Joao Baptista de Oliveira Figueiredo temporarily gives up his position one day after suffering a heart attack.

21   **Belize,** a Central American nation, becomes independent of Great Britain.

24   **President Reagan appeals** for additional spending cuts of $13 billion.

25   **Sandra Day O'Connor** is sworn in as the first woman justice of the U.S. Supreme Court.

28   **The Supreme Court of Canada** rules that the federal government may submit to the British Parliament a resolution that would allow Canada to amend its constitution.

30   **China asks Taiwan** to join in talks on the reunification of China.

Oct. 6

October

				1	2	3
4	5	6	7	8	9	10
11	12	13	14	15	16	17
18	19	20	21	22	23	24
25	26	27	28	29	30	31

2   **Reagan proposes** building 100 M-X missiles and 100 B-1 long-range bombers.

4   **The eight nations** of the European Monetary System change the relative values of their currencies.

5   **France freezes** the prices of certain goods and services.
Iranian voters elect Hojatolislam Mohammed Ali Khamenei president.
Sudan's two parliaments are dissolved by President and Prime Minister Gaafar Mohamed Nimeiri.

5-8   **Sears, Roebuck and Company** agrees to buy Coldwell, Banker & Company, the largest U.S. real estate brokerage firm, and Dean Witter Reynolds Organization, Incorporated, the fifth-largest securities company.

6   **Egypt's President and Prime Minister** Anwar el-Sadat is assassinated while watching a military parade in a suburb of Cairo.

7   **Lech Walesa** is re-elected chairman of Solidarity.

8   **A Canadian parliamentary subcommittee,** after a one-year study, urges government action to curb acid rain.

10   **About 250,000 people demonstrate** in Bonn, West Germany, against the North Atlantic Treaty Organization's plan to install new nuclear missiles in Europe.

13   **Mohamed Hosni Mubarak** is sworn in as president of Egypt.

18   **Wojciech Jaruzelski,** Poland's Council of Ministers chairman, replaces Stanislaw Kania as Communist Party first secretary.
Andreas Papandreou's Panhellenic Socialist Movement defeats Greek Prime Minister George Rallis' New Democracy Party in parliamentary elections.

19   **President Reagan** and France's President Mitterrand attend a re-enactment of the historic British surrender at Yorktown, Va., on Oct. 19, 1781.

22-23   **Leaders** of 14 developing nations and eight industrial countries discuss Third World issues in Cancún, Mexico.

25   **Alberto Salazar** wins the New York City Marathon in a world-record time of 2 hours 8 minutes 13 seconds. Allison Roe breaks the women's record, finishing in 2:25.28.

27   **Russian submarine** runs aground near a Swedish naval base.
Finland's President Urho Kekkonen resigns because of illness.

28   **Los Angeles Dodgers** win the World Series, defeating the New York Yankees, four games to two.
U.S. Senate approves the sale of five AWACS radar aircraft to Saudi Arabia.

29   **OPEC sets a single price** of $34 per barrel of crude oil.

Nov. 12

Nov. 20

Nov. 6

November

1	2	3	4	5	6	7
8	9	10	11	12	13	14
15	16	17	18	19	20	21
22	23	24	25	26	27	28
29	30					

1   **Antigua and Barbuda,** an island nation in the Caribbean Sea, becomes independent of Great Britain.

4   **Libya says** its troops will leave Chad.

5   **Canada's federal government** and the nine English-speaking provinces agree on a plan for a new national constitution.
Buckingham Palace announces that the Princess of Wales is expecting a baby in June.

6   **Russian submarine** leaves Swedish waters after running aground in a restricted area on October 27.
Reagan discloses that he has given up hope of balancing the budget by 1984.

9   **The International Monetary Fund** approves its largest loan ever, $5.8 billion for India.

12   **David A. Stockman,** director of the Office of Management and Budget, offers to resign after a magazine article quotes him as saying that he doubts the Administration's economic program will work. Reagan keeps him on the job.
Egypt indicts four accused killers of Sadat.

Denmark's government falls when parliament fails to support a jobs plan.
Four balloonists complete the first manned balloon flight across the Pacific Ocean.

13   **Richard V. Allen,** President Reagan's national security adviser, is under investigation for accepting $1,000 from a Japanese magazine, the White House announces.

14   **U.S. space shuttle** *Columbia* returns to earth, completing a mission that was cut short by a fuel-cell failure.
U.S. paratroopers bail out over Egypt, beginning the largest U.S. military exercises in the Middle East since World War II.

17   **Kathryn J. Whitmire** is elected as Houston's first woman mayor.

18   **Reagan proposes** to cancel a plan to install new nuclear missiles in Europe if Russia will dismantle comparable weapons.

20   **World chess champion** Anatoly Karpov of Russia keeps his title, defeating Viktor Korchnoi, a Russian defector.

22   **Greece announces** it will set a timetable for the removal of U.S. bases from the country.

23   **Reagan vetoes** a bill that would have provided money to pay for current operations of the federal government. Congress then votes to continue spending at the current rate until December 15.

25   **Arab League summit meeting** in Fez, Morocco, collapses after eight of the 21 member heads of state fail to attend.

30   **Arms-reduction talks** between the United States and Russia begin in Geneva, Switzerland.
Israel and the United States sign an agreement on threats to the Middle East.

Dec. 1

December

		1	2	3	4	5
6	7	8	9	10	11	12
13	14	15	16	17	18	19
20	21	22	23	24	25	26
27	28	29	30	31		

1 **Yugoslav jet crashes** into a mountain in Corsica, killing all 178 people aboard.

2 **Polish police break up** a sit-in by about 300 cadets at a fire fighters' academy in Warsaw.

3 **Terrorists trained in Libya** have entered the United States in a plot to assassinate President Reagan or other members of the Administration, federal officials say.

4 **Solidarity threatens** to lead a national protest strike if Poland's government enacts an emergency powers bill.

8 **Dissident Russian physicist** Andrei D. Sakharov ends a 17-day hunger strike after Soviet officials say that his daughter-in-law may leave Russia.

9 **President Reagan cancels a ban** on federal jobs for flight controllers who were fired during an illegal strike in August.

10 **Reagan asks** U.S. citizens to leave Libya.
   China and India open talks to resolve border disagreements.

11 **Javier Pérez de Cuéllar** of Peru is nominated for the post of secretary-general of the UN.

Argentina's President Roberto Eduardo Viola is removed from office by the military junta.

12 **Solidarity's National Commission** calls for a day of protest on December 17 and a referendum on replacing the government.

13 **Poland declares martial law,** sets up a Military Council of National Salvation to run the country, bans public gatherings and strikes, and arrests Solidarity leaders.

14 **Israel annexes** the Golan Heights, a plateau that it took from Syria in 1967.

15 **Congress passes** a $200-billion military spending bill, the largest in U.S. history.

17 **U.S. Brigadier General** James L. Dozier is kidnapped in Italy by the Red Brigades, a left wing terrorist organization.
   Albania's Prime Minister Mehmet Shehu commits suicide.
   UN Security Council unanimously declares Israel's annexation of the Golan Heights "null and void."

18-20 **The United States suspends** the strategic agreement that it signed with Israel in November. Israel's Prime Minister Begin angrily says that he considers the pact to be canceled.

19 **Poland's ambassador** to the United States, Romuald Spasowski, asks for political asylum.

23 **A federal judge rules** that Congress acted unconstitutionally in 1978 when it extended the deadline for ratifying the proposed Equal Rights Amendment until June 30, 1982.
   Reagan announces suspension of major economic ties with Poland.

29 **The United States imposes** limited economic sanctions against Russia.

The Year
in Focus

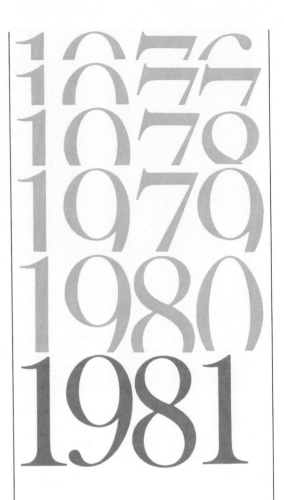

The meaning of some of the important events
and trends of 1981 is discussed by the members
of THE YEAR BOOK Board of Editors:

Harrison Brown, Director, the
East-West Resource Systems Institute, the
East-West Center, Honolulu, Hawaii.
Lawrence A. Cremin, President, Teachers
College, Columbia University.
James J. Kilpatrick, columnist for the
Universal Press Syndicate.
Sylvia Porter, columnist for the
Universal Press Syndicate.
Carl T. Rowan, columnist for the Field
Newspaper Syndicate.

Seated: Brown, Porter; standing, left to right, Rowan, Kilpatrick, Cremin.

Lawrence A. Cremin

James J. Kilpatrick

Sylvia Porter

Carl T. Rowan

A Faltering
Economy,
an Uneasy
World

**In the United States, a new President had to cope
with "an economic affliction of great proportions."
Elsewhere, the Middle East and Poland were hot spots**

The YEAR BOOK Board of Editors met in Washington, D.C., in mid-November 1981, about 10 months into the presidency of Ronald Reagan. During their all-day discussion, the board members talked about what President Reagan considered his first priority — strengthening the faltering U.S. economy. How was he dealing with it? What were his prospects for success? They then turned their attention to two of the most critical areas on the international scene — the perpetual hot spot of the Middle East and the uneasy situation in Poland. Joining the discussion were Ralph Schey, chairman, president, and chief executive officer of The Scott Fetzer Company; William H. Nault, editorial director of World Book, Inc.; and Wayne Wille, executive editor of THE WORLD BOOK YEAR BOOK.

Harrison Brown

Wayne Wille

William H. Nault

Ralph Schey

William H. Nault: As we meet here in Washington today, the 40th President of the United States, Ronald Reagan, has been in office about 10 months. Some would say that in terms of his economic program he's been in office about 40 days, or just since the beginning of the 1982 fiscal year. We want to talk about how he has used that time, especially about his efforts to aid the ailing U.S. economy. We also want to explore some of the year's important events on the world scene—specifically, the always smoldering Middle East and the uneasy situation in Poland.

Sylvia, in President Reagan's inaugural address, he said, "These United States are confronted with an economic affliction of great proportions." He said that his first priority would be "to reawaken this industrial giant, to get government back within its means, and to lighten our punitive tax burden." Reagan devoted a great deal of his time to those domestic priorities during his first 10 months. Sylvia, what is his record on the economy so far? What has he done, and what are the prospects for success, as you view them?

Sylvia Porter: What he has done is help inaugurate a slump that, as of now, is of unknown duration, width, and depth. This is so far the only visible result of what is known as supply-side economics, which was introduced by Reagan as his basic cure for the economic affliction that does indeed beleaguer our country. Supply-side economics is a fairly unfamiliar term. I define it as a combination of policies that, on the face of it, are impossibly in conflict and cannot be put together to make work. One of those policies, as the Reagan Administration pursues its version of supply-side, is a tremendous three-year tax cut. Another is an increase in military spending. Simultaneously, the President has fought for a great cut in overall government spending, in this case concentrating mostly on social welfare programs, which admittedly have gotten out of hand. And the sum of all this is supposed to be a balanced federal budget. The theory is that if we cut individual and corporate income tax rates sufficiently, we increase new investment by American industry, and this encourages increased productivity, which then expands the economy. This, in turn, creates more revenue, which offsets what the government lost by cutting the tax rates. So now we are off to the races with a balanced budget. The rate of inflation would decline because of the increased productivity. We also would have lower interest rates because interest rates would not have to go up if the Federal Reserve didn't encourage higher rates to control inflation.

So that's supply-side economics, what is being called these days "Reaganomics." People get big tax cuts, and they can look forward to a balanced budget, lower interest rates, declining inflation, and an improved economy.

James J. Kilpatrick: Well, why is all of this impossible?

Porter: It just strikes me as defying reason. I can understand your defending a theory that, as you might say, has not really had a chance to work yet. But my feeling as I try to put these things together is that they don't make sense. Wall Street—which is not Wall Street at all;

it's the sum total of the thinking of millions of investors and thousands of stockbrokers – couldn't see the logic of it either. Stock prices have not gone up as they should have if Wall Street really had confidence in the program. "I don't believe it," said the stock market. Nor do I, Jack Kilpatrick, nor do I. Reagan's economic program to date has been – my instinct is to say it has been a disaster, but I think I'll just say that it has been an enormous disappointment. Supply-side economics may not even have a chance to be really tested, because the American people won't permit it to be tested. I personally think that the quicker we dismiss Reaganomics and get back to principles we are a little more capable of understanding, the better off we'll be.

Kilpatrick: As you can imagine, I am in nearly total disagreement with my friend Sylvia over there. First off, I think it is unfair to charge that Reagan helped us into this slump or recession. I can't look back over these 10 months and see what Reagan has done or the Congress has done with his leadership that would have helped us into this slump. On the contrary, my own strong feeling is that we would be in

Rowan: "The tight-money policies that were supposed to control inflation have brought the automobile and housing industries to the brink of disaster."

far worse shape if it had not been for Reagan's leadership and the actions of the Congress over these past 10 months.

His program hasn't had an opportunity to have an appreciable impact on the economy. I think we must simply wait and see what happens. I don't see anything wrong with the basic supply-side theory. It makes a lot of sense to me. I think it is demonstrable in terms of classic economics that if you cut the tax rates enough, you will generate so much additional business activity that in the course of time—not immediately, but in the course of time—your total revenues are going to be greater than they were.

I am not nearly as pessimistic as you are, Sylvia. I think that this recession we're in now, in November 1981, is not going to be a long one. I don't think it is going to be a fearfully deep one.

Harrison Brown: I agree that you can't blame the whole thing on Reagan. His program has barely gotten started. But I think we have to ask ourselves—are these steps that the Reagan Administration is taking going to ease the situation, or are they going to make it worse?

I am convinced that we are going through a time, or heading for a time, that is not unlike that of the Vietnam War, only worse. You'll recall that during President Lyndon B. Johnson's years, military expenditures skyrocketed because of Vietnam, and there were no

Porter: "What Reagan has done is help inaugurate a slump that, as of now, is of unknown duration, width, and depth."

compensatory steps taken to balance this. As a result, inflation was well underway in the Johnson days—and went even further in President Carter's time, because there is a tremendous amount of momentum involved in what happens in the U.S. government.

Today, the acceleration of military spending greatly exceeds what happened during Vietnam. And at the same time, we have cut taxes. I fail to see how we are going to avoid the continuation of high inflation rates. Maybe there will be a miracle, but I think the military spending part of things is going to be our undoing.

Looking at the nonmilitary cuts, what disturbs me greatly is that one takes a simple-minded goal—that of balancing the budget—and just says, "All right, we're going to cut everything we can possibly cut in order to do that." Now, I agree with the effort—there are a lot of things that should be cut. But to just go across the board and slash and slash without asking what one is slashing and what will be the consequences in terms of human lives, and in terms of the welfare of our country, I think is a very grievous error.

Nault: Carl, what is your view of Reagan's progress?

Carl T. Rowan: Everything I have seen suggests to me that Bush [George H. W. Bush, now Vice-President] knew what he was talking about during the Republican Party primaries of 1980 when he

Brown: "To just go across the board and slash and slash without asking what one is slashing and what will be the consequences in terms of human lives is a very grievous error."

described Reaganomics as "voodoo economics." The old voodoo isn't working, and I don't think it will ever work. It is just plain folly to assume that we can spend $1.6 trillion on the military over the next five years – at a time when we are heading into one of the largest tax cuts in our history – and, just because we cut some domestic programs, wind up with a situation where the economy blossoms. I never believed it could work. I don't believe it now. I see nothing in this country that tells me that American business believes that this 25 per cent tax cut is going to cause a flowering of the economy. I do see that economists of every political description I know – from the very liberal ones to the conservative ones – are saying that this recession is wider and deeper than anybody thought.

We know, for example, that the tight-money policies that were supposed to control inflation have brought the automobile and the housing industries to the brink of disaster. And the economists now are discovering that it is much wider, that this recession touches all kinds of small businesses. Only two months ago, the White House people were saying to me, "You are wrong. There is no way unemployment is going to get to 8 per cent." Well, it is there now; that is the national figure. And in some of the communities in America, it is a *de*pression – 16.7 per cent unemployment among black Americans. That means that 1 black out of every 6 looking for a job can't find one. This has got to have a devastating impact on the cities of America.

Now, I – like other Americans – look at what has happened in the cost of Medicaid and Medicare, and I say, "How did it get this high this fast?" I look at the cost of food stamps and welfare costs, and I can understand why the American public would say, "We've got to put some kinds of controls on the social programs." But I say, as Harrison has said, that you just cannot do this with a cleaver, by cutting across the board. I just do not believe, for example, that we have to cut a nutrition program for poor, pregnant women, particularly when I hear the chairman of the Senate Appropriations Committee, Mark Hatfield, saying that the cost overrun on the Patriot missile alone would cover the nutrition program for 700,000 poor, pregnant women. I do not believe that we have to try to cut spending in such a way as to penalize the working poor – to literally make it advantageous for a woman heading a household with two children to sit home and live on welfare rather than go out and try to have some pride by holding a job.

So, not only are we looking at a program that will not work economically, but we're also looking at a program that is going to create some social tragedies and some social chaos in this country.

Nault: Larry, how has the Reagan program affected education?

Lawrence A. Cremin: I think the cuts in funds for college loans alone will make it difficult – indeed, impossible – for almost a million young people who would have gone to college to go to college. Yes, there were abuses in the college loan program that needed to be corrected. Well-to-do families were taking government loans at low interest rates, and either the youngsters or the parents were reinvest-

Porter: "Stock prices have not gone up as they should have if Wall Street really had confidence in the Reagan program."

ing the money at very high interest rates. That needed to be corrected, but it seems to me it is harmful to have the kind of correction that goes so far in the other direction that a million young Americans end up unable to go to college.

More broadly, we've been talking about President Reagan's economic policies and the recession our country is in, but I think we have to understand that nobody is going to reawaken any industrial giant without being primarily concerned with people. We can reindustrialize. We can produce new machines. But unless we are deeply concerned with the most precious of our resources, the human beings who make up the American society, we're not really going to reawaken the United States economically.

Here I think the several goals the President announced in his inaugural speech may be inconsistent. I don't think we can cut taxes and thereby – particularly in the fiscal years 1983 and 1984, given the tax cuts that are coming – live within the federal budget, considering the increased military expenditures. We can't cut down the social and nonmilitary expenditures the way they're going to have to be cut to live within that budget and still reawaken the American industrial giant.

We tend to use the term *social welfare programs*, and the word *welfare* casts an unfortunate color upon these programs. I'd rather think of many of them as human-resource programs. They are programs that enable people to develop to the fullness of their capacities. They are programs that the states and localities have been unable to mount and that the federal government has helped to subsidize in a way that, I think, has produced incalculable benefits for American society.

Kilpatrick: "I think it is unfair to charge that Reagan helped us into this slump or recession. His program hasn't had an opportunity to have an appreciable impact on the economy."

Now, a great deal of attention has been directed to the Japanese economy. If we look at some of the elements in this so-called Japanese industrial miracle, two things stand out. One is the education of the Japanese people. For years in the United States, we've been immensely proud that America holds its children in school longer than any other society. That is no longer true. The Japanese now hold about 92 per cent of their 18-year-olds through graduation from secondary school. In the United States, we have about 75 per cent. Moreover, the Japanese are insisting that *all* their young people take more work in mathematics, the sciences, language, and the social studies than we require. The fact is, the Japanese are giving their children a better academic education than we Americans are giving our children, and this has everything to do with the quality of Japan's awakened industrial giant. I would say the same with respect to the second important element – the Japanese government's stimulation of research and development activity, particularly as it has come out in the electronics industry in Japan, where they have pushed far ahead of American industry in some respects.

Nault: Ralph, as head of a major American business, what mark would you give Reagan?

Ralph Schey: I give him high marks. Our business system operates on confidence as much as it does on statistical facts. I think

Cremin: "Unless we are deeply concerned with the most precious of our resources, the human beings who make up the American society, we're not really going to reawaken the United States economically."

there are segments of Reagan's program – as with any program – that you can criticize, but I think it was what we did in the past that created the economic horror we have today. Some years back, I bought small companies that needed to be turned around to be profitable. I found it was impossible to start reorganizing a company by letting people defend what they wanted to keep. They didn't want to cut anything, and the business remained unprofitable. It was only by doing some real surgery that we cured the patient. That's the situation Reagan has found himself in with the economy – it needs some surgery.

America faces a tremendous dilemma today. We simply are not competitive in the world markets. All you need to do to see that is look at the kinds of products we manufacture. We've talked about Japan – if you really look at the gut issues between Japan and America, a key one is the fact that they build better quality products than we do. Or at least they do in the mind of the purchaser. If you look at an automobile, it is hard to define quality in quantitative terms, but the fact is that our buying public thinks Japan's is better. And Japan does build good products. One of the most important reasons for the Japanese success is the quality and superior training of their work force, compared with the American work force.

I used to be with a company that had a small plant in Japan with 500 employees. Every year we had to hire 40 apprentices. In our U.S. company we had 8,000 employees, and we didn't have 40 apprentices in the entire company. This was 12 or 13 years ago. Apprenticeship programs that would provide a constant flow of trained workers have been difficult to support in this country, and some of the incentives to rebuild industry have not been present. So, if anything, the Reagan Administration hasn't gone far enough with steps like improving the investment tax credit, changing depreciation schedules, and providing help on research and development.

I think we should have even greater incentives to support research and development at colleges and universities. We should dramatically increase the number of people who will stay in doctoral programs to be teachers — to train the people who are going to have to live and work during the electronic age, because we are not ready for it. Japan — with half our population — graduates more engineers than we do. If you look at what the Russians are doing in their engineering programs, it is equally astounding. What I like about Reagan's program is that it is dramatic. It headlines the issues of industrialization. It does create incentives for investment.

Porter: You have put your finger, Ralph, on an issue with which none of us would disagree, and that is the importance of stimulating industry investing in new plants and modernized equipment. But this is what I think the program that Congress passed under Reagan's very smooth push does not do enough of. Every one of us would have approved depreciation clauses, incentive clauses — all kinds of incentives — without a murmur. But three years of an enormous tax cut? Three years, without waiting to see what would happen after the first year? We didn't need that kind of tax cut. We needed what Ralph is talking about. We needed the kind of tax cut that would have sent Wall Street into a state of sheer delight.

As Ralph pointed out, it's a matter of confidence. But confidence on the part of industry has not been expressed by your fellow businessmen, Ralph. They have made it clear that they do not like this tax cut. They do not like much at all about supply-side economics.

Nault: Ralph, you have been quoted as saying that this is a time of almost unparalleled opportunity for American business.

Schey: To quote what I said — "Business has the greatest opportunity it has had in 50 years. We better not ruin it." What I mean by that is that there is a different feeling today among business, labor, and government. A lot of it has to do with what Reagan is trying to do to reduce the amount of regulation that is stifling business. As a businessman, I find that I spend almost half my time with lawyers and accountants on unproductive matters, many of them having to do with regulations. It is not a question of whether they should be reduced, because they have got to be reduced.

In the area of labor there also are a lot positive things happening

Brown: "Maybe there will be a miracle, I don't know, but I think the military spending part of things is going to be our undoing."

today. American labor, for a variety of reasons, did become less productive, not the least of these reasons being the management of that labor. I think that the auto industry over the years was wrong in giving wage increases for increased productivity when, in fact, they weren't getting that higher productivity. Building cost-of-living pay adjustments into union contracts was another mistake for which we are paying dearly. The control of auto design by the marketing people and the stylists rather than the engineering people contributed to the lack of quality in our cars. Both management and labor contributed to our demise.

My feeling of confidence today is based on the belief that we have a government that is more receptive to what has to be done to expand our industrial base. Labor unions will support productivity-improvement programs. I believe the American worker senses that he must compete with the Japanese and West German workers in a way that he's never had to before. Finally, we have management that is becoming less autocratic and more democratic. Becoming so is going

Kilpatrick: "We would
be in far worse shape
if it had not been
for Reagan's leadership
and the actions of
the Congress over
the past 10 months."

to help the worker – if we adopt different attitudes about arbitrary layoffs and arbitrary cutbacks and start looking at labor as being part of the entire management process. So my view is that I have never seen a climate that is more conducive to reindustrializing America since I've been in business during the last 30 years.

Cremin: I agree with Ralph about where business stands with respect to opportunity. One of my colleagues, P. Michael Timpane, recently made a survey of the attitude of business leaders toward the public schools. He found a tremendous interest, a tremendous concern. More importantly, he found a tremendous readiness to help in upgrading the schools. One problem is that the schools frequently are unaware of the needs of business. They're teaching the best programs of the 1940s and 1950s and not the best programs needed for the 1980s and beyond. So, first, he found a tremendous interest by industry in getting the kind of education we need for young people.

Second, he found that industry is becoming aware that it has a responsibility, in collaboration with labor, for the continuing education of the people who work in business and industry. A company like American Telephone and Telegraph, for example, runs a bigger internal education program, going from apprenticeships up through executive training, than any college or university in the United States. More and more companies are recognizing that they have a responsibility for the continuing education of their employees if, indeed, we're going to have the kind of increased productivity we need to compete in the international markets.

Nault: Let's turn to the international scene. The Middle East has been a hot spot for many years, and 1981 certainly was no exception. There has been continuing turmoil in Lebanon, the Palestine Liberation Organization's terrorist activities, the Israeli bombing of the nuclear reactor in Iraq. But perhaps the most unsettling event of the year was the assassination of Egypt's President Anwar el-Sadat. Apparently the killing had nothing to do with his efforts to make peace with Israel — at least, that is the opinion of some observers — but his death did remove a major figure from the world scene. Carl, what did Sadat's death mean to the peace process in the Middle East?

Rowan: Well, as we sit here, we have high-level British officials saying that the Camp David peace process is dead. We have the U.S. Administration saying that it has only one peace plan, and that is the Camp David peace plan, and they are pushing Israel and the new president of Egypt, Hosni Mubarak, to go forward with the talks to keep that process alive. But my guess is that the Camp David process is virtually dead. I think Mubarak will be relatively quiet until April 1982, when the Sinai is supposed to be returned to Egypt by Israel. After that, I don't think you will get much in the way of progress. I think Mubarak is going to be a different kind of fellow from Sadat. I think he *does* believe that Sadat's overtures toward Israel had a lot to do with his having been assassinated.

Porter: "Three years of an enormous tax cut, without waiting to see what would happen after the first year? We needed the kind of tax cut that would have sent Wall Street into a state of sheer delight."

I think myself that it had a lot to do with the assassination. I think Mubarak knows, as the leaders of some of the other Arab countries have been saying, that if he continues the Sadat peace process, he will come to the same fate as Sadat. What I am saying is that I think you will see efforts in Egypt to move back to some degree of closeness with the other Arab countries. Sadat was a pariah to the other Arab leaders. Even the Saudis, who are always spoken of as moderate, were doing their best to squeeze him economically, and they are now in a movement to get Mubarak to come back into the Arab fold.

Kilpatrick: One of the complicating factors in this situation is the outcome of the June election in Israel, which restored Prime Minister Menachem Begin to power by the slimmest possible margin — depending upon some hard-liners and some fundamentalist religious parties to make up his parliamentary majority. This has made his position in Israel shakier than it was before, and it has caused the hard-liners, the opponents of Camp David, to come to the forefront. That is bound to make peace negotiations more difficult. Then, with Sadat's assassination and the new leadership in Egypt, a volatile situation has been made even more uncertain. You also have the emergence of the eight-point plan for peace put forward by Saudi Arabia. The Israelis have rejected it. Others appear to be embracing it, including Reagan to a degree, though they still insist at the White House that there have been no changes in United States policy.

Rowan: You know, this is one of the things that makes it so difficult to figure out what our foreign policy is. We know that this Administration looks favorably on point seven of the Saudi plan, which speaks of the right of all states in this area to live in peace. The President and the secretary of state obviously want to read this as a willingness on the part of Saudi Arabia to recognize Israel at some point down the road. But just yesterday, when the White House chief of staff was asked about our Middle East policy, he came back with this line: "We have only one policy." Meaning Camp David.

Great Britain and the other Common Market countries very clearly want to deal with this Saudi plan, but — in my view — it can never go forward as it is, because it flatly requires Israel to go back to its 1967 boundaries. Even those, myself included, who believe that there has to be some Israeli withdrawal from areas that were occupied during the Six-Day War of June 1967 are not foolish enough to believe that Israel will ever go back to the pre-June 1967 boundaries. That would mean Syria putting guns on the Golan Heights, virtually hanging over the homes of the towns and villages of Israel below.

Wayne Wille: It would also mean giving up East Jerusalem — which had been Jordan's half of the city until 1967, when Israel took it over and made it an official part of Israel.

Rowan: Yes, that's right. That is one of the points of the plan, too, so it is a gloomy situation.

Nault: Any discussion of the Middle East would be lacking if we didn't talk a minute about the U.S. sale of Airborne Warning and Control Systems aircraft and other military equipment to Saudi Arabia — the AWACS deal.

Rowan: That is one of the subjects where Jack and I found ourselves uncommonly in agreement.

Kilpatrick: But I still think I'm right, Carl. That was the President's first major foreign policy test — the AWACS vote in the House and in the Senate. The conditions were such that the sale would go through unless both houses of Congress disapproved it. The House adopted its resolution of disapproval overwhelmingly by a margin of 3 to 1. Then it was up to the Senate, where all of the President's persuasive powers were brought to bear on a few senators, who changed their minds. Finally, Reagan won by a vote of 52 to 48.

My own feeling was that the Administration's decision was sound. These are essentially defensive weapons, not offensive weapons. They will help to protect the oil fields that are vital to the whole of the Western world. I didn't see that the presence of these weapons would represent any new or significant danger to Israel. I never truly understood the vehemence of the opposition to the sale.

Nault: Some commentators called the Senate vote a Pyrrhic victory, one that was won at very great cost to the President.

Schey: "We have to increase the number of people who will stay in doctoral programs to be teachers — to train the people who are going to have to live and work during the electronic age, because we are not ready for it."

Kilpatrick: It may turn out to be that way, but I don't think he gained as much by winning as he would have lost by losing. Had he lost that vote, his ability to negotiate with foreign countries would have been handicapped for a time — not fatally handicapped, but it would have been an embarrassment. We don't know exactly the price the White House paid for those last few votes. He did put a lot of chips on the line — and he has been putting them on the line. He put a lot on the line in getting the budget measure and the tax program through Congress by very narrow votes, too. This is part of leadership — to lead — and he has led successfully.

Wille: Would you say that the AWACS sale will advance or hinder the Middle East peace process?

Kilpatrick: I hope that it advances the peace process.

Rowan: That is one of the great gambles, you see. I think the Administration believes that there is no way you can ever have peace in the Middle East without having the involvement of Saudi Arabia and some of the other so-called moderate Arab states, such as Jordan. The Administration is gambling that through this sale they can say to the Saudis, "You see, we are pursuing an evenhanded policy. We do respect you for some of the things you've done. Now come on in and help us some more in pushing the peace process forward."

That is a big gamble. Nobody can really be sure that the Saudis are going to do what we hope they will do. Nor is it too likely that many other Arab states will buy the Saudi peace plan. But I think there is a little more to it than pursuing the peace process. I think the sale of those AWACS was step number one in the United States achieving the equivalent of some military bases in Saudi Arabia as part of our plan to protect Persian Gulf oil supplies.

Cremin: "The fact is, the Japanese are schooling their children better than we Americans are schooling our children, and this has everything to do with the quality of Japan's awakened industrial giant."

Brown: I feel quite strongly that the AWACS sale and other military sales that have been made and will be made in the future far transcend what we call the peace process. It involves very simply the fact that it is very much in our interest that the government of Saudi Arabia — our largest foreign supplier of oil — not be overturned. We had better see to it that our channels for getting Middle Eastern oil, particularly Saudi Arabian oil, remain open. It is in that general area of oil supplies that I think we're going to find the great volatility in the Middle East during the next five years or so.

Cremin: There is one other situation regarding the Arab countries that we should have in mind for the long term, and that is the movement of large sums of Middle Eastern money into American business, industry, and land ownership.

Wille: What are some of the implications of the transfers of these funds, which I imagine are mostly from the members of OPEC — the Organization of Petroleum Exporting Countries?

Brown: Some of the OPEC money is being invested in factories, and so forth, but most of it is still invested in short-term loans with our banks. Now, the banks — in turn — have been lending great amounts of money to developing countries. And should there be massive defaults by these countries — which is entirely possible — this would place us in a very, very difficult financial position because of all the money the banks owe on those loans from the OPEC countries.

Porter: There is more to it than that. The transfer of vast amounts of OPEC money has brought into the open the question of who controls our banks and our corporations. To what extent are we willing to let a potentially dangerous enemy come in and control the most sensitive institutions that we have? I have been told by the heads of some of the largest banks that my worries are misplaced. I have been told that I should not worry about the Middle Eastern money coming in and buying the big banks or banking systems. Then I tell these people, "Now wait a minute. You know that buying those banks gives them knowledge of every conceivable thing they might want to know about our big corporations and about individuals." When you open up a bank account, as you know, when you take out a loan, you have to give the bank all sorts of details, whether you're an individual or a corporation. These bankers who try to reassure me aren't worried about other countries knowing that much about our business. They think they ought to be trusted. Well, I think it is a misplaced trust, and I think this is something we should be worried about.

Schey: "I give Reagan very high marks. There are segments of his program that you can criticize, but I think it was what we did in the past that created the economic horror that we have today."

In addition to buying banks, these Middle Eastern countries are sending their money in to buy our corporations. Well, I know, the answer to that is that we can use the money. It builds factories. It builds things we need and the companies need, and it is stimulating to our economy. The other side of it is that it makes thinking Americans nervous. In short, how long before the tiger turns?

Wille: There are those, though, who say that turnabout is fair play — that for decades and decades we've poured our money into overseas corporations, and now that the same thing is happening to us, we say, "Not fair."

Porter: Now wait a minute. In England, for example, no outside interest can come in and buy more than 49 per cent of a "money" bank. But English interests can come over here and buy any percentage of our banks they want.

Schey: Shouldn't we be treated the same way as they are treated here? Let me take Japan, for example. It is extremely difficult for a foreign business to get a controlling interest in a Japanese company, yet the Japanese are marching in here buying automobile plants, appliance factories, and so on. In the process they are adopting

Rowan: "One black out of every six looking for a job can't find one. This has got to have a devastating impact on the cities of America."

certain practices that we would be forbidden to adopt in Japan that make Japan very difficult to compete with here in America. There must be some way to assure that we are treated in foreign countries as foreign countries are treated here.

Nault: Looking at the Middle East again, how can the United States maintain its special close relationship with Israel and at the same time improve its relations with the Arab nations?

Kilpatrick: Not easily, but I think that skilled diplomacy may bring it off. In the end, the rewards will be great, because the dependency of Israel on the United States is very large. I think there is room for our government to maneuver now, especially with the death of Sadat, to try to get a little bit of tilt toward some of the Arab states and not be perceived as so completely under the influence of Israel. I think the President said as much in one of his kind of offhand comments about the appearance that Israel was dictating our foreign policy.

Rowan: Yes, he did. I think one of the reasons he fought so hard to go ahead with the AWACS sale was that he perceived this as one of the steps toward improving our relations with Arab states without diminishing our support for Israel.

Nault: "Perhaps the most unsettling event of the year in the Middle East was the assassination of Egypt's President Anwar Sadat."

Nault: For more than a year now, the entire world has been watching Poland as it has had a series of surprising strikes, a number of government shakeups, and some important concessions from the government – including approval for the trade union Solidarity. It's still very uncertain, the end result of all these efforts at democratic reform. Jack, do you rank the situation in Poland as a very serious one, compared with the Middle East?

Kilpatrick: Yes. I can pass on something that Secretary of State Alexander Haig told me not too long ago. I asked him to list the greatest areas of concern to the United States. His first one was Poland, and the second was Iran. This was about six weeks ago, just before Solidarity's second conference in Gdańsk. The Solidarity conference, remember, was divided into two parts. And during the first part, they had urged other Eastern European nations – satellites of the Soviet Union – to follow their leadership in setting up free trade unions. I think Haig was very uncertain whether the Soviet Union was going to intervene actively in Poland if the second conference got out of hand. He thought something very drastic could happen.

Well, as it turned out, both sides have pulled back, and it looks as though things have settled down there somewhat. But there was a point when – in the view of the U.S. secretary of state – Poland was our number-one concern in the world.

Rowan: I doubt the situation has changed a great deal, because I still believe that the Soviets are going to move into Poland. There is certainly nothing on the horizon to suggest that the problems that have caused all the turmoil in Poland are going away. The economy is just absolutely in chaos. People are standing in line to buy almost anything and everything, and usually there is nothing there when they get to the head of the line. I think it was a measure of the magnitude of this crisis in Poland that you could get the leader of

Brown: "We had better see to it that our channels for getting Middle Eastern oil, particularly Saudi oil, remain open."

Solidarity, the head of the government, and the head of the Roman Catholic Church there to sit down and talk to each other about what could be done to defuse the situation. I just don't see it being defused, and I think our leaders really do believe that there is a serious danger of the Soviet Union moving into Poland with force. And that, very likely, would create a situation that we could not do much about.

Brown: The Soviet Union's perception of the Polish situation is very critical, because the Soviets may see it as signaling a breakdown of the entire buffer-state system they have established in Eastern Europe. I personally would be surprised if the Russians didn't go in. Now, they can go in in a number of ways, of course, not just militarily, but I suspect that they will go in. And we're going to take a beating because of that from a public relations point of view because of our inability to prevent it — but what can we do about it?

Kilpatrick: Very little. If they go in economically, simply by cutting off their trade with Poland or reducing it to some insignificant level, that would be just as effective as sending in troops.

Poland has a $25-billion to $27-billion debt that has been burdening the government. National income is 15 per cent under 1980; coal

Kilpatrick: "The June election in Israel, which restored Prime Minister Menachem Begin to power by the slimmest possible margin, has caused the opponents of Camp David to come to the forefront."

production is off 20 per cent; copper, grain, cattle production – all down. Exports are off 20 per cent. Carl mentioned those lines for food. If they have a brutally hard winter this year, it will be very serious.

Wille: This ties in with what you and Sylvia and Harrison were talking about earlier – the Middle Eastern money invested in the United States. Much of that Polish foreign debt you mentioned is owed to Western banks. I imagine the Soviet leaders have to take that into consideration as they think about how to handle Poland.

Kilpatrick: Yes – about $16 billion of the debt is owed to banks.

Rowan: This also ties in with our earlier discussions about how we spend our money, how much we put into the military. I asked Caspar Weinberger – our secretary of defense – "Suppose they move into Poland. Is there anything we can do?" He said, "Well, I will tell you the truth. We do not have the conventional military forces to do anything, and that is why I am so strongly in favor of this military build-up. We have got to build up our conventional forces so that we have some way of responding other than a resort to nuclear war."

Nault: "For more than a year now, the world has been watching Poland. And what the result of all the efforts at democratic reform will be is still uncertain."

Nault: Harrison, how do you view this nuclear arms build-up, the missile race, that seems to be developing – and that has caused so many massive protests in Western Europe?

Brown: I am very apprehensive about the whole situation, which you have to talk about in several contexts. First, with respect to what you might call the deterrent forces – which we have relied upon for a long time to keep from getting into a nuclear war. The theory is that if one side launches an attack, it knows full well that it is going to be destroyed itself in the process. The question that is being debated in the United States now is whether the Soviet Union has the power to carry out a first strike and so destroy our forces that we will not be able to strike back effectively. I think statements to the effect that they are capable of carrying out such a strike successfully are considerably exaggerated. There is more than one reason for this, but the main reason is that it is extremely difficult to get at submarines, and submarines are a major part of our own strike force.

There also has been a lot of fuzzy talk concerning what a deterrent is. To have a deterrent to Soviet attack, does this mean we have to be able to destroy every single city in the Soviet Union? As far as I am concerned, if I were a Russian and the U.S. threat was to destroy only 100 cities, that would deter me pretty well from making a first strike. You probably could even narrow it down to five or six cities.

Let me carry this one step further and talk about the large, very expensive complexes of land-based missiles designed to be very hard, or protected from attack. My own feeling is that these are not needed. I would much rather see the money put into the submarine operation, if we feel that we need more of a deterrent force than we now have.

So that is the first part – do we need the big, long-range missiles? The second part involves intermediate-range missiles. The Soviet Union's missiles are aimed directly at Western Europe, and we are attempting to counter that with more missiles of our own in Europe. As long as the Soviets' are aimed at Europe, I think we have to counter that. This is a dangerous situation. I see no way that – once all the missiles are in place – you are going to avoid using them if a war breaks out. I think the only hope lies in a negotiated settlement to reduce the number of such weapons in Europe.

So we have all the demonstrations in Western Europe against the deployment of more missiles by the North Atlantic Treaty Organization, as you've mentioned, Bill. I think it would be a shame if the demonstrators win, simply because it would create a terribly one-sided situation – the Russians already having their missiles there.

Nault: To end the day, I'd like to ask each of you your general reaction to the year that is coming to a close and your feeling about what 1981 might mean for the months or years ahead.

Kilpatrick: I think 1981, like most other years, has been a good year and a bad year. We've talked perhaps not enough about the good things that have happened. I look back over the year and think of *Voyager 2* – a fantastic achievement for American science and technology to have sent that spacecraft all the way to Saturn to send back those

Rowan: "It was a measure of the magnitude of this crisis in Poland that you could get the leader of Solidarity, the head of government, and the head of the Roman Catholic Church there to sit down and talk about what could be done to defuse the situation. But I still believe that the Soviets are going to move into Poland."

magnificent pictures of a part of the universe we'd known very little about before. I also would put on the side of good news the fact that the Supreme Court of the United States finally has its first woman justice, Sandra Day O'Connor.

I do have some deep concerns about 1981. I am perhaps most concerned domestically about our system of education. The public schools are not doing the job, somehow. What the reasons are, I don't know, but the continuing steady decline in the achievement levels of our high school graduates is a cause for concern.

If I had another national concern to express, it would be over the degree of violent crime in our society. People are afraid to go out of their houses at night in our major cities. Something has happened to our national mores. It is also reflected in the figures on illegitimacy. The number of illegitimate births as a percentage of all births is going up rapidly. The stigma that used to be attached to having a child out of wedlock or living together out of wedlock is just about gone. Something fundamental is changing in our society in that regard. I don't think it is changing for the good, so I have a certain sympathy for the people in the Moral Majority, so-called, who are deeply concerned about the erosion of these old social and moral values.

Rowan: One of my concerns about 1981 centers around the fact that people are so eager to fight inflation or to reindustrialize America that they forget the human components of what is going on in this society. Jack mentioned crime. The crime rate is going up, and I don't think it is going down soon, because we have in this society millions of Americans who not only feel alienated, but are alienated. They are in America, but they are not part of America. We have millions of youngsters who see violence – not just on the television, not just in the movies, but in their real life, their real families. They never see much of anything else, and they have no hope. I can tell you that there are millions of Americans who more or less accept this as part of the American way of life. They assume that a segment of this population is uneducable, so they don't worry about whether or not we are really educating these people. I know what racial conflict did in the 1960s. I do not want the economic programs of 1981 to become the basis for class conflict in America, which would be even more destructive.

Brown: First of all, I agree with Jack about *Voyager 2*. The *Voyager* achievement is just beyond belief from a technological point of view. No other people, including the Russians, have accomplished that, and we can feel very proud. But I would suggest that certain things – certain budgetary things – that have happened in 1981 may decrease our capability of achieving such things in the future – may tend to decrease that capability from the point of view of education, from the point of view of research and development appropriations.

Secondly, my main concern involves prospects of nuclear war, and I suggest that maintaining a dialogue with the Russians is the most important single thing that we can do. We've got to negotiate at all levels – intercontinental ballistic missiles, short-range missiles, our armaments in Europe, and so forth.

Cremin: I think the revolution that we began in the 1770s was a revolution to bring into being a kind of society that could give John Doe and Mary Roe and Mr. Average Person or Unaverage Person as good a life as each could conceivably make. That has been the meaning of our revolutionary ideal around the world in competition with other revolutions and other ideals. We have made enormous strides in enabling the average person to realize his or her capabilities.

During the 1920s and 1930s, we faced a crossroads in our society — involving whether we would like each person to try to make it on his or her own. If you made it, you had the goods of society. If you didn't make it, you fell by the wayside. In the 1930s, we decided that some problems are so big that we have got to collaborate as a society to help everybody get as far as everybody can get. But now, under the Reagan Administration, I think we are going back to a time when individualism becomes the rule again, and we say to people, "Everybody has a chance. Try it. If you make it, fine. If you don't make it, you fall by the wayside." I would like to see a better balance than we've had over the past year between a reassertion of that individualism and our societal responsibility for seeing that everybody gets as far as he or she can get in society.

Brown: "My main concern involves the prospect of nuclear war, and I suggest that maintaining a dialogue with the Russians is the most important single thing that we can do."

Porter: To me, inflation has been a profound challenge that we as a nation ignored far too long. Inflation at a rate in the double digits would mean the destruction of our dollar in a short period, leading to the possible destruction of our system. When 1981 began, there was a great hope on the part of the United States that we had found some kind of answer in our new Administration. I think we have not found the answer we hoped for. Inflation is indeed coming under control to some extent, but at the same old price of an economic downturn. What I fear more than anything else, as a result, is class warfare – to bring up what you were warning about, Carl. I see a danger of the rich against the poor. I see the fire next time breaking out in a different sort of way – not in terms of color or race, as last time, but in terms of class. I am worried about the kind of warfare and pulling apart that I thought was long behind us.

Schey: I have two concerns as I look at America. They have already been expressed here today, but in a different way. As I've said, I think business and our economy are built on a foundation of confidence. In fact, our form of democratic government is based on that same confidence, on the ability to believe strongly that we can, as a nation, cope with the problems that confront us and that we can at the same time provide individual opportunity for people. My first concern is that I see an erosion of that self-confidence. I see doubts about where we're going and how we're going to get there. My second and greater concern is that out of that loss of confidence, out of that doubt, the upper class – the so-called rich – will elect into public office a leader who will help solve the problems of crime, of class warfare, of social injustice, by the power of his office, not by more democratic, legitimate means. He will say, "I'll make you feel secure. I will put four National Guardsmen at every corner." To bring to office that type of person might serve some useful social or economic purpose in the short run. But the loss of freedom we would experience, and the loss of our free enterprise system as we know it, would be the greatest tragedy history could record.

Nault: And on that cautionary note, Ralph, I think we'll end today's discussion. I want to thank all of you for gathering here in Carl Rowan's home, as we've ranged broadly over some of the important issues of 1981 – in the United States, in the Middle East, and in Poland – and tried to see how those issues may resolve themselves in the years to come.

For further reading:

Numerous articles in THE WORLD BOOK ENCYCLOPEDIA provide valuable background information on some of the matters discussed in this Focus article. These articles include BUDGET (Government Budgets); ECONOMICS; GOVERNMENT REGULATION; MIDDLE EAST; NATIONAL DEFENSE; ORGANIZATION OF PETROLEUM EXPORTING COUNTRIES (OPEC); POLAND; TAXATION; and WELFARE.

Special Reports

1976
1977
1978
1979
1980
1981

Six articles give special treatment to subjects of current importance and lasting interest.

54 **Leader for These Times,**
an interview with President Ronald Reagan, conducted by Hugh Sidey
74 **The Plight of the Panda,**
by Nancy Nash
92 **The Threats to Our Water Supply**
by Peter Gwynne
108 **Shuttle Opens New Space Era**
by Marsha F. Goldsmith
122 **The Airport's Unseen City**
by Mark Perlberg
138 **A Robot in Your Future?**
by William J. Cromie

See "The Plight of the Panda," page 90.

Leader for
These Times

An interview with President Ronald Reagan,
conducted by Hugh Sidey

**Reagan talks about his first year as President – why he
wanted the job, what he likes most about it, what he
likes least, and what in his life prepared him for it**

Ronald Reagan pops a cough drop into his mouth with apologies.
He has been talking all day long and his voice is now raspy, he says.
And now he is getting ready for another hour's conversation about his
work, his life – his presidency. He is number 40 in the American
caravan of power that has stretched beyond two centuries. Most
Presidents have succeeded. A handful have been great. No President
has really failed, though some have been only fair, and one was
disgraced. The country still runs; the shop is open for business. The
United States remains strong, though worried about Soviet power.
The United States continues to be the hope of all free nations, the
secret envy of Communist societies, though the United States is
nervous about its economic health.

The author and interviewer:
Hugh Sidey is contributing editor for *Time* magazine and writes a column on the presidency.

Ronald Reagan, a former Iowa sportscaster and motion-picture actor, is leader for these times. For this reporter, who grew up listening to "Dutch" Reagan's broadcasts, it is an extraordinary event to encounter him in the Oval Office of the White House. His voice is much the same as it was nearly half a century ago. A few wrinkles have been added to his face in those five decades, but he appears remarkably as he did then.

Reagan, at age 69, was the oldest President to assume office. His background makes him one of the most unique persons to enter the presidential fraternity. And his impact on Washington, D.C., in his first year was perhaps the most impressive of any President since Franklin D. Roosevelt in 1933. Still, capturing the respect of Washington and winning legislative victories in Congress, all of which Reagan did with unexpected skill in 1981, are only the first steps in that long, tough road of governing a nation of 230 million people in a dangerous world. Reagan's task now is to capture the minds and hearts of the people of the United States, to turn his speeches and the parchment of statutes into real events in the lives of all Americans.

Such a task is difficult under the best of conditions, but Reagan came to the White House in a time of singular crisis. The United

As key members of the Executive Office of the U.S. government, top White House aides and Vice-President George H. W. Bush meet with the President frequently.

States faces another nation that is deeply hostile to it and that may be more powerful. That nation is the Soviet Union. And the United States in the past few years has begun to reach the limits of its resources and wealth. It must import nearly half of its oil and some supplies of many critical minerals. The exuberance of the post-World War II years in which everything seemed possible — "We can have both guns and butter," said President Lyndon B. Johnson — gave way to the realization that the federal government could not do all of the things it wanted to do or was asked to do by the people who formed it. Indeed, Reagan won power by his promise to reduce the burden and the hand of big government and to guide America to renewed global influence.

The crisis that Reagan encountered was far different from others so familiar to the nation's capital. It was a crisis of spirit, of trust. Was the American dream lost? Could the United States capture its old vitality? The political labels of Democrat and Republican and the philosophical shadings of liberal and conservative meant far less than before in the shifting sands of global and national events that are brought with stunning speed to almost everyone's awareness by television, the modern stage for power politics. The complexities of today's economies and the peril in weapons added undreamed-of dimensions to the challenge for this new President.

In a city that has seen other crises and always found a solution, hope never dies. Thousands gathered on Pennsylvania Avenue the night in 1963 they brought John F. Kennedy's body back from Dallas, wondering if the government would falter under the tragedy. It did not. The city was scorched and looted in the aftermath of the assassination of Martin Luther King, Jr., in 1968, but it steadied itself and trudged back to work the next week. When Richard M. Nixon went on television on a humid August night in 1974 to announce that he would resign from the presidency, those people who wield authority in Washington watched and wondered once again. In the end, they marched off under a new man, under a new banner.

Now it is Ronald Reagan's turn. His battle cry is for more elbow-room for each citizen. His watchword is for a stronger America ready again to use its strength to hold freedom's borders around the globe.

On this day late in 1981, he is gracious, ready with a few of his

As chief of state, the President is ceremonial head of the government. *Below,* Reagan decorates *Columbia* space shuttle astronauts John W. Young, at Reagan's left, and Robert L. Crippen, center, after their successful flight.

inexhaustible stories about his Iowa days or his years making movies. Here and there in the Oval Office are the first marks of his own tenure. A jar of his favorite jellybeans is on a table. Pictures of his family are behind the desk. But much remains the same in this special place. The mounds that President Thomas Jefferson had graded on the south lawn to add interest to the landscape still rise gracefully below the White House. The huge elm tree that President John Quincy Adams planted in 1826 has shed its leaves, but its proud trunk stands as sentinel for the White House. Far beyond the windows of the Oval Office rises the stark spike of the Washington Monument, and Jefferson's own graceful memorial is in the distance. The heritage for Ronald Reagan is rich. The duties are immense. He talks about them both.

Hugh Sidey: When did you decide that you could be President of the United States?

President Ronald Reagan: I could say, being the kind of guy who always hates to predict a victory, probably on the day that I stood there with a towel around me and heard the President [Jimmy Carter] on the phone congratulating me. But, no, I know that the general belief is that I started way back in 1968, and that isn't true. I never lifted a finger in '68. I had only become governor [of California]

As chief of state, the President also receives foreign heads of state. In August, Reagan held a dinner, *below,* for Egypt's President Anwar el-Sadat. After Sadat's assassination in October, Reagan says, his first reaction was "the horror of the event." Then he felt "a very great personal sense of loss."

He doesn't think the presidency is too big a job for one person, Reagan tells THE YEAR BOOK: "I think it got that reputation . . . only because the federal government has usurped too many things that it shouldn't be doing."

in January 1967. What happened in '68 was very strange. Against my wishes, I was persuaded to be a favorite-son candidate [for the presidential nomination] only to prevent — in the aftermath of the '64 debacle and all its bitterness — another party-splitting primary in California.

There were people who kept insisting, with regard to '76 — which is why I got into it then. Again, I will have to say, no one prayed harder than I did that Jerry [President Gerald R. Ford] would be so far out in front that there wouldn't be any need for anyone to do it.

Sidey: Why did you feel that you wanted to step in at that point?

Reagan: It came from the people. I've always said that they tell you whether you should be a candidate or not. This pressure began coming in, and it was just based on the fact that they believed they wanted a choice. They expressed that, and so I finally said I'd run.

Sidey: At some point, Mr. President, you must have had a notion that you could do it as well as the fellow in the office. Did that occur to you?

Reagan: Yes, it did during the last four years, based on my experience in California. I always felt that I had taken that job at a time when the situation was a duplicate at the state level of what's going on here at the federal level — that the state was spending more than it was taking in. The state government had grown about 2½ times the rate of the increase in population, and it was one of the fastest-growing states in the country. And some of the things that we did there worked – in fact, many of them. And I did feel then that there was an answer to the problems here.

Sidey: Presidents have been assassinated, frustrated, driven from office, their health destroyed – you knew all that and yet you still got into that race. Why?

Reagan: Because I felt that we couldn't go on the way we were, and I felt maybe that's what the California experience was all about. Maybe we could do something about it.

Sidey: You've been in office about a year. What has helped you the most?

Reagan: I suppose all of us are the sum total of all the things that have happened to us back through our lives. The most obvious preparation as to actual understanding of the job and the responsibilities came in the eight years of being governor of the largest state in the Union. Now, it almost seems as if there must have been some planning.

Of course, the state doesn't have a foreign policy; but while I was governor, the President sent me on several international missions, not just the ribbon-cutting things. For example, I was in Taiwan meeting with Chiang Kai-shek while Henry [Henry A. Kissinger] was making the final details in Peking for Nixon's visit [to the People's Republic of China]. And I was there to convince them that this did not mean we were abandoning our old friends. When we saw each other for the first time after that, Henry said to me, "Never again." He said, "Every morning the Chinese were waiting for me with what you'd said in Taiwan." And he said, "All I can say to them is that in America anyone can say anything." I was sent again, this time to six countries in Europe and to the NATO [North Atlantic Treaty Organization] headquarters and met with the heads of state.

And following that there were two other trips. The first one was not as serious as the other trips. That one was to the Philippines for the opening of the great cultural center there. But then we came back to Australia and New Zealand, took a trip to Japan, to Taiwan, to Singapore, to Thailand, to Saigon [South Vietnam] – when Saigon was still standing – and to South Korea. And that had to give me something that would have been missed normally.

I have to go back to Hollywood days for something else. Shortly after I was in Hollywood, the Screen Actors Guild had a vacancy on the board, and I was appointed. I was just a young newcomer with Warner Brothers. It ended up that probably for the better part of 25 years, I was on the committee that negotiated the contract every couple of years when it would expire. In the last several years, I was in charge of the negotiations. I have to say I can't discount how much I learned about sitting across the table and negotiating.

Somebody may say, "Well, you can't compare Hollywood to a summit conference." I don't know. Those old robber barons that built the motion-picture industry were still in charge then, and they were pretty formidable competition.

Sidey: Is the job of being President tougher than you had imagined?

Reagan: No. As a matter of fact, I find I sleep well nights.

Sidey: Is there anything particularly different about it from what you had perceived from the outside?

Reagan: Again, I would have to say that maybe California prepared me for this. You have to remember that a great many Presidents in recent years have come by way of the legislative process. It used to be, in the old days, that the ranks of the governors were where you looked for Presidents. The fact that every day I get a piece of paper late in the day that tells me what I'm going to be doing every 15 minutes the next day — well, I'm used to that. I remember one day looking at that schedule, and I finally called in the young lady that was in charge of scheduling there, and I said, "When do I have time to be governor?" — you know, thinking maybe she was to blame. I said, "Tell me, how many requests for appointments do you turn down for every one I do?" She said, "Forty." I quit complaining.

Sidey: Do you see, from the inside now, that the presidency is really impossible, or that it is too big for a single person?

Reagan: No.

Sidey: Would you change anything?

Reagan: The one thing I would change is what we are trying to change. I think it got that reputation as possibly too big only because the federal government has usurped too many things that it shouldn't be doing.

I know I have talked about it and it is a cliché, but this country was established to be a federation of sovereign states. The person next in line in the country in protocol, to the President, is no one in Washington. It is the 50 governors. That is the protocol setup of our nation. And I think that if we can restore some responsibilities back to where they belong, at levels of government closer to the people — as the 10th Amendment [to the United States Constitution] calls for — we will get rid of that idea that it is too much.

I don't mean to sound smug, as if it were hard for everyone but me, but we developed in California a cabinet system that I don't believe has ever been tried nationwide. That is, for all of the issues that confront us, instead of just being between me and the Cabinet member under whose province that particular problem comes, we have regular Cabinet meetings with an agenda. And those things go out on the table and, like a board of directors, we round-table them and everybody pitches in with their views. The only difference between those meetings and a board of directors is, we don't take a vote. I realize when I've heard enough, I have to make the decision.

Sidey: You are the chairman.

Reagan: Yes.

Sidey: I'm sure you are familiar with Jefferson's definition of the office as the "splendid misery," which suggests that he loved the power but abhorred the public buffeting. You are in a season of criticism. Is that too tough?

Reagan: You can get frustrated sometimes, annoyed sometimes,

As the nation's chief executive, Reagan named Sandra Day O'Connor to be the first woman on the U.S. Supreme Court, *above left.* Because the U.S. Constitution says the President must see that the laws are "faithfully executed," Reagan had letters sent firing air-traffic controllers who were striking illegally, *above.*

because you'll find yourself being criticized for something and you can't respond because you know all the facts. You can't reveal the facts in order to respond to the criticism. So you have to sit and take it.

When it gets too tough, I always think back. The best picture that I was ever in was a thing called *Kings Row*. I have never been in a picture that was as badly panned by the critics as *Kings Row*. Today, they talk about it as one of the 10 great pictures of all time, and so forth. I don't know why, but the critics just said it was a picture about people you wouldn't want to know, and no one could understand why it was made. Everybody hated it but the audience, and they loved it.

Sidey: So that brings you through.

Reagan: I think that role brings that back sometimes.

Sidey: What is the most difficult part of the job as you see it after a year?

Reagan: Well, in that do you mean. . . .

Sidey: I am talking about just what seems to be the hardest thing. Whether it is to get your point of view across, or to get our viewpoint into foreign capitals? Just what seems to cause you the most trouble?

Reagan: The reason I asked you that was because I didn't know whether you meant it that way, or whether you meant what is the heaviest thing on your back here. I suppose it is dealing with the legislature, with the Congress. That is true, I guess, out there in the 50 states.

Sidey: Does it take more of your time and energy, the congressional relationship?

Reagan: There are an awful lot of claims on your time, that is true. But the President is the only elected official in Washington who represents all the people. Senators have been sent here to represent their states. Congressmen are sent here, and their first representation is to their districts. You go up here [to Congress] with something that single-mindedly you believe is of benefit to the country, and you are talking to individuals who are sincere but are weighing it from the angles of, well, "What does it do to my state?" or, "What does it do to my district? Where does my first loyalty lie?"

Now, it's true we all say our first loyalty is to the government as a whole and to the country as a whole. But, still, an individual who represents a particular district has to say, "Well, my share of the country has a very definite view on this." And if it's counter to what you're trying to do, he feels he's got to explain how he could go with you and not with them.

Sidey: So it's this business of trying to keep the national interest focused.

Reagan: Yes. I think I am the lobbyist for the people. All of them.

"We have regular Cabinet meetings with an agenda," says Reagan. "The only difference between those meetings and a board of directors is, we don't take a vote. I realize when I've heard enough, I have to make the decision."

Sidey: When you were shot, Mr. President, did you have any second thoughts — either then, in that fleeting moment, or later — about having become President?

Reagan: No. I felt that possibly there'd be a change in my life from then on. Of course, you know, at first I didn't know I was shot. When I got out of the car and walked into the hospital, I still thought that the Secret Service man had broken my rib. I was coughing up blood, and I thought, "Well, the broken rib's punctured my lung." And I walked in, and — to the first young lady that came rushing to meet me — I said, "I'm having trouble breathing." And at this time, more blood. It wasn't until they peeled me that they found out I'd been shot.

Sidey: But in that recovery period, when you reflected on the hazards of the job, did it alter any of your attitudes?

As commander in chief of the armed forces, the President attends graduation ceremonies at the U.S. Military Academy at West Point.

Reagan: No. I found myself wondering about things. I've always enjoyed the crowd, and I've always felt a responsibility to them. I remember here in Washington before the inauguration that I would come out of Blair House, and there'd be a crowd always across the street.

I used to like to put my foot up when the door of the car was open so that I could at least recognize the people who had waited there to see me. I felt a responsibility to stand up and wave back. And I found myself thinking, "Well, I guess that's something that I won't be able to do because I was just coming out of a building and right there from among the press this fellow shot me."

And so I thought some things would be changed. But, no, I never had any feelings like, "Get me out of here."

Sidey: What about things like your faith, your religious belief, your sense of mission in the presidency? Did those alter any?

Reagan: No. I've always believed that there is a plan for everybody. My mother raised me and my brother with an abiding faith that no matter what happened in our childhood — and many unhappy things did happen — everything that happened happened for a reason and for the best. And you might not be able to understand why at the time, but if you put up with it, there would come a day when you'd look back and say, "Well, yes, I can see why this happened."

Sidey: I think you've answered my next question. I was going to ask you how come you don't get discouraged as I've seen other Presidents. I guess that might be rooted in that parental training.

Reagan: I think so.

Sidey: Is there anything, as you look back over this year, that really surprised you in events in the world or encounters with other leaders or developments on Capitol Hill?

Reagan: Oh, now, I'm trying to think back. There are so many stupendous things that have happened worldwide. The tragedies like Sadat [Egypt's President Anwar el-Sadat, who was assassinated in October], who was just here and all. Things of that kind.

Sidey: Have the Russians been tougher than you had thought?

Reagan: No. Here again is a funny thing. And, again, this is going to sound strange, trying to draw a parallel between Hollywood and world affairs. But there has been a great rewriting of history since the early post-World War II days. I found myself president of the Screen Actors Guild at the time when all of the things broke in Hollywood in the so-called blacklisting.

The real blacklisting was done by Communists. They destroyed careers of people that wouldn't go along with them. And they finally called a jurisdictional strike. They had gotten control — I think there are 43 unions — of the picture business. And a little group of them, kind of rebelling against the AFL and the CIO, had formed a thing called the Hollywood Conference of Studio Unions. This came into being during World War II, while most of us were gone.

I was not a Red-baiter. As a matter of fact, I was a stubborn resister to that. I came back, and even when my own brother tried to tell me

"The President is the only elected official in Washington who represents all the people," says Reagan. In his State of the Union address, *left,* he speaks before members of Congress, who represent their states or districts.

Presidents usually are active in influencing legislation. They may, for example, meet with congressional leaders or send Congress special messages or, *as at left,* drafts of bills they want passed. They also may veto bills they oppose.

As the leader of his political party, the President appears at a gathering in Virginia to support a Republican Party candidate in the November 1981 election.

that these things had gone on in Hollywood, I couldn't believe it. And I was a New Deal Democrat at the time. I said, "Don't give me all of that."

They claimed it was a jurisdictional strike. Management was helpless because this was a fight between two unions – involved only 350 people in the whole picture business, as to whether they should be in this union or that union.

I had proposed that the guild ask both factions and management to sit at a table with us as the neutral party – noninvolved, who could guarantee fairness – and see if we could not arrive at a solution that would keep our people from all being laid off. At these meetings, it was like Panmunjom [site of the truce talks to end the Korean War]. These meetings went on for seven months, daily. And we kept the studios open. We made a decision early that the Screen Actors Guild had to abide by its contract at the studios, and we went through the [picket] lines. Finally, those mass picket lines were made up of waterfront workers that Harry Bridges [long-time president of the International Longshoremen's and Warehousemen's Union] provided. And you'd go through thousands of them. You'd meet early in the morning at buses. You'd get a call at midnight, telling you where your bus would be in the morning. They wouldn't even tell you the day before. And I remember I got to our bus one day, and everybody was standing around waiting for another bus because ours was still on fire from the bomb that had been thrown at it. And this went on in Hollywood.

But time after time, we would arrive at what we thought was just right on the edge of settling, and everybody good-naturedly would go home in the evening and say, "We'll come back at 10 o'clock in the morning for these meetings and wind it up." Then, at 10 o'clock in the morning, they'd be in there with 17 new demands that had never before been introduced.

And this is where I learned. This was where I got an education also, because it is documented. It was a Communist undertaking. And I have found that internationally, the tactics aren't much different. They follow the same tactics.

I even found myself on the board of directors of a Communist-front organization. And several of us discovered this and finally decided to make sure — "Well, is it true or not?" This included people like [playwright and producer] Dore Schary, [President Franklin D. Roosevelt's son] James Roosevelt, [actress] Olivia de Havilland, myself, and several others. So we introduced a statement — a policy statement — that we knew no domestic Communist could ever support, and we presented it, and we were the only votes for it. And we resigned from the organization's board, and — believe it or not — the organization went out of existence. We were the front behind which they could hide.

Sidey: Over this last year, Mr. President, was there a worst moment?

Reagan: A worst moment? The whole budget-and-tax thing. We were supposed to be even further behind on that as the day of voting came than we were on AWACS [congressional approval of the sale of Airborne Warning and Control System airplanes to Saudi Arabia]. On both of them, when the day dawned for the voting, we were behind. It was easy to be awfully low then and you start to say, you know, "Where do we pick it up and start over again to come out with a victory?"

Your next question is, when was the highest moment?

Sidey: Yes.

Reagan: I was in Los Angeles when the word came that we had made it on that first vote, on the economic package. I had been sitting there. I had to go to L.A., but I was on the phone calling individual representatives. When the word came, when it happened, it was like a fourth-quarter win.

I'll tell you, there was a dark moment with Sadat also, because I discovered something else in this job. Your first reaction is the horror of the event, and then Nancy and I sat down and looked at each other and realized that we also felt a very great personal sense of loss. I don't know whether it is that you meet in a highly charged relationship. But in just those couple of days [during Sadat's visit to Washington] — and I found it true of many other meetings — you become friends and feel real friendship so quickly. Maybe it is all that you have in common, maybe it is the issues that must be discussed and settled between you, and the knowledge that you have of each other before you meet. But we discovered then that for both Anwar and his wife, that our feeling was — it was a personal sense, as if it was some close friend of long standing that this had happened to.

Sidey: Some of the observers of both the Ottawa and Mexican summit meetings, Mr. President, say that your personal work or rapport with those other leaders was responsible for the success of those meetings. Is this the thing that you are talking about? You get a sort of fraternity spirit when that group that runs the world, or part of it, gets together?

Reagan: I think so, and I like people.

Sidey: You haven't found any that you don't like?

Reagan: Yes, but I always try to be understanding and see why they are doing what they are doing.

Sidey: You have had power for a year. What would you say are the one, or two, or three specific things that you have accomplished in this year?

Reagan: I have wanted a closer relationship with our two neighbors than I think that our country has had. I have had some ideas about why it might not have been closer, particularly Mexico. We were the great behemoth of the North, and we were not always sensitive to that fact when we met with leaders of other countries. I think that the relationship that has been established personally with Prime Minister Pierre Trudeau of Canada and President Lopez Portillo of Mexico is better. Both have testified to that for some time.

I think that we have a better relationship worldwide than we have had. I have had over 70 meetings now, bilateral and multilateral, with heads of state and foreign secretaries — most of Asia, Southeast Asia, Europe, and a number of the African states — and I think that we have made great progress.

A specially equipped U.S. Air Force plane becomes the "flying White House" when the President takes a trip.

The economic package – I believed very strongly for many years that this is where I gradually found myself abandoning my position as a New Deal Democrat and going the other way. I found that to be able to deal with things like the economy, to get that biggest budget cut in history, the biggest tax-rate reduction in history, was a major accomplishment.

Sidey: I can see that our time is running out. The matter of living in the White House, being a symbol in the country – has it been enjoyable?

Reagan: Yes, although I learned early why Presidents found it pleasant to get to Camp David. You are kind of a bird in a gilded cage. You take the elevator home, and when you get out, that is it. You are confined there. Lovely surroundings and comfortable quarters, no question about that. But you long to be, by the end of the week, in a place where you can walk out the door and take a walk if you want to, which you can do at Camp David. You might say, "Can't you take a walk outside here?" Well, you can, but you suddenly notice that there have been a great number of [security] individuals deployed around the grounds if you do it.

Sidey: How do you keep your energy level up? We don't hear much anymore about your being 70 years old.

Reagan: I know. I am kind of relaxed and relieved about that. But I ride sometimes on a Wednesday afternoon. We kind of look to a Wednesday, if we can clear that, because it is only 20 minutes by helicopter from here to Quantico [Marine Corps Base], if we ride there. And now we have trails that you can ride at Camp David, and we trailer the horses up. But also we have restored something that used to be in the White House and seemed to have disappeared, and that is a little gymnasium. I have a daily workout that I do up there. I have never felt better in my life.

Sidey: You could still recommend that young Americans aspire to this job and get healthy?

Reagan: Yes.

Sidey: You have been called the great persuader. That is kind of a new category in that whole list of things that they have attributed to presidential power. Are you satisfied with that? Does that define you?

Reagan: I hope that it is not premature. I hope that I can continue. In this last one [the AWACS vote], all the usual clichés were applied – twisting arms, putting on pressure, and so forth. But I think that if you talk to any of the senators that you will find that all I did was try as honestly as I could to explain to them why I felt this was important, being able to bring about peace in the Middle East. They usually came in very concerned, either worried excessively about whether we were giving away some technology that we should not or whether we were reducing Israel's position in relation to us. I tried to convince them that we had protected the technology, and I could give them the evidence why. The other reason was that I felt that it was the best thing that we could do for Israel. This country has a moral obligation that it is never going to forsake with regard to Israel. But

"The presidency is an institution . . . and you are given temporary custody of it," Reagan tells THE YEAR BOOK in the Oval Office interview.

the greatest security for Israel lies in peace. They cannot go on forever as an armed camp surrounded by enemies that outnumber them 100 to 1. We have seen one enemy that had fought recurrent wars with them – Egypt – actually turn to a peace treaty. They are getting along. You have to assume that other countries can be persuaded to do this too. So this is what I used for persuasion.

You said something about how I viewed the presidency and so forth, and view the job. I have always felt that the presidency is an institution in and of itself, and you are given temporary custody of it. That is why I have always felt that there are certain things that go with it. They might be personally kind of embarrassing and make you self-conscious. But you have no right to change those things, because they are not yours. They belong to the office. For example, "Hail to the Chief," and so forth. If that is the tradition and the thing that goes with it, then all right. That goes with the job, and it is not yours personally to do with as you choose.

Sidey: The power and the establishment are on loan.

Reagan: Those traditions have grown up, yes, and they must be there for a reason. I would not think, for example, that if I did not like Camp David I would have a right to sell it. It belongs with the institution. If I don't want to use it, then I don't use it. I *do* use it — I enjoy it.

Sidey: What would you like the history books to say about you?

Reagan: I guess that I would like for them to be approving and maybe to say that I made individual freedom a little more secure. I know that we have got to go. But you didn't ask what I liked least about the job.

Sidey: What is that?

Reagan: There is one thing, seriously. I think that the hardest thing to bear with — and maybe this was brought home more on March 30th [when Reagan was shot] — is the security aspect. Not that these men are not wonderful. They are magnificent, these security men. It is not that. They are not in the way at all. They do everything in their power to give you as much freedom as you can have, so it is not from that angle.

What I mean is the knowledge that as much as you might want to walk into that happy-faced crowd that has waited and waited to see you or to shake your hand, you have to abide by the restrictions that they place on you — because they know and you don't. I mean your security men. You represent a risk to others. You know, I came out just about better than anyone else who was hit.

You would be a threat to others, for example, in today's world, to go to a football game or something of that kind. That, I think, is one thing that you are conscious of and that bothers you. There are things that I am reluctant to do, not because of me, but because I might get somebody else hurt.

Sidey: Thank you, Mr. President.

As always in these interviews, the time rushes by too quickly. Questions remain unanswered and answers remain ungiven, which is the perpetual state of that office. Events propel the life of a President. Every minute of his working time is scheduled. Now, the office fills with nervous aides who must move him along to other duties. Reagan is still smiling, warm, and accommodating. "You haven't gotten through all your questions," he notes, realizing that it just cannot be, but he wants to offer a touch of sympathy. He has small jars of jelly-beans for his guests, and a firm handshake. Then he turns briskly and without hesitation moves out of this brief, calm interlude back into the clamorous and impatient world.

For further reading:

Heineman, Ben W., Jr., and Hessler, Curtis A. *Memorandum for the President.* Random House, 1980.

Neustadt, Richard E. *Presidential Power.* John Wiley & Sons, 1980.

Reedy, George E. *Twilight of the Presidency.* New American Library, 1971.

Rose, Richard. *Managing Presidential Objectives.* The Free Press, 1976.

Rossiter, Clinton. *The American Presidency.* Harcourt Brace Jovanovich, 1960.

Schlesinger, Arthur M., Jr. *The Imperial Presidency.* Houghton-Mifflin, 1973.

Sickels, Robert J. *The Presidency.* Prentice-Hall, 1980.

Tourtellot, Arthur B. *The Presidents on the Presidency.* Doubleday & Co., 1964.

The Plight of the Panda

By Nancy Nash

Efforts to ensure the survival of one of the world's most endearing – but endangered – animals are going into high gear

High on a steep slope in the mountainous territory of southwest China, a female giant panda peered through the bars of a trap. Although she was uninjured, she was unhappy about her confinement. Bleating plaintively, she gazed at a small group of biologists standing a few feet away in a fall of fresh snow. The biologists – a team of scientists from the People's Republic of China and the United States – were as apprehensive as their captive. Their job was to fit the bearlike creature with a miniature radio collar. The panda – later named Zhen-Zhen, meaning Precious – would be only the second of its species to wear such a collar and transmit round-the-clock information about panda life in the wild. The same scientific team had captured and radio-collared a male a few days earlier.

There was an element of danger in what the scientists were doing. First, the panda had to be sedated, and the use of a drug always presents some risk. Too much might kill the animal; too little could leave her only groggy but still able to injure the biologists. Furthermore, although the group observing her was experienced and prepared with fine equipment, they were acutely aware that they were not dealing with just any animal. Here was a wild panda, an individual of a very rare species, a national treasure of China, and the symbol of the World Wildlife Fund – a conservation group dedicated to the rescue of all endangered species.

The scientists calculated that Zhen-Zhen's weight was about 220 pounds (100 kilograms). One of them drew the proper dose of sedative into a syringe attached to the end of a pole. The pole, pushed through the bars of the cage, was aimed at the animal's thigh; as the syringe was plunged home, the panda roared. For a moment, tension lessened among the people clustered around the cage. Then the biologists exchanged wry looks; the heavy-duty needle had been bent double on Zhen-Zhen's thick hide. Another try brought success, however, and after a few minutes the animal nodded. But she remained awake. Finally, after a small additional dose, Zhen-Zhen sank into a deep sleep, and her captors went into action.

The scientists had to move quickly before the sedative wore off. Zhen-Zhen was weighed; she tipped the scales at about 190 pounds (86 kilograms) – a bit short of the 220-pound calculation. She was measured: 65 inches (166 centimeters) from her black nose to the tip of her stumpy white tail; 32 inches (81 centimeters) tall at the shoulder. One team member carefully examined her for *ectoparasites* – parasites that live on the surface of the body. There were none. Other biologists recorded physical features: Zhen-Zhen's four nipples were dark and worn – evidence that she had borne and nursed offspring, though not recently; several teeth were missing from her lower jaw; the contours of her hipbones were visible under her woolly hide. All of these findings were clues to her age. Pandas are reckoned to have a life expectancy of 25 to 30 years. On the evidence, the scientists decided that Zhen-Zhen was getting old.

It was an exciting and gratifying 30 minutes for the team that cold day in March 1981. They had spent months in Szechwan Province (Sichuan in the phonetic Pinyin alphabet that China now uses) scouring trails, examining banks of streams, and exploring thick brush for panda tracks. They had searched for droppings and for chewed bamboo stems. Weeks had been occupied piecing together the evidence they were able to collect. Traps had to be checked frequently. Now their search had been rewarded.

Throughout the examination, the scientists monitored Zhen-Zhen's pulse and breathing for any signs of overreaction to the drug. Now, finally, they fastened a collar around her neck, loose enough for comfort but tight enough to prevent it from being pawed off. Three

The author:
Nancy Nash, a free-lance writer living in Hong Kong, has made several trips into panda country.

Author Nancy Nash, sixth from left, poses with scientists, local officials, and the team that is designing the new panda research and conservation center in China's Wolong Reserve.

hours had elapsed from the moment the team had left camp to clamber up a mountainside and over a ridge to find Zhen-Zhen. And now she was sending signals from her new collar – 75 pulses per minute, indicating sleep, rest, or – in this case – a drugged doze. An hour later, however, the panda's pulse beat quickened to 100 per minute. Zhen-Zhen had come to – alert, steady on her feet, free – and trotted off. The miniature radio collar, a device already used successfully for studies of many other mammal species, joined a growing list of tools for research and conservation of the giant panda.

The use of radio collars is strongly endorsed by George B. Schaller, director of the New York Zoological Society's Animal Research and Conservation Center. Schaller, who is famous for his studies of the Serengeti lion, the mountain gorilla, and other large mammals, is also the first foreigner to share field work on pandas with Chinese scientists. Ideally, he explains, collared animals should be tracked continuously on a 24-hour-a-day schedule. "But this is clearly impractical," he says. "Instead, once a day we locate each animal and determine its location on a map. This will ultimately reveal the size of home range, extent of seasonal movement, and other data. Radios also reveal activity, information about a daily routine otherwise impossible to collect because pandas are shy and live in difficult terrain."

Such information is urgently needed if the rare giant panda is to be removed from the endangered species list. Pandas once ranged widely in China. Fossils have been found in the far north with the remains of prehistoric Peking man. Just inside the Burmese side of the southern Chinese border, a well-preserved skull of an extinct animal believed to be an ancestor of the giant panda was discovered and dated back 2 million years. With the encroachment of China's steadily increasing human population, however, and the subsequent clearing of bamboo forests and expansion of agricultural areas, pandas and other wild

The panda's "sixth finger" enables it to grasp food and hold it for eating while the animal is in a sitting position.

creatures have retreated into more remote, rugged areas. Today, when pandas are found at all, they inhabit isolated pockets of bamboo wilderness 5,000 to 10,000 feet (1,500 to 3,000 meters) above sea level in only three Chinese provinces — Szechwan, Kansu (Gansu), and Shensi (Shaanxi).

This paradise for pandas is dramatically beautiful. The forests include not only bamboo, but also numerous species of fir, pine, spruce, and mosses. There are flowering plants — flamboyant rhododendrons, vivid azaleas, and exotic orchids among them. Clear streams cut through ravines. Rivers flow through valleys. From high points, you can see the mountain ranges that rise westward to the Tibetan tablelands and peaks. The views are spectacular. At least 25 other endangered animal species — including the golden-haired monkey, the white-lipped deer, and the golden cat — share this paradise with the giant panda, as do rare bird species and many rare plants and herbs. But conditions for human intruders are difficult. Outsiders rarely venture there. The few farm families in the region are seemingly conditioned to a climate in which skies are often leaden with snow in winter or overcast with rain in other seasons. The few existing trails are narrow and treacherous.

The inaccessibility of the panda's habitat has enhanced the ani-

The Panda's Shrinking Territory

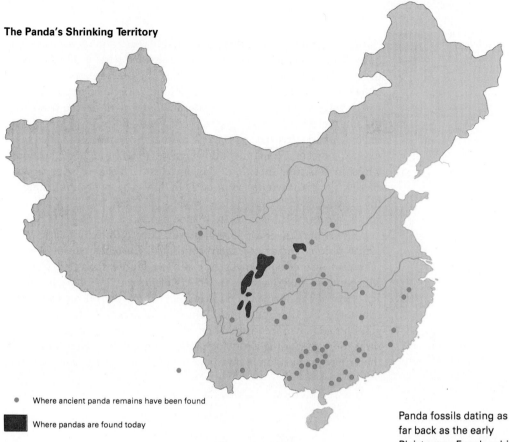

●   Where ancient panda remains have been found

■   Where pandas are found today

Panda fossils dating as far back as the early Pleistocene Epoch, which began about 1.7 million years ago, show that pandas once ranged widely in China. Today, pandas live in only three Chinese provinces.

mal's mystery, even though it has appeared under various names in ancient Chinese chronicles dating back to 2000 B.C., when a panda skin was presented as tribute from the Kingdom of Chen (now Szechwan) to the Kingdom of Yu. A Szechwan legend, so ancient that its origins are lost in prehistory, records that the panda got its black markings when it mourned the death of a human friend. The animal is also mentioned in several T'ang dynasty (A.D. 618-907) records, and a famous poet of that time wrote of the animal as having magical qualities: A screen with pandas painted on it would ward off evil when placed in front of a door. Documents from A.D. 685 indicate that the emperor of China had sent the ruler of Japan two live pandas and 70 skins. In the late 1200s, Marco Polo, the Venetian trader and traveler, saw the skins of "black and white bears" in the Imperial Palace in Peking (Beijing). But not until 1869 was the animal's existence noted in scientific textbooks in the West. That year, native hunters in Szechwan presented Jean-Pierre Armand David, a Jesuit missionary, with two giant panda carcasses that he named *Ursus melanoleucos*, or black and white bear. Père David sent these specimens to zoologist Alphonse Milne-Edwards in Paris for further study. After careful examination of the bone and dental structure of the strange beasts, Milne-Edwards concluded that pandas resembled bears only superficially. They were, he decided, more closely related to raccoons than to bears. Consequently, Milne-Edwards classified what is now known as the giant panda in a new *genus* (a group of closely related animals or plants) – *Ailuropoda*, meaning "panda foot" – because of the animal's "sixth finger," an amazingly dexterous outgrowth on the wrist with the characteristics of an opposable thumb. Because of this "sixth finger," pandas are among the few mammals, humans included, able to grasp objects in a manner allowing food to be brought to the mouth while in a sitting position. Zoologists still disagree over how to classify the giant panda. Most of them, however, believe it belongs to the raccoon family, *Procyonidae*. Some, however, put it in the bear family *Ursidae*. Still others say it should be in a family of its own.

Pandas, perhaps, have always been relatively rare, but early in the 1900s serious threats to their continued existence arose. Western scientists wanted specimens to examine. Hunters wanted trophies. Museums wanted displays. In 1929, Kermit and Theodore Roosevelt Jr., sons of the former U.S. President who were on an expedition sponsored by Chicago's Field Museum of Natural History, shot a giant panda in Szechwan. Soon after, a European hunter bagged three more, including a nursing mother and a baby. Later hunters, in the bring-'em-back-alive tradition, took up the challenge of capturing

Scientists found this panda den, *below*, in a fir tree. Rugged forest areas like those in the Wolong Reserve, *right*, are home not only to pandas, but also to many other species of plants and animals.

and transporting live pandas. In 1936, Ruth Harkness, an American who took over a panda expedition when her husband died in China, presented a cub to Chicago's Brookfield Zoo. Su-Lin, as it was called, was the first live panda seen outside of China. "Panda-monium," as the public's instant affection for the playful creature was described in news reports, broke out in the Western world.

It was a love affair that has never died. Su-Lin was followed by Happy, who, justifying his name, good-naturedly toured Europe with a German keeper, crossing the continent in a cage strapped to the top of a car and enchanting crowds wherever he appeared. Happy ended up in the St. Louis, Mo., Zoo. Then there were the London Zoo's Ming, who was shy, and later Chi-Chi, who was gregarious. And there were others – Pandora and Pan in New York City's Bronx Zoo, Mei-Lan in Chicago's Brookfield, Ping-Ping and An-An in Moscow. Each of these rare individuals kept admissions turnstiles clicking and public affection growing. Giant pandas became internationally known and admired as cuddlesome, playful creatures. But the animals had been taken out of China when the nation was in political turmoil, when Chinese authorities who might have wished to stop both "hunting-to-kill" and "hunting-to-capture" expeditions had no control over events. How many pandas were wounded in the chase?

Much of panda country is wildly beautiful, with clear rushing streams, twisted underbrush, and forests of bamboo, fir, pine, and spruce.

Sir Peter Scott, British naturalist and chairman of the World Wildlife Fund, fourth on the trail, *left*, leads the first group of foreigners invited to Wolong Reserve, in 1980. Workers build a hut for panda researchers, *below*, while a scientist radio-tracks a panda, *bottom*.

Scientists interested in
saving the panda need
to know more about the
animal's habits and the
food it depends on. Here,
a panda munches dinner,
right, while a researcher
weighs a bamboo sample,
above. Another scientist
measures a bamboo stem,
far right, while panda
droppings are collected
for analysis, *below*.

How many mothers were killed for their cubs? How many were captured and expired from thirst, inappropriate diet, or stress? No one knows.

Nor does anyone know very much about giant pandas themselves. Anatomically, the animal is unique, hence its own genus. The jaws of a giant panda could be powerful weapons, yet the animal appears to be mostly shy, solitary, and harmless. Panda's have jaws capable of cracking the bones of animals their own size and even larger, and their powerful teeth suggest that panda ancestors were probably *carnivorous* (feeding mostly on flesh). Today's giant pandas have been known to feed on fish and small rodents, but basically pandas have evolved into vegetarians with a specialized, one-item menu — bamboo. It is a dish, it turns out, with a hitch. Pandas may eat as much as 20 pounds (9 kilograms) of food per day. Once every 80 to 100 years, however, certain bamboo species in panda territory flower, produce seeds, and wither away. It then takes a few years for the seeds to produce new plants suitable as panda food. This kind of life history is unique among flowering plants, and botanists are unable to explain either why the cyclic flowering and dying occurs or the mechanism that triggers it. When this happens but only one of several species of bamboo that are growing in an area dies, the panda might lose its favorite dish, but it will still find a meal. But when this happens and kills off the one bamboo species that exists in some areas, the result is disaster for the pandas.

Such a disaster occurred in the Wanglang Reserve in Szechwan in the winter of 1975-1976. Early on, alarming reports of starving pandas had reached Chinese conservation officials. Responding quickly, they mobilized some 3,000 people to do emergency survey and rescue work. But despite their efforts, at least 138 pandas died of starvation.

How many are left? The answer underscores how little is known about the animal. Estimates range from 400 to 1,000, with most experts quoting the higher number while warning that even this number is dangerously low for any animal, and especially for an animal like the panda.

The danger is real. Giant pandas are rare to begin with, and they mature slowly. Little is known about their breeding habits, but it is generally believed they breed infrequently even in the best conditions, and produce few young even if fertile and active sexually. And, of course, their specialized diet of bamboo shoots poses a constant threat to their survival, especially today. Bamboo that bloomed widely, then died off, in southwest China in the 1880s reportedly is blooming again in the 1970s and 1980s, raising the possibility of a reduced food supply. Another serious threat to the panda's survival is *Ascaris schroederi*, a parasitic worm that shows up in half of the autopsies performed on panda carcasses. Furthermore, so little is known about the animal's life cycle — its existence in the wild, its diet, diseases, and reproductive biology — that there may well be other, more ominous threats to the panda's survival than have surfaced.

Studying the animal in its natural habitat is one key to saving it. Professor Hu Jin Chu, a native of Szechwan Province and a lifelong naturalist, has probably seen and studied more pandas — in captivity and in the wild — than anyone now or before. He explains why China, with the formidable goal of achieving modernization by the year 2000, and its struggle to feed and improve the living standards of perhaps a billion Chinese, is nevertheless concentrating considerable effort and money on an animal.

"The panda is as much a part of our cultural heritage as language or literature or the Great Wall," says Professor Hu. The animal, he notes, has been described in official documents as not only the precious property of the Chinese people, but also a precious natural heritage of concern to people all over the world. Next, he speaks as a naturalist: "Pandas are rare, but they are survivors in spite of many pressures; they may be able to teach humans something about survival. Also, when you study nature, you realize that every living thing seems to have a niche in the delicate balance of all life. Losing one leads to losing perhaps many others, and we lose it all at our own peril."

In 1980, the Chinese government pledged approximately $9 million for panda protection. Supplementary regulations were instituted to reinforce the protection from hunting and capture that the panda has had in China since the early 1950s. A system of well-planned and policed reserves is growing. Of China's present 75 reserves (compared with 55 in 1980 and fewer than 40 in 1975), 10 are primarily for the protection of the giant panda and its environment. Wolong Reserve, in Szechwan Province, with about 500,000 acres (200,000 hectares), is the largest of the 10. It is also the one least disturbed by human interference, and one of the few natural panda habitats with more than one species of bamboo. For these reasons, Wolong was selected as the site of the first international cooperative project to ensure the survival of the species — a joint China-World Wildlife Fund project that includes the field work Schaller is already engaged in with Hu and other Chinese colleagues. The fund is contributing $1 million to the project; China, $3 million.

Construction on the project, which is known as the Wolong Research and Conservation Centre, was to begin in 1981. When completed in 1983, it will be a world headquarters for panda research. It will also serve as a coordination point for exchange of information among scientists representing many disciplines, many countries, and zoos with pandas. William Conway, general director of the New York Zoological Society and probably the world's foremost expert on captive facilities for wild animals, visited Wolong in June 1980 to work with the design team on blueprints, at the invitation of the Chinese organizations responsible for the project. Conway describes

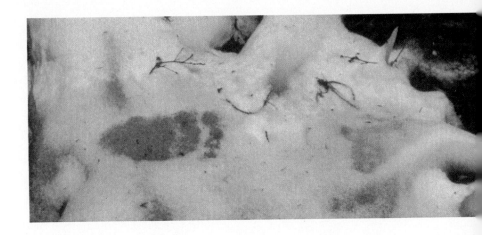

the series of low buildings that will occupy terraces and riverbanks of the reserve's main valley as practical and sophisticated. There will be laboratories for biochemistry, nutrition, and reproductive biology; libraries; and rooms for veterinary and clinical care. The most important installation will also be the largest — a series of breeding facilities that will include special cubbing dens, nurseries, and pens allowing wild pandas to mate with captives.

It is not unusual for panda females to give birth to two cubs, but in captivity in any case, only one ever survives at best. In the wild? No one knows for sure, but female pandas in the wild are thought to breed every year if the young from the previous year die. If the cub survives, however, the mother probably will breed only every other year at most. Females weighing about 250 pounds (110 kilograms) give birth to infants of about 3.5 ounces (100 grams), which are blind for more than two weeks, nearly hairless for weeks, and totally dependent on the mother for several months — several cold, dangerous, winter months.

If pandas hibernated, as bears do, the young could be assured of a measure of warmth, nourishment, and protection from predators such as leopards and a native breed of wild dog. But pandas do not hibernate. Nursing mothers, in fact, are known to travel about, without the convenience of a pouch similar to those possessed by *marsupials* — animals such as kangaroos, koalas, and opossums — whose young are raised in a *marsupium* (pouch) in the mother's body. Instead, pandas hobble along on three legs, with an offspring cradled in a forepaw. The helpless cub won't miss a meal that way, but its safety is far from that enjoyed by a baby kangaroo in a pouch, or that which a baby panda might enjoy if left in a secure den. It has been suggested, only partially tongue-in-cheek, that if pandas had been designed with pouches, whether they give birth to one or two cubs, the species might be less endangered.

The phenomenon of the perambulating panda was a subject of discussion one evening in early 1981 when Professor Hu, Schaller,

Hunting for a panda, researchers find a pawprint in the snow, *far left*. One of the hunters prepares to bait a panda trap with charred pig bones, *left*. Their efforts a success, the hunters carry their captive, *below left*.

and others gathered around a cozy fire in the midst of a tent camp perched in thick vegetation in the Choesweigo area of Wolong. Hu recalled an incident that had occurred some years earlier in Pao-hsing (Baoxing) county, another panda habitat two days travel from Wolong. Villagers there had noticed a panda walking on three legs. They thought it was injured, Hu explained, and they followed it. Information programs have educated the Chinese public to leave the creatures alone – in or outside the reserves – but to feed or help them if they seem hungry or unwell. The Pao-hsing panda became nervous and bolted, running away on all four legs. The villagers, following its trail, found a newborn panda, so tiny it was carried back to the village curled up inside a man's hat. Forestry ministry officials were notified,

and they arrived expecting to find a dead specimen but one that might yield information. Instead they found an infant with markings just beginning to show pale grey – thriving on food from the commune's kitchen.

The forestry officials left it there and later transported it, as a 100-pound (45-kilogram) cub, to Peking Zoo. In 1972, the young adult male, now named Hsing-Hsing, became a "diplomatic" panda and traveled, with a female, Ling-Ling, to the National Zoological Park in Washington, D.C., as a gift from China to President Richard M. Nixon. Unfortunately, Hsing-Hsing has been unable or reluctant to mate with Ling-Ling, but his place in panda scientific history is assured, according to Professor Hu. He is the first panda successfully hand-reared from infancy.

Why can't, or won't, Hsing-Hsing perform during mating season? "This is his natural home," says Hu, indicating with a sweep of his hand the Ch'iung-lai (Qionglai) mountain range, halfway around the world from the capital of the United States. Perhaps he is reacting naturally, as might any panda reared by humans and living in a zoo far from his native home, says Hu. Or perhaps, Hu adds, pandas – like humans and some other animals – are choosy about their mates. Or maybe something about his diet dampens his sexual drive. Or perhaps the relationship between individual male and female pandas has a delicate but critical balance. During the rare occasions when wildlife biologists have observed wild pandas during their brief spring mating season, they have noted that females in heat attract more than one potential partner before choosing a mate. It could be that in order to mate successfully, Hsing-Hsing needs first to be free-living, at liberty to wander through bamboo groves, and then, as a further stimulus, some competition with other males for Ling-Ling's favors.

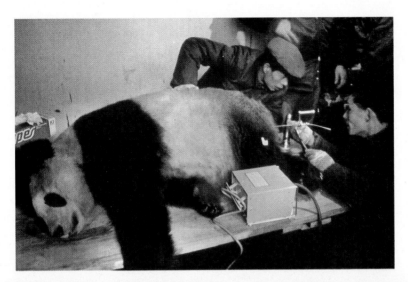

Removed from the wild, some pandas delight crowds like those at the Peking Zoo, *far left*. Meanwhile, in the lab, scientists work to refine artificial insemination techniques, *left*. Yuanjing, the first panda born as a result of such techniques, plays with its mother, Juan Juan, in 1978, *below*.

Growing up in the Peking Zoo, Yuanjing, the world's first panda baby conceived through artificial insemination, investigates the flag of the World Wildlife Fund, *above*. Far from the zoo and – it is hoped – far from extinction, a panda clings to a tree trunk in China's Wanglang Reserve, *above right*.

No one knows the answers to this critical mating question, but conservationists know that pandas, like 1,000 other animal species and 25,000 plant species, are on the brink of extinction; they may or may not survive such pressures as a shrinking habitat, specialized food requirements, susceptibility to disease, human depredation, or even the uncertainties of natural selection. If people had the power to take pandas back to the drawing board, Hu concedes, pouches would not be out of place. "But," he adds, "nature is the best designer. Pandas are the way they are for reasons prescribed by nature. It is our task to discover those reasons." There will be no fast and easy answers. Studying any little-known animal is slow, meticulous work. But there is a pioneering atmosphere to this project that gives each item of information, each glimpse of a wild panda, special excitement.

Efforts to save the giant panda from extinction include exploring ways to breed it in captivity. In 1978, Chinese scientists managed to artificially impregnate a captive female and, in September of that year, two cubs were born, one of which, Yuanjing, survived. The same female, Juan Juan, again gave birth to two cubs in September

1981, but again only one survived. A try at artificial insemination failed at the National Zoological Park in Washington, D.C., in 1980, but efforts are continuing throughout the world. Over the years, efforts to mate pandas in zoos outside China always resulted in failure. Then, in Mexico City, Mexico, the Chapultepec Zoo's Ying-Ying was successfully mated with Pe-Pe, the London Zoo's male. In August 1980, Ying-Ying gave birth to the first panda cub ever naturally conceived in captivity and the first ever born outside China. The cub was accidentally smothered by its mother eight days after birth, but Ying-Ying became pregnant again and, on July 21, 1981, gave birth to a second cub.

Far from the zoos, the mating calls of male and female pandas were heard in the wild in 1981. Even old Zhen-Zhen had enough sex appeal to attract two suitors. Her radio collar, plus strident whines and barks, allowed Schaller, panda expert Zhu Jing, and members of their team to find the animals and observe a trio during two days of a mating selection process that involved climbs up trees and chases across valleys. Finally, they saw Zhen-Zhen, having accepted one of the males, mating. In October, she gave birth to a cub.

With any luck, 1982 may see a panda "baby boom," but anxious scientists are not relying on luck. Artificial insemination equipment and procedures are being reviewed and refined. More — and more detailed — tests are being made of the panda's biology. There is increasingly careful study of the creature's life cycle. In panda habitats with only one species of bamboo, other species are being introduced experimentally. A rescue program is being worked out in case there is a disastrous blooming of bamboo. But for all of the newly introduced technology and expanded laboratory information, experts point out, much of the most important progress is going to be slow in coming. And it will be obtained painstakingly, by accumulating information in the wild. Time is short, but people dedicated to the survival of the *Da Xiong Mao* (literally, Giant Bear Cat) — as the animal is now known in China — are determined not to fail. "A world without pandas," says Hu, echoing a sentiment expressed in many ways by many people around the world, "would be a much less colorful and happy home for all of us."

For further reading:

Fagen, Robert. *Animal Play Behavior*. Oxford University Press, 1981.

Gould, Stephen Jay. "The Panda's Peculiar Thumb," *Natural History*, November 1978.

Morris, Desmond, and Morris, Ramona. *Men and Pandas*. McGraw-Hill, 1966.

Perry, Richard. *The World of the Giant Panda*. Taplinger, 1969.

"With a Little Help from Science, Panda Has Blessed Event," *Smithsonian*, September 1979.

The Threats to Our Water Supply

By Peter Gwynne

The United States faces a drier future if industry, government, agriculture, and the public fail to deal with a host of serious water-supply problems

Many Americans worry about the high price of gasoline and wonder whether there will be adequate supplies of this precious fuel in years to come, regardless of the cost. But a water shortage is actually "the most serious long-range problem now confronting the nation," according to Gerald D. Seinwill, acting director of the Water Resources Council, an agency of the United States government. "By the turn of the century," Seinwill warns, "almost every section of the country [will face] water shortages unless the nation recognizes that we cannot continue to waste and mistreat precious, finite resources."

The cause of Seinwill's concern is actually several problems that have already confronted the United States. During the past few years, nearly every American citizen has felt their impact. Let us look briefly at these problems before examining them in greater detail.

■ The movement of increasing numbers of people to the Southwest is causing water wars between dry, growing cities and moist, sparsely

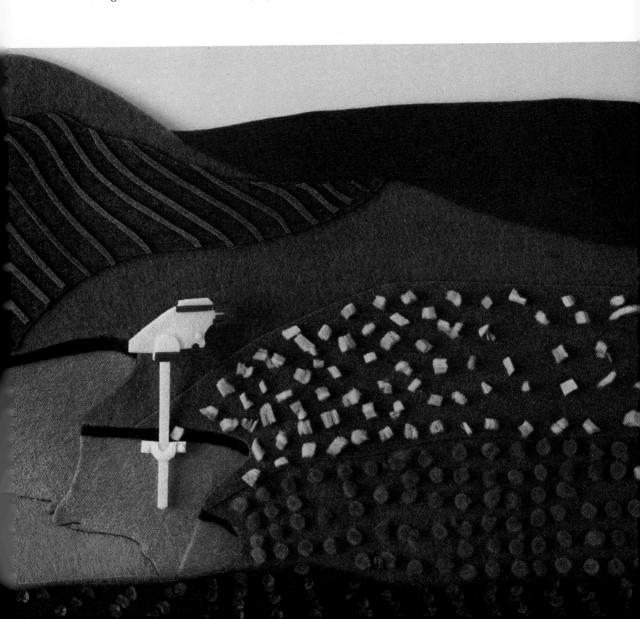

populated rural areas. Proposals to divert water from rivers have even caused conflicts among states.

■ In several parts of the nation, pollution has made supplies of drinking water less reliable than they used to be. Long-lasting chemicals from various sources are polluting underground reservoirs.

■ Even the rain is contaminated in some places. Certain pollutants released from tall factory smokestacks in the Midwest react with moisture in the air, resulting in *acid rain*.

Such problems, whether shortages or pollution, do not affect all areas of the country equally. While residents of Los Angeles, Phoenix, and other Western centers of population must be ever vigilant about their water supplies, residents of Chicago, Philadelphia, Washington, D.C., and other Eastern and Midwest cities can, in most years, use water almost without caring. In addition, most areas of the United States have avoided the worst forms of chemical contamination in their water supplies. And only those regions that are unfortunate enough to stand downwind of large industrial centers suffer the ill effects of acid rain.

Water shortages are not caused only by people, however. Nature frequently adds to the problem by providing its own shortfalls in the form of droughts. During a drought, the amount of rainfall over a particular region decreases markedly below normal levels for weeks, months, or even years. As a result, water supplies in reservoirs and water levels in rivers and lakes fall drastically, so that the amount of water available for human use drops sharply. The definition of a drought often depends on location and frequency. Desert dwellers routinely survive in areas with just a few inches of annual rainfall, while residents in the Eastern United States start to worry if fewer than 30 inches (76 centimeters) of precipitation falls in a year.

People who rely heavily on rainfall face grave danger during periods of drought, as illustrated by the stretch of subnormal precipitation in the United States that started in June 1980. By the spring of 1981, 46 states suffered from drought. The water shortage was particularly severe in two-thirds of the nation's crop-growing areas. Tractor drivers planting spring wheat in Montana sent up towering clouds of dust behind their vehicles. Iowa corn growers saw small creeks that wind through their land dry up, leaving the soil crumbly and arid instead of clumpy and moist. Long-time landowners spoke fearfully of a return to the Dust Bowl days of the 1930s, when drought and poor farming practices destroyed topsoil and the mineral content of the soil on thousands of farms on the Great Plains.

People who live in normally wet areas suffer almost as much during prolonged droughts as people who live in dry areas. The 1980-1981 drought, for example, drained upstate New York reservoirs, which New York City residents depend heavily on, to less than one-third of their capacity. New York City officials had to restrict water use accordingly. The city prohibited residents from washing their cars,

The author:
Peter Gwynne is a free-lance writer and was formerly science editor of *Newsweek* magazine.

watering their lawns, and filling their swimming pools. Mayor Edward I. Koch posed for publicity pictures shaving with a sinkful of water, rather than with running water. As a result of the conservation efforts, the city's water consumption dropped 20 per cent — from 1.5 billion to 1.2 billion gallons (5.7 billion to 4.5 billion liters) per day.

Southern Florida suffered even more severely than the Northeast during the 1980-1981 drought. It received almost no trace of the February 1981 rains that had eased the Northeast's drought. The Florida rainy season, which usually dumps 32 inches (81 centimeters) of rain between May and October, did not materialize in 1981. Lake Okeechobee dropped to the lowest level ever recorded. Citrus trees turned brown, the volume of the sugar cane crop fell drastically, and boating and fishing on the lake almost ceased. But Clarence W. Knecht, chief engineer of the United States Sugar Corporation, argued that the drought was not entirely responsible for the misery. "People are what's causing the problem," he said. "The population pressure brings a high demand for potable [drinkable] water. Now here we are with a lack of rainfall last year coupled with a lack this year while the demand is greater and greater."

The problem of drought, like other water problems, is not limited to the United States, of course. A drought in much of western Europe in 1976 turned green lawns into dusty brown stretches of scrub. As the water level in the underground reservoirs dropped, the ground itself settled, opening cracks in the foundations of buildings that had been weakened by bombing during World War II. Even the hardy nomads of the Sahel region on the southern edge of Africa's Sahara could not deal with a drought that gripped the desert region from 1968 until 1974. The sparse vegetation died. Animals. that had overgrazed the Sahel in relatively moist years perished by the hundreds of thousands. Eventually, the people themselves succumbed. An estimated 1 million people in Chad, Mali, Mauritania, Niger, Senegal, the Sudan, Upper Volta, and other nations died of malnutrition and other diseases caused by the drought.

Meteorologists — scientists who study weather — warn that periodic droughts must be expected. In addition, some experts say that the overall climate on the earth seems to be entering a less predictable era after about 60 years of generally stable weather. They expect more periods of abnormally low rainfall, and they expect such periods to last longer than they do now.

But climate deserves only a small part of the blame for modern water shortages, emphasize *hydrologists* — scientists who study water. Proper management of water supplies should enable even the driest communities to survive occasional droughts. However, people have wasted and contaminated water supplies and thus guaranteed hard times during lean years.

It is sometimes difficult to think of the United States as having a serious water problem because the nation as a whole has far more than enough water to go around. Estimates of water availability and use vary because of practical difficulties in measuring water throughout the country. But the United States Water Resources Council says that the nation, except for Alaska and Hawaii, receives a total of about 4.2 trillion gallons (16 trillion liters) of precipitation on a typical day. About 2.8 trillion gallons (11 trillion liters) evaporates, and about 1.3 trillion gallons (4.9 trillion liters) trickles into streams, rivers, and lakes. Most of the river water eventually flows — unused — into the oceans, where salt destroys its freshness. About 61 billion gallons (230 billion liters) of the daily precipitation drains into natural underground reservoirs. These reservoirs, called *aquifers*, are enormous traps of sand, gravel, and silt deposited by rivers about 1.75 million to 14 million years ago. Rock underlies the traps. Rain water seeps through the soil into the aquifers, and the underlying rock prevents most of it from escaping.

The United States uses only a small fraction of the water that it receives. But more water is pumped out of underground reservoirs than seeps into them. (Statistics are for the 48 contiguous states.)

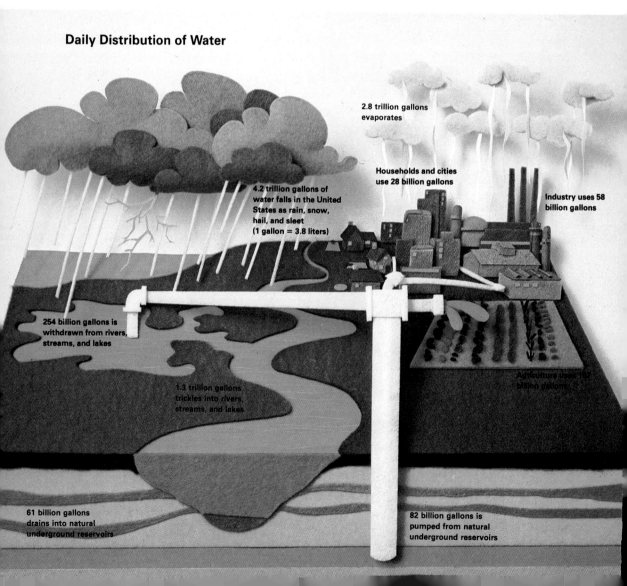

Daily Distribution of Water

2.8 trillion gallons evaporates

Households and cities use 28 billion gallons

4.2 trillion gallons of water falls in the United States as rain, snow, hail, and sleet (1 gallon = 3.8 liters)

Industry uses 58 billion gallons

254 billion gallons is withdrawn from rivers, streams, and lakes

1.3 trillion gallons trickles into rivers, streams, and lakes

Agriculture uses 167 billion gallons

61 billion gallons drains into natural underground reservoirs

82 billion gallons is pumped from natural underground reservoirs

The largest aquifer in the United States is the Ogallala. It spreads beneath about 225,000 square miles (583,000 square kilometers) of land that stretches from western Texas to northern Nebraska. The Ogallala contains 650 trillion gallons (2.5 million billion liters) of water. It provides drinking water for 2 million people and irrigation water to sustain rich agriculture on land that is too arid to rely on rain water alone.

Farmers, industrialists, and city dwellers, however, are straining the capacity of the Ogallala. The aquifer's water level is dropping 2 to 5 feet (0.6 to 1.5 meters) per year in places. Nobody expects the Ogallala to run dry, but hydrologists predict that its water will become increasingly difficult and expensive to obtain.

During a typical day in 1965, about 270 billion gallons (1.022 trillion liters) of water was withdrawn from aquifers, rivers, streams, and lakes in the United States, except for Alaska and Hawaii, according to the U.S. Water Resources Council. By 1975, the year of the latest report, this figure had risen to 336 billion gallons (1.272 trillion liters), of which 82 billion gallons (310 billion liters) came from aquifers and 254 billion gallons (962 billion liters) was withdrawn from surface sources.

But the people themselves use little of this water directly. Agriculture is the biggest user of water in the United States — about 157 billion gallons (594 billion liters) per day. Water that is pumped far from rainfall or rivers literally makes deserts bloom in parts of the West and Midwest. One agriculture expert says that farmers in Nebraska's Sand Hills region are growing corn "on sand that is no different from that at Miami Beach, except for the salt content." Irrigated crop acreage in the United States has almost tripled during the past 30 years to about 40 million acres (16 million hectares). The reliance of crops on water is astonishing. A bushel of wheat, for example, consumes almost 15,000 gallons (57,000 liters) of water from the time it is planted to the time it is eaten as bread. Even 1 pound (0.45 kilogram) of cotton requires about 150 gallons (570 liters) as it grows.

Next in line for water use comes industry. Industrial plants either use water in its natural state to cool equipment and products or convert it into steam to provide heat and generate electrical power. Ore extraction and manufacturing plants use 58 billion gallons (220 billion liters) of water every day. Steam electric generators use an additional 89 billion gallons (337 billion liters) a day. Power companies have been spurred by the shortage and increasing cost of oil to seek alternate fuels. But they have found that water scarcity can limit their efforts to obtain energy from other sources. For example, it takes from two to four barrels of water to produce one barrel of synthetic fuel from shale or coal. A planned pipeline that will move a mixture of coal and water from Wyoming to Arkansas will use 6.5 billion gallons (25 billion liters) of water per year.

Water losses can create unearthly landscapes. In northern California, *above*, water withdrawn for arid Los Angeles lowered Mono Lake 44 feet (13 meters) and exposed rock towers that once were covered by water. On a Midwestern farm, *right*, a long drought turned valuable topsoil into powder.

A drought left boats high and dry along a cracked riverbed in France, *above*. Houses and cars fell into a sinkhole in Florida, *left*, after too much water was pumped out of a natural limestone reservoir during a long dry spell. Pumping the reservoir dry weakened it so much that it caved in.

Households and municipalities in the United States use a total of 28 billion gallons (106 billion liters) of water daily for drinking, bathing, running such appliances as washing machines, and other purposes. The 21,000 municipal water-supply systems in the United States serve about 180 million people, or about 80 per cent of the U.S. population. These systems are virtually unmatched in the world in their ability to deliver great amounts of clean water inexpensively to large numbers of people. The typical American family uses 60 gallons (230 liters) of water per day, 50 per cent more than an average European family uses. Many European households lack such appliances as dishwashers that Americans take for granted.

People moving to the United States Southwest, however, are putting fresh pressures on scarce water supplies. The region will have to get whatever additional supplies are needed from large projects that will divert water from distant sources. For example, in 1985, a $2-billion system of aqueducts and tunnels called the Central Arizona Project will start to transport water from the Colorado River more than 300 miles (480 kilometers) to Phoenix and Tucson. Unfortunately, treaties among seven Southwestern states and Mexico already provide for the distribution of more water than the river contains in all but the wettest years.

Plans for other diversion projects have led to political disagreements. In California, controversy rages over the Peripheral Canal. The canal is the main feature of a $5-billion network designed to begin moving water in the late 1980s from the fairly moist northern part of the state to the parched south. The canal would make up for water that will no longer be available to southern California from the Colorado River after the Central Arizona Project is completed. Los Angeles officials insist that their city desperately needs the canal. But San Franciscans maintain that taking the water from the north will turn the Sacramento River Delta into a salty wasteland unable to support freshwater life.

Arkansas state legislators criticized Texas Governor William P. Clements, Jr., for suggesting that his state should consider importing water from Arkansas. They feared that Texas would gain a right to withdraw an annual quota of water that Arkansas might need later.

Other states and other countries also argue about water distribution. Iowans worry about a proposal to divert water from the Missouri River to Texas and Nebraska. Russian authorities in the cotton-growing area of central Asia are studying a scheme to increase irrigation in the area by piping in water from the Ob and Irtysh rivers about 1,600 miles (2,600 kilometers) away. The rivers drain into the Arctic Ocean. Ecologists fear that the scheme could reduce temperatures inside the Arctic Circle and perhaps set off a new Ice Age. British planners have outlined a scheme to build a barrier across the River Thames in London so that drinking water can be taken from a region that has always been tidal and salty. However, environmentalists fear that the barrier might transform the area into a stagnant pool.

Even when problems of distribution are solved and when nature cooperates by providing plentiful rain, usable water sometimes is less plentiful than it should be. The reason is pollution. More and more Americans are finding that they cannot trust the water from their wells or from city water systems. Almost 300 families in northern Michigan's Fonda Lake area have used bottled water rather than the lake water since 1978, when road salt from a state highway dump polluted the lake. Some families in the community of Lake Carmel, N.Y., have relied on neighbors' wells since July 1979, when tests showed that their own wells contained some components of gasoline. Tap water in Boston's well-to-do Beacon Hill neighborhood sometimes contains high proportions of lead from the ancient pipes that carry the water to the houses. The pipes are leaky as well as tarnished. According to one estimate, Boston's water system loses 2 gallons for every 1 gallon that it delivers.

The U.S. Environmental Protection Agency (EPA) reported in July 1981 that streams and rivers at 34 locations are so contaminated with toxic chemicals that they probably require special cleaning procedures to prevent them from threatening public health. The locations range from the Delaware River near Philadelphia to Oregon's Lake River and from the Mississippi River near Minneapolis-St. Paul to a series of bayous near Beaumont, Tex. The sources of pollution are equally widespread. "Industrial discharges, agricultural and urban run-off, and accidental spills have combined to make many of our rivers and streams a lethal soup of organic chemicals," says former EPA Administrative Assistant Eckardt Beck.

Worse yet, the pollution goes deeper than rivers and streams. Scientists have evidence that some dangerous chemicals have seeped into aquifers, the sources of drinking water for much of the U.S. population. Unlike surface waterways, aquifers cannot clean themselves by flowing so rapidly that they deposit the chemicals in silt. After a pollutant penetrates an aquifer, it begins to spread throughout the water. "Once contaminated, groundwater can remain so for hundreds or thousands of years,"

A Massachusetts woman buys pure water for drinking and cooking. Her household supply is contaminated so, like her ancestors, she must carry bottles to and from a central source of the vital fluid.

according to a study by the President's Council on Environmental Quality. Efforts to undo the damage to aquifers seem destined for failure. "You can't correct overnight a problem that took 30 years to generate," explains John Frisco, head of the Hazardous Waste Unit at the EPA's New York City office. "It may take just as long to clean it up." No one has even determined exactly how to clean a polluted aquifer. The contaminated water would have to be diluted by pumping in clean water to mix with it, or the contaminated water would have to be pumped out. Either way would be expensive. Furthermore, some pollutants may have spread so far that they could not be diluted significantly or pumped out.

Even some rain water is polluted. The pollutants are *oxides* (compounds containing oxygen) of sulfur and nitrogen that are carried high into the air from tall factory smokestacks. The gases react with water vapor in clouds and form acids. Some clouds become as acidic

Wise use of water can prevent shortages. Communities can divert river water for use, and desalination plants can change seawater into fresh water. Industry can recycle almost all of its supply. Farmers can irrigate with water that drips through pipes and can cover crops to minimize evaporation.

as lemon juice. Pushed along by prevailing winds, the clouds drop their acid rain or acid snow great distances away. When the acids drain into lakes, they kill fish and other wildlife. Acid rain has already helped kill wildlife in more than 200 lakes in the Adirondack Mountains in New York.

Because of the great distances from the smokestacks to the lakes, acid rain is an interstate and international problem. In the spring of 1981, for example, the Canadian province of Ontario went to court to persuade the EPA not to reduce the strict federal pollution standards imposed on certain Midwestern power plants. Pollutants from these plants are contaminating lakes in Ontario. In Europe, smoke from factories in the British Midlands produces acid rain that pollutes lakes and forests in Norway and Sweden.

Can anything be done to conserve the world's supplies of fresh water? The obvious approach is to persuade farmers, industrialists,

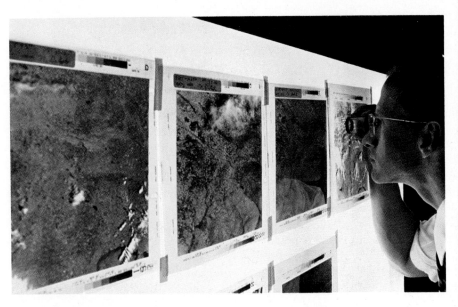

New tools help scientists determine water requirements and water quality. A crop specialist, *above*, studies infrared photographs taken by a satellite to learn which fields need water. A biologist, *right*, uses an underwater laboratory to measure the effects of pollution.

and people in general to use less water and to use it more efficiently. People can water their lawns and wash their cars less often, take short showers instead of baths, and generally use water as if it cost as much as gasoline. Industry can save large amounts of water by recycling it. Factories consume only about 2 per cent of the water that they use by adding it to such products as soft drinks and by converting it to steam. Industry could recycle the remaining water, including almost all the cooling water.

Farmers can use advanced technology to save water. For example, a technique known as *drip irrigation* delivers precisely measured amounts of water directly to the roots of fruits and vegetables, instead of wastefully spraying the plants. Scientists at the U.S. Water Conservation Laboratory in Phoenix have developed an infrared sensor that indicates when plants need water. The device measures the temperatures of leaves, which become warmer as they dry.

Other scientists are doing research on food crops that thrive in salty soil. A team at the University of Arizona in Tucson has searched the world for edible salt-tolerant plants. Some of these plants, such as atriplex, promise to yield as much nutritive value as conventional plants. The juicy young leaves of atriplex, also called *orach*, are already a favorite among American and Canadian coastal residents who enjoy wild foods. About 2.5 billion acres (1 billion hectares) of the world's land lie above aquifers whose water is too salty for most plants that are grown commercially for human consumption. Therefore, if growing edible salt-tolerant species in salty soil became

Water-conservation equipment for the consumer includes a solar blanket — a plastic sheet that prevents evaporation from a swimming pool — *above*, and machinery, tanks, and filters that recycle all of a home's supply, *right*.

Conventional irrigation, *left,* soaks a large part of a field quickly, but wastes water through evaporation from the exposed crop and ground. But in parts of Israel that are extremely dry, farmers cover crops to seal in moisture and water them slowly by hand, *below.*

commercially practical, the new crops could greatly relieve the burden on freshwater supplies.

Another way to relieve this burden is to increase the supply of fresh water. *Desalination processes* produce fresh water by removing the salt from seawater or *brackish* (slightly salty) water. Desalination factories now supply such countries as Saudi Arabia and South Africa with fresh water, but in extremely limited amounts. All the desalination plants in the world provided about 2 billion gallons (7.6 billion liters) of fresh water per day in 1981. By contrast, New York City alone consumed 1.5 billion gallons (5.7 billion liters) of fresh water per day. Desalinated water costs upwards of $1 per 1,000 gallons (3,800 liters), which is too expensive for most communities at present. But desalination does open otherwise dry coastal areas to settlement, farming, and industrialization. And there may come a day when people who live in areas that are now moist will need more fresh water, no matter what the cost.

One promising approach to increasing freshwater supplies is *cloud seeding*. Small airplanes shoot tiny particles of silver iodide into clouds, producing rain. The process is simple and much less expensive than desalination. The sky serves as the factory, and nature brings in the moisture. However, the technique can be used only when nature cooperates by providing clouds to seed. In addition, cloud seeding is unreliable. Sometimes, no rain falls, despite the seeding. At other times, it falls too heavily. And even when the rain comes down at the desired rate, it may fall in the wrong place. But Israeli scientists recently developed an experimental method of cloud seeding that uses substances derived from certain bacteria in place of silver iodide. The seeding agent promises to be less expensive and more reliable than silver iodide.

It was no surprise that a group of Israeli scientists developed the new method of cloud seeding. Israel receives less than 25 inches (64 centimeters) of rain per year, which would be considered drought status in the Northeastern United States. Some parts of Israel receive almost none. Yet a combination of scientific ingenuity and public persuasion ensures adequate supplies of fresh water for the whole country. Wells along the coastline trap fresh water before it drains into the sea. Airplanes regularly seed clouds. Farmers use drip irrigation backed up by computers that monitor air temperature, humidity, and wind speed. Plants thus receive the exact amount of water they need. Israeli botanists have classified plants according to their salt tolerance, enabling farmers to conserve fresh water in another way. They mix fresh water with brackish supplies to irrigate salt-tolerant fruits and vegetables. The Israeli people themselves conserve water as much as possible, persuaded by monthly water bills that rise steeply if a household uses more than a certain amount.

The United States and other nations may not be able to use all of Israel's water conservation techniques. However, that small country is setting an example for the day when all of us must begin to heed Gerald Seinwill's warning.

For further reading:

"America the Dry," *Life*, August 1981.
Boslough, John. "The Electric River," *Science 81*, July-August 1981.
Boslough, John. "Rationing a River," *Science 81*, June 1981.
"The Browning of America," *Newsweek*, Feb. 23, 1981.
Second National Water Assessment Summary Volume. U.S. Water Resources Council, 1979.
"Water in America: Solving the Quandary," *The New York Times*, Aug. 9-13, 1981.
"Water: Will We Have Enough to Go Around?" *U.S. News & World Report*, June 29, 1981.

Shuttle Opens New Space Era

By Marsha F. Goldsmith

**The flawless maiden flight of space shuttle *Columbia*,
which will ferry people and freight to and from orbit,
excites the hopes of scientific and commercial pioneers**

"What a way to come to California!" exulted pilot Robert L.
Crippen as he helped commander John W. Young bring the remarkably successful space shuttle *Columbia* in for a perfect landing at
Edwards Air Force Base in the Mojave Desert. Touchdown occurred
at 1:22 P.M. (E.S.T.) on April 14, 1981. That was 54 hours 22
minutes – and 36 earth orbits – after the world's first reusable spacecraft lifted off from the National Aeronautics and Space Administration's (NASA) Kennedy Space Center in Cape Canaveral, Fla., at 7
A.M. (E.S.T.) on April 12. Worldwide acclaim greeted *Columbia*'s
achievement, and people throughout the United States experienced a
reawakened sense of pride and national prestige as America showed
itself magnificently fit to open a new era of extraterrestrial endeavor.

"Prepare for exhilaration!" is the command at Mission Control at Johnson Space Center in Houston when television consoles show space shuttle *Columbia*'s landing trajectory is exactly on target. Precision is the keynote as flight controllers on the ground support the pioneering astronauts.

The author:
Marsha F. Goldsmith is a Senior Editor for THE WORLD BOOK YEAR BOOK and SCIENCE YEAR.

Columbia, the result of a 10-year, almost $10-billion program to develop the first Space Transportation System (STS), completed perfectly a mission that no previous spacecraft could accomplish. Its three-part configuration enabled it to take off from the earth like a rocket, operate in orbit like a spacecraft, and land on a hard-surfaced runway like an airplane. Though it has been characterized as a space truck, a workhorse, and the prairie schooner or Conestoga wagon of the new frontier, the shuttle resembles none of these.

The STS includes the sleek orbiter, a delta-winged craft about as long—122 feet (37 meters)—as a DC-9 jet plane. It is "the first true spaceship"—with a 78-foot (23.8-meter) wingspan—and it is the heart of the shuttle operation. Its main section is a cargo bay. The forward section is a two-level cabin—the upper level is the flight deck, and the lower level, called the mid-deck, contains the living area for crew and passengers.

But the orbiter would never get off the ground without the other two parts of the system. A blimplike, expendable fuel tank, 154 feet (47 meters) long, that supplies 0.5 million gallons (2 million liters) of liquid fuel to *Columbia*'s main engines is secured to the orbiter's underside. Two reusable solid-fuel rocket boosters, longer and wider than railroad tank cars, are attached to the sides of the throwaway tank. After a launch, they are recovered by ship and reconditioned.

NASA is building three more of these space transportation systems, and each, like the first, will have a 100-mission life. Missions will differ in detail while the spacecraft are in orbit, but the space agency will be more than content if they all begin and end with the amazing precision of *Columbia*'s maiden flight.

An unprecedented burst of smoke and flames accompanied the ascent of STS-1 from Kennedy Space Center's pad 39A. As Young and Crippen braced for the mild three-times-gravity pull of liftoff and half a million launch watchers shouted encouragement, the most powerful rocket engines and solid-rocket boosters ever built delivered 6.5 million pounds (30 million newtons) of thrust to impel the huge

Commander John Young, left, and pilot Robert Crippen, right, guide *Columbia*'s operations by means of a vast array of controls and displays. More than 2,000 switches, lights, gauges, and dials in the orbiter's highly computerized cockpit are used to fly the ship and take charge of payloads.

vehicle upward. After 2 minutes 11 seconds, the two solid-fuel boosters fell away and dropped by parachute back to earth. After 8 minutes 42 seconds, the three main rocket engines in the rear of the orbiter cut off. Then, after 9 minutes 2 seconds, the liquid-fuel tank was dropped; most of it was destroyed when it re-entered the atmosphere, though some pieces fell into the Indian Ocean. At 10 minutes 36 seconds into the flight, two smaller orbital maneuvering rocket engines fired, and *Columbia* achieved orbit about 150 miles (240 kilometers) above the earth. Ascent flight team director Neil Hutchinson was pleased. Eyes intent on his console at Mission Control in Houston, he announced, "Right on the money — beautiful!"

That sentiment fortunately described the entire shuttle debut. *Nominal*, meaning "right on plan," is NASA's word for it. As tense flight controllers tersely applied the term *nominal* to each successive phase of the mission, the spirits of everyone connected with the long-awaited triumph soared with the smooth-sailing ship.

Attention focused on the astronauts, of course. Young was a 50-year-old veteran of two *Gemini* and two *Apollo* flights, and Crippen a 43-year-old rookie who had waited 15 years for his chance. They performed on STS-1 essentially as test pilots checking out a design at

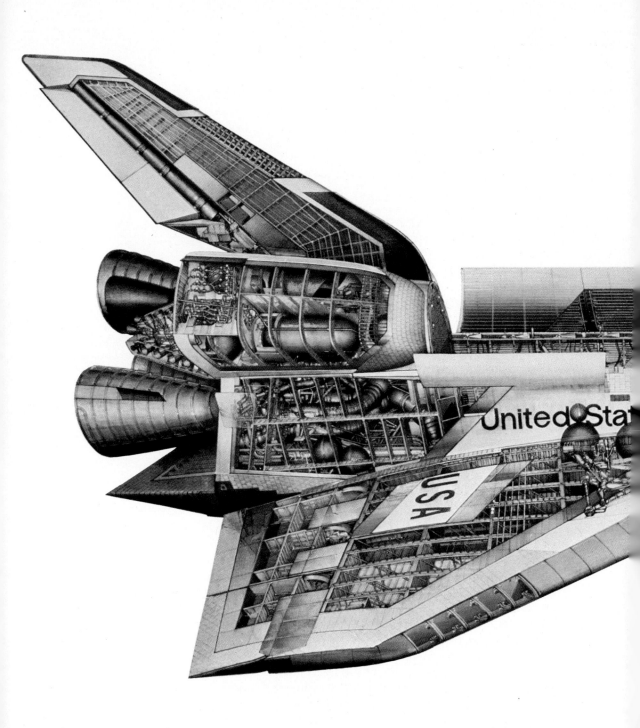

The First True Spaceship

Almost everything about the orbiter, the heart of the Space Transportation System, exceeds what was recently thought extraordinary. Only science fiction readers believed in a craft that could be shot into orbit around the earth, serve as home to a flight crew of three and as a laboratory for four experimenters, then land on earth intact. On April 12, 13, and 14, 1981, science fiction became science fact. *Columbia* does all that and more. The 165,000-pound (75,000-kilogram) ship has a cargo bay 60 feet (18.3 meters) long and 15 feet (4.6 meters) in diameter to hold research and manufacturing payloads more than one-third of the ship's own weight.

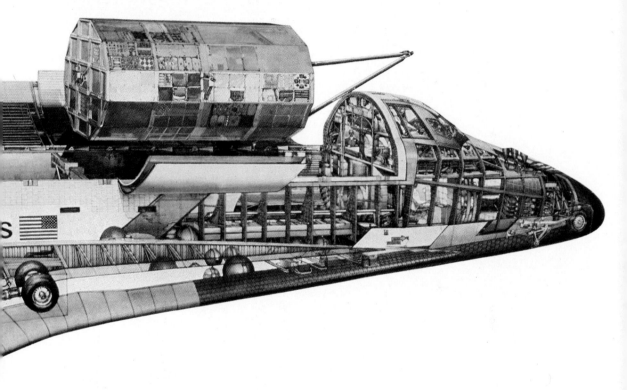

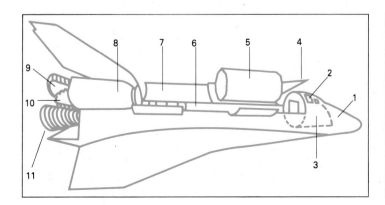

1. Forward control thrusters
2. Flight deck
3. Mid-deck (living area)
4. Manipulator arm
5. Spacelab
6. Payload bay
7. Payload bay doors
8. Fuel tanks
9. Maneuvering engines (2)
10. Aft control thrusters
11. Main engines (3)

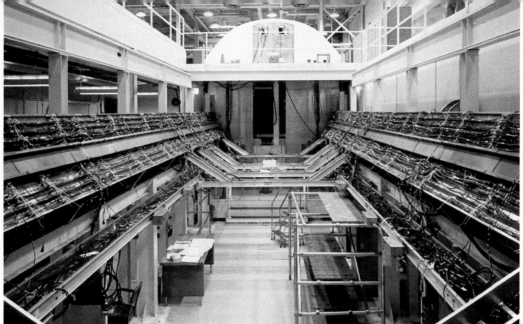

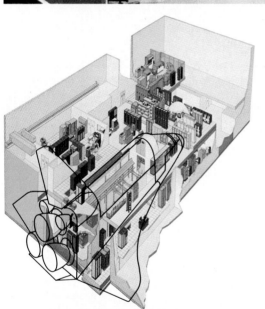

The wire-crammed avionics integration laboratory, *above*, allows on-the-ground appraisal of the maze of electronic interconnections that stretch through the orbiter, *left.* The ship's every move is controlled through a "fly-by-wire" system, in which five computers receive data on such factors as the craft's performance, attitude, and velocity from a great many instruments. After processing the data, the computers issue commands to various parts of the spaceship. But people are still needed to make the parts and assemble them. A technician modifies an engine manifold, *below left*, while others ready one of the three rocket engines, *below.*

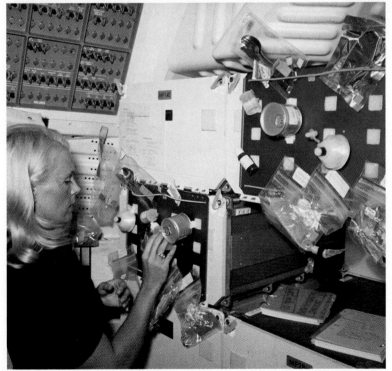

Just as parts of the STS
machine must be prepared
for a trip into space,
the human components
undergo training tasks.
Crippen, *above*, wearing
a new extravehicular
mobility unit, maneuvers
in a zero-gravity airplane.
Scientist-astronaut Rhea
Seddons, *left*, practices
assembling a meal in a
mock-up of orbiter galley.

Retaining heat-resistant tiles was crucial to the orbiter's success. After opened cargo-bay doors revealed that only 16 were missing, *above*, elation was keen. Live transmission of the reassuring sight reaches Director Christopher C. Kraft, Jr., at Johnson Space Center, *right*, relieving him of some concern about *Columbia*'s eventual safe return.

Columbia's crew snapped a heavenly view of clouds over the Pacific Ocean, *above*, knowing they were the first U. S. space travelers who would not "splash down." Instead, after their 36th orbit, they headed southwest over Utah and Arizona, *left*, aiming for a runway landing on a dry lakebed at Edwards Air Force Base in California's Mojave Desert.

Scientists and technicians who will work in Spacelab train in a mock-up of the module, *above*. NASA teaches these payload specialists how to live and work in orbit. Hoping the experience will remain only an exercise, a trainee tries out the proposed personal-rescue enclosure, *left*, an inflatable sphere for carrying stranded astronauts between spacecraft. Scientist-astronaut Anna L. Fisher, *below*, looks trim in the "constant-wear garment" that will be standard attire on shuttle missions.

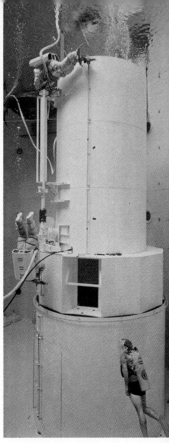

The shuttle will launch and service the Space Telescope, *above left*, a 10-ton instrument that will have 10 times better resolution than any earth-based observatory. Technicians test a mock-up of the telescope in a water-filled neutral buoyancy simulator, *above*. The Canadian-built manipulator arm, *left*, will launch and retrieve payloads from the shuttle.

Aimed at the unknown like a sailing ship of old, *Columbia* is committed to a future of discovery as bold as the vision and courage of its crews.

the technological frontier. Never before had men taken a spacecraft on its first flight. Five on-board computers helped them make the incredibly complex maneuvers, but the astronauts had the option of flying the orbiter manually, as Young confidently did during re-entry.

Young and Crippen also monitored *Columbia*'s behavior under the varying conditions of space and atmospheric flight, and checked especially on such things as the operation of the cargo-bay doors and the condition of the protective insulating tiles that cover 70 per cent of the orbiter. More than 30,000 silica-fiber tiles were required to disperse the intense heat caused by friction as the shuttle re-entered the atmosphere, and so keep the orbiter from burning up. However, bonding the tiles to the orbiter's surface proved difficult and caused some concern. About 100 tiles had fallen off the orbiter when a modified Boeing 747 jet carried it from California to the Kennedy Space Center in 1980. But only 16 tiles fell off during *Columbia*'s launch, with no ill effects. Indeed, the astronauts experienced no problems at any time during the flight. Crippen summed up their feeling of fulfillment when he said, "I think we're back in the space business to stay."

Business is what the shuttle is all about. Earlier space flights, which required the vast expense of completely new craft and launch facilities for every trip into orbit, held no lure for industry. But the sturdy shuttle was designed to appeal to far-thinking people who can envision the advantages of manufacturing or doing scientific research in the low-gravity, high-vacuum environment of space.

After *Columbia*'s four scheduled trials, on which only pilot astronauts will fly, the shuttle will begin its real work. Early in 1983, the first scientist-astronaut, or mission specialists, will join the two-member crew. NASA is also training payload specialists – nonastronauts who will be experts on specific experiments.

In addition to ferrying scientific and industrial payloads between the earth and space, the shuttle will carry up to five mission and payload specialists – men and women who will not need the intensive training given to pilot astronauts because they will simply be doing a job in space, not operating a spaceship. They will be trained to do such things as inspect orbiting spacecraft and repair them if necessary, conduct rescue missions, collect film and data from satellites, and build new space facilities. Mission specialists will also be in charge of such "housekeeping" tasks as preparing meals and keeping gear in order. More than 40 private contractors have booked space on future shuttle flights. Some companies have studied using the shuttle to place in space solar collectors that could furnish electricity for manufacturing in orbit, or even beam power back to earth.

On 20 to 30 per cent of all shuttle missions, a removable modular laboratory called Spacelab will become part of the orbiter, fitting into the cargo bay. One of Spacelab's main elements is a pressurized laboratory. There, scientists working not in space suits but in special trim uniforms designed with no flapping parts to catch on switches in the weightless environment will perform research. The other major part of Spacelab is the pallet, an open, instrument-laden platform that exposes materials and equipment directly to space.

Spacelab was financed and developed by 10 countries – Austria, Belgium, Denmark, France, Great Britain, Italy, the Netherlands, Spain, Switzerland, and West Germany – as part of the joint Spacelab program of NASA and the European Space Agency. Spacelab scientists will perform a number of short-term studies. For example, they might study the sun and the solar wind, measure the earth's electromagnetic environment, experiment with the manufacture of industrial and biomedical products in space, and study the effects of space conditions on cells, plants, and animals. A 96-inch (244-centimeter) telescope is scheduled to be carried into space by the shuttle and deployed in earth orbit in 1985.

The space shuttle *Columbia* was named for the first United States ship to sail around the world, between 1787 and 1790. Each of the other spaceships in NASA's planned fleet – *Challenge*, *Discovery*, and *Atlantis* – honors a naval vessel that played a role in some significant scientific initiative here on earth. Their names symbolize a continuity of our commitment to exploration, this time probing the boundless possibilities in the vast new ocean of space.

For further reading:

Allaway, Howard. *The Space Shuttle at Work*. NASA, 1979.
Boelke, Michael. "Space Shuttle," *Astronomy*, August 1981.
Young, John and Crippen, Robert. "Our Phenomenal First Flight," *National Geographic*, October 1981.

The Airport's Unseen City

By Mark Perlberg

A major airport is actually a city of thousands of people and hundreds of facilities — many of which we do not see — working to make air travel pleasant and safe

The big silver jet hovers above the crowded expressway, seemingly close enough to touch. It inspires a soft chorus of "oohs" and "wows" from the back seat of the yellow subcompact automobile that is heading for the airport's parking garage. It could be any one of the seven or eight major United States international airports – such as those in Atlanta, Ga.; Dallas-Fort Worth; Los Angeles; New York City; or San Francisco – or one of those in other countries, such as Tokyo International Airport, Toronto International, London's Heathrow, Rome's Leonardo da Vinci, or Paris' Orly.

But, in fact, the airport toward which the yellow car is driving this warm summer afternoon is Chicago-O'Hare International Airport. It is the world's busiest airport, handling more passenger traffic and more take-offs and landings than any other airport.

Airplanes today are the chief means of long-distance travel. In 1947, ocean liners carried two-thirds of the passengers who crossed

Departing passengers bound for various destinations line up to check their bags and receive seat assignments, *above.* Tourists from India, *above right,* like all passengers arriving on international flights, have their bags inspected by U.S. customs agents.

The author:
Mark Perlberg is a Chicago-based editor and free-lance writer.

the North Atlantic Ocean. Today, those ocean liners have almost disappeared. In 1947, scheduled airlines carried 24.3 million passengers. Today, that total has swelled to well over 600 million, and chartered airlines carry additional millions. Yves Lambert, secretary-general of the International Civil Aviation Organization, wrote in 1978, "Aviation has become one of the major means for international exchange, shattering man's concept of time and distance. . . . No other achievement of our century has made such a profound impact on the lives of people everywhere as aviation."

As the role of aviation has expanded, airports such as Chicago's O'Hare have grown in importance as transportation terminals. Except for its great volume of traffic, however, O'Hare airport — behind the scenes — is much like the other major world airports. And, thanks to the fictional family in the yellow car — let's call them the Canigas — we're going to go behind the scenes in this article to see what it takes to keep such an airport operating efficiently and safely.

As the Canigas watch, the plane banks to the left and disappears behind a row of low buildings. The Canigas soon will be on a similar plane, en route to visit relatives in Phoenix, Ariz. Like most Chicago-area residents, the Canigas are familiar with the airport. Tony, an engineer for an international paper company, makes a number of trips each year to Latin America. As a product manager for a detergent company, his wife, Martha, flies extensively throughout the

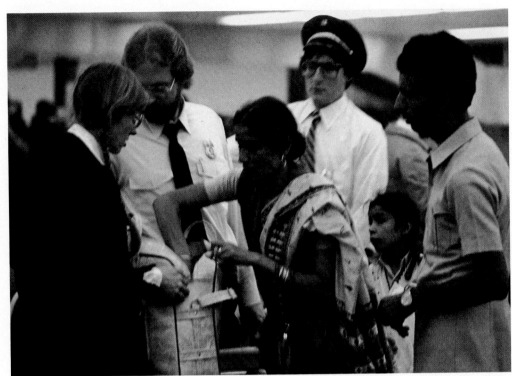

Midwest. Matt, a high-school sophomore, once took a regional airline to canoeing camp in Minnesota. Even 7-year-old Elizabeth has traveled by air alone — to visit her grandparents in Florida.

Although they are seasoned travelers, the Canigas feel a sense of excitement as they near O'Hare. As they turn off toward the parking garage, they can see beyond it the three boxy glass-and-steel passenger terminals and the low-curving airport hotel. They drive into the six-level garage, go slowly up a winding ramp, and find an empty parking space. Martha writes the location of the parking space — level 4, row H-J — in her pocket notebook, while Tony unloads the hatchback and Matt and Elizabeth pull the smaller pieces of colorful nylon luggage from the back seat. The Canigas load their luggage into the elevator, and Matt pushes the button marked "terminal." The elevator makes its slow, humming descent. When it reaches the "terminal" level, the Canigas walk the short distance to a moving sidewalk. The moving track carries them, along with their mound of baggage, to the terminal building.

The Canigas have entered a small city — one, in fact, that is about the size of Palatine, the Chicago suburb in which they live. O'Hare has a permanent "population" of 33,000 people who work around the clock to keep the facility serving the 125,000 passengers who fly in and out of O'Hare on an average day. Not all of these people work in the passenger terminals. Many work in buildings that few visitors to the

O'Hare, like all major
airports, offers many
facilities to serve
people waiting for
flights. Here, sailors
enjoy a few hands of
cards at the USO rest
station. Fast-food
counters provide a
place to sit down and
have a snack. Travelers
find souvenirs of the
city in one of the
airport's gift shops.

airport see. The vast, 7,000-acre (2,800-hectare) plot that is O'Hare is crisscrossed with roads lined with such buildings.

Two nondescript, windowless, concrete structures house the airport's electrical system. The awesome jumble of conduit feeds enough electric power into O'Hare to light the entire city of Las Vegas, Nev. There is enough wiring in the airport's control tower to link the telephones in a city of 80,000 people.

A gleaming single-story glass box contains O'Hare's heating and cooling system. Its transparent walls reveal a maze of colored pipes composing a monumental work of abstract art. However, this art form was definitely constructed with its function in mind — each pipe takes its precisely heated or cooled water from enormous storage tanks to a destination prescribed by its color.

The "city" of O'Hare is serviced by two strategically located police stations, charged with keeping order and enforcing airport regulations. It has three fire stations, two of which have paramedics who can reach any point on the grounds in less than three minutes. Because the President of the United States often passes through O'Hare, they must be prepared to see that the President is treated and whisked off by helicopter to the presidential suite at a nearby hospital should he be injured or fall ill while at the airport.

Like any city its size, O'Hare must supply certain goods and services. To do so, it maintains an enormous warehouse with miles of shelves holding orderly arrangements of products needed to maintain the airport: cleaning solvents, mops, and pails; stores of light bulbs, paper towels, and toilet tissue; brooms, floor buffers, and vacuums. It has a large garage to maintain trucks and snow-removal equipment.

The far-flung airport grounds even contain three lakes, the foundations of farmhouses built by German settlers in the mid-1800s, and three tree farms run by the city of Chicago. There is even an old cemetery tucked away on the southwest corner of the field. The lettering on the weathered headstones is almost impossible to read, but the cemetery is well cared for.

Back in the 1940s, O'Hare's predecessor — a small airport and an aircraft factory — was in the midst of farmland, and there was a forest preserve nearby that still exists. Hence, deer, ducks, skunks, and pheasants live on the airport grounds.

Although the Canigas probably will never see any of these sights or even learn that they are there, they are more aware than most travelers of many of the service facilities that are located in the terminal. They gained this awareness the hard way, during the evening of Sunday, Jan. 14, 1979, when they were still living in Des Moines, Iowa. Tony had just accepted a job with a Chicago firm, and the family had come to the city for a weekend to look at houses. However, a 21-inch (53-centimeter) snowfall that began on Saturday morning closed O'Hare, cancelling their Sunday-afternoon flight back to Des Moines. Luckily, they were able to extend their airport

Many of the facilities that keep O'Hare running are unfamiliar to passengers. Snow-removal vehicles, *opposite page, above,* keep the runways clear in winter. Pipes in the temperature-control plant are color-keyed to indicate their functions, *opposite page, below.* Fuel stored in enormous tanks, *above,* is piped to pumps. Fire fighters at O'Hare test their equipment, *below.*

hotel reservations, while hundreds of other would-be passengers had to camp out in the terminal buildings.

After a full-course dinner at one of the terminal's restaurants, Martha and Elizabeth Caniga retired to their hotel room, while Matt and his father took turns monitoring the flight listings to see whether any flights to Des Moines would be rescheduled.

During his first break, Matt found a science-fiction paperback at one of the newsstands and went to the coffee shop to read and sip hot chocolate. However, he soon became restless and decided to explore.

As Matt explored the airport that wintry night, he found a fascinating array of facilities that he had never seen before. In one wing of the terminal he passed a circular stainless-steel counter. On closer inspection, he saw that the counter held hundreds of telephone books in metal covers. Filed in alphabetical order, they were the "white" and "yellow" pages of all of the major cities in the United States. A row of clocks gave the correct time in each zone; a computer display carried long-distance telephone rates. A telephone operator was stationed at the counter to help travelers call any place in the world.

In the same wing, a glass enclosure draped with colorful flags and pennants played host to service personnel representing every branch of the United States military. As they waited to make connections,

A maintenance worker washes down the sleek body of a passenger jet, *left*. In a remote section of the airfield, a cargo plane is loaded with bales of freight, *above*.

these sailors and soldiers were guests of the United Service Organizations (USO), the same group that has served and entertained U.S. troops since World War II. The USO maintains a way station for weary service personnel in many airports throughout America.

Matt discovered that O'Hare also had its own barbershop and shoeshine parlor. However, he easily resisted his father's constant entreaty to "get a haircut."

Not far from the barbershop, Matt found a bustling office that was surprisingly busy for 10 o'clock on a Sunday night. It was the nursing station, where nurses and paramedics were treating an elderly woman who had fainted and a baby with diaper rash. The nursing stations are normally not as busy as that weekend, when the overcrowded terminal put a heavy demand on their staff. They more typically provide a place for people in poor health to rest, privacy for nursing mothers, and medical care to anyone injured at the airport.

Looking out of a window, Matt watched as the airport's snow-removal crews struggled vainly to clear runways so that the airport could resume operations. As it turned out, O'Hare was shut down for 42 hours that stormy 1979 weekend.

Now, however, more than two years later, it is 60 minutes before the Caniga family's flight to Phoenix is scheduled to take off. While

Tony and Martha get in line to check in at the ticket counter, Matt takes Elizabeth with him to one of the airport's eight fast-food stands. It has been only a few hours since lunch, and the Canigas are booked on a dinner flight, but Matt feels a hunger pang. He buys a hot dog and a root beer for himself and a small ice cream cone for Elizabeth.

O'Hare's food-service operation is well equipped to provide a quick bite for travelers like Matt. During an average year, the fast-food stands – along with the coffee shop, restaurant, two cafeterias, and a pancake house – sell 127,000 pounds (57,600 kilograms) of hot dogs, 4 million soft drinks, and 320,000 gallons (1.2 million liters) of coffee.

After Matt and Elizabeth finish their snacks, they meet their parents at the ticket counter. The computerized reservation system made it possible for the agent to verify the Canigas' reservations within seconds. It also facilitated a choice of seats. The family was able to get four seats together in their plane's "no smoking" section.

Their baggage had been tagged and sent along a conveyor belt to await loading in the cargo section of the plane. They kept out two bags that were small enough to fit under the seats.

It is now about 45 minutes before take-off time. The Canigas check the large computer display overhead for the concourse and gate where their plane will be loading. The gate, E-11, is some distance from the terminal, so they decide to walk there to wait. On the way they pass one of the airport's several gift shops, which carry everything from

An air traffic controller in the radar room deciphers a mass of lines and lights to track the progress of aircraft as they arrive and depart.

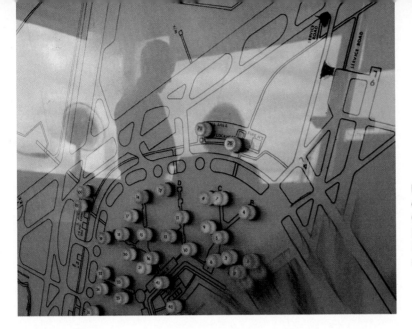

Personnel in the central operations tower at O'Hare are reflected in the electronic alarm board that monitors the entire airport for fire.

sweatshirts to sewing kits to stuffed animals. Most of the items seem to be souvenirs, many displaying the name "Chicago."

Before they can proceed to their gate, the Canigas must walk through a short oval tunnel that is, in fact, a metal detector where they are electronically searched for concealed weapons. Detectors were installed at most airports in the early 1970s, during an epidemic of airplane hijackings by passengers who had smuggled weapons or bombs aboard. As an additional precaution, the Canigas must also place their carry-on luggage and Martha's purse on a short conveyor belt that passes through an X-ray machine. Elizabeth watches the monitor screen to see the "insides" of her mother's handbag.

Matt complains a little when a guard asks to inspect the rolled-up newspaper he is carrying, but his father reminds him that such searches are a necessity. Tony is used to much more rigorous inspections. When he returns from one of his business trips to Latin America, he must pass through a facility operated by the U.S. Customs Service in O'Hare's international terminal. There, all passengers entering the United States must present their baggage to be inspected for illegal substances as well as for items that are subject to import taxes or duties.

As the Canigas take a leisurely stroll to meet their plane, airline crews are working briskly to ready it for the flight to Phoenix. Jim Perry is directing the operation. He sits before a small computer screen in a glass-walled tower above the American Airlines ramp — the area where the planes park at the boarding gates. At O'Hare, American and United Airlines have their own towers on their ramps.

Unlike our fictional Caniga family, Perry is a real person. He has been with American Airlines for 35 years. As ramp manager, it is his responsibility to see that all of the airline's schedules are met at O'Hare, and if not, that they are exceeded by as short a time period as possible. As he coordinates operations in the tower, he must see that there is a gate ready for an arriving plane, and ensure that the plane is serviced efficiently while it is in the airport.

While federal air traffic controllers monitor all planes in the air, Perry controls his airline's planes on the ground. If there are not enough open gates to handle all of American's planes at the gates, he will have to decide which planes will be delayed. He will try to do this in a way that will cause the least amount of confusion and delay to passengers in the plane. For example, if a plane is carrying 50 passengers who must make a connecting flight, he sends it to the next available gate. He will give it precedence over a plane whose passengers' final destination is O'Hare.

Once the plane is on the ground and at the appropriate gate, the action begins. A maintenance man meets the plane and talks to the captain to take any servicing requests. If the captain has noticed any mechanical problems, such as a flashing generator light, he will want to take advantage of O'Hare's ability to provide full servicing.

Meanwhile, the plane's doors have been thrown open by passenger-service personnel. After the passengers leave the plane, the cabin-service personnel go on board and meet with the flight attendants to see what they need for the next flight. They bring in new pillows and replace magazines and stereo headphones. Caterers remove the left-over food from the last flight and bring on the food to be served on the next one. Finally, the service crew cleans the cabin and the lavatories.

Small trucks carrying cargo-service representatives also pull up. They open the cargo bellies, take off the baggage, and deliver it to the baggage room for passengers to claim. Items shipped by air freight are taken to the air-freight terminal. The crew also removes mail carried to Chicago. The mail goes to the U.S. Post Office on O'Hare's grounds – the largest postal facility at a U.S. airport.

Perry must coordinate all of these operations – plus the loading operations needed for the flight to Phoenix – so that everything is finished by the scheduled departure time. When the plane is ready, after all the passengers have boarded and their baggage and outgoing mail has been stored in the cargo bellies, a small truck called a tug pushes the plane away from the gate. The plane's captain starts the engines and rolls the gleaming jet onto the taxiway.

Perry and his staff had to put in a lot of advance work to get the plane to this point. Several hours before the flight, a member of his staff called the post office at the field to find out how much mail the plane would be expected to carry to Phoenix. The staff also determined the weight of the fuel and freight planned for the flight, and the number of passengers scheduled to be aboard. This information enabled them to calculate the weight of the loaded plane and its distribution so that the plane could be properly balanced for flight.

An hour before flight time, the members of the flight crew arrived and checked in. The captain and co-pilot picked up their flight plans and weather information. Most major airlines have a weather station

As departure time nears, airline personnel make the final preparations for a safe and pleasant flight. The flight crew reviews weather conditions, *left*; a flight attendant's makeup is skillfully applied, *above*; and dinner entrees are packed, *below*.

It's flight time. A passenger gets a good-by kiss, *below*. The ground crew directs a plane onto the runway, *right*. And a jumbo jet soars aloft, *below right*.

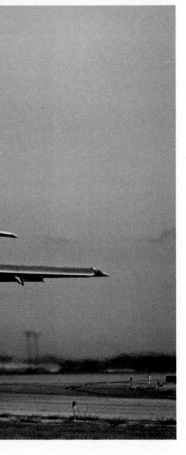

at O'Hare to furnish pilots with detailed reports about weather conditions. The National Weather Service station at O'Hare provides this kind of information for many small airlines, international flights, and private planes, and general reports for the Chicago area.

While all of this activity is in progress, other vital preparations are being made in another area of the field, in a 200-foot (60-meter) control tower. Here, the Federal Aviation Administration (FAA) controls airline traffic in the air as well as on the ground. The FAA controllers clear airplanes to take off and land, issue flight plans, and control the traffic threading through the skies within a radius of 35 miles (56 kilometers) of the airport.

The traffic controllers sit in a glass-walled area near the top of the tower. They monitor the planes by means of a computerized system that produces a digital readout, much like the time on a clock radio, on a big radar screen known as the Automated Radar Terminal Service (ARTS). The airplane appears as a set of vital statistics. For example, "AA553 069 170H" means American Airlines, flight 553; altitude 6,900 feet (2,100 meters); airspeed 170 miles (272 kilometers) per hour; heavy aircraft. This information moves across the screen as the plane approaches the airport. In addition, ARTS projects flight paths of incoming planes and, if necessary, issues verbal warnings to controllers if planes are on a collision course.

While the control booth is the nerve center of the air operation at O'Hare, it is not a scene of animated frenzy. The controllers sit hunched over their terminals as though they were playing electronic chess. They speak evenly as they deliver instructions to pilots, even when the airways are extremely crowded. O'Hare's safety record — only four serious accidents in more than 14 million take-offs and landings — attests to the air controllers' skill under pressure.

It is two minutes to take-off. The Canigas are aboard their plane and are fastening their seat belts. The ground crew has latched the plane's exterior doors, and the flight attendants make certain that all of the passengers are properly seated and belted in.

The captain receives clearance from the air controller. As the plane begins to roar down the runway, the co-pilot calls off the aircraft speed. Once the plane reaches take-off speed, the co-pilot calls out, "Rotate!", the captain pulls back on the "stick," and the great plane, loaded with its precious cargo, lifts off the ground at just the right moment. Within seconds, the only reminder of the silver jet is a faint pink streamer melting into a cloud bank above O'Hare.

The thousands of pieces — people, equipment, and facilities — that make up a major airport have fallen into place, from the skycaps who carry a passenger's baggage, to the snack bars and newsstands, to the taxicabs that throng the roadway in rush hours, to the workers who keep the runways in good condition, to those who work in the control tower, to the city police and fire fighters, to the flight crew in the big jet. The Canigas are on their way to Phoenix.

A Robot in Your Future?

By William J. Cromie

Nobody expects robots to become smarter than people and take over all our jobs, but many people do work that robots could do

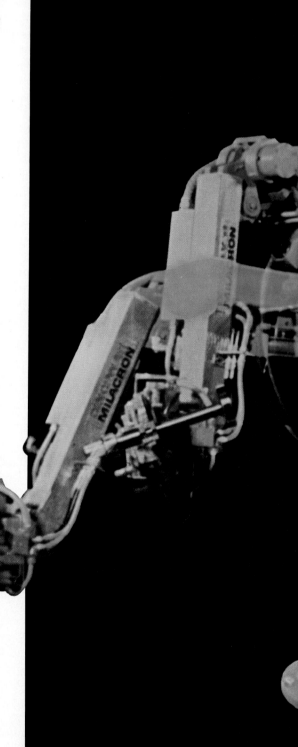

Everyone at the Ford Motor Company stamping plant in Chicago where he works knows Clyde and admires him. When he suffered a breakdown, they sent him cards and flowers. The company newspaper ran a story and a photograph of Clyde's co-workers with their arms around him at a get-well party. This would not have been worthy of special note except for one fact – Clyde is a robot. His real name is Unimate 4000B, but everyone at the plant calls him Clyde the Claw.

Clyde exemplifies the irresistible tendency to give robots human characteristics and emotions.

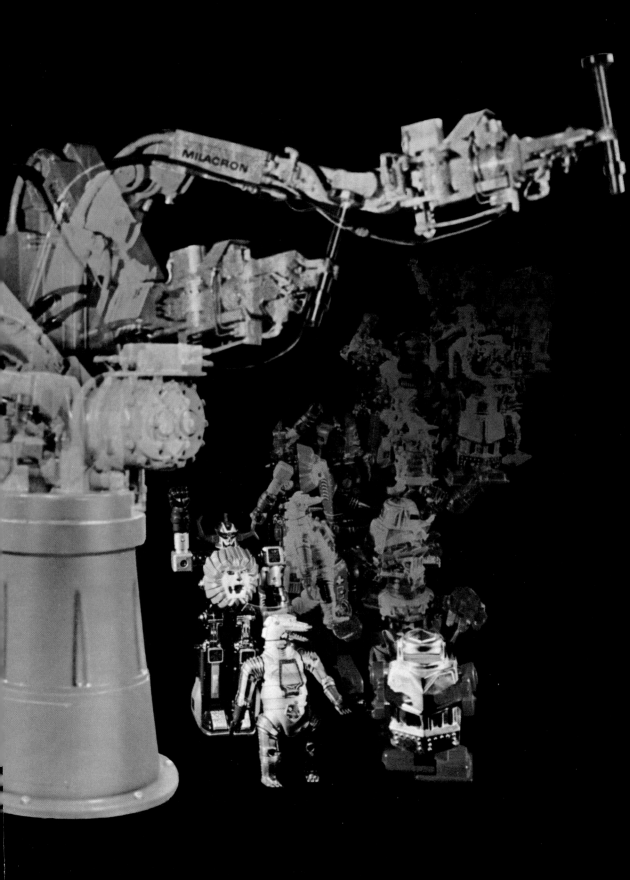

Because they are made to replace people, it is difficult to think of them as mindless and without character. We envision them as sinister beings – capable of attacking their human masters, like HAL in the motion picture *2001: A Space Odyssey* (1968). Or we see them as benevolent companions who cheerfully help us with dreary or difficult tasks, like R2-D2 in *Star Wars* (1977).

In factories around the world, robots perform hard, hazardous, and boring work. Clyde, for example, loads heavy chunks of hot metal into a machine that stamps them into useful shapes. Often, the worker replaced by one of these industrial robots gets the job of maintaining the machine, and "the worker usually makes the robot a kind of buddy," says Charles A. Rosen, president of Machine Intelligence Corporation in Palo Alto, Calif. "Once the rest of the workers no longer feel threatened, they think of the robot as one of them."

Between 17,000 and 18,000 robots worked in the world's factories in 1981, some 4,000 of them in the United States. Western Europe employs about 2,500, and most of the rest are in use in Japan. None of them fits the common image of a mechanical person that walks, talks, pilots a spaceship, or vacuums rugs. Today's industrial robots are brainless, immobile for the most part, and virtually blind. They consist mainly of a torso, shoulder, arm, wrist, and clawlike hand. They turn, bend, and grab in repetitive actions, such as welding, paint-spraying, moving material from one place to another, loading and unloading machines, and doing simple assembly work. One robot expert describes them as "powerful but docile, slow-witted but untiring workers . . . barely *sensate* [able to perceive by the senses]." Even in the most advanced research laboratories, no robot is smart enough to find a ball in a box of diversely shaped objects, or skillful enough to wash dishes.

The author:
William J. Cromie is executive director of the Council for the Advancement of Science Writing.

Visions of creation and the created: In 1511, Michelangelo painted *The Creation of Adam.* In 1938, designer Buckminster Fuller described human beings in robotlike terms: "A self-balancing, 28-jointed adapter-base biped . . . stowages of special energy extract in storage batteries, for subsequent actuation of thousands of hydraulic and pneumatic pumps with motors attached. The whole, extraordinary complex mechanism guided with exquisite precision from a turret in which are located telescopic and microscopic self-registering and recording range finders. . . ."

Sistine Chapel, The Vatican, Rome

Despite their limitations, industrial robots have undergone a population explosion since 1961, when the first one went to work in a General Motors Corporation (GM) plant. Joseph F. Engleberger, president of Unimation Incorporated, largest robot manufacturer in the United States, estimated in mid-1981 that annual worldwide sales of robots had reached $300 million, up from $130 million the previous year. Projections of U.S. sales in 1981 ranged from $75 million to $90-million. Engleberger noted that Unimation's business "doubled from 1980 to 1981, and I expect it to double again in 1982." Financial analysts predict an annual growth of 35 per cent a year for the industry, resulting in U.S. sales of $2 billion by 1990. Engleberger forecasts a total of $3 billion in sales for Western Europe and the United States by the end of the century.

Robots range in price from $10,000 for the weakest and simplest to $150,000 or more for the strongest and smartest. If you need a robot that can see, new vision systems coming on the market average $30,000. Extra joints, such as a wrist that turns in a complete circle, run $5,000 each.

Although industrial robots have existed for only two decades, and the word *robot* was not coined until 1921, people have made mechanical images of themselves for thousands of years. Archaeologists unearthed the remains of mechanical "dolls" more than 2,500 years old among the ruins of ancient Egypt. Daedalus, the architect in Greek mythology who designed the famous Labyrinth in Crete, constructed life-sized moving statues to guard it. A mechanical orchestra found in China dates from 202 B.C. The German scholar Albertus Magnus, who lived in the A.D. 1200s, built one of the first household robots, which opened doors. His student, the theologian Thomas Aquinas, thought it was made by the Devil and smashed it.

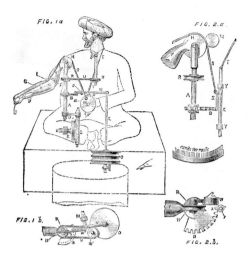

An inventor, Maskelyne, *in photo at right,* created the automaton "Psycho" in the late 1800s. The robot, which amused crowds with its ability to do card tricks, was operated by a bellows, levers, pulleys, and several sets of clockwork.

In the 1600s and 1700s, artisans created many mechanical thing-umajigs that talked, wrote letters, played music, performed in miniature theaters, or just clanked around for the amusement of onlookers. An Austrian, Joseph Faber, spent 25 years constructing a humanoid that recited the alphabet, asked questions, laughed, and spoke English with a German accent. The best known of these early robots were three automatons built in the late 1700s by Pierre and Henri-Louis Jacquet Droz for French royalty. One, made in the likeness of a young boy, wrote letters; a second "boy" drew four different pictures; a third figure, a "girl," played the piano. These mechanical puppets still can be seen at the Fine Arts and History Museum in Neuchâtel, Switzerland. Mary Wollstonecraft Shelley wrote the novel *Frankenstein, or the Modern Prometheus* (1818) a year after seeing them, notes robot expert James S. Albus of the National Bureau of Standards (NBS). He proposes that the dolls may have suggested to Shelley the idea of "artificial life gone amok, an idea that still plagues robotics."

Czech dramatist Karel Čapek took up this theme in his 1921 play *R.U.R.* (*Rossum's Universal Robots*), about a company that mass-produced synthetic men and women to replace the world's factory workers. Čapek called these mechanical people "robots," taking the name from the Czech word *robotit*, which some interpret to mean *worker* and others to mean *drudge*. In the play, the robots rebel against humans and destroy them.

The first industrial robot developed from a conversation at a 1956 cocktail party in Danbury, Conn., when Engleberger met engineer-inventor George C. Devol. "George described an idea and some patents he had for a teachable machine which was more versatile than anything made at the time," says Engleberger. "If you want to make

one product in quantities of 500,000 or more a year – ballpoint pen barrels or beer bottles, for example – you construct a special machine for the task. That's called fixed or hard automation. However, most manufacturing involves smaller runs, and manufacturers need to change styles in response to innovations and changing consumer demand. Devol looked at what people do in factories and discovered that they mostly pick and place things. They pick a part out of a box and put it on a conveyor, or they may put raw stock into a machine tool and take out a finished product. Devol wanted to build a robot that picked and placed a variety of objects used in different kinds of manufacturing operations. It still sounded like a good idea the morning after the party, so we went into business."

Five years later, the first Unimate robot went to work for GM, loading hot metal into a casting machine. That robot is now on display at the Smithsonian Institution in Washington, D.C. At first, industry resistance to these new types of workers ran high. Unimation and its backers spent $14 million before the corporation made a profit in 1974. By 1981, Unimation had built 4,900 robots, and "industry's attitude," says Engleberger, is "one of feverish acceptance."

Other early robotlike creations included the Droz "scribe," *top left*, built in 1770, which could write messages up to 40 letters long. Mechanical clock figures, *above left*, toll each quarter-hour. The walking tin man, built in Canada in the late 1800s, *above*, was powered by steam and walked in circles.

Robots in comic books or motion pictures can take almost any shape and do almost anything. Bunda the Great has a "clutching claw" on a comic-book cover, *above*, while the robot in the film *The Invisible Boy* is friendlier, *above right*.

The advantages of robots are no longer questioned. "During the severe 1978-1979 winter, we suffered from tardiness, absenteeism, and shutdowns," reports Chuck Symonds, general manager of Du-Wel Metal Products in Dowagiac, Mich. "But the robots in our plant worked every day and produced parts for three shifts with no coffee breaks." Robots designed to work 40,000 hours are still on the job after 65,000 hours. That is equivalent to 30 worker-years without a pay raise, strike, or vacation. Corporations – from such giants as GM to small family-owned businesses – cite increased productivity as the main benefit of robots. Automakers say that the consistent work of robots eliminates many "lemons" produced on Friday afternoons and Monday mornings when workers are tired and either looking forward to weekends or suffering from their aftereffects.

People who use robots are more in accord about their advantages than about their definition. For example, the Japanese classify an automatic tree climber that cuts off branches as a robot. "It doesn't qualify because it cannot be taught or programmed to do tasks other than prune trees," insists Donald Vincent, former manager of the Robot Institute of America (RIA), a trade association. A true robot, such as Clyde the Claw, can switch from loading and unloading a stamping machine one day to spraying paint or welding the next. The Japanese tree climber, automatic lathes, and some other machines lack one specification in the U.S. definition of robots: electronic circuits that allow the machine to be reprogrammed to do new tasks. Many also do not have multiple articulation, or joints that allow them to turn, twist, or move up and down, in and out, and side to side. The RIA says that about 10,000 Japanese machines fit its strict definition of robot as "a reprogrammable multifunctional manipulator designed to move material, parts, tools, or specialized devices through variable programmed motions for the performance of a variety of tasks." Many people in the robotics field agree with Engleberger when he says, "I can't define a robot, but I know one when I see it."

Automobile manufacturers in the United States, Japan, and Western Europe also know robots when they see them. They weld the bodies of GM's new J cars, for example. GM is "applying suitable commercial robots as rapidly as they are developed as well as designing in-house robotics systems," comments GM engineer Alex Joyce. Robots do 98 per cent of the 3,000 spot welds made in the assembly of Chrysler Corporation's K cars. Twenty-four Unimates make 700 welds on each of the 75 Plymouth Horizons and Dodge Omnis produced every hour in the company's Belvidere, Ill., plant. Italy's Fiat Motors says its Strada is "hand-built by robots."

"The Communist countries are very interested in robots," notes Engleberger. Poland has about 400 robots, mostly built in the United States, and Russia uses Japanese-made models in at least one truck-assembly plant. Some companies are developing in-house robots for special uses. Seiko Industries of Japan builds an automaton that positions a part to a hair-splitting 0.0008 inch (0.02 millimeter) in the assembly of watches. "Texas Instruments designs its own robots to do very simple assembly work, such as putting together integrated circuits," says Virge W. McClure, manager of the Dallas corporation's technical center. "We also have a sizable number of machines that 'see' well enough, via cameras, to inspect and reject some finished products." These robots use a television "eye" coupled with a computer "brain" to tell the robot what it is seeing and what to do.

Robotists categorize most of the robots and robotlike machines actually working today in plants as "first generation." Generally, these machines consist of a single arm with three to six joints, which reaches out from a revolving base. The robots are "taught," or programmed, to do a task by people who lead them through the required motions manually or by remote control. The movements are recorded in memory circuits so that the robots can later perform the movements by themselves.

"First-generation robots work like people with rote memory," explains electrical engineer Eugene Bartell of Carnegie-Mellon University in Pittsburgh. "They go through the programmed movements whether or not the objects they are supposed to work with are there or in the correct position." Such a robot, programmed to screw light bulbs into an automobile dashboard, will screw away even though the dashboard or light bulb is absent or out of alignment.

Manufacturers are overcoming these limitations by constructing second-generation robots controlled directly by computers. Small computers integrated with the robot instruct it to take alternate action if parts are missing or out of position. For example, they adjust themselves to changes in the speed of a conveyor belt.

Second-generation robots still lack adequate means to sense what goes on around them. Those equipped with vision see the world as a series of silhouettes. The vision systems now used in manufacturing plants produce only two-dimensional, black-and-white images at best. Usually a computer converts the image to a map of numbered dots. For example, 0 signifies white, 5 represents black, and the numbers 1 to 4 represent shades of gray. The electronic brain compares this map with maps stored in its memory in order to identify a scene. Such systems inspect finished products, determine the orientation of objects, identify pieces to be picked up, and guide arc welders to follow seams.

Second-generation robots do not possess the sense of touch, the dexterous hands, and the finely controlled muscles necessary for most assembly work. Therefore, robotists are developing third-generation robots that are smart and skillful enough to put together many of the products made in the world's factories, such as toasters, television sets, calculators, electric motors, valves, pumps, and compressors. More than 75 per cent of such products are made in diverse sizes and styles and in quantities too small to justify the construction of a custom-made machine for their manufacture.

Few third-generation robots are mature enough to work in a factory, but many more of them are "growing up" in industrial and academic laboratories, particularly in the United States. A large part of this effort centers on vision research. Researchers at universities are constructing television-computer combinations that produce stereo or 3-D images, thus giving a robot depth perception. However, the computers are large and costly and may take as long as several minutes to analyze a picture. Costs must be reduced from hundreds of thousands of dollars to thousands of dollars and image-processing time must be cut to a fraction of a second to make these computers competitive with human workers. Michael Brady of the Massachusetts Institute of Technology (M.I.T.) Artificial Intelligence Laboratory believes that this will be accomplished in the mid-1990s.

Researchers are developing devices to make robots more dexterous. A flexible wrist that allows a mechanical hand to wobble a bolt into a hole — the way a human would when the two do not exactly line up — was invented by robotists James L. Nevins and Daniel E. Whitney at the Charles Stark Draper Laboratory in Cambridge, Mass. A study by Nevins and Whitney revealed that the insertion of peg-shaped objects into holes and the installation of screws are the tasks most frequently performed in the assembly of a large variety of items, from bicycle brakes to electric toaster-ovens. Using this "remote center compliance device," as the flexible wrist is known, Draper engineers constructed a robot that assembles an automobile alternator in 65 seconds, compared with 90 seconds for a human.

Hitachi Limited of Japan makes a three-fingered "Hi-Ti" hand that wiggles slightly misaligned parts together and is dexterous

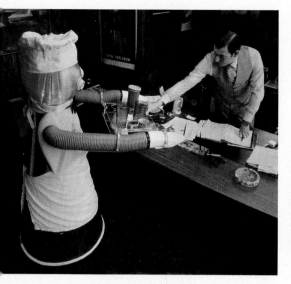

Robots with limited capabilities are already at work in offices and in homes, where they perform such tasks as serving coffee and playing chess.

enough to twirl a baton. Researchers at Carnegie-Mellon University have integrated a similar flexible hand with a television camera and computer. The camera and computer determine the best way to grasp different objects and then send the proper commands to the hand. Electrical engineer John Birk and his colleagues at the University of Rhode Island in Kingston are working on a rubber hand that molds itself to the shape of a part and picks it up by suction. M.I.T. scientists are experimenting with fingers covered with an artificial "skin" sensitive enough to distinguish between a pencil and a screw. The skin consists of pressure sensors controlled by computer and is responsive enough to pick up a paper cup without crushing it.

Researchers are also working on speech-recognition systems to produce robots that understand voice commands – and even answer back. Texas Instruments' McClure expects to develop voice-actuated robots with a limited vocabulary in less than five years. The toy forerunners of voice-controlled robots that respond to such commands as "stop" and "go" are already marching around playrooms.

Scientists have been working since the mid-1960s on programming computers to learn from experience and to reason by comparing a new situation to a known situation. At SRI International, a private research institution in Menlo Park, Calif., scientists built a robot named Shakey in 1971. Shakey resembled a small, round trash can on wheels, but it could solve at least one important type of problem. It knew – with the help of a computer – the properties of every object in the laboratory. One day, researchers ordered Shakey to push a box off a platform. This was a challenge for the armless Shakey, who could

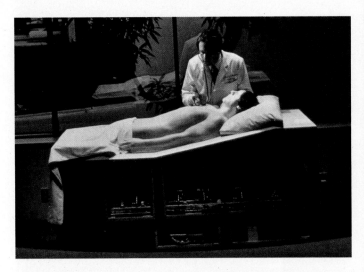

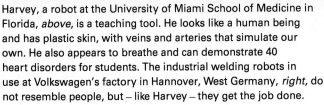

Harvey, a robot at the University of Miami School of Medicine in Florida, *above*, is a teaching tool. He looks like a human being and has plastic skin, with veins and arteries that simulate our own. He also appears to breathe and can demonstrate 40 heart disorders for students. The industrial welding robots in use at Volkswagen's factory in Hannover, West Germany, *right*, do not resemble people, but — like Harvey — they get the job done.

not roll up or climb up onto the platform. The robot "recalled" that there was a ramp in the room, located it, pushed it against the platform, then rolled up the incline and shoved the box onto the floor.

Many robotists regard Shakey as an impractical toy, and some dismiss efforts to create "thinking" robots as pie in the sky. "The field at first produced a lot of Ph.D. theses but no practical results," comments one researcher. "However, the AI [Artificial Intelligence] people now seem to be settling down to realistic goals." "We don't have to make robots that do everything that people do," adds M.I.T.'s Brady. "If we restrict the environment to a limited number of things that can go wrong, we can design programs which give robots a substantial degree of intelligence in a restricted problem-solving domain. The possibility of doing this increases as the price of computers decreases. We now do for $50,000 computations that cost $500,000 ten years ago. Ten years from now the same capability may cost only $5,000."

The pot of gold at the end of the robot rainbow is the completely automatic factory. "The Japanese are getting close to doing this," Albus believes. He cites Nissan Motors' Zama plant, where robots and automatic machines assemble 2,200 Datsun auto bodies per day with the help of only about 80 people. In a suburb of Milwaukee, Allis-Chalmers Corporation constructed a $6-million tractor plant

where automatic carts carry parts to and from robots and computerized metal-forming machines. One NBS project involves designing a machine shop where robots that do everything from inventory control to inspection of the finished product will run a night shift without human guidance.

Future robots, as they become more intelligent and skillful, will not be confined to blue-collar jobs. Engleberger believes they will work as miners, deepwater divers, explorers of other planets, and military combatants — perhaps with laser eyes and missile-launching arms. Engelberger predicts that robots will perform services now done by gas-station attendants, garbage collectors, and server-cashiers in fast-food restaurants. "Eventually, we will have to bend our human habits to this new class of slave labor," he believes, "for example, having the correct change at a gas station, or compacting our garbage and placing it at a precise spot for pickup."

Engleberger guesses it would cost an extra $100,000 to build a house of the future that would employ a domestic robot. Kitchens, laundry rooms, and appliances would have to be designed so that they could be maintained by the "robutler." Engleberger envisions single-family houses built on one level because a robot that can cope with stairs is likely to be too expensive. (Elevators would have to be designed for operation by apartment-dwelling mechanical servants.)

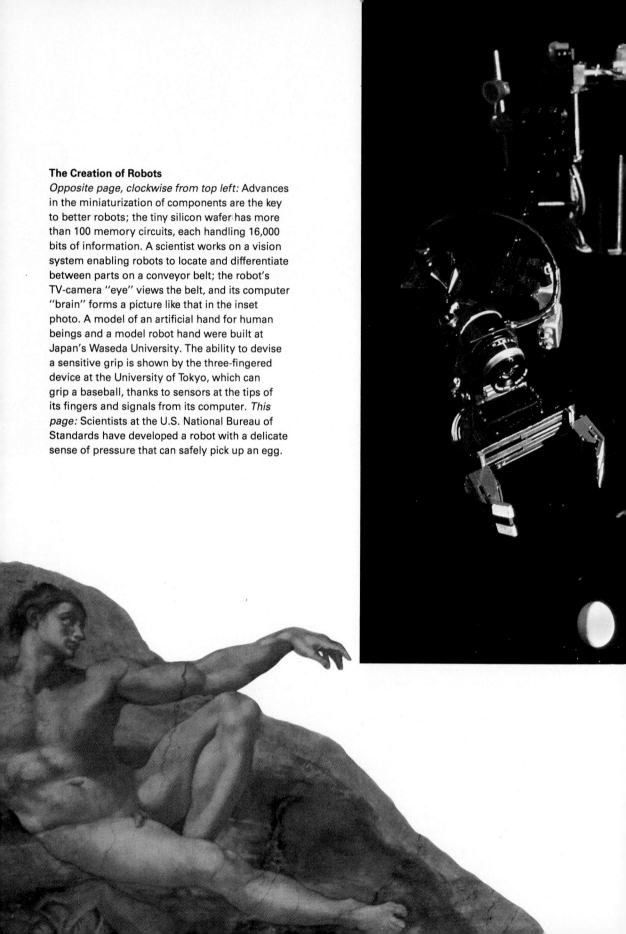

The Creation of Robots
Opposite page, clockwise from top left: Advances in the miniaturization of components are the key to better robots; the tiny silicon wafer has more than 100 memory circuits, each handling 16,000 bits of information. A scientist works on a vision system enabling robots to locate and differentiate between parts on a conveyor belt; the robot's TV-camera "eye" views the belt, and its computer "brain" forms a picture like that in the inset photo. A model of an artificial hand for human beings and a model robot hand were built at Japan's Waseda University. The ability to devise a sensitive grip is shown by the three-fingered device at the University of Tokyo, which can grip a baseball, thanks to sensors at the tips of its fingers and signals from its computer. *This page:* Scientists at the U.S. National Bureau of Standards have developed a robot with a delicate sense of pressure that can safely pick up an egg.

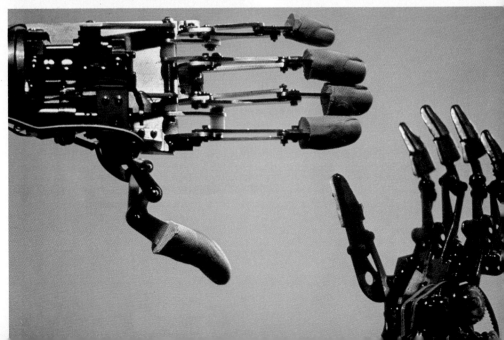

The robutler would be kept in a storeroom with its spare parts, tools, and controlling computer. Besides scrubbing floors, vacuuming, dusting, washing windows, cleaning bathrooms, cutting grass, and shoveling snow, a domestic robot could hold a complete household inventory in its memory. Its computer would be in communication with a supermarket, a drugstore, and a master-mechanic computer to help it make repairs. The robutler could awaken the family in case of fire, fight the fire, and nab intruders. It would refuse entry into the house to people whose voices it did not recognize.

In its 1981 Christmas catalog, Neiman-Marcus Company, a Dallas-based retailing and mail-order firm, offered two "domestic robots." The $15,000 standard model featured a smoke detector, fire extinguisher, wireless telephone, and black-and-white television. The deluxe model for $17,500 included color television and other extras.

The first robutlers may be built to help the handicapped. "A good solution for many of the problems of paraplegics and quadriplegics is to provide them with a robot," Engleberger suggests. A "robotaid," or microcomputer-controlled arm and hand that can be operated by voice or turning the head, is under development.

Robotized assembly lines and hamburger cooks conjure up an image of robots that "walk, talk, have flashing lights, and take your job," says Vincent. The question of robots taking jobs from people is an immediate concern. No robotists believe that mechanical workers will ever completely displace people. But there is widespread disagreement over how much of the work force will be replaced and how fast this will occur.

"We plan to hire 50,000 to 100,000 new employees to meet future production goals," says Texas Instruments' McClure. "Without robots and other forms of automation, we would need 300,000." "There's no question that robots replace humans in the job market; they're not successful unless they do," Engleberger admits. "However, it is the hard, dangerous, demeaning, and stultifying jobs that they take. Some adults are willing to do such work, but their kids want no part of it."

In the automobile industry, retraining and attrition have prevented significant problems so far. But economic factors threaten to tip this balance. "In 1961, when the first robot was installed, an employee in an auto-assembly plant received $3.80 an hour, including fringe benefits," Engleberger remarks. "Today, that same worker costs $17 an hour, and by 1982 this will rise to $20. In contrast, a robot costs about $5 an hour, including depreciation, maintenance, and electricity."

The Society of Manufacturing Engineers predicts that 50 per cent of all automobile-assembly work will be done by robots and other machines by 1995. Harley Shaiken, an M.I.T. research fellow, speculates that, by 1990, some 32,000 robots will replace more than 100,000 auto workers. He sees computer technology, as symbolized by robots, as perhaps the main collective-bargaining issue of the 1980s. Surprisingly, the labor union that would be affected most does not worry about such forecasts. "Our membership favors the introduction of robots as part of our overall support of technological advancements," comments Thomas L. Weekley of the United Automobile, Aerospace and Agricultural Implement Workers of America (UAW). "These advances increase productivity, and employees recognize that wages, working hours, fringe benefits, and safety improve when this happens. To date, increased productivity has paid for the robots, not replacement of workers. When this no longer holds true, we will negotiate shorter working hours without reduction in pay." Some union leaders, however, fear that the robot population will increase faster than it is possible to create new and better jobs. William P. Winpisinger, president of the International Association of Machinists, warns that "the union worker is the endangered species in the robot revolution."

Engleberger estimates that about 80 million people in the U.S. and Europe now do the kinds of work that could be done by robots. "I see a 5 per cent penetration in 50 years, or robots replacing 4 million workers by 2030," he says. Others predict a greater displacement.

Weekley points out that, "as jobs are being eliminated in one industry they are being created in another. Somebody has to make robots." The "somebody" might be other robots. What then?

None of the experts expect robots to become smarter than people and take over all the work that people do. Robots will be limited, they say, to specialized intelligence to deal with specific situations, such as assembling machines or dispensing hamburgers and French fries. In these situations, they probably will be smarter or quicker than people. "But robots never will have the broad, general intelligence and sensitivity of humans," Engleberger declares. "We'll never have the ability or the economic incentive to make robots that do abstract painting or lead their team to victory in the Super Bowl."

A recent incident at the Stanford University Artificial Intelligence Laboratory in Palo Alto illustrates this. A robot, busily assembling automobile water pumps, ran out of screws at its work station. It immediately called a master computer, which instructed the robot to get more screws from a nearby rack. The robot found the rack empty and called back the master computer for instructions. The latter seemed annoyed as it sent this reply via a television screen, "Call a human, you dummy!"

For further reading:

Geduld, H.M. and Gottesman, R., editors. *Robots Robots Robots*. Little, Brown, 1978.

Malone, Robert. *The Robot Book*. Jove Publishers (Harcourt, Brace, Jovanovich), 1978.

Reichardt, Jasia. *ROBOTS, Fact, Fiction, and Prediction*. Penguin Books, 1978.

A Year in Perspective

1876
1877
1878
1879
1880

1881

THE YEAR BOOK casts a backward glance at the furors, fancies, and follies of yesteryear. The coincidences of history that are revealed offer substantial proof that the physical world may continually change, but human nature — with all its inventiveness, amiability, and even perversity — remains fairly constant, for better or worse, throughout the years.

See page 156.

What Was News Is Still News

By Paul C. Tullier

Political assassinations, royal weddings, shrinking pension funds, and peace in South Africa were topics of interest during the year

If news values could be measured on a scale of 1 to 10, many events of the year would have scored high. A few would even have hit the 10 mark. Many of the 10-mark hitters of 1881 were remarkably similar to the top scorers 100 years later, thus providing the kind of coincidence that led an anonymous 17th-century philosopher to conclude that though "everything changes, everything remains the same."

In 1881, two world leaders died at the hands of assassins. One was a United States President, James A. Garfield. The other was a European head of state, Alexander II, czar of Russia. There were two glittering royal weddings in Europe. One united Crown Prince Frederick Wilhelm of Prussia to Princess Victoria of Schleswig-Holstein, a niece of Great Britain's Queen Victoria. (The Prince of Wales, who married in 1981, is Victoria's great-

The scene of the Russian czar's assassination forms a gruesome background for three other 1881 events: the death of President Garfield, a royal wedding in Germany, and victory by Boers in the Transvaal.

great-great-grandson.) The other marriage united Crown Prince Rudolph of Austria with Princess Stephanie, the daughter of Leopold II, king of the Belgians. Rudolph's gift to the bride was a wedding ring that had belonged to his great-great-great-great-grandmother, the Empress Maria Theresa; the bride's gift to him was a $450,000 dowry.

In Germany, anti-Semitism was on the rise. A petition bearing 255,000 signatures that was submitted to Chancellor Otto von Bismarck demanded legislation to curtail activities by Jews in banking and social circles. In France, the government's finances were in such disarray that the Budget Commission announced it would auction off state treasures to raise funds. The items included a horde of diamonds collected by generations of kings. Romania's Senate and Chamber of Deputies, dissatisfied with the nation's status as a principality, voted unanimously in March to become a kingdom. Prince Karl, the ruler, became King Carol I. In Africa, there was peace at last in the strife-torn Transvaal (South Africa). The British government had surrendered to the Boers, the Dutch farmers who had risen in revolt in 1880.

New Zealand was experiencing an influx of Chinese immigrants. To control the flow, the government enacted a Chinese Immigrants Act similar to legislation that had been introduced in Australia in 1880. The United States, too, was having difficulties with China over U.S. immigration policies the Chinese considered discriminatory.

While trying to soothe China's ruffled feelings, the United States was concerned about an outbreak of guerrilla warfare in Central America, where Guatemala's determined efforts to form a union with Nicaragua and El Salvador had angered Honduras and Costa Rica. The U.S. secretary of state, concerned by reports that the guerrillas' arms were being supplied by Spain, invited the Central and South American countries to a Pan-American conference. It would have been the hemisphere's first, but it was canceled. Once-cold U.S. relations with Mexico were thawing; to facilitate trade relations, a rail link was established between the two countries. On November 20, the first locomotive crossed the temporary bridge erected over the Rio Grande at Laredo, Tex.

Other news that came close to hitting the 10 mark during the year included a report of "enigmatic holes" — 20 feet (6 meters) wide and 20 feet deep — opening in several places in Paris. Gondoliers in Venice, Italy, angered by the introduction of noisy, wave-making steamboats on the canals, petitioned Pope Leo XIII to ban them.

The state of the world found an echo in the state of the United States. On July 2, President James A. Garfield was shot in Washington, D.C. He lingered over the summer and died on September 19, after only 200 days in office. Vice-President Chester A. Arthur succeeded him as President. Charles J. Guiteau, his assassin, who was a disappointed office seeker, was hanged in 1882.

The author:
Paul C. Tullier is former Managing Editor of THE WORLD BOOK YEAR BOOK.

President Arthur inherited formidable problems, including a balky Congress in which, complained *The New York Times*, "it is every man for himself and devil take the hindmost." Other newspapers were also pointed in their criticism, *Leslie's Illustrated Weekly Newspaper* among them. "Today we have a legislative body so intent on pursuing private interests," said *Leslie's*, "that it has allowed 7,000 bills to accumulate on its Calendar." Among them, according to *Leslie's*, were bills to fund a beef-up in U.S. naval strength, increase shore fortifications, expand and upgrade U.S. consular and diplomatic posts, reform the civil service, and cut government waste. In the latter category, critics included such extravagances as a "masticator which had been installed at the Treasury to shred soiled and worn-out federal currency." Some critics even branded as waste Congress's decision to honor the nation's heroes of the past with monuments cast at government expense. The first such monument — a heroic bronze statue of Admiral David G. Farragut — was unveiled in Washington, D.C., on April 25. Other critics condemned further funding of the Washington Monument, which in 1881 stood only 40 feet (12 meters) high.

Leslie's criticized Congress for the waste and the legislative bottleneck, but it felt the voters were equally to blame. "Several states have antitramp laws," said *Leslie's*. "If they would only enforce them against the political vagrants who are now misrepresenting them in the halls of Congress a real service would be done to end the graft and corruption that are depleting the government's coffers."

One cause for alarm was the drain on the Treasury's pension account. "It is growing almost intolerable," said an editorial in a New York City newspaper. "It is estimated at the Pension Bureau that, considering the large number of claims allowed and the rate at which they are being paid off, the $50 million appropriated for paying pensions will be exhausted on the first of January next [even though] the amount was intended to cover the entire fiscal year. Evidently something must be done to compel a closer scrutiny of claims and if possible balk the rapacious assaults upon the Treasury."

Many Americans agreed, though a large number felt that it was the government itself that was rapacious. Rising taxes coupled with high inflation, low wages, and tight credit were a heavy drain on the typical family's pocketbook. About 7,000 bankruptcies were reported in 1881. But in Charlotte, N.C., a man named Charles Didenover came up with a novel way to avoid bankruptcy. He mortgaged his body, including all rights and title to himself, to secure a debt he owed the mortgagee. The mortgage was duly witnessed in the presence of Mrs. Didenover. Didenover's lawyer, who had drawn up the paper, saw great potential in the scheme. "If a man can mortgage himself and convert his body into legal collateral," he said, "it will open up a new class of security which will be hailed with great pleasure by all impecunious [poor] men." The courts ruled otherwise and voided the unusual contract.

The Didenover plan was widely publicized. It scored high in news of the day. But as usual, events of far greater importance were barely mentioned in the press. The widening of educational opportunities in the United States was an example. Technical education received a boost in 1881 with the establishment of the nation's first Manual Training School in St. Louis. A course in forestry was instituted at the University of Michigan. Formal training for a career in business was offered by the Wharton School of Finance and Economy, the nation's first business college. A psychology laboratory was established at Johns Hopkins University. The cause of education for blacks was furthered with the founding of Tuskegee Normal and Industrial Institute for men and women in Alabama. Its organizer was Booker T. Washington.

Joining in efforts to encourage the spread of knowledge, Pittsburgh steel magnate Andrew Carnegie began offering free public libraries to cities that would supplement his $250,000 contribution with an annual $15,000 appropriation for maintenance costs. Carnegie's generosity was limited to the buildings; his donations were given on condition that libraries be supplied with books by communities in which they were built.

A probable candidate for any library in 1881 was American novelist Henry James's *The Portrait of a Lady*, a novel that, according to one critic, "reflected the excessive refinement in social behavior of Americans abroad." Social behavior of another sort was the subject of Helen Hunt Jackson's exposé *A Century of Dishonor*. In it, she denounced the U.S. government for its cruel treatment of American Indians. Her indignation was such that she distributed copies of the book to members of Congress at her own expense. Jefferson Davis, the former president of the Confederate States of America, published *The Rise and Fall of the Confederate Government*, a two-volume history that he had first been urged to write while in prison awaiting trial for high treason. Oliver Wendell Holmes, Jr., a co-editor of the *American Law Review*, brought out

In the background, music lovers listen to opera by telephone. Also in 1881, a statue of Admiral Farragut is erected, the Washington Monument is still unfinished, and violinist Dengremont debuts.

The Common Law. For children, there was *Five Little Peppers and How They Grew*, which Harriet Mulford Stone Lothrop had written under the pen name Margaret Sidney. A best seller among the get-rich-quick set was *How To Win on Wall Street, by a Successful Operator*, a 25-cent paperback published in Chicago. Wall Street watchers also were aided by new Western Union offices in New York City, which transmitted prices of stocks and gold to buyers and sellers.

More and more publishers were widening the range of subjects covered in the pages of their publications. And more and more magazines catering to specialized readership were being introduced. A weekly literary review, *The Critic*, made its bow in 1881. *Judge*, a weekly humor magazine, was introduced in New York City, as was *The Studio and Musical Review*. The first magazine devoted exclusively to fishing as a sport, *The American Angler*, was published in October as a monthly. Within a year, it had become a weekly. *The Working Man* appeared in 1881, coinciding with the founding in Pittsburgh, Pa., of the Federation of Organized Trades and Labor Unions of the United States and Canada. (Five years later it was renamed the American Federation of Labor.) But *The Atlantic Monthly* remained unquestionably the leading periodical of the times. In its March 1881 issue, it published Henry Demarest Lloyd's "The Story of a Great Monopoly." The article provided revealing insights into the business practices of John D. Rockefeller, who had just put the finishing touches on what would become, in 1882, the first modern "oil trust."

The one publishing event of the year that became a "must" for the book-buying public was the appearance of a revised version of the New Testament. It represented the combined work of dozens of American and British scholars over a 15-year period. About 200,000 copies were sold in New York City alone in the first week after publication. There was some carping: "The revisers have made alterations which will excite some consternation and not a little regret among all those who are familiar with the authorized version," said a well-known minister. Despite this faultfinding, interest was widespread. On May 20, the Western Union office in New York City, in a remarkable feat of telegraphy, began transmitting the new version to a Chicago newspaper eager to publish it in installments. The first transmission, enough to fill 33 columns, comprised 28 chapters of the book of Matthew, 16 of Mark, 7 of Luke, and 5 of John. Altogether, 83,715 words were transmitted in seven hours.

The speed with which the New Testament was transmitted "holds untold promise for the newspaper profession and will perhaps redeem its now-besmirched image as the mighty standardbearer of truth." This observation, made by an editorial writer in *The New York Herald*, was prompted by a scandal that had rocked the press in April. "There is reason for public alarm," reported the *Herald*, "in the discovery and exposure by the Associated Press of a great conspiracy of liars embracing some of the most prominent newspapers in the land and extending from New York to San Francisco." According to the paper, "a league has been formed consisting of a Wall Street newspaper as well as one morning and one evening newspaper in New York City. Chicago and San Francisco newspapers are also in the conspiracy. For a fee, their financial editors impose false reports on the public and thus depress the prices of grain and other produce as well as stocks. They and their co-conspirators then purchase stocks at cheaper prices before the bad news can be contradicted. Later, when the false reports have been refuted and the stocks have returned to their high value, the co-conspirators sell at a large profit."

According to the false newspaper reports, the voracious army worm had attacked vegetable farms, vineyards, and plant nurseries in northern New York; New Jersey's potato crop had been hard-hit by potato bugs; and cornfields in Illinois and Arkansas were being devastated by locusts. However, one news report about California's vineyards and fruit trees was all too true. A hundred years before the Medfly invasion of 1981, vineyards in the Sonoma Valley were being attacked by plant lice, while scale and moths were damaging fruit trees in the San Jose Valley. Consequently, the California legislature on March 4 passed a plant quarantine law – the nation's first – in which it established rules and regulations for the protection of fruit and fruit trees in both interstate and intrastate shipments.

False news reports were the exception, then as in 1981. Most newspapers tried to be as honest in their reporting as they were comprehensive in what they reported on. It was through the news media that the general public learned that a man named John Tammany of Cambridge, Mass., had been granted a patent for his "mechanical musical instrument" – a forerunner of the automatic piano player – and that the first cold-storage plant operated by mechanical refrigeration opened in Boston in 1881. There were also reports in the press of the launching of the nation's first steel-hull ferryboat, the *Lackawanna*, which had cost $76,000 to build and which speeded up travel between Hoboken, N.J., and New York City. In Atlantic City, N.J., work was completed on the first ocean pier built not only to serve the fishing fleet, but also to provide a promenade for the citizens. It extended 650 feet (200 meters) seaward from the foot of Kentucky Avenue. It was promptly christened Howard's Pier after its builder, Colonel George W. Howard of Washington, D.C.

One press report dismayed many people. A fiscal institution known as The Ladies' Deposit came to a disgraceful end in Boston. Mrs. S. E. Howe, the "projector and manager" of the bank, had encouraged deposits by promising to pay 8 per cent interest per month. She stipulated that only women could deposit, provided they were "unprotected" – unmarried or widowed. No deposit of less than $200 or more than $1,000 would be accepted in any one month. Over a three-year period, according to investigators, The Ladies' Deposit received $500,000 from depositors. But only one-sixth of the sum was paid out in interest. Most of the rest had gone to support Mrs. Howe's taste for luxurious living. Mrs. Howe, as it turned out, was not only a swindler, but also a fortuneteller, a thief, and a bigamist, and had spent two years in an insane asylum.

The Howe scandal was deplored in a statement issued by members of the National Woman Suffrage Association, which held its 13th annual convention in Boston in June. They considered the press's treatment of the affair as a "snide attempt to denigrate women in general and the association in particular." Elizabeth Cady Stanton presided over the convention, which now boasted representatives from 10 states — an increase of five over the previous year. Prominent among those attending was Louise Blanchard Bethune of Buffalo, N.Y., the first woman to enter the architectural profession and the first to eventually become a member of the American Institute of Architects. Two other women shared the spotlight with her. One was Belva Lockwood, the first woman admitted to practice before the Supreme Court of the United States. To her great indignation, Lockwood had just been refused admission to the bar in Carroll County, Maryland. Another was Kate Kane, a lawyer from Milwaukee, who berated Wisconsin's state legislature for failing to pass a law directing that a female deputy sheriff be appointed for Milwaukee County with a yearly salary of $800. Not present was a woman admired by all — Clara Barton, who had established the American Red Cross on May 21 and had been elected its first president by acclamation.

Barton and her organization won an endorsement from the American Medical Association when it held its 32nd annual session in Richmond, Va., on May 30. About 500 delegates from every state and every important city in the United States attended. The delegates agreed unanimously that "the time has now arrived when the twin curse of pernicious drugs and fraudulent gimcrackery should be thoroughly exposed so that the most

In the background, new steamboats ply the Venice canals. Also in 1881, old currency is fed into a new shredder, a magnetic healer practices his trade, and a railroad links the United States and Mexico.

164

THE MAGNETIC HEALER

illiterate are in a position to understand the character of diseases, together with treatment upon a truly scientific basis." It was a medical statement many considered long overdue; quack remedies and cure-all panaceas were being sold not only in drugstores, but also by door-to-door peddlers. There was "magnetic healing," for example, in the shape of waist belts, chest shields, headbands, and back pads that were "guaranteed" to cure everything from nervous indigestion to kidney, liver, stomach, and heart disorders.

At the medical association's final session, the delegates issued an endorsement of the nation's first Pure Food and Drug Law, which had been enacted earlier in the month by the New York legislature. Some members of the medical association undoubtedly were aware of two significant advances in medicine in other countries in 1881: France's Louis Pasteur developed a vaccine to prevent the disease anthrax in sheep and hogs, and Spanish bacteriologist Jaime Ferran had just discovered a cholera serum. A third contribution to the advancement of medical science came from a Cuban physician named Carlos Juan Finlay, who published a paper in 1881 suggesting that yellow fever might be spread by mosquitoes. (His suspicion proved accurate.)

Finlay's paper on yellow fever had been prompted by observations he had made in Panama, where preparations were underway to build a canal across the isthmus. The magnitude of the project required not only all of the engineering skill available, but also vast supplies of equipment. A partial list of the equipment needed to begin the project included 32 steam shovels; 1,000 shovels specially designed for scooping the ash out of the steam-shovel boilers; 3,000 flat cars, dirt trucks, steam launches, tugs, coal lighters, and dredges; as well as 50 locomotives and 80 miles (130 kilometers) of track. Each of the locomotives was said to be fitted with a newly invented electric headlight to facilitate night work. It was yet another use for Thomas A. Edison's invention – the electric light bulb – which created a sensation in London in 1881 when it was used to illuminate the Savoy Theatre, the first public building in England lit entirely by electricity.

The use of Alexander Graham Bell's telephone was also spreading. Music lovers at an "electrical exhibition" in Paris could listen to opera by telephone. In July, the press reported that the first international conversation held over a telephone took place between a man in Calais, Me., and another in the Canadian town of St. Stephen, N.B. The telephone also played a starring role in the theatrical season of 1881 when *Our German Senator* opened at the Park Theatre in Brooklyn, N.Y., in January. The farce, which starred comedian Gus Williams, began and ended with a telephone conversation between Williams and – presumably – a "congressman" in Washington, D.C. Imitators, professional and amateur, quickly adopted the telephone monologue. But no one dared attempt an imitation of the inimitable French actress Sarah Bernhardt, who completed her first American tour in May.

Another U.S. box-office draw that season was *The Professor*, a play written by William Gillette, a matinee idol who had temporarily forsaken the grease paint for the role of playwright. Abroad, Edwin Booth was entrancing British audiences with his portrayal of Iago in *Othello*. During the play's run, Booth arranged a morning visit to Charles Darwin, the aging and ailing naturalist. In a letter to *The Times* of London, Darwin had confused Edwin Booth with John Wilkes Booth, who had assassinated U.S. President Abraham Lincoln in 1865. Booth assured him that John Wilkes had been the only Booth family member involved in the assassination.

The sensation of Britain's theatrical season was Lillie Langtry, who made her debut in Twickenham, England, as Lady Clara St. John in *A Fair Encounter*. The critics, aware of the special status she enjoyed with the Prince of Wales, were cautious in their reviews. One critic wrote carefully that "she gave evidence of histrionic ability." The year's disappointment in theatrical circles was the long-awaited first performance of the Norwegian dramatist Henrik Ibsen's new play, *Ghosts*. The critics found the play's theme unspeakably vulgar.

Theatergoers had their favorites. The same was true of sports lovers. Horse racing was becoming increasingly popular in the United States, and rejoicing was great when Iroquois, a colt owned by Pierre Lorillard of Jersey City, N.J., became the first American-bred horse to win the English Derby. The Kentucky Derby was won by Hindoo.

In addition to horse racing, sports-minded Americans had a wide variety of recreational activities to choose from. In August, the U.S. National Lawn Tennis Association was formed at a meeting of representatives of the Eastern clubs. The association sponsored the first U.S. Men's National Championship in Newport, R.I., in August. Richard S. Sears won the title. In baseball, a new rule increased the distance of the pitcher from home plate from 45 feet (13.7 meters) to 50 feet (15.2 meters). Chicago won the National League baseball pennant with a season record of 56 victories and 28 defeats. The team's manager, first baseman Cap Anson, led the league in batting with a .399 average.

Boston's music lovers were treated to the inaugural concert of the Boston Symphony Orchestra. Major Henry Lee Higginson, its founder and principal backer, was a confirmed lover of music by German composers with one major exception – he thoroughly disliked Richard Wagner's works. He also disdained most "modern" composers, whose works, he said, were "by and large trash." One such composer he considered "modern," along with Wagner, was Johannes Brahms, who, in 1881, published the score of his *Academic Festival* overture. Instant acclaim was given to Jacques Offenbach's *The Tales of Hoffmann*, which was produced at Paris' Opéra Comique on February 10; Offenbach had died in 1880. Charles Gounod's new opera *The Slave Sale*, however, was a flop and was dropped from the repertory.

Gounod's once-soaring reputation was in fact in decline, but that of

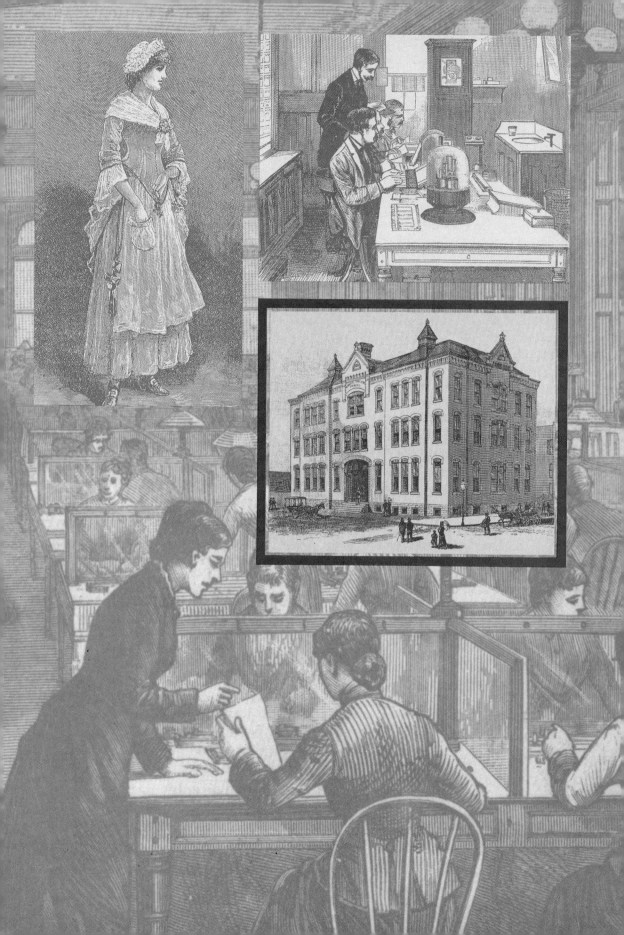

Franz Liszt remained high. On October 23, an all-Liszt concert was given in Rome to celebrate the pianist-composer's 70th birthday. Earlier, in May, a memorial concert for Hector Berlioz was given in New York City, where 500 musicians and 1,500 singers performed his *Requiem*. It was as sensational as the U.S. debut of violinist Maurice Dengremont, a 15-year-old prodigy from Rio de Janeiro, Brazil, who had been giving concerts in Europe since he was 6 years old.

Dengremont's debut on March 28, 1881, coincided with the death of Russian composer Modest Mussorgsky in St. Petersburg. Both events scored high on the 10-mark scale, as did the deaths that year of Russian novelist Fyodor Dostoevsky, Scottish historian Thomas Carlyle, and English statesman Benjamin Disraeli. But no public notice was given to the births in that same year of Hungarian composer Béla Bartók, British author P. G. Wodehouse, Spanish painter Pablo Picasso, or French philosopher Pierre Teilhard de Chardin.

The seemingly unnewsworthy births belied an insightful remark made by Mark Twain at a lecture in Hartford, Conn., in 1881. "Those who seek next year's news," he said, "need only read this week's newspapers." And there were indeed news items that, in retrospect, bear out Twain's comment. One example in a report that appeared in *Leslie's* in 1881 will suffice. In an article headlined "An Interesting Substance," *Leslie's* reported: "A new material has been introduced in Germany for ornamental and other purposes. The substance, which is of a neutral shade, is sufficiently pliable to be pressed into various shapes and used for the production of bas-reliefs and other figures, or worked by hand into models. When allowed time to set, it hardens into a stonelike unbreakable form. It has been found suitable for the production of medallions, salvers, buttons, combs, knives, handles . . . card cases, boxes and pen holders as well as door knobs and frames for hand mirrors. The substance, which is produced from nitrocellulose, camphor and alcohol, is called plastic."

Western Union's new New York City office forms the background for other 1881 scenes: Lillie Langtry's debut, a room where gold and shares of stock are traded, and a manual-training school in St. Louis.

1976
1977
1978
1979
1980
1981

The Year on File

Contributors to THE WORLD BOOK YEAR BOOK report on the major developments of 1981. The contributors' names appear at the end of the articles they have written, and a complete roster of contributors, listing their professional affiliations and the articles they have written, is on pages 6 and 7.

Articles in this section are arranged alphabetically by subject matter. In most cases, the article titles are the same as those of the articles in THE WORLD BOOK ENCYCLOPEDIA that they update. The numerous cross-references (in **bold type**) guide the reader to a subject or information that may be in some other article or that may appear under an alternative title. "See" and "See also" cross-references appear within and at the end of articles to direct the reader to related information elsewhere in THE YEAR BOOK. "In WORLD BOOK, see" references point the reader to articles in the encyclopedia that provide background information to the year's events reported in THE YEAR BOOK.

WELCOME
BACK TO
FREEDOM

EXIT

OPEN

See "Iran," page 348.

ADVERTISING

ADVERTISING in 1981 was one of the first industries in the United States to be affected by the election victory of President Ronald Reagan and other conservative candidates. In February, conservative Christian action groups such as Jerry Falwell's Moral Majority Incorporated and Donald E. Wildmon's Coalition for Better Television began calling for a "cleanup" of sex, violence, and profanity in the programs aired on television, which is the most pervasive entertainment – and advertising – medium in the United States. Threatened with a possible boycott of their products, several major television advertisers capitulated and urged the networks to eliminate things that conservative groups found objectionable. However, despite the hue and cry, the fall 1981 season started with sex and violence still widely in evidence.

On a totally different front, cable television was a big newsmaker in 1981. By year-end, it was estimated to have penetrated into one-third of all U.S. households. The rapid expansion of cable and satellite transmission appeared to be ushering in a new era for the broadcast medium. Fare for the newly opened channels is heavy on motion pictures, sporting events, and news, but other programs are planned. Because of the likelihood of different channels choosing to specialize in different subjects, the medium that from its beginning was called "broadcasting" may one day be called "narrowcasting."

Food and Travel. Fast food became even faster in 1981. New outlets sprouted, seemingly overnight; new menu items were added too rapidly to count; and advertising – already omnipresent – became even more so. To cap off all this strenuous activity, McDonald's Corporation, the giant of the industry, startled the advertising world in October when it moved its more than $50-million account from Needham, Harper & Steers Incorporated, its agency for the past 11 years, to another Chicago agency, Leo Burnett Company Incorporated.

The airline industry fairly flew from one agency to another. Already plagued by steep rises in fuel costs, coupled with the strike by the Professional Air Traffic Controllers Organization that started in August, many airlines seemed to feel that the only way they could improve their lot was to change their advertising approach, via a new ad agency. Nevertheless, no clear-cut creative breakthroughs in airline advertising resulted from agency changes. Instead, as 1981 wound down, print and broadcast media were filled with fare-cutting advertising as carriers tried desperately to fill dozens of empty seats. See AVIATION.

In Detroit, rebate time came early. Beleaguered carmakers started saturating the media with rebate offers shortly after new-model introductions, the earliest that such ads ever appeared. General Motors Corporation, Ford Motor Company, and Chrysler Corporation all reported enormous losses in the third quarter. They were banking on the proper mixture of effective advertising, substantial rebates – and an attractive product – to solve their current woes. See AUTOMOBILE.

Advertising Revenue. At the end of 1980, the outlook for ad revenues for the upcoming year was uncertain for most advertising media. They had been hit with a sharp economic recession, the cancellation of the Summer Olympic Games, and an actors' strike that affected most key network-TV series. It seemed evident that the expansion in advertising demand that started in 1976 had lost its momentum, and in early 1981 some media fared no better than they had in 1980. Others, however, began posting dramatic gains early in the year. By September, Robert J. Coen, senior vice-president of McCann-Erickson Worldwide, said in his annual study of ad revenue, "It appears quite possible that a rising trend is setting in and this year will ultimately turn out to be much better than many had hoped just nine months ago." Coen added that if this strengthening in ad usage continued, most media could look forward to an excellent year in 1982, with volume approaching $70 billion. Estimated ad volume for 1981 was more than $61 billion.

Advertising agencies posted another record year

Teen-age actress Brooke Shields lends her beauty to advertising aimed at deterring other young people from smoking cigarettes.

in 1980, reporting to *Advertising Age* gross income of $4.7 billion on worldwide billings of $31.8 billion. This was a 13.9 per cent increase over the $4.1-billion in gross income reported in 1979, and a 14 per cent jump in billings over the $27.9 billion figure of 1979. New York City's J. Walter Thompson Company, long-time holder of the gross worldwide income crown, was dethroned by Young & Rubicam Incorporated. With its list of subsidiary agencies, the latter posted combined gross worldwide income for 1980 of $340.8 million on billings of $2.3 billion.

Procter & Gamble Company again was the number-one advertising spender. It invested $649.6 million in 1980, according to the annual study conducted by *Advertising Age*. Sears, Roebuck and Company moved past General Foods Corporation into the second spot, with a total of $599.6-million in national advertising. General Foods's expenditure was $400 million. The 100 top national advertisers spent an estimated $13 billion for 1980, up 11 per cent from the $11.7 billion in 1979. The most interesting addition to the list of 100 top spenders was Hershey Foods Corporation. From its founding in 1905 until 1970, Hershey spent nothing on advertising. It is now the 93rd largest advertiser in the United States.   Jarlath J. Graham

In WORLD BOOK, see ADVERTISING.

AFGHANISTAN. The war between Afghan resistance groups and the Russian occupation forces supporting the regime of Revolutionary Council President Babrak Karmal continued during 1981. The resistance groups, who called themselves *mujahedeen* (fighters for the faith), had opposed the "radical" social programs pursued by Karmal's predecessors. The mujahedeen considered these programs, which included women's education and land reform, to be a threat to Afghanistan's traditional Islamic way of life. The Soviet Union's invasion of December 1979 provided the rebels with an additional goal of ridding the country of foreign atheist forces.

Soviet forces held Kabul, the capital, and other Afghan cities in a tight grip. But they failed to establish secure control over the countryside, despite their superiority in equipment and their policy of totally destroying villages suspected of aiding the mujahedeen. The Soviets were further hampered by the continued defection of regular Afghan Army units, many with Russian weapons, to the guerrillas.

Rebel Alliance Formed. An unintended result of the Soviet invasion was that for the first time in history traditional tribal rivalries gave way in 1981 to the national struggle against the invader. In June, three mujahedeen groups formed a new alli-

Members of an Afghan resistance group prepare to fire a 75-millimeter gun against Russian troops who have occupied Afghanistan since December 1979.

ance, the Islamic Unity of the Mujahedeen, with headquarters in Peshawar, Pakistan. Its declared objectives were the liberation of Afghanistan, self-determination for the Afghan people, and an elected government. Two representatives from each of Afghanistan's 29 provinces would be elected to a 58-member Grand Council, under the Afghan system of the *Loya Jirga*, or Great Tribal Assembly. The Islamic Unity alliance stood a better chance of success than its predecessors. It had the advantages of better communications across the largely open Afghan-Pakistani border and greater coordination among the mujahedeen groups inside Afghanistan.

The War Took a Heavy Toll among the Afghan civilian population, as an average of 15,000 to 20,000 refugees per week poured into temporary camps in Pakistan. The Pakistani government estimated that more than 2 million refugees had fled Afghanistan since 1978.

The Afghan economy — what was left of it — was more and more closely tied to the Soviet Union's. For example, Afghanistan exported to the Soviet Union its total natural gas output of 3.5 billion cubic meters (124 billion cubic feet) at a higher-than-normal price of $80 per 1,000 cubic meters (35,300 cubic feet).   William Spencer

See also ASIA (Facts in Brief Table). In WORLD BOOK, see AFGHANISTAN.

AFRICA. African nations in 1981 made only limited progress toward solving five major, persistent problems — achieving political independence for Namibia; ending civil war in Angola; reducing racial conflict in South Africa; resolving the territorial dispute between Somalia and Ethiopia; and ending the war between Morocco and nationalist guerrillas for control of the Western Sahara. In another problem spot — the new multiracial state of Zimbabwe — the black-majority government attempted to reassure the white minority and, at the same time, deal with strong conflicts among rival black factions.

Namibia, also known as South West Africa, has been a colonial possession of South Africa since 1920. Over 80 per cent of its population is black, and, since 1966, the major black political party, the South West Africa People's Organization (SWAPO), has waged a guerrilla war against white South Africa for control of Namibia. In the late 1970s, the United Nations (UN) attempted to work out a program for Namibian independence, and, at the end of 1980, South Africa's government appeared ready to accept a UN-supervised cease-fire and subsequent elections. However, negotiations ended on Jan. 14, 1981, when South Africa's representatives rejected the plan as "premature." They argued that UN supervisors would favor SWAPO at the expense of other political parties.

Throughout 1981, diplomats from five Western countries — the United States, Great Britain, Canada, France, and West Germany — negotiated with South Africa to find a basis for peaceful settlement. As the year closed, there were indications that their current proposal, which included special guarantees for Namibia's white minority, would be acceptable to South Africa. See NAMIBIA.

While participating in these negotiations, South Africa's government continued to wage war against SWAPO guerrillas, launching several attacks against SWAPO bases in southern Angola. In the largest incursion, which lasted from August 24 to September 4, South African forces reportedly killed more than 1,000 enemy fighters.

Angola. In addition to South African attacks, Angola's central government had to cope with a continuing rebel movement in the southeast region of the country. The National Union for the Total Independence of Angola (UNITA), led by Jonas Savimbi, claimed in July to have 15,000 troops and to occupy an area in southeastern Angola in which 40 per cent of the country's population lived.

The Administration of United States President Ronald Reagan showed signs of preparing to grant UNITA military aid. On March 19, Reagan asked Congress to repeal 1976 legislation that prohibited military aid to factions fighting in Angola's civil

Troubled Nations of Southern Africa

Symbolizing the continuing strife in southern Africa, South African tanks move across the Angolan desert in August, after attacking guerrilla bases.

war. If the law were repealed, Savimbi, an avowed anti-Communist, seemed likely to receive U.S. aid against Angola's Marxist central government. The Reagan Administration was particularly concerned with the presence of from 15,000 to 20,000 Cuban troops in Angola.

The U.S. Senate voted to repeal the law. The repeal effort faced strong opposition in the House of Representatives, however, and it remained on the House floor at year-end. See ANGOLA.

South Africa. The National Party, which has ruled South Africa since 1948, retained control of the government by winning parliamentary elections on April 29. It lost considerable electoral support, however, to both the Progressive Federal Party and the Reconstructed National Party.

Only whites were allowed to participate in those elections. Blacks demonstrated their opposition by boycotting businesses and sabotaging public facilities. See SOUTH AFRICA.

On December 4, Ciskei became the fourth tribal "homeland" to gain formal political independence from South Africa. Under the National Party's policy of *apartheid* (separate development), each black ethnic group in South Africa has been assigned to one of 10 such tribal areas, or homelands. Together, the homelands comprise only 15 per cent of South Africa's area, though blacks constitute about 70 per cent of the population. See CISKEI.

Zimbabwe. In South Africa's neighboring state of Zimbabwe, which achieved independence in 1980, the black-majority government took steps to reassure the white minority. Prime Minister Robert Mugabe fired a black Cabinet officer – accused of murdering a white farmer but acquitted on a technicality – from his Cabinet position on January 10 and from his post as secretary-general of the ruling Zimbabwe African National Union Party on August 6.

Mugabe's government made economic, as well as political, concessions to whites. White farmers benefited from higher government-set prices for their crops.

Armed clashes between Zimbabwe's major black ethnic groups erupted in 1981. About 150 people died in February in fighting between tribal forces in Bulawayo, the country's second-largest city. Political rivalries were also heated. Mugabe's political party swept the municipal elections in Salisbury, Zimbabwe's capital city, on March 28 and 29, but lost on June 7 in Bulawayo, which is dominated by a rival tribe. See ZIMBABWE.

Warfare over Disputed Territory. Throughout 1981, Somalia continued to provide military assistance to separatist guerrillas in the Ogaden region of southeastern Ethiopia, where most of the population are ethnic Somalis. The separatists are seeking to detach the Ogaden from Ethiopia and join it

Facts in Brief on African Political Units

Country	Population	Government	Monetary Unit*	Foreign Trade (million U.S. $) Exports†	Imports†
Algeria	21,086,000	President Chadli Bendjedid; Prime Minister Mohamed Ben Ahmed Abdelghani	dinar (4.3 = $1)	9,545	8,537
Angola	7,402,000	President Jose Eduardo dos Santos	kwanza (32.3 = $1)	800	720
Benin	3,757,000	President Mathieu Kerekou	CFA franc (279.2 = $1)	230	435
Bophuthatswana	1,719,000	President Lucas Mangope	rand (1 = $1.03)	no statistics available	
Botswana	872,000	President Quett K. J. Masire	pula (1 = $1.30)	520	694
Burundi	4,662,000	President Jean-Baptiste Bagaza	franc (83.3 = $1)	65	167
Cameroon	8,807,000	President Ahmadou Ahidjo; Prime Minister Paul Biya	CFA franc (279.2 = $1)	1,129	1,271
Cape Verde	339,000	President Aristides Pereira; Prime Minister Pedro Pires	escudo (50 = $1)	2	45
Central African Republic	2,565,000	National Recovery Committee President Andre-Dieudonne Kolingba	CFA franc (279.2 = $1)	79	61
Chad	4,718,000	President Goukouni Weddeye	CFA franc (279.2 = $1)	91	180
Ciskei	600,000	President Lennox Sebe	rand (1 = $1.03)	no statistics available	
Comoros	353,000	President Ahmed Abdallah; Prime Minister Salim Ben Ali	CFA franc (279.2 = $1)	12	17
Congo	1,615,000	President Denis Sassou-Nguesso; Prime Minister Louis-Sylvain Goma	CFA franc (279.2 = $1)	119	242
Djibouti	333,000	President Hassan Gouled Aptidon; Prime Minister Barkat Gourad Hamadou	franc (279.2 = $1)	5	72
Egypt	43,876,000	President Mohamed Hosni Mubarak	pound (1 = $1.45)	3,046	4,860
Equatorial Guinea	382,000	Supreme Military Council President Obiang Nguema Mbasogo	ekuele (153.8 = $1)	37	12
Ethiopia	32,664,000	Provisional Military Government Chairman Mengistu Haile-Mariam	birr (2.3 = $1)	418	567
Gabon	605,000	President Omar Bongo; Prime Minister Leon Mebiame	CFA franc (279.2 = $1)	1,106	616
Gambia	632,000	President Sir Dawda Kairaba Jawara	dalasi (2.2 = $1)	53	280
Ghana	12,394,000	Military Junta headed by Jerry J. Rawlings	cedi (2.7 = $1)	1,096	993
Guinea	5,257,000	President Ahmed Sekou Toure; Prime Minister Lansana Beavogui	syli (16 = $1)	410	380
Guinea-Bissau	861,000	Revolutionary Council President Joao Bernardo Vieira; Vice-President Victor Saude Maria	peso (37.6 = $1)	14	61
Ivory Coast	8,555,000	President Felix Houphouet-Boigny	CFA franc (279.2 = $1)	2,515	2,493
Kenya	16,840,000	President Daniel T. arap Moi	shilling (9 = $1)	1,104	1,658
Lesotho	1,406,000	King Moshoeshoe II; Prime Minister Leabua Jonathan	loti (1 = $1.03)	35	262
Liberia	1,984,000	Head of State Samuel K. Doe	dollar (1 = $1)	537	487
Libya	3,227,000	Leader of the Revolution Muammar Muhammad al-Qadhafi; General People's Congress General Secretary Muhammad al-Zarruq Rajab; General People's Committee Chairman (Prime Minister) Jadallah Azzuz al-Talhi	dinar (1 = $3.41)	16,085	5,311
Madagascar	9,393,000	President Didier Ratsiraka; Prime Minister Desire Rakotoarijaona	franc (274.5 = $1)	394	641

Country	Population	Government	Monetary Unit*	Foreign Trade (million U.S. $) Exports†	Imports†
Malawi	6,283,000	President H. Kamuzu Banda	kwacha (1 = $1.10)	295	439
Mali	7,029,000	President Moussa Traore	franc (400 = $1)	177	180
Mauritania	1,718,000	President Mohamed Khouna Ould Haidalla; Prime Minister Maayouia Ould Sid Ahmed Taya	ouguiya (48.4 = $1)	194	295
Mauritius	977,000	Governor General Sir Dayendranath Burrenchobay; Prime Minister Sir Seewoosagur Ramgoolam	rupee (8 = $1)	429	609
Morocco	21,090,000	King Hassan II; Prime Minister Maati Bouabid	dirham (5.3 = $1)	2,403	4,185
Mozambique	10,966,000	President Samora Moises Machel	metical (28.6 = $1)	129	278
Namibia (South West Africa)	1,063,000	Administrator-General D. J. Hough	rand (1 = $1.03)	no statistics available	
Niger	5,577,000	Supreme Military Council President Seyni Kountche	CFA franc (279.2 = $1)	494	555
Nigeria	89,118,000	President Shehu Shagari	naira (1 = $1.54)	18,073	12,399
Rwanda	5,340,000	President Juvenal Habyarimana	franc (89.3 = $1)	115	190
São Tomé & Príncipe	88,000	President Manuel Pinto da Costa	dobra (40.1 = $1)	23	14
Senegal	6,033,000	President Abdou Diouf; Prime Minister Habib Thiam	CFA franc (279.2 = $1)	627	1,006
Seychelles	67,000	President France Albert Rene	rupee (6.4 = $1)	17	100
Sierra Leone	3,651,000	President Siaka Stevens	leone (1.1 = $1)	205	297
Somalia	3,830,000	President Mohamed Siad Barre	shilling (11.8 = $1)	111	249
South Africa	30,815,000	President Marais Viljoen; Prime Minister Pieter Willem Botha	rand (1 = $1.03)	9,618	8,336
Sudan	19,330,000	President & Prime Minister Gaafar Mohamed Nimeiri	pound (1 = $1.75)	581	869
Swaziland	617,000	King Sobhuza II; Prime Minister Prince Mabandla Dlamini	lilangeni (1 = $1.03)	220	356
Tanzania	19,973,000	President Julius K. Nyerere; Prime Minister Cleopa David Msuya	shilling (8.1 = $1)	523	1,084
Togo	2,670,000	President Gnassingbe Eyadema	CFA franc (279.2 = $1)	290	448
Transkei	5,916,000	President Kaiser Matanzima; Prime Minister George Matanzima	rand (1 = $1.03)	no statistics available	
Tunisia	6,677,000	President Habib Bourguiba; Prime Minister Mohamed Mzali	dinar (1 = $2.07)	2,201	3,536
Uganda	14,620,000	President Milton Obote; Prime Minister Erifasi Otema Alimadi	shilling (80 = $1)	306	370
Upper Volta	7,234,000	Chief of State Saye Zerbo	CFA franc (279.2 = $1)	85	593
Venda	320,000	President Patrick Mphephu	rand (1 = $1.03)	no statistics available	
Zaire	30,438,000	President Mobutu Sese Seko; Prime Minister Nsinga Udjuu	zaire (5.4 = $1)	1,324	597
Zambia	6,209,000	President Kenneth David Kaunda; Prime Minister Nalumino Mundia	kwacha (1 = $1.21)	1,377	755
Zimbabwe	7,870,000	President Canaan Banana; Prime Minister Robert Mugabe	dollar (1 = $1.50)	1,194	940

*Exchange rates as of Dec. 1, 1981. †Latest available data.

to Somalia. Ethiopia retaliated with aerial bombings of border cities and villages inside Somalia. See SOMALIA.

Morocco and the Polisario Front continued to fight for control of the Western Sahara, a former Spanish colony. Morocco had annexed the northern two-thirds of the Western Sahara in 1976 and the southernmost one-third in 1979. Polisario had been fighting since 1975 to establish a separate state, to be called the Sahara Arab Democratic Republic, for the entire territory. In 1981, more than 70 countries recognized Polisario's claims to the territory.

King Hassan II of Morocco on June 26 announced his willingness to hold an internationally supervised referendum on the status of the territory. However, Morocco and Polisario could not agree on who would be allowed to vote.

On October 13, Polisario guerrillas attacked a 2,000-man Moroccan garrison at Guelta Zemmour. Morocco claimed that these guerrillas had infiltrated from Algeria and Mauritania and had used Russian tanks and ground-to-air missiles. On November 27, Polisario said it had occupied Guelta Zemmour and another outpost, Bir Anzaran, since November 9.

Violence over Cameroon's claims to land in eastern Nigeria flared briefly in 1981. On May 16, a Cameroon coast guard boat fired on a patrol of Nigerian soldiers along a river claimed by both countries, killing five and injuring three. Cameroon's government formally apologized on May 24 and subsequently offered to pay reparations. Nonetheless, it maintained that the Nigerian patrol had been 20 miles (32 kilometers) inside territory that rightfully belonged to Cameroon. On August 1, Nigeria's Foreign Minister Ishayu Audu announced that the dispute would be arbitrated.

Unions of States. Chad's President Goukouni Weddeye on January 6 announced plans to merge his country with Libya. The announcement came after Libya had sent about 5,000 troops to help his government defeat rebel forces in December 1980. However, on June 27, 1981, the Organization of African Unity (OAU) agreed to replace the Libyan troops in Chad with an inter-African peacekeeping force, which arrived in mid-November. By year-end, almost all of the Libyan troops had withdrawn, and the merger plans appeared to have been shelved. See CHAD.

Senegal and Gambia announced plans to unite after Senegalese forces helped to put down a Gambian uprising in August. A unification treaty signed on December 18 established a confederation called Senegambia. See GAMBIA.

U.S. Relations with Africa. In its first year in office, the Reagan Administration made several important changes in U.S. African policy. Unlike his predecessor, President Jimmy Carter, who empha-

sized U.S. aid to African governments, Reagan sought to encourage private business investments.

The new Administration also vowed to work for a "more constructive relationship with South Africa." On April 30, the United States joined Great Britain and France to veto four UN Security Council resolutions calling for economic and political sanctions against South Africa. The resolutions were designed to pressure South Africa into granting independence to Namibia. On August 31, the United States was the only Security Council member to veto a resolution condemning South Africa for its 12-day military incursion into Angola. Despite opposition from the OAU and public protests within the United States, the Administration permitted South Africa's national rugby team to play matches in the United States in September.

The OAU Summit was held in Nairobi, Kenya, from June 23 to 27 and attended by heads of state from 30 of the 50 member countries. The conference set up an "action committee" to work with Mauritania, Morocco, and Polisario for a popular referendum to determine the status of the Western Sahara, and approved the creation of the OAU peacekeeping force sent to Chad.

Attempted Coups. Two former members of Mauritania's ruling Military Committee for National Salvation, allegedly backed by Morocco, led an unsuccessful coup against the government on March 16. One leader was killed in the brief fighting; the other was arrested and later executed with several accomplices. In December 1980, the Military Committee had appointed a civilian, Sidi Ahmed Ould Bneijara, as prime minister, as a step toward phasing out military rule. However, after the abortive coup, a military career officer, Colonel Maayouia Ould Sid Ahmed Taya, became the new prime minister in April.

Members of Gambia's small security forces, led by Marxist politician Kukli Samba Sanyang, seized Banjul, the capital city of Gambia, on July 30 while President Sir Dawda Kairaba Jawara was attending the royal wedding in London. Jawara flew to Senegal on July 31 and called on that nation to help him put down the rebellion. About 2,000 Senegalese troops were dispatched, and by August 6 the uprising was crushed.

Seychelles was also the site of a failed coup in 1981. Officials there on November 26 announced the defeat of an uprising led by white mercenaries. Forty-four of the mercenaries hijacked an Air India jet and escaped to South Africa. In Liberia, the deputy leader and four members of the military government were arrested on August 9 for plotting to overthrow Head of State Samuel K. Doe. They were executed on August 14. See LIBERIA.

Two coups were successful, however. On September 2 in the Central African Republic, Army Chief of Staff Andre Kolingba ousted civilian President David Dacko. On December 31 in Ghana, former Air Force Lieutenant Jerry J. Rawlings, who had headed the government briefly in 1979, overthrew civilian President Hilla Limann.

The civilian regime established in Uganda in December 1980 elections survived despite widespread unrest during 1981. Opposition party leaders claimed that the election-vote counts were fraudulent; rebel groups conducted sabotage campaigns; and government soldiers were accused of frequent lootings and indiscriminate killings. Moreover, most of the Tanzanian troops who had helped to maintain order in 1979 and 1980 were withdrawn by mid-1981. See UGANDA.

Famine. The breakdown of law and order, as well as a drought, substantially reduced harvests, contributing to mass starvation in the remote Karamoja region of Uganda, where as many as 30,000 nomads may have starved to death in the 18 months ending in March 1981. Food supplies were also dangerously low in Somalia, where about 1.3 million refugees from neighboring Ethiopia were reported to be living. J. Dixon Esseks

In WORLD BOOK, see AFRICA.

AGRICULTURE. See FARM AND FARMING.

AIR FORCE. See ARMED FORCES.

AIR POLLUTION. See ENVIRONMENT.

ALABAMA. See STATE GOVERNMENT.

ALASKA. See STATE GOVERNMENT.

ALBANIA and Yugoslavia quarreled over the status of Yugoslavia's Kosovo province in 1981. About 80 per cent of Kosovo's people are ethnic Albanians, yet the province is part of Serbia, one of the six republics that make up Yugoslavia. Ethnic Albanians in Kosovo want Yugoslavia to elevate the province to the status of a republic.

Students in Priština, Kosovo's capital, demonstrated and rioted over university policies and the province's poor economy in March. The rioting soon spread to the general public and was compounded by nationalist tensions.

Albania's Communist Party newspaper *Zeri i Popullit* (*Voice of the People*) accused Yugoslav authorities of using excessive force against the rioters. The main Albanian-language newspaper in Kosovo then accused Albania of "flagrant interference" in Yugoslavia's affairs. On May 17, *Zeri i Popullit* rejected this accusation and supported the demand that Kosovo become a republic.

Mehmet Shehu, prime minister since 1974, committed suicide on December 17. The Albanian press agency said he had "a nervous breakdown."

Albania's Communist Party First Secretary Enver Hoxha told delegates at the party congress in November that relations with Greece and Italy were excellent. Chris Cviic

See also EUROPE (Facts in Brief Table). In WORLD BOOK, see ALBANIA.

ALBERTA, locked in a bitter dispute with the federal government in Ottawa, Ont., over oil pricing and the division of revenues, carried out two production cutbacks of 60,000 barrels a day, on March 1 and June 1, 1981. The province imposed the cutbacks to affirm its right to control oil production. Canada's Prime Minister Pierre Elliott Trudeau and Alberta's Premier Peter Lougheed signed an agreement on September 1 that averted a third cutback.

Forest fires, most caused by lightning, raged in August. At month's end, 22 fires burned out of control, destroying hundreds of thousands of acres of timberland. A forest fire in the Swan Hills oil fields in mid-August forced three oil companies to shut down their wells temporarily.

The Budget, announced on April 14, forecast a deficit of $336 million (Canadian dollars; $1=U.S. 84 cents as of Dec. 31, 1981), the first such shortage in five years. The deficit resulted from a drop in natural gas production combined with declines in oil revenues caused by reduced exploration. The deficit was registered after 30 per cent of oil and gas revenues had been transferred into the Alberta Heritage Savings Trust Fund, which was expected to total $11 billion by the end of the 1981-1982 fiscal year. David M. L. Farr

See also CANADA. In WORLD BOOK, see ALBERTA.

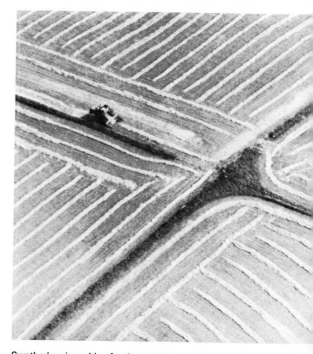

Swathed grain waiting for the combine on an Edmonton, Alta., farm makes the 1981 crop a record picture of plenty for the province.

ALGERIA. The government of President Chadli Bendjedid played a crucial role in the negotiations between Iran and the United States that led to the release of the 52 American hostages on Jan. 20, 1981. Three Algerian officials served as intermediaries in the negotiations. The Algerian central bank controlled the escrow account used for the return of Iranian assets frozen in the United States by President Jimmy Carter following seizure of the hostages. As a nonaligned Islamic nation with links to Iran's regime and economic ties with the West, Algeria was well suited for its intermediary role.

The government was also active in efforts to resolve two African conflicts — Libya's intervention in Chad and the ongoing war between Morocco and the Algerian-backed Polisario Front in the Western Sahara. A conference of Saharan nations on February 18 in Algiers recommended a nonaggression pact for the region. Initiatives by Bendjedid also resulted in an Organization of African Unity (OAU) recommendation in June for a referendum in the Western Sahara (see MOROCCO).

The Political Scene. Reorganization and expansion of the political bureau of the ruling National Liberation Front (FLN) completed Bendjedid's efforts to establish his authority as Algeria's leader. Opposing factions had hampered his efforts since the death of President Houari Boumediene in 1978. The bureau was expanded to 10 members — 5 Cabinet ministers, who are all army commanders; 4 civilians; and Bendjedid. Two close associates of Boumediene who had been rivals of Bendjedid for the presidency were dropped — former Foreign Minister Abdelaziz Bouteflika and FLN Secretary-General Mohammed Salah Yahiaoui.

The expected improvement in relations between Algeria and the United States because of Algeria's mediation in the hostage crisis failed to develop, as the United States wavered between support for its long-time ally Morocco and its economic interests in Algeria. In February, Algeria proposed a price increase for natural gas from $4.50 to $6 per 1,000 cubic feet (28 cubic meters) in order to resume deliveries to El Paso Company, a leading U.S. importer. The company rejected the new price, but Great Britain and Belgium accepted increases.

The Algerian Economy, based on exports of oil and natural gas, continued to expand. The 1981 budget was balanced at $17 billion, a 33 per cent increase over 1980.

Three ammonium nitrate plants went into operation in May at Arzew and Annaba (Bone) seaports. This made Algeria a net exporter of ammonium nitrate and phosphate fertilizers, since production met domestic needs.   William Spencer

See also AFRICA (Facts in Brief Table). In WORLD BOOK, see ALGERIA.

AMERICAN LEGION. See COMMUNITY ORGANIZATIONS.

AMERICAN LIBRARY ASSOCIATION (ALA) held its 100th annual conference in San Francisco from June 26 to July 2, 1981. More than 12,500 librarians, trustees, and friends of libraries heard Executive Director Robert Wedgeworth report on a year of unprecedented growth for the association. ALA's income topped $8 million, and membership reached a record high of 39,000. Also, the association moved into new headquarters in Chicago.

Conference Events spotlighted outgoing ALA President Peggy Sullivan's theme, "Libraries and the Pursuit of Happiness." A film featuring author and interviewer Studs Terkel focused on "the life in libraries and the place of libraries in life." A multimedia extravaganza celebrated the 25th anniversary of the Library Services and Construction Act, the federal program for improving and expanding public library services in the United States. Speakers at the conference included authors Stephen King and P. D. James; Senator S. I. Hayakawa (R., Calif.); and Michael Farris, the executive director and legal counsel for the Moral Majority of Washington state, a conservative political action group.

Censorship issues made 1981 a year of unusual activity for ALA's Office for Intellectual Freedom. Its director, Judith Krug, explained ALA's anticensorship stand in all the major news media.

Elizabeth W. Stone, dean of the Graduate Department of Library and Information Science at Catholic University of America in Washington, D.C., took office as the new ALA president. She announced that her theme would be "Responsiveness: Key to developing library awareness; Awareness: Key to meeting fiscal challenges."

National Awards. The Statistics Section of the Library Administration and Management Association won the 1981 Bailey K. Howard-World Book Encyclopedia-ALA Goals Award. It will finance a meeting to produce goals and specifications for a field test of the Draft Revision of American National Standard for Library Statistics Z39.7.

The Public Library Association (PLA) Goals, Guidelines, and Standards for Public Libraries Committee won the 1981 J. Morris Jones-World Book Encyclopedia-ALA Goals Award. It will support a three-day seminar to evaluate and edit 11 performance measures for a PLA manual to help librarians assess the quality of their service.

Katherine Paterson, author of *Jacob Have I Loved*, won the 1981 Newbery Medal for the most distinguished contribution to American literature for children. Arnold Lobel, illustrator and author of *Fables*, won the 1981 Caldecott Medal for creating the most distinguished American picture book for children.   Margaret Barber

See also CANADIAN LIBRARY ASSOCIATION (CLA); LIBRARY; LITERATURE FOR CHILDREN. In WORLD BOOK, see AMERICAN LIBRARY ASSN.

ANDORRA. See EUROPE.

South African troops display Russian-made arms captured from SWAPO forces in Angola as evidence of Soviet interest in southern Africa's conflict.

ANGOLA continued to endure attacks from South Africa in 1981 as each nation supported rebel movements against the other's government. The South Africans made repeated incursions into southern Angola from neighboring Namibia to attack bases of the South West Africa People's Organization (SWAPO), a black nationalist movement. SWAPO guerrillas have been fighting for Namibia's independence from South African rule and have been supported by Angola's government.

The most extensive South African incursion began on August 24 and lasted to September 4. The South Africans claimed to have captured $214-million in military equipment and to have killed approximately 1,000 soldiers — about 600 of whom were Angolans.

Namibia's Importance. South Africa has also been providing military supplies to the rebel movement, the National Union for the Total Independence of Angola (UNITA), across the Namibian-Angolan border. As a result, Angola's President Jose Eduardo dos Santos had a vested interest in the Namibian independence negotiations that continued throughout 1981. Dos Santos expected that an independent Namibia under a black-majority government would no longer be a passageway for South African aid to UNITA. See NAMIBIA.

UNITA Forces maintained control of most of southeastern Angola during 1981. In the country's central region, they kept the vital east-west Benguela railroad closed.

The Administration of United States President Ronald Reagan showed an interest in providing UNITA with military aid. On March 19, Reagan asked Congress to repeal 1976 legislation barring U.S. assistance to any faction in Angola's civil war. The Senate voted to repeal the law, but the repeal effort remained on the floor of the House of Representatives at year-end.

If the law were repealed, UNITA seemed likely to receive U.S. aid against Angola's Marxist central government. On March 27, President Reagan criticized the dos Santos government for being "dominated" by the Cuban military presence in Angola. During 1981, about 15,000 to 20,000 Cubans were reported to be stationed in the country. Angola contended that the troops were needed to protect Angola against South African attacks.

The federally owned United States Export-Import Bank agreed in July to lend Angola $86-million to help fund an oil-development project. The venture would be owned by Angola's government and Gulf Oil Corporation.   J. Dixon Esseks

See also AFRICA (Facts in Brief Table). In WORLD BOOK, see ANGOLA.

ANGUILLA. See WEST INDIES.

ANIMAL. See CAT; CONSERVATION; DOG; ZOOLOGY; ZOOS AND AQUARIUMS.

ANTHROPOLOGY

ANTHROPOLOGY. In February 1981, anthropologist John W. K. Harris of the University of Wisconsin in Milwaukee announced the dating of what may be the world's oldest tools made by human beings. Dating of the volcanic ash just below the implements suggested that the tools were at least 2.5 million years old, 500,000 years older than the earliest previously known tools. Harris had excavated the artifacts in 1977 while working as part of a joint French and United States anthropological expedition in northeastern Ethiopia. The tools, made from volcanic rock, consisted mostly of simple flakes used for cutting. Fragments of animal bone lay with the tools. Harris suggested that the area may have been an ancient campsite. No hominid fossils were found there, however.

Early Human Beings in the New World. Debate over when human beings arrived in the Americas from Asia continued in the August 28 issue of *Science* magazine. In 1974, chemists Jeffrey L. Bada and Roy Schroeder of Scripps Institution of Oceanography in La Jolla, Calif., reported a date of 70,000 years ago for some human fossils found in California. They studied a human skeleton found near Del Mar and other fossilized human remains found near Sunnyvale. Utilizing a new, unproved dating method known as *amino acid racemization,* which involves analysis of changes in the amino acids in bone, the Scripps scientists estimated the Del Mar skeleton to be about 48,000 years and the Sunnyvale fossils to be about 70,000 years old. If Bada and Schroeder are right, it would mean that human beings came to the Americas from Asia as early as 70,000 years ago, rather than only 20,000, as most scientists believe.

In the 1981 *Science* report, however, geologists James L. Bischoff and Robert J. Rosenbauer of the United States Geological Survey seriously questioned the age estimates of Bada and Schroeder. Using dating techniques based on the radioactive decay of uranium, Bischoff and Rosenbauer claimed that the Del Mar skeleton was only 11,000 years old, and the Sunnyvale fossils a mere 8,300.

Slow or Fast? Controversy over the pace at which evolution proceeds continued during 1981. The traditional theory of evolution holds that new species evolve out of existing ones by the gradual accumulation of small changes. But a growing number of scientists believe in an idea called the *punctuated equilibrium theory.* The theory holds that most species go through long periods of evolutionary stability or equilibrium "punctuated" by short periods of rapid change.

In the July 9-15 issue of *Nature,* four anthropologists presented evidence supporting the traditional idea of gradual evolution. The scientists were John E. Cronin of Harvard University in Cambridge, Mass.; Noel T. Boaz of New York University in New York City; Christopher B. Stringer of the British Museum in London; and Yoel Rak of Tel Aviv University in Israel. They analyzed the fossil record for the last 4 million years and concluded that human evolution was characterized by gradual changes in cranial capacity and other skeletal features. Their findings appear to contradict the punctuated equilibrium theory.

Other Developments. Anthropologist Donald C. Johanson left the Cleveland Museum of Natural History in November to become founding director of the International Institute for the Study of Human Origins. The institute, in Berkeley, Calif., is the first research organization in the United States dedicated to the study of human origins.

Chinese scientists announced in 1981 the discovery of a late Pleistocene skull that they called Dali man. The skull shares many primitive characteristics with Peking man, a member of the early human species *Homo erectus.* However, the Dali skull also displays more advanced features characteristic of *Homo sapiens,* the modern human species. Dali man, therefore, may provide an important link between *Homo erectus* and *Homo sapiens.* Donald C. Johanson

See also ARCHAEOLOGY. In WORLD BOOK, see ANTHROPOLOGY; PREHISTORIC PEOPLE.

ANTIGUA AND BARBUDA. See LATIN AMERICA (Facts in Brief Table); WEST INDIES.

AQUARIUM. See ZOOS AND AQUARIUMS.

Anthropologist John W. K. Harris in February displays photographs of stone tools about 2.5 million years old, the oldest yet found.

ARCHAEOLOGY. Archaeologists continued to make spectacular discoveries in 1981 at the tomb of Shih Huang Ti (Shi Huang Di), also called Chin Shih Huang (Qin Shi Huang), the emperor who unified China in 221 B.C. The site, which covers about 500 acres (200 hectares) near Sian (Xian), is one of the greatest archaeological finds in history.

In 1974, excavations at the site unearthed the first of what proved to be an army of more than 6,000 life-sized terra-cotta statues of soldiers and horses standing in formation. The center of the site is a towering mound of earth, where presumably the emperor himself lies buried. On the assumption that the tomb was planned to be symmetrical, Chinese archaeologists measured the distance from the clay figures to the mound and then dug an equal distance away on the opposite side. This time the statues they found were made of bronze. By October 1981, archaeologists had uncovered five chariots, each with a driver and four horses about half life-size.

The main burial mound remains to be investigated, but excavations of other tombs revealed that some of the bodies buried at Sian were flesh and blood, not clay or bronze. Archaeologists found the graves of generals, courtiers, and servants as well as the skeletons of horses and dismembered corpses of the royal family. Historical accounts say the

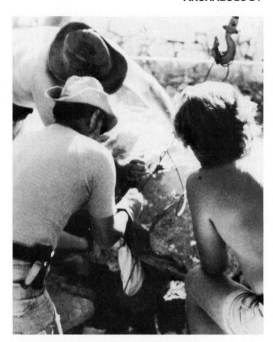

Archaeologists excavate what may be part of a holy ark from the ruins of a temple dating from the A.D. 300s near Zefat, Israel, in July.

The half-ton limestone fragment discovered in Israel, *top picture,* has a gabled roof decorated with relief sculptures of two lions.

emperor's successor killed all possible rivals, which may explain the royal corpses.

Raiders of the Lost Ark, one of the most successful motion pictures of 1981, had a parallel in real life when a team of archaeologists discovered what may be a portion of the oldest sacred ark yet found. In the film, the archaeologist hero, Indiana Jones, discovers the original Ark of the Covenant. According to tradition, the original Ark was made by the ancient Hebrews to hold the stone tablets of the Ten Commandments and has been lost for centuries. However, every Jewish temple has its own ark, in which the Torah is kept.

The newly discovered fragment, which may be part of an ark, was found in the remains of a fourth century A.D. synagogue at Nabratein, near Zefat, Israel. A team of archaeologists sponsored by Duke University and the American Schools of Oriental Research uncovered the relic.

Excavations at Ebla, near Aleppo, Syria, continued to yield treasures. The discovery of more than 15,000 clay tablets there in 1975 was enough to make the site one of the most important in the Near East. The palace in which those tablets were found, destroyed in about 2250 B.C., belongs to the first of what now appear to be two important phases of Ebla's history. The second is represented by another, larger palace, which archaeologist Paolo Matthiae of the University of Rome and his colleagues have studied for several years. About 1600 B.C., the second palace was burned and pillaged, but its destroyers missed the royal tombs beneath its floors. There, members of the royal family lay buried along with their prized possessions. In 1981, Matthiae's team found about 20 kilograms (44 pounds) of unworked lapis lazuli, a semiprecious stone, at Ebla. The stone can have come only from Afghanistan, which suggests the Eblaites had a trading network wider than archaeologists thought.

Controversy continued over what the Eblaite tablets, written centuries before the Bible, have to do with the world of the Old Testament. Two major books on Ebla published in 1981 took opposite sides in the debate. In *The Archives of Ebla*, Giovanni Pettinato, the expert who was first called upon to read the tablets, suggests that there are many similarities between names on the Eblaite tablets and names in the Old Testament, particularly those of people and places. But Matthiae and many other experts deny the validity of Pettinato's claims. In *Ebla: An Empire Rediscovered*, Matthiae discusses the tablets and the other discoveries at Ebla.

Ancient Shrine. During the summer, a team of American and Spanish archaeologists discovered what may be the oldest religious monument. The shrine, which dates from 14,000 years ago, lies near Santander, Spain. It includes a sculptured stone head that may be that of a god.   Paul E. Zimansky

In WORLD BOOK, see ARCHAEOLOGY; EBLA.

ARCHITECTURE. More than 7,000 architects gathered in Minneapolis, Minn., from May 17 to 22, 1981, for the annual meeting of the American Institute of Architects (AIA). At the 1981 meeting, as in recent years, AIA speakers concentrated more on the practical applications of design than on aesthetics. Keynote speaker Ralph Knowles of the University of Southern California in Los Angeles referred to the effects of energy conservation on design forms, but he primarily discussed ways to avoid problems of shade in the design of buildings with solar collectors.

Other speakers also concentrated on the necessity of incorporating energy-efficient features into a building's design. Architect Richard Stein of New York City said, "The impact of energy on the design process will have a more profound and lasting effect on the shape and appearance of our buildings, our cities, and our suburban and rural areas than any other single factor." Robert MacNeil, co-anchor of the Public Broadcasting Service's "MacNeil-Lehrer Report," questioned a panel of architects about the depth of the profession's commitment to energy conservation. The general response was that energy-conscious design had not yet permeated the profession.

Architectural Awards. The AIA's prestigious annual awards for building design were divided into two categories in 1981—new structures and restored or recycled buildings. Skidmore, Owings & Merrill's Chicago office received a new-structures award for its design of three bank buildings in and around Guatemala City, Guatemala. The judges praised the "highly successful relationship of the structures to their urban surroundings." Other recipients of that award included I. M. Pei & Partners of New York City for the East Building at the National Gallery of Art in Washington, D.C.; Hartman-Cox Architects of Washington, D.C., for the National Permanent Building, an office building in that city; Gruzen & Partners of New York City and The Wold Association, Incorporated, of St. Paul, Minn., for the Ramsey County Adult Detention Center in St. Paul—a jail with a spectacular view; Sert, Jackson & Associates, Incorporated, of Cambridge, Mass., for a residential community on Roosevelt Island, New York City; Fay Jones & Associates of Fayetteville, Ark., for Thorncrown Chapel in Eureka Springs, Ark.—a woodland church clad in glass and lattice work; Peters, Clayberg & Caulfield of San Francisco for St. Mary's Gardens, a housing project for the elderly in Oakland, Calif.; and Bohlin Powell Larkin Cywinski of Wilkes-Barre, Pa., for a home built inside an old barn in Coatesville, Pa.

There were seven winners in the category of restored or recycled buildings: Nagle, Hartray Associates, Limited, of Chicago for its conversion of a 1926 hotel in Oak Park, Ill., into apartments for the elderly and handicapped; Chrysalis Corporation of Milwaukee for the interior remodeling of a Chicago town house; Hardy Holzman Pfeiffer Associates of New York City for merging an old motion-picture theater with new construction in Madison, Wis.; Rosekrans and Broder, Incorporated, of San Francisco for restoring the Crocker Art Gallery in that city; Moore Grover Harper of Essex, Conn., for harmoniously incorporating high-tech biological research areas into a historic building at Cold Spring Harbor, N.Y.; Taft Architects of Houston for embellishing a blank wall on an 1859 building in Galveston, Tex.; and Sargent-Webster-Crenshaw & Folley of Syracuse, N.Y., and Architectural Resources Cambridge, Incorporated, of Cambridge, Mass., for the interior of the Hall of Languages at Syracuse University.

The third annual $100,000 Pritzker Architecture Prize went to Scottish architect James Stirling. His firm—James Stirling, Michael Wilford & Associates—has produced designs for the Engineering School at the University of Leicester in Leicester, England, and the History Faculty Building at Cambridge University in Cambridge, England. Architects consider both of these buildings international landmark structures. In the United States, Stirling has three institutional buildings under construction: an addition to the School of Architecture at Rice University in Houston, a chemistry building for Columbia University in New York City, and an expansion of Harvard University's William Hayes Fogg Art Museum in Cambridge, Mass.

On June 6, Maya Yang Lin, a 21-year-old undergraduate at Yale University School of Architecture in New Haven, Conn., received a $20,000 prize for her design of a Vietnam War Memorial for Constitution Gardens in Washington, D.C. Lin's design was chosen over those submitted by hundreds of established architects in a nationwide competition. It featured two long, low, black-granite walls forming a wide V. The walls are to be engraved with the names of the war dead.

Notable New Buildings. The Gerald R. Ford Presidential Museum in Grand Rapids, Mich., was dedicated on September 18. Designed by Marvin DeWinter Associates of Grand Rapids, the two-story, triangular structure has a 300-foot (91-meter) glass wall facing the Grand River.

Construction began during the summer on Columbia Center, a $120-million office tower in Seattle. At 76 stories, it will be the tallest building on the United States West Coast. It was designed by Chester L. Lindsey Architects of Seattle.

I. M. Pei & Partners followed their celebrated East Building addition to the National Gallery with the West Wing of the Museum of Fine Arts in Boston. The wing opened on July 22.   Rob Cuscaden

In WORLD BOOK, see ARCHITECTURE.

The New Residential Community in New York City is one of many attractive urban developments designed by 1981 AIA Gold Medalist Josep Lluis Sert.

Supporters in Buenos Aires celebrate former President Isabel Perón's departure for Madrid, Spain, in July after five years of house arrest.

ARGENTINA. General Roberto Eduardo Viola, commander in chief of the army, became president of Argentina on March 29, 1981. He was selected by the nation's military leaders to succeed President Jorge Rafael Videla, who held that office since the military seized power in 1976. In November, Viola temporarily stepped down from the presidency for health reasons. The military junta, increasingly concerned about the state of the economy, asked Viola to resign. He refused, and the military replaced him by elevating General Leopoldo F. Galtieri to the presidency. Galtieri was inaugurated on December 22.

The Economy of Argentina was a shambles in 1981. In February, Sasetru, the nation's largest conglomerate, declared bankruptcy, sending shock waves throughout the economy. In May, a remark by Minister of Trade Carlos Garcia Martinez that the economy was on the verge of collapse prompted a $400-million run on Argentina's foreign-exchange reserves as Argentines rushed to buy U.S. dollars.

Viola divided responsibility for the economy among five members of his Cabinet. The concentration of economic power in a single minister in the previous administration was blamed in part for the nation's economic ills. Despite the reorganization, domestic production had fallen by 10 per cent by September, and unemployment was rising.

Regardless of its suspicions of multinational companies, Argentina's military government invited several such firms to help develop the nation's oil resources. Argentina imports 20 per cent of the oil it uses, though it is said to have proven reserves of 2.4 billion barrels and potential reserves of at least 10 billion barrels.

Argentina's Image Abroad was damaged by the publication of *Prisoner Without a Name, Cell Without a Number,* a book written by Jacobo Timerman, an Argentine newspaper editor. Timerman reported brutality and anti-Semitism on the part of his captors during a 20-month imprisonment by the nation's military.

Former President Isabel Perón, third wife and successor to President Juan D. Perón, was released on parole on July 6 and sought exile in Spain. She had been held under house arrest for five years awaiting trial on charges of corruption.

Signs of a Deepening Split within the Argentine military over the timetable for an eventual return to democracy were seen during 1981. Political activity remained officially banned, but political parties met openly and pressed their demand for elections in 1984.   Nathan A. Haverstock

See LATIN AMERICA (Facts in Brief Table). In WORLD BOOK, see ARGENTINA.

ARIZONA. See STATE GOVERNMENT.

ARKANSAS. See STATE GOVERNMENT.

ARMED FORCES. On Oct. 2, 1981, President Ronald Reagan unveiled a weapons program that defense analysts described as the most sweeping overhaul of United States strategic forces in the nation's history. Reagan declared that the program, which would cost $180.3 billion over six years, was needed to close a "window of vulnerability" to nuclear attack by Russia.

Reagan's plan to expand U.S. military defenses included revival of the B-1, a long-range supersonic bomber that had been canceled by President Jimmy Carter. Reagan announced that he would also proceed with development of the Stealth bomber, a plane with absorbent surfaces, a special shape, and other features to avoid enemy radar detection. He proposed that the first land-based M-X missiles, a more advanced type of intercontinental ballistic missile (ICBM), be ready by 1986.

Reagan's weapons program also called for accelerated development of a more powerful, more accurate submarine-launched ICBM called Trident 2. He ordered that several hundred jet-powered missiles called cruise missiles, equipped with nuclear warheads, be ready for launching from attack submarines by 1984. In addition, he provided for substantial improvements in strategic communications and control systems and in the air defenses of the North American continent.

M-X Missile Plans. The major surprise in the weapons package was Reagan's unexpected decision on where to base the controversial M-X missile. The Carter Administration had planned to continually shift 200 of the missiles among 4,600 shelters in remote areas of Utah and Nevada. To knock out the missiles, an attacker would have to guess which shelters to hit. Reagan scrapped this plan, claiming that it would be too vulnerable to a Soviet nuclear strike.

Reagan deferred a permanent decision about basing the M-X until 1984, when more technical information would be available. However, production of 100 M-X missiles would begin immediately upon congressional approval of the plan. The first 36 missiles would be housed in existing underground shafts called silos, now used for Titan missiles. The aging Titans would be deactivated, and their silos hardened to provide more protection.

Additional Build-Ups. To strengthen the U.S. airborne deterrent force until the Stealth bomber can be built in the 1990s, Reagan planned to put 3,000 cruise missiles on existing B-52 bombers in 1982 and on B-1 bombers when the new planes become available. He proposed to obtain additional F-15 jet fighters, which can travel at more than twice the speed of sound, and more of the sophisticated radar reconnaissance aircraft called AWACS (Airborne

A prototype of the supersonic B-1 bomber makes a test flight in California in May. President Ronald Reagan called for revival of the canceled B-1.

GI
General

Foot soldiers, who judge generals as severely as baseball fans rate managers, loved General of the Army Omar N. Bradley. The unassuming World War II field commander wore general issue (GI) clothing, a strong contrast to the more flamboyant costume of, say, General George S. Patton, Jr. Bradley was, in the words of *The New Yorker* magazine correspondent A. J. Liebling, "the least dressed-up commander of an American army since Zachary Taylor, who wore a straw hat."

Bradley was soft-spoken and polite, two qualities not always found in military commanders. Most of all, Bradley was a skilled tactical leader who was economical of both men and machines. He spared his soldiers when he could and used them well when he had to.

His skills carried him from the dusty camps and schools of the pre-World War II Army to the highest military rank the United States can give. When he died in 1981, he was the last of the five-star generals of the Army created during and shortly after World War II.

Omar Nelson Bradley was born on Feb. 12, 1893, in Clark, Mo. His father, a schoolteacher, died when Bradley was 13 years old, and the boy's youth in Moberly, Mo., was impoverished. His Sunday school superintendent suggested that the U.S. Military Academy at West Point, N.Y., was a good place for a poor boy to gain an education.

Bradley entered West Point and graduated in the class of 1915, which became known as the "class the stars fell on" because more than 30 members of the class became generals.

Young Second Lieutenant Bradley married a high school classmate, Mary Elizabeth Quayle, in December 1916. Over the next 25 years or so, his wife followed Bradley to 28 Army posts. Bradley saw no action in World War I. His Army career was a succession of posts and training schools as he honed his military skills.

In February 1941, the United States was gathering its strength to enter World War II, and Bradley was appointed brigadier general in command of the Army's Infantry School at Fort Benning, Ga. He became the first in his 1915 class, which included Dwight D. Eisenhower, to receive a general's star.

Bradley had been a soldier for more than 30 years when he first heard hostile gunfire, in North Africa in February 1943. He served as a field aide to Eisenhower and then as commander of the Second U.S. Army Corps. Some units of the Second Corps — particularly the 34th Infantry Division — had been badly mauled by the German Army at Kasserine Pass in Tunisia and were thoroughly demoralized. Bradley restored their self-esteem. Years later, he remembered, "I put them at [Hill] 609. . . . It was almost a cliff. But the 34th went up it [and defeated the Germans]. . . ."

Bradley's troops went on to help defeat the enemy in North Africa and Sicily. Bradley himself was soon sent to London to help prepare for the D-Day invasion of France.

He was on the beaches of Normandy within 24 hours of the invasion on June 6, 1944. As commander of the more than 1.3 million soldiers of the Twelfth Army Group, Lieutenant General Bradley wore his three stars across France and into Germany.

Troops under Bradley's command crossed the Rhine River in March 1945, bringing the war to German soil. His soldiers met the westbound Russian Army on April 25, and the war in Europe came to an end on May 9.

Omar Bradley served as Army chief of staff from 1948 to 1953, with two terms as chairman of the Joint Chiefs of Staff. He gained his fifth star in 1950.

In 1958, Bradley became chairman of the board of the Bulova Watch Company. His wife died in 1965, and he married Esther Buhler in 1966. In his last years, Bradley lived at Fort Bliss in El Paso, Tex. Like the other men who held five stars, Bradley never retired from the U.S. Army. He was considered a general on active duty when he died on April 8, 1981, in the 89th year of his life and the 70th year of service to his country.   Edward G. Nash

"He can't be a real general. He said please."

Warning and Control System) planes. He also ordered stepped-up research and development on a new generation of antiballistic missiles.

Defense officials claimed the Reagan program, when fully implemented by the year 2000, would double the number of U.S. weapons able to survive a surprise attack. But some defense hard-liners complained it was only a stopgap solution, and other critics claimed it would ignite a new arms race with the Soviet Union. On November 30, U.S. and Russian negotiators in Geneva, Switzerland, began talks on limiting nuclear weapons in Europe.

The Sale of AWACS Planes to Saudi Arabia was approved by the Senate on October 28 by a 52 to 48 margin in a stunning political victory for Reagan. The President wanted to sell five AWACS planes and other military hardware to Saudi Arabia for $8.5 billion, but he needed approval of at least one house of Congress to do so. Many members of Congress believed the sale would threaten Israel. The House of Representatives had rejected the deal on October 14.

Libyan Dogfight. On August 19, two U.S. Navy F-14 jet fighters from the aircraft carrier U.S.S. *Nimitz* shot down two Libyan fighter planes after one of the Libyan planes fired on them. It was the first aerial combat by U.S. armed forces since the end of the Vietnam War in 1975. The dogfight occurred about 60 miles (96 kilometers) from the Libyan coast during U.S. naval maneuvers in the Gulf of Sidra. Libya claims the gulf as territorial waters, but the United States regards it as international waters.

Defense Budget. President Carter submitted his final Department of Defense budget request to Congress on Jan. 15, 1981. The budget request asked for $180 billion for the 1982 fiscal year, which runs from Oct. 1, 1981, to Sept. 30, 1982. That amount was $22.4 billion more than the previous year's outlays.

The incoming Reagan Administration, reflecting the new President's view that a major build-up of U.S. military power was overdue, added $4.8 billion to the budget request on March 4. The new request included funds for a new strategic bomber, the reactivation of two moth-balled battleships and an aircraft carrier, a military pay raise, and sizable increases in the purchases of major weapons.

A larger-than-expected federal budget deficit, however, forced the Reagan Administration to announce on September 23 a reduction in planned military spending of $13 billion over three years, including a $2-billion cut from the defense budget for fiscal 1982. The cutbacks would be accomplished by phasing out the aging Titan missiles, reducing one Army division to skeleton status, shrinking the fleet by 29 ships, and canceling the Roland missile program. In addition, planned purchases of M-1 tanks, infantry fighting vehicles,

A-10 attack planes, and F-15 jet fighters would be reduced. On December 15, Congress approved a $200-billion defense spending bill, and Reagan signed it on December 29.

Readiness Problems. The armed forces' maintenance and personnel problems eased somewhat in 1981. In 1980, the problems had been so severe that some members of Congress and other critics asserted that U.S. military forces were no longer a sufficient deterrent to aggression.

All the services continued to report sizable shortages of skilled career personnel during 1981, but two substantial military pay raises helped reduce the shortages. Members of the armed forces received a 5.3 per cent raise in July. In October, enlisted personnel got an additional raise of 10 to 17 per cent, and officers got 14.3 per cent.

The Army exceeded its enlistment and re-enlistment quotas for the second consecutive year, partly due to an economic slump that made military service an attractive alternative for thousands of unemployed workers. Shortages of skilled technicians and spare parts kept many Air Force and Navy fighter planes grounded, but five of the six Army divisions judged unfit for combat in 1980 were rated combat-ready by the end of 1981.

The Pentagon's personnel problems and the huge increase in the size of the armed forces planned by the Reagan Administration intensified pressure to resume the draft. Some defense officials began to lobby publicly for a return to conscription, but the Pentagon officially resisted the idea.

On September 30, troop strength stood at 2,083,000, an increase of 32,000 from the previous year. More than 491,000 troops were overseas.

On June 25, 1981, the Supreme Court of the United States ruled that women may be excluded from military draft registration. The court concluded that the "military context" of the case placed it in a different category from most alleged sex-discrimination cases.

Command Changes. The entire civilian leadership of the Defense Department changed hands with the incoming Reagan Administration in January. The new secretary of defense was Caspar W. Weinberger, a long-time Reagan confidant and secretary of health, education, and welfare under President Richard M. Nixon (see WEINBERGER, CASPAR W.). John O. Marsh, Jr., was named secretary of the Army; Verne L. Orr was appointed secretary of the Air Force; and John F. Lehman, Jr., became secretary of the Navy. General David C. Jones continued as chairman of the Joint Chiefs of Staff.   Thomas M. DeFrank

In WORLD BOOK, see the articles on the branches of the armed forces.

ARMY. See ARMED FORCES.

ART. See ARCHITECTURE; DANCING; LITERATURE; MUSIC, CLASSICAL; POETRY; VISUAL ARTS.

ASIA

Afghans who fled the Russian occupation
of their country sit on relief supplies at
a camp in northern Pakistan in January.

Guerrilla wars flared from the Philippines to Iran, refugees fled conflict and oppression, and floods and other natural disasters tormented the already impoverished people of Asia in 1981. But the average Asian lived quietly, eking out a bare living on a bit of farmland, far from modern politics, and little aware of the turmoil on the vast, diverse continent.

Most Asians realized, however, that the continent's continued population increase was straining their scarce resources. Old people could remember when a plot of land had to grow food for only half as many people, and firewood was easier to find. During 1981, the population of Asia increased by 50 million and reached about 2.5 billion. World Bank projections forecast a population of 3.3 billion by the end of the century and predicted that growth would continue until the 22nd century, when 5.2 billion people – 800 million more than the present population of the world – would jostle for space and food on the continent.

Population pressure contributed to natural disasters. The destruction of forests and the planting of previously uncultivated land to increase food production also increased erosion. The year 1981 saw the worst floods in decades in the Chinese province of Szechwan (Sichuan). They were blamed on deforestation that caused rain to run off rapidly instead of soaking into the soil.

Refugee Movements. Great economic hardship, caused partly by natural conditions and partly by mismanagement, drove some Asians to other countries in hopes of new opportunities. Poverty was a major cause of the continuing exodus from Vietnam, Cambodia, and Laos during 1981. Some 600,000 people from these countries had been resettled since 1975 as political refugees. Tens of thousands left their homelands in tiny boats and risked their lives at sea as "boat people." Others fled overland to Thailand. In 1981, nearby nations began to take a more hostile attitude toward the fleeing people. They felt the refugees were seeking better economic conditions rather than escaping persecution and so did not deserve special aid.

The war of resistance by the Afghan people against Russian occupation caused a more clearly political problem. Russia had invaded Afghanistan in December 1979 and installed a Soviet-controlled puppet government there. Afghanistan became the world's largest source of refugees during 1981. Pakistan was sheltering more than 2 million Afghan refugees. Estimates of Afghan refugees in Iran ranged from 100,000 to 1 million. About 20 per cent of the population claimed by Afghanistan's puppet government had fled its control.

Internal Wars and Border Disputes. In addition to the Afghan conflict, scattered fighting occurred in Cambodia and Laos, in Vietnam's highlands, on the Vietnam-China border, and between Iran and Iraq. At year-end, all these conflicts ground on without an end in sight. New international efforts to resolve the Iran-Iraq war came to nothing. Proposals for the withdrawal of Soviet troops from Afghanistan broke down over Soviet reluctance to allow the Soviet-backed government of Babrak Karmal to collapse. China maintained military pressure on Vietnam to help relieve pressure on the Khmer Rouge, a group of Cambodian Communists who were fighting the Vietnamese occupation of Cambodia.

Efforts by Ethnic Minorities to win greater self-rule also caused conflict in a number of Asian countries. Resistance to Indonesian control smoldered on the western half of New Guinea island. Muslim rebels in the southern Philippines made guerrilla attacks against Philippine troops in an effort to win independence from the predominantly Roman Catholic nation. Nagas and other tribal groups in the hills of eastern India continued a decades-old struggle to escape Indian rule, and similar tribes in the Chittagong Hills area of Bangladesh fought the control of that country. The attempt by some members of a minority group called the Tamils to win independence in Sri Lanka produced violence there, but a similar separatist movement in the Pakistani province of Baluchistan was fairly quiet after years of fighting. Kurds and other minorities in Iran fought against Iranian control, with the Kurds managing to maintain a separate territory. And on Taiwan, an underground independence movement struggled to survive police suppression. It opposed the view of both Taiwan's ruling Kuomintang party and the mainland Chinese government that the island is part of China and should be reunited with it.

The Major World Powers played roles in some of Asia's troubles. The United States, China, and other countries reportedly sent weapons to Afghan guerrillas. The Soviet Union was extremely active. It not only controlled Afghanistan, but also increased its involvement in Indochina. While criticizing Vietnam for wasting its aid, the Soviet Union sent more aid and advisers to Cambodia and Laos. Instead of just helping the Vietnamese, whose puppet regimes ran those two countries, Russia seemed eager to increase its own influence and, in effect, compete with Vietnam.

The Soviet Union and China vied for commercial and political influence throughout Asia. In Southeast Asia, such countries as Malaysia and Singapore showed growing concern over Soviet naval activities and spying. But there was mixed reaction to prospects that Japan might build up its military power. Japanese commercial power already worried many countries of Southeast Asia.

Japan increased its 1982 defense budget but gave no other sign of expanding its military role, though some Japanese people urged that their country do more for its own defense. Controversy over the defense issue forced Japan's Foreign Minister Masayoshi Ito to resign on May 16, 1981, after a joint U.S.-Japanese communiqué referred to an "alliance" between the two countries. Critics said this sounded like greater military cooperation than the Japanese people would accept.

Soviet military pressure on China's border continued during 1981, but in September Moscow proposed reopening talks on border disputes. On December 10, China and India began talks in an effort to resolve an old border dispute between the two countries.

Governmental Changes. Asia, a continent often shaken by revolutions and military coups d'état, experienced no successful coups in 1981. A military group in Thailand attempted a coup in April, but King Bhumibol Adulyadej's refusal to accept the coup leaders helped Prime Minister Prem Tinsulanonda rally support and force the soldiers to back down. An abortive coup attempt by army officers

Facts in Brief on the Asian Countries

Country	Population	Government	Monetary Unit*	Foreign Trade (million U.S. $) Exports†	Imports†
Afghanistan	16,681,000	Revolutionary Council President Babrak Karmal; Prime Minister Sultan Ali Keshtmand	afghani (49.3 = $1)	494	686
Australia	15,032,000	Governor General Sir Zelman Cowen; Prime Minister Malcolm Fraser	dollar (1 = $1.15)	22,053	20,332
Bangladesh	93,849,000	President Abdus Sattar; Prime Minister Shah Azizur Rahman	taka (15.7 = $1)	662	1,530
Bhutan	1,374,000	King Jigme Singye Wangchuck	Indian rupee and ngultrum (9.1 = $1)	1	1
Burma	35,133,000	President U San Yu; Prime Minister U Maung Maung Kha	kyat (7.1 = $1)	390	292
Cambodia (Kampuchea)	9,303,000	People's Revolutionary Party Secretary General & Council of State President Heng Samrin; Premier Pen Sovan (Khmer Rouge government: President & Prime Minister Khieu Samphan)	riel (4 = $1)	1	20
China	969,665,000	Communist Party Chairman Hu Yaobang; Premier Zhao Ziyang	yuan (1.7 = $1)	13,800	14,500
India	692,860,000	President Neelam Sanjiva Reddy; Prime Minister Indira Gandhi	rupee (9.1 = $1)	7,608	9,546
Indonesia	160,210,000	President Suharto; Vice President Adam Malik	rupiah (630 = $1)	21,909	10,834
Iran	40,663,000	President Ali Khamenei; Prime Minister Hosein Musavi-Khamenei	rial (79 = $1)	19,872	9,738
Japan	120,448,000	Emperor Hirohito; Prime Minister Zenko Suzuki	yen (216.5 = $1)	129,248	140,528
Korea, North	18,918,000	President Kim Il-song; Premier Yi Chong-ok	won (1.8 = $1)	1,320	1,300
Korea, South	39,556,000	President Chun Doo Hwan; Acting Prime Minister Duck-woo Nam	won (688 = $1)	17,548	22,292
Laos	3,884,000	President Souphanouvong; Prime Minister Kayson Phomvihan	kip (400 = $1)	15	80
Malaysia	14,798,000	Paramount Ruler Ahmad Shah Ibni Al-Marhum Sultan Abu Bakar; Prime Minister Mahathir bin Mohamed	ringgit (2.3 = $1)	11,280	9,416
Maldives	158,000	President Maumoon Abdul Gayoom	rupee (3.1 = $1)	5	22
Mongolia	1,767,000	People's Revolutionary Party First Secretary & Presidium Chairman Yumjaagiyn Tsedenbal; Council of Ministers Chairman Jambyn Batmonh	tughrik (3.1 = $1)	258	336
Nepal	14,595,000	King Birendra Bir Bikram Shah Dev; Prime Minister Surya Bahadur Thapa	rupee (13 = $1)	80	342
New Zealand	3,156,000	Governor General Sir David Stuart Beattie; Prime Minister Robert D. Muldoon	dollar (1.2 = $1)	5,414	5,464
Pakistan	87,497,000	President Mohammad Zia-ul-Haq	rupee (9.8 = $1)	2,588	5,350
Papua New Guinea	3,306,000	Governor General Sir Tore Lokoloko; Prime Minister Sir Julius Chan	kina (1 = $1.45)	964	788
Philippines	51,992,000	President Ferdinand E. Marcos; Prime Minister Cesar E. Virata	peso (8.1 = $1)	5,393	7,789
Russia	269,591,000	Communist Party General Secretary & Supreme Soviet Presidium Chairman Leonid Ilich Brezhnev; Council of Ministers Chairman Nikolay Aleksandrovich Tikhonov	ruble (1 = $1.41)	76,481	68,523
Singapore	2,471,000	President Devan Nair; Prime Minister Lee Kuan Yew	dollar (2 = $1)	19,376	24,008
Sri Lanka	15,173,000	President J. R. Jayewardene; Prime Minister R. Premadasa	rupee (18.5 = $1)	924	2,029
Taiwan	18,524,000	President Chiang Ching-kuo; Premier Sun Yun-hsuan	new Taiwan dollar (37.9 = $1)	16,100	14,800
Thailand	49,981,000	King Bhumibol Adulyadej; Prime Minister Prem Tinsulanonda	baht (23 = $1)	6,509	9,212
Vietnam	54,427,000	Communist Party Secretary General Le Duan; National Assembly Chairman Nguyen Huu Tho; Prime Minister Pham Van Dong	dong (2.2 = $1)	300	900

*Exchange rates as of Dec. 1, 1981. †Latest available data.

in Bangladesh on May 30 killed President Ziaur Rahman, whose leadership had given that impoverished country one of the world's most effective development programs. Abdus Sattar won election on November 15 as Bangladesh's new president.

Continuing turmoil in Iran decimated that country's leadership. President Abol Hasan Bani-Sadr was forced from office in June by opponents in the clergy-controlled Islamic Republican Party. His successor, Mohammed Ali Rajai, died on August 30 in a wave of terrorist attacks that killed a number of government leaders. Ali Khamenei was then elected president in October. The virtual civil war in Iran, plus Kurdish and other separatist movements, and the fight against Soviet control in Afghanistan made those two countries the most disturbed in Asia.

Other governmental changes were more peaceful. President Benjamin Henry Sheares of Singapore died in May and was succeeded by Devan Nair. President U Ne Win of Burma retired in November after 19 years in office. U San Yu became president, but Ne Win kept the leadership of the dominant political party. Malaysia's Prime Minister Hussein Onn retired, and in July Mahathir bin Mohamed became prime minister. China brought a long leadership struggle to at least a temporary end when its Communist Party removed Hua Kuo-feng (Hua Guofeng) as party chairman and gave that position to Hu Yaobang.

Regional Cooperation flourished. The five members of the Association of Southeast Asian Nations (ASEAN) — Indonesia, Malaysia, the Philippines, Singapore, and Thailand — worked without success to bring peace to Cambodia. Vietnam, Cambodia, and Laos coordinated their policies under Vietnam's control, partly to counteract ASEAN. China and Japan moved toward closer economic ties.

Seven nations of southern Asia — Bangladesh, Bhutan, India, Maldives, Nepal, Pakistan, and Sri Lanka — took the first steps toward a regional forum. Foreign secretaries of these countries held a meeting in Colombo, Sri Lanka, in April. They set up study groups on cooperation in agriculture, rural development, telecommunications, meteorology, and health and family planning.

Asia's Economy. World prices for many of the commodities sold by Asian countries declined during 1981, but the prices of imported industrial goods continued to climb, and there was little relief from the high cost of imported oil. These factors caused severe economic problems for several Asian countries. Lower rubber prices hurt Malaysia, for instance, and a slump in coconut prices devastated Philippine farmers. However, good harvests relieved some economic strains.   Henry S. Bradsher

See also the various Asian country articles. In the WORLD BOOK SUPPLEMENT section, see KUALA LUMPUR; MALAYSIA. In WORLD BOOK, see ASIA.

ASTRONOMY. The highlight of the year came on Aug. 25, 1981, as the National Aeronautics and Space Administration's (NASA) planetary probe *Voyager 2* swept past Saturn 101,000 kilometers (63,000 miles) above its cloud tops — 23,000 kilometers (14,000 miles) closer than *Voyager 1* in November 1980. *Voyager 2* took four years to travel from Earth to Saturn on a journey of more than 2 billion kilometers (1.2 billion miles) at an average speed of 64,000 kilometers (40,000 miles) per hour. It will reach Uranus in January 1986.

Astronomers believe an unexpected improvement in the clarity of *Voyager 2* pictures was caused by an accidental variation in the quality of vidicon tubes used in the equipment for transmitting pictures from both *Voyager* spacecraft. This and other, planned variations helped them gain much new information from the second probe. *Voyager 2* was specially targeted to study the structure of Saturn's ring system. One experiment delivered unprecedented detail of the rings by tracking the variation of light from the star Delta Scorpii as it shone through the rings to the spacecraft. Computers converted data on a strip chart into high-resolution views of the rings impossible to obtain from the probe's cameras. *Voyager 1* photos had shown that the rings consist of at least thousands of small "ringlets," but *Voyager 2* data revealed that there are hundreds of thousands.

Radio Waves beamed through the ring system allowed scientists to estimate the size and distribution of ring particles, which consist mainly of water ice. The largest particles seem to be about 10 meters (33 feet) in diameter, with about 120 to 200 of these per square kilometer (310 to 520 per square mile). Smaller particles, down to about 3 meters (10 feet) in diameter, are more numerous. Below that size, the radio data were inconclusive. However, astronomers became convinced that the patterns of bright and dark "spokes" that *Voyager 1* photos showed forming and dissolving are due to dust or ice grains.

The narrow F ring, which showed mysterious "braids" in *Voyager 1* photos, showed no such irregularities in the *Voyager 2* pictures. *Voyager 2* successfully photographed the narrow G ring, which lies somewhat farther outside the main ring system than the F ring. Its existence had been inferred from shadows it cast on passing moons and from particle counts. The E ring, located even farther out, is extremely tenuous and extended. The *Voyager* imaging team confirmed two more small moons in 1981, bringing Saturn's total to 17 moons — nine major moons and eight so-called rocks.

Voyager 2 produced the first close-up views of Enceladus, whose surface showed evidence of five geologic eras of bombardment and surface activity. The most recent era dates back only about 100 million years — so recent in geologic terms that

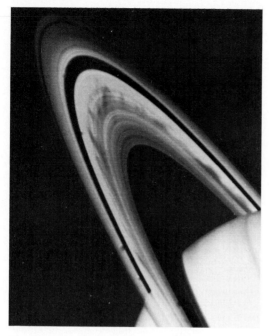

The *Voyager 2* probe in August returned photos
of Saturn's B ring that suggest its mysterious
dark spokes are dust particles hovering over it.

Enceladus is presumed to be still geologically active. *Voyager 2* also showed Tethys more clearly, revealing a huge 400-kilometer (250-mile) crater and a long rift valley.

Voyager 1 had not photographed at close range the three moons orbiting beyond Titan, so their pictures were full of surprises for the *Voyager 2* team. Hyperion, shaped like a battered watermelon, has a spin that is strangely out of equilibrium. Iapetus is an exotic "black-and-white" moon. Its leading face is dark, reflecting only 5 per cent of the sunlight falling on it. Its trailing face is bright, reflecting 50 per cent of the sunlight that strikes it.

Phoebe, Saturn's outermost moon, was found to have a diameter of 200 kilometers (120 miles) and a surprisingly round shape for so small a moon. Its color is much darker than the other moons, which are generally icy and bright. Astronomers observed Phoebe's spin for the first time. Its period of 9 to 10 hours means that Phoebe does not keep one face always turned toward Saturn as its companions do. Its retrograde, or opposite, orbit is considerably inclined to the orbits of the other moons. All these strange characteristics, combined with Phoebe's enormous distance from Saturn's center — 12,930,000 kilometers (8,030,000 miles) — suggest that this outermost satellite of Saturn is really a captured asteroid or comet nucleus and did not form naturally with the Saturn system.

Neptune. Planetary astronomers Harold J. Reitsema, William B. Hubbard, Larry A. Lebofsky, and David J. Tholen may have found a third moon of Neptune on May 24, 1981. Using two University of Arizona telescopes, they watched Neptune pass almost directly in front of a distant star. Although Neptune just missed cutting off the light of the star, both telescopes recorded an 8-second decrease in brightness. The astronomers ruled out the possibility that the decrease was caused by an unknown asteroid, an unknown ring of Neptune, or by Neptune's atmosphere. Therefore, they suggested that an unknown third moon of Neptune was responsible. They calculated that the third moon, if it exists, is at least 180 kilometers (110 miles) in diameter and orbits about 50,000 kilometers (31,000 miles) from the planet.

Pulsars. All of the collapsed, fast-spinning stars known as pulsars discovered until recently have been tiny neutron stars about 16 kilometers (10 miles) in diameter. Small areas of a neutron star's surface emit a high-energy beam of radiation that is detected by X-ray telescopes. As the star spins and the beam swings past the observer, it is recorded as a sudden pulse of electromagnetic energy — hence the name *pulsar*. Joseph O. Patterson of Harvard University in Cambridge, Mass., and João Steiner of the University of São Paulo in Brazil reported that they discovered in June three pulsars that are white dwarf stars. These stars are about 1,000 times larger than neutron stars but emit a much weaker beam.

Galaxies in Collision. Astronomer Peter Quinn of Australian National University in Canberra reported in November that he had produced computer models showing that the collision of two spiral galaxies produces an elliptical or spherical galaxy with a faint shell-like shape near the outer edge. Stars in galaxies are so far apart that individual star collisions are extremely rare. However, the gravitational pull of two galaxies can drastically deform their shapes and so result in their merging.

According to Quinn's picture of galactic evolution, or change in structure, galaxies first form as spirals. When two of them collide and merge, an elliptical galaxy with a shell is formed. Most of these elliptical galaxies lose their shells in later collisions. However, about 10 per cent show existing shells, and most of these lie in isolated locations where further collisions are unlikely.

During the past two years, other astronomers had discovered very faint outlying shells of stars around some, but not all, elliptical galaxies. The fit between these unexplained observations and Quinn's computer result is impressive and may lead to a new conception of why galaxies develop the shapes they do.   Eric D. Carlson

See also SPACE EXPLORATION. In WORLD BOOK, see ASTRONOMY; articles on the planets.

AUSTRALIA enjoyed political stability and prospects of massive investment in minerals and energy but suffered a decline in export sales in 1981. Prime Minister Malcolm Fraser's Liberal-National Country coalition remained in office. Minister for Industrial Relations Andrew Peacock resigned on April 15, accusing Fraser of "disloyalty," but there were no immediate repercussions.

The Fraser government's freedom to legislate was limited after July 1, when senators elected in 1980 took office. The Australian Democrats had elected five senators and thus gained the ability to swing the balance of power, depending on whether they voted with the government's 31 senators or with the Australian Labor Party's 27. One Independent was also elected. The only state race in 1981 took place in New South Wales, where Neville Wran's Labor government won re-election on September 19.

Prime Minister Fraser led the Commonwealth Heads of Government Meeting in Melbourne from September 30 to October 7. The meeting concentrated on problems of so-called North-South economic relations, or relations between the industrialized and the developing nations. Fraser identified Australia with the economic needs of developing countries. He also opposed national tours by such South African sports teams as the Springboks, South Africa's national Rugby team, whose visit to New Zealand from July to September had created controversy because of South Africa's racial policies. By August, Australian foreign aid had increased to $662.3 million, up $104 million. (All money values in this article are expressed in Australian dollars; $1=U.S. $1.13 as of Dec. 31, 1981.)

Australia's prime minister took several steps to cement friendly relations with the new Administration of U.S. President Ronald Reagan. He supported the United States positions on Afghanistan and El Salvador. At the end of October, Fraser accepted U.S. proposals made in May that Australia contribute to the international peacekeeping force that would supervise the Israeli withdrawal from the Sinai Desert. Australian agreement was conditional on British and Canadian participation. Fraser announced on March 11 that U.S. B-52 strategic bombers and other aircraft based on Guam would be allowed to land at Darwin in the Northern Territory on surveillance and training flights. However, they would require Australian consent if they carried nuclear weapons. The government on September 17 called on the United States to commit itself to final negotiations at the United Nations (UN) Law of the Sea Conference, which had been meeting for eight years. Australia stressed the importance of these negotiations to Pacific Island nations.

The Economy continued to improve in 1981. Unemployment fell below 6 per cent, and inflation was down to 8.8 per cent in July. Fraser's government continued to make reducing inflation its main task. The budget presented by Treasurer John Howard on August 18 aimed at cutting the government deficit by almost $1 billion in the 1981-1982 fiscal year. The government continued to enforce limits on spending and remained hostile to proposals for a 35-hour workweek.

The Conciliation and Arbitration Commission, which in 1975 had instituted cost-of-living wage increases, abandoned the practice of indexing wages to prices on July 31, 1981. The Congress of the Australian Council of Trade Unions (ACTU) expressed limited opposition and voted on September 8 for a system of salary raises that would adjust wages to prices on a quarterly basis.

The 24-nation Organization for Economic Cooperation and Development (OECD) predicted in July that Australia would have the fastest growth rate of all member countries in 1982. It forecast the rate of increase in gross domestic product at 5.25 per cent, compared with 2.0 per cent for the OECD as a whole. Much of this optimism was based on investment in minerals and energy. The federal government received 1,212 proposals for foreign investment, mainly in those fields, in the fiscal year ending June 30, 1981, compared with 1,106 a year earlier. Of these proposals, 710 were approved unconditionally, 462 approved with conditions, and only 40 rejected. Those approved totaled $6.6-billion.

There were encouraging oil finds in South Australia's Cooper Basin. On February 9, the Strzelecki field recorded the biggest onshore flow that had yet been discovered in Australia – 3,600 barrels per day.

Exports Were Disappointing in 1981. Shipments of coal, meat, and wool declined, though sugar exports stayed the same. In addition, farmers in eastern Australia suffered from a prolonged drought. The depressed state of the world's aluminum market in October caused Australia's three major producers to reduce production and lower domestic prices. International lead and zinc markets were in a similar position.

Social Changes. New Zealanders were required for the first time on July 1 to have passports when entering Australia. The quota for refugees, most of whom came from Indochina, was set at 15,000 for 1981-1982. The ACTU Congress voted overwhelmingly on September 11 to support free, legal abortions for working women. On July 27, the Labor Party's national conference adopted the policy that Australia should become a republic. On August 24, the sections of the Church of England in Australia formed a single entity – the Anglican Church of Australia.   J. D. B. Miller

See also ASIA (Facts in Brief Table). In WORLD BOOK, see AUSTRALIA.

AUSTRIA continued to struggle with its growing trade deficit, which amounted to nearly $2 billion at the beginning of 1981. The country had little chance of cutting this figure because the costs of its fuel imports continued to rise.

The results of a 1978 referendum prevented Austria from using its only nuclear power plant. Chancellor Bruno Kreisky accepted Austria's need for nuclear power, but he refused to try to override the referendum until Great Britain, Russia, and the United States agreed on an international agency to deal with nuclear waste. Trade unions and industry favored nuclear power, but the political parties were divided on the issue.

Death Plot. Egypt's President Anwar el-Sadat canceled a visit to Austria on August 6 because of fears that a Palestinian terrorist had plotted to kill him. Austrian authorities suspected that the officially recognized Palestine Liberation Organization (PLO) representative in Vienna, Ghasi Hussain, was involved.

Hussain had been waiting to meet two Arabs at the Vienna airport a week earlier. But Austrian police arrested the Arabs at the airport and found a submachine gun, 4 rifles, 6 hand grenades, and 500 rounds of ammunition in their luggage. Hussain claimed that he had nothing to do with a plot, but Austria's Interior Minister Erwin Lanc called for Hussain to be expelled.

Wage Moderation. The 24-nation Organization for Economic Cooperation and Development (OECD) reported in February that a "unique social partnership reflected in wage moderation" had helped the Austrian economy to absorb rising oil prices without a major loss of jobs. But the OECD expected some job losses in 1981. Unemployment might rise above 2 per cent, but it was likely to remain among the lowest in Western Europe. Anton Benya, president of Austria's trade union federation, agreed in 1981 that trade unions would accept wage increases that matched the 6.5 per cent inflation rate.

Minister of Finance Hannes Androsch resigned on January 6. He had announced he would resign in December 1980 following charges that he had been involved in a hospital-financing scandal. However, the government had asked him to stay through January 1981. On January 14, Kreisky named Minister of Health Herbert Salcher to succeed Androsch.

Steel Crisis. The world steel crisis hit Austria hard in February, when more than 4,000 of the nation's 19,000 steelworkers had their hours cut. Orders from Eastern Europe and China declined, and industrialists complained that the economy could not support six plants that made special kinds of steel. Kenneth Brown

See also EUROPE (Facts in Brief Table). In WORLD BOOK, see AUSTRIA.

AUTOMOBILE. The automobile industry in the United States, already reeling from a depressingly persistent two-year sales slump, suffered its worst year in 20 years in 1981. United States automakers laid off nearly 215,000 workers, abandoned or postponed factory construction or modernization plans, delayed the introduction of new models, and demanded wage and benefit concessions from auto workers. Industry officials blamed plunging auto sales on the recession, high interest rates, and competition from imported cars. But experts also cited adverse consumer reaction to hefty sticker-price increases that have pushed the average cost of a new car to $10,000.

Nevertheless, prices for 1982-model cars continued to rise. General Motors Corporation (GM) posted a tentative 5.8 per cent increase of $617 per car on its 1982 models. Ford Motor Company upped its prices 4.8 per cent or $430 per car, and Chrysler increased its prices 7.7 per cent or $662 per car. Among the smaller companies, American Motors Corporation increased prices on its domestic models and on the Renault imports it sells by an average of 3.8 per cent or $332 per car, while Toyota Motor Company hiked prices 6.8 per cent or $451 per car.

Auto Sales. Record rebate offers in 1981 seemed to do little to revive sagging auto sales. United States auto manufacturers sold 6.21 million cars in 1981, a drop of about 5 per cent from 6.58 million cars sold in 1980 and the lowest domestic sales figure since 1961. All U.S. automakers except Chrysler reported lower sales. Sales of Chrysler cars in 1981 rose 10.5 per cent over 1980. During October, the first full month of the 1982-model year, sales of domestically produced cars were the worst for any October since 1958 and 26 per cent lower than sales in October 1980.

Imported cars maintained their firm hold on the U.S. market, totaling an estimated 2.32 million units sold, or a record 27.1 per cent of the market, from 2.38 million in 1980 or 26.6 per cent. Total car sales in the United States during the year fell to about 8.52 million, from 8.96 million in 1980.

Production. United States automakers cut production and laid off workers as the number of unsold cars jamming company and dealer lots during the final quarter of 1981 reached 1.5 million, an 84-day supply. A 60-day supply is considered normal. During the past two years, Chrysler, Ford, and GM cut their U.S. work force by nearly 25 per cent and closed 16 of about 220 manufacturing plants. The Department of Commerce estimated in December that more than 1 million people were out of work because of the auto slump. In 1981, automakers also canceled or delayed a number of capital-spending programs. GM, for example, announced in November that it had delayed for one year the construction of a controversial

Automaker John Z. De Lorean sits atop his new $25,000 De Lorean sports car. Made in Northern Ireland, it features a stainless-steel finish and gull-wing doors.

$500-million assembly plant in Hamtramck, Mich. Neighborhood groups in Hamtramck had opposed GM's efforts to acquire and clear land for the plant. The company also dropped plans to build a $500-million assembly plant in Kansas City, Kans.

Finances. United States auto manufacturers lost a staggering $1 billion after taxes in the third quarter of 1981. GM's higher-than-expected $468-million loss after taxes was the first quarterly loss for the world's largest automaker since the third quarter of 1980. American Motors reported a $16.8-million loss for the period, and Ford lost $334.5 million – the result, said Ford's Chairman Philip Caldwell, of "weak economic conditions worldwide."

Chrysler announced a third-quarter loss of $149.3 million, compared with a $489.7-million loss for the same period a year earlier. The company's lower-than-expected loss, coupled with its $12-million profit during the second quarter – the first in two years – led Chrysler's Chairman Lee A. Iacocca to announce that the company would not ask the federal government for the $300 million remaining from the $1.5-billion loan package approved by Congress in 1979. Although GM was expected to earn a profit in 1981, the United States auto industry as a whole was expected to show losses of $1.4 billion, much less than 1980's $4.2-billion loss.

Labor Talks. During 1981, U.S. auto manufacturers repeatedly pressed the United Automobile Workers (UAW) to renegotiate existing contracts, arguing that wage and benefit concessions were necessary in order to make U.S. autos competitive with imported cars. UAW President Douglas A. Fraser called the demands "shenanigans." However, in December, the UAW dropped its opposition to renegotiation. Citing the dismal condition of the auto industry, the UAW's executive council voted to allow bargaining councils at individual companies to decide whether to reopen their contracts. Existing contracts between the UAW and Ford and GM expire in September 1982. The contract between the UAW and American Motors ends in September 1983. In January, union workers at Chrysler had agreed to accept $622 million in wage and benefit concessions as part of the government-backed bailout plan for the company.

In mid-December, Ford and GM announced cuts in benefits for their white-collar workers. The UAW had insisted that automakers must reduce benefits for salaried workers before union members would agree to similar concessions. On December 17, UAW leaders at American Motors agreed to begin talks on the company's proposal to defer scheduled pay raises for union employees. On December 21, UAW bargaining councils at Ford and GM also agreed to discuss contract revisions.

AUTOMOBILE

Japanese Cutback. On May 1, Japan, acting under the threat of import quotas, agreed to a three-year plan to "voluntarily" curb auto shipments to the United States. The pact limited Japanese auto imports to no more than 1.68 million cars between April 1, 1981, and March 31, 1982. In 1980, Japan sold 1.82 million cars in the United States. No quota was set for the second year of the agreement, and U.S. officials said it was unlikely that the pact would be extended when it expired in August 1984. United States automakers had argued that quotas were needed to increase domestic car sales and raise the money needed to retool for the production of smaller, more fuel-efficient cars. In 1981, Japan also agreed to limit auto imports to West Germany and Canada.

Airbags Abandoned. On October 23, the National Highway Traffic Safety Administration abandoned the controversial requirement that auto manufacturers must equip cars with airbags or other automatic restraints. Automatic restraints were to have been required in large cars in the 1982-model year and in all cars thereafter. But in July 1980, Congress postponed implementing the safety standard for one year. The decision to scrap the requirement drew criticism from safety groups and the insurance industry.   Charles C. Cain III

In WORLD BOOK, see AUTOMOBILE.

AUTOMOBILE RACING. In 1981, for the first time ever, the winner of the Indianapolis 500, the world's richest automobile race, was disqualified. Four and a half months later, that driver, Bobby Unser of Albuquerque, N. Mex., was reinstated as winner of the race.

The race was held at the Indianapolis Motor Speedway in Indianapolis on May 24. Unser, driving a Penske-Cosworth, started from the inside position of the first row in the field of 33 cars because he had the best time in the qualification trials. Mario Andretti of Nazareth, Pa., in a Wildcat-Cosworth, started from the last row.

On the 149th lap of the 200-lap race, Unser, Andretti, and other drivers went into the pits during a yellow, or caution, flag. They took on fuel and new tires and then returned to the field.

The rules required drivers returning to the field on a yellow flag to blend in with traffic and maintain their position. They were not permitted to improve their position by passing other cars.

According to race stewards, when Unser left the pit after that stop, he passed eight or nine cars. Roger Penske, who owned Unser's car, said Unser had obeyed the rules. He said Andretti, who left the pits behind Unser, had passed three cars.

Unser finished first in the race, 5.3 seconds ahead of Andretti, in the second-closest Indianapo-

Danny Ongais' car explodes into flames after hitting a wall on the 64th lap of the Indianapolis 500 on May 24. Ongais suffered multiple fractures.

lis finish ever. The next morning, when the stewards posted the official results, they penalized Unser one lap for illegally passing cars. The penalty dropped him to second place and made Andretti the winner.

Penske lost one appeal to a board of stewards. But on October 9, a three-member appeals panel appointed by the United States Auto Club (USAC), which had sanctioned the race, ruled that the penalty against Unser was too severe.

The panel said the infraction should have been called during the race. It voted to fine Unser $40,000, but it revoked the one-lap penalty, which meant that Unser was the winner after all.

In another ruling, the USAC decreed that only stock-block engines would be allowed for the Indianapolis 500 starting in 1982. In the 1981 race, 29 of the 33 cars were powered by eight-cylinder Cosworth engines from Great Britain, which cost about twice as much as stock-block engines.

NASCAR Series. For 15 years, there had been few changes in the large, late-model sedans that competed on the 31-race Grand National series of the National Association for Stock Car Auto Racing (NASCAR). In 1981, the large sedans, which measured 115 inches (292 centimeters) between their axles, were replaced by medium-sized cars with a 110-inch (279-centimeter) wheelbase.

Darrell Waltrip of Franklin, Tenn., won 12 races in the 1981 NASCAR series and Bobby Allison of Hueytown, Ala., won five. Waltrip narrowly defeated Allison for the series title.

Richard Petty of Randleman, N.C., captured the year's most important stock-car race in the United States. Driving a Buick, he won NASCAR's Daytona 500 on February 15 in Daytona Beach, Fla.

Grand Prix. The international series of Grand Prix races for the world drivers' championship was threatened in 1981 by a power struggle between the car builders and the sport's administrators. Until a compromise was reached, two rival series for the sophisticated Formula One cars seemed possible.

One series of 15 Grand Prix races was finally approved. Nelson Piquet of Brazil edged out Carlos Reutteman of Argentina for the title, 50 points to 49. Piquet, in a Brabham, won races in Argentina, San Marino, and West Germany. Reutteman, in a Williams-Ford, was first in Brazil and Belgium.

Alan Jones of Australia won two Grand Prix races – the Toyota Grand Prix of Long Beach on March 15 in Long Beach, Calif., and the new Las Vegas Grand Prix on October 17 in Las Vegas, Nev. Jacques Laffite of France took the Canadian Grand Prix on September 27 in Montreal, Canada.

In the major international endurance competition, Jacky Ickx of Belgium and Derek Bell of England, in a Porsche, won the 24 Hours of Le Mans on June 14 in France.   Frank Litsky

In WORLD BOOK, see AUTOMOBILE RACING.

AVIATION in 1981 was plagued with a lagging economy in the United States, customer resistance to fare increases, financial distress from fare discounts, and an air-traffic controllers strike that hampered operations. Major United States airlines stretched their crash-free record beyond two years in November.

United States domestic-airline passenger traffic through October was off 5.6 per cent from the first 10 months of 1980, air freight declined 1.6 per cent, and international air freight fell 5.1 per cent. The International Air Transport Association (IATA) said that airlines carried 2 per cent more paying passengers on North Atlantic routes in the first eight months of 1981 than in the same period in 1980, and cargo was up 1.9 per cent. International traffic carried by U.S. airlines was down 0.2 per cent through October.

George W. James, the U.S. airline industry's chief economist, estimated in December that any U.S. scheduled carriers' profits would be minimal in 1981. After earnings of $18 million in 1980, he saw another operating loss. The sales of some hotels and other assets helped produce profits. In addition, easing fuel costs, cuts in capacity and in the work force, and basic fare increases aided earnings. However, James pointed out that fare discounting cut into profits.

President Ronald Reagan appointed Clinton Dan McKinnon, owner of several San Diego and Texas radio and television stations, as chairman of the Civil Aeronautics Board (CAB). McKinnon took office in October. The Lockheed Corporation announced on December 7 that it would stop making L-1011 Tristar jetliners after it finishes manufacturing Tristars that were on order on that date. Lockheed will deliver the last Tristar in 1984. The company said that it had lost $2.5 billion on the L-1011 since 1968.

Controller Shortage. A strike disrupted air traffic in 1981. On July 29, the Professional Air Traffic Controllers Organization (PATCO) rejected a contract offer from the Federal Aviation Administration (FAA). Some 12,000 PATCO members struck on August 3. Strikes by federal employees are illegal, so President Reagan warned the strikers that they would be fired unless they returned to work by 11 A.M. on August 5. When time ran out, the government began firing the strikers.

The FAA kept planes flying by borrowing a number of military controllers and using nonstrikers and supervisors as controllers. The FAA also stepped up the training of controller recruits, reduced the number of airline flights by 25 per cent, and severely restricted general aviation use of the control system.

Airlines lost $200 million in revenues in August, the IATA said. Many people did not fly because they were afraid the flight they wanted might be

Two members of the Professional Air Traffic Controllers Organization (PATCO) picket New York City's La Guardia Airport in August.

canceled. But carriers dropped many marginal flights, and most planes carried a full load of passengers. FAA Administrator J. Lynn Helms said in December that operations might not return to normal for three years or more.

International Airlines continued to suffer big losses in 1981. In December, the IATA said that 1981 losses would amount to $900 million, with $650-million lost on North Atlantic routes alone. At the IATA meeting in Cannes, France, in October, airline representatives called for restraint in fare cutting. Airlines agreed to pursue that goal, especially over North Atlantic routes. President Reagan urged the CAB to postpone the effective date of a ruling that barred U.S. airlines from participating in fare-setting conferences for North Atlantic routes. In September, the CAB moved the date back to Jan. 15, 1982.

Air France halted direct flights of the supersonic Concorde transport between Washington, D.C., and Paris on March 29. Instead, Concordes flew to New York City. Some then flew on to Washington, D.C., or Mexico. On November 20, Reagan approved a CAB order that suspended for one week flights between Washington and Moscow by Aeroflot, Russia's national airline. The U.S. Department of State had accused Aeroflot of deliberately leaving its usual route to fly over "sensitive" areas of New England.

On December 29, Reagan suspended all flights by Aeroflot to the United States. The suspension was part of a package of sanctions that he imposed against Russia for its involvement in Poland's internal crisis. See POLAND; PRESIDENT OF THE UNITED STATES; RUSSIA.

Fare Changes. United States airlines boosted basic fares to cover rising expenses, but the increases decreased passenger demand instead. By late November, domestic coach airfares had risen 11.2 per cent, the CAB said. On October 1, allowable fares for international routes had increased over 1980 levels by amounts that ranged from about 7 per cent on routes between the United States and Latin America to about 19 per cent for Atlantic routes. In addition, carriers were given much leeway to boost fares in individual markets above those standard domestic and international levels. In March, airlines said that they would raise fares on North Atlantic routes 10 to 33 per cent.

But carriers frequently tried to increase business by offering travelers special fare bargains. Discounting broke out along the busy Boston-New York City-Washington corridor, along New York City-Florida routes, and in some Pacific Coast, Midwest, and other Northeast markets. Continental Air Lines, United Airlines, and others engaged in a price war for transcontinental routes.

Airline Turbulence. PanAm had trouble merging its operations with those of National Airlines, which it had bought in 1980. The difficult merger left PanAm in financial distress. Braniff Airways had money problems after expanding considerably under deregulation and being forced to pull back. Both airlines made major management changes in 1981 and took financial steps to stay in the air. A few smaller airlines quit flying. Many carriers reported sizable losses in the third quarter.

The short-term impact of the controllers strike aggravated problems caused by a lagging economy and the drag on profits from fare changes. Carriers asked employees to take wage cuts or salary freezes and turned to big layoffs.

Texas International Airlines spent most of the year trying to take over Continental, and it finally won when President Reagan gave his approval on October 12. The CAB also approved Air Florida's take-over of Air California in March.

Air Safety. Commercial airlines reported 21 fatalities through late November, compared with 15 in all of 1980, according to the National Transportation Safety Board. Most of those deaths occurred in commuter-airline accidents. None involved a major airline crash. The last fatal accident of a passenger jet operated by a major U.S. airline occurred on Oct. 31, 1979.   Albert R. Karr

See also TRANSPORTATION; TRAVEL. In the Special Reports section, see THE AIRPORT'S UNSEEN CITY. In WORLD BOOK, see AVIATION.

AWARDS AND PRIZES presented in 1981 included the following:

Arts Awards

Academy of Motion Picture Arts and Sciences. *"Oscar" Awards: Best Picture,* Ordinary People, Ronald L. Schwary, producer. *Best Actor,* Robert De Niro, *Raging Bull. Best Actress,* Sissy Spacek, *Coal Miner's Daughter. Best Supporting Actor,* Timothy Hutton, *Ordinary People. Best Supporting Actress,* Mary Steenburgen, *Melvin and Howard. Best Director,* Robert Redford, *Ordinary People. Best Original Screenplay,* Bo Goldman, *Melvin and Howard. Best Screenplay Adaptation,* Alvin Sargent, *Ordinary People. Best Cinematography,* Geoffrey Unsworth and Ghislain Cloquet, *Tess. Best Film Editing,* Thelma Schoonmaker, *Raging Bull. Best Original Musical Score,* Michael Gore, *Fame. Best Original Song,* "Fame," from *Fame,* music by Michael Gore, lyrics by Dean Pitchford. *Special Achievement for Visual Effects, The Empire Strikes Back. Best Foreign Language Film, Moscow Does Not Believe in Tears,* Mosfilm Studio Productions (Russia). *Best Documentary Feature, From Mao to Mozart: Isaac Stern in China,* the Hopewell Foundation, Murray Lerner, producer. *Best Documentary Short Subject, Karl Hess: Toward Liberty,* Roland Halle and Peter W. Ladue, producers. *Best Animated Short Subject, The Fly,* Pannonia Film, Budapest, Hungary. *Honorary,* Henry Fonda. See DE NÍRO, ROBERT; SPACEK, SISSY.

American Dance Festival. *Samuel H. Scripps American Dance Festival Award,* choreographer Martha Graham.

American Institute of Architects. *Honors, New Buildings:* Skidmore, Owings & Merrill, Chicago, for three bank buildings in Guatemala; I. M. Pei & Partners, New York City, for the East Building at the National Gallery of Art in Washington, D.C.; Hartman-Cox Architects, Washington, D.C., for the National Permanent Building in that city; Gruzen & Partners, New York City, and the Wold Association, Incorporated, St. Paul, Minn., for the Ramsey County Adult Detention Center in St. Paul; Sert, Jackson & Associates, Incorporated, Cambridge, Mass., for a residential community on Roosevelt Island, New York City; Fay Jones & Associates, Fayetteville, Ark., for Thorncrown Chapel, Eureka Springs, Ark.; Peters, Clayberg & Caulfield, San Francisco, for St. Mary's Gardens, a housing project for the elderly in Oakland, Calif.; Bohlin Powell Larkin Cywinski, Wilkes-Barre, Pa., for a home in Coatesville, Pa. *Honors, Restored or Recycled Buildings:* Hardy Holzman Pfeiffer Associates, New York City, for the Madison (Wis.) Civic Center; Rosekrans and Broder, Incorporated, San Francisco, for the Crocker Art Gallery in that city; Moore Grover Harper, Essex, Conn., for the Jones Laboratory in Cold Spring Harbor, N.Y.; Taft Architects, Houston, for a wall in Galveston, Tex.; Sargent-Webster-Crenshaw & Folley, Syracuse, N.Y., and Architectural Resources Cambridge, Incorporated, Cambridge, Mass., for the Hall of Languages at Syracuse University; Nagle, Hartray Associates, Limited, Chicago, for an apartment building in Oak Park, Ill.; Chrysalis Corporation, Milwaukee, for a town house in Chicago.

Antoinette Perry (Tony) Awards. *Drama: Best Play, Amadeus,* by Peter Shaffer. *Best Actor,* Ian McKellen, *Amadeus. Best Actress,* Jane Lapotaire, *Piaf. Best Featured Actor,* Brian Backer, *The Floating Light Bulb. Best Featured Actress,* Swoosie Kurtz, *The Fifth of July. Best Director,* Peter Hall, *Amadeus. Musical: Best Musical, 42nd Street,* directed by Gower Champion. *Best Actor,* Kevin Kline, *The Pirates of Penzance. Best Actress,* Lauren Bacall, *Woman of the Year. Best Featured Actor in a Musical,* Hinton Battle, *Sophisticated Ladies. Best Featured Actress in a Musical,* Marilyn Cooper, *Woman of the Year. Best Director,* Wilford Leach, *The Pirates of Penzance. Best Choreography,* Gower Champion, *42nd Street. Best Book,* Woman of the

Year, by Peter Stone. *Best Score, Woman of the Year,* by John Kander and Fred Ebb. *Best Revival of a Play or Musical, The Pirates of Penzance. Special Awards,* Lena Horne, and Trinity Square Repertory Company, Providence, R.I.

Cannes International Film Festival. *Golden Palm Grand Prize, Man of Iron* (Poland). *Best Actor,* Ugo Tognazzi, *The Tragedy of a Ridiculous Man* (Italy). *Best Actress,* Isabelle Adjani, *Quartet* and *Possession* (France). *Special Jury Prize,* Alain Tanner, *The Years of Light* (Switzerland).

Capezio Dance Foundation. *Capezio Dance Award,* Dorothy Alexander, founder of the Atlanta (Ga.) Ballet, for "her idealism and concern for high standards [that] have helped make dance one of the great American arts."

Hyatt Foundation. *Pritzker Architecture Prize,* James Stirling, Great Britain, for a lifetime of creative achievement.

John F. Kennedy Center for the Performing Arts. *Honors,* for artistic achievement, Count Basie, bandleader; Cary Grant, actor; Helen Hayes, actress; Jerome Robbins, choreographer; and Rudolf Serkin, pianist.

National Academy of Recording Arts and Sciences. *Grammy Awards: Record of the Year,* "Sailing," Christopher Cross. *Album of the Year,* "Christopher Cross," Christopher Cross. *Song of the Year,* "Sailing," Christopher Cross. *Best New Artist of the Year,* Christopher Cross. *Best Jazz Vocal Performance, Female,* Ella Fitzgerald, "A Perfect Match/Ella & Basie." *Male,* George Benson, "Moody's Mood." *Best Jazz Instrumental Performance, Solo,* Bill Evans, "I Will Say Goodbye." *Group,* Bill Evans, "We Will Meet Again." *Big Band,* Count Basie, "On the Road." *Best Pop Vocal Performance, Female,* Bette Midler, "The Rose." *Male,* Kenny Loggins, "This Is It." *Duo or Group with Vocal,* Barbra Streisand and Barry Gibb, "Guilty." *Instrumental,* Bob James and Earl Klugh, "One on One." *Best Rhythm and Blues Vocal Performance, Female,* Stephanie Mills, "Never Knew Love Like This Before." *Male,* George Benson, "Give Me the Night." *Duo or Group with Vocal,* Manhattans, "Shining Star." *Instrumental,* George Benson, "Off Broadway." *Best Rhythm and Blues Song,* "Never Knew Love Like This Before," by Reggie Lucas and James Mtume. *Best Country Vocal Performance, Female,* Anne Murray, "Could I Have This Dance?" *Male,* George Jones, "He Stopped Loving Her Today." *Duo or Group with Vocal,* Roy Orbison and Emmylou Harris, "That Lovin' You Feelin' Again." *Instrumental,* Gilley's "Urban Cowboy" Band, "Orange Blossom Special/ Hoedown." *Best Country Song,* "On the Road Again," by Willie Nelson. *Best Rock Vocal Performance, Female,* Pat Benatar, "Crimes of Passion." *Male,* Billy Joel, "Glass Houses." *Duo or Group with Vocal,* Bob Seger and the Silver Bullet Band, "Against the Wind." *Instrumental,* Police, "Regatta de Blanc." *Best Album, Original Score for a Motion Picture or Television Special, The Empire Strikes Back,* John Williams, composer. *Best Original Cast Album, Evita — Premier American Recording,* Andrew Lloyd Webber, composer, and Tim Rice, lyrics. *Album of the Year, Classical, Berg: Lulu,* Pierre Boulez, conductor. *Best Orchestra Performance, Bruckner: Symphony No. 6 in A Major,* Sir Georg Solti, conductor. *Best Opera, Berg: Lulu,* Pierre Boulez, conductor. *Best Classical Choral Performance, Mozart: Requiem,* Carlo Maria Giulini, conductor. *Best Chamber Music Performance,* Itzhak Perlman and Pinchas Zuckerman, *Music for Two Violins. Best Instrumental Solo Performance with Orchestra,* (tie) Itzhak Perlman, *Berg: Concerto for Violin and Orchestra* and Stravinsky: *Concerto in D Major for Violin and Orchestra;* and Itzhak Perlman and Mstislav Rostropovich, *Brahms: Concerto in A Minor for Violin and Cello. Best Instrumental Solo Performance,* Itzhak Perlman, *The Spanish Album. Best Classical Vocal Solo Performance,* Leontyne Price, *Prima Donna, Volume 5 — Great Soprano Arias from Handel to Britten.*

National Academy of Television Arts and Sciences. *Emmy Awards: Outstanding Comedy Series,* "Taxi." *Outstanding Actor in a Comedy Series,* Judd Hirsch, "Taxi." *Outstanding Actress in a Comedy Series,* Isabel Sanford, "The Jeffersons." *Outstanding Drama Series,* "Hill Street Blues." *Outstanding Actor in a Drama Series,* Daniel J. Travanti, "Hill Street Blues." *Outstanding Actress in a Drama Series,* Barbara Babcock, "Hill Street Blues." *Outstanding Limited Series,* "Shōgun." *Outstanding Drama Special, Playing for Time. Outstanding Actor in a Limited Series or Special,* Anthony Hopkins, *The Bunker. Outstanding Actress in a Limited Series or Special,* Vanessa Redgrave, *Playing for Time. Outstanding Variety, Music, or Comedy Program, Lily: Sold Out.*

New York Drama Critics Circle Awards. *Best New Play, A Lesson from Aloes,* by Athol Fugard. *Best New American Play, Crimes of the Heart,* by Beth Henley. *Special Citations, Lena Horne: The Lady and Her Music* and *The Pirates of Penzance.*

Journalism Awards

American Association for the Advancement of Science (AAAS). *AAAS-Westinghouse Science Writing Awards: Science Writing in Newspapers with More Than 100,000 Daily Circulation,* Mark Bowden, *Philadelphia Inquirer. Science Writing in Newspapers with Under 100,000 Circulation,* David Crisp, *Palestine* (Tex.) *Herald-Press. Science Writing in General Circulation Magazines,* G. P. Gilmore, *Popular Science.*

American Society of Magazine Editors. *National Magazine Awards: Public Service, The Reader's Digest. General Excellence, Circulation over 1 Million, Glamour; Circulation of 400,000 to 1 Million, Business Week; Circulation of 100,000 to 400,000, Audubon; Circulation Under 100,000, ARTnews. Design, Attenzione. Fiction, North American Review. Reporting, National Journal. Essays and Criticism, Time. Single Topic Issue, Business Week.*

Long Island University. *George Polk Memorial Awards: Editorials,* the editorial board of *The New York Times,* for "keen perspectives on local, national, and world developments." *Local Reporting,* the local staff of *The Miami* (Fla.) *Herald,* for an investigation of police conduct toward the black community of Miami. *National Reporting,* Jonathan Neumann and Ted Gup, *The Washington Post,* for articles on conflicts of interest in the awarding of consulting contracts by federal regulatory agencies. *Regional Reporting, The Charlotte* (N.C.) *Observer,* for a series on brown lung disease among cotton workers. *Foreign Reporting,* Shirley Christian, *The Miami* (Fla.) *Herald,* for coverage of political violence in Guatemala and El Salvador. *News Photography,* Oscar Sabetta, United Press International, for a picture of a boy carrying an elderly woman to safety under gunfire on a San Salvador street. *Commentary,* Roger Angell, *The New Yorker,* for "literate and engrossing essays on sports events and personalities." *Satiric Drawings,* Edward Sorel, for originality and perceptiveness. *Cultural Reporting, ARTnews* magazine, for "persistent and revealing investigations of ill-doings in the esoteric world of art." *National Radio Reporting,* National Public Radio, for daily reporting of national and world news. *Local Radio Reporting,* KMOX, St. Louis, for reports on crime within the black community of St. Louis. *Political Reporting,* Bill Moyers for "Bill Moyers' Journal: Campaign Report." *Local Television Reporting,* Stephen Talbot and Jonathan Dann, KQED-TV, San Francisco, for a documentary on hazards of nuclear weapons stored in the Bay Area. *National Television Reporting,* Charles Kuralt, CBS News, for the "wit and wisdom" of his reporting.

The Newspaper Guild. *Heywood Broun Award,* Barb Brucker and Jim Underwood, *Mansfield* (Ohio) *News-Journal,* for a series on police brutality toward prisoners and a cover-up by authorities.

The Society of Professional Journalists, Sigma Delta Chi. *Newspaper Awards: General Reporting, The Longview* (Wash.) *Daily News,* for its coverage of the eruption of Mount St. Helens. *Editorial Writing,* William Hallstrom, Betsy Poller, and Louis J. Salome, *The Miami* (Fla.) *News,* for editorials on the criminal justice system, on race riots, and on Cuban refugees. *Washington Correspondence,* Joseph Albright, Cox Newspapers, for a series of articles on the United States nuclear command and control network. *Foreign Correspondence,* Edward Girardet, *The Christian Science Monitor,* for articles on Afghan resistance to the Soviet occupation. *News Photography,* Giovanni Foggia, the Associated Press, for photographs of the earthquake that struck southern Italy in November 1980. *Editorial Cartooning,* Paul Conrad, *The Los Angeles Times,* for cartoons that "cover the gamut of American life." *Public Service in Newspaper Journalism, The Independent, Press-Telegram,* Long Beach, Calif., for its investigation of the Emergency Aid Program in Los Angeles County. *Magazine Awards: Reporting,* Penny Lernoux, *The Nation,* for her articles on Latin America. *Public Service in Magazine Journalism, Philadelphia* magazine for its article "Tunnel of Terror" about Philadelphia's subway system. *Radio Journalism: Reporting,* WHDH Radio, Boston, for its coverage of a toxic chemical spill resulting from a railroad collision. *Public Service in Radio Journalism,* WIND Radio, Chicago, for a series of editorials about motorists stranded on expressways. *Editorializing on Radio,* Lesley Crosson, WEEI Radio, Boston, for a series of editorials on condominium conversions. *Television Journalism: Reporting,* Bill Blakemore and Greg Dobbs, ABC-TV News, for their coverage of the Italian earthquake. *Public Service in Television Journalism,* KSL-TV, Salt Lake City, Utah, for its study of nursing homes. *Television Editorializing,* Bill Moyers, for a program about the New Right on "Bill Moyers' Journal: Campaign Report." *Research in Journalism,* John Lofton, St. Louis, for his book *The Press as Guardian of the First Amendment.*

Literature Awards

Academy of American Poets. *Lamont Poetry Selection Award,* Carolyn Forché, for her book *The Country Between Us. Walt Whitman Award,* Alberto Rios, for his book, *One Night in a Familiar Room.*

Academy of the American Book Awards. *The American Book Awards: Autobiography-Biography, Walt Whitman,* by Justin Kaplan. *Fiction, Plains Song,* by Wright Morris. *General Nonfiction, China Men,* by Maxine Hong Kingston. *History, Christianity, Social Tolerance, and Homosexuality,* by John Boswell. *Science, The Panda's Thumb,* by Stephen Jay Gould. *Poetry, The Need to Hold Still,* by Lisel Mueller. *Children's Fiction, The Night Swimmers,* by Betsy Byars. *Children's Nonfiction, Oh, Boy! Babies!,* by Alison Cragin Herzig and Jane Lawrence Mali. *Translation, The Letters of Gustave Flaubert 1830-1857,* translated by Francis Steegmuller; and Arno Schmidt's *Evening Edged in Gold,* translated by John E. Woods. *The National Medal for Literature,* Kenneth Burke.

American Library Association (ALA). *Bailey K. Howard — World Book Encyclopedia — ALA Goals Award,* to the statistics section of the Library Administration and Management Association. *J. Morris Jones — World Book Encyclopedia — ALA Goals Award,* to the Goals, Guidelines, and Standards for Public Libraries Committee of the Public Library Association. *Newbery Medal,* for the most distinguished contribution to children's literature, Katherine Paterson for *Jacob Have I Loved. Caldecott Medal,* for illustration, Arnold Lobel, author and illustrator of *Fables.*

Canadian Library Association. *Amelia Frances Howard-Gibbon Illustrator's Award,* Douglas Tait for his illustrations in *The Trouble with Princesses. Book of the Year for Children Award,* Donn Kushner for *The Violin-maker's Gift.*

Columbia University. *Bancroft Prizes,* Walter Lippmann and the American Century, by Ronald Steel; and Alice James: A Biography, by Jean Strowe.

MacDowell Colony. *Edward MacDowell Medal,* writer John Updike.

National Arts Club. *Gold Medal of Honor for Literature,* writer Leon Edel for "his contributions to the art of biography."

National Book Critics Circle. *National Book Critics Circle Awards: Fiction,* The Transit of Venus, by Shirley Hazzard. *General Nonfiction,* Walter Lippmann and the American Century, by Ronald Steel. *Poetry, Sunrise,* by Frederick Steel. *Criticism, Part of Nature, Part of Us: Modern American Poets,* by Helen Vendler.

Yale University Library. *Bollingen Prize in Poetry,* Howard Nemerov and May Swenson.

Nobel Prizes. See NOBEL PRIZES.

Public Service Awards
Albert Einstein Peace Prize Foundation. *The Albert Einstein Peace Prize,* George F. Kennan, former United States ambassador to Russia, for his continuing efforts to ease tensions between the two nations.

Boys Clubs of America. *Herbert Hoover Award,* Charles L. Brown, chairman of the board of American Telephone and Telegraph Company. *National Boy of the Year Award,* John Magee, North Little Rock, Ark.

National Association for the Advancement of Colored People. *Spingarn Medal,* Mayor Coleman A. Young of Detroit.

The Templeton Foundation. *Templeton Prize,* Dame Cicely Saunders, English physician who founded the modern system of hospices to care for dying patients.

United States Government. *Medal of Freedom,* for contributions to world peace, the security of national interest, or in cultural or other significant public or private endeavors: Roger Baldwin, founder of the American Civil Liberties Union; Harold Brown, secretary of defense; Zbigniew Brzezinski, national security adviser; Warren M. Christopher, deputy secretary of state; Walter Cronkite, television news anchorman; Kirk Douglas, actor; Margaret McNamara, founder of Reading Is Fundamental; Karl Menninger, psychiatrist; Edmund S. Muskie, secretary of state; Esther Peterson, special assistant to the President for consumer affairs; Gerald C. Smith, former director of the Arms Control and Disarmament Agency; Robert S. Strauss, former special trade representative; Earl Warren, chief justice of the United States (posthumous award); Andrew J. Young, Jr., former United States ambassador to the United Nations.

Pulitzer Prizes
Journalism. *Public Service,* The Charlotte (N.C.) Observer, for a series of articles on brown lung disease among cotton workers. *General Local Reporting,* The Longview (Wash.) Daily News, for its coverage of the eruption of Mount St. Helens. *Special Local Reporting,* Clark Hallas and Robert B. Lowe, The Arizona Daily Star, for an investigation of the University of Arizona's athletic program. *National Reporting,* John M. Crewdson, The New York Times, for an investigation of United States immigration problems. *International Reporting,* Shirley Christian, The Miami (Fla.) Herald, for reports on Central America. *Feature Photography,* Taro M. Yamasaki, The Detroit Free Press, for photographs of the State Prison of Southern Michigan. *Editorial Cartooning,* Mike Peters, The Dayton (Ohio) Daily News, for a variety of cartoons. *Distinguished Commentary,* Dave Anderson, The New York Times, for his columns on sports. *Distinguished Criticism,* Jonathan Yardley, The Washington Star, for his book reviews. *Feature Writing,* Teresa Carpenter, The Village Voice.

Letters. *Biography,* Robert K. Massie, for Peter the Great. *Drama,* Beth Henley, for Crimes of the Heart. *General Nonfiction,* Carl E. Schorske, for Fin-de-Siècle Vienna: Politics and Culture. *History,* Lawrence A. Cremin, for American Education: The National Experience 1783-1876. *Poetry,* James Schuyler, for The Morning of the Poem.

Science and Technology Awards
American Association for the Advancement of Science (AAAS). *AAAS Socio-Psychological Prize,* Bibb Latané of Ohio State University, Stephen G. Harkins of Northeastern University, and Kipling D. Williams of Drake University. *AAAS-Newcomb Cleveland Prize,* Fred Noel Spiess of Scripps Institution of Oceanography, University of California at San Diego, and Kenneth C. Macdonald of the University of California at Santa Barbara, in association with Charles S. Cox, James W. Hawkins, Jr., Rachel Haymon, Robert R. Hessler, Miriam Kastner, J. Douglas Macdougall, Stephen Miller, and John Orcutt of Scripps Institution of Oceanography, University of California at San Diego; Tanya M. Atwater and Bruce P. Luyendyk of the University of California at Santa Barbara; Robert Ballard of Woods Hole Oceanographic Institution; Arturo Carranza, Diego Cordoba, Victor M. Diaz Garcia, and Jose Guerrero of the Universidad Nacional Autónoma de México; Jean Francheteau of the Centre Océanologique de Bretagne, France; Thierry Juteau of the Université Louis Pasteur, France; Roger Larson of Lamont-Doherty Geological Observatory, Columbia University; William R. Normark of the United States Geological Survey; and Claude Rangin of the Université de Paris, France.

American Chemical Society. *Arthur C. Cope Award,* Frank H. Westheimer, Harvard University. *Priestley Medal,* Bryce L. Crawford, Jr., University of Minnesota.

American Geophysical Union. *William Bowie Medal,* Herbert Friedman, Naval Research Laboratory. *Maurice Ewing Medal,* Manik Talwani, Lamont-Doherty Geological Observatory, Columbia University.

American Institute of Physics (AIP). *AIP Prize for Industrial Applications,* Alec N. Broers, International Business Machines Corporation. *AIP-United States Steel Foundation Science Writing Awards, Scientist,* Eric J. Chaisson, Harvard University. *Journalist,* Leo Janos, Science '80 magazine. *Karl T. Compton Award for Outstanding Statesmanship in Physics,* Melba Phillips, University of Chicago. *Dannie N. Heinemann Prize for Astrophysics,* Riccardo Giacconi, Harvard-Smithsonian Center for Astrophysics. *Dannie N. Heinemann Prize for Mathematical Physics,* Jeffrey Goldstone, Massachusetts Institute of Technology. *John N. Tate International Medal for Distinguished Service to Physics,* Pierre Aigrain, Thomson-Brandt.

Aspen Institute for Humanistic Studies. *Humanism and Technology Award,* Masaru Ibuka, cofounder of the Sony Corporation of Japan.

Columbia University. *Louisa Gross Horwitz Prize,* Aaron Klug, Medical Research Council, Cambridge University, England. *Vetlesen Prize,* M. King Hubbert, United States Geological Survey.

Geological Society of America. *Penrose Medal,* John Rodgers, Yale University. *Arthur L. Day Medal,* Donald Lawson Turcotte, Cornell University.

Albert and Mary Lasker Foundation. *Albert Lasker Basic Medical Research Award,* Barbara McClintock, Carnegie Institution of Washington. *Albert Lasker Clinical Medical Research Award,* Louis Sokoloff, National Institute of Mental Health.

National Medal of Science. Philip Handler, president of the National Academy of Sciences.   Sara Dreyfuss

BAHAMAS. See LATIN AMERICA (Facts in Brief Table).

BAHRAIN. See MIDDLE EAST.

BALDRIGE, MALCOLM (1922-   ), a Connecticut industrialist, was confirmed by the United States Senate on Jan. 22, 1981, as secretary of commerce under President Ronald Reagan. Business leaders generally praised the nomination of Baldrige, who pledged to promote productivity, tax cuts, and less government regulation of business.

Baldrige was born in Omaha, Nebr., on Oct. 4, 1922, and graduated from Yale University in 1944. He served three years in the U.S. Army, rising to the rank of captain. He then went to work as a shop foreman at a Connecticut iron foundry in 1947, and became president of the company in 1960.

In 1962, Baldrige joined Scovill, Incorporated, of Waterbury, Conn., then a small brass-button company. He served as chairman of the firm from 1969 until his nomination as commerce secretary. Baldrige helped build Scovill into a worldwide manufacturer of small appliances. He also gained a reputation as a supporter of minority rights.

A close friend of Vice-President George H. W. Bush, Baldrige headed Bush's presidential campaign committee in Connecticut in 1980. He served as a national vice-chairman for business in the 1980 Reagan-Bush presidential campaign.

"Mac" Baldrige — as he is called by friends — is a rugged individualist who competes as a steer roper in rodeos.   William T. Graham

BALLET. See DANCING.

Soldiers in Dacca, Bangladesh, lower the coffin of Bangladesh President Ziaur Rahman, who was assassinated on May 30 in an attempted coup.

BANGLADESH. Rebel soldiers shot and killed President Ziaur Rahman of Bangladesh, together with two aides and six bodyguards, on May 30, 1981, in an attempted military coup d'état. The president, known as Zia, was visiting Chittagong on one of his frequent journeys around the country to solve problems, oversee development projects, and urge people to work.

Major General Mohammed Abul Manzur, the army commander in Chittagong, led Zia's killers. Manzur failed to win widespread army support. The army chief of staff, Lieutenant General H. M. Ershad, rallied troops in other parts of Bangladesh, and those in Chittagong began to desert Manzur. He fled to a rural area, was captured by loyal soldiers, and was killed while in custody. Thirty-one other officers were tried for their part in the murders, and 12 were executed on September 23.

Zia's personal leadership was given credit for the valiant effort that Bangladesh has made in recent years to solve its immense economic problems with meager resources. His death cast new doubt on whether the nation would reach its goal of becoming self-sufficient in food by 1985. A record grain harvest of 15 million short tons (13.6 million metric tons) for 1980-1981 provided nearly enough food, but crops declined later in 1981.

Abdus Sattar, former Supreme Court judge and vice-president of Bangladesh, assumed the duties of acting president. He said he would not run for the presidency because he was 75 years old and in poor health. However, Sattar changed his mind because no other leader could keep Zia's political party, the Bangladesh National Party, united.

Sattar's chief rival for president was Kamal Hossain, the candidate of the Awami League, the largest opposition party. The league had been headed by Bangladesh's first president, Sheik Mujibur Rahman, who led Bangladesh to independence in 1971. Mujib was murdered by soldiers in 1975. Hossain had been Mujib's foreign minister, and Mujib's daughter, Hasina Wajed, led his campaign. The election therefore pitted the memory of Zia against that of Mujib.

Sattar was elected president on November 15 with nearly 66 per cent of the vote. Mirza Nurul Huda became vice-president.

Relations with India were strained in 1981. Tribes in the Chittagong Hill Tracts, a hilly jungle area in southeastern Bangladesh, carried out guerrilla attacks against settlers who came there from other parts of the country. Bangladesh accused India of helping the tribes. The two nations also continued to argue over control of the waters of the Ganges and Brahmaputra rivers, which flow from India into Bangladesh.   Henry S. Bradsher

See also ASIA (Facts in Brief Table). In WORLD BOOK, see BANGLADESH.

BANKS AND BANKING. High and fluctuating interest rates marked 1981 as the Federal Reserve Board (Fed) struggled to control inflation in the United States. The Fed aimed to slow the growth rate of the money supply, making it hard to get loans.

The money supply is defined in several ways. Narrowly defined "money to spend" is called M1A and M1B. M1A consists of currency in the hands of the public and noninterest-bearing checking-account balances in banks. M1B consists of M1A and interest-bearing checking-account balances in banks, savings and loan associations (S&L's), credit unions, and similar institutions. Widely defined "money to hold" is called M2 and consists of M1B plus savings-account balances, balances in money market funds (MMF's), and less familiar kinds of assets. M1A began 1981 at $384 billion, falling steadily from the beginning of December 1980 through the end of January 1981, and hovered for the rest of the year between $360 billion and $370 billion. M1B, by contrast, rose from $415-billion at the beginning of 1981 and fluctuated between $430 billion and $440 billion from the beginning of April to the end of the year. This was caused by the public transferring money from noninterest-bearing accounts that are counted in M1A to negotiable order of withdrawal (NOW) and automatic transfer service (ATS) checking accounts that pay interest and are counted in M1B.

The more broadly defined money supply, M2, includes balances in MMF's, which pay much higher rates of interest than the 5¼ per cent or 5½ per cent the Fed allows NOW and ATS accounts to pay. M2 rose much faster than M1B during 1981. It began the year at $1.67 trillion and rose at an annual rate of 13 per cent through April, when the rise slowed to the 5 per cent to 7 per cent range. The growth of M2 became faster in September.

The high short-term interest rates responsible for the dramatic growth of M2 rose and fell sharply through 1981. With bank reserves rising slowly, according to the Fed's plan, the federal funds rate – the interest rate at which banks lend one another reserves on an overnight basis – reached a record-breaking peak of 20 per cent during the second week in January. The rate varied through the year, dropping to less than 14 per cent by the end.

The 90-day Treasury bill (T-bill) rate had peaked at 16.8 per cent in the middle of December 1980. It fell to less than 13 per cent in late March and early April, then peaked again at 16.8 per cent in late May. The rate fluctuated around 15 per cent until the beginning of September and then fell below 11 per cent by early December.

The most conspicuous interest rate is the *prime rate,* the rate banks charge their best corporate customers for short-term loans. The prime rate began January at a record-high 21.5 per cent, fell to 17 per cent in April, rose again and hov-

All-savers certificates, one-year savings certificates that pay up to $1,000 interest free of federal tax, go on sale October 1.

ered between 20 per cent and 20.5 per cent from June to September, and fell for the rest of 1981.

Inflation and Interest Rates. Falling interest rates in the last quarter of 1981 had two causes. First, inflation had slowed because of the lower rate of money growth. But slowing money growth often has the consequence of slowing economic growth. The real gross national product (GNP) – the actual amount of goods and services that are produced expressed in constant dollars – fell slightly during the second and third quarters of the year. This decline may have slowed the demand for loans.

The policy of slowing money growth announced by the Fed on Oct. 6, 1979, had finally brought inflation down to the single-digit level in the first half of 1981. Inflation, which ran between 14 per cent and 16 per cent during 1979 as measured by the Consumer Price Index, had been held to 10 per cent to 12 per cent in 1980. By the first half of 1981, inflation dropped to an 8.5 per cent rate. Although it soared again during August and September to about 13 per cent, before dropping under 10 per cent again in October and November, inflationary expectations had been reduced.

Slowing the rate of growth of the money supply has two effects on interest rates. On the one hand, slower growth of bank reserves makes banks less willing to make new loans and drives rates up for a time. On the other hand, slower growth of money in relation to the supply of consumer goods lowers the currently measured inflation rate along with expectations of future inflation. Every interest rate is composed of two parts: the expected inflation rate, to make up for the change in the value of money; and the "real" rate of interest, to pay the lender for giving up the use of money while it is loaned out. If lenders expect less inflation in the future, they will lower the inflation premium and ask for lower interest rates.

By historical standards, the real rate of interest was very high all year. Short-term rates were 5 per cent to 7 per cent above the inflation rate. Economists had expected short-term rates to go down with the rate of inflation early in 1981, because the real rate had not been above 3 per cent for the past 20 years. In fact, interest rates were below inflation rates for most of the 1970s. One possible explanation of this puzzle is that high real rates of interest, which slow economic growth, reflect increasing uncertainty in the world at large.

The Plight of the Savings and Loans. High interest rates strike hardest at the housing industry and the S&L's that finance it. Mortgage interest rates were high in 1981, as were all other interest rates. Conventional mortgages began the year at 15 per cent and rose to more than 17 per cent by July. High mortgage rates and the threat of recession caused housing starts to fall to depression levels and lowered the demand for mortgages.

What really hurt the S&L's was current high interest rates coupled with the much lower rates of past years. S&L's raise money by issuing short-term savings certificates and passbook accounts that pay current interest rates and then investing in long-term mortgages. Most mortgages held by S&L's have rates below 10 per cent. Some old mortgages have rates as low as 3 per cent. However, to finance these old mortgages, S&L's must continually borrow by issuing certificates of deposit that pay at least the T-bill rate – a minimum of 13 per cent in 1981.

S&L's began losing money in 1979. By 1981, an alarming number were failing and being merged into healthier institutions by the Federal Savings and Loan Insurance Corporation (FSLIC). The FSLIC had to dip into its fund to avoid losses to depositors in eight cases in the first half of 1981.

S&L's, along with commercial banks that had also lost money on old mortgages, began ensuring that they would not fall into the same trap again by getting permission to issue variable-rate or renegotiable-rate mortgages. The rates of these instruments change over the life of the mortgage as the lender's cost of funds changes. Congress helped out by creating the all-savers certificate, which banks and S&L's began selling on Oct. 1, 1981. The all-savers certificate pays 70 per cent of the one-year T-bill rate, with up to $1,000 of interest

per individual free of federal income tax. The rate on October 1 was 12.6 per cent.

The Changing Banking Business. In 1981, the Fed and Congress continued the process begun by the Depository Institutions Deregulation and Monetary Control Act of 1980 by allowing all banks and S&L's to offer NOW and ATS accounts. However, the major change in the banking business was not in new services but in new entrants to the business. S&L's could now invade banks' territory by offering personal and commercial loans. This prompted such giant diversified companies as Sears, Roebuck and Company and the American Express Company to purchase S&L's and investment banks. They began to take deposits and pay interest as well as sell corporate securities, set up MMF's, and engage in other transactions forbidden by law to commercial banks.

Free-Trade Zone. In a move supporters said would make New York City the world's foremost financial center, the state of New York opened on December 4 a free-trade zone in international banking. Banks based in the zone can accept deposits and make loans without paying state and local income taxes or conforming to certain federal banking regulations. Donald W. Swanton

See also ECONOMICS. In WORLD BOOK, see BANKS AND BANKING.

BARBADOS. See WEST INDIES.

BASEBALL. The 1981 major-league baseball season may be remembered for the Los Angeles Dodgers' comeback in three postseason competitions, culminating in their World Series victory over the New York Yankees. It may also be remembered for the stunning rookie season of Fernando Valenzuela, the Dodgers' 20-year-old pitcher from Mexico. The season may be remembered, too, for the milestones achieved by some veteran players.

But most of all, the 1981 baseball season will be remembered for a player strike that wiped out the middle third of the schedule and created, for the first time in major-league history, a split season.

The Strike resulted from a disagreement between the club owners and the players over compensation for the signing of free agents.

In 1976, the players won the right for certain veterans to become free agents and sign with another team. The team losing a free agent would receive an amateur draft choice as compensation.

Many club owners, unhappy with the high salaries brought on by the free agent system, insisted on restraints in the form of "professional compensation." If a club signed a free agent, these owners said, the club that lost the player should get another professional player in return.

In February 1981, the owners implemented a new compensation plan they had designed in 1980. It entitled a team losing a free agent to professional compensation. One week later, the players announced their intention to strike over the issue. They set a May 29 strike deadline but agreed on May 28 to a delay. On June 12, the players struck.

The owners, who were covered by $50 million in strike insurance, seemed in no hurry to end the strike. Each club received a $100,000 insurance payment for every unplayed game, starting with the 155th unplayed date on the league schedule.

On July 31, seven weeks after the strike began, it ended. The players and the owners reached a complex agreement that established professional compensation, but only for certain top players.

The season resumed on August 9 with the postponed All-Star Game in Cleveland, and all 26 clubs played on August 10. The strike caused the cancellation of 713 games. It cost the players about $28 million in salaries. The clubs lost an estimated $116 million in ticket and concession revenue, but they collected $44 million in strike insurance.

Standings in Major League Baseball

The 1981 season was interrupted by a players' strike from June 12 to August 9. After the regular season, first- and second-half winners from each division played a best-of-five series that determined which teams advanced to the pennant play-offs.

American League

First-Half Final Standings

Eastern Division	W.	L.	Pct.	GB.
New York	34	22	.607	
Baltimore	31	23	.574	2
Milwaukee	31	25	.554	3
Detroit	31	26	.544	3½
Boston	30	26	.536	4
Cleveland	26	24	.520	5
Toronto	16	42	.276	19

Western Division	W.	L.	Pct.	GB.
Oakland	37	23	.617	
Texas	33	22	.600	1½
Chicago	31	22	.585	2½
California	31	29	.517	6
Kansas City	20	30	.400	12
Seattle	21	36	.368	14½
Minnesota	17	39	.304	18

Second-Half Final Standings

Eastern Division	W.	L.	Pct.	GB.
Milwaukee	31	22	.585	
Boston	29	23	.558	1½
Detroit	29	23	.558	1½
Baltimore	28	23	.549	2
Cleveland	26	27	.491	5
New York	25	26	.490	5
Toronto	21	27	.438	7½

Western Division	W.	L.	Pct.	GB.
Kansas City	30	23	.566	
Oakland	27	22	.551	1
Texas	24	26	.480	4½
Minnesota	24	29	.453	6
Seattle	23	29	.442	6½
Chicago	23	30	.434	7
California	20	30	.400	8½

Offensive Leaders

Batting Average–Carney Lansford, Boston	.336
Runs–Rickey Henderson, Oakland	89
Home Runs–Tony Armas, Oakland; Dwight Evans, Boston; Bobby Grich, California; Eddie Murray, Baltimore (tie)	22
Runs Batted In–Eddie Murray, Baltimore	78
Hits–Rickey Henderson, Oakland	135
Stolen Bases–Rickey Henderson, Oakland	56

Leading Pitchers

Games Won–Dennis Martinez, Baltimore; Steve McCatty, Oakland; Jack Morris, Detroit; Pete Vuckovich, Milwaukee (tie)	14
Win Average–Pete Vuckovich, Milwaukee (14-4) (110 or more innings)	.778
Earned-Run Average–Steve McCatty, Oakland	2.32
Strikeouts–Len Barker, Cleveland	127
Saves–Rollie Fingers, Milwaukee	28

Awards

*Most Valuable Player–Rollie Fingers, Milwaukee
*Cy Young–Rollie Fingers, Milwaukee
*Rookie of the Year–Dave Righetti, New York
†Manager of the Year–Billy Martin, Oakland

National League

First-Half Final Standings

Eastern Division	W.	L.	Pct.	GB.
Philadelphia	34	21	.618	
St. Louis	30	20	.600	1½
Montreal	30	25	.545	4
Pittsburgh	25	23	.521	5½
New York	17	34	.333	15
Chicago	15	37	.288	17½

Western Division	W.	L.	Pct.	GB.
Los Angeles	36	21	.632	
Cincinnati	35	21	.625	½
Houston	28	29	.491	8
Atlanta	25	29	.463	9½
San Francisco	27	32	.458	10
San Diego	23	33	.411	12½

Second-Half Final Standings

Eastern Division	W.	L.	Pct.	GB.
Montreal	30	23	.566	
St. Louis	29	23	.558	½
Philadelphia	25	27	.481	4½
New York	24	28	.462	5½
Chicago	23	28	.451	6
Pittsburgh	21	33	.389	9½

Western Division	W.	L.	Pct.	GB.
Houston	33	20	.623	
Cincinnati	31	21	.596	1½
San Francisco	29	23	.558	3½
Los Angeles	27	26	.509	6
Atlanta	25	27	.481	7½
San Diego	18	36	.333	15½

Offensive Leaders

Batting Average–Bill Madlock, Pittsburgh	.341
Runs–Mike Schmidt, Philadelphia	78
Home Runs–Mike Schmidt, Philadelphia	31
Runs Batted In–Mike Schmidt, Philadelphia	91
Hits–Pete Rose, Philadelphia	140
Stolen Bases–Tim Raines, Montreal	71

Leading Pitchers

Games Won–Tom Seaver, Cincinnati	14
Win Average–Tom Seaver, Cincinnati (14-2) (110 or more innings)	.875
Earned-Run Average–Nolan Ryan, Houston	1.69
Strikeouts–Fernando Valenzuela, Los Angeles	180
Saves–Bruce Sutter, St. Louis	25

Awards

*Most Valuable Player–Mike Schmidt, Philadelphia
*Cy Young–Fernando Valenzuela, Los Angeles
*Rookie of the Year–Fernando Valenzuela, Los Angeles

*Selected by Baseball Writers Association of America.
†Selected by *The Sporting News*.

The Split Season. The chief problem facing the owners after the strike ended was what to do about the season as a whole. They decided on a split season, a solution that angered many people.

Edward Bennett Williams, owner of the Baltimore Orioles, called the split season a "terrible disaster." Joe McGuff, writing in the Kansas City *Star,* said it was "baseball's greatest embarrassment since the Black Sox scandal."

Club owners came up with the following plan: The four teams that led their divisions when the strike began – the Dodgers, the Philadelphia Phillies, the Yankees, and the Oakland A's – were declared the first-half winners. They would play the second-half winners for the division championships. If one team won both halves, it would play the division rival with the best overall season record.

The plan seemed to make sense until a loophole was found. It was discovered that a situation could develop in which a team might intentionally lose games in order to help put itself or a rival team into the division play-offs at the expense of another club.

The embarrassed club owners said that this possibility had never occurred to them. They then changed the plan so such a situation could not occur. Under the revised plan, if one team won both halves, its opponent in the division play-offs would be the club with the second-best record in the second half of the season.

Still, the revised play-off format produced oddities. The Cincinnati Reds, with the best overall won-lost record (66-42) among the major-league clubs, did not make the play-offs. The Kansas City Royals, with a losing record (50-53), did.

Postseason Competition. In the National League, the Montreal Expos won the Eastern Division title, Canada's first baseball championship of any kind. The Expos beat the Philadelphia Phillies, 3 games to 2. In the Western Division play-off, Los Angeles won the last three games to defeat the Houston Astros, 3 games to 2. The Dodgers then won the last two games of the pennant play-off to beat Montreal, 3 games to 2.

In the American League, Oakland swept by Kansas City in the Western Division play-off, 3 games to 0. The Yankees eliminated the Milwaukee Brewers in the Eastern Division play-off, 3 games to 2. In the pennant play-off, the Yankees swept Oakland in three games.

The World Series started as a runaway for the Yankees. They won the first two games, 5-3 and 3-0. Then the Dodgers turned it around. They took the next four games, 5-4, 8-7, 2-1, and 9-2, and won the series, 4 games to 2.

Individual Stars. No player attracted more attention than pitcher Fernando Valenzuela, the Dodgers' stocky left-hander. He won his first eight games, matching the major-league record for rookies. He finished the season with a 13-7 record and received the Cy Young Award as the National League's outstanding pitcher. Valenzuela led the major leagues in strikeouts (180).

Len Barker of the Cleveland Indians pitched a perfect game against the Toronto Blue Jays in May. It was the first perfect game in the major leagues since Oakland's Jim (Catfish) Hunter threw one in 1968. In September, Nolan Ryan of the Astros hurled his fifth career no-hit game, a record. The Milwaukee Brewers' 35-year-old Rollie Fingers became the first relief pitcher to be voted the American League's Most Valuable Player. He also won the league's Cy Young Award. Pete Rose, Philadelphia's 40-year-old first baseman, broke Stan Musial's National League record of 3,630 hits.

Hall of Fame. Pitcher Bob Gibson was elected by veteran baseball writers to the National Baseball Hall of Fame in Cooperstown, N.Y., in 1981. In 17 seasons with the St. Louis Cardinals, from 1959 to 1975, Gibson posted a 251-174 record, a 2.91 earned-run average, and 3,117 strikeouts.

Johnny Mize and Andrew (Rube) Foster were selected to the Hall of Fame by a veterans' committee. From 1936 to 1953, Mize, a first baseman, hit a total of 359 home runs for the Cardinals, the New York Giants, and the Yankees. Foster pitched in the Negro leagues from 1897 to 1926.   Frank Litsky

In WORLD BOOK, see BASEBALL.

BASKETBALL. The Boston Celtics and the Indiana University Hoosiers, basketball champions in 1976, reigned again in 1981. The rebuilt Celtics won their 14th National Basketball Association (NBA) title after a scare from the Philadelphia 76ers in the Eastern Conference finals. Indiana won the National Collegiate Athletic Association (NCAA) title.

NBA Free Agents. The major development of the year in the NBA was a new system governing the signing of free agents. Previously, when a free agent signed with a new team, that team had to compensate his former team. The new system gave the "right of first refusal" to the former team, which could thus keep a free agent by matching his highest offer from another team. If it declined to match the offer, it lost the player and received no compensation.

The new system paid quick dividends for several players. Mitch Kupchak had been earning $160,000 a year as a forward for the Washington Bullets. He signed a seven-year contract with the Los Angeles Lakers for $800,000 a year. The Cleveland Cavaliers signed center James Edwards of the Indiana Pacers and forward Scott Wedman of the Kansas City Kings, each for $750,000 a year for four years. Cleveland also offered Kansas City guard Otis Birdsong a five-year contract starting at $800,000 a year and rising to $975,000 a year. But

Kansas City matched the offer, signed Birdsong, and then traded him to the New Jersey Nets.

The escalating salaries of free agents benefited other players as well. Earvin (Magic) Johnson, in the second year of a five-year contract with Los Angeles, had become one of the premier players in the league. The 6-foot 8-inch (203-centimeter) guard signed a new 25-year contract that will pay him $1 million a year, first as a player and then as a coach or general manager. The contract, to take effect in 1984, was the richest in sports history.

Such astronomical salaries in a sport that already had high salaries worried many basketball people. The NBA reported that its teams lost $13-million in 1979-1980, the latest season for which

figures were available. Cleveland, so active in the free-agent market, lost $1.2 million in 1979-1980 and had the league's lowest attendance (5,475 per game) in 1980-1981. Overall, NBA attendance dropped 4.9 per cent in 1980-1981.

The Pro Season. The 23 NBA teams, including the new Dallas Mavericks, played 82 games from October 1980 to March 1981. Atlantic Division rivals Boston and Philadelphia (each 62-20) had the best records. Boston won the division title because it had a better record against teams in the Eastern Conference. The Milwaukee Bucks, San Antonio Spurs, and Phoenix Suns won the other division titles.

The greatest excitement in the play-offs came

National Basketball Association Final Standings

Eastern Conference

Atlantic Division	W.	L.	Pct.
Boston	62	20	.756
Philadelphia	62	20	.756
New York	50	32	.610
Washington	39	43	.476
New Jersey	24	58	.293

Central Division			
Milwaukee	60	22	.732
Chicago	45	37	.549
Indiana	44	38	.537
Atlanta	31	51	.378
Cleveland	28	54	.341
Detroit	21	61	.256

Western Conference

Midwest Division	W.	L.	Pct.
San Antonio	52	30	.634
Houston	40	42	.488
Kansas City	40	42	.488
Denver	37	45	.451
Utah	28	54	.341
Dallas	15	67	.183

Pacific Division			
Phoenix	57	25	.695
Los Angeles	54	28	.659
Portland	45	37	.549
Golden State	39	43	.476
San Diego	36	46	.439
Seattle	34	48	.415

Leading Scorers	G.	FG.	FT.	Pts.	Avg.
Dantley, Utah	80	909	632	2,452	30.7
Malone, Houston	80	806	609	2,222	27.8
Gervin, San Antonio	82	850	512	2,221	27.1
Abdul-Jabbar, Los Angeles	80	836	423	2,095	26.2
Thompson, Denver	77	734	489	1,967	25.5
Birdsong, Kansas City	71	710	317	1,747	24.6
Erving, Philadelphia	82	794	422	2,014	24.6
Mitchell, Cleveland	82	853	302	2,012	24.5
Free, San Diego	65	516	528	1,565	24.1
English, Denver	81	768	390	1,929	23.8

Women's Professional Basketball League

Central Division	W.	L.	Pct.
Nebraska	27	9	.750
Chicago	18	18	.500
St. Louis	14	21	.400
Minnesota	7	28	.200

Coastal Division			
Dallas	26	9	.743
New Jersey	22	14	.611
New Orleans	18	19	.486
San Francisco	14	22	.389

College Champions

Conference	School
Atlantic Coast	Virginia (regular season)
	North Carolina (ACC tournament)
Big East	Boston College (regular season)
	Syracuse (Big E tournament)
Big Eight	Missouri (regular season)
	Kansas (Big 8 tournament)
Big Sky	Idaho
Big Ten	Indiana
East Coast	American (regular season)
	St. Joseph's (EC tournament)
Eastern 8	Duquesne-Rhode Island
	(tie) (regular season)
	Pittsburgh (E-8 tournament)
Ivy League	Princeton
Metro Seven	Louisville
Mid-American	Ball State-Bowling Green-
	Northern Illinois-
	Toledo-Western Michigan
	(tie) (regular season)
	Ball State (MA tournament)
Mid-Eastern Athletic	North Carolina A. & T. (regular season)
	Howard (MEA tournament)
Midwestern City	Xavier (Ohio) (regular season)
	Oklahoma City (MC tournament)
Missouri Valley	Wichita State (regular season)
	Creighton (MV tournament)
Ohio Valley	Western Kentucky
Pacific Coast Athletic	Fresno State
Pacific Ten	Oregon State
Southeastern	Louisiana State (regular season)
	Mississippi (SEC tournament)
Southern	Tennessee (Chattanooga)
Southland	Lamar
Southwest	Arkansas
Sun Belt	Virginia Commonwealth-South
	Alabama (tie) (regular season)
	Virginia Commonwealth
	(SB tournament)
Trans-America Athletic	Houston Baptist (regular season)
	Mercer (TA tournament)
West Coast Athletic	San Francisco
Western Athletic	Utah-Wyoming (tie)

College Tournament Champions
NCAA Division I: Indiana
NCAA Division II: Florida Southern
NCAA Division III: Potsdam State (New York)
NAIA (Men): Bethany Nazarene (Oklahoma)
  (Women): Kentucky State
NIT: Tulsa
AIAW (Women) Division I: Louisiana Tech
AIAW Division II: William Penn (Iowa)
AIAW Division III: Wisconsin–La Crosse
Junior College: Westark (Arkansas)

Isiah Thomas of Indiana University soars over Sam Perkins of the University of North Carolina as Indiana wins the NCAA championship in March.

after Philadelphia had taken a lead of three games to one over Boston in their best-of-seven series. Philadelphia then dissipated leads of 10, 17, and 11 points in the next three games, and Boston won them all, the final by a 91-90 score. Boston then beat the Houston Rockets, four games to two, in the championship series.

The Celtics had been rebuilt after Harry Mangurian became sole owner in April 1979. They signed forward Larry Bird out of college in 1979 and obtained center Robert Parish from the Golden State Warriors in 1980.

Julius Erving, a Philadelphia forward, was voted the league's Most Valuable Player. He was the first noncenter to receive the award since the 1963-1964 season. The all-star team consisted of Erving and Bird at forward, Kareem Abdul-Jabbar of Los Angeles at center, and Dennis Johnson of Phoenix and George Gervin of San Antonio at guard.

The College Season. One leader after another stumbled in the final weeks of the college season. Virginia, unbeaten in 23 games, was ranked number one nationally until it lost on February 22 to Notre Dame, 57-56. Oregon State then became number one and had a 26-0 record before it lost on March 7 to Arizona State, 87-67. The final wire-service polls ranked DePaul first. But in its first game of the NCAA tournament, on March 14, DePaul lost to St. Joseph's of Philadelphia, 49-48.

The 48-team tournament concluded on March 28 and 30 in Philadelphia. In the semifinals, North Carolina upset Virginia, 78-65, and Indiana beat Louisiana State, 67-49. In the final, Indiana defeated North Carolina, 63-50.

Indiana, coached by the volatile Bobby Knight, was an unlikely champion. The team had finished the regular season with 26 victories and nine losses, the most defeats ever for an NCAA titlist. Indiana's star was Isiah Thomas, a sophomore guard who averaged 23 points per game.

Ralph Sampson, Virginia's 7-foot 4-inch (223-centimeter) center, was chosen as player of the year in most polls. Others named to many all-America teams included Thomas, Mark Aguirre of DePaul, Danny Ainge of Brigham Young, and Rolando Blackman of Kansas State.

Women. Louisiana Tech was the stand-out college team. It finished the regular season with a 30-0 record and then won the Association for Intercollegiate Athletics for Women championship. It defeated Tennessee, 79-59, in the final.

The Women's Professional Basketball League collapsed after the 1980-1981 season. The league started the 1980-1981 season with nine teams and finished with eight. The Dallas Diamonds and the Nebraska Wranglers won the division titles. Nebraska beat Dallas, three games to two, in the play-off finals.   Frank Litsky

In WORLD BOOK, see BASKETBALL.

BELGIUM changed governments twice in 1981. Christian Democrat Prime Minister Wilfried Martens' six-party coalition resigned on March 31 after failing to cure the country's economic ills, including an unemployment rate of 10.6 per cent – the second highest in the European Community (EC or Common Market).

A heavy speculative run on Belgium's monetary unit, the franc, brought down the government when the coalition failed to agree on Martens' proposals for avoiding devaluation. Martens wanted to suspend the indexing of incomes to inflation until January 1982, and he wanted to remove gasoline, tobacco, and liquor from the list of items whose prices the government would use to determine the inflation rate.

Mark Eyskens, Christian Democrat foreign minister, became prime minister on April 6, leading the center-left coalition that had failed under Martens. But Eyskens resigned on September 21, when the Cabinet failed to agree on how to help the troubled Cockerill-Sambre Steel Company, located in southern Belgium's French-speaking Walloon area.

The Christian Democrats lost 21 seats in the 212-member House of Representatives in national elections on November 8. The loss dropped their total to 61 seats. The Socialists gained 3 seats for a total of 61, while the Liberals added 15 seats to give them 52. On November 12, King Baudouin I asked Herman Vanderpoorten, a Liberal, to try to find the basis for a new government. On November 24, the king asked Willy de Clerq, the Liberal Party leader, to form a government. De Clerq's attempt failed. On December 1, King Baudouin asked Charles-Ferdinand Nothomb, foreign minister in the Eyskens Cabinet, to form a government. Nothomb gave up on December 7.

On December 14, Martens announced that he had formed a center-right coalition with the Liberals. He said that the new government would seek emergency powers until the end of 1982. These powers would allow the Cabinet to apply some of its economic programs without submitting them to the House of Representatives.

Money Problems. The year began with efforts to freeze wages, causing strikes in February in the steel, textile, and public transportation industries.

On October 4, the value of the franc changed within the European Monetary System, a program that eight nations set up in 1979 to stabilize the relative values of their currencies. The Netherlands and West Germany increased the values of their currencies by 5.5 per cent relative to those of Belgium, Denmark, Ireland, and Luxembourg, while France and Italy lowered their currencies by 3 per cent. Kenneth Brown

See also EUROPE (Facts in Brief Table); EYSKENS, MARK. In WORLD BOOK, see BELGIUM.

BELIZE, a small country on the Caribbean coast of Central America, became independent from Great Britain on Sept. 21, 1981. Prince Michael of Kent, the personal representative of Queen Elizabeth II, formally handed over the instruments of independence to Belize's prime minister, George Price, at Belmopan, the country's capital. Belize, a parliamentary democracy, will remain in the Commonwealth of Nations. Formerly called British Honduras, the country had been a self-governing territory since 1964.

Not everyone celebrated Belize's independence, however. The local chamber of commerce, fearful that the new country will not be able to stand alone, boycotted the ceremonies. Guatemala has long claimed Belize as part of its own national territory and refused to recognize the new nation.

According to Price, the first goal of Belize was to reduce its negative trade balance and improve the standard of living of its 174,000 citizens. The average annual income in Belize is about $1,000. The government expected that foreign aid and closer ties with the United States would help energize the economy. Military assistance came from Great Britain, which agreed to station troops in Belize for an indefinite period. Nathan A. Haverstock

See also LATIN AMERICA (Facts in Brief Table). In WORLD BOOK, see BELIZE.

Newly Independent Belize

★ National capital

BELL, TERREL HOWARD (1921-   ), a Utah educator, was confirmed by the United States Senate on Jan. 22, 1981, as secretary of education under President Ronald Reagan. Reagan's nomination of Bell as education secretary had been ironic. During his 1980 presidential campaign, Reagan pledged to abolish the Department of Education, which was created by Congress in 1979. Although Bell had strongly advocated the creation of the department, he promised to carry out Reagan's plan to dismantle it.

Bell was born in Lava Hot Springs, Ida., on Nov. 11, 1921. After serving four years in the U.S. Marine Corps, he earned a B.A. degree from Southern Idaho College of Education in 1946. In 1961, he received a doctorate in educational administration from the University of Utah.

From 1963 to 1970, Bell served as superintendent of public instruction in Utah. He became U.S. commissioner of education in 1974 under President Richard M. Nixon but resigned in 1976 for a higher-paying job as Utah's commissioner of education. Bell has a reputation as a tough-minded administrator and has written five books on educational philosophy.

Bell married Betty Ruth Fitzgerald in 1957. They have four sons.   William T. Graham

BENIN. See AFRICA.

BHUTAN. See ASIA.

BIOCHEMISTRY. Scientists in 1981 made strides toward using recombinant-DNA technology to manufacture valuable medical products. Recombinant-DNA technology involves splicing selected genes of other organisms into genetic material in bacteria or yeast. A group of West German scientists announced in February that they had developed the first vaccine produced with recombinant-DNA techniques.

The West German researchers and later U.S. scientists at the Plum Island Animal Disease Center in New York and at Genentech, Incorporated, of South San Francisco, Calif., spliced into bacteria the gene for a single protein of the coat of the virus that causes foot-and-mouth disease. This is a severe, highly contagious illness that affects more than 30 species of animals. The bacteria reproduced and, in doing so, produced copies of the protein. When used in a vaccine, the protein stimulates the animal's defense system to develop immunities to the virus. Tests by the U.S. Department of Agriculture showed that the new vaccine is effective against a common form of the virus.

Scientists from Genentech announced in January that, for the first time, yeast had been genetically engineered to produce a human protein. The protein was interferon, the natural substance thought to boost the human immune system against viruses and cancer. Scientists believed that yeast would have advantages over bacteria for large-scale production of protein because techniques for growing yeast commercially are already in use in bread, beer, and wine production.

In August, biochemist William Rutter of the University of California at San Francisco announced that he and his colleagues had moved the gene for the coat protein of the hepatitis B virus first into bacteria and then from bacteria into yeast. The genetically engineered yeast produced a more complex protein than did the bacteria. The protein produced by the yeast appeared identical to particles purified from the blood of hepatitis patients. These particles were recently shown to be effective as a vaccine against hepatitis B.

Agricultural Problems also became a focus of genetic-engineering research in 1981. Scientists at Cornell University in Ithaca, N.Y., reported a major advance in conferring upon plants the ability to fix nitrogen. Some plants, such as soybeans and peas, have root nodules containing bacteria that extract nitrogen from the atmosphere and pass it along to the plants. These plants do not need additional nitrogen fertilizers. The Cornell group transferred a complete set of 17 genes that carry information essential to nitrogen fixation from the original free-living bacterium into a laboratory bacterium and then into yeast. If these genes can eventually be transferred to plants, the plants could fix nitrogen without housing bacteria.

Scientists at the University of Wisconsin in Madison performed genetic-engineering operations on a higher form of plant. They transferred the gene for a major seed-storage protein from French beans to cells from a sunflower. Theoretically, this action may increase the nutritive value of the seeds by increasing their storage capacity.

In September, scientists at Ohio University in Athens claimed the first successful transfer of functional genetic material between two species of mammals. They injected a gene for a rabbit blood protein into newly fertilized mouse eggs. The blood of a few of the mice that developed from the eggs contained the rabbit form of the protein as well as the mouse form. Two of these mice were subsequently mated. Their offspring inherited the rabbit gene and thus could make the rabbit protein.

Recombinant-DNA Rules. On March 22, biologist Samuel I. Kennedy was charged with violations of the National Institutes of Health (NIH) guidelines regulating recombinant-DNA research. Kennedy had used a disease-causing virus before it was approved for recombinant-DNA experiments at the University of California at San Diego. He resigned from his post before the NIH investigation was completed, and thus he was no longer receiving NIH funding.

Martin J. Cline, a specialist in blood disorders at the University of California at Los Angeles, received a harsh NIH penalty for conducting controversial experiments in 1980. Cline used recombinant-DNA techniques to insert genes for normal red blood cell production into bone marrow cells and injected the cells into patients suffering from blood diseases in Israel and Italy. These experiments violated federal guidelines for protection of human subjects as well as NIH guidelines for use of recombinant DNA. Cline was stripped of two NIH grants, and given heavy restrictions on a third. He must also receive prior NIH approval for any research with human subjects or with recombinant DNA during the next three years.

An NIH committee on recombinant-DNA research proposed on September 10 the elimination of the regulatory aspects of the guidelines. Adherence to standards would be recommended – but not required – for any laboratory, with no penalties for scientists who disregard them.

The proposal also simplified the system for assigning safety measures to experiments. In most cases, the scientists would simply be asked to proceed with methods appropriate for the organisms they are using, assuming no special danger because of the use of recombinant-DNA techniques. The proposal did not prohibit any specific experiments, as the guidelines did. The proposal was open to comment pending a final vote in 1982. Julie Ann Miller

In WORLD BOOK, see BIOCHEMISTRY; CELL.

BIOLOGY. In June 1981, scientists convened in the United States to discuss therapsids, mammallike reptiles that dominated animal life for more than 40 million years and are thought by many scientists to be the ancestors of all mammals. This first major scientific meeting on therapsids was sponsored by the National Institute of Mental Health's Laboratory of Brain Evolution and Behavior and the Smithsonian Institution's National Museum of Natural History. Biologists know far less about therapsids, which lived about 250 million years ago, than about the dinosaurs, which came slightly later. Scientists searching for the origins of familiar mammalian traits have begun to focus their attention on therapsids.

Scientists believe that mammallike reptiles may have developed from large reptiles called pelycosaurs and that they eventually ranged in size from that of a rhinoceros to that of a rat. According to this theory, they progressed from a crawling lizardlike posture to a more erect walk, with all four limbs swinging under the body. Some therapsids were carnivorous, and some herbivorous; some fleet-footed, and some plodding. The scientists at the conference suggested that the later therapsids, at least, generated their own heat and had well-developed hearing and specialized teeth. They also developed the ability to communicate through smell by emitting chemicals called pheromones.

Most species of therapsids disappeared, leaving only a few types of small nocturnal animals. Scientists had blamed this disappearance on the dinosaurs. But recent evidence indicates that even during their years of dominance, the therapsids were developing into smaller and smaller forms. As with more recent extinctions, however, scientists are still trying to piece together the full story.

Video Microscopy. Cell biologists began flocking to dealers in electronic equipment in 1981 to upgrade their microscopes. The new, relatively inexpensive video equipment allows microscopists to see structures as narrow as 25 nanometers (one-billionth of an inch) and to record images a thousand times faster than previous photographic methods at a fraction of the cost. The system used includes a closed-circuit television camera aimed through a light microscope, a monitor, and a videotape recorder.

The biologists who developed the technique – Robert D. Allen of Dartmouth College in Hanover, N.H., and Shinya Inoué of the Marine Biological Laboratory at Woods Hole Oceanographic Institution in Massachusetts – said the method allows scientists to view previously invisible changes in structures in living cells. The earliest observations with the technique included views of an activated sea cucumber sperm that sends out a minute projection, the rotating flagella of a single bacterium, the action of cilia in the balance organ of a snail, and the movement of particles within an algal cell.

Morphine in the Milk. Scientists from Wellcome Research Laboratories in Research Triangle Park, N.C., reported in August that both cow's milk and human milk are naturally spiced with a small amount of the narcotic morphine. The researchers found that hay, lettuce, and other plants, in addition to the poppy, contain measurable amounts of morphine. Such plants, eaten by cows and nursing mothers, are a likely source of morphine in milk.

Although the amount of morphine measured in a quart of milk is only a small fraction of the dose of morphine used as a painkiller, it may play a more subtle role. The human body has morphine receptors – molecules that attract morphine and take it into the cell. A search for the "body's own morphine" had led scientists to the discovery in 1975 of enkephalins and endorphins – which are natural substances important in pain perception and other physiological processes. With the discovery of morphine in milk and in plant-derived foods, it began to seem likely that the natural function of the morphine receptors is, perhaps, to bring the morphine from various plant sources into body cells. Julie Ann Miller

In WORLD BOOK, see BIOLOGY.
BIRTHS. See CENSUS; POPULATION.
BLINDNESS. See HANDICAPPED.

BLOCK, JOHN RUSLING (1935-   ), was confirmed by the Senate on Jan. 22, 1981, as United States secretary of agriculture. When President-elect Ronald Reagan nominated him for the agriculture post in late 1980, Block was director of the Illinois Department of Agriculture. His nomination pleased many farmers, who felt that Block — himself a farmer — would promote policies favorable to them. Some farmers were concerned, however, that Block's lack of experience in Washington, D.C., would limit his effectiveness.

Block was born in Galesburg, Ill., on Feb. 15, 1935, and grew up on a farm in nearby Gilson. After graduating from the United States Military Academy at West Point, N.Y., in 1957, he served in the U.S. Army's 101st Airborne Division.

In 1960, Block left the Army and took over his family's farm, which he gradually expanded from 300 acres (120 hectares) to 3,000 acres (1,200 hectares). He became active in farm organizations and received the United States Jaycees Outstanding Young Farmer Award in 1969. He was appointed Illinois Director of Agriculture in 1977 by Governor James R. Thompson. In that post, Block traveled widely, meeting with agriculture officials from China, Russia, and other nations.

Block married Suzanne Rathje in 1958. They have three children.   William T. Graham

BOATING. Scandal shook United States yachting in 1981. The first three finishers overall in the Southern Ocean Racing Conference (SORC) series were accused of competing with improper handicap ratings. The SORC, held in February off Florida and the Bahamas, attracted 90 yachts from 13 nations. The yachts carried handicap ratings based on such factors as size, weight, and sail area. The ratings were intended to make smaller, slower yachts competitive with larger, faster yachts.

Louisiana Crude, a 43-foot (13.1-meter) sloop owned by Tom Dreyfus of New Orleans and Dick Jennings of Chicago, was at first declared series champion. *Acadia,* a 40-foot (12.2-meter) sloop owned by Burt Keenan of Lafayette, La., was second, and *Williwaw,* a 48-foot (14.6-meter) sloop owned by Seymore Sinett of Plainfield, N.J., third.

A month later, the United States Yacht Racing Union (USYRU), the governing body for American yacht racing, reported that it had uncovered irregularities. Union officials said that when *Acadia* and *Williwaw* were remeasured, their handicap ratings rose considerably.

The SORC then declared that, under its rules, *Louisiana Crude* and *Williwaw* had not taken part in the race because they lacked proper handicap rating certificates. The SORC also placed *Acadia* lower in the standings.

High waves and strong winds buffet yachts at the start of the third race of the Southern Ocean Racing Conference series in February.

After a 14-week investigation, the USYRU said Harvey Ward, *Williwaw*'s professional captain, had testified that the boat's bilges were filled with water ballast and that extra gear was stowed on board before measurement. The USYRU suspended Sinett, *Williwaw*'s owner, from races under its jurisdiction for two years – believed to be the most severe penalty ever leveled in American yacht racing. The USYRU suspended Keenan, *Acadia*'s owner, for one year.

The USYRU said Dreyfus stated that *Louisiana Crude* carried 11 sails when measured, though only six were allowed. According to his lawyer, Dreyfus was not aware of the six-sail limit.

Powerboats. Dean Chenoweth of Tallahassee, Fla., driving *Miss Budweiser*, won the national unlimited hydroplane series for the second straight year. Bill Muncey, of La Mesa, Calif., the winningest driver in unlimited-hydroplane history, was killed in a racing accident on October 18 in Acapulco, Mexico.

Betty Cook of Newport Beach, Calif., won her third national offshore championship. She drove *Michelob Light*, a 38-foot (11.6-meter) Scarab powered by twin 700-horsepower Kaama engines. Joel Halpern of Tarrytown, N.Y., the 1976 and 1977 champion, was killed on March 28 in New Orleans in a two-boat collision.   Frank Litsky

In WORLD BOOK, see BOATING; SAILING.

BOLIVIA. In September 1981, Bolivia installed its third government in little more than a year. General Celso Torrelio Villa, commander of the Bolivian Army, was sworn in as president on September 4. A military junta, composed of Torrelio and the commanders of the navy and air force, had ruled since August 4, when they overthrew the government of General Louis Garcia Meza Tejada.

Torrelio took office as Bolivia was struggling to recover from near-bankruptcy. In July and August, foreign banks refused to honor checks issued by the Bolivian government. Throughout the year, inflation and unemployment were both at an annual rate of 30 per cent or more. World prices had declined for some of Bolivia's major mineral exports, and the government-run mining company reported that 13 of its 14 production subsidiaries were losing money.

Promising reductions in government spending and stern measures to increase the profitability of the government-dominated economy, the Torrelio Administration requested financial aid from the International Monetary Fund and the World Bank. Neither agency came to the rescue, both insisting, as they had earlier, that Bolivia first put its economic house in order.

Drug Traffic. The only booming part of Bolivia's economy in 1981 was the illicit trade in drugs, mainly cocaine. The drug trade seemed to be centered in Santa Cruz, where powerful landowners and drug traffickers appeared to have enlisted the aid of some military and civilian leaders. Leaders of the Meza Administration had been linked with the drug traffic, and the United States and most international financial agencies reduced their aid to Bolivia because of the government's failure to curb this trade. In August, the U.S. government estimated that Bolivia earns at least $1.5 billion annually from its illegal drug trade – more than it does from any other export. According to the report, most of these earnings are invested abroad, but about $300 million returns to Bolivia and is put into the black market.

Human Rights. Torrelio promised to end political oppression and police brutality. There were reports, however, of harsh treatment of political dissidents. During 1981, the U.S. government continued to insist that a normalization of its relations with Bolivia would depend largely on the success of Torrelio's efforts to restore civil liberties and put an end to the drug trade.   Nathan A. Haverstock

See also LATIN AMERICA (Facts in Brief Table). In WORLD BOOK, see BOLIVIA.

BOND. See STOCKS AND BONDS.

BOOKS. See CANADIAN LITERATURE; LITERATURE; LITERATURE FOR CHILDREN; POETRY; PUBLISHING.

BOPHUTHATSWANA. See AFRICA.

BOTANY. Scientists in 1981 reported two new ways in which plants avoid being eaten by insects and other animals. John P. Bryant of the Institute of Arctic Biology at the University of Alaska in Anchorage demonstrated that many trees and shrubs that snowshoe hares feed on will, over time, develop a flavor unpleasant to the hares. Bryant found that newly formed shoots of such trees as quaking aspen, balsam, poplar, paper birch, and green alder contained high concentrations of certain unpalatable resins. These resins were present, but in much lower concentrations, in the older parts of the same trees. Moreover, these high resin concentrations existed only in shoots of trees growing in areas where the hares had fed extensively.

Bryant linked this observation to cycles in snowshoe hare populations. The number of hares in a given area peaks every 10 years and then drops. Bryant hypothesized that when hare populations are at a peak, their increased feeding stimulates the production of the unpalatable resins. The increase in resins, which makes the shoots inedible and thus reduces the hare's food supply, may be responsible for the population declines.

Zoologists Kathy S. Williams and Lawrence E. Gilbert of the University of Texas in Austin found that a certain variety of passionflower, *Passiflora cyanea*, protects its leaves from butterfly larvae in a roundabout way. The plant produces leaf structures that look like the eggs laid by butterflies of the species *Heliconius cydno*. Egg-bearing female *Heliconius* butterflies avoid passionflower vines on which eggs appear to have been laid. They do so because the larvae that hatch from the eggs feed on the leaves, and there will be more food if fewer larvae hatch on a given plant. The butterflies therefore by-pass the passionflower vines sporting egglike leaf structures.

Flower Fossils. In 1981, scientists made a significant addition to the knowledge of the structure of some of the earliest flowers. E. M. Friis of the University of London in England and A. Skarby of the Geological Institute in Stockholm, Sweden, found well-preserved flower structures in sedimentary rocks in southern Sweden. The tiny fossils, which measure only 0.08 inch (2 millimeters) long, are of flowers that lived about 100 million years ago during the Cretaceous Period. Although a number of leaf and pollen fossils from that period had been found previously, few fossils of flower structures had been discovered. The Swedish discovery furnished the first real evidence that flowers of the Cretaceous Period had highly developed structures. The fossil flowers resemble those of the present-day order *Saxifragales*, which includes sedum and hydrangea. Barbara N. Benson

In WORLD BOOK, see BOTANY.
BOTSWANA. See AFRICA.

BOWLING. Professional bowlers set new earnings records in 1981. Earl Anthony of Dublin, Calif., won four tournaments and was the year's leading money winner with a record $164,735. Randy Lightfoot of St. Charles, Mo., won the richest prize ever for a pro bowler. He earned $35,000 by taking the American Bowling Congress Masters title in May in Memphis.

The PBA Tour. The Professional Bowlers Association (PBA) tour consisted of 34 tournaments from January to November with purses totaling more than $4.75 million. The richest competition was the $150,000 Firestone Tournament of Champions, held from April 21 to 25 in Akron, Ohio.

Earl Anthony and Tom Baker of Torrance, Calif., each won three tournaments in four weeks. Anthony's streak in February and March included the $135,000 PBA national championship in Toledo, Ohio. Baker's streak in June and July included the PBA Doubles Classic in Las Vegas, Nev., which he won with Joe Hutchinson of Denver.

Marshall Holman of Medford, Ore., had three victories in the first three months of the year. In February, he won the $131,000 United States Open in Houston. He beat Roth, 200-179, in the final.

Roth also won three tournaments. Wayne Webb of Tucson, Ariz., the outstanding bowler of 1980, won two. Mac Acosta of Hayward, Calif.; Steve Cook of Roseville, Calif.; Mike Durbin of Chagrin

Falls, Ohio; Hutchinson; and Steve Martin of Kingsport, Tenn., also won twice. Cook took the Tournament of Champions by overwhelming Pete Couture of Windsor Locks, Conn., 287-183, in the final. The all-America team chosen by *The Bowlers Journal* consisted of Anthony, Roth, Baker, Holman, and Webb. Anthony was named for a record 10th consecutive year. The women's team comprised Donna Adamek of Duarte, Calif.; Pam Buckner of Reno, Nev.; Pat Costello of Union City, Calif.; Nikki Gianulias of Vallejo, Calif.; and Virginia Norton of South Gate, Calif.

Women. The Women's PBA disbanded and was replaced by the Ladies Professional Bowlers Tour. The new organization conducted 10 tournaments carrying $405,000 in prize money. Its major tournament was the U.S. Open, held from April 25 to May 2 in Rockford, Ill. Adamek won it by defeating Gianulias, 201-190, in the final, and she was the year's leading money winner among women with $41,270 in prize money. Costello captured her 21st pro tourney in October, a record for a woman bowler.

Katsuko Sugimoto of Japan won the Women's International Bowling Congress (WIBC) Queens title, becoming the first non-American champion in the tournament's 21-year history. Sugimoto beat Norton, 166-158, in the final. Frank Litsky

In WORLD BOOK, see BOWLING.

BOXING. The most publicized fight of 1981 turned out to be an artistic as well as a financial success. The bout, for the undisputed welterweight title of the world, was held on September 16 in Las Vegas, Nev. It matched 25-year-old Sugar Ray Leonard of Palmer Park, Md., recognized as champion by the World Boxing Council (WBC), and 22-year-old Thomas Hearns of Detroit, the World Boxing Association (WBA) champion. Leonard, behind in the scoring, knocked down the previously unbeaten Hearns in the 13th round and stopped him in the 14th, when the referee ended the fight.

The fight grossed $37 million, far surpassing the boxing record of $24.7 million for the 1980 title fight in Montreal, Canada, between Leonard and Roberto Duran of Panama. Leonard earned a record purse of more than $11 million, and Hearns received $5 million.

Holmes, Ali, and Weaver. Larry Holmes of Easton, Pa., the WBC heavyweight champion, dominated his weight class. In title fights, he outpointed Trevor Berbick of Halifax, Canada, on April 11 in Las Vegas; knocked out Leon Spinks of St. Louis in three rounds on June 12 in Detroit; and knocked out Renaldo Snipes of White Plains, N.Y., in 11 rounds on November 6 in Pittsburgh.

Former heavyweight champion Muhammad Ali came out of retirement at age 39 to fight Berbick on December 11 in Nassau, the Bahamas. But Ali,

World Champion Boxers

Division	Champion	Country	Year Won
Heavyweight	†Larry Holmes	U.S.A.	1978
	*Mike Weaver	U.S.A.	1980
Cruiserweight	†Carlos DeLeon	Puerto Rico	1980
	*No champion		
Light-heavyweight	†Dwight Braxton	U.S.A.	1981
	*Michael Spinks	U.S.A.	1981
Middleweight	Marvin Hagler	U.S.A.	1980
Junior-middleweight	†Wilfrid Benitez	Puerto Rico	1981
	*Tadashi Mihara	Japan	1981
Welterweight	Ray Leonard	U.S.A.	1980
Junior-welterweight	†Saoul Mamby	U.S.A.	1980
	*Aaron Pryor	U.S.A.	1980
Lightweight	†Alexis Aguello	Nicaragua	1981
	*Arturo Frias	U.S.A.	1981
Junior-lightweight	†Rolando Navarrete	Philippines	1981
	*Samuel Serrano	Puerto Rico	1981
Featherweight	*Eusebio Pedroza	Panama	1978
	†Salvador Sanchez	Mexico	1980
Junior-featherweight	†Wilfredo Gomez	Puerto Rico	1977
	*Sergio Palma	Argentina	1980
Bantamweight	†Lupe Pintor	Mexico	1979
	*Jeff Chandler	U.S.A.	1980
Junior-bantamweight	†Kim Chul Ho	South Korea	1981
	*Gustavo Ballas	Argentina	1981
Flyweight	†Antonio Avelar	Mexico	1981
	*Juan Herrera	Mexico	1981
Junior-flyweight	†Hilario Zapata	Panama	1980
	*Katsuo Tokashiki	Japan	1981

†Recognized by World Boxing Council.
*Recognized by World Boxing Association.

who said that he earned more than $3 million for the fight, lost in a unanimous 10-round decision. He said he would retire again.

Mike Weaver of Pomona, Calif., the WBA heavyweight champion, called off a lucrative title fight against Gerry Cooney of Huntington, N.Y. The WBA had insisted that Weaver first defend his title against James (Quick) Tillis of Chicago. Weaver did, outpointing Tillis on October 3 in Rosemont, Ill. Cooney knocked out Ken Norton of San Diego in 54 seconds on May 11 in New York City.

Other Champions. There were 27 world champions in the 15 weight divisions. The WBC, the WBA, promoters, and television networks thrived on separate champions because more champions meant more title bouts and thus more money for all concerned. The only universally recognized champions were welterweight (Leonard) and middleweight (Marvin Hagler of Brockton, Mass.).

Hagler knocked out three challengers in title fights during the year—Fulgencio Obelmejias of Venezuela on January 17 in Boston; Vito Antuofermo of New York City on June 13 in Boston; and Mustafo Hamsho of Bayonne, N.J., on October 3 in Rosemont. Leonard won the WBA junior middleweight title in June, but gave it up.   Frank Litsky

In WORLD BOOK, see BOXING.
BOY SCOUTS. See YOUTH ORGANIZATIONS.
BOYS CLUBS. See YOUTH ORGANIZATIONS.

BRAZIL. On Sept. 23, 1981, Aureliano Chaves became the first civilian in 17 years to serve as Brazil's president. Vice-President Chaves assumed the powers of the presidency on a temporary basis after President Joao Baptista de Oliveira Figueiredo suffered a heart attack on September 18. The elevation of Chaves was widely interpreted as additional assurance that Brazil was moving toward the eventual restoration of a democratic form of government. Twelve years earlier, under similar circumstances, Brazil's military leadership named a military junta to fill in for an incapacitated president, disregarding constitutional provisions for the elevation of the vice-president. Chaves continued as acting president during Figueiredo's convalescence. Figueiredo reassumed the presidency on November 12.

Throughout 1981, Figueiredo continued to lead Brazil through his program of *abertura* (the Portuguese word for *opening*), a gradual return to elections and civilian democratic government. Military hard-liners in Brazil opposed Figueiredo, insisting on a continuation of the military rule that has given Brazil stability and economic progress. At the same time, moderate business, labor, and church leaders argued for a speedier return to democracy. Brazil's first free elections in 15 years were scheduled for 1982.

Industrial Growth. Despite concern over the size of Brazil's foreign debt—the country paid $8.5-billion in interest alone on its debts in 1981—there was little doubt that Brazil has joined the ranks of the world's industrialized nations. In 1981, manufactured goods comprised 60 per cent of Brazil's total exports and earned about $24.5 billion. Brazil has also become the world's second most important builder of ships, after Japan. Planned deliveries of new vessels in 1983 are expected to earn Brazil $1.1 billion.

During the past five years, Brazil has also developed a brisk trade in armaments. In 1981, exports of aircraft, missiles, and armored vehicles were worth $1.6 billion and accounted for nearly 11 per cent of the nation's total manufactured exports. Brazil also sold 70 of its two-engine turboprop airplanes to airlines in the United States.

Symbolic of its rise as a competitor in high technology, Brazil won out over Japanese and European competitors in 1981 in bidding for the construction of a steel rolling mill in the United States. The $67-million mill will be located near Paducah, Ky. Brazil is also finding U.S. markets for its high-performance pistons used in light-aircraft engines; traction motors and chassis for subway systems; and high-strength steel.

Brazil Moved Ahead on two important projects during 1981. One project is the construction of a pipeline to carry natural gas from fields near Santa Cruz, Bolivia, to São Paulo, Brazil, the foremost industrial area of South America. The other project is the development of the mineral resources of a 35,000-square-mile (90,700-square-kilometer) area in the states of Pará and Maranhão. This area is believed to have 18 billion short tons (16.3 billion metric tons) of iron ore; 60 million short tons (54.4 billion metric tons) of manganese; and substantial quantities of bauxite, nickel, tin, and gold. Brazil hopes to earn $12 billion annually by bringing this area into production.

Brazilians continued to complain about rising prices, high interest rates, and the widening gap between the rich and the poor in 1981. A severe drought in the densely populated northeast brought hardship for the millions of subsistence farmers there. In Brazil's major cities, there was growing uneasiness about rising crime rates. According to the 1980 census, the populations of these cities grew by 50 to 75 per cent during the 1970s.

The weekly news magazine *Veja*, a frequent critic of the government, praised Brazil's Ministry of Debureaucratization, calling it "the smallest, cheapest and most successful of all government agencies." The two-year-old ministry is credited with eliminating 400 million forms in government paperwork per year. Nathan A. Haverstock

See also LATIN AMERICA (Facts in Brief Table). In WORLD BOOK, see BRAZIL.

BRIDGE. See BUILDING AND CONSTRUCTION.

BRIDGE, CONTRACT. The United States defeated Pakistan to win the world team championship in Port Chester, N.Y., in October. On the team were Thomas Sanders of Nashville, Tenn., the nonplaying captain; Jeff Meckstroth of Columbus, Ohio; Eric Rodwell of Lafayette, Ind.; Russ Arnold and Robert Levin of Miami, Fla.; and Bud Reinhold of Highland Park, Ill. Great Britain won the women's team championship, defeating the United States.

Elsewhere, players of all ages made bridge news in 1981. B. Jay Becker, 76, led his son Michael Becker, Edgar Kaplan, and Ron Rubin, all of New York City, and Norman Kay of Narberth, Pa., to victory in the Harold A. Vanderbilt knockout team championship in Detroit in March. Steve Weinstein, 17, of Accord, N.Y., became the youngest player ever to win an American Contract Bridge League (ACBL) national title when he and his teacher-partner, Fred Stewart, also of Accord, captured the Life Master Pairs championship during the ACBL summer championships in Boston in July. And Doug Hsieh of New York City became the youngest Life Master in history by winning points in Montreal, Canada, on September 27 at the age of 11 years, 10 months, and 4 days.

In international play, Pakistan won the first Middle East championship. Poland won in Europe, and Argentina won in South America. Henry G. Francis

In WORLD BOOK, see BRIDGE, CONTRACT.

BRITISH COLUMBIA in 1981 honored the memory of Terry Fox, the 22-year-old student who ran a marathon across Canada in 1980, after he had lost his right leg to cancer. The government established the Terry Fox Trust Fund in March, a few months before Fox's death on June 28. It will support biomedical and pharmaceutical research.

Higher taxation characterized the March 9 budget of Finance Minister Hugh Curtis. The province increased the retail sales tax from 4 per cent to 6 per cent, raised corporate income taxes, and placed a surtax on provincial personal income tax in excess of $3,500 (Canadian dollars; $1=U.S. 84 cents as of Dec. 31, 1981). Total spending was forecast at $6.64 billion, with large sums to be raised by borrowing for northeastern coal development and rapid-transit improvements in the Vancouver area.

The Burgess Shale Fossil Site, a 530-million-year-old fossil deposit in the Rocky Mountains 47 miles (75 kilometers) west of Banff, Alta., was dedicated as a United Nations Educational, Scientific and Cultural Organization World Heritage Site on July 16. The site, which is covered by snow 10 months of the year, contains forms of life never found elsewhere. David M. L. Farr

See also CANADA. In WORLD BOOK, see BRITISH COLUMBIA.

Mount Terry Fox in Prince George is named in September and dedicated to the memory of a brave and remarkable young British Columbian.

BRUNDTLAND, GRO HARLEM (1939-   ), a physician turned politician, became Norway's first woman prime minister on Feb. 4, 1981, heading a Labor Party government. She succeeded Odvar Nordli, also a Laborite, who resigned in January. But national elections on September 13 and 14 gave opposition conservative parties a majority in the *Storting* (parliament). Conservative Kaare Willoch succeeded Brundtland on October 14. See NORWAY; WILLOCH, KAARE.

Brundtland was born into a political family on April 20, 1939. Her father is also a physician and a former Cabinet minister, and her mother works at the Labor Party Group Secretariat in the Storting.

Brundtland became a physician in 1963 and obtained a master's degree in public health in 1965. She then served as junior medical officer at the National Directorate of Health's Office of Hygiene. From 1969 until 1974, she was assistant medical superintendent in the office of Oslo's school medical superintendent.

Brundtland was named Norway's minister of environment in 1974 and remained in the post until 1979. She was elected vice-chairman of the Labor Party in 1975 and became a member of the Storting in 1977.

Her husband, Arne O. Brundtland, is a political scientist and a member of the Conservative Party. The Brundtlands have four children.   Jay Myers

BUILDING AND CONSTRUCTION. Increases in construction spending, contracts awarded, and planned building projects in the United States signaled a recovery in 1981 from the previous year's sharp decrease in activity. The annual rate of construction spending, as estimated by the Department of Commerce in June 1981, totaled $236-billion, up from $230 billion in 1980. The value of new structures put in place increased from $17-billion in January 1981 to $21.5 billion in June. However, this figure does not include housing starts of single-family homes, which were at the lowest level in six years in September 1981 (see HOUSING).

For the first time in 12 years, money spent on private building outweighed that for public works. Nonresidential private construction accounted for $56 billion of the 1981 estimate, up from $52-billion in 1980. Public-sector building, which includes highways and sewers, fell from $55 billion in 1980 to $51 billion in 1981.

Construction-contract awards also reflected this change. Private projects made up 58 per cent of all new contracts through June. During the same period in 1980 and 1979, public construction accounted for 54 per cent of the contract awards. Economists attributed the shift to budget cutting by President Ronald Reagan's Administration and to revenue pressures put on state and local governments by a sluggish economy. The value of the new contract awards totaled almost $59 billion during the first 41 weeks of 1981, up 9 per cent from the same period in 1980. Nonresidential private building represented $29.5 billion of the contracts, a 13 per cent increase over 1980. Public awards rose 3 per cent to $21.5 billion. The value of planned new construction projects reached almost $122 billion in October 1981, an increase of 11 per cent over the October 1980 total.

Skilled workers in the construction industry earned an average of $17.66 per hour in October 1981, up 11 per cent from the previous year. Wages for nonskilled labor were 11.4 per cent higher than in 1980. The cost of structural steel increased 13.8 per cent in 1981 over 1980; ready-mix concrete, 8.5 per cent; and asphalt paving, 37.4 per cent.

Codes and Specifications. The city of Los Angeles passed an ordinance in 1981 requiring the strengthening or elimination of unreinforced brick and stone structures that were built before building codes were first introduced in 1934. The collapse of brick and stone structures causes most of the deaths during earthquakes, and inspectors enforcing the new law quickly cited nearly 1,000 buildings as unsafe.

Building codes do not specifically treat elevated walkways, such as those that collapsed at the Hyatt Regency Hotel in Kansas City, Mo., on July 17, 1981, killing 113 persons. The three codes in effect in Kansas City treat such walkways as corridors or exit facilities. Representatives of the three code-writing groups said that any revision of the codes must await determination of the cause of the walkway failures. Engineers theorize that the two so-called skyways fell onto a crowded dance floor because two box beams from which they were suspended did not meet strength standards set by the steel industry. The hotel reopened in October with a single walkway supported by 10 columns in place of the three skyways that once hung from the ceiling.

Dams. Chinese engineers building the first dam on the Yangtze (Chang Jiang) River successfully closed the river's main channel in January. The dam is about 3 miles (5 kilometers) upstream from I-ch'ang (Yichang) in southeast China and stands 131 feet (40 meters) high. It forms part of a concrete and earthen structure that will cross a shallow section of the river 6,560 feet (2,000 meters) wide. Part of the huge Gezhouba hydroelectric and flood-control project, the $2-billion dam in July withstood the worst Yangtze River floods since 1905. Flows as large as 2.4 million cubic feet (68,000 cubic meters) per second were reported. The first turbine-generator set installed in the complex began to deliver electric power in August.

In April, the Supreme Court of the United States let stand a lower court ruling that the federal

Ironworkers cut Brooklyn Bridge cables in July preparatory to replacing old and dangerously sagging cables with new, safer retainers.

government cannot be sued for damages stemming from the 1976 collapse of Teton Dam in southeastern Idaho. The federal government, under special legislation, repaid uninsured losses caused by the water unleashed when the dam failed, but it did not reimburse insurance companies for their payments to customers. The companies, claiming that the dam collapse was due to government negligence, sued in federal court.

Bridges. A 1981 study by the U.S. General Accounting Office found at least 200,000 bridges throughout the country to be structurally or functionally deficient. This total represents about 35 per cent of America's 566,000 spans. Data from the National Highway Administration showed that about 98,000 bridges are structually weak and must be closed, restricted to light vehicles, or immediately rehabilitated to prevent further deterioration and failure. The other 102,000 bridges were labeled functionally obsolete because they are too narrow or have inadequate underclearance, insufficient load-carrying capacity, or poor alignment with roadways.

The $180-million Humber Bridge near Hull in northeast England opened in June, eight years after construction began. The bridge has the world's longest main span—4,626 feet (1,410 meters). This span is 366 feet (112 meters) longer than that of the former recordholder, New York City's

Verrazano-Narrows Bridge. The bridge, which crosses the Humber River estuary, has a total length of 7,283 feet (2,220 meters), compared with 13,700 feet (4,176 meters) for the Verrazano-Narrows Bridge. Cost of the structure escalated from an estimated $56 million to about $180-million. Completion ran about four years behind schedule because of problems that were encountered in sinking tower-supporting caissons, bad weather, strong winds and tides, labor difficulties, and inflation.

Tunnels. A planned bridge across Maryland's Baltimore Harbor, near historic Fort McHenry, became a tunnel instead after local residents protested that a bridge would obstruct the view of the fort. Workers have begun construction of tunnel sections containing twin tubes, each of which will accommodate two lanes of traffic. The sections measure 320 feet (98 meters) long, 82 feet (25 meters) wide, and 42 feet (13 meters) high. They will be aligned in pairs in a trench 115 feet (35 meters) deep to form an eight-lane passage 5,400 feet (1,646 meters) long. The Fort McHenry tunnel, which is part of a $980-million project to complete a 1.7-mile (2.7-kilometer) stretch of interstate highway 95, is scheduled to be opened for traffic in 1985.   William J. Cromie

In WORLD BOOK, see BRIDGE; BUILDING CONSTRUCTION; DAM; TUNNEL.

BULGARIA celebrated the 1,300th anniversary of the founding of the first Bulgarian state throughout 1981. The high point of the celebration was a meeting in Sofia on October 22, attended by delegates from all over the world. Speaking at the meeting, Communist Party General Secretary and State Council Chairman Todor Zhivkov repeated a call for a nuclear-free zone in the Balkans.

Bulgaria's anniversary celebrations aggravated its relations with Yugoslavia. That country interpreted Bulgaria's celebrations as another denial of separate nationhood for the Macedonians who live in Bulgaria. In February, the Yugoslav press attacked an article in the Bulgarian magazine *Vekovi* about Bulgarian-Yugoslav relations from 1941 to 1944, when Bulgaria ruled the part of Macedonia that is now in Yugoslavia. The two countries quarreled over the killing of a Bulgarian civilian by a Yugoslav frontier guard on Aug. 30, 1981. Yugoslavia refused to send a representative to the October celebrations in Sofia and canceled several traditional assemblies for people who live along the border between the two countries.

Lyudmila Zhivkova, Zhivkov's daughter, died of a brain hemorrhage on July 21. She had been an influential member of the Politburo, the most powerful part of the Communist Party's central committee, and she had organized the anniversary celebrations.

New Prime Minister. Zhivkov was re-elected leader of the Communist Party for five years on April 4 at the party congress in Sofia. On June 16, the National Assembly elected Grisha Filipov as prime minister. He succeeded Stanko Todorov, who moved to the less important post of president of the National Assembly. Filipov had been in the Politburo since 1974.

Four Turks diverted the flight of a domestic Turkish airliner with 112 passengers aboard to Burgas, Bulgaria, on May 24. The hijackers demanded $500,000 and the release of 47 prisoners in Turkish jails. On May 25, Bulgarian security officials lured two of the hijackers off the aircraft and captured them. Passengers then overcame the other two hijackers. On September 2, a court sentenced the hijackers to three years in prison.

The Economy. Industrial production increased by 6 per cent and foreign trade by 19.7 per cent in the first six months of 1981. Bulgaria's first polypropylene plant was completed at Burgas. The plant can produce 80,000 metric tons (88,000 short tons) of polymers per year. Georgi Dyulgerov replaced Misho Mishev as head of the trade unions in March. Party leaders expected that the change would improve the manner in which the unions carried out party policies.   Chris Cviic

See also EUROPE (Facts in Brief Table). In WORLD BOOK, see BULGARIA; MACEDONIA.

BURMA. President U Ne Win resigned on Nov. 9, 1981, from the position he had held since he seized power in Burma in 1962. He had personally selected the 475 candidates who were elected in October to the People's Assembly, Burma's parliament. All were members of the Burma Socialist Program Party (BSPP), Burma's only political party. The assembly then voted for new leaders that Ne Win had chosen. He remained BSPP chairman and continued to dominate Burmese affairs.

U San Yu, a 63-year-old former general, became president. He had held, at various times, most of the high army, government, and political party posts in Burma. Another army leader, Aye Ko, became deputy chairman of the BSPP. U Maung Maung Kha remained prime minister.

Economic growth continued in 1981. After years of rejecting foreign aid and investment, Burma began to cautiously welcome them again in the late 1970s. High-yield varieties of rice increased rice production by 45 per cent. Good rice crops were a major factor in turning the economy around after years of stagnation. In the fiscal year ending in 1981, the economic growth rate reached 8.3 per cent, the highest since the 1940s.   Henry S. Bradsher

See also ASIA (Facts in Brief Table). In WORLD BOOK, see BURMA.

BURUNDI. See AFRICA.

BUS. See TRANSIT; TRANSPORTATION.

BUSH, GEORGE H. W. (1924-   ), was sworn in as the 43rd Vice-President of the United States on Jan. 20, 1981. Shortly thereafter, President Ronald Reagan began to define Bush's role in his Administration. On January 22, President Reagan named Bush to a Cabinet-level post as head of the Task Force on Regulatory Relief.

The White House announced on February 25 that in the absence of the President, Bush would be responsible for handling sudden foreign crises. White House Press Secretary James S. Brady revealed on March 24 that the President had chosen Bush to head the newly formed "crisis management team" to respond to "emergency situations, both foreign and domestic."

Stands In for President. Bush was in Texas for a speaking engagement on March 30 when he was notified that President Reagan had been shot and wounded. Bush returned to Washington, D.C., at 7 P.M. to preside over a Cabinet meeting. The next day, he substituted for the President in meetings at the White House with Netherlands Prime Minister Andreas A. M. van Agt. On April 1, he began to preside over White House staff meetings.

On April 2, after meeting with Chief Deputy Premier Mieczyslaw Jagielski of Poland at the White House, Bush announced that the United States would provide Poland with $70 million in surplus food to ease that nation's food crisis.

As President Reagan's Envoy, Bush met with President François Mitterrand of France in Paris on June 24 to discuss relations between the United States and France. Bush expressed U.S. "concern" that four Communists were named to the French Cabinet.

The Vice-President represented the United States at the inauguration of Philippine President Ferdinand E. Marcos in Manila on June 30. He drew criticism from those who consider the Marcos government repressive when he praised its "adherence to democratic principles."

Bush addressed the annual conference of the National Urban League in Washington, D.C., on July 20, defending the Administration's programs and calling for support for its efforts to solve the nation's problems. On August 11, he defended the Administration's economic program in an address to the National Governors Association's annual meeting in Atlantic City, N.J. Bush represented the United States at Mexico's 171st Independence Day celebration on September 16. While in Mexico City, he met with Mexico's President Jose Lopez Portillo to discuss the political and economic situation in Latin America.   Carol L. Thompson

See also PRESIDENT OF THE UNITED STATES. In WORLD BOOK, see VICE-PRESIDENT OF THE UNITED STATES.

BUSINESS. See BANKS AND BANKING; ECONOMICS; LABOR; MANUFACTURING.

CABINET, UNITED STATES. In a series of votes taken from Jan. 20 to Jan. 23, 1981, the United States Senate confirmed all but one of President Ronald Reagan's Cabinet appointments. The Senate made its final Cabinet confirmation, that of Raymond J. Donovan as secretary of labor, on February 3.

Cabinet members taking office in January were Secretary of State Alexander M. Haig, Jr.; Secretary of the Treasury Donald T. Regan; Secretary of Defense Caspar W. Weinberger; Attorney General William French Smith; Secretary of the Interior James G. Watt; Secretary of Agriculture John R. Block; Secretary of Commerce Malcolm Baldrige; Secretary of Health and Human Services Richard S. Schweiker; Secretary of Housing and Urban Development Samuel R. Pierce, Jr.; Secretary of Transportation Andrew L. Lewis, Jr.; Secretary of Energy James B. Edwards; and Secretary of Education Terrel H. Bell.

Donovan's confirmation was delayed pending the outcome of a Federal Bureau of Investigation (FBI) inquiry into charges his construction company had made illegal payments to union officials. The FBI cleared Donovan of the charges in January, but a special prosecutor was appointed to reopen the case in December. See the biographies of individual Cabinet members.

The Succession Question. A short-lived controversy over the line of succession to the presidency erupted after President Reagan was shot in an assassination attempt on March 30. During the confusion of the first few hours following the shooting, Secretary of State Haig announced to a television audience that, pending the return of Vice-President George H. W. Bush from a speaking engagement in Texas, he was "in control . . . at the White House." Haig, who implied that the line of command passed from the President to the Vice-President to the secretary of state, was challenged by Secretary of Defense Weinberger, who maintained that he was empowered to act as the agent of the President and Vice-President in military matters. By an executive order, military authority in an extraordinary emergency passes first from the President to the Vice-President, then to the secretary of defense.

The Presidential Succession Act of 1886 and its 1947 amendment detail the line of succession in the event that both the President and Vice-President die or become disqualified. The law states that the speaker of the House and then the president *pro tempore* of the Senate are next in line. The secretary of state follows them. Beverly Merz

In WORLD BOOK, see CABINET.

CALIFORNIA. See LOS ANGELES; STATE GOV'T.

President Ronald Reagan's Cabinet meetings are equipped to ward off hunger pangs. The crystal jar holds a supply of his favorite jellybeans.

CALVO SOTELO Y BUSTELO, LEOPOLDO (1926-), became Spain's prime minister on Feb. 10, 1981, succeeding Adolfo Suarez Gonzalez, who resigned in January. Calvo Sotelo had been deputy prime minister in charge of economic affairs. See SPAIN.

Leopoldo Calvo Sotelo y Bustelo was born on April 14, 1926. He obtained a doctor's degree in civil engineering and then worked in the chemical industry until 1967, when he was named president of the national railway system.

Calvo Sotelo became a member of the *Cortes* (parliament) in 1971. After dictator Francisco Franco died in 1975, Prime Minister Carlos Arias Navarro appointed Calvo Sotelo minister of commerce. Suarez became prime minister in 1976 and named Calvo Sotelo minister for public works.

Calvo Sotelo left the Cabinet before the June 1977 parliamentary election – Spain's first open general election in 41 years – to organize the successful campaign of the Union of the Democratic Center coalition, led by Suarez. Suarez named Calvo Sotelo minister in charge of relations with the European Community (EC or Common Market) in 1978 and deputy prime minister in September 1980.

Calvo Sotelo is married to Pilar Ibáñez-Martín Mellado, daughter of a former education minister. They have eight children.   Jay Myers

CAMBODIA (Kampuchea) was still occupied in 1981 by Vietnamese troops, who had overthrown the Communist Khmer Rouge regime of Pol Pot in 1979 and installed a government of rival Cambodian Communists. Cambodia's civil war also continued with scattered fighting. But the Vietnamese-backed government made efforts to restore order, including the holding on May 1, 1981, of the first national elections since the Vietnamese invasion.

In the Elections, the candidates were designated by the Communist Party, which changed its name to the People's Revolutionary Party of Kampuchea (PRPK). The government reported that 99 per cent of the voters approved the PRPK candidates, who were elected to a 117-member National Assembly. On June 27, the Assembly named Heng Samrin as president of the council of state. Pen Sovan became president of the council of ministers.

Sovan was confirmed as the country's most powerful leader on May 29, when a PRPK congress elected him secretary-general of the party. On December 5, however, it was announced that Pen Sovan had resigned from the PRPK post, reportedly because of illness. The party's Central Committee appointed Heng Samrin to succeed Pen Sovan as secretary-general.

Peace Proposals. The Association of Southeast Asian Nations met on June 17 and 18 to search for a solution to the continuing civil war in Cambodia.

It proposed that the United Nations (UN) send a peacekeeping force to Cambodia, that the 200,000 Vietnamese troops there withdraw, and that the other warring factions be disarmed.

The United Nations held a conference on Cambodia in New York City from July 13 to 17. Cambodia, Vietnam, and more than 20 other nations boycotted the conference. The 92 nations that did participate called for the withdrawal of Vietnamese troops and for elections under UN supervision.

Three Former Cambodian Leaders met in Singapore from September 2 to 4 in an attempt to join forces against the Vietnamese occupation of their country. The leaders were Prince Norodom Sihanouk, the former king of Cambodia; Khieu Samphan, president and prime minister of the exiled Khmer Rouge regime of Pol Pot; and Son Sann, a former Cambodian premier who heads a group called the Khmer People's National Liberation Front. The three leaders formally agreed to cooperate against the Vietnamese-backed government, but cooperation proved difficult. The Khmer Rouge later announced that they had abolished their Communist Party.   Henry S. Bradsher

See also ASIA (Facts in Brief Table). In WORLD BOOK, see CAMBODIA.

CAMEROON. See AFRICA.

CAMP FIRE. See YOUTH ORGANIZATIONS.

Cambodian voters cast their ballots in 1981 in the first nationwide elections held since the Vietnamese invaded Cambodia (Kampuchea) in 1979.

CANADA

Canada, like other Western industrial nations, experienced economic difficulties in 1981. Interest rates higher than 20 per cent and energy prices nearing world levels led to greater inflation and the highest unemployment rate since 1978. Liberal Prime Minister Pierre Elliott Trudeau took a detached attitude toward the country's economic problems. His government's response came only in a budget presented on Nov. 12, 1981. Trudeau concerned himself with topics closer to his heart, such as the adoption of a "made-in-Canada" constitution and efforts to breathe life into the faltering dialogue between the rich, industrialized nations of the North and the poorer, developing ones of the South. His efforts met with mixed success in a year of recession and uncertainty.

Trudeau and the Premiers. Canada is governed under the 1867 British North America Act, which is a statute of the British Parliament and so can be changed only in London. In October 1980, Trudeau proposed a resolution establishing a formula for amending the act in Canada. He also suggested a charter setting forth civil, political, and linguistic rights that would apply across Canada. Adoption of the resolution by the Canadian Parliament and subsequent final approval by the British Parliament would complete Canada's sovereignty by removing the last vestige of British legislative authority over Canada.

The Progressive Conservative (PC) Party denounced Trudeau's plan, especially the strategy for adopting it, as being contrary to Canadian custom. They said that because the proposals would affect the powers of the provinces, Trudeau should obtain provincial approval before sending them to London. The PC also wanted Trudeau to refer the proposals to the Supreme Court of Canada for a test of their legality. Eight provincial premiers joined in the PC's resistance. Only Ontario and New Brunswick supported Trudeau.

Trudeau's resolution was sent to a 25-member special committee drawn from the Senate and House of Commons for detailed study. After the committee accepted the broad lines of the proposal on February 13, a bitter debate took place in the full House of Commons. On March 31, an agreement was reached whereby the Liberals accepted additional changes in the charter of rights, most notably affecting the position of women and native

groups, and agreed to Supreme Court consideration of the proposals. The PC accepted a limitation on further debate on the resolution.

The Supreme Court handed down its judgment on the issue on September 28. The nine justices ruled 7 to 2 that Canada's Parliament had the legal power to patriate the British North America Act with a Canadian amending procedure. At the same time, six judges agreed and three disagreed that provincial consent was necessary, by custom and convention, for fundamental constitutional change. This decision meant that legally Trudeau could now proceed, though morally he should obtain provincial agreement for his changes. Trudeau and his Cabinet decided to go ahead. The prime minister offered to meet once more with the opposing premiers beginning on November 2.

Finally, on November 5, the Canadian government and every province except Quebec reached agreement on proposals for a new constitution. The Canadian House of Commons on December 2, and the Senate on December 8, overwhelmingly supported a resolution calling on the British Parliament to transfer the British North America Act, along with the power to amend it, to Canada. On Thursday, December 10, a Canadian delegation presented the resolution to Queen Elizabeth II in London. The British Parliament was expected to consider it in early 1982. Trudeau gained a long-sought victory by settling the constitutional impasse. He said he was pleased that after 114 years, "Canada becomes, in the technical and legal sense, an independent country."

Internal Affairs. Joseph (Joe) Clark, PC leader since 1976, received the support of only 66 per cent of party delegates at a convention in Ottawa, Ont., on February 27. His showing reflected the party's unhappiness with Clark's 1980 electoral defeat after his nine-month term as prime minister. It also indicated that many party members felt he should be replaced by a more appealing leader.

Results of the five by-elections held in 1981 left party standings in the 282-seat House of Commons as follows: Liberals, 147; PC, 102; and New Democratic Party (NDP), 33. The Liberals held on to three of five vacant seats during 1981; saw the PC retain their only Quebec seat; and lost a supposedly safe seat in Toronto, Ont., to the NDP. Trudeau slightly reconstructed his Cabinet on September 22, adding four new ministers and changing the responsibilities of several others. The resulting 36-member Cabinet was the largest since Canadian Confederation in 1867.

A four-year inquiry into the activities of the famed Royal Canadian Mounted Police (RCMP) ended on August 25, when Canadian Solicitor General Robert Kaplan released a final report by a three-member royal commission. The report, written by Alberta Supreme Court Judge David C.

Prime Minister Pierre Trudeau welcomes Margaret Thatcher, his British counterpart, to the Ottawa economic summit in July.

CANADA

McDonald, criticized the RCMP for committing a number of illegal acts and for deceiving Cabinet ministers and Parliament about the scope of its operations. The commission recommended that a civilian security agency authorized to operate at home and abroad be set up apart from the RCMP.

The Canada Post Office became a Crown, or public, corporation on October 16, changing its status from a government department. The change was to increase efficiency through better management and financial structures and to improve labor relations in the organization, which had been plagued by strikes in recent years. A strike of "inside" workers from June 30 to Aug. 10, 1981, resulted in "outside" workers being laid off.

Federal Spending in Canada

Estimated Budget for Fiscal 1982*

	Billions of Dollars†
Health and welfare	20.958
Public debt	12.350
Economic development and support	6.875
Defense	7.045
Transportation and communications	4.045
Fiscal transfer payments to provinces	3.766
General government services	2.946
Education assistance	2.144
Internal overhead expenses	1,846
Foreign affairs	1.284
Culture and recreation	1.295
Total	64.554

*April 1, 1981, to March 31, 1982

†Canadian dollars; $1 = U.S. 85 cents as of Dec. 1, 1981.

Spending Since 1976

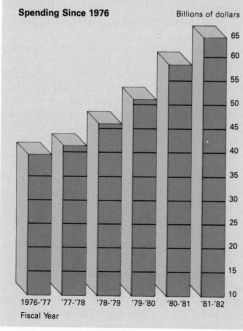

Billions of dollars

1976-'77 '77-'78 '78-'79 '79-'80 '80-'81 '81-'82

Fiscal Year

Source: Treasury Board of Canada

Canada's Economy performed reasonably well in the first half of 1981 despite the brake imposed by high interest rates. It weakened during the summer, as indicated by the unemployment rate's sharp rise to 8.3 per cent in October. The third quarter of the year saw little or no growth as interest rates remained high and the world economy stagnated. The Bank of Canada's prime lending rate, which sets the standard for chartered bank rates, reached 21.2 per cent on August 6, falling to 15 per cent by December. Although external trade was strong until August, the housing market collapsed as prohibitive mortgage rates discouraged building or buying. Personal spending and retail trade also declined. The gross national product (GNP) was expected to amount to $324-billion (Canadian dollars; $1 = U.S. 84 cents on December 31) on an annual basis in 1981, with growth after the middle of the year leveling off following a 5 per cent increase in the first six months.

The Canadian dollar was under pressure for most of 1981 as investors moved money out of Canada to take advantage of higher interest rates elsewhere. Its value hovered between 80 and 84 U.S. cents for most of the year—the lowest rate since the depression of the 1930s. Inflation ran about 13 per cent.

Prime Minister Trudeau and Premier Peter Lougheed of Alberta announced an encouraging development on September 1. This was the settlement of the 18-month dispute between the federal government in Ottawa and the Alberta provincial government over oil pricing and the sharing of oil and gas revenues. Alberta gained a price close to the world level for its new oil and a larger share in revenue from energy resources. Ottawa took more in taxes and royalties. The oil companies profited through technical changes in pricing arrangements. In the end, the Canadian consumer paid the higher prices, with an additional $32 billion for oil purchases expected over the next five years.

Finance Minister Allan MacEachen unveiled the Trudeau government's answer to difficult economic conditions on November 12 when he presented his second budget to Parliament. He emphasized the need to maintain high interest rates and a strong fiscal policy in order to contain inflation. He committed himself to reduce the federal deficit to $10.5 billion in 1982-1983, a drop of almost $3 billion. Changes were introduced to restore "equity and fairness" in the tax system. Loopholes by which wealthier taxpayers had benefited were closed; overall federal tax rates were reduced slightly; and assistance was offered homeowners, farmers, and business people suffering from high interest rates.

World Affairs. Leaders of the seven principal industrial nations—Canada, France, Great Britain,

Visitors inspect an assembly line at the Windsor, Ont., Essex Engine Plant, the Ford Motor Company's first North American producer of V-6 car engines.

Italy, Japan, the United States, and West Germany — converged on Canada from July 19 to 21 for the seventh Economic Summit Conference. Meeting at the picturesque Chateau Montebello near Ottawa, they discussed subjects ranging from inflation, unemployment, trade barriers, and interest rates to tensions in the East-West relationship. Prime Minister Trudeau, who chaired the meeting, was determined that it face the urgent question of inequities in the economic interchange between industrialized Northern nations and developing Southern countries. His efforts in this direction resulted in a tentative commitment among the leaders to begin negotiations with the developing world "in whatever forums may be appropriate." They agreed to continue the discussion at the Cancún meeting in Mexico on October 22 and 23.

After visiting 10 countries to promote North-South dialogue, Trudeau tried again at Cancún to focus attention on ways to help the quarter of the world's population that lives in poverty. Leaders from 22 countries and United Nations (UN) Secretary-General Kurt Waldheim attended the Cancún meeting. Co-chairman Trudeau served along with Mexico's President Jose Lopez Portillo. Trudeau made a sincere effort to hammer out a consensus among the participants. However, the Cancún summit produced a closing statement that was far from his hopes. The conference agreed only to start preparatory talks leading to global negotiations on North-South issues, using the UN as the forum for these talks. This was a disappointingly modest advance over the position reached at the Montebello conference.

U.S. Relations became strained after Canada announced its National Energy Program in October 1980. The program had three objectives: independence for Canada from the world oil market, increased federal revenues from oil and gas, and "Canadianization" of the petroleum industry. The third target was to be achieved by making room for Canadian oil and gas companies in the petroleum industry, 80 per cent of which was owned by nonresidents in the early 1970s. The goal of Canadianization was to increase the 1980 figure of 26 per cent Canadian ownership to 50 per cent by 1990 through tax concessions, grants, and pricing and purchasing incentives. The program stimulated Petro-Canada, the national oil company, to buy control of Petrofina Canada Incorporated from its Belgian parent company for $1.46 billion. Dome Petroleum Limited, a private company, purchased a controlling interest in Hudson's Bay Oil and Gas Company Limited from its U.S. parent, Conoco Incorporated, for about $1.68 billion. The United States sharply criticized the National Energy Program, calling it discriminatory and unfair. Threats of retaliation included prohibiting Canadian com-

The Ministry of Canada*
In order of precedence

Pierre Elliott Trudeau, prime minister
Allan Joseph MacEachen, deputy prime minister and minister of finance
Jean-Luc Pepin, minister of transport
Jean Chrétien, minister of justice and attorney general of Canada and minister of state for social development
John Munro, minister of Indian affairs and northern development
H. A. Olson, minister of state for economic development
Herbert Gray, minister of industry, trade, and commerce
Eugene Francis Whelan, minister of agriculture
André Ouellet, minister of consumer and corporate affairs and postmaster general
Marc Lalonde, minister of energy, mines and resources
Raymond Joseph Perrault, leader of the government in the Senate
Roméo LeBlanc, minister of fisheries and oceans
John Roberts, minister of state for science and technology and minister of the environment
Monique Bégin, minister of health and welfare
Jean-Jacques Blais, minister of supply and services and receiver general of Canada
Francis Fox, minister of communications
Gilles Lamontagne, minister of national defence
Pierre De Bané, minister of regional economic expansion
Hazen Argue, minister of state for the Canadian Wheat Board
Gerald Regan, secretary of state of Canada
Mark MacGuigan, secretary of state for external affairs
Robert Kaplan, solicitor general of Canada
James Fleming, minister of state for multiculturalism
William Rompkey, minister of national revenue
Pierre Bussières, minister of state for finance
Charles Lapointe, minister of state for small business
Edward Lumley, minister of state for trade
Yvon Pinard, president of the queen's privy council for Canada
Donald Johnston, president of the Treasury Board
Lloyd Axworthy, minister of employment and immigration
Paul Cosgrove, minister of public works
Judy Erola, minister of state for mines
Jacob Austin, minister of state
Charles L. Caccia, minister of labor
Serge Joyal, minister of state
W. Bennett Campbell, minister of veterans affairs

*As of Dec. 31, 1981.

Premiers of Canadian Provinces

Province	Premier
Alberta	Peter Lougheed
British Columbia	William R. Bennett
Manitoba	Howard Pawley
New Brunswick	Richard B. Hatfield
Newfoundland	Brian Peckford
Nova Scotia	John Buchanan
Ontario	William G. Davis
Prince Edward Island	James M. Lee
Quebec	René Lévesque
Saskatchewan	Allan Blakeney

Commissioners of Territories

Northwest Territories	John H. Parker
Yukon Territory	Douglas Bell, Administrator

panies from gaining mineral leases on U.S. federal land and forcing Canadian companies interested in taking over American companies to observe the same financing guidelines as U.S. corporations.

Canada denied that the impact of its policies was discriminatory, pointing out that many U.S. regulations were nationalistic in their intent. Trudeau said that American companies were not being nationalized by Canadian federal action or forced to sell their Canadian holdings, but could still operate profitably in Canada. He said retaliation would hurt both countries, whose economies were so closely integrated. Finally, Trudeau appealed to U.S. President Ronald Reagan to restrain U.S. rhetoric in the dispute.

Reagan struck a calming note on March 10 and 11 when he and his wife, Nancy, paid the first state visit of his Administration to Canada. In meetings with Trudeau and his officials and in an address to the Canadian Parliament, Reagan stressed the importance of good will and frank discussion in working out solutions for Canadian-American problems. Specific issues were not resolved during the meeting, though the two leaders renewed the life of the North American Air Defense Command (NORAD) for five years.

Fisheries remained a sore point between the North American neighbors. Progress was made in agreements respecting the albacore tuna and salmon on the Pacific coast. However, the management of cod, haddock, and scallop stocks in the valuable North Atlantic fishing ground of Georges Bank remained unsettled. Two treaties signed in 1979 were subjected to severe scrutiny. The Reagan Administration withdrew the first agreement, concerning the management of Atlantic fish stocks, from the U.S. Senate but recommended approval of the second, which called for binding arbitration of the two nations' claims for a maritime boundary across the disputed coastal area. The Senate voted 91 to 0 to send the boundary issue to the International Court of Justice in The Hague, the Netherlands, for settlement. Fishing industry leaders feared that the Georges Bank fisheries would be seriously depleted unless both sides took immediate temporary conservation measures.

Acid Rain is a serious form of pollution in a large area extending north and east of the Great Lakes. Sulfur dioxide and nitrogen oxides released into the air from smelters, power plants, and factories that burn coal combine with falling rain and form weak acids. This acid rain pollutes lakes and streams and may threaten the growth of trees and other plants. Both Canada and the United States emit large quantities of sulfur and nitrogen oxides into the atmosphere each year. Both countries lacked adequate pollution-restraining safeguards in 1981 despite lengthy talks between Ottawa and Washington. A Canadian parliamentary committee,

Canada and Provinces
Population Estimates

	1980	1981
Alberta	2,068,800	2,160,400
British Columbia	2,626,400	2,710,600
Manitoba	1,027,100	1,031,000
New Brunswick	705,700	710,600
Newfoundland	578,200	585,800
Northwest Territories	42,800	43,200
Nova Scotia	851,600	857,100
Ontario	8,558,200	8,624,900
Prince Edward Island	124,000	124,300
Quebec	6,298,000	6,340,000
Saskatchewan	967,400	979,700
Yukon	21,400	21,900
Canada	**23,869,700**	**24,189,400**

City and Metropolitan
Population Estimates

	Metropolitan Area June 1, 1980, estimate	City 1976 Census
Toronto	2,883,100	633,300
Montreal	2,827,300	1,080,500
Vancouver	1,200,900	410,200
Ottawa-Hull	753,300	304,500
Edmonton	610,800	461,400
Winnipeg	590,900	560,900
Quebec	565,700	177,100
Calgary	543,800	469,900
Hamilton	542,100	312,000
St. Catherines-Niagara	309,500	123,400
Kitchener	288,000	131,900
London	276,800	240,400
Halifax	274,500	117,900
Windsor	244,900	196,500
Victoria	231,900	62,600
Regina	167,500	149,600
Sudbury	151,700	97,600
St. John's	149,900	86,600
Saskatoon	144,100	133,800
Oshawa	143,500	107,000
Chicoutimi-Jonquiere	130,700	60,700
Thunder Bay	121,800	111,500
Saint John	120,400	86,000

calling for tougher regulation of Canadian sources of sulfur dioxide, emphasized that the harm done by acid rain would not be corrected until both countries acted.

Facts in Brief: Population: 24,189,400. Government: Governor General Edward Richard Schreyer; Prime Minister Pierre Elliott Trudeau. Monetary unit: the Canadian dollar. Foreign trade: exports, $64,252,000,000; and imports, $58,545,000,000.　　　　　　　　David M. L. Farr

See also Canadian provinces articles; CANADIAN LIBRARY ASSOCIATION (CLA); CANADIAN LITERATURE; SCHREYER, EDWARD RICHARD; TRUDEAU, PIERRE ELLIOTT. In WORLD BOOK, see CANADA; CANADA, GOVERNMENT OF.

CANADIAN LIBRARY ASSOCIATION (CLA) urged Canada's Parliament to pass freedom-of-information legislation in a March 24, 1981, appearance before Parliament's Justice and Legal Affairs Committee. Bill C-43 – the Access to Information Act – would increase public access to government documents, records, and files.

The CLA asked for revisions to the bill before it becomes law, however. One change would require the government to publish a list of the documents that it would not disclose because disclosure might jeopardize national security, or for other reasons. The original Bill C-43 would require the government to list only accessible documents. Thus, the public would be unaware of the existence of material that the government had decided to withhold. An ordinary individual would not be in a position to challenge the withholding of a document.

Federal Aid. The CLA called for greater federal assistance to libraries in an appearance before the Federal Cultural Policy Review Committee in Edmonton, Alta., on May 27. The CLA told the committee that libraries further the national good, and so the federal government should play a strong role in developing library service nationally and in promoting equal opportunity of access. The committee was established by the government to recommend directions for cultural activity.

Conference. The CLA attracted 1,553 delegates to its 36th annual conference in Hamilton, Ont., from June 10 to 16. The association approved resolutions that called for improving library services to disabled persons and establishing a national network of legal information centers for the public. Marianne Scott, director of libraries for McGill University in Montreal, Que., took office as president of the CLA for a one-year term.

Awards. The CLA awarded the Howard V. Phalin-World Book Graduate Scholarship in Library Science to Judith Saltman of Vancouver, B.C.; the H. W. Wilson Education Foundation Scholarship to Jocelyn Ayers of Williamstown, Ont.; and the Elizabeth Dafoe Scholarship to Kathleen Esdaile of Montreal.

The CLA Outstanding Service to Librarianship Award went to Frances Morrison for her work as chief of the Saskatoon (Sask.) Public Library, from which she retired in December 1980. The Award for Special Librarianship went to Olga Bishop of London, Ont.; and Mary Coggin of New Westminster, B.C., received the Margaret B. Scott Award of Merit for school library service.

The CLA presented the Book of the Year for Children Award to Donn Kushner for *The Violinmaker's Gift* (Macmillan). The Amelia Frances Howard-Gibbon Illustrator's Award went to Douglas Tait for *The Trouble with Princesses* by Christie Harris (McClelland and Stewart). 　Paul Kitchen

In WORLD BOOK, see CANADIAN LIBRARY ASSN.

CANADIAN LITERATURE enjoyed a buoyant and artistically triumphant year in 1981, particularly in the area of fiction. Many of Canada's major novelists emerged with outstanding new works. In addition, an array of significant nonfiction books demonstrated that Canadian publishers – despite the nation's sluggish economy and a trend toward marketing commercially profitable titles – felt a responsibility to serious readers.

Fiction. Several new novels explored feminist issues. Margaret Atwood's fifth novel, *Bodily Harm,* was an inventive satire in which a writer who suffers from breast cancer attempts to come to terms with her past as well as her bleak present. Marian Engel's *Lunatic Villas,* a comic novel about a middle-aged divorced mother, spun variations on a similar theme. Brian Moore's *The Temptations of Eileen Hughes* told the story of an innocent 20-year-old Irish girl plunged into a sophisticated and profane world. Aritha Van Herk's *The Tent Peg* was a complex, intriguing tale of a young woman cook in a Yukon mining camp.

Robertson Davies' first novel in four years, *The Rebel Angels,* described the rivalries and sexual jealousies of academic life. Timothy Findley's *Famous Last Words,* perhaps the outstanding literary work of the year, resurrected Hugh Selwyn Mauberley – a character created by poet Ezra Pound – and cast him as a figure caught in the rise of fascism in Europe. Other noteworthy novels included Matt Cohen's *Flowers of Darkness,* Marie-Claire Blais's *Deaf to the City,* W. O. Mitchell's *How I Spent My Summer Holidays,* Jack Hodgins' *The Barclay Family Theatre,* and George Jonas' *Final Decree.* The best collections of short stories included Mavis Gallant's *Home Truths* and W. P. Kinsella's *Born Indian.* Janet Hamilton wrote the best first novel, *Sagacity,* a complex, experimental story in which Queen Victoria plays the major role.

Biographies and Memoirs. Portraits of business and political figures provided the inspiration for some fine biographies during the year. Peter Newman's *The Acquisitors,* the sequel to his best-selling *The Canadian Establishment,* examined the burgeoning new group of financial and corporate leaders in western Canada. Claude Bissell's *The Young Vincent Massey* traced the early career of the man who served as governor general of Canada from 1952 to 1959. J. L. Granatstein's *A Man of Influence* chronicled the life of Norman Robertson, a high-ranking civil servant who helped shape Canada's foreign and domestic policies under Prime Ministers W. L. Mackenzie King and Lester B. Pearson. Other biographies included H. Jefferson Lewis' *Something Hidden,* the story of brain surgeon Wilder Penfield; Betty Keller's *Pauline Johnson,* a look at the famous Indian poet; and David Livingstone's *The Story So Far,* the life of singer Anne Murray.

Most prominent among a cluster of intriguing memoirs was Charles Ritchie's diary excerpts, *Diplomatic Passport,* about his rise from minor civil servant to Canada's ambassador to West Germany. Hugh L. Keenlyside, another influential diplomat, wrote *Hammer the Golden Day,* the first volume of a two-part autobiography. *The Good Fight* was a posthumously published account of political leader David Lewis' rise to national prominence.

History. Many works took up the theme of war. Pierre Berton's *Flames Across the Border,* his second volume on the War of 1812, was one of the best sellers of the year. Four books dealt with World War II. Roy MacLaren's *Canadians Behind Enemy Lines* documented the little-known, clandestine activities of Canadian spies and saboteurs during that war. Two books, George Gabori's *When Evils Were Most Free* and Anita Meyer's *One Who Came Back,* told the story of the Holocaust – the Nazi campaign against the Jews – from the point of view of those who survived. Anne Gomer Sunahara's *The Politics of Racism* analyzed the wartime expulsion of Japanese Canadians from Canada's west coast and their incarceration. Other books about war included Richard Rohmer's *Patton's Gap,* Grace Morris Craig's *But This Is Our Way,* Bill Mathieson's *My Grandfather's War,* and Brian Nolan's *Hero.*

Histories dealing with more contemporary subjects included *The Canadian Caper* by Claude Adams and Jean Pelletier. Pelletier is the Quebec journalist who broke the story of Canada's role in helping six American hostages to escape from Iran in 1980. Robert Bothwell, Ian Drummond, and John English co-authored *Power, Politics and Provincialism,* an analysis of economic and political issues affecting Canada since 1945. Historian C. P. Stacey surveyed Canada's domestic and foreign fortunes from 1921 to 1948 in *Canada and the Age of Conflict.*

A number of authors gave gloomy views of Canada's past and present. Peter Desbarats sounded the alarm of doom in *Canada Lost, Canada Found.* June Callwood assessed the Canadian tendency to value security over individual liberty in *Portrait of Canada.* Thomas Berger considered Canada's treatment of minority groups and dissenters in *Fragile Freedoms.*

Poetry. New collections by Miriam Waddington, P. K. Page, Ralph Gustafson, Raymond Souster, Al Purdy, Daryl Hine, Irving Layton, Robert Kroetsch, and Stephen Scobie demonstrated the diversity of Canadian poetry. A retrospective edition of the poems of F. R. Scott honored a writer who helped nurture the blooming of modern Canadian poetry in the 1920s. The best of the collections was Margaret Atwood's *True Stories,* a powerful work about political and sexual violence.

Miscellaneous. Two books discussed how such economic problems as inflation and the weak dollar imperiled Canada's cultural climate – David Helwig's *The Human Elements* and Paul Audley's *Voices* *of Our Own.* In the year's most interesting sports book, *The Game of Our Lives,* journalist-broadcaster Peter Gzowski gave a highly personal account of a season spent following National Hockey League star Wayne Gretzky.

Governor General's Literary Awards for books published in 1980 went to George Bowering for *Burning Water* (English fiction); Jeffrey Simpson for *Discipline of Power* (English nonfiction); Stephen Scobie for *McAlmon's Chinese Opera* (English poetry); Pierre Turgeon for *La première personne* (French fiction); Maurice Champagne-Gilbert for *La famille et l'homme à délivrer du pouvoir* (French nonfiction); and Michel van Schendel for *De l'oeil et de l'écoute* (French poetry).

Larry Shouldice won the Canada Council Translation Prize for *Contemporary Quebec Criticism,* an English translation of essays by 10 Quebec writers and critics; and Yvan Steenhout won for her French translation of *The Complete Log House Book* by Americans Dale Mann and Richard Skinulis.

Gary Lautens won the Stephen Leacock Memorial Award for humor for his book of essays, *Take My Family . . . Please!* Margaret Atwood won the Molson Prize, in recognition of her outstanding contribution to the arts in Canada.   Ken Adachi

See also LITERATURE. In WORLD BOOK, see CANADIAN LITERATURE.

CAPE VERDE. See AFRICA.

CARTER, JAMES EARL, JR. (1924-   ), the 39th President of the United States, delivered his farewell speech to the nation from the White House on Jan. 14, 1981. In his address, President Carter urged the American people to work to prevent a nuclear war, to preserve human rights, and to protect the environment.

He submitted his final State of the Union message in writing to Congress on January 16. The 76-page document assessed the nation as sound but warned that serious problems – unemployment, inflation, the energy shortage, and challenges from Russia – were yet to be solved. Carter's final budget message proposed federal expenditures of $739.3 billion and a deficit of $27.5 billion for fiscal 1982. However, expenditures were slashed to $695-billion in a budget-cutting bill signed by President Ronald Reagan on August 13.

Hostages Released. Carter sought to free the 52 Americans held hostage in Iran before he left office, working around the clock in his last two days as President, as negotiations to free the hostages dragged on. Due to last-minute delays, the hostages – whose continuing captivity had contributed heavily to Carter's defeat in the November 1980 election – were not flown out of Teheran until 36 minutes after Ronald Reagan took the oath of office. Thus, it was as a private citizen that Jimmy Carter flew to Wiesbaden, West Germany, to greet the former hostages before they returned to the United States. See IRAN (Close-Up).

Retirement. Carter signed a contract to publish his memoirs with Bantam Books Incorporated on March 17. Bantam scheduled a hard-cover edition for publication in 1982 and a paperback for 1983. Carter said that he was preparing his manuscript on a word processor using notes transcribed from recordings he made daily in the White House.

On a 10-day trip to China and Japan in late summer, Carter met with Communist Party Chairman Hu Yaobang and appeared on Chinese television. In a public statement on September 3, he noted that differences over Taiwan were a major obstacle to better relations between the United States and China. On September 4 in Japan, Carter warned of the danger of a world oil crisis.

Carter and former Presidents Gerald R. Ford and Richard M. Nixon flew to Egypt as members of the U.S. delegation to the funeral of President Anwar el-Sadat on October 10. Ford and Carter reportedly overcame long-standing personal differences and issued a joint statement declaring that the United States would eventually have to negotiate with the Palestine Liberation Organization to bring peace to the Middle East.   Carol L. Thompson

See also PRESIDENT OF THE UNITED STATES. In WORLD BOOK, see CARTER, JAMES EARL, JR.

Former President Jimmy Carter writes the memoirs of his Administration at a computer terminal in his home in Plains, Ga.

CAT. Persian cats continued to dominate the cat show scene in the United States in 1981. A cream-and-white male Persian, Grand Champion Lee's Let the Sunshine In, was chosen National Best Cat by the Cat Fanciers' Association, Incorporated (CFA), America's largest organization that registers purebred cats. Sunshine, as he is called, was bred and is owned by William and Gayle Lee of Grand Rapids, Mich. He competed in 32 of the 240 CFA shows in the 1980-1981 show year and was the fifth Persian in five years named Best Cat.

The title of Best Kitten went to another Persian, Grand Champion Ann-Ge's Cool Million of Windborne, a white male bred by George and Ann Beal of Albuquerque, N. Mex., and owned by the Beals and Vicki Dickerson of Phoenix. Best Altered Cat was Nepenthes Timur, a Ruddy Abyssinian that was bred by Alfred and Joan Wastlhuber of San Francisco and is owned by Jack and Fran Stevenson of Ellisville, Mo. A total of 60,000 entries vied for the various awards offered by the CFA.

In 1980, 34 breeds of cat were registered with the CFA. Persians led in the number of registrations. Following Persians in order of popularity were Himalayans, Siamese, Abyssinians, and Burmese. The breed most recently accepted for registration was the Singapura, a short-haired breed from Singapore. Thomas H. Dent

In WORLD BOOK, see CAT.

CENSUS. The flood of statistics released by the United States Bureau of the Census in 1981 revealed an American population undergoing tremendous changes. The 20th Decennial Census of Population and Housing in 1980 found that Americans are marrying later and divorcing more often. Although the decline in the American birth rate appears to have stopped, American women are waiting longer to have children. The overall population growth rate in 1980 remained about the same as in 1970 – 1.1 per cent per year – though the number of blacks and Hispanic Americans grew at a much faster rate. The population of the United States on Census Day, April 1, 1980, was 226,504,825 – an 11.4 per cent increase over 1970. (The Census Bureau said on Jan. 1, 1982, that the U.S. population at the end of 1981 was about 230.5 million.) The growth rate during the 1970s was the slowest for any decade covered by a census, except for the decade of the Great Depression, the 1930s. Population figures for states, counties, metropolitan areas, and cities are listed in the special Census Section beginning on page 521.

Americans in 1980 were more educated and generally more affluent than they were a decade earlier. For the first time in 160 years, small towns and rural areas grew faster than metropolitan areas. And although most Americans in 1980 still lived in urban areas, the nation's cities continued to lose population. The 1980 census also provided additional evidence of the sizable migration of Americans from the Northeastern and North-Central states of the Frost Belt to the Sunbelt states of the West and South.

The 1980 census counted and surveyed all residents of the United States, Puerto Rico, the Virgin Islands, Guam, American Samoa, and the Trust Territories of the Pacific Islands. The Census Bureau announced that the 1980 census was the most complete and accurate count of Americans ever taken. It also became the most controversial as many cities challenged its accuracy.

An Aging Population. The population of the United States is growing older, according to the 1980 census. Between 1970 and 1980, the median age of all Americans rose from 28.1 years to 30 years. The Bureau of the Census attributed the rise to a decline in the birth rate, the aging of those born during the post-World War II baby boom between 1945 and 1964, and greater longevity.

Changes in the country's population mix also reflected this trend. For example, the number of Americans aged 14 or younger dropped by 11.5 per cent during the 1970s. However, the number of Americans between 25 and 34 years old jumped by 48.8 per cent, while the number aged 55 to 64 grew by 16.7 per cent. Most startling of all was the 28 per cent increase in the number of Americans 65 or older. From 1970 to 1980, that group swelled from 20.1 million, or 9.9 per cent of the population, to 25.5 million, or 11.3 per cent.

Census figures also revealed an increased gap between the number of older women and men. During the 1970s, the number of women aged 65 or older jumped from 11.7 million to 15.2 million, while the number of men in that age group increased from 8.4 million to 10.3 million.

Living Alone. The growing number of young, single people and divorced or separated people living alone was cited as the chief reason for a huge jump in the number of American households and the sharp decline in the size of those households. Although the U.S. population increased by only 11.4 per cent between 1970 and 1980, the number of households rose by 27 per cent to 80.4 million. In addition, the number of people living alone rose from 10.9 million to 17.8 million. During the same period, the average number of persons per household shrank from 3.11 to 2.75. Experts also attributed the drop in household size to a declining birth rate.

Sunbelt Shift. The 1980 census showed a restless American population still on the move. The Sunbelt in the South and West emerged as the big winner in the shift, with 90 per cent of the country's net population growth occurring in that region. Florida, California, and Texas showed especially high population gains.

United States Population Changes from 1970 to 1980

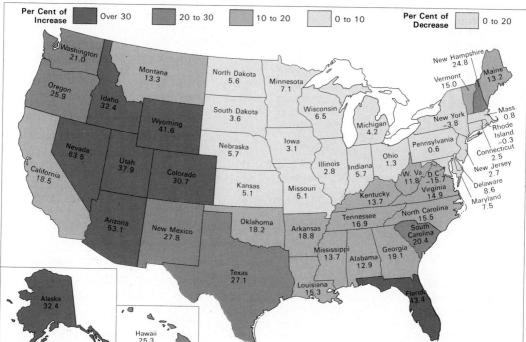

Source: U.S. Department of Commerce

With only a few exceptions, population in the Northeastern and North-Central states grew more slowly than the national average of 11.4 per cent. As a result, for the first time in U.S. history, the nation's population center crossed the Mississippi River (see map on page 234). Because of the population shift, the Northeast and Midwest will lose 17 congressional seats to the South and West in 1982. Florida will pick up the most seats, 4; New York will lose the most, 5.

Reverse Migration. For the first time since 1820, rural areas and small towns in the United States grew faster than metropolitan areas. Census figures showed that population in the country's nonmetropolitan areas grew by 15.4 per cent, compared with a metropolitan growth rate of 9.5 per cent. In contrast, during the 1960s, the population of U.S. metropolitan areas grew by 17 per cent, while nonmetropolitan areas grew by only 4 per cent. The shift, however, was to small towns and rural areas, not back to the farm. During the 1970s, the number of U.S. farmworkers continued to decline. Experts attributed the population reshuffling to the relocation of businesses and industries in small towns, the growth of recreation and retirement communities in rural areas, and the revival of the mining industry.

By region, the greatest nonmetropolitan population growth took place in the West, which showed a 31.8 per cent increase. In the Northeast, the population of nonmetropolitan areas rose by 12.4 per cent; in the Midwest, by 7.8 per cent; and in the South, by 17.1 per cent. However, the South was the only region whose cities and suburbs grew faster than its small towns and rural areas.

City Growth, Decline. Despite the sizable movement to nonmetropolitan areas, 3 of every 4 Americans lived in a metropolitan area at the time of the 1980 census. During the 1970s, metropolitan populations grew by 13.6 million to 162.4 million.

New York City, Chicago, and Los Angeles retained their positions as the country's first, second, and third most populous cities. Of the nation's six cities with 1 million or more inhabitants, only Los Angeles and Houston gained population. Los Angeles' population increased by 5.5 per cent; Houston's by 29.2 per cent. Other large cities showed population losses: New York City was down 10.4 per cent; Chicago, 10.8 per cent; Philadelphia, 13.4 per cent; and Detroit, 20.5 per cent.

On the other hand, 13 U.S. cities with 100,000 or more inhabitants showed population increases of more than 50 per cent. Such cities included Anchorage, Alaska, whose population jumped by 259.8 per cent; Mesa, Ariz., which increased by 141.8 per cent; Aurora, Colo., which grew by 115.5 per cent; and Lexington-Fayette, Ky., which reported an 88.8 per cent increase.

CENSUS

The New York City metropolitan area, with more than 9 million residents, remained the most populous U.S. metropolitan area, while also showing a 9 per cent population loss, the sharpest loss for any large metropolitan area. The Los Angeles-Long Beach area edged out the Chicago metropolitan area for the number-two position. However, during the 1970s, both regions registered population gains—5.7 per cent for the Los Angeles area and 1.2 per cent for Chicago. For the first time since 1950, no metropolitan area doubled in population during the 10 years surveyed by a census.

Minority Increases. Minority populations in the United States grew at a much faster rate than the country's overall growth rate of 11.4 per cent. The number of blacks increased by 17 per cent, from 22.6 million in 1970 to 26.5 million in 1980. Blacks in 1980 represented 11.7 per cent of the American population, up from 11.1 per cent a decade earlier.

According to the Census Bureau, the migration of blacks to Northern and Western cities has slowed or stopped. Philadelphia; San Francisco; Cleveland; St. Louis; and Washington, D.C., showed decreases in the number of blacks. However, the migration of whites from many large cities left blacks in the majority in Baltimore; New Orleans; Detroit; Atlanta, Ga.; and Washington, D.C.

Census figures showed a 61 per cent increase since 1970 in the number of Hispanic Americans. More than 60 per cent of the 14.6 million Hispanic Americans in the United States lived in California, New York, and Texas in 1980. They made up a majority of the population in San Antonio, Tex., and outnumbered blacks in New York City, Los Angeles, San Diego, Phoenix, San Francisco, and Denver. The Census Bureau attributed the high growth rate among blacks and Hispanic Americans chiefly to improved counting methods.

The American Indian population more than doubled between 1970 and 1980 to 1,362,000. In 1980, half of all American Indians lived in California, Oklahoma, Arizona, New Mexico, and North Carolina. California replaced Oklahoma as the state with the highest Indian population. In 1980, Eskimos and Aleuts were counted separately for the first time. The Census Bureau counted 42,149 Eskimos and 14,177 Aleuts, most of them living in Alaska.

The number of Chinese in the United States grew so rapidly during the 1970s that they replaced Japanese as the country's leading Asian population. Between 1970 and 1980, the Chinese population increased 85.3 per cent to 806,627. The number of Filipinos also grew rapidly, making them the country's second most numerous Asian population

U.S. Population Distribution in 1980

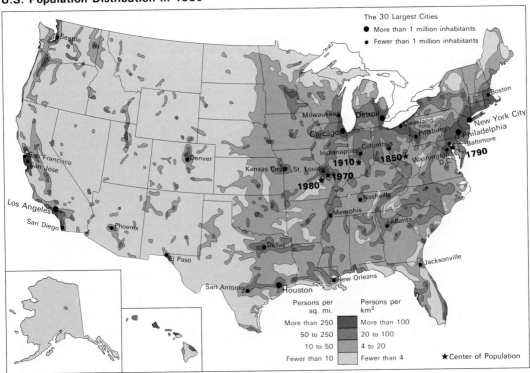

The 30 Largest Cities
● More than 1 million inhabitants
• Fewer than 1 million inhabitants

Persons per sq. mi.
- More than 250
- 50 to 250
- 10 to 50
- Fewer than 10

Persons per km²
- More than 100
- 20 to 100
- 4 to 20
- Fewer than 4

★ Center of Population

The Population of the United States

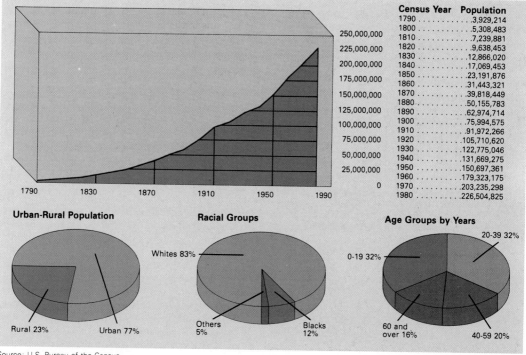

Census Year	Population
1790	3,929,214
1800	5,308,483
1810	7,239,881
1820	9,638,453
1830	12,866,020
1840	17,069,453
1850	23,191,876
1860	31,443,321
1870	39,818,449
1880	50,155,783
1890	62,974,714
1900	75,994,575
1910	91,972,266
1920	105,710,620
1930	122,775,046
1940	131,669,275
1950	150,697,361
1960	179,323,175
1970	203,235,298
1980	226,504,825

Urban-Rural Population — Rural 23%, Urban 77%

Racial Groups — Whites 83%, Others 5%, Blacks 12%

Age Groups by Years — 20-39 32%, 0-19 32%, 60 and over 16%, 40-59 20%

Source: U.S. Bureau of the Census.

with 774,640. Also during the 1970s, the Korean population in the United States soared by 413 per cent to 354,529. The Census Bureau said the increases reflect the surge in immigration that began with the lifting of restrictive quotas on Asians in the late 1960s.

Undercount Lawsuits. United States courts of appeals in New York City and in Cincinnati, Ohio, overturned in June 1981 lower court decisions ordering the Bureau of the Census to increase population totals for Detroit, New York City, and other major cities by at least 5 million. A number of large cities had challenged the Census Bureau's figures, claiming that their minority populations had been seriously undercounted. The cities said that such errors not only would cost them millions of dollars in federal funds, but also would reduce their representation in the U.S. House of Representatives.

In Cincinnati, the federal appeals court ruled that Detroit and other plaintiffs had not demonstrated a "judicially cognizable injury." The New York appeals court ordered a new trial on the basis that the lower court ruling had failed to protect the rights of other states that might be affected by a revision of census data. Arthur E. Mielke

See also POPULATION. In WORLD BOOK, see CENSUS; POPULATION.

CENTRAL AFRICAN REPUBLIC. See AFRICA.
CEYLON. See SRI LANKA.

CHAD. About 10,000 Libyan troops called in to help Chad's President Goukouni Weddeye defeat rebel forces at the end of 1980 began withdrawing from Chad in November 1981. Their yearlong presence in Chad had concerned leaders of other African countries, who feared that Libya would try to dominate the country. Such fears were heightened on January 6, when Libya and Chad announced an agreement to merge into one state.

A special summit meeting of the Organization of African Unity (OAU) on January 14 urged the two countries not to unite and called on Libya to withdraw its troops. Weddeye needed military aid to suppress three rival factions that threatened to renew Chad's civil war. October reports indicated that a faction led by former Defense Minister Hissene Habre had 4,000 troops and got Egyptian military aid through Sudan.

At its annual summit conference in Nairobi, Kenya, from June 24 to 27, the OAU authorized the creation of a Chad peacekeeping force. In late October, Weddeye formally asked Libya to withdraw its troops. The first contingent of the OAU force, 700 soldiers from Zaire, had arrived in Chad's capital, N'Djamena, by November 16. The OAU was expected to provide more than 5,000 troops from six African countries. J. Dixon Esseks

See also AFRICA (Facts in Brief Table); LIBYA. In WORLD BOOK, see CHAD.

CHARLES, PRINCE (1948-   ), heir apparent to the British throne, married 20-year-old Lady Diana Spencer on July 29, 1981, in St. Paul's Cathedral in London. Some 2,500 guests attended the wedding, while about 1 million people lined the route from Buckingham Palace to the cathedral. About 700 million people throughout the world watched the ceremony on television. The couple spent their honeymoon at Broadlands, the Mountbatten country home in Hampshire, and on board the royal yacht *Britannia*, cruising the Mediterranean Sea. See GREAT BRITAIN (Close-Up).

On November 5, Buckingham Palace announced that the new princess was expecting a baby in June 1982. The child would stand second in line of succession to the throne.

Charles Philip Arthur George was born on Nov. 14, 1948, the son of Princess Elizabeth and Philip Mountbatten, formerly Prince Philip of Greece. Prince Charles became heir apparent on Feb. 6, 1952, after his grandfather, King George VI, died and his mother ascended the throne as Queen Elizabeth II. The queen named him Prince of Wales in 1958.

The prince was educated at Cheam, a preparatory school near London; Gordonstoun, a school in Scotland; and Trinity College at Cambridge University. He became a member of the House of Lords in 1970.   Jay Myers

CHEMICAL INDUSTRY sales in the United States did not match the expected pattern in 1981. After the slow fourth quarter of 1980, the industry expected a sluggish start in 1981, followed by slow growth and a fast finish at the end of the year.

Business followed the script in the first quarter. Earnings slumped by 12 per cent, compared with the first quarter of 1980. Experts blamed the slump on increasing costs of energy and raw materials and on weak sales to foreign customers.

The weakness in foreign markets continued in the second quarter. Nevertheless, the 10 largest chemical companies increased their earnings by an average of 33 per cent over the second quarter of 1980. The next 10 companies' earnings were up 18 per cent. Third-quarter earnings were up solidly for major chemical companies despite depressed housing and automobile markets and some decline in chemical sales. As the entire U.S. economy slowed down in the last quarter, however, chemical industry gains moderated.

Capital Spending. The industry had predicted in late 1980 that it would spend about $12 billion on new plants and equipment in 1981, an increase of 16 per cent. By early 1981, however, chemical companies had begun to trim their budgets, and industry experts forecast only a 9 per cent increase. They were more optimistic in March, when they predicted a gain of almost 13 per cent. However,

economic statistics released by the government at midyear caused chemical industry managers to reduce their spending plans again. By August, surveys showed that 1981 spending probably would top 1980 outlays by less than 1 per cent.

Superfund. Environmentalists complained during 1981 that the U.S. Environmental Protection Agency (EPA) was moving too slowly in implementing the so-called superfund program. In December 1980, Congress had approved a bill creating a $1.6-billion fund for cleaning up chemical spills and abandoned hazardous-waste dumps. Most of the money was to come from taxes on chemicals used as raw materials and on crude oil going to refineries. By September 1981, the EPA had committed only $9.8 million of the $68 million that it was authorized to spend up until then. Nevertheless, the EPA claimed in September that it had identified 9,600 hazardous sites, completed 2,800 investigations, and undertaken emergency action at 52 sites.

Plans by the Administration of President Ronald Reagan to apply cost-benefit analysis to federal regulations suffered a setback in June, when the Supreme Court of the United States handed down a decision on a 1978 cotton-dust standard. The court ruled that the Occupational Safety and Health Administration could not use cost-benefit

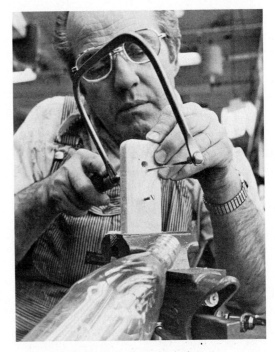

A carpenter saws a block of wood-substitute made by recycling polyester containers like the soft-drink bottle in the foreground.

analysis in enforcing certain major regulations. Later that month, the court refused to review a lead standard that had been pending since 1978, so the standard went into effect. See SAFETY.

Combining Sources. The chemical industry praised the EPA's new policy that allows industry to consider a plant or group of plants as one unit for the purpose of measuring their emissions. Under the old policy, a company had to consider each source of pollution separately. If EPA regulations called for reducing a certain type of pollution by a set percentage within a year, the company had to cut the amount of that pollutant coming from each source in a plant by that percentage.

Under the new policy, however, the company may consider all of the sources at the plant as one source. Thus, the company can comply with EPA regulations by decreasing by the required percentage the total amount of the pollutant coming from the plant as a whole.

E. I. du Pont de Nemours & Company announced in September that applying this new concept to one of its plants would cost only one-third as much as the company would have had to pay under the old EPA policy. Du Pont would control the emissions at only seven major smokestacks rather than have to treat more than 100 sources of pollution. Frederick C. Price

In WORLD BOOK, see CHEMICAL INDUSTRY.

CHEMISTRY. Two groups of scientists reported in July 1981 that they had discovered a new amino acid and synthesized it in the laboratory. Amino acids are fundamental building blocks of proteins.

Scientists do not know the biological role of the new amino acid, called beta-carboxyaspartic acid. However, its job might be similar to that of a related compound known as gamma-carboxyglutamic acid. That acid plays a major role in human blood clotting and kidney function.

Chemists M. Robert Christy, Robert M. Barkley, and Tad H. Koch of the University of Colorado in Boulder and John J. Van Buskirk and Wolff M. Kirsch of the University of Colorado Health Sciences Center in Denver reported that they had found beta-carboxyaspartic acid in the ribosomes of *Escherichia coli* bacteria and had synthesized the acid. Ribosomes contain ribonucleic acids that help build proteins and enzymes.

Van Buskirk and Kirsch first suspected that the ribosomes contained beta-carboxyaspartic acid when they analyzed experiments that they had performed on ribosomes. They had used two kinds of chemicals – an acid and a base – to break ribosome proteins into amino acids. The scientists found that the acid produced slightly more aspartic acid, a common amino acid, than did the base.

They suspected that beta-carboxyaspartic acid was responsible for the larger amount of aspartic

acid. They knew that beta-carboxyaspartic acid would react with an acid, but not a base, to form aspartic acid.

The Denver scientists checked their theory by running ribosome protein mixtures through an instrument called an amino acid analyzer. First, the amino acids flow down through a column of solid chemicals that attracts them, thus slowing their flow. The strength of the attraction and therefore the flow rate through such a column depends upon the composition of the flowing chemicals. Some acids are attracted more strongly than others, so the acids move down the column at different speeds. Because of the speed differences, the various acids separate from one another. The acids then pass by an electronic detector, which emits a certain electrical signal for each kind of acid. Christy, Barkley, and Koch synthesized beta-carboxyaspartic acid in their laboratory and found that this amino acid passed through the analyzer in exactly the same way as the Denver scientists' amino acid.

Meanwhile, another research group was also making beta-carboxyaspartic acid in the laboratory. Researchers Edward B. Henson, Paul M. Gallop, and Peter V. Hauschka of Children's Hospital Medical Center in Boston also reported a synthesis of the acid in July 1981. Neither group knew of the other's work.

Large-Cavity Molecules. Chemists Donald J. Cram, Roger C. Helgeson, and Jean-Paul Mazaleyrat of the University of California at Los Angeles (UCLA) reported in July 1981 that they had synthesized organic (carbon-containing) molecules called spherands. These molecules have charged gaps that can bind, or chemically hold, other organic molecules or metal ions.

The UCLA scientists began with an organic compound made up of two naphthalene groups. Each group has 10 carbon atoms arranged in two hexagons that share one side.

The chemists produced compounds that had large cavities. One spherand was made up of 6 of the four-ring groups, another contained 8 such units, and the third had 10 units.

Experiments performed in 1981 showed that the 8-unit spherand strongly adsorbed a cesium ion and bound the organic molecule cyclohexane; the 10-unit spherand did not bind the cesium ion well. The 6-unit compound was expected to bind the sodium ion, which is smaller than cesium.

Similar spherands that could bind useful ions or molecules might have medical value. The spherands would prevent medicines from dissolving until they reached the part of the body where they were needed. There, a chemical reaction would break the spherands, releasing the medicines that were trapped inside them. Lawrence P. Verbit

In WORLD BOOK, see CHEMISTRY.

CHESS. Anatoly Karpov of Russia successfully defended his world championship in a match that began on Oct. 1, 1981, in Merano, Italy. His opponent was Viktor Korchnoi, a Russian now living in Switzerland. Karpov gained an early lead by taking advantage of weak play by Korchnoi, and went on to win on November 20, 6 games to 2, with 10 draws. Korchnoi had won the right to challenge Karpov by defeating grandmaster Robert Hübner of West Germany in January.

Women's world champion Maya Chiburdanidze defended her title against veteran women's grandmaster Nana Alexandria in September in various places in the Soviet Union's Georgian Soviet Socialist Republic, the home of both players. The match ended in a draw, and so Chiburdanidze kept her title.

U.S. Championship. As Karpov and Korchnoi prepared their match strategies, the world championship cycle was starting again. Sixteen top United States chess masters met in South Bend, Ind., in July for the 1981 U.S. chess championship and zonal qualifier. Besides the coveted championship, at stake were three spots in the 1982 interzonal tournaments, the next stage in the world championship cycle.

Grandmasters Walter Browne of Berkeley, Calif., and Yasser Seirawan of Seattle shared first place. Grandmasters Larry Christiansen of Modesto, Calif.; Lubomir Kavalek of Reston, Va.; and Samuel Reshevsky of Spring Valley, N.Y., tied for third and went into a play-off in September in Jacksonville, Fla. All six games ended in draws, with Christiansen advancing on a tie-break.

Other Tournaments. Romanian grandmaster Florin Gheorghiu won the 1981 U.S. Open championship in August in Palo Alto, Calif., on a tie-break ahead of Christiansen; international master Nick deFirmian of Oakland, Calif.; FIDE master John Meyer of Washington, D.C.; and national master Jeremy Silman of San Francisco. Jay Whitehead of San Francisco won the 1981 U.S. Junior championship in July in Scottsdale, Ariz., while Diane Savereide of Santa Monica, Calif., won the 1981 U.S. Women's championship in Brigham City, Utah. Korchnoi made a surprise visit to the United States in April, winning the 1981 Louis Statham Tournament in Lone Pine, Calif.

The World Open drew about 700 players to New Paltz, N.Y., in July. International masters Joel Benjamin of New York City and Michael Rohde of New Haven, Conn.; FIDE master Dimitri Gurevich of New York City; and Canadian champion Igor Ivanov of Repentigny, Que., shared first place.

The International Association of Chess Journalists awarded Karpov the Chess Oscar as the outstanding player of 1980. It was his record seventh Oscar. Peter C. Prochaska

In WORLD BOOK, see CHESS; HOBBY.

CHICAGO managed to keep its mass-transit system running, its schools open, and its budget balanced in 1981 with the help of new city taxes and several onetime infusions of cash.

The Transit System, which carries about 800,000 passengers a day, came perilously close to shutting down in the spring as Chicago's Mayor Jane M. Byrne, Illinois Governor James R. Thompson, and Illinois legislators tried, without success, to agree on a state subsidy. When the legislature ended its regular session on July 2, Chicago remained the only big city in the United States without state funding for daily transit operations.

To keep the system running and meet other city needs, the City Council passed a $213-million tax package on July 20. It approved a new 1 per cent city sales tax – raising Chicago's total state and local sales tax to 7 per cent – doubled the cigarette tax to 10 cents per pack, and passed a new 1 per cent tax on fees for services, such as those rendered by doctors, lawyers, and architects. However, the service tax was declared unconstitutional by the Illinois Supreme Court on November 16. After putting $20 million of city funds into mass transit, Mayor Byrne announced that she would use the $103 million raised by the surviving new taxes for city expenses other than transportation.

The mayor also created a 13-member commission to direct the course of the Chicago Transit Authority (CTA) , which operates buses and elevated trains in Chicago and 36 suburbs. On July 6, the CTA raised its fare to 90 cents, a 50 per cent increase over the 60-cent fare prevailing in January. It later began reducing the number of employees and bus routes.

Chicago Public Schools raised enough money to wipe out a projected $74.7-million budget deficit and to open on schedule on September 9. State law prohibits the Chicago schools from opening with a budget deficit. The school system rushed property-tax collections to bring in a onetime bonus of $65-million. To raise additional revenue, it sold Midway Airport to the city for $16.5 million in cash and a permanent exemption from city water and sewer charges. In a one-year contract agreement approved on August 31, Chicago teachers received no salary increase, but would have pension contributions – an amount equal to 7 per cent of salaries – paid.

The Board of Education's desegregation plan, submitted to Federal District Judge Milton I. Shadur on April 29, set a ceiling of 70 per cent on white enrollment at any Chicago public school to be achieved by September 1983. The board changed school attendance boundaries and encouraged students to transfer voluntarily, but did not require busing. The plan was criticized by the United States Department of Justice in a July 21 statement, which said the proposal did not ade-

Chicago Mayor Jane M. Byrne and husband, Jay McMullen, move into an apartment in a high-crime housing project in March to try to improve conditions there.

quately promote the desegregation of predominately black schools. However, the department withdrew its opposition in August. The board presented a final desegregation plan on December 31.

Byrne's Balanced Budget. Mayor Byrne's $1.87-billion city operating budget for fiscal 1982, submitted on Nov. 13, 1981, was balanced, despite the anticipated loss of $100 million in federal funds. The budget, which was 12.7 per cent higher than the previous year's, called for adding 200 police officers to the force of 12,200 and for police pay increases of 20 per cent over two years. The budget did not provide pay increases for the city's 5,000 fire fighters, but city officials said it would be amended later to give fire fighters the same raises as police officers. Other city workers were to receive pay raises of from 4 to 10 per cent.

Housing Project. On March 31, Mayor Byrne and her husband, Jay McMullen, drew worldwide attention by moving into an apartment in the Cabrini-Green Homes, a 14,000-tenant public-housing project that had been the scene of 10 murders in the preceding nine weeks. Byrne vowed to stay "as long as it takes to clean it up." The couple moved out after spending 26 nights there, but the housing project continued to receive increased police protection and improved city services.   John Camper

See also CITY. In WORLD BOOK, see CHICAGO.

CHILD WELFARE in the United States in 1981 suffered a dramatic turnaround in federal spending policies affecting its programs. After much review of President Ronald Reagan's fiscal 1982 budget proposals, Congress hammered out a budget that Reagan signed into law on Aug. 13, 1981. Although the child welfare cuts were not as drastic as the Administration had requested, many people feared that their implementation would prove harmful to the welfare of children.

The Administration proposed replacing many so-called categorical grants with a few larger block grants. *Categorical grants,* previously established by Congress, are individually directed toward programs dealing with such specific problems as child abuse or adolescent pregnancy. They carry specific federal guidelines for each program. The *block grants* mandated by the fiscal 1982 budget consolidate many of these programs into relatively few problem areas. A block grant automatically repeals federal guidelines for the programs it covers and allows each state to decide how to divide the reduced appropriation. The new budget is set at 75 per cent of the 1981 appropriation for the covered programs. Block grants fit in with the Reagan Administration's political philosophy of government decentralization.

Handicapped and Disadvantaged Children. During its summer deliberations, Congress rejected

239

proposals to consolidate major programs for the handicapped into block grants. Rehabilitation, special education, and developmental disabilities programs were retained as categorical programs with minor or no cuts. Compensatory aid programs, which are designed to help schools meet the needs of minority and underprivileged children, also remained as categorical grants.

Congress also protected some health programs that affect children's welfare by keeping them as categorical grants. Such programs include family planning, immunization, migrant-worker health, adolescent pregnancy, and research on alcoholism and drug abuse. However, the health block grants covered a host of other services designed to meet children's needs, including those of crippled children. Within the social service block grants are day-care programs, family counseling, aid to the mentally retarded, and other basic services.

Further Cuts. In September, President Reagan requested various additional budget cuts, including a 12 per cent reduction in the operating costs of all federal departments and services. Although many members of Congress reportedly opposed the additional cuts, some further paring of appropriations appeared inevitable.   Frances A. Mullen

In WORLD BOOK, see CHILD WELFARE.

CHILDREN'S BOOKS. See LITERATURE FOR CHILDREN.

CHILE. General Augusto Pinochet Ugarte formally assumed an eight-year term as president of Chile on March 11, 1981. Pinochet had been named president in 1973 by the military junta that overthrew Socialist President Salvador Allende Gossens in a bloody coup.

Under the military government of Pinochet, Chile has opened its doors to foreign investment. During the first half of 1981, the government reported, financial institutions in the United States, Great Britain, Spain, Panama, and other countries invested $355 million in Chile. The government-owned copper corporation, the world's largest producer of copper, announced in 1981 that it had pledges of $1.4 billion in investments for the next five years. The investments should help increase output at four large mines. Several South African companies and a Chilean firm invested $8 million in Chile's fishing fleet.

Chilean factories assembled 20,000 vehicles in the first six months of the year, under arrangements with automakers in the United States, Italy, and France. Chile dramatically increased its exports of fresh fruits to other South American countries and Europe.

Continuity and Stability will be the keystones of Pinochet's regime, he emphasized in a speech in September. He reaffirmed his government's anti-Communist stance, serving notice that Chileans who have been forcibly exiled will not be allowed to return. "If we permitted the return of these Communist agents, we would be betraying the ideals of our men and women who died in action," he said, referring to the domestic violence that rocked Chile in 1973. Pinochet also said that the ban on political activity in Chile would continue for the foreseeable future.

As a move toward its announced eventual goal of restoring democracy, however, the government formally recognized the Democratic Union of Workers on April 24. The union, which will represent 780,000 workers of 46 affiliated unions, said it would pursue a moderate course in its promotion of workers' rights.

The Cost of Living Index rose at an annual rate of only 5.5 per cent in the first half of 1981, but interest rates were high and the money supply was tight. Goods were more plentiful in Chilean stores and markets, and there was an apparent growth of the nation's middle class, but there was also restiveness among the poor.

Chile's international image, however, was marred by continuing accusations by Chileans who have voluntarily or forcibly gone into exile and who accuse the military government of human rights violations.   Nathan A. Haverstock

See also LATIN AMERICA (Facts in Brief Table). In WORLD BOOK, see CHILE.

CHINA, PEOPLE'S REPUBLIC OF. China completed the installation of new, more moderate Communist leadership in 1981. The Communist Party's Central Committee chose the new leaders at a meeting in Peking (Beijing in the phonetic Pinyin alphabet) from June 27 to 29. The appointments ended more than four years of maneuvering by party Vice-Chairman Teng Hsiao-p'ing (Deng Xiaoping), China's dominant political leader, to transfer power to individuals who agreed with his practical approach to politics.

Hu Yaobang replaced Hua Kuo-feng (Hua Guofeng) as chairman of the Communist Party. The deposed Hua had risen into the national leadership during the 1960s as a protégé of Mao Tse-tung (Mao Zedong). The Central Committee adopted a resolution on party history reassessing the work of Mao and his followers. The document said Hua blindly obeyed "whatever policy decisions Chairman Mao made, and . . . whatever instructions Chairman Mao gave," even though Mao introduced wrongful policies during the last decade before his death in 1976. Under Hua's leadership, the resolution said, "it is impossible to correct 'left' errors within the party, and all the more impossible to restore the party's fine traditions."

Hu, Hua's successor, was a veteran of the famous Long March in 1934 and 1935, in which Mao led the Chinese Communists to Shensi (Shaanxi)

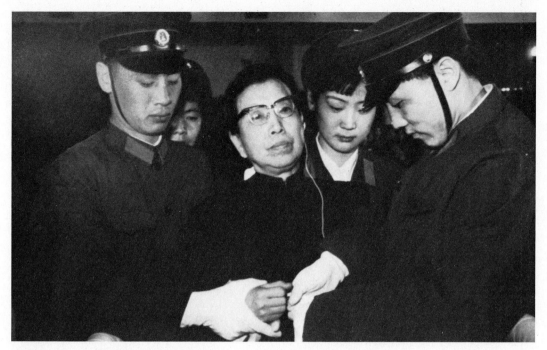

Chinese guards handcuff Chiang Ching (Jiang Qing), the widow of Mao
Tse-tung (Mao Zedong). She received a suspended death sentence in January.

Province. The ordeal of the march welded the survivors into a tight group under Mao's leadership. Hu became Teng's protégé during China's civil war in the late 1940s, when he served as a political officer in army units under Teng. See HU YAOBANG.

In other appointments at the June meeting, the Central Committee named China's Premier Zhao Ziyang, another protégé of Teng's, a party vice-chairman. Former Chairman Hua also received the title of vice-chairman, but he ranked lowest of six people holding that title. Teng replaced Hua as chairman of the party's military commission, which controls the army.

The History Resolution, issued on June 30 after the meeting, was a compromise statement following years of argument over how to evaluate Mao's contributions to China. Much of the debate surrounded Mao's role in the Cultural Revolution, a 10-year period of purges and turmoil during which leftist radicals in the Communist Party attempted to put China back on a revolutionary path. Victims of the purges wanted to condemn Mao's policies, but leftists and many military leaders defended him. The army newspaper warned before the meeting that "defaming Chairman Mao can only demean the party and our socialist motherland."

The history resolution assessed Mao as "a great Marxist and a great proletarian revolutionary, strategist, and theorist. It is true that he made gross mistakes during the Cultural Revolution, but if we judge his activities as a whole, his contributions to the Chinese revolution far outweigh his mistakes. His merits are primary and his errors secondary. He rendered indelible meritorious service in founding and building up our party . . . ."

But, the resolution said, Mao then became arrogant and "acted more and more arbitrarily and subjectively . . . ." He "imagined that his theory and practice were Marxist and that they were essential for the consolidation of the dictatorship of the proletariat. Herein lies his tragedy."

The resulting Cultural Revolution caused "the most severe setback and the heaviest losses suffered by the party, the state and the people since the founding of the People's Republic," the document said. It "did not, in fact, constitute a revolution or social progress in any sense . . . ."

The Gang of Four. The Cultural Revolution was defined by the history resolution as lasting from May 1966 to October 1976. The final date was when Mao's widow, Chiang Ching (Jiang Qing), and three of her leftist allies, dubbed the Gang of Four, were arrested. The four were tried for treason along with leftist Chen Po-Ta (Chen Poda), who was one of Mao's top aides, and five generals who had been associated with Defense Minister Lin Piao (Lin Biao), Mao's designated heir, who died

China hopes to make more goods, such as these washing machines in Peking (Beijing), to become a modern industrialized nation by the year 2000.

mysteriously in 1971 after reportedly trying to kill Mao. The trial of the 10 defendants by a special court lasted from Nov. 20 to Dec. 29, 1980.

On Jan. 25, 1981, the court delivered a 34-page judgment on the Gang of Four and the other six defendants. The document said two counterrevolutionary groups, headed by Chiang Ching and Lin Piao, had "framed and persecuted" state and party leaders, "conspired to overthrow the government and sabotage the army," and committed other crimes. The generals "plotted to stage an armed coup d'état and conspired" to murder Mao, and Chiang Ching's group "plotted to stage an armed rebellion in Shanghai," the judgment said.

Chiang Ching, who frequently shouted protests during the trial in defiance of the court's authority, claimed she had only followed Mao's instructions. She was sentenced to death. So was another Gang of Four member, Chang Chun-chiao (Zhang Chunqiao), a former mayor of Shanghai. Both death sentences were suspended for two years to give the prisoners a chance to "reform." In theory, they would be shot in 1983 if they remained defiant, but it was more likely they would spend the rest of their lives in prison — unless another political reversal restores leftists to power.

Wang Hung-wen (Wang Hongwen), another member of the Gang of Four, who had in 1973 been elevated by Mao to the number-three position in

China's leadership, was sentenced to life imprisonment. The fourth, Yao Wen-yuan (Yao Wenyuan), got 20 years in prison. Chen and the generals received sentences ranging from 16 to 18 years. The Supreme People's Court confirmed the verdicts on March 3.

Discontent in the Armed Forces about Teng's policies was intensified by the generals' trial. Many high-ranking officers believed Teng's policies threatened the army's traditionally important social, political, and economic role in China and reduced the prestige that Mao had given it. There was concern that the government considered the armed forces a low financial priority. The government did cut the military budget in 1981 as part of a general belt-tightening.

Commenting on the trial, the Communist Party newspaper *People's Daily* warned that the armed forces must give up their "feudal and patriarchal ways." The paper announced on March 3 that soldiers would be required to swear a new loyalty oath to the party leadership. On March 6, Geng Biao, a Long March veteran who had left the army in 1949, became China's first civilian defense minister. By appointing a civilian to the defense post and by making Teng chairman of the military commission, China's leadership attempted to put the armed forces firmly under civilian control.

Other Grumbling came from leftists who had benefited from the Cultural Revolution and wanted to restore its prestige. *Red Flag*, a Communist Party journal, said on February 18 that some dissidents, calling for a second "cultural revolution," had established illegal organizations and magazines. The journal demanded a crackdown on people holding secret meetings to "conspire to spread chaos . . . ." *Red Flag* said, "Although their numbers are small, they are like a malignant, contagious disease."

China's Sluggish Economy caused discontent. "A pessimistic wave of sabotage, protests, and despair has been sweeping the country," *Red Flag* said on January 31. "It is bound to ruin our hard-earned stability." There were reports of bombings, strikes, and demonstrations to protest economic conditions. Troops were called out in Shanghai in April when some 1,000 persons demonstrated against unemployment. An estimated 20 million of China's people, about 2 per cent of the population, were unemployed in 1981. In November, the government announced that it would no longer guarantee every able-bodied citizen a job. The government also called for more private enterprise to relieve unemployment.

Deputy Premier Yao Yilin announced on February 28 that government spending would be cut 13 per cent and capital construction 45 per cent, while farmers and small private businesses would be given more freedom to produce what they wanted.

Inflation was 7.5 per cent, and the foreign-trade balance showed a deficit.

After China opened up some of its long-secret financial accounts, the International Monetary Fund, an agency of the United Nations (UN), decided on March 2 to make available $915 million in credits and trust funds. In June, the World Bank, another UN agency, approved a $200-million loan to improve Chinese education and technology as the beginning of an $800-million lending program. These two decisions opened a new era as China, long a giver of aid to others, joined the ranks of the developing countries in need of international help.

A World Bank survey found that China ranked among low-income countries with an estimated per capita annual income of $260 in 1979. The agency noted, however, that "the physical quality of life of the bulk of the Chinese people is strikingly better than in most other low-income countries."

Natural Disasters hampered China's economic efforts. Floods in Hupeh (Hubei) Province in 1980 were followed by drought there in 1981, and Hopeh (Hebei) Province also suffered drought. In July, the worst floods in Szechwan (Sichuan) Province since 1949 killed 768 people and left 1.5 million homeless. Severe flooding hit Shensi Province two months later.

Foreign Relations were agitated over Taiwan. China ordered the Dutch ambassador on January 19 to leave Peking because the Netherlands planned to sell Taiwan two submarines. China also protested proposals by the Administration of U.S. President Ronald Reagan to sell advanced weapons to Taiwan.

United States Secretary of State Alexander M. Haig, Jr., announced on June 16 that America would begin selling weapons to China, but China was slow to follow up with orders. The next day, U.S. officials disclosed that Russian missile tests had been monitored for more than a year by Chinese technicians using American equipment, with the data shared.

Pope John Paul II sought to re-establish ties with the Roman Catholic Church in China. The Chinese government had nationalized churches in 1957 and broken ties with the Vatican. On June 6, the pope appointed as archbishop of Canton Monsignor Dominic Tang Yiming, a bishop who had been released in 1980 from 22 years in prison for refusing to join the official Chinese church. Chinese officials rejected the appointment and stripped Tang of his church titles.   Henry S. Bradsher

See also ASIA (Facts in Brief Table); RELIGION; TAIWAN. In WORLD BOOK, see CHINA.

CHRONOLOGY. See pages 8 through 21.

CHURCHES. See EASTERN ORTHODOX CHURCHES; JEWS AND JUDAISM; PROTESTANTISM; RELIGION; ROMAN CATHOLIC CHURCH.

CISKEI on Dec. 4, 1981, became the fourth tribal "homeland" to be given political independence by South Africa's government. It followed Transkei, which became independent in October 1976; Bophuthatswana, in December 1977; and Venda, in September 1979. Under South Africa's system of *apartheid* (the separate development of races), each of the country's black ethnic groups has been assigned to one of 10 homelands. Ciskei is the homeland of the Xhosa-speaking people.

Together the homelands comprise only about 13 per cent of South Africa's area, while the 23 million blacks who are to live in the homelands make up more than 70 per cent of the country's population. None of the independent homelands has been recognized by any nation other than South Africa.

Ciskei has a territory of about 2,000 square miles (5,200 square kilometers) in the southeastern part of South Africa. Approximately 600,000 people live within its borders. However, Ciskei is also the designated homeland of some 1.4 million additional Xhosa-speaking people living elsewhere in South Africa. South Africa can deport these Xhosa to Ciskei or some other country.

Ciskei is a poor country. Its per capita income in 1976 was only $275.   J. Dixon Esseks

See also AFRICA (Facts in Brief Table); SOUTH AFRICA. In WORLD BOOK, see SOUTH AFRICA.

Ciskei—Newest Independent Homeland

★ National capital

▪ Independent homelands

▫ Other homelands

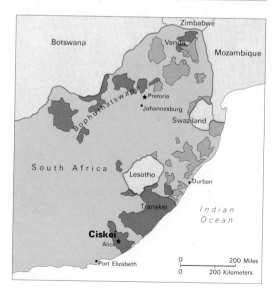

CITY. Many cities in the United States were forced to raise taxes, dismiss employees, and reduce services in 1981 as sources of municipal funds shrank. In addition to cuts in federal aid, older cities in the Northeast and Midwest were faced with declining local tax bases as industries and middle-class residents moved to the Sunbelt.

State of the Cities. The Joint Economic Committee of Congress, reporting on May 16 on a survey of 275 American cities, said that half of all cities with populations of over 10,000 were spending more for operations than they were taking in. The committee concluded that "because of the magnitude of the proposed federal cuts and the abruptness with which they are likely to be implemented, many economic development initiatives will be reversed, the population of many cities will be forced to forgo certain services and to pay more for others, and an increasing number of cities will find themselves on the brink of fiscal collapse."

Federal Cuts. The biggest jolt to U.S. cities in 1981 came from the new federal spending law, known as the Omnibus Budget Reconciliation Act of 1981, which took effect on October 1. The legislation reduced federal aid to state and local governments by about $7 billion from the 1981 level of $95.1 billion. Federal aid to mass transit, for example, was reduced $1.3 billion below the

$5.1 billion that would have been spent if previous federal policies had remained unchanged, according to projections by the Congressional Budget Office. The law also eliminated the 300,000 public service jobs financed by the Comprehensive Employment and Training Act (CETA) and reduced the budget of the Economic Development Administration – which makes low-interest loans and guarantees loans in depressed city neighborhoods – from $1 billion to $290 million. The law removed some federal restrictions from certain federal aid programs in the areas of health, social services, education, and community development by incorporating them into block grants – funds to be administered by the states.

President Ronald Reagan signed the bill on August 13. On September 24, as the projected federal deficit mounted, he asked Congress to cut federal aid to states and localities, including the $4-billion general revenue-sharing program, by an additional 12 per cent. Congress approved domestic cuts averaging about 4 per cent on December 11. The President called the action "only another installment in a long and hard program to get the federal budget under control."

In late December, however, President Reagan bowed to pleas by urban officials to reject a proposal to cut all new spending for Community Develop-

Henry G. Cisneros won support from both Hispanics and non-Hispanics in San Antonio to become the first Mexican American mayor of a major U.S. city.

ment Block Grants and Urban Development Action Grants after 1983. The President countered the proposal with one that allowed programs to operate through 1984 with annual budgets of $3.8-billion, a slight reduction from the 1982 budget.

High Interest Rates also bedeviled cities in 1981, preventing many of them from selling bonds to raise operating cash or finance capital improvements. Interest rates began to come down late in the year. However, New York City still could not sell $200 million in notes, and Chicago failed to market $140 million in mass-transit bonds.

Mayors complained that the new federal tax law, which took effect on October 1, diminished cities' borrowing power in two ways. First, it lowered the tax rate on upper incomes, giving wealthy people less incentive to seek tax-free income from municipal bonds. Second, it enabled savings institutions to offer tax-exempt all-savers certificates, which the mayors feared would also draw investors' money away from city bonds.

Some city officials hoped that Congress would help spur urban development by passing a law offering federal tax breaks to businesses that locate in decaying city neighborhoods called "enterprise zones." Two congressmen from New York — Republican Jack F. Kemp and Democrat Robert Garcia — introduced such legislation on June 3, but the bills did not get through Congress in 1981.

Rising Taxes. Many cities, particularly the older ones in the Northeast and Midwest, raised taxes and cut expenditures even before the federal cuts took effect. In Cleveland, which had defaulted on $15.5 million of notes in 1978, residents voted on February 17 to raise the city income tax by one-third — from 1.5 to 2.0 per cent. It was the second 0.5 percentage point income tax increase approved by Cleveland voters in two years.

Detroit residents, facing a projected $270-million city budget deficit, voted on June 23 to raise the city income tax from 2.0 to 3.0 per cent and to raise the income tax on commuters from 0.5 to 1.5 per cent. The city's major municipal employees' unions accepted a two-year wage freeze.

The Chicago City Council on July 20 raised the combined state-local sales tax from 6.0 to 7.0 per cent, doubled the cigarette tax to 10 cents per pack, and approved a new 1.0 per cent tax on professional services. The service tax, however, was later declared unconstitutional.

Shrinking City Services. Dallas voters on January 17 rejected a proposal that would have cut local property taxes by almost 30 per cent and forced a reduction in city services. Another referendum to reduce property taxes, known as Proposition 2½, caused severe budget problems for Massachusetts cities after the state's voters approved it on Nov. 4, 1980. The measure reduced Boston's income for the 1981-1982 fiscal year by an estimated $87-

50 Largest Cities in the World

Rank	City	Population
1.	Shanghai, China	10,820,000
2.	Mexico City, Mexico	8,988,230
3.	São Paulo, Brazil	8,407,500
4.	Tokyo, Japan	8,219,888
5.	Moscow, Russia	7,831,000
6.	Peking (Beijing), China	7,570,000
7.	New York City, N.Y., U.S.A.	7,071,030
8.	London, England	7,028,200
9.	Seoul, South Korea	6,889,502
10.	Cairo, Egypt	6,133,000
11.	Bombay, India	5,970,575
12.	Jakarta, Indonesia	5,490,000
13.	Hong Kong	4,966,000
14.	Rio de Janeiro, Brazil	4,857,716
15.	Bangkok, Thailand	4,835,000
16.	Teheran, Iran	4,716,000
17.	Tientsin (Tianjin), China	4,280,000
18.	Leningrad, Russia	4,073,000
19.	Santiago, Chile	3,899,495
20.	Karachi, Pakistan	3,515,402
21.	Ho Chi Minh City, Vietnam	3,460,500
22.	Delhi, India	3,287,883
23.	Madrid, Spain	3,201,234
24.	Calcutta, India	3,148,746
25.	Berlin (East & West), East & West Germany	3,038,689
26.	Chicago, Ill., U.S.A.	3,005,072
27.	Buenos Aires, Argentina	2,983,000
28.	Baghdad, Iraq	2,969,000
29.	Los Angeles, Calif., U.S.A.	2,966,763
30.	Lima, Peru	2,941,473
31.	Rome, Italy	2,868,248
32.	Bogotá, Colombia	2,850,000
33.	Sydney, Australia	2,765,040
34.	Yokohama, Japan	2,723,940
35.	Osaka, Japan	2,600,001
36.	Istanbul, Turkey	2,547,364
37.	Pyongyang, North Korea	2,500,000
38.	Melbourne, Australia	2,479,422
39.	Madras, India	2,469,449
40.	Pusan, South Korea	2,453,173
41.	Shen-yang (Shenyang), China	2,411,000
42.	Alexandria, Egypt	2,320,000
43.	Singapore, Singapore	2,308,200
44.	Paris, France	2,299,830
45.	Lahore, Pakistan	2,169,742
46.	Wu-han (Wuhan), China	2,146,000
47.	Kiev, Russia	2,144,000
48.	Ch'ung-ch'ing (Chongqing), China	2,121,000
49.	Budapest, Hungary	2,093,187
50.	Nagoya, Japan	2,080,666

Sources: 1980 Bureau of the Census final results for cities of the United States; censuses and estimates from governments or UN *Demographic Yearbook, 1979* for cities of other countries.

50 Largest Cities in the United States

Rank	City	Population (a)	Per cent change in population since 1970 census	Mayor or City Manager (b)
1.	New York City	7,071,030	− 10.4	Edward I. Koch (D, 1/86)
2.	Chicago	3,005,072	− 10.8	Jane M. Byrne (D, 4/83)
3.	Los Angeles	2,966,763	+ 5.5	Tom Bradley (NP, 6/85)
4.	Philadelphia	1,688,210	− 13.4	William J. Green (D, 1/84)
5.	Houston	1,594,086	+ 29.2	Kathryn J. Whitmire (NP, 1/84)
6.	Detroit	1,203,339	− 20.5	Coleman A. Young (D, 1/86)
7.	Dallas	904,078	+ 7.1	Jack Evans (NP, 5/83)
8.	San Diego	875,504	+ 25.5	Pete Wilson (R, 12/84)
9.	Baltimore	786,775	− 13.1	William Donald Schaefer (D, 12/83)
10.	San Antonio	785,410	+ 20.1	Henry G. Cisneros (NP, 5/83)
11.	Phoenix	764,911	+ 30.9	Margaret M. Hance (NP, 1/84)
12.	Indianapolis	700,807	− 4.9	William H. Hudnut III (R, 12/83)
13.	San Francisco	678,974	− 5.1	Dianne Feinstein (NP, 1/84)
14.	Memphis	646,356	+ 3.6	Wyeth Chandler (I, 12/83)
15.	Washington, D.C.	637,651	− 15.7	Marion S. Barry, Jr. (D, 1/83)
16.	San Jose	636,550	+ 38.4	Janet Gray Hayes (D, 12/82)
17.	Milwaukee	636,212	− 11.3	Henry W. Maier (D, 4/84)
18.	Cleveland	573,822	− 23.6	George V. Voinovich (R, 11/83)
19.	Columbus, Ohio	564,871	+ 4.6	Tom Moody (R, 12/83)
20.	Boston	562,994	− 12.2	Kevin H. White (D, 1/84)
21.	New Orleans	557,482	− 6.1	Ernest N. Morial (D, 5/82)
22.	Jacksonville, Fla.	540,898	+ 7.3	Jake M. Godbold (D, 7/83)
23.	Seattle	493,846	− 7.0	Charles Royer (NP, 1/86)
24.	Denver	491,396	− 4.5	William H. McNichols, Jr. (D, 6/83)
25.	Nashville	455,651	+ 7.0	Richard H. Fulton (D, 9/83)
26.	St. Louis	453,085	− 27.2	Vincent L. Schoemehl, Jr. (D, 4/85)
27.	Kansas City, Mo.	448,159	− 11.7	Richard L. Berkley (NP, 4/83)
28.	El Paso	425,259	+ 32.0	Jonathan Rogers (NP, 4/83)
29.	Atlanta	425,022	− 14.1	Andrew J. Young, Jr. (D, 1/86)
30.	Pittsburgh	423,938	− 18.5	Richard S. Caliguiri (D, 1/86)
31.	Oklahoma City	403,213	+ 9.5	*Scott Johnson (1981)
32.	Cincinnati	385,457	− 15.0	*Sylvester Murray (1979)
33.	Fort Worth	385,141	− 2.1	*Robert L. Herchert (1978)
34.	Minneapolis	370,951	− 14.6	Donald M. Fraser (D, 1/86)
35.	Portland, Ore.	366,383	− 3.6	Francis D. Ivancie (D, 11/84)
36.	Honolulu	365,048	+ 12.4	Eileen Anderson (D, 1/85)
37.	Long Beach	361,334	+ 0.7	*John E. Dever (1977)
38.	Tulsa	360,919	+ 9.3	James M. Inhofe (R, 5/82)
39.	Buffalo	357,870	− 22.7	James D. Griffin (D, 12/85)
40.	Toledo	354,635	− 7.4	*David Boston (1981)
41.	Miami	346,931	+ 3.6	Maurice A. Ferre (11/85)
42.	Austin	345,496	+ 36.3	*Nicholas Meiszer (10/81)
43.	Oakland	339,288	− 6.2	*Henry Gardner (1981)
44.	Albuquerque	331,767	+ 35.7	Harry E. Kinney (R, 12/85)
45.	Tucson	330,537	+ 25.7	*Joel D. Valdez (1974)
46.	Newark	329,248	− 13.8	Kenneth A. Gibson (D, 7/82)
47.	Charlotte	314,447	+ 30.2	H. Edward Knox (D, 12/83)
48.	Omaha	311,681	− 10.2	Michael Boyle (NP, 6/85)
49.	Louisville	298,451	− 17.5	Harvey Sloane (D, 12/85)
50.	Birmingham	284,413	− 5.5	Richard Arrington, Jr. (NP, 11/83)

Sources:
(a) 1980 census (U.S. Bureau of the Census).
(b) *Asterisk before name denotes city manager; all others are mayors. Dates are those of expiration of term for mayors and dates of appointment for city managers.
D—Democrat, R—Republican, NP—Nonpartisan, I—Independent.
(National League of Cities; *Municipal Yearbook 1981*, International City Management Association).

Average cost of living (family of 4) (c)	Unemployment rate (d)	Revenue (e)	Gross debt outstanding (e)	Per capita income (f)	Sales tax rate (g)
$26,749	8.1	$17,797,473	$10,645,307	$ 9,839	8.25%
23,387	8.0	1,934,014	1,069,891	10,455	6%
22,500	6.5	2,689,271	2,810,740	10,606	6%
24,364	7.6	1,940,816	1,835,152	8,958	6%
21,572	4.8	760,129	1,415,707	10,638	5%
23,168	11.4	1,383,918	896,855	10,433	4%
20,766	9.4	475,259	581,960	9,931	5%
22,727	6.8	418,743	116,815	8,908	6%
23,389	8.5	1,088,317	614,969	8,967	5%
n/a	7.3	612,111	988,573	7,518	5%
n/a	5.1	411,911	494,576	9,322	5%
n/a	7.9	419,502	326,550	9,361	4%
24,704	5.8	1,336,167	704,633	11,741	6½%
n/a	8.1	957,633	602,792	8,041	6%
25,203	5.1	960,667	1,660,893	11,313	6%
n/a	5.7	259,627	175,074	11,064	6½%
24,028	7.2	405,164	311,039	9,715	4%
23,429	8.4	434,410	432,790	10,167	5½%
n/a	7.7	290,584	650,449	8,639	4½%
27,029	6.7	995,359	594,312	9,351	5%
n/a	7.6	421,959	456,131	8,605	7%
n/a	5.9	586,714	675,481	7,808	4%
23,392	7.5	465,138	517,191	10,788	5.4%
22,813	4.5	524,625	390,577	10,133	6%
n/a	6.3	680,994	636,804	8,510	6¾%
22,248	7.8	449,689	157,096	9,171	4⅝%
22,504	6.2	353,036	276,577	9,632	4⅛%
n/a	8.0	151,445	54,085	6,207	5%
21,131	5.5	390,776	1,001,138	9,294	4%
22,492	6.3	259,015	191,358	9,218	6%
n/a	2.6	244,714	384,578	9,306	4%
22,681	8.2	357,828	184,225	8,995	4½%
20,766	9.4	181,940	215,798	9,931	5%
23,630	3.9	280,523	437,749	10.025	5%
n/a	7.7	211,499	282,984	10,067	—
28,488	4.7	377,551	235,973	9,573	4%
22,500	6.5	346,074	106,536	10,606	6%
n/a	2.7	207,345	412,627	9,436	5%
23,995	10.0	435,934	255,795	8,401	7%
n/a	10.8	173,006	161,547	8,962	4½%
n/a	6.2	183,457	148,735	9,714	4%
n/a	3.9	323,897	865,256	8,560	5%
24,704	5.8	223,049	247,164	11,741	6½%
n/a	7.2	174,350	269,059	8,062	3.75%
n/a	5.2	173,087	143,749	8,319	6%
n/a	7.1	407,126	140,260	10,500	5%
n/a	4.7	170,841	200,419	8,890	4%
n/a	5.3	145,503	128,510	8,510	4½%
n/a	8.3	210,038	243,139	8,810	5%
n/a	9.8	151,036	314,701	8,429	5%

(c) Estimates for autumn, 1980, for Standard Metropolitan Statistical Areas (U.S. Bureau of Labor Statistics). n/a—not available.
(d) August 1981 figures for Standard Metropolitan Statistical Areas (U.S. Bureau of Labor Statistics).
(e) Figures in thousands of dollars for 1979–1980 (U.S. Bureau of the Census).
(f) 1979 figures for Standard Metropolitan Statistical Areas (U.S. Bureau of Economic Analysis).
(g) Total sales tax rate, including state, county, city, school district, and special district taxes (The Tax Foundation).

million. In the 13 months following passage of Proposition 2½, Boston reduced its work force – through layoffs and attrition – by 2,700, including 900 police officers and fire fighters. Boston had spent its entire snow-removal budget for the 1981-1982 winter by mid-December.

Transit Troubles. Birmingham, Ala., shut down its bus system on March 1, leaving 30,000 daily riders without public transportation after state and local governments failed to provide funds to erase the system's $800,000 deficit. About 63 per cent of the service was restored on June 1 when local communities agreed to contribute $64,000 to the transit system.

Youngstown, Ohio, shut down its bus system from November 1 to December 1 after voters rejected a property tax increase to subsidize it. The nation's two largest transit systems – New York City and Chicago – raised fares in 1981 in an effort to stay in business. New York City's fare rose from 60 to 75 cents; and Chicago's, from 60 to 90 cents.

Municipal Strikes added to the woes of many cities. Philadelphia weathered three – a five-day strike by school maintenance workers and bus drivers that ended on February 6, a 19-day strike by transit workers that ended on April 2, and a 50-day strike by city schoolteachers that ended on October 27.

Interns and residents struck eight New York City municipal hospitals from March 16 to 23 to dramatize their demands for larger staffs and better equipment. In California, 789 San Diego County sheriff's deputies struck from July 1 to 9, and county voters showed their displeasure by voting on November 3 to fire any county employee who strikes in the future.

Municipal workers in San Jose, Calif., struck for eight days over the issue of equal pay for women. The strike ended on July 14 after the city agreed to raise the pay of female employees.

Police struck in Riverside, Calif., and in Terre Haute, Ind. Fire fighters staged two brief strikes in Milwaukee. Police officers, fire fighters, and other municipal workers struck in Yonkers, N.Y., and in Steubenville, Ohio. New York City endured an 18-day strike by private garbage collectors, and Providence, R.I., suffered through a 15-day strike by more than 1,000 city workers.

Elections. Despite the many urban problems, voters generally stuck by their mayors in 1981 elections. Incumbent mayors re-elected in 1981 included Edward I. Koch of New York City, Thomas A. Bradley of Los Angeles, Coleman A. Young of Detroit, Margaret M. Hance of Phoenix, George V. Voinovich of Cleveland, Richard S. Caliguiri of Pittsburgh, Donald M. Fraser of Minneapolis, and Charles Royer of Seattle. However, Houston Mayor Jim McConn was unseated by City Controller Kathryn J. Whitmire.

Population Shift. While cities of the Northeast and Midwest raised taxes and reduced services, many communities in the South and West had an easier time, largely because of expanding population and industrial growth. The U.S. Bureau of the Census reported on March 19 that every one of the nation's fastest-growing metropolitan areas in the 1970s was in the South or West, while 30 of the 32 metropolitan areas that lost population were in the Northeast or North-Central regions.

This trend did not go unnoticed by the President's Commission for a National Agenda for the Eighties. "Cities are not permanent," the commission said in a report released on January 16. The commission advised that instead of trying to "revitalize obsolete industries" in the older urban centers, the federal government should "assist those [people] who wish to relocate to areas where employment opportunities abound."

Representatives of the older cities criticized the report. The Northeast-Midwest Congressional Coalition questioned whether cities of the South and West will be able to afford the "huge public expenditures for new roads, housing, schools, hospitals, and water systems, duplicating facilities already built but now being abandoned in the Northeast and Midwest."   John Camper

See also articles on individual cities. In WORLD BOOK, see CITY and articles on individual cities.

CIVIL RIGHTS in 1981 suffered setbacks in Egypt, a nation where such rights had made significant progress in recent years. President Anwar el-Sadat, whose 12-year regime had broadened civil liberties in that nation, initiated several measures during September to restrict his domestic opponents. On September 3 and 4, he arrested about 1,600 religious activists, journalists, lawyers, and professors, accusing them of "irresponsible and suspicious acts" in the name of religion. On September 5, he removed Shenuda III as patriarch of Egypt's 6 million Coptic Christians and exiled him to a remote monastery. The religious affairs ministry announced on September 7 that the government would gradually put the country's 40,000 mosques under state supervision.

Sadat also closed *Al Daawa*, a Muslim fundamentalist newspaper; the newspaper of the Socialist Labor Party; and five other newspapers. However, Sadat's precautions did not prevent his assassination as he reviewed a military parade in Cairo on October 6. The attack was attributed to Muslim fundamentalists.

In contrast, some improvements occurred in several countries where civil rights had been severely curtailed. In the Philippines, President Ferdinand E. Marcos ended eight years of martial law on January 17 and released 341 political prisoners. Marcos promised that people arrested in the future would be tried in civilian courts but stipulated that all decrees issued under martial law would remain in effect. In South Korea, President Chun Doo Hwan commuted the death sentence of leading dissident Kim Dae Jung to life imprisonment on January 23. The next day, Chun lifted martial law.

Switzerland moved toward ending discrimination against women on June 14 by adopting a constitutional amendment that strengthened guarantees of equality between the sexes.

Black-Rights Organizations in the United States in 1981 devised strategies to save the civil rights that they perceived as threatened by President Ronald Reagan's budget cuts and an increasingly conservative national climate. Delegates to the national convention of the National Association for the Advancement of Colored People (NAACP) were unswayed by Reagan's June 29 address inviting them to join his "coalition for change" to enable business and industry to bring about an "economic emancipation" for the deprived. Instead, delegates supported the call of NAACP Executive Director Benjamin L. Hooks. Hooks urged them to insist on extension of the Voting Rights Act of 1965.

The two largest black-rights organizations lost their top leaders in 1981. Roy Wilkins, the executive secretary of the NAACP for 22 years, died on September 8. Vernon E. Jordan, Jr., head of the National Urban League, resigned effective December 31. John E. Jacob, the league's vice-president, was named to succeed him.

School Desegregation and school busing remained prominent civil rights issues, particularly because President Reagan had made clear his opposition to mandatory busing. On May 4, the U.S. Department of Justice and the St. Louis School Board proposed an alternative. Their program would reward students who voluntarily switched primary or secondary schools to further desegregation by paying part of their college tuition. But the Administration backed away following criticism that the plan was a "bribe" and an "insult." Attorney General William French Smith, in a speech on May 22, called for "more innovative and effective approaches" to school integration but did not mention the St. Louis plan.

The school-busing dispute in Los Angeles ended when the city's school board voted to dismantle the mandatory program and allow students to return to their neighborhood schools. After years of legal battles and contradictory court decisions, the program came to an end on November 30 when a California superior court returned all jurisdiction over the case to the Los Angeles Board of Education. On April 29, the Chicago school board adopted a plan that delayed mandatory busing until 1983, leaving hundreds of schools with predominantly white, black, or Hispanic student bodies.

Thousands of demonstrators march on the Mobile, Ala., courthouse in April to urge renewal of the Voting Rights Act of 1965.

On September 10, the Justice Department reversed a position it had taken during President Jimmy Carter's Administration by requesting the Supreme Court to uphold a 1978 Washington state antibusing law. The law had been designed to end an integration program voluntarily adopted by school boards in Seattle and two other cities. In 1979, lower courts invalidated the law.

Voting Rights. The struggle over the renewal of the Voting Rights Act of 1965 – widely regarded as the most important civil rights issue before the 97th Congress – began in earnest on April 7. On that date, members of both parties in Congress introduced bills to extend the act, scheduled to expire on Aug. 6, 1982, for 10 years. The Reagan Administration endorsed a modified extension of the act, though several conservatives opposed extending parts of the law on grounds that they represented a federal intrusion into local affairs.

Vice-President George H. W. Bush announced on August 12 that the Reagan Administration would review affirmative action rules and other federal guidelines ensuring equal rights to minorities. On August 24, the Administration proposed new regulations to relax antidiscrimination rules for federal contractors. Civil rights leaders denounced the proposals.

Women's Rights. A coalition of women's groups and other organizations on March 26 assailed President Reagan's budget cutbacks in antipoverty programs as endangering rights "for which women have struggled over the last several years." Legislation to strengthen the economic rights of women in such areas as pensions, insurance, inheritances, child care, and military service was introduced in Congress in April. The bill was considered a partial substitute for the Equal Rights Amendment, which at year-end still needed ratification by three additional states to become law.

Children's Rights. On October 16, the United States granted permanent resident status to 14-year-old Walter Polovchak, who had been given asylum in the United States in 1980 after he refused to return to Russia with his parents. On October 21, Polovchak's sister and cousin filed suit in U.S. District Court in Chicago to block all measures to return the boy to his native country.

On December 30, the Illinois Appellate Court ruled that Walter was no longer a ward of the state. The decision would allow Walter's parents to retain custody of him if they return to the United States. However, the Justice Department had said in August it would not permit the boy to be returned to Russia against his will.   Louis W. Koenig

See also COURTS AND LAWS; EDUCATION; SUPREME COURT OF THE UNITED STATES. In WORLD BOOK, see CIVIL RIGHTS.

CLOTHING. See FASHION.

COAL. The National Coal Association (NCA) predicted on March 1, 1981, that United States exports of coal will grow throughout the 1980s, perhaps doubling by 1990. The NCA, a group of coal producers, forecast that a world plagued by high oil prices and potential oil supply disruptions will become increasingly eager to buy coal.

The NCA said exports could increase to 142 million short tons (129 million metric tons) per year by 1990 and could reach 160 million short tons (145 million metric tons). Exports in 1980 were 89.9 million short tons (81.5 million metric tons).

The most dramatic increases are expected to occur in overseas shipments of steam coal, which is used to fire boilers in electric generating stations and industrial plants. In the past, U.S. coal exports have consisted largely of metallurgical coal, which is used for steel production. In 1980, 16 million short tons (15 million metric tons) of steam coal were exported, primarily to Europe. The NCA forecast that steam-coal exports could reach 79 million short tons (72 million metric tons) by 1990.

Coal Transportation Problems. The NCA noted that insufficient port capacity is the single most important factor limiting overseas exports of U.S. coal. The association called for new and enlarged coal-port facilities, dredging of deeper channels to accommodate larger ships, and other measures to improve coal transportation.

The Seafarers' International Union of North America also expressed concern about inadequate coal transportation. Union President Frank Drozak told a Senate subcommittee on April 28 that the United States is forfeiting millions of dollars in international trade and risking the loss of future overseas markets because it has no comprehensive coal-transportation policy. He urged a new financial commitment to boost international coal sales by improving railways, inland waterways, ports, and commercial oceangoing vessels.

A 72-Day Coal Strike ended on June 6 with a new wage settlement between coal operators and the United Mine Workers of America (UMW). The strike began on March 27, when the existing contract expired. On March 31, UMW members rejected the initial wage offer. The final pact provided an increase of 37.5 per cent over 40 months.

The strike had cut coal production in half and sparked concern among overseas buyers about the stability of the U.S. coal supply. The strike also contributed to an estimated 3.5 per cent decrease in coal production for 1981. According to the NCA, 795 million short tons (721 million metric tons) would be mined, compared with 824 million short tons (747 million metric tons) in 1980.

A Car Fueled by Powdered Coal was unveiled by General Motors Corporation (GM) on June 3 in a

Coal cars stand empty at Chelyan, W. Va., near Charleston, during a 72-day strike by the United Mine Workers of America that ended on June 6.

demonstration of coal's potential for easing U.S. dependence on petroleum. The experimental vehicle is powered by a turbine engine that burns coal ground to a dustlike powder. The coal is fed to the engine in a stream of compressed air. GM said cars powered by coal dust probably will not go into mass production until the 21st century.

Domestic Coal Reserves totaled 475 billion short tons (431 billion metric tons) in 1981, according to estimates released by the U.S. Department of Energy (DOE) on May 13. The May estimate was 8 per cent higher than the last official estimate of 438 billion short tons (397 billion metric tons), issued in 1976. The DOE said that about 318 billion short tons (288 billion metric tons) could be mined with traditional underground methods, and about 156 billion short tons (141 billion metric tons) could be mined from the surface.

British Coal Miners returned to work on February 19 after Prime Minister Margaret Thatcher abandoned plans to close down antiquated coal mines. Union leaders estimated that about 25 per cent of Great Britain's 230,000 coal miners had joined a strike that began on February 17. The strikers feared the mine closings, part of the government's modernization program for the industry, would put thousands out of work.   Michael Woods

See also ENERGY; MINING. In WORLD BOOK, see COAL.

COIN COLLECTING. Rare coins continued to fetch high prices in 1981 despite lower market prices for precious metals. Yale University in New Haven, Conn., sold the centerpiece of its $3-million coin collection, a Brasher's doubloon, to an anonymous collector for $650,000 on January 11. The coin is one of seven surviving specimens struck by the New York goldsmith Ephraim Brasher in 1787.

Another Brasher's doubloon sold for $625,000 on March 28 in the final round of coin sales from the Garrett collection owned by Johns Hopkins University in Baltimore. That auction also brought $200,000 for an early American penny — the highest price ever paid for a copper coin. The Garrett collection was sold in four rounds for a total of $25.2 million — the highest sum ever paid at auction for a single rare-coin collection.

Setbacks for Collectors. Some measures enacted by the United States government in 1981 had implications that many coin dealers viewed as unfavorable. A rider attached to President Ronald Reagan's tax-cut bill eliminated coin purchases as acceptable investments under Keogh and Individual Retirement Account plans. Although coin companies united to fight the provision, it remained in the version of the bill that passed both houses of Congress and that Reagan signed on August 13.

The U.S. Tax Court in Washington, D.C., ruled in January that gold coins must be considered property rather than currency and that their worth must be determined by market value instead of face value. This ruling subjected coin collectors to higher personal property taxes.

The price of silver dropped from as much as $48 per troy ounce (31.1 grams) in 1980 to $8 to $10 in 1981. As a result, many coin collectors and dealers who had invested in silver coins primarily because of the metal's value suffered great losses.

New Coins. Congressmen Doug Barnard (D., Ga.) and Frank Annunzio (D., Ill.) sponsored a bill to issue a new silver half dollar in 1982 to commemorate the 250th anniversary of George Washington's birth. President Reagan signed the bill into law on December 23.

On May 20, Senator Alan Cranston (D., Calif.) introduced a coinage bill designed to provide funds for the 1984 Summer Olympic Games to be held in Los Angeles. The bill specifies a $100 gold piece and 28 other coins to be sold at premium prices.

On July 15, the Department of the Treasury began selling two gold medallions honoring American authors: a Mark Twain medallion weighing 1 troy ounce (31.1 grams) and a Willa Cather medallion weighing 0.5 troy ounce (15.55 grams). The second set in a series of 10 medallions to be issued over a five-year period, the coins were priced at $14 and $7 above prevailing gold prices.   Lee Martin

In WORLD BOOK, see COIN COLLECTING.

COLOMBIA. Rebel groups continued their guerrilla activities in Colombia during 1981, rejecting a government offer of amnesty to those who laid down their arms. On March 7, the dominant terrorist group, the Movement of April 19, also known as M-19, killed an American linguist and lay missionary, Chester A. Bitterman III. Bitterman worked for the Summer Institute of Linguistics, a field agency of Wycliffe Bible Translators of Huntington Beach, Calif. The terrorists had kidnapped Bitterman on January 19, claiming that he was a spy for the United States Central Intelligence Agency (CIA) and that the institute was a front for the CIA.

On March 23, Colombia suspended its diplomatic relations with Cuba. President Julio Cesar Turbay Ayala charged that at least 60 per cent of the guerrillas captured in Colombia were trained in Cuba. Colombia's military leaders have appealed for increased supplies of arms from the United States to combat guerrilla activities. On July 22, the government's four-month offer of unrestricted amnesty for guerrillas who laid down their arms expired, and no truce was in sight.

Colombian authorities were also hard-pressed to cope with illicit trafficking in drugs. Estimates indicated that in 1981, illegal drugs were Colombia's most valuable export, earning one peso for every peso earned in a legitimate business activity.

Development Projects. On June 1, the Colombian government announced that a $1.3-billion hydroelectric power plant will be built at Guavio, 35 miles (56 kilometers) east of Bogotá. The project, scheduled for completion in 1988, will be financed by the World Bank, the Inter-American Bank, and commercial banks. The new plant will provide about 15 per cent of Colombia's electric power.

Colombia has also undertaken, with the World Bank's assistance, a program aimed at developing the heavily populated area around the headwaters of the Magdalena River. The poverty-stricken areas of Huila and Tolima are also slated for the development of coffee, vegetable, fruit, rice, cotton, and cacao production.

1982 Elections. Politicking for the 1982 elections began in 1981 with indications that Colombia could see a realignment of political forces. A broad field of candidates jockeyed for position in both the Liberal and Conservative parties, which have dominated politics for 30 years. The leader of the M-19 guerrillas, Jaime Bateman Cayon, proposed talks between the rebels and the government, vowing to sabotage the spring elections if the government refuses to talk.   Nathan A. Haverstock

See also LATIN AMERICA (Facts in Brief Table). In WORLD BOOK, see COLOMBIA.

COLORADO. See STATE GOVERNMENT.

COMMON MARKET. See EUROPE.

COMMUNICATIONS in the United States was dominated in 1981 by technological growth and continuing uncertainty about the direction of national policy. Throughout the year, federal officials and business firms struggled to come to grips with the implications of the information age.

However, Congress, with the help of the Administration of President Ronald Reagan, took a dramatic step toward resolving years of regulatory and judicial conflict. On October 7, the Senate approved the Telecommunications Competition and Deregulation Act of 1981 by a 90 to 4 vote. The vote marked the first time either house of Congress acted on a major rewrite of communications regulations since the Federal Communications Act became law in 1934. The new bill is designed to end federal regulation of many areas of the telecommunications business, though regulation of local and long-distance telephone service would remain.

The most controversial section of the bill would permit the American Telephone and Telegraph Company (A.T. & T.), the largest corporation in the world and the dominant firm in the communications industry, to sell such unregulated products as data-processing equipment for the first time. However, a plan designed to bar the company from using money from telephone subscribers to finance the new ventures provides that A.T. & T. could sell those products only through a subsidiary.

A.T. & T. and the Department of Justice continued in 1981 to confront each other in Washington, D.C., courts on another issue. The Justice Department charged the communications giant with massive antitrust violations and sought to break up the firm. The government closed its case in September, after U.S. District Court Judge Harold L. Greene denied an A.T. & T. motion to dismiss it. Greene said he expected to issue his final decision in July 1982, though the Reagan Administration pledged to dismiss the suit if legislation is passed that clearly sets up a competitive industry.

Cable Television grew rapidly in 1981, and its cross-country spread was the most significant development in the communications industry. Almost 30 per cent of all U.S. households had access to cable systems by late 1981, and the figure was expected to exceed 90 per cent by 1990. Many major cities awarded cable franchises during the year, and others began the complex process.

As cable television spread, small systems and larger networks were bought by even larger companies. For example, Time Incorporated purchased an interest in USA Network, a sports cable network. The Westinghouse Electric Corporation completed its purchase of Teleprompter Corporation on August 18 for $646 million. It was the largest merger in history of U.S. communications

Microprocessor-equipped pay phones that compute the cost of a call and make change are being installed throughout Great Britain.

companies. As the cable business gained momentum, the antagonism the three major TV networks had long displayed toward it eroded. Each network made moves to enter the business. For example, CBS Inc. offered cultural programming for cable, and American Broadcasting Companies, Incorporated (ABC), produced similar material.

Communications Satellites retained and increased their vital role in 1981. In addition to cable-television firms using them to connect local systems, other companies began to use satellites to beam their signals directly to households and businesses. Communications Satellite Corporation (COMSAT), Aetna Life and Casualty Company, and International Business Machines Corporation (IBM) began providing high-speed voice, data, and video services through a $1-billion partnership called Satellite Business Systems.

The Federal Communications Commission (FCC) on April 21 gave interim approval to COMSAT for development of a direct-broadcasting satellite (DBS) service. The service would bring television programming directly from satellites to subscribers' rooftop receiving antennas. The Reagan Administration urged quick approval of the plan, but final authorization awaited decisions on technical questions.   Merrill Brown

In WORLD BOOK, see COMMUNICATION; COMMUNICATIONS SATELLITE.

COMMUNITY ORGANIZATIONS. The American Red Cross marked 100 years of service on May 21, 1981. The centennial slogan was "Red Cross: Ready for a New Century!" To celebrate its first 100 years, the organization issued a pictorial history book and a long-playing record narrated by entertainer Arthur Godfrey. Exhibits commemorating the centennial appeared at Red Cross national headquarters, the Smithsonian Institution, and the Corcoran Gallery of Art, all in Washington, D.C.

The Salvation Army. Meeting in London in October, the Salvation Army's High Council elected Jarl Wahlstrom of Finland as the army's general, or international commander. He succeeded Arnold Brown of Canada, who retired in December.

The army announced that its headquarters in the United States would move from New York City to Verona, N.J., by the end of 1981. The move was intended to unite the central administration with other U.S. functions at separate locations.

YMCA of the USA, the national organization of Young Men's Christian Associations in the United States, moved its headquarters from New York City to Chicago in May. The YMCA served more than 11 million members and participants in 1981, of whom approximately 43 per cent were women. Programs continued to emphasize health enhancement, family life, and international understanding.

The Young Women's Christian Association of the USA (YWCA) had a membership of about 2.5 million people in 1981. YWCA programs, attuned to the changing roles of women and girls, emphasized affirmative action workshops and preparing women for jobs traditionally held by men.

Service Organizations. Kiwanis International reported its 1981 membership at more than 300,000 in 8,000 clubs in 75 nations. E. B. McKitrick, an accountant from Edmonton, Canada, was elected president in October. He announced a program called "Share Good Health," dedicated to enhancing basic health services.

Lions Clubs International elected Kaoru (Kay) Murakami of Japan as president in June. Murakami, the first president from Asia, chose as his theme "People at Peace," connoting both peace of mind and friendly relations among nations. Membership stood at more than 1.3 million in 35,000 clubs.

Rotary International had about 19,500 clubs with 900,000 members in 156 countries in 1981. The Rotary Foundation sponsored immunization projects in India and the Philippines and a polio rehabilitation program in Malawi. The foundation also granted more than 1,200 international scholarships at a cost of $14.5 million.

Veterans' Organizations. Robert P. Nimmo, a World War II pilot and retired colonel in the National Guard, was sworn in as the new Veterans Administration (VA) chief. At his swearing-in, Nimmo disputed charges that veterans of the Vietnam War have been treated with less sensitivity than other veterans.

Nonetheless, treatment of Vietnam veterans remained a sensitive issue. Proposals by the Administration of President Ronald Reagan to eliminate Operation Outreach, a counseling program for Vietnam veterans, aroused a storm of protest from the American Legion, the Veterans of Foreign Wars of the United States, Vietnam Veterans of America, AMVETS, and Disabled American Veterans. The counseling program operates 91 storefront centers and has served 55,000 veterans since it started in October 1979. On July 22, VA Administrator Nimmo announced a three-year extension of the program with an increase of $8.6 million for the 1982 fiscal year.

Controversy continued about Agent Orange, an herbicide containing a poison called dioxin, which was used to defoliate forests during the Vietnam War. On June 16, Congress approved legislation to provide federally financed treatment for veterans exposed to Agent Orange.   Virginia E. Anderson

In WORLD BOOK, see the articles on various community organizations.

COMOROS. See AFRICA.

CONGO (BRAZZAVILLE). See AFRICA.

CONGO (KINSHASA). See AFRICA.

CONGRESS OF THE UNITED STATES. The first session of the 97th Congress convened on Jan. 5, 1981. For the first time since 1932, different political parties controlled the two houses. While Democrats held a 243 to 192 majority in the House of Representatives, Republicans dominated the Senate 53 to 46, with 1 independent. However, conservative Democrats — so-called boll weevils — voted consistently with Republicans in the House, and Congress cooperated with President Ronald Reagan in reducing the size and cost of the federal government. Bill by bill, the Administration persuaded Congress to whittle away 50 years of federal regulations, agencies, and programs.

Congressional Leaders. Vice-President George H. W. Bush served in his constitutional role as president of the Senate. Howard H. Baker, Jr., of Tennessee was majority leader; Theodore F. Stevens of Alaska, majority whip; and Strom Thurmond of South Carolina, president pro tem. West Virginia's Robert C. Byrd was minority leader; and California's Alan M. Cranston, minority whip.

Thomas P. (Tip) O'Neill, Jr., a Massachusetts Democrat, was speaker of the House; James C. Wright, Jr., of Texas was majority leader; and Thomas S. Foley of Washington was majority whip. Robert H. Michel of Illinois was minority leader; and Trent Lott of Mississippi, minority whip.

The Budget. On January 15, President Jimmy Carter sent Congress his $739.3-billion budget for fiscal year 1982, which began on Oct. 1, 1981. The Carter budget included an estimated deficit of $27.5 billion.

On February 18, speaking to a joint session of Congress, President Reagan invoked his "mandate for change" and urged legislators to approve a new economic program cutting proposed federal spending and reducing federal taxes. To reduce projected federal spending in fiscal 1982, Reagan suggested cuts of $41.4 billion in 83 major programs. On March 10, he proposed a budget for fiscal 1982 of $695.3 billion, with a deficit of $45 billion. At the same time, he urged a personal income tax cut of 10 per cent per year for three years.

In the months that followed, Congress clashed repeatedly with the President on the size and distribution of the budget cut. But on May 20, the Democrat-controlled House voted 244 to 155 — with key Democrats deserting their party leadership — to approve the revised fiscal 1982 budget target of $695.4 billion, and the following day the Senate voted 76 to 20 to approve it. The target budget specified that $36 billion be cut from health, social, and education programs. It also provided for additional defense spending of $25-billion in the military budget of $188.8 billion. Congress was to decide specifically what to cut.

An angry debate over where to make cutbacks followed. On June 16, the President called on Congress to pass his budget before the August recess. He accused House Speaker O'Neill of "sheer demagoguery," charging that Democrats in the House were making an "unconscionable" effort to defeat his budget. Chairman of the House Rules Committee Richard Bolling (D., Mo.) responded, scoring the President for trying to impose "totalitarian" rule over Congress. On June 24, the President revealed that he had telegraphed all the Republicans and Democrats who had supported his budget proposal in May, urging them to vote on the budget as a single package and avoid piecemeal amendments. In a procedural vote on June 25, the House voted 217 to 210 to consider the budget as a single package. On June 26, it voted 217 to 211 to approve the Omnibus Budget Reconciliation Act of 1981 — a single bill that contained $38.2 billion in budget cuts for fiscal 1982. The Senate approved a slightly different version on June 25. After the two versions were reconciled by a conference committee, the final budget act was approved on July 31 by a voice vote in the House and a vote of 80 to 14 in the Senate. In its final form, the bill called for budget cuts of $35.2 billion for fiscal 1982.

Unfortunately, the cuts won in July were not sufficient to meet the overall target for fiscal 1982 and to achieve a balanced budget by fiscal 1984. In a televised address on September 24, the President urged public support for further cuts of $13 billion for fiscal 1982 and called for legislation to close tax loopholes to produce $3 billion more in revenue. He presented a revised estimate of the 1982 fiscal deficit — $43.1 billion. The budget of the Department of Defense was to be cut $2 billion.

The appropriations bills to implement the President's budget encountered heavy opposition as Congress balked at making cuts in federal allocations. Thus, the 97th Congress turned to stopgap funding to run the federal government while the debate over cuts continued. The first stopgap bill ran from October 1 to November 20. After federal funding ran out at midnight on November 20, President Reagan vetoed a $428-billion stopgap spending bill on November 23 because it did not include an additional 4 per cent spending cut. That same day, Congress passed a three-week extension of government spending at the current level. On December 15, the President signed a $413-billion measure to keep the government running through March 31, 1982.

Tax Cuts. Before adjourning for a five-week summer recess, the House on July 29 voted 238 to 195 to approve the new tax law, which included a 25 per cent across-the-board cut in personal income taxes. That same day, the Senate approved a slightly different version of the bill. On August 3, the Senate approved the compromise version of the bill, 67 to 8. The next day, the House completed

Members of the United States Senate

The Senate of the second session of the 97th Congress consisted of 53 Republicans, 46 Democrats, and 1 independent when it convened in January 1982. Senators shown starting their term in 1981 were elected for the first time in the Nov. 4, 1980, elections. Others shown ending their current terms in 1987 were re-elected to the Senate in the same balloting. The second date in each listing shows when the term of a previously elected senator expires. For organizational purposes, the one Independent will line up with Democrats.

State	Term	State	Term	State	Term
Alabama		**Louisiana**		**Ohio**	
Howell T. Heflin, D.	1979—1985	Russell B. Long, D.	1948—1987	John H. Glenn, D.	1975—1987
Jeremiah Denton, R.	1981—1987	J. Bennett Johnston, Jr., D.	1972—1985	Howard M. Metzenbaum, D.	1977—1983
Alaska		**Maine**		**Oklahoma**	
Theodore F. Stevens, R.	1968—1985	William S. Cohen, R.	1979—1985	David L. Boren, D.	1979—1985
Frank H. Murkowski, R.	1981—1987	George J. Mitchell, D.	1980—1983	Donald L. Nickles, R.	1981—1987
Arizona		**Maryland**		**Oregon**	
Barry Goldwater, R.	1969—1987	Charles McC. Mathias, Jr., R.	1969—1987	Mark O. Hatfield, R.	1967—1985
Dennis DeConcini, D.	1977—1983	Paul S. Sarbanes, D.	1977—1983	Robert W. Packwood, R.	1969—1987
Arkansas		**Massachusetts**		**Pennsylvania**	
Dale Bumpers, D.	1975—1987	Edward M. Kennedy, D.	1962—1983	H. John Heinz III, R.	1977—1983
David H. Pryor, D.	1979—1985	Paul E. Tsongas, D.	1979—1985	Arlen Specter, R.	1981—1987
California		**Michigan**		**Rhode Island**	
Alan Cranston, D.	1969—1987	Donald W. Riegle, Jr., D.	1977—1983	Claiborne Pell, D.	1961—1985
S. I. Hayakawa, R.	1977—1983	Carl M. Levin, D.	1979—1985	John H. Chafee, R.	1977—1983
Colorado		**Minnesota**		**South Carolina**	
Gary Hart, D.	1975—1987	David F. Durenberger, R.	1978—1983	Strom Thurmond, R.	1956—1985
William L. Armstrong, R.	1979—1985	Rudolph E. Boschwitz, R.	1979—1985	Ernest F. Hollings, D.	1966—1987
Connecticut		**Mississippi**		**South Dakota**	
Lowell P. Weicker, Jr., R.	1971—1983	John C. Stennis, D.	1947—1983	Larry Pressler, R.	1979—1985
Christopher J. Dodd, D.	1981—1987	Thad Cochran, R.	1979—1985	James Abdnor, R.	1981—1987
Delaware		**Missouri**		**Tennessee**	
William V. Roth, Jr., R.	1971—1983	Thomas F. Eagleton, D.	1968—1987	Howard H. Baker, Jr., R.	1967—1985
Joseph R. Biden, Jr., D.	1973—1985	John C. Danforth, R.	1977—1983	James R. Sasser, D.	1977—1983
Florida		**Montana**		**Texas**	
Lawton Chiles, D.	1971—1983	John Melcher, D.	1977—1983	John G. Tower, R.	1961—1985
Paula Hawkins, R.	1981—1987	Max Baucus, D.	1979—1985	Lloyd M. Bentsen, D.	1971—1983
Georgia		**Nebraska**		**Utah**	
Sam Nunn, D.	1972—1985	Edward Zorinsky, D.	1977—1983	Edwin Jacob Garn, R.	1975—1987
Mack Mattingly, R.	1981—1987	J. James Exon, D.	1979—1985	Orrin G. Hatch, R.	1977—1983
Hawaii		**Nevada**		**Vermont**	
Daniel K. Inouye, D.	1963—1987	Howard W. Cannon, D.	1959—1983	Robert T. Stafford, R.	1971—1983
Spark M. Matsunaga, D.	1977—1983	Paul Laxalt, R.	1975—1987	Patrick J. Leahy, D.	1975—1987
Idaho		**New Hampshire**		**Virginia**	
James A. McClure, R.	1973—1985	Gordon J. Humphrey, R.	1979—1985	Harry F. Byrd, Jr., Ind.	1965—1983
Steven D. Symms, R.	1981—1987	Warren B. Rudman, R.	1981—1987	John W. Warner, R.	1979—1985
Illinois		**New Jersey**		**Washington**	
Charles H. Percy, R.	1967—1985	Harrison A. Williams, Jr., D.	1959—1983	Henry M. Jackson, D.	1953—1983
Alan J. Dixon, D.	1981—1987	Bill Bradley, D.	1979—1985	Slade Gorton, R.	1981—1987
Indiana		**New Mexico**		**West Virginia**	
Richard G. Lugar, R.	1977—1983	Pete V. Domenici, R.	1973—1985	Jennings Randolph, D.	1958—1985
J. Danforth Quayle, R.	1981—1987	Harrison H. Schmitt, R.	1977—1983	Robert C. Byrd, D.	1959—1983
Iowa		**New York**		**Wisconsin**	
Roger W. Jepsen, R.	1979—1985	Daniel P. Moynihan, D.	1977—1983	William Proxmire, D.	1957—1983
Charles E. Grassley, R.	1981—1987	Alfonse M. D'Amato, R.	1981—1987	Robert W. Kasten, Jr., R.	1981—1987
Kansas		**North Carolina**		**Wyoming**	
Robert J. Dole, R.	1969—1987	Jesse A. Helms, R.	1973—1985	Malcolm Wallop, R.	1977—1983
Nancy Landon Kassebaum, R.	1979—1985	John P. East, R.	1981—1987	Alan K. Simpson, R.	1979—1985
Kentucky		**North Dakota**			
Walter Huddleston, D.	1973—1985	Quentin N. Burdick, D.	1960—1983		
Wendell H. Ford, D.	1975—1987	Mark Andrews, R.	1981—1987		

Members of the United States House of Representatives

The House of Representatives of the second session of the 97th Congress consisted of 243 Democrats and 192 Republicans (not including representatives from American Samoa, the District of Columbia, Guam, Puerto Rico, and the Virgin Islands) when it convened in January 1982, compared with 242 Democrats, 192 Republicans, and 1 independent when the first session convened. This table shows congressional district, legislator, and party affiliation. Asterisk (*) denotes those who served in the 96th Congress; dagger (†) denotes "at large."

Alabama
1. Jack Edwards, R.*
2. William L. Dickinson, R.*
3. William Nichols, D.*
4. Tom Bevill, D.*
5. Ronnie G. Flippo, D.*
6. Albert Smith, R.
7. Richard C. Shelby, D.*

Alaska
† Don Young, R.*

Arizona
1. John J. Rhodes, R.*
2. Morris K. Udall, D.*
3. Bob Stump, D.*
4. Eldon Rudd, R.*

Arkansas
1. Bill Alexander, D.*
2. Ed Bethune, R.*
3. John Paul Hammerschmidt, R.*
4. Beryl F. Anthony, Jr., D.*

California
1. Eugene A. Chappie, R.
2. Don H. Clausen, R.*
3. Robert T. Matsui, D.*
4. Vic Fazio, D.*
5. John L. Burton, D.*
6. Phillip Burton, D.*
7. George Miller, D.*
8. Ronald V. Dellums, D.*
9. Fortney H. Stark, D.*
10. Don Edwards, D.*
11. Tom Lantos, D.
12. Paul N. McCloskey, Jr., R.*
13. Norman Y. Mineta, D.*
14. Norman D. Shumway, R.*
15. Tony Coelho, D.*
16. Leon E. Panetta, D.*
17. Charles Pashayan, Jr., R.*
18. William M. Thomas, R.*
19. Robert J. Lagomarsino, R.*
20. Barry M. Goldwater, Jr., R.*
21. Bobbi Fiedler, R.
22. Carlos J. Moorhead, R.*
23. Anthony C. Beilenson, R.*
24. Henry A. Waxman, D.*
25. Edward R. Roybal, D.*
26. John H. Rousselot, R.*
27. Robert K. Dornan, R.*
28. Julian C. Dixon, D.*
29. Augustus F. Hawkins, D.*
30. George E. Danielson, D.*
31. Mervyn M. Dymally, D.
32. Glenn M. Anderson, D.*
33. Wayne R. Grisham, R.*
34. Dan Lungren, R.*
35. David Dreier, R.
36. George E. Brown, Jr., D.*
37. Jerry Lewis, R.*
38. Jerry M. Patterson, D.*
39. William E. Dannemeyer, R.*
40. Robert E. Badham, R.*
41. Bill Lowery, R.
42. Duncan L. Hunter, R.
43. Clair W. Burgener, R.*

Colorado
1. Patricia Schroeder, D.*
2. Timothy E. Wirth, D.*
3. Ray Kogovsek, D.*
4. Hank Brown, R.
5. Ken Kramer, R.*

Connecticut
1. Barbara B. Kennelly, D.
2. Samuel Gejdenson, D.
3. Lawrence J. DeNardis, R.
4. Stewart B. McKinney, R.*
5. William R. Ratchford, D.*
6. Toby Moffett, D.*

Delaware
† Thomas B. Evans, Jr., R.*

Florida
1. Earl D. Hutto, D.*
2. Don Fuqua, D.*
3. Charles E. Bennett, D.*
4. William V. Chappell, Jr., D.*
5. Bill McCollum, R.
6. C. W. Young, R.*
7. Sam M. Gibbons, D.*
8. Andy Ireland, D.*
9. Bill Nelson, D.*
10. L. A. Bafalis, R.*
11. Dan Mica, D.*
12. Clay Shaw, R.
13. William Lehman, D.*
14. Claude D. Pepper, D.*
15. Dante B. Fascell, D.*

Georgia
1. Ronald Ginn, D.*
2. Charles F. Hatcher, D.
3. Jack T. Brinkley, D.*
4. Elliott H. Levitas, D.*
5. Wyche Fowler, Jr., D.*
6. Newt Gingrich, R.*
7. Lawrence P. McDonald, D.*
8. Billy Lee Evans, D.*
9. Ed Jenkins, D.*
10. Doug Barnard, D.*

Hawaii
1. Cecil Heftel, D.*
2. Daniel K. Akaka, D.*

Idaho
1. Larry Craig, R.
2. George Hansen, R.*

Illinois
1. Harold Washington, D.
2. Gus Savage, D.
3. Martin A. Russo, D.*
4. Edward J. Derwinski, R.*
5. John G. Fary, D.*
6. Henry J. Hyde, R.*
7. Cardiss Collins, D.*
8. Dan Rostenkowski, D.*
9. Sidney R. Yates, D.*
10. John Edward Porter, R.*
11. Frank Annunzio, D.*
12. Philip M. Crane, R.*
13. Robert McClory, R.*
14. John N. Erlenborn, R.*
15. Tom Corcoran, R.*
16. Lynn Martin, R.
17. George M. O'Brien, R.*
18. Robert H. Michel, R.*
19. Thomas F. Railsback, R.*
20. Paul Findley, R.*
21. Edward R. Madigan, R.*
22. Daniel B. Crane, R.*
23. Charles Melvin Price, D.*
24. Paul Simon, D.*

Indiana
1. Adam Benjamin, Jr., D.*
2. Floyd J. Fithian, D.*
3. John P. Hiler, R.
4. Daniel R. Coats, R.
5. Elwood H. Hillis, R.*
6. David W. Evans, D.*
7. John T. Myers, R.*
8. H. Joel Deckard, R.*
9. Lee H. Hamilton, D.*
10. Philip R. Sharp, D.*
11. Andrew Jacobs, Jr., D.*

Iowa
1. James Leach, R.*
2. Thomas J. Tauke, R.*
3. Cooper Evans, R.
4. Neal Smith, D.*
5. Tom Harkin, D.*
6. Berkley Bedell, D.*

Kansas
1. Pat Roberts, R.
2. James E. Jeffries, R.*
3. Larry Winn, Jr., R.*
4. Dan Glickman, D.*
5. Robert Whittaker, R.*

Kentucky
1. Carroll Hubbard, Jr., D.*
2. William H. Natcher, D.*
3. Romano L. Mazzoli, D.*
4. Marion Gene Snyder, R.*
5. Harold Rogers, R.
6. Larry J. Hopkins, R.*
7. Carl D. Perkins, D.*

Louisiana
1. Robert L. Livingston, R.*
2. Lindy Boggs, D.*
3. Billy Tauzin, D.*
4. Charles Roemer, D.
5. Jerry Huckaby, D.*
6. W. Henson Moore, R.*
7. John B. Breaux, D.*
8. Gillis W. Long, D.*

Maine
1. David F. Emery, R.*
2. Olympia J. Snowe, R.*

Maryland
1. Roy Dyson, D.
2. Clarence D. Long, D.*
3. Barbara A. Mikulski, D.*
4. Marjorie S. Holt, R.*
5. Steny H. Hoyer, D.
6. Beverly Butcher Byron, D.*
7. Parren J. Mitchell, D.*
8. Michael D. Barnes, D.*

Massachusetts
1. Silvio O. Conte, R.*
2. Edward P. Boland, D.*
3. Joseph D. Early, D.*
4. Barney Frank, D.
5. James M. Shannon, D.*
6. Nicholas Mavroules, D.*
7. Edward J. Markey, D.*
8. Thomas P. O'Neill, Jr., D.*
9. John J. Moakley, D.*
10. Margaret M. Heckler, R.*
11. Brian J. Donnelly, D.*
12. Gerry E. Studds, D.*

Michigan
1. John Conyers, Jr., D.*
2. Carl D. Pursell, R.*
3. Howard E. Wolpe, D.*
4. Mark D. Siljander, R.
5. Harold S. Sawyer, R.*
6. Jim Dunn, R.
7. Dale E. Kildee, D.*
8. Bob Traxler, D.*
9. Guy Vander Jagt, R.*
10. Donald J. Albosta, D.*
11. Robert W. Davis, R.*
12. David E. Bonior, D.*
13. George W. Crockett, Jr., D.
14. Dennis M. Hertel, D.
15. William D. Ford, D.*
16. John D. Dingell, D.*
17. William M. Brodhead, D.*
18. James J. Blanchard, D.*
19. William S. Broomfield, R.*

Minnesota
1. Arlen Erdahl, R.*
2. Thomas M. Hagedorn, R.*
3. Bill Frenzel, R.*
4. Bruce F. Vento, D.*
5. Martin O. Sabo, D.*
6. Vin Weber, R.
7. Arlan Stangeland, R.*
8. James L. Oberstar, D.*

Mississippi
1. Jamie L. Whitten, D.*
2. David R. Bowen, D.*
3. G. V. Montgomery, D.*
4. Wayne Dowdy, D.
5. Trent Lott, R.*

Missouri
1. William L. Clay, D.*
2. Robert A. Young, D.*
3. Richard A. Gephardt, D.*
4. Ike Skelton, D.*
5. Richard Bolling, D.*
6. E. Thomas Coleman, R.*
7. Gene Taylor, R.*
8. Wendell Bailey, R.
9. Harold L. Volkmer, D.*
10. Bill Emerson, R.

Montana
1. Pat Williams, D.*
2. Ron Marlenee, R.*

Nebraska
1. Douglas K. Bereuter, R.*
2. Hal Daub, R.
3. Virginia Smith, R.*

Nevada
† James Santini, D.*

New Hampshire
1. Norman E. D'Amours, D.*
2. Judd Gregg, R.

New Jersey
1. James J. Florio, D.*
2. William J. Hughes, D.*
3. James J. Howard, D.*
4. Christopher H. Smith, R.
5. Millicent Fenwick, R.*
6. Edwin B. Forsythe, R.*
7. Marge S. Roukema, R.
8. Robert A. Roe, D.*
9. Harold C. Hollenbeck, R.*
10. Peter W. Rodino, Jr., D.*
11. Joseph G. Minish, D.*
12. Matthew J. Rinaldo, R.*
13. James A. Courter, R.*
14. Frank J. Guarini, D.*
15. Bernard J. Dwyer, D.

New Mexico
1. Manuel Lujan, Jr., R.*
2. Joe Skeen, R.

New York
1. William Carney, R.*
2. Thomas J. Downey, D.*
3. Gregory W. Carman, R.
4. Norman F. Lent, R.*
5. Raymond McGrath, R.
6. John LeBoutillier, R.
7. Joseph P. Addabbo, D.*
8. Benjamin S. Rosenthal, D.*
9. Geraldine A. Ferraro, D.*
10. Mario Biaggi, D.*
11. James H. Scheuer, D.*
12. Shirley Chisholm, D.*
13. Stephen J. Solarz, D.*
14. Frederick W. Richmond, D.*
15. Leo C. Zeferetti, D.*
16. Charles Schumer, D.
17. Guy Molinari, R.
18. S. William Green, R.*
19. Charles B. Rangel, D.*
20. Ted Weiss, D.*
21. Robert Garcia, D.*
22. Jonathan B. Bingham, D.*

23. Peter A. Peyser, D.*
24. Richard L. Ottinger, D.*
25. Hamilton Fish, Jr., R.*
26. Benjamin A. Gilman, R.*
27. Matthew F. McHugh, D.*
28. Samuel S. Stratton, D.*
29. Gerald B. Solomon, R.*
30. David Martin, R.
31. Donald J. Mitchell, R.*
32. George Wortley, R.
33. Gary A. Lee, R.*
34. Frank Horton, R.*
35. Barber B. Conable, Jr., R.*
36. John J. LaFalce, D.*
37. Henry J. Nowak, D.*
38. Jack F. Kemp, R.*
39. Stanley N. Lundine, D.*

North Carolina
1. Walter B. Jones, D.*
2. L. H. Fountain, D.*
3. Charles Whitley, D.*
4. Ike F. Andrews, D.*
5. Stephen L. Neal, D.*
6. Eugene Johnston, R.
7. Charles Rose, D.*
8. W. G. Hefner, D.*
9. James G. Martin, R.*
10. James T. Broyhill, R.*
11. William M. Hendon, R.

North Dakota
† Byron L. Dorgan, D.

Ohio
1. Willis D. Gradison, Jr., R.*
2. Thomas A. Luken, D.*
3. Tony P. Hall, D.*
4. Michael G. Oxley, R.
5. Delbert L. Latta, R.*
6. Bob McEwen, R.
7. Clarence J. Brown, R.*
8. Thomas N. Kindness, R.*
9. Ed Weber, R.
10. Clarence E. Miller, R.*
11. J. William Stanton, R.*
12. Bob Shamansky, D.
13. Donald J. Pease, D.*
14. John F. Seiberling, D.*
15. Chalmers P. Wylie, R.*
16. Ralph S. Regula, R.*
17. John M. Ashbrook, R.*
18. Douglas Applegate, D.*
19. Lyle Williams, R.*
20. Mary Rose Oakar, D.*
21. Louis Stokes, D.*
22. Dennis E. Eckart, D.
23. Ronald M. Mottl, D.*

Oklahoma
1. James R. Jones, D.*
2. Michael L. Synar, D.*
3. Wes Watkins, D.*
4. Dave McCurdy, D.
5. Mickey Edwards, R.*
6. Glenn English, D.*

Oregon
1. Les AuCoin, D.*
2. Denny Smith, R.
3. Ron Wyden, D.
4. James Weaver, D.*

Pennsylvania
1. Thomas M. Foglietta, D.
2. William H. Gray III, D.*
3. Joseph F. Smith, D.
4. Charles F. Dougherty, R.*
5. Richard T. Schulze, R.*
6. Gus Yatron, D.*
7. Robert W. Edgar, D.*
8. James K. Coyne, R.
9. Bud Shuster, R.*
10. Joseph M. McDade, R.*
11. James Nelligan, R.
12. John P. Murtha, D.*
13. Lawrence Coughlin, R.*
14. William J. Coyne, D.
15. Donald L. Ritter, R.*
16. Robert S. Walker, R.*
17. Allen E. Ertel, D.*
18. Doug Walgren, D.*
19. William F. Goodling, R.*
20. Joseph M. Gaydos, D.*
21. Don Bailey, D.*
22. Austin J. Murphy, D.*
23. William F. Clinger, Jr., R.*
24. Marc L. Marks, R.*
25. Eugene V. Atkinson, R.*

Rhode Island
1. Fernand J. St. Germain, D.*
2. Claudine Schneider, R.

South Carolina
1. Thomas F. Hartnett, R.
2. Floyd D. Spence, R.*
3. Butler C. Derrick, Jr., D.*
4. Carroll A. Campbell, Jr., R.*
5. Ken Holland, D.*
6. John L. Napier, R.

South Dakota
1. Thomas A. Daschle, D.*
2. Clint Roberts, R.

Tennessee
1. James H. Quillen, R.*
2. John J. Duncan, R.*
3. Marilyn Lloyd Bouquard, D.*
4. Albert Gore, Jr., D.*
5. William H. Boner, D.*
6. Robin L. Beard, Jr., R.*
7. Ed Jones, D.*
8. Harold E. Ford, D.*

Texas
1. Sam B. Hall, Jr., D.*
2. Charles Wilson, D.*
3. James M. Collins, D.*
4. Ralph M. Hall, D.
5. James Mattox, D.*
6. Phil Gramm, D.*
7. Bill Archer, R.*
8. Jack Fields, R.
9. Jack Brooks, D.*
10. J. J. Pickle, D.*
11. Marvin Leath, D.*
12. James C. Wright, Jr., D.*
13. Jack Hightower, D.*
14. William Patman, D.
15. Eligio de la Garza, D.*
16. Richard C. White, D.*
17. Charles W. Stenholm, D.*
18. Mickey Leland, D.*
19. Kent Hance, D.*

20. Henry B. Gonzalez, D.*
21. Thomas G. Loeffler, R.*
22. Ronald E. Paul, R.*
23. Abraham Kazen, Jr., D.*
24. Martin Frost, D.*

Utah
1. James V. Hansen, R.
2. Dan Marriott, R.*

Vermont
† James M. Jeffords, R.*

Virginia
1. Paul S. Trible, Jr., R.*
2. G. William Whitehurst, R.*
3. Thomas J. Bliley, Jr., R.
4. Robert W. Daniel, Jr., R.*
5. Dan Daniel, D.*
6. M. Caldwell Butler, R.*
7. J. Kenneth Robinson, R.*
8. Stanford E. Parris, R.
9. William C. Wampler, R.*
10. Frank R. Wolf, R.

Washington
1. Joel Pritchard, R.*
2. Al Swift, D.*
3. Don Bonker, D.*
4. Sid Morrison, R.
5. Thomas S. Foley, D.*
6. Norman D. Dicks, D.*
7. Mike Lowry, D.*

West Virginia
1. Robert H. Mollohan, D.*
2. Cleve Benedict, R.
3. Mick Staton, R.
4. Nick J. Rahall, D.*

Wisconsin
1. Les Aspin, D.*
2. Robert W. Kastenmeier, D.*
3. Steven Gunderson, R.
4. Clement J. Zablocki, D.*
5. Henry S. Reuss, D.*
6. Thomas E. Petri, R.*
7. David R. Obey, D.*
8. Toby Roth, R.*
9. F. James Sensenbrenner, Jr., R.*

Wyoming
† Richard B. Cheney, R.*

Nonvoting Representatives

American Samoa
Fofo Sunia, D.

District of Columbia
Walter E. Fauntroy, D.*

Guam
Antonio Won Pat, D.*

Puerto Rico
Baltasar Corrada, D.*

Virgin Islands
Ron de Lugo, D.

Senate expulsion proceedings were brought against
Harrison A. Williams, Jr. (D., N.J.), convicted of
bribery and conspiracy in the Abscam case in May.

action on the bill with a vote of 282 to 95. And on
August 13, at his ranch in California, the vacation-
ing President Reagan signed the new tax program
into law. The Economic Recovery Tax Act of 1981
provided a 5 per cent tax cut effective on October
1; an additional 10 per cent cut on July 1, 1982;
and a further 10 per cent cut on July 1, 1983.

The new tax law also offered working couples
some gradual relief from the so-called marriage
penalty, raised the maximum child-care credit,
lowered tax rates on long-term capital gains, and
encouraged dividend reinvestment. Estate and gift
taxes were to be reduced gradually.

Business tax relief was included to encourage
investment. Oil companies received reduced taxes
on windfall profits and other tax credits.

Social Security. The Omnibus Budget Reconciliation Act provided for the elimination of the minimum Social Security payment of $122 a month as
part of the Administration's effort to restructure
America's Social Security system. In a separate
proposal on May 12, the Administration asked that
benefits for those who chose to retire at age 62 be
cut to 55 per cent of full benefits, rather than 80 per
cent, and to phase in a gradual 23 per cent cut in
benefits for future retirees. On May 20, in a "sense
of the Congress" resolution, the Senate refused to
support the Reagan plan to cut Social Security
benefits for early retirees.

On July 31, the House voted 404 to 20 to restore
the Social Security minimum payment of $122 per
month. In a slightly different version, the Senate
restored a major portion of the cut on October 15
in a 95 to 0 vote. The compromise measure was
passed by both houses of Congress in December
and signed by Reagan on December 29.

Federal Debt. The Reagan Administration was
committed to balancing the federal budget and
reducing the growing federal debt. But the spiraling costs of government, the prospect of reduced
revenues, rising interest rates on the current federal
debt, and a continuing recession forced the 97th
Congress to approve two increases in the temporary national debt-limit ceiling in 1981. On February 5, the House voted 305 to 104 to increase the
temporary ceiling by $50 billion, to $985 billion.
The Senate approved the increase the following
day. On September 29, to enable the federal government to meet its October 1 payroll, the Senate
voted 64 to 34 to complete congressional action on
a bill raising the debt limit to $1.079 trillion.

On November 10, Reagan admitted that the
budget would not be balanced in 1984. On December 7, he predicted that the 1982 federal deficit
might reach a record $109 billion.

Farm Price Supports. As part of its drive to trim
federal spending, the Administration urged Congress to reject a proposed rise in dairy price supports and to eliminate price subsidies on all the
nation's major crops, specifically wheat, corn, soybeans, barley, rice, and upland cotton. In addition,
Reagan urged eliminating price supports for tobacco and peanuts and the abolition of low-interest
agricultural loan programs. On March 21, the
President signed a bill that blocked a 7 per cent
increase in dairy price supports scheduled for April
1 – a rise that would have cost the government
$147 million in 1981.

Congress was under pressure from the Administration to cut farm spending and from farmers to
increase agricultural aid. On September 18, the
Senate approved a $10.6-billion bill that provided
most of the cuts asked by the Administration. The
House passed a $16.6-billion version of the bill on
October 22. On December 8, a conference committee released an $11-billion measure that authorized
sugar and tobacco price supports, changed the
method of calculating price supports for milk, and
eliminated government restrictions on peanut
growing. The Senate approved the bill on December 10; the House, on December 16. The President
signed it on December 22.

The AWACS Sale. On March 6, the Reagan Administration agreed to sell Saudi Arabia some $8.5-
billion in military equipment, including Airborne
Warning and Control System (AWACS) planes, 62
F-15 fighters, Sidewinder missiles, and other supplies. The President announced the sale on April

21, raising a storm of protest from Israelis, who saw the deal as a threat to their security. The President was required to submit the agreement to Congress for approval. A negative vote in both houses of Congress would have blocked the proposed sale.

The battle in Congress was bitter. The President staked his prestige on the sale and openly attacked the pro-Israel lobby for opposing the deal. The Saudis lobbied openly for it, and many American business and military interests threw their considerable support behind the sale.

The House on October 14 voted 301 to 111 to block the sale. But, on October 28, in another victory for the Administration, the Senate voted 52 to 48 against a resolution rejecting the sale.

Other Action. On October 7, Congress approved a pay increase of 10.7 to 17 per cent for enlisted military personnel and 14.3 per cent for officers. Reagan signed the measure on October 14.

On June 2, the House voted unanimously to grant the Veterans Administration funds to provide medical and hospital care to Vietnam War veterans who had been exposed to the herbicide Agent Orange. The Senate approved the bill unanimously on June 16, and the President signed it on November 3.

In November, President Reagan signed legislation adding almost $1 billion in veterans benefits. On November 13, the Senate voted 61 to 21 to refuse to eliminate funding for legal aid to the poor and voted 47 to 33 to continue the program for one year with a 25 per cent cut in funding. The House had approved the measure in September. A bill to extend key provisions of the Voting Rights Act of 1965, passed by the House on October 5, awaited a Senate vote at year-end.

On December 29, the President signed 35 bills into law, including a $200-billion defense appropriations bill and an $11.5-billion foreign aid bill.

Abscam Aftermath. In further fallout from the Federal Bureau of Investigation's Abscam investigation, Representative Raymond F. Lederer (D., Pa.) on January 9 and former Representative Richard Kelly (R., Fla.) on January 26 were convicted on charges of bribery and conspiracy. Lederer resigned from Congress on April 28. On May 1, a U.S. district court in Brooklyn, N.Y., found Senator Harrison A. Williams, Jr. (D., N.J.), guilty of the same charges. On August 24, the Senate Select Committee on Ethics recommended unanimously that Williams be expelled because of his "ethically repugnant" conduct. On November 30, however, Senate leaders agreed to postpone expulsion efforts until January 1982.   Carol L. Thompson

See also FARM AND FARMING; PRESIDENT OF THE UNITED STATES; TAXATION; UNITED STATES, GOVERNMENT OF THE; WELFARE. In WORLD BOOK, see CONGRESS OF THE UNITED STATES.
CONNECTICUT. See STATE GOVERNMENT.

CONSERVATION. Environmental organizations in the United States attacked the pro-development policies of Secretary of the Interior James G. Watt throughout 1981. Gaylord A. Nelson, formerly a Democratic senator from Wisconsin and now chairman of the Wilderness Society, called Watt "unfit to hold public office." On July 14, the largest United States conservation organization, the National Wildlife Federation, announced a poll showing that its members overwhelmingly opposed Watt's policies. Senator Alan Cranston (D., Calif.) called for Watt's ouster on July 24. See WATT, JAMES G.

The conservationist Sierra Club launched an "oust Watt" drive in April. On October 19, the club presented petitions demanding Watt's ouster to congressional leaders on the steps of the Capitol in Washington, D.C. More than 1 million people had signed the petitions.

However, Watt was popular in the Western states. Westerners viewed Watt's policy of opening up public lands to oil and gas operators and other developers as a victory over what they called the "lockup" of resources under President Jimmy Carter's Administration.

President Ronald Reagan said on August 13 that Watt had his full support. "I think we have been victimized by some individuals that I refer to as environmental extremists," Reagan said. "I can assure you Jim Watt does not want to destroy the beauty of America. He just wants to recognize that people are ecology, too."

The *Denver Post* commented on September 13 that many Americans appeared to have heard only one side of the story about Watt's policies. "It would be good if more Americans realized that Watt's task is more difficult than environmental lobbies would have them believe," the *Post* declared. "It is important that we should protect scenery, recreational lands, and the general natural heritage. But it is also important to the national welfare that oilmen drill the public lands of the rich Overthrust Belt. So what we're after is wise use. A land lockup is easy. So is a policy that turns a blind eye to development. Maybe after Watt responds to Western concerns we can move toward a middle ground." The Overthrust Belt is a geologic formation rich in oil and gas stretching from New Mexico to the Canadian Rockies.

Watt won substantial support from Western political leaders during a visit to six Western states in September and October. However, the national conflict over energy development seemed certain to continue.

National Parks. Environmental groups began their attack on Watt when Reagan nominated him on Dec. 22, 1980. They objected to Watt's background as president of the Mountain States Legal Foundation, which had fought conservation groups

Marine conservationist Norine Rouse studies the endangered hawksbill species of sea turtle in the Gulf Stream, its natural environment.

in court. The environmentalists sharpened their attack when Watt proposed that the government stop buying land for national parks. He testified at Senate hearings on May 7 in favor of diverting funds that had been set aside for buying new land for parks. Watt said that the government should use the money to take better care of existing park areas. Watt cited a General Accounting Office (GAO) estimate that showed a $1.6-billion backlog in needed maintenance of park buildings and roads and charged that the National Park System had deteriorated into a "shameful" condition. He asked Congress to divert $105 million earmarked for new land purchases into a crash maintenance program.

William A. Turnage, executive director of the Wilderness Society, replied that Watt based his argument on misleading studies. Turnage said that the major park problem was overcrowding, which could be relieved by adding land to the system.

Wilderness Versus Energy. Watt's determination to encourage exploration and development in wilderness areas created the sharpest conflicts with the environmental movement. The House Committee on Interior and Insular Affairs ordered three wilderness areas in Montana withdrawn from leasing on May 21. Watt complied with the order, but questioned its constitutionality. The Mountain States Legal Foundation challenged the order in court. The Department of Justice also announced

that it would oppose the moratorium on mineral exploration.

Test Case. Conservationists expected a conflict over the use of part of a national forest in Wyoming to lead to a major federal court case in 1981 or 1982. The region, known as the Washakie area of Shoshone National Forest, is in a section of the Overthrust Belt that may contain a large amount of oil. The federal government declared the 687,000-acre (278,000-hectare) Washakie area a wilderness in 1972. Companies that want to explore for oil have filed almost 150 applications to lease parcels of land in the area.

The U.S. Forest Service, an agency of the Department of Agriculture, must decide whether to recommend that the Interior Department issue leases. "What is at issue is the whole future of the wilderness concept," said Bruce Hamilton, the Sierra Club's representative in the Wyoming region, on August 29. "The idea of wilderness is just not compatible with oil and gas activity."

Energy interests argue that they can search for oil and eventually bring it to the surface without damaging the environment. "A lot of environmentalists refuse to take into account the need for energy," the Mountain States Legal Foundation said. "There must be a balance struck between the values of these resources and the values of wilderness." A court case on the Washakie area could set a precedent for deciding future conflicts between energy companies and environmentalists over the use of wilderness areas.

Industry pressed Congress to extend the deadline for mineral-leasing in wilderness areas. Congressman James Santini (D., Nev.) introduced legislation to extend the deadline for mining in wilderness areas for 10 years. Mining is potentially much more destructive than oil development. However, a 1977 law permits mining only if the mining companies restore wilderness characteristics to the land after they finish their work.

On November 19, Watt pledged that his department would grant oil and gas leases in wilderness areas only after notifying the public well in advance of the proposed leasing date, consulting with Congress, and making a full environmental assessment.

Whale Hunting. On July 25, the International Whaling Commission (IWC) virtually banned the hunting of sperm whales. The IWC again defeated a proposal, backed by the United States, for a moratorium on all commercial whaling. Since the IWC was formed in 1946, the annual limit set on the catch of all whales has fallen from about 46,000 to less than 15,000 throughout the world. However, several species on the international endangered species list are still fair game.

Endangered Species. The U.S. Fish and Wildlife Service (FWS) announced on January 30 that it would concentrate on saving species already found to be endangered rather than on adding new species to the endangered list. The policy went into effect before Watt took office, according to FWS officials, but the new assistant secretary for fish and wildlife and parks, G. Ray Arnett, endorsed it. "There'll never be enough money to save all the animals and plants," he said on September 16, "so I am leaving it up to the biologists to decide which species we should concentrate our efforts on."

Topsoil Crisis. The loss of topsoil in the United States and other countries is so severe it could trigger food shortages in the 1980s, according to Lester Brown, president of the Worldwatch Institute, a nonprofit organization that researches problems of worldwide concern. On October 10, Brown called the widespread loss of topsoil the most serious single threat humanity now faces. He said that the doubling of world food output since 1950 was achieved at the expense of severe land abuse.

In January, 60 environmentalist groups held a conference on "The Global 2000 Report to the President," a federal study of how current social and economic trends might influence the quality of human life in the year 2000. The groups issued a joint statement that urged more public attention to the impact of population growth on the environment and on the quality of life.   Andrew L. Newman

In WORLD BOOK, see CONSERVATION.

CONSTITUTION OF THE UNITED STATES. Three proposed amendments to the Constitution made little progress toward adoption in 1981. The Constitution specifies that a proposed amendment must be passed by both houses of Congress or drafted by convention—and then adopted by three-fourths of the states—to become law.

The Equal Rights Amendment (ERA), which would prohibit discrimination on the basis of sex, remained three states short of the 38 needed for ratification. Although the deadline for its passage was extended in 1978 to June 30, 1982, no state has ratified it since Indiana did so in January 1977. Moreover, on December 23, a U.S. district court in Boise, Ida., declared the deadline extension unconstitutional. ERA supporters planned to appeal the decision, which would kill the amendment.

The drive to call a convention to propose a constitutional amendment requiring a balanced federal budget was only slightly more successful. The legislatures of 34 states must pass resolutions to convene the convention, and at year-end, only 30 had done so.

An amendment to secure voting rights for District of Columbia residents was ratified by a single state, Oregon, in 1981, bringing the total of states that had approved it to 10.   Beverly Merz

In WORLD BOOK, see CONSTITUTION OF THE UNITED STATES.

CONSUMERISM. A recession in late 1981 began to provide some relief from the double-digit inflation that had plagued consumers in the United States for many years. The U.S. government's Consumer Price Index, the most widely used measure of inflation, rose at an annual rate of 9.2 per cent from January to November 1981, amid growing signs that prices were moderating.

Hopes for Price Relief. Good weather brought record or near-record crops of corn, wheat, soybeans, and other food products. The large supplies sent some key farm prices tumbling. The price of a bushel of corn, for example, dropped from $3.17 in June to $2.57 in mid-September, according to the U.S. Department of Agriculture. Increased production of meat forced poultry prices down and kept beef prices at 1980 levels. See FARM AND FARMING.

During spring and summer, buyer resistance to high prices and high interest rates on automobile loans forced U.S. car manufacturers to offer a series of rebates and special deals in an effort to boost sagging sales. By November, with sales at a 23-year low, automakers began to consider actual price cuts. See AUTOMOBILE.

Gasoline prices also leveled off during the year as an increasing number of motorists cut back on travel or switched to fuel-saving cars. For the first time, a U.S.-made automobile topped 40 miles per gallon (17 kilometers per liter) of gas. A 1982 Chevrolet Chevette hit the magic figure in tests reported on September 10 by the U.S. Environmental Protection Agency. However, foreign cars continued to maintain their fuel superiority, with several exceeding the Chevette mark.

Housing prices also lost their upward momentum as construction of new houses dropped to one of the lowest points in history. But interest costs for home mortgages rose most of the year to average nearly 18 per cent. Although the prime rate, the interest rate banks charge their best business customers, dropped substantially in the fall, mortgage rates fell much less. See HOUSING.

Regulatory Changes. As a presidential candidate, Ronald Reagan frequently promised to reduce the number and complexity of government regulations, maintaining that their cost and paperwork were hampering business. Once in office, President Reagan followed through with massive cutbacks. He started in January by freezing all pending rules for 60 days and setting up a Task Force on Regulatory Relief headed by Vice-President George H. W. Bush to screen out any "unnecessary rules."

In March, Bush announced that more than 100 pending regulations were being held up for review, revision, or postponement. Almost all dealt with safety, environment, or other consumer matters. The main criterion for keeping a regulation, Bush said, was whether it was cost effective – that is, whether benefits anticipated from the regulation exceeded the cost of carrying it out. See SAFETY.

The regulations slated for postponement included restrictions on oil drilling in environmentally sensitive areas off the California coast and elsewhere, requirements that surface-mining firms restore mined areas to prime farmland or approximate the original contour, and rules to control the discharge of industrial wastes into municipal sewage systems. The regulations designated for review included guidelines for limiting water pollutants from industrial sources; rules governing the generation, handling, and disposal of hazardous wastes in dumps and landfills; and requirements that drug manufacturers enclose with their products "patient inserts," leaflets similar to those given physicians warning about possible side effects.

On August 12, more than 30 federal regulations were held up for possible elimination or change. They included requirements that manufacturers provide the government with certain information about new chemicals before marketing them, fire safety standards for construction of mobile homes, and automobile bumper standards prohibiting damage to the body of the car in crashes at speeds of 5 miles (8 kilometers) per hour or less.

In October, the government ended a nine-year effort to require automatic seat belts or airbags in new cars. The National Association of Independent Insurers, an insurance group, had protested the action in court, claiming it would increase highway fatalities.

The Reagan Administration also used budget cuts to lessen government regulation. It persuaded Congress to reduce funds for numerous regulatory agencies, including the Consumer Product Safety Commission, whose budget was cut by 30 per cent for the 1982 fiscal year; and the National Highway Traffic Safety Administration, cut by more than 33 per cent. As a result, the consumer agency was forced to close five of its 10 regional offices, and the highway safety agency stopped issuing safety standards for motor vehicles.

The Federal Trade Commission (FTC), the government's chief consumer-protection agency, wound up with a relatively small reduction of 11 per cent for fiscal 1982. Congress had already reined in the agency in 1980 through severe restrictions on its powers and a provision that Congress could overturn any FTC rule by a vote in both houses within 90 days after the FTC issued it.

As a result of pressures from both Congress and the White House, the FTC relaxed many long-pending rules, including regulations designed to restrict certain practices of funeral directors and used-car dealers. The agency also dropped an eight-year-old lawsuit alleging antitrust violations by the nation's largest oil companies. An FTC administrative law judge also dismissed the agency's nine-year-old case charging three large breakfast-cereal manufacturers with conducting a "shared monopoly" to control prices and supplies.

Publications Cutbacks. A wide variety of government publications for consumers went on the chopping block. Among them was *The Car Book,* a compendium of crash-test data, repair costs, and other information about specific automobile models, published by the Department of Transportation. Automakers had charged that the book was full of errors. The decision to discontinue publication came despite brisk public demand for the book.

Also discontinued was *The Energy Consumer,* a monthly issued by the Department of Energy that had run an article that reportedly displeased the nuclear power industry. The Occupational Safety and Health Administration dropped some educational materials alleged to be biased against business. The White House also set up a clearance procedure for new publications.

Consumer Groups reacted slowly to all the changes, appearing stunned into inaction after so many successes in earlier Administrations. It was not until October that the Alliance for Justice, a coalition of public-interest groups, launched a protest. In a 68-page study, *Undermining Public Protections,* the coalition accused the Reagan Administration of ignoring the public interest and of using a "sledge-hammer" approach to deregulation.

Changes in the Market Place. Increased deregulation freed financial institutions to offer a variety of new services. Beginning in January, banks and savings and loan associations nationwide began paying interest on money in negotiable order of withdrawal (NOW) accounts. On October 1, savings institutions began offering all-savers certificates, one-year tax-exempt savings certificates authorized by the Economic Recovery Tax Act of 1981, the tax-cutting law enacted on August 13. See BANKS AND BANKING.

Despite their new freedom, commercial banks fell behind a number of large conglomerates that began to offer banking services along with a variety of other services that banks were not authorized to provide. Among services offered by these firms were insurance, real estate selling, investments, car rental, and cash management. Leading the race to diversify was Sears, Roebuck and Company, which acquired a large real estate brokerage house and an investment firm in October. The mergers put Sears, the nation's leading retailer, ahead of the American Express Company in variety of services offered, according to a survey by *The Wall Street Journal.*

Arthur E. Rowse

In WORLD BOOK, see CONSUMERISM.

COSTA RICA. See LATIN AMERICA.

COURTS AND LAWS. Seven years of negotiations at the United Nations Law of the Sea Conference in Geneva, Switzerland, suffered a major reversal on Aug. 5, 1981, when the Administration of President Ronald Reagan suddenly withdrew United States support from the draft treaty. On March 3, only a week before a meeting at which ratification was expected, the Administration announced it would seek a "sweeping review" of the document. All ranking members of the U.S. delegation were dismissed, but two were later reinstated. See OCEAN.

The Hostage Accord. The most complicated arbitration procedure in history was set up in the January 19 agreement freeing the remaining 52 hostages captured at the United States Embassy in Teheran, Iran, on Nov. 4, 1979. After returning some $8 billion in Iranian assets frozen in U.S. banks, the United States deposited an additional $2 billion in a bank in the Netherlands to be distributed by the Iran-United States Claims Tribunal housed at The Hague. Some 600 claims of $250,000 or more were expected to be filed against Iran by U.S. companies before the January 1982 deadline. Another 3,000 smaller claims were to be negotiated in a group presentation by U.S. government officials. See IRAN (Close-Up).

Court Trends. Conservatism continued to make inroads in political thought in the United States during 1981, and both court and criminal justice

Headmistress Jean S. Harris leaves jail on March 20 to be sentenced for the 1980 murder of Herman Tarnower, cardiologist and *Scarsdale Diet* author.

procedures were targets of criticism. In a February 8 speech at the American Bar Association (ABA) Convention in Houston, Chief Justice of the United States Warren E. Burger blasted allegedly overly elaborate procedures safeguarding the rights of criminal defendants. He said, "Our search for justice must not be twisted into an endless quest for technical errors, unrelated to guilt or innocence." He added that stiffer crime-control measures are necessary to deal with "a reign of terror in American cities."

Both President Reagan and Attorney General William French Smith voiced agreement with Burger on several occasions during the year. In August, Reagan called for "reform" of bail-bond abuses and abolition of the exclusionary rule, which bars use in court of evidence obtained illegally by police. In October, Smith urged Congress to set minimum mandatory sentences and to abolish parole, under certain circumstances, to deal with rising crime. He also promised that the Reagan Administration would seek greater judicial restraint in such areas as abortion rights, school desegregation, sexual and racial quotas in the workplace, environmental protection, and the constitutional rights of aliens and prisoners.

Several well-backed efforts to limit court powers were mounted in Congress, worrying some bar leaders, civil rights activists, and constitutional experts. Senator Jesse A. Helms (R., N.C.) led forces opposed to Supreme Court rulings striking down state anti-abortion laws, prohibiting state-sponsored prayer in public schools, and ordering busing to desegregate schools. Their proposal for new legislation to strip the high court's authority over such matters brought an immediate reaction. ABA President David R. Brink warned in a November 11 speech that passage of such a law would threaten the very existence of the judicial branch of government.

Budget Cutbacks advocated by Reagan during 1981 included eliminating the nationwide Legal Services Corporation, an agency created by Congress in 1974 to provide the poor with legal aid in civil cases, and distributing reduced funding to states inside a block grant. Congress refused to abolish the agency, but slashed its budget from $321 million in the 1981 fiscal year to $241 million in fiscal 1982.

The venerable United States Fifth Circuit Court of Appeals, responsible for desegregating the Deep South over the past 25 years, was split in half on October 1 to facilitate case management. After the action, 14 judges remained in the Fifth Circuit, comprising Louisiana, Mississippi, Texas, and the Panama Canal Zone, while 12 judges sat in a new Eleventh Circuit, covering Georgia, Alabama, and Florida.

Major Trials. In 1981's most publicized trial, Jean S. Harris, the headmistress of a private school, was found guilty on February 24 of the second-degree murder of Herman Tarnower, cardiologist and author of *The Complete Scarsdale Diet*, at his Purchase, N.Y., home on March 10, 1980. Harris was sentenced on March 20, 1981, to a minimum of 15 years in prison. The slaying of another prominent cardiologist and author, Michael J. Halberstam of Washington, D.C., was resolved on April 10 with the conviction of Bernard C. Welch, Jr., a habitual criminal. Welch, who was captured when the mortally wounded Halberstam struck him with a car, received a mandatory life sentence as a repeat offender.

In State Supreme Court in New York City on August 24, Mark David Chapman was sentenced to 20 years to life in prison. Chapman shot and killed singer John Lennon on Dec. 8, 1980. Craig S. Crimmins, a stagehand at the Metropolitan Opera House, was sentenced to at least 20 years in prison after his conviction on June 4 for murdering violinist Helen Hagnes. The only U.S. judicial proceeding stemming from the Nov. 18, 1978, tragedy in Jonestown, Guyana, in which 911 people died, ended inconclusively on Sept. 26, 1981, when the murder-conspiracy case against Larry J. Layton was declared a mistrial.   David C. Beckwith

See also CRIME; SUPREME COURT OF THE UNITED STATES. In WORLD BOOK, see COURT; LAW.

CRIME. A wave of violent attacks on national and religious leaders swept across the world in 1981. On March 30, United States President Ronald Reagan was shot in the chest outside the Washington (D.C.) Hilton Hotel. Presidential Press Secretary James S. Brady and two security officers were also wounded. The alleged assailant, John W. Hinckley, Jr., was indicted on 13 counts on August 24. See PRESIDENT OF THE UNITED STATES.

Pope John Paul II was shot in St. Peter's Square in Rome on May 13. On July 22, Mehmet Ali Agca, an escaped Turkish killer, was convicted of attempting to murder the pope and sentenced to life imprisonment. See ROMAN CATHOLIC CHURCH.

Iran's Chief Justice Ayatollah Mohammed Beheshti died when a terrorist bomb exploded in Teheran on June 28. Another bomb blast in Teheran killed President Mohammed Ali Rajai and Prime Minister Mohammed Jad Bahonar on August 30 (see IRAN). A small group of Islamic extremists assassinated Egypt's President Anwar el-Sadat on October 6 while he was watching a military parade in a Cairo suburb (see EGYPT).

Airliner Hijackings. Three armed men sympathetic to the regime of Pakistan's former Prime Minister Zulfikar Ali Bhutto seized a domestic Pakistani airliner on March 2 and ordered it to Kabul, Afghanistan. The hijackers held more than 100 passengers hostage in Kabul and demanded that Pakistan release 92 political prisoners. On March 9, the hijackers forced the crew to fly the plane to Damascus, Syria.

Pakistan agreed on March 12 to release 54 prisoners in exchange for the release of the hostages. Eventually, the prisoners were flown to Damascus, and the hostages were released. The hijackers surrendered on March 14, but Syria refused to return the hijackers and the freed prisoners to Pakistan.

A similar hijacking in Southeast Asia ended in bloodshed. Five armed Islamic fundamentalists forced a domestic Indonesian airliner to go to Bangkok, Thailand, on March 28 and held 55 passengers and crew members hostage. On March 31, Indonesian commandos attacked the aircraft, freed the hostages, and killed four of the hijackers.

U.S. Crime Rate. The Federal Bureau of Investigation (FBI) reported on October 30 that the crime rate in the United States increased 3 per cent during the first six months of 1981, compared with the same period in 1980. Crimes against property, such as burglary, larceny, and motor-vehicle theft, rose 2 per cent in the first six months of 1981. Violent crimes generally were up 7 per cent. Specifically, murder increased 4 per cent, robbery 11 per cent, and forcible rape and aggravated assault 1 per cent each.

Four gunmen overpowered two employees in a Tucson, Ariz., bank on April 23 and drove away

A poster in Atlanta, Ga., publicizes a task force investigating the deaths of 28 black youths. A suspect went on trial in December.

with $3.3 million. It was the largest cash haul from a bank in U.S. history.

Murders. Wayne B. Williams went on trial on December 28 for the murder of two black youths in one of the most puzzling mass murder episodes in U.S. history – the slaying of 28 young blacks in Atlanta, Ga., over a two-year period. Williams, a black free-lance photographer, was arrested after police, who were staking out a bridge over the Chattahoochee River, heard a loud splash and saw Williams' car move slowly over the bridge. Williams claimed that he had thrown garbage over the bridge, but the body of a strangulation victim was found in the river a few hours later.

One of the most unusual crime stories of any year centered on Jack Henry Abbott, a convicted criminal who became acquainted with author Norman Mailer. Mailer helped Abbott publish *In the Belly of the Beast*, a book about his almost lifelong prison experiences, and win parole. Only a few months later, Abbott allegedly stabbed a man to death in New York City and, after a nationwide manhunt, was captured and returned to prison.

Mark David Chapman, who killed rock musician John Lennon of the Beatles in December 1980, received a prison sentence of 20 years to life on August 24.   David C. Beckwith

See also COURTS AND LAWS. In WORLD BOOK, see CRIME; TERRORISM.

CUBA. Reaction to Cuban intervention in the internal affairs of neighboring Latin American countries gained momentum during 1981. Most of the region's military dictatorships had long been opposed to Cuba, but in 1981, the elected governments of Colombia, Ecuador, Jamaica, Peru, and Venezuela took steps to break ties with Cuba. Even previously friendly countries, such as Panama and Mexico, cooled toward Cuba. Mexico's President Jose Lopez Portillo welcomed Cuba's President Fidel Castro Ruz on an official visit in August, but denied him an invitation to a summit conference between industrialized and developing nations in Cancún, Mexico, in October. United States President Ronald Reagan said he would not attend if Castro was invited.

U.S.-Cuban Relations were further strained in February when the United States Department of State released evidence that seemed to indicate Cuba was heavily involved in supplying arms to guerrillas seeking to overthrow the government of El Salvador.

The Reagan Administration acknowledged its intention to thwart Cuban subversion and support for terrorism in Latin America. In October, Secretary of State Alexander M. Haig, Jr., said his department was studying policy options that would make the risks to Cuba of meddling in Latin America "more costly than the advantages."

The United States tightened its economic embargo of Cuba, publicly identifying U.S., Panamanian, and Jamaican companies that have fronted for Cuban trade. The U.S. government did little to discourage the activities of anti-Castro Cuban groups that were openly training in the United States for eventual military action to overthrow Cuba's government.

Many Americans were angered by the high cost of caring for some 125,000 Cubans who sought refuge in the United States after a mass exodus from Cuba in 1980. Particularly troublesome was the prospect of coping with hardened criminals and social misfits who had been released from Cuban prisons and institutions and added to the refugee flow.

Castro Lashed Out at the United States on July 26 in a speech marking the 28th anniversary of the Cuban revolution. Castro accused the United States of causing an outbreak of dengue fever, a highly infectious, mosquito-carried disease that swept the island in 1981. More than 270,000 cases of dengue fever and more than 100 deaths from the disease were reported. United States officials denied Castro's charges and suggested that the disease may have been introduced by Cuban troops returning from Africa.   Nathan A. Haverstock

See also LATIN AMERICA (Facts in Brief Table). In WORLD BOOK, see CUBA.

CYPRUS. See EUROPE.

CZECHOSLOVAKIA

CZECHOSLOVAKIA remained a loyal member of the Eastern bloc in 1981. At the Communist Party congress held from April 6 to 10 in Prague, Russia's Communist Party General Secretary and Supreme Soviet Presidium Chairman Leonid Ilich Brezhnev praised the Czechoslovak party as a "militant and mature social force that has accumulated a wealth of valuable experience of political struggle." Delegates at the congress re-elected General Secretary Gustav Husak for five years and re-elected the entire 11-member Presidium, the policymaking body of both the party and the government. They added one member to the Presidium – Milos Jakes, who had been in charge of the party purge after the 1968 occupation by Russia and other Eastern nations. Jakes was put in charge of the party's economic policy, replacing Josef Kempný, who was said to be ill.

Double Agent. Prime Minister Lubomir Strougal visited Austria on May 25 for talks with Chancellor Bruno Kreisky. Strougal planned to visit that country again in October. But he had to cancel his plans in September, after Austria said that the visit would be "inopportune." Austrian officials were angry over the case of Josef Hodic, a member of Czechoslovakia's intelligence service. Hodic had gone to Austria in 1978, pretending to be a persecuted and active member of the Charter 77 human rights movement. The Austrian government found a job for him and allowed him to become an Austrian citizen. But in June 1981, he returned to Czechoslovakia. Hodic declared in press conferences and radio discussions in Prague that he had exposed the political activities of Czechoslovak emigrants in the West and had discovered their alleged links with Western intelligence organizations, including those of Austria.

Czechoslovakia began a new crackdown on dissidents on July 9, sentencing Jiri Gruntorad, a 28-year-old construction worker, to four years in prison for helping to publish a paper on the persecution of dissidents. On July 28, Rudolf Battek, a 57-year-old sociologist and a spokesman for Charter 77, received a prison sentence of 7½ years. In September, six Roman Catholics, including two priests, were sentenced to prison terms ranging from 10 months to three years for illegally publishing religious magazines and other materials.

The Grain Harvest in Czechoslovakia in 1981 amounted to 8.8 million metric tons (9.7 million short tons), 12 per cent less than the 1980 crop. Industrial production in the first six months of 1981 was 1.8 per cent higher than in the first half of 1980, while exports to the West were 6.2 per cent higher. Chris Cviic

See also EUROPE (Facts in Brief Table). In WORLD BOOK, see CZECHOSLOVAKIA.

DAIRYING. See FARM AND FARMING.

DAM. See BUILDING AND CONSTRUCTION.

DANCING. The wealth of activity in the United States dance world continued in 1981 despite administrators' gloomy forecasts about the financial stability of the dance community. Impending cuts in the performing-arts budgets of federal and state agencies were indeed a grim reality, but their effects were not yet felt.

Of special interest was American Ballet Theatre's (ABT) debut year under the artistic direction of Mikhail Baryshnikov. The company performed in New York City in April, May, and June and danced before a broad range of audiences and under varying performing conditions on its travels.

Critics were nearly unanimous in their appraisals of the troupe's new profile. The casting policy initiated by Baryshnikov drew the most praise. An increasing number of dancers from the company's *corps de ballet*, some of them very young, were given major roles in new productions.

Dance critics described the ensemble as newly vigorous and carefully rehearsed. They felt that the new director's repertory policy was conservative, yet sensible. Instead of offering new ballets of unproven worth, Baryshnikov concentrated on revivals. He presented ballets by master choreographers Marius Petipa, George Balanchine, Sir Frederick Ashton, and Kenneth MacMillan. Modern dance was represented by the work of Paul Taylor and Merce Cunningham. Baryshnikov him-

Dancers of Montreal's Les Grands Ballets Canadiens re-create *Soaring,* a 1920 work, at New York City's Lehman College in February.

self began revamping such classics as *Swan Lake* and *Giselle.*

The New York City Ballet presented a spate of new creations in 1981. They were prepared for the group's Tchaikovsky Festival, the brainchild of artistic director Balanchine, which was held from June 4 to 14 at the New York State Theater in New York City. The festival premièred a dozen new ballets choreographed to the music of Russian composer Peter Ilich Tchaikovsky by such company associates as Jerome Robbins, John Taras, Peter Martins, and of course Balanchine.

The artistic level of the new ballets varied, with Balanchine supplying the most interesting ones. His *Mozartiana* provided an astounding vehicle for ballerina Suzanne Farrell, while his pageant to the last movement of Tchaikovsky's *Symphony No. 6* – the "Pathétique" – astounded the public with its intense religiosity. Robbins came up with a popular hit in *Piano Pieces,* a jaunty suite of dances.

The most spectacular, and perhaps most controversial, feature of the festival was not the choreography but the "crystal palace" décor. Designed by architects Philip C. Johnson and John Burgee, it

served for the entire festival and the duration of the spring season, through June 28. Some critics found the set cold or an example of dated modernism. Others described the subtle play of light through the structure's transparent tubings as "ravishing."

Avant-Garde Techniques, or what is often called "new dance" or "post-modern dance," received increased attention in 1981. Several organizations featured special avant-garde festivals. The American Dance Festival in Durham, N.C., commissioned new works for an "Emerging Generation" series, held from July 7 to 12. In mid-October, New York City's Brooklyn Academy of Music embarked on a "Next Wave" program with experimentalists Laura Dean, Trisha Brown, and Lucinda Childs. The American Theater Laboratory, a small theater in New York City, made big waves by granting extended seasons to relatively unknown but talented dance innovators. Among them were Karole Armitage, Charles Moulton, Kenneth Rinker, and David Gordon. A virtual gathering of the clan took place from October 3 through 11 at the Walker Art Center in Minneapolis, Minn. Although the Walker has long been a staunch supporter of new dance, its New Dance USA festival was a landmark.

Exponents of the new dance tend to draw small audiences, but experimental choreographer Twyla Tharp wants a large public. In her desire to reach the mainstream, she joined forces with Bill Gra-

U.S. ballerina Amanda McKerrow, winner of the junior women's competition of an international dance contest, performs in Moscow in June.

ham, a producer usually connected with rock concerts, for an engagement in San Francisco in March. Graham also helped produce Tharp's month-long stand on Broadway, beginning on September 22 – the longest run a modern dance group has sustained on Broadway.

Although not as aggressive a wooer of the mass audience as Tharp, Paul Taylor found himself with a box-office success in *Arden Court*. This work premièred on April 15 during the Taylor company's three-week season at New York City Center. Set to the baroque music of William Boyce, *Arden Court* is an all-out showstopper for male dancers. The combination of spectacular dancing with the discreet, charming music proved a pleasing irony. *Arden Court* was later filmed for the Public Broadcasting Service (PBS) series "Dance in America."

Visitors from Abroad. The most glamorous company to visit the United States was Great Britain's Royal Ballet, celebrating its 50th anniversary. The company opened at the Metropolitan Opera House in New York City on June 15 for three weeks and performed during July in Toronto, Canada; Washington, D.C.; and Boston. The much-anticipated visit turned out to be disappointing because of what many critics perceived as a decline in the general level of dancing. Although the repertory had a gratifying number of ballets by Ashton, including his *Rhapsody*, the dancers appeared ill at

ease with a style that had always been synonymous with the Royal Ballet. Better performances graced works by MacMillan, but several critics noted that unfortunately the caliber of the dancing rose for choreography of fairly low quality. Indeed, MacMillan's new full-evening *Isadora* was condemned as a travesty of the life and work of Isadora Duncan, the famous American dancer.

One company that showed marked improvement over its last visit to the United States was the Israel Ballet, which began a two-month tour of North America on April 15 in Atlantic City, N.J. A visit to New York City's Metropolitan Opera House in July by The Hague's Nederlands Dance Theater aroused excitement. Jiri Kylian, its resident choreographer, presented ballets that had a profound emotional impact. But probably the most extraordinary event was a brief encounter in July with an Australian Aboriginal dance ensemble.

The People's Republic of China, inaccessible until recently, grew closer to the United States through cultural exchange programs. An instructor from the Peking (Beijing) Dance Academy taught at the San Francisco Ballet School in the summer, and several Chinese students enrolled at the Houston Ballet's dance school for a year's work. The Houston Ballet, in turn, toured China for six weeks during the summer.   Nancy Goldner

In WORLD BOOK, see BALLET; DANCING.

DEATHS of notable persons in 1981 included those listed below. An asterisk (*) indicates the person is the subject of a biography in THE WORLD BOOK ENCYCLOPEDIA. Those listed were Americans unless otherwise indicated.

Addonizio, Hugh J. (1914-Feb. 2), Democratic congressman from 1949 to 1962 and mayor of Newark from 1962 to 1970.

Albertson, Jack (1910?-Nov. 25), actor and comedian who played the crotchety garage owner in the TV series "Chico and the Man."

*Algren, Nelson (Nelson Algren Abraham) (1909-May 9), writer whose novels described life in the Chicago slums of the 1930s. His works include *The Man with the Golden Arm* (1949) and *Chicago: City on the Make* (1951).

Alice, Princess (1883-Jan. 3), countess of Athlone (Great Britain), the last surviving grandchild of Queen Victoria.

Anderson, Jack Z. (1905-Feb. 9), Republican congressman from California from 1939 to 1953.

Astaire, Adele (1898-Jan. 25), dancer who charmed audiences of 1920s musical comedies with her partner and brother, Fred Astaire.

Auchinleck, Field Marshal Sir Claude John E. (1884-March 23), British commander in chief in the Middle East and India during World War II.

Bagnold, Enid (1890-March 31), British writer whose works included the novel *National Velvet* (1935) and the play *The Chalk Garden* (1956).

Baldwin, Roger (1884-Aug. 26), founder of the American Civil Liberties Union and its director from 1920 to 1950 – a crusader for the cause of freedom everywhere.

*Barber, Samuel (1910-Jan. 23), composer whose works included *Adagio for Strings* and the opera *Vanessa*.

Beard, Matthew (Stymie) (1925-Jan. 8), actor who played the baldheaded kid with the derby in the 1930s *Our Gang* films.

Benchley, Nathaniel (1915-Dec. 14), novelist and humorist whose book *The Off-Islanders* became the motion picture *The Russians Are Coming, the Russians Are Coming*.

Bennett, Robert Russell (1894-Aug. 18), composer and conductor who orchestrated such hit musicals as *Oklahoma!* (1943) and *My Fair Lady* (1956).

Berman, Émile Z. (1902-July 3), trial lawyer whose notable cases included the defense of Sirhan Sirhan, killer of Senator Robert F. Kennedy (D., N.Y.).

Betancourt, Rómulo (1908-Sept. 28), president of Venezuela from 1945 to 1948 and from 1959 to 1964.

Bliss, Ray C. (1907-Aug. 6), national chairman of the Republican Party from 1965 to 1969.

Böhm, Karl (1894-Aug. 14), Austrian conductor, one of the most esteemed musicians of his generation.

Bondi, Beulah (1888-Jan. 12), actress who played elderly women on the stage, on film, and on TV for more than 50 years.

Boone, Richard (1917-Jan. 10), actor best known for his role as the hired gunman Paladin in the "Have Gun, Will Travel" TV series.

*Bradley, General Omar N. (1893-April 8), brilliant military leader during World War II, last of America's five-star generals. See ARMED FORCES (Close-Up).

Breuer, Marcel (1902-July 1), Hungarian-born Bauhaus architect who played a major role in shaping modern architecture.

*Brink, Carol Ryrie (1895-Aug. 15), author of many children's books, including *Caddie Woodlawn*, winner of the 1936 Newbery Medal.

Brodie, Fawn (1915-Jan. 10), historian whose books included the best-selling *Thomas Jefferson: An Intimate History* (1974).

Brown, Christy (1932-Sept. 6), Irish author whose autobiography, *Down All the Days* (1970), was translated into 14 languages. Severely handicapped by cerebral palsy, he typed with the little toe of his left foot.

Cadieux, Marcel (1915-March 19), Canadian diplomat and ambassador to the United States from 1969 to 1975.

*Carmichael, Hoagy (Hoagland) (1899-Dec. 27), songwriter famous for such songs as "Stardust," "Lazy River," and "Old Rockin' Chair."

Celler, Emanuel (1888-Jan. 15), Democratic congressman from New York from 1923 to 1972.

Chapin, Harry (1942-July 16), pop singer and composer of the hit ballads "Taxi" and "Sequel."

Chase, Mary (1907-Oct. 20), playwright best known for *Harvey* (1944), a whimsical play about an invisible rabbit.

Chayefsky, Paddy (Sidney) (1923-Aug. 1), playwright and screenwriter who won three Oscars—for *Marty* (1955), *The Hospital* (1971), and *Network* (1976).

*Clair, René (1898-March 15), French film director, noted for his satirical philosophical themes in *Under the Roofs of Paris* (1929) and other films.

Cole, Cozy (William R.) (1909-Jan. 29), jazz drummer who played with Cab Calloway, Louis Armstrong, and Benny Goodman during the big-band era.

Coleman, Bill (1904-Aug. 24), jazz trumpeter who played with Fats Waller in 1935.

Cotter, William R. (1926-Sept. 8), Democratic congressman from Connecticut since 1970.

Coon, Carleton S. (1904-June 3), anthropologist and archaeologist.

*Cronin, A. J. (1896-Jan. 6), Scottish writer and physician whose novels included *Hatter's Castle* (1931), *The Citadel* (1937), and *The Keys of the Kingdom* (1941).

Crowther, Bosley (1905-March 7), film critic for *The New York Times* from 1940 to 1967.

Harold Urey, who won the 1934 Nobel Prize for Chemistry.

Roy Wilkins, noted civil rights leader.

Omar Torrijos Herrera, the long-time leader of Panama.

Anita Loos, a well-known playwright.

Curran, Joseph (1906-Aug. 14), labor leader who founded the National Maritime Union and served as its president from 1937 to 1973.

Daniels, Jonathan W. (1902-Nov. 6), press secretary to President Franklin D. Roosevelt in 1945 and editor of *The Raleigh* (N.C.) *News and Observer* from 1933 to 1942.

Davis, Jim (1915-April 26), actor best known as the tough Jock Ewing in the TV series "Dallas."

*Dayan, Moshe (1915-Oct. 16), military hero and political leader who directed Israel's campaign in the 1967 six-day war.

Dean, Paul (Daffy) (1913-March 17), baseball player who pitched the St. Louis Cardinals to the World Series championship in 1934 with his brother, Dizzy Dean.

Dean, General William F. (1899-Aug. 24), highest-ranking U.S. officer to be taken prisoner during the Korean War. He spent three years in North Korean prisoner-of-war camps.

Delbrück, Max (1906-March 9), German-born molecular geneticist, co-winner of the 1969 Nobel Prize for Physiology or Medicine for his work with *bacteriophages*, viruses that destroy bacteria.

DiSalle, Michael V. (1908-Sept. 5), Democratic governor of Ohio from 1959 to 1963.

Dominick, Peter H. (1915-March 18), Republican senator from Colorado from 1962 to 1974 and congressman from 1960 to 1962.

Doubrovska, Felia (Felizata Dluzhnevska) (1896-Sept. 18), Russian-born ballerina who danced with Sergei Diaghilev's Les Ballets Russes.

Natalie Wood, gifted
Hollywood actress.

Melvyn Douglas, a popular
Hollywood star since the 1920s.

Frank E. Fitzsimmons,
Teamsters president.

Moshe Dayan, Israeli military
hero and political leader.

*Douglas, Donald W., Jr. (1892-Feb. 1), aeronautical engineer and founder of the Douglas Company, now part of the McDonnell Douglas Corporation. His development of the DC-3 in 1936 brought mass airline travel to the world.

Douglas, Melvyn (Melvyn Edouard Hesselberg) (1901-Aug. 4), debonair film actor of the 1920s and 1930s who developed into a forceful character actor, winning Oscars for best supporting actor in *Hud* (1963) and *Being There* (1979).

Durant, Ariel (1898-Oct. 28), Russian-born writer who collaborated with her husband, Will Durant, on the 11-volume *The Story of Civilization*.

*Durant, Will (William James) (1885-Nov. 7), historian and philosopher who won the Pulitzer Prize for nonfiction in 1968 for *Rousseau and Revolution,* part of the 11-volume *The Story of Civilization.*

Eberly, Bob (1916-Nov. 17), singer with the Dorsey Brothers Orchestra in the 1930s. His hit recordings included "Tangerine" and "Green Eyes."

Elson, Bob (Robert A.) (1904-March 10), radio announcer, the voice of the Chicago White Sox baseball team for 37 seasons.

Fawzi, Mahmoud (1900-June 12), Egyptian politician, prime minister of Egypt from 1970 to 1972.

*Fitzsimmons, Frank E. (1908-May 6), president of the Teamsters Union since 1971.

Fox, Carol (1926-July 21), opera producer and co-founder of the Lyric Opera of Chicago. She helped to make the Lyric Opera one of North America's finest.

Fox, Terry (1959-June 28), Canadian college student who ran halfway across Canada to raise money for cancer research after he lost his right leg to cancer.

Fraser, Admiral Bruce Austin (1888-Feb. 12), British naval officer, noted for the sinking of the German battle cruiser *Scharnhorst* off Norway during World War II.

Frederika, Queen (Louise) (1917-Feb. 6), queen of Greece from 1947 to 1964.

Friedhofer, Hugo (1902-May 17), composer who wrote the music for many Hollywood films and won an Oscar for his work in *The Best Years of Our Lives* (1947).

Gance, Abel (1889-Nov. 10), French filmmaker whose *Napoleon* (1927) is still acclaimed by audiences throughout the world.

Gayn, Mark (1909-Dec. 17), Manchurian-born chief writer on foreign affairs for the *Toronto* (Canada) *Star* and long-time contributor of Asian country articles to THE WORLD BOOK YEAR BOOK.

George, Chief Dan (1899-Sept. 23), actor and Indian chief of the Tel-lal-watt section of the Coast Salish tribe of British Columbia. He was best known for his performance in the film *Little Big Man* (1970).

Golden, Harry (1903-Oct. 2), editor and publisher of *The Carolina Israelite* from 1942 to 1968. He fought bigotry with humor. His books include *Only in America* (1958).

Grahame, Gloria (1925-Oct. 5), sultry blonde film actress who won an Oscar in 1952 as best supporting actress for her performance in *The Bad and the Beautiful.*

*Grasso, Ella T. (1919-Feb. 5), governor of Connecticut from 1975 to 1980 and the first woman to be elected governor who did not succeed her husband in office.

*Green, Paul E. (1894-May 4), playwright noted for his folk plays and pageants. His play *In Abraham's Bosom* won a 1927 Pulitzer Prize.

Guion, David W. (1895-Oct. 17), composer who transcribed American folk music into such fiddle tunes as "Turkey in the Straw."

Guyer, Tennyson (1913-Apr. 12), Republican congressman from Ohio since 1972.

Haden, Sara (1897-Sept. 15), Hollywood film actress who played such crabby characters as the spinster Aunt Molly in the Andy Hardy series.

Hagerty, James C. (1909-Apr. 11), journalist, White House press secretary under President Dwight D. Eisenhower from 1953 to 1961.

Haley, Bill (1925-Feb. 9), singer and guitarist whose trail-blazing recording of "Rock Around the Clock" has sold 22.5 million copies since 1955.

Haley, James A. (1899-Aug. 6), Democratic congressman from Florida from 1953 to 1977.

Handler, Philip (1917-Dec. 29), president of the National Academy of Sciences for 12 years.

*Hanson, Howard H. (1896-Feb. 26), composer and conductor, director of the Eastman School of Music in Rochester, N.Y., from 1924 to 1964.

Harburg, Edgar Y. (Yip) (1896-March 5), lyricist whose songs included "Over the Rainbow," "April in Paris," and "Brother Can You Spare a Dime?"

Harding, Ann (1901-Sept. 1), stage and film actress who played beautiful, aristocratic women in such films as *The Condemned* (1929) with Ronald Colman.

Hayden, Russell (Lucky) (1912-June 19), actor who starred in many Westerns.

Hays, Brooks (1898-Oct. 12), Democratic congressman from Arkansas from 1942 to 1958.

Hays, Lee (1914-Aug. 26), bass singer with the Weavers, a quartet that helped to start the folk-singing boom of the 1950s.

Head, Edith (1907-Oct. 24), doyenne of motion-picture costume designers. She won eight Academy Awards.

Hendrix, Wanda (1928-Feb. 1), Hollywood actress who made some 20 films in the 1940s and 1950s, including *Confidential Agent* (1945) and *The Prince of Foxes* (1949).

Farewell to the Brown Bomber

Joe Louis (1914-1981)

The record books show that Joe Louis held the world heavyweight boxing championship longer than anyone else – 11 years and 8 months. They also show that Louis made more title defenses than any other heavyweight, that he retired while he was still the champion, and that he failed in two comeback attempts.

But no collection of facts and figures can show Joe Louis' impact in lessening racial tensions in the United States during the 1930s and 1940s. The son of a poor black sharecropper, the Brown Bomber – as he was known – provided the nation's financially deprived black community with the kind of hero that white people could also appreciate. James J. Walker, the flamboyant mayor of New York City, expressed the feelings of many Americans by telling him, "Joe Louis, you laid a rose on Abraham Lincoln's grave." When he died on April 12, 1981, Louis was mourned as few athletes before him.

Joe Louis was born Joseph Louis Barrow in 1914 in Alabama. He was raised in a shack without electricity or indoor plumbing, and his education ended in sixth grade.

As a teen-ager, Joe moved with his family to Detroit, where he entered a vocational school. He took up boxing at a classmate's urging, won a national amateur championship in 1934, and then turned professional.

Louis earned $52 for his first professional fight, $54 for his second. He became heavyweight champion in 1937 and eventually earned $4.6 million in the ring, but he saved none of his winnings. He gave money freely to friends and would-be friends and spent a lot on good times.

In 1942, during World War II, Louis gave his purse from one fight to the Navy Relief Fund and the purse from his next fight to the Army Relief Fund. He joined the U.S. Army later that year. In three years as a soldier, he staged 96 boxing exhibitions for American troops.

Louis announced his retirement from boxing in 1949. But he soon returned to the ring because he needed money. He tried to regain the heavyweight title from Ezzard Charles in 1950, but was beaten in 15 rounds. A final comeback bid ended in 1951, when Rocky Marciano knocked him out.

From the mid-1950s to the mid-1960s, the federal government hounded Louis for $1.25 million in back taxes and penalties. To the distress of his fans, he refereed wrestling matches and worked at other small-time jobs to pay his debts.

Louis' speed and power in the ring helped make him one of the all-time great heavyweights. James J. Braddock, from whom he won the title, described Louis' ability this way: "The first jab he nails you, you know what it's like. It's like someone jammed an electric bulb in your face and busted it."

Louis was the first black heavyweight champion since Jack Johnson, who reigned from 1908 to 1915 and who had infuriated whites. In the 1930s, much of white America still was not ready for a black boxing hero. But Louis tempered the animosity of whites with simple dignity. Jackie Robinson, who in 1947 became the first black player in major-league baseball, said Louis had paved the way for his acceptance.

Black Americans venerated Louis as a demigod. "He gave inspiration to downtrodden and despised people," wrote Chester Higgins in *Ebony* magazine. "When Joe Louis fought, blacks in ghettos across the land were indoors glued to their radios, and when Louis won, as he nearly always did, they hit the streets whooping and hollering in celebration. For Joe's victory was their victory, a means of striking back at an oppressive and hateful environment. Louis was the black Atlas on whose broad shoulders blacks were lifted, for in those days there were few authentic black heroes."

Louis became an authentic hero. He visited President Franklin D. Roosevelt in the White House. He paid his sister's way through Howard University, his proudest achievement. An arena in Detroit was named for him. At the request of President Ronald Reagan, Joe Louis was buried with other American heroes in Arlington National Cemetery in Arlington, Va.   Frank Litsky

Will and Ariel
Durant, historians.

William Saroyan, a noted
novelist and playwright.

Jim Davis, actor who
played in "Dallas."

Harry Chapin, a popular
songwriter and composer.

Hirsch, Joseph (1910-Sept. 21), artist noted for bold realistic paintings that often depicted social injustice and corruption.

Hirshhorn, Joseph H. (1899-Aug. 31), Latvian-born financier and art collector who founded the Hirshhorn Museum and Sculpture Garden in Washington, D.C.

Hite, Robert (1943-April 6), lead singer of the rock group Canned Heat.

Holden, William F. (1918-Nov. 16), film actor whose 40-year career included starring roles in such films as *Golden Boy* (1939) and *Sunset Boulevard* (1950). He won an Oscar in 1953 for his performance in *Stalag 17*.

Hollowood, Bernard (1910-March 28), British economist and journalist who was editor of the humor magazine *Punch* from 1957 to 1968.

Hulme, Kathryn C. (1900-Aug. 25), author of the bestselling *The Nun's Story* (1956).

Humes, Helen (1913-Sept. 13), singer of ballads and blues with Count Basie's band.

Ilg, Frances L. (1902-July 6), pediatrician, cofounder of the Gesell Institute of Human Development in New Haven, Conn.

Ireney, Metropolitan (1892-March 18), primate of the Orthodox Church in America from 1965 to 1977.

Jessel, George (1898-May 24), comedian who started in vaudeville and became known as the "toastmaster-general of the United States."

Johnson, Pamela Hansford (1912-June 18), British novelist and biographer, widow of the novelist C. P. Snow. Her most recent novel was *The Firebird* (1981).

Joslyn, Allyn M. (1901-Jan. 21), actor of stage, radio, and film who appeared in such films as *Heaven Can Wait* (1943) and *Titanic* (1953).

Kelly, Patsy (Sarah Veronica Rose) (1910-Sept. 24), character actress and comedian who played in dozens of knockabout comedies in the 1930s and 1940s.

Kieran, John (1892-Dec. 10), *New York Times* sports columnist and a regular on radio and TV's "Information Please."

Knight, John S. (1894-June 16), founder of the Knight newspaper-publishing empire. His column, "The Editor's Notebook," won a 1968 Pulitzer Prize.

Koehler, Don A. (1925-Feb. 25), listed in the *Guinness Book of Records* as the world's tallest man at 8 feet 2 inches (249 centimeters). He weighed 300 pounds (136 kilograms) and wore a size 22 shoe.

Kondrashin, Kiril (1914-March 7), Russian conductor who directed the Moscow Philharmonic from 1960 to 1978, when he defected to the West.

*Krebs, Sir Hans Adolf (1900-Nov. 22), German-born biochemist who won the Nobel Prize in Physiology or Medicine in 1953.

Lane, Lola (Dorothy Mulligan) (1906-June 22), actress who appeared in 38 Hollywood films. She co-starred with two of her sisters, Rosemary and Priscilla, in *Four Daughters* (1938), *Four Wives* (1939), and *Four Mothers* (1941).

Lasker, Edward (1885-March 23), German-born engineer who was a five-time winner of the United States Open Chess Championship.

Lee, Bernard (1908-Jan. 16), British actor best known for his role as the spy chief M in 12 James Bond films.

Lenya, Lotte (Karoline Blamauer) (1900-Nov. 27), German-born actress and singer acclaimed for her performance as Jenny in *The Threepenny Opera*.

Levin, Meyer (1905-July 9), writer, best known for *Compulsion* (1956), based on the 1920s Leopold-Loeb murder case.

Lewis, David (1909-May 23), Polish-born Canadian politician, a founder of the New Democratic Party and an eloquent champion of social change.

Lidell, Alvar (1908-Jan. 7), British Broadcasting Corporation announcer from 1932 to 1969, noted for his measured tones and impeccable delivery of the news.

Liebman, Max (1902-July 21), Austrian-born television producer who brought the glitter of Broadway musicals to the TV screen in "Your Show of Shows."

Lilienthal, David E. (1899-Jan. 15), chairman of the Tennessee Valley Authority from 1933 to 1946 and of the Atomic Energy Commission from 1946 to 1950.

Lindsay, Margaret (1910-May 8), Hollywood actress who played in 88 films in 30 years.

Lindstrom, Fred (1905-Oct. 4), baseball player, third baseman and outfielder with the New York Giants and a member of baseball's Hall of Fame (1976).

*Link, Edwin A. (1904-Sept. 7), inventor who developed the Link flight simulator in 1929 – a mechanical trainer to train pilots in instrument flying.

*Loeb, William (1905-Sept. 13), publisher of New Hampshire's *Manchester Union Leader* and *New Hampshire Sunday News*.

Loos, Anita (1888-Aug. 18), playwright and novelist best known for *Gentlemen Prefer Blondes* (1925), which became an American classic.

*Louis, Joe (Joseph Louis Barrow) (1914-April 12), boxer who held the heavyweight boxing championship of the world longer than any other man – from 1937 to 1949 (see Close-Up).

Ludden, Allen E. (1917-June 9), host of the TV game shows "GE College Bowl" and "Password."

Lynch, David (1929-Jan. 2), singer with the original Platters rhythm and blues group in the 1950s.

Markey, Enid (1890?-Nov. 15), actress who created the role of Jane in the first Tarzan movie in 1918.

Marley, Bob (1945-May 11), Jamaican musician, best-known and most influential star of reggae music, and leader of The Wailers group.

Martin, Ross (1920-July 3), Polish-born actor best known for his role as Artemus Gordon in the TV series "The Wild, Wild West."

Matthews, Anne E. (1899-Jan. 29), actress who played Stella Dallas on the radio serial of that name from 1939 to 1955.

McHugh, Frank (1898-Sept. 11), actor known for his supporting roles in such films as *Dodge City* (1939), *The Fighting 69th* (1940), and *The Last Hurrah* (1958).

Montale, Eugenio (1896-Sept. 12), Italian poet who won the 1975 Nobel Prize for Literature in spite of his modest output of five books in 50 years.

Montgomery, Robert (1904-Sept. 27), film actor, director, and producer who starred in more than 60 films, including *Night Must Fall* (1937).

Moses, Robert (1888-July 29), politician who changed the skyline of New York City in 44 years of public service and influenced many city planners.

Nissim, Yitzhak (1896-Aug. 9), Iraqi-born former chief rabbi of Israel.

Northrop, John K. (1895-Feb. 18), aeronautical engineer who founded the Northrop Corporation. His pioneering designs included the original Lockheed Vega and the World War II P-61, known as the *Black Widow*.

O'Connell, Arthur (1908-May 18), actor of stage and screen, acclaimed for his performance as Howard Evans, the reluctant suitor in the film *Picnic* (1955).

Oldfield, Sir Maurice (1915-March 10), former chief of Great Britain's Secret Service network. He was believed to be the inspiration for George Smiley in John Le Carré's spy novels and for M in Ian Fleming's James Bond books.

Padover, Saul K. (1905-Feb. 22), Austrian-born political scientist who wrote more than 30 books, many of them on Thomas Jefferson and Karl Marx.

Piccard, Jeannette R. (1895-May 17), high-altitude balloonist and one of the first American women to become an Episcopal priest.

***Ponselle, Rosa M.** (1897-May 25), dramatic soprano, noted for her richness of tone. She sang with the Metropolitan Opera from 1918 to 1936.

Popov, Dusko (1912-Aug. 21), Yugoslav-born double agent for Great Britain during World War II, thought by many to be the model for Ian Fleming's fictional spy James Bond.

Powell, Wesley (1915-Jan. 6), Republican governor of New Hampshire from 1959 to 1963.

Presser, William (1907-July 18), a leader of the Teamsters Union for more than 50 years.

Procope, Russell (1908-Jan. 21), clarinetist and saxophonist, a star soloist with Duke Ellington's orchestra.

Raymond, James C. (1917-Oct. 14), artist who worked on the "Blondie" comic strip for 40 years.

Richter, Karl (1926-Feb. 16), German conductor and organist.

Roldos Aguilera, Jaime (1940-May 24), president of Ecuador since 1979.

Roosevelt, John A. (1916-April 27), banker, youngest son of President Franklin D. Roosevelt.

***Roszak, Theodore** (1907-Sept. 3), Polish-born sculptor, known for his welded steel sculptures of savage birds and animals.

Russell of Liverpool, Lord (Edward F. L. Russell) (1895-April 10), British military jurist best known for his controversial book about Nazi war crimes — *The Scourge of the Swastika* (1954).

***Sadat, Anwar el-** (1918-Oct. 6), president and prime minister of Egypt. See MIDDLE EAST (Close-Up).

***Saroyan, William** (1908-May 18), writer and playwright. He won and rejected the Pulitzer Prize in 1939 for his play *The Time of Your Life*.

Sauter, Edward (Eddie) (1914-April 21), jazz composer, trumpet player, and arranger.

Sharp, Zerna (1889-June 17), teacher who created the concept of Dick and Jane reading textbooks.

***Soong Ching-ling (Madame Sun Yat-sen)** (1890-May 29), Chinese Communist leader; widow of Sun Yat-sen.

Soupart, Pierre (1923-June 10), Belgian-born biochemist and gynecologist, the first researcher to publish evidence of successful human fertilization in the laboratory.

Speer, Albert (1905-Sept. 1), Nazi architect and administrator who directed war production and forced labor for Adolf Hitler during World War II. He served 20 years in West Berlin's Spandau Prison.

Taurog, Norman (1899-April 8), film director who won an Oscar in 1930 for *Skippy,* starring Jackie Cooper.

Teague, Olin E. (1910-Jan. 23), Democratic congressman from Texas from 1946 to 1977.

Thatcher, Torin (1905-March 4), Indian-born British actor of stage and screen whose 70 movies included *Major Barbara* (1941) and *Great Expectations* (1946).

***Thomas, Lowell** (1892-Aug. 29), news commentator, globe-trotter, and author of many books. He gave radio listeners a folksy digest of the day's news for 46 years.

Torrijos Herrera, Omar (1929-Aug. 1), head of Panama's government from 1968 to 1978.

Trippe, Juan T. (1890-April 3), pioneer in international air travel and founder of Pan American World Airways.

***Urey, Harold C.** (1893-Jan. 5), winner of the 1934 Nobel Prize for Chemistry for his discovery of *deuterium* (heavy hydrogen).

General Omar N. Bradley, an Army leader in World War II.

DeWitt Wallace, a noted publisher.

William Holden, popular actor and long-time Hollywood star.

Bob Marley, leading star of reggae music.

Lowell Thomas, a noted commentator.

Barbara Ward, a brilliant economist.

Terry Fox, courageous marathon runner.

Stefan Cardinal Wyszyński, Catholic primate of Poland.

Vanderbilt, William H. (1901-April 14), Republican governor of Rhode Island from 1938 to 1940.

Vera-Ellen (Vera-Ellen Rohe) (1926-Aug. 1), dancer in such Hollywood musicals as *Words and Music* (1948) with Gene Kelly, *Three Little Words* (1950) with Fred Astaire, and *White Christmas* (1954).

Vinson, Carl (1883-June 1), Democratic congressman from Georgia from 1914 to 1964, the longest-serving congressman on record.

Von Zell, Harry (1906-Nov. 21), radio announcer and comic actor, best known for his work in the "Burns and Allen" radio and TV shows.

Walker, Mickey (1901-April 28), boxer who won the world welterweight boxing title in 1922 and the world middleweight boxing title in 1926.

Wallace, DeWitt (1889-March 30), publisher who founded *The Reader's Digest* magazine in 1922.

Walsh, Bishop James E. (1891-July 29), Roman Catholic priest and missionary who spent 12 years in a Chinese prison on charges of spying and subversion.

Walsh, Raoul (1887-Jan. 3), motion-picture director for nearly 50 years. His films included *Sadie Thompson* (1928) and *High Sierra* (1941).

Wangensteen, Owen (1898-Jan. 13), surgeon who helped develop open-heart surgery.

*__Ward, Barbara (Baroness Jackson of Lodsworth)__ (1914-May 31), British economist who promoted social justice and the needs of developing countries.

Warren, Harry (Salvatore Guaragna) (1893-Sept. 22), composer of more than 300 songs including "I Only Have Eyes for You," "Shuffle Off to Buffalo," and "Chattanooga Choo Choo."

*__Waugh, Alec__ (1898-Sept. 3), British novelist and travel writer, best known for *Island in the Sun* (1955).

*__Wilkins, Roy__ (1901-Sept. 8), secretary of the National Association for the Advancement of Colored People from 1955 to 1977, often called "Mr. Civil Rights."

Williams, Eric E. (1911-March 29), prime minister of Trinidad and Tobago since 1962.

Williams, Mary Lou (1910-May 28), composer, pianist, first woman to be ranked with the greatest of the jazz musicians.

Wood, Natalie (Natasha Gurdin) (1938-Nov. 29), Hollywood film actress who began her career when she was a child, notably in *Miracle on 34th Street* (1947), and went on to starring roles in such films as *West Side Story* (1961) and *Gypsy* (1962).

Wurf, Jerry (Jerome) (1919-Dec. 10), president of the American Federation of State, County, and Municipal Employees.

*__Wyler, William__ (1902-July 27), French-born film director whose many films included the Oscar winners *Mrs. Miniver* (1942), *The Best Years of Our Lives* (1946), and *Ben-Hur* (1959).

*__Wyszyński, Stefan Cardinal__ (1910-May 28), Roman Catholic primate of Poland since 1948, a strong defender of the Roman Catholic Church.

*__Yukawa, Hideki__ (1907-Sept. 8), Japanese physicist, noted for his contributions to theoretical nuclear physics, including his prediction in 1935 of the existence of the *meson*, an atomic particle.

Ziaur Rahman (1936-May 30), president of Bangladesh, who assumed power by coup in 1975 and named himself president in 1977.   Irene B. Keller

DELAWARE. See STATE GOVERNMENT.

DEMOCRATIC PARTY leaders in 1981 tried to develop a strategy that would enable their party to recover from its resounding defeat in the 1980 general election. In that election, Democrats lost the White House to Ronald Reagan and saw Republicans take control of the United States Senate. The Democratic Party's immediate goals were to preserve its majority in the House of Representatives and to regain control of the Senate in the 1982 elections.

The Democratic National Committee (DNC), meeting in Washington, D.C., on February 27, elected Los Angeles lawyer Charles T. Manatt as its new chairman. In his address to the meeting, Manatt said that the Democrats had been "out-conceptualized, out-organized, out-televised, out-coordinated, out-financed, and out-worked" by the Republicans. He asserted that the DNC needed closer ties to state and local parties and a bigger campaign chest to overcome the Republican advantage. Manatt also called upon the DNC to expand its direct-mail solicitations for funds. He hoped to raise between $6 million and $8 million in 1981. The DNC owed approximately $740,000 in campaign debts.

The February meeting was marked by controversy over the selection of members to serve at-large on the 371-member DNC. Manatt, who was elected with strong labor backing, allocated 15 of the committee's 25 at-large seats to members of the American Federation of Labor and Congress of Industrial Organizations (AFL-CIO). He drew complaints from black and Hispanic groups, who claimed that they were underrepresented.

Leading Democrats met again on October 16 and 17 in Baltimore to map out a comeback program. Although the U.S. economy had slipped into recession by then, the Democrats generally agreed not to count on the failure of President Reagan's economic program to provide them with a winning issue in 1982. Several speakers urged Democrats to unite behind a more positive approach, one advocating alternatives to Reagan's programs. Former Vice-President Walter F. Mondale and Senator Edward M. Kennedy of Massachusetts – both possible candidates for the Democratic presidential nomination in 1984 – took part in the session.

Election Results in a few off-year contests were not particularly decisive in most cases. The most notable Democratic victory of 1981 came on November 3 in Virginia, where Lieutenant Governor Charles S. Robb defeated state Attorney General J. Marshall Coleman and so ended 12 years of Republican control of the state house. Robb put together a coalition of old-line Democrats, blacks, and union members, which helped him to win by more than 100,000 votes. Robb is a son-in-law of President Lyndon B. Johnson, who inaugurated massive federal spending programs. Nevertheless, Robb endorsed President Reagan's proposed cuts in the federal budget.

Democrats lost in New Jersey, however, in the only other gubernatorial election of 1981. Republican candidate Thomas H. Kean claimed victory on November 3, after a canvass showed him with a lead of 1,677 votes out of more than 2 million cast. Kean's victory margin held up in a November 30 recount. The Democratic candidate, Representative James J. Florio, campaigned on his opposition to Reagan's economic policies. Kean – a former speaker of the New Jersey Assembly – cautiously embraced the President's program. The Republican National Committee spent more than $1 million on Kean's behalf – over 10 times as much as the DNC provided for Florio.

The Democrats picked up one House seat in a series of congressional elections. Democrat Wayne Dowdy upset the favored GOP candidate, Liles B. Williams, to capture the Mississippi seat vacated by Republican Jon Hinson, who resigned from Congress after his arrest on morals charges. In a heavily Republican Ohio district, Republican Michael Oxley narrowly defeated Democrat Dale Locker. A former Democratic state senator, Steny Hoyer, overcame a major Republican campaign effort and defeated Audrey Scott, the mayor of Bowie, Md., in the congressional district formerly represented by Democrat Gladys N. Spellman,

Los Angeles lawyer Charles T. Manatt addresses the Democratic National Committee after his election as national party chairman in February.

whose seat was declared vacant because of her disabling illness.

Democrat Joseph F. Smith, elected as an independent with Republican backing over organization Democrat David B. Glancey in Pennsylvania, joined the Democratic caucus in the House. He replaced Democrat Raymond F. Lederer, who resigned after he was convicted of bribery in the Abscam scandal. Conservative Republican Mark Siljander kept the Michigan seat vacated by David A. Stockman, who left Congress to become director of the United States Office of Management and Budget.

Other Losses. In a rare political development, two Democratic members of Congress announced they would run as Republicans in the future. On September 24, Representative Bob Stump of Arizona disclosed his change in party affiliation. Representative Eugene V. Atkinson of Pennsylvania did so at a White House ceremony on October 14.

The Democratic Party was also faced with the prospect of lost congressional seats from redistricting according to the results of the 1980 census. Most of the states gaining seats are in the traditionally conservative South and Southwest; those losing seats are in traditionally Democratic areas in the Northeast and Midwest.   William J. Eaton

See also ELECTIONS. In WORLD BOOK, see DEMOCRATIC PARTY.

DE NIRO, ROBERT (1943-   ), received the Academy of Motion Picture Arts and Sciences Award for best actor on March 31, 1981. He won the Oscar for his performance in *Raging Bull,* the story of boxer Jake LaMotta, who used his aggression and his ability to withstand pain in the ring as a means of dealing with his anxieties outside it. De Niro had twice before been nominated for the award, for his roles in *Taxi Driver* (1976) and *The Deer Hunter* (1978). He won the 1974 Academy Award for best supporting actor for playing the young Vito Corleone in *The Godfather, Part II.*

Robert De Niro was born to artist parents on Aug. 17, 1943, in New York City. He studied acting in his early teens. At the age of 16, he began to study acting with Stella Adler and appeared in off-Broadway and workshop productions.

His first major film role was in the satire *Greetings* in 1968. In 1970, De Niro appeared with Shelley Winters in *Bloody Mama.* He played a demoralized Vietnam War veteran in *Hi, Mom!* in 1970, appeared in *Born to Win* and *The Gang That Couldn't Shoot Straight* in 1971, and then returned briefly to the stage.

De Niro first drew critical acclaim for his role as a dying baseball player in *Bang the Drum Slowly* (1973). He won the New York Film Critics Circle's Best Supporting Actor Award for his role in the 1973 film *Mean Streets.*   Jay Myers

DENMARK. Prime Minister Anker Henrik Jorgensen's Social Democratic minority government fell on Nov. 12, 1981, when the *Folketing* (parliament) rejected its plan to create jobs. Denmark's unemployment was expected to reach 250,000, or 9 per cent of the work force, by the end of 1981.

Jorgensen's plan called for managers of pension funds to cash in high-interest but nonproductive government bonds and then to place the money in so-called active investments. These investments were supposed to create 50,000 jobs per year.

The defeated prime minister scheduled parliamentary elections for December 8. The Social Democrats lost heavily in the elections, and Jorgensen resigned. Jorgensen then formed a minority coalition government with the small Radical Liberal Party, and his new Cabinet was sworn in on December 30.

Depressed Economy. Denmark's worst depression since the 1930s continued in 1981, even though the Danes enjoyed the highest standard of living in the European Community (EC or Common Market). Danish farmers faced their worst crisis in 30 years because of high inflation, high interest rates, heavy taxes, spiraling costs, and increased competition from other EC countries. Denmark exports two-thirds of its farm products. These products make up about 30 per cent of the country's exports.

On October 4, the value of the krone, Denmark's unit of money, changed within the European Monetary System, a program that eight nations set up in 1979 to stabilize the relative values of their currencies. The Netherlands and West Germany increased the values of their currencies by 5.5 per cent relative to those of Denmark, Belgium, Ireland, and Luxembourg, while France and Italy lowered theirs 3 per cent.

Defense Debate. On August 13, Denmark ended a debate on defense spending that had lasted more than a year. On that date, the government and four centrist and rightist parties agreed to increase defense spending by about $20 million per year for three years. This amounts to an annual increase of 2 per cent after adjusting for inflation.

The Social Democrats had proposed to freeze spending until 1985, except for increases to keep pace with inflation. However, the Liberals and Conservatives claimed that a freeze would seriously weaken Denmark's defenses. When the government offered a 1 per cent annual increase, opponents pointed out that Denmark, as a member of the North Atlantic Treaty Organization (NATO), was committed to a 3 per cent hike in *real* spending, after inflation. Denmark's armed forces had demanded a 5 per cent increase.   Kenneth Brown

See also EUROPE (Facts in Brief Table). In WORLD BOOK, see DENMARK.

DENTISTRY. The 52 Americans held hostage in Iran did not suffer serious dental problems during their captivity, according to three U.S. Air Force dentists who examined them upon their release in January 1981. More than half of the hostages had needed some dental treatment at the beginning of their ordeal, but they managed to maintain their oral health at a reasonably acceptable level. Many of the hostages practiced oral hygiene almost compulsively during captivity, brushing their teeth as often as six times a day. When supplies of American toothpaste gave out, the hostages were given an Iranian toothpaste they considered foul tasting.

Other dental supplies were not replenished, however. The hostages used twigs and chicken bones to replace worn toothbrushes. When their dental floss ran out, they cleaned their teeth and gums with nylon strands from the ropes used to bind their hands and feet, with wool fibers pulled from blankets, or with cellophane strips from cigarette packages.

The Canker Sore Connection. Scientists have found that canker sores, painful ulcers in the mouth, may be related to a person's genetic make-up. David Wray of the National Institute of Dental Research in Bethesda, Md., reported in March that there may be a connection between canker sores and molecules called human leucocyte antigens (HLA), which identify all body cells as be-

British children learn how to avoid "black holes" in their teeth in the "Solar Molar Module," a space age dental hygiene laboratory.

DETROIT, with its economy buffeted by high unemployment and slumping automobile sales in 1981, suffered through its worst fiscal crisis since the 1930s. It regained its financial balance, however, when Mayor Coleman A. Young successfully carried out a complex and controversial bailout plan.

The City's Fiscal Woes were directly linked to declining sales of American automobiles, upon which the city's economy is heavily dependent. Sales of U.S.-built cars in 1981 totaled about 6.2 million, down 5.6 per cent from 1980, but about 20 per cent less than in 1979 – the industry's last healthy year. The number of auto workers laid off indefinitely fluctuated between 168,000 and 197,000 throughout 1981, and the city's unemployment rate hovered around 14 per cent – nearly double the national average.

On January 29, Young, acknowledging that the city's financial problems were out of control, formed a special panel of business executives, bankers, labor union representatives, and other civic leaders to advise him on the crisis. On February 11, Detroit officials announced that the city's projected deficit for the fiscal year that began on July 1, 1980, was $135 million, the largest in Detroit's history, and that the deficit for fiscal 1982 was projected at $147 million.

On April 13, Young unveiled his rescue plan, which took the recommendations of the advisory panel into account. Young proposed several measures to liquidate the deficit – a 1 per cent increase in the city's income tax on all people employed or living in the city, wage concessions by 20,000 city employees, and the sale of more than $100 million in bonds. He predicted massive layoffs of city workers, wholesale cuts in services, and eventual bankruptcy if his plan was not approved.

In late May, the Michigan legislature narrowly authorized the income tax hike, on condition that it win voters' approval and that bond sales and wage cuts also be instituted. In a special election on June 23, 64 per cent of Detroit voters approved the tax increase. Throughout July and August, the city negotiated agreements for a two-year wage freeze with 55 municipal unions, frequently threatening large-scale layoffs if the freeze were rejected. On August 13, two city pension systems and a consortium of seven local banks agreed to buy $113-million in municipal bonds. That day, the Michigan State Administrative Board, which was charged with reviewing the city's finances, declared Detroit's budget to be balanced and allowed the income tax hike, making it retroactive to July 1, 1981, the start of the current fiscal year.

Elections. The solution of the fiscal crisis robbed Detroit's municipal election of its most compelling issue. None of the city's major politicians chose to challenge Young, and he was easily re-elected to a third 4-year term on November 3.

longing to a certain individual. At least 32 types of HLA molecules have been discovered, and the cells of each person carry eight different types.

In studying the families of 50 patients with canker sores, Wray found that the disease often occurred in two successive generations of a family, and that canker sore sufferers had a higher incidence of two particular HLA types. Family inheritance patterns suggested that a recessive gene linked to the two HLA types may also be responsible for the development of canker sores. If the gene is recessive, only people who inherit two copies of it – one from each parent – will be afflicted with canker sores.

Diabetes and Gum Disease. Insulin-dependent juvenile diabetics stand a greater than normal chance of developing advanced gum disease after reaching puberty, according to dental scientists at the State University of New York in Buffalo. This susceptibility may be due to hormonal changes that make it more difficult to control diabetes during puberty and therefore lower the patient's resistance to infections, including gum disease. The researchers recommended that routine dental checkups of juvenile diabetics include examination for gum disease, which, if untreated, can result in serious jawbone damage and subsequent tooth loss.

Lou Joseph

In WORLD BOOK, see DENTISTRY.

In an election held the same day, voters in Wayne County, which includes Detroit, approved a new charter aimed at streamlining the county's debt-ridden government. The charter, effective Jan. 1, 1983, provides for an elected county executive, reduces the size of the county's legislative body, and eliminates its board of auditors.

Transit Plans. A plan to build a 10-mile (16-kilometer) rapid-transit line and a 2.9-mile (4.7-kilometer) downtown people-mover system, financed primarily with federal funds, was jeopardized when the Administration of President Ronald Reagan proposed large cutbacks in federal funding for transportation projects. Funds for the people mover were restored to the 1982 federal budget, allowing the project to proceed. But the status of the more costly and controversial rapid-transit line remained in doubt.

Despite Protests from local residents, the city cleared a 450-acre (180-hectare) site in a residential neighborhood on its east side and turned it over to General Motors Corporation on May 1 for construction of an automobile-assembly plant. A total of 3,438 residents, 150 businesses, and 16 churches were uprooted by the project. The $500-million plant, scheduled to open in 1984, will employ 3,000 to 6,000 workers and will replace two older plants on the city's west side.   Ken Fireman

See also CITY. In WORLD BOOK, see DETROIT.

DIANA, PRINCESS OF WALES (1961-   ). Lady Diana Spencer married Charles, Prince of Wales and heir to the British throne, on July 29, 1981. She has no official powers or duties as the Princess of Wales, but she acquired the following titles and accompanying privileges by her marriage: Princess of Wales and Countess of Chester, Duchess of Cornwall, Duchess of Rothesay, Countess of Carrick, and Baroness of Renfrew. She is the first Englishwoman to marry an heir to the throne in more than 300 years. On November 5, Buckingham Palace announced that Diana was expecting a baby in June 1982.

Lady Diana Frances Spencer was born on July 1, 1961, at Park House in Sandringham, on the royal estate of Queen Elizabeth II. She was educated at West Heath School in Kent and at a finishing school in Switzerland. Lady Diana taught at a kindergarten in London from 1979 until she became engaged in February 1981.

Diana comes from a wealthy family that traces its ancestry to King James I and King Charles II. Diana's parents were divorced in 1969, and both remarried. Her father is the eighth Earl Spencer. Her mother, Frances Roche, the daughter of the fourth Baron Fermoy, is now Mrs. Peter Shand-Kydd.   Sandra Streilein

See also GREAT BRITAIN (Close-Up).

DICTIONARY. See DICTIONARY SUPPLEMENT.

DISASTERS. Two earthquakes rocked strife-ridden Iran in the summer of 1981, adding to that nation's woes. The quakes, which devastated a wide area of Kerman province in southeastern Iran, left 2,500 people dead and more than twice that number injured.

In the United States, a freak accident claimed the lives of 113 people when concrete walkways above the lobby of the Hyatt Regency Hotel in Kansas City, Mo., collapsed during a tea dance. Victims included spectators observing the festivities from the walkways as well as dancers on the floor below.

Disasters that resulted in 10 or more deaths in 1981 included the following:

Aircraft Crashes

Feb. 7 – Leningrad, Russia. As many as 70 Soviet military officers, including three top commanders of Russia's Pacific fleet, died in a plane crash on the outskirts of the city.

Feb. 26 – Subic Bay Naval Base, the Philippines. A U.S. Air Force C-130 plane crashed into the South China Sea, killing 23 of 24 American, Philippine, Australian, and New Zealand military personnel aboard.

March 2 – Near Al Qasr, Egypt. Egypt's Defense Minister Ahmed Badowi Hilal and 13 others were killed when their helicopter crashed during military exercises.

April 17 – Near Loveland, Colo. A twin-engine commuter airliner and a small private craft carrying sky divers collided, killing 15 people.

May 6 – Walkersville, Md. All 21 crew members aboard a U.S. Air Force C135-A jet died when the plane exploded over a farm.

May 26 – Off Jacksonville, Fla. A U.S. Marine Corps EA-6B electronic combat jet crashed on the deck of the aircraft carrier U.S.S. *Nimitz,* killing 14 men, destroying 3 fighter planes, and damaging 16 other planes.

July 21 – Mogadiscio, Somalia. A Somali Airlines passenger plane crashed within minutes after take-off, killing all 49 people aboard.

July 28 – Chihuahua, Mexico. Thirty-two people were killed and 36 injured when an Aeromexico DC-9 crashed and burst into flames while landing in heavy wind and rain.

Aug. 23 – Taipei, Taiwan. A Taiwanese jetliner crashed, killing 110 persons in the worst air disaster in Taiwan's history.

Sept. 22 – Near Babaeski, Turkey. A Turkish air force combat jet crashed in a bivouac area while practicing a diving run, killing 26 people.

Oct. 6 – Near Rotterdam, the Netherlands. Fierce winds ripped off the wing of a Dutch Fokker F-28 Fellowship passenger plane and caused it to crash, killing all 17 people on board.

Nov. 8 – Near Altamirano, Mexico. All 18 people aboard a Mexican DC-10 died when the jet crashed on a mountain slope.

Dec. 1 – Near Ajaccio, Corsica. A Yugoslav DC-9 got lost in fog and crashed into a mountain peak, killing all 178 people on board.

Dec. 5 – Pearl Harbor Naval Base, Hawaii. A twin-engine Beechcraft airplane carrying sky divers to a jump at a football game plunged into Pearl Harbor, killing 11 of 12 people on board.

Bus and Truck Crashes

Feb. 18 – Quantico, Va. A commuter bus crashed through guardrails and hurtled down a steep embankment, killing at least 10 passengers.

Fourteen crew members were killed and 43 injured when a jet crashed on the deck of the United States Navy aircraft carrier *Nimitz* on the night of May 26.

April 25 – Culiacán, Mexico. Some 30 people died when a crowded bus traveling from Tijuana to Mexico City crashed into a truck.

May 12 – New Delhi, India. A bus packed with people bound for three separate weddings overturned and caught fire, killing at least 25 people.

July 18 – Bangkok, Thailand. A bus carrying 70 worshipers to a Buddhist temple swerved off the road and plunged into a reservoir, killing 34 passengers.

July 18 – Bulawayo, Zimbabwe. A Zimbabwean Army truck taking schoolchildren to a sports festival crashed, killing 11 children and injuring 61.

Nov. 16 – Near Gaya, India. A bus crashed into a truck and rolled into a brook, killing 13 people.

Nov. 27 – Near San Carlos, Chile. A truck collided with a bus on the Pan American Highway, killing 32 people.

Earthquakes

Jan. 23 – Irian Jaya, Indonesia. An earthquake that destroyed 14 villages in the region claimed the lives of approximately 250 people.

Feb. 24 – Athens, Greece. Fifteen people died in a series of earthquakes that jolted the city, damaging the Parthenon and other historic structures.

June 11 – Kerman Province, Iran. An earthquake that shook southeastern Iran left more than 1,000 people dead.

July 28 – Kerman Province, Iran. Approximately 1,500 people died in the second earthquake to rock the Iranian province in seven weeks.

Sept. 12 – Northern Pakistan. An earthquake that triggered landslides resulted in a death toll of 212 people.

Fires

Jan. 9 – Keansburg, N.J. Thirty people were killed when fire roared through a two-story home for the elderly.

Jan. 17 – London. An all-night birthday party ended with the deaths of 10 celebrants as a blaze swept through a three-story house.

Feb. 7 – Bangalore, India. Fire consumed a circus tent, killing 66 people.

Feb. 14 – Dublin, Ireland. Fire broke out in a crowded discothèque, claiming the lives of 48 people.

March 14 – Chicago. Nineteen people perished as fire swept through a four-story residential hotel on the city's North Side.

Floods

April 25-26 – Caracas, Venezuela. Flooding and mud slides resulting from heavy tropical rains killed 20 people and left 4,000 homeless.

May 25 – Austin, Tex. Flash floods swept through the city, killing 17 people.

July 12-20 – Szechwan (Sichuan) Province, China. Floods in the upper reaches of the Yangtze (Chang Jiang) River left 753 persons dead.

Aug. 19 – Szechwan Province, China. Fifteen people were killed and 100 injured in the second series of floods to strike Szechwan during the summer.

October – Kwangtung (Guangdong) Province, China. Flooding in the Chan-chiang (Zhanjiang) district killed 70 people and left thousands homeless.

Dec. 12-13 – Rio de Janeiro, Brazil. Landslides and floods caused by torrential rains in the state of Rio de Janeiro killed 28 people, raising the death toll from December flooding to 80.

Hurricanes, Tornadoes, and Other Storms

Feb. 9-13 – Northeast United States. Icy rains, heavy snows, and subzero temperatures were responsible for a death toll of 53 people in the winter's worst storm.

April 17 – Bay of Bengal, India. A tornado flattened four villages, killing 120 people.

DISASTERS

July 1 – Philippines. Tropical Storm Kelly lashed through the islands, killing 120 people in floods and mud slides.

Aug. 2-7 – West Indies. Hurricane Allen tore through the Caribbean, killing 272 people.

Aug. 23 – North-Central Japan. Typhoon Thad smashed across the area, unleashing high winds and heavy rains. Fourteen persons died in the storm.

Nov. 2 – Arabian Sea, off India. Approximately 470 people were lost in a hurricane that sank at least 11 fishing boats.

Nov. 18-19 – Midwestern United States. At least 12 people died in a severe storm that blanketed Minnesota and neighboring states with heavy snow.

Nov. 24 – Philippines. Typhoon Irma battered the northern part of the island of Luzon, killing more than 50 people.

Dec. 11 – Eastern India and Bangladesh. A typhoon killed at least 93 people and left 2 million homeless.

Dec. 14-17 – Eastern United States. At least 21 people died in a series of severe storms that dumped up to 9 inches (23 centimeters) of snow on the eastern half of the nation.

Dec. 26 – Philippines. Typhoon Lee swept across the Philippines, killing 50 people and leaving nearly 200,000 homeless.

Mine Disasters

April 15 – Redstone, Colo. A powerful explosion rocked the Dutch Creek No. 1 coal mine, killing 15 workers.

Sept. 3 – Zaluzi, Czechoslovakia. Sixty-five coal miners died in a pit explosion. It was Czechoslovakia's worst mining disaster in 20 years.

Oct. 16 – Yubari, Japan. A series of explosions in a coal mine killed at least 44 people.

Shipwrecks

Jan. 6 – Near Macapá, Brazil. An overloaded ferry over-

A tea dance ended in a shower of glass and steel on July 17 at the Hyatt Regency Hotel in Kansas City, Mo., when walkways collapsed, killing 113.

turned in treacherous waters in a tributary of the Amazon River, drowning 311 people.

Jan. 27 – Java Sea. Approximately 500 people died when the passenger ship *Tamponas II* sank in a storm.

April 8 – Off Costa Rica. Seventeen people drowned when a small British freighter bound for Ecuador sank in the Pacific.

May 8 – Off Bermuda. As many as 25 people died when the Israeli freighter *Mezada* sank.

July 3 – Off Newfoundland. The Canadian survey ship *Arctic Explorer* sank, killing 13 people.

Sept. 19 – Obidos, Brazil. More than 300 people drowned when an Amazon riverboat sank while in port.

Sept. 20 – Philippines. The Philippine Navy destroyer *Datu Kalantlaw* ran aground, killing at least 40 sailors.

Oct. 26 – Off Miami, Fla. Thirty-three emigrating Haitians drowned when their small craft capsized in choppy waters of the Gulf Stream.

Nov. 26 – Off Bermuda. Twenty-two crew members were lost when the West German container ship *Elma Tres* capsized in stormy waters.

Train Wrecks

Feb. 15 – Banaras, India. Fourteen people were killed when a passenger train rammed another after a traveler in the lead train mistakenly pulled an emergency brake cord.

March 8 – Coronel Brandsen, Argentina. A train carrying tourists home from a beach resort collided with two derailed freight cars, killing at least 45 people.

June 6 – Mansi, India. Approximately 400 people aboard an overcrowded passenger train died when seven cars tumbled into the Bagmati River after the train braked suddenly on a bridge.

June 24 – Gagry, Russia. Approximately 70 people were killed when an express and a local train collided near the popular Black Sea resort.

July 31 – Bahawalpur, Pakistan. Six coaches of a passenger train derailed, killing 43 people.

Aug. 2 – Near San Luis Potosí, Mexico. A train carrying hydrochloric acid hurtled off its track and crashed, killing at least 12 people.

Other Disasters

January – Northern India. More than 270 people died during a month-long cold wave that brought heavy snows.

Feb. 8 – Piraeus, Greece. At least 24 soccer fans were trampled to death when a crowd of 40,000 stampeded as they left the stadium.

March 10 – Beni Suef, Egypt. Two neighboring houses collapsed, killing 23 people.

March 22 – Near Belgrade, Yugoslavia. A landslide swept two railroad cars into the Morava River, killing 12 people aboard.

March 27 – Cocoa Beach, Fla. Eleven construction workers died when the five-story building on which they were laboring collapsed.

June 21 – Mount Rainier, Wash. Cascading ice boulders that broke from a glacier buried 10 mountain climbers and their guide.

July 17 – Kansas City, Mo. Two concrete walkways spanning the lobby of the Hyatt Regency Hotel collapsed while a dance was underway, killing 113 people.

Nov. 15 – Mérida, Mexico. Forty-eight people were killed when a wall collapsed at a political rally in a bull ring and caused a panic.

Nov. 19 – Taif, Saudi Arabia. The roof of a building collapsed during a wedding, killing 50 people.

Dec. 4 – New Delhi, India. Forty-five persons, most of them schoolchildren, were killed in a crush of sightseers trying to get down a narrow stairway in an Islamic monument. Beverly Merz

DJIBOUTI. See AFRICA.

DOG. A pug named Champion Dhandy's Favorite Woodchuck was selected best-in-show out of 2,910 dogs at the Westminster Kennel Club show in New York City on Feb. 10, 1981. It was the first time a pug had taken top honors in the Westminster contest, which is the oldest and most highly regarded dog show in the United States.

The pug's owner, Robert A. Hauslohner of Rosemont, Pa., did not follow tradition and retire his dog after it won the Westminster show. Instead, he continued to exhibit Woodchuck. By July 1981, the little dog had won more than 25 other contests.

More than 1 million purebred dogs were registered with the American Kennel Club, the chief organization of U.S. dog breeders, in 1980. Poodles led in number of registrations. Following poodles in order of popularity were Doberman pinschers, cocker spaniels, German shepherds, Labrador retrievers, golden retrievers, beagles, miniature schnauzers, dachshunds, and Shetland sheepdogs. Cocker spaniel registrations rose more than 10,000 since 1979.

Cases of *canine parvovirus*, an illness that killed thousands of dogs in 1980, decreased in 1981. Widespread vaccination and public awareness helped control its spread. Roberta Vesley

In WORLD BOOK, see DOG.

DOMINICAN REPUBLIC. See LATIN AMERICA.

Champion Dhandy's Favorite Woodchuck, a pug, won top honors at the Westminster Kennel Club dog show in New York City in February.

DONOVAN, RAYMOND JAMES (1930-   ), became United States secretary of labor on Feb. 4, 1981. Donovan was vice-president of a New Jersey construction company when President-elect Ronald Reagan nominated him for the Cabinet post on Dec. 16, 1980. His confirmation was delayed by hearings by the Senate Labor and Human Resources Committee into allegations that he had made illegal payments to unions to buy labor peace for his company. The charges were not proved, and the committee sent his nomination to the Senate for confirmation, which came on February 3.

Under Donovan's leadership, the Labor Department began in 1981 to cut support of government-sponsored training and employment programs. The department also began to modify or eliminate various health and safety standards.

Raymond James Donovan was born on Aug. 31, 1930, in Bayonne, N.J. He graduated from Notre Dame Seminary in New Orleans in 1952. In 1959, he joined Schiavone Construction Company in Secaucus, N.J., as a vice-president with responsibilities in finance, management, and labor relations. He became executive vice-president in 1971.

Donovan is married to the former Catherine Sblendorio. They have three children. Sandra Streilein

DROUGHT. See WATER; WEATHER. In the Special Reports section, see THE THREATS TO OUR WATER SUPPLY.

DRUGS. The first major government-sponsored tests of the controversial drug Laetrile concluded in 1981 that the apricot-pit derivative was useless as a cancer treatment. On April 30, researchers from four medical centers in the United States reported "no substantive benefit" from Laetrile in curing cancer, slowing its advance, or relieving its symptoms. Of the 156 patients in the Laetrile trial, supervised by the National Cancer Institute, 50 per cent worsened within a month and 90 per cent after three months. By the ninth month of the study, 102 of the patients had died, and cancer had spread further in 49 of the 54 survivors.

Arthur H. Hayes, Jr., a physician and expert in therapeutic drugs, was appointed director of the Food and Drug Administration (FDA) in April 1981. Hayes pledged to accelerate the FDA's drug-approval process. In August, the FDA approved the artificial sweetener aspartame, ending an eight-year controversy over its safety.

New Drugs. The FDA approved several new therapeutic drugs in 1981. One of these drugs, verapamil, is one of a group of cardiac drugs called calcium-blockers that have been used outside the United States for 10 years. In March, researchers at the University of Texas Health Science Center in Dallas announced that verapamil had proved effective in relieving *angina* (chest pain caused by an inadequate flow of blood to the heart).

Another newly available drug is amoxapine, an antidepressant that relieves biological symptoms of depression, such as fatigue and loss of appetite, within days. Conventional antidepressants may require weeks to take effect.

Zomepirac sodium, another new drug, is a powerful pain reliever that poses no danger of long-term users developing tolerance or addiction. According to a report in the July 24 *Journal of the American Medical Association,* zomepirac is more powerful than either aspirin or codeine alone.

Experimental Drugs. The discovery of a "super-drug" that seems to slow aging and prevent cancer and obesity was reported by microbiologist Arthur G. Schwartz of Temple University in Philadelphia at the annual meeting of the American Association for the Advancement of Science in January. The drug, dehydroepiandrosterone (DHEA), is a steroid secreted by the adrenal gland.

In tests with laboratory mice, DHEA increased their life span by 50 per cent and prevented obesity without interfering with appetite. DHEA also reduced susceptibility to breast cancer in mice with a genetic predisposition to the disease. Clinical tests of DHEA began in 1981 with women at high risk of developing breast cancer.

Another new drug, acyclovir, proved effective against the herpes simplex virus, according to re-

A new artificial sweetener, aspartame, sold under the trade name Equal, was approved for use in August after eight years of controversy.

searchers at Johns Hopkins University School of Medicine in Baltimore. Clinical trials with cancer patients showed that acyclovir can prevent the herpes simplex virus from producing sores. Cancer patients are especially vulnerable to herpes because their immune response may be lowered by chemotherapy. Acyclovir may someday provide relief to an estimated 20 million Americans with genital herpes, a venereal disease.

Drugs and Pregnancy. In July 1981, the U.S. surgeon general advised pregnant women and even those trying to become pregnant to avoid all alcohol because of potential danger to the fetus. The new caution extended previous warnings that heavy drinking during pregnancy can cause severe mental retardation and growth deficiency in the child. The dangers of lighter drinking are not firmly established but may include increased risk of miscarriages and of low birth weight in infants.

Bendectin, a drug used to relieve nausea during pregnancy, was reported safe in June 1981. It had been suspected of causing birth defects, such as cleft palate and heart abnormalities.

Pregnant women concerned about other drugs may benefit from a new test reported in May by researchers at Johns Hopkins University. The lab test shows how the liver breaks down a drug to determine whether it can cause birth defects.

Drug Abuse. Drug use among teen-agers in the United States has declined markedly, according to a report to Congress by psychiatrist William Pollin, head of the National Institute of Drug Abuse. There was a significant decrease in cigarette smoking and marijuana use among the high school students surveyed, but an increased percentage of the students admitted using drugs other than marijuana, primarily stimulants. The report added that teen-agers in the United States still use more marijuana and other drugs than teen-agers in any other industrialized nation.

"Look-alike" pills that contain potentially deadly combinations of substances found in over-the-counter drugs were being sold as amphetamines to drug users during 1981. Look-alike pills contain the same ingredients as cold remedies, diet pills, and stimulants, but in much greater quantities. Look-alikes were implicated in the deaths of at least 14 people in 1980 and 1981.

On September 16, the Select Committee on Narcotics Abuse and Control of the House of Representatives reported a "shocking level" of drug abuse in the U.S. armed forces. According to a survey cited by the committee, 49 per cent of those questioned in the Navy used drugs or alcohol regularly, as did 42 per cent of Army respondents, 34 per cent of Marine Corps respondents, and 17 per cent of Air Force respondents.   Dianne Hales

In WORLD BOOK, see DRUG; DRUG ABUSE.
EARTHQUAKE. See DISASTERS.

EASTERN ORTHODOX CHURCHES in 1981 marked the 1,600th anniversary of the Second Ecumenical Council held in Constantinople (now Istanbul, Turkey) in 381, at which the Nicene Creed was finalized. This creed became the universal creed of the Christian church. The anniversary was celebrated in Istanbul on June 6, with representatives of all Orthodox churches participating in the liturgy at the patriarchal Church of St. Georges.

During 1981, a crisis developed in the relationship between the World Council of Churches (WCC) and its Orthodox members. At the August meeting of the WCC Central Committee in Dresden, East Germany, Orthodox churches expressed their desire for more representation on WCC committees and greater attention to Orthodox theology in WCC undertakings. The Orthodox members feared that the theological directions the WCC is taking in its study of Christian ministry and sacraments will be unacceptable to Eastern Orthodoxy.

On Dec. 19, 1980, the patriarch of Jerusalem, Benedictos I, died at the age of 88. He had served as patriarch since 1957. His successor, Deodoros, was installed as patriarch of Jerusalem on Feb. 16, 1981. Deodoros had served since 1962 as the patriarchal representative of Jordan.

Persecutions of Russian Orthodox dissenters in the Soviet Union were reported to be rising in 1981. According to Keston College in Great Britain, which monitors all information concerning religion in Eastern Europe, the number of Christian prisoners in Russia grew from 180 in 1979 to 307 in January 1981.

Other reports indicated that the number of monks at Mount Athos in eastern Greece, the traditional center of Orthodox monasticism, increased from 1,145 in 1971 to 1,232 in 1978.

In the United States. In August 1981, Archbishop Philip, head of the Antiochian Orthodox Christian Archdiocese of North America, stated that efforts to achieve unity among the various Orthodox jurisdictions in the United States had "failed utterly." He delivered his remarks in Los Angeles, at a convention of his archdiocese. The archbishop directed his main criticism at the Standing Conference of Orthodox Bishops in America, which was formed in 1960 for the promotion of such unity. Archbishop Philip also said, however, that discussions on cooperation between his jurisdiction and the Orthodox Church in America (OCA) will continue, with "eventual unity . . . in mind."

Metropolitan Ireney, the first primate of the Orthodox Church in America, died on March 18 at the age of 88. He became head of OCA when it gained *autocephaly* (administrative independence) from the Russian Orthodox Church in 1970. He had retired in 1977.   Alexander Schmemann

In WORLD BOOK, see EASTERN ORTHODOX CHURCHES.

ECONOMICS

ECONOMICS. Inflation eased, unemployment rose, interest rates hit new highs before falling late in the year, and the United States appeared to be in a recession during 1981. All of these conditions occurred against the backdrop of President Ronald Reagan's program of tax cuts, decreased federal budget deficits, and increased expenditures for the national defense.

Reagan's economic program gave rise to vigorous discussion and debate in Congress and among economists. After first projecting a budget deficit of $42.3 billion for the fiscal year beginning October 1981, the President acknowledged later that high interest rates and lower tax revenues resulting from the recession would widen the deficit, perhaps to as much as $109 billion. He also stated that these factors, combined with increased defense expenditures, would make a balanced budget impossible by 1984, as originally promised.

Inflation, as measured by the Consumer Price Index (CPI), slowed to an annual rate in 1981 of approximately 9 per cent, the lowest level since 1979. Nevertheless, prices were about three times as high as they had been in 1967. In addition, there was almost no indication that the upward price spiral could be stopped, though it might be slowed. The U.S. gross national product (GNP) – the total of all goods and services produced during the year – ran at an annual rate of $2.65 trillion, measured in current inflated prices. Measured in 1972 dollars, however, the GNP totaled only slightly more than $1.5 trillion.

Interest-Rate Fluctuations during the year were unusually wide. The Federal Reserve Board (Fed) maintained its "tight money" policy in its efforts to choke off inflation. The *prime rate* – the rate at which major banks lend to their most creditworthy commercial customers – was 20.5 per cent at the start of 1981, dropped to 17 per cent in early April, and rose again to 20.5 per cent in July. It remained at 20.5 per cent for the next two months. The prime rate then began a steady and relatively sharp decline. In early December, it stood at its lowest point of the year – 16 per cent.

Other interest rates followed a similar pattern, with interest on conventional mortgages peaking at more than 18 per cent in August. Hardest hit were builders of single-family dwellings and manufacturers of automobiles. New housing starts fell in October to an annual rate of 857,000, the lowest level in 15 years. In November, they rose very slightly, up 0.8 per cent from the previous month, to an annual rate of 871,000. Housing starts for the year totaled slightly more than 1.1 million, the lowest since 1975. Only about 6 million cars were built by U.S. producers in 1981. Sales of heavy farm equipment also fell sharply as consumers and producers either refused or were unable to meet the carrying costs imposed by high interest.

Expenditures for new plants and equipment totaled about $320 billion in 1981, slightly above 1980. After correction for inflation, however, the real expenditures were only marginally ahead of those for 1980. Business executives obviously found that modernization of plants and equipment was necessary if they hoped to avoid the fate of the car manufacturers, who continued to face tough competition from Japan. An illustration of this is the increasing use of robots in American manufacturing, though it is reported that the Japanese have several times as many of these automatons in operation as there are in the United States. In the Special Reports section, see A ROBOT IN YOUR FUTURE?

There was great pressure on the Fed in 1981 to lower interest rates by making more reserves available to the banks and thus increasing the money supply. Nevertheless, the Fed continued its policy of permitting only a modest growth in the money supply in an effort to prevent renewed inflationary pressures when the economy moved into its recovery phase. At least a partial justification for the Fed's position was given by the so-called misery index – the total of the unemployment rate and the rate of inflation as measured by the CPI. For 1981, the misery index showed a drop of approximately four percentage points from the 1980 rate. The Fed further argued that high interest rates resulted partly from inflationary expectations and that the best thing it could do was to choke off inflation even at the cost of slowing economic activity.

Unemployment. How long the Fed would maintain such a position in the face of sharply rising unemployment – 8.9 per cent in December – was uncertain. On the brighter side, however, about 91 million people were employed in the United States in 1981, nearly a million more than in 1980. In addition, more than 70 per cent of the unemployed had been out of work for less than 15 weeks. Unemployment rates for experienced workers and married men with a family were significantly below the general unemployment rate. On the other hand, the rates for teen-agers, blacks and other ethnic minorities, and women were higher than the average. The rate was especially high for black teen-agers in metropolitan centers, where 40 to 50 per cent of these young people were out of work.

An important cause of the relatively high unemployment rates is the lack of skills among the jobless. For example, there are acute shortages of machinists and tool and die makers, with relatively small numbers in training for such positions. Because a training period of at least six years is needed to produce the necessary skills, these shortages are likely to continue for some time. They may become even more serious as the United States begins a military build-up, which includes highly sophisticated weapons. Furthermore, the armed forces must spend large sums to bring the literacy of new recruits up to a level where they can operate increasingly sophisticated weapons. For some time, United States public schools have been producing ever-lower levels of achievement, and enrollment has been decreasing in mathematics and other subjects that lie at the heart of much advanced technology. For this reason, as well as others, there has been considerable talk of abandoning the all-volunteer Army and reinstituting the draft to bring individuals with higher qualifications into the ranks of the military.

Personal and Business Income. One measure of the basic well-being of the ordinary American citizen is per capita income after personal taxes. In 1981, such income rose to $8,600 – a 1 per cent increase in real terms over 1980. Average hourly earnings climbed to $7.34. The purchasing power of these earnings, however, was virtually the same as in 1980.

Corporate profits fell in 1981, and farm income rose very slightly. But in real terms, the corporate profits and farm income were far below the level of 1973. Interest income climbed in 1981 because of higher interest rates. Transfer payments, consisting largely of Social Security benefits, increased sharply. Common stock prices were about 8 per cent lower at year-end than at the beginning of 1981,

also largely the result of high interest rates. And the United States continued to run a small balance-of-payments surplus on current accounts, which includes exports and imports of goods and services, foreign aid, and tourist spending.

The Economy Abroad. During 1981, Japan and West Germany again had the best records on the inflation front among the major industrialized nations, 5 and 6 per cent, respectively. The inflation rate in Great Britain dropped from about 18 per cent in 1980 to 12 per cent in 1981, but that country suffered the worst unemployment in almost 50 years. Industrial growth generally slowed in Western Europe. France, Italy, and Great Britain all showed significant declines in production. Even the usually rapidly growing Japanese economy slowed somewhat, though it managed a 1 or 2 per cent gain in industrial production for 1981.

Little information was available about the economy in Communist countries during 1981. However, the difficulties in Poland as a result of strikes and sharply lowered production became a familiar story. With the formation of the trade union Solidarity, the Poles largely broke with the Communist tradition of government-dominated unions. Widespread strikes, both authorized and unauthorized, disrupted Poland, and it was an open question at year-end whether a free trade union could exist in

The sun shines in June on Director of the Office of Management and Budget David A. Stockman, but in November he weathered a severe political storm.

Selected Key U.S. Economic Indicators

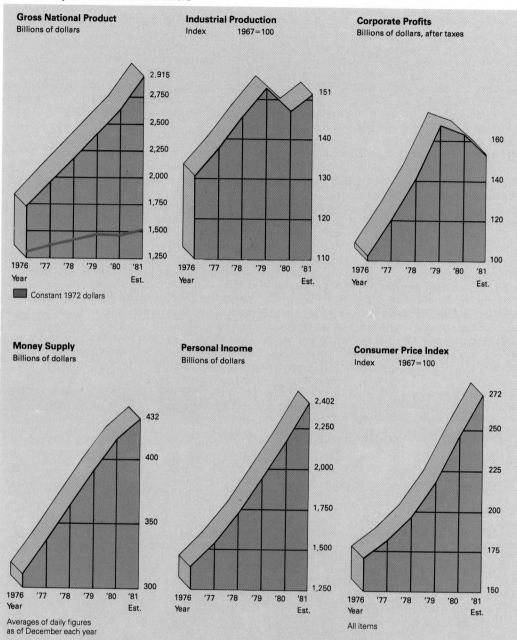

Gross National Product
Billions of dollars

2,915
2,750
2,500
2,250
2,000
1,750
1,500
1,250

1976 '77 '78 '79 '80 '81
Year   Est.

■ Constant 1972 dollars

Industrial Production
Index   1967=100

151
140
130
120
110

1976 '77 '78 '79 '80 '81
Year   Est.

Corporate Profits
Billions of dollars, after taxes

160
140
120
100

1976 '77 '78 '79 '80 '81
Year   Est.

Money Supply
Billions of dollars

432
400
350
300

1976 '77 '78 '79 '80 '81
Year   Est.

Averages of daily figures
as of December each year

Personal Income
Billions of dollars

2,402
2,250
2,000
1,750
1,500
1,250

1976 '77 '78 '79 '80 '81
Year   Est.

Consumer Price Index
Index   1967=100

272
250
225
200
175
150

1976 '77 '78 '79 '80 '81
Year   Est.

All items

The most comprehensive measure of the nation's total output of goods and services is the *Gross National Product* (GNP). The GNP represents the dollar value in current prices of all goods and services plus the estimated value of certain imputed outputs, such as the rental value of owner-occupied dwellings. *Industrial Production* is a monthly measure of the physical output of manufacturing, mining, and utility industries. *Corporate Profits* are quarterly profit samplings from major industries. *Money Supply* measures the total amount of money in the economy in coin, currency, and demand deposits. *Personal Income* is current income received by persons (including nonprofit institutions and private trust funds) before personal taxes. *Consumer Price Index* (CPI) is a monthly measure of changes in the prices of goods and services consumed by urban families and individuals. CPI includes selected goods and services. All 1981 figures are *Year Book* estimates.

an almost totally planned economy. However, the Polish government's imposition of martial law on December 13 seemed to provide a negative answer.

Poland has a huge foreign debt. It is largely owed to Western banks, which extended considerable credits in previous years. The fall-off in exports has made it impossible for Poland to meet the interest and principal repayment requirements of its debt. In November, Poland applied to join the International Monetary Fund to obtain temporary relief from the country's external financial problems. At the same time, Western banks were trying to determine how Poland's debt could be restructured to avoid a complete default.

Russia experienced its third successive poor grain harvest in 1981. The severity of internal economic problems increased the possibility that significant Soviet arms limitations, or even reduction, might be considered so that more money would be available to alleviate these pressures.

For the first time in several years, gasoline prices fell in 1981 as reduced consumption and continued high crude-oil output by Saudi Arabia caused a surplus that strained storage facilities. Late in the year, members of the Organization of Petroleum Exporting Countries met and agreed on a unified price structure that significantly reduced the premiums that countries with high-quality light oil had been charging. At the same time, they agreed that these prices would remain fixed during 1982. After years of uncertainty, there was a prospect that some stability would be introduced into gasoline prices for the American consumer.

Supply-Side Economics. The basic economic concepts behind the Reagan Administration's proposals – sometimes called supply-side economics – were that high marginal rates of taxation on income destroy the incentive to produce and to invest, and that reduction in such rates would result in greater productivity. The increased productivity would come from additional efforts by the labor force and through the increased investment that would flow from the higher returns available to capital. The net results would be more employment and greater revenue accruing to the government from the stimulated economic activity. The more enthusiastic proponents of this concept went so far as to argue that these results would be simultaneous with the introduction of the Administration's proposed tax cuts. Therefore, they said, the government would not, in fact, lose any revenue as a result of the cuts. However, most economists, though agreeing with the basic premises of supply-side economics, believed that the desired effects would take time, and that their initial impact would reduce government revenues. Opinion was divided as to whether the then-existing marginal rates of taxation in the United States were high enough to inhibit effort and investment. Most

© 1981 by Herblock in
The Washington Post

"I hear it's letting up a little."

economists probably agreed that, at least concerning investment, the rates were high enough to reduce the availability of funds for productive enterprise. The fact that the United States has one of the lowest savings rates (as a proportion of national income) and the lowest investment rates (as a proportion of GNP) among the industrialized nations of the world seems to support that belief.

Whatever their merits or demerits, these arguments were overtaken by the course of events. When Congress finally passed the tax cut on August 4, the economy appeared to be expanding. But when second-quarter results were known, the GNP was seen to be declining at an annual rate of 2.4 per cent. Economists predicted that the then-unconfirmed recession, which most people expected, would continue through the first half of 1982. If the recession were to last that long, the increased deficit that would result would stimulate the economy and help moderate the recession – which no one expected to be very severe or lengthy. But the effect as the economy recovered would probably be to put upward pressure on prices, or at least prevent them from falling as far as they otherwise would have a tendency to do.

Demand Management. What did seem certain was that the United States seemed headed for a more or less continuing debate over the appropriate role of government in the country's economy.

Ever since the passage of the Full Employment Act of 1946, the popular view has been that government should "manage demand" by manipulating taxes or expenditures, or both, to maintain a low level of unemployment. A budgetary surplus was achieved in only two years since 1946, with the net result that the national debt stood at more than $1-trillion in 1981.

The recent rapid acceleration of prices and the failure to combat unemployment have made many economists question the concept of "demand management." Also in doubt is the whole role of government in attempting to manage the economy by regulation. As the Reagan Administration eliminates many regulations, it appears that the next few years will see a vigorous test of the idea that a relatively free market is the best guarantee against inflation and unemployment. While this test is going on, there will be continuing debate over how to allocate scarce government revenues among a variety of possible uses. It seems impossible to have both "guns" and "butter" without suffering the pains of inflation and all its distortions and hardships. Warren W. Shearer

See also INTERNATIONAL TRADE AND FINANCE and individual country articles. In the WORLD BOOK SUPPLEMENT section, see INFLATION. In WORLD BOOK, see ECONOMICS; GROSS NATIONAL PRODUCT.

ECUADOR. Vice-President Oswaldo Hurtado Larrea assumed the presidency of Ecuador after the death of President Jaime Roldos Aguilera in an airplane crash on May 24, 1981. The 42-year-old Hurtado is a Christian Democrat, lawyer, and sociologist who shares his predecessor's generally liberal outlook on social issues.

Once in office, Hurtado moved quickly to put together a working majority in the nation's Congress. He was helped by the elevation to the vice-presidency of Leon Roldos Aguilera, brother of his predecessor. Hurtado had worked closely with his new vice-president in the previous administration.

Ecuador's Economy suffered in 1981 from a drop in the price of oil, which accounts for 60 per cent of Ecuador's export earnings. Declines in cacao and coffee prices also hurt the economy, and the losses were especially hard on the many impoverished farmers in the heavily populated highland and coastal areas of Ecuador, who depend on these crops for their livelihood. The value of Ecuador's agricultural exports was down 8.8 per cent in the first five months of 1981.

Hurtado declared that improving Ecuador's petroleum reserves was his top priority, but in boosting oil production, he faced stiff opposition in Congress, where foreign oil companies have long been held suspect. Texaco Incorporated is the only major international oil company that has contin-

ued its operations in Ecuador; other companies have left the country, and potential investors have been frightened off by what they consider inconsistent oil policies.

In February, the government earmarked 17 per cent of new taxes for the development of Ecuador's Amazon region. The funds will be used for roads, forestry development, and colonization.

Like other nations dependent on oil earnings, Ecuador was hard put to control inflation and to dull its impact on the ordinary citizen. By mid-1981, the country had approved a 50 per cent increase in the minimum wage, boosting it to the equivalent of $160 per month for a 40-hour week.

Tensions Flared in late January in a boundary dispute between Ecuador and Peru. In February, there were still reported incidents of clashes in the disputed area of the Cordillera del Condor mountains. Ecuador moved in armored vehicles and placed orders for Israeli-built fighter planes.

On February 22, Ecuador recalled its diplomatic mission to Cuba after Cuban security forces entered the Ecuadorean Embassy in Havana. Ecuador had promised diplomatic immunity to a group of 29 Cubans who had sought refuge in the embassy on February 13. Nathan A. Haverstock

See also LATIN AMERICA (Facts in Brief Table). In WORLD BOOK, see ECUADOR.

Community development through self-help projects aims at improving living conditions in Ecuador. Villagers built this communal wash basin.

EDUCATION. The mood among educators in the United States was somber in 1981 because of the efforts of President Ronald Reagan's Administration to reduce federal spending for education. The educators faced cuts in support in virtually every area, from programs for the disadvantaged to loans and grants for college students. Of the total of $198 billion to be spent on all levels of education in 1981-1982, an estimated $20 billion, or 10 per cent, was to come from the federal government. This was about $4 billion less than in 1980-1981.

The American Council on Education expressed concern over the projected cut of more than $560-million in federal student aid for 1982. The cut meant that more than a million aid awards for low- and middle-income students might be eliminated. In addition, educators expressed concern because the Department of Education (DOE), which began operations on May 4, 1980, was slated for dismantling, possibly to be replaced by an independent organization comparable to the National Science Foundation, without Cabinet status.

On August 26, Secretary of Education Terrel H. Bell responded to widespread concern over the decline of educational quality in schools and colleges by appointing an 18-member National Commission on Excellence in Education. He asked the commission to "make practical recommendations for action" in 18 months.

Total Enrollment in U.S. schools and colleges declined for the ninth consecutive year in 1981. The DOE expected an estimated 57.6 million persons to enroll in formal education programs from kindergarten through graduate school in the 1981-1982 academic year. Estimated enrollment thus declined about 850,000 from the previous year's 58.4 million. Nevertheless, the total number of Americans engaged directly in education, as students or teachers, remained at more than 61 million. In a nation of 230 million people, about 27 per cent are direct participants in education.

Elementary grades enrolled 31 million children. Of those, about 27.3 million were in public schools, a decline of 1.3 per cent from 1980 and a continuation of a downward trend that began in 1970. The DOE predicted that the trend might be reversed in the mid-1980s because of an increase in births that began in 1977. Nonpublic schools followed the downward trend, with a slight enrollment decrease of approximately 10,000.

High schools were expected to enroll 14.4 million students, down 3.4 per cent from 1980's total of 14.9 million. High school enrollments peaked at 15.7 million in 1976 and have fallen every year since. Further declines are expected throughout most of the 1980s. The number of students enrolled in public high schools in 1981 was expected to be 12.8 million.

Enrollment in institutions of higher education reached an all-time high of 12.1 million in 1980. Public institutions accounted for 9.5 million. Only a nominal increase was expected in the fall of 1981. A decrease is expected in the U.S. college-age population after 1981, and a small annual drop in the number of college students is projected for the rest of the 1980s.

The Graduates. About 3 million students graduated from public and private high schools in 1981, and the 1982 graduating class was expected to drop only slightly below the 3-million mark. The peak year for high school graduates was 1977, with 3,161,000 diplomas conferred.

Colleges and universities were expected to award 945,000 bachelor's degrees, 300,000 master's degrees, 33,000 doctor's degrees, and 72,000 first professional degrees in 1981-1982. These estimates for bachelor's and first professional degrees are at or near their all-time highs. The figures for master's and doctor's degrees are down slightly from peaks reached in 1977 and 1973, respectively.

The U.S. Bureau of the Census reported that there were approximately 110 million high school graduates in the United States in 1980. Nearly 24 million of these had also completed four or more years of college. The median number of school years completed by persons age 25 years or older was 12½, compared with nine years in 1949. The number of adults with less than five years of schooling decreased by about 54 per cent from 1930 to 1980, from 9.45 million to 4.32 million.

The Teachers. An estimated 2.4 million elementary- and secondary-school teachers were involved in classroom instruction, a small decrease from a year earlier. In addition, 300,000 teachers were working as superintendents, principals, and supervisors. Colleges and universities employed about 840,000 teachers.

The National Education Association estimated that, as a result of budgetary pressures, about 55,000 teachers would lose their jobs during the 1981-1982 school year, the largest number ever in a single year.

Education Expenditures at all levels for the 1981-1982 school year were estimated by the DOE at $198 billion, compared with outlays totaling about $181 billion in 1980-1981. Most of the increase was attributed to inflation. Higher education was to receive $71 billion; public elementary and secondary schools, $112.8 billion. Public institutions at all levels were expected to spend about $161 billion, with the private sector spending about $37-billion.

In addition to the $20 billion in federal funds for 1981-1982, state governments were to contribute $77 billion, or 39 per cent. Local governments' share amounted to about $50 billion, or 25 per cent. Funds from a variety of private sources — including tuition and fees, earnings from endow-

Some proposed federal regulations on bilingual education were revoked in February as being harsh, inflexible, unworkable, and costly.

greater stress on the teaching of basic skills and to public pressure for increased attention to educational standards. Minimum-competency tests to determine students' achievements have been introduced in most states. The policy of automatically promoting students from grade to grade has given way to promotion based on achievement in several school systems, including the nation's largest, in New York City.

Public Attitudes toward the schools, as measured by a 1981 Gallup Poll and a study by the Charles F. Kettering Foundation, showed that the majority of Americans want more demanding curriculums, more control over student behavior, and more attention to ethics. But the surveys also detected a growing feeling that parents are more deficient than schools in the upbringing of their children.

The polls also showed that the public's willingness to support the schools financially continues to decline. Only 30 per cent of those polled favored raising taxes if the schools need more money; 60 per cent rejected tax increases.

A California Judge Ruled on March 6 that the state's policy on science textbooks does not violate the rights of people who object to the teaching of the theory of chemical evolution. Kelly Segraves of San Diego, director of the Creation-Science Research Center, had brought suit against the California Department and Board of Education. He charged that his children's religious freedom was violated by state guidelines for the preparation of science textbooks, which hold that living forms developed from nonliving matter by the process of chemical evolution. Segraves asked that students be taught that there are a number of other theories of how life began, including the Biblical doctrine of creation.

Superior Court Judge Irving Perluss ruled that the textbook guidelines did not violate the children's rights. He also ruled, however, that state education authorities should give wide circulation to an official policy that forbids *dogmatism* (the emphatic assertion of opinion) in the teaching of the origins of life. Perluss said copies of the policy should be sent to California schools, textbook publishers, and others who had received a copy of the guidelines.

Desegregation and Bilingualism. Amid growing hostility toward busing to achieve school integration, the U.S. Department of Justice prepared to seek nonbusing remedies to provide minority students with "an education of comparable quality." Such approaches would include voluntary student transfers, magnet schools, and improved course content and instruction.

At the same time, however, a study sponsored by the DOE's Office for Civil Rights and the National Institute of Education reported that school deseg-

ments, gifts, and grants — were expected to total $51 billion, or 26 per cent.

Higher Education's Cost continued to rise. A number of high-prestige colleges now charge more than $10,000 per year for tuition and board. At the same time, corporate gifts to higher education increased by 25 per cent in 1980, reaching an estimated total of $696 million. A smaller increase was forecast for the 1981 fiscal year, however. Total voluntary support from all sources was estimated to be $3.8 billion in 1980. Faculty salaries in the 1980-1981 academic year were up 8.7 per cent, an increase that almost matched the inflation rate.

Student Achievement appeared to be taking a turn for the better. The College Entrance Examination Board announced in September that the downward slide in high school seniors' scores on the Scholastic Aptitude Test had been halted. For students who graduated in 1981, the average scores for college-bound seniors remained at 424 in verbal skills and at 466 in mathematics. The tests are scored on a scale ranging from 200 to 800 points. Since 1963, the scores had declined from a high of 478 in verbal skills and 502 in mathematics.

Many school systems also reported improved educational achievements. In New York City, for example, reading scores improved markedly. The entire state of New Jersey reported similar gains. Many educators attributed the upward trend to regation has been shown capable of improving educational achievements as well as race relations. To be effective, the study said, desegregation must start at the earliest possible grade, and students must be expected to meet high standards.

On February 3, Education Secretary Bell revoked regulations on bilingual education that had been proposed by President Jimmy Carter's Administration. Under the regulations, if 25 students in a school district did not speak English, the district would have had to offer instruction in their native language as well as in English. Bell said the regulations were "harsh, inflexible, burdensome, unworkable, and incredibly costly." He added that the DOE would rewrite the regulations to "protect the rights of children who do not speak English well, but we will do so by permitting school districts to use any way that has proved successful."

Electronics and the Schools. More than 500 colleges had said by the end of 1981 that they will offer academic credits to adults who enroll in television courses carried by stations that are members of the Public Broadcasting Service.

The Sloan Foundation issued a report in 1981 on "The New Liberal Arts." The report stressed the need to include applied mathematics and knowledge of computers in the general education of all students.   Fred M. Hechinger

In WORLD BOOK, see EDUCATION.

EDWARDS, JAMES BURROWS (1927-   ), was sworn in as United States secretary of energy on Jan. 23, 1981. At his confirmation hearing, Edwards told the Senate Energy and Natural Resources Committee that he would like to help "get the nuclear industry back on track again." He promised federal help for all forms of energy, including nuclear, and said he was rethinking the Republican Party's 1980 campaign pledge to dismantle the Department of Energy. Instead, he said, he would prefer to dismantle "the regulations of the department."

Edwards was born on June 24, 1927, in Hawthorne, Fla. He served with the U.S. Maritime Service during World War II and with the U.S. Navy from 1955 to 1957.

Edwards received a bachelor of science degree from the College of Charleston in South Carolina in 1950 and a doctor of dental medicine degree from the University of Louisville in Kentucky in 1955.

From 1972 to 1974, Edwards was a member of the South Carolina state Senate. He served as governor from 1975 to 1979. As governor, he created South Carolina's Energy Research Institute; in 1978 he was chairman of the National Governors' Association Subcommittee on Nuclear Energy.

Edwards and his wife, the former Ann Norris Darlington, have a son and a daughter. Wayne Wille

EGYPT. The assassination of President Anwar el-Sadat on Oct. 6, 1981, during a military parade in Cairo stunned the world and cast a cloud of uncertainty over the peace process with Israel begun by Sadat with Israel's Prime Minister Menachem Begin in 1977. Sadat was gunned down as he sat in a reviewing stand. A group of men in military uniform leaped from one of the trucks in the parade and opened fire on the reviewing stand with automatic weapons and grenades.

There were a number of casualties, but Vice-President Mohamed Hosni Mubarak, seated next to Sadat, received only superficial wounds. Ironically, the parade marked the eighth anniversary of the October 1973 war with Israel, when rapid military success restored Egypt's self-confidence after three disastrous wars.

Despite the shock of the assassination, the country remained calm. The transfer of power was orderly. On October 7, the People's Assembly unanimously endorsed Mubarak to succeed Sadat. And, on October 13, the electorate approved Mubarak in a referendum. See MUBARAK, MOHAMED HOSNI.

On November 21, four Muslim fundamentalists went on trial for Sadat's assassination. Twenty others went on trial for complicity.

Many Questions remained unanswered, but the assassination underscored the extent of opposition to Sadat and his policies among hard-line Muslim fundamentalists. The leader of the death squad, Army Lieutenant Khaled Ahmed Shawki al-Istanbuli, was linked to *Al Takfir Wal Hijra* (Repentance and Flight from Sin), a group that advocates the restoration in Egypt of a purified Islamic society, by violence if necessary. Other militant groups, such as the Islamic Liberation Organization and the Muslim Brotherhood, opposed Sadat for favoring Western capitalism, straying from the path of Islam, and making peace with Israel. Two days after the assassination, Muslim militants seized police headquarters in Asyut and fought gun battles with police.

Crackdown on Foes. Sadat may have contributed to his demise with a sweeping crackdown on the opposition in early September. About 1,600 persons were arrested. They included not only fundamentalists, but also journalists, lawyers, Muslim clerics, Coptic Christian bishops, and leaders of Egypt's two small but legal opposition parties, Socialist Labor and National Progressive Union.

Sadat also deposed the Coptic patriarch, Shenuda III, leader of Egypt's 6 million Coptic Christians. Sadat said Shenuda had incited sectarian feelings that had developed into clashes in June between Muslims and Copts. Authority over the Coptic Church was transferred to a council of five bishops.

In addition, Sadat accused Russian and Hun-

Minutes before his assassination on October 6, Egypt's President Sadat, right, chats with his vice-president and successor, Hosni Mubarak.

garian embassy staffs of instigating sectarian strife and plots against his regime. On September 5, the Soviet ambassador, six members of his staff, and more than 1,000 Soviet technical advisers to Egypt's heavy industry program were expelled.

A series of new laws were put into effect to root out religious unrest and deal with "indiscipline," described by Sadat as a major cause of Egypt's problems. Some 40,000 privately owned mosques were transferred to government control; six provincial governors were replaced; Islamic societies on university campuses were dissolved; and an additional $1.3 million in loans and services was allocated to needy students.

Egypt's New President pledged himself to continue the peace process with Israel, to restore order, and to improve living conditions for all Egyptians. Mubarak promised to deal ruthlessly with "those who play with fire and threaten people's freedom." Continuing arrests of fundamentalists and others suspected of complicity in the assassination brought the total of persons under detention to more than 3,000 by early November. Strict new directives prohibited Egyptians from sheltering suspected terrorists and required registration of all weapons. Universities were closed and heavy security was placed around public buildings as Cairo became almost an armed camp.

In the long run, to reunite the country around

his leadership, the new president will have to resolve the same economic problems that bedeviled his predecessor. Sadat's policy was to encourage private enterprise and the free inflow of large amounts of foreign capital, while providing government subsidies to hold down the prices of basic commodities to benefit the poor.

The budget that took effect on July 1 increased food subsidies to $2.8 billion, or 20 per cent of the $14-billion budget. The minimum wage was raised from $29 to $36 per month, with university graduates scheduled to receive $64 per month instead of $47. An additional 25,000 positions in the universities were set aside for new graduates in an effort to alleviate Egypt's critical shortage of jobs.

The Economy benefited from expanded oil production and increased remittances from Egyptian workers abroad – $2.8 billion a year, enough to cover the food subsidies. A major oil field was discovered by Mobil Oil Corporation in January in its offshore concession in the Gulf of Suez. Production in the Morgan and October fields that Israel returned to Egypt after the 1979 peace treaty increased to 823,000 barrels per day. Cotton exports also increased. In June, the People's Republic of China agreed to purchase 150,000 bales of cotton, one-third of Egypt's total crop. William Spencer

See also MIDDLE EAST (Facts in Brief Table). In WORLD BOOK, see EGYPT.

ELECTIONS. Off-year elections in the United States in 1981 were virtually a stand-off between Republicans and Democrats despite President Ronald Reagan's dominance of the national political scene. Reagan personally intervened in the Virginia and New Jersey governors' races, which were decided on November 3.

In Virginia, Charles S. Robb, a Democrat, won the governor's race with an impressive margin of more than 100,000 votes. Robb, the lieutenant governor of Virginia and a son-in-law of Democratic President Lyndon B. Johnson, did not make Reagan's controversial budget and tax cuts an issue in the race against the Republican candidate, Virginia Attorney General J. Marshall Coleman. Instead, the campaign was a battle of personalities and television advertising dollars, with President Reagan traveling to the state on Coleman's behalf and the Republican National Committee spending heavily to try to retain the statehouse, which had been held by Republicans for 12 years.

In New Jersey, Republican gubernatorial candidate Thomas H. Kean was the beneficiary of $1-million in campaign funds from the Republican National Committee and personal appearances by President Reagan. Nonetheless, Kean barely squeaked into the governor's office after a tough battle with Democratic Representative James J. Florio. According to a canvass, Kean won by only

1,677 votes out of more than 2.2 million ballots cast. He maintained that margin in a recount.

Congressional Elections. In a series of special congressional elections, Democrats picked up one seat previously held by a Republican; two seats remained under GOP control; and Democrats held on to two other seats.

In Mississippi, Democrat Wayne Dowdy on July 7 upset Republican Liles B. Williams. Dowdy won the seat left vacant by the resignation in April of Representative Jon Hinson (R., Miss.) after his arrest on morals charges in February.

In other House contests, Republican Mark Siljander on April 21 won a special election in Michigan to replace David A. Stockman, who resigned to become director of the Office of Management and Budget. Republican Michael Oxley on June 25 won a close race in Ohio to succeed Republican Tennyson Guyer, who died in April.

In Maryland, Democrat Steny H. Hoyer on May 19 defeated GOP candidate Audrey Scott, mayor of Bowie, Md., in a contest to fill the seat left vacant by Gladys N. Spellman, a Democrat who was disabled by illness. In Pennsylvania, dissident Democrat Joseph F. Smith, running as an independent with Republican backing, on July 21 defeated Philadelphia Democratic Party Chairman David B. Glancey in a heavily Democratic district. Smith was elected to the seat vacated by Democrat Raymond F. Lederer, who resigned in April after his conviction for bribery in the Abscam scandal.

In an unusual development, two Democratic members of Congress announced they would run for re-election as Republicans in 1982. The party-switchers were Bob Stump of Arizona and Eugene V. Atkinson of Pennsylvania.

Mayoral Elections were, as usual, dominated by Democrats. One notable exception was George V. Voinovich, a Republican, who won a second two-year term in Cleveland.

There were a number of firsts recorded in 1981 mayoral contests. In San Antonio, Democrat Henry G. Cisneros became the first Mexican American to be elected mayor of a major U.S. city. In Houston, City Controller Kathryn J. Whitmire became the city's first woman mayor (see HOUSTON). In Hartford, Conn., Thurman L. Milner was the city's first black to be elected mayor. And in New York City, Edward I. Koch, the first candidate to win both Democratic and Republican nominations, was re-elected with 75 per cent of the vote (see NEW YORK CITY).

Other mayors re-elected in 1981 included Richard Caliguiri of Pittsburgh, Pa.; Charles Royer of Seattle; Margaret Hance of Phoenix; Maurice A. Ferre of Miami, Fla.; Donald M. Fraser of Minneapolis, Minn.; and Coleman A. Young of Detroit (see DETROIT). Thomas A. Bradley of Los Angeles was elected to a third term (see LOS ANGELES).

Former UN Ambassador Andrew J. Young, Jr., greets supporters at his campaign headquarters after his election as mayor of Atlanta on October 28.

Former U.S. Ambassador to the United Nations Andrew J. Young, Jr., won a first term as mayor in Atlanta. City Council member Vincent L. Schoemehl, Jr., was elected mayor in St. Louis. In Albany, N.Y., Erastus Corning 2nd, the dean of American mayors, won an unprecedented 11th term.

Tax Referendums were on the ballot in several cities in 1981. Voters in Detroit on June 23 responded to Mayor Young's plea and approved a $96-million increase in city taxes to avert municipal bankruptcy. In Cleveland, in an effort to alleviate the persistent financial crunch, voters on February 17 approved an increase from 1.5 to 2.0 per cent in the city income tax. Los Angeles voters, however, on June 2 rejected a proposed tax increase to expand the city's police force.

San Diego got a turnout of 60.8 per cent of registered voters in a referendum in which voters, who balloted by mail, turned down a $224-million convention center. Washington, D.C., voters rejected, by a margin of more than 8 to 1, a plan that would have allowed tax credits of up to $1,200 per child to parents who paid tuition to private or out-of-city schools. In Washington state, a proposal to allow voters to veto financing for five nuclear plants was approved.   William J. Eaton

See also DEMOCRATIC PARTY; REPUBLICAN PARTY. In WORLD BOOK, see ELECTIONS.
ELECTRIC POWER. See ENERGY.

ELECTRONICS manufacturers continued to develop very-large-scale integrated (VLSI) circuits in 1981. A VLSI circuit provides the equivalent of more than 100,000 transistors on a chip of silicon about the size of a thumbnail. This development strengthened two major trends. Companies that built VLSI circuits became more dependent upon computers programmed to design complex circuits, while firms building products that use VLSI circuits increased their reliance on people who could write programs for their machines.

One popular product of VLSI technology is the microprocessor, a tiny integrated circuit that does the work of a computer. Bell Laboratories in Murray Hill, N.J.; Hewlett-Packard Company's Desktop Division in Fort Collins, Colo.; and Intel Corporation in Santa Clara, Calif., introduced microprocessors in 1981 that can handle 32 *bits* at one time. (A *bit* is the basic unit of information in digital computers.) The new microprocessors will replace slower 16-bit machines in industrial robots and other devices. In the Special Reports section, see A ROBOT IN YOUR FUTURE?

For microprocessors to succeed in the market place, a large number of programs – or software – must be available to potential buyers. However, the computer industry has suffered for some time from a shortage of people who can write programs.

A partial solution appeared in 1981 with the growing popularity of Ada, a computer language that is easy to learn. However, supporters of an older, more difficult computer language called Pascal and its variations still influence programmers.

Faraway Places. The VLSI circuits increased the capabilities of computer terminals, the computer operator's work station. These machines control more powerful devices such as large computing circuits and gigantic memory banks to which they are connected electrically by wires. Thus, office workers who operate terminals in individual work areas scattered throughout a big company can share powerful equipment housed in a single computer room. Manufacturers call a system of terminals and central equipment a *local network*. Such networks continued to increase demand for equipment storing large amounts of information.

The Personal-Computer Boom continued at full speed in 1981. Manufacturers introduced at least 16 of these machines. All of them are built around 8- or 16-bit microprocessors. Their memories can handle approximately 48,000 to 128,000 letters or digits from the user. These computers also use some form of mass storage such as a floppy disk. The disk, which looks like a small phonograph record, stores information magnetically. Personal computers display data and illustrations on an ordinary television screen or on a special picture tube. Most cost about $3,000.

Finer Lines. CBS Inc.; Sony Corporation of Japan; and Japan's broadcasting company, NHK, introduced an experimental TV set whose picture is made up of 1,125 lines. This picture provides much more detail than does the 525-line picture used in the United States. However, a TV channel that carried a program for 1,125-line screens would need broadcast frequencies about five times as wide as today's frequencies. Therefore, adopting the 1,125-line screen as standard would decrease the number of channels available in the range of frequencies that are presently set aside for TV.

Manufacturers prepared to crowd even more circuits onto memory chips in 1981. They had developed chips that hold 65,536 bits in one type of device known as random access memory (RAM) and chips that store 262,144 bits in another kind of device called read-only memory (ROM).

To avoid scrapping a chip that has a small number of faulty individual circuits, some companies built extra circuits into their chips. Although some RAM manufacturers have rejected this technique, known as redundancy, all firms agree that they will need to use redundancy to build a 262,144-bit RAM chip. The remaining issue is whether to remove bad circuits by isolating them with electrical fuses or by burning them away with lasers.   Gerald M. Walker

In WORLD BOOK, see ELECTRONICS.

Huge earphones attract the eye and then treat the observer to stereophonic sound at a radio and television exposition in Switzerland.

EL SALVADOR. Assurances of United States support from President Ronald Reagan soon after he took office in January 1981 buoyed the spirits of El Salvador's embattled ruling junta, headed by Jose Napoleon Duarte, a Christian Democrat. The United States provided 54 military advisers and stepped up economic and military aid to $161-million in 1981 to help end widespread violence.

Leftist guerrillas mounted what they called a "final offensive" in January to topple the Duarte government, and fighting between the rebels and government troops intensified. Two American citizens employed by the American Institute for Free Labor Development, sponsored by U.S. labor unions, were assassinated on January 3 in San Salvador, El Salvador's capital, where they were advising the Salvadoran Communal Union on peasant cooperatives.

Throughout the first half of 1981, there was a steady stream of reports about atrocities committed by the armed forces, and by rightist and leftist extremists. El Salvador's land reform program was assailed as ineffective, and the grave condition of the country's poor was widely reported.

In a Bold Gesture to counter what he called an international campaign to discredit his regime, Duarte toured the United States in September. He explained his government's plan of action in a highly publicized but unofficial visit with Reagan, at meetings with members of the U.S. Congress, and in appearances on television news programs. Duarte steadfastly declared that the junta sought an end to violence in El Salvador as the preliminary step to holding elections.

Shortly before Duarte's trip, his opponents in the country's Democratic Revolutionary Front, an alliance of leftist, Marxist, and non-Marxist groups, sent representatives to the United Nations and to selected countries of Latin America, Western Europe, and Africa. The representatives sought international support for a negotiated settlement to the conflict in El Salvador, which has already cost more than 30,000 lives.

A negotiated settlement, however, would imply recognition of the armed guerrilla groups, and the Duarte junta continued to insist that all guerrillas lay down their arms as a precondition for holding elections. In September, the U.S. Senate voted to make further U.S. military aid to El Salvador dependent on progress by the Duarte government in ending oppression.　　　Nathan A. Haverstock

See also LATIN AMERICA (Facts in Brief Table). In WORLD BOOK, see EL SALVADOR.

EMPLOYMENT. See ECONOMICS; EDUCATION; LABOR; SOCIAL SECURITY; WELFARE.

ENDANGERED SPECIES. See CONSERVATION.

Salvadoran soldiers open fire on rebel strongholds near El Jocotillo, El Salvador. The country limped through another year of civil war in 1981.

ENERGY. President Ronald Reagan, following through on a campaign pledge, approved on Dec. 16, 1981, a proposal to dismantle the Department of Energy (DOE) and abolish some of its functions. Most of the DOE's remaining responsibilities would be transferred to the Department of Commerce, where they would be carried out by a semiautonomous agency called the Energy Research and Technology Administration. As part of its responsibilities, the new agency would oversee the production of nuclear weapons, which accounts for about half the DOE's proposed $14.4-billion budget for fiscal 1983. The Reagan Administration contended the move will save the federal government several billion dollars over the next two years. If the proposal is approved by Congress, the DOE would become the first U.S. Cabinet department ever to be eliminated. The Department of Energy was created in 1977 by President Jimmy Carter.

Nuclear Power Problems. The beleaguered nuclear power industry in the United States experienced additional difficulties in 1981. On November 19, the Nuclear Regulatory Commission (NRC) suspended the operating license of the Diablo Canyon nuclear power plant near San Luis Obispo, Calif. The license, which permitted the plant to load fuel and conduct low-power testing, was to remain suspended until the plant passed a series of tests verifying the effectiveness of its earthquake-protection equipment.

A number of design errors related to seismic safety were discovered after the plant was licensed to test its reactors in September. The Diablo Canyon plant was the target of protests and an attempted shutdown by demonstrators who alleged the plant is unsafe because it lies near a geologic fault. In announcing the suspension, Nunzio J. Palladino, chairman of the NRC, said "a significant number" of other nuclear plants in the United States also had "construction-related deficiencies." In November, the NRC fined the Cincinnati Gas & Electric Company a record $200,000 for what the agency called "a widespread breakdown in the utility's quality assurance program" in the construction of the unfinished Zimmer nuclear power plant at Moscow, Ohio.

In July, the NRC warned the operators of 17 nuclear plants that steam generators in the plants were corroding much faster than expected. The generators, bundles of tubing that carry hot, radioactive water from the reactor's uranium core, were designed to last for 40 years, the expected lifetime of a plant. The problem forced the shutdown of at least five plants for repairs.

In July, NRC officials warned the operators of 44

A solar collector bowl near Crosbyton, Tex., collects energy to power a new commercial solar-power plant, the first to use steam to produce electricity.

nuclear plants that radiation was making the steel shell surrounding the plants' uranium core susceptible to cracks. In September, officials said that the shells at eight plants were becoming brittle so rapidly that without substantial repairs, some of the plants may become unsafe to operate by the end of 1982. A crack in the shell would permit the water cooling the core to leak out. Without the coolant, the core might melt down, causing a nuclear catastrophe.

On September 25, officials at Three Mile Island nuclear power plant near Harrisburg, Pa., announced the completion of the first significant decontamination of the plant since the accident there in 1979. Officials said 15,000 gallons (56,800 liters) of the 600,000 gallons (2.3 million liters) of highly radioactive water in Nuclear Unit Number 2's containment building had been decontaminated.

Agency Opposition. In February, the Reagan Administration told the World Bank it would not help finance the establishment of a proposed energy affiliate intended to provide loans for energy projects in developing countries. President Jimmy Carter had agreed to U.S. participation. The proposed agency would, during the 1980s, finance up to $500 billion in energy projects to help developing countries expand their production of oil and natural gas and develop renewable energy sources. The United States stated its opposition to the agency at the first United Nations Conference on New and Renewable Energy, held in Nairobi, Kenya, in August. However, the United States announced that in fiscal 1982 it would double to $70 million its energy aid to developing countries.

Synfuel Projects. In July and August, the DOE approved federal loan guarantees totaling $3.1 billion for the first major projects in the $20-billion synthetic-fuels (synfuels) program approved by Congress in 1980. At the same time, the DOE relinquished its role as interim synfuels authority for the United States to the Synthetic Fuels Corporation. One loan guarantee, for $2.02 billion, was approved on August 6 for construction of the Great Plains coal-gasification plant in Beulah, N. Dak. The plant will convert lignite, or brown coal, into 125 million cubic feet (3.5 million cubic meters) of synthetic gas each day. The plant, to be built by a consortium of natural gas companies, will be the first large commercial coal-gasification plant in the United States.

Also on August 6, the DOE approved a second loan guarantee, for $1.1 billion, for a plant that will produce 48,300 barrels of crude oil daily from oil shale. The oil-shale project, to be located in Garfield County, Colorado, is a joint venture of Exxon Corporation and the Tosco Corporation. Earlier, on July 29, the DOE approved $400 million in loan guarantees for another oil-shale project in Garfield County, to be built by the Union Oil Company.

However, Gulf Oil Company and Standard Oil Company of Indiana announced on November 13 that they were delaying for at least two years plans to build a $330-million oil-shale plant in Rio Blanco County, Colorado. The companies cited rising costs, moderating oil prices, and the need for additional research as the reasons.

Gasohol. On August 14, the DOE gave preliminary approval for $706 million in federal loan guarantees for 11 alcohol fuels projects. Together, the plants, which would produce 365 million gallons (1.38 billion liters) of ethyl alcohol, or ethanol, per year from corn, would double current U.S. production capabilities. The Reagan Administration attempted to block funding for the projects, but Congress ordered the DOE to proceed with the guarantees. The use of gasohol has been widely promoted as a way to reduce U.S. reliance on foreign oil.

However, on October 19, Texaco, Incorporated, announced its decision to halt sales of gasohol at most of its service stations. Texaco, the largest U.S. gasohol dealer and the oil industry's most vocal advocate of the fuel, halted all gasohol sales in 14 Northeastern states, where transportation costs made sales uneconomical. Texaco service stations in five Midwestern states planned to replace gasohol with a premium grade of unleaded gasoline that uses grain alcohol as an octane booster.

Abandoned Projects. On March 20, Exxon announced that it had abandoned development of what it once considered a revolutionary energy-saving device – the alternating-current synthesizer. The device was intended to allow large industrial electric motors to draw a reduced amount of current when running at less than full capacity.

The National Research Council on July 2 recommended against government funding for the development of a solar power satellite system. The proposed system consisted of 60 satellites, each about the size of Manhattan Island, that could have generated 300 billion watts of electricity. The NRC, which advises the government on science and technology, said the system's $3-trillion price tag was too costly and the technology required too difficult.

U.S. Energy Consumption during the first half of 1981 totaled 37.5 quadrillion British Thermal Units (BTU's), according to the DOE. The total was 3 per cent less than was consumed during the same period in 1980. Petroleum consumption dropped 6.7 per cent, while coal consumption rose by 5.4 per cent. The average daily consumption of energy from other sources, including hydroelectric, nuclear, and geothermal power, and wood and waste, fell by 0.2 per cent. Michael Woods

See also COAL; PETROLEUM AND GAS. In WORLD BOOK, see ENERGY SUPPLY.
ENGINEERING. See BUILDING & CONSTRUCTION.

ENVIRONMENT. The Congress of the United States voted to continue providing money to enforce the Clean Air Act of 1970 but formally allowed the act to expire on Oct. 1, 1981. Industry had called for a substantial revision of the act. On July 28, the Business Roundtable's Environmental Task Force, an industry group, released a study charging that the act was "unnecessarily burdensome, costly and time-consuming." The report said that the act required new plants to be so clean that businesses were better off keeping older, dirtier plants in operation. In December, the Senate Environment and Public Works Committee voted to delay amending the act until 1982.

Both sides agreed that the law had helped to improve air quality. Government reports showed that total particulates in the atmosphere decreased by 32 per cent between 1969 and 1979.

Revision Delayed. Both Congress and the Administration of President Ronald Reagan feared that the debate over the Clean Air Act would develop into one of the toughest and most divisive congressional battles in many years. The Administration had planned to announce its proposals by June 30. However, Representative Henry A. Waxman (D., Calif.), chairman of the House subcommittee reviewing clean air legislation, released draft recommendations for an Administration bill on June 19. The recommendations called for sweeping changes, including the elimination of specific goals and deadlines for reducing pollution in areas with dirty air. Waxman called the proposal "nothing less than a blueprint for the destruction of our clean air laws."

The draft recommendations ran counter to public opinion. Louis Harris and Associates, Incorporated, a polling organization, released the results of a survey showing that 86 per cent of the United States public opposed weakening the Clean Air Act. The Administration denied that the Cabinet had even considered the draft.

On October 1, Congress approved a resolution that provided money for current clean air programs until Congress reauthorizes the act. Environmentalists welcomed the delay because they believed that Congress would be more likely to listen to grass-roots support in the election year of 1982.

Acid Rain remained one of the thorniest problems in rewriting the Clean Air Act. On March 30, John Roberts, Canada's minister of the environment, said that about 70 per cent of the acid rain falling on eastern Canada comes from the United States. U.S. Secretary of Energy James B. Edwards confirmed on July 18 that Canadian diplomats had charged the Reagan Administration with failure to

Thousands of Greeks protest against air pollution in Athens on April 21. Airborne pollutants sometimes hang over the city like a cloud.

comply with an August 1980 agreement on acid rain. The United States had promised to try to reduce pollution from factories that burned large amounts of coal.

The Sagebrush Rebellion, an effort by some Western states to have the federal government give the states control of 400 million acres (160 million hectares) of public land, virtually ended in 1981. State leaders attending the Western Governors' Conference in Jackson, Wyo., on September 11 agreed that the rebellion had run its course. The movement had begun in 1979, when Nevada enacted legislation to seize 49 million acres (20 million hectares) of federal land. Four other states passed similar legislation, but such bills failed in five states.

Members of the Senate Energy and Natural Resources Committee questioned James G. Watt, Reagan's choice for secretary of the interior, closely on the rebellion during confirmation hearings in January. Watt's answers surprised some of the senators, because both he and Reagan had described themselves as "sagebrush rebels." "The solution to the rebellion does not need to be massive transfers of federal lands to the states," Watt said. "Instead, the solution is good management that will put aside the oppressive landlord attitude."

At the September 11 governors' conference, Watt said that his "good neighbor" policy toward the West was working and that the sagebrush rebellion had been defused. "The President continues to be a sagebrush rebel and so does Jim Watt," he said. "But I hope to be a rebel without a cause."

Offshore Leases. On February 11, Watt proposed to include four areas off the shore of central and northern California in a May sale of oil and gas leases. Watt's proposal brought a storm of angry protests. California's Governor Edmund G. Brown, Jr., and many California congressmen argued that oil development was too risky along the scenic coastline.

Secretary of the Interior Cecil D. Andrus had removed the four areas from the sale list in October 1980, just before the November national elections. Environmentalists who opposed Watt cited Andrus' conclusion that the risk of ecological damage outweighed the potential benefit of recovering the small supply of oil that geologists said might be in the areas.

Watt said that offshore exploration was safe and that the United States should develop new domestic sources of oil and gas to reduce the nation's dependence on imports. "The greatest potential for new oil discoveries is on public land, and 80 per cent of that oil is expected to be found offshore," he said.

California Republican leaders warned Watt that selling leases in the four areas might help Demo-

Secretary of the Interior James G. Watt rides along a shallow river during an inspection of Yellowstone National Park in September.

cratic candidates. Watt announced on August 7 that he would not pursue leasing the areas until certain legal issues were settled.

On July 15, the Interior Department proposed an offshore oil- and gas-leasing program that would run from 1982 through 1986. The program would shorten the environmental-impact study process and allow early leasing in areas thought to contain large amounts of oil, especially regions off the coast of Alaska. The department expected that the program would allow it to offer about 200 million acres (80 million hectares) per year. By contrast, the department currently offers about 8 million acres (3.2 million hectares) per year.

Pesticide Problem. California officials declared victory over the Mediterranean fruit fly (Medfly) on September 23 after a month without new major infestations. Governor Brown's initial opposition to the aerial spraying of the pesticide malathion on infested areas appeared to damage him and the environmental movement politically. A poll taken in late August showed that 60 per cent of California's voters disapproved of Brown's handling of the infestation. *The Wall Street Journal* said on September 1 that Brown had "generated unfounded hysteria over the health effects of the pesticide and seems to have become the first politician hoist by his own environmentalist petard." California harvested bumper crops despite the infestation, but officials estimated the total cost of fighting the Medfly and its damage to crops at $100 million.

Four environmental organizations asked the federal government to ban the pesticide endrin on September 29 after wild ducks and geese in Montana were found to have been contaminated by it. Endrin, which is 225 times as poisonous as malathion, was sprayed on 262,000 acres (105,000 hectares) of wheat fields in Colorado, Montana, South Dakota, Wyoming, and possibly Utah to counteract cutworms. Montana considered canceling its duck-hunting season but decided on September 25 to permit hunting. See HUNTING.

EPA Cuts. The Senate Committee on Environment and Public Works halted action on environmental legislation on September 30 so that it could investigate proposals for cutting the budget of the Environmental Protection Agency (EPA). The proposals would decrease the EPA's funding and personnel by 50 per cent by the end of 1984. Conservationists worried about cuts in funds for enforcing rules that govern the pollution of air by industry and for implementing legislation that calls for safely disposing of the 40 million short tons (36 metric tons) of hazardous waste generated annually in the United States.   Andrew L. Newman

See also CONSERVATION. In WORLD BOOK, see ENVIRONMENT; ENVIRONMENTAL POLLUTION.

EQUATORIAL GUINEA. See AFRICA.

ETHIOPIA. See AFRICA.

EUROPE. Poland shocked the world on Dec. 13, 1981, by imposing martial law; banning public gatherings; arresting leaders of the independent labor union Solidarity and former leaders of the government and the Communist Party; and instituting the most effective news blackout in Europe since World War II. United States Secretary of State Alexander M. Haig, Jr., said that the United States was "seriously concerned" about the imposition of martial law and repeated the West's warning to Russia not to interfere in the crisis. Russia's official news agency, Tass, said that the imposition was an internal Polish affair and that the West should stay out of it. On December 23, President Ronald Reagan suspended major economic ties with Poland and threatened Russia with sanctions if "the outrages in Poland" did not end. On December 29, Reagan imposed economic sanctions against Russia and warned that "further steps may be necessary and I will be prepared to take them" (see PRESIDENT OF THE UNITED STATES).

Dissension between European nations and the United States reached new peaks in 1981. United States Secretary of Defense Caspar W. Weinberger announced on August 10 that President Reagan had decided to assemble neutron warheads, apparently without consulting his Western allies. The news sparked demonstrations in Belgium, Great Britain, the Netherlands, Sweden, and West Germany. West German leaders feared that Reagan's decision would damage the prospects of détente with Russia.

A neutron warhead contains a nuclear weapon that emits a large amount of radiation when it explodes. This radiation could penetrate the armor of tanks, killing their crews without causing massive damage to the surrounding area.

France Moves Left. After 23 years of center-right government, the French voted President Valéry Giscard d'Estaing out of office on May 10 and replaced him with Socialist François Mitterrand. Parliamentary elections in June gave the Socialists a majority in the National Assembly.

Greek voters followed suit on October 18, rejecting the New Democratic Party government of Prime Minister George Rallis. Andreas Papandreou of the victorious Pan Hellenic Socialist Movement succeeded Rallis.

Belgium, Italy, the Netherlands, and Portugal suffered crises of confidence in their governments. Spain's Prime Minister Adolfo Suarez Gonzalez resigned on January 29. His deputy and successor, Leopoldo Calvo Sotelo y Bustelo, overcame an attempted right wing coup d'état in February.

Heir Marries. Europe's social event of the year was the July 29 wedding of Charles, Prince of Wales and heir to the British throne, and Lady Diana Spencer. Most of Europe's royal families, whether in power or in exile, were represented.

West German protesters march over John F.
Kennedy Bridge on the way to Bonn during an
October demonstration against nuclear weapons.

Pope Shot. The world was shocked on May 13,
when Turkish terrorist Mehmet Ali Agca shot Pope
John Paul II in St. Peter's Square. Two bullets hit
the pope as he was riding in an open car welcoming
pilgrims. After undergoing surgery, he made a slow
recovery and finally left the hospital on August 14.
See ROMAN CATHOLIC CHURCH.

Strong Dollar. Leaders of Canada, France, Great
Britain, Italy, Japan, the United States, and West
Germany held their annual economic summit

meeting from July 19 to 21 near Ottawa, Canada.
British Prime Minister Margaret Thatcher called
the meeting "a very successful summit," and a
joint communiqué declared a "determination and
ability to tackle our problems in a spirit of shared
responsibility." But some of the leaders came away
discouraged by major disagreements over political
and economic issues.

The summit had shown no sign of agreement on
bringing down high U.S. interest rates, which
stood at about 20 per cent at that time. In addition,
U.S. plans to toughen restrictions on trade with
Russia had angered West German leaders.

By August 3, the British pound had slipped to its
October 1977 value of $1.79, and the French franc

had fallen to a record 6 francs to $1. European and Japanese central banks intervened on August 4 through 6 to halt the dollar's advance against their currencies. The banks of Great Britain, Switzerland, and West Germany sold dollars heavily with little immediate effect, but the dollar fell slightly in later weeks.

New Values. The finance ministers of the European Monetary System (EMS), a program established by eight nations to stabilize their exchange rates, announced four changes on October 4. The Netherlands and West Germany raised the values of their currencies by 5.5 per cent, while France and Italy lowered theirs by 3 per cent, relative to the currencies of Belgium, Denmark, Ireland, and Luxembourg.

France's inflation rate of 20 per cent and a 13.5 per cent rate in Italy had caused the prices of those countries' goods to rise sharply in West Germany, their largest foreign market. Consequently, both France and Italy had built up large trade deficits. The October 4 changes helped the two countries by making their products 8.5 per cent less expensive in the Netherlands and West Germany and 3 per cent cheaper in the other EMS nations.

NATO Alarmed. Ministers of the North Atlantic Treaty Organization (NATO) agreed in Rome on May 5 to implement their 1979 decision to install new nuclear missiles in Europe. They also pledged to try to negotiate limits on these missiles with Russia. In Moscow, a Soviet official said that Russia would not passively accept NATO's attempt to upset the nuclear balance in Europe by installing the missiles. But the United States insisted that NATO must catch up with the latest Russian missile installations. NATO estimated that Russia had installed on its own soil some 450 SS-20 missiles capable of striking Western Europe. Russia also had 210 mobile missiles.

NATO wanted to begin installing 464 cruise missiles and 108 Pershing II ballistic missiles in Belgium, Great Britain, Italy, the Netherlands, and West Germany in 1983. West Germany repeated its willingness to have nuclear missiles on its soil, and Chancellor Helmut Schmidt did his best to persuade the Netherlands and Belgium to follow suit. But the antinuclear movement was growing, and demonstrations occurred in many cities.

Reagan Proposed on November 18 to cancel the new missiles if Russia would dismantle comparable weapons. Thatcher and Schmidt praised the proposal, but Russia said Reagan was trying to scuttle disarmament talks and to weaken the antinuclear movement.

Schmidt held arms talks with Russia's Communist Party General Secretary and Supreme Soviet Presidium Chairman Leonid Ilich Brezhnev in Bonn from November 22 to 25. After the talks, Schmidt said Brezhnev had convinced him that Russia wanted to reduce arms. However, Brezhnev would not acknowledge that Reagan wanted peace.

Budget Debate. Gaston Thorn – the new president of the Commission, the governing body of the European Community (EC or Common Market) – threatened legal action against Belgium, France, and West Germany unless they paid their full contributions to the EC's 1980 supplementary budget and to its 1981 budget. The countries finally paid their dues.

In 1981, Thatcher found a new ally in Schmidt. The two were concerned about being the largest contributors to the EC budget. They demanded an early start on restructuring the budget and changing the Common Agricultural Policy, the system of price supports that took most of the money.

The Commission asked for a 16 per cent spending hike to $23 billion. The budget included a 12.8 per cent increase in spending on agriculture and higher grants for depressed areas. The EC compromised on July 24, cutting the increase in total spending to 4.4 per cent.

Tenth Member. On Jan. 1, 1981, Greece became the 10th nation to join the EC. Prime Minister George Rallis said that the main beneficiaries would be Greek farmers, who could count on $430-million per year. The EC continued entry negotiations with Spain and Portugal, which hoped to join the Common Market in 1984.

Parliament's Workplace. Luxembourg; Brussels, Belgium; and Strasbourg, France, continued their competition to become the European Parliament's single workplace. Luxembourg announced on July 15 that it intended to take Parliament before the Court of Justice over its decision to hold all its sessions in Strasbourg. Party leaders in Parliament decided to ask the Council of Ministers, the policy-making body of the EC, to decide the issue by secret ballot.

Unemployment in the EC rose from 8.4 million at the start of 1981 to 8.5 million by June, an increase of 1.2 per cent, compared with a 7.7 per cent increase for all of 1980.

Peace Moves. The EC continued its involvement with countries outside Europe by encouraging Middle East peace moves and proposing a peace plan for Afghanistan. President Anwar el-Sadat of Egypt began three days of talks with EC leaders in Luxembourg on February 9 to promote a European peacemaking role in the Middle East. He called on the European Parliament to support the right of the Palestinian people to self-determination.

On June 30, the EC proposed an international conference in the autumn to secure the withdrawal of Russian troops from Afghanistan and to end that country's internal political crisis. Lord Carrington, the British foreign secretary, took the idea to Moscow on July 6, but Russia told him that it was unacceptable.

Facts in Brief on the European Countries

Country	Population	Government	Monetary Unit*	Foreign Trade (million U.S. $) Exports†	Foreign Trade (million U.S. $) Imports†
Albania	2,875,000	Communist Party First Secretary Enver Hoxha; People's Assembly Presidium Chairman Haxhi Lleshi	lek (7 = $1)	151	173
Andorra	34,000	The bishop of Urgel, Spain, and the president of France	French franc & Spanish peseta	no statistics available	
Austria	7,529,000	President Rudolf Kirchschlaeger; Chancellor Bruno Kreisky	schilling (15.5 = $1)	17,508	24,495
Belgium	9,909,000	King Baudouin I; Prime Minister Wilfried Martens	franc (37.6 = $1)	64,066 (includes Luxembourg)	71,185
Bulgaria	8,992,000	Communist Party General Secretary & State Council Chairman Todor Zhivkov; Prime Minister Georgi Stanchev Filipov	lev (1 = $1.18)	10,372	9,650
Czechoslovakia	15,569,000	Communist Party General Secretary & President Gustav Husak; Prime Minister Lubomir Strougal	koruna (11.7 = $1)	14,891	15,148
Denmark	5,180,000	Queen Margrethe II; Prime Minister Anker Henrik Jorgensen	krone (7.2 = $1)	16,485	19,363
Finland	4,795,000	Acting President Mauno Koivisto; Acting Prime Minister Eino Uusitalo	markka (4.3 = $1)	14,155	15,580
France	54,446,000	President François Mitterrand; Prime Minister Pierre Mauroy	franc (5.6 = $1)	111,251	134,912
Germany, East	16,645,000	Communist Party Secretary General & State Council Chairman Erich Honecker; Prime Minister Willi Stoph	mark (2.4 = $1)	17,312	19,082
Germany, West	60,935,000	President Karl Carstens; Chancellor Helmut Schmidt	Deutsche mark (2.2 = $1)	192,930	188,001
Great Britain	56,019,000	Queen Elizabeth II; Prime Minister Margaret Thatcher	pound (1 = $1.94)	115,350	120,095
Greece	9,663,000	President Constantine Karamanlis; Prime Minister Andreas Papandreou	drachma (56.7 = $1)	5,143	10,531
Hungary	10,839,000	Communist Party First Secretary Janos Kadar; President Pal Losonczi; Prime Minister Gyorgy Lazar	forint (29.5 = $1)	8,677	9,235
Iceland	235,000	President Vigdis Finnbogadottir; Prime Minister Gunnar Thoroddsen	krona (7.8 = $1)	931	1,000
Ireland	3,440,000	President Patrick J. Hillery; Prime Minister Garret FitzGerald	pound (1 = $1.59)	8,489	11,192
Italy	58,159,000	President Alessandro Pertini; Prime Minister Giovanni Spadolini	lira (1,191.5 = $1)	77,667	99,452
Liechtenstein	26,000	Prince Franz Josef II; Prime Minister Hans Brunhart	Swiss franc	no statistics available	
Luxembourg	365,000	Grand Duke Jean; Prime Minister Pierre Werner	franc (37.6 = $1)	64,066 (includes Belgium)	71,185
Malta	370,000	President Anton Buttigieg; Prime Minister Dom Mintoff	pound (1 = $2.58)	497	938
Monaco	26,000	Prince Rainier III	French franc	no statistics available	
Netherlands	14,467,000	Queen Beatrix; Prime Minister Andreas A. M. van Agt	guilder (2.4 = $1)	73,871	76,881
Norway	4,154,000	King Olav V; Prime Minister Kaare Willoch	krone (5.7 = $1)	18,476	16,957
Poland	36,190,000	Communist Party First Secretary & Council of Ministers Chairman Wojciech Jaruzelski; President Henryk Jablonski	zloty (33.2 = $1)	16,998	18,871
Portugal	10,286,000	President Antonio dos Santos Ramalho Eanes; Prime Minister Francisco Pinto Balsemao	escudo (64 = $1)	3,468	6,086
Romania	22,742,000	Communist Party General Secretary & President Nicolae Ceausescu; Prime Minister Ilie Verdet	leu (4.4 = $1)	12,230	13,200
Russia	269,591,000	Communist Party General Secretary & Supreme Soviet Presidium Chairman Leonid Ilich Brezhnev; Council of Ministers Chairman Nikolay Aleksandrovich Tikhonov	ruble (1 = $1.41)	76,481	68,523
San Marino	23,000	2 captains regent appointed by Grand Council every 6 months	Italian lira	no statistics available	
Spain	38,420,000	King Juan Carlos I; President Leopoldo Calvo Sotelo y Bustelo	peseta (94.2 = $1)	20,721	34,080
Sweden	8,369,000	King Carl XVI Gustaf; Prime Minister Thorbjorn Falldin	krona (5.5 = $1)	30,914	33,441
Switzerland	6,291,000	President Fritz Honegger	franc (1.8 = $1)	29,634	36,356
Turkey	47,999,000	Head of State Kenan Evren; Prime Minister Bulend Ulusu	lira (127.4 = $1)	2,445	5,802
Yugoslavia	22,709,000	President Sergej Kraigher; Prime Minister Veselin Djuranovic	dinar (33.3 = $1)	8,367	14,029

*Exchange rates as of Dec. 1, 1981. †Latest available data.

France's President Mitterrand and Prime Minister Thatcher of Great Britain announce new joint studies on building a tunnel under the English Channel.

Farmers' Siege. Riot police used tear gas in Brussels on March 31 to scatter thousands of farmers, mainly French and Italian, who had besieged EC headquarters to demand higher farm support prices. Emotions were inflamed when a French farmer outside the building was knocked down and killed by a car. Farmers threw rotten eggs, vegetables, stones, and bottles at police. Inside EC headquarters, the European Commission was ending weeks of argument by agreeing on a 9 per cent increase in farm support prices. The farmers wanted at least 15 per cent.

Russian Energy. On November 20, Russia and Ruhrgas A.G., a West German gas company, signed an agreement that was expected to lead to the construction of a $10-billion pipeline to carry gas from Siberia to Czechoslovakia. Other pipelines would convey the gas to Western Europe. The United States expressed fears that the pipeline would make Western Europe too dependent on Russia.

Eastern Troubles. Poland's continuing labor crisis and grave economic problems overshadowed the annual conference of the Communist bloc's Council for Mutual Economic Assistance (COMECON) in Sofia, Bulgaria, from July 2 through 4. Poland failed to meet its 1980 commitment to supply its COMECON neighbors with $40 million worth of coal, sulfur, and machinery, and faced even greater failures in 1981. Poland's problems affected the COMECON nations' economies so severely that the delegates had to postpone crucial decisions on the countries' five-year plans until 1982. The delegates recognized that Poland would not be able to meet its trade commitments for several years.

Steel Crisis. On February 27, the EC Commission ordered the steel companies in the EC to cut their production by 18 to 25 per cent of 1979 levels. The commissioners hoped that this move would lead to higher prices.

EC industrial ministers agreed on March 27 to subsidize only those companies that took steps to upgrade their equipment and cut their production capacity. The EC agreed to end all steel subsidies by the end of 1985.

Iceland's Inflation spurred that nation's government to freeze prices on January 1. Leaders hoped this action would lower the inflation rate to 40 per cent per year by the end of 1981. Before the freeze, the government raised postage rates and the charges of the state-run bus, electrical, and telephone service by 10 per cent. Kenneth Brown

See also the various European country articles; CHARLES, PRINCE; DIANA, PRINCESS OF WALES; ECONOMICS. In WORLD BOOK, see EUROPE; EUROPEAN COMMUNITY.

EXPLOSION. See DISASTERS.

EYSKENS, MARK (1933-   ), a Christian Democrat, served as prime minister of Belgium from April 6 to Sept. 21, 1981. He succeeded Wilfried Martens but resigned after five months when his Cabinet failed to agree on financial aid for a troubled Belgian steel company. See BELGIUM.

Mark Eyskens was born in Louvain in the Flemish part of Belgium on April 29, 1933. His father, Gaston Eyskens, was prime minister under three governments: from 1949 to 1950, from 1958 to 1961, and from 1968 to 1972. Mark graduated from Louvain Catholic University with a bachelor's degree and a doctorate in laws and economic sciences. He also received a master's degree in economics from Columbia University in New York City.

Eyskens began his career in 1962 as economic adviser to the finance minister. From 1966 to 1969, he served on commissions to study economic expansion and ports. He became a deputy senator in 1974 and a member of Parliament in 1977.

Under the first government of Prime Minister Leo Tindemans, Eyskens served as secretary of state for Flemish regional economy, territory development, and housing from October 1976 to June 1977. From June 1977 to April 1979, he was secretary of state for the budget, along with economy and development. He later served as minister for cooperation in development and became minister of finance in October 1980.   Marsha F. Goldsmith

FARM AND FARMING. For farmers in the United States, 1981 was as disappointing as 1980. In 1980, farm income dropped sharply because of increased production costs and lowered output resulting from erratic weather. In 1981, farmers harvested bumper crops but were squeezed between falling prices for their crops and continued increases in costs due to inflation and high interest rates. As income fell, farmers' savings, seriously depleted in 1980, dropped further. In addition, nearly all federal farm legislation was up for renewal in 1981. As farm programs were threatened by pressures to cut federal spending and legislation dragged on throughout most of the year, farmers became even more restive. Nevertheless, the number of farms in the United States increased in 1981 for the first time since 1935.

Farm Bill. Congressional debate over the farm bill dragged on for months and cracked the traditionally solid farm bloc. Lawmakers were caught between pressure from the Administration of President Ronald Reagan to cut farm spending and demands by farmers to increase aid. On September 18, the Senate approved a four-year, $10.6-billion bill, which exceeded Administration spending targets but gave the Administration most of the spending cuts it had requested. On October 22, however, the House passed its own $16.6-billion version of the bill.

After more than a month of haggling, a Senate-House conference committee agreed on December 8 to a compromise $11-billion measure. The bill slowed the growth of price support loans and income subsidies for wheat, corn, cotton, and rice, and abandoned the use of parity in determining support levels for milk. Parity is a 1914-based index that attempts to reflect the prices farmers receive compared with their costs. The measure also re-established the sugar price-support system, eliminated restrictions on peanut growing, preserved the tobacco price-support system, and cut $700 million from the food-stamp program.

The Senate approved the compromise bill on December 10. Democratic leaders predicted a tough fight in the House, which had rejected the sugar and peanut provisions of the bill in October. Nevertheless, the Reagan Administration eked out a narrow victory as the House passed the measure on December 16 by a two-vote margin.

Production and Prices. Farmers in the United States in 1981 harvested record crops of wheat, corn, and rice as well as bumper crops of soybeans, cotton, sugar, and peanuts. Overall farm production rose 8 per cent. Total livestock output was up 2 per cent, and total crop output climbed a whopping 14 per cent. Sorghum led the increase at 49 per cent. Cotton was up 41 per cent; rice, 26 per

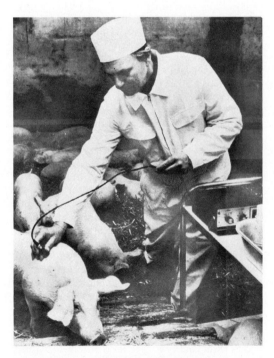

A veterinary assistant in Munich, West Germany, uses ultrasound to measure the layer of fat on a pig. Such examinations help ensure meat quality.

Fear that the Mediterranean fruit fly would enter the San Joaquin Valley led California officials in August to quarantine a nearby infested area.

cent; corn, 22 per cent; soybeans, 16 per cent; wheat, 16 per cent; tobacco, 14 per cent; and oats, 11 per cent. Broilers were up 6 per cent, and turkeys rose 6 per cent. Beef, veal, and milk rose 3 per cent, and lamb and mutton rose 6 per cent. Pork dropped 5 per cent, and eggs fell 1 per cent.

Overall prices received by farmers advanced during the first part of 1981, rising as much as 14 per cent in the first quarter over the same period in 1980. But by the fourth quarter, livestock prices had fallen 7 per cent, and crop prices were down 13 per cent, resulting in an overall price drop of 10 per cent. Compared with 1980 prices, prices in November 1981 were down 19 per cent for cotton, 27 per cent for sorghum, 25 per cent for corn, 27 per cent for soybeans, 12 per cent for wheat, and 15 per cent for rice. Prices for oranges and grapefruit, damaged by a severe freeze in Florida in January, rose early in the year but were near 1980 levels at year-end. On September 2, Secretary of Agriculture John R. Block ordered a 15 per cent reduction in the amount of land planted with wheat in 1982 as a means of halting the continuing decline in wheat prices and of holding down the cost of federal subsidies for wheat farmers.

U.S. Farm Finances. Net farm income dropped 13 per cent in 1981 to $19 billion. Inflation increased the value of farmers' assets, so that 1981 income, adjusted for inventory value increases, actually improved over 1980 levels. But because 1981 was their second year of depressed incomes, many farmers experienced severe cash-flow problems. Although cash receipts in 1981 rose 6 per cent, production expenses climbed 9.5 per cent. In addition, the gap between the prices farmers received for their products and retail food prices widened in 1981.

In early 1981, the total value of farm assets stood at $1.09 trillion, up 9 per cent from 1980 levels. Total liabilities equaled $175 billion, and farmers' equity stood at $916 billion. Farm debt rose 10 per cent in 1981. Many farmers were caught in a credit crunch as interest rates soared to record levels.

Agricultural Trade. Although considerably below expectations, U.S. agricultural exports increased for the 12th straight record year, rising 8 per cent to $43.8 billion during the 1981 fiscal year. However, export volume actually dropped 1 per cent, partly because of the partial embargo on sales of wheat and corn to the Soviet Union. Agricultural imports remained approximately at the 1980 level of $17 billion. Thus, the fiscal 1981 agricultural trade surplus exceeded $26 billion, up from about $23 billion in fiscal 1980.

In 1981, wheat and flour exports rose 22 per cent; feed grains, 14 per cent; rice, 31 per cent; fruits, vegetables, and nuts, 14 per cent; and sugar and tropical products, 66 per cent. Exports of livestock and livestock products rose 13 per cent. Oilseeds, including peanuts and cotton seeds, and oilseed products were down 6 per cent; cotton fell 26 per cent; soybeans dropped 16 per cent; and tobacco was essentially unchanged.

Japan remained the number-one outlet for U.S. agricultural exports in 1981. Mexico replaced the Soviet Union in second place, and China moved up to third. The industrialized nations received 48 per cent of U.S. agricultural exports. The centrally planned countries, such as the Soviet Union and China, took 14 per cent. Developing countries took 37 per cent, a 19 per cent increase over fiscal 1980 that accounted for nearly the total increase in U.S. agricultural exports in fiscal 1981.

World Production. World grain production in 1981 rose 4 per cent to a record high of 1.62 billion metric tons (1.79 billion short tons) of wheat, coarse grains, and rough rice. Record U.S. crops accounted for most of the increase. Production gains in Canada and Brazil were offset by reductions in Argentina and Russia, which had its third consecutive bad harvest. Production in Western Europe also dropped sharply. In Canada and Eastern Europe, a larger amount of planted land and improved yields helped boost production.

World production of individual crops varied from 1980 levels, with coffee up 15 per cent; soybeans, 11 per cent; sugar, 15 per cent; cotton, 9 per cent; wheat and rice, 3 per cent; and corn, 8 per cent. Meat production remained at 1980 levels. Poultry production rose slightly, but the increase was offset by a decline in pork production.

Global Food Problems. The first World Food Day was observed in 140 countries on October 16. Sponsored by the Food and Agriculture Organization (FAO) of the United Nations, the observance was intended to call attention to the severity of world hunger. World hunger also was on the agenda at several international conferences, including the summit between industrialized and developing countries in Cancún, Mexico, in October and the FAO Conference in Rome in November.

Increases in food production in China in 1981 and in some Latin American countries were overshadowed by many problems elsewhere. In July, India announced that for the first time in four years, it would import food. Famine continued to rage in Somalia, Ethiopia, and Uganda and in parts of Asia. At year-end, world food stocks had fallen to only about 17 per cent of annual world consumption, an amount considered a minimum.

Embargo Lifted. On April 24, President Reagan fulfilled a campaign promise by lifting the 15-month partial ban on sales of grain to the Soviet Union. The embargo had been imposed by President Jimmy Carter on Jan. 4, 1980, because of Russia's invasion of Afghanistan. Farmers in the United States had strongly opposed the embargo.

They felt that they were being forced to shoulder an unfair part of the cost of U.S. foreign policy.

On August 5, the United States and the Soviet Union agreed to a one-year extension of an existing contract that commits Russia to buy at least 6 million metric tons (6.6 million short tons) of grain per year. The two countries agreed to the extension after failing to reach a new long-term grain-purchasing agreement.

On October 1, the United States announced that the Soviet Union would be allowed to purchase up to 23 million metric tons (25.3 million short tons) of grain during the next 12 months. On December 29, Reagan postponed negotiations on the long-term purchasing agreement.

Agricultural Statistics, 1981

World Crop Production
(million units)

Crop	Units	1980	1981*	% U.S. 1981*
Corn	Metric tons	402.9	434.7	47.3
Wheat	Metric tons	438.6	448.1	16.7
Rice (milled)	Metric tons	265.7	275.5	2.2
Barley	Metric tons	162.5	162.1	6.4
Oats	Metric tons	44.3	45.6	16.2
Rye	Metric tons	25.3	24.7	1.8
Soybeans	Metric tons	80.9	90.0	62.8
Cotton	Bales**	65.4	70.9	22.0
Coffee	Bags***	84.3	96.9	****
Sugar (centrifugal)	Metric tons	86.6	95.8	6.1

*Preliminary
**480 lbs. (217.7 kilograms) net
***132.276 lbs. (60 kilograms)
****Less than 1 per cent

Output of Major U.S. Crops
(millions of bushels)

Crop	1962-66*	1980	1981**
Corn	3,876	6,648	8,097
Sorghum	595	588	876
Oats	912	458	509
Wheat	1,229	2,370	2,750
Soybeans	769	1,792	2,077
Rice (rough) (a)	742	1,451	1,826
Potatoes (b)	275	303	329
Cotton (c)	140	111	156
Tobacco (d)	2,126	1,782	2,028

*Average; **Preliminary
(a) 100,000 cwt. (4.54 million kilograms)
(b) 1 million cwt. (45.4 million kilograms)
(c) 100,000 bales (50 million lbs.) (22.7 million kilograms)
(d) 1 million lbs. (454,000 kilograms)

U.S. Production of Animal Products
(millions of pounds)

	1957-59*	1980	1981**
Beef	13,704	21,470	22,063
Veal	1,240	379	408
Lamb & Mutton	711	310	328
Pork	10,957	16,431	15,585
Eggs (a)	5,475	5,806	5,717
Turkeys	1,382	2,303	2,447
Total milk (b)	123	128.4	132.3
Broilers	4,430	11,089	11,733

*Average; **Preliminary
(a) 1 million dozens
(b) Billions of lbs. (454 million kilograms)

War on the Medfly. California fruit growers brought in largely undamaged harvests in 1981 despite an infestation of the Mediterranean fruit fly that spread to seven counties and threatened the state's $14-billion agricultural industry. At times, however, the $56-million battle against the pest seemed to be only a part of a larger war that pitted state officials against federal officials and agricultural organizations against community and environmental groups.

Mediterranean fruit flies, or Medflies, were first discovered in California in June 1980 in Santa Clara County and in the Los Angeles area. California officials suspected that the flies had entered the state in fruit smuggled from Hawaii. The Medfly lays its eggs in more than 200 varieties of fruits and vegetables. The maggots that hatch from the eggs cause the fruit and vegetables to rot.

State officials quickly eradicated the pests in the Los Angeles area by applying insecticide to infested trees and by releasing sterile male Medflies to sabotage the flies' reproductive cycle. However, the fly was more tenacious in northern California. Plans for aerial spraying of infested areas with the pesticide malathion were halted after a storm of protest by community and environmental groups. They opposed the use of the pesticide because some experts believed it might cause birth defects in the unborn and cancer. Instead, Governor Edmund G. Brown, Jr., imposed a quarantine over three infested counties and ordered massive ground spraying. State workers also stripped thousands of tons of fruit from trees in the area. By August, the quarantined area had been expanded to more than 3,000 square miles (7,770 square kilometers).

Brown repeatedly resisted demands by growers to order aerial spraying of infested areas until July. On July 10, Agriculture Secretary Block threatened to impose a quarantine on all California produce unless Brown ordered aerial spraying. Spraying began on July 14, after the California Supreme Court refused to block the move. State workers eventually sprayed a 1,300-square-mile (3,365-square-kilometer) area.

On August 4, Medflies were discovered near Tampa, Fla., but the infestation was quickly eliminated. In early October, California officials announced that eradication efforts seemed to be working because no fertile Medflies had been found in sprayed areas for a long period. However, the discovery in late October of two fertile Medflies in an area that had been repeatedly sprayed delayed plans to end aerial spraying.

Farm Increase. The number of farms in the United States increased in 1981 for the first time in 46 years, the United States Department of Agriculture (USDA) announced in December. The agency reported that there were an estimated 2,436,000 farms in the United States, 8,000 more than in 1980. The last rise in the number of U.S. farms occurred in 1935, when the government reported an increase to 6,810,000. The decline had been steady since then.

According to the USDA, the total amount of farmland in use in the United States in 1981 was 1.045 billion acres (423 million hectares), up from 1.042 billion acres (422 million hectares) in 1980. The average U.S. farm was 429 acres (174 hectares).

Genetic Engineering. The USDA announced on June 18 that a safe, effective vaccine against foot-and-mouth disease had been developed using gene-splicing techniques. Gene splicing involves the transfer of genes from one organism to another. The vaccine consists of a protein, found on the surface of the virus that causes the disease, that is capable of immunizing animals against the disease. Genetic material carrying instructions for producing the protein is spliced into the genes of commonly used laboratory bacteria, which then manufacture the protein.

On June 29, the USDA announced that scientists had developed a genetic-engineering process for moving genes from one plant species to another. Researchers had transferred a gene from a French bean into a sunflower cell. Charles E. French

See also FOOD. In WORLD BOOK, see AGRICULTURE; FARM AND FARMING.

FASHION. Permissiveness was the rule in fashion in 1981 as lengths and shapes of clothes varied within designers' collections as well as in women's wardrobes. There was no longer any need to measure hemlines in terms of inches from the floor or from the waistline. The choice of hemline was up to the individual, and it varied from above the knees to almost skimming the ankles. What prevailed, however, was a middle ground, hovering around the knee. Some avant-garde dressers wore tunic-length sweaters over heavy tights and thick, knitted leg warmers during cold weather, while others opted for calf-length skirts.

Fashion designers, spearheaded by Giorgio Armani, Valentino, and Karl Lagerfeld in Europe, and by James Galanos in the United States, made a strong effort to change the contour of trousers in wildly inventive ways in 1981. Balloon pants, breeches, Bermuda shorts, and styles that were puffy over the hips and tapered down the legs were shown in many lengths. These were more readily adopted by fashion-conscious women in European cities, such as Paris and Milan, Italy, than they were in the United States, where culottes, or divided skirts, were widely accepted. The shape of the culottes was also diversified. Some of them were cut so full that they could scarcely be distinguished from skirts, while others more nearly resembled trousers.

Sportswear was the prevailing mode of dressing, which meant that different tops — camisoles, sweaters, blouses, and jackets of all lengths — were paired with different bottoms. This allowed women to put clothes together in an individual way. Many of the separate parts were interchangeable for day or evening, and for casual or more formal occasions. Rising prices of all apparel contributed to the appeal of multiple-purpose clothes.

Sweatshirts made final their drift during the past few years up from the football stadium into the realm of women's fashion. Versions appeared hand-painted, gilt-decorated, and of fine fabrics.

Metal and Leather aroused new interest. Gold, copper, brass, and other metallic fashions, such as blouses or skirts, appeared. Gleaming accessories, such as handbags, shoes, and belts, were worn with warm-weather and cool-weather clothes, giving a spark of glamour to otherwise sober outfits. Leather became a stylish material, used alone or in combination with silk, linen, cotton, or wool fabrics. New processing made leather as supple as silk. In pastel and strong colors, it was considered appropriate for all seasons.

Elegance Re-Enters. There was also a general upgrading in the caliber of clothes worn by fashionable women, sparked by the taste of President Ronald Reagan's wife, Nancy, and her penchant for formal entertaining at the White House. This contrasted with the homier atmosphere of President Jimmy Carter's Administration. The first lady's patronage of top-flight designers, such as Galanos, Adolfo, and Bill Blass, spurred interest in higher-priced clothing.

In London, the July wedding of Lady Diana Spencer to Charles, Prince of Wales, also stimulated a lively interest in dressing up. It focused attention on David and Elizabeth Emanuel, the young designers who made the bridal gown. They promptly introduced a perfume to capitalize, like many other designers, on their name.

In Paris, the couture or made-to-order part of the fashion industry brought out dazzlingly extravagant collections, as if in defiance of the recently elected Socialist regime of France's President Francois Mitterrand. Only a very small percentage of their work was destined for French people, however. The bulk of the clients at most couture houses were from the oil-rich countries of the Middle East, and from South America.

Of all the world's fashion centers, Milan and New York City fared best. Clothes originating there were easy, unpretentious, and in the modern spirit. With designers like Armani, Missoni, and Fendi, the Milanese fashion message spread throughout the world. New York designers, concentrating on the needs of the working woman, also became more influential internationally.   Bernadine Morris

In WORLD BOOK, see FASHION.

First lady Nancy Reagan's opulent, beaded inaugural gown by designer James Galanos epitomized the return to evening elegance.

FINLAND. President Urho Kekkonen, 81, resigned on Oct. 27, 1981, after 25 years in office. He had been suffering from memory lapses and absent-mindedness caused by hardening of the arteries. The government announced that the people would select an electoral college on Jan. 17 and 18, 1982, and that the electoral college would choose a new president on January 26. Prime Minister Mauno Koivisto had been serving as acting president since September 11.

Koivisto won a power struggle that threatened to topple his coalition government on April 10, 1981. The Communists in the coalition had caused a crisis over the 1981 wages and prices agreement by insisting on changes in the health insurance plan. However, Koivisto's Social Democrats and the Center Party, which together held 97 of the 200 seats in the *Eduskunta* (parliament), supported the plan.

Communist Party Chairman Aarne Saarinen discussed the disagreement with Kekkonen and then reported that Kekkonen thought Koivisto should be replaced. Koivisto fought back. "Only parliament can dismiss the prime minister," he said. His stand forced the coalition to patch up its differences. Kenneth Brown

See also EUROPE (Facts in Brief Table). In WORLD BOOK, see FINLAND; KEKKONEN, URHO.

FIRE. See DISASTERS.

FISHING. Fishing enthusiasts from as far away as Maine flocked to the Bighorn River on the Crow Indian reservation in Montana on Aug. 20, 1981, for the first public fishing in six years on what many regard as the finest trout stream in the United States. The river had been closed to public fishing in 1975 by the Crow, who claimed they had the right to manage fishing on the 50-mile (80-kilometer) stretch that flows through their reservation. However, the Supreme Court of the United States ruled in March that the state had jurisdiction over the Bighorn.

Many early-arriving anglers were prevented from fishing by a blockade that angry Indians had set up across an access road. Later in the day, a federal court ordered the blockade removed.

Anglers reported many catches in excess of 20 inches (51 centimeters) and 5 pounds (2.3 kilograms). Lunkers were said to strike at every cast.

Some anglers, however, were worried that heavy fishing could deplete the Bighorn's trout population, despite state regulations limiting the number of fish taken. They feared that too many young fish would be harvested, reducing the number of fish that would be spawned in future years.

New Records. Dianne North of Whangarei, New Zealand, set a new all-tackle world record in February, when she landed an 802-pound (364-kilogram) thresher shark after a four-hour battle off Tutukaka, New Zealand. Jim Anson of Miami, Fla., broke a record in April by taking a 30-pound 4-ounce (13.7-kilogram) *permit* (large pompano) on a fly rod at Key West, Fla.

Other Developments. In June, the American Fishing Tackle Manufacturers Association (AFTMA) charged that federal and state agencies misuse millions of dollars in funds provided by U.S. anglers each year. The AFTMA contended that the money, which should be invested in projects that improve sports fishing, is used to fund such projects as monuments and tennis courts. Sixty million American anglers spent $175 million for license fees, permits, and excise taxes on fishing tackle in 1980.

The largest source of funds to improve sports fishing is the Dingell-Johnson fisheries tax, which has apportioned more than $300 million to the states since it was set up in 1952. AFTMA Vice-President Tom Schedler acknowledged that the federal fund has played a vital role in improving sport fisheries, but he said closer scrutiny is needed to ensure that the funds are used for the proper purposes.

On July 9, the International Game Fish Association (IGFA) announced the establishment of a 2-pound (0.9-kilogram) line-class category for freshwater world records. Andrew L. Newman

In WORLD BOOK, see FISHING.

FISHING INDUSTRY. The United States trade deficit could be reduced by $1.7 billion annually by eight major fishery resources scheduled for development during the 1980s, according to an official of the National Oceanic and Atmospheric Administration (NOAA). These resources are to be developed within the U.S. fishery conservation zone, which extends 200 nautical miles off the coasts.

Terry L. Leitzell, NOAA assistant administrator for fisheries, told the U.S. House of Representatives subcommittee on fisheries on June 2, 1981, that the fisheries' annual trade deficit was $2.5-billion. He estimated that development of such resources as Pacific mackerel, Atlantic whiting, and Gulf of Mexico groundfish will increase domestic landings by 2.5 million metric tons (2.8 million short tons) per year. This would bring an additional $782 million yearly in vessel revenues, create more than 43,000 jobs, and add $1.2 billion annually to the gross national product.

The U.S. Fish Catch rose for the third consecutive year in 1980, reaching a record 6.5 billion pounds (2.9 billion kilograms). The domestic fisheries' share of the U.S. seafood market rose from 46.5 per cent in 1976 to 57.1 per cent in 1980. The remainder was supplied by imports. Menhaden, salmon, crabs, and tuna led in quantity caught and value.

Disputes and Distress. President Ronald Reagan pledged during his March 1981 visit to Canada

A Nantucket scalloper carries fishing dredges from his icebound dory in January. The severe winter weather made scallop prices soar.

that efforts to protect the rich Georges Bank fishing grounds off Cape Cod would continue while the two countries' dispute over maritime boundaries there is arbitrated by the International Court of Justice at The Hague in the Netherlands. Georges Bank provides about 17 per cent of the United States fish supply. Canadian Prime Minister Pierre Elliott Trudeau told Reagan that Canada was distressed by the United States decision on March 6 to scrap a treaty to share and manage fish stocks off the Atlantic coast. The Reagan Administration had been unable to win congressional support for the treaty.

Oil from Troubled Waters. A drill bit from an oil rig pierced the ocean floor in the Georges Bank fishing grounds for the first time on July 24. The event climaxed a six-year battle between energy companies on one side and the U.S. Department of the Interior and fishing crews on the other. Fishing crews and environmental groups had bitterly opposed offshore oil development in the area because it might damage or destroy fishery resources.

The Department of the Interior will try to protect the fishery with the most stringent safeguards ever imposed on oil exploration. A biological task force will monitor drilling activities to detect any signs of damage to the ecology from drilling muds. See ENVIRONMENT. Andrew L. Newman

In WORLD BOOK, see FISHING INDUSTRY.

FITZGERALD, GARRET MICHAEL DESMOND (1926-), head of the *Fine Gael* (Gaelic People) party since 1977, became prime minister of Ireland on June 30, 1981. He succeeded Charles J. Haughey, leader of the *Fianna Fáil* (Soldiers of Destiny) party.

Garret FitzGerald was born on Feb. 9, 1926, in Dublin. Both his Roman Catholic father and his Protestant mother were strong Irish nationalists, so the boy grew up in a political atmosphere. FitzGerald went to school in Bray and Waterford and then completed his education in Dublin. He received his bachelor's degree from Belvedere College, his doctorate in economics from University College, and his law degree from King's Inns.

From 1948 to 1958, FitzGerald worked as research and schedules manager at Aer Lingus, the Irish national airline. He was a lecturer in political economics at University College from 1959 to 1973 and wrote for several newspapers. Among his books is *Towards a New Ireland* (1972).

FitzGerald served in the Irish Senate from 1965 to 1969. He was elected to the House of Deputies, which makes Ireland's laws, in 1969. He served as Prime Minister Liam Cosgrave's minister for external affairs from 1973 to 1977. Marsha F. Goldsmith

FLOOD. See DISASTERS.
FLORIDA. See STATE GOVERNMENT.
FLOWER. See GARDENING.

FOOD

FOOD. Lower-than-expected increases in meat prices helped slow the overall rise in food prices in the United States in 1981. Retail food prices rose approximately 8 per cent, slightly less than the 1980 increase. The Agricultural Research Service of the U.S. Department of Agriculture (USDA) estimated that a moderate meal plan for an American family of four in 1981 cost $90 per week.

Food Program Cuts. Federally funded food programs were cut as President Ronald Reagan moved ahead with plans to reduce government spending. Funds for child-nutrition programs, including the national school breakfast and the national school lunch programs, were cut 30 per cent from 1980 levels. In addition, the USDA tightened eligibility requirements for these programs, thereby eliminating an estimated 1.6 million children, who otherwise would have been eligible, from the school lunch program. The Reagan Administration also cut $1.3 billion from the food stamp program, though more people became eligible for benefits because of rising unemployment and inflation.

Food Consumption in the United States remained high in 1981. However, per capita consumption declined slightly from 1980. Experts attributed the decrease to such factors as higher food prices and concerns about health and nutrition.

Pork consumption fell 7 per cent, chiefly because of production cutbacks and a 10 per cent price increase. However, beef and veal consumption increased 0.4 pound (0.18 kilogram) per person, reversing a two-year decline. Beef production also rose, helping hold price increases to less than 2 per cent. In addition, poultry consumption was up.

Egg consumption fell during 1981 to the lowest level since 1935. The drop was attributed to the increased use of other foods as protein sources and consumer concern about dietary cholesterol. The consumption and prices of most other dairy products remained stable. The demand for milk continued to decline.

Price increases for vegetables and fruits dampened consumer demand for those items. Prices jumped 20 per cent for fresh vegetables, 5 per cent for fresh fruits, and 12 per cent for processed fruits and vegetables. A freeze in January destroyed 20 per cent of Florida's orange crop, resulting in higher prices for orange juice and concentrate.

Following a sharp decline in 1980, consumption of sugar and other sweeteners in the United States rose to an estimated 125.9 pounds (57 kilograms) per person in 1981. Falling sugar prices – the result of record production – and greater use of high-fructose corn syrup contributed to the increase.

World Food Production. During 1981, production in the major food-exporting countries continued to expand, while production in developing nations remained variable or static. Good weather and an expansion of tilled land led to a large increase in the worldwide production of wheat, coarse grain, and rice. However, most of the increase occurred in the United States, where crop production rose 14 per cent.

The United States exported more than 100 million short tons (91 million metric tons) of food in 1981. About 5 per cent went to the Food for Peace program for shipment to developing countries. The rest was sold commercially, mainly to European nations, Russia, Japan, China, and oil-exporting countries, primarily for use as animal feed.

Infant Formula Controversy. A U.S. vote against the adoption of a nonbinding international code of ethics curtailing the promotion of infant formula created a storm of protest. In May, the United States cast the only negative vote against the code at a meeting of the United Nations World Health Organization in Geneva, Switzerland, on the grounds that the code would unfairly restrict private companies and limit advertisers' freedom of speech. Supporters of the code had argued that the use of infant formulas, especially under unsanitary conditions in developing countries, contributed to the deaths from malnutrition and infant diarrhea of up to 1 million infants each year.

New Sweetener. On July 15, the Food and Drug Administration (FDA) approved a new artificial sweetener, called aspartame, for dry food products and table use. The sweetener, sold under the brand name "Equal," was developed by G. D. Searle & Company of Skokie, Ill. Saccharin is the only other sugar substitute approved by the FDA.

Nitrite Findings. On December 10, a panel of scientists evaluating the safety of nitrites and nitrates as food additives reported that cured meats provide only a small proportion of human exposure to these compounds. The panel was convened by the National Academy of Sciences at the request of the FDA and the USDA.

Nitrites and, to a lesser extent, nitrates are added to bacon, ham, and other cured meats to prevent botulism and to add flavor and a pink color. Their safety has been challenged in recent years, after it was discovered that the compounds can be converted in the body to cancer-causing nitrosamines. The panel reported that cigarette smoke, cosmetics, new car interiors, cereals, and some vegetables contain significant levels of nitrites. Nevertheless, the panel recommended a reduction in the use of nitrites and nitrates.

Salt Talks. Concern about *hypertension* (high blood pressure) led the FDA in June to ask food processors to voluntarily restrict the amount of sodium in foods and to label the sodium content of their products. Studies have connected high sodium intake in the diet with hypertension, which can lead to heart attack and stroke.   Katherine L. Clancy

See also FARM AND FARMING; NUTRITION. In WORLD BOOK, see FOOD; FOOD SUPPLY.

FOOTBALL. There were similarities in professional and college football in the United States in 1981. On the field, winning teams suddenly became losers. Off the field, the organizations that conducted the sport fought off challenges to their authority.

In the National Football League (NFL), the old order of haves and have-nots changed drastically as the 1981 season produced what the league called parity and critics called mediocrity. Forty per cent of NFL games were decided by seven points or less and 26 per cent by three points or less.

At season's end, the division champions were the San Francisco 49ers (13-3 won-lost record), the Dallas Cowboys (12-4), and the Tampa Bay Buccaneers (9-7) in the National Football Conference (NFC); and the Cincinnati Bengals (12-4), the Miami Dolphins (11-4-1), and the San Diego Chargers (10-6) in the American Football Conference (AFC). These teams advanced to the play-offs with four wild-card teams—the Philadelphia Eagles (10-6), the New York Giants (9-7), the New York Jets (10-5-1), and the Buffalo Bills (10-6).

San Francisco and Cincinnati, which led their conferences in victories, finished 6-10 the year before. Tampa Bay was 5-10-1 in 1980, and the Giants and the Jets were 4-12. On the other hand, such 1980 leaders as the Cleveland Browns, the Atlanta Falcons, the Houston Oilers, and the Los Angeles Rams fell badly. So did the Oakland Raiders, who dropped from an 11-5 record and a Super Bowl victory in January 1981 to 7-9.

The Play-Offs. In the AFC wild-card game on December 27 in New York City, Buffalo held off a furious fourth-quarter rally by the New York Jets and won, 31-27. On Jan. 2, 1982, in Miami, Fla., San Diego defeated Miami in a thriller, 41-38, on Rolf Benirschke's 29-yard field goal after 13 minutes and 52 seconds of overtime. The next day in Cincinnati, Ohio, the Bengals eliminated Buffalo, 28-21. In the AFC championship game played on Jan. 10, 1982, in Cincinnati in bitterly cold weather, the Bengals beat San Diego, 27-7.

The New York Giants opened the NFC play-offs by upsetting the Eagles, 27-21, on Dec. 27, 1981, in Philadelphia. Dallas trampled Tampa Bay, 38-0, on Jan. 2, 1982, in Irving, Tex. On January 3 in San Francisco, the 49ers beat the Giants, 38-24. The 49ers defeated Dallas in the NFC title game on January 10 in San Francisco, 28-27, on a touchdown pass from Joe Montana to Dwight Clark with 51 seconds remaining.

In Super Bowl XVI, held on January 24 in the Silverdome in Pontiac, Mich., San Francisco beat Cincinnati, 26-21, as Montana completed 14 of 22 passes for 157 yards and one touchdown and Ray Wersching kicked four field goals.

NFL in Court. Before the 1981 season, the NFL spent three months in a federal court in Los Angeles fighting a challenge from one of its members,

1981 College Conference Champions

Conference	School
Atlantic Coast	Clemson
Big Eight	Nebraska
Big Sky	Idaho State
Big Ten	Iowa, Ohio State (tie)
Ivy League	Dartmouth, Yale (tie)
Mid-American	Toledo
Missouri Valley	Drake, Tulsa (tie)
Ohio Valley	Eastern Kentucky
Pacific Coast	San Jose State
Pacific Ten	Washington
Southeastern	Alabama, Georgia (tie)
Southern	Virginia Military Institute
Southland	Texas-Arlington
Southwest	Southern Methodist
Southwestern	Jackson State
Western Athletic	Brigham Young
Yankee	Massachusetts, Rhode Island (tie)

Major Bowl Games

Bowl	Winner	Loser
Amos Alonzo Stagg (Div. III)	Widener (Pa.) 17	Dayton (O.) 10
Bluebonnet	Michigan 33	UCLA 14
Blue-Gray	Blue 21	Gray 9
California	Toledo (O.) 27	San Jose State 25
Cotton	Texas 14	Alabama 12
Fiesta	Penn State 26	Southern California 10
Garden State	Tennessee 28	Wisconsin 21
Gator	North Carolina 31	Arkansas 27
Hall of Fame	Mississippi State 10	Kansas 0
Holiday	Brigham Young 38	Washington State 36
Hula	West 26	East 23
Independence	Texas A&M 33	Oklahoma State 16
Japan	West 28	East 17
Liberty	Ohio State 31	Navy 28
Olympia Gold	National 30	American 21
Orange	Clemson 22	Nebraska 15
Palm (Div. II)	Southwest Texas 42	North Dakota State 13
Peach	West Virginia 26	Florida 6
Pioneer (Div. I-AA)	Idaho State 34	Eastern Kentucky 23
Rose	Washington 28	Iowa 0
Senior	South 27	North 10
Shrine	West 20	East 13
Sugar	Pittsburgh 24	Georgia 20
Sun	Oklahoma 40	Houston 14
Tangerine	Missouri 19	Southern Mississippi 17
NAIA Division I	Elon (N.C.) 3	Pittsburg (Kans.) 0
NAIA Division II	Concordia (Minn.) 24	Austin (Tex.) 24 (tie)

All-America Team (as picked by AP)

Offense

Wide receivers—Anthony Carter, Michigan; Julius Dawkins, Pittsburgh
Tight end—Tim Wrightman, UCLA
Tackles—Ed Muransky, Michigan; Terry Tousch, Texas
Guards—Kurt Becker, Michigan; Sean Farrell, Penn State
Center—David Rimington, Nebraska
Quarterback—Jim McMahon, Brigham Young
Running backs—Marcus Allen, Southern California; Herschel Walker, Georgia
Place kicker—Gary Anderson, Syracuse

Defense

Ends—Billy Ray Smith, Arkansas; Andre Tippett, Iowa
Tackles—Jeff Gaylord, Missouri; Kenneth Sims, Texas
Middle guard—Tim Krumrie, Wisconsin
Linebackers—John Cooks, Mississippi State; Bob Crable, Notre Dame; Sal Sunseri, Pittsburgh
Defensive backs—Terry Kinard, Clemson; Mike Richardson, Arizona State; Tommy Wilcox, Alabama
Punter—Reggie Roby, Iowa

Player Awards

Heisman Trophy (best player)—Marcus Allen, Southern California
Lombardi Award (best lineman)—Kenneth Sims, Texas
Outland Award (best interior lineman)—David Rimington, Nebraska

the Oakland Raiders. The Raiders wanted to move to Los Angeles to play in Los Angeles Memorial Coliseum, where they would have more seating capacity.

After the 1979 season, the Los Angeles Rams had moved their games from the Coliseum to Anaheim Stadium in Anaheim, a suburb 30 miles (48 kilometers) south of Los Angeles. Al Davis, the managing general partner of the Raiders, then sought to move his team to the Coliseum 400 miles (640 kilometers) to the south.

In March 1980, the club owners voted 22-0, with five abstentions, against allowing the Raiders to move. Davis sued the league for $160 million, and the Coliseum sued the league for $53 million. The Raiders and the Coliseum contended that NFL teams were individual and competitive business enterprises, and thus the league's refusal to allow the Raiders to move violated federal antitrust laws. The NFL said that it was one business entity with 28 independent partners, not competitors. It said that if it lost the suit, teams could move anywhere they wished whenever they wished, sign as many players as they wished, and negotiate their own television contracts.

On Aug. 13, 1981, Judge Harry Pregerson declared a mistrial because the jury, after 13 days of deliberations, could not reach a unanimous verdict. Pregerson started arrangements for a retrial while trying to get the parties to settle out of court.

Standings in American Football Conference

Eastern Division	W.	L.	T.	Pct.
Miami	11	4	1	.719
New York Jets	10	5	1	.656
Buffalo	10	6	0	.625
Baltimore	2	14	0	.125
New England	2	14	0	.125

Central Division	W.	L.	T.	Pct.
Cincinnati	12	4	0	.750
Pittsburgh	8	8	0	.500
Houston	7	9	0	.438
Cleveland	5	11	0	.313

Western Division	W.	L.	T.	Pct.
San Diego	10	6	0	.625
Denver	10	6	0	.625
Kansas City	9	7	0	.563
Oakland	7	9	0	.438
Seattle	6	10	0	.375

American Conference Individual Statistics

Scoring	TDs.	E.P.	F.G.	Pts.
Jim Breech, Cincinnati	0	49	22	115
Nick Lowery, Kansas City	0	37	26	115
Chuck Muncie, San Diego	19	0	0	114
Pat Leahy, New York	0	38	25	113
Rolf Benirschke, San Diego	0	55	19	112

Passing	Att.	Comp.	Yds.	TDs.	Int.
Ken Anderson, Cincinnati	479	300	3,754	29	10
Craig Morton, Denver	376	225	3,195	21	14
Dan Fouts, San Diego	609	360	4,802	33	17
Terry Bradshaw, Pittsburgh	370	201	2,892	22	14
Jim Zorn, Seattle	397	236	2,788	13	9

Receiving	No. Caught	Total Yds.	Avg. Gain	TDs.
Kellen Winslow, San Diego	88	1,075	12.2	10
Steve Largent, Seattle	75	1,224	16.3	9
Dan Ross, Cincinnati	71	910	12.8	5
Frank Lewis, Buffalo	70	1,244	17.8	4
Charlie Joiner, San Diego	70	1,188	17.0	7

Rushing	Att.	Yds.	Avg. Gain	TDs.
Earl Campbell, Houston	361	1,376	3.8	10
Chuck Muncie, San Diego	251	1,144	4.6	19
Joe Delaney, Kansas City	234	1,121	4.8	3
Mike Pruitt, Cleveland	247	1,103	4.5	7
Joe Cribbs, Buffalo	257	1,097	4.3	3

Punting	No.	Yds.	Avg.	Longest
Pat McInally, Cincinnati	72	3,272	45.4	62
Ray Guy, Oakland	96	4,195	43.7	69
Craig Colquitt, Pittsburgh	84	3,641	43.3	74
Steve Cox, Cleveland	68	2,884	42.4	66
Rich Camarillo, New England	47	1,959	41.7	75

Punt Returns	No.	Yds.	Avg.	TDs.
James Brooks, San Diego	22	290	13.2	0
Paul Johns, Seattle	16	177	11.1	0
J. T. Smith, Kansas City	50	528	10.6	0
Tommy Vigorito, Miami	36	379	10.5	1
Larry Anderson, Pittsburgh	20	208	10.4	0

Standings in National Football Conference

Eastern Division	W.	L.	T.	Pct.
Dallas	12	4	0	.750
Philadelphia	10	6	0	.625
New York Giants	9	7	0	.563
Washington	8	8	0	.500
St. Louis	7	9	0	.438

Central Division	W.	L.	T.	Pct.
Tampa Bay	9	7	0	.563
Detroit	8	8	0	.500
Green Bay	8	8	0	.500
Minnesota	7	9	0	.438
Chicago	6	10	0	.375

Western Division	W.	L.	T.	Pct.
San Francisco	13	3	0	.813
Atlanta	7	9	0	.438
Los Angeles	6	10	0	.375
New Orleans	4	12	0	.250

National Conference Individual Statistics

Scoring	TDs.	E.P.	F.G.	Pts.
Ed Murray, Detroit	0	46	25	121
Rafael Septien, Dallas	0	40	27	121
Mick Luckhurst, Atlanta	0	51	21	114
Joe Danelo, New York	0	31	24	103
Wendell Tyler, Los Angeles	17	0	0	102

Passing	Att.	Comp.	Yds.	TDs.	Int.
Joe Montana, San Francisco	488	311	3,565	19	12
Danny White, Dallas	391	223	3,098	22	13
Steve Bartkowski, Atlanta	533	297	3,829	30	23
Lynn Dickey, Green Bay	354	204	2,593	17	15
Joe Theismann, Washington	496	293	3,568	19	20

Receiving	No. Caught	Total Yds.	Avg. Gain	TDs.
Dwight Clark, San Francisco	85	1,105	13.0	4
Ted Brown, Minnesota	83	694	8.4	2
William Andrews, Atlanta	81	735	9.1	2
Joe Senser, Minnesota	79	1,004	12.7	8
James Lofton, Green Bay	71	1,294	18.2	8

Rushing	Att.	Yds.	Avg. Gain	TDs.
George Rogers, New Orleans	378	1,674	4.4	13
Tony Dorsett, Dallas	342	1,646	4.8	4
Billy Sims, Detroit	296	1,437	4.9	13
Wilbert Montgomery, Phil.	286	1,402	4.9	8
Ottis Anderson, St. Louis	328	1,376	4.2	9

Punting	No.	Yds.	Avg.	Longest
Tom Skladany, Detroit	64	2,784	43.5	74
Dave Jennings, New York	97	4,198	43.3	62
Larry Swider, Tampa Bay	58	2,476	42.7	62
Frank Corral, Los Angeles	89	3,735	42.0	67
Carl Birdsong, St. Louis	69	2,883	41.8	75

Punt Returns	No.	Yds.	Avg.	TDs.
LeRoy Irvin, Los Angeles	46	615	13.4	3
Jeff Fisher, Chicago	43	509	11.8	1
Jeff Groth, New Orleans	37	436	11.8	0
Mike Nelms, Washington	45	492	10.9	2
Stump Mitchell, St. Louis	42	445	10.6	1

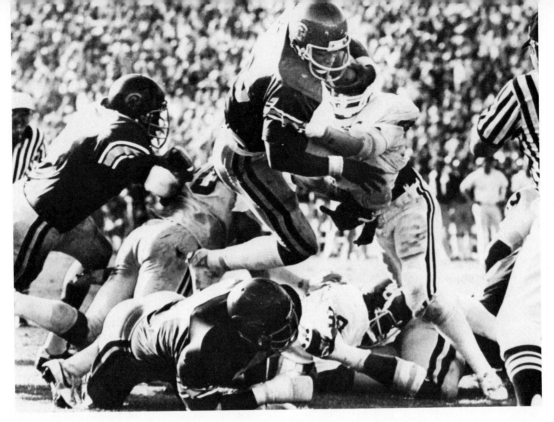

Tailback Marcus Allen of Southern California rushed for 2,342 yards in 11 games and won the 1981 Heisman Trophy as college football's best player.

Canadian Football. Vince Ferragamo, who had quarterbacked the NFL Los Angeles Rams to an 11-5 record in 1980, defected to the Montreal Alouettes of the Canadian Football League (CFL) in 1981. Ferragamo, who was paid $400,000 by the Alouettes, had so many problems with his new team that he was demoted to third string and not allowed to suit up for late-season games. The Alouettes finished the 1981 season with a 3-13 record.

The Edmonton Eskimos had the CFL's best regular-season record (14-1-1). In the Grey Cup championship game on November 22 in Montreal, Edmonton won for the fourth straight year by defeating the Ottawa Rough Riders, 26-23, in the last three seconds.

College Feud. The major college football powers, like the Oakland Raiders of the NFL, sought more control over their future. They belonged to the National Collegiate Athletic Association (NCAA), and in 1976 many of them formed the College Football Association (CFA), an organization within in an organization.

Traditionally, the NCAA negotiated a television contract with one network that covered the regular-season games of all member colleges. On July 30, 1981, it signed agreements with two networks – ABC and CBS – worth $263.5 million over four years, starting in 1982. Ten days later, the CFA rebuked the NCAA by signing a four-year contract with NBC for $180 million. The CFA contended that television rights belonged to the colleges, not to the NCAA.

The most important of the NCAA's 450 football-playing colleges made up Division I-A, with lesser teams in divisions I-AA, II, and III. The CFA's 61 members included most major football powers. The CFA said that smaller colleges among Division I-A's 139 members had too great a voice. Many CFA members were dissatisfied, but no more than five or six were willing to commit themselves to the NBC television package, and it collapsed.

The College Season. Except for Clemson, 1981 was a difficult year for teams ranked first in the United States. Michigan, Notre Dame, Southern California, Texas, Penn State, and Pittsburgh were all ranked number one during the season, and each was defeated and knocked from its perch. Clemson (11-0) ended the regular season as number one and the only major team undefeated and untied. It assured itself of the unofficial national championship by beating Nebraska, 22-15, in the Orange Bowl on Jan. 1, 1982, in Miami.

Georgia, Pittsburgh, and Southern Methodist finished the regular season at 10-1. Alabama was 9-1-1, and its 28-17 victory over Auburn on November 28 gave Paul (Bear) Bryant 315 victories as a coach, a record.   Frank Litsky

In WORLD BOOK, see FOOTBALL.

FORD, GERALD RUDOLPH (1913-   ), 38th President of the United States, spoke out on international issues, traveled abroad, and attended to numerous business interests in 1981.

Foreign Travel. Ford met with Chinese Communist Party Vice-Chairman Teng Hsiao-p'ing (Deng Xiaoping) in Peking (Beijing) on March 23. He told the Chinese leader that President Ronald Reagan wanted to continue to improve relations between the People's Republic of China and the United States.

Ford joined former Presidents Jimmy Carter and Richard M. Nixon as a member of the U.S. delegation to the funeral of Egyptian President Anwar el-Sadat on October 10. Returning from Cairo after the funeral, Ford and Carter held a joint press conference on *Air Force One.* In an unusual show of unity, they declared that the United States would eventually have to negotiate with the Palestine Liberation Organization to achieve peace in the Middle East. Characterizing Libya's Muammar Muhammad al-Qadhafi as a "bully," Ford said that United States pressure might help the moderate Arab nations to "disengage from the radicals."

Chatting on the return flight, Ford and Carter apparently overcame their personal differences. Ford declared that the meeting of the three former Presidents was "a plus for the country."

Dedications. Two institutions housing memorabilia of the Ford Administration were dedicated in 1981. The Gerald R. Ford Library, a repository for presidential papers and documents, was dedicated at Ford's alma mater, the University of Michigan in Ann Arbor, in April.

On September 18, President Reagan, Canada's Prime Minister Pierre Elliott Trudeau, and Mexico's President Jose Lopez Portillo joined Ford at the dedication of the $11-million Gerald R. Ford Museum in Grand Rapids, Mich.

Business Ventures. The former President is a member of the board of directors of several corporations, including AMAX, Incorporated; GK Technologies; Pebble Beach Corporation; Shearson Loeb Rhodes, Incorporated; Texas Commerce Bancshares, Incorporated; and Tiger International, Incorporated. In 1981, he became affiliated with two additional firms. He joined the board of directors of Twentieth Century-Fox Film Corporation in July and was hired as a consultant to The Charter Company — an oil, insurance, and communications conglomerate — in February.

As a senior fellow of the American Enterprise Institute, a conservative think tank, Ford lectured in political science at 10 colleges and universities in 1981.   Carol L. Thompson

In WORLD BOOK, see FORD, GERALD RUDOLPH.

The former President speaks to the press following the dedication in April of the Gerald R. Ford Library at the University of Michigan in Ann Arbor.

FOREST AND FOREST PRODUCTS. The United States timber industry and environmental organizations engaged in 1981 in several skirmishes that were part of a larger and so far indecisive battle over limiting the extent of wilderness areas where logging would be banned.

Environmental groups criticized President Ronald Reagan's selection of John B. Crowell, Jr., as assistant secretary of agriculture for natural resources and environment. Crowell had been serving as general counsel to the Louisiana Pacific Corporation, a large buyer of timber grown on federal lands. The environmentalists charged that his appointment to a position in which he would supervise the U.S. Forest Service constituted a conflict of interest and would tilt Forest Service policies in favor of industry.

Senator S. I. Hayakawa (R., Calif.) had introduced legislation on April 21 that would allow logging and mining of lands recommended by the Forest Service for preservation as wilderness. The lands could be logged only if Congress did not designate them as wilderness by January 1985. In hearings before the Senate's Committee on Energy and Natural Resources on June 17, 1981, Crowell gave Administration support to the legislation.

The lumber industry would like to increase the harvest from national forests substantially. The Forest Service offered the industry 11.9 billion board feet (28 million cubic meters) in the 1981 fiscal year and expects to offer between 11 billion and 12.5 billion board feet (26 million and 29.5 million cubic meters) annually by 1985. Industry would like the offerings to total 15 billion board feet (35 million cubic meters) by 1985. Industry demands for more logging in the national forests conflict with environmentalists' demands for more wilderness and recreation areas. This conflict, which has smoldered for years, seemed certain to burst into flames during the 1980s.

The Pacific Northwest. The housing industry slump, caused by high interest rates, battered the lumber and wood-products industry in the Pacific Northwest. The Western Wood Products Association reported on October 2 that 138 of 750 sawmills in 12 Western states had closed, and that almost one-third of 102,000 employees were out of work. A sharp upswing in imports of wood products from Canada and diversion of domestic timber to Japanese mills also contributed to the severe downturn.

Lumber prices dropped in August as a month-long strike in Canada's British Columbia forest industry ended. The strike by three unions almost halted the province's huge pulp and lumber production, which contributes about 25 per cent of U.S. lumber supplies. Andrew L. Newman

In WORLD BOOK, see FOREST; FOREST PROD-UCTS; FORESTRY.

FOUR-H CLUBS. See YOUTH ORGANIZATIONS.

FRANCE moved sharply to the left politically in 1981. The voters ended 23 years of center-right government in the second round of presidential elections on May 10, rejecting President Valéry Giscard d'Estaing in favor of Socialist François M. Mitterrand. Mitterrand received 52 per cent of the votes to 48 per cent for Giscard. Parliamentary elections on June 14 and 21 then gave the Socialists control of the National Assembly and handed the Communists a surprising defeat. The Socialists won 296 of the 491 seats in the National Assembly, but the Communists lost 43 of the 86 seats they had previously held. See MITTERRAND, FRANÇOIS M.

Two Rounds. In the first round of presidential voting on April 26, Giscard and Mitterrand emerged as front-runners, but Georges Marchais and his Communist Party did worse than at any time since the Popular Front elections of 1936. Marchais then called on the 4.5 million people who had voted for him to support Mitterrand in the second round. Giscard received support from Jacques Chirac, former Gaullist mayor of Paris, who had won 18 per cent of the first-round vote.

Franc Falls. France's move to the left caused the franc to plunge more than 4 cents against the United States dollar on May 12. The franc thus became the weakest currency within the European Monetary System (EMS), a group of eight nations

President François Mitterrand of France lays a wreath at the Tomb of the Unknown Soldier shortly after his inauguration on May 21.

working to stabilize their exchange rates. By May 13, shares traded on the Paris stock market dropped $7.3 billion in value. On October 4, France and Italy lowered the values of their currencies by 3 per cent, while the Netherlands and West Germany raised theirs by 5.5 per cent, relative to the currencies of the other EMS nations.

New Era. Mitterrand took office on May 21 and appointed Pierre Mauroy, Socialist mayor of Lille, as prime minister. Mauroy's first task was to announce financial controls to boost the franc and prevent a flight of capital out of the country.

Mauroy's Cabinet resigned on June 22 so that Mitterrand could appoint a Cabinet that reflected the results of the parliamentary elections. As expected, Mitterrand reappointed Mauroy prime minister. But he also named four Communists to Cabinet posts. Mitterrand recognized that the Communists controlled France's biggest labor union, and he badly needed a labor pact on wages.

EC Payments. France aroused the anger of the European Community (EC or Common Market) by refusing to pay its full contribution to the 1980 supplementary budget, claiming it had been passed by an irregular procedure. The EC also demanded that France cease to "illegally" subsidize the incomes of French farmers. France finally paid its dues and cut farm subsidies.

New Deal. Mitterrand lost no time in changing government policies. He gave top priority to putting the nation's 1.8 million unemployed to work. On June 17, the government announced plans to train young people and provide incentives to firms to hire them.

On July 30, Mitterrand honored an election pledge by canceling work on France's biggest nuclear power station, at Plogoff, Brittany. In August, the government borrowed $1.3 billion to stimulate the economy, in spite of an inflation rate that had reached 14.4 per cent.

Wealth Tax. On June 10, the Cabinet proposed to increase taxes on the rich to pay for jobs and better pensions for the poor. Social measures that would cost $1.2 billion were expected to create some 54,000 public sector jobs. Gasoline prices would be increased, income taxes would go up, and a windfall profits tax would be levied.

Shorter Week. The French Employers' Federation agreed on July 6 to reduce the workweek from 40 to 39 hours and to grant workers a fifth week of paid vacation each year. The National Assembly approved a bill on September 12 giving more power to local governments.   Kenneth Brown

See also EUROPE (Facts in Brief Table). In WORLD BOOK, see EUROPEAN MONETARY SYSTEM; FRANCE.

FUTURE FARMERS OF AMERICA (FFA). See YOUTH ORGANIZATIONS.

GABON. See AFRICA.

GAMBIA. Factions of Gambia's 900-member security force rebelled against the government of President Sir Dawda Kairaba Jawara on July 30, 1981. The rebellion occurred while Jawara, leader of Gambia since it became independent from Great Britain in 1965, was attending the wedding of Prince Charles and Lady Diana Spencer in London. Notified of the uprising, Jawara immediately asked neighboring Senegal for military aid and flew to Senegal on July 31. Senegal sent about 2,000 troops to aid the Gambian forces still loyal to Jawara. British counterterrorist experts assisted.

Rebel leaders gained control of Gambian radio and announced their intention to establish a "Marxist-Leninist dictatorship of the proletariat." However, Senegalese forces and loyalist Gambians won control of the capital city, Banjul, on August 2 and ended rebel resistance in its suburbs by August 6. More than 500 civilians were reported to have died in the fighting, though some sources reported as many as 2,000 deaths.

Following the abortive coup, Jawara and Senegal's President Abdou Diouf began to discuss the possible formation of a confederation of their countries. In mid-November, the two presidents announced the pending formation of "Senegambia," a confederation with Diouf as president and Jawara as vice-president.   J. Dixon Esseks

See also AFRICA. In WORLD BOOK, see GAMBIA.

GAMES AND TOYS. The United States toy industry's sales were stable in 1981. Three trends that contributed to gains made during 1980 — growth in basic toy purchases, added interest in home entertainment, and increasing year-round sales — continued and accelerated. Consumers looked for toys that were durable and versatile.

Major toy trends of 1981 included video games played on a TV screen and the solution-defying puzzle called Rubik's Cube, which spawned several imitations and also a number of explanatory books. Among best-selling dolls was "Strawberry Shortcake," a whimsical character doll that smelled like strawberries, and her "fruit-scented friends." Also highly popular were die-cast vehicles, particularly those fashioned after a car seen in "The Dukes of Hazzard" television series, and playthings mirroring the adult world, such as imitation cosmetics. Such basics as activity toys, stuffed playthings, and craft and model car kits also remained in demand.

Electronic Offerings. Adventure games helped bolster year-round sales and the adult toy market in 1980. The most popular, dealing with medieval and fantasy themes, successfully crossed over to electronics in 1981. Adaptations extended to video game systems and electronic board games.

Although sales of electronic games continued to be strong, they did not mushroom as they did when

Erno Rubik, creator of the baffling puzzle that was a 1981 sensation, contemplates one of his cube's 42.3 quintillion possible configurations.

such games were introduced in the late 1970s. Consumers appeared to favor those offering multiple games and varying skill levels, which the whole family could enjoy. Handheld and video-cartridge versions of coin-operated arcade games were most popular.

Licensing continued to be a significant sales factor in the toy industry. Lines of playthings licensed to depict characters from popular books, comic strips, motion pictures, television shows, and even greeting cards appealed to many toy purchasers. Almost every category in the toy industry featured at least one successful product that tied in with a character license. Toys and games accounted for an estimated 40 per cent of all retail sales of licensed products in 1981.

Product Safety Standard 72-76 was undergoing a mandatory five-year review in 1981. The United States toy industry's products continued to be among the safest in the world, partly because most manufacturers adhered to an industry-wide voluntary safety standard that applies to all aspects of a toy's design, function, engineering, and production. The standard was developed by Toy Manufacturers of America, Incorporated, the toy industry trade association, and published by the Department of Commerce's National Bureau of Standards in 1976. Donna M. Datre

In WORLD BOOK, see DOLL; GAME; TOY.

GARDENING. Awareness of the urgent need to protect and propagate endangered plant species increased among United States horticultural groups in 1981. At the end of 1980, the U.S. Fish and Wildlife Service released a list of 3,000 North American plants that may qualify for protection under the Endangered Species Act of 1973. The act shields rare wildlife from being collected, hunted, or otherwise threatened. However, only about 60 plants have been officially accepted as endangered, compared with more than 700 animals. In an article in the October-November 1980 issue of *American Horticulturist,* botanist Bruce MacBryde said 355 species on the plants list may already be extinct. He added that about 10 per cent of North American plants, about 2,100 kinds, were probably in danger of extinction, as were almost 50 per cent of Hawaiian plants, nearly 1,100 kinds.

Garden Club of America (GCA), a national organization of some 180 garden clubs, issued 151 post cards of endangered plants. The GCA also publishes pamphlets on endangered species and supplies speakers on the subject for schools and civic groups. The Lake Minnetonka (Minn.) Garden Club contributed $16,000 to the Minnesota Nature Conservancy for the purchase of 80 acres (32 hectares) of marshy prairie to be set aside as a wildlife area. The area has the state's largest concentration of the small white lady's-slipper, *Cypripedium candidum,* an increasingly rare flower of the orchid family.

Frost Protection for seedlings and transplants can be provided by a simple, inexpensive system developed by researchers at the University of New Hampshire in Durham. The researchers made protective domes from sturdy wire hoops and clear plastic. Vents in the plastic prevent overheating on warm days. The soil can be kept even warmer by covering it with black plastic, which can be left in place to control weeds and retain moisture after the clear plastic is removed.

New Horticultural Encyclopedia. The New York Botanical Garden's *Illustrated Encyclopedia of Horticulture* by Thomas H. Everett was published by Garland Publishing Incorporated in 1981. Reviewers hailed the 10-volume encyclopedia as a new standard reference work. It has more than 3 million words, 10,000 photographs, and 7,000 entries.

Honeysuckle Pest. An aphid native to Russia that was first observed in the United States in 1979 near Chicago-O'Hare International Airport was killing entire hedges in the Chicago area by 1981. The pest attacks *Lonicera tatarica* and *L. Korolkowii,* two species of bush honeysuckle native to Russia.

New Plants. All-America Selections, an organization that tests new flower and vegetable seed varieties, awarded bronze medals to two flowers and one pepper plant in 1981. Impatiens Blitz became the first variety of impatiens to win an

This sign near a national park forbids collecting of cacti and other specimens. Illegal gathering of cacti is increasing as cactus prices rise.

GEOLOGY. Mount St. Helens, the volcano in Washington state that erupted with devastating force in May 1980, was relatively quiet in 1981. However, a lava dome in the volcano's crater grew rapidly during the year, and the mountain still puffed smoke and steam. On October 20, the United States Forest Service announced that an area that had been damaged by the 1980 eruption had been set aside for public education, recreation, and research.

A Number of New Techniques continued to make the search for oil and gas more productive in 1981. Several of the new techniques were variations of the reflection seismic method, in which geologists set off dynamite explosions in shallow drill holes. The sound waves generated by the explosions travel into the rock layers below. Where there are differences between adjacent rock layers, some of the sound waves bounce back to the surface. At the surface, an array of detectors record the reflected sound. The reflection seismic method enables oil prospectors to find underground rock formations that might contain oil.

The original reflection seismic technique has been modified in two major ways. One modification is to replace the dynamite with huge vibrators mounted on heavy trucks. The other change has been the use of computers to analyze data.

award in the 49 years of All-America Selections. The plant has orange-scarlet flowers and a compact shape. The other bronze medal winners were Apricot Brandy, a dwarf plume celosia that reaches 18 inches (46 centimeters) in height and bears apricot-orange flowers, and Sweet Pepper Gypsy, which bears yellow fruits 3 to 4 inches (7.6 to 10 centimeters) long.

All-America Rose Selections, an organization of commercial rose growers, awarded its 1982 All-America designation to four new roses. Mon Cheri, a hybrid tea rose in shades of red and pink, was originated by Jack Christensen of Ontario, Calif. A fragrant hybrid tea with golden-yellow blooms, Brandy, was produced by Herbert C. Swim, also of Ontario. An All-America grandiflora in shades of orange, salmon, and coral was called Shreveport after Shreveport, La., which is nicknamed the *City of Roses*. Reimer Kordes of Sparrieshoop, West Germany, produced the rose. French Lace, a white floribunda with a spicy fragrance, was developed by William A. Warriner of Tustin, Calif.

After 15 years of selection and crossbreeding, Charles Unwin of Cambridge, England, developed a frilled sweet pea in a rich new salmon shade. The flower was named Frances Perry in honor of the internationally known garden writer.   Phil Clark

In WORLD BOOK, see FLOWER; GARDENING.

GAS AND GASOLINE. See ENERGY; PETROLEUM.

A researcher gathers rocks in February inside the crater of Mount St. Helens in Washington. The volcano's lava dome grew rapidly in 1981.

Improvements in Seismic Methods make it possible to look for oil in 1981 in areas once considered too difficult to explore. For example, the techniques have helped geologists locate oil fields within the Canadian Rockies.

Oil-rich geologic formations like the strip under the Canadian Rockies are known as *overthrust belts*. They formed millions of years ago, when one geologic plate thrust over another, trapping pockets of oil and gas. Until recently, geologists in the oil industry avoided overthrust belts. The rock structures were so complex that it was difficult to map underground formations, and any oil was so deep that expensive wells were needed to reach it.

Today, however, oil geologists have had spectacular successes in western Wyoming, which lies on the western overthrust belt that stretches from New Mexico to Canada. Oil geologists also are looking at belts in Arizona and the Appalachians.

Another new technique is *seismic stratigraphy,* which uses reflection seismic methods to look for single layers of rock that might contain oil. Most petroleum geologists think seismic stratigraphy is the most promising technique to be developed in many years. Using it, geologists from Shell Oil Company explored northern Michigan and located many small oil fields.   Kenneth S. Deffeyes

In WORLD BOOK, see GEOLOGY.

GEORGIA. See STATE GOVERNMENT.

GERMANY, EAST. On Feb. 15, 1981, Communist Party Secretary General and State Council Chairman Erich Honecker mentioned the possibility of reunifying East Germany and West Germany, the first such mention by an East German official in many years. Honecker told party leaders in East Berlin that he would approve of unification if West Germany turned "socialist."

Honecker held talks with West German Chancellor Helmut Schmidt in East Germany on December 12. This was the first full-scale meeting between leaders of the two countries since 1970. Honecker said that future relations between the countries depended upon West Germany's reaction to United States plans to install new nuclear missiles in Europe. "Good neighborliness cannot flourish in the shadow of U.S. atomic missiles," said Honecker.

Polish Crisis. The crisis in Poland was the main topic at a three-day conference of the 10 member nations of the Council for Mutual Economic Assistance (COMECON), the Communist economic group, in July in Sofia, Bulgaria. Delegates faced the fact that Poland will not be able to keep its trade commitments for several years.

COMECON postponed a decision on coordinating its members' economic plans. The delay forced East Germany to base hopes for increasing its exports on stepping up trade with the West.

Japan Visit. The country's most profitable exchange of views took place during Honecker's six-day visit to Japan in late May. Honecker was shopping for advanced technology and industrial robots that would help East Germany make highly technical products to sell in the West.

Honecker also wanted to persuade Japan to help East Germany build a $500-million petrochemical plant in Schwedt. But Japan said that increased trade and cooperation between the two countries would depend upon East Germany's abiding by the 1975 Helsinki declaration on human rights.

Five-Year Plan. The government set extremely high targets for the five-year plan that began in 1981. The plan called for national income to rise by 105 per cent, industrial production by 105.8 per cent, labor productivity by 105 per cent, and retail sales and net income by 104 per cent. The plan included modernizing 174,500 apartments for 500,000 people.

Wall Anniversary. East Germany turned out its troops, armed factory workers, bands, and crowds to celebrate the 20th anniversary of the building of the Berlin Wall on August 13. At least 70 people have been killed trying to cross the wall to escape to the West.   Kenneth Brown

See also EUROPE (Facts in Brief Table). In WORLD BOOK, see GERMANY.

Ceremonies in East Berlin on August 13 mark the 20th anniversary of a so-called "act of freedom" – the building of the Berlin Wall.

GERMANY, WEST. Chancellor Helmut Schmidt struggled throughout most of 1981 to keep his coalition government of Social Democrats and Free Democrats intact. His first fight occurred on May 10 in West Berlin's city elections. There, a series of scandals and allegations of misgovernment prompted voters to end 33 years of almost continuous Social Democratic rule. The Christian Democrats received 47.9 per cent of the vote and 65 seats in the 132-seat house of representatives to the Social Democrats' 38.4 per cent and 52 seats.

Budget Split. Schmidt faced the next threat on June 2, when the Social Democrats opposed welfare cuts suggested by the Free Democrats. A compromise settled this issue.

Schmidt breathed more easily when Hamburg's city parliament approved Social Democrat Klaus von Dohnanyi as mayor on June 24. Von Dohnanyi succeeded Hans-Ulrich Klose, who had resigned on May 25 rather than agree to delay a decision on whether to build a nuclear power plant in nearby Brokdorf. The Social Democrats agreed when they elected Von Dohnanyi that they would delay the decision until after city elections in 1982.

U.S. Relations. West Germany's relations with the United States were shaky in 1981. Foreign Minister Hans-Dietrich Genscher went to Washington, D.C., in March to try to soften what West Germany felt was the tough and uncompromising line taken by President Ronald Reagan and Secretary of State Alexander M. Haig, Jr., toward Russian peace overtures. Genscher said the Americans "expressed willingness to negotiate in all fields."

On November 18, Reagan proposed canceling plans to install new U.S. nuclear missiles in Western Europe if Russia would dismantle comparable weapons. Schmidt praised the proposal, calling it "America's peace plan."

Schmidt and Russia's Communist Party General Secretary and Supreme Soviet Presidium Chairman Leonid Ilich Brezhnev held arms talks in Bonn in November. At the end of the talks on November 24, Schmidt said that Brezhnev had convinced him of Russia's interest in arms reduction, but that Brezhnev would not acknowledge Reagan's desire for peace.

Schmidt visited East Germany's Communist Party Secretary General and State Council Chairman Erich Honecker on December 12.

Pressure on Currency. West Germany's Council of Economic Advisers and the 24-nation Organization for Economic Cooperation and Development called on July 6 for a rise in the value of the Deutsche mark to help stimulate West Germany's economy. In separate reports, they urged a higher base for the West German currency in the European Monetary System (EMS), a program that eight nations set up in 1979 to stabilize the prices of their currencies.

The EMS made a change on October 4. West Germany and the Netherlands raised the values of their currencies by 5.5 per cent, while France and Italy lowered theirs by 3 per cent, relative to the values of the currencies of Belgium, Denmark, Ireland, and Luxembourg.

Schmidt blamed cuts in the 1982 defense budget on high interest rates in the United States. The Cabinet agreed on July 30 to raise West Germany's defense spending by 4.2 per cent, but the country's inflation rate was 5 per cent. Thus, West Germany would not meet the North Atlantic Treaty Organization's target of a spending increase of 3 per cent in terms of real purchasing power.

Spending Cuts. Schmidt warned on July 23 that high U.S. interest rates were "destructive for business and employment." Observers said that West Germany's 30 "fat years" were over when Schmidt announced austerity measures on July 30.

West Germany marked the 20th anniversary of the building of the Berlin Wall on August 13 by laying wreaths on the Western side. Since the wall went up, more than 3,000 East Germans had tried to escape to the West. Kenneth Brown

See also EUROPE (Facts in Brief Table). In WORLD BOOK, see GERMANY.

GHANA. See AFRICA.

GIRL SCOUTS. See YOUTH ORGANIZATIONS.

GIRLS CLUBS. See YOUTH ORGANIZATIONS.

GOLF. Bill Rogers of Texarkana, Tex., and Tom Kite of Austin, Tex., had the most success on the 1981 Professional Golfers' Association (PGA) tour for men.

The 29-year-old Rogers won three tour events, including the World Series of Golf and its first prize of $100,000, and he was named as the PGA's Player of the Year for 1981. But his biggest win came in the British Open, one of the world's four major tournaments, held from July 16 to 19 in Sandwich, England. Rogers' 72-hole score of 276 beat Bernhard Langer of West Germany by four strokes.

Although he had only one tournament victory in 1981, the 32-year-old Kite won a four-man struggle for the money-winning title. His earnings for the year were $375,699. Next were Ray Floyd with $359,360, Tom Watson with $347,660, and Bruce Lietzke with $343,446.

The Men's Tour ran from January to October and comprised 44 tournaments with prize money exceeding $13 million. Floyd, Watson, and Lietzke won three tournaments each. Jerry Pate, Jay Haas, Hale Irwin, Larry Nelson, David Graham, and Johnny Miller won twice each.

Graham became the first Australian to win the United States Open, held from June 18 to 21 in Ardmore, Pa. He rallied from three shots behind on the final round with a brilliant 67 for a 273 that beat Rogers and George Burns by three strokes.

Jerry Pate dives happily into the lake at the 18th green after winning the Danny Thomas Memphis Classic in June, his first victory in five years.

Watson, who had been Player of the Year for the four previous years, won the Masters in April in Augusta, Ga. His 280 beat Miller and Jack Nicklaus by two strokes.

Larry Nelson took the PGA championship in August in Duluth, Ga., with a 273, defeating Frank (Fuzzy) Zoeller by four strokes. Nicklaus tied for fourth there and tied for sixth in the U.S. Open.

Tour officials faced many problems. Television ratings were low. Many sports fans seemed uninterested. Sponsors complained that many leading players did not enter their tournaments.

The players rejected a proposal to establish two separate but equal tours. They rejected another proposal to create two concurrent tours — one major, one lesser.

In November, the tour's policy board established new qualifying standards for tournaments, starting in 1983. Monday qualifying for lesser players will be eliminated. Instead, an all-exempt tour will be created with at least 200 eligible players — chiefly the previous year's 125 top money winners and the 50 leaders in the tour's qualifying school.

Tour officials made one change for identification and marketing reasons. Most of the members of the PGA were club professionals who never or seldom played on the tour. So the PGA Tour, which involved 355 professionals in all, changed its name to the Tournament Players Association (TPA) Tour.

The Women's Tour. In 1965, the Ladies Professional Golf Association (LPGA) offered 33 tournaments worth $356,316. Kathy Whitworth was the leading money winner with $28,658. In 1981, women golfers competed in 40 tournaments worth $5.8 million, and Whitworth was still playing and still winning.

The 41-year-old Whitworth became the first woman golfer to reach $1 million in career earnings in 1981 when she finished third in the United States Open, held from July 23 to 26 in La Grange, Ill. Later in the year, Donna Caponi and JoAnne Carner also reached $1 million.

Caponi captured six tournaments during the year; Carner won four; and Jan Stephenson, Nancy Lopez-Melton, Sally Little, and Beth Daniel won three each. The leading money winners among the women were Daniel with $206,977 for the year and Carner with $206,648.

Pat Bradley won the United States Open; Caponi, the LPGA championship; Lopez-Melton, the Colgate-Dinah Shore; and Daniel, her second straight World Championship of Women's Golf.

Stephenson made history in the Mary Kay Classic, held from August 14 to 16 in Dallas. She finished with a 54-hole score of 198, the first time a woman had broken 200 for three rounds. Frank Litsky

In WORLD BOOK, see GOLF.

GOVERNORS, U.S. See STATE GOVERNMENT.

GREAT BRITAIN

Political turbulence and the problems of unemployment and urban violence were forgotten for a day when Prince Charles and Lady Diana Spencer were married in St. Paul's Cathedral on July 29, 1981. The ceremony was televised and watched by some 700 million people throughout the world. Early in November came the news that Diana, now the Princess of Wales, was expecting a royal heir in June 1982. See Close-Up.

Despite rebellion in the ranks of her ruling Conservative Party, Great Britain's Prime Minister Margaret Thatcher pursued her tough economic policies in 1981. But the most notable feature of the year was the birth and remarkable growth of the Social Democratic Party (SDP), a new center party that rapidly captured much of the political middle ground abandoned by the Conservatives and the Labour Party.

The SDP was formally launched on March 26 by four former ministers in Labour governments, known as the "gang of four," who had left Labour because of what they described as its "drift to extremism." The four were Roy Jenkins, a former deputy leader of the Labour Party and president of the European Economic Commission; David Owen, former foreign secretary; Shirley Williams, former education minister; and William Rodgers, former transport minister. In January, the four had founded the Council for Social Democracy without officially leaving the Labour Party. They finally made the break after a special Labour Party conference in the Wembley section of London on January 24, called to debate and vote on new rules.

The SDP Started with the support of 14 members of Parliament (MP's) in the House of Commons, 13 of whom had transferred their allegiance from Labour, and one from the Conservatives. Later the number rose to 23. While the new party's policies remained vague in some areas, they included continued membership in the European Community (EC or Common Market) and the North Atlantic Treaty Organization (NATO), multilateral arms control, a mixed economy with private ownership of most businesses, and possible government price and income control. The SDP rejected both the leftist policies of Labour and the "survival of the fittest" philosophy of Thatcher. As an immediate aim, it sought to introduce proportional representation into British elections.

St. Paul's Cathedral in London is the site as Prince Charles and Lady Diana Spencer are wed on July 29 by the archbishop of Canterbury.

A Royal Wedding

Buckingham Palace issued an announcement on the morning of Feb. 24, 1981, that put an end to months of intense speculation. It said: "It is with the greatest pleasure that the Queen and the Duke of Edinburgh announce the betrothal of their beloved son, the Prince of Wales, to the Lady Diana Spencer, daughter of the Earl Spencer and the Honourable Mrs. Shand-Kydd."

Charles had chosen for his bride an "English rose." The innocent, fair-haired 19-year-old, the youngest of four children by Earl Spencer's first marriage, was to be the first English bride of an heir to the British throne since 1659. She was also of royal Stuart descent. Harold Brooks-Baker of Debrett's Peerage Limited, a publishing company that keeps track of noble doings (and misdoings), said, "She descends five times from Charles II, four times on the wrong side of the blanket and once on the right side!"

Immediately after the announcement of her forthcoming marriage, Diana moved out of the West London apartment she shared with two other young women and gave up her job as a kindergarten teacher. She moved into Clarence House, the home of the Queen Mother, Queen Elizabeth, to prepare for the big day.

The wedding took place on Wednesday, July 29, in St. Paul's Cathedral, built by the English architect Sir Christopher Wren between 1675 and 1710. It was the most public of weddings, attended by 2,500 guests inside the cathedral, heard over loudspeakers by 1 million people lining the procession route, and watched by another 700 million throughout the world in probably the most popular television program ever transmitted.

By early morning on the warm, muggy day, a forest of red-white-and-blue flags and periscopes covered the route. First came eight of the reigning monarchs of Europe. Next, the British royal family proceeded in strength, ending with the bridegroom himself in the full-dress uniform of a naval commander. But it was the first appearance of Diana and her wedding dress that every-

Prince Charles and
the Princess of Wales

body was waiting for. It was only when the bride stepped out of her glass coach at the cathedral that its true magnificence was revealed. The fairy-tale-lovely princess-to-be wore a wildly romantic creation of ivory taffeta and old lace with 25 feet (7.6 meters) of train that cascaded behind her down the cathedral steps.

Robert A. K. Runcie, the archbishop of Canterbury, performed the ceremony according to the rites of the Church of England. He was assisted by clergymen of other denominations. Wedding-day nerves made the couple muff their lines. She mistakenly reversed the order of his first two names and promised to take "Philip Charles Arthur George." He endowed her with "thy goods" instead of "all my worldly goods." But nobody cared, and a huge cheer went up at 11:20 A.M. from the crowd outside as the archbishop pronounced them man and wife. After signing the cathedral register, the Prince of Wales and the Princess of Wales, as she would henceforth be called, retraced the processional route in a regal-looking open carriage, a 1902 state landau. While the royal family entertained their 120 family guests at a wedding breakfast, the barriers came down in the tree-lined Mall, permitting the vast crowd to surge forward to the railings of Buckingham Palace. On the balcony, Charles held Diana's hand and bestowed on her what the audience wanted to see — a kiss.

Later, as the prince and princess drove to Waterloo Station, their carriage trailed a clutch of silver balloons and a "Just Married" sign, the work of Charles's brothers, Prince Andrew and Prince Edward. The couple then traveled by train to Romney in Hampshire, to spend a few days at the home of Charles's great-uncle, the late Lord Louis Mountbatten. Their story seemed to slake the world's thirst for romance, and when the prince and princess flew to Gibraltar that Saturday to begin a Mediterranean honeymoon cruise aboard the royal yacht *Britannia*, they took with them every good wish for a future lived "happily ever after."

Ian Mather

The SDP fought its first parliamentary by-election on July 16 at Warrington, a working-class town in northern England that is usually a solid Labour stronghold. Jenkins, with Liberal support, ran a sensational second, reducing Labour's majority to a mere 1,759 from 10,274 at the last general election. The two parties made arrangements to avoid putting up candidates against each other, and at the next parliamentary by-election, on October 22, William Pitt, a local Liberal running with SDP backing, won. He took Croydon North West, a London residential suburb, from the Conservatives despite having polled very few votes at two previous general elections. A string of local council by-election successes by the SDP-Liberal alliance appeared to confirm predictions of imminent change in British politics. Shirley Williams caused a sensation when she overturned a Conservative majority of more than 19,000 in a by-election at Crosby, Lancashire, on November 27 and became the first SDP member of Parliament.

Monetarist Policy Remains. Meanwhile, Thatcher continued to demonstrate why she was called the "Iron Lady" by scorning suggestions of a turnaround in her monetarist economic policies, despite sustained opposition from moderates within her own party, known as "wets." She insisted that the battle against inflation could be won only by tight control of government spending, even if this meant cuts in social services, and she maintained that British industry was becoming more efficient and competitive. The government reported on November 13 that the annual inflation rate rose to 11.7 per cent in September.

Thatcher demonstrated her toughness on September 14 when she "dried out" her Cabinet by sacking three prominent "wets," reshuffling some other ministers, and bringing in more hard-liners. As a result, all key economic posts were occupied by monetarists. But the "wets," joined by former Conservative Prime Minister Edward Heath, continued their attacks.

Despite the government's claim that its policies were the only long-term solution, everything indicated that the situation was getting worse. Thirteen Conservative MP's issued *Changing Gear,* a treatise that rejected Thatcher's declaration that there was no alternative to monetarism. The "wets" argued that with unemployment at almost 3 million and with record interest rates, Great Britain was in a worse situation than at any time since the 1930s. They called on the government to spend $7 billion to $9 billion on capital projects to revive the economy, and to lighten the financial burden on employers through reductions in the national insurance contributions they paid. However, Thatcher stood firm, arguing that more government borrowing to pay for such projects would simply make matters worse.

A "Labour Solidarity Campaign" was launched after the party's Wembley conference by more than 100 Labour MP's to try to reverse what they called "the narrow and intolerant decisions and views which unrepresentative minorities have been allowed to impose upon us." Nobody opposed party leader Michael Foot, but in the early hours of April 2 during an all-night session of the House of Commons, left wing leader Tony Benn announced that he would contest the deputy leadership against Denis Healey, former chancellor of the exchequer and a leading right winger. Intensive lobbying preceded the contest. John Silkin, a former agriculture minister and also a left winger, was a third candidate, but he was eliminated after the first ballot. In the end, Healey won on September 27 by a desperately close margin of less than 1 per cent of the vote. Healey declared, "My hope is that now we can put our miserable years behind us and concentrate on getting Mrs. Thatcher out."

At its annual conference, held in late September and early October, Labour voted for unilateral nuclear disarmament and withdrawal from the EC without a referendum, but in favor of remaining in NATO. The "moderates" then recaptured a majority on the National Executive Committee. It looked as if the struggle for the soul of the Labour Party would continue.

Urban Violence swept through more than 30 British cities in mid-July. Earlier in 1981, serious rioting had broken out in Brixton, a multiracial area of south London. In three nights of violence, from April 10 to 12, buildings and cars were vandalized and set on fire, shops were looted, and 224 people were arrested. On July 3, disturbances broke out in Southall, an Asian immigrants' area west of London, heralding 13 consecutive nights of rioting in many parts of Great Britain. The worst rioting took place in Toxteth, in the dockside area of Liverpool, one of the worst unemployment areas. Some people blamed unemployment and social deprivation, others blamed agitators. But government and police officials generally agreed that the incidents were not race riots as such because the violence was perpetrated largely by young people of various races. Nearly all the disturbances occurred in inner-city areas where serious social problems were made worse by strained relations between the police and the local population. An alarmed Thatcher responded quickly. She announced a special package of antiriot measures to improve physical protection for police in riots, and set up a public inquiry under Lord Scarman, a retired appeals court judge. Thatcher also announced government plans to spend between $760-million and $950 million during the rest of 1981 to help unemployed youths. She gave Environment Minister Michael Heseltine the temporary portfolio of minister for inner cities and sent him to

Rioting by unemployed youths in Great Britain in July symbolized to many the nation's economic problems. Damage in Brixton was about $4.7 million.

Liverpool in search of solutions. Lord Scarman's report, delivered on November 25, said the riots were an expression of resentment against the police by young blacks. It recommended immediate action to end racial inequality in Great Britain.

Other Developments. On January 5, Peter Sutcliffe, a young truckdriver, was charged with the November 1980 murder of Jacqueline Hill, who had been the 13th victim of what came to be known as the "Yorkshire Ripper." Sutcliffe was convicted and began a sentence of life in prison on June 2.

On November 1, employees of BL Limited, Great Britain's only domestic automaker, went on strike for higher wage increases. The company, which manufactures such cars as the Jaguar and the Triumph, had warned that it would go out of business if the strike was held.

Thatcher met with Ireland's Prime Minister Garret FitzGerald in London on November 6. They agreed to create a joint "intergovernmental council" to find ways to forge closer links between their two countries. Their meeting was held under tight security because of several recent bombings by the Irish Republican Army that had killed three people in London. See IRELAND; NORTHERN IRELAND.   Ian Mather

See also CHARLES, PRINCE; DIANA, PRINCESS OF WALES; EUROPE (Facts in Brief Table). In WORLD BOOK, see GREAT BRITAIN.

GREECE moved to the left in national elections on Oct. 18, 1981. Andreas Papandreou's Pan Hellenic Socialist Movement (Pasok) received 47.5 per cent of the votes to 36.7 per cent for Prime Minister George Rallis' New Democracy Party and 10.6 per cent for the Communists. Papandreou's election platform had been anti-American but, within days of taking office as prime minister, he assured United States President Ronald Reagan that the Greek government wanted to forge closer links with the United States. See PAPANDREOU, ANDREAS.

Joins EC. Greece became the 10th member of the European Community (EC or Common Market) on January 1. President Constantine Karamanlis and the ambassadors of Greece's EC partners attended the admission ceremony in Athens on January 5, but the main Greek opposition parties boycotted it.

Prime Minister Rallis said that joining the EC would provide the greatest benefit to Greek farmers, who would gain $576 million per year. The EC Regional Development Fund would provide $184-million in the first year.

U.S. Bases. Parliament recessed on July 2, postponing negotiations over the future of U.S. military bases in Greece until after the general election. The United States and Greece had discussed the bases for five months. In return for the bases, Greece wanted the United States to pledge to continue

ΠΡΩΤΕΥΣ

Former King Constantine kisses the ground as he returns to Greece in February to attend his mother's funeral after a 14-year absence.

granting military aid to Greece and Turkey in a way that would preserve the balance of power between them. The United States, however, did not seem to want to give such assurances.

The talks stalled on June 4 when Greece rejected a U.S. offer to supply advanced military equipment in exchange for use of the bases. Greece finally broke off negotiations on June 17, hoping that their firm stand would help the New Democracy Party in the elections. The Pasok vowed to make the United States give up the bases if the Socialists won in October.

Papandreou Announced his program on November 22. The government would set a timetable for U.S. withdrawal from the bases, remove all nuclear arms from Greek soil, and pull Greek forces out of the military wing of the North Atlantic Treaty Organization. Rallis warned that the Pasok foreign policy would plunge Greece into "dangerous adventures." Parliament approved the government program on November 24.   Kenneth Brown

See also EUROPE (Facts in Brief Table). In WORLD BOOK, see GREECE.

GRENADA. See LATIN AMERICA (Facts in Brief Table); WEST INDIES.

GUATEMALA. See LATIN AMERICA.

GUINEA. See AFRICA.

GUINEA-BISSAU. See AFRICA.

GUYANA. See LATIN AMERICA.

HAIG, ALEXANDER MEIGS, JR. (1924-   ), became United States secretary of state on Jan. 21, 1981. His nomination to that post by President-elect Ronald Reagan was controversial because Haig had served as White House chief of staff for President Richard M. Nixon during the final months of the Watergate scandal. However, the Senate confirmed Haig by a 93-6 vote.

Haig was born on Dec. 2, 1924, in Philadelphia. He graduated from the U.S. Military Academy in 1947 and was commissioned an Army lieutenant. In 1962, he received a master's degree in international relations from Georgetown University.

Following a number of military assignments, Haig was named in January 1969 to the staff of Henry A. Kissinger, Nixon's assistant for national security affairs. Haig was Army vice chief of staff when Nixon appointed him to his personal staff in May 1973. He retired from the Army when he later was named chief of staff in the White House. He served there until October 1974, when President Gerald R. Ford recalled him to active duty as commander in chief of U.S. forces in Europe. Two months later he was also appointed supreme commander of Allied forces in Europe. He retired from the Army again in 1979 and was elected president of United Technologies, a position he held until becoming secretary of state.   Wayne Wille

HAITI. See LATIN AMERICA (Facts in Brief Table).

HANDICAPPED. The United Nations (UN) proclaimed 1981 the International Year of Disabled Persons (IYDP). The theme of IYDP was "Full Participation and Equality." Its goal was to promote rehabilitation of the estimated 450 million persons in the world who suffer from some form of handicap. See UNITED NATIONS (Close-Up).

In the United States, the U.S. Council for IYDP worked with community groups and business organizations to promote awareness of IYDP and to encourage activities benefiting the estimated 35 million disabled Americans. A wide variety of programs highlighted the year.

Orange County, California, arranged for performances by the National Theater of the Deaf. Sunrise, Fla., established an information network, a job-placement service, and a local job bank for handicapped workers. Erie, Pa., held a series of workshops where attitudes about disability were discussed. Tacoma, Wash., planned a weekly newspaper column on disability and a yearlong program honoring local contractors and architects for buildings free of barriers to the handicapped.

The U.S. government set up the Federal Interagency Committee for IYDP to ensure federal observance. Agencies improved accessibility to their facilities and reviewed hiring practices to increase opportunities for handicapped persons.

Many disabled persons celebrated the year in unique ways. Itzhak Perlman, a renowned violinist disabled by polio, invited 100 guests from the Institute of Rehabilitation Medicine of New York University Medical Center to a rehearsal of his New Year's Eve recital at Carnegie Hall in New York City. Perlman walks with leg braces and crutches. On August 26, Phil Carpenter of Holiday, Fla., and George Murray of Tampa, Fla., reached New York City after rolling in wheelchairs across the United States from Los Angeles.

A "Bill of Rights" for the mentally retarded was effectively repealed on April 20 by the Supreme Court of the United States. The legislation, part of the Developmentally Disabled Assistance Act and Bill of Rights of 1975, declared the right of a retarded person to "appropriate treatment" in the "least restrictive" setting possible. The court ruled that the law was too vague to be enforceable.

Regulatory Changes. On July 17, Secretary of Transportation Andrew L. (Drew) Lewis, Jr., revoked rules requiring cities receiving federal mass transit funds to build wheelchair lifts into all new buses and to install elevators in existing rapid transit systems. Lewis called the rules, which were established under Section 504 of the Rehabilitation Act of 1973, "an inordinate, inflexible burden on local communities." He said that communities should decide how best to meet the transportation needs of the disabled until the Transportation Department issues new rules after public hearings.

Disabled climbers, including five who are blind and one with an artificial leg, conquer Mount Rainier, Washington's highest peak, on July 3.

On December 1, a federal board on architectural and transportation barriers relaxed rules that would have required the remodeling of many federally financed buildings. As a result of the decision, fewer elevators, ramps, and other special facilities will be installed in buildings to make them accessible to the handicapped.

The Jerry Lewis Telethon for the benefit of victims of muscular dystrophy on September 6 and 7 brought objections from a coalition of disability rights groups. The groups claimed that Lewis' program, in which he frequently referred to muscular dystrophy sufferers as "my kids," evoked pity for the disabled rather than respect.

Robert Sampson, a member of the Muscular Dystrophy Association Board of Directors and himself a victim of muscular dystrophy, responded that he has found Lewis' approach dignified and successful in focusing attention on the disease.

The Handicapped American of the Year, chosen by the President's Committee on Employment of the Handicapped, was Thomas McDonnell of Clinton, Iowa. McDonnell, who is paralyzed as the result of polio, was cited for making facilities accessible for the disabled in Clinton, where he serves on the town council. Virginia E. Anderson

In WORLD BOOK, see HANDICAPPED.

HARNESS RACING. See HORSE RACING.

HAWAII. See STATE GOVERNMENT.

HEALTH AND DISEASE. Long-time users of oral contraceptives were warned in August 1981 that they may face a greater than usual risk of heart attack, even after they stop taking the pills. In a study directed by pediatrician Dennis Slone of Boston University Medical School, a group of 556 women, aged 25 to 49, who had suffered heart attacks was compared with a random sample of 2,036 women of the same age span. The researchers found that the rate of heart attacks increased two to three times in women who had used oral contraceptives for more than 10 years. The researchers also reported that the increased risk of heart attack for long-time users may persist up to nine years after they discontinue use of the pills.

Passive Smoking Dangers? The debate over the hazards to nonsmokers of inhaling the cigarette smoke of others heated up in January 1981 because of a study that was directed by epidemiologist Takeshi Hirayama of the National Cancer Center Research Institute in Tokyo. Hirayama reported that a husband's smoking habits could be hazardous to his wife's health. According to the study, nonsmoking wives of men who smoked 20 or more cigarettes every day were found to have 2.08 times greater risk of lung cancer than nonsmoking women married to nonsmokers. The survey was based on a sample of more than 265,000 Japanese people over the age of 39.

The findings of the Japanese study were challenged in June by Lawrence Garfinkel, vice-president for epidemiology and statistics at the American Cancer Society. His analysis of data on lung cancer deaths, collected over 12 years, showed that nonsmoking women married to smokers were at no greater risk of dying of lung cancer than those wed to nonsmokers.

Vasectomy Risks. There were also conflicting reports in 1981 on possible links between *vasectomy* (a sterilization procedure performed on men) and heart disease. At an American Heart Association seminar in February, researchers reported that vasectomized monkeys fed high-cholesterol diets had much greater cholesterol build-up than nonvasectomized monkeys fed the same diet. Monkeys that had been vasectomized nine to 14 years previously and given low-fat, no-cholesterol diets also had more widespread cholesterol build-up than those that had not been sterilized.

However, a study reported in the British medical journal *Lancet* indicated that the actual incidence of heart attacks in almost 5,000 vasectomized men was about the same as in 24,000 men who did not have the operation.

Cancer Risks. At the American Association for the Advancement of Science meeting in January 1981, a Canadian physiologist reported that Vali-

U.S. Surgeon General Julius Richmond in January asks cigarette companies for information on the additives they use, which may cause cancer.

Members of hiking clubs arrive at the Capitol in Washington, D.C., in May after their cross-country trek from the West Coast to promote good health.

um, a tranquilizer that has become the most widely prescribed U.S. drug, seemed to promote the growth and spread of cancer in laboratory rats.

Another widely used substance – coffee – was also implicated as a cancer risk. Epidemiologists at the Harvard University School of Public Health reported in March that they found a strong statistical association between coffee and pancreatic cancer when they compared the habits of 369 patients with this cancer to a control group of 644 hospital patients with other disorders. The report did not cite coffee as a cause of pancreatic cancer.

Progress Against Disease. The first synthetic forms of interferon and insulin were used in patient trials in 1981, marking the beginning of a new era in treating disease. Synthetic interferon produced by genetic engineering proved no more and no less effective than natural interferon in cancer experiments. Interferon, a chemical substance produced in the cells of human beings, is being tested as a treatment for virus infections and cancer. Synthetic insulin, given to diabetics in a national trial, showed promise as a cheaper alternative to natural insulin obtained from the pancreas of oxen, pigs, and sheep. Synthetic insulin eliminates any risk of allergic reaction.

Researchers at Emory University in Atlanta, Ga., unraveled part of the mystery of adult muscular dystrophy, a disease that cripples thousands of people each year. In April, the Atlanta researchers reported that adults suffering from this disease have a deficiency of growth hormone – a substance that stimulates bone and muscle growth. (Children with muscular dystrophy have a different form of the disease and do not have low levels of growth hormone.) The discovery may eventually lead to a form of treatment or a means of detecting adult muscular dystrophy before symptoms develop.

In late 1980, the results of a two-year trial of a hepatitis B vaccine showed that the vaccine gave nearly total protection against this viral disease of the liver and caused few side effects. The Food and Drug Administration approved a hepatitis B vaccine, called Heptavax-B, in November 1981. The vaccine is made from blood plasma of people who have contracted the disease.

The National Cooperative Gallstone Study reported that oral therapy with a drug called chenodeoxycholic acid dissolves gallstones safely and effectively. In tests with the drug, gallstones were dissolved completely most often in thin patients and in those who had smaller stones or levels of cholesterol in their blood at the high end of the normal range. Dianne Hales

See also DRUGS; MEDICINE; PUBLIC HEALTH. In WORLD BOOK, see HEALTH; DISEASE.
HIGHWAY. See BUILDING AND CONSTRUCTION; TRANSPORTATION.

HOBBIES. Crafts and modelmaking continued to enjoy great popularity in the United States in 1981. Factors contributing to this popularity included the increased availability of many types of supplies, the introduction of new products, and the existence of a wide range of information on making and assembling various items.

Such long-popular pursuits as cross-stitch embroidery, crocheting, and macramé continued to lead the list of commonly practiced crafts, but other forms of handiwork attracted interest. An adaptation of the 18th-century art of tole painting enabled the hobbyist to use easy-to-apply acrylic paints to decorate pots, trays, and other metalware. Hobbyists used kits and patterns for silk flowers to construct bouquets that closely resembled living blossoms. Miniatures—particularly dollhouses and their furnishings—increased in popularity because they could be built from kits at a fraction of the cost of preassembled models.

Models, especially those of trains, airplanes, and cars, continued to capture the interest of both children and adults. Although antique train kits remained best sellers, the most successful plane and car models capitalized on current events. Sales leaders in 1981 included kits for the F-14 Tomcat fighter—the United States Navy plane that shot down two Libyan jets in August—and for replicas of the customized cars that careened through the weekly television series "The Dukes of Hazzard."

Collections. Coins and stamps were by far the most popular collectors' items in 1981, as they had been for many years. However, doll collecting, particularly of older dolls, was increasing rapidly. Collectors also expressed great interest in Americana—a term that applies to a wide assortment of items originating in the United States, from baseball cards to documents.

Historic documents commanded the highest prices among Americana in 1981. In March, an anonymous commodities trader paid more than $500,000 for copies of the first and second drafts of the Constitution of the United States.

A letter written by President Ronald Reagan, in which he defended his friendship with singer Frank Sinatra, sold at auction for $22,500 on January 22. It was said to be the highest price ever paid for a letter while the author was still living. Another Reagan document, a $50 check dated Sept. 14, 1948, sold for $3,800 at a New York City auction on March 5. The check was made payable to Americans for Democratic Action, a liberal public-interest group. Joyce Bennett

See also COIN COLLECTING; GAMES AND TOYS; STAMP COLLECTING. In WORLD BOOK, see HOBBY.

Autograph hound Emil Dern displays some of the 70,000 signatures and pictures of celebrities that he has collected since he was 13 years old.

HOCKEY

HOCKEY. The New York Islanders won the Stanley Cup in 1981, their second consecutive cup. Wayne Gretzky, the Edmonton Oilers' precocious 20-year-old center, won his second straight Hart Trophy as the Most Valuable Player in the National Hockey League (NHL).

Gretzky began his major-league career at age 17 in the now-defunct World Hockey Association. In the 1979-1980 season, his first in the NHL, he tied Marcel Dionne of the Los Angeles Kings for the league's scoring title. In the 1980-1981 season, he won the title outright with a record output.

During the 80-game regular season from early October 1980 to early April 1981, Gretzky amassed 55 goals and 109 assists for 164 points. His point total broke the NHL record of 152 set by Phil Esposito in the 1970-1971 season. His assist total eclipsed the record of 102 set by Bobby Orr in 1970-1971. His 29-point margin over Dionne, the second-highest scorer, was the widest ever. His average of 2.05 points per game was also a record.

Mike Bossy, a right wing for the Islanders, scored 50 goals in his first 50 games, equaling the achievement of Maurice (Rocket) Richard of the Montreal Canadiens in the 1944-1945 season, when 50 games constituted a season. Charlie Simmer of Los Angeles almost duplicated Bossy's feat by scoring 49 goals during the first 50 games.

Butch Goring of the New York Islanders slips a shot past Minnesota North Stars goalie Don Beaupre in the Stanley Cup play-off finals.

Standings in National Hockey League

Clarence Campbell Conference

Lester Patrick Division	W.	L.	T.	Pts.
New York Islanders	48	18	14	110
Philadelphia	41	24	15	97
Calgary	39	27	14	92
New York Rangers	30	36	14	74
Washington	26	36	18	70

Conn Smythe Division				
St. Louis	45	18	17	107
Chicago	31	33	16	78
Vancouver	28	32	20	76
Edmonton	29	35	16	74
Colorado	22	45	13	57
Winnipeg	9	57	14	32

Prince of Wales Conference

Charles F. Adams Division	W.	L.	T.	Pts.
Buffalo	39	20	21	99
Boston	37	30	13	87
Minnesota	35	28	17	87
Quebec	30	32	18	78
Toronto	28	37	15	71

James Norris Division				
Montreal	45	22	13	103
Los Angeles	43	24	13	99
Pittsburgh	30	37	13	73
Hartford	21	41	18	60
Detroit	19	43	18	56

Scoring Leaders	Games	Goals	Assists	Points
Wayne Gretzky, Edmonton	80	55	109	164
Marcel Dionne, Los Angeles	80	58	77	135
Kent Nilsson, Calgary	80	49	82	131
Mike Bossy, N.Y. Islanders	79	68	51	119
Dave Taylor, Los Angeles	72	47	65	112
Peter Stastny, Quebec	77	39	70	109
Charlie Simmer, Los Angeles	65	56	49	105
Mike Rogers, Hartford	80	40	65	105
Bernie Federko, St. Louis	78	31	73	104
Jacques Richard, Quebec	79	52	51	103
Bryan Trottier, N.Y. Islanders	73	31	72	103
Rick Middleton, Boston	80	44	59	103

Leading Goalies (25 or more games)	Games	Goals against	Avg.
Richard Sevigny, Montreal	33	71	2.40
Rick St. Croix, Philadelphia	27	65	2.49
Pete Peeters, Philadelphia	40	115	2.96
Don Edwards, Buffalo	45	133	2.96
Bob Sauve, Buffalo	35	111	3.17

Awards

Calder Trophy (best rookie)–Peter Stastny, Quebec
Hart Trophy (most valuable player)–Wayne Gretzky, Edmonton
Lady Byng Trophy (sportsmanship)–Rick Kehoe, Pittsburgh
Masterton Trophy (perseverance, dedication to hockey)–
   Blake Dunlop, St. Louis
Norris Trophy (best defenseman)–Randy Carlyle, Pittsburgh
Ross Trophy (leading scorer)–Wayne Gretzky, Edmonton
Selke Trophy (best defensive forward)–Bob Gainey, Montreal
Smythe Trophy (most valuable in Stanley Cup)–
   Butch Goring, N.Y. Islanders
Vezina Trophy (leading goalie)–Richard Sevigny, Denis Herron,
   Michel Larocque, Montreal

Bossy, who had the quickest shot in the NHL, also led the league in goals (68), power-play goals (28), and game-winning goals (10).

Islanders. The key players for the Islanders were Bossy, center Bryan Trottier, defenseman Denis Potvin, and goalie Billy Smith. During the regular season, the Islanders had the best record – 48 victories, 18 defeats, and 14 ties for 110 points. The other division winners were the St. Louis Blues, the Buffalo Sabres, and Montreal.

Sixteen teams qualified for the Stanley Cup playoffs. The Islanders advanced to the final round by eliminating Toronto, 3 games to 0; Edmonton, 4 games to 2; and the New York Rangers, 4 games to 0. They then faced the Minnesota North Stars, who had reached the finals for the first time in their 14-year history. The Islanders beat the North Stars, 4 games to 1, as Bossy set play-off records for scoring (35 points in 18 games) and power-play goals (9). Butch Goring of the Islanders won the Conn Smythe Trophy as the Most Valuable Player in the play-offs.

The all-star team for the regular season consisted of Mike Liut of St. Louis in goal, Randy Carlyle of Pittsburgh and Potvin on defense, Gretzky at center, and Bossy and Simmer at wing. The season ended unhappily for Simmer, who broke a leg with a month remaining.

The excitement provided by Gretzky and Bossy and a league-wide increase in scoring helped set a regular-season attendance record of 10,725,134. An average of 7.69 goals were scored per game, about half a goal per game more than the average of the previous season. The number of penalty minutes served by players also increased, mainly because of a new rule that provided for two 10-minute misconduct penalties on all players on the ice who fail to skate away from a fight.

International Competition. The year 1981 saw two major international competitions – the eight-nation world championship held from April 12 to 26 in Göteborg, Sweden, and the six-nation Canada Cup held from September 1 to 13 in four Canadian cities.

Russia won the world championship competition. Canada, using players from NHL teams, finished fourth. The United States, which had to start from scratch after its 1980 Olympic championship team disbanded, placed fifth.

Players from the NHL made up most of the Canadian team and the American team for the Canada Cup series, which also involved Czechoslovakia, Finland, Russia, and Sweden. Canada won all five games in the preliminary round robin and beat the United States, 4-1, in the semifinals. But Russia won the tournament by trouncing Canada in the final game, 8-1.   Frank Litsky

In WORLD BOOK, see HOCKEY.

HONDURAS. See LATIN AMERICA.

HORSE RACING. John Henry, a 6-year-old gelding who sold for $1,100 as a yearling, became the leading money winner in the history of thoroughbred racing in 1981. His victory in the Jockey Club Gold Cup at Belmont Park near New York City on October 10 brought his career earnings to $2,805,310. This total surpassed Spectacular Bid's world record of $2,781,607.

John Henry ran only in stakes events during the year and won eight of 10 races. His richest victory came in the first $1-million thoroughbred race, the Arlington Million, held on August 30 at Arlington Park in Illinois. He earned $600,000 in that race, a 1¼-mile (2-kilometer) turf event that attracted 12 horses from the United States and Europe. His only defeat occurred in June in the Hollywood Gold Cup at Hollywood Park in California.

John Henry's main rival for Horse of the Year honors was Pleasant Colony, who nearly captured the Triple Crown in 1981. The horse won the Kentucky Derby on May 2 and the Preakness on May 16, but finished third to Summing in the Belmont Stakes on June 6. Two days before a highly anticipated showdown with John Henry in the Jockey Club Gold Cup, Pleasant Colony injured a leg and was retired.

Before Dawn, a 2-year-old filly, was undefeated in five races against other female horses of her age.

Major Horse Races of 1981

Race	Winner	Value to Winner
Arlington Million	John Henry	$600,000
Belmont Stakes	Summing	170,580
Benson & Hedges Gold Cup (England)	Beldale Flutter	157,160
Epsom Derby (England)	Shergar	314,700
Grand National Steeplechase (England)	Aldaniti	112,900
Irish Sweeps Derby	Shergar	175,600
Jockey Club Gold Cup	John Henry	340,800
Kentucky Derby	Pleasant Colony	317,200
King George VI & Queen Elizabeth Diamond Stakes (England)	Shergar	221,723
Marlboro Cup Handicap	Noble Nashua	240,000
Preakness	Pleasant Colony	200,800
Prix de l'Arc de Triomphe (France)	Gold River	363,000
Prix du Jockey-Club (France)	Bikala	175,400
Rothmans International	Open Call	185,250
Santa Anita Handicap	John Henry	238,150
Washington, D.C., Int'l	Providential	150,000
Woodward Stakes	Pleasant Colony	137,400

Major U.S. Harness Races of 1981

Race	Winner	Value to Winner
Cane Pace	Wildwood Jeb	$130,847
Hambletonian	Shiaway St. Pat	419,000
Little Brown Jug	Fan Hanover	90,198
Meadowlands Pace	Conquered	500,000
Messenger Stakes	Seahawk Hanover	78,734
Roosevelt International	Ideal du Gazeau	125,000
Woodrow Wilson Memorial Pace	McKinzie Almahurst	880,000

John Henry, left, with jockey Bill Shoemaker driving him hard, charges
past The Bart and wins the Arlington Million horse race on August 30.

But she finished second to Timely Writer when she challenged male horses in the Champagne Stakes at Belmont Park on October 10.

Bill Shoemaker, the world's leading jockey, recorded his 8,000th career victory in May. In September, Laffit Pincay, Jr., became the third jockey to win 5,000 races. Only Shoemaker and Johnny Longden had ridden as many winners.

Horse buyers paid world record prices at the yearling sale at Keeneland in Lexington, Ky., on July 20. A son of Northern Dancer, the 1964 Kentucky Derby winner, sold for $3.5 million, more than twice the previous record for a yearling.

Harness Racing. Fan Hanover won the Little Brown Jug on September 24 in Delaware, Ohio, thus becoming the first filly to win the race. Shiaway St. Pat won the first Hambletonian run at the Meadowlands in New Jersey. The race had been held at Du Quoin, Ill., from 1957 to 1980. McKinzie Almahurst earned $880,000 by winning the $1.76-million Woodrow Wilson Memorial Pace at the Meadowlands on August 3.

Quarter Horse Racing. The richest race for quarter horses, the $1.3-million All-American Futurity at Ruidoso Downs, N. Mex., was won on September 7 by Special Effort. The 2-year-old colt earned $528,000.   Jane Goldstein

In WORLD BOOK, see HARNESS RACING; HORSE RACING.

HOSPITAL. Studies reported in the *New England Journal of Medicine* (*NEJM*) in 1981 indicated that infection, adverse reactions to medicine, and mistakes in the operating room can make hospital care hazardous to the patient's health.

In the March 12 issue of the *NEJM*, a study made at Boston University Medical Center reported that 36 per cent of patients suffered illnesses directly resulting from the drugs, therapy, or diagnostic procedures they received. In 9 per cent of patients, such illnesses were life-threatening or produced considerable disability. Two per cent of patients died because of the care they received. In another article in the same issue of the *NEJM*, a one-year review of surgical mistakes at the Peter Bent Brigham Hospital in Boston found 36 operating-room mistakes among 5,612 surgical patients, resulting in 11 deaths and 5 serious impairments. The researchers said the mistakes resulted from overoptimism, needless haste, and an urge for perfection on the part of doctors.

A report published in the June 11 issue of *NEJM* charged that poor hygienic practices by doctors and nurses contributed to infections acquired by hospital patients. Researchers at the University of Washington Veterans Administration Medical Center in Seattle found that hospital personnel washed their hands after contact with patients less than 50 per cent of the time. Physicians were the worst offenders, washing their hands only 14 to 28 per cent of the time.

Outpatient Surgery. In February 1981, Walter J. McNerney, president of the Blue Cross and Blue Shield associations, asked the associations' 110 member organizations to help keep certain patients out of hospitals by promoting outpatient surgery. McNerney said that such "walk-in" surgery is more convenient for doctors and patients, reduces psychological trauma – especially for children – and may cut costs by 30 to 50 per cent.

One of the newest procedures to be performed on an outpatient basis is a diagnostic test for heart disease called *cardiac catheterization,* in which a dye is injected into the blood vessels of the heart to create X-ray images. At the American Heart Association meeting in Dallas in November, cardiologist Earl Perrigo of Sandusky, Ohio, reported that outpatient catheterization was safe and cut costs by 20 to 30 per cent.

Hospital Costs, which had increased by 13.3 per cent in 1980, continued to soar in 1981, despite the American Hospital Association's Voluntary Effort cost-control program. In September, officials of the voluntary program projected an 18 per cent increase in hospital costs in 1981.   Dianne Hales

In WORLD BOOK, see HOSPITAL.
HOSTAGES. See IRAN (Close-Up).

HOUSING. Record-high interest rates for home mortgage and construction loans in 1981 kept the housing industry in the United States in its most prolonged slump since 1946. New housing starts in 1981 were expected to reach only 1.07 million – the lowest total in 35 years and a drop of almost 50 per cent from a peak of 2 million new units in 1978. Total starts in 1980 numbered 1.29 million – 853,000 single-family houses and 441,000 multi-unit dwellings, representing about $102 billion in construction costs. In November 1981, the seasonally adjusted annual rate of new starts fell to 871,000. This rate was the third lowest since the federal government began to compile such statistics in 1959. Sales of existing homes were the lowest in six years, falling to an estimated 2.5 million units. Building permits, which indicate future activity, dropped to a seasonally adjusted annual rate of 844,000 units in September, 44 per cent below the prevailing rate in 1980.

The slump was reflected in high rates of unemployment and business failure. Unemployment in the construction trades reached 16.3 per cent in September – more than double the overall rate. This figure represented about 828,000 jobless workers. The rate of failure among housing-related businesses increased 53 per cent, and the number of realtors declined by 80,000 from 1980, according

Construction on the first luxury housing development in New York City's Battery Park proceeded in 1981, belying a disastrous year for builders.

By permission of Bill Mauldin
and Wil-Jo Associates, Inc.

"You haven't referred to house
trailers as eyesores lately."

tober 1. Legislation creating these certificates specifies that financial institutions selling them must
use 75 per cent of the money for home-mortgage
and farm loans.

The certificates provide tax-free interest of up to
$1,000 for those persons filing an individual federal
income tax return and up to $2,000 for those filing
a joint return. Because lending institutions pay
relatively low interest on the certificates — 10.77
per cent in November — they can obtain funds at a
lower cost. This should enable them to lower mortgage rates. Bankers want the certificates to be
made permanently available instead of only
through Dec. 31, 1982, as scheduled. A USLSA
official said "we are reluctant to put one-year
money into 30-year mortgages."

Financial institutions also hope that the certificates will reduce mortgage delinquencies, which
stood at $6.4 billion at the end of August. This
represented a delinquency rate of 0.99 per cent,
compared with the normal 0.6 per cent to 0.7 per
cent rate. Foreclosures also were rising. The Federal Housing Administration (FHA), which insures
about 10 per cent of all home mortgages, reported
more than 23,000 foreclosures against FHA-
covered properties in the 11 months ending September 30 — 30 per cent more than the total for the
previous 12 months.   William J. Cromie

In WORLD BOOK, see HOUSE; HOUSING.

to the National Association of Home Builders
(NAHB). The U.S. League of Savings Associations
(USLSA) reported in October that many home-
builders stopped working, and unsold new homes
exceeded 300,000.

Fewer privately owned and financed multifamily
rental units were started in 1980 and 1981 than in
the early 1970s. The national rental vacancy rate
dropped below 5 per cent for the first time in recent
years. The vacancy rate was as low as 2 per cent in
many urban areas, according to the U.S. Bureau of
the Census.

Home Prices. The median price of a new single-
family home was $67,100 in September, up from
the $64,600 annual median in 1980 and $25,600 in
1969. Regional median prices in August ranged
from $82,800 in the Northeast and $82,200 in the
West to $73,700 in the Midwest and $63,900 in the
South.

Mortgage payments for these houses were almost
double those of three years ago due to increased
interest rates. At annual interest rates of 9 per cent,
available in 1978, a $60,000, 30-year home loan
cost $483 per month. The same loan in 1981, with
interest of 17½ per cent, required payments of $880
per month.

Mortgage Money, in short supply despite high
interest rates, was expected to be boosted by all-
savers certificates, which became available on Oc-

HOUSTON elected its first woman mayor on Nov.
17, 1981, when City Controller Kathryn J.
Whitmire defeated Harris County Sheriff Jack
Heard in a runoff vote. Whitmire captured 62.4 per
cent of the votes cast. Whitmire and Heard had led
a field of 15 candidates, including incumbent
Mayor Jim McConn, in a nonpartisan election on
November 3. Both candidates criticized the city's
failure to provide adequate services for its residents
despite its continued economic prosperity. They
cited Houston's rising crime rate, traffic conges-
tion, pothole-riddled streets, inadequate garbage
pickup, and insufficient mass transportation. In
the November 17 election, Houston voters also
rejected limiting the property tax rate to 50 cents
for each $100 of assessed value.

Despite its problems, Houston's expanding
economy attracted an estimated 75,000 new residents in 1981. Many were from the North and
Midwest, with a large percentage from Detroit,
where jobs in the declining automobile industry
were drying up rapidly (see DETROIT). The city
issued an unprecedented number of building
permits — for more than $3 billion in new
construction — during the year.

Favors to Business. On February 17, a federal
court found that Mayor McConn, the city of Houston, and a local cable-television company conspired to violate federal antitrust laws when the

City Controller Kathryn J. Whitmire acknowledges victory in a November 17 runoff election as she becomes the first woman elected mayor of Houston.

city contracted for five cable-TV franchises in 1978. The jury awarded $6.3 million in damages to the plaintiff, Affiliated Capital – a cable-TV company that had been unsuccessful in obtaining one of the franchises. On July 7, however, U.S. District Judge Carl O. Bue upheld the conviction but overturned the jury's award, saying he could not find sufficient evidence to show that the conspiracy to limit competition had resulted in Affiliated Capital's failure to obtain a franchise. In the same opinion, the judge was extremely critical of the city officials, stating that they had contracted for the franchises without considering the best interests of the residents of Houston. During the trial, McConn testified that he voted for the five successful franchises "to keep certain influential political groups content." Some of the city's most powerful residents held interests in the cable-TV companies that received franchises.

On September 10, State District Judge Arthur Lesher, Jr., appointed a special master, Houston attorney Joe E. Coleman, to oversee the city's tax department. Coleman's appointment grew out of a lawsuit filed against the city by Noble Ginther, Jr., a candidate for mayor who alleged that the city was giving tax breaks to some of Houston's biggest businesses. At the hearings preceding Lesher's ruling, city tax appraisers testified that city officials encouraged them to accept the property values

submitted by some corporations and to disregard their own appraisals, which were usually higher – in one instance by $223 million.

The Houston Independent School District's taxes, collected by the city, are assessed on the basis of city property appraisals. Coleman will aid the city in placing additional property on city and school-district tax rolls.

Schools Desegregated. On June 17, U.S. District Judge Robert O'Conor, Jr., ruled that the Houston Independent School District was a desegregated system in which all traces of dual black and white systems had been eliminated. The ruling, in effect, ended a lawsuit filed in 1956 on behalf of two black students who were refused admission to white schools in Houston.

On August 27, the United States Department of Justice announced that it would drop its 1980 suit to integrate Houston's public school system with 22 suburban school districts – the federal government's first attempt to achieve cross-district school desegregation – and would not appeal Judge O'Conor's June 17 ruling. However, two other parties to the Houston Independent School District's 1956 integration suit – the Houston Teachers' Association and the National Association for the Advancement of Colored People – filed appeals. Pat Reed

See also CITY. In WORLD BOOK, see HOUSTON.

HU YAOBANG (1915-) was named chairman of the Communist Party in the People's Republic of China in June 1981 by Teng Hsiao-p'ing (Deng Xiaoping), the powerful deputy premier. Hu succeeded Hua Kuo-feng (Hua Guofeng), who had been chosen for the position by his predecessor, Mao Tse-tung (Mao Zedong) in 1976. See CHINA, PEOPLE'S REPUBLIC OF.

Hu Yaobang was born in 1915 into a poor peasant family in Hunan Province in south-central China. As a youth, he had scant formal education but later taught himself to read. When he was 14 years old, Hu left home to become one of the "little red devils," or child soldiers, who formed part of the Red Army at its first base in the mountains of northwestern China.

Hu's long friendship with Teng began in 1941 when both were army political officers. They worked together in Szechwan (Sichuan) Province in 1949, and both were sent to Peking (Beijing) in 1952. During the 1950s and 1960s, Hu ran the Communist Youth League.

Hu's political fortunes rose and fell with the tides of the Cultural Revolution of 1966 to 1976. After Mao's death in 1976, both Teng and Hu regained power. Hu became head of the Communist Party's organization department in 1978 and head of propaganda in 1979. In 1980, he became the party's general secretary. Marsha F. Goldsmith

HUNGARY continued to reform its economy in 1981. On January 1, the government combined three so-called branch ministries of industry into a single ministry, the only one of its kind in Eastern Europe. The government told the new Ministry of Industry to supervise state-owned businesses, but not to direct them as the branch ministries had done. Another government decree gave 40 manufacturing businesses the right to deal with foreign enterprises.

On August 28, Hungary declared that it would allow private businesses to employ up to 100 full-time workers and some part-time workers, including pensioners and students. The government abolished the Ministry of Labor on September 30 and replaced it with a small office for employment. On October 29, Hungary also broke up its poultry, brewery, and various agricultural monopolies into smaller enterprises.

Industrial Output from January through September was 2.2 per cent higher than in the first nine months of 1980. Food production increased 3.9 per cent, but investments were down 3 per cent. Construction was also off 3 per cent. Both imports and exports were up 5.1 per cent during the first half of 1981. Exports to the West increased 7 per cent, while imports rose 6 per cent.

Hungary announced in November that it would allow private citizens to take one trip to the West per year, instead of one every two years. Tourists traveling to Western countries and Yugoslavia would be permitted to buy 15,000 forint (about $500) worth of hard currency instead of 10,000 forint (about $340). People going to Eastern countries could purchase 12,000 forint (about $400) worth instead of 8,000 (about $270).

Political Crackdown. Communist Party First Secretary Janos Kadar said on March 15 that the national political situation was "stable," but he warned that "certain irresponsible elements" had become more active. In the same month, the government broke up a young writers' club called Attila Jozsef Circle for being too critical of government political positions.

Mihaly Kornidesz, head of the party's education and science division, warned in the September issue of the party magazine *Partelet* (*Party Life*) that the party would not stand by while a small group of intellectuals opposed the party line. This comment was taken as a reference to the activities of an antipoverty organization called Szeta. Some intellectuals had circulated privately the work of Istvan Bibo, a non-Communist intellectual. Bibo had been a member of Premier Imre Nagy's government, which introduced the multiparty system in Hungary in 1956 and proclaimed its intention of leaving the Warsaw Pact.   Chris Cviic

See also EUROPE (Facts in Brief Table). In WORLD BOOK, see HUNGARY.

HUNTING. Wildlife officials in 17 states along the Central and Pacific migratory flyways in the United States decided to open fall waterfowl hunting seasons in 1981, despite fears that ducks had been contaminated by endrin, a highly toxic pesticide.

High levels of endrin, which had been sprayed on wheatland in eastern Montana in April, were found in ducks in that state in early September. The finding caused fears that duck hunting might be banned throughout the West. But on September 25, the Montana Fish and Game Commission unanimously voted to allow the migratory waterfowl season to open as planned on October 3. Federal and state wildlife officials said endrin contamination posed little danger to hunters who properly clean their game. Following the Montana decision, other Western states also opened their waterfowl seasons, though some adopted special restrictions to reduce possible health hazards.

A drought affecting duck habitats in the north-central United States in 1981 lowered the number of waterfowl in fall migratory flights.

On August 13, the U.S. Fish and Wildlife Service designated portions of 26 states "steel shot zones." The ban against lead shot, which was to remain in effect indefinitely, was part of a continuing effort by the service to reduce the incidence of lead poisoning in waterfowl.   Andrew L. Newman

In WORLD BOOK, see AMMUNITION; HUNTING.

ICE SKATING. Scott Hamilton of Haverford, Pa., whose growth was stunted by a childhood illness, became the men's world figure-skating champion in 1981. American speed skating suffered from the retirement of Eric Heiden and his sister, Beth.

Figure Skating. The world championships were held from March 3 to 7 in Hartford, Conn. The men's competition became a battle between the 22-year-old Hamilton and 23-year-old David Santee of Park Ridge, Ill. Whichever of the two skaters finished first in the free skating, which counted for 50 per cent of the final score, would win. Hamilton won the battle and the gold medal. Santee took the silver medal.

As a youngster, Hamilton suffered from Schwachman's syndrome, an inability of the body to absorb food. He started skating at the age of 8 with his physician's children. The illness disappeared a year later, and Hamilton eventually grew to 5 feet 3½ inches (161 centimeters).

Denise Biellmann of Switzerland won the women's world title. Her graceful routine included the acrobatic Biellmann spin, in which she rotated on her right skate while holding her left leg behind her back and then over her head.

Fifteen-year-old Elaine Zayak of Paramus, N.J., did seven triple jumps in her four-minute free-skating program and finished second. No woman had ever tried as many triples in a competition.

Fifteen-year-old Elaine Zayak of Paramus, N.J., wins a silver medal for her acrobatic routine at the world figure-skating championships.

IMMIGRATION. President Ronald Reagan's Administration on July 30, 1981, recommended a package of legislation to stem the recent tidal wave of illegal immigration into the United States. The U.S. Bureau of the Census estimated that 3 million to 6 million persons were living in the United States without proper immigration papers on January 1 – about 50 per cent of whom were Mexicans. To check the inflow, the Administration proposed a federal law banning the hiring of illegal aliens, except in businesses that have fewer than four workers on the payroll. Fines of $500 to $1,000 would be imposed on employers who knowingly hired anyone who had entered the United States illegally.

The plan, announced by U.S. Attorney General William French Smith, would grant temporary residency rights to illegal aliens who had been in U.S. territory since Jan. 1, 1980. However, these aliens would be barred from receiving welfare, food stamps, unemployment insurance, and other social benefits. After 10 years, they would be eligible to become permanent-resident aliens and to apply for U.S. citizenship. As permanent-resident aliens, they could receive government benefits. Cubans and Haitians who entered the United States before 1981 would be eligible for permanent-resident status after five years.

Hamilton and Zayak won the United States championships held from February 3 to 8 in San Diego. Santee finished second in the men's competition, extending his nonwinning record in the nationals to four second places and two thirds in six years. Peter and Caitlin (Kitty) Carruthers, a brother-and-sister team from Wilmington, Del., won the pairs title.

Speed Skating. In the year's six world championships – men's overall, sprint, and junior and women's overall, sprint, and junior – the United States won only two of the 24 medals. Both went to 16-year-old Sarah Docter of Madison, Wis.

Thirty skaters from 11 nations took part in the women's overall championship in February in Ste.-Foy, Canada. Natalia Petruseva of Russia won for the second consecutive year. Docter finished third.

In the women's junior championships held on February 28 and March 1 in Elverum, Norway, Docter easily captured the gold medal. She won three races and finished third in the fourth.

Amund Sjoebrend of Norway won the men's overall title in February. Four American men took part in the competition, but none qualified for the 10,000 meters, the last of the four races. Frank Litsky

In WORLD BOOK, see ICE SKATING.

ICELAND. See EUROPE.

IDAHO. See STATE GOVERNMENT.

ILLINOIS. See CHICAGO; STATE GOVERNMENT.

An enormous American flag is unfurled as 10,000 people – the largest number ever to be naturalized at one time – become U.S. citizens in Los Angeles in June.

INCOME TAX

Proposed Pilot Program. The Administration's proposal would set up a two-year pilot program to allow 50,000 Mexican "guest-workers" into the United States annually. These aliens would spend from 9 to 12 months working in the United States and then return to their homeland. In addition, the annual quota for Mexican and Canadian immigrants would be doubled to 40,000 persons from each country. Finally, the United States would tighten the enforcement of immigration laws at its borders. This would involve turning back boats carrying would-be immigrants who have not been granted permission to enter the country.

To enforce the latter provision, the United States and Haiti on September 30 announced an agreement under which the United States may intercept ships suspected of carrying illegal immigrants in international waters off the coast of Haiti. Previously, the United States could challenge only vessels that had entered U.S. territorial waters.

On Nov. 17, President Reagan appointed Alan C. Nelson as commissioner of the Immigration and Naturalization Service. Nelson, a lawyer, had served in Reagan's cabinet when Reagan was governor of California. William J. Eaton

In WORLD BOOK, see IMMIGRATION AND EMIGRATION.

INCOME TAX. See TAXATION.

INDIA recorded a population of 684 million in its official 1981 census, at least 12 million more than the government had expected. The United Nations and other population experts estimated that the population was closer to 700 million, however. The figures indicated that the government's family-planning efforts had reduced India's birth rate no faster than improved nutrition and health facilities had reduced the nation's death rate.

Efforts to Overcome Poverty were hindered by population growth. Almost 50 per cent of the population lived below India's low poverty level, being unable to buy adequate food. The 1980-1985 economic-development plan, introduced only in 1981 because government planning lagged behind schedule, aimed to reduce the proportion below the poverty line to 30 per cent. But inflation, which raged at more than 25 per cent in the 18 months from 1980 to mid-1981, hurt the poor.

The World Bank announced on January 3 that it was canceling a $250-million loan to build two fertilizer plants because India had refused, reportedly for political reasons, to use the consulting firm that the World Bank had approved to advise on the construction. On November 9, the International Monetary Fund (IMF) approved a $5.8-billion loan to India to reduce its foreign-trade deficit. India's foreign-currency reserves were falling by

India's Prime Minister Indira Gandhi visits an exhibition on health and child welfare in New Delhi. The man at the left is an Indian health official.

$100 million per month because of the high price of imported oil. To meet IMF conditions for the loan, India reduced domestic subsidies on fertilizer, oil products, and certain other items.

India's Prime Minister Indira Gandhi announced on July 12 that the government had been unable to buy enough grain from Indian farmers to replenish its reserve, despite an estimated record crop of 133.5 million metric tons (147.2 million short tons) in the 1980-1981 crop season. To prevent hoarding and price fixing, she said, India would import food for the first time in four years.

Farmers in several states agitated for higher guaranteed prices for their crops. To counter this pressure, Gandhi supporters organized India's largest rally. Some 2 million farmers gathered in New Delhi on February 16 to back her policies.

Gandhi's Only Surviving Son, Rajiv, supervised the farm rally as his first major political venture. He abandoned his career as a commercial pilot and yielded to pressure to replace his brother, Sanjay — who died in 1980 — as Gandhi's chief deputy.

On June 15, Rajiv won a special election to fill Sanjay's parliamentary seat. Working behind the scenes, the quiet, reserved Rajiv began building up a network of supporters. This caused speculation that Rajiv, whose grandfather Jawaharlal Nehru was India's first prime minister, might become the third generation of his family to lead India.

Internal Unrest. Linguistic, caste, religious, and political problems continued to plague India in 1981. Students in Assam state agitated to drive out Bengali settlers, most of whom were immigrants from neighboring Bangladesh. The Assamese resented the competition for jobs and social services. Nearly 300 people in Assam died in outbreaks of violence against the immigrants in June. However, oil began to flow from Assam to the rest of India again in January. A strike staged by Assamese students had disrupted the flow since May 1980.

At least 25 persons were killed in Gujarat state in January and February 1981, in protests against admission of lower-caste students to medical classes. Five days of clashes between Hindus and Muslims in Bihar state in April and May killed at least 48 persons.

Foreign Relations. A high-ranking Chinese official visited India for the first time since the two countries fought in 1962 over Himalayan territorial claims. On December 10, Chinese and Indian representatives began talks in Peking (Beijing), China, in an effort to resolve the border dispute.

On July 28, India barred United States diplomat George G. B. Griffin from taking up an assignment at the U.S. Embassy in New Delhi. Communists in India had accused Griffin of being an agent of the Central Intelligence Agency.   Henry S. Bradsher

See also ASIA (Facts in Brief Table). In WORLD BOOK, see INDIA.

INDIAN, AMERICAN. United States Secretary of the Interior James G. Watt on July 15, 1981, named a five-member Commission on Fiscal Accountability of the Nation's Energy Resources to investigate oil thefts from federal and Indian tribal lands. The action was inspired by mounting evidence that an estimated $2 billion in crude oil was being stolen annually from federal leases. Unpaid royalties on legally obtained oil as well as on stolen oil may have cost Indian tribes hundreds of millions of dollars over the years.

Since the early 1960s, the General Accounting Office has periodically reported that federal supervision of royalty collections from Indian and other federal lands was slipshod. However, the outright thefts of oil did not come to the attention of federal officials until June 1980, when an employee of the U.S. Geological Survey (USGS) — the agency responsible for collecting royalties on tribal lands — stopped a truck filled with stolen oil on the Wind River Indian Reservation in Wyoming.

Although royalties paid to the federal government and Indian tribes in 1981 are expected to exceed $4 billion, they may be losing a combined sum of as much as $1 million per day, according to testimony presented to the commission on August 28. Charles Thomas, a former USGS inspector now employed by the Blackfeet Indians, charged at the hearings that USGS officials were not investigating discrepancies in information provided by the companies that lease oil fields from the Indians.

The Standard Oil Company of Indiana (AMOCO) presented a check for $763,605 to the Wind River tribe on July 30 as compensation for unpaid royalties. The payment was believed to be the first in a series of similar compensations.

Claim Disputes. The Supreme Court of the United States ruled on March 24 that the state of Montana — not the Crow Indians — owns a 52-mile (84-kilometer) stretch of the Bighorn River that flows through the Crow Reservation. The decision revoked the Crow's right to regulate hunting and fishing on the reservation. The tribe claimed it had jurisdiction over the Bighorn River under treaties with the United States government signed in 1851 and 1868. However, the court ruled that the title to the river had passed to the state when Montana joined the union in 1889.

The Montana Fish and Game Commission decided in July to open the river to public fishing on August 20 despite the tribe's plea that it needed more time to set up a management plan. The Crows blockaded a bridge on August 20, preventing hundreds of anglers from reaching the river. The tribe removed the blockade under an order by a U.S. District Court in Billings, Mont.

The Oglala Sioux on August 14 filed a petition with the Supreme Court urging a reversal of lower court decisions that had rejected the tribe's claim to the mineral-rich Black Hills of South Dakota. In the appeal, the tribe refused $105 million in compensation that it and seven other Sioux tribes had won from the Indian Claims Commission.

On September 8, a group of Oglala Sioux vacated a campsite that they had established at Sheridan Lake in the Black Hills to protest the handling of Indian claims. The Indians voted to abandon the protest after officials of the U.S. Department of the Interior promised to negotiate the return to the tribe of some land for religious purposes.

Claim Settlements. A federal law dividing a 1.8-million-acre (730,000-hectare) tract of land in northeast Arizona equally between the Navajo and Hopi tribes went into effect on April 18. To implement the measure, which involved relocating from 3,000 to 6,000 Navajo and 100 Hopi, the Bureau of Indian Affairs seized Navajo livestock grazing in Hopi territory and moved them to Navajo land.

The Canadian government announced on August 22 that, after six years of negotiations, it had settled a claim by the Wagmatcook Indians of Nova Scotia. The tribe received $1.2 million for the loss of 1,660 acres (672 hectares) that were sold without the tribe's permission. It was the first land settlement involving an Indian tribe in the Atlantic Provinces.   Andrew L. Newman

In WORLD BOOK, see INDIAN, AMERICAN.

INDIANA. See STATE GOVERNMENT.

INDONESIA increased its agricultural production in 1981. The yield of rice, the country's most important food, was about 50 per cent higher than a decade earlier. The use of new "miracle" rice, more fertilizer, and improvements in irrigation systems produced the bumper crop. Indonesia's President Suharto claimed on August 15 that farmers' incomes had risen and that wealth was being more fairly distributed among the nation's 160 million people.

An estimated 70 per cent of the rural inhabitants of the island of Java remained below the poverty line, however, and Indonesia still had to import rice. Rice production has been increasing about 4 per cent per year, but the population has grown by about 2.3 per cent annually. The demand for rice has increased even more as people switch to rice from less popular foods.

Soaring exports of oil and liquefied natural gas (LNG) helped pay for rice and other imports. Oil and LNG exports reached an annual rate of $17-billion. Oil reserve estimates rose from 10 billion barrels to 14 billion barrels, and gas from 30 trillion cubic feet (840 billion cubic meters) to 55 trillion cubic feet (1,540 billion cubic meters). With domestic oil consumption rising 12 per cent a year, however, officials worried that the country might have none to export by the early 1990s.

Indonesia continued to need foreign aid as oil prices leveled off worldwide and income from other exports dropped. A group of countries and agencies promised $2.1 billion in aid in 1981, the same amount as in 1980.

Hijacking. Five men hijacked an Indonesian airliner on March 28 and ordered it to Bangkok, Thailand, where they held 55 hostages on the plane. In exchange for the hostages, the hijackers demanded the release of about 80 prisoners, including several Indonesian Muslim extremists who had attacked police stations and bombed churches and motion-picture theaters. A team of Indonesian antiterrorist commandos, who had been trained and specially equipped by the United States, flew to Bangkok. With Thai cooperation, the commandos stormed the plane early on March 31, freed the hostages, and killed four of the hijackers. The plane's captain died of wounds.

The hijacking focused attention on a revival of Muslim fundamentalism in Indonesia. Although 90 per cent of Indonesia's people are considered Muslims, many Indonesians combine ancestor and nature worship with Islam. The government is officially secular. Religion has become a form of protest by educated young people, who call for the overthrow of the Suharto government and its replacement by a Muslim state.   Henry S. Bradsher

See also ASIA (Facts in Brief Table). In WORLD BOOK, see INDONESIA.

INSURANCE. The problems of inadequate rate levels and higher costs of settling claims that characterized the United States property and liability fields during the late 1970s intensified in 1981. Underwriting losses of $2.76 billion by midyear were expected to reach $4.5 billion by year-end, making 1981 the least profitable year since 1975. The 1980 underwriting loss was $3.4 billion.

Investment income offset some of the loss, providing a $6.33-billion gain for insurers by mid-1981. After deducting losses, the industry had pretax earnings of $3.37 billion. Analysts projected a $13-billion investment gain by the end of 1981, compared with $11.2 billion in 1980.

Premium income was expected to reach $100-billion by the end of the year – about $10 billion more than in 1980. Much of the 1981 increase came from higher rates for automobile and homeowner's insurance, increased property values, and new classes of risks covering such growing hazards in the United States as environmental damage and hazardous waste disposal.

The price competition for high-premium commercial business continued unabated despite warnings of dire consequences from some industry leaders and state regulatory officials. Insurers showed increasing willingness to accept risks at severely inadequate rates in order to take in dollars they could then invest in high-interest money markets.

In the past, the industry itself carefully guarded the combined ratio of underwriting losses and operating expenses so that it would not exceed 96 cents for every premium dollar. Although this ratio was expected to reach 115 per cent in 1981, few executives appeared disturbed.

Catastrophe Losses, defined as those of at least $1 million each, totaled 23 by mid-1981. Property and liability insurers paid out $589 million on these disasters. During the same period in 1980, insurers paid out a similar amount for only 21 incidents. Insured catastrophe losses were expected to reach $1.1 billion by the end of 1981. Starting in 1982, "catastrophe" will, by definition, mean a minimum insured loss of $2 million.

The worst catastrophe during the first half of 1981 was the series of tornadoes that struck Texas, Oklahoma, Kansas, and Louisiana from May 7 to May 10. The tornadoes caused $200 million in insured losses, not counting flood losses on fixed property covered by federal flood insurance.

The most costly nonweather-related catastrophe in the first half of 1981 was a fire at the Las Vegas Hilton Hotel on February 10. The fire, set by an arsonist, killed eight persons and injured at least 200 others. Property damage was estimated at $60-million. On July 17, two walkways above a crowded lobby of the Hyatt Regency Hotel in Kansas City, Mo., collapsed, killing 113 persons and injuring about 200 others. More than 100 lawsuits were filed almost immediately, and property and liability claims were estimated at $3 billion.

Legislation. Congress renewed for one year the federal flood, crime, and riot insurance programs that were to expire on October 1. The action was part of the Omnibus Budget Reconciliation Act of 1981, the budget-cutting measure that President Ronald Reagan signed into law on August 13. However, the Holtzman Amendment was allowed to die. The amendment was enacted in 1978 to prohibit Free Access to Insurance Requirements (FAIR) plans — designed to cover otherwise uninsurable risks — from charging higher rates than those of the voluntary market.

On Sept. 25, 1981, President Reagan signed the Product Liability Risk Retention Act of 1981. It permits manufacturers, sellers, and distributors of products to establish group self-insurance programs or to purchase coverage as a group, outside the scope of state regulatory authorities.

On October 17, Reagan signed the Overseas Private Investment Corporation (OPIC) Amendments Act of 1981, extending until Sept. 30, 1985, OPIC authority to issue investment insurance, loans, and loan guarantees. The agency insures U.S. firms operating in other countries against such political risks as revolution and take-overs. Its fiscal 1981 coverage was $1.48 billion. Emanuel Levy

In WORLD BOOK, see INSURANCE.

INTERNATIONAL TRADE AND FINANCE. Recession prevailed throughout most of the industrial world during 1981. Only Japan and Canada recorded modest economic growth. The economies of the other major industrialized countries, including the United States, either declined or showed negligible growth. The growth rate of the developing nations, though slowing to about 4 per cent, exceeded that of the industrialized countries. However, economic stagnation persisted in many developing countries.

Unemployment increased. In the United States, more than 9 million workers, over 8 per cent of the labor force, were jobless — the highest number since the Great Depression of the 1930s. Unemployment in the 10-nation European Community (EC or Common Market) also exceeded 9 million. In Great Britain alone, the number of jobless workers approached 3 million, about 12 per cent of the labor force.

Inflation eased somewhat in the United States, Britain, Italy, and Japan but still averaged about 10 per cent in the industrialized countries. The average inflation rate in the developing nations approached 35 per cent, a slight rise over 1980.

Perhaps the most encouraging sign in 1981 was an improvement in the energy sector. Industrialized nations used less energy per unit of output and made greater use of nonpetroleum energy sources.

President Ronald Reagan's decision on April 24 to end the partial grain embargo against Russia spurs brisk trading at the Chicago Board of Trade.

Hundreds of Japanese cars sit at a dockside in Newark, N.J. In May,
Japan agreed to limit auto exports to the United States for three years.

Crude oil prices fell in 1981 from a peak of more than $35 a barrel early in the year to below $34 by autumn, contributing greatly to the slowing of inflation rates. See PETROLEUM AND GAS.

U.S. Dollar Soars. Monetary and fiscal policy in the United States dominated much of the international economy in 1981. Tight monetary controls caused interest rates to rise, in real terms, to their highest level since the 1860s. Foreign leaders claimed that the high rates, coupled with U.S. tax cuts, forced them to raise their nations' interest rates to compete for investment funds. They also said the tax cuts would prolong the high rates.

Spurred by the high U.S. interest rates, the dollar soared on foreign-exchange markets. The Administration of President Ronald Reagan, in a U.S. policy change, announced it would intervene in the markets only in extreme cases.

Trade Deficits. The industrialized nations reduced their combined deficit in the current account, one category of the balance of payments, in 1981 to an estimated $30 billion from $46 billion in 1980. The current account includes exports and imports, foreign aid, income on investments, and tourist spending. However, one country — Japan — accounted for most of the improvement. Japan's sharply higher trade surplus raised new concern over possible protectionist reactions in the United States and Europe. As a result, the United States,

Japan, Great Britain, Italy, West Germany, and France agreed at an economic summit held near Ottawa, Canada, in July to meet periodically to try to anticipate future trade problems.

Adding to the concern were signs that world trade in 1981 appeared headed for a decline for the first time since 1975. In general, the major nations refrained from new protectionist measures. However, under the threat of import quotas, the Japanese government "voluntarily" made a series of agreements to restrict the export of automobiles to Canada, West Germany, and the United States.

Grain Embargo Lifted. Bowing to demands by American farmers, the United States lifted on April 24 the limited embargo on grain shipments to the Soviet Union and in August agreed to a one-year extension of a contract that commits the Soviets to buy at least 6 million metric tons (6.6 million short tons) of grain per year. The United States then offered the Soviets an additional 15 million metric tons (16.5 million short tons) of grain during the 1981-1982 marketing year.

Tight controls continued, however, on exports of advanced technology to the Soviet Union. On December 29, Reagan imposed sanctions against Russia in response to the imposition of martial law in Poland. The sanctions included the suspension of export licenses for computers, electronics, and other high-technology items and for gas and oil production equipment (see PRESIDENT OF THE U.S.). By contrast, the United States relaxed its controls on such exports to China.

International Investment Policies became increasingly controversial in 1981, particularly in the United States and Canada. Canadian companies tried to acquire several large U.S. firms. In addition, the Canadian government proceeded with plans to take over a bigger share of its domestic energy industry, despite U.S. protests that the moves discriminated against U.S. investors in Canada. In response, the United States began reviewing its own policies to determine whether more safeguards were needed to protect major U.S. corporations against acquisition by foreign investors.

On December 4, a free-trade zone in international banking opened in New York City, a move supporters said would make the city the world's international financial center. Banks based in the zone can accept deposits and make loans without paying state and local income taxes and without conforming to certain federal banking regulations.

Cancún Summit. President Reagan suggested that the world's poorer countries should rely more heavily on private investment rather than on foreign aid to develop their economies. At the annual meeting of the World Bank and International Monetary Fund (IMF) in September and at a summit conference in Cancún, Mexico, in October, Reagan extolled "the magic of the market place."

The Cancún summit dealt with so-called North-South relations – those between industrialized and poorer nations. The developing nations seemed to win a small concession when the United States endorsed the possibility of holding "global negotiations" on food, energy, trade, and finance. The United States renewed its opposition, however, to such proposals as the establishment of a World Bank "energy affiliate," the easing of restrictions on loans from the IMF and World Bank, and more voting power for the developing nations in those organizations.

Increasing Debts. During 1981, the foreign debt of the developing countries grew to nearly $500-billion, straining the capacity of some countries to pay. Debts were rescheduled in about 10 nations, mainly those in central and southern Africa.

The IMF, an agency of the United Nations, played a larger role in helping developing countries in 1981. Through November, the agency had provided nearly $17 billion in loans. The biggest loan – $5.8 billion – went to India to help finance investments in basic industries. In 1981, Saudi Arabia agreed to lend the IMF about $10 billion over two years. Thirteen industrialized countries lent an additional $1.3 billion.   Richard Lawrence

See also ECONOMICS. In WORLD BOOK, see INTERNATIONAL TRADE.

IOWA. See STATE GOVERNMENT.

IRAN. In 1981, two years after the fall of Shah Mohammad Reza Pahlavi, the revolution unleashed by his overthrow was still unable to sort itself out. During 1981, Iran made – and unmade – three presidents, saw its top leadership almost destroyed several times, and continued to wage a small-scale war with Iraq. And, as if these were not enough, the country also endured a seemingly endless cycle of violence.

The one constant factor in the revolutionary turmoil was the personality and final authority of Ayatollah Ruhollah Khomeini, the *faqih* or "supreme Islamic guide" of the republic as written into the revolutionary Constitution. Khomeini stood above the fray, but the excesses committed in his name by his supporters turned the revolution's dream of a just society ruled by Islamic laws into a nightmare for most Iranians.

The one positive action taken by the government in 1981 was the release on January 20 of the 52 Americans held hostage since Nov. 4, 1979 (see Close-Up). In accordance with the terms of the release agreement, Iran received on January 20 about $2.9 billion of the $12 billion in assets that President Jimmy Carter had frozen in the United States after the hostages were taken. An additional $5.1 billion was set aside to pay claims against Iran by American banks. On August 18, the United

Mourners weep as the body of Iran's Chief Justice Ayatollah Mohammed Beheshti, killed by a bomb on June 28, is taken for burial.

The Hostages Come Home

The American people breathed a collective sigh of relief on Jan. 20, 1981, as one of the most important foreign trade agreements in United States history went into effect. Representatives of U.S. President Jimmy Carter had concluded price talks with the revolutionary government of Iran. They had not haggled over the price of American weapons or of Persian Gulf oil, but rather over the price of freedom for 52 U.S. citizens—hostages taken at the U.S. Embassy in Teheran on Nov. 4, 1979.

What ended, almost coolly, as a business deal, had begun as a violent act of retaliation. Some 400 self-styled Iranian militants—followers of Ayatollah Ruhollah Khomeini—had seized the embassy to protest the admission of the deposed Shah Mohammad Reza Pahlavi to the United States for medical care. The militants demanded that the United States hand over the ailing shah in return for the hostages. President Carter summarily refused.

With the American electorate clamoring for the hostages' release, Carter began to exert pressure upon Iran. He stopped delivery on military equipment, deported Iranian students and diplomats, diverted an aircraft carrier from the Indian Ocean to the Arabian Sea, and froze $8 billion in Iranian assets held in U.S. banks. Iran did not respond.

On December 15, the shah left the United States for Panama. On December 25, the hostages spent their first Christmas in Iran.

The stalemate continued until February 1980, when newly elected Iranian President Abol Hasan Bani-Sadr outlined his conditions for the hostages' release—that the United States acknowledge its "past crimes" against Iran, recognize Iran's right to extradite the shah and recover his wealth, and promise not to interfere in Iranian affairs. Only the last condition was remotely acceptable to Carter, and the lines between Washington and Teheran went silent.

The dialogue resumed in April, when Khomeini announced that the question of the hostages' fate would be postponed until the newly elected *Majlis* (parliament) convened. Car-

ter responded by bringing full U.S. diplomatic might against Iran. He severed diplomatic relations, banned Iranian imports, prohibited travel to Iran, and pressured the European Community and Japan to do the same. He hinted at military force.

Carter's hint became an unfortunate reality on April 24, when an American commando team staged a rescue mission that was aborted after three of the eight helicopters involved succumbed to mechanical failure. Eight U.S. servicemen died in the retreat when a helicopter collided with a C-130 cargo plane. A dispirited Carter could do little more than wait for Iran's next move.

A lull set in during the summer as Iran's domestic situation began to work in the United States favor. Inflation had passed the 50 per cent mark; 30 per cent of the work force was unemployed; and a border skirmish with Iraq was developing into a full-fledged war. Bani-Sadr was eager to dispense with the hostage question and tackle these pressing matters. The shah was no longer an issue—he had died on July 27.

On September 12, Khomeini pronounced new terms for freeing the hostages—the United States must cancel its claims against Iran, return the late shah's wealth, release the frozen Iranian assets, and pledge noninterference. These conditions, acceptable "in spirit" to Carter, were ratified by the Majlis on November 2. Still unsettled was the value of the assets to be "thawed."

Carter appointed Deputy Secretary of State Warren M. Christopher to work out the details. Christopher worked through the holidays while the hostages spent their second Christmas in captivity. By Jan. 15, 1981, he had brought the Iranians down from their original demand of $24 billion to the considerably lower sum of $8 billion. The final agreement, signed on January 19, offered Carter hope that he might welcome the hostages home while in office. However, it was early afternoon the next day when the hostages crossed the Iranian border—minutes after Ronald Reagan became President of the United States.   Beverly Merz

The ordeal ends

States transferred about $2 billion in frozen Iranian assets to a bank in the Netherlands. On October 20, about 3,000 U.S. companies and individuals began filing claims against Iran for property losses or for money due them because of contracts signed with the shah's government. An international tribunal was formed to arbitrate the claims, with successful judgments to be paid out of the $2 billion.

Bani-Sadr Ousted. The regime turned from violence against supporters of the shah to destroying its own people when rivals of President Abol Hasan Bani-Sadr joined forces in June to oust him from office. Bani-Sadr had threatened earlier to resign and had used his veto power to block legislation in the *Majlis* (parliament) and the appointment to Cabinet positions of his opponents in the clergy-dominated Islamic Republican Party (IRP). These actions cost him Khomeini's support. On June 10, Khomeini dismissed Bani-Sadr as commander in chief of the armed forces. On June 13, Bani-Sadr was reported to be in hiding, fearing for his life. On June 21, the Majlis declared him guilty of "political incompetence" and impeached him by a vote of 177-1. The next day, Khomeini removed him from office. On July 29, Bani-Sadr escaped to France and joined the anti-Khomeini exile movement there.

Violence Escalates. Bani-Sadr's downfall left Iran open to a confrontation between the IRP and the leftist *Mujahedeen* (Fighters for the Faith), a guerrilla group whose goal is a nonreligious Islamic republic. The Mujahedeen drew first blood with the June 28 bombing of IRP headquarters in Teheran. The bomb killed about 70 party leaders, including Chief Justice Ayatollah Mohammed Beheshti. A second bomb attack on August 30 killed Prime Minister Mohammed Jauad Bahonar and President Mohammed Ali Rajai, who had been elected in July to succeed Bani-Sadr. Assassinations by the well-armed Mujahedeen of IRP leaders, *mullahs* (religious leaders), and public figures associated with the regime continued without letup throughout the year. The IRP's Revolutionary Guards and allied *Hezbollahis* (Servants of God) retaliated with mass executions. An estimated 1,400 persons had been executed by revolutionary courts by late October, and 100 IRP leaders had been assassinated by the Mujahedeen.

The Long-Suffering Iranians marched to the polls again on October 2 and elected the new head of the IRP, Ali Khamenei, as their third president of the year. Khamenei became the first mullah to hold the office. His first choice as prime minister was rejected by the Majlis. On October 30, however, his appointment of Hosein Musavi-Khamenei to be prime minister was approved. Musavi named a 21-member Cabinet on November 2 and pledged to crack down on leftist opponents of the government and to press the war with Iraq.

President Bani-Sadr has to take cover during a March visit to the Iran-Iraq war front. He was impeached in June and fled to France in July.

The war had ground on with no decision, almost forgotten in the political upheavals. An Iranian offensive in the Susangerd area in January failed to gain ground, but Iranian forces partially broke the Iraqi siege of the oil refinery city of Abadan in October. Heavy fighting was reported in Khuzistan province in late November.

Economic Progress. Despite the nation's political instability, Iran's economy managed to show progress in some areas. Oil exports were resumed in February, and new contracts were signed with Turkey, Spain, and India. The Isfahan refinery resumed production in March. A 5 per cent price increase to $37 per barrel of oil, plus these new contracts, improved the country's economic prospects.

The lucrative trade with Japan also resumed. On February 17, five Japanese banks reopened their offices in Teheran. A Japanese-built power line from the Caspian Sea to Teheran went into operation in March. In May, assembly plants for Honda and Yamaha motorcycles began production. They will produce 21,000 assembled units a month.

On July 15, the Majlis approved the 1981 budget of $39.9 billion. The expected $8-billion deficit was to be covered by increased oil sales, bank loans, and improved tax collection. William Spencer

See also MIDDLE EAST (Facts in Brief Table). In WORLD BOOK, see IRAN.

IRAQ entered the second year of its war with Iran in September 1981, with neither a political nor a military settlement in sight. Iraq halted a major Iranian counteroffensive launched in January in the Susangerd area of Iran's Khuzistan province. Iraqi troops continued to hold most of the Iranian territory captured during the early months of the war. An exception was the withdrawal of Iraqi forces in September from the east bank of the Karun River outside the besieged Iranian refinery port of Abadan.

Despite Casualties estimated at 30,000, including 10,000 dead, the Iraqi population generally supported the war. The most popular film of the year in Baghdad was *Al-Qadisiyah,* a screen version of the battle in which the Arabs defeated the Persians in A.D. 637, which brought Iran into the Islamic world. Tough security measures coupled with the absolute authority of the ruling Baath Party over Iraqi life kept opposition to a minimum.

Other reasons for the popularity of the war effort lay in the personality of President Saddam Hussein, viewed by most Iraqis as a kind of charismatic elder brother, and the continued economic benefits dispensed by his regime.

Nuclear Reactor Bombed. The destruction of the French-built Osirak nuclear reactor near Baghdad by Israeli warplanes on June 7 reduced Iraq's isolation from other Arab states. Saudi Arabia agreed to pay all costs of rebuilding the reactor, which both Iraq and France said was intended for peaceful scientific research.

The Economy resumed its progress after a brief halt during the first months of the war. Blockage of the main ports of Basra and Umm Qasr brought about a major shift to truck transport. The Iraq-Jordan Overland Transport Company was formed in July. It put 700 new trucks in use on the new asphalt highway from Al Aqabah, Jordan, to Baghdad. This highway served as Iraq's main link with the outside world for imports of consumer goods and weapons.

In July, the government approved the 1981-1985 five-year plan. It set expenditures at $133 billion, with most of the funds to come from oil exports. Top priorities included health, rural education, and the construction of 350,000 units of housing and 6,500 kilometers (4,000 miles) of roads.

Work on a 32-kilometer (20-mile) Baghdad subway began in April. Along with new expressways, new hotels, and an urban "face-lift" by British architects, the subway is intended to make Iraq's capital the "Paris of the East" in time for the nonaligned nations conference scheduled to be held there in September 1982.   William Spencer

See also MIDDLE EAST (Facts in Brief Table). In WORLD BOOK, see IRAQ.

IRELAND. A general election on June 11, 1981, held in the shadow of hunger strikes in Northern Ireland and severe economic problems in the Republic of Ireland, resulted in the ouster of Prime Minister Charles J. Haughey and his replacement by Garret FitzGerald.

Announcing the dissolution of the Irish Parliament on May 21 as a prelude to the election, Haughey said the government needed a "clear and definite mandate," particularly to pursue its efforts to achieve a political solution to the problem of Northern Ireland. He hoped the electorate would be impressed by the dialogue he had begun with British Prime Minister Margaret Thatcher.

However, such economic issues as 17 per cent inflation, an economy in disarray, and fears that the country might have to appeal to the International Monetary Fund for aid dominated the election. The prosperity that membership in the European Community (EC or Common Market) had brought to Irish agriculture was evaporating.

Neither of the two major parties emerged an outright election winner. The results were: *Fianna Fáil* (Soldiers of Destiny), 78 seats; *Fine Gael* (Gaelic People), 65; Labour, 15; and independents (including two Irish Republican Army members imprisoned in Northern Ireland), 8. After a period of political uncertainty, economist and former Foreign Minister Garret FitzGerald led Fine Gael to

A 1979 photograph shows the partially built nuclear reactor near Baghdad, Iraq, that was destroyed by Israeli warplanes on June 7.

Garret FitzGerald, left, leader of Ireland's
Fine Gael party, leaves the Irish Parliament
after being elected prime minister on June 30.

ISRAEL. Prime Minister Menachem Begin somewhat unexpectedly won a narrow victory and a
second term in office in national elections on June
30, 1981. Begin's win came after a stormy election
campaign that had seen his Likud Party coalition
trailing well behind challenger Shimon Peres'
Labor Party early in the year.

The Likud won 48 seats in the *Knesset* (parliament) to 47 for Labor. The remainder of the seats
in the 120-member Knesset were divided among
various minority parties. The largest minority
party, the National Religious Party (NRP) headed
by Interior Minister Yosef Burg, retained only 6 of
its 13 seats. But together with two other religiously
oriented minority parties, Agudat Israel (4 seats)
and Tami (3 seats), the NRP provided Begin with
13 votes. Added to Likud's 48 votes, this gave
Begin a 2-vote majority in the Knesset, 61-59.

The Campaign was marked by heated public de-
bates, vandalism, and personal attacks on each
other by the candidates. Peres accused Begin of
character assassination and appeals to voter emotions. Begin, in turn, denounced Peres as a "sabo-
teur" for publicly criticizing the June 7 Israeli raid
on the Osirak nuclear reactor in Iraq (see IRAQ).

A number of factors contributed to Begin's victory at the polls. The most important was the
government's new economic policy. After the resig-

form a coalition with Labour. The coalition issued
a joint policy document, *Programme for Government
1981-1986.* Among its proposals were a wealth tax, a
special tax on bank profits, tougher measures
against tax avoidance, continuation of the Anglo-
Irish talks, maintenance of Irish neutrality, creation of an all-party committee to study marital
law, and abolition of capital punishment. FitzGerald was elected prime minister on June 30, though
without a majority (see FITZGERALD, GARRET).

On September 27, FitzGerald announced he was
hoping to introduce such changes to the Irish
Constitution as removing the ban on divorce and
the claims of jurisdiction over Northern Ireland in
order to make it more attractive to northern Protestants. The Senate endorsed FitzGerald's call for a
review of the Constitution on October 16. However, Fianna Fáil's continuing opposition cast doubts
on his chances of winning such a referendum.

The Irish Arts received encouragement on March
16 with the announcement that 150 Irish writers
and artists would be given tax-free salaries and
annual pensions of $7,000 (4,000 Irish pounds).
A self-governing artistic assembly, the *Aosdana,*
meaning "a collective of wise men" in Gaelic,
would be formed to implement the grants. Ian Mather

See also GREAT BRITAIN; NORTHERN IRELAND.
In WORLD BOOK, see IRELAND.

IRON AND STEEL. See STEEL INDUSTRY.

Israel's Prime Minister Begin prays at the
Wailing Wall in Jerusalem after being asked to
form a new government. He won in June elections.

Mounted police chase ultra-Orthodox Jews who were protesting an archaeological dig in Jerusalem. The protesters said the digging was desecrating a cemetery.

nation of Finance Minister Yigael Hurwitz on January 11, his successor, Yoram Avidor, reduced sales taxes on many consumer goods, including imports of luxury items. At the same time, the government increased its subsidies on basic commodities and gasoline to hold down prices. Civil servants were given a 20 per cent salary increase in March. Excise taxes on some automobiles were reduced. The end of restrictions on color-TV broadcasting was also popular with voters. One critic saw all these measures as "election bribery."

Begin also profited by a split in the Labor Party between Peres and former Prime Minister Yitzhak Rabin. The decision of former Foreign Minister Moshe Dayan to form a new party, Telem (Movement for National Renewal), damaged Labor more than Likud because it reduced the possibility of Labor's forming a majority coalition.

To Form His Knesset Majority, Begin had to make concessions to the three religious parties to bring them into a coalition. The promises included strict observance of the Jewish Sabbath, which meant a shutdown of El Al airline flights on that day. It also meant a stoppage of Saturday work at the ports of Haifa, Ashdod, and Elat, which handle all of Israel's freight and cruise-ship traffic. Begin also earmarked $58 million in the 1981 budget of $3.8 billion for new seminaries and religious schools.

Progress toward a solution of critical foreign-policy issues affecting Israel was suspended during the elections. Begin's resistance to full self-rule for the Palestinians on the West Bank of the River Jordan and the Gaza Strip and his toughness in dealing with Israel's Arab neighbors gained him the election support of the Oriental, or Sephardic, Jews – those originally from Arab, Mediterranean, or Asian countries. The Sephardim form a slight majority of the Israeli population over the European, or Ashkenazic, Jews and advocate a "no compromise" foreign policy. The bombing of the Iraqi nuclear reactor and the pursuit by Israeli warplanes of Palestinian guerrillas into Lebanon contributed to the Begin government's popularity among the Sephardim.

Other Developments. The Knesset in January voted against the annexation of the Golan Heights, Syrian territory that Israel has occupied since 1967. But on December 14, it reversed itself and rushed through a law imposing Israeli "law, jurisdiction, and administration" on the region. Syria and Egypt immediately condemned the action.

After the assassination of Egypt's President Anwar el-Sadat in October, Begin pledged that Israel would continue the negotiations on Palestinian autonomy begun at Camp David. Israel's interpretation of autonomy – or self-rule – differed sharply from that of Egypt and that of the Palestinians themselves. In the more narrow Israeli view, the authority of the proposed Palestine Self-Governing Authority would be limited to local affairs, while Israeli military authorities would continue to be responsible for defense and internal security. Talks resumed in Cairo, Egypt, on November 11.

Relations with the new United States Administration of President Ronald Reagan were strained in October, when the U.S. Senate approved the Administration's sale of five Airborne Warning and Control System (AWACS) planes and other advanced air equipment to Saudi Arabia. The Israeli Cabinet on October 29 issued a statement of regret over the sale. On November 30, the United States and Israel announced a strategic-cooperation agreement. On December 14, however, Israel unexpectedly annexed the Golan Heights, taken from Syria in 1967. In response, the United States suspended the agreement on December 18. Begin, in turn, said the United States was treating Israel like "a banana republic."

The government's drastic pre-election economic measures slowed inflation somewhat, though the improvement was offset by rising costs for raw materials. Exports totaled $3.1 billion for the first half of the year, a slight increase over the first six months of 1980. William Spencer

See also MIDDLE EAST (Facts in Brief Table). In WORLD BOOK, see ISRAEL.

ITALY. Mehmet Ali Agca, a right wing Turkish terrorist, shocked the world on May 13, 1981, when he shot Pope John Paul II in St. Peter's Square in Rome. The pope, in an open car, was welcoming 10,000 pilgrims and tourists when Agca opened fire, wounding him in the abdomen, right arm, and left hand. Surgeons at Gemelli Hospital removed sections of the pope's intestines and put him in intensive care until his 61st birthday, five days later. After a second abdominal operation, the pope returned to the Vatican on August 14. Agca, an assassin who had escaped from Turkey, was jailed for life by the Rome Court of Assizes on July 22. See ROMAN CATHOLIC CHURCH.

On December 17, United States Army Brigadier General James L. Dozier was kidnapped from his home in Verona by members of the Red Brigades, a terrorist organization. At year's end, he was still in captivity.

Masonic Scandal. Italy was rocked by a scandal that toppled Prime Minister Arnaldo Forlani's coalition of Christian Democrats, Socialists, Social Democrats, and Republicans. Forlani had to resign on May 26 when the activities of a Masonic lodge called Propaganda Two (P-2) became known.

Masonic lodges were not illegal in Italy, but secret organizations were. P-2's leader, Grandmaster Licio Gelli, kept its membership list secret, so investigating magistrates considered the lodge ille-

gal. Two Cabinet ministers were members of P-2.

New Government. Italy's powerful Communist Party refused to help Forlani form a new government. The task then fell to Giovanni Spadolini, 56, secretary of the small Republican Party. On June 28, Spadolini formed a five-party coalition dedicated to dealing with four emergencies: inflation, terrorism, public scandals, and the worsening international situation. See SPADOLINI, GIOVANNI.

Economic Troubles. Spadolini inherited a weak economy. Italy's balance-of-payments deficit had soared to a record $5 billion in the first five months of 1981, compared with $6.5 billion for all of 1980. Inflation reached 20 per cent, and the budget deficit threatened to top $50 billion. Industrial production was down 5.4 per cent.

On October 4, Italy and three other countries changed the values of their currencies within the European Monetary System, a program that eight nations set up in 1979 to stabilize the prices of their currencies. Italy and France decreased the values of their currencies by 3 per cent, while the Netherlands and West Germany raised theirs by 5.5 per cent, relative to the currencies of Belgium, Denmark, Ireland, and Luxembourg. Kenneth Brown

See also EUROPE (Facts in Brief Table). In WORLD BOOK, see ITALY; MASONRY.

IVORY COAST. See AFRICA.

JAMAICA. See WEST INDIES.

JAPAN. Disputes over defense and trade continued between Japan and the United States, making 1981 perhaps the most difficult year in Japanese-American relations since World War II. U.S. officials pressed Japan to increase defense expenditures and reduce exports to the United States.

Japan's Defense Responsibilities were the major topic of discussion between Japan's Prime Minister Zenko Suzuki and President Ronald Reagan when the two leaders met in Washington, D.C., on May 7 and 8. Suzuki and the President issued a joint communiqué following their meeting expressing concern over Russia's involvement in Afghanistan and the possibility of any "intervention in Poland." The statement also reaffirmed the two nations' "solidarity, friendship, and mutual trust" and mentioned a Japanese-American "alliance."

On May 16, Japan's Foreign Minister Masayoshi Ito resigned after a furor erupted over the word *alliance* in the communiqué. The Japanese press interpreted the word as referring to a military alliance between the two nations against the Soviet Union. Suzuki criticized Ito for releasing the communiqué without including Suzuki's subsequent comments in which he said that Japan could do little to increase defense spending. On December 28, however, Japan's Cabinet approved a 7.7 per cent increase in military spending for the 1982-1983 fiscal year.

Collision at Sea. Two Japanese crew members died on April 9 when the U.S. nuclear-powered submarine *George Washington* struck and sank a small Japanese freighter in the East China Sea. The American submarine left the scene of the accident without assisting the survivors. Later, the U.S. government assumed responsibility for the collision and agreed to pay compensation to the families of the victims.

Protests over Nuclear Weapons. On May 17, former U.S. Ambassador to Japan Edwin O. Reischauer revealed that a secret "oral agreement" had existed between the United States and Japan since 1960. Under the agreement, U.S. ships carrying nuclear weapons were allowed to visit Japanese ports regularly. Official Japanese policy forbids the introduction of nuclear weapons into Japan, as well as the production or possession of such weapons. The revelation caused a political uproar.

On June 5, the U.S. aircraft carrier *Midway* made a routine call at its home port of Yokosuka, Japan. Political groups who claimed the ship was carrying nuclear weapons held protest rallies.

Trade with the United States and Canada. The United States continued to be concerned in 1981 about the increasing deficit in its trade with Japan. The estimated deficit for 1981 was a record $15-billion, topping the previous record of $11.6 billion

in 1978. Much of the deficit was due to U.S. imports of Japanese automobiles, electronic products, and other manufactured goods.

On May 1, the Japanese government announced that it would voluntarily limit automobile exports to the United States for three years. The plan limited exports to the United States to 1.68 million cars during Japan's 1981-1982 fiscal year, which ran from April 1, 1981, to March 31, 1982. That represented a 7.7 per cent reduction from the 1.82 million cars sold to U.S. buyers in 1980-1981.

On June 4, the Canadian government announced a similar agreement. Japan consented to cut automobile exports to Canada by 6 per cent during the 1981-1982 fiscal year.

Relations with Other Countries. Suzuki conferred from January 7 to 20 with leaders of Indonesia, Malaysia, the Philippines, Singapore, and Thailand – the five members of the Association of Southeast Asian Nations. In June, he spent 13 days in Europe, meeting with leaders of six Western European countries. The discussions dealt with the impact of Japanese exports on European markets. During the trip, Japan and West Germany reached an agreement to limit the growth of Japanese automobile exports to West Germany to 10 per cent a year. Suzuki was also one of the seven leaders of industrialized countries attending the economic

Japanese children display entries in a Tokyo contest for calligraphy, the art of beautiful writing, which the Japanese consider much like painting.

summit conference near Ottawa, Canada, from July 19 to 21.

On October 4, Japan and Russia announced that they would begin talks on "various pending questions" by the end of 1981. A major topic of discussion was to be Japan's demand that Russia return the southern four of the Kuril Islands northeast of Japan. The Soviet Union occupied the islands after World War II, but Japan claims them. Suzuki dramatized the issue on September 10 by visiting the eastern tip of Hokkaido, from which he could view the closest of the disputed islands.

Pope John Paul II traveled in Japan in February, the first visit to the country by any pope. He visited Hiroshima and Nagasaki and Tokyo, where he was received by Emperor Hirohito.

Japan's Economy remained healthy in 1981. Economic experts predicted in late September that the real rate of economic growth for the current fiscal year would be about 5 per cent, the highest growth rate among major industrialized nations. They predicted that by 1990 Japan's per capita gross national product (GNP) would be $29,100, compared with $27,730 for the United States. Per capita GNP, determined by dividing the GNP by the nation's population, is considered a good measure of a nation's standard of living.   John M. Maki

See also ASIA (Facts in Brief Table). In WORLD BOOK, see JAPAN.

JARUZELSKI, WOJCIECH (1923-   ), was elected leader of Poland's Communist Party on Oct. 18, 1981, making him one of the most powerful men in Polish history. He had been Poland's defense minister since 1968 and its prime minister since Feb. 9, 1981. After the Communist Party election, he held nearly complete power as head of the party, the armed forces, and the government.

Wojciech Witold Jaruzelski was born on July 6, 1923, into a landowning family in Kurow. In 1939, at the start of World War II, the Russians invaded the area. Jaruzelski, then only 16 years old, was deported to the Soviet Union as a forced laborer.

Jaruzelski began his military career in the Soviet Union. He attended infantry officer training school at Ryazan, and joined the First Polish Army in 1943. He served in combat until the end of World War II in 1945. From 1945 to 1947, he fought against the anti-Communist resistance movement in Poland. The Polish Army sent him to general staff college, and Jaruzelski rose quickly through the ranks. By 1957, he commanded a division. In 1968, he became a general.

Jaruzelski's political career also grew. He became deputy defense minister in 1962. In 1964, he was elected to the party's Central Committee. He became an alternate member of the Politburo, the party's most powerful decision-making body, in 1970 and a full member in 1978.   Sara Dreyfuss

JEWS AND JUDAISM. The historic conflict between religion and state erupted again in Israel in 1981. Orthodox followers of the chief rabbi protested against archaeological diggings in the City of David near the Old City of Jerusalem, claiming that the graves of ancient Jews were being violated. Permission to excavate the site had been granted by Israel's Ministry of Religious Affairs. In September, the Israeli Supreme Court upheld the digging, ruling that the rabbinate has no legal right to determine state policy.

Prime Minister Menachem Begin of Israel made several concessions on religious legislation in 1981 to gain the support of several small Orthodox parties and so form his coalition government (see ISRAEL). Begin agreed to a two-year deadline to resolve the controversial "Who is a Jew?" amendment to Israel's Law of Return. Orthodox supporters of the amendment would require that conversion to Judaism be performed in the traditional Halachic manner. Conversions performed by Conservative and Reform rabbis in the United States would then not be recognized for purposes of immigration to Israel.

Jewish Emigration from Russia declined sharply in 1980, according to figures released in January 1981 by the National Conference on Soviet Jewry. A bitter controversy flared between the Jewish Agency for Israel and the U.S.-funded Hebrew Immigrant Aid Society over the right of Russian Jews to immigrate to the country of their choice. The Jewish Agency wants the U.S. organization to stop helping Russian Jews immigrate to the United States, unless they have spouses, children, or parents there. Israel is troubled by the numbers of Jewish immigrants moving to Western Europe and the United States, rather than to Israel.

Survivors of the Holocaust, the mass murder of Jews by the Nazis during World War II, gathered in Jerusalem for four days in June to commemorate the dead and reaffirm their faith in the future. More than 4,000 survivors and children of survivors attended the ceremonies.

A new U.S. commission on the Holocaust was announced in September. The commission, headed by Arthur J. Goldberg, a former associate justice of the Supreme Court of the United States, will inquire into certain aspects of American foreign policy during World War II. For example, it will try to determine what President Franklin D. Roosevelt and the U.S. Department of State knew about the Nazi campaign against the Jews, how soon they knew it, and what they did about it.

California Supreme Court Judge Thomas T. Johnson took "judicial notice" of the Holocaust in October. He stated that "Jews were gassed to death in Auschwitz in Poland in the summer of 1944." Johnson was acting on a suit filed by an Auschwitz survivor, Mel Mermelstein of Long

Beach, Calif., who sued the Institute of Historical Review, a right wing group that claims the Holocaust is a fabrication. The institute had offered $50,000 to anyone who could prove the Holocaust had occurred. Mermelstein contended the institute had not paid him, though it had seen his proof.

The First Reform Commentary on the Torah was published in the United States in September. The chief author of the work, *The Torah — A Modern Commentary,* was Rabbi W. Gunther Plaut of Toronto, Canada. Rabbi Bernard Bamberger of New York City wrote the commentary on Leviticus.

Anti-Semitism. On October 20, a bomb exploded near a synagogue in Antwerp, Belgium, killing two people and injuring about 100 others. On August 29, two Arabs tossed grenades at a synagogue in Vienna, Austria, during a bar mitzvah, killing two people. A B'nai B'rith Anti-Defamation League report recorded a sharp rise in anti-Semitic incidents, such as firebombing and swastika painting, in the United States during 1981. There were 974 such incidents in 1981, compared with 377 in 1980. However, an American Jewish Committee study reported in July that prejudice against Jews in the United States had declined significantly since 1964.   Arnold G. Kaiman

See also MIDDLE EAST. In WORLD BOOK, see JEWS; JUDAISM.

JORDAN remained largely aloof from inter-Arab conflicts and the general Arab-Israeli conflict during 1981. King Hussein I played host to an Arab summit conference in Amman in January, however, and continued to insist on Israeli withdrawal from the West Bank and recognition of Palestinian rights there.

A major exception to Jordanian aloofness occurred when the government accused Syria of being involved in the February 6 kidnapping of Hisham al-Mohaisen, a Jordanian diplomatic official in Lebanon. Jordan claimed that the kidnapping was organized by the head of the Syrian security forces, who is a brother of Syria's President Hafiz al-Assad. The kidnapping was apparently done in retaliation for a Jordanian grant of asylum for seven Syrian pilots opposed to Assad who defected in 1980. Jordan closed its border with Syria and expelled several Syrians. Mohaisen's release in April eased the tension, and the border was reopened.

Hussein continued to cultivate good relations with the United States. He visited Washington, D.C., in March and November. Relations with Iraq also improved as Jordan supported the Iraqis in their war with Iran. Military hardware and other imports were funneled to Iraq through Jordan after Iranian air raids shut Iraqi ports.

Survivors of the Holocaust light candles at Jerusalem's Wailing Wall during ceremonies in June to commemorate those who died in concentration camps.

Jordan's King Hussein, front, watches a graduation parade at Britain's Royal Military Academy, Sandhurst. His son was among the graduates.

KENYA. Several incidents in 1981 marred Kenya's reputation as one of Africa's most stable nations. On March 5, Andrew Mungai Muthemba, a Nairobi businessman, and Dickson Kamau Muiriri, a cousin of Home Affairs Minister Charles Njonjo, were accused of plotting to overthrow the government of President Daniel T. arap Moi. However, the two were acquitted on May 20.

On May 22, police arrested the editor and five staff members of the *Nation,* a daily newspaper, for the paper's coverage of government handling of a physicians' strike. After Nairobi University students demonstrated in favor of the strike, as well as against the government's treatment of a former vice-president of Kenya, Jaramogi Oginga Odinga, the government responded on May 18 by closing the university for almost two months.

Odinga had clashed with former President Jomo Kenyatta and had been jailed for 15 months during Kenyatta's rule. Still very popular among the Luo, one of Kenya's largest ethnic groups, Odinga was encouraged by President Moi to make a political comeback. However, he embarrassed Moi by publicly criticizing Kenyatta in a speech in April. Moi then vetoed Odinga's candidacy for a vacant parliamentary seat. 　　　　　　J. Dixon Esseks

See also AFRICA. In WORLD BOOK, see KENYA.
KIRIBATI. See PACIFIC ISLANDS.

Economic Growth. Other Arab countries continued to provide massive infusions of aid under the principle of support for Jordan as a front-line state in the war with Israel. This aid spurred economic growth. In July, Saudi Arabia, Iraq, and the United Arab Emirates paid a second installment of $197.5 million that was pledged at the 1978 Arab summit conference following the Camp David peace negotiations between Egypt and Israel. Kuwait paid Jordan an equal amount in August.

Aside from Arab aid, Jordan did quite well on its own. The country's 1981-1985 five-year plan forecast a 10.4 per cent annual economic growth rate. Per capita income, which was $580 in 1975, reached $1,425 in 1981.

Economic growth resulted mainly from expansion of the production of Jordan's major mineral resources, potash and phosphates, which are used in fertilizers. In September, Jordan became the world's third-largest producer of phosphates, with 9.1 per cent of the market. 　　　William Spencer

See also MIDDLE EAST (Facts in Brief Table). In WORLD BOOK, see JORDAN.
JUDAISM. See JEWS AND JUDAISM.
JUNIOR ACHIEVEMENT (JA). See YOUTH ORGANIZATIONS.
KAMPUCHEA. See CAMBODIA.
KANSAS. See STATE GOVERNMENT.
KENTUCKY. See STATE GOVERNMENT.

Kenya's President Daniel T. arap Moi, right, confers with Uganda's President Milton Obote at an OAU meeting in Nairobi in June.

KIRKPATRICK, JEANE JORDAN (1926-   ), was appointed United States permanent representative to the United Nations (UN) by President Ronald Reagan on Jan. 29, 1981. She is the first woman to hold the position, in which she succeeded Ambassador Donald F. McHenry.

Jeane Duane Jordan was born on Nov. 19, 1926, in Duncan, Okla., and grew up in Oklahoma and Illinois. She received an A.A. degree from Stephens College in Columbia, Mo., in 1946. In New York City, she earned a B.A. from Barnard College in 1948 and an M.A. in political science from Columbia University in 1950. She studied political science at the University of Paris in 1952 and 1953 and received a Ph.D. from Columbia University in 1968.

During her career, Kirkpatrick has held a series of positions as professor, lecturer, and researcher at various colleges, universities, and foundations. Prior to her UN appointment, she was a professor of government at Georgetown University and resident scholar at the American Enterprise Institute for Public Policy Research, both located in Washington, D.C.

She is married to Evron M. Kirkpatrick, executive director of the American Political Science Association. They have three sons.   Marsha F. Goldsmith

KIWANIS INTERNATIONAL. See COMMUNITY ORGANIZATIONS.

KOREA, NORTH. In an effort to overcome its economic problems, North Korea's Communist government, headed by President Kim Il-song, modified its long-standing policy of self-reliance in 1981. The government began to encourage trade with other countries and to explore the possibility of joint ventures in which foreign companies would produce goods in North Korea.

North Korea carries on most of its foreign trade by barter with other Communist nations. Its avoidance of trade with the West, combined with heavy military spending, gives it little Western currency with which to pay its debts. Many plants stand idle or in disrepair for lack of money. The new foreign trade policy was intended to relieve that problem.

One export flourished, however—that of arms and military advisers. North Korea continued to send weapons and military experts to a variety of countries. More than 100 North Korean advisers arrived in Zimbabwe on August 8 to train an army brigade.

The United States said North Korea fired an antiaircraft missile at a U.S. SR-71 reconnaissance plane flying in South Korean and international airspace on August 26. The missile missed the plane. North Korea said the plane had violated its airspace.   Henry S. Bradsher

See also ASIA (Facts in Brief Table). In WORLD BOOK, see KOREA.

KOREA, SOUTH. Chun Doo Hwan, a former general who seized power in 1979 through a military coup and became interim president in 1980, was elected president of South Korea in 1981. Some 80 per cent of the nation's 20 million voters turned out on February 11 to select 5,278 members of an electoral college, a group of representatives chosen to elect the president. This system of indirect election had been established under South Korea's new Constitution, approved the previous October. On January 24, the government lifted the state of martial law, imposed when President Park Chung Hee was assassinated in 1979, to permit campaigning. Chun's newly created Democratic Justice Party won 69.9 per cent of the vote. The electoral college met on February 25 and gave Chun 90 per cent of its votes for a seven-year term as president. Yoo Chi Song of the Democratic Korea Party ran second.

The Democratic Justice Party also won 151 out of 276 seats in a new National Assembly elected on March 25. The Democratic Korea Party became the main opposition group with 81 seats, and the Korean National Party won 24. The remaining 20 seats went to other parties and independents.

"A Just Society" was the theme of Chun's inaugural address on March 3. He criticized the pervasive corruption of South Korea's political life, promised clean government and honest civil servants, and said the distribution of wealth would become more equitable. Ho Sam Su, a retired general, ran a purification campaign that had begun in 1980 with the firing of more than 8,000 civil servants and other workers accused of corruption or inefficiency. The cleanup drive continued with efforts to simplify regulations, thus reducing temptations to circumvent them dishonestly, and with measures to reward honesty.

On July 11, No Tae Woo, a strong supporter of Chun's who had succeeded him as head of the Defense Security Command, was promoted to full general. Five days later, No retired from the army to become minister for national security and foreign affairs. Some observers interpreted these events as signs that Chun wanted No to succeed him in 1988.

Opposition Political Leaders continued to suffer repression under the Chun government. Many former leaders were still banned from politics at the time of the elections. Some, including Kim Young Sam, former leader of the New Democratic Party, were later released from restrictions.

Chun's most prominent political opponent, Kim Dae Jung, remained in prison. Kim was sentenced to death in September 1980 on charges of trying to overthrow the government. The Supreme Court of South Korea affirmed the sentence on Jan. 23, 1981, but later that day Chun commuted Kim's sentence to life imprisonment.

South Korea's President Chun Doo Hwan, front, addresses the National Assembly on April 11. Behind Chun is the speaker of the Assembly.

On several occasions during 1981, Chun granted amnesty to political and other prisoners. However, some 15,000 dissidents were reportedly still held without trial or formal charges. Chun's opponents charged that the prisoners were beaten regularly and that some were killed.

Relations with the United States. The sparing of Kim's life and the lifting of martial law were widely seen as efforts to cultivate good relations with the new Administration of United States President Ronald Reagan, whose military support remained vital to South Korea's security. Chun visited Reagan in Washington, D.C., on February 2 and 3. South Koreans regarded the visit as a symbolically important U.S. endorsement of Chun.

South Korea's Economy recovered in 1981 from a recession that had plagued it in late 1979 and 1980. Government officials admitted that the slump was partly a result of government mismanagement of the economy. The government's five-year economic development plan for 1982 to 1986, released on August 21, forecast a 7.6 per cent annual growth in the gross national product (GNP) after inflation. The plan shifted emphasis from the development of industries to better social services for the poor.   Henry S. Bradsher

See also ASIA (Facts in Brief Table). In WORLD BOOK, see KOREA.

KUWAIT. See MIDDLE EAST.

LABOR. When 1981 began, 7.8 million workers in the United States were jobless, and forecasts of economic activity for the rest of the year ranged from average to somewhat pessimistic. The jobless rate remained at about 7.3 per cent of the labor force until fall, when the nation appeared to sink into recession. The unemployment rate rose to 8.4 per cent in November – the highest level in six years – with a continued rise forecast.

Industries that were once bellwethers of economic growth suffered severe setbacks in activity and jobs in 1981. Construction companies and automobile manufacturers were savaged by record-high interest rates (see AUTOMOBILE; BUILDING AND CONSTRUCTION). Steel and rubber manufacturers continued to be troubled by obsolescent plants and by slackened activity in the transportation equipment industry and other industries that use their products. And in the white-collar sector, where stability and steady growth in employment had been the rule, the thrift industry – particularly savings and loan institutions – suffered unprecedented buffeting as high interest rates siphoned off revenues. See BANKS AND BANKING; MANUFACTURING.

Despite the troubled economy, pay increases in collective-bargaining settlements covering 1,000 workers or more ran somewhat higher in the first nine months of 1981, compared with the same period in 1980. Preliminary data issued by the

Roy Lee Williams addresses members of the
Teamsters Union after being elected president
at the union's June convention in Las Vegas, Nev.

Bureau of Labor Statistics (BLS) showed average wage increases of 11.5 per cent in the first contract year and 9.3 per cent over the life of the contract. As in the past, settlements in the construction industry led the way, averaging 13.9 per cent in the first year, compared with 10.1 per cent in other industries. Also as in the past, wage bargains in major contracts containing cost-of-living-adjustment (COLA) clauses were lower – 7.9 per cent in the first year and 6.4 per cent over the contract's life – than in agreements without such clauses, where they were 12.4 per cent in the contract's first year and 10 per cent over its life. Wage and benefit settlements in contracts covering 5,000 workers or more averaged 11.8 per cent in the first year and 10 per cent over the contract's life.

BLS estimates of major employment changes are summarized below:

	1980	1981*
	(in thousands)	
Total labor force	**106,821**	**108,573**
Armed forces	2,102	2,140
Civilian labor force	104,719	106,433
Total employment	97,270	98,551
Unemployed	7,448	7,979
Unemployment rate	7.1%	7.5%
Change in real weekly earnings (Worker with 3 dependents – private nonfarm sector)	−5.0%	−4.7%†
Change in output for all persons	0.3%	0.8%‡

*January through November average, seasonally adjusted except for armed forces data.
†For 12-month period ending Oct. 31, 1981.
‡Third quarter of 1981, compared with third quarter of 1980.

Air Traffic. The year's most dramatic collective bargaining involved relatively few employees. They were the 17,000 workers – mostly union members – who control air traffic at United States airports. Bargaining against a strike deadline, the Professional Air Traffic Controllers Organization (PATCO) and the Department of Transportation's Federal Aviation Administration agreed on an average wage and benefit package estimated to cost $108 million. However, PATCO's executive board recommended rejection, and the 15,000-member union later rejected the accord by a margin of 19 to 1. PATCO struck on August 3 despite warnings of penalties, including a three-year bar from federal government employment, because the strike violated federal law.

President Ronald Reagan immediately entered the dispute and gave the strikers 48 hours to return to work. Some controllers returned, but about 11,500 remained on strike and were fired.

The government kept air traffic moving by reducing the number of flights and substituting supervisors, nonstriking civilian controllers, and military controllers. On October 22, the Federal

Labor Relations Authority decertified PATCO as bargaining agent for the controllers. PATCO called off the strike and expressed willingness to resume negotiations. But the government declined to negotiate and continued to train new controllers to replace those who were discharged. See AVIATION.

Coal. In early April, the United Mine Workers of America (UMW) rejected by a 2 to 1 margin a March 23 settlement raising wages about 36 per cent. On June 6, after a 72-day strike, the miners approved a 40-month pact by the same margin. The new agreement restored a royalty payment requiring mine operators to contribute to the union pension fund for each ton of "nonunion" coal mined by the operators. It also provided wage increases of 37.5 per cent over 40 months, a $150 "back-to-work" bonus, and a slightly reduced pension for miners' widows. The return to work of 60,000 of the miners was hampered by the continuing strike of mine-construction workers, also members of the UMW. On June 24, they ratified an agreement paralleling that of the coal miners, thus ending the 1981 bargaining round in the coal fields.

Postal Service. On August 25, the American Postal Workers Union and the National Association of Letter Carriers, which together represent 500,000 postal workers, agreed with the United States Postal Service on a three-year contract. It provided pay increases of $300 each year, a $150 bonus for ratifying the agreement, and minimum bonuses of $350 each year for productivity improvements. The COLA formula, which generated a pay increase of $3,619 over the previous three years, was retained. An agreement was reached to fold the COLA increase into base pay in October 1984, the end of the new contract.

Baseball. The most unusual contract negotiations in 1981 involved a strike by 650 major-league baseball players, a few of whom make more than $1-million per year. Two months were clipped from the middle of the April-to-October season when the Major League Baseball Players Association and the team owners could not agree on the sensitive issue of compensation for teams in the free-agent system, which allows top players to play out their contracts and then sign with other teams. Aided by federal mediator Kenneth E. Moffett, the parties agreed on a formula on July 31, after a 49-day walkout. It would compensate the "losing" team from a pool of players, rather than by direct compensation from the "gaining" team – the method team owners had sought. The season resumed on August 9 with the All-Star Game. A revised play-off format was devised for the league championships leading to the 1981 World Series. See BASEBALL.

UMW coal miners angrily reject a proposed contract in March. They changed their tune in June and accepted a 37.5 per cent wage increase over 40 months.

LABOR

An illegally striking San Francisco air
traffic controller wears prisonlike garb to
dramatize demand for a new contract in August.

Other Agreements. On February 12, the United Steelworkers of America settled on a three-year agreement covering 20,000 workers with the Continental Group Incorporated, American Can Company, National Can Corporation, and Crown Cork & Seal Company. It increased wages 25 to 49 cents per hour the first year, 20 to 44 cents in the second year, and 15 to 27 cents in the third, and retained the cost-of-living arrangement.

Although sometimes involved in stormy negotiations in the past, the West Coast Longshoremen and the Pacific Maritime Association agreed on July 2 on a three-year pact. It raised pay an average 35 per cent, added two paid holidays, and increased pensions to a top of $780 per month.

Concessions. In a turnabout from traditional practice, union employees in some economically ill industries agreed to a reduction or elimination of scheduled wage and benefit improvements – or they accepted cuts in current wages – to help their company survive. Representative of such concessions – which occurred in the automobile, rubber, airline, trucking, and other industries and in public employment – was the acceptance by the United Automobile Workers (UAW) of $622 million in cutbacks of previously negotiated wage and benefit increases. The cutbacks were the union's contribution to an effort to save the Chrysler Corporation, which was threatened with bankruptcy.

On December 9, the UAW said it would look into the possibility of reopening contracts in the automobile and agricultural-equipment industries in an effort to aid financially ailing businesses.

Difficulties in the trucking industry, in which about 100,000 truckdrivers were laid off, led the International Brotherhood of Teamsters (Teamsters Union) to agree to early negotiations on their contract, due to expire in March 1982, and so replace it ahead of schedule. Some Teamsters locals had already agreed to pay concessions.

In Detroit, unions representing 20,000 city employees agreed in August to a wage freeze until 1983. The Detroit Police Department accepted a wage freeze in exchange for a guarantee of no layoffs over the contract's life and retirement at any age after 25 years of service.

AFL-CIO. At its winter executive council meeting in Bal Harbour, Fla., in February, the American Federation of Labor and Congress of Industrial Organizations (AFL-CIO) attacked the Administration's program as "inequitable" and expressed disbelief in its "euphoric promises." The council proposed tax cuts for middle- and lower-income families most ravaged by inflation and tax cuts and other incentives for industries either buffeted by the economic conditions or expanding – or with the potential for expanding – and creating jobs.

At its spring meeting, the council called for a Solidarity Day during which workers and others

362

could protest the Reagan Administration's economic and social policies. On September 19, about 260,000 people gathered in Washington, D.C., to hear speeches by union and political leaders and to voice their concerns.

Ending a 13-year separation, the United Automobile Workers rejoined the AFL-CIO on July 1. The return of the 1.2-million-member UAW to the "House of Labor" raised the federation's membership to 15 million.

The AFL-CIO declined to invite President Reagan to address its biennial November convention in New York City. It was the first time in the federation's 100-year history that the convention failed to invite an incumbent President. By contrast, the convention heard from Robert E. Poli, president of PATCO, who apologized to his fellow union leaders for not consulting them before going on strike in August.

Barbara B. Hutchinson, an attorney and official of the American Federation of Government Employees, the largest union of federal workers, became the first black woman ever to serve on the AFL-CIO executive council. She was elected at the November convention.

Legal Decisions. Ending a seven-year equal-employment lawsuit brought by the Equal Employment Opportunity Commission (EEOC), the Ford Motor Company agreed on Nov. 25, 1980, to a $13-million out-of-court settlement. The award will be distributed to 14,000 women and members of minority groups as follows: $8 million to unsuccessful applicants; $3.5 million to salaried minority and women workers; and $1.5 million to women in hourly rated jobs. In addition to providing $18-million for "upward mobility" programs within the company, Ford agreed to increase the proportions of minorities in supervisory jobs and women in hourly rated jobs.

After losing for the third time on discrimination suits concerned with questions of race and national origin brought in federal circuit courts, the EEOC agreed to an out-of-court settlement with Sears, Roebuck and Company on June 4, 1981. Only minor changes were made in Sears's affirmative action plan, and there was no back pay award or other monetary settlement.

Death. Frank E. Fitzsimmons, 73, who had been president of the Teamsters Union since 1971, died in La Jolla, Calif., on May 6. The union's executive board chose Roy Lee Williams, 66, head of the Central Conference of Teamsters in Kansas City, Mo., to succeed him. Williams was embroiled almost immediately in a controversy over his fitness to assume leadership of the union because of his alleged ties to organized crime (see WILLIAMS, ROY LEE). Robert W. Fisher

See also CITY; COAL; ECONOMICS. In WORLD BOOK, see LABOR; LABOR FORCE.

LAOS continued to be dominated by Vietnam during 1981, causing a steady trickle of civil servants, members of the hill tribe known as the Meo or Hmong, and other refugees to flee across the Mekong River into Thailand. An estimated 5,000 Vietnamese advisers virtually ran the government of Laos, and several divisions of Vietnamese troops were stationed in the country. China, which continued to have border clashes with Vietnam, charged that Vietnamese soldiers disguised as Laotians had made several attacks across its border with Laos.

Prince Souvanna Phouma, the last prime minister of Laos before the Communist take-over in 1975, worked as a political and economic adviser to the new Vietnamese-backed Laotian government.

Former Laotian Leaders tried to put together a united front of those opposing Vietnamese control of their country. The leaders included Phoumi Nosavan, a right wing general and political leader of the 1960s; Sisouk na Champassak, a former defense minister; and Vang Pao, a Hmong leader. They agreed to establish the United Lao National Liberation Front. Its goals were to drive the Vietnamese out of Laos, dissolve the Communist government, and hold elections under United Nations supervision. Although scattered fighting against the Vietnamese still continued in Laos, the front had little military power.

Vang Pao, who had led a Hmong army controlled by the U.S. Central Intelligence Agency (CIA), said that there had been talk of his leading a new army with Chinese backing to fight the Vietnamese in Laos. But there was nothing official, he said, and he remained in exile in the United States. Unconfirmed reports said that China was training some members of northern Lao tribes in guerrilla warfare at a camp inside China.

Chemical Warfare. The United States government said in September that the Vietnamese, with Russian backing, had used poison gas on hill tribes in Laos. The U.S. government identified a "yellow rain" reported by witnesses as containing mycotoxins, poisons derived from fungi that cause death by internal hemorrhage.

United States government officials disclosed on May 21 that American civilians under CIA supervision had helped organize, finance, and train Laotian exiles in Thailand who made at least two excursions into Laos in search of American prisoners of war missing since the Vietnam War ended in 1975. The patrols were carried out in response to reports that a few of the 2,528 men still missing in Southeast Asia might be in Laotian labor camps. Satellite photos had seemed to show white men in the camps. But the patrols found no Americans or other Westerners. Henry S. Bradsher

See also ASIA (Facts in Brief Table). In WORLD BOOK, see LAOS.

LATIN AMERICA

Peruvian soldiers position a tank in Tumbes, Peru, near the Ecuador border, after a long-standing boundary dispute flared early in 1981.

Economic issues dominated the attention of Latin Americans in 1981, as governments and families struggled to balance their budgets and preserve the value of their income during the deepening global recession. The squeeze was particularly acute among Latin America's middle-class people, whose take-home pay failed to keep pace with rising prices. Rents especially continued to skyrocket in the overcrowded cities, where most Latin Americans now live.

Declining world prices for Latin America's all-important food and mineral exports caused great concern in 1981. For example, the international price for sugar dropped from 27 cents per pound (0.45 kilogram) in January to 15 cents per pound in July, and coffee fell from $1.24 per pound to $1.17. Mineral prices followed a similar decline. Tin prices fell from $6.50 per pound in January to $5.74 in July; copper prices went from 84 cents to 79 cents; and bauxite dropped from 88 cents to 76 cents. Reduced export earnings meant leaner government budgets, even in such petroleum-exporting nations as Venezuela and Ecuador. Oil prices also leveled off in 1981, as the world market experienced an oversupply of petroleum.

In 1981, the combination of large trade deficits and growing foreign debt eroded the large gains made by Latin American economies during the 1970s, according to the annual report of the Inter-American Development Bank (IADB). The IADB report, released in October, noted that Latin America's growth as a producer of manufactured goods was slowing down as a result of tight money and high interest rates. Food production lagged behind the region's· population growth and increased the need for costly food imports.

The mass movement of rural Latin Americans to the large cities has also hurt food production. In 1961, more than 50 per cent of the region's people lived in rural areas. But by 1981, nearly 70 per cent of the population lived in cities. Antonio Ortiz Mena, president of the IADB, called this shift "the most profound socioeconomic transformation which has taken place in modern history." He warned that food supplies to cities must increase 60 per cent over the next 20 years to feed a projected urban population of 450 million by the year 2000 at present per capita consumption levels.

Flight of Capital. The central banks of Latin America found it difficult to compete with the high interest rates offered by financial institutions in the United States in 1981. The result was a flight of capital from Latin America — particularly from strife-torn Guatemala and El Salvador but also in large volume from more stable countries, such as Argentina and Venezuela. Buying real estate in the United States, especially condominiums in Miami, Fla., and New York City, became a trend among wealthy Latin Americans. There was also mounting evidence that much of the profit from Latin America's illicit trade in drugs was ending up in U.S. banks, thereby robbing Latin American countries of funds needed for investment in legitimate business activities. The drug trade has become a principal foreign-exchange earner in Bolivia, Colombia, and Jamaica.

A Willingness for Collaboration among the countries of Latin America was evident in 1981. Venezuela and Mexico sold oil on bargain terms to some of their poorer oil-importing Caribbean neighbors. In April, Venezuelan President Luis Herrera Campins and Mexico's President Jose Lopez Portillo announced the extension of the oil-purchase arrangement to include Haiti and Belize, bringing to nine the number of small Caribbean nations in the trade agreement.

In September, representatives of Venezuela, Colombia, Ecuador, Bolivia, and Chile discussed steps to revive the failing Andean Common Mar-

ket. The representatives agreed to allow bilateral agreements to boost trade within the market, and to delay the more difficult goal of reaching multilateral decisions of universal application for market members.

The Treaty of Montevideo of 1980, which created the Latin American Integration Association to replace the Latin American Free Trade Association, became effective on March 18. The new association, which consists of Mexico and 10 South American nations, permits separate negotiations between two or more member countries in dismantling trade barriers and providing incentives for business development.

A "Subtle Revolution" is occurring among Latin American women, according to the Inter-American Development Bank. In its annual report, the IADB noted that a growing number of Latin American women are working outside the home. The number of working women is expected to rise from 23 million in 1975 to more than 55 million by the year 2000.

Many of Latin America's working women are also heads of households, according to the IADB. Within Caribbean areas formerly belonging to Great Britain, approximately 35 per cent of all heads of households are women. Within the urban slums of Brazil, Venezuela, El Salvador, and Honduras, women are the heads of about 45 per cent of the households.

The United Nations (UN) also documented a dramatic increase in the number of women attending Latin American institutions of higher learning. In a study of six Latin American nations, the UN found that women made up 40 per cent of the students enrolled in universities.

"Microenterprises" in Latin America gained recognition in 1981. The term microenterprise was coined by the Northeast Union for Assistance to Small Organizations, a Brazilian organization that found that within poor areas of Recife, in northeastern Brazil, there are 40,000 tiny — mostly family-operated — enterprises. They produce goods, such as clothing, shoes, and household wares, and provide services in areas of the city poorly served by conventional business enterprises. Very few of the microenterprises are chartered, and thus most are not eligible to participate in national or commercial credit programs.

In Colombia, the Carvajal Foundation in Cali provides training in business operation to microenterprise owners. During 1981, its program was duplicated by nonprofit foundations in eight other Colombian cities. The success of these programs resulted in increased pressure on the Colombian government to open participation in the economic system to people formerly excluded.

International financial aid agencies have a poor record of reaching down to the level of such small businesses, but in 1981 the IADB provided funding for the Colombian programs to make loans to microenterprise operators.

An Arms Build-Up was seen in several Latin American countries during the year, as governments of the right, left, and center all sought to prepare to meet perceived threats. Nicaragua's forces were increased to three times the level they reached under the rule of dictator Anastasio Somoza. Cuba, with President Fidel Castro Ruz proclaiming that an invasion by the United States was imminent, increased its defenses. Both Nicaragua and Cuba received arms from Russia.

Arms suppliers rushed to fill orders from Latin American countries, including Venezuela, Ecua-

dor, Peru, Chile, Argentina, and El Salvador. In October, United States Department of State officials told Congress that West Germany, France, Israel, and Italy had all outpaced the United States as arms merchants in the Americas. Within Latin America, industrialized Brazil has developed its own arms export trade, earning more than $1-billion annually.

The reasons for the arms build-ups were varied. Some governments were wary of what appeared to be increasing strength in international terrorism, and other governments feared Russian and Cuban intervention. Flare-ups of violence in territorial disputes between Peru and Ecuador and between Venezuela and Guyana led to increased arms pur-

Facts in Brief on Latin American Political Units

Country	Population	Government	Monetary Unit*	Foreign Trade (million U.S. $)	
				Exports†	Imports†
Antigua & Barbuda	79,000	Governor General Sir Wilfred Ebenezer Jacobs; Prime Minister Vere C. Bird	dollar (2.7 = $1)	no statistics available	
Argentina	27,785,000	President Leopoldo Fortunato Galtieri	peso (9,875 = $1)	7,810	6,713
Bahamas	252,000	Governor General Sir Gerald C. Cash; Prime Minister Lynden O. Pindling	dollar (1 = $1)	3,495	3,949
Barbados	280,000	Governor General Sir Deighton Harcourt Lisle Ward; Prime Minister J. M. G. Adams	dollar (1.9 = $1)	219	521
Belize	174,000	Governor General Minita Gordon; Prime Minister George Cadle Price	dollar (2 = $1)	67	103
Bolivia	5,876,000	President Celso Torrelio Villa	peso (24.7 = $1)	942	814
Brazil	128,892,000	President Joao Baptista de Oliveira Figueiredo	cruzeiro (114.5 = $1)	20,131	25,000
Chile	11,486,000	President Augusto Pinochet Ugarte	peso (39 = $1)	4,820	5,720
Colombia	28,637,000	President Julio Cesar Turbay Ayala	peso (57.4 = $1)	3,410	3,365
Costa Rica	2,372,000	President Rodrigo Carazo Odio	colón (15 = $1)	1,002	1,457
Cuba	10,330,000	President Fidel Castro Ruz	peso (1 = $1.28)	4,700	5,000
Dominica	87,000	President Aurelius Marie; Prime Minister Mary Eugenia Charles	dollar (2.7 = $1)	8	24
Dominican Republic	5,764,000	President Silvestre Antonio Guzman Fernandez	peso (1 = $1)	995	1,433
Ecuador	8,930,000	President Oswaldo Hurtado Larrea	sucre (28.4 = $1)	2,013	1,986
El Salvador	4,877,000	Revolutionary Governing Junta President Jose Napoleon Duarte	colón (2.4 = $1)	1,032	1,012
Grenada	111,000	Governor General Sir Paul Godwin Scoon; Prime Minister Maurice Bishop	dollar (2.7 = $1)	22	42
Guatemala	7,423,000	President Fernando Romeo Lucas Garcia	quetzal (1 = $1)	1,270	1,504
Guyana	895,000	President Forbes Burnham; Prime Minister Ptolemy A. Reid	dollar (2.5 = $1)	291	317
Haiti	5,174,000	President Jean-Claude Duvalier	gourde (5 = $1)	145	236
Honduras	3,939,000	President Policarpo Paz Garcia	lempira (2 = $1)	806	1,019
Jamaica	2,273,000	Governor General Sir Florizel Glasspole; Prime Minister Edward Seaga	dollar (1.8 = $1)	769	1,010
Mexico	76,924,000	President Jose Lopez Portillo	peso (25.9 = $1)	15,321	19,433
Nicaragua	2,743,000	3-member Government of National Reconstruction Junta	córdoba (10.1 = $1)	567	360
Panama	2,092,000	President Aristides Royo	balboa (1 = $1)	292	1,187
Paraguay	3,239,000	President Alfredo Stroessner	guaraní (125 = $1)	310	494
Peru	18,787,000	President Fernando Belaunde Terry; Prime Minister Manuel Ulloa Elias	sol (480.1 = $1)	3,474	2,090
Puerto Rico	3,672,000	Governor Carlos Romero Barcelo	U.S. $	2,454	6,044
St. Lucia	126,000	Governor General Sir Allen Montgomery Lewis; Prime Minister Winston Cenac	dollar (2.7 = $1)	28	78
St. Vincent & the Grenadines	118,000	Governor General Sir Sydney Gunn-Munro; Prime Minister R. Milton Cato	dollar (2.7 = $1)	15	46
Surinam (Suriname)	396,000	President & Prime Minister Henk R. Chin A Sen	guilder (1.8 = $1)	444	411
Trinidad & Tobago	1,188,000	President Ellis Emmanuel Innocent Clarke; Prime Minister George Chambers	dollar (2.3 = $1)	4,077	3,178
Uruguay	2,950,000	President Gregorio Alvarez	peso (11.4 = $1)	788	1,231
Venezuela	14,811,000	President Luis Herrera Campins	bolívar (4.3 = $1)	14,159	9,618

*Exchange rates as of Dec. 1, 1981. †Latest available data.

El Tiempo/Bogotá

chases by those nations. The flare-ups were kindled by rumors of possible oil deposits in the disputed areas.

Despite the rush to buy arms, 1981 was a relatively peaceful year in Latin America. The exceptions were El Salvador and Guatemala – countries that have only a tiny fraction of Latin America's total population. Elsewhere, there was a marked decrease in terrorism and political violence, though crime was on the rise in the major cities of several Latin American countries.

U.S. Relations. Soon after taking office in January 1981, U.S. President Ronald Reagan took a hard line against Soviet-Cuban intervention in El Salvador. The United States stepped up its arms shipments to the Revolutionary Governing Junta of El Salvador, headed by President Jose Napoleon Duarte, and sent U.S. military advisers to help train the Salvadoran Army. Two U.S. military advisers to Honduras were wounded by terrorist gunfire in Tegucigalpa on September 23.

To quiet critics within the United States who feared another "Vietnam" in Central America, the U.S. State Department released a report on February 23 based on captured guerrilla documents. The report charged that Russia, Cuba, and Nicaragua were involved in supplying arms to the guerrillas in El Salvador.

The Reagan Administration de-emphasized

human rights in U.S. foreign policy in an effort to patch up relations with the military-run governments of Chile and Argentina. Relations between the United States and those two countries had frequently been strained by allegations of civil liberties violations but were restored to normal in 1981. Amnesty International and other private organizations were left to lead the fight against human rights abuse.

Two Explosive Issues in U.S.-Latin American relations – drug traffic and illegal immigration – remained unsolved in 1981. Despite U.S. pressures on Latin American countries that produce drugs, the trade continued. Within Latin America, some of the profits from the drug trade were used to bribe government officials. The corruption existed at local and national levels, making crackdowns on drug traffic even more difficult.

The illegal immigration issue was dramatized in October by the drowning of 33 Haitian refugees off the coast of Florida. The victims were trying to reach the United States in a wooden sailboat that was swamped by high waves less than 60 yards (56 meters) from land. Thirty of the refugees survived.

On September 29, President Reagan had ordered the U.S. Coast Guard to deter illegal entry to the United States by sea. He had also requested extraordinary emergency powers to cope with the illegal immigration problem. The Reagan Administration had been criticized for its apparent lack of ability to control the United States borders. See IMMIGRATION.

Two New Nations came into existence in Latin America in 1981 – Belize in Central America and Antigua and Barbuda in the West Indies. Both had been self-governing territories of Great Britain (see BELIZE; WEST INDIES). The increasing number of predominantly black, English-speaking ministates in Latin America has added muscle to the black nations' power bloc in such international agencies as the Organization of American States and the United Nations General Assembly, which operate on the principle of one nation, one vote.

Leadership Losses. Airplane crashes took the lives of two Latin American leaders in 1981. President Jaime Roldos Aguilera of Ecuador was killed in a crash in May, and Panamanian National Guard Commander Omar Torrijos Herrera in July. Two other Latin American leaders died during the year. Former Venezuelan President Rómulo Betancourt died in September; and Eric E. Williams, the scholarly prime minister of Trinidad and Tobago, died in March.   Nathan A. Haverstock

See also articles on the various Latin American countries. In WORLD BOOK, see LATIN AMERICA and articles on the individual countries.

LAW. See CIVIL RIGHTS; COURTS AND LAWS; CRIME; SUPREME COURT OF THE UNITED STATES.

A bulldozer clears away rubble of buildings that were destroyed when Israeli planes bombed guerrilla strongholds in Beirut in July.

LEBANON. The intermittent civil war that has divided the country since 1975 and paralyzed its economy threatened to expand into regional warfare in April 1981. Syrian troops of the Arab peacekeeping force attacked the Christian Falange stronghold of Zahlah in the Al Biqa – or Bekaa – Valley. The city was besieged for three months and suffered heavy casualties before Saudi Arabia and other Arab countries arranged a cease-fire. The Falange, along with other Christian groups, objected to the presence of the peacekeeping force as constituting a Syrian occupation of Lebanon. In January, the Arab League extended the force's mandate for another year. There were further complications in May and June, when Syria moved surface-to-air missiles into Lebanon to counter Israeli support for the Christians.

Israeli raids on Palestine Liberation Organization (PLO) bases imposed further hardships on the Lebanese people. On July 15, PLO guerrillas fired dozens of rockets at northern Israeli towns. On July 16 and 17, apparently in retaliation, Israeli planes attacked PLO targets throughout southern Lebanon and for the first time bombed Beirut, the capital. The Lebanese government said 400 persons were killed and 800 wounded in the attacks.

The endless cycle of violence not only made life difficult for most Lebanese, but it also contributed to political chaos. It was estimated that nearly 100

factions – cutting across sectarian lines – were represented in the population, ranging in size from several hundred members to the 15,000-member Falange. The Lebanese Army of 18,000, charged with maintaining order, continued to be unequal to the task.

The Economy. Despite the violence and the political uncertainty, Lebanon's economy showed a slight recovery, helped by aid from other Arab states. In July, Saudi Arabia paid Lebanon's debt of $120 million to the Trans-Arabian Pipeline Company (Tapline) for oil purchases. In September, Kuwait gave $30 million as part of its support pledged after the 1975 civil war. In June, Algeria purchased the entire Lebanese tobacco crop, valued at $14 million. Remittances from Lebanese workers abroad generated a balance-of-payments surplus of $728 million for the year.

But without the emergence of a strong central government or unification of competing groups, the country's long-term economic prospects remained dim. The budget approved in June forecast a $347-million deficit, 29 per cent of expenditures. More than $300 million was expected to be lost in customs revenues alone, due to control of Lebanese ports by various militia units.   William Spencer

See also MIDDLE EAST (Facts in Brief Table). In WORLD BOOK, see LEBANON.

LESOTHO. See AFRICA.

LEWIS, ANDREW LINDSAY (DREW), JR. (1931-
), was sworn in as United States secretary
of transportation on Jan. 23, 1981. He had been
named to the post by President-elect Ronald Reagan on Dec. 11, 1980. Lewis had been active in
Reagan's presidential campaign as deputy chairman of both the Reagan-Bush Campaign Committee and the Republican National Committee.

Drew Lewis was born in Philadelphia on Nov. 3,
1931. He graduated from Haverford College near
Philadelphia in 1953 and received a master's degree in business administration from Harvard University in Cambridge, Mass., in 1955. In that year,
Lewis joined the Philadelphia contracting firm of
Henkels & McCoy, Incorporated. He worked for
the National Gypsum Company from 1960 to 1969.
During the early 1970s, he served as president of
both Simplex Wire and Cable Company and
Snelling and Snelling, Incorporated, a major employment agency. He headed his own consulting
firm from 1975 until his Cabinet appointment.

From 1971 to 1977, Lewis served as one of two
court-appointed trustees of the bankrupt Reading
Company, a transportation firm in Philadelphia.
He helped reorganize the Reading Railroad and
oversaw its eventual transfer to the Consolidated
Rail Corporation (Conrail).

Lewis married Marilyn S. Stoughton in 1950.
They have three children.   Edward G. Nash

LIBERIA. The government of Samuel K. Doe reportedly withstood two plots against it in 1981.
Thirteen soldiers were arrested in May for allegedly planning to overthrow Doe. All of them were
executed in June. A second, higher-ranking group
of military men was accused of treason in August.
Five members of the ruling People's Redemptive
Council were arrested and charged with plotting to
kill Doe. They were executed on August 14.

These plots may have delayed Liberia's return to
civilian rule. Following the second plot, Doe
drafted the 11 civilian members of his government
into the military. Doe's action appeared to jeopardize the mission of a 25-member committee drafting
a new Liberian constitution. Doe had appointed
the committee on April 12, the first anniversary of
his violent coup against the late President William
R. Tolbert, Jr.

Liberia's government also faced severe financial
difficulties. In an effort to reduce the $100-million
government deficit, Doe on July 17 announced new
taxes and the end of a long-established government
subsidy of rice prices. Without the subsidy, the
price of rice rose about 20 per cent. The United
States upped aid to Liberia from $8 million in
1979, Tolbert's last year in power, to $68.3 million
in 1981.   J. Dixon Esseks

See also AFRICA (Facts in Brief Table). In
WORLD BOOK, see LIBERIA.

LIBRARY. Rising costs and cuts in state and local
funding forced many libraries in the United States
to reduce their services and programs in 1981.
Empty shelves, shrunken staffs, forced closings,
and shortened hours affected libraries throughout
the nation.

A reduction in city funding forced the Boston
Public Library to shorten hours of operation at its
central library and branches, to eliminate service
to hospitals, and to close its multilingual library.
The Nassau County Library System in New York
reduced its staff from 108 to 71, with more layoffs
expected. The St. Louis Public Library closed four
branches. A moratorium on book purchases continued at Detroit's 26 branch libraries. The Tucson
(Ariz.) Public Library cut hours of service in five of
its 17 branches. The Denver Public Library closed
its central branch on Thursdays, and the Chicago
Public Library Cultural Center shut its doors on
Sundays.

Canadian Libraries fared better. Ontario's Culture and Recreation Ministry increased grant support of public library service by 9.3 per cent.
Alberta's libraries received an 11 per cent boost in
financial assistance.

Theft and Vandalism became increasing problems for libraries. Canada's Metro Toronto Library, for example, reported that more than 12,000
books, films, and musical scores were damaged or
stolen in 1980. The loss equaled about 20 per cent
of the library's budget for materials. Many libraries have installed electronic systems to keep rare
and expensive collections under close watch.

New Buildings. The Gerald R. Ford Library at
the University of Michigan in Ann Arbor was
dedicated on April 27 (see FORD, GERALD R.). The
building has an area of 46,000 square feet (4,270
square meters). It includes a research room, processing and storage space for archives and audio-
visual materials, an auditorium, and offices.

The Orlando (Fla.) Public Library announced
plans to build a new $22-million central library.
Construction of the new central building for the
Dallas Public Library continued on schedule. The
664,000-square-foot (61,690-square-meter) facility
was expected to open in April 1982.

Library Meetings. The Canadian Library Associ-
ation's annual conference was held in Hamilton,
Ont., in June. The International Federation of
Library Associations and Institutions' general con-
ference was held in Leipzig, East Germany, from
August 17 to 23.

The 100th annual conference of the American
Library Association was held in San Francisco
from June 26 to July 2. The theme was "Libraries
and the Pursuit of Happiness."   Robert J. Shaw

See also AMERICAN LIBRARY ASSOCIATION; CA-
NADIAN LIBRARY ASSOCIATION. In WORLD BOOK,
see LIBRARY.

LIBYA. Leader of the Revolution Muammar Muhammad al-Qadhafi scored a foreign policy breakthrough in January 1981 when he and President Goukouni Weddeye of Chad agreed to work toward the merger of their countries into a single nation. Libya and Syria had made the same kind of agreement in September 1980, but nothing had come of it. The January 1981 move followed the collapse of antigovernment forces in Chad as the intervention of 8,000 to 15,000 Libyan troops turned the tide in the Chadian civil war. The announcement of the proposed merger specified full unity between the two countries, with government by joint popular committees as defined under Qadhafi's "power to the people" concept of government. See CHAD.

Qadhafi's Initial Success offset a number of failures in recent years in his efforts to achieve a greater role for Libya in Arab-African and Islamic affairs. But the accomplishment had its price. Many African states denounced the intervention. In November, Libyan troops began to withdraw from Chad.

Ostracism by many African states had little effect on Qadhafi's popularity at home, however, or on the continuing implementation of his program of popular government. Neither did the international embarrassment caused by the loss of two Libyan jets shot down on August 19 by United States fighter planes over the Gulf of Sidra, which Libya claims as part of its territorial waters (see ARMED FORCES). On December 10, President Ronald Reagan asked American firms to pull their U.S. citizens out of Libya. He also invalidated U.S. passports for travel to Libya. Earlier in December, there were reports that Libya had sent assassination teams to the United States to kill top government officials.

In January 1981, the General People's Committee, in theory the nation's chief decision-making body, approved a general mobilization plan. Under the plan, Libya's educational institutions would become military camps "to defend the nation." Students would be subject to military law and would be given ranks, uniforms, and military pay.

Another element in Qadhafi's program of building an Islamic socialist state became a reality in March and April with a series of decrees aimed at abolishing the country's remaining private businesses by the end of 1981.

The Economy. With a worldwide oil glut and Libya losing customers because of its high price of $40 per barrel, the government put a priority on development of the nonpetroleum sector of the economy.   William Spencer

See also AFRICA (Facts in Brief Table). In WORLD BOOK, see LIBYA.

LIECHTENSTEIN. See EUROPE.

LIONS INTERNATIONAL. See COMMUNITY ORGANIZATIONS.

LITERATURE. The continuing economic slump reduced the number of books produced by United States publishers during 1981. The consequences for quality literature, however, were not as harsh as had been feared in 1980. Hard-cover first novels of quality managed to bob up in the increasing flood of trashy mass-market books, produced mostly by paperback houses. And even hard-cover short-story collections, which are slow sellers, held their own. Most heartening was the overall high quality of hard-cover fiction published during 1981, a year that saw much distinguished work from American writers, both young and old.

American Fiction. Among novelists of established reputation, John Updike and Philip Roth produced their finest works in years. Updike's *Rabbit Is Rich,* the third novel featuring Rabbit Angstrom, was an acute examination of middle-class manners and mores. Roth's *Zuckerman Unbound* explored with satisfying high comedy the life of a writer seemingly based on that of Roth himself.

In *Sauce for the Goose,* satirical novelist Peter De Vries extended his astonishing range by challenging the increasingly comfortable tenets of feminism. Joyce Carol Oates's 12th novel, *Angel of Light,* was a political work based on the fall of the mythical House of Atreus. Other distinguished novels included *Tar Baby,* by Toni Morrison; *Reinhart's*

Author James Clavell continued to please readers in 1981. His *Noble House,* a novel set in Hong Kong, became a best seller.

Women, by Thomas Berger; *Darconville's Cat,* by Alexander Theroux; and *The Temptation of Eileen Hughes,* by Canadian Brian Moore.

A number of young writers of repute also produced outstanding novels. Robert Stone explored imperialism and religion in Central America in *A Flag for Sunrise,* a powerful work of politics and ideas. William Wharton's sinewy second novel, *Dad,* successfully melded humor and pathos as a dying father reflected on his own mortality. In *The Company of Women,* Mary Gordon successfully examined women's relation to male power. Leonard Michaels, known as a short-story writer, made his mark as a novelist with *The Men's Club,* a psychological satire of feminist attitudes. David Plante's *The Country* and Francine du Plessix Gray's *World Without End* enhanced the two authors' reputations.

The year's most interesting experimental novel was Russell Hoban's *Riddley Walker.* Hoban wrote this cautionary tale of a future England after a nuclear holocaust in a remarkably rich and evocative language based on 20th-century English. Marilynne Robinson's *Housekeeping* was a brooding but exhilarating first novel, the best debut of 1981.

The year was strong in short-story collections. They included Donald Barthelme's *Sixty Stories;* Joyce Carol Oates's *A Sentimental Education;* Mark Helprin's *Ellis Island and Other Stories;* Richard Yates's *Liars in Love; The Stories of Elizabeth Spencer;* and *The Stories of Ray Bradbury.*

Fiction in English from Other Lands was also bountiful in 1981. From Great Britain, the most notable was *The White Hotel,* D. M. Thomas' stunning novel about Freud and the erotic dreams of a young woman. Britain also sent Iris Murdoch's *Nuns and Soldiers;* Doris Lessing's *The Sirian Experiments,* the third of her futurist *Canopus in Argos: Archives* novels; Elizabeth Bowen's *Collected Stories;* Muriel Spark's *Loitering with Intent;* Beryl Bainbridge's *Winter Garden;* William Trevor's *Other People's Worlds;* and G. B. Edwards' posthumously published *The Book of Ebenezer Le Page,* a stunning traditional novel set on the Channel Island of Guernsey.

South Africa was represented by Athol Fugard's novel *Tsotsi* and Nadine Gordimer's *July's People.* Ireland's best export was Frank O'Connor's *Collected Stories.*

Translated Works included two important novels from West Germany: Günter Grass's *The Meeting at Telgte* and Gregor von Rezzori's *Memoirs of an Anti-Semite.* Russia's best offering was Alexander Zinoviev's *The Radiant Future,* a scathingly funny satire of Soviet life. Italy was represented by Italo Calvino's *If on a Winter's Night a Traveler.* Argentina sent *Borges: A Reader,* by Jorge Luis Borges, and *On Heroes and Tombs,* by Ernesto Sabato. Finally, Czeslaw Milosz, the Lithuanian-born Polish poet and 1980 Nobel laureate who lives in California,

Historian Dumas Malone examines *The Sage of Monticello,* published July 4, 1981, the last book in his series *Jefferson and His Time.*

saw the appearance of the first English translation of his splendid 1955 novel, *The Issa Valley.*

Biography. It was not a particularly fruitful year for biography, but there was no drought. Two ambitious literary biographies were Margaret Brenman-Gibson's *Clifford Odets,* an exemplary study of the troubled American playwright, and Paul Mariani's *William Carlos Williams,* an excellent critical work that came close to placing its subject as "the single most important American poet of the 20th century." Other notable literary lives included Frank MacShane's *The Life of John O'Hara,* Jenni Calder's *Robert Louis Stevenson,* Robert Martin's *Tennyson: The Unquiet Heart,* Bernard Crick's *George Orwell,* Gay Wilson Allen's *Waldo Emerson,* and Raymond Nelson's *Matthew Arnold: A Life.*

Two British poets—Dame Edith Sitwell and W. H. Auden—inspired a pair of biographies each. The Sitwell lives, both titled *Edith Sitwell,* were produced by Victoria Glendinning and Geoffrey E. Elborn. Edward Mendelson wrote *Early Auden,* and Humphrey Carpenter illuminated the poet's career in *W. H. Auden.*

Milton Rugoff's biography *The Beechers* explored how American ethics changed during the 19th century. William S. McFeeley's *Grant* ably dealt with both the brilliant military career and the abysmal political career of that U.S. general. David McCullough's *Mornings on Horseback* was a fascinat-

The fourth book by Scottish veterinarian James Herriott, *The Lord God Made Them All*, proved to be just as popular as the first three.

ing adventure into the early life of Theodore Roosevelt. Robert V. Remini issued the second volume of his excellent presidential biography, *Andrew Jackson and the Course of American Freedom, Vol. 2: 1822-1832*. Dumas Malone put the capstone on his distinguished career with *The Sage of Monticello*, the sixth volume of *Jefferson and His Time*.

Autobiography, Memoirs, and Letters. The year's most interesting memoir was *Journey Around My Room: The Autobiography of Louise Bogan*. It was not a real autobiography but a fascinating mosaic assembled from the journals, poems, letters, and criticism of the American writer by Ruth Limmer.

Other important literary memoirs were Isaac Bashevis Singer's *Lost in America*, Wright Morris' *Will's Boy*, Graham Greene's *Ways of Escape*, John Osborne's *A Better Class of Person*, Clive James's *Unreliable Memoirs*, and Maya Angelou's *Heart of a Woman*. *Personal Impressions* was the fourth and final volume of the *Selected Writings* of Isaiah Berlin, one of the great thinkers of our age.

Hope Cooke's *Time Change* was the remarkably thoughtful autobiography of the American woman who married the crown prince of Sikkim. John Kenneth Galbraith told of his career as economist and diplomat in *A Life in Our Times*.

Musicology became enriched by *Cosima Wagner's Diaries: Vol. 2, 1878-1883* and *The Diary of Richard Wagner, 1865-1882*. American history was illuminat-

ed by the diaries of a Southern aristocrat in *Mary Chesnut's Civil War*, edited by C. Vann Woodward.

Selected Letters of James Thurber and *Ernest Hemingway: Selected Letters* were the year's most important collections of literary correspondence. *Letters of Nunnally Johnson* gave interesting insights into the career of the notable Hollywood screenwriter. *Selected Letters of Raymond Chandler* brought to light some little-known facts about the creator of the private investigator Philip Marlowe.

Criticism. Very few enlightening books in this category were published in 1981. The most important was *Shaw's Music*, edited by Dan H. Laurence. The work consisted of the complete music criticism of George Bernard Shaw. It reminded the world that Shaw was a top-flight critic as well as a brilliant playwright. Vladimir Nabokov's *Lectures on Russian Literature* was by turns cantankerous and engaging. James K. Lyon's *Bertolt Brecht in America* was a useful discussion of aspects of the German playwright's career.

History. After a comparatively dull 1980, the history category picked up steam in 1981, especially in the areas of moral and ethical history. George M. Fredrickson's *White Supremacy: A Comparative Study in American and South African History* was a brilliant exercise. Walter Laqueur's *The Terrible Secret* told how the world ignored the evidence of Adolf Hitler's "Final Solution" (to the "Jewish Problem") during World War II. Michael R. Marrus and Robert O. Paxton revealed a shameful national relationship in *Vichy France and the Jews*.

The upward revision of the reputation of Dwight D. Eisenhower as President continued in 1981 in several works. They were *The Eisenhower Diaries*, edited by Robert H. Ferrell; *Eisenhower the President*, by William Bragg Ewald, Jr.; *Eisenhower and the Cold War*, by Robert A. Divine; and *The Declassified Eisenhower*, by Blanche Weisen Cook.

Excellent specialized American histories included Ray Allen Billington's *Land of Savagery/Land of Promise*, Garry Wills's *Explaining America: The Federalist*, and Joanna L. Stratton's *Pioneer Women*.

Russia in the Age of Catherine the Great, by Isabel de Madariaga, was a stunningly majestic history. *The Lisle Letters*, edited by Muriel St. Clare Byrne, offered six volumes of remarkable letters that shed light on the reign of King Henry VIII of England.

Hiroshima and Nagasaki, by the Committee for the Compilation of Materials on Damage Caused by the Atomic Bombs in Hiroshima and Nagasaki, was a final, horrible accounting of the destruction.

Contemporary Affairs. The most affecting and controversial book in this category in 1981 was *Prisoner Without a Name, Cell Without a Number*. It was written by Jacobo Timerman, a former Buenos Aires newspaper publisher now living in Israel, who charged that anti-Semitism in Argentina is deep and violent.

Two excellent studies of China were Orville Schell's *"Watch Out for the Foreign Guests!"* and Jonathan Spence's *The Gate of Heavenly Peace.* Spence's book told how three little-known Chinese helped shape the modern nation. *Nam,* by Mark Baker, and *Everything We Had,* by Al Santoli, were illuminating oral histories of the Vietnam War.

James H. Jones's *Bad Blood* revealed the shameful Tuskegee (Ala.) syphilis experiment of the 1930s, in which treatment was withheld from hundreds of black victims of the disease. In *John Muir and His Legacy,* Stephen Fox told the history and prospects of the American conservation movement.

V. S. Naipaul's *Among the Believers,* a powerful and controversial account of the novelist's travels through four ultraconservative Islamic countries, forecast continued turmoil and bloodshed. James Fallows' masterly *National Defense* was a shocking exploration of the confusing and wasteful world of arms procurement.

Two books on the booming Japanese economy were popular among American business executives: *The Art of Japanese Management,* by Richard Tanner Pascale and Anthony G. Athos, and *Theory Z,* by William G. Ouchi.

Jonathan Raban's *Old Glory* was a highly amusing and edifying account of the English literary critic's travels down the Mississippi River.

Science and Social Science. Among important books in this category were *Lucy: The Beginnings of Mankind,* by Donald C. Johanson and Maitland Edey; *The Making of Mankind,* by Richard E. Leakey; *The Hour of Our Death,* by Philippe Aries; *Basin and Range,* by John McPhee; *Psychoanalysis: The Impossible Profession,* by Janet Malcolm; and *The Mismeasure of Man,* by Stephen Jay Gould.

Paperbacks. The 11 best-selling paperbacks of 1981 were *If There Be Thorns, Petals on the Wind,* and *Flowers in the Attic,* all commercial novels, published as paperback originals, by V. C. Andrews; *Rage of Angels,* by Sidney Sheldon; *Princess Daisy,* by Judith Krantz; *The Rubik's Cube: A Simple Solution* by James Nourse; *No Love Lost,* by Helen Van Slyke; *Firestarter,* by Stephen King; *Shadowland,* by Peter Straub; *Come Pour the Wine,* by Cynthia Freeman; and *The Key to Rebecca,* by Ken Follett.

Hard-Cover Best Sellers. The three top-selling novels of 1981 were Martin Cruz Smith's *Gorky Park,* James Clavell's *Noble House,* and Joseph Wambaugh's *Glitter Dome.* Leading the nonfiction list were Richard Simmons' *Never Say Diet Book;* James Herriot's *The Lord God Made Them All;* and Carl Sagan's *Cosmos,* published in 1980. Henry Kisor

See also AWARDS AND PRIZES (Literature Awards); CANADIAN LITERATURE; LITERATURE FOR CHILDREN; POETRY; PUBLISHING. In WORLD BOOK, see LITERATURE.

LITERATURE, CANADIAN. See CANADIAN LIBRARY ASSOCIATION; CANADIAN LITERATURE.

LITERATURE FOR CHILDREN. Reflecting what statistics and observers of society in the United States have reported, many of the children's books published in 1981 portrayed children from broken homes. Not only were the parents divorced in the books, but both mothers and fathers also were portrayed as working and much more concerned with their own affairs than with their children's concerns.

Also of note in 1981 were the many books with distinguished illustrations in only one color, a positive result from the financial restrictions that have forced less multicolor printing.

Some outstanding books of 1981 were:

Picture Books

On Market Street, pictures by Anita Lobel, words by Arnold Lobel (Greenwillow). This appealing alphabet book has charming illustrations of figures made from market wares. All ages.

Babar's Anniversary Album, six favorite books by Jean and Laurent de Brunhoff (Random House). Celebrating the 50th anniversary of the first Babar book, this volume has three titles by each author and De Brunhoff family photographs. All ages.

Light, by Donald Crews (Greenwillow). Beautiful full-color paintings of city lights, glimmering lights, and starlight are accompanied by only a word or two of text on each page. Ages 2 to 6.

Peony's Rainbow, by Martha Weston (Lothrop). Peony the pig had always wanted a rainbow and when her chance came, she took it. The surprising — and colorful — happenings that follow are fun for the young listener or reader. Ages 3 to 6.

Mrs. Pig's Bulk Buy, by Mary Rayner (Atheneum). Delightful illustrations show Mrs. Pig's humorous solution when her children want to put catchup on everything they eat. Ages 3 to 7.

The Seven Days of Creation, adapted from the Bible and illustrated by Leonard Everett Fisher (Holiday House). This pictorial representation of the Biblical story of the Creation is original, majestic, and beautiful. Ages 4 and up.

Yussel's Prayer, a Yom Kippur Story, retold by Barbara Cohen, illustrated by Michael J. Deraney (Lothrop). Notable illustrations distinguish this story of a boy who pipes a tune that opens the gates of heaven. Ages 4 to 9.

Cooper, by Nancy Winslow Parker (Dodd). The pictures provide an amusing counterpoint to this story of an endearing and funny dog that persuades his family to keep him, despite his shortcomings. Ages 4 to 8.

Encore for Eleanor, by Bill Peet (Houghton). When old Eleanor the elephant falls off her stilts in her circus act, she is retired to the zoo. She finds this dull until she discovers a new talent. Ages 4 to 8.

I'll Bet You Thought I Was Lost, by Shirley Parenteau, pictures by Lorna Tomei (Lothrop).

"The Camel Dances," *above*, is an illustration from *Fables*, a picture book by Arnold Lobel that won the Caldecott Medal in 1981.

Sandy tries to keep his cool when he gets separated from his dad in the supermarket. Ages 4 to 8.

Night Story, by Ethel and Leonard Kessler (Macmillan). Nighttime scenes show activities of animals and people and give children an idea of the things that go on while they sleep. Ages 4 to 8.

Dear Sarah, by Elizabeth Borchers, illustrated by Wilhelm Schlote (Greenwillow). Translated and adapted from a German story by Elizabeth Shub, this is a collection of eight delightful letters Sarah's papa writes to her. Each letter has a short story or imaginative account of events that conveys her father's affection. Ages 5 to 9.

The Wish Card Ran Out, by James Stevenson (Greenwillow). When Charlie finds a Wish Card, the exciting and humorous results are fun for everyone. Ages 5 to 10.

Angus and the Mona Lisa, by Jacqueline Cooper (Lothrop). Angus, an American cat, helps his French cousin and her friends to trap thieves stealing the famous *Mona Lisa* painting in this book filled with cats, cats, and more cats. Ages 5 to 9.

The Thingumajig Book of Manners, by Irene Keller, illustrations by Dick Keller (Ideals and Children's Press). Rollicking rhymes and humorous full-color pictures illustrate the value of good manners. Ages 4 to 8.

A Halloween Happening, by Adrienne Adams (Scribners). Delightful illustrations show what happens when some witches decide to build a pumpkin tower and invite children to a Halloween party. Ages 5 to 8.

One Zillion Valentines, by Frank Modell (Greenwillow). Good friends Marvin and Milton have not received any valentines, and when they realize that they must send some to get some, they decide to make a zillion valentines. Ages 5 to 10.

Three Days on a River in a Red Canoe, by Vera B. Williams (Greenwillow). Written and illustrated as though by one of the child participants, this book offers an appealing and realistic account of the delights of a canoe trip. Ages 5 to 10.

Hot-Air Henry, by Mary Calhoun, illustrated by Erick Ingraham (Morrow). By mistake, Henry the Siamese cat ends up soloing in a hot-air balloon. His exciting adventure is illustrated by remarkable paintings. Ages 5 to 10.

Tilly's Rescue, by Faith Jaques (McElderry/Atheneum). Vivid watercolors with a wonderful doll's-eye view help tell the story of a brave doll, Tilly, and her rescue of her friend Edward Bear. Ages 5 to 9.

Jumanji, by Chris Van Allsburg (Houghton). Stunning black-and-white illustrations show the results of a magic game in this remarkable picture book. Ages 5 to 10.

A Very Mice Joke Book, by Karen Jo Gounaud, illustrated by Lynn Munsinger (Houghton). This delightful book of puns and line drawings of mice in all sorts of unlikely situations is fun for all ages.

Fun Things to Do

Holidays on Stage: A Festival of Special Occasion Plays, by Virginia Bradley (Dodd). The 10 plays in this collection approach the holidays from a new and unusual point of view while still considering their traditions. Suggestions for staging, costumes, and props are included. Ages 10 to 14.

The Easy Ice Skating Book, by Jonah and Laura Kalb, illustrated by Sandy Kossin (Houghton). Its easy language and amusing cartoon pictures should make this book valuable to beginning skaters, from the fitting of their first skates to the performance of jumps. Ages 8 and up.

Discovering the Guitar: Teach Yourself to Play, by Linda Swears, diagrams by Gene Azzam, photographs by Keith Derrickson (Morrow). This introduction to the guitar is for children with no experience in reading music or playing the guitar. It includes many simple melodies. Ages 8 to 12.

Better Synchronized Swimming for Girls, by Janet Chiefari and Nancy Wightman, photographs by Ann Hagen Griffiths (Dodd). A swimming teacher discusses basic skills, suggests practice exercises, and tells how to make up routines and prepare for performances. Ages 8 to 14.

Science Magic Tricks: Over 50 Fun Tricks That Mystify and Dazzle, by Nathan Shalit, illustrated by

Helen Cerra Ulan (Holt). This book not only shows tricks using math, physics, and chemistry, but it also suggests accompanying patter for performances. Ages 8 and up.

Lettie Lane Paper Dolls, by Sheila Young (Dover). Appearing in the *Ladies' Home Journal* from 1908 to 1918, these paper dolls show clothes, hairstyles, toys, and furnishings of the time. Ages 8 and up.

Superstars of Women's Track, by George Sullivan (Dodd). This high-interest, low-vocabulary introduction to six outstanding runners discusses each woman's background, races, coaches, and awards. Photographs show each athlete in action. Ages 8 and up.

Animals, Places, and Things

Bermuda Petrel: The Bird That Would Not Die, by Francine Jacobs, illustrated by Ted Lewin (Morrow). An encouraging account of efforts to ensure the survival of a species of bird that was thought to be extinct, but was discovered alive. This book shows that even one person can help to rescue an endangered species. Ages 6 to 10.

The Weaver's Gift, by Kathryn Lasky, photographs by Christopher G. Knight (Warne). The photographs and text of this fascinating book start with a newborn lamb and end with the weaving of a child's blanket. Ages 8 to 12.

Extraordinary Stories Behind the Invention of Ordinary Things, by Don L. Wulffson, illustrated by Roy Doty (Lothrop). Fascinating and amusing information about the invention of such everyday items as the shopping cart and the safety pin make this an entertaining book. All ages.

African Countries and Cultures; A Concise Illustrated Dictionary, by Jane M. Hornburger and Alex Whitney, illustrated by Hameed Benjamin (McKay). For pleasure or research, this book provides a surprising amount of information about languages, history, geography, customs, and famous people associated with Africa. Ages 12 and up.

Flight: A Panorama of Aviation, by Melvin B. Zisfein, illustrated by Robert Andrew Parker (Pantheon). Large full-color illustrations and brief text by the deputy director of the Smithsonian Institution's National Air and Space Museum provide an overview of unusual and historically important flying machines. Ages 10 and up.

Fiction

Taking Care of Carruthers, by James Marshall (Houghton). Told in a matter-of-fact style that makes it even funnier, this book relates the adventures of a bear (Carruthers), a turtle (Eugene), and a pig (Emily) on a boating trip. Ages 8 to 10.

Out of the Bug Jar, by Kathleen Thomas, illustrated by Tom O'Sullivan (Dodd). Tom catches Marvin the tooth fairy under his pillow and puts

Katherine Paterson's *Jacob Have I Loved,* the story of twin sisters growing up in the 1940s, won the 1981 Newbery Medal for children's books.

him in a bug jar, not knowing what a big change it will make in his life. Realistic characters and imaginative situations make this a fun story. Ages 8 to 11.

Ramona Quimby Age 8, by Beverly Cleary, illustrated by Alan Tiegreen (Morrow). A long-time favorite, Ramona Quimby continues to be her own zestful, unique, totally believable self in this humorous account of her year in third grade. Ages 8 to 12.

Me and the Weirdos, by Jane Sutton, illustrated by Sandy Kossin (Houghton). After Roger Snooterman tells Cindy that her family is weird, she notices how unusual they are and begins a campaign to "unweird" them. Ages 7 to 10.

Chasing After Annie, by Marjorie Weinman Sharmat, illustrated by Marc Simont (Harper). Using excerpts from the diaries of Richie and Annie—often contradictory reports of the same event—this amusing book relates Richie's attempts to get Annie to be his friend. Ages 8 to 11.

A Jar of Dreams, by Yoshiko Uchida (McElderry/Atheneum). Eleven-year-old Rinko and her family were excited about the visit of her aunt from Japan, but no one guessed the changes that would take place in this Japanese-American household. The importance of family, friends, and self-respect are woven into this story, seen through the eyes of Rinko. Ages 9 to 12.

Summer Home, by Cynthia D. Grant (Atheneum). A realistic and comic look at a family's summer in a camping area as seen by 11-year-old Max, who finds the behavior of his 13-year-old sister quite puzzling. Ages 10 to 15.

A Different Kind of Gold, by Cecily Stern, illustrated by Ruth Sanderson (Harper). Ten-year-old Cara and her family work to protect their home from commercial development in this quiet book, which describes the wild beauties of Alaska and a believable, happy family relationship. Ages 10 and up.

Apple Is My Sign, by Mary Riskind (Houghton). Harry and the rest of his family are deaf. This book tells about Harry's experiences at a school for the deaf and his first visit home from school. Filled with enthusiasm and joy, Harry is a very real and appealing little boy. Ages 10 to 14.

Soul-Singer of Tyrnos, by Ardath Mayhar (Atheneum). At the school for the Singers of Souls, the youngest Singer is told that she may be the chosen one of her generation, destined to face evil forces and great tasks. The original, imaginative story and expressive language make this narrative an outstanding fantasy. Ages 12 and up.

Giftwish, by Graham Dunstan Martin (Houghton). Through trickery, the peasant boy Ewan is forced to play the part of a prophesied champion and go into the Forbidden City. This exciting adventure includes a quest, a battle of wizards, and many other elements of fantasy. Ages 12 and up.

Homecoming, by Cynthia Voigt (Atheneum). Dicey decides to take charge after learning that her mother has left her and her younger sister and brothers. Dicey keeps the family together and leads them on a difficult journey to find the only other relative they have ever heard of. Dicey's courage and resourcefulness lead to an unexpected and satisfying solution. Ages 12 and up.

No Safe Harbors, by Stephanie S. Tolan (Scribners). Amanda's secure world as the mayor's daughter is shattered when her adored father is accused of taking a bribe. Well-drawn characters and a serious theme make this a worthwhile and engrossing book. Ages 12 and up.

Mind-Call, by Wilanne Schneider Belden (Atheneum). Drawn by dreams and mental summons, a group of children gradually collect at the home of a powerful, insane millionaire. The suspense mounts as they learn why they are there and how to combat the evil seeking to control them. Ages 14 and up.

Anna to the Infinite Power, by Mildred Ames (Scribners). Set 20 years in the future, this story's implications begin to dawn on the reader with the realization that Anna is a clone. Ages 12 and up.

A Fabulous Creature, by Zilpha Keatley Snyder (Atheneum). James, who is almost 16 years old, finds his summer dominated by two fabulous creatures – a magnificent stag and a beautiful, self-centered 15-year-old girl whose appeal he finds hard to handle. Ages 14 and up.

The Voyage Begun, by Nancy Bond (McElderry/Atheneum). The reader is already involved in this terse, realistic adventure before realizing that it is set 30 or 40 years in the future on a Cape Cod that is crumbling and barren. An unlikely partnership between 15-year-old Paul and Mickey, a tough 11-year-old girl, leads them into danger as they try to help an old man. Ages 14 and up.

Awards in 1981 included:
American Library Association/Association for Library Services to Children Awards: The *Newbery Medal* for "the most distinguished contribution to American literature for children" was awarded to Katherine Paterson for *Jacob Have I Loved.* The *Caldecott Medal* for "the most distinguished American picture book for children" went to Arnold Lobel for *Fables,* and the *Mildred L. Batchelder Award* cited Morrow for its publication of *The Winter When Time Was Frozen* by Els Pelgrom, which was translated from the Dutch by Raphael and Maryka Rudnik.   Sandra Streilein

See also CANADIAN LITERATURE; LITERATURE; POETRY. In WORLD BOOK, see CALDECOTT MEDAL; LITERATURE FOR CHILDREN; NEWBERY MEDAL.

LIVESTOCK. See FARM AND FARMING.

LOS ANGELES celebrated its 200th anniversary on Sept. 4, 1981. That same day, the city's residents were shaken by an offshore earthquake that began at 8:15 A.M. and rumbled across southern California. The earthquake, registering 5.1 on the Richter scale, was the strongest to strike Los Angeles since Feb. 9, 1971, when a quake registering 6.4 killed 64 people, injured 1,000, and caused more than $1-billion in damage. However, the bicentennial earthquake caused only minor damage, and no injuries were reported.

City Elections. Mayor Thomas A. Bradley captured 64 per cent of the vote to defeat former Mayor Samuel W. Yorty and 17 other challengers in a nonpartisan primary election on April 14. Yorty had defeated Bradley in the 1969 mayoral election but had lost to him in 1973. By capturing more than 50 per cent of the votes cast, Bradley avoided a runoff election. In doing so, he became the first Los Angeles mayor to win a third term in the primary.

In the June 2 general election, Los Angeles voters elected two new council members, a new city attorney, and a new controller. They also defeated a measure to impose a special residential and commercial property tax to finance the hiring of 1,354 additional police officers.

An End to Busing. The Los Angeles Board of Education voted on March 16 to end court-ordered busing in the city's school system, the second largest in the United States. The mandatory busing program had affected nearly 22,000 students and 153 elementary and junior high schools. The vote came after the state Supreme Court on March 11 refused to hear an appeal of a lower court's decision that upheld an antibusing amendment approved by California voters in 1979. Los Angeles Superior Court Judge Robert B. Lopez on November 30 issued a final ruling on the city's lengthy school-desegregation case, throwing out all previous lower-court orders. Lopez ruled that the proposed desegregation program would satisfy the school board's legal obligations to reduce segregation in its 665 schools. The program is based on establishing magnet schools—those with superior facilities—to attract students of all races to formerly segregated neighborhoods. Opponents of the ruling appealed the decision.

Budget Cuts. In adopting a record $4.66-billion budget on July 3, the Los Angeles County Board of Supervisors agreed to cut $75 million from health-care programs. The cuts called for the layoff of 2,000 health-service workers from several county hospitals and health clinics. However, a lawsuit filed by several patients, public interest lawyers, and health workers postponed some of the cuts.

The city's proposed "downtown people mover" system—a 2.9-mile (4.7-kilometer) elevated transit line—was also a victim of budget reductions. Officials of the federal Urban Mass Transportation Administration on April 14 notified the city that it would end federal grants for the people mover. On June 16, the City Council voted to abandon the $175-million program because the federal government was no longer willing to share the costs.

Another Transit Project—the long-awaited Century Freeway that would link Los Angeles International Airport with southeastern Los Angeles County—moved closer to reality in 1981. The $1.5-billion cost of the 17-mile (27.4-kilometer) freeway is to be financed with federal, state, and local funds. However, the Environmental Protection Agency (EPA) had blocked the release of federal funds in response to objections from local governments that emissions from freeway traffic would increase air pollution along its route. The EPA dropped its objection after federal, state, and local governments signed a consent decree on September 22, agreeing to allow freeway construction to begin in 1982.

Nonetheless, the future of the freeway remained in dispute. Courts had yet to act upon suits seeking to block construction because it would displace thousands of residents. Victor Merina

See also CITY. In WORLD BOOK, see LOS ANGELES.

LOUISIANA. See STATE GOVERNMENT.
LUMBER. See FOREST AND FOREST PRODUCTS.

LUXEMBOURG lost its bid to become a permanent meeting place of the European Parliament, the advisory legislative branch of the European Community (EC or Common Market), on July 7, 1981. Parliament decided to hold committee meetings in Brussels, Belgium, and meetings of the entire body in Strasbourg, France. Luxembourg threatened to stop supporting Parliament financially.

Luxembourg claimed that the decision violated certain treaties giving EC leaders the right to decide where to locate Parliament. In 1980, the EC's policymaking body, the Council of Ministers, had called on Parliament to choose a single location.

Steel Peace. Luxembourg and Belgium settled their argument over competition between their steel industries on January 25. Luxembourg's Foreign Minister Colette Flesch announced that the Arbed steel company's new rolled-steel mill at Dudelange would produce 650,000 metric tons (710,000 short tons) of steel per year, rather than 1.2 million metric tons (1.3 million short tons) as originally planned.

Unemployment rose by 50 per cent in the year ending in May. However, it amounted to only 1 per cent of the work force. Kenneth Brown

See also EUROPE (Facts in Brief Table). In WORLD BOOK, see LUXEMBOURG.
MADAGASCAR. See AFRICA.

Prince Henri, Luxembourg's heir apparent, walks down the aisle with his bride, Maria Teresa Mestre of Switzerland, in February.

MAGAZINE. The combined circulation per issue of the 100 leading magazines in the United States increased 3.9 per cent during the first six months of 1981 over the same period in 1980, according to an Audit Bureau of Circulations (ABC) survey. Average paid-subscription circulation per issue increased 3.0 per cent, though average paid single-copy circulation per issue decreased by 4.2 per cent. The ABC survey indicated that there were 63 magazines with circulations of 1 million or more in 1981, up from 52 in 1975.

Advertising revenues for magazines in the United States exceeded $3 billion in 1981. This was an increase of about 10 per cent over a record 1980.

New Magazines. Among the 240 new magazines introduced in 1981 was *It's Me,* a five-times-a-year publication by Lane Bryant, Incorporated, bearing the inscription, "Not for Little Women." *Pro!,* introduced in August by National Football League (NFL) Properties, is to be published monthly from August to February and features in-depth articles about NFL teams and players. Straight Arrow Publishers, Incorporated, originator of *Rolling Stone,* in November launched *The Record,* a 24-page rock-music tabloid. *Science Fiction Digest,* a bimonthly featuring condensed versions of original science-fiction novels in each issue, was introduced in October by Davis Publications, Incorporated.

Carol Burnett's expressive face registers delight as a jury decides a libel suit against the *National Enquirer* in her favor in March.

Changes. A few magazines changed hands in 1981, while others were given new life, new names, or new faces at the helm. Several magazines died. The American version of *GEO* magazine, the glossy "human geography" publication, was sold in September by Gruner + Jahr USA, Incorporated, to Knapp Communications Corporation, publishers of *Architectural Digest* and *Bon Appétit.* The New Yorker Magazine, Incorporated, and Eliot Wadsworth II, owner of White Flower Farms, a mail-order nursery in Litchfield, Conn., announced in September that they had signed an agreement to acquire *Horticulture* magazine, which for years has been the official publication of the Massachusetts Horticultural Society.

Condé Nast Publications, Incorporated, in July announced that it will revive *Vanity Fair,* a magazine of "wit and critical intelligence," as a monthly in January 1983. It was published for 22 years before it died during the Great Depression of the 1930s. With the April issue, Meredith Corporation's *Apartment Life* magazine was renamed *Metropolitan Home,* and *Dun's Review* became *Dun's Business Month* with the September issue.

Triangle Publications, publishers of *TV Guide,* ceased publication of its slick, four-color monthly, *Panorama,* with the June issue. Johnson Publishing Company Incorporated, the nation's largest black-owned publishing firm, folded its entertainment monthly, *Black Stars,* with the July issue. The British newsweekly *Now* died in April.

Awards. Robert A. Burnett, president and chief executive officer of the Meredith Corporation, was named by the Magazine Publishers Association as the 1981 recipient of the Henry Johnson Fisher Award, which is the industry's most prestigious honor. National Magazine Awards, sponsored by the American Society of Magazine Editors, were presented in April. Among the winning publications were *Attenzione* for design; *Business Week* for a single-topic issue; *National Journal* for reporting; *North American Review* for fiction; *The Reader's Digest* for public service; and *Time* for essays and criticism. Four publications cited for general excellence in categories based on circulation were *Glamour* (circulation of over 1 million), *Business Week* (400,000 to 1 million), *Audubon* (100,000 to 400,000), and *ARTnews* (under 100,000).

Damages. Entertainer Carol Burnett was awarded $1.6 million on March 27 by a Los Angeles Superior Court jury in a libel suit against the *National Enquirer.* The jury ruled that the tabloid had knowingly printed false, defamatory information about Burnett. The damages were later reduced to $800,000. Gloria Ricks Dixon

See also PUBLISHING. In WORLD BOOK, see MAGAZINE.

MAINE. See STATE GOVERNMENT.

MALAWI. See AFRICA.

MALAYSIA. Prime Minister Hussein Onn underwent heart surgery in February 1981. After the operation, he resigned as prime minister. Mahathir bin Mohamed, Malaysia's deputy prime minister, was elected on June 26 to succeed Hussein as president of the United Malays National Organization (UMNO), the most powerful political party in a coalition called the National Front. The party president, by tradition, becomes prime minister, and Mahathir took office on July 16.

Mahathir, who was then 55 years old, represented a new generation in Malaysian politics. He was the first head of government to have held office under the British colonial government or to have participated in negotiations that led to Malaysia's independence in 1957. Mahathir, an ethnic Malay and a strong Malay nationalist, had been temporarily expelled from the UMNO in 1969 after riots between Malays and Chinese. Party leaders felt then that his fiery views conflicted with efforts to unite Malaysia's ethnic groups into one nation. Mahathir returned with a more moderate attitude and won wide enough backing to gain the party presidency without a real contest.

Three days before Mahathir became prime minister, the Malaysian government arrested his political secretary, Siddiq Mohamad Ghouse, accusing him of acting for a foreign power. The government also expelled three Russian diplomats charged with spying.

Apprehension about activities of a Russian-backed political group called the Communist United Front caused the Malaysian government to pass legislation on April 8 permitting only politicians and registered political parties and societies to make public comments on government affairs.

China, rather than the Soviet Union, however, caused the most worry about interference in Malaysian affairs. The long-time figurehead chairman of the Communist Party of Malaya (CPM), Musa Ahmad, returned home after more than 20 years in China. In a television appearance on January 6, he said China still directed the CPM and hoped eventually to make Malaysia a satellite. About 3,000 CPM guerrillas remained in the jungles under leadership of ethnic Chinese Malaysians and continued to fight the Malaysian armed forces.

Malaysia's Economy slumped a bit but remained relatively good. In a move to gain control over a key sector of the economy, the government on September 7 took over the Guthrie Corporation, a British-based company that manages rubber, palm oil, cocoa, and tea plantations.   Henry S. Bradsher

See also ASIA (Facts in Brief Table). In the WORLD BOOK SUPPLEMENT section, see KUALA LUMPUR; MALAYSIA.

MALDIVES. See AFRICA.

MALI. See AFRICA.

MALTA. See EUROPE.

MANITOBA voters returned the New Democratic Party (NDP) to power on Nov. 17, 1981, after four years of Progressive Conservative (PC) rule. NDP leader Howard Pawley became the province's new premier. His party won 34 of the 57 seats in the Manitoba parliament; the PC took 23.

A bizarre case involving a member of the legislature convicted of drug trafficking ended in June when the Supreme Court of Canada dismissed a final appeal from Robert Wilson of Winnipeg, the accused politician. After he was sentenced to a seven-year prison term for conspiring to import marijuana from Florida, Wilson refused to give up his legislative seat pending appeals. The assembly then passed a bill to bar any member sentenced to five or more years in prison from sitting in the legislature.

Finance Minister Brian Ransom presented a cautious budget on behalf of the PC government on April 14. A budget of $2.4 billion (Canadian dollars; $1= U.S. 84 cents as of Dec. 31, 1981) left a deficit of $219 million, the largest since 1977.

Pearl McGonigal, the second woman to be appointed lieutenant governor of a province, took office on October 23. The former deputy mayor of Winnipeg had been elected to the City Council five times since 1969. She also wrote a weekly newspaper column, "Frankly Feminine."   David M. L. Farr

In WORLD BOOK, see MANITOBA.

MANUFACTURING. On Oct. 18, 1981, President Ronald Reagan reluctantly conceded that the United States was in a "slight" recession. The Administration had predicted a brief recession as its measures to combat the downturn—which included a first stage of tax cuts for individuals and businesses and a decline in interest rates—began to take effect. Administration economists considered record-high interest rates a main reason for the slump, especially in two bellwether industries—cars and housing (see AUTOMOBILE; BUILDING AND CONSTRUCTION; HOUSING). By mid-November, the *prime rate*—the interest rate at which banks lend to their best commercial customers—at some of the leading U.S. banks had dropped to 16.5 per cent.

However, other economists were in sharp disagreement with the Administration's assessment of the recession. Howard Sharpe of Purcell, Graham & Company, a firm of stockbrokers, who had predicted that the Department of Commerce's composite index of leading economic indicators would decline in September by 2.7 per cent—which is exactly what happened—said it would be the "worst recession since World War II." Also pointing to a severe recession was the inventory accumulation of manufactured goods, which stood at a historically high $23.3-billion annual rate in the first quarter of 1981. Third-quarter predictions of a rise of only $2.4 billion grossly underestimated

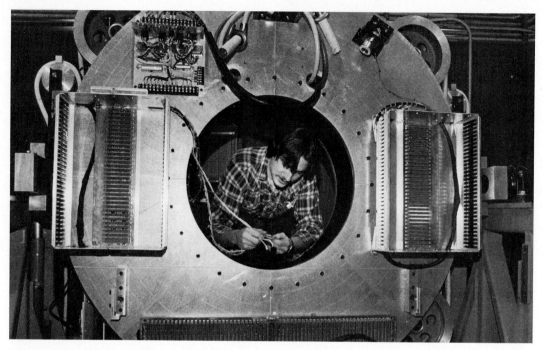

A CAT scanner, a computerized X-ray machine used for diagnosis, is made in a mobile version so that small hospitals can share its use – and high cost.

the actual rate at which inventories grew – a $17.6-billion annual rate. This indicated that companies would have to cut production to work off excess stocks, something that could send the economy into more than a "slight" recession.

A look at some of the production figures in the leading indicators for September showed the quickening pace of the slump. Average hours worked by factory employees slipped to 39.1 hours per week after holding steady at 40 hours for several months; the layoff rate in manufacturing was 1.7 per cent, up from 1.5 per cent in August and 1 per cent in July. New plant and equipment spending, a bulwark of the economy, dropped steadily – down 9 per cent from June and 17 per cent from December 1980.

In November, Secretary of Commerce Malcolm Baldrige acknowledged that the downturn had spread beyond housing and automobiles and permeated the economy. This was reflected in the drop in factory production for October, down 1.5 per cent from September for the greatest drop since June 1980. The October industrial production index stood at 149.5 (taking the 1967 production rate as 100), 2.5 per cent less than the high point in July 1981.

New Factory Orders fell 0.9 per cent, and the situation would have been worse except for an increase in defense orders, according to a Commerce Department report in September. New orders decreased to a seasonally adjusted $168.54-billion, after a revised decline of 1.5 per cent in August to $170.06 billion. The Commerce Department was particularly distressed by the decline in orders for nondefense spending, a steep 8 per cent drop, which indicated a retreat in capital-spending plans. This was confirmed when new orders for manufacturers' durable goods plummeted 2.9 per cent in September to a seasonally adjusted $84.57-billion, prompting Robert Ortner, chief economist for the Commerce Department, to say that the report was "not good for the immediate outlook for capital spending."

With the build-up in inventories and the fall-off in new orders, plant utilization dropped to 76.9 per cent of capacity in October. This was the lowest level since August 1980, the end of the 1980 recession, but above the 74.9 per cent of July 1980, the bottom of the 1980 recession.

Industry's sluggishness did little to stimulate capital spending. According to the Department of Commerce, a survey conducted in July and August indicated that capital spending would be "about the same as in 1980" – $326.63 billion, according to the McGraw-Hill Economics Department. Allen Sinai, senior economist for Data Resources Incorporated, a forecasting firm, said, "We're seeing two years of back-to-back stagnation in business spending, and that's very negative for the long-term health of the economy."

Employees felt the sting of the downturn. The United States unemployment rate was up to 8.4 per cent in November, the highest level since the recession of 1974-1975. Total employment was 98 million, down slightly, but nonagricultural payroll employment dropped significantly. See LABOR.

Another indicator of the weakened economy was the decline in the output per hour in American businesses, excluding farms. Productivity dropped at a seasonally adjusted rate of 1.6 per cent in the third quarter, following a productivity increase of 1.4 per cent in the second quarter. For the year, unit labor costs showed little improvement from those of 1980, which rose by 10.3 per cent.

Research and Development (R & D) spending climbed some 3.8 per cent to about $68.6 billion in 1981 despite the downturn and continued high inflation rates, according to Battelle Columbus Laboratories, an independent research concern. This marked the fourth consecutive year of real gains. The National Science Foundation claimed that basic research accounted for 13.6 per cent of R & D in the United States in 1980, the highest proportion in more than 15 years. The renewed emphasis on R & D prompted Battelle to predict that outlays for it throughout the 1980s would rise an average of 3 per cent annually; the average rise on a year-to-year basis during the 1970s was 1 per cent. The interest U.S. companies showed in R & D came from growing confidence in the profit potential of basic research and the accelerating threat of foreign competition.

The renewed vigor of U.S. industry, despite the downturn, was seen in its commitment to "make a stunning leap into total automation," according to a special report on automation in the August 3 issue of *Business Week* magazine. Many business leaders believe the United States will pass Japan and West Germany in the contest to automate and will successfully turn back their threat to U.S. technological and industrial supremacy. The big push was predicted to come in capital spending, with industry tripling its annual automation investments to more than $5 billion by 1985.

About 4,000 robots were at work in U.S. factories in 1981, up from 1,300 as recently as 1979. Some forecasters envisioned as many as 120,000 robots by 1990. Robots in the pioneering generation were programmed mainly to forge, weld, spray paint, handle materials, cast dies, load machines, and inspect automobile bodies. But by 1981, robots with rudimentary vision and touch abilities were being put to such jobs as assembling small parts. In the Special Reports section, see A ROBOT IN YOUR FUTURE?

Machine Tools. For machine tool builders, 1981 was not a good year. In September, machine tool orders dropped to the lowest level in five years, down 50 per cent to $188.1 million from $374.8-million in 1980, and 12 per cent below August's $214.4 million. For the entire third quarter, machine tool builders were able to book only $597.3-million in new orders, down 34 per cent from the same period in 1980. It was the weakest quarter since the second quarter of 1976, according to the National Machine Tool Builders Association. The weakened position of the industry was also seen in the order backlog, which was $3.69 billion at the end of September, compared with $5.48 billion a year earlier.

Rubber. While so much of U.S. industry was down, tire manufacturers rebounded from a very poor year in 1980, despite 1981 being a poor year in automobile sales. Production in 1981 was estimated at 190 million passenger car, truck, and bus tires by the Rubber Manufacturers Association, compared with only 159 million produced in 1980. One reason for the improvement was that manufacturers began the year with leaner tire inventories. By the start of 1981, manufacturers had also eliminated much of the industry's overcapacity. From 1978 through 1980, some 23 per cent of the industry's tire-making capacity had been eliminated. The facilities that remained were more efficient. Uniroyal Incorporated reported that blemished tires were no longer a problem. The Firestone Tire and Rubber Company centralized responsibility for manufacturing and product development, and Goodyear Tire & Rubber Company received concessions from the United Rubber Workers at its Wichita, Kans., plant that allowed the company to make work rules more flexible.

Electrical Equipment sales were up a mere 1.2 per cent from 1980, according to the National Electrical Manufacturers Association. The only bright spot in an otherwise dim performance by the industry was a 10.3 per cent increase in the sale of medical diagnostic and therapy equipment. Computer development continued to hold center stage in the electrical field. IBM, the giant of the industry, introduced its most powerful computer, the 3081 Group K, which is up to 40 per cent faster than the first 3081 Series H, introduced in 1980. According to IBM, the new model can execute 14 million instructions per second. New architectural features of the machine give it the capacity to handle 2 billion characters of internal memory, compared with 32 million for the Series H.

In a step toward the automated office, Xerox Corporation introduced a computer designed to overcome the reluctance of white-collar workers with no computer experience to use electronic terminals. The 8010 Star Information System is a video-display terminal that can be used to print and edit documents, create graphs and charts, retrieve documents stored in electronic files, and send and receive electronic messages. The operator moves a pointer on the screen to symbols representing various functions, rather than having to type special commands and code words, as is required on other terminals. For example, to remove a file, the operator moves the pointer to a picture of a filing cabinet and presses one key; to print a document, the pointer is moved to a picture of a printer.

Paper and Paperboard. Although forest-product companies had a dismal year in 1981 because of the decline in housing construction, their paper divisions thrived. The American Paper Institute reported that production of paper and paperboard was up to an annual rate of 65.1 million short tons (59.0 million metric tons) for the July and August period, and reached an annual rate of 65.7 million short tons (59.6 million metric tons) for the January through August period. These figures were about 2.5 per cent above the 1980 average and 1 per cent above the previous high established in the full year of 1979.   George J. Berkwitt

In WORLD BOOK, see MANUFACTURING.

MARINE CORPS, U.S. See ARMED FORCES.

MARYLAND. See STATE GOVERNMENT.

MASSACHUSETTS. See STATE GOVERNMENT.

MAURITANIA. See AFRICA.

MAURITIUS. See AFRICA.

MAYOR. See CITY.

MEDICINE. In January 1981, the World Health Organization (WHO) reported increases in coronary deaths in several eastern European countries and decreases in a few industrialized nations. The United States was the only nation to show a decrease of 3 per cent or more in fatal heart attacks among men. Israel, Japan, Switzerland, and the United States showed 3 to 4.9 per cent fewer heart attacks among women between 1968 and 1977.

The WHO report was only part of the good news about the health of Americans' hearts in 1981. On September 17, the National Heart, Lung and Blood Institute reported "huge and dramatic" progress against heart disease, the number-one killer of American adults. According to the institute, deaths due to heart disease fell by 25 per cent and deaths due to stroke fell by 40 per cent during the 1970s. During those 10 years, an estimated 1 million lives were saved because of advances in the recognition and treatment of high blood pressure, earlier and more precise diagnosis of heart problems, more effective therapies for treatment of heart disease, and changes in the life style of many Americans. These changes include less smoking, more exercise, and decreased consumption of foods high in saturated fats and cholesterol.

A breakthrough in treating heart disease came on March 9, when a surgery team headed by Norman E. Shumway and Bruce A. Reitz of Stan-

ford University in California completed the first successful transplant of both a heart and a pair of lungs. The recipient was Mary D. Gohlke, age 45, from Arizona – the fourth person in the world to receive such a transplant. Similar operations had been attempted in the late 1960s and early 1970s, but the longest survival period until 1981 was 23 days. On May 1, Charles Walker, age 30, received the fifth heart-lung transplant.

New Treatments for Heart Disease. On July 23, Denton Cooley, a surgeon at the Texas Heart Institute in Houston, implanted an artificial heart in Willebrordus A. Meuffels, a 36-year-old Dutch bus driver who had suffered a massive heart attack after by-pass surgery. The electrically powered plastic heart kept Meuffels alive for two days until he received a human heart transplant. He died a week later. The artificial-heart operation was controversial because it was performed without permission from the Food and Drug Administration, which approves new medical devices.

A report by researchers at the University of Pennsylvania in Philadelphia presented at the International Cardiovascular Society meeting in Dallas in June indicated that a technique called balloon angioplasty may be as effective as surgery in treating blocked blood vessels and reducing the risk of heart attack. In balloon angioplasty, a tiny

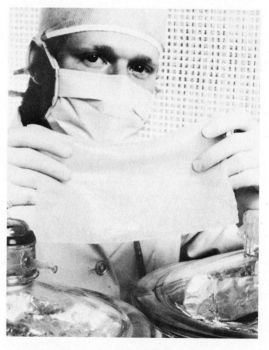

An experimental artificial skin offers new hope for burn victims. The artificial skin is made from cowhide, plastic, and shark cartilage.

balloon is threaded through an obstructed blood vessel and inflated to restore normal blood flow. In patients suffering from blocked blood vessels, more than 90 per cent of the arteries cleared by balloon angioplasty remained open a year later, and more than 80 per cent remained open after two years.

Battle Against Cancer. The American Cancer Society reported on March 24 that its yearlong trial of the chemical substance interferon in the treatment of cancer showed disappointing results. Interferon was given to patients with breast cancer, melanoma, lymphoma, or multiple myeloma. Fewer than 40 per cent responded favorably, and those in remission relapsed after six months. Interferon also produced some of the same unfortunate side effects as conventional chemotherapy, including nausea, sudden fever, and lethargy.

According to a study by Italy's National Cancer Institute published in July, radical mastectomy (surgical removal of a breast and the underlying chest muscle) is no more effective for women with small tumors than less drastic surgery combined with radiation and chemotherapy treatments.

A study conducted at 68 medical centers in the United States showed dramatic success in treating breast cancer with a new combination of drugs plus surgical removal of the tumor and lymph nodes. Physicians added a chemical called tamoxifen to the usual two-drug treatment called PF (for L-phenylalanine mustard and 5-fluorouracil). This new treatment cut the expected recurrence rate in women whose cancer had spread beyond the breast from 45 per cent to 5 per cent.

An implanted pump that bathes liver cancers with continuous chemotherapy extended the life of patients with primary liver tumors and liver malignancies caused by colorectal cancer. According to a report by the National Institutes of Health in August, the continuous chemotherapy provided by the pumps in 61 patients shrank nearly 90 per cent of the liver cancers and extended life expectancy by at least 18 months.

Bone Powder. A research team at Harvard University Medical School in Boston reported in May that they had made successful facial repairs in 44 patients by using specially treated bone from cadavers. Most of these repairs corrected cleft palate or other birth defects. The bone was ground into powder, soaked in hydrochloric acid to remove all minerals, dried, and sterilized. Physicians transformed the powder into a paste by adding water and then molded the paste to reconstruct or correct skeletal deformities. Cartilage and new bone appeared within six months of the implant.

Prenatal Treatments. In April, a medical team at the University of California in San Francisco performed the first known successful surgical treatment of an unborn baby. The physicians had detected through sonograms (pictures similar to X

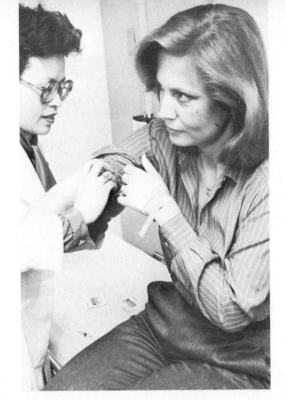

Joan Kanfotas of Northbrook, Ill., is the first cancer patient to receive synthetic interferon in a clinical study in a Houston hospital in January.

rays produced by ultrasound) that two fetuses were in the mother's womb. One fetus had a blocked urinary system that was causing a potentially fatal build-up of waste products. During the last weeks of the pregnancy, surgeons inserted a tube through the mother's abdomen and uterus into the bladder of the fetus to drain its urinary system. The baby boy and his twin sister were both healthy at birth.

In another pioneering attempt at the University of California in San Francisco to treat problems before birth, physicians diagnosed and treated a fetus suffering from a life-threatening hereditary deficiency of biotin, a crucial B vitamin.

Medical Politics. Delegates at the annual meeting of the American Medical Association (AMA) in June took their strongest stand ever against smoking and federal subsidies for tobacco products. Criticized for holding $1.4 million in tobacco stocks as part of an investment, the AMA announced in September that it had sold the stock.

The Senate confirmed the nomination of pediatrician C. Everett Koop, 65, for the post of surgeon general of the United States on November 16, after a long delay caused by controversy about his age and his opposition to abortion and homosexuality. Koop was already serving as deputy assistant secretary for health.   Dianne Hales

See also HEALTH AND DISEASE; PUBLIC HEALTH. In WORLD BOOK, see MEDICINE.

MENTAL HEALTH. A new technique called *positron emission tomography* (PET) was hailed in 1981 as a major advance in diagnosing certain mental disorders. In a PET scan, the patient either inhales or is injected with a glucoselike substance containing a radioactive chemical that emits positively charged particles. A scanning device can detect these particles, called *positrons*, when they combine with negatively charged electrons normally found in the body's cells and emit gamma rays. A computer translates the information into a black-and-white or color image that indicates the intensity of metabolic activity in different regions of the brain.

In 1981, researchers used PET scans to study the brains of people suffering from schizophrenia, manic-depressive disorder, and senile dementia. Preliminary reports indicated different patterns of glucose metabolism for each disorder.

The Elderly. In a task force report prepared for the White House Conference on Aging that began in November, the American Psychiatric Association (APA) said that most Americans over 65 years of age are well-functioning individuals with little or no evidence of mental disorder. Compared with the rest of the population, however, elderly people are more apt to develop depression; organic mental disorders, such as dementia; mental reactions as side effects to medication; and certain paranoid disorders. Although the elderly make up only 11 per cent of the U.S. population, they account for 20 per cent of suicides. The incidence of psychosis increases after age 65 and rises even more after age 75. An estimated 15 to 25 per cent of older Americans show significant symptoms of mental illness.

Young Adults. A series of articles in the July issue of *Hospital and Community Psychiatry* reported an alarming increase in the number of severely mentally ill patients between the ages of 18 and 35. The patients were born during the post-World War II "baby boom" and had reached the age when mental problems most often begin to manifest themselves. The articles, which focused on the problems of these young adults, characterized them as rootless, unemployed individuals who use alcohol and other drugs heavily and resist help.

Depression, the most common mental disorder, was the focus of considerable research in 1981. In the November 26 issue of *New England Journal of Medicine,* researchers reported that certain genes influence susceptibility to depression. This discovery raised the possibility of early detection of persons likely to develop a clinically significant depression.

A five-year investigation of the biological nature of depression, reported in June, underscored the extremely diverse nature of the disorder. According to the report's coordinator, psychopharmacologist Stephen H. Koslow, the most promising finding was the possibility of using laboratory tests of various substances in a patient's urine, blood, or cerebrospinal fluid to diagnose and classify the depression and to prescribe treatment. One such test measures the production of cortisol by the body after administration of *dexamethasone,* a cortisol-suppressing steroid. Unlike healthy persons, depressed people continue to produce cortisol.

At the APA meeting in May, a group of psychiatrists from Children's Hospital in Washington, D.C., and the National Institute of Mental Health in Bethesda, Md., reported that depression in childhood may not be a passing problem but a forerunner of significant mental disorders in adolescence. The psychiatrists noted that more than 50 per cent of the depressed children surveyed still experienced depression three to five years after it was first diagnosed. The remainder developed a variety of nondepressive emotional disorders.

Runner's High. A report by researchers at Massachusetts General Hospital in the September 3 issue of *New England Journal of Medicine* showed that strenuous exercise increases levels of *endorphin* (a natural narcoticlike painkiller) in the brain. This finding might explain the euphoria experienced by many athletes, particularly runners.   Dianne Hales

See also DRUGS. In the WORLD BOOK SUPPLEMENT section, see MENTAL ILLNESS. In WORLD BOOK, see MENTAL HEALTH; MENTAL ILLNESS.

Kambiz/Nebelspalter/Zurich

MEXICO. A decline in world petroleum prices cut into Mexico's oil revenues in 1981, but substantial new investments in oil and gas production helped make up the losses. The Mexican economy showed a growth rate of about 7 per cent for the year, and foreign investment doubled, as in the previous three years.

Mexico has become the world's fourth-largest producer of oil, and it has proven reserves of 130 billion barrels. As the government moved to develop further its oil resources, Mexico became the second-largest market for United States exports of goods and services.

Although Mexico has tried to keep its economy diversified and not heavily dependent on oil exports, oil revenues accounted for 70 per cent of all its exports in 1981. Inflation was running at an annual rate of about 30 per cent, and government spending was also high.

Speculation on the Political Successor to President Jose Lopez Portillo, whose term expires in December 1982, received unusual international attention, owing to the nation's growing economic power. According to Mexico's Constitution, a president may not seek a second term.

On September 25, the country's ruling Institutional Revolutionary Party (IRP) announced the selection of 46-year-old Miguel de la Madrid Hurtado, planning and budget minister in the Portillo Administration, as its candidate for president. The announcement of his candidacy was equivalent to his election because the IRP candidate has won every presidential election since it was established in 1929. The elections will be held on July 4, 1982.

The selection of de la Madrid was also a signal for the traditional government public-relations campaign aimed at persuading voters that Mexico is in good hands under the control of the IRP. Traditionally, voters are told of the government's accomplishments and assured that the new leader will follow in his predecessor's footsteps. These traditions, forged from the Mexican revolution in 1910, are geared to preserve stability and provide for the continuation of government policies.

Curbing Corruption. Portillo proposed legislation, in his annual message to the National Congress on September 1, to control gifts to Mexican public officials, including the president, in an effort to curb corruption. Portillo's speech brought a standing ovation. To show that he meant what he said, Portillo turned down a $2.4-million ranch offered to him by a group of business supporters in gratitude for his services to Mexico. His public refusal of the gift was a dramatic demonstration in a political system in which presents, bribes, conflict of interest, and outright embezzlement are common practices. If adopted and enforced, the code limiting gifts to public figures would have great impact on Mexico's political system. Attor-

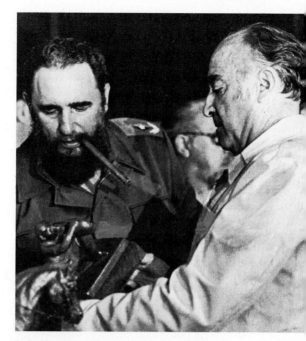

Cuban President Fidel Castro, left, and Mexican President Jose Lopez Portillo exchange gifts at an August meeting in Cozumel, Mexico.

ney General Oscar Flores Sanchez claimed that about 4,000 people – including 2,360 government officials – have been charged with corruption involving public funds within the past five years.

World Attention Turned to Cancún, Mexico, as 22 leaders of industrialized and developing nations gathered there for a summit meeting held from October 22 to 23. The leaders discussed ways in which the industrialized Northern countries could help the developing Southern countries. Portillo and Canadian Prime Minister Pierre Elliott Trudeau were co-chairmen of the conference.

Domestic Problems. Mexico continued its struggle to develop an effective strategy for coping with its fast-growing population. The problems of pollution and overcrowding were particularly severe in the capital, Mexico City, whose present metropolitan-area population of more than 14 million is expected to reach from 23 million to 32 million by the year 2000. An estimated four-fifths of Mexico City's people live in slum conditions.

Another major problem in Mexico is the widening gap between the upper class and the millions of subsistence farmers. It has been estimated that about 10 million Mexican children under 6 years of age suffer from malnutrition.   Nathan A. Haverstock

See also LATIN AMERICA (Facts in Brief Table). In WORLD BOOK, see MEXICO.

MICHIGAN. See DETROIT; STATE GOVERNMENT.

MIDDLE EAST

The scene is one of confusion as assassins pour gunfire into the Cairo reviewing stand where Egypt's President Sadat is killed on October 6.

The assassination of Egypt's President Anwar el-Sadat by Muslim extremists in the armed forces during a military parade in Cairo on Oct. 6, 1981, capped a year of violence and conflict in the Middle East and underscored the region's strategic and economic importance to the world. The assassination also provided further evidence of the emergence of Islamic fundamentalism as a political force throughout the Arab states. In Egypt, the fundamentalists opposed Sadat because of his peace treaty with Israel and what they saw as his excessive dependence on Western capitalism and technology. But behind their opposition lay deep concern with preserving Islamic values, which were believed threatened by the secularism of Islamic governments and the influence of foreign culture.

These circumstances, plus the normal turmoil in the region, created a difficult situation for the United States as it sought to develop an effective Middle East policy. America was trying to forge a policy geared to the protection of its own national interests yet flexible and evenhanded enough to meet conflicting Arab and Israeli demands. The difficulty of achieving this end became apparent in the congressional debate over the proposal by President Ronald Reagan's Administration to sell five Airborne Warning and Control System (AWACS) aircraft to Saudi Arabia. The AWACS planes were designed for radar warning and surveillance rather than attack, but Israel and its supporters in the United States—fearing that the planes could be used against Israeli targets—mounted a vigorous campaign against the sale. The sale would not have gone through if both houses of Congress opposed it. In October, the Senate endorsed the sale after the House of Representatives voted against it. But many observers believed the Senate endorsement was more a showing of support for Reagan's management of foreign policy than approval of the sale.

American Hostages Freed. The year began on a positive note with Iran's release on January 20 of the 52 Americans who had been held hostage since Nov. 4, 1979. Mediation by Algeria was crucial in the hostages' release. Iran accepted Algeria as a mediator because of its Islamic ties to Iran and its economic links to the United States.

Neither Algeria nor Iran gained significantly from the resolution of the hostage crisis, however. Algeria had hoped for increased U.S. support for the Algerian-backed Polisario Front, which has been contesting Moroccan sovereignty over the Western Sahara since 1975 (see MOROCCO). These hopes went unfulfilled, as the United States continued to back both Morocco and Algeria and even increased arms shipments to Morocco. Iran did gain in terms of an end to the international economic boycott imposed after the hostages were seized, and the release of Iranian assets frozen in the United States (see IRAN).

Iranian Power Struggle. Resolution of the hostage crisis and the resulting reduction of international pressure on Iran brought little relief to that revolution-wracked country. In June, President Abol Hasan Bani-Sadr was impeached by the *Majlis* (parliament) on grounds of political incompetence and interference with the progress of the revolution. Bani-Sadr's impeachment and his subsequent escape to France set off a violent power struggle between the dominant Islamic Republican Party (IRP), controlled by the clergy, and the *Mujahedeen* (Fighters for the Faith)—a coalition of Marxists, European-educated moderates, and others. The Mujahedeen advocate a secular Islamic socialist republic in Iran.

The Iran-Iraq War. Iran's preoccupation with its internal problems helped keep its war with Iraq from broadening to involve other countries in the region. After Iraqi forces repulsed a strong Iranian counterattack on Iraqi positions in Iran's Khuzi-

stan province in January, the war settled down. There was little action beyond intermittent artillery exchanges until late November, when heavy fighting again was reported in Khuzistan province.

War-damaged refineries and other installations in both countries resumed production during the year. Continued closure of Iraqi ports hampered the Iraqi war effort, however, by forcing the government to depend on long overland routes through Turkey and Jordan for supplies and military equipment. Efforts by Saudi Arabia and other countries to mediate the war proved futile.

Other Wars in the Region remained localized. The Soviet Union's military occupation of Afghanistan continued to draw worldwide criticism but brought little aid to the Afghan resistance groups. Despite steady casualties, the Soviet Union continued to reject all proposals for mediation and withdrawal of its troops, which Russia said were in Afghanistan to help the government put down an internal uprising. See AFGHANISTAN.

President Goukouni Weddeye of Chad was more successful than the Afghan resistance fighters in removing foreign occupiers. In January, Libyan troops occupied N'Djamena, Chad's capital, and Weddeye joined Libya's head of state, Leader of the Revolution Muammar Muhammad al-Qadhafi, in announcing the merger of the two countries into one Islamic republic. Neighboring African states denounced the action. They feared Qadhafi's ambition to expand Libya's influence throughout the continent and forge a Libyan-dominated coalition of Arab and African countries. The United States joined France in pressuring Weddeye to remove the Libyan troops, and Qadhafi began to withdraw them in November. See CHAD.

Cooperation Efforts. The revived interest by the United States and Russia in the strategic and economic importance of the Middle East, and their rivalry for regional control, led to increased efforts among some Middle Eastern countries toward greater cooperation. In May, six oil-producing states—Bahrain, Kuwait, Oman, Qatar, Saudi Arabia, and the United Arab Emirates—formally inaugurated the Gulf Cooperation Council (GCC). The GCC's objectives were cooperation in the areas of oil policy, economic and social planning, finance and trade, and social services and culture. The six states agreed to aid one another against outside attack and internal subversion. The council also offered economic aid to Yemen (Aden), the only Persian Gulf state fully allied with the Soviet Union, in return for GCC membership, but Yemen rejected the offer.

On December 3, Yemen (Aden) and Yemen (Sana) said they had signed a pact providing political and economic cooperation.

Islamic Fundamentalism, though not in control in any Middle Eastern country except Iran, contin-

Debate in Congress over the sale of AWACS planes to Saudi Arabia pointed up the difficulty of developing an effective U.S. Middle East policy.

ued to exert strong influence on the internal policies of most states in the area. In February, five fundamentalists won seats in the elections for a new National Assembly in Kuwait, the first since the Assembly was dissolved by the ruling emir in 1976 for political subversion. Ironically, the fundamentalists were Western-educated and trained in technological and managerial skills.

Fundamentalist groups, such as *Silfiyyin* (New Breed) and the Muslim Brotherhood, gained control of universities in Kuwait, Egypt, Jordan, and other Arab countries. These groups increasingly challenged their governments with a platform advocating a return to the principles of Islam and its social requirements.

The extent of fundamentalism in Egypt was demonstrated in the wake of Sadat's assassination. Sadat's massive roundup of Muslim and Coptic Christian extremists along with other opponents of his regime in September probably accelerated the plot to kill him. The Egyptian Army remained loyal, however, and Vice-President Mohamed Hosni Mubarak succeeded Sadat without opposition. An additional crackdown on disloyal extremist elements followed, and four accused assassins and 20 co-conspirators went on trial on November 21. See EGYPT.

Camp David Talks. Perhaps the greatest irony of Sadat's death was that it provided the opportunity for a breakthrough in the stalled Camp David talks between Israel and Egypt about future Palestinian autonomy. It also provided an opportunity, though, for the Arab states to unite in their policy toward Israel. Sadat had largely isolated himself from other Arab leaders by failing to force Israel into concessions on the Palestinian issue and concentrating instead on the recovery of the Sinai, which benefited only Egypt.

The re-election of Israeli Prime Minister Menachem Begin on June 30 was seen by some observers as a blow to the Camp David talks. Begin's narrow majority in the *Knesset* (parliament) was achieved through concessions to minority religious parties, firmness on the issue of continued Jewish settlements on the occupied West Bank, and a tough stance toward the Arabs, all of which won him the support of the Oriental, or Sephardic, majority of Israel's population, who fear the Arab states more than do European Jews. The Camp David talks resumed in Cairo, however, on November 11.

U.S.-Israeli Relations. Begin's tough policy and Israel's concern with security led to several actions during the year that adversely affected its normally close relationship with the United States. On June 7, Israeli warplanes destroyed the Osirak nuclear reactor under construction near Baghdad, Iraq. Israel claimed that Iraq planned to use the reactor to make atomic bombs for possible use against

Israel. Iraq insisted that the reactor was intended only for peaceful nuclear research.

The attack put the United States in a difficult position. American-built jets had carried out the raid in violation of the U.S.-Israeli arms agreement requiring Israel to use American military equipment purely for defense. The delivery of 10 U.S. F-16 jet fighters to Israel was suspended after the reactor raid. Congress appropriated $1.4 billion in arms sales to Israel for the 1981-1982 fiscal year, however, with repayment of $500 million "forgiven" and an additional $800 million earmarked for construction of new air bases to replace those to be returned to Egypt under the peace treaty.

Further cracks appeared in the wall of tradition-al Israeli-American mutual alliance with the approval of the sale of the AWACS aircraft to Saudi Arabia in October. On November 30, however, the United States and Israel announced an agreement on strategic cooperation aimed at threats "caused by the Soviet Union or Soviet-controlled forces" from outside the Middle East. The United States suspended the agreement on December 18, though, after Israel annexed the Golan Heights, taken from Syria in 1967. Begin responded by accusing the United States of treating Israel like "a banana republic" and said the agreement was canceled. Alexander M. Haig, Jr., U.S. secretary of state, described the situation as "a difference among good friends."

Facts in Brief on the Middle East Countries

Country	Population	Government	Monetary Unit*	Foreign Trade (million U.S. $) Exports†	Imports†
Bahrain	451,000	Amir Isa bin Salman Al-Khalifa; Prime Minister Khalifa bin Salman Al-Khalifa	dinar (1 = $2.66)	2,492	2,481
Cyprus	623,000	President Spyros Kyprianou	pound (1 = $2.29)	525	1,202
Egypt	43,876,000	President Mohamed Hosni Mubarak	pound (1 = $1.45)	3,046	4,860
Iran	40,663,000	President Ali Khamenei; Prime Minister Hosein Musavi-Khamenei	rial (79 = $1)	19,872	9,738
Iraq	14,114,000	President Saddam Hussein	dinar (1 = $3.41)	19,800	8,700
Israel	4,116,000	President Yitzhak Navon; Prime Minister Menachem Begin	shekel (14.5 = $1)	5,265	7,910
Jordan	3,398,000	King Hussein I; Prime Minister Mudhar Badran	dinar (1 = $3.02)	550	2,291
Kuwait	1,519,000	Emir Jabir Al-Ahmad Al-Sabah; Crown Prince & Prime Minister Saad Al-Abdullah Al-Sabah	dinar (1 = $3.55)	18,252	5,204
Lebanon	3,325,000	President Elias Sarkis; Prime Minister Shafiq al-Wazzan	pound (4.2 = $1)	723	2,749
Oman	948,000	Sultan Qaboos bin Said	rial (1 = $2.86)	3,299	1,424
Qatar	181,000	Amir & Prime Minister Khalifa bin Hamad Al-Thani	riyal (3.6 = $1)	5,761	1,445
Saudi Arabia	8,853,000	King & Prime Minister Khalid ibn Abd al-Aziz Al Saud	riyal (3.4 = $1)	109,111	30,177
Sudan	19,330,000	President & Prime Minister Gaafar Mohamed Nimeiri	pound (1 = $1.75)	581	869
Syria	9,210,000	President Hafiz al-Assad; Prime Minister Abd al Ra'uf al-Kassem	pound (3.8 = $1)	2,108	4,124
Turkey	47,999,000	Head of State Kenan Evren; Prime Minister Bulend Ulusu	lira (127.4 = $1)	2,445	5,802
United Arab Emirates	1,196,000	President Zayid bin Sultan Al-Nahayyan; Prime Minister Rashid ibn Said al-Maktum	dirham (3.7 = $1)	13,652	6,960
Yemen (Aden)	1,886,000	Supreme People's Council Presidium Chairman & Council of Ministers Chairman Ali Nasir Muhammad	dinar (1 = $2.90)	46	387
Yemen (Sana)	6,114,000	President Ali Abdallah Salih; Prime Minister Abdul Karim al-Iryani	rial (4.4 = $1)	2	1,374

*Exchange rates as of Dec. 1, 1981. †Latest available data.

From War to Peace

Anwar el-Sadat (1918-1981)

"No more war, no more bloodshed," was the slogan bestowed upon the Middle East by Egypt's President Anwar el-Sadat and his fellow peacemaker, Israel's Prime Minister Menachem Begin. The watchword was coined in conjunction with the Egyptian leader's dramatic journey to Israel in November 1977, when for 44 spectacular hours the world witnessed the birth of a new relationship in which two ancient nations, Egypt and Israel, ended 29 years of intermittent warfare and began a negotiating process that culminated in a peace treaty on March 26, 1979.

No one knows what inspired this military man. Indeed, it was the same President Anwar el-Sadat who, as supreme commander of his country's armed forces, gave the fateful order for Egyptian troops to cross the Suez Canal on Oct. 6, 1973, and to fight the Israelis in the Sinai.

He may have been motivated by the loss of a brother in combat. Perhaps he felt that there was no point in prolonging the fruitless military struggle with Israel, or he may have been driven by concern over a shift in foreign policy in which the United States advocated a joint diplomatic initiative with Russia to resolve the Middle East crisis. Sadat, who had ousted the Soviet Union's military advisers from Egypt, did not want to see a restoration of Russia's influence on Middle Eastern affairs.

Sadat came from a rural background and grew up in an atmosphere steeped in colorful Egyptian folklore – attributes reflected in his brilliant Arabic oratory. He was born on Dec. 25, 1918, in the Nile River Delta village of Mit Abu'l Kum, 60 miles (100 kilometers) north of Cairo. Despite coming from a Muslim family, Sadat attended a Coptic Christian school. His ambition was to become an army officer. This goal became feasible when the Anglo-Egyptian accord of 1936 opened the doors of Egypt's military academies to men from less affluent families. Sadat studied in the class of 1938, which eventually became known in Egypt as the "class of revolutionaries" because 11 of its 40 members later joined the Revolu-

tionary Command Council that overthrew King Faruk in 1952.

During World War II, Sadat's anti-British feelings drove him to cooperate with Nazi agents who had infiltrated Egypt. As a result, the British arrested and imprisoned him twice during the 1940s.

On the day of Faruk's overthrow – July 23, 1952 – Sadat's mentor and colleague in the revolution, Colonel Gamal Abdel Nasser, assigned Sadat to proclaim to the Egyptian nation over the radio that the monarchy had been abolished.

Throughout Nasser's rule, Sadat remained active in government, ultimately rising to the vice-presidency. He became president after Nasser's death on Sept. 28, 1970.

Observers doubted at the time that the relatively unknown Sadat could hold on to the reins of power in the face of several popular rivals. But Sadat acted swiftly and shrewdly to neutralize the various "centers of power" ranged against him.

The dire straits of the Egyptian economy constantly haunted Sadat. One of the world's highest birth rates and an obsession with military expenditures kept Egypt in stagnant condition, with vital public services deteriorating.

Once Sadat had succeeded in restoring national pride through the successful canal crossing in 1973, he shifted the emphasis to economic reconstruction. The peace initiative fitted perfectly into this scheme, bringing massive sums of American government aid in its wake.

Throughout his life, Sadat maintained a fervent personal commitment to Islam. He often prayed with his fellow Egyptian Muslims in mosques throughout the country.

However, when Muslim fundamentalists turned against his life style, if not against his policies, Sadat reacted by imprisoning their leaders. This may have precipitated his downfall, because it was a squad of fundamentalists in Egyptian military uniforms who on Oct. 6, 1981, gunned Sadat down during a military parade marking the eighth anniversary of the "Yom Kippur War" against Israel.   Jay Bushinsky

Saudi Peace Plan. Saudi Arabia, seeking greater involvement in the Middle East peace process, announced an eight-point peace plan in August. The plan included Israeli withdrawal from all occupied Arab territories, the dismantling of Jewish settlements in those territories, the establishment of a Palestinian state with East Jerusalem as its capital, and compensation for Palestinian refugees. The plan's seventh point called for recognition of the territorial integrity and political independence of all states in the region.

The six members of the GCC endorsed the Saudi plan, and the seventh point caused some favorable comment in Washington, D.C. Even Yasir Arafat, leader of the Palestine Liberation Organization (PLO), described it as a "good basis" for starting negotiations, though there was strong opposition to it from within the PLO. An Arab League meeting in Fez, Morocco, however, broke up only hours after it opened on November 25, primarily because Syria opposed the plan.

The Saudi peace plan was not necessarily dead, and King Hassan II of Morocco said there would be another meeting to discuss it in 1982. But as 1981 ended, it seemed that some 30 years of Middle Eastern conflict were very little closer to a resolution.   William Spencer

In WORLD BOOK, see MIDDLE EAST and individual Middle Eastern country articles.

MINING. The new Administration of President Ronald Reagan moved on several fronts during 1981 to stimulate the United States mining industry and reduce U.S. dependence on foreign sources of strategic minerals. At his confirmation hearing on January 7 and 8, James G. Watt, who became the new secretary of the interior, pledged to open to mineral exploration millions of acres of public lands and wilderness areas now closed to mining.

Watt acted to implement the new policy by proposing to relax controls on exploration and development on all public lands being considered for addition to the federal wilderness system and on portions of five national recreation areas in the West. On May 13, Watt began a reorganization of the Department of the Interior's Office of Surface Mining Reclamation and Enforcement (OSM) in an effort to ease what the Reagan Administration considered excessive regulation of surface-mining operations.

Watt also began to review decisions, made during President Jimmy Carter's Administration, to ban exploratory drilling for oil in four areas off the California coast and to prohibit strip mining near Bryce Canyon National Park in Utah. These and other actions by Watt drew sharp criticism from environmentalists.

The Supreme Court of the United States upheld on June 15 the constitutionality of the federal strip-mining law that imposes strict environmental regulations on mine owners and states. The Surface Mining Control and Reclamation Act of 1977 had been challenged by the mining industry and the governments of Virginia and Indiana.

Strategic Minerals. For the first time in more than 20 years, the United States began rebuilding the national stockpile of strategic minerals. The stockpile, which contains 93 minerals, would be used to supply defense and industrial needs if imports were disrupted because of political unrest or war in supplying countries. The United States imports more than 90 per cent of these metals.

The National Oceanic and Atmospheric Administration (NOAA) reported on October 6 the discovery of an undersea deposit of copper-containing ore, estimated to be worth billions of dollars, in the Pacific Ocean off the coast of Ecuador. The newly discovered deposit, located about 200 miles (320 kilometers) east of the Galapagos Islands in an undersea geologic formation known as the Galapagos Ridge, reportedly contains at least 25 million short tons (23 million metric tons) of ore.

Treaty Objections. The Reagan Administration presented its objections to the draft of the sea-law treaty at the United Nations Law of the Sea Conference in Geneva, Switzerland, on August 5. The Administration objected chiefly to the establish-

A gigantic hydraulic shovel with a capacity of 27.5 cubic yards (21 cubic meters) is displayed at a trade fair and mining congress in West Germany.

ment of an international seabed authority to regulate mining on the ocean floor, claiming that such a move would harm American mining interests. See OCEAN.

The United Mine Workers of America and the soft-coal industry reached an agreement on a new contract on June 6, ending a 72-day strike. See COAL; LABOR.

Foreign Purchases. A surge in attempts by foreign-owned companies to buy American mining companies during 1981 aroused concern among industry executives and government officials. Big oil companies also increased their investment in the mining industry. Standard Oil Company of Ohio, whose majority owner is British Petroleum Company Limited, bought the Kennecott Corporation, the largest U.S. copper producer. Consolidated Gold Fields Limited of London in November acquired a quarter interest in Newmont Mining Corporation, a producer of copper and gold. Société Nationale Elf Aquitaine, an oil company whose majority owner is the French government, on September 25 acquired Texasgulf Incorporated, a producer of sulfur and rock phosphate.   Michael Woods

See also DISASTERS (Mine Disasters). In WORLD BOOK, see MINING.

MINNESOTA. See STATE GOVERNMENT.

MISSISSIPPI. See STATE GOVERNMENT.

MISSOURI. See STATE GOVERNMENT.

MITTERRAND, FRANÇOIS (1916-   ), a long-time socialist, was elected president of France on May 10, 1981. His election marked a shift to the left in French politics and the end of 23 years of right wing and right-centrist rule in the Fifth Republic, established by Charles De Gaulle in 1958. See FRANCE.

François Maurice Mitterrand was born on Oct. 26, 1916, in Jarnac in southwestern France. He graduated from the University of Paris in 1938 and served in the French Army from 1939 to 1940, during World War II. He was captured by the Germans and held a prisoner of war for 18 months before escaping. He fought in the French Resistance until France was liberated in 1944.

The new president has been active in French politics since 1946, when he was elected to the National Assembly. He served in that body until his election as president, except for the years 1959 to 1962, when he was a senator. Mitterrand held numerous Cabinet posts. He ran unsuccessfully for the presidency in 1965 against De Gaulle and against Valéry Giscard d'Estaing in 1974.

Mitterrand was secretary-general of the Socialist Party from 1971 to January 1981 and has written several books about socialism.   Edward G. Nash

MONACO. See EUROPE (Facts in Brief Table).

MONGOLIA. See ASIA.

MONTANA. See STATE GOVERNMENT.

MONTREAL in 1981 tried to struggle back from blows dealt to its economy by restrictive language laws passed by the province of Quebec. Residents of the city were also hard hit by sharply higher property taxes enacted to finance the debt remaining on facilities built for the 1976 Summer Olympic Games.

Language Laws. In 1981, the final provision of legislation that was enacted in 1977 to make French the chief language in all aspects of Quebec life went into effect. It bars the display of any public or commercial sign in English. Two other provisions had gone into effect earlier. A 1977 provision stipulates that most Quebec children must be educated in French, and a 1978 provision requires that all legal communications originating in Quebec be in French.

The language laws have driven many English-speaking businesses and residents from Montreal. In addition, firms based in the city have been unable to recruit skilled workers from the United States, Great Britain, or Australia or from the other Canadian provinces because these potential employees are unwilling to have their children educated solely in French. Moreover, service firms and shops may not advertise in English. They thus cannot reach the English-speaking residents, who still comprise nearly 30 per cent of the city's population. Of Canada's 300 largest companies, only 60 were headquartered in Montreal in 1981, a 30 per cent decline since 1976.

The exodus of English-speakers from Montreal has resulted in a 34 per cent decline in new construction since 1976. In 1976, building permits were issued for new construction valued at $1.76-billion (Canadian dollars; $1=U.S. 84 cents as of Dec. 31, 1981). By 1981, the figure had dropped to an estimated $1.16 billion.

Montreal's Total Debt stood at $1.04 billion in 1981, up slightly from 1980. To help reduce this deficit, the city enacted unusually high property taxes. In 1981, the tax on a Montreal house valued at $50,000 totaled $1,600 — about 60 per cent more than the tax on comparable houses in other Canadian cities.

Much of Montreal's debt was attributed to expenditures on facilities for the 1976 Summer Olympics. The most costly single facility — the $800-million sports stadium — still had no roof in 1981, though engineers had warned city officials that the stadium might collapse without the addition of a $150-million roof.

City officials in 1981 announced plans to spend $151 million on other capital and construction projects in 1982 — a 53 per cent increase over 1981. The city plans to pay for the projects with $21-million in subsidies from the province of Quebec and with $130 million borrowed on international money markets.

On the Brighter Side, investment in Montreal's manufacturing industry reached $825 million in 1981, up $100 million from 1980. The city's aerospace industry in particular enjoyed a boom, with sales of $1.2 billion in 1981 – an increase of 50 per cent since 1979.

Higher fuel prices gave the Port of Montreal its best year since 1945. The inland port attracted shippers who wanted to get their products as close to market as possible on ships, which use fuel more efficiently than trucks or trains and thus have comparatively low freight rates.

Labor Problems continued to plague Montreal in 1981. A nationwide postal strike, in which the militant Montreal chapter of the Canadian Union of Postal Workers played a major part, held up all mail delivery from June 29 to August 10. The strike cost the national economy an estimated $3 billion.

Montreal was also still reeling in 1981 from a bitter 41-day municipal strike in 1980 that left the city without garbage collection, snow removal, or other maintenance services. Under the terms of the settlement, the 5,600 workers received an average 21 per cent pay increase in 1981. In addition, the city was required to compensate supervisory personnel who were injured or had property damaged during the strike.   Kendal Windeyer

See also CANADA; QUEBEC. In WORLD BOOK, see MONTREAL.

MOROCCO. Hopes for an end to Morocco's five-year war with the Polisario Front guerrillas fighting for independence of the Western Sahara brightened in July 1981. Mediation by the Organization of African Unity produced a provisional cease-fire agreement in July after King Hassan II said his government would accept the results of a referendum in the disputed territory. The people there could choose between independence and continued Moroccan rule, he said. Previously Hassan had insisted that the Western Sahara was historically part of Morocco and had refused to negotiate with the Polisario.

On October 13, however, guerrilla units armed with missile-equipped tanks attacked Guelta Zemmour, Morocco's main Saharan base. Hassan said the attack, which came from Mauritanian territory, restored to Morocco "a total freedom of action." The attack left the referendum's status in doubt. In November, the Polisario Front said it had occupied Guelta Zemmour and Bir Anzaran, another outpost.

Economic Woes. The end of the Saharan war would bring considerable relief to a Moroccan economy hard-hit by severe drought and the high cost of military preparedness. Because of the drought, grain production was down 50 per cent, and 30 per cent of the livestock were lost. The International Monetary Fund granted Morocco a stand-by credit of $1.2 billion, but it criticized the country for its low agricultural growth rate of 2 per cent annually, unnecessarily high subsidies for basic foodstuffs, and poor long-range planning in the vital phosphate industry.

Aside from heavy military expenditures, Morocco's principal economic weakness continued to be its dependence on oil imports. In January, the government committed $1 billion to a program to extract petroleum from oil shale. Phosphate prices were increased from $32 to $52 per short ton (0.9 metric ton) to pay the investment costs.

Price Hikes Cause Riots. On June 20 and 21, rioting broke out in Casablanca during a general strike protesting sharp price increases set by the government on such basic foods as tea, sugar, milk, and coffee. Police and army units restored order, but not until 66 people were dead and 110 injured, according to official figures. The government blamed the riots on the opposition Socialist Union of Popular Forces (USFP), the only political party that had refused to join the "national reconciliation" of 1977. About 1,000 USFP members were arrested. In July, 11 USFP leaders were sentenced to prison. Apparently recognizing the economic justice of the riots, the government cut the price increases in half.   William Spencer

See also AFRICA (Facts in Brief Table). In WORLD BOOK, see MOROCCO; OIL SHALE.

MOTION PICTURES. For the motion-picture industry, 1981 was a year of contradictory trends. Usually, ticket sales follow a worldwide trend. If the movies have a good year at the box office in one country, the industry can expect to do well in other countries. The same pattern holds for the number of motion pictures produced in a given year. Production volume expands and contracts fairly uniformly. However, attendance and production volume varied considerably from country to country in 1981.

In Great Britain, for example, ticket sales continued to dwindle. In Italy, however, which had lost about 50 per cent of its moviegoing audience over a four-year period, a sharp drop in attendance had leveled off. Ticket sales had also faltered in France in recent years, but attendance increased about 5 per cent in 1981. Attendance was also up in West Germany, though production declined. The reverse was true in such countries as Mexico and Japan, where attendance was down, but the number of films being made was on the rise.

Complicating the situation further were the varied fortunes of United States films in other countries. In Japan, for instance, U.S. imports fared much worse than usual, while domestic films increased their share of the market from 47 per cent to 54 per cent. And in Italy, for the first time in years, domestic rather than U.S. films accounted

Harrison Ford as archaeologist and adventurer
Indiana Jones defends himself and a friend
in the blockbuster *Raiders of the Lost Ark.*

for a majority of the tickets sold. American films
retained their drawing power in West Germany,
however, accounting for 54 per cent of revenues.

The Fate of Foreign Films in the United States
also changed. West German films had been highly
acclaimed in previous years, but they made a poor
showing in 1981. Even *Lili Marleen*, a World War II
romance directed by the prestigious Rainer Werner
Fassbinder, generated little critical or box-office
interest.

Australian films, too, had much less impact than
in 1980. Of the several imported, only one managed to find some following – Peter Weir's *Gallipoli*,
a lavish production about Australia's tragic participation in the famous World War I battle. But the
film's reception was far below that of the earlier
Breaker Morant and *My Brilliant Career*.

Perennially popular Italian films performed with
even less distinction. Federico Fellini's amusing,
surreal *City of Women* had been extremely successful
in Italy and sparked great interest at the Cannes
International Film Festival in France, but its reception in the United States was mild. However,
the French produced several fairly well-received
imports. The most popular was François Truffaut's

The most significant import and the year's most important film, however, was none of these. Ironically, it was *Napoleon*, a 54-year-old silent classic, much of whose footage was believed lost. *Napoleon* was the work of Abel Gance, who died on November 10. The film was legendary for sequences that required simultaneous projection on three screens. Film historian Kevin Brownlow painstakingly reconstructed the 4½-hour epic, and Carmine Coppola composed and conducted a new score.

Napoleon was booked into Radio City Music Hall in New York City for three days in January, with tickets set at an astounding $25. Contrary to expectations, the huge house was not only sold out, but audiences were so enthusiastic that the run was extended. After the Radio City run, *Napoleon* played in major cities throughout the United States. It became the highest-grossing foreign film of 1981, with receipts of more than $6 million.

Ups and Downs. A truly extraordinary work, *Napoleon* seemed even more extraordinary in contrast to the drab products surrounding it. The films released in the first five months of 1981 were so poor that ticket sales hit a 10-year low during the normally lucrative spring-vacation period.

However, in a turnaround typical of the unstable year, sales shot up during the next four months. The two highest-grossing weeks in movie history were registered during June. By September, industry experts were predicting that 1981 might well break the record high gross of $2.9 billion set in 1979.

Sales plummeted again in October and November, however, and the optimism faded. Christmas promised some relief but held little hope for a cure. It seemed likely that 1981's gross, adjusted for inflation, would fall a few percentage points short of that of 1980, thus continuing 1980's downward spiral.

Heavy Hitters. Nevertheless, 1981 had its blockbusters. The most notable was *Raiders of the Lost Ark*. It was conceived and produced by George Lucas, who had produced *Star Wars*, and directed by Steven Spielberg, famous for *Jaws*. *Raiders* was a witty, expensive version of the action-packed movie serials of the 1930s and 1940s. The film was released in June and took in $125 million during the summer season. The summer's other box-office bonanza was *Superman II*, which grossed over $100-million. Critics said that *Superman II* was better than its predecessor. Also contributing generously to summer receipts was the year's James Bond movie, *For Your Eyes Only*. Critics reviewed the film unfavorably, but it managed to earn close to $40-million.

Several comedies were popular at the box office. They included *Stripes*, starring Bill Murray, television's "Saturday Night Live" star; *Arthur*, an old-fashioned romance featuring Dudley Moore and

The Last Metro, a sentimental drama about theatrical life during the German occupation of France in World War II. The film earned more than $3-million at U.S. box offices.

British movies, after years of artistic decline, suddenly found new vigor. Robert Enders' *Stevie*, a delicate film featuring superb performances by Glenda Jackson as poet Stevie Smith and Mona Washbourne as her aunt, won unanimous acclaim. And so did Hugh Hudson's *Chariots of Fire*, a moving exploration of the motivations of two track stars at the 1924 Olympic Games. Also of considerable interest were Polish director Andrzej Wajda's *Man of Marble* and its sequel, *Man of Iron*, timely films about the problems of Polish workers.

The man of steel smashed the movie industry's box-office record for a single week's ticket sales as *Superman II* earned $24 million.

Liza Minnelli; *The Four Seasons*, a domestic comedy about three middle-aged couples, written by and starring Alan Alda; and *Time Bandits*, a Monty Python spoof.

Young and Old. All the money-makers, except for *Arthur* and *The Four Seasons*, were aimed at the youth market. But more movies than usual were directed toward mature audiences: *On Golden Pond*, starring Katharine Hepburn, Henry Fonda, and Jane Fonda, and depicting the difficulties of coming to terms with old age; *Ghost Story*, a thriller with venerable actors Melvyn Douglas, Douglas Fairbanks, Jr., Fred Astaire, and John Houseman; and *Atlantic City*, celebrating an old-time numbers runner, superbly played by Burt Lancaster, and his dreams of days of yore. Even *Mommie Dearest*, the highly melodramatic Joan Crawford biography with an overstated but compelling performance by Faye Dunaway, seemed clearly addressed to moviegoers who could recall the old-time star.

The year seemed to have more than its share of lightweight entertainment, though just as many of the films were serious in intentions. These included Sidney Lumet's flawed but powerful *Prince of the City*, based on the true story of a New York City policeman who agrees to become an informer, and *Whose Life Is It Anyway?*, an adaptation of the play about a quadriplegic, with a brilliant performance by Richard Dreyfuss. In a similarly serious vein, but greatly disappointing, was *True Confessions*, a pretentious police story with existential overtones that wasted the talents of Robert De Niro and Robert Duvall.

Adaptations. *True Confessions* was based on John Gregory Dunne's respected novel. But the finest adaptation and one of the year's few superior films was *The French Lieutenant's Woman*, an American-British production. Playwright Harold Pinter adapted John Fowles's best seller on Victorian manners and mores. The result was both highly romantic in tone and complex and suggestive in structure. Actress Meryl Streep turned in an impeccable performance. *Ragtime*, in contrast, emerged as the most disappointing film of the year. Director Milos Forman and scenarist Michael Weller not only missed the tone and import of E. L. Doctorow's novel but also created a thoroughly lifeless work.

Beatty's Baby. *Ragtime* and *The French Lieutenant's Woman* were large-scale productions, as were *Raiders of the Lost Ark* and *Superman II*. None, however, came close in size and scope to the long-awaited *Reds*, starring Warren Beatty, who also produced and directed the film. An epic romance set against the background of the Russian Revolution and inspired by the lives of John Reed and Louise Bryant (played by Diane Keaton), this exquisitely mounted movie was dismissed by some critics, highly praised by others, and emerged as the most

Alan Alda wrote, directed, and starred with Carol Burnett in *The Four Seasons*, a motion picture about the relationships among three couples.

controversial film of the year. In December, it was voted best picture of the year by the New York Film Critics Circle.

Some of the controversy over *Reds* was predictably political. The Communist revolutionary Reed struck some critics as an inappropriate hero for an American epic. But much of the controversy was inspired by the film's astounding $33-million cost. In the wake of the 1980 *Heaven's Gate* disaster, general sentiment was strongly against such extravagant productions.

Sympathy lay instead with the low-budget features, some of which were made for less than $1-million. Among these were *Heartland*, an independent feature about a pioneer woman; and *Ticket to Heaven*, a movie about religious cults in California. And herein lay perhaps the year's greatest contradiction. For despite the fact that the industry had sworn to tighten its belt, and the public had indicated strong dissatisfaction with Hollywood's wasteful expenditures, movies themselves seemed to be getting bigger, longer, and more costly. And it was precisely these hugely scaled productions that moviegoers selected to attend and turned into blockbuster money-makers.   Joy Gould Boyum

See also AWARDS AND PRIZES (Arts Awards); DE NIRO, ROBERT; SPACEK, SISSY. In WORLD BOOK, see MOTION PICTURE.

MOZAMBIQUE. See AFRICA.

MUBARAK, MOHAMED HOSNI (1928-   ), became president of Egypt on Oct. 14, 1981. He succeeded Anwar el-Sadat, who was assassinated on October 6. Like Sadat, Mubarak was considered a staunch anti-Communist and a friend of the United States. See EGYPT.

Mubarak was born on May 4, 1928, in the province of Minufiya in northeastern Egypt. He graduated from Egypt's national military academy in 1949 and joined the Egyptian Air Force. He trained as a pilot at the Air Force Academy and then took advanced flight training in Russia. Sadat first met him in the early 1950s, when Mubarak was a young bomber pilot.

Mubarak was appointed chief of staff of the air force in 1969 and became its commander in 1972. As commander, he helped plan and direct a successful surprise attack against Israel on Oct. 6, 1973, the Jewish holiday of Yom Kippur. Mubarak's handling of the air battle in the resulting war, called the October War or the Yom Kippur War, helped him gain national prominence. During the fighting, Egypt regained the Suez Canal and other Egyptian territory that had been seized by Israel. Sadat appointed Mubarak vice-president of Egypt on April 15, 1975.

Mubarak enjoys playing squash and reading. He and his wife, Suzanne, live in Heliopolis, a suburb of Cairo, Egypt. They have two sons.   Sara Dreyfuss

MUSEUM

MUSEUM. Federal budget cuts and other changes in government policies affected nearly all museums in the United States during 1981. The Administration of President Ronald Reagan reduced the budgets of the Institute of Museum Services, the National Endowment for the Arts, the National Endowment for the Humanities, and the science-education programs of the National Science Foundation. Changes in federal tax laws affecting charitable donations, capital gains, and inheritances threatened to discourage private donations to museums. Changes in the federal government's program of revenue sharing also reduced the ability of state and local governments to fund museums.

Museums responded to these policy changes by stepping up efforts to win support in both the public and private sectors. In keeping with the philosophy of the new Administration, museums worked to gain more support from private sources to compensate for lessening federal support. Individual museums adjusted to their new financial situations by reassessing their priorities and carrying on long-range planning.

"Rodin Rediscovered," the largest show ever dedicated to French sculptor Auguste Rodin, was held at the National Gallery of Art in Washington, D.C. The show featured nearly 400 of Rodin's works, as well as a reconstruction of a Paris salon of the 1870s.

Professional Standards continued to be a major emphasis of the American Association of Museums (AAM). The AAM's accreditation program had accredited or reaccredited nearly 500 museums by 1981. To help smaller museums qualify for accreditation, the AAM began a Museum Assessment Program with the cooperation of other museum organizations and funding from the Institute of Museum Services.

The U.S. arm of the International Council of Museums, AAM/ICOM, initiated International Partnership Among Museums, the first structured exchange of staff members between U.S. and foreign museums. The group's Technical Assistance Program also offers advice on foreign museum building projects.

New Buildings. The Boston Museum of Fine Arts opened its new West Wing, designed by architect I. M. Pei, on July 22. The new wing provides galleries for the museum's permanent collection of 20th century art and for traveling exhibits. In New York City, the Asia Society dedicated its new headquarters, Asia House, on April 14. The building has space for the John D. Rockefeller III collection of Asian art and for loan exhibits. Discovery Place, a new science museum in Charlotte, N.C., opened on October 31. The San Antonio Art Museum opened in the renovated Lone Star Brewery on February 28.   Kenneth Starr

In WORLD BOOK, see MUSEUM.

MUSIC, CLASSICAL. Musicians in the United States in 1981 sought to restore cuts that were made in appropriations for the National Endowment for the Arts as part of President Ronald Reagan's effort to reduce the federal budget. The President, while expressing his support for the arts, insisted that the arts should rely more heavily on private funding. The battle was fought vigorously on Capitol Hill by artists from every field. Among them was soprano Leontyne Price, who sang her testimony ("Save the performing arts, arts that I love") before a congressional committee to the tune of Irving Berlin's "God Bless America." Price received a standing ovation, but the cutting continued and America's musical organizations faced a tighter financial squeeze and the prospect of more curtailments and cancellations.

In 1981, labor disputes disrupted the seasons of the Kansas City Philharmonic and the Baltimore Symphony. Musicians insisted on more money to keep up with the cost of living, and management pleaded for mercy because their ledgers were all in red ink. The New Jersey Symphony, silenced since August 1980, began a shortened season in November 1981. The Detroit Symphony announced that its reserve funds were wiped out and reported a $1-million deficit.

Musicians and managements sought new approaches to fund-raising. Radio marathons became popular. Radio syndication spread, bringing opera and orchestra performances to millions around the country and extra funds to the performers. The Metropolitan Opera in New York City called upon renowned pianist Vladimir Horowitz to play a benefit recital. The Milwaukee Symphony took its act into the neighborhoods to gain new audience support, and the Denver Symphony played in Mile High Stadium. At Lincoln Center for the Performing Arts in New York City, such show-business personalities as Mickey Rooney and Ruby Keeler helped stage "Broadway Salutes the New York City Opera."

Another possible solution to the financial crunch began to emerge as cultural cable-television services debuted: Bravo! in December 1980, ABC Alpha Repertory Television Services (ARTS) in April 1981, and CBS Cable in October. CBS featured a festival of the music of Ludwig van Beethoven performed by the Vienna Philharmonic under the direction of Leonard Bernstein. ABC ARTS presented several opera performances from La Scala Opera House in Milan, Italy. More cultural programming was planned for 1982 and 1983, and the cable services are expected to bring needed funds to struggling arts organizations.

Notes on Musicians. Johanna Meyer, a Chicago soprano, became the first American to sing the part of Isolde in *Tristan and Isolde* at the Bayreuth Wagner Festival in West Germany. In April, the son

398

Andre-Michel Schub, left, of New York City receives his first-place award at
the sixth Van Cliburn International Piano Competition, in Fort Worth, Tex.

and grandson of Russian composer Dimitri Shostakovich defected to the West. Son Maxim, a conductor, and grandson Dimitri, a pianist, asked for
political asylum after a performance with the Soviet Radio and Television Symphony Orchestra in
Fürth, West Germany. They settled in New York
City.

Lorin Maazel, music director of the Cleveland
Orchestra, was named general manager of Austria's Vienna State Opera. Ardis Krainik became
general manager of the Lyric Opera of Chicago,
replacing Carol Fox, cofounder of the organization,
who resigned in January and died in July. Philippe
Entremont was appointed music director of the
New Orleans Philharmonic, and the Milwaukee
Symphony named composer Lukas Foss as its new
music director. Kurt Herbert Adler marked his
28th and last year as general manager of the San
Francisco Opera.

Protest and Discovery. In October, protests
caused conductor Zubin Mehta to halt a performance in Tel Aviv-Yafo, Israel, of the Prelude and
Love Death from *Tristan and Isolde*. Richard Wagner's music has been banned by the Israel Philharmonic since 1939 because it was a favorite of Adolf
Hitler's and was played in Nazi concentration and
death camps. Mehta had hoped to end the ban.

No such controversy surrounded the May 1981
performance in a castle near Munich, West Germa-

ny, of a newly discovered symphony by Wolfgang
Amadeus Mozart. The *Symphony in F major* had
been found earlier in the year in a packet of manuscripts and had been sold to the Bavarian State
Library. Mozart wrote the work in 1765, when he
was 9 years old. The symphony premièred in the
United States in July at the White House.

Premières. Three composers conducted world
premières of their own works: Stanislaw Skro-
waczewski conducted his *Clarinet Concerto* with the
Minnesota Orchestra. Rafael Kubelik conducted
his *Orphikon: Music in Three Movements*, and Ravi
Shankar performed his new *Concerto No. 2 for Sitar*,
with the New York Philharmonic.

It was a big year for premières. Works introduced by instrumental groups included: Donald
Erb's *Concerto for Keyboards and Orchestra* (Akron,
Ohio) and *Trumpet Concerto* (Baltimore); Theodore
Antoniou's *Circle of Thanatos and Genesis*, Peter Max-
well Davies' *Symphony No. 2*, Steven Starer's *Violin
Concerto*, and Roger Sessions' *Concerto for Orchestra*
(all in Boston); Ned Rorem's *Double Concerto for
Cello and Piano* (Cincinnati); Morton Gould's *Burch-
field Gallery* (Cleveland); Martin Scot Kosins' *Ren-
dezvous Concerto* (Detroit); David Noon's *Star-
Captains* (Houston); Billy Taylor's *Let Us Make a
Joyful Noise to the Lord* (Indianapolis); and Ezra
Laderman's *Symphony No. 4* (Los Angeles) and *Concerto for String Quartet* (Pittsburgh). Other new

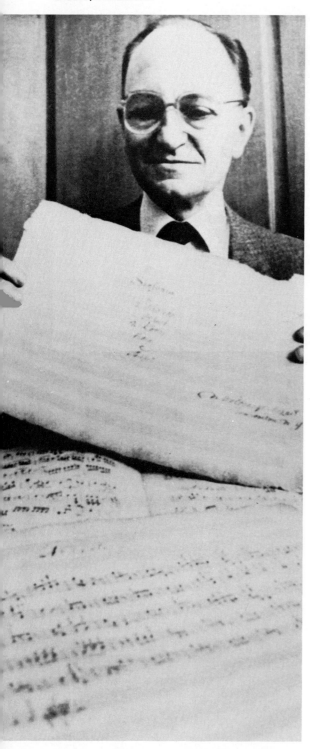

A newly discovered symphony by Wolfgang Amadeus Mozart, composed when he was 9, is displayed at the Bavarian State Library in Munich, West Germany.

works were Heinz Werner Zimmermann's *Missa Profana* and Ivana Themmen's *Guitar Concerto* (Minnesota); George Walker's *In Praise of Folly* (New York City); Peter Mennin's *Flute Concerto* (New York City) and *Sinfonia Capricciosa* (Washington, D.C.); David Del Tredici's *All in the Golden Afternoon* (Philadelphia); Eugene Phillips' *Prelude, Adagio, and Toccata* (Pittsburgh); and John Williams' *Violin Concerto,* David Amram's *Violin Concerto,* and Rhian Samuel's *Elegy-Symphony* (St. Louis).

New Operas drawn from literature were Carlisle Floyd's *Willie Stark,* based on *All the King's Men* by Robert Penn Warren and presented in April by the Houston Opera; *Miss Havisham's Wedding Night* by Dominick Argento, based on Charles Dickens' *Great Expectations* and introduced in May by the Minnesota Opera in Minneapolis; and Iain Hamilton's *Anna Karenina,* based on the novel by Leo Tolstoy and produced in May by the English National Opera in London. Other noteworthy opera premières included Karlheinz Stockhausen's *Thursday* (Milan, April); Mauricio Kagel's *Aus Deutschland* (Berlin, May); and Friedrich Gerha's *Network* (Vienna, May) and *Baal* (Salzburg, August).

United States opera companies continued to surprise audiences with imaginative programming. The Michigan Opera presented the American première of *Anoush* by Armenian composer Armen Tigranian. The Opera Theatre of St. Louis offered two Western Hemisphere premières: Minoru Miki's *An Actor's Revenge* and Frederick Delius' last opera, *Fennimore and Gerda.* Two Philip Glass operas had their U.S. introductions: his madrigal opera *The Panther* by the Houston Opera and his *Satyagraha* at the Brooklyn Academy of Music in New York City.

The San Francisco Opera opened its first summer season with the U.S. première of Aribert Reimann's *Lear.* Composer George Antheil finally had his 1930 jazz opera, *Transatlantic, the People's Choice,* produced in his homeland – in fact, in his hometown of Trenton, N.J. Two rarely heard works by Gioacchino Rossini gained attention: *Mosé,* given its American première by the Opèra Company of Philadelphia; and *La Donna del Lago,* given in Houston in its first U.S. staging in 150 years. Dimitri Shostakovich's *Lady Macbeth of the Mtsensk District* was introduced in San Francisco, as was Karol Szymanowski's *Król Roger* in Seattle.

David Del Tredici's new piece, *Final Alice,* as recorded by Sir Georg Solti and the Chicago Symphony, became in October the first new work to top the classical album sales chart of *Record World* magazine. Another first was the concurrent appearance on best-seller lists of two books on musical figures – *Pavarotti – My Own Story* by Luciano Pavarotti and *Maria Callas: The Woman Behind the Legend* by Arianna Stassinopoulos.   Peter P. Jacobi

In WORLD BOOK, see MUSIC; OPERA.

MUSIC, POPULAR. Lionel Richie, a member of the Commodores soul group, achieved success on his own in 1981. While still performing with the veteran singing group, he branched out to become a successful pop-music producer and songwriter, working with Kenny Rogers and Diana Ross. Richie wrote such hits for the Commodores as "Easy," "Lady You Bring Me Up," and "Three Times a Lady." He produced Kenny Rogers' LP "Share Your Love" and wrote four of the album's songs, including the hit "I Don't Need You." He also composed the title tune for the movie *Endless Love* and sang it with Diana Ross on her recording.

Members of other prominent groups also launched individual projects, causing some concern that the creative glue that keeps pop bands together was losing its hold. The most talked-about example was Mick Fleetwood, founder of Fleetwood Mac. He went to Ghana to record his first solo LP, which included both African rhythms and pop music. Two other members of the band, Stevie Nicks and Lindsey Buckingham, also released solo LP's. Nicks's "Bella Donna" became the number-two single in the United States.

Don Henley and Glenn Frey of the Eagles, Michael McDonald of the Doobie Brothers, and Donald Fagen of Steely Dan all recorded solo LP's. Carl Wilson of the Beach Boys, charging his associates with a lack of creativity, also became a soloist. Deborah Harry of the band Blondie succeeded with a solo LP. On the other hand, Grace Slick, who left Jefferson Starship in 1980 to work alone, rejoined the group to record and tour.

New Stars. Kim Carnes and Judy Kay (Juice) Newton became celebrities in 1981. Carnes succeeded with her husky interpretation of the offbeat novelty song "Bette Davis Eyes." Newton's success in the country pop field came after 10 years of struggle. Her hits ranged from a remake of the 1968 song "Angel of the Morning" to a new rockabilly tune, "Queen of Hearts." Another woman, blind vocalist Terri Gibbs, made a name for herself in the country field with the popular single "Somebody's Knockin'."

Surf Music and Beach Music exploded anew in different parts of the United States. The surf music revival centered in the San Diego area. Singer Dick Dale and several local surf bands led the revival of this brand of 1960s rock music. Beach music, a blend of rhythm and blues tempos and lyrics from the 1940s through the 1960s, gained renewed popularity in Southern States.

The Rolling Stones returned to the United States after a three-year absence. They played to huge crowds during a 25-city tour from September through December.

Pop music's first U.S. television soap opera hero was Rick Springfield, an Australian singer turned actor. While playing Noah Drake on "General

Singer and television star Barbara Mandrell won the Academy of Country Music's Entertainer of the Year award in Los Angeles in April.

Hospital," he found time to record for RCA Corporation and to produce the hit LP numbers "Working Class Dog" and "Jessie's Girl."

Comebacks. A major surprise in 1981 was the reunion of Paul Simon and Art Garfunkel after 11 years of performing separately. In September, they performed a free concert in New York City's Central Park, drawing nearly 500,000 people. The Carpenters ended their self-imposed exile from show business, begun in 1978, with the LP "Made in America" and the single "Touch Me When We're Dancing." The Baja Marimba Band also made a comeback, starting its own BJ label and releasing the single "Shout." The group had been second only to the Tijuana Brass as a successful A&M Records act in the 1960s.

The punk-rock fad faded as negative reactions to the violence and antisocial behavior of some of its followers overcame the dynamics of the music. Disco, however, rebounded from the loss in popularity it suffered during 1980. Disco night spots began playing rock and country music in addition to disco recordings. Several clubs added big-name live entertainment.

Yoko Ono, John Lennon's widow, finally had a hit LP in 1981. After three previous solo albums, her Geffen LP, "Season of Love," drew international recognition.

The Oak Ridge Boys, a veteran touring group of

Mick Jagger, lead singer of the Rolling Stones, belts out a rock
number during the British group's 12-week tour of the United States.

gospel singers, entered the pop field. After succeeding with the single "Elvira," they began playing major outdoor shows.

Reggae. Bob Marley's death from lung cancer in May drew attention to his crusade to bring Jamaican reggae music to the United States. The music's hybrid sound of Caribbean rhythms and urban lyrics, with their references to revolution, were not well received by U.S. radio stations that specialize in playing so-called black music. Nonetheless, Marley had remained a top concert attraction.

After Marley's death, a controversy sprang up with the release of an LP of his earlier works. Rita Marley, the singer's widow, said that the album did not reflect his true ability, but Island Records, the releasing company, denied that the LP would injure Marley's name and standing.

Music of the Swing Era infatuated many pop artists in 1981. Joe Jackson recorded an LP of big-band tunes of the 1930s and 1940s. Rock producer Richard Perry cut a modernized version of big-band music called "Swing," featuring three vocalists and a group of top contemporary studio musicians, notably jazz-and-rock saxophonist Tom Scott.

Christopher Cross surprised everyone by winning five Grammy Awards: top album, record, and song of the year; best new artist; and best arrangement for a vocalist.

Jazz. The most discussed jazz event of the year was the return of trumpeter Miles Davis after a five-year absence because of illness. Davis drew large crowds and mixed reviews at concerts in the United States and Japan.

Jazz festivals continued to proliferate. The two-night Playboy Jazz Festival drew capacity audiences to the Hollywood Bowl in Los Angeles. The Monterey Jazz Festival in California was sold out for the first time in its 24-year history. The 11-day Kool Jazz Festival in New York City was almost as successful. Its producer, George Wein, also presented a festival at Newport, R.I., for the first time since 1971.

Tania Maria, a Brazilian-born singer and pianist, was praised for her lively personality and creative style at U.S. festivals and clubs. Also new to the United States was Canada's leading orchestra, Rob McConnell and the Boss Brass Big Band, which drew unanimous critical praise at Monterey and other California locales. Air — a trio consisting of a saxophonist, bassist, and drummer — remained the most respected avant-garde group, playing new and compelling mixtures of melodic jazz and free-form music.   Leonard Feather and Eliot Tiegel

See also AWARDS AND PRIZES (Arts Awards); RECORDINGS. In WORLD BOOK, see COUNTRY AND WESTERN MUSIC; JAZZ; POPULAR MUSIC; ROCK MUSIC.

NAMIBIA. Early in 1981, negotiations for Namibia's independence from South Africa suffered a setback. On January 13, South Africa rejected as "premature" an independence plan presented by the "contact group" of five Western nations – the United States, Canada, France, Great Britain, and West Germany – that worked together on Namibian negotiations since 1978.

UN Plan. The contact group developed a plan for the United Nations (UN) to supervise a cease-fire in the war between Namibian nationalists and South Africa. The plan also called for UN supervision of elections for an assembly that would draw up a constitution in preparation for Namibia's independence. South Africa's government objected to the plan, however. It feared that the UN would not be impartial but would favor the South West Africa People's Organization (SWAPO), the majority Namibian black political party. SWAPO has waged a guerrilla war against South African rule since 1966.

On April 23, however, the contact group agreed to a new peace plan designed to overcome South Africa's objections. The plan provided that the UN peacekeeping forces would consist mostly of soldiers from white Western nations. It also guaranteed representation in the constitutional assembly of Namibia's white minority, who comprise about 12 per cent of the total population, as well as other ethnic groups. Approval of the constitution would require a two-thirds vote of the assembly. The previous plan had given the majority party complete authority in drafting the constitution.

A delegation from the contact group met on October 26 with representatives of 16 minority Namibian political parties, both black and white. At the meeting, most parties approved the new plan. South Africa's government reportedly also endorsed it, at least in principle, on October 29. SWAPO's leader, Sam Nujoma, announced his party's acceptance of the new Western plan on November 19.

Angola's Involvement. The United States, in an effort to gain South Africa's support for the contact group's plan, proposed in April that the approximately 15,000 to 20,000 Cuban troops stationed in Angola be withdrawn as a condition of the peace plan. Angolan leaders had previously stated that, with Namibia independent under a democratically elected government, there would be no need for Cuban soldiers in their country. They maintained that Cuban forces were there only to defend Angola against South African attacks, launched from Namibia, on SWAPO bases and other military facilities in southern Angola. The most damaging South African incursion lasted from August 24 to September 4. See ANGOLA.   J. Dixon Esseks

See also AFRICA (Facts in Brief Table); SOUTH AFRICA. In WORLD BOOK, see NAMIBIA.

NATIONAL PTA (NATIONAL CONGRESS OF PARENTS AND TEACHERS) in 1981 issued its sixth *TV Program Review Guide*, which gave its evaluations of prime-time television programs seen during fall 1980. The 10 shows considered best for family viewing were "Those Amazing Animals," "Little House on the Prairie," "60 Minutes," "Lou Grant," "The Waltons," "NBC Magazine," "20/20," "Disney's Wonderful World," "Eight Is Enough," and CBS Specials.

New President. At the 1981 National PTA Convention held in Orlando, Fla., in May, members elected Mary Ann Leveridge of East Bernard, Tex., to serve as president for 1981 and 1982. Reaffirming the PTA's role as advocate for children and young people, the new president included among her priorities strengthening the parent-teacher alliance and building community participation in programs dealing with drug abuse, nutrition, health, and safety. The PTA conducted Parent Seminars on Adolescent Sexuality in cooperation with the March of Dimes Birth Defects Foundation in 29 states.   Virginia E. Anderson

In WORLD BOOK, see NATIONAL CONGRESS OF PARENTS AND TEACHERS; PARENT-TEACHER ORGANIZATIONS.

NAVY. See ARMED FORCES.

NEBRASKA. See STATE GOVERNMENT.

NEPAL. See ASIA.

NETHERLANDS. A general election on May 26, 1981, left the Netherlands without a majority government until September. The Christian Democrats and Liberals, parties in the ruling center-right coalition, lost their two-seat majority in the 150-member Second Chamber of the States-General (lower house of parliament).

Prime Minister Andreas A. M. van Agt's Christian Democrats lost one seat, finishing with 48. The Liberals dropped from 28 seats to 26, while the Labor Party slipped from 53 to 44 seats. Democrats '66, a left wing party, gained nine seats for a total of 17.

Nuclear Missiles. The main issue in the election was whether to allow the North Atlantic Treaty Organization to install nuclear missiles on Dutch soil. The Netherlands had said that it would give an answer by the end of 1981. Van Agt wanted to install the missiles, but members of his party opposed him in the States-General. The Labor Party also opposed the missiles. Other major issues included nuclear power, rising unemployment, and the level of social benefits.

New Government. The Christian Democrats, Labor, and Democrats '66 finally agreed to form a center-left coalition that would say as little as possible on the missile issue. The coalition took office on September 11 with Van Agt as prime minister. Observers felt the coalition had an uncer-

Dutch police use water cannons in February to scatter demonstrators protesting the eviction of squatters from empty houses in Amsterdam.

NEW BRUNSWICK. Premier Richard B. Hatfield's Progressive Conservative (PC) administration continued to govern New Brunswick during 1981. Liberal Party member Robert McCready switched allegiance several times, finally proclaiming himself a Conservative in July. The Hatfield government pressed ahead with legislation to give fishermen collective-bargaining power. It also proposed to change the public school system to provide group as well as individual rights for the French-speaking Acadians who make up 33 per cent of New Brunswick's population.

As one of only two provincial premiers who early supported the federal constitutional proposals, Hatfield was involved in much activity outside New Brunswick during 1981. Critics demanded that he pay more attention to the province's problems, especially financial ones. The April 7 budget revealed that the province faced a deficit of $10-million (Canadian dollars; $1=U.S. 84 cents as of Dec. 31, 1981) on expenditures of $1.96 billion. The province increased taxes on cigarettes and corporate profits but eliminated taxes on wood stoves and furnaces.   David M. L. Farr

In WORLD BOOK, see NEW BRUNSWICK.
NEW HAMPSHIRE. See STATE GOVERNMENT.
NEW JERSEY. See STATE GOVERNMENT.
NEW MEXICO. See STATE GOVERNMENT.
NEW YORK. See NEW YORK CITY; STATE GOV'T.

NEW YORK CITY. Edward I. Koch, the first New York City mayor to capture both Democratic and Republican nominations, easily won a second term on Nov. 3, 1981. Koch's victory reflected his success in overseeing New York City's financial recovery from a brush with municipal bankruptcy in 1975. Koch promised that his second-term priorities would be to improve municipal services and to repair the city's deteriorating facilities.

However, the election of all 43 City Council members, originally scheduled for November 3, was postponed indefinitely after the United States Department of Justice ruled on October 27 that the council's redistricting plan did "not fairly reflect minority voting strength" in the boroughs of Manhattan, Brooklyn, and the Bronx. The election was the first in a Northern state to be canceled under the Voting Rights Act of 1965. The City Council subsequently agreed not to contest the ruling. At year-end, no acceptable plan had been drafted and no election date set.

Out of the Red. The city finished the 1981 fiscal year on June 30 with its first truly balanced budget ever. The budget surplus of $128 million was attributed to high receipts from taxes imposed upon sales, personal income, and businesses. As a result, the city was able to spend an additional $193-million to compensate for $272 million in federal budget cuts.

tain future because the three parties could not agree on the issues of nuclear power, unemployment, and public spending cuts. Van Agt wanted to cut spending, while Joop den Uyl, the Labor Party leader, wanted to decrease unemployment.

A disagreement over unemployment and spending broke up the coalition, and so the government resigned on October 16. However, the three parties reached a compromise on November 4. They agreed to levy an income tax in 1982 to raise $205-million for the creation of jobs. Van Agt withdrew the coalition's resignation on November 5.

China Protested the Netherlands' decision in February to sell two submarines to Taiwan. Van Agt said that China had known of the deal in advance, but China denied it. China had recalled its ambassador to the Netherlands because of the dispute in October 1980. On February 27, China ordered the Dutch to recall their ambassador.

Aid to Industry. The Netherlands decided in 1981 how to invest its income from selling gas to foreign firms. The government would loan up to $536 million to industry during 1981 and 1982, at interest rates based on company profits. An additional $248 million would be set aside to cover defaults and lost interest.   Kenneth Brown

See also EUROPE (Facts in Brief Table). In WORLD BOOK, see NETHERLANDS.
NEVADA. See STATE GOVERNMENT.

New York City's financial health enabled it on March 24 to hold the first public sale of long-term bonds in six years. However, the city's economy began to show signs of sluggishness toward the end of 1981. Hotel occupancy and retail sales – major factors in the city's rebound from the mid-1970s recession – declined.

Fares and Wages. Subway and bus fares rose from 60 cents to 75 cents on July 3. But a projected $1 fare was averted when the state legislature enacted a $792-million transit-tax package. The sales tax increased by a quarter of a percentage point in New York City and seven suburban counties served by mass or commuter transit. The city's sales tax rose to 8.25 per cent as a result.

The city made progress in "gain-sharing" productivity agreements with municipal labor unions. Sanitation workers on new two-person trash-collection trucks were given a productivity bonus of $11 per work shift after agreeing to meet productivity goals in teams of two, rather than three.

Building Breakthroughs. The city made breakthroughs on three long-stalled construction projects in 1981. On November 4, Olympia & York Properties Limited of Toronto, Canada, signed an agreement to develop a $1-billion commercial complex, Battery Park City, on 14 acres (5.7 hectares) of landfill on the Lower West Side of Manhattan. Ground was broken on December 3. The new complex will include six towers with 6 million square feet (560,000 square meters) of office space and other facilities. Battery Park City is expected to provide 25,000 permanent jobs and form the nucleus of a new downtown Manhattan community. On August 16, the city announced that it had signed a contract with six teams of developers to build 2,000 housing units in Battery Park City.

As the first step in a push to rebuild another part of Manhattan's West Side, the city announced a plan to raze parts of deteriorated streets and targeted new office, hotel, and retail construction for the Times Square area. On September 8, three state and city agencies reported that 30 developers had submitted bids on a plan to redevelop West 42nd Street. The plan involves returning architecturally valuable motion-picture houses to their original function as theaters for stage plays.

Mayor Koch and New York Governor Hugh L. Carey on July 31 agreed on terms for Westway – a 4.2-mile (6.8-kilometer) federal highway surrounded by parklands – between the lower tip of Manhattan and West 42nd Street. Westway's cost was estimated in 1979 at $1.8 billion – 90 per cent of which is to come from the federal Highway Trust Fund. President Ronald Reagan on September 7 delivered a check for $85 million as a down payment on the highway.   Owen Moritz

See also CITY. In WORLD BOOK, see NEW YORK CITY.

New Yorkers welcome the freed hostages home from Iran as they parade down Broadway on January 30 in a hail of ticker tape and confetti.

NEW ZEALAND suffered unprecedented civil disorders from July through September 1981 caused by a tour of the South African Springboks Rugby team. More than 1,000 protesters were arrested and hundreds of police and demonstrators injured. Opponents claimed the tour signified acceptance of South Africa's *apartheid* (separate development) system, but supporters claimed private sports contacts with South Africa should be retained.

The Economy continued a slow recovery in 1981 after five difficult years, with real output growing by about 2 per cent. However, inflation at about 15 per cent in 1981 and unemployment of 3 per cent were unacceptably high. A keystone of economic recovery was the government's growth strategy, or "Think Big" policy, based on a few large investment projects designed to reduce dependence on energy imports and strengthen the nation's export base. Major projects included a synthetic oil plant, an aluminum smelter, and expansion of New Zealand's only oil refinery and steel plant. The total investment involved was estimated at more than $3.5 billion. At the end of 1981, however, some projects were running into economic and environmental difficulty, and the feasibility of financing them was questioned. The government also continued its emphasis on forestry development as a major export industry to supplement the tradition-al major exports – wool, meat, and dairy products.

The 1981 budget, designed to stimulate economic activity, provided for an increase in government outlays of 17 per cent to $14 billion and a deficit before borrowing of $2 billion. The budget reduced income taxes slightly but increased taxes on land, alcohol, and tobacco.

The government tried unsuccessfully to negotiate a policy with the trade union movement under which unions would restrain wage demands in return for tax cuts. Government-union relations remained tense throughout the year, and a series of large anti-union demonstrations indicated widespread public feeling against union activities.

The General Election on November 29 narrowly returned the incumbent conservative National Party led by Prime Minister Robert D. Muldoon, who had held that office since 1975. His party won 47 of the 92 seats in the unicameral House of Representatives. The result had been difficult to predict because of considerable voter dissatisfaction with both major parties. The moderate-left opposition Labour Party, led by former Prime Minister Wallace E. Rowling, and the Social Credit Party, led by Bruce E. Beetham, received much support during the campaign.   David A. Shand

See also ASIA (Facts in Brief Table). In WORLD BOOK, see NEW ZEALAND.

Christchurch police arrest many of the 500 anti-apartheid demonstrators who protested the appearance of South Africa's Springboks Rugby team in August.

NEWFOUNDLAND. Federal draft legislation presented in Ottawa, Ont., in June 1981 offered a way out of the long-standing dispute between Newfoundland and Quebec over the export of hydroelectric power from Labrador's Churchill Falls. The legislation would authorize the National Energy Board to grant Newfoundland a power corridor through Quebec, which would eliminate the need to use that province as an intermediary in the sale of Newfoundland's power.

Newfoundland suffered a disastrous fishing season for the second successive year. With one-fourth of all workers earning at least part of their income from fishing, the cod catch was only half the government quota.

Premier Brian Peckford's Progressive Conservative government, holding a 33-19 majority over the Liberals, established new taxes on tobacco, gasoline, and licenses in its April 14 budget.

The Canadian Coast Guard found the remains of a secret German weather station near Cape Chidley on the northern tip of Labrador in July. The ruined station was probably established in late 1943 by a crew from a German submarine. This discovery provided the first indication that Germany set up any installation in North America during World War II. David M. L. Farr

See also CANADA. In WORLD BOOK, see NEWFOUNDLAND.

NEWSPAPER. The shaky economy in the United States in 1981 held down circulation and advertising revenues and took heavy tolls on three metropolitan dailies. The 128-year-old *Washington Star* in Washington, D.C., published its last edition on August 7. It had suffered losses of more than $35-million since its purchase by Time Incorporated in 1978. The morning *New York Daily News* folded its year-old afternoon *Tonight* edition on August 28. Union employees at the Philadelphia *Bulletin* on August 16 agreed to wage concessions of $4.9-million and the layoff of 113 workers in an attempt to salvage the 134-year-old afternoon daily paper. The four-year-old *Philadelphia Journal,* however, published its last edition on December 16 after unions refused to accept pay cuts and layoffs.

Electronic Publishing attracted dozens of newspapers during 1981. By November, approximately 30 dailies were transmitting some form of printed news over cable television, and many others were awaiting approval from the Federal Trade Commission to operate low-power television stations. Field Enterprises, Incorporated, publishers of the *Chicago Sun-Times,* in September test-marketed the nation's first British teletext system – a subscription news service – in Chicago. Dow Jones & Company, publisher of *The Wall Street Journal* and the *Danbury* (Conn.) *News-Times,* announced plans to test the French teletext system in Danbury.

The *Washington Star* carries its own obituary in August as it becomes the latest in a series of major afternoon newspapers to cease publication.

NICARAGUA

Acquisitions and Mergers. Australian publisher Rupert Murdoch on February 13 purchased *The Times* of London and its affiliated publications from the International Thomson Organization Limited for $15 million after reaching an agreement with employees' unions. Murdoch agreed to provide $13.6 million in severance payments for 563 staff members whose jobs would be eliminated by *The Times*'s switch to electronic typesetting in 1981.

Gannett Company in Rochester, N.Y., owner of the largest newspaper chain in the United States, made several additions to its roster in 1981. It acquired *The Times* of Gainesville, Ga.; *The Knoxville* (Tenn.) *Journal; El Diario-La Prensa*, New York City's Hispanic daily; and *The Norwich* (Conn.) *Bulletin.*

The Des Moines (Iowa) Register and Tribune Company and the Minneapolis (Minn.) Star and Tribune Company on September 9 announced plans to merge. The two communications companies, owned by separate branches of one family, have annual revenues of about $300 million.

Pulitzer Declined. *The Washington Post* in April declined to accept a Pulitzer Prize awarded to reporter Janet Cooke for an article about an 8-year-old heroin addict. Cooke resigned from the paper after admitting that she had fabricated many details in the story.   Celeste Huenergard

In WORLD BOOK, see JOURNALISM; NEWSPAPER.

NICARAGUA. On Sept. 9, 1981, Daniel Ortega Saavedra, head of Nicaragua's leftist Government of National Reconstruction Junta, declared a one-year state of social and economic emergency. He announced further nationalizations of private companies and belt-tightening steps for the nation's economy. These steps included a 5 per cent cut in the $87-million national budget, a 10 per cent cut in government subsidies for food and public transportation, and a tax of 30 to 100 per cent on luxury imports. The junta also threatened jail terms for acts of "economic sabotage," said to include strikes by workers and price hikes by manufacturers without government approval.

The downward swing of the Nicaraguan economy was documented in 1981 by the World Bank, an agency of the United Nations, which estimated that 10 years might be needed to bring the country back to the 1977 level of per capita production. A growing international disenchantment with Nicaragua's revolution was evidenced by the failure of any foreign leader to attend the second anniversary celebration of the revolution. United States aid to Nicaragua was suspended in January because of Nicaragua's alleged involvement in arms shipments to rebels in El Salvador.   Nathan A. Haverstock

See also LATIN AMERICA (Facts in Brief Table). In WORLD BOOK, see NICARAGUA.

NIGER. See AFRICA.

NIGERIA. During 1981, Nigeria's political system was strained by conflicts between and within political parties. On July 7, the Nigerian People's Party (NPP) withdrew from its alliance with President Shehu Shagari's National Party of Nigeria (NPN), the party with the largest representation in parliament. However, six of the 77 NPP deputies and two of the ministerial appointees decided to continue supporting the Shagari government. Neither the NPN nor the NPP held a majority of seats in either house of parliament. But, as a two-party coalition, they had controlled the legislature since 1979.

The state of Kaduna – where the NPN held two-thirds of the legislative seats but Alhaji Musa Balarabe of the People's Redemption Party (PRP) held the governorship – was also a site of continued conflict between the executive and legislative branches of government. As a result, the NPN impeached Balarabe on June 23. His successor, an NPN member, was sworn in on July 5.

The PRP also held the governorship in the state of Kano. However, Kano's governor, Mohammed Abubakar Rimi, belonged to the Eagle Faction, a left wing group within his party. After Rimi sent an allegedly insulting note to the emir of Kano – an influential Muslim leader – rioting broke out on July 10. Two people were reported killed, and fire damaged many properties, including the state radio station and the legislative building. Opponents of Rimi and the Eagle Faction were believed to have instigated the riots to embarrass him.

More Serious Disturbances occurred in the city of Kano from Dec. 18, 1980, to Jan. 3, 1981. During that period, about 1,000 people were killed in fighting involving security forces, members of a fanatical Muslim sect called Yen Izla, and other residents of Kano. The violence erupted when police tried to prevent a confrontation between sect members and orthodox Muslim worshipers at Kano's grand mosque. Cultists reportedly killed four policemen and rampaged through the city, attacking residents with daggers, knives, and bows and arrows. They then retreated to a part of the city they had fortified so well that regular army units had to dislodge them with artillery, machine guns, and bazookas. Yen Izla leader Muhammadu Marwa died in the fighting. Some government sources believed Libya backed the insurgents.

Oil Prices and Problems in 1981 had a particularly serious impact on Nigeria, which derives 90 per cent of its export earnings from petroleum. As demand for oil weakened, oil exports dropped from an average of 1.9 million barrels per day (bpd) in January to fewer than 500,000 bpd in September. Nigeria's agency for marketing oil tried to increase sales by lowering prices. On August 26, Nigeria cut its price to $36 per barrel.   J. Dixon Esseks

See also AFRICA (Facts in Brief Table). In WORLD BOOK, see NIGERIA.

NIXON, RICHARD MILHOUS (1913-   ), 37th President of the United States, remained in the public eye in 1981, as he traveled to the Middle East, lost a court battle, and tried to establish a library for his presidential papers.

Foreign Travel. As a member of the U.S. delegation to the funeral on October 10 of Egyptian President Anwar el-Sadat, Nixon traveled to Cairo on the presidential plane, *Air Force One*, with former Presidents Gerald R. Ford and Jimmy Carter. Afterward, Nixon undertook a personal trip through the Middle East and North Africa, conferring with leaders in Jordan, Saudi Arabia, Tunisia, and Morocco. White House spokespersons insisted that Nixon carried no official messages from the U.S. government and was traveling as a private citizen.

Legal Difficulties continued to plague the former President. In a 4-4 ruling on June 22, the Supreme Court of the United States affirmed a 1979 U.S. Court of Appeals ruling that rejected Nixon's claim of absolute immunity for himself and three others — Henry A. Kissinger, former secretary of state and national security adviser; former Attorney General John N. Mitchell; and H. R. Haldeman, former White House chief of staff. The four were charged with unconstitutional surveillance for the placing in 1969 of an illegal wiretap on the home telephone of Morton Halperin, a former Kissinger aide, in an attempt to trace news leaks. The case, *Kissinger v. Halperin,* was sent to a U.S. District Court in Washington, D.C., for trial. If they lose, Nixon and the other defendants will have to pay damages to the Halperin family.

Papers filed on August 13 in connection with the Halperin case revealed that in 1980 Nixon paid A. Ernest Fitzgerald, an official of the Department of Defense, $144,000 in an out-of-court settlement. Fitzgerald sued the former President because he was fired for exposing military accounting errors during the Nixon Administration.

New Homes. The former President also ran into difficulty in his efforts to find a home for his presidential papers at Duke University in Durham, N.C., where he received his law degree. Despite protests from students and faculty, the executive committee of the university's board of trustees voted on September 4 to provide land next to the campus for a Nixon presidential library.

On June 10, Nixon and his wife, Pat, purchased a 15-room house in Saddle River, N.J., for more than $1 million. They moved into their new home during the summer. The Nixons' New York City town house was sold to the Syrian government for $2.6 million in September. They had bought the home for $750,000 in 1979.   Carol L. Thompson

In WORLD BOOK, see NIXON, RICHARD M.

Former President Richard M. Nixon complies with an autograph request before addressing a Republican fund-raiser in Columbus, Ohio, in February.

NOBEL PRIZES

NOBEL PRIZES in peace, literature, economics, and various sciences were awarded in 1981 by the Norwegian *Storting* (parliament) in Oslo and by the Royal Academy of Science, the Caroline Institute, and the Swedish Academy of Literature, all in Stockholm, Sweden.

Peace Prize, given in recognition of "the best work for fraternity between nations," was awarded to the Office of the United Nations (UN) High Commissioner for Refugees. In naming the organization, which also had won the Peace Prize in 1954 for its work in post–World War II Europe, the Nobel committee cited the agency's excellent record in dealing with "a veritable flood of human catastrophe and suffering."

Literature Prize was won by Elias Canetti, 76, a writer of Sephardic Jewish ancestry who was born in Bulgaria; was educated in Switzerland, Germany, and Austria; and lives in London. This cosmopolitan background evidently contributed to his work, as the Swedish Academy of Literature cited Canetti for his "writings marked by a broad outlook, a wealth of ideas and artistic power." The academy also said he had "one native land, and that is the German language." Canetti's most important works are a novel, *Die Blendung* (published in 1935 and translated as *Auto-da-Fé* and *The Tower of Babel*), and *Masse und Macht* (*Crowds and Power*,

1960), an examination of mass political movements. Canetti, described as "a very private man," also has written plays, essays, and memoirs.

Chemistry Prize was shared by a Japanese and an American who developed similar theories concerning chemical reactions though separated by miles of space and decades of time. Kenichi Fukui, 63, professor of physical chemistry at Kyoto University in Japan, began his work in the 1950s and was largely ignored by his traditionalist colleagues. Roald Hoffman, 44, John A. Newman Professor of Physical Science at Cornell University in Ithaca, N.Y., on the other hand, was encouraged by two men who themselves had won the Nobel Prize for Chemistry: William N. Lipscomb, Jr., in 1976; and Robert B. Woodward, in 1965. The two 1981 prizewinners each pioneered a way of applying the theories of quantum mechanics to predict the course of chemical reactions.

Economics Prize went to James Tobin, 63, a professor of economics at Yale University in New Haven, Conn., for his analysis of the relationship between financial markets, such as stocks and bonds, and the "real" markets involved in consumption, prices, production, and investment. The Nobel selection committee said Tobin's pioneering studies, technically known as Portfolio Selection Theory, "unquestionably inspired substantial research during the 1970s on the effects of monetary policy, the implications of budget deficits, and stabilization policy in general."

Physics Prize rewarded two Americans and a Swede for their work using different types of spectroscopy as an analytical tool for investigating the properties of matter. Nicolaas Bloembergen, 61, of Harvard University in Cambridge, Mass., and Arthur L. Schawlow, 60, of Stanford University in Palo Alto, Calif., were cited "for their contribution to the development of laser spectroscopy." Kai M. Siegbahn, 63, of Uppsala University in Sweden was chosen for "his contribution to the development of high-resolution electron spectroscopy."

Physiology or Medicine Prize was shared by three scientists whose research is essential to understanding the organization and function of the brain. The work of Roger W. Sperry, 68, of the California Institute of Technology in Pasadena, established that the functions performed by the right and left hemispheres of the human brain are different from, and sometimes independent of, each other. David H. Hubel, 55, and Torsten N. Wiesel, 57, have worked together since 1959 at Harvard University studying the way the brain handles visual information.   Marsha F. Goldsmith

In WORLD BOOK, see NOBEL PRIZES.
NORTH ATLANTIC TREATY ORGANIZATION (NATO). See EUROPE.
NORTH CAROLINA. See STATE GOVERNMENT.
NORTH DAKOTA. See STATE GOVERNMENT.

Literature winner Elias Canetti was rewarded for writings that "are held together by a most original and vigorously profiled personality."

NORTHERN IRELAND was dominated in 1981 by anguish over a hunger-strike campaign by jailed members of the Irish Republican Army (IRA) that lasted 216 days. During that time, 10 men starved themselves to death against a background of violence unusual even by Northern Irish standards.

The hunger strikes began on March 1 as an attempt by imprisoned IRA members to force the British government to restore their "special category" status, which Great Britain abolished in March 1976. The men in the Maze Prison near Belfast claimed five "rights": to wear their own clothes; to do no compulsory prison work and have free time for education; to associate freely with other "political" prisoners; to receive one letter, parcel, or visit per week; and to have reduced sentences for good behavior, lost through prison protests, restored.

Bobby Sands, a 25-year-old prisoner and the first hunger striker, was elected to the British House of Commons in a by-election in Fermanagh and South Tyrone on April 9. Without ever being able to take his seat, Sands died on May 5, the 66th day of his fast. He became an IRA hero, and 50,000 people attended his funeral. On May 12, Francis Hughes became the second hunger striker to die, and eight more followed. They were Raymond McCreesh and Patrick (Patsy) O'Hara, who died on May 21; Joseph McDonnell, on July 8; Martin Hurson, on July 13; Kevin Lynch, on July 31; Kieran Doherty, on August 2; Thomas McElwee, on August 8; and Michael Devine, on August 20.

The British government refused to make any concessions, but it indicated some changes would be made in the prison regime if the fasts ceased. The hunger strikes were called off on October 3. James Prior, the new secretary of state for Northern Ireland, promptly announced partial concessions but said they would apply to all 2,500 prisoners in the Maze.

Another Death followed the end of the hunger strike. On November 14, IRA gunmen in Belfast killed Robert J. Bradford, a Protestant member of the British Parliament. Bradford, an outspoken critic of the IRA, was a member of Northern Ireland's Democratic Unionist Party (DUP). Two days later, three DUP members, including Ian Paisley, its head, were ousted from the House of Commons in London and suspended after they shouted abuse during a hearing on the Bradford killing. On January 21, gunmen killed Sir Norman Stronge, speaker of Northern Ireland's Parliament for 24 years, and his son James.   Ian Mather

See also GREAT BRITAIN; IRELAND. In WORLD BOOK, see NORTHERN IRELAND.

Members of the outlawed Irish Republican Army join Bobby Sands's family at his funeral in May in Belfast. He was the first of 10 hunger strikers to die.

NORTHWEST TERRITORIES oil pipelines were again in the news in 1981. On April 22, Canada's National Energy Board approved the construction of a 538-mile (866-kilometer) pipeline to carry south the products of an expanded field at Norman Wells. Designed to transport up to 25,000 barrels of oil and natural gas liquids per day, the line will run to Zama City in northern Alberta, where it will link with the southern distribution system. The line will cover about half the route that would have been followed by the Mackenzie River pipeline rejected by a royal commission in 1977. Native land claims must be settled before it is begun. An ambitious mining project on Little Cornwallis Island in the Arctic, 75 miles (120 kilometers) from the North Magnetic Pole, neared completion. The lead and zinc mine's concentrator, powerhouse, and offices were constructed on a 100- by 400-foot (30- by 120-meter) barge, which was then towed about 2,500 miles (4,000 kilometers) from Quebec to the Arctic island in August. When it reached the island, the barge was lowered onto a prepared site and enclosed with landfill to protect it from the ice-filled Arctic Ocean. The mine, to employ 250 people, is expected to produce over 225,000 short tons (204,000 metric tons) of lead and zinc concentrates annually. David M. L. Farr

See also CANADA. In WORLD BOOK, see NORTHWEST TERRITORIES.

NORWAY moved to the right in general elections on Sept. 13 and 14, 1981, rejecting Prime Minister Gro Harlem Brundtland's Labor Party government. Brundtland had become Norway's first woman prime minister on February 4, when she replaced Odvar Nordli, who resigned. See BRUNDTLAND, GRO HARLEM.

Nonsocialist parties won 85 of the 155 seats in the *Storting* (parliament). The Conservative Party, Christian People's Party, and Center Party had a total of 80 seats and tried to form a majority government. However, they could not agree on abortion and oil policies. Kaare Willoch formed a minority government of Conservatives in October. See WILLOCH, KAARE.

Tax Relief. Willoch had promised to lower taxes but maintain Norway's social programs and increase defense spending by 4 per cent per year over inflation. His first job was to reduce the country's 15 per cent inflation rate. On August 7, the minority Labor government had frozen all domestic prices until the end of 1981.

Gas Pipeline. Norway's state-owned oil company, Statoil, asked the government to develop a natural-gas pipeline system in the North Sea. Great Britain was already building a $3.6-billion project that will link 12 North Sea oil fields, but Statoil wanted an independent system. Statoil plans to deliver gases suitable for production of

Gro Harlem Brundtland became Norway's first woman prime minister in February, but was rejected in national elections in September.

petrochemicals to Norway and to pipe heating gases to Emden, West Germany. Oil and gas provide about 15 per cent of Norway's gross national product and 25 per cent of its exports. Norway expects eventually to double its production to 90 million metric tons (100 million short tons) per year.

Norway and Sweden signed a 20-year economic agreement on March 26. Under the pact's terms, Sweden will provide Norway with the equivalent of 2 million kilowatt hours of electricity per year in return for 3 million metric tons (3.3 million short tons) of Norwegian oil.

Nuclear-Free Zone. Foreign ministers of Norway, Sweden, and Finland met in Stockholm, Sweden, on September 6 to discuss setting up a so-called Nordic nuclear-free zone. President Urho Kekkonen of Finland first mentioned establishing the zone in 1963. Countries in such a zone would not allow nuclear missiles to be installed on their soil. The 1979 North Atlantic Treaty Organization (NATO) agreement on land-based missiles in Europe did not call for placing these weapons in Norway, the only one of the three nations that is a NATO member.

The Storting voted by 54 votes to 24 on June 3 to ban professional boxing in Norway.   Kenneth Brown

See also EUROPE (Facts in Brief Table). In WORLD BOOK, see NORWAY.

NOVA SCOTIA gave strong support to Premier John Buchanan's government in an election on Oct. 6, 1981, awarding the Progressive Conservatives 37 of the 52 seats in the legislature. All of Buchanan's ministers were re-elected. The Liberals lost 7 per cent of their popular vote from 1978, electing 13 members. The New Democratic Party increased its share of the popular vote but elected only Alexa McDonough, the party's new leader. One independent also won office.

The federal government promised new life to the Sydney Steel Corporation on March 20 when it announced the financing of 80 per cent of a two-year modernization project for the 80-year-old plant on Cape Breton Island. The project will cost a total of $96 million (Canadian dollars; $1=U.S. 84 cents as of Dec. 31, 1981).

A strike in the Cape Breton coal mines that lasted almost three months was settled on October 8 when 4,000 miners accepted a new contract raising basic weekly wages from $295 to $350. The provincial budget of April 10 revealed an operating deficit of $139 million, three times as large as the 1980 figure. Much of the deficit resulted from the start of the largest job-creation projects in Nova Scotia's history.   David M. L. Farr

See also CANADA. In WORLD BOOK, see NOVA SCOTIA.

NUCLEAR ENERGY. See ENERGY.

NUTRITION. Massive reductions in the funding of federal nutrition programs were among the budget cuts passed by the Congress of the United States on July 31, 1981. The spending cuts, which President Ronald Reagan called "the most sweeping cutbacks in the history of the federal budget," included reductions of more than $3 billion in food-stamp and child-nutrition programs for the fiscal year starting Oct. 1, 1981.

Diet and Cancer. Diet accounts for 35 per cent of cancer deaths in the United States, according to British cancer specialists Sir Richard Doll and Richard Peto of Oxford University. In a report published in June 1981, the two scientists recommended intensive research to determine exactly which dietary modifications would be most beneficial against cancer.

A study presented at a 1981 workshop on cholesterol and death from causes other than heart disease failed to support earlier reports that low levels of cholesterol in the blood may cause an increased risk of death from cancer. The workshop was sponsored by the National Cancer Institute and the National Heart, Lung and Blood Institute of the National Institutes of Health. Experts at the workshop unanimously recommended that persons with elevated blood cholesterol levels, which have been linked to heart disease, should try to reduce those levels through a diet that is low in saturated fat and cholesterol.

Nutrition and Birth Defects. In July, the Surgeon General's office issued a strongly worded warning to women to avoid alcohol completely if they are pregnant or even considering pregnancy. Alcohol consumption during pregnancy increases the risk of spontaneous abortion. It also may result in the birth of babies with low birth weight or a cluster of mental and physical defects known as fetal alcohol syndrome.

In September 1980, investigators at the United States Food and Drug Administration (FDA) had reported finding birth defects and delayed skeletal development in the offspring of rats fed various doses of caffeine during pregnancy. Other researchers, in a study published in June 1981, reported three children with missing fingers and toes, a rare birth defect. The children had been born to women who were heavy coffee drinkers during pregnancy. Although the researchers lacked conclusive evidence linking caffeine to birth defects in human beings, the FDA recommended that pregnant women avoid caffeine. The substance is found in many over-the-counter drugs as well as in coffee, tea, chocolate, and a number of soft drinks.

An Infant-Formula Marketing Code gained approval on May 21 at a meeting of the World Health Organization (WHO), a specialized agency of the United Nations (UN). The code recommended voluntary guidelines to regulate marketing of commercially prepared formulas. Bottle-feeding with such formulas has replaced breast-feeding as the most common method of feeding babies in many countries. But formula-feeding is hazardous if poverty and unsanitary conditions cause parents to use overdiluted or contaminated formula. It may result in infant malnutrition, diarrhea, and even death. The United States, claiming the marketing code would unfairly restrict private companies and limit advertisers' freedom of speech, was the only nation of 119 at the World Health Assembly to oppose the code. It was sponsored by WHO and the UN Children's Fund (UNICEF) and supported by consumer, religious, and health groups from many nations. In June, the U.S. Senate and House of Representatives passed resolutions urging the Reagan Administration to support the basic aims of the code and to cooperate with other nations in implementing it.

World Food Day took place on Oct. 16, 1981, with special events and activities throughout the world. It was the first time such a day had been designated internationally to focus public attention on the severity of world hunger. The UN Food and Agriculture Organization sponsored the observance.   Jean Weininger

See also FOOD. In WORLD BOOK, see DIET; FOOD; FOOD SUPPLY; NUTRITION.

OCEAN. The Deep Sea Drilling Project (DSDP) ship *Glomar Challenger* completed one of its most challenging expeditions in January 1981. Scientists worked for 60 days at a drill site 300 miles (480 kilometers) east of Fort Lauderdale, Fla., to retrieve the oldest rocks ever taken from the deep ocean. The rocks were buried beneath 3 miles (4.8 kilometers) of water and 1 mile (1.6 kilometers) of young sediment. The scientists estimated that the samples are 150 million years old. Thus, they would have existed when the North Atlantic Ocean began to form just after North America started to drift away from Africa.

To reach the deeply buried layers, the scientists lowered a re-entry cone – a pipe attached to a large cone-shaped platform – to the sea floor. They then drilled with a *casing string* (a series of encased, connected pipes) that was 1,708 feet (521 meters) long – the longest casing string ever run into the sea floor. The researchers used six drill bits to reach the final depth of 5,404 feet (1,647 meters).

A funding squeeze prompted the National Science Foundation (NSF) on August 5 to propose retiring the *Challenger* in 1983. The NSF provides most of the money for the DSDP. The *Challenger*'s replacement, the more powerful and more expensive *Glomar Explorer,* would concentrate its drilling in offshore areas. Scientists had hoped that both

A safe recovered in 1981 from the luxury liner *Andrea Doria,* which sank in 1956, arrives in the United States. It was to be opened on live TV in 1982.

the DSDP and the *Explorer*'s offshore drilling program could be supported in the 1980s.

Deep-Sea Vents. The first deep-sea hot spring, or vent, off the United States coast was discovered in September during a 10-day voyage of the oceanographic research ship *S. P. Lee*. Researchers found the vent on the Juan de Fuca Ridge, off the Oregon coast, at a depth of 8,000 feet (2,440 meters). Similar vents were found near the Galapagos Islands in 1976, off Mexico in 1978, and along the East Pacific Rise off Peru in 1981.

As hot, mineral-rich water rises from these vents and cools, metallic sulfides solidify and fall to the ocean floor. The *S. P. Lee*'s dredge recovered about 2 short tons (1.8 metric tons) of material containing 20 pounds (9 kilograms) of minerals rich in zinc and silver. The environment around the vents produces strange living things, such as colonies of sulfur-consuming bacteria that inhabit giant worms. The bacteria provide food and energy for the worms in a manner never before observed. Some scientists consider these finds the greatest discovery of animal communities in the history of biology. Others rank the vents among the major geologic discoveries of the decade.

Scientists aboard a submersible craft explored the area around the Galapagos vents in August. They found vast deposits of copper-rich sulfides.

Georges Bank Drilling. After six years of bitter legal wrangles, oil companies began exploratory drilling on July 24 on Georges Bank off Massachusetts—one of North America's richest fisheries. Starting in the mid-1970s, New England fishing crews, state governments, and environmentalists sued to block or delay drilling until tighter safeguards were enacted. The Department of the Interior and the Department of Commerce, along with 22 oil companies, argued that the need for domestic energy supplies outweighed the risk to fishing. They said that present environmental safeguards would protect the fish and their habitat from oil pollution.

Sea Law Blocked. The United States announced on March 3 that it would delay approval of an international agreement on sea law drawn up at the ninth session of the United Nations (UN) Law of the Sea Conference in 1980. The Reagan Administration wanted to review negotiations that had taken place before it took office.

The United States presented objections to the agreement at the August session in Geneva, Switzerland. James L. Malone, assistant secretary of state for oceans and environmental affairs, said that the law might harm U.S. mining interests and probably would not pass the U.S. Senate. The delegates then scheduled a "final decision-making session" for 1982.　　　　　Arthur G. Alexiou

In WORLD BOOK, see DEEP SEA DRILLING PROJECT; OCEAN.

O'CONNOR, SANDRA DAY (1930-　　), was sworn in as the first woman justice of the Supreme Court of the United States on Sept. 25, 1981. She had been nominated by President Ronald Reagan on July 7 to replace retiring Associate Justice Potter Stewart. See SUPREME COURT OF THE UNITED STATES (Close-Up).

Sandra Day was born on March 26, 1930, in El Paso, Tex., the daughter of Harry and Ada Mae Day. She spent her early childhood on her family's ranch, the Lazy B, near Duncan, Ariz. She entered Stanford University at the age of 16 and received her bachelor's degree in 1950 and law degree in 1952. She married John J. O'Connor III, a fellow Stanford law student, in 1952.

From 1953 to 1956, O'Connor worked for the U.S. Army in Frankfurt, West Germany. In 1957, she settled in Phoenix and devoted most of the next eight years to her family. In 1965, she entered public life as assistant state attorney general. She was appointed to an unexpired term in the Arizona state Senate in 1969 and was elected to the Senate in 1970 and 1972. In 1974, she was elected to the Superior Court of Maricopa County, Arizona. O'Connor was appointed to the Arizona Court of Appeals in 1979. O'Connor and her husband, a lawyer, have three sons.　　　　Edward G. Nash

OHIO. See STATE GOVERNMENT.

OKLAHOMA. See STATE GOVERNMENT.

OLYMPIC GAMES. The International Olympic Committee (IOC) voted in 1981 to award the 1988 Summer Olympics to Seoul, South Korea, and the 1988 Winter Olympics to Calgary, Canada. The committee had previously awarded the 1984 Summer Olympics to Los Angeles and the 1984 Winter Olympics to Sarajevo, Yugoslavia.

The only candidates for the 1988 Summer Olympics were Seoul and Nagoya, Japan. Three cities—Calgary; Falun, Sweden; and Cortina d'Ampezzo, Italy—bid for the 1988 Winter Olympics.

The committee relaxed its standards of amateurism in 1981, allowing international sports federations to set their own eligibility rules, subject to IOC approval. Responding to that action, the International Amateur Athletic Federation made it permissible for track-and-field athletes to accept payments for endorsing products. The athletes' national federations would hold these payments in escrow and use them for training expenses.

The IOC also helped resolve a dispute between the People's Republic of China and Taiwan. China had refused to join the IOC until the Taiwanese Olympic committee removed the words *Republic of China* from its name, flag, and emblem. In March, Taiwan's Olympic committee agreed to use the name *Taipei* instead.　　　　Frank Litsky

In WORLD BOOK, see OLYMPIC GAMES.

OMAN. See MIDDLE EAST.

ONTARIO. The Progressive Conservatives (PC) in Ontario extended their record as Canada's longest-lived provincial administration on March 19, 1981, when they won a resounding electoral victory, their 12th in 38 years. Led by Premier William G. Davis, in office since 1971, the PC took 70 seats in the legislature. The Liberals won 34; and the New Democratic Party, 21.

The newly elected Davis government hit taxpayers with a tough budget on May 19, 1981. Treasurer Frank Miller brought in higher health-insurance premiums as well as tax increases on personal income, cigarettes, and alcoholic beverages. Taxes on gasoline and cigarettes changed from a flat rate to a percentage, or *ad valorem*, rate.

Ontario entered the petroleum business on October 13, when it announced the purchase of 25 per cent of the shares of Suncor Incorporated (Sunoco) for $650 million (Canadian dollars; $1=U.S. 84 cents as of Dec. 31, 1981). Participation by the Ontario government was intended to attract other Canadian investment in order to bring Canadian ownership in the company to 51 per cent. This change would qualify Suncor for National Energy Policy incentives for further exploration in frontier areas of Canada.   David M. L. Farr

In WORLD BOOK, see ONTARIO.

OPERA. See MUSIC, CLASSICAL.

OREGON. See STATE GOVERNMENT.

PACIFIC ISLANDS. Increasing pressure on France to grant independence to nickel-rich New Caledonia was the major development in the Pacific Islands in 1981. New Caledonia first came into the spotlight in February. Barak Sope, a leading Melanesian politician from newly independent Vanuatu, arrived in New Caledonia for a congress of the Independence Front, a group that champions the rights of New Caledonia's 55,000 native Melanesians. The Melanesians make up 43 per cent of the population; the rest of the people are locally born and immigrant French, Polynesians, and Asians. Although the French Embassy in Vanuatu had granted Sope a visa, he was told in New Caledonia that it was no longer valid. Vanuatu reacted by expelling the French ambassador within 24 hours and cutting the embassy staff. The French, in turn, balked at signing an aid agreement.

Although the aid agreement was later signed and France was asked for a new ambassador, Vanuatu's Prime Minister Walter Lini took every opportunity to press for New Caledonia's independence. At a meeting of the South Pacific Forum — Australia, New Zealand, and the independent Pacific nations — it was decided to send a delegation, led by Fiji's Prime Minister Ratu Sir Kamisese Mara, to Paris to urge President François Mitterrand to decolonize New Caledonia, French Polynesia, and the Wallis and Futuna Islands.

Pierre Declerq, secretary-general of New Caledonia's pro-independence *Union Caledonienne* party, was assassinated by a fellow Frenchman. His murder created new tensions and brought New Caledonia's problems to the notice of the Commonwealth Heads of Government Meeting (CHOGM) in Melbourne, Australia, in October. Later, CHOGM formally welcomed the forum's plan to put pressure on Mitterrand.

Islands Plan Halted. A plan that had been made by the Administration of President Jimmy Carter for the United States to cease administering the Mariana, Caroline, and Marshall islands in 1981 came apart after President Ronald Reagan's inauguration in January. Reagan ordered a "full review" of all agreements on the future status of those islands.

The United States has administered the islands since 1947 as the United Nations (UN) Trust Territory of the Pacific Islands. Since 1969, however, delegates from several island groups have negotiated agreements for various forms of autonomy. For example, the Palau Islands in the Caroline Archipelago became the Republic of Belau on Jan. 1, 1981. The Mariana Islands voted in 1975 to become a commonwealth in "political union" with the United States, and other island groups chose republican and federation status in "free associa-

New Island Nation Born

Facts in Brief on Pacific Island Countries

Country	Population	Government	Monetary Unit*	Exports† (million U.S. $)	Imports† (million U.S. $)
Australia	15,032,000	Governor General Sir Zelman Cowen; Prime Minister Malcolm Fraser	dollar (1 = $1.15)	22,053	20,332
Fiji	657,000	Governor General Ratu Sir George Cakobau; Prime Minister Ratu Sir Kamisese Mara	dollar (1 = $1.12)	350	562
Kiribati	51,000	Governor General Reginald James Wallace; President Ieremia Tabai	Australian dollar	21	18
Nauru	8,000	President Hammer DeRoburt	Australian dollar	50	32
New Zealand	3,156,000	Governor General Sir David Stuart Beattie; Prime Minister Robert D. Muldoon	dollar (1.2 = $1)	5,414	5,464
Papua New Guinea	3,306,000	Governor General Sir Tore Lokoloko; Prime Minister Sir Julius Chan	kina (1 = $1.45)	964	788
Solomon Islands	245,000	Governor General Sir Baddeley Devesi; Prime Minister Solomon Mamaloni	dollar (1 = $1.19)	67	57
Tonga	93,000	King Taufa'ahau Tupou IV; Prime Minister Prince Fatafehi Tu'ipelehake	pa'anga (1 = $1.15)	8	29
Tuvalu	7,000	Governor General Sir Fiatau Penitala Teo; Prime Minister Tomaso Puapua	Australian dollar	0.1	1
Vanuatu	113,000	President Ati George Sokomanu; Prime Minister Walter Lini	Australian dollar & New Hebrides franc	33	45
Western Samoa	161,000	Head of State Malietoa Tanumafili II; Prime Minister Taisi Tupuola Efi	tala (1 = $1.07)	15	61

*Exchange rates as of Dec. 1, 1981. †Latest available data.

tion" with the United States. For most practical purposes, the agreements are already in effect, and the islands are self-governing. But until the UN Security Council approves the agreements and terminates the trusteeship arrangement, the United States will remain the administering power.

Legal Actions. People of the Marshall Islands sued the United States for enormous sums during 1981 in claims relating to nuclear testing in their area. Representatives of Bikini Atoll launched a legal action in March for $450 million, alleging their homeland was twice taken from them illegally. The first time was in 1946 for nuclear tests; the second was in 1979 when their atoll was deemed unsafe because of radiation.

Gold Tooth Mine. The Papua New Guinea government took a 20 per cent interest in a huge mining project at Ok Tedi in the remote Star Mountains near its border with Indonesia. Australian, United States, and West German companies will develop the mine under an agreement signed in March. Geologists say Ok Tedi is shaped like a huge gold-capped tooth with copper roots. Its gold and copper deposits may be 37 million and 414 million short tons (34 million and 376 million metric tons), respectively.   Robert Langdon

In the WORLD BOOK SUPPLEMENT section, see VANUATU. In WORLD BOOK, see PACIFIC ISLANDS.
PAINTING. See VISUAL ARTS.

PAKISTAN was politically unsettled during 1981 as various groups struggled against the military government of President Mohammad Zia-ul-Haq. The Russian Army's presence in neighboring Afghanistan also created problems and deep uneasiness for Pakistan. Russia had invaded Afghanistan in 1979.

President Zia, who had seized power from Prime Minister Zulfikar Ali Bhutto in 1977 and executed him for murder in 1979, continued to postpone elections. Pakistan's last elections had been held in 1977, before Zia's coup. Some of Bhutto's former followers and other opponents of Zia's government formed a group called the Movement for the Restoration of Democracy (MRD). On February 6, the MRD demanded that the government hold elections by May. After large demonstrations, the government arrested several opposition leaders.

On December 24, Zia announced that he would not hold elections. Instead, he established a 350-member council to help him rule Pakistan.

Political Violence. On March 2, three men hijacked a Pakistani airliner with 148 passengers aboard and forced the pilot to fly to Afghanistan, then to Syria. The hijackers threatened to blow up the plane unless the Pakistani government released a number of prisoners, almost all connected with Bhutto's political party. Pakistan agreed on March 12 to release 54 prisoners, and the hijackers surrendered to Syrian authorities on March 14.

Pakistani hijackers give themselves up to Syrian authorities on March 14 after holding a Pakistani plane, its passengers, and its crew since March 2.

Bhutto's son, Murtaza Bhutto, claimed to have organized the hijacking. He said that he headed an organization called Al Zulfikar, which sought the violent overthrow of Zia's government.

The hijacking discredited Zia's opposition. The MRD canceled a nationwide strike scheduled for March 23. Zia had many more opposition leaders arrested. On March 25, Zia fired Chief Justice Anwar ul-Haq of the Supreme Court and eight other judges for refusing to take an oath upholding his authority to change the Constitution or to endorse other powers he claimed to have.

Afghan refugees continued to flood into Pakistan throughout 1981. Zia said on October 28 that the number had reached 2.4 million.

Aid Agreement. On September 15, Pakistan formally accepted a United States offer of $3.2 billion in aid over five years beginning in October 1982. The aid, divided equally between military and economic help, was intended to strengthen Pakistan's defenses against a threat from the Soviet troops in Afghanistan. The United States also promised to speed delivery of 40 F-16 jet fighters that Pakistan had agreed to buy. However, on October 21, the Congress of the United States voted that aid to Pakistan would be halted if the country exploded a nuclear device.   Henry S. Bradsher

See also ASIA (Facts in Brief Table). In WORLD BOOK, see PAKISTAN.

PALEONTOLOGY. A new discovery of mastodon fossils announced in October 1981 indicated that mastodons, the furry prehistoric relatives of living elephants, ranged more widely across North America and lived at higher elevations than paleontologists once thought. Wade E. Miller, chairman of the Department of Geology at Brigham Young University in Provo, Utah, announced the find. Discovered on the Wasatch Plateau south of Price, Utah, the fossils consisted of skulls, ribs, foot bones, and other skeletal remains of two young mastodons. It was the first time mastodons had been found in Utah and the first discovery ever of mastodons at elevations as high as 10,000 feet (3,000 meters). Most have been found in the East and at elevations below 1,000 feet (300 meters).

The Origin of Species. A persistent problem in paleontology has been the absence of transitional forms — that is, fossils that bridge the gaps between species. The British naturalist Charles R. Darwin theorized that new species evolved out of existing ones by gradual changes over long periods of time. Darwin explained the gaps in the fossil record by saying the record was incomplete.

Today, many paleontologists believe that the explanation lies not with the incomplete fossil record but with the way species form. These paleontologists think new species do not develop by gradual, small changes but by rapid, major ones. This

Paleontologists clean the skeletons of prehistoric camels, horses, and rhinoceroses found in a 10-million-year-old fossil bed near Orchard, Nebr.

belief is called the *punctuated equilibrium theory* because it holds that most species go through long periods of equilibrium – during which they remain basically the same – punctuated by sudden bursts of change.

Support for the punctuated equilibrium theory was provided by a study reported in the October 8-14 issue of *Nature* by Peter G. Williamson of the Museum of Comparative Zoology at Harvard University in Cambridge, Mass. Williamson studied fossil freshwater snails and clams in about 400 meters (1,300 feet) of sediment near Lake Turkana (formerly Lake Rudolf) in Kenya. Williamson found that he could trace the history of 13 species of mollusks through successive layers of sediment in the beds. Williamson found no gradual change in any of the species. Instead, each species persisted unchanged through a thick sequence of deposits. When a species did disappear, it would quickly be replaced by a new species apparently derived from the ancestral form. The transitional forms between species occupied only a thin section of deposits, representing perhaps 5,000 to 50,000 years. According to Williamson, this pattern strongly supports the punctuated equilibrium theory.

In a reply to Williamson's work, geneticist J. S. Jones of University College at the University of London pointed out that 5,000 to 50,000 years is not a short time in genetic research. From 5,000 to 50,000 generations of clams and snails could live during that time. Genetic researchers can develop new species in as few as 20 generations.

More Baby Dinosaurs. John R. Horner, a vertebrate paleontologist at Princeton University Natural History Museum in New Jersey, continued to make news with his unprecedented discoveries of dinosaur eggs, babies, and nest sites. Since 1978, Horner and Robert Makela, a high school science teacher from Rudyard, Mont., have spent summers collecting dinosaur fossils in Montana.

In 1981, Horner and Makela found another nest with bones of young duckbill dinosaurs, a nearly complete baby duckbill skeleton (perhaps the first ever found), and an assortment of other duckbill bones. Duckbill dinosaurs, also called *duckbilled dinosaurs* or *hadrosaurs*, were plant-eating creatures with broad bills. The scientists also found bones and eggs of a dinosaur called *Troödon*, which may have been meat-eating.

The collecting site, which was an upland area during the age of dinosaurs, has already produced more baby dinosaur bones than any other place in the world. In the past, most paleontologists looked for dinosaur fossils in areas that were formerly lowlands. Horner suggested that many dinosaurs moved to higher elevations to lay eggs. Ida Thompson

In WORLD BOOK, see DINOSAUR; FOSSIL; PALEONTOLOGY; PREHISTORIC ANIMAL.

PANAMA. The death of National Guard Commander Omar Torrijos Herrera in a plane crash on July 31, 1981, set off a scramble for power in Panama. As head of the country's National Guard, Torrijos had ruled Panama since October 1968, when he took control in a military coup. In 1978, Panama returned to a civilian government, but Torrijos retained most of his power.

The highlight of Torrijos' Administration was the renegotiation of the 1903 treaty that gave the United States control over the Panama Canal Zone. In 1977, the United States and Panama signed treaties to end U.S. control.

Players in the Power Struggle that followed Torrijos' death included senior military officers and the present civilian president, Aristides Royo, whom Torrijos had hand-picked for the job. With real power in Panama concentrated in the National Guard, however, speculation centered on which officer would attempt to fill Torrijos' shoes. The new commander of the 9,000-member National Guard, Colonel Florencio Florez Aguilar, though near retirement age, made several tours of the country and stepped up his schedule of public appearances. His potential challengers included four lieutenant colonels: Rubén Darío Paredes, who served as minister of agricultural development from 1972 to 1978; Armando Contreras, the liaison

officer with the U.S. Southern Command for coordination of the canal's defense; Roberto Díaz Herrera, secretary of the National Guard and a cousin of Torrijos; and Manuel Antonio Noriéga, head of Panama's intelligence services.

In August, the general staff of the National Guard assumed responsibility for decision making in a $2-billion copper-development project at Cerro Colorado. Paredes was named head of the copper-development team. Observers generally saw the National Guard's actions as an attempt to pull the rug out from under President Royo in key decisions.

Canal Traffic. During 1981, Panama became increasingly concerned about competition for canal traffic. An oil pipeline across the Isthmus of Panama, scheduled for completion in 1982, is expected to carry all Alaskan crude oil shipments and reduce transits of the canal by more than 1,000 ships annually. Another challenge to canal traffic is the rail route for containerized cargo that Mexico has nearly completed across its own Isthmus of Tehuantepec. The new rail route is expected to cut the shipment of container cargo through the Panama Canal by 10 per cent. During 1981, Japan reiterated its interest in helping Panama construct a second canal, at sea level.   Nathan A. Haverstock

See also LATIN AMERICA (Facts in Brief Table). In WORLD BOOK, see PANAMA.

PAPANDREOU, ANDREAS (1919-   ), became prime minister of Greece after his Pan Hellenic Socialist Movement (Pasok) defeated Prime Minister George Rallis' New Democracy Party in national elections on Oct. 18, 1981. Papandreou said during his campaign that Greece should end its close relationship with the West. See GREECE.

Andreas George Papandreou was born on Feb. 5, 1919, on the island of Khios. His father, George, was prime minister of Greece from 1963 to 1965.

Andreas Papandreou received his early education in Athens. In 1938, however, his political activities got him into trouble with the military dictatorship, and he fled to the United States. He received a doctor's degree in economics from Harvard University in Cambridge, Mass., in 1943. In 1944, he joined the United States Navy and became a U.S. citizen.

After World War II, Papandreou taught economics in the United States. He renounced his U.S. citizenship in 1964 and ran successfully for the Greek parliament. He became minister of economic coordination in his father's government.

Army officers took over Greece in 1967 and sent Papandreou into exile. He taught in Sweden and Canada and then returned to Greece after democracy was restored there in 1974. In the same year, he was elected to parliament.   Jay Myers

PAPUA NEW GUINEA. See ASIA; PACIFIC ISLANDS.

Mourners line the streets of Panama City as the coffin bearing National Guard Commander Omar Torrijos Herrera is carried to the cemetery.

PARAGUAY. The tightly controlled economy of Paraguay continued to show vigor during 1981. According to figures released at midyear by the United Nations Economic Commission for Latin America, Paraguay's economy was the most dynamic in all Latin America. Ongoing construction at two huge hydroelectric power plants provided plentiful employment in 1981. Paraguay jointly manages one of the plants with neighboring Brazil and the other with neighboring Argentina. When the first stages of the power plants go into operation by 1983, Paraguay will have significantly reduced its dependence on imported oil and become an important exporter of electric power.

An Inflow of Financing from such international institutions as the World Bank and the Inter-American Development Bank also helped Paraguay's economy. Aided by such financing, the country pushed ahead with an impressive array of public works, including road, airport, and telecommunications projects and the construction of a bridge over the Paraguay River at Concepción. The bridge will be named in honor of the nation's long-time ruler, President Alfredo Stroessner.

In 1981, Paraguay budgeted $20 million to increase production on its farms and ranches and $40-million to build more than 80 community health centers and sanatoriums. To improve education, Paraguay invested $30 million to build 60 schools. An additional $80 million has been earmarked for sanitation and urban-development programs.

Political Controls. The government of Paraguay continued to take a hard line on political opposition. On June 24, Luis Alfonso Resck, president of the Christian Democratic Party and a prominent member of the National Consensus coalition, was arrested and expelled from the country.

The government also took steps to reduce political opposition in the future. A new law prohibited alliances among political parties. The law also provided penalties for parties that maintain international links and raised the number of signatures required for a party to register for elections from 10,000 to 20,000.

In 1981, the Stroessner regime came under continued international criticism for alleged violations of human rights. There was also increasingly vocal opposition within Paraguay to government economic policies. Opponents charged that government-controlled increases in the minimum wage have failed to keep pace with increases in the cost of living.   Nathan A. Haverstock

See also LATIN AMERICA (Facts in Brief Table). In WORLD BOOK, see PARAGUAY.

PARENTS AND TEACHERS, NATIONAL CONGRESS OF. See NATIONAL PTA (NATIONAL CONGRESS OF PARENTS AND TEACHERS).

PENNSYLVANIA. See PHILADELPHIA; STATE GOVERNMENT.

PÉREZ DE CUÉLLAR, JAVIER (1920-   ), was chosen by the United Nations (UN) General Assembly on Dec. 15, 1981, to succeed Kurt Waldheim as secretary-general. See UNITED NATIONS (UN).

Javier Pérez de Cuéllar was born in Lima, Peru, on Jan. 19, 1920. He attended Roman Catholic schools and received a law degree from the Catholic University of Lima in 1944.

Pérez de Cuéllar joined Peru's foreign ministry in 1940, while still a student. Starting in 1944, he served as secretary in embassies in France, Great Britain, Bolivia, and Brazil. From 1964 to 1966, Pérez de Cuéllar was ambassador to Switzerland and Austria. From 1969 to 1971, he was Peru's first ambassador to Russia and concurrently ambassador to Poland. From 1977 to 1979, he served as ambassador to Venezuela.

Pérez de Cuéllar became Peru's permanent representative to the UN in 1971. As special representative on the UN peacekeeping force in Cyprus, he initiated talks between Greek and Turkish leaders in 1976. He impressed world leaders with his able supervision of elections in Zimbabwe in 1980. In 1981, he attempted to persuade Russia to withdraw its troops from Afghanistan.

The new secretary-general also taught diplomatic law at Peru's Diplomatic Academy and wrote two textbooks, *Recognition of States and Government* and *Diplomatic Law*.   Marsha F. Goldsmith

PERSONALITIES OF 1981 included the following:

Astaire, Fred, 82, dancing star of such musicals as *Flying Down to Rio* (1933), *Easter Parade* (1948), and *Finian's Rainbow* (1968), received the American Film Institute's ninth Life Achievement Award on April 11. The actor was cited as an individual "whose talent has in a fundamental way advanced the film-making art . . . and whose work has stood the test of time." In 1981, Astaire co-starred with three other great screen veterans—Melvyn Douglas, Douglas Fairbanks, Jr., and John Houseman—in the film *Ghost Story*.

Borge, Victor, 72, a pianist who would rather play for laughs than serious critical acclaim, collected an unusual accolade in October. Borge, a Dane of Jewish descent, received his fourth Scandinavian knighthood. The Finnish Order of the White Rose followed similar honors from Denmark, Norway, and Sweden in recognition of various aid programs Borge has provided their citizens. He did so, he said, to "give thanks for the selfless help the Scandinavians provided their Jewish brothers during the Holocaust."

Bossert, Patrick, 13, a schoolboy in London, figured out the secret of the tricky Rubik's Cube in just five days. Then he wrote up a four-page instruction sheet and sold copies for 45 cents each to his less logic-minded friends. According to *Scientific American* magazine, which featured the puzzle in its

Singer Lena Horne, 64, highlights a brilliant career with the May opening on Broadway of her one-woman show, *The Lady and Her Music*.

March 1981 issue, mastering the cube is "a three-dimensional problem of restoring the scrambled colored pieces of a 3 × 3 × 3 cube to their proper positions." The pieces can slip into 42.3 quintillion possible positions. David Singmaster, professor of mathematical sciences and computing at the Polytechnic of the South Bank in London, wrote the definitive treatise on the tough toy. Called *Notes on Rubik's "Magic Cube,"* it is highly technical and read mostly by mathematicians. Young Bossert's

instruction sheet became a best-selling paperback called *You Can Do the Cube.*

Butts, Alfred, 82, celebrated the 50th anniversary of a great idea in August. Back in 1931, he invented a game he first called Lexico, then Criss Cross, until the right word finally formed — Scrabble. Since then, the little tiles have brought fun and fury to millions, but Butts is not among them. He said, "I have always been described as an indifferent player. I am a poor speller."

Carey, Hugh L., 62, governor of New York, married Evangeline Gouletas, 44, a Chicago real estate executive, on April 7, and they invited more than 700 guests to the reception. Politicians, industrialists, entertainers, and New York society joined

nies in July, he said, "I don't believe a country can survive without understanding history and who the real heroes are."

Clements, George, 49, a Roman Catholic priest in Chicago, became a father on July 6. The black clergyman had preached to his parishioners about the need to find families for homeless black children. When he discovered 13-year-old Joey in an orphanage and decided to adopt the boy himself, the archdiocese admitted it was an unusual step, but did not oppose him. And that's how Father Clements of Holy Angels became "Joey's dad."

Erickson, John, 26, a Chicago physical education teacher, got a lot of exercise on August 11 and 12. Starting from Shakespeare Beach in Dover, England, Erikson swam to Cap Gris Nez in France, back to Folkestone near Dover, then finally back to France to become the first person to swim the English Channel three times nonstop. Erikson was allowed 10 minutes on the beach between stages, and his total time for the feat was 38 hours 27 minutes. A spokesman for the Channel Swimming Association said, "We are absolutely in awe of it because we didn't think it could be done."

Goodwin, Dan, 25, a mountain climber from Kennebunk, Me., twice scaled the heights in Chicago in 1981 but fell to low esteem in the opinion of a Windy City judge. "Spider Dan," using mountaineering gear, climbed to the top of the 110-story Sears Tower on May 30. Police were amazed but not amused. They arrested Goodwin, and a Circuit Court judge ordered him not to repeat his offense. He did not. But on November 11, despite the intervention of police and fire fighters, he reached the roof of the 100-story John Hancock Center. Thousands of Chicagoans cheered his agile, if illegal, ascent. However, a week later, Goodwin was sentenced to a year's probation for contempt of court, and the judge told him, "Your stunt for publicity resulted in expense for all taxpayers." Goodwin gracefully accepted the sentence, saying, "Judges only do what they think is right."

Gould, Chester, 80, is now a retired cartoonist in Woodstock, Ill., but his most famous character celebrated 50 years in business in October. Dick Tracy is "a little more handsome than he was in 1931," according to Gould, and finally wed to patient blonde Tess Trueheart. But he is still one step ahead of assorted evil-looking villains, and likely to remain so as long as Rick Fletcher and Allan Collins, who took over from Gould in 1977, can keep him alive.

Harriman, W. Averell, 90, was honored for almost 50 years of public service on his birthday on November 15. Such political notables as John Kenneth Galbraith, Clark Clifford, Senator Edward M. Kennedy, Lady Bird Johnson, and Walter F. Mondale recalled the roles Harriman played in the administrations of Democratic presidents Franklin

Mayor Edward I. Koch in wishing the couple "120 years of luck."

Chronopoulos, Tassos, 42, a restaurateur in Palos Heights, Ill., and a naturalized American citizen of Greek descent, believes in restoring honor to heroes. He felt that while the world constantly lauds current celebrities, no one seemed interested in providing a lasting tribute to the eight Americans who died in an attempt to rescue the hostages in Iran. So Chronopoulos took on the job. He designed a marble monument inscribed with their names, raised and donated funds, and persuaded the City Council to place the memorial on land near the town's City Hall. It all took a lot of effort, but it was well worthwhile to Chronopoulos. At ceremo-

"Beatle loves Bach" might startle some pop music fans, but it was true on April 27 when former Beatle Ringo Starr wed actress Barbara Bach.

D. Roosevelt, Harry S. Truman, John F. Kennedy, Lyndon B. Johnson, and Jimmy Carter. Harriman optimistically said he is "looking forward to a job in the next Democratic administration," adding, "I've had experience."

Hesburgh, Theodore M., 64, president of the University of Notre Dame in South Bend, Ind., has a namesake marking a place for him in the heavens. Astronomy Professor Frank K. Edmondson of Indiana University proposed that a small asteroid orbiting between Mars and Jupiter be named "1952-Hesburgh" in honor of the educator. The Minor Planet Center of the International Astronomical Union, the group in charge of such cosmic events, approved the name in January, and Father Hesburgh said he felt "great."

Lowen, Daniel, 17, a student at Cocoa Beach High School in Florida, challenged an answer and raised the scores of 240,000 takers of the Preliminary Scholastic Aptitude Test. Following a new policy, the Educational Testing Service of Princeton, N.J., sent students a copy of their test results and an answer sheet. When Daniel received his, he found that his answer to a question involving the placement of pyramids, designed to measure "analytical reasoning," was marked wrong. He set out to correct the situation. Daniel's father, a mechanical engineer who works on the space shuttle, backed up his son's answer with two mathematical

proofs, and the College Entrance Examination Board analytically reasoned that the Lowens – and everyone who saw things the Lowens' way – were right.

MacCready, Paul B., 56, of Pasadena, Calif., creator of the first human-powered aircraft, was flying high in February. The Association for the Advancement of Invention and Innovation named MacCready Inventor of the Year, and he was honored at the ninth National Inventors Day celebration at the United States Patent and Trademark Office in Arlington, Va. MacCready's pedal-operated planes, the *Gossamer Condor* and *Gossamer Albatross,* were patented in June 1980. In July 1981, his *Solar Challenger* became the first aircraft to fly – across the English Channel – powered only by solar cells.

Mackal, Roy P., 56, head of the University of Chicago's office of management and conservation, would like to manage and conserve the last dinosaurs left on earth. But first he has to find one. Mackal, who directed the search for Scotland's Loch Ness monster from 1965 to 1975, has been called an adventurer encumbered only by dreams. Encouraged by a scouting expedition in the African Congo in 1980, when Pygmies in the Likuoala Region rain forest reported familiarity with a brontosauruslike creature they call *Mokele-Mbembe,* Mackal left Chicago on October 16 to look for proof that dinosaurs still exist. He expected the search to be difficult, but said, "I do these things for the romance, the adventure. It's worth every bit of danger." He returned to Chicago without the proof he sought, but vowed to try again.

Reed, Arthur, 121, of Oakland, Calif., has had more authenticated birthdays than anyone else in the world. According to Social Security Administration records, he was born on June 28, 1860. Alert and well and answering reporters' questions on June 28, 1981, Reed said he had lived so long because "they took the time and made me good."

Stanwyck, Barbara, 73, star of such films as *Double Indemnity* (1944), *Sorry, Wrong Number* (1949), and *Cattle Queen of Montana* (1956) and of several television series in the 1960s, received a glowing tribute to her versatility. At a dinner in her honor given on April 13 by the Film Society of Lincoln Center in New York City, director Frank Capra said, "It's this gift of hers to communicate the truth of a role which has made Barbara the great actress she is . . . . Her many faces are all different, and all dazzling."

Tudor, Betty, 50, of Exeter, England, discovered she had little in common with an earlier Tudor — Elizabeth I. While the 16th-century queen of England steered a country, the 20th-century landlady of the Golden Lion Inn could not even steer a car.

After investing 19 years in 273 driving lessons, failing seven tests, and having one instructor land in a mental hospital, Tudor said, "I'm afraid I'm never going to make a driver." She bought a moped instead.

Updike, John, 49, became the 22nd winner of the Edward MacDowell Medal in August. The award, which is rotated among composers, visual artists, and writers, is presented annually at the MacDowell Colony in Peterborough, N.H., a woodsy retreat for creative people. Author Updike, who has produced popular as well as critically acclaimed novels, short stories, criticism, and poems, said writers were "disreputable, incorrigible, early to decay and late to bloom." But, he added, "they do try to tell the truth." Updike accepted the medal "with particular pleasure and pride for this particular pat."

Wallenberg, Raoul, a Swedish diplomat who disappeared after Soviet agents seized him in Hungary in 1945, was made an honorary United States citizen on Oct. 5, 1981. President Ronald Reagan said Wallenberg's achievements in saving 100,000 Hungarians from the Germans in World War II were of "Biblical proportions." There is speculation that Wallenberg may still be alive, and the honorary citizenship will enable the U.S. Department of State to search for him.　Marsha F. Goldsmith

At White House ceremonies in January, President Jimmy Carter gives Walter Cronkite the Medal of Freedom, America's highest civilian honor.

PERU. Good management and the discovery of additional oil resources lifted the fortunes of Peru during 1981. Since taking office in July 1980, President Fernando Belaunde Terry has led Peru back from the edge of bankruptcy.

Peru boosted its financial reserves to more than $1 billion in 1981. The annual inflation rate was 50 per cent in 1981, compared with 80 per cent in 1979. Banking sources in Lima, Peru's capital, said the inflation rate would have been even lower if the government had not lifted controls on food prices and interest rates.

Petroleum Boost. New discoveries of oil in Peru transformed it from a $200-million-per-year importer of oil in 1978 to a small exporter of oil in 1981. New oil resources are known to exist within Peru's Amazon territory, and additional deposits are thought to exist offshore. The Belaunde government signed long-term exploration contracts with several international oil companies. Under these contracts, the oil companies will receive up to 50 per cent of the oil they find and develop, or 42 per cent if production exceeds 300,000 barrels per day.

Other minerals, including silver, copper, zinc, and lead, continued to figure importantly in the Peruvian economy, though the value of mineral exports dropped in 1981 because of declines in world prices.

Encouraging foreign investment has been a priority of the Belaunde government, some of whose top officials had worked for the World Bank while they were in exile under the previous military regime. The Belaunde government enhanced investment opportunities by rewriting nationalistic provisions that had scared off foreign investors, and by adding new incentives on taxes and profits.

The Problems of the Poor were increasingly left to local authorities in Peru. In Lima, Mayor Eduardo Orrega, an architect and city planner who serves without salary, worked with community and church organizations in a citywide improvement campaign. The rate of unemployment in Lima was 25 per cent in 1981.

Tourism, a growing source of jobs and earnings in Peru, was hard-hit in 1981 when Brian Brady of the U.S. Bureau of Mines predicted that devastating earthquakes would strike the Lima area. The earthquakes did not materialize in July as predicted and Brady withdrew his forecast, but it was too late to prevent the damage to Peru's tourist industry during some of the best months of the year.

In December, Peru's representative to the United Nations (UN), Javier Pérez de Cuéllar, was chosen to succeed Kurt Waldheim as UN secretary-general.   Nathan A. Haverstock

See also LATIN AMERICA (Facts in Brief Table); PÉREZ DE CUÉLLAR, JAVIER. In WORLD BOOK, see PERU.

PET. See CAT; DOG.

PETROLEUM AND GAS. Under pressure from Saudi Arabia, the world's leading oil exporter, the Organization of Petroleum Exporting Countries (OPEC) agreed on Oct. 29, 1981, to set the base price of crude oil at $34 per barrel. The agreement, to remain in effect until December 1982, ended a bitter two-year price dispute among the 13 members of the oil cartel. OPEC oil ministers also set a ceiling of $38 per barrel on crude oil that commands a higher price because of quality or nearness to consumers. In addition, Saudi Arabia, which produces about one-third of OPEC's output, announced it would reduce oil production by about 10 per cent or 1 million barrels per day (bpd).

According to the settlement, Saudi Arabia agreed to raise the base price of its crude oil by $2 per barrel, while some producers — including Algeria, Nigeria, and Libya — agreed to lower theirs. It was the first time OPEC had agreed to officially reduce the prices charged by most members. Saudi Arabia had pressed for the agreement to stabilize and reduce world oil prices because of its concern that high oil prices were forcing consumers to seek alternate energy sources, particularly coal.

The Saudi production cutback was expected to end the world oil glut. Energy experts estimated that the price increase and the Saudi cutback would raise the price of gasoline in the United States by about 3 cents per gallon (3.8 liters).

Faced with a continuing oversupply of oil and a worldwide economic slowdown, OPEC agreed on December 11 to cut the price of its best crude oil to $37 per barrel. It trimmed the price of some inferior grades by 20 to 70 cents per barrel.

The World Oil Glut resulted in a gasoline surplus in the United States in 1981. The surplus led to the closing of some refining facilities and a reduction in some wholesale gasoline prices. Because of conservation measures and poor economic conditions that reduced demand, U.S. imports of oil reached an eight-year low in April 1981, according to the American Petroleum Institute. The U.S. Department of Energy (DOE) reported that crude oil imports for the first seven months of 1981 averaged 4.2 million bpd, down greatly from the 5.5 million bpd imported during the same period in 1980. The United States also imported an average of 1.4 million bpd of refined petroleum products in 1981, a slight decrease from the previous year.

United States production of crude oil averaged 8.57 million bpd for the seven-month period, compared with 8.64 million bpd for the same period in 1980. United States production of natural gas during the period totaled 11.3 trillion cubic feet (320 billion cubic meters), 1.1 per cent less than the previous year. Imports of natural gas totaled 494 billion cubic feet (14 billion cubic meters) for the period, down 18.2 per cent from a year earlier.

In February, the United States began exploiting

Roschkov/*Toronto Star*

the oil glut by making record purchases of crude oil to help fill the Strategic Petroleum Reserve – five huge underground salt domes in Texas and Louisiana. These salt domes will eventually store 750 million barrels of crude oil for use if the flow of foreign oil to the United States is disrupted. By mid-November, the reserve contained 217 million barrels, up from 100 million barrels in January. On September 1, the United States and Mexico began implementing a five-year, $3.5-billion agreement that will put up to 110 million barrels of Mexican oil into the stockpile.

Government Action. President Ronald Reagan abolished remaining federal price controls on United States crude oil on January 28, fulfilling a campaign pledge to end what he regarded as counterproductive regulation of the petroleum and natural gas industry. The order allowed oil companies to raise to world price levels the price of the 25 per cent of U.S. crude oil still controlled. According to a timetable set by President Jimmy Carter, controls would have expired on September 30.

The Reagan Administration also prepared a plan for early decontrol of natural gas prices. Controls were due to expire in 1985.

Wilderness Leases. The Interior Department's Bureau of Land Management issued the first leases for oil and gas exploration in a federal wilderness area on November 17. The leases cover 9,000 acres

(3,600 hectares) in New Mexico, including 700 acres (280 hectares) in the Capitan Wilderness. Under pressure from Representative Manuel Lujan, Jr. (R., N. Mex.), however, Interior Secretary James G. Watt pledged on November 19 that no future oil and gas leases would be granted in federal wilderness areas without a full environmental impact study and consultation with Congress.

Alaska Pipeline. A fiercely debated financing package for a proposed 4,800-mile (7,700-kilometer) natural gas pipeline from Alaska was approved by the Senate on November 19 and the House of Representatives on December 9. The package included a provision that would allow gas companies to add surcharges to gas bills to help pay off loans on completed portions of the pipeline. Supporters said the measure was necessary to tap the gas reserves on Alaska's North Slope. Opponents said the bill could cost consumers billions of dollars before any gas is delivered or even if the pipeline is never completed.

The First U.S. Deepwater Port for handling oil supertankers opened on May 5 on a trial basis in the Gulf of Mexico, about 19 miles (31 kilometers) off the coast of Louisiana. The $700-million Louisiana Offshore Oil Port (LOOP) took 10 years to plan and build. Before LOOP opened, no American port could handle the biggest oil tankers. The cargo from supertankers docking at LOOP is pumped onshore by undersea pipelines. LOOP was expected to be fully operational by mid-1982.

Libyan Shutdown. Exxon Corporation relinquished all its oil-producing interests in Libya on November 12. Exxon gave no explanation for its action, but oil-industry analysts cited the worsening relations between the United States and Libya as a major factor. On December 10, President Reagan asked U.S. oil companies operating in Libya to withdraw their American employees.

Take-Overs. E. I. du Pont de Nemours & Company, a manufacturer of chemical products, on August 4 acquired Conoco Incorporated, the nation's ninth largest oil company. The merger, the largest in history, cost Du Pont $7.54 billion.

On October 30, Mobil Oil Corporation, an unsuccessful bidder for Conoco, offered to buy Marathon Oil Company for $5.1 billion. Marathon fought the attempt. In November, Marathon and United States Steel Corporation announced an alternative plan under which U.S. Steel would acquire the oil company for up to $6.8 billion.

On December 9, Mobil announced that it had informed U.S. Steel it intended to purchase up to 25 per cent of the steel company's stock. On December 11, the Federal Trade Commission (FTC) filed an antitrust suit against Mobil. The FTC indicated it would drop the suit if Mobil agreed to divest itself of Marathon's transportation, storage, and marketing operations.

On December 23, a federal appeals court in Cincinnati upheld lower court rulings that Mobil's bid for Marathon would violate antitrust laws. But it also ruled that parts of U.S. Steel's bid were illegal. Mobil appealed the case to the Supreme Court of the United States on December 29, but the high court refused to intervene.

Russian Gas Deal. West Germany agreed on November 13 to buy more than $44 billion worth of natural gas from Russia over a 15-year period beginning in 1984. The gas will be delivered to Western Europe by a proposed 3,500-mile (5,600-kilometer) pipeline from Siberia to Czechoslovakia. Other pipelines will carry the gas from there to West Germany. The United States opposed the deal, claiming Western European dependence on Soviet gas would weaken the Western alliance. On December 29, President Reagan blocked the export to Russia of about $200 million in gas and oil production equipment as part of economic sanctions on Russia because of Poland's imposition of martial law. See PRESIDENT OF THE U.S.

Kuwaiti Petroleum Corporation, Kuwait's state-owned oil company, agreed on October 5 to buy Santa Fe International Corporation, a major U.S. petroleum concern, for $2.5 billion. The transaction was the largest single investment of Middle East oil revenues in the United States. Michael Woods

In WORLD BOOK, see PETROLEUM; GAS.

PHILADELPHIA weathered major school and transit strikes, witnessed heated battles between its mayor and City Council, and registered continuing signs of economic decline during 1981.

School Strikes. A walkout of nonteaching employees that closed Philadelphia schools from February 2 to 6 foreshadowed a 50-day teachers' strike that began on September 8. The teachers' union struck to protest the layoffs of 3,500 members and the cancellation of the 10 per cent pay raise that it had won after a 22-day strike in 1980. The school district, on the brink of bankruptcy, had taken these measures to reduce a budget deficit of more than $223 million.

During the dispute – the city's fifth teachers' strike since 1970 – teachers were arrested, the union was fined, two councilmen brawled, and a citywide general strike was narrowly averted.

The bitter strike ended on October 27 when a Commonwealth Court ordered the 22,000-member union back to work under the 1980 contract. The court also voided provisions for the second year of that contract because the school district did not have the funds to finance them, and ordered the union and the school district back into mediation.

Mayor William J. Green called for a long-term solution to the school system's perennial fiscal crisis, urging a 10 per cent property-tax increase

Philadelphia's spring transit strike resulted in such heavy commuter traffic that express lanes, right, resembled a parking lot, foreground.

and the sale of city bonds. However, both of those proposals were tabled indefinitely by the City Council.

A Transit Strike that left 400,000 commuters without public transportation for 19 days was settled on April 2, after Pennsylvania Governor Richard L. Thornburgh pressed the Southeastern Pennsylvania Transit Authority to drop its demand to hire part-time employees. The 4,900 transit workers ratified a $23.5-million package that included a 14.5 per cent wage increase over two years. Leaders of four suburban governments on October 26 rejected the mayor's proposal for a 1 per cent regional sales tax to aid the transit authority. Transit officials forecast that, as a result, bus and subway fares would reach $1 and commuter train service would cease within a year.

The State of the City. Philadelphia entered fiscal 1982, which began on July 1, 1981, in a relatively healthy financial state. The City Council on May 29 approved a $1.2-billion operating budget that restored many services cut in 1980 in an austerity move. The budget included two new tax measures — an increase in the real estate transfer tax from 2 to 3 per cent of the selling price of a house, and an unprecedented 2 per cent tax on gasoline sales by wholesale distributors.

The city's economic picture was not entirely promising, however. The volume of international freight handled by the Delaware River ports — including Philadelphia; Wilmington, Del.; and Camden, N.J. — fell 15.9 per cent in 1980, according to statistics released in April by the Delaware River Port Authority. The decline, attributed primarily to a drop-off in bulk petroleum cargo, was the largest suffered by any of the competitive East Coast ports, including New York City and Baltimore.

Mayor-Council Disagreements. The Philadelphia City Council took officials of Mayor Green's administration to court for refusing to put into effect a council ordinance freezing real estate assessments at the 1980 level until they are equalized. The assessments ran as low as 17 per cent of market value in some city neighborhoods and as high as 80 per cent in others. The suit was settled on May 18 when Common Pleas Court Judge Harry A. Takiff approved an agreement calling for the reassessment of all 560,000 individual properties in Philadelphia by the end of 1986. Under the six-year agreement, increases in individual property taxes would be held to less than 15 per cent.

The council also preliminarily opposed the mayor's plan for a single citywide cable-television system. It favored instead a proposal to divide the city into separate franchise areas, each of which could be serviced by a different system.   Jan Schaffer

See also CITY. In WORLD BOOK, see PHILADELPHIA.

PHILIPPINES President Ferdinand E. Marcos ended more than eight years of martial law on Jan. 17, 1981. On January 19, Marcos turned over to the National Assembly legislative powers he had held during the period of martial law.

A new "Philippines-style" presidential system was established by constitutional amendments that won 79 per cent voter approval in a plebiscite on April 7. The changes provided for a Cabinet to handle daily government business but left Marcos most of the powers he had exercised under martial law.

In a presidential election on June 16, Marcos, who ran almost unopposed, won a new six-year term with 88 per cent of the vote. The major opposition groups boycotted the election. Marcos, who had held the title of prime minister in addition to that of president since 1978, appointed Finance Minister Cesar E. Virata as prime minister.

Economic Plans. The new government's first budget, presented on August 4 for the 1982 fiscal year, raised spending 12.9 per cent. It continued to subsidize increased food production and consumption and to encourage better nutritional habits. But the new budget put more emphasis on encouraging rural enterprise and developing natural resources.

The government sought to steer industrial investment into more efficient use of money and to increase exports of manufactured goods to reduce the large foreign-exchange deficit. Government planners worked closely with the International Monetary Fund and the World Bank, two international development agencies.

Guerrilla Wars. Marcos claimed on January 17 that a "formidable secessionist war" in the southern islands had been "effectively terminated." Muslim rebels there had been fighting for years for independence from the Philippines, which is mostly Roman Catholic. Marcos said that over 37,000 rebels had surrendered and received amnesty. But on February 12, the war flared up again when about 120 soldiers were killed by Muslim guerrillas on Pata Island.

The Philippine Army also fought a guerrilla force called the New People's Army (NPA), the military branch of the outlawed Philippine Communist Party. The NPA was blamed for the death of 15 persons when a grenade exploded on April 19 during Easter Mass at a Roman Catholic cathedral in Davao.

United States Vice-President George H. W. Bush, attending Marcos' June 30 inauguration, said, "We love your adherence to democratic principles and to the democratic process." His statement angered opponents of Marcos, who charged that Marcos had violated civil rights.   Henry S. Bradsher

See also ASIA (Facts in Brief Table). In WORLD BOOK, see PHILIPPINES.

PHONOGRAPH. See RECORDINGS.

PHOTOGRAPHY

PHOTOGRAPHY. Sony Corporation of Japan in August 1981 demonstrated a new, truly instant-photography camera that uses video technology to make still pictures. Called Mavica (*Ma*gnetic *vi*deo *ca*mera), it makes 50 color photographs electronically on a small magnetic disk. The photographs are viewed on a television set. The Mavica looks much like a conventional single-lens reflex camera and has interchangeable lenses. Sony said it might be available in late 1982 and that accessories will include a device to make paper copies of the images.

Sales of videotape and video-cassette recorders climbed sharply. Recorder sales were expected to approach 1.5 million, almost double the 1980 figure. Videodisc players were advertised widely. Video-camera systems finally seemed to be underway in 1981. By October, besides larger-format video-camera/recorder systems, at least four miniature systems using ¼-inch, or 6-millimeter (mm), videotape had been announced. None of the new systems were compatible with any of the other three small units. At the same time, sales of conventional 8-mm movie cameras continued to drop.

Major Camera Manufacturers introduced many new conventional still cameras in 1981 as competition sharpened. Canon's New Fl—so called to distinguish it from the Fl it replaced—features interchangeable viewfinders and focusing screens. The Canon AE-1 Program camera offers a totally automatic programmed exposure mode plus shutter-preferred automation.

Minolta's XG-M and the Pentax ME-F were also announced. The Pentax features an advanced electronic focus-control system within the camera to speed and increase the accuracy of manual focusing with standard Pentax lenses. It also provides automatic focusing with a new series of lenses designed for it. The Minolta went on the market in 1981, but the Pentax was scheduled for 1982.

So-called compact-35-mm cameras, most of which can slip easily into a pocket, became increasingly popular in 1981. These cameras make full-frame 35-mm pictures and are focused by estimation, scale, or range finder. Most do not have interchangeable lenses; however, the most expensive models feature automatic focusing.

Makers of instant-photography film and cameras continued to introduce new products. Polaroid's 600 Sun System offers two electronically advanced cameras that balance flash and natural light automatically. These cameras are used with a special new 600-ASA-speed instant film.

Interest in Darkroom Activity remained high, and the year saw continuing research into the processing of both color and black-and-white mate-

Joe Rosenthal, retiring after 51 years as a photographer, poses with his historic photo of the flag-raising on Iwo Jima during World War II.

rials to make them longer lived. Two notable devices to simplify color printing were offered in 1981. Polaroid produced a slide copier that makes either color prints or black-and-white prints and negatives from color slides, depending on the type of Polaroid pack film used with it. Eastman Kodak Company introduced its Ektaflex PCT color-print-making system, which requires only one processing solution. The first printing paper offered by the system is used with color negatives for 5- by 7-inch (13- by 18-centimeter) or 8- by 10-inch (20- by 25-centimeter) prints.

Lenses continued to appear in quantity from major camera makers as well as independent producers. New zoom lenses featured shorter focal lengths and greater ranges as well as macro-focusing modes for close-up work. Ricoh's and Canon's autofocusing lenses reached the market. Pentax brought out the world's first 400- to 600-mm mirror-reflex zoom lens.

Photographs for collecting continued to grow in importance. In New York state, a law was passed to protect buyers of art objects produced in multiple copies — including photographs — from unethical sellers. For example, sellers must provide prospective buyers of photo prints with six important kinds of information about the works to establish their authenticity and background.   Kenneth Poli

In WORLD BOOK, see CAMERA; PHOTOGRAPHY.

PHYSICS. Small, imaginative experiments conducted in 1981 revealed important details of how light, electrons, and molecules behave. A research team from the University of Washington in Seattle and a group from the University of California, Berkeley, both produced results that support the Weinberg-Salam theory of physical forces. This theory was proposed in the late 1960s by physicists Steven Weinberg and Sheldon L. Glashow of Harvard University in Cambridge, Mass., and Abdus Salam, head of the International Center for Theoretical Physics in Trieste, Italy.

According to the Weinberg-Salam theory, two forces that previous theories had described as fundamentally different are merely two forms of a single force. One of the forces, the electromagnetic force, makes electricity flow and magnets attract one another. The other force, known as the weak force, makes such subatomic particles as neutrons and protons come apart under certain conditions.

The Seattle and Berkeley scientists based their experiments on a prediction made by the Weinberg-Salam theory about how metal vapors absorb light. Light consists of pointlike bundles of radiation called photons. A photon spins in one of two directions as it travels through space. The old laws of electromagnetism say that a metal vapor will absorb photons regardless of their spin direction. Physicists explain this tendency by a principle

called conservation of parity. But the Weinberg-Salam theory predicts that the vapors will violate parity, preferring to absorb photons of one of the two spin directions.

Parity Violation had been revealed by previous experiments with high-energy photons. These experiments thus supported the Weinberg-Salam theory, but the theory also predicts that low-energy photons should exhibit a small parity violation. Except for a 1979 experiment in Novosibirsk, Russia, previous attempts to observe such a violation produced inconsistent results.

The Seattle and Berkeley experimenters bombarded hot metallic vapor with photons of varying spin direction. Measurements of absorption indicated differences that confirmed the Novosibirsk experiment and agree with the Weinberg-Salam theory.

Tighter Bonds. Experimenters at International Business Machines (IBM) Corporation's research laboratory in San Jose, Calif., announced on January 26 that they had discovered a way to strengthen the bonds between molecules of certain solids. Molecules form solids when positive electrical charges in one type of molecule and negative charges in another type attract one another so strongly that they form bonds, holding the molecules in place.

Weak bonds form in solids between molecules that are neutral — that is, neither positive nor negative. These molecules attract one another because of the positions of their internal electrical charges. A molecule of this type has equal numbers of protons and electrons, so it is electrically neutral. But certain parts of the molecule have more electrons than protons and therefore are negatively charged. Protons dominate other areas, which are thus positively charged. The positive regions of certain molecules attract the negative zones of others.

A stronger kind of bond forms when one type of molecule gives up an electron to another type. This process creates positively and negatively charged molecules that attract one another.

Some neutral organic molecules attract others almost enough to enable an electron to jump from one type of molecule to the other, forming an ionic bond. The IBM scientists identified a number of such pairs of molecules. They then determined that reducing the spacing between the pairs slightly might change neutral bonds to ionic bonds.

The researchers began their experiment by building up crystals with alternating layers of two types of molecule. Then they squeezed the crystals mechanically to about 40,000 times atmospheric pressure (14.7 pounds per square inch or 1.03 kilograms per square centimeter). The change in bonding was dramatic in most cases. Thomas O. White

In WORLD BOOK, see PHYSICS.

PIERCE, SAMUEL RILEY, JR. (1922-   ), became secretary of the United States Department of Housing and Urban Development (HUD) on Jan. 23, 1981. During his confirmation hearing, he told the Senate Banking Committee that "inflation is public enemy number one" and that it could force a reduction in HUD's spending.

Pierce was born in Glen Cove, N.Y., on Sept. 8, 1922. During World War II, he served three years in North Africa and Italy with the U.S. Army's Criminal Investigation Division.

He graduated from Cornell University in 1947 and received a law degree there in 1949. In 1952 he received a master of laws degree in taxation from New York University.

From 1949 to 1953 he was an assistant district attorney for New York County, then served two years as an assistant U.S. attorney for the southern district of New York. From 1955 to 1956 he was assistant to the undersecretary of the U.S. Department of Labor, and in 1956 and 1957 he was associate counsel and later counsel of the Subcommittee on Antitrust of the House of Representatives' Committee on the Judiciary. At the time of his nomination to HUD, Pierce was a senior partner in the New York City law firm of Battle, Fowler, Jaffin, Pierce & Kheel, specializing in labor issues.

He is married to the former Barbara Penn Wright.   Wayne Wille

Poet Czeslaw Milosz, a Polish exile living in the United States, visits Gdańsk, Poland, in June. He won the 1980 Nobel Prize for Literature.

POETRY. A diversity of themes and styles earned critical praise for established poets in 1981. James Schuyler won the Pulitzer Prize for Poetry for *The Morning of the Poem*, a long, candid autobiographical work. He received the award on April 13 in New York City. Lisel Mueller's elegant views of art, civilization, family, and womanhood in *The Need to Hold Still* earned the first American Book Award for Poetry. The award, one of a group of literary honors sponsored by the Association of American Publishers, was presented at a ceremony in New York City on April 30. Other contenders included Philip Booth's naturalistic *Before Sleep*, Isabella Gardner's personal journeys in *That Was Then*, and Mark Strand's *Selected Poems*. The National Book Critics' Circle honored Frederick Seidel's meditations on urban dilemmas in *Sunrise*.

May Swenson and Howard Nemerov shared the 1981 Bollingen Prize for Poetry. Mona Van Duyn was cited by the Academy of American Poets "for distinguished poetic achievement." Kenneth Burke won the National Medal for Literature and its accompanying $15,000 prize.

Among significant new works were John Ashbery's inventive and lyrical *Shadow Train* and A. R. Ammons' *A Coast of Trees*, a fragmented vision of man in the world. The jazzy, oracular writing in Gerald Stern's *The Red Coal* led one critic to call Stern "the most startling and tender poet to emerge in America in a decade." Michael Ryan's *In Winter*, a book about loneliness and desire, was the finest volume to come from the National Poetry Series. Michael Van Walleghen won the Lamont Prize for his ironic ruminations in *More Trouble with the Obvious*. Distinctive collections from veteran poets included David Wagoner's *Landfall*, Louis Simpson's *Caviare at the Funeral*, and *The Glass Houses* from John N. Morris. Notable first works were John Bensko's *Green Soldiers; Work, for the Night is Coming* by Jared Carter; Sydney Lea's *Searching the Drowned Man*; and *Satan Says* by Sharon Olds.

From Other Countries. Bulgarian poet Lyubomir Levchev addressed the rites of war and freedom in *The Mysterious Man*. From Canada, Margaret Atwood's *Two-Headed Poems* considered cultural malaise and the condition of women. Russian exile Joseph Brodsky wrote of human heights and misfortune in *A Part of Speech*.

Important translations included John E. Woods's version of German poet Arno Schmidt's *Evening Edged in Gold*; Lillian Vallee's rendering of *Bells in Winter* by Polish exile Czeslaw Milosz, winner of the 1980 Nobel Prize for Literature; and the eminent Russian poet Osip Mandelstam's *Stone* by Robert Tracy. The year's major critical work was Helen Vendler's appreciation of contemporary poetry in *Part of Nature, Part of Us*.   G. E. Murray

In WORLD BOOK, see POETRY.

POLAND cracked down suddenly and harshly on the independent labor union Solidarity on Dec. 13, 1981. Communist Party First Secretary and Council of Ministers Chairman Wojciech Jaruzelski declared martial law, banned public gatherings, and ordered Solidarity leaders, strikers, and some former government leaders arrested. The government set up a Military Council of National Salvation to run the country during the period of martial law.

Workers defied the crackdown, but soldiers broke up strikes throughout the country. Poland's ambassador to the United States, Romuald Spasowski, asked for political asylum on December 19 and declared the next day that "specially trained units and security police" had begun "an unprecedented reign of terror." Warsaw Radio reported that the last major strikers, coal miners at the Piast Pit, ended their sit-in on December 28.

United States President Ronald Reagan suspended major economic ties with Poland on December 23 and warned that the United States would take economic and political action against Russia "if this repression continues." On December 29, Reagan imposed limited economic sanctions against Russia. The Polish government said on December 30 that eight people had been killed during the period of martial law and that security forces had arrested or confined 5,500 people.

Solidarity and the government had struggled for power throughout the year. On January 10 and 24, millions of Poles stayed off their jobs to express their demand for a 40-hour workweek. On January 31, Solidarity leader Lech Walesa and Deputy Prime Minister Mieczyslaw Jagielski agreed on a 42-hour week until the end of 1981, with a reduction to 40 hours "as soon as possible."

Jozef Pinkowski was dismissed as Council of Ministers chairman on February 9 and was succeeded by Jaruzelski, then minister of defense. One day later, Poland's Supreme Court rejected an application for official status from Rural Solidarity, a union representing 3.5 million independent farmers. On May 6, however, the *Sejm* (parliament) made the union legal. A Warsaw court officially recognized Rural Solidarity on May 12.

Russia tried to slow down Poland's liberalization. Mikhail Suslov, Russia's top ideologist, visited Poland in April. In June, the Central Committee of the Communist Party of the Soviet Union sent a letter to its Polish counterpart pointing out Russia's concern over the program of "antisocialist forces" in Poland and criticizing the Polish United Workers' Party (PZPR), the Communist party of Poland, for not doing enough to stop them.

Party Meeting. The PZPR held an emergency congress from July 14 to 20. The delegates to the

Lech Walesa skillfully guided Poland's independent labor organization Solidarity until December, when the government began to crush the union.

Poland's Roman Catholics suffered a heavy blow in May when the country's primate, Stefan Cardinal Wyszyński, died at the age of 79.

congress had been chosen in contested elections throughout the country. Communist Party First Secretary Stanislaw Kania was re-elected in the first contested election for the party leadership.

Solidarity held its first national congress in two sessions, from September 5 to 10 and from September 26 to October 7. The delegates adopted a program that called for a gradual increase in prices, monetary changes to control inflation, and cuts in military spending. Walesa was re-elected national chairman.

Kania Resigned on October 18, and Jaruzelski replaced him. Jaruzelski remained Council of Ministers chairman. See JARUZELSKI, WOJCIECH.

On November 4, Jaruzelski, Walesa, and the Roman Catholic primate of Poland, Archbishop Jozef Glemp, held an unprecedented meeting to try to solve the nation's problems. Glemp was named primate on July 7 after the death of his predecessor, Stefan Cardinal Wyszyński.

On December 12, Solidarity leaders meeting in Gdańsk threatened a general strike if the government enacted an emergency powers bill. They also proposed holding a national referendum on setting up a non-Communist government. Martial law was declared the next day.   Chris Cviic

See also EUROPE (Facts in Brief Table). In WORLD BOOK, see POLAND.

POPULAR MUSIC. See MUSIC, POPULAR.

POPULATION. World population continued to rise rapidly in 1981. In its annual report issued in mid-June, the United Nations (UN) Fund for Population Activities estimated that total world population had reached 4.4 billion and was increasing at the rate of 1.7 per cent per year. According to the report, world population would stabilize at 10.5 billion by the year 2110.

Growth Rates. UN projections indicated that the industrialized nations, which accounted for 24 per cent of the world's population in 1980, would account for only 13 per cent of the population by the year 2110. The nonindustrialized countries would account for the remainder, with South Asia and Africa alone accounting for 60 per cent.

Africa, with a population of 478 million, had the highest annual growth rate – 2.9 per cent; South America, with 252 million, was growing by 2.3 per cent; and Asia, with 2.7 billion, was increasing at the rate of 1.8 per cent. Europe, with 690 million, had only a 0.4 per cent growth rate – the world's lowest. North America, with 375 million, had a growth rate of 0.7 per cent, while Australia and the Pacific Islands, with 26 million, showed a growth rate of 1.3 per cent.

The People's Republic of China, with a population of 970 million, was the world's most populous nation in 1981. India, with 693 million, was second. Russia ranked third with 270 million, followed by the United States with 230 million.

Niger had the world's highest birth rate – 51.4 live births for every 1,000 persons. West Germany, with 9.8 per 1,000, had the lowest birth rate. Birth rates in the United States and Canada were 15.2 and 16.0 respectively.

Life Expectancy for men continued to rise. In Japan, the average life span for males born between 1975 and 1980 was estimated at 72.7 years, the world's highest. Sweden, with 72.3, and Canada, with 70.1, followed. The United States, with a 69.1 year life span, ranked fourth. Life expectancy for females was considerably higher throughout the world. Sweden had the world's highest average, 77.9 years, followed by Japan with 77.4. Canada and the United States tied for third with 77.0 years.

There were some indications, however, that the average annual increase in life expectancy was beginning to decline worldwide. The Overseas Development Council, a global population-study group, reported that life-expectancy gains in the world's poorer nations were beginning to decline after a generation of rapid advances. According to the council, infectious diseases previously had been the leading cause of death in the poorer countries. But their near-eradication had been followed by a growth in "respiratory problems, diarrheal diseases, and malnutrition that did not yield easily to modern medical treatment."   Paul C. Tullier

In WORLD BOOK, see POPULATION.

PORTUGAL. Prime Minister Francisco Pinto Balsemao resigned on Aug. 11, 1981, after a bitter argument with critics in his Social Democratic Party (SDP). He had become prime minister on January 9, succeeding Francisco Sa Carneiro, who died in an airplane crash on Dec. 4, 1980.

Balsemao's center-right coalition with the Christian Democrats and Popular Monarchists met its first challenge in June. Right wing Social Democrats claimed that he was not taking proper care of the Sa Carneiro "inheritance." Balsemao's problems stemmed from a severe drought, long strikes against the government, and a dispute with the Revolutionary Council, the military advisory body that has supervised Portugal's transition to civilian rule since 1974. The council vetoed a bill that would have permitted private ownership of banks and insurance companies. Balsemao called a special meeting of the SDP's national council on June 14 and received a vote of confidence.

Minister Resigns. Minister of Social Affairs Carlos Macedo resigned on July 27, causing another crisis within the SDP. He and other conservative critics in the SDP objected to Balsemao's attempts to work with the left wing Revolutionary Council and President Antonio dos Santos Ramalho Eanes. They wanted Balsemao to confront Eanes, as Sa Carneiro had. But Balsemao refused. Instead, he interrupted his vacation and returned to Lisbon to confront his critics.

The party leaders argued for 30 hours. Finally, on August 11, Balsemao resigned. No suitable successor emerged, so the Social Democrats asked him to stay on. They gave him a vote of confidence, 58 votes to 1, with 3 abstentions. Balsemao said that this vote showed a "significant modification" within his party. On August 25, Eanes asked him to form a new government. Eanes approved Balsemao's new Cabinet on September 2.

Spending Cuts. On July 17, the government introduced measures that would make more money available for paying foreign debts and buying oil. Portugal paid $12.5 billion more for oil in 1981 than it did in 1980. Its foreign debt amounted to $950 million at the end of February. The measures included cuts in public spending, tighter and more expensive credit, and higher energy prices, including a 10 per cent increase in the price of gasoline. Finance Minister Joao Morais Leitao admitted that the measures would push inflation beyond the year's target of 16 per cent.

Into the EC. Portugal prepared to enter the European Community (EC or Common Market) in 1985, two years later than originally planned. The 24-nation Organization for Economic Cooperation and Development reported in July that Portugal's growth rate was declining. Kenneth Brown

See also EUROPE (Facts in Brief Table). In WORLD BOOK, see PORTUGAL.

POSTAL SERVICE, UNITED STATES. Facing mounting deficits as its payroll climbed sharply, the U.S. Postal Service raised postal rates twice in 1981 in an effort to stay in the black. On March 10, the Postal Service's Board of Governors approved an increase in first-class postage from 15 cents to 18 cents, effective March 22. The cost of mailing a post card rose from 10 cents to 12 cents at the same time, with corresponding increases for other classes of mail. On September 30, less than seven months later, the Board of Governors approved another postage increase – from 18 cents to 20 cents for a first-class letter and from 12 cents to 13 cents for a post card. Postage rates for most other classes of mail also were raised, effective November 1.

The 20-cent stamp was approved despite the opposition of the independent Postal Rate Commission, which had three times rejected the Postal Service's request for such an increase. The Board of Governors was allowed by law to put the raise into effect even without the commission's approval. Greeting-card companies and other mail users filed suit to block the increase.

The November jump was the sixth increase in postage rates since 1971, when it cost only 6 cents to mail a letter. Robert L. Hardesty, chairman of the Postal Service's Board of Governors, said the independent agency lost nearly $126 million in the

By permission of Bill Mauldin and Wil-Jo Associates, Inc.

"This takes care of the bills, but how will we pay the postage?"

first five months of the 18-cent stamp. With the 20-cent stamp, Hardesty said, the postal service should reap an additional $1 billion in revenues and actually have an operating profit of $100 million for the year ending in February 1982. "Your local supermarket cannot sell you milk and bread and groceries at 1978 prices because it has to pay more for its goods, its wages, and its utilities," Hardesty told reporters. "For the same reasons, the Postal Service cannot continue to deliver mail at 1978 prices."

Deficit After Surplus. Postmaster General William F. Bolger announced on Feb. 2, 1981, that the Postal Service ended its 1980 fiscal year with a deficit of $306 million, after registering a surplus of $470 million during fiscal 1979. The deficit occurred despite the fact that the Postal Service handled a record 106.3 billion pieces of mail in the year that ended on Sept. 30, 1980. Nevertheless, President Ronald Reagan proposed a reduction of $632 million in federal subsidies to the Postal Service in the year starting Oct. 1, 1981. These subsidies had been reduced by $250 million during the preceding fiscal year.

Payroll costs, which account for 85 per cent of Postal Service expenses, increased after a new three-year contract was ratified on August 25 by the American Postal Workers Union and the National Association of Letter Carriers of the United States of America. The agreement provided for a $2,100 increase in pay over three years, and cost-of-living increases tied to the Consumer Price Index. Bolger said the package would add $4.8 billion to the Postal Service's payroll. The settlement, reached during a 30-hour bargaining session ending on July 21, came after threats of an illegal strike by leaders of the two unions. Before the new contract took effect, the average postal worker earned $21,146 per year.

The Nine-Digit ZIP Code, which would send mail directly to an individual letter carrier's route instead of just to a postal station, encountered heavy opposition. The Postal Service said that the change would save $571 million per year by 1987, when it would be in full effect, but protests from Congress and the White House delayed the planned start of the system. First, it was postponed from February to June 1981. Next, the nine-digit code was to be used on a "completely voluntary" basis by business firms starting on June 28. Finally, Congress postponed the introduction of the new system for other mailers until Oct. 1, 1983, at the earliest. The Postal Service notified large mailers of plans for the nine-digit ZIP codes, but households were not scheduled to get this information until 1982. Meanwhile, the five-digit ZIP code was to remain in effect indefinitely. William J. Eaton

In WORLD BOOK, see POST OFFICE; POSTAL SERVICE, UNITED STATES.

PRESIDENT OF THE UNITED STATES. Ronald Reagan was inaugurated as the 40th President of the United States on Jan. 20, 1981. He pledged to revitalize the U.S. economy, balance the federal budget, and reduce the size and scope of the federal government. The President survived an assassination attempt on March 30 and recovered quickly from serious bullet wounds. He went on to persuade Congress to enact his new economic program, reverse a 50-year trend toward greater federal participation in social programs, and approve a six-year, $1.48-trillion military-spending package.

Assassination Attempt. President Reagan was shot in the chest as he left the Washington (D.C.) Hilton Hotel after addressing a labor meeting on March 30. The President's press secretary, James S. Brady, and two security men were also wounded in the attack. The President was rushed to George Washington University Hospital where, after two hours of chest surgery, he was pronounced in "good" condition. He remained in the hospital until April 11, and by mid-June had made a complete recovery.

Vice-President George H. W. Bush, in Texas for a speaking engagement at the time of the shooting, returned to Washington on the evening of March 30 and assumed many of the President's duties while he was hospitalized. See BUSH, GEORGE H. W.

John W. Hinckley, Jr., a 25-year-old college dropout from Evergreen, Colo., was arrested immediately after the shooting, and on August 24 was indicted for attempting to kill the President. Hinckley made two suicide attempts while in custody. At year-end he was in a federal prison awaiting trial.

Reaganomics. President Reagan addressed the nation on February 5, asking for support for sweeping budget and tax cuts. The President urged a joint session of Congress on April 28 to pass his 1982 fiscal budget. On July 31, Congress approved the President's package of budget cuts totaling more than $35 billion. On August 4, Congress approved Reagan's plan to reduce personal and corporate income taxes by 25 per cent over three years, the largest tax cut in U.S. history.

On September 24, the President asked for an additional $13 billion in federal spending cuts for fiscal 1982 so that he could achieve his goal of a balanced budget in fiscal 1984. On November 6, Reagan abandoned his goal of balancing the federal budget by 1984 but refused to consider raising taxes or cutting defense spending. President Reagan exercised his first veto on November 23 in rejecting a $428-billion stopgap spending bill

Struck by gunfire on March 30 as he waves to onlookers, *top,* President Reagan draws upright, *center,* then is shoved into his limousine, *bottom.*

Ronald Reagan is sworn in as 40th President
by Chief Justice Warren E. Burger on January
20 as Reagan's wife, Nancy, looks on.

prohibiting strikes against the federal government. The President warned PATCO members on August 3 that they were breaking the law and ordered them back to work. On August 5 he directed the FAA to fire all striking controllers, and on August 17 the FAA began to replace the PATCO strikers.

The striking controllers did not win wide labor support, but many union members became wary of the President's approach to labor unions and strikes. On September 19, at a Solidarity Day demonstration in Washington, D.C., organized by the American Federation of Labor and Congress of Industrial Organizations (AFL-CIO), some 260,000 people protested the President's budget cuts in social programs.

Presidential Advisers were often a cause for concern and embarrassment during the year. Secretary of State Alexander M. Haig, Jr., was involved in several conflicts with other Cabinet officers and White House staff members over his role in emergency and security affairs. He voiced a "lack of enthusiasm" for the appointment on March 24 of Vice-President Bush as head of the crisis management team designed to respond to federal emergency situations; challenged Secretary of Defense Caspar W. Weinberger over the chain of military command after President Reagan was shot on March 30; and hinted that national security adviser Richard V. Allen was trying to undermine his authority in November. The President reprimanded Haig and Allen for "feuding" on November 5.

Allen became a further source of controversy in November when it was revealed that he had accepted $1,000 from a Japanese magazine in return for arranging an interview with the President's wife, Nancy. Allen took a leave of absence from his position on November 29 pending an investigation by the Department of Justice. Although cleared by the investigation, he resigned, at President Reagan's request, on Jan. 4, 1982.

David A. Stockman, director of the Office of Management and Budget, said he had exercised "poor judgment and loose talk" in a series of interviews with *The Atlantic* magazine in which he criticized the Administration's economic programs. Reagan reprimanded Stockman, but refused to accept his resignation.

Foreign Policy. On January 29, Reagan charged that Russia's leaders "reserve for themselves the right to commit any crime, to lie, to cheat," and on April 5, the President wrote to Communist Party General Secretary and Supreme Soviet Presidium Chairman Leonid Ilich Brezhnev warning against Soviet intervention to suppress labor unrest in Poland. Following a declaration of martial law in Poland on December 13, Reagan warned that the United States and its allies would take seriously any direct Soviet intervention in Poland.

On December 29, President Reagan imposed

passed by Congress because it contained less than 25 per cent of the $8.5 billion in cuts he had requested. On the same day, Congress passed and the President signed a three-week extension of current spending levels. On December 15, he signed a $413-billion federal-funding bill to keep the government running through March 31, 1982.

Federal Regulation. President Reagan acted quickly to implement his campaign promises to relax federal regulation of business in an effort to free money for investment and cut bureaucratic paperwork. On January 22, the President named Vice-President Bush to a Cabinet-level post as the head of a Task Force on Regulatory Relief. On January 28, the President ended remaining price and allocation controls on crude oil produced in the United States. The following day, in his first press conference, Reagan announced the abolition of the Council on Wage and Price Stability and ordered a 60-day freeze on all pending government regulations. Reagan signed an executive order on February 17 requiring federal agencies to list alternatives, including costs and benefits, when proposing regulations.

The President's Labor Policies. President Reagan responded quickly when the Professional Air Traffic Controllers Organization (PATCO) voted on July 29 to walk off their jobs with the Federal Aviation Administration (FAA) in defiance of a law

Four U.S. Presidents – Gerald R. Ford, Richard M. Nixon, Ronald Reagan, and Jimmy Carter – meet in October to mourn the death of Egypt's Anwar el-Sadat.

limited economic sanctions against the Soviet Union, charging it with "heavy and direct responsibility for the repression in Poland." He halted negotiations on long-term grain agreements; suspended maritime negotiations; halted exports of electronics and oil equipment; and banned the Soviet airline, Aeroflot, from the United States.

Arms Build-Up. The President refused to consider cuts in the defense budget, declaring that the United States must strengthen its military to close the "window of vulnerability" that might permit the Soviet Union to attack the United States in the 1980s. On August 10, Secretary of Defense Weinberger revealed that President Reagan had ordered the production of neutron weapons. The decision reversed a policy of the Administration of President Jimmy Carter.

On October 2, the President revealed a $180.3-billion defense program. His plan to strengthen the nation's strategic nuclear arsenal included the deployment of 100 M-X intercontinental missiles, many in existing missile silos that would be "super-hardened" to withstand nuclear attack; the construction of 100 B-1 long-range bombers; more powerful and more accurate missiles for Trident submarines; and the establishment of an improved military communications network.

On June 16, in a surprising reversal of policy, the Administration announced that it would sell arms to the People's Republic of China as part of the widening cooperation between the two countries. Some observers believed that the announcement indicated that the two countries were moving closer to forming an anti-Soviet alliance.

Arms Control. On November 18, in a major address on arms control, President Reagan offered a proposal that would limit missiles and conventional forces in Europe. The key proposal was an offer to cancel plans for deployment of new American intermediate-range missiles in Western Europe if the Soviet Union would dismantle its comparable missiles aimed at Western Europe. Reagan also proposed that a new round of arms-control negotiations – the Strategic Arms Reduction Talks (START) – begin soon. On November 30, U.S. and Russian negotiators in Geneva, Switzerland, began talks on limiting nuclear weapons in Europe.

Middle East Policy. The sale of Airborne Warning and Control System (AWACS) surveillance planes to Saudi Arabia reflected the Administration's determination to strengthen its military presence throughout the world. The Senate on October 28 approved the sale after it was overwhelmingly defeated in the House. The approval of only one chamber was needed. Israel viewed the sale as a serious threat to its security, but President Reagan wrote to Israel's Prime Minister Menachem Begin on October 28 that the United States was "fully committed" to guaranteeing Israel's "military and technological edge" over the Arabs. U.S. relations with Israel became strained in December when Israel annexed the Golan Heights, taken from Syria in 1967. The United States suspended a strategic-cooperation agreement made with Israel after the AWACS sale. In response, Begin said the agreement was canceled. See MIDDLE EAST.

Relations with Israel were, in fact, strained throughout 1981. Israel's bombing on June 7 of Iraq's Osirak nuclear reactor near Baghdad angered the President, and he ordered that the shipment of four F-16 planes sold to Israel be held up. The ban on shipment was lifted on August 17, and the planes were delivered to Israel on September 1. President Reagan also criticized the July 17 Israeli air raids on Palestinians in Beirut, Lebanon, in which a reported 300 civilians were killed. In May, President Reagan dispatched former Assistant Secretary of State Philip C. Habib to Jerusalem, Israel; Damascus, Syria; and Beirut to try to arrange a cease-fire between Israelis and soldiers of the Palestine Liberation Organization (PLO), who were fighting across Lebanon's borders. Despite friction between the United States and Israel, Habib succeeded in arranging a cease-fire between Israel and the PLO on July 24.

On August 19, two U.S. Navy F-14 fighter planes shot down two Soviet-built Libyan jets that had attacked them 60 miles (100 kilometers) off the coast of Libya. The President defended the American action, declaring that the U.S. planes flew into the airspace to challenge Libya's claims to international waters.

Foreign Aid. Reversing Carter Administration policy, the President in July instructed delegates to international development banks to vote in favor of loans to Chile, Argentina, Paraguay, and Uruguay despite these nations' recognized violations of human rights. In January, the United States had begun to send military aid to El Salvador, another nation accused of violating its citizens' rights, to counter the left wing offensive there.

On September 29, addressing the opening session of the 36th annual meeting of the World Bank and the International Monetary Fund, the President declared that incentives for private enterprise rather than outright foreign aid are the key to economic advancement in the developing nations. He sounded a similar theme at the International Meeting on Cooperation and Development – a summit of eight industrialized Northern nations and 14 developing Southern nations – in Cancún, Mexico, on October 22 and 23.   Carol L. Thompson

See also CONGRESS OF THE UNITED STATES; REAGAN, RONALD WILSON; UNITED STATES, GOVERNMENT OF THE. In the Special Reports section, see LEADER FOR THESE TIMES. In WORLD BOOK, see PRESIDENT OF THE UNITED STATES.

PRINCE EDWARD ISLAND. Premier Angus MacLean announced his retirement on Aug. 7, 1981, after 30 years as an elected politician – 25 of them in Canada's House of Commons. MacLean led the Progressive Conservative Party to office in the island province in 1979 and won re-endorsement through a by-election victory on July 13. The Conservatives held 22 of the legislature's 32 seats, and the Liberals held 10. A leadership convention on November 7 chose James M. Lee, 44, as MacLean's successor. Lee was sworn in as premier of the province 10 days later.

The budget presented by Finance Minister Lloyd MacPhail on March 12 showed heavy dependence on transfer payments from the federal government. The budget forecast revenues of $352-million (Canadian dollars; $1=U.S. 84 cents as of Dec. 31, 1981). About 53 per cent would come from two federal measures due to expire in March 1982. An illustration of Prince Edward Island's dependence upon Ottawa came on October 23. That day, the province announced that it would have to lay off 161 civil servants whose salaries were being paid by a federal department under a 15-year development plan. Ottawa intended to cut the final phase of the project in half, completing most of it on the federal level.   David M. L. Farr

See also CANADA. In WORLD BOOK, see PRINCE EDWARD ISLAND.

PRISON. United States prisons became even more overcrowded in 1981. Prisons held a record 328,695 inmates at the beginning of 1981, and courts added another 20,000 in the first six months of the year. The annual growth rate for the first six months was a record 12.8 per cent. The previous growth record was 10 per cent in 1975.

Federal prisons accounted for only a small part of the increase, with a net jump of 1,370 prisoners that reversed a three-year downward trend. Tough new state laws caused much of the increase. These laws specified minimum prison sentences for certain offenses and tightened parole policies.

Several state prisons housed twice their rated capacity, while others tried to ease overcrowding by using tents, prefabricated buildings, and local jails as well as early-release programs. Iowa and Michigan passed laws that allowed officials to roll back sentences, releasing inmates when a prison population ceiling was exceeded. A federal judge forced Alabama to release 222 prisoners on July 25 after declaring state facilities hopelessly inadequate. This was the first ruling of its kind.

The Supreme Court of the United States ruled on June 15 that prison officials could house more than one prisoner in a cell built for one inmate without violating constitutional prohibitions against cruel and unusual punishment, as long as other prison facilities were adequate and humane. On October

20, the court ruled that prisoners must take their appeals to state courts before appealing to the federal court system. The court decided on June 17 that convicts serving life terms do not have a constitutional right to parole.

Steven T. Judy became the fourth prisoner to be executed in the United States since the Supreme Court reinstated capital punishment in 1977. Judy was electrocuted on March 9 at Indiana State Prison in Michigan City. Judy, 24, had raped and murdered a woman and drowned her three young children in 1979.

Riots in four Michigan prisons caused $5 million in property damage and more than 50 injuries in May. James Earl Ray, assassin of Martin Luther King, Jr., was stabbed 22 times and critically injured on June 4 by fellow inmates at Brushy Mountain State Prison in Petros, Tenn.

A report issued on July 6 by South Africa's National Institute for Crime Prevention and Rehabilitation of Offenders revealed that South Africa has the highest prison population per capita in the Western world—440 inmates per 100,000 residents. By contrast, the United States holds 189 of each 100,000 persons in prison.   David C. Beckwith

In WORLD BOOK, see PRISON.

PRIZES. See AWARDS AND PRIZES; CANADIAN LIBRARY ASSOCIATION; CANADIAN LITERATURE; NOBEL PRIZES.

Workers assemble a bronze sculpture of praying hands at the City of Faith medical complex in Tulsa, Okla., built by evangelist Oral Roberts.

PROTESTANTISM. Conflict marked 1981 for some of the younger and smaller Protestant churches in the United States, while older and larger denominations worked toward reconciliation after years of tension. The Salvation Army, an international religious group well known for its work among the poor, withdrew in protest from the World Council of Churches (WCC) in September 1981. The Salvation Army, which helped found the largely Protestant and Eastern Orthodox council in 1948, had charged for several years that the WCC was growing too supportive of violent Third World guerrilla movements. The WCC leadership claimed that it was only giving support to people who were acting out the Biblical drama of the poor overthrowing the powerful and oppressive. The Salvation Army was also concerned about trends by the council to stress sacramental unity, because the army does not practice the sacraments of baptism and the Lord's Supper.

Other churches experienced internal stresses in 1981. The Church of Jesus Christ of Latter-day Saints, centered in Utah, found itself arguing with the smaller Missouri-based Reorganized Church of Jesus Christ of Latter Day Saints over the origins and authority of their two church bodies. Missouri Mormon leaders have long claimed that they are the rightful heirs of Mormon founder Joseph Smith and that the Mormons who moved to Utah under

the leadership of Brigham Young had followed a usurper. In March 1981, a Utah Mormon antique dealer, Mark Hoffman, reported his discovery of a document dated Jan. 17, 1844. In this document, Joseph Smith clearly expressed his desire that his son, Joseph Smith III—who became the leader of the reorganized church in Missouri—should be his successor and spiritual heir. The Utah Mormon leaders acknowledged the authenticity of the document but announced that its discovery would not alter their policies.

The Seventh-Day Adventists also debated an issue of authenticity during the year. Most of the 3.5 million Adventists throughout the world ascribe a sort of "scriptural" authority to the visions written down by their 19th-century leader Ellen Gould White. Before her death in 1915, White claimed some 2,000 such visions. An Adventist pastor, Walter Rea of Long Beach, Calif., produced evidence in 1981 allegedly showing that White had plagiarized her visions from the published writings of others. Rea said that 80 per cent of White's material was unoriginal and contended, "Now we know it is all false." He was defrocked.

The Adventist leadership also had to respond to a 991-page document of evidence presented by Australian Adventist theologian Desmond Ford—now in the United States—alleging that White had departed from the Biblical book of Daniel in her

The archbishop of Canterbury, Robert Runcie, center, watches a Vietnamese children's group in Garden Grove, Calif., during his U.S. tour in May.

view of the end of history and the Second Coming of Jesus. Robert Olson, who directs the White estate and serves as custodian of her papers, was unruffled as he spoke for Adventist leadership, "The church's confidence in the prophetic leadership of Ellen White is unimpaired."

Another Protestant church body, the conservative Christian Reformed Church, was also beset by dissension. An ultraconservative group of pastors in Iowa announced plans to start a "protest seminary." They charged that teachings at the denominational school — Calvin Seminary in Grand Rapids, Mich. — were too liberal and compromising. The church leadership and the majority of pastors and members vigorously denied the charge.

Reconciliation was the keynote at conventions of three major Lutheran church bodies in the United States in 1981. Polls of the 18,504 delegates to the conventions of the Lutheran Church in America, the American Lutheran Church, and the Association of Evangelical Lutheran Churches showed that 86 per cent favored the formation of a single Lutheran church. Advocates of unity hoped that a merger could occur as early as 1987.

A Lutheran group that opposed such a merger, The Lutheran Church — Missouri Synod, concentrated on developing internal unity at its convention in 1981. President J. A. O. Preus, whose election in 1969 brought 12 years of extremely conservative policies, chose not to stand for re-election. The Missouri Synod elected as its president another archconservative with a more moderate manner — Ralph A. Bohlmann, president of Concordia Seminary in St. Louis. Bohlmann expressed hope that the synod would find ways to cooperate with other Lutherans on some levels. He concurred, however, with synod delegates who voted to break off fellowship with their largely Midwestern partner, the American Lutheran Church (ALC). The Missouri Synod objects to the ALC ordination of women and claims that the ALC is not sufficiently traditionalist in its understanding of Biblical authority. The Missouri Synod believes in Biblical "inerrancy" in matters of science and historical detail.

The conservative and stress-filled Southern Baptist Convention also worked toward internal harmony in 1981. Some of the reconciliation efforts resulted from an impressive showing by moderates at a Los Angeles convention in June. Presidents of the Southern Baptist Convention traditionally succeed themselves for one additional term, but moderates at the convention gained the support of some 40 per cent of the delegates for challenger Abner V. McCall, chancellor of Baylor University in Waco, Tex. The moderates' challenge led President Bailey Smith, an Oklahoma pastor, to rein in the church body's tendency to purge seminary professors and other moderate leaders who are unacceptable to extreme conservatives.

The United Presbyterian Church in the U.S.A. also did some patching up during its 1981 general assembly. Protest over church policies of ordaining women and being too lax over homosexuality and too liberal in theology had led some ultraconservative congregations to leave the denomination. But the assembly delegates acted to help defuse the protest and perhaps slow the walkout of dissenters by voting overwhelmingly in support of historic Presbyterian teachings as formulated in the 1500s and 1600s. This action put the liberal leadership on its guard and was seen as a sign of that leadership's moderation.

The New Christian Right Movement, which became controversial during the national elections of 1980, continued to make news in 1981. One element of this movement pressed hard to get equal time in public schools for a literal Biblical approach to universal and human origins. These "scientific creationists" claimed that the theory of evolution was being taught as fact and supported with religious fervor, and thus had become privileged – against the will of the public. In March, a California judge directed school districts to give more publicity to a 1973 policy statement that urged schools to stress that evolution is a theory (see EDUCATION). The Arkansas state legislature passed a resolution in March requiring that equal time be given to "creation science" whenever evolution was taught in public schools. This resolution was challenged in court by other Protestant, Roman Catholic, and Jewish leaders as an unconstitutional establishment of religion.

Another group of the conservative Christian movement, the Coalition for Better Television, threatened to boycott companies that sponsor television programs offensive to them, such as shows that feature sex or violence. Several major advertisers announced new policies that would show more sensitivity to these viewers and their values.

The Moral Majority, led by evangelist Jerry Falwell, expressed support throughout 1981 for President Ronald Reagan and some of the new conservative tendencies in government. But it protested noisily the Reagan Administration's reluctance to put such issues as abortion, school prayer, and legislation to support "the traditional family" ahead of economic and defense agendas. The political activities of the Moral Majority and similar groups inspired counterorganization by People for the American Way and some church groups that oppose the stands taken by the New Christian Right. Both sides girded themselves for the 1982 elections.   Martin E. Marty

See also RELIGION. In WORLD BOOK, see PROT-ESTANTISM and articles on Protestant denominations.

PSYCHOLOGY. Chemicals that affect human intelligence made news in 1981. Herbert Weingartner and five colleagues at the National Institute of Mental Health (NIMH) in Bethesda, Md., reported in the February 6 issue of *Science* magazine that a proteinlike substance called 1-desamino-8-D-arginine vasopressin (DDAVP) influences human learning and memory. DDAVP is found in natural form near the hippocampus, a part of the brain involved in memory. Previous research showed that laboratory animals that were given DDAVP outperformed control animals that were not given the substance in simple tests of learning and memory performance.

The NIMH researchers gave small groups of college students DDAVP or a neutral solution in a nasal spray three times per day. On the days the students received DDAVP, their performance on memory tests improved markedly, sometimes by 20 per cent or more. On days when the students received the nasal spray without DDAVP, their performance was normal.

Alzheimer's Disease, a common cause of senility in old people, was the subject of a conference held in January 1981 at the National Institutes of Health in Bethesda. Six groups of researchers all reported that old people who suffer symptoms of senility are deficient in choline acetyltransferase, an enzyme vital to the manufacture of acetylcholine, an important brain chemical.

Senility is a major problem of old age, affecting 1 out of 6 people over the age of 65. According to researchers, 60 to 80 per cent of nursing home patients show the disease symptoms of forgetfulness, irritability, and confusion. Although scientists knew that widespread degeneration of brain cells causes the symptoms, the absence of acetylcholine in patients suffering from Alzheimer's disease is the first consistent, marked biochemical abnormality they have found. Peter Davies of Albert Einstein College of Medicine in New York City said the new finding gives researchers a tool they can use to find the cause and cure of Alzheimer's disease.

Neurologists Gary E. Gibson and Christine Peterson of Cornell University Medical College in White Plains, N.Y., and pharmacologist Donald J. Jenden of the University of California at Los Angeles (UCLA) School of Medicine in August reported the results of an experiment that appeared to confirm the tie between acetylcholine and senility. The researchers tested the ability of mice aged 3 months, 10 months, and 30 months to walk across a miniature tightrope. When they killed the mice and examined their brains, the scientists found decreased levels of acetylcholine in the brains of older mice. In almost every case, the less acetylcholine a mouse had in its brain, the more difficult it had been for the mouse to walk the tightrope.

The Possible Long-Term Effects of marijuana on intelligence were studied by a group of researchers at UCLA School of Medicine. Psychiatrists Jeffrey Schaeffer, Therese Andrysiak, and J. Thomas Ungerleider reported their findings in the July 24 issue of *Science*. They had studied members of a religious sect who use marijuana "in a continuous and ritualistic manner throughout virtually all waking hours." The sect members smoke a potent form of the drug with a tetrahydrocannabinol (THC) content of more than 8 per cent. THC is the active ingredient in marijuana and hashish.

Schaeffer and his colleagues gave the smokers a battery of psychological tests, including the Michigan Neuropsychological Test Sequences, the Wechsler Adult Intelligence Scale, the Rey Auditory-Verbal Learning Test, and Raven's Progressive Matrices. They found that "none of the neuropsychological test data indicated impairment of cognitive functioning." Language intelligence and nonlanguage intelligence were unimpaired, and general intellectual functioning was equal to or better than average. The researchers also located intelligence quotient (IQ) scores of the sect members in school records dating back 15 to 20 years, well before their use of marijuana. These IQ scores were virtually identical to the cult members' present scores. Russell A. Dewey

In WORLD BOOK, see PSYCHOLOGY.

PUBLIC HEALTH. A mysterious epidemic, finally traced to a substance sold as cooking oil, killed more than 200 persons and sickened another 15,000 in Spain in 1981. The first death occurred on May 1 in Madrid. The disease – characterized by severe muscular pain, fever, skin rashes, and impaired nerve function – was initially termed an "atypical pneumonia" by Spanish health officials. As it spread through the provinces around Madrid, however, the disease was linked to use of an oil that had originally been imported for industrial purposes, then reprocessed and sold door-to-door as cooking oil. International teams of physicians were unable to explain how the oil caused the disease, and no effective remedy was found.

U.S. Health Trends. The decline in life expectancy in the United States in 1980, the first such dip since 1968, reflected a 14 per cent increase in deaths from influenza and pneumonia, according to a report issued by the National Center for Health Statistics in October 1981. The life expectancy at birth for Americans in 1980 was 73.6 years, down from a record high of 73.8 in 1979.

In 1981, however, there were several indicators of improving national health. For example, the infant mortality rate reached its lowest point in U.S. history. Only about 1.2 per cent of babies born in the United States died during the first year of life – about half the rate in 1960.

In September, a Gallup Poll reported a decline in the percentage of smokers in the United States. Thirty-five per cent of the respondents to the poll said they smoked, the lowest percentage in 37 years. The number of people who smoked more than two packs a day declined from 13 per cent in 1977 to 2 per cent in 1981.

Venereal Disease. An October report from the Venereal Disease National Hotline, a venereal disease (VD) information and referral service, challenged the stereotype of VD victims as young, nonwhite, urban, and poor. The report said that only 18 per cent of callers to the hotline were under 20 years old, more than 50 per cent earned at least $15,000 a year, and 83 per cent were white.

The Centers for Disease Control (CDC) in Atlanta, Ga., strongly recommended routine tests for penicillin-resistant gonorrhea, a problem that was spreading across the United States. Until 1980, most cases of this gonorrhea, which resists standard medications, had been brought from overseas by returning servicemen. But Stuart T. Brown, CDC coordinator for international VD-control activities, reported in July that the disease had risen sharply in Florida and California.

Among heterosexual white Americans, the most common venereal disease was *chlamydia trachomatis*, a bacterial infection. Paul Weisner, director of CDC's venereal disease control activities, estimated that 2.5 million to 3 million Americans had chlamydia and that each year more than 100,000 babies born to women with chlamydia developed pneumonia or eye infection as a result.

Other Diseases. The first reported case of human rabies in the United States in nearly two years killed a 27-year-old man in Oklahoma City, Okla., in July. There was no known cause of the rabies.

Rocky Mountain spotted fever, a disease that is transmitted by wood ticks, increased by 25 per cent during the first six months of 1981, according to CDC officials. The disease has a mortality rate of 5 per cent.

The campaign to eliminate measles by late 1982 was proceeding on schedule, according to the CDC. In 1980, 13,430 cases of measles were reported, 170 fewer than in 1979. More than 75 per cent of the counties in the United States had no cases.

Researchers at Massachusetts Public Health Biological Laboratories developed an antiserum that prevents chicken pox in infants and children who are unusually susceptible to the disease. The antiserum, called varicella zoster immune globulin, became available through Red Cross blood centers in February. It consists of concentrated chicken pox antibodies that are obtained from the blood of people who have developed immunity to the disease. Dianne Hales

See also HEALTH AND DISEASE; MEDICINE. In WORLD BOOK, see PUBLIC HEALTH.

PUBLISHING. The United States book industry faced continued threats of censorship during 1981. On April 17, for example, Georgia Governor George D. Busbee signed a bill making it a misdemeanor to sell, lend, or distribute books and other materials containing descriptions or depictions of "illicit sex or sexual immorality" to minors.

The Supreme Court of the United States on October 13 agreed to decide whether students could sue school board members for banning books from public schools. A lower court had previously dismissed the case in question – a 1976 suit against members of a Long Island, N.Y., school board who removed 11 books they deemed obscene or antireligious from a high school library.

Acquisitions and Sales. European companies figured prominently in sales of publishing companies during 1981. In an unprecedented take-over announced in January, the French industrial conglomerate Matra acquired a controlling interest of 41 per cent in Hachette, the largest publishing group in France. Previously, no single organization had owned more than a small fraction of Hachette's stock. International Thomson Organization Limited of Toronto, Canada, on April 1 acquired the Litton Industries publishing division – its fourth purchase of a U.S. book publishing firm in less than four years. On May 15, New

English Library – a subsidiary of Times-Mirror of Los Angeles in the United Kingdom – was sold to the British publishing firm Hodder and Stoughton for $4.7 million.

Other changeovers occurred between U.S. companies. Hearst Corporation acquired all of the outstanding stock of William Morrow & Company – the 55-year-old publishing house – from SFN Companies Incorporated of Chicago for $25.3 million on May 1. CBS Inc. agreed on June 19 to divest itself of Popular Library, ending a three-year antitrust suit by the United States Department of Justice. CBS kept its major publishing subsidiary, Fawcett Publications Incorporated.

Writers' Fees. In what was claimed to be the largest advance for a work not yet in manuscript, Simon & Schuster paid $2 million for the hardcover and paperback rights to Carl Sagan's novel *Contact.* However, most writers fared considerably worse. According to a study released on June 15 by Columbia University in New York City, the median income for writers in 1981 was only $4,775 per year. The Writers' Congress meeting in New York City in October voted unanimously to form a national union to work for higher pay for free-lance book and magazine writers. Celeste Huenergard

See also CANADIAN LITERATURE; LITERATURE; MAGAZINE; NEWSPAPER; POETRY. In WORLD BOOK, see BOOK; PUBLISHING.

PUERTO RICO experienced political turmoil in 1981, as narrowly re-elected Governor Carlos Romero Barcelo sought to govern with a slim popular mandate. Barcelo faced a legislature dominated by the opposition party.

The cuts in federal spending approved in 1981 by the Congress of the United States at the prodding of President Ronald Reagan were expected to have dire consequences for Puerto Rico, which relies on federal revenues for one-third of its gross domestic product. Puerto Rico will lose an estimated $500 million to $700 million annually in U.S. aid.

A pro-independence terrorist group called the Macheteros claimed responsibility for the bombing and destruction of nine U.S. military jets stationed at the Muniz Air National Guard base near San Juan on January 12.

In August, the United Nations (UN) Special Committee on Decolonization approved a resolution to return Puerto Rico to the list of territories having colonial status. If the UN General Assembly approves the resolution, the United States would be required to submit a yearly report of its conduct on the island. Nathan A. Haverstock

See also LATIN AMERICA (Facts in Brief Table). In WORLD BOOK, see PUERTO RICO.

PULITZER PRIZES. See AWARDS AND PRIZES.

QATAR. See MIDDLE EAST.

Australian publisher Rupert Murdoch displays a copy of *The Times* of London as he announces in January his forthcoming purchase of the paper.

Supporters of Prime Minister René Lévesque celebrate his election win in April. His Parti Québécois took 80 seats in Quebec's legislature.

QUEBEC voters surprisingly re-elected the separatist government of Prime Minister René Lévesque on April 13, 1981. Since coming to power late in 1976, Lévesque's Parti Québécois (PQ) had suffered 11 successive by-election defeats. It also had seen its objective of sovereignty-association — an independent Quebec — rejected in a 1980 referendum. But in 1981, after Lévesque assured voters he would not hold another referendum on Quebec's future if he won a second term, the PQ won 80 of the 122 seats in the National Assembly.

The Liberals under Claude Ryan took 42 seats, a gain of eight. The chief loser was the once-powerful Union Nationale party, which lost all five of its seats and saw its share of the popular vote plummet from 18 to 4 per cent. For the first time, the PQ elected two English-speaking members, possibly indicating that the isolation of English Quebeckers was beginning to break down.

The Constitutional Proposals of Canada's Prime Minister Pierre Elliott Trudeau were bitterly attacked by Lévesque, both alone and with the seven other provincial premiers who opposed them. Lévesque called a special three-day session of the National Assembly to adopt a resolution condemning federal action on the constitution as impairing the rights and powers of Quebec. The motion was approved by a vote of 111 to 9 on October 2. When all 10 provincial premiers met with Trudeau in November, all except Lévesque finally supported the constitutional proposals.

Income and Outgo. Finance Minister Jacques Parizeau's fifth budget, presented on March 10, tried to meet mounting deficits by reaching out for new sources of revenue. Hydro-Québec, a massive state-owned utility that paid no provincial income tax, was to be charged a "royalty" on its income for 1982. In 1979, Hydro-Québec's net income was $746 million (Canadian dollars; $1 = U.S. 84 cents as of Dec. 31, 1981), with more profit expected to be reported for 1980. The royalty concept was inspired by Alberta's levy on oil and gas production. Other provincially owned companies would also pay dividends to the state at a rate of about 20 per cent of earnings. Even with these changes in taxation, the Parizeau budget forecast a deficit for the province of almost $3 billion on $20 billion in expenditures.

Demographers announced that Quebec was losing population to the booming western provinces at a higher rate than Ontario. In 1980, more than 13,000 families left Quebec, twice the number that moved in. This exodus meant the loss of about 30,500 people during the year.   David M. L. Farr

See also CANADA. In WORLD BOOK, see QUEBEC.

RACING. See AUTOMOBILE RACING; BOATING; HORSE RACING; ICE SKATING; SKIING; SPORTS; SWIMMING; TRACK AND FIELD.

Anthony Daniels, left, and Mark Hamill re-create their roles as C-3PO and Luke Skywalker in an adaptation of *Star Wars* for National Public Radio.

RADIO. In 1981, the radio industry in the United States underwent sweeping deregulation. On January 14, the Federal Communications Commission (FCC) voted 6 to 1 to free the country's 9,089 radio stations from many regulations involving advertising, programming, and record keeping.

The New Freedoms. Radio stations no longer had to limit advertising messages to 18 to 20 minutes per hour. The FCC removed advertising limits on the theory that competition among the stations would prevent them from becoming overly commercialized. The FCC also dropped all rules governing the amount of news and public affairs programming a station must broadcast. Formerly, stations had to devote 6 to 8 per cent of their programming to news and public affairs.

Deregulation also freed radio broadcasters from having to keep comprehensive logs of the programs they broadcast. In addition, station officials no longer had to use certain procedures to ascertain community programming needs every three years.

The Supreme Court of the United States on March 24 handed down a decision supporting further deregulation. The court voted 7 to 2 in support of an FCC ruling that a station's program format is not to be considered in judging whether to grant or renew its license.

The FCC in 1981 petitioned Congress for approval of several other changes. On July 31, Congress approved an increase in the term of radio licenses from five years to seven years.

The FCC also asked Congress to change license-renewal procedures so that the commission would not have to review challenges to broadcasting licenses unless there was evidence that the license holder was unfit. FCC proposals to abolish two other regulations were still pending in Congress at year-end. One regulation required stations to give equal time to major candidates for public office, and the other required stations to give balanced coverage to important public issues.

The FCC voted on August 4 to drop a proposal to reduce the space between AM radio frequencies and thereby create 200 to 400 new stations. The FCC determined that the revised spacing could cost the radio industry up to $46 million in conversion costs and cause interference on the airwaves.

FM Popularity continued to increase in 1981 as the 4,460 FM stations in the United States expanded their share of the radio audience to 54.9 per cent, up from 51.4 per cent in 1980. FM stations, which have clearer signals than AM stations and the ability to broadcast stereophonic sound economically, featured a preponderance of musical programming. AM radio, though still dominated by stations with musical formats, was beginning to feature other types of programming.   Ron Alridge

In WORLD BOOK, see RADIO.

RAILROAD systems in the United States increased their profits in 1981. Harvey A. Levine, chief economist for the Association of American Railroads (AAR), credited sharply improved earnings to "increases in coal traffic, greater operating efficiency, and rapid recovery of inflationary cost increases" under a 1980 law that deregulated U.S. railroads. Business began to decline in the closing weeks of 1981, however.

The AAR said that United States railroad firms earned $977 million in the first six months of 1981, compared with a profit of $439 million in the first half of 1980. Operating revenues were $15.2 billion, 11 per cent higher than a year earlier. Second-quarter earnings totaled $341 million, 96 per cent above the 1980 second quarter, from 9 per cent greater revenues. Freight traffic was nearly unchanged by December.

Rate-Adjusting Flexibility given the industry by the deregulation act allowed railroads to raise freight rates quickly each quarter according to an AAR cost formula. The Interstate Commerce Commission allowed quarterly increases and special rate hikes based on fuel costs totaling about 9 per cent in 1981. Rate flexibility also permitted railroads to cut rates in an attempt to increase business.

Railroads also gained from labor peace. Six unions representing 240,000 employees agreed on a new contract on November 10. The 39-month contract called for a 32.5 per cent pay increase and some benefit gains.

Cutting Conrail Loose. The Administration of President Ronald Reagan pushed hard for legislation that would allow it to sell Consolidated Rail Corporation (Conrail). In August, Congress approved a plan that would allow the government to sell Conrail as a single unit any time it could find a buyer. However, the government could sell segments of Conrail no earlier than Nov. 1, 1983, and only if it was not making a profit.

Conrail Chairman L. Stanley Crane had warned in March that Conrail needed much more federal financing to keep running. However, Conrail earned profits in the second and third quarters of 1981. Crane credited the improvement to cost-reduction moves.

Passenger Traffic. The National Railroad Passenger Corporation (Amtrak) survived an Administration attempt to reduce its route system. Congress approved $735 million for Amtrak for the 1982 fiscal year. Amtrak ridership in 1981 was about equal to the 21.3 million passengers carried in 1980. Amtrak raised fares 9 per cent on April 26 and 6.5 per cent on October 26.   Albert R. Karr

In WORLD BOOK, see RAILROAD.

The new French T.V.G. (high-speed train), which will link Paris and Lyon, set a world speed record of 380 kilometers (236 miles) per hour in February.

President Reagan and his wife, Nancy, congratulate their son Ron on May 18 after his performance with the Joffrey II Dancers in Washington, D.C.

REAGAN, RONALD WILSON (1911-   ), 40th President of the United States, was sworn into office on Jan. 20, 1981, in a setting of pomp and glitter that contrasted markedly with the home-spun inauguration of his predecessor, Jimmy Carter. Republicans celebrated the change of administration with nine inaugural balls and four days of dinners, fireworks, and formal receptions.

Assassination Attempt. On March 30, President Reagan was shot in the chest as he left the Washington Hilton Hotel after speaking at a conference of labor leaders. The alleged assailant, John W. Hinckley, Jr., was seized and arrested immediately after the shooting. Press Secretary James S. Brady, Secret Service agent Timothy J. McCarthy, and Thomas Delahanty, a Washington, D.C., police officer, were also wounded. The President was rushed to George Washington University Hospital, where a bullet was removed from his left lung. He returned to the White House on April 11. Hinckley was awaiting trial at the end of 1981.

Relaxed Style. The 40th President was a relaxed chief executive. The oldest man (at 69) to win the presidency, Reagan clearly enjoyed his first year in office and his enormous personal popularity.

The President downplayed the widely publicized infighting among members of his Cabinet and the White House staff, particularly the conflict between Secretary of State Alexander M. Haig, Jr.,

and National Security Adviser Richard V. Allen. He also refused to fire David A. Stockman, director of the Office of Management and Budget, after Stockman's doubts about the Reagan economic program appeared in *The Atlantic* magazine.

Reagan delegated a great deal of authority to his three-man White House staff—Edwin Meese III, James A. Baker III, and Michael K. Deaver. He routinely reached his office at 8:45 A.M. and left before 6 P.M., spending the evening in his private quarters watching television or reading.

On August 6, the Reagans flew to their 688-acre (278-hectare) ranch near Santa Barbara, Calif., for a four-week holiday. The 28-day vacation was the longest taken by any U.S. President since Richard M. Nixon's in 1969.

Financial Disclosures. On January 30, the White House announced that Reagan had placed his assets in a blind trust, to be managed by Raymond J. Armstrong, president of the Starwood Corporation, an investment company. Reagan's financial disclosure report for 1980 revealed that his net worth was $4 million. The President's federal income tax return for 1980 reported an adjusted gross income of $227,968. He and his wife paid $69,563 in federal income tax for 1980.

Redecorating Controversy. The Reagans sparked controversy in March by using $735,912 in private donations to redecorate their private living quarters in the White House. Criticism again erupted when the first lady purchased new china for the official residence with a $209,000 contribution by a private donor.

The First Family. Nancy Reagan visited New York City to watch the Reagans' son Ron perform with the Joffrey II Dancers on March 15. On July 29, she attended the wedding of Prince Charles and Lady Diana Spencer in Great Britain. Patti Davis, the Reagans' actress daughter, appeared in two NBC television productions in 1981 under the terms of her exclusive contract signed with NBC Entertainment in December 1980. Maureen Reagan, the President's daughter by his first wife, actress Jane Wyman, was married to law clerk Dennis Revell on April 25. In the fall, she announced plans to enter the California senatorial race on the Republican ticket. On May 20, Michael Reagan, the President's son adopted during his first marriage, resigned his executive sales position with Dana Ingalls Profile Incorporated after he was sharply criticized for using President Reagan's name in a sales letter soliciting government contracts.   Carol L. Thompson

See also PRESIDENT OF THE UNITED STATES. In the Special Reports section, see LEADER FOR THESE TIMES. In WORLD BOOK, see REAGAN, RONALD WILSON.

RECORDINGS. The average cost of a long-playing record (LP) by an established performer rose to $8.98 in the United States in 1981. LP's by many new acts sold for $7.98.

Two-record LP sets lost popularity for the first time because of their price of $13 to $17. CBS Inc. became the first United States record company to abolish the virtually meaningless "suggested list price," allowing stores to set their own price for albums. The annual volume of illegally copied records and tapes in the United States had risen to $560 million by the beginning of 1981, up from $400 million a year earlier.

The mini-LP, a 7- or 12-inch (17.8- or 30.5-centimeter) disk spinning at 33⅓ revolutions per minute, was introduced by five more labels, bringing the total number of companies issuing them to nine. Mini-LP's sold for $4.98 and $5.98, an attractive price for young people. Record companies expected the disks to help new rock acts become popular.

LP Rental became the newest listening fad. Single-disk LP's rented for an average of $2 at a growing number of stores. The fad began at a store called Rena's Rent-A-Record in Toronto, Canada. In 1981, the store opened franchise outlets in Providence, R.I.; Los Angeles; Detroit; Chicago; and New York City.

President Reagan carves the turkey as wife, Nancy, and daughter Maureen help prepare Thanksgiving dinner at the Reagans' California ranch.

Singer Christopher Cross won five Grammy awards at the National Academy of Recording Arts and Sciences ceremony in February.

Mobile Fidelity Lab, a Chatsworth, Calif., company that sells extremely high-quality records, tapes, and players, introduced the first $40 LP in the United States. This kind of record is made in Japan from an extremely pure, heavy vinyl, and the disk weighs 7 ounces (200 grams), twice as much as a regular LP. The artists performing in this historic release were Pink Floyd, Supertramp, and Earl Klugh. The company planned a limited pressing of 5,000 copies of the LP.

In a move to stay abreast of the growing market for high-quality equipment, CBS introduced a system called CX that it claims eliminates surface noise on records and brings out high and low frequencies. However, users needed a special device called a decoder to enjoy these benefits.

Awards. The National Academy of Recording Arts and Sciences presented five Grammy awards to Christopher Cross at ceremonies in New York City's Radio City Music Hall in February. Cross won for best arrangement for a vocalist and for best recording, song, and album with "Sailing." He was also named best new artist of 1981. George Benson won Grammys for best rhythm and blues (R & B) male vocalist, best R & B instrumental, and best male jazz vocalist. Leonard Feather and Eliot Tiegel

See also MUSIC, CLASSICAL; MUSIC, POPULAR. In WORLD BOOK, see PHONOGRAPH.

RED CROSS. See COMMUNITY ORGANIZATIONS.

REGAN, DONALD THOMAS (1918-), was sworn in as secretary of the United States Department of the Treasury on Jan. 22, 1981. In his confirmation hearing, Regan told the Senate Finance Committee that reductions of federal regulation and government spending were the most important parts of President Ronald Reagan's economic program. Before joining the Reagan Administration, Regan was chairman and chief executive officer of Merrill Lynch & Company, Incorporated, a holding company.

Regan was born in Cambridge, Mass., on Dec. 21, 1918. He graduated from Harvard University with a bachelor of arts degree in 1940 and joined the Marine Corps. He left military service at the end of World War II as a lieutenant colonel.

Regan joined the brokerage firm of Merrill Lynch, Pierce, Fenner & Beane in 1946 as an account executive trainee. He became a general partner in 1954, and from 1955 to 1960 managed its Philadelphia office. He transferred to New York City in 1960 and in 1964 was elected the firm's executive vice-president. He became president of the company in 1968 and was elected chairman and chief executive officer in January 1971. He assumed the same positions in Merrill Lynch & Company when it was formed in 1973.

Regan and his wife, the former Ann Buchanan, have four children. Wayne Wille

RELIGION. News of religious reawakening in the People's Republic of China claimed the attention of observers of global religious trends during 1981. Since the Chinese revolution of 1949, Western scholars have known little about the survival in China of Christianity and the ancient Chinese philosophies and faiths, such as Confucianism, Taoism, and Buddhism. Reports from travelers and analysts in 1981 revealed new government attitudes toward religion in China.

In the spring of 1981, churches reopened in China that had been closed for years, and religious groups were again permitted to worship in public. Official policies appeared to be changing after three decades of repression.

Bishop Ting Kuang-hsun (Ding Guangxuan), head of Nanking (Nanjing) Theological College and vice-president of Nanking University, distinguished between the Chinese government's *attitude* toward religion — highly opposed — and its *policy* — grudgingly more generous. In this way, Ting said, the government allows for different religious outlooks among the Chinese people as long as they all work for a "united front" in the nation's modernization programs.

Ting also reported the revival after a 20-year lapse of a national organization of Protestant churches called the Three-Self Patriotic Movement ("self-government, self-support, and self-propaga-

U.S. Membership Reported for Religious Groups with 150,000 or More Members*

African Methodist Episcopal Church	2,050,000
African Methodist Episcopal Zion Church	1,134,176
American Baptist Association	1,500,000
American Baptist Churches in the U.S.A.	1,600,521
The American Lutheran Church	2,353,229
The Antiochian Orthodox Christian Archdiocese of North America	152,000
Armenian Church of America, Diocese of the (including Diocese of California)	450,000
Assemblies of God	1,732,371
Baptist Missionary Association of America	224,533
Christian and Missionary Alliance	189,710
Christian Church (Disciples of Christ)	1,177,984
Christian Churches and Churches of Christ	1,063,254
Christian Methodist Episcopal Church	786,707
Christian Reformed Church in North America	213,995
Church of God (Anderson, Ind.)	176,429
Church of God (Cleveland, Tenn.)	435,012
Church of God in Christ	425,000
Church of God in Christ, International	501,000
The Church of Jesus Christ of Latter-day Saints	2,811,000
Church of the Brethren	170,839
Church of the Nazarene	484,276
Churches of Christ	1,600,000
Community Churches, National Council of	190,000
Conservative Baptist Association of America	225,000
The Episcopal Church	2,786,004
Free Will Baptists	227,888
General Association of Regular Baptist Churches	243,000
Greek Orthodox Archdiocese of North and South America	1,950,000
Jehovah's Witnesses	565,309
Jews	5,920,000
Lutheran Church in America	2,923,260
The Lutheran Church—Missouri Synod	2,625,650
National Baptist Convention of America	2,688,799
National Baptist Convention, U.S.A., Inc.	5,500,000
National Primitive Baptist Convention	250,000
Orthodox Church in America	1,000,000
Polish National Catholic Church in America	282,411
Presbyterian Church in the United States	838,485
Progressive National Baptist Convention	521,692
Reformed Church in America	345,532
Reorganized Church of Jesus Christ of Latter Day Saints	190,087
The Roman Catholic Church	50,449,842
The Salvation Army	417,359
Seventh-day Adventists	571,141
Southern Baptist Convention	13,600,126
United Church of Christ	1,736,244
The United Methodist Church	9,584,711
United Pentecostal Church, International	465,000
The United Presbyterian Church in the U.S.A.	2,423,601
Wisconsin Evangelical Lutheran Synod	407,043

*Majority of the figures are for the years 1980 and 1981.
Source: National Council of Churches, *Yearbook of American and Canadian Churches* for 1982.

Classes are held again at the Nanking (Nanjing) Theological College in March as the government of China relaxes its restrictions on religion.

tion"). The movement's Roman Catholic counterpart—the Catholic Patriotic Association—met during May in Peking (Beijing). Both the Catholic and Protestant organizations, which are supervised by the government, are trying to link up with the many informal "underground" churches formed during the Cultural Revolution.

Religion and Violent Conflicts. Egypt's President Anwar el-Sadat was assassinated on Oct. 6, 1981, reportedly by Muslim fundamentalists or fanatics. Earlier in the year, Sadat had cracked down on both Muslim fundamentalists and militant Christian Copts, charging that both extremes threatened the stability of Egypt. See EGYPT.

Violence raged throughout 1981 in Iran, where the clergy-dominated Islamic Republican Party continued to hold power. Many assassinations were carried out by Muslim factions religiously and politically either to the right or to the left of the government led by Ayatollah Ruholla Khomeini.

In Afghanistan, Muslim tribal groups called *mujahedeen* (fighters for the faith) continued to resist Russian troops that had invaded Afghanistan in 1979. These tribal groups are fairly small bands that tend to fight one another when not unified in their struggle against the Russians. The mujahedeen see their military action against the invaders as part of a *jihad*, a holy struggle against unbelievers. See AFGHANISTAN.

In Israel, Prime Minister Menachem Begin and his Likud Party formed a coalition government in 1981 based on an alliance with small political parties dominated by Orthodox rabbis. To gain their votes, Begin made concessions, mainly on religious legislation. For example, he supported legislation requiring that the Israeli airline and government-owned companies eventually cease work on the Jewish Sabbath. The concessions set off a storm of protest from non-Orthodox and liberal Israelis. In August, Orthodox rabbis and their followers protested archaeological digs at the City of David near the Old City of Jerusalem. They claimed the digging disturbed the graves of ancient Jews and thus violated Jewish law. The courts disagreed, and the digging continued.

In India, Jainism, one of India's historic faiths, conducted ceremonies that occur every 12 to 14 years during the ritual washing of a statue. Thousands of pilgrims who pay for the privilege of sharing the ritual cleansing gathered in March at Shravanabelagola, at the 1,000-year-old stone statue of Lord Bahubali, whom they believe to be the only mortal in this epoch to achieve *nirvana* (spiritual liberation).   Martin E. Marty

See also EASTERN ORTHODOX CHURCHES; JEWS AND JUDAISM; PROTESTANTISM; ROMAN CATHOLIC CHURCH. In WORLD BOOK, see RELIGION and articles on various religions.

REPUBLICAN PARTY strategists in 1981 concentrated on making the GOP the majority party in the United States. On March 27, Richard Richards, the party's national chairman, spoke to the executive committee of the Republican National Committee (RNC) in Arlington, Va. He cited President Ronald Reagan's enormous popularity and the Republicans' possession of "the finest political money machine in the country" as assets in the drive for political dominance. Richards, a Utah lawyer, became RNC chairman in January, succeeding William E. Brock III, who became a special U.S. trade representative.

The Party's Immediate Goal was to gain control of Congress in 1982. Although the President's landslide victory in the 1980 election swept the party into a Senate majority for the first time since 1954, Democrats kept control of the House of Representatives. To get control of the House, the Republicans need a net gain of 27 seats in 1982, a feat that would be virtually unprecedented. Not since 1934 has the party in the White House gained congressional seats in an off-year election.

The national Republican campaign committees had budgeted $90 million for the 1982 elections, according to plans announced on October 28. This sum, a record amount for either party, would be in addition to funds raised locally by state and regional candidates. The Democratic national committees had planned to pour only $20 million into the campaign.

The Republican Party calculated that it would have another advantage in the 1982 election. The redistricting following the 1980 census is expected to shift 10 to 12 House seats from traditionally Democratic areas in the Northeast and Midwest to areas in the South and Southwest that usually vote Republican. To protect these gains, the RNC planned to spend $1 million in 1981 to help state Republican parties gain "fair" redistricting.

Republicans were also seeking to recruit Democrats in the House to switch parties. Two House Democrats did so in 1981. Bob Stump of Arizona announced in September that he would run for re-election as a Republican in 1982. And, with greater fanfare, Eugene V. Atkinson of Pennsylvania switched allegiance on October 14 in the White House Rose Garden.

Off-Year Elections, however, proved somewhat disappointing. In Virginia, 12 years of GOP control in the statehouse ended on November 3, when the gubernatorial contender, state Attorney General J. Marshall Coleman, lost to Democrat Charles S. Robb, Virginia's lieutenant governor and a son-in-law of President Lyndon B. Johnson. President Reagan campaigned in the state for Coleman, and the RNC spent heavily on his behalf. However,

Chairman Richard Richards and Co-Chairman Betty Heitman of the Republican National Committee were elected to office in January.

Coleman, a moderate, never seemed to win the full backing of Virginia's most conservative Republicans, and he lost the race by more than 100,000 votes.

In New Jersey, Republican candidate Thomas H. Kean, who also had the benefit of Reagan's personal campaigning, squeaked to victory over Democratic Representative James J. Florio in the closest race for governor in the state's history. Kean, who had a lead of only 1,677 of more than 2.2 million votes cast, survived a recount with approximately the same margin of victory. Florio had made the President's economic program his major campaign issue.

The Republicans lost one seat to Democrats in a series of special congressional elections. GOP candidate Liles B. Williams, running with Reagan's strong backing, lost to Democrat Wayne Dowdy in a Mississippi race for the seat vacated by Republican Jon Hinson, who resigned after his arrest on morals charges in February. The GOP retained seats in Michigan and Ohio but failed to win seats held by Democrats in Maryland and Pennsylvania.

Disputes and Disclosures. The Republican Party suffered in late fall as the Reagan Administration was rocked by disputes and disclosures. David A. Stockman, director of the Office of Management and Budget, had criticized the President's economic program in a series of interviews for *The Atlantic* magazine. Stockman offered his resignation, but the President refused to accept it.

Another controversy, involving National Security Adviser Richard V. Allen, also inflicted political damage. Allen was accused of accepting $1,000 in cash from a Japanese magazine in return for his help in securing an interview with President Reagan's wife, Nancy. Allen resigned on Jan. 4, 1982.

The Republican Party high command was divided in 1981 by a dispute over the role of independent political action committees. RNC Chairman Richards deplored the tactics of such groups as the National Conservative Political Action Committee, charging that their sharp personal attacks on Democrats "create all kinds of mischief." But Lyn Nofziger, Reagan's top political adviser, defended the harshly critical advertising against Democratic incumbents, saying: "You have to establish the negatives."

Richards came under fire in December for publicly declaring that Stockman and Allen would be dismissed from their jobs in the near future. President Reagan reprimanded him, and observers predicted that Richards would be stripped of his authority in the RNC. *William J. Eaton*

See also ELECTIONS. In WORLD BOOK, see REPUBLICAN PARTY.

RHODE ISLAND. See STATE GOVERNMENT.

RHODESIA. See ZIMBABWE.

ROADS. See TRANSPORTATION.

ROMAN CATHOLIC CHURCH. World attention turned in shock and dismay to Rome on May 13, 1981, when Pope John Paul II was shot in an assassination attempt. The pope was riding in an open car in St. Peter's Square, acknowledging the cheers of 10,000 tourists and religious pilgrims, when he was struck by two bullets from a 9-millimeter pistol. He was rushed by ambulance to nearby Gemelli Hospital and underwent 5½ hours of surgery to repair serious intestinal wounds and less dangerous wounds in his left hand and right arm. Two women tourists – an American and a Jamaican – were wounded by two other bullets, one critically. Both survived.

Moments after the shooting, angry bystanders and police seized the gunman. The police later identified him as Mehmet Ali Agca, 23, a militant Turkish terrorist and convicted murderer. Agca had escaped from prison in Turkey in 1979 and had threatened in a letter to assassinate the pope during John Paul's visit to Turkey that year.

The pope was released from the hospital on June 3, but he returned on June 20 for treatment of an infection and again in August for further surgery. After a period of convalescence, the pope was pronounced fit in October.

On July 22, an Italian court found Agca guilty of attempting to kill the pope. He was sentenced to life imprisonment. The Italian police could not connect Agca's action with any conspiracy, but an Italian newspaper, *Il Tempo,* said Agca had been part of a plot contrived by Russia's secret police agency, the KGB. According to the newspaper, the Soviet government feared the pope's influence with the people of Poland, where political unrest was brewing over Solidarity, the labor union involved in a power struggle with the Polish government. Vatican officials replied there was no evidence that the KGB had participated in any conspiracy.

Papal Asian Tour. On Feb. 15, 1981, before the shooting, the pope embarked on another world pilgrimage. His 12-day tour included stops in Pakistan, the Philippines, Japan, and Guam. The pope's visit to Karachi, Pakistan, was marred by the explosion of a bomb near a reviewing stand about 20 minutes before the pope's appearance. The explosion killed the man carrying the bomb.

In Manila, capital of the Philippines, where about 80 per cent of the population is Roman Catholic, the pope delivered a talk on human rights. For years, Philippine President Ferdinand E. Marcos has been involved in controversy over alleged human rights violations and political repression under his government. John Paul said,

Pope John Paul II sings a Polish folksong at a "Pope with the Youth" meeting in Tokyo during his 12-day tour of Asian countries in February.

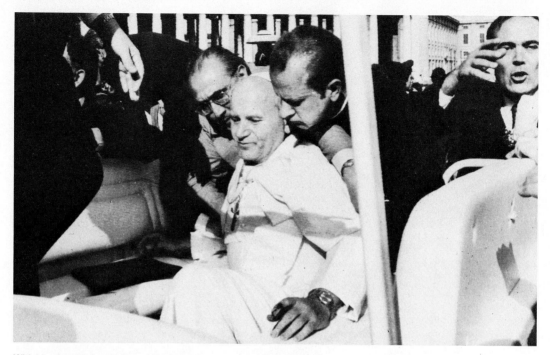

With blood on his hands, Pope John Paul II falls into the arms of his aides moments after being shot in Rome's St. Peter's Square on May 13.

"Even in exceptional situations that may at times arise, one can never justify any violation of the fundamental dignity of the human person or the basic rights that safeguard this dignity."

After a stop in Guam, the pope went on to Japan, arriving in Tokyo on February 23. During his visits to Hiroshima and Nagasaki, the two Japanese cities devastated by nuclear bombs in 1945 during World War II, the pope made an appeal for worldwide commitment to peace.

Church Policies. Pope John Paul II published an *encyclical* (a letter from the pope to his bishops stating church policy) on September 15 entitled *Laboren Exercens*. The Vatican gave it the English title *On Human Work*. The pope had intended to publish it on May 15, the 90th anniversary of Pope Leo XIII's encyclical *Rerum Novarum* (*Of New Things*), but the wounds he suffered in the assassination attempt delayed his work. In his encyclical, John Paul stressed that the human being is an image of God, and human work is an image of God's creativity; that labor has "priority" over capital; and that work is a social enterprise and must be seen within the scope of social groupings. The pope also wrote that labor unions are "an indispensable element" of modern industrialized society and an instrument "for the struggle for social justice."

Vatican officials emphasized the broad views and general language used in the encyclical and cautioned against applying it lightly to specific economic situations. In particular, the Vatican denied that the document specifically supported Solidarity. However, the pope's sympathies were known to lie with the Polish workers of Solidarity, and he gave an audience to Lech Walesa, Solidarity's leader, in the Vatican in January 1981. The pope also counseled restraint and nonviolence in his references to events in Poland.

The pope continued his policy of tightening church doctrine and practice during 1981. He denounced the "hasty" annulments granted by some church marriage tribunals. He also said that artificial birth control methods make women merely sex objects. The pope's representative in the United States, Archbishop Pio Laghi, complained to American bishops that Catholic newspapers often printed the work of writers who "did harm to the faith." Officials of the Catholic Press Association responded by citing Vatican appeals for free speech and pointed out the widespread support in the Catholic press for official church actions.

New Archbishops in Poland and China. On May 28, 1981, Stefan Cardinal Wyszyński, archbishop of Gniezno and Warsaw, died after serving more than 30 years as the head of Poland's Roman Catholic Church. Pope John Paul named Bishop Jozef Glemp of Warmia as Wyszyński's successor.

Glemp had served as an aide to Wyszyński from 1967 to 1978, when he was appointed bishop of Warmia. The Roman Catholic Church in Poland has great influence because the overwhelming majority of the people are Catholics.

The pope named Monsignor Dominic Tang Yiming as archbishop of Canton on June 6, 1981. The Patriotic Catholic Association of China, which split with the Roman Catholic Church after the 1949 Chinese revolution, had previously named Tang as its bishop of Canton. The appointment by the pope was seen by some observers as an effort by the Vatican to repair its split with the Patriotic Catholic Association. The Vatican does not recognize bishops ordained by the Chinese church, and the Chinese church does not recognize the authority of the pope. The Chinese government rejected Tang's appointment.

In the United States, Catholic groups took stands on various social and political issues during 1981. Several Catholic leaders criticized President Ronald Reagan's budget cuts in social programs for poor Americans. A number of American Catholic bishops publicly criticized the construction and maintenance of nuclear arms by the government.

On April 2, the United States Catholic Conference, which implements policies set forth by U.S. bishops, proposed a list of moral principles to be followed in energy production, use, and waste disposal. A report by the Center for Applied Research in the Apostolate published in March stated that most Catholic churches in the United States saw women only in traditional roles. The report recommended that seminarians study the experiences of women in history and in contemporary life; that all dioceses offer training in the ministry to anyone, regardless of sex; and that a study be conducted to suggest ways in which nonordained persons of either sex might preach.

Ecumenical Efforts. The Vatican named Bishop Bernard F. Law of Springfield and Cape Girardeau, Mo., to direct efforts to receive into the Roman Catholic communion Anglican priests who disapprove of the ordination of women by the Anglican Church. This effort offended some Episcopalians, but Anglican and Roman Catholic scholars in Great Britain reported progress in unity discussions. Unity discussions were also held between representatives of the Catholic Church and leaders of the Lutheran, United Methodist, and Presbyterian churches.

Representatives of the Roman Catholic Church and the Eastern Orthodox Churches also met for discussions about unity. The split between these two churches dates back to 1054. Numerous differences in doctrine and practice exist between the two faiths, but both groups agreed to continue the talks. Owen Campion

In WORLD BOOK, see ROMAN CATHOLIC CHURCH.

ROMANIA was active in international diplomacy in 1981. The Polish crisis posed a dilemma for Romanian leaders. They worried that Russia might intervene in Poland, establishing a precedent for an intervention in Romania. However, they insisted that Poland had a right to settle its problems without outside interference. After the Polish labor union Solidarity held its national congress in September and October, Romania began to denounce it sharply as an "antisocialist movement."

Relations with Russia and other Warsaw Pact nations improved, then worsened. Romania's Communist Party General Secretary and President Nicolae Ceausescu visited Russia's Communist Party General Secretary and Supreme Soviet Presidium Chairman Leonid Ilich Brezhnev in the Crimea on July 31. After the meeting, they announced that trade between the two countries would double in the period from 1981 to 1985 and that Romania would help to build a gas pipeline and dig an iron mine in Russia.

But relations deteriorated in the autumn. Ceausescu demanded a summit meeting to discuss the economic problems of the Communist bloc's Council for Mutual Economic Assistance (COMECON). But Russia disapproved of such a meeting. Ceausescu angered the Russians in November by welcoming United States President Ronald Reagan's offer to cancel plans to install new nuclear missiles in Western Europe. Ceausescu opposed Russia's demand for a world conference of Communist parties on peace and disarmament. Romania clashed with Russia at a meeting of Warsaw Pact nations' foreign ministers in Bucharest on November 30 and December 1.

Food Problems. On January 1, the government raised prices of raw materials and fuel delivered to industry and agriculture, but promised that food prices would remain unchanged. Food shortages worsened throughout the year, however. On October 9, the government made food hoarding punishable by imprisonment for up to five years. On October 17, Romania limited the consumption of wheat and corn products and outlawed feeding grain to animals. The decree led to a complex system of rationing bread that caused disturbances throughout the country. Ceausescu announced in November that the grain harvest was short of the planned 23.7 million metric tons (26.1 million short tons).

Romania's hard-currency debt, estimated at $8.4 billion near the end of 1981, worried Western creditors. Chris Cviic

See also EUROPE (Facts in Brief Table). In WORLD BOOK, see ROMANIA.

ROTARY INTERNATIONAL. See COMMUNITY ORGANIZATIONS.

ROWING. See SPORTS.

RUBBER. See MANUFACTURING.

457

RUSSIA feuded with the United States throughout 1981, but drew closer to West Germany, both diplomatically and economically. Russian propaganda accused United States President Ronald Reagan of renewing the arms race to achieve military superiority over the Soviet Union. On November 18, Reagan offered Russia the so-called zero option. Reagan said that the North Atlantic Treaty Organization (NATO) would cancel its plan to install cruise and Pershing II nuclear missiles in Europe if Russia would dismantle its new medium-range, triple-warhead SS-20 missiles and its older SS-4s and SS-5s. Russian media said that the offer was a propaganda exercise designed to impress the peace movement in Western Europe. But on November 30, the United States and Russia opened talks in Geneva, Switzerland, about reduction of medium-range nuclear weapons in Europe.

The Polish Problem. Russia tried to stop the liberalizing trend in Poland. On June 5, the Communist Party Central Committee sent a strong letter to the Polish Central Committee expressing concern about the Polish government's loss of control over events and criticizing it for not doing enough. Russia's Foreign Minister Andrei A. Gromyko visited Warsaw, Poland's capital, from July 3 to 5.

As the situation deteriorated in early December, the Soviet press printed reports indicating ever-greater concern. The Soviet news agency Tass said that "patriotic forces" in Poland had made an "increasingly more resolute demand that a rebuff be given to the enemies of socialism, a rebuff they deserved by their criminal action."

Russian leaders did not comment directly when Polish authorities imposed martial law on December 13. However, Tass said that the imposition was an internal Polish affair and that the West should not interfere. See POLAND.

On December 23, Reagan suspended major economic ties with Poland and warned that the United States would take economic and political action against Russia "if this repression continues." Reagan imposed limited economic sanctions against Russia on December 29. The measures included a halt to negotiations on a long-term pact for sales of U.S. grain to Russia; the suspension of the issuance or renewal of export licenses for U.S.-made high-technology items, including computers and other electronic equipment; and the cancellation of all flights to the United States by Russia's state-owned airline Aeroflot. See PRESIDENT OF THE U.S.

Other Foreign Relations. Russia's relations with France cooled after the election of President François Mitterrand in May, but its relations with West Germany improved. Communist Party General Secretary and Supreme Soviet Presidium

Russian conductor Maxim Shostakovich and his son announce their defection to the West in April. Maxim's father, Dimitri, was a major Russian composer.

Chairman Leonid Ilich Brezhnev visited Bonn from November 23 to 26 for talks with West German Chancellor Helmut Schmidt. The two leaders did not agree on broad political and strategic issues, but they decided to set up a Russian-West German panel on arms control.

Russia's relations with Egypt continued to deteriorate in 1981. In September, Egypt expelled Russia's ambassador and other personnel on the grounds that they had been involved in a plot against the government. In October, Russia extended full diplomatic recognition to the Palestine Liberation Organization (PLO). On September 25, Russia proposed to reopen border talks with China. The two countries had broken off talks early in 1980 after Russia invaded Afghanistan. Guerrilla attacks in Afghanistan inflicted heavy casualties on Russian troops throughout 1981.

Gas Pipeline. On November 20, Russia signed an agreement on gas sales with a private West German company, Ruhrgas A. G. of Essen. Russia will supply 10.5 billion cubic meters (370 billion cubic feet) of natural gas per year to a group of West German companies. Shipment will begin in 1984 and continue for 25 years. Russia promised to use some of the money that it receives for the gas to buy steel piping and other equipment for a new pipeline. The pipeline will carry gas 3,500 miles (5,600 kilometers) from Siberia to Czechoslovakia. Russia also contracted to supply an additional 30 billion cubic meters (1.06 trillion cubic feet) per year to Austria, Belgium, France, Italy, the Netherlands, and Switzerland. The United States strongly opposed the deal on the grounds that it would make Western Europe dangerously dependent on Russian energy supplies.

Sub Runs Aground. Russia attempted to reduce NATO's influence in Scandinavia but suffered a setback on October 27, when a Russian submarine ran aground close to a restricted naval base in Swedish waters. Russia claimed that the submarine's navigational equipment had failed. The Swedes detected radioactivity coming from the sub, indicating that there were nuclear weapons aboard. Swedish vessels finally escorted the submarine out to sea on November 6, though Russia did not provide a satisfactory explanation of what the sub had been doing in Swedish waters.

The main political event of the year in Russia was the Communist Party Congress held in Moscow from February 23 to March 3. Brezhnev was re-elected general secretary for another five years. In addition, the entire 14-member Politburo, the party's policymaking body, was re-elected.

Dissident Scientist Andrei D. Sakharov and his wife, Yelena G. Bonner, began a hunger strike on November 22 to protest against the government's refusal to allow their daughter-in-law to emigrate. Yelizaveta K. Alekseyeva wanted to move to the

Russian officials dedicate a historical museum in Kiev on May 9 as a memorial to the struggle against German invaders during World War II.

United States to join her husband, Alexey Semyonov, Bonner's son by a previous marriage.

Sakharov, a nuclear physicist and dissident leader, had broken with the government, charging that it violated basic human rights. Sakharov won the 1975 Nobel Prize for Peace for his efforts to promote human rights and world peace. In January 1980, the government had exiled him to Gorki, a city out of bounds to Western visitors. Sakharov said when he began his fast that he considered Alekseyeva a hostage to his political activities.

On December 9, Alekseyeva was told that the government would allow her to leave. Sakharov and Bonner then ended their fast. Alekseyeva arrived in the United States on December 20.

From January through September, only 8,282 Jews were allowed to leave Russia, compared with 18,369 in the first nine months of 1980. In all of 1980, 21,000 Jews had emigrated, compared with 51,000 in 1979.

Industrial Production rose 3.3 per cent in the first nine months of 1981, while labor productivity increased 2.6 per cent compared with the same period in 1980. On September 15, gasoline prices for private motorists were doubled to about $1.60 to $2.10 per gallon (3.8 liters). The price of wine and vodka rose 17 to 27 per cent. Prices of luxury items, such as jewelry, cut glass, furs, leather goods, and porcelain, increased 25 to 30 per cent.

The government announced in November that the price of coal and gas supplied to industry would rise on Jan. 1, 1982. The increase was intended to force inefficient factories to save fuel. The price of gas was scheduled to increase 45 per cent, while coal would cost 42 per cent more. Prices of raw materials were also due to rise on January 1 — timber by 40 per cent and nonferrous metals by 14 per cent.

Poor Harvest. The 1981 grain harvest was expected to total about 170 million metric tons (187 million short tons), compared with the target of 235 million metric tons (259 million short tons) and the 1980 harvest of 189 million metric tons (208 million short tons). Brezhnev acknowledged on November 16 that both inefficiency and poor weather were to blame for the bad harvest.

On January 18, the Communist Party Central Committee and the government issued a joint decree intended to stimulate food production. The decree authorized state farms and collective farms to make voluntary contracts to buy meat and other animal products from farmers who worked on private plots. State and collective farms may use these products to fulfill their output quotas. The decree legalized a practice that farms had used for more than 20 years. Chris Cviic

See also EUROPE (Facts in Brief Table). In WORLD BOOK, see RUSSIA.

RWANDA. See AFRICA.

SAFETY. Concern about public safety escalated in the United States during 1981 chiefly because of efforts by the Administration of President Ronald Reagan to reduce government regulations. Shortly after taking office in January, Reagan imposed a 60-day "freeze" on almost all pending safety rules. He also set up a Task Force on Regulatory Relief under Vice-President George H. W. Bush to screen out "unnecessary rules."

In March, Bush announced that more than 100 regulations were being reviewed to eliminate those that were not "cost effective" – that is, those that would cost more to carry out than the benefits they would yield. The rules up for review included nearly all those of the Occupational Safety and Health Administration (OSHA).

Worker Safety. In March 1980, the American Textile Manufacturers Institute and 12 major textile companies filed a suit challenging an OSHA regulation that limits the level of cotton dust in textile mills. The regulation was passed in 1978 to reduce the incidence of *byssinosis,* commonly known as *brown lung disease,* which labor groups claimed attacked as many as 150,000 workers exposed to cotton dust. Compliance with the regulation would have required the companies to install expensive air-filtering equipment in their mills. In 1981, in an unusual action, the Reagan Administration asked the Supreme Court of the United States not to decide the case until the government completed an analysis weighing the cost of complying with the cotton dust restrictions against the benefits they achieved. The Supreme Court refused the Administration's request and ruled in June that safety, not cost, must be the determining factor in setting safety standards. The decision was a major blow to the Administration's plans for using cost-benefit analyses to ease other safety rules.

Administration officials also asked the Supreme Court to set aside a lower-court decision that upheld rules regarding lead exposure on the job. The rules required employers to transfer workers with high levels of lead in their blood. In June, the court affirmed the validity of those rules. Rather than enforce the rules, however, OSHA lowered its limits on lead exposure and granted 21 companies exemptions from the rules.

An estimated 21 million American workers are exposed to substances on the job that seriously endanger their health. But many workers do not realize the dangers because only about 20,000 of some 86,000 trade-name substances are subject to federal regulation. OSHA officials in 1981 nullified a regulation requiring employers to identify and clearly label all trade-name substances used in the workplace. In another action, OSHA relaxed restrictions on the amount of noise in work areas.

Vehicle Safety. Government efforts to reduce motor-vehicle hazards virtually ended in 1981.

Reagan Administration officials claimed that further safety rules would be too costly to the economically depressed automobile industry. The government discontinued its announcements of vehicle recalls for safety defects and stopped saying whether cars passed or failed crash tests.

In October, the National Highway Traffic Safety Administration withdrew a regulation that would have required automobile manufacturers to install airbags or automatic seat belts in new cars. The regulation was to take effect with 1982 models.

Product Safety. Budget cuts forced the Consumer Product Safety Commission to close five of its 10 regional offices. In October, the commission voted to postpone indefinitely the implementation of standards for making upholstered furniture more fire-resistant.

Nuclear Safety. Despite reports of new safety problems in dozens of nuclear power plants during the year, the Nuclear Regulatory Commission decided to cut back numerous safety regulations and speed up the licensing process for new plants (see ENERGY). Arthur E. Rowse

In WORLD BOOK, see SAFETY.

SAILING. See BOATING.

SALVATION ARMY. See COMMUNITY ORGANIZATIONS; RELIGION.

SAN MARINO. See EUROPE.

SÃO TOMÉ AND PRÍNCIPE. See AFRICA.

SASKATCHEWAN expected to benefit economically from an energy-pricing and revenue-sharing agreement signed with the federal government on Oct. 26, 1981. The agreement was designed to take account of Saskatchewan's large number of marginal oil wells, most of which produce less than 35 barrels per day. The province's Crown land royalties, the highest in western Canada, were reduced to give the oil industry a larger share of the revenue coming from higher prices.

While prospects looked good for oil, the potash industry faced oversupply. This condition led the province to forbid the expansion of a privately owned potash mine near Saskatoon.

The Saskatchewan government formed an airline, Saskair, through the purchase of aircraft, hangars, equipment, and routes for $5.2 million (Canadian dollars; $1 = U.S. 84 cents as of Dec. 31, 1981) from Norcanair, a Saskatchewan company. The successful example of the Alberta government's Pacific Western Airlines probably influenced Saskatchewan's decision to re-enter air transport after a false start in the 1940s.

A balanced budget was presented to the legislature on March 5. Small reductions in taxes were promised in a budget showing revenues of $2.28-billion. David M. L. Farr

See also CANADA. In WORLD BOOK, see SASKATCHEWAN.

SAUDI ARABIA. The intensity of the debate in the United States Congress over selling Airborne Warning and Control Systems (AWACS) aircraft and other military equipment to Saudi Arabia to bolster its defense system underscored that country's steadily increasing importance in 1981 to American foreign policy in the Middle East. With four AWACS already in Saudi Arabia – though flown by U.S. pilots – the Saudis could not understand congressional reluctance to support President Ronald Reagan's plan to send more. In their view, the planes would add significantly to Saudi Arabia's ability to defend Middle East oil fields against sudden attack and were suited purely for defense. The U.S. House of Representatives voted against the sale, but the Senate approved it on October 28, so the sale went through.

Growing Influence. Aside from its strategic value to the United States and its importance as a major oil supplier to the industrialized nations, Saudi Arabia played an increasingly influential role in regional and international economic affairs in 1981. In August, Saudi Arabia put forward an eight-point Middle East peace plan as a substitute for the Camp David process (see MIDDLE EAST). In May, the government agreed to provide $10-billion to the International Monetary Fund (IMF) over two years.

Saudi Arabia's foreign minister, Prince Saud, meets with Alexander M. Haig, Jr., during the U.S. secretary of state's visit to Riyadh in April.

The Saudis also picked up a funding deficit of $20 million for the Palestine Liberation Organization, paid for some of Lebanon's oil imports, and contributed $381 million to Yemen (Aden) and $120 million to Jordan as part of its aid program to other Arab states.

Booming Economy. The enormous outflow of Saudi capital, $20 billion since 1976, barely made a dent in the country's continued prosperity and did not slow down the pace of domestic development.

The 1981 budget approved by the Council of Ministers in May was $87.65 billion, a new high. Despite the heavy expenditures, oil revenues were expected to reach $12.5 billion even with planned production cutbacks, announced in September, from 10.3 million barrels per day to 9.3 million.

With oil reserves likely to be exhausted in 30 to 50 years, the nation's principal objective remained one of economic self-sufficiency and diversification. Several components of the huge industrial port complexes planned at Yanbu on the Red Sea and Al Jubayl on the Persian Gulf went into production during the year, including a methanol plant, hydrocarbon refineries, and a desalination plant. A pipeline from gas fields to the Yanbu refinery was completed in September. William Spencer

See also MIDDLE EAST (Facts in Brief Table). In WORLD BOOK, see SAUDI ARABIA.

SCHOOL. See CIVIL RIGHTS; EDUCATION.

SCHREYER, EDWARD RICHARD (1935-   ), Canada's 22nd governor general and the queen's representative in the country, joined Canadians in mourning the death of Terry Fox on June 28, 1981. Schreyer had awarded Fox the Order of Canada for running halfway across Canada in a Marathon of Hope from April to September 1980 – despite having lost his right leg to cancer. Fox's effort raised millions of dollars for cancer research and inaugurated an annual Marathon of Hope. The first run took place in 800 communities on Sept. 13, 1981.

The governor general represented Canada at many state occasions during the year. He attended the wedding of Prince Charles and Lady Diana Spencer in London on July 29 and the funeral of Egypt's President Anwar el-Sadat in Cairo on October 10. United States President Ronald Reagan and his wife, Nancy, stayed at Government House, the Schreyers' official residence, when they visited Ottawa, Ont., on March 10 and 11. Schreyer also received Prime Minister Zenko Suzuki of Japan on May 9.

Schreyer traveled extensively within Canada – from the Arctic and the Canadian Northwest, where he inspected the Syncrude plant built to extract oil from the Athabascan tar sands, to Halifax, N.S., on the Atlantic coast, where he went to sea in a Canadian submarine. David M. L. Farr

See also CANADA.

SCHWEIKER, RICHARD SCHULTZ (1926-   ), was sworn in as United States secretary of health and human services (formerly health, education, and welfare) on Jan. 22, 1981. At his confirmation hearing, Schweiker told the Senate Finance Committee that his first priority would be to strengthen the financing of the troubled Social Security system (see SOCIAL SECURITY).

Schweiker was born in Norristown, Pa., on June 1, 1926. He was valedictorian of his Norristown High School class in 1944, then served in the U.S. Navy for two years as an electronics technician aboard an aircraft carrier. He earned a bachelor of arts degree from Pennsylvania State University in 1950. Schweiker worked in his family's ceramic tile company from 1950 to 1960, becoming president. In 1960, he was elected to the U.S. House of Representatives, where he served on the Government Operations and Armed Services committees. Schweiker was elected to the Senate in 1968 and 1974. He did not seek re-election in 1980.

In 1976, Ronald Reagan selected Schweiker as his running mate in Reagan's unsuccessful campaign for the Republican Party's presidential nomination. Wayne Wille

SCOTLAND. See GREAT BRITAIN.

SCULPTURE. See VISUAL ARTS.

SENEGAL. See AFRICA.

SEYCHELLES. See AFRICA.

SHIP AND SHIPPING. Shipbuilding increased in many parts of the world in 1981 but continued to slump in the United States. Lloyd's Register of Shipping reported that 1,823 merchant ships were under construction throughout the world on June 30, up 3 per cent from a year earlier. Orders, including ships being built, rose to 3,291 from 3,111. Tonnage of vessels on order increased to 37.5 million gross tons, 15 per cent higher than at mid-1980 and the highest in nearly four years.

Construction Decline. United States shipbuilders held orders of about $10.8 billion. The Maritime Administration of the U.S. Department of Transportation said that commercial-ship orders were valued at $2.1 billion on September 1, down from $2.7 billion a year earlier. Forty-one ships were scheduled for completion by 1984, seven fewer than on Sept. 1, 1980. Avondale Shipyard Incorporated in April received a contract to build three ocean tankers for Exxon Corporation at a total cost of about $300 million. However, Admiral Harold E. Shear, who became maritime administrator in October, noted in a November 5 speech that subsidy-rule changes permit U.S. lines to buy ships built in foreign countries. "Whether we like it or not," he said, "a number of modern U.S. flag ships are going to be built abroad." Sun Company planned to phase out shipbuilding and tentatively agreed on November 23 to sell the assets of its Sun Ship

Incorporated subsidiary to Levingston Shipbuilding Company.

The Shipbuilders Council of America estimated that U.S. Navy orders amounted to $8.6 billion at the end of 1981. In May, the Navy awarded a combined $522.5-million contract to Todd Shipyards Corporation and Bath Iron Works for six guided-missile frigates.

Rescue Mission. The Administration of President Ronald Reagan studied ways of helping the troubled merchant marine as another company, Seatrain Lines Incorporated, plunged into bankruptcy proceedings in February. However, Administration budget cuts included the elimination of subsidies for ship construction, and Shear said that "all other forms of federal maritime assistance are under increasing scrutiny."

In June, the United Nations Conference on Trade and Development urged adoption of a resolution to phase out "flags of convenience." According to the resolution, a country would no longer allow foreign ships to fly its flag for a registration fee. Instead, the country would control all ships that fly its flag.   Albert R. Karr

In WORLD BOOK, see SHIP.

SHOOTING. See HUNTING; SPORTS.

SIERRA LEONE. See AFRICA.

SINGAPORE. See ASIA.

SKATING. See HOCKEY; ICE SKATING; SPORTS.

SKIING. Phil Mahre of White Pass, Wash., gained the major men's skiing honor in 1981. He became the first American skier ever to win the World Cup overall title. Marie-Thérès Nadig of Switzerland took the women's championship.

World Cup competition ran from December 1980 to March 1981 in the United States, Japan, and seven European countries. There were 31 events for men and 28 for women. The men's title was decided in the final event, a giant slalom on March 28 in Laax, Switzerland.

Ingemar Stenmark of Sweden was the overall leader entering that race. But under the complex scoring system, he already had scored the maximum number of points allowed in giant slalom events. Mahre could win the season championship by finishing third or higher in the race. He finished second and ended the season with 266 points to 260 for Stenmark. Aleksandr Zhirov of Russia came in third with 185 points, and Steve Mahre, Phil's twin, was fourth with 155. Steve Podborski of Canada finished ninth and won three consecutive downhill races.

Stenmark won the overall title in 1976, 1977, and 1978 by skiing only in slaloms and giant slaloms, never in downhills. Officials then changed the rules to favor all-around skiers rather than specialists. Still, Stenmark raced in only one downhill race in the 1980-1981 season. Phil Mahre

competed in several downhills, and the points he scored in them helped earn him the season title.

Nadig totaled 289 points to 251 for Erika Hess of Switzerland and 241 for Hanni Wenzel of Liechtenstein, the 1979-1980 champion. American women made their best showing ever. Christin Cooper of Sun Valley, Ida., was fourth with 198 points; Tamara McKinney of Olympic Valley, Calif., sixth with 176; and Cindy Nelson of Lutsen, Minn., eighth with 168. McKinney won three giant slalom races and became season champion in that discipline. Hess won the last six slaloms, a record streak.

Other Competition. The United States Nordic championships were held from February 1 to 8 in Lake Placid, N.Y. They had been moved there from Anchorage, Alaska, because of a lack of snow. Alison Owen of Lake Fork, Ida., won two individual races, placed second in another, and led off the winning relay. The victories gave her a total of 11 national women's titles. Bill Koch of Putney, Vt., won two men's races.

André Arnold of Austria won his fourth straight world professional title. He earned $92,333 in prize money and raised his total of career victories to 36, a record. Toril Forland of Norway gained her third women's pro championship in four years and led in earnings with $15,575.   Frank Litsky

In WORLD BOOK, see SKIING.

Phil Mahre of White Pass, Wash., careens down a slope in Sweden in February. In 1981, he became the first American to win the men's World Cup.

SMITH, WILLIAM FRENCH (1917-   ), took the oath of office as the 74th attorney general of the United States on Jan. 23, 1981, three days after the inauguration of President Ronald Reagan. Smith, who had been Reagan's personal attorney for more than 15 years, thus became the highest-ranking law-enforcement officer in the new Administration.

William French Smith was born on Aug. 26, 1917, in Wilton, N.H. He graduated with highest honors from the University of California at Los Angeles in 1939 and received a law degree from Harvard University in Cambridge, Mass., in 1942. From 1942 to 1946, he served in the Navy.

In 1946, Smith joined Gibson, Dunn & Crutcher, a prestigious Los Angeles law firm. He was a senior partner with the same firm when Reagan named him attorney general on Dec. 11, 1980.

Smith had been active in California politics and civic affairs for many years. As a close friend of Reagan's, he was among the wealthy conservative Californians who helped launch Reagan's successful run for governor of California in 1966. Reagan appointed him to the Board of Regents of the University of California in 1968. Smith served as chairman of that board from 1970 to 1972, 1974 to 1975, and in 1976. Smith married Jean Webb Vaughan in 1964. He has four children by a previous marriage.   Edward G. Nash

Rudy Glenn scores the decisive goal as the Chicago Sting beat the New York Cosmos in a shoot-out, 1-0, in the 1981 Soccer Bowl.

SOCCER. The North American Soccer League (NASL) continued its efforts to gain public acceptance in 1981. The league also struggled with the Fédération Internationale de Football Association (FIFA), soccer's international governing body, over rules used in NASL play.

In 1980, the then 24-team NASL lost $30 million, and no team made a profit. After that season, teams in Washington, D.C.; Houston; and Rochester, N.Y., disbanded. Four other teams moved — Detroit to Washington, D.C.; Philadelphia to Montreal, Canada; New England to Jacksonville, Fla.; and Memphis to Calgary, Canada.

In 1981, despite fewer teams, the league's losses mounted to about $35 million. Every team lost at least $1 million. After the season, six more teams (Washington, Calgary, Atlanta, California, Minnesota, and Los Angeles) dropped out, and Dallas merged with Tampa Bay.

The NASL uses special rules to encourage scoring and make the game more attractive to a North American public that generally dislikes low scoring in any sport. Instead of awarding teams two points for a victory and one for a tie, as the rest of the soccer world does, the NASL gives six points for a victory and one bonus point per goal to a maximum of three per game. Tie games have been abolished by creating a tie-breaking shoot-out. The offside line has been moved from midfield to the 35-yard line to encourage the offense. Each team is allowed three substitutions instead of two.

In 1981, the FIFA told the United States Soccer Federation (USSF), the governing body for U.S. soccer, to make the NASL abandon its offside and substitution rules or the USSF would face expulsion. Finally, the FIFA decided to allow the NASL to use its own rules again in 1981.

Each of the 21 NASL teams played 32 games from March to August. The defending champion Cosmos (23-9, 200 points), who played in East Rutherford, N.J., and the Chicago Sting (23-9, 195 points) had the best regular-season records. Chicago won the championship by beating the Cosmos, 1-0, in a shoot-out in the Soccer Bowl held on September 26 in Toronto, Canada.

Indoor Soccer. Two major indoor leagues played from November 1980 to March 1981. The Edmonton (Canada) Drillers became champions of the NASL's 19-team league by beating the Chicago Sting, 9-6 and 5-4, in the two-game final. The New York Arrows won the 12-team Major Indoor Soccer League title for the third straight year. They defeated the St. Louis Steamers, 6-5, in the final.

International Competition. Teams representing Argentina, Brazil, Italy, Uruguay, West Germany, and the Netherlands competed in the World Gold Cup held in January in Uruguay. Uruguay defeated Brazil, 2-1, in the final.   Frank Litsky

SOCIAL SECURITY financial problems, which had existed for years, reached crisis proportions in the United States in 1981. The Social Security program began in 1935, during the upheaval of the Great Depression. The program helped stabilize the nation then, and it since has become an accepted fact of American life. About 36 million Americans, most of them over the age of 65, rely on monthly benefits from Social Security for part or most of their income.

Social Security benefits are financed by taxes paid by workers and employers. The government distributes the tax money to three trust funds: one for Old Age and Survivors Insurance (OASI); one for Disability Insurance (DI); and one for Hospital Insurance (HI).

Projections in 1981 showed that the OASI trust fund, which pays retirement benefits, would run out of money by late 1982 without additional financing. In December, Congress solved the immediate problem by authorizing a transfer of money from the DI and HI funds.

In 2005, a second, more serious shortage could begin. The percentage of elderly people in the population is expected to increase sharply after 2005 as persons born during the "baby boom" of 1945 to 1964 reach retirement age. There will be fewer workers paying taxes to support a much larger number of Social Security recipients.

Senior citizens gather near the U.S. Capitol on July 21 to demand that Congress restore the $122-a-month minimum Social Security benefit.

Social Security Cuts. On May 12, the Administration of President Ronald Reagan proposed reducing Social Security benefits for everyone who retired after Jan. 1, 1982. Workers who retired at 62 instead of 65 were to receive 55 per cent of full benefits for the rest of their lives – rather than 80 per cent as at present. Benefits for those who retired at 65 also were to be smaller because of changes in how benefits would be calculated. This would have been the first significant benefit reduction in the program's 46-year history. A storm of protest met the proposal, and the Senate rejected it on May 20 by an overwhelming vote of 96 to 0.

The Omnibus Budget Reconciliation Act of 1981, the budget-cutting bill that was enacted into law on August 13, included some reductions in Social Security benefits, however. The cuts included ending benefits for parents of dependent children when the children reach the age of 16, rather than 18; phasing out benefits for 18- to 21-year-old students; and eliminating the minimum $122-per-month benefit. In December, the President signed legislation to restore the minimum benefit.

Other Developments. On December 16, President Reagan appointed a 15-member bipartisan commission to recommend changes in the Social Security system to solve its long-range financial problems. Virginia E. Anderson

In WORLD BOOK, see SOCIAL SECURITY.

SOMALIA continued throughout 1981 to provide military aid to the Western Somalia Liberation Front, a separatist guerrilla movement that operates in the Ogaden region of southeastern Ethiopia. Almost all of the Ogaden region's population is ethnically Somali, and the front's goal is to join that region to Somalia. Ethiopia retaliated with aerial bombings of cities and villages in Somalia's central provinces from June 7 to 14.

The guerrilla war in the Ogaden brought a constant flow of refugees into Somalia. The number of refugees was estimated in March to average 4,000 people a day. As fighting slowed, the refugee influx dropped to between 50 to 100 people daily in September. Nevertheless, Somalia estimated that it had 1.3 million refugees at year-end, though other estimates ranged as low as 300,000 refugees.

Efforts to bring food and other supplies to the refugees were hindered by floods that came in early May after a 30-month drought. Overflowing rivers flooded six refugee camps and cut off access to at least four others. Somalia asked the United States private relief agency CARE to monitor supplies in an effort to prevent mounting thefts.

On April 27, President Mohamed Siad Barre dismissed 10 members of Somalia's military government. J. Dixon Esseks

See also AFRICA (Facts in Brief Table). In WORLD BOOK, see SOMALIA.

SOUTH AFRICA. The white-controlled government of South Africa on Jan. 13, 1981, began a policy of compulsory education for black children up to the age of 16. In 1981, only black children in first grade had to attend school. However, the requirement would be expanded at yearly intervals to include children in the next highest grade.

Residential Rights. In other areas, however, the legal status of blacks did not improve. Under South African law, blacks may not own land outside of 10 tribal "homelands," which together make up only about 15 per cent of the country's total area. Although blacks may legally live outside the homelands with government permission, many do so illegally.

In July and August, the government cracked down on illegal residents in the Cape Town area. In several raids in the black townships of Nyanga and Langa during July, police evicted hundreds of blacks without permits from their residences and ordered them back to their homelands. However, many of the evicted did not leave the area but set up makeshift shelters in a field near Nyanga. On August 19, the police arrested about 2,000 of these "squatters" and tore down their shelters.

Most of the squatters were from Transkei, a tribal homeland now formally independent of South Africa. As citizens of a "foreign country," they were deported back to Transkei. On December 4, Ciskei became the fourth homeland to gain independence. See CISKEI.

Parliamentary Elections. The South African government's majority party made a relatively poor showing in the April 29 parliamentary elections. Although the National Party won 131 out of 165 seats, its share of the total popular vote dropped to 59 per cent – down from 64 per cent in 1977, when the last election was held. The liberal Progressive Federal Party increased the number of seats it held from 17 to 26. The conservative Reconstituted National Party won no seats but raised its share of the votes from less than 4 per cent in 1977 to almost 14 per cent. Only whites could elect representatives to and serve in Parliament.

The President's Council, established to advise the government on constitutional changes, convened in February. No blacks were appointed to the council, even though about 70 per cent of the country's population is black. However, South Africa's Indian, other Asian, and colored – or racially mixed – populations are represented on the council.   J. Dixon Esseks

See also AFRICA. In WORLD BOOK, see SOUTH AFRICA.

SOUTH AMERICA. See LATIN AMERICA and articles on Latin American countries.

SOUTH CAROLINA. See STATE GOVERNMENT.

SOUTH DAKOTA. See STATE GOVERNMENT.

SOUTH WEST AFRICA. See NAMIBIA.

SPACE EXPLORATION. United States astronauts completed the first round trip in history in a used spacecraft when they landed the space shuttle *Columbia* in the Mojave Desert on Nov. 14, 1981. Controllers had to shorten the flight from a scheduled 124 hours to 54 hours because one of *Columbia*'s three fuel cells failed. Fuel cells supply electricity and water to the spacecraft.

The $10-billion effort to operate the first reusable spacecraft was plagued with problems. *Columbia*'s first launch, on April 12, occurred more than three years late because of problems with the main engines and with silica tiles that protect the craft against the heat of re-entry into the Earth's atmosphere. Astronauts John W. Young and Robert L. Crippen flew the first mission for 54 hours 22 minutes, landing on April 14 on a dry lake bed at Edwards Air Force Base in California.

The National Aeronautics and Space Administration (NASA) planned to relaunch *Columbia* on September 30, with astronauts Joe H. Engle and Richard H. Truly aboard. However, a fuel spill dissolved glue that held 70 tiles in place, postponing the liftoff until November 4. Technical difficulties, including high oil pressure caused by a clogged oil filter, produced an additional delay of eight days.

The two flights proved that a space-transportation system based on a reusable spacecraft is feasible. However, the delays and federal budget cuts prompted NASA to trim the shuttle schedule from 44 missions to 28 over the next four years. In the Special Reports section, see SHUTTLE OPENS NEW SPACE ERA.

Soviet Activities in 1981 indicated that the Soviet Union intends to build a space station run by as many as 12 cosmonauts. Communist Party General Secretary and Supreme Soviet Presidium Chairman Leonid Ilich Brezhnev said on June 17 that his country's next step in space would be "the creation of permanent orbital complexes with changeable crews." Two days later, the 13,500-kilogram (29,800-pound) satellite *Cosmos 1267* docked automatically with the *Salyut 6* space station. The newest *Soyuz T* spacecraft consists of two modules. One can be left as a room addition to an orbiting station while cosmonauts return to Earth in the other.

Vladimir Kovalyonok and Victor Savinykh landed in a T-type re-entry module near Dzhezkazgan, Kazakhstan, on May 26, after 75 days in space, most of them aboard *Salyut 6*. They were visited earlier in May by Leonid Popov and Romanian Dumitru Prunariu, who made the last flight in the old model *Soyuz*. Two other cosmonauts visited Kovalyonok and Savinykh in March.

Saturn Encounter. The U.S. spacecraft *Voyager 1* ended its encounter with Saturn on Dec. 15, 1980, after taking more than 17,500 photographs and

The space shuttle orbiter *Columbia* comes in for a landing at Edwards Air Force Base in California on April 14, completing its first mission.

obtaining scientific data about the ringed planet and its moons. *Voyager 2* continued the exploration, skirting the clouds at a distance of 101,000 kilometers (63,000 miles) on August 25 after a four-year journey that covered 1.9 billion kilometers (1.2 billion miles). See ASTRONOMY.

Multinational Launches. The European Space Agency (ESA) launched a multiple payload on June 19 aboard its *Ariane 3* rocket. The booster orbited a European weather satellite called *Meteosat 2*, India's *Apple* communications satellite, and a data capsule.

Arcad 3, a Russian scientific satellite, carried French- and Soviet-built equipment and instruments into orbit on September 21. The instruments will transmit information about the magnetic field that surrounds the Earth to ground stations in France and Russia.

U.S. Launches. *Intelsat V-A*, the largest commercial communications satellite ever built, lifted off on Dec. 6, 1980, but it malfunctioned and was replaced by *Intelsat V-B* in May 1981. *Comstar D-4*, fourth in a series of advanced domestic communications satellites, was launched on February 19. A Delta booster sent two *Dynamics Explorer* satellites into orbit on August 3 to study how energy from the Sun affects radio transmission and weather on Earth.   William J. Cromie

In WORLD BOOK, see SPACE TRAVEL.

SPACEK, SISSY (1949-   ), won the Academy of Motion Picture Arts and Sciences Award for best actress in 1981. She received the Oscar for her role in *Coal Miner's Daughter,* a film biography of country singer Loretta Lynn. Spacek portrayed Lynn's rise from a rural Kentucky girl to a Nashville star of country music. Spacek herself sang Lynn's hit ballads in the movie.

Mary Elizabeth Spacek was born on Christmas Day, 1949, in Quitman, Tex. Her two brothers nicknamed her Sissy. After graduating from high school, Spacek moved to New York City to pursue a career in music. She met with little success, turned to acting, and attended the Lee Strasberg Theatrical Institute in New York City.

Spacek made her professional motion-picture debut in *Prime Cut* (1972), playing a teen-ager sold into white slavery. Her next major role was the girlfriend of a psychotic teen-age murderer in *Badlands* (1974).

In the title role of the horror film *Carrie* (1976), Spacek achieved stardom. Critics and movie audiences applauded her chilling portrayal of a maladjusted girl who uses supernatural powers to destroy the people who make her life miserable. Her other film credits include *Welcome to L.A.* (1977), *Three Women* (1977), and *Heart Beat* (1980).

Spacek married Jack Fisk, a film art director, in 1974.   Sandra Streilein

SPADOLINI, GIOVANNI (1925-   ), was sworn in as prime minister of Italy on June 28, 1981. He became the first person from outside the dominant Christian Democratic Party since 1945 to hold that post. Spadolini, the secretary of the Republican Party, formed his five-party coalition government – Italy's 41st government since World War II – on June 19, ending a 33-day political crisis. The previous government collapsed in the wake of a scandal involving government officials who were members of a secret Masonic lodge accused of illegal activities. See ITALY.

Giovanni Spadolini was born on June 21, 1925, in Florence. He earned a degree in law from the University of Florence. He was the editor of a Bologna newspaper from 1955 to 1968 and edited the Milan daily *Corriere della Sera* from 1968 to 1972.

Spadolini entered politics in 1972 with his election as a Republican senator and soon became his party's leader in the Senate. He served as minister of cultural heritage from 1974 to 1976 and became minister of education in 1979. That same year, he was appointed secretary-general of the Republican Party. In June 1981, he became president of the council of ministers.

Spadolini also has taught history at the University of Florence and is a recognized expert on the relationship between the Italian state and the Roman Catholic Church.   Barbara A. Mayes

SPAIN survived an attempted coup d'état against its democratic government on Feb. 23, 1981. About 200 civil guards led by Lieutenant Colonel Antonio Tejero Molina entered the meeting place of the Chamber of Deputies, the lower house of the *Cortes* (parliament), while the members were voting on the appointment of Leopoldo Calvo Sotelo y Bustelo as prime minister. The guards fired machine guns and ordered everyone to the floor.

King Juan Carlos I ordered chiefs of staff and government undersecretaries into a permanent session at the Zarzuela Palace "to ensure the governability of the country by civilian and constitutional means." Behind the coup attempt was a hard-line supporter of the old Franco dictatorship, Lieutenant General Jaime Milans del Bosch, head of the Valencia military region in eastern Spain. Del Bosch ordered a state of emergency and moved tanks into the center of Valencia.

Surrender. The guards held the deputies captive for 18 hours. Tejero finally gave up just after noon on February 24. Del Bosch was dismissed from his post and arrested. As the 350 deputies emerged to freedom, weary and unkempt, Francisco Fernández Ordóñez, minister of justice, shouted, "Long live democracy!" The civil guards were jailed.

Prime Minister Resigns. Adolfo Suarez Gonzalez, prime minister since 1976, had resigned on January 29 in face of growing opposition from the right wing of his Union of the Democratic Center. The rightists complained about Suarez' "indecisive and ineffective" style of government. He was succeeded by his deputy, Calvo Sotelo. On February 26, Calvo Sotelo formed a Cabinet entirely from members of his own party, refusing a coalition offer from the Socialists. See CALVO SOTELO Y BUSTELO, LEOPOLDO.

Continuing Terrorism threatened Spain's fragile democracy. Guerrillas killed 23 security officials and civilians between February and May. In Madrid, a left wing organization named GRAB gunned down a brigadier general and a policeman in the street.

Basque separatists continued their terrorist activities. In January, the Basque Homeland and Liberty Organization (ETA) kidnapped José María Ryan, a nuclear engineer, in an attempt to stop work at a nuclear power plant near Bilbao. The ETA threatened to kill Ryan unless the plant was dismantled. The organization carried out its threat on February 6, then announced a murder campaign against officials of the company building the plant. On February 9, at least 100,000 people demonstrated against ETA violence in Bilbao.

A suspected member of the ETA died in a Madrid prison hospital on February 13. Official reports suggested that the police had tortured him to death. Thousands of people demonstrated against the death in San Sebastián and Vitoria on February 14, and riots broke out in Bilbao on February 15. People throughout the Basque region observed a general strike on February 16. The incident also led to the resignation of the director-general of Spain's police force, five security chiefs, and 200 senior police officers on February 17.

Poisoning Scandal. More than 200 people died of poisoning and 15,000 others were treated in hospitals after consuming an industrial oil that was sold as cooking oil. The scandal, which began in May, damaged Spain politically and economically.

Italy and France blocked certain food exports from Spain until health experts could determine what chemical substance had caused the deaths. By October 16, Spanish police had arrested 22 people in connection with the poisoning scandal.

Gibraltar Snub. King Juan Carlos declined to attend the wedding of Charles, Prince of Wales, and Lady Diana Spencer in London on July 29. The king stayed home because Prince Charles and his bride planned to start their honeymoon cruise from Gibraltar – the disputed British dependency located on a tiny peninsula that juts out from the Spanish mainland. Spain wants to annex Gibraltar. However, the people of Gibraltar voted for continued British rule in 1967. Negotiations failed to solve the problem in 1981.   Kenneth Brown

See also EUROPE (Facts in Brief Table). In WORLD BOOK, see SPAIN.

SPORTS. Pay-television, which offers special programs to television viewers for a fee, extended its influence on sports in the United States in 1981. Experts predicted that the role of pay-TV in sports would continue to grow dramatically.

For the richest and most publicized fight of the year — the welterweight boxing title bout between Sugar Ray Leonard and Thomas Hearns on September 16 in Las Vegas, Nev. — $5.5 million of the $37-million gross came from people who paid a fee to watch the fight on home television. The Seattle SuperSonics of the National Basketball Association (NBA) sold a pay-TV package of eight preseason and 82 regular-season games for $120 per home. Wichita State University in Kansas sold a pay-TV package of 15 basketball games for $78 per home.

The major commercial networks continued to dominate the televised sports market, however. The networks paid $166 million to telecast pro football games, $41 million for major-league baseball games, and $18.5 million for pro basketball games. In addition, local TV and radio stations paid $49 million for major-league baseball games.

The National Collegiate Athletic Association (NCAA) negotiated lucrative new contracts with commercial networks in 1981. The contracts will pay NCAA member colleges an average of $66-million a year for regular-season college football games and $16 million a year for the NCAA basketball tournament.

The high expense of conducting athletic programs troubled many colleges in 1981. For example, Villanova University in Pennsylvania, where varsity football had been played for 87 years, dropped the sport in the middle of spring practice.

Professional franchises were sold for large amounts — $30.2 million for the Philadelphia Phillies and $20.5 million for the Chicago Cubs in baseball, $30 million for the Denver Broncos in football, and $13.5 million for the San Diego Clippers and $12 million for the Philadelphia 76ers in basketball.

Storm Bird, an English horse sired by 1964 Kentucky Derby winner Northern Dancer and purchased for $1 million at the 1979 Keeneland yearling sales in Kentucky, was syndicated for stud duty for a record $28 million in 1981.

Eric Heiden of Madison, Wis., who won five gold medals in speed skating at the 1980 Winter Olympics, received the Sullivan Award in February as America's outstanding amateur athlete. He was the first speed skater ever to win the award.

Among the Winners in 1981 were the following:

Fencing. Russia won four of the eight titles in the world championships in July in Clermont-Ferrand, France. The United States made its best showing since 1976. Its men's saber and men's foil teams placed in the top eight.

Gymnastics. Russia won the four major titles in the world championships in November in Moscow — men's team, women's team, men's all-around (Yuri Korolev)

Off-road racing cars parade through Las Vegas, Nev., at the start of a race on May 2. They compete on a track in the nearby desert.

and women's all-around (Olga Bicherova). Bronze medals were won by Tracee Talavera of Walnut Creek, Calif., in the women's balance beam and Julianne McNamara of Walnut Creek in the women's uneven parallel bars.

Rowing. East Germany, as expected, dominated the world championships in August and September in Munich, West Germany. Scott Roop of Syracuse, N.Y., won the gold medal in lightweight single sculls.

Shooting. Lones Wigger of Fort Benning, Ga., won the small-bore three-position title for the sixth straight year in the national championships at Camp Perry, Ohio. He also took the small-bore free rifle and the English match titles in the international championships in Phoenix. Mary Stidworthy of Prescott, Ariz., won the national title in small-bore rifle, prone position.

Weight Lifting. Russia won five gold, three silver, and two bronze medals in the 10 weight classes of the world championships at Lille, France, in September. Anatoly Pisarenko of Russia won the super-heavyweight title.

Wrestling. Russia won five of the 10 free-style titles and seven of the 10 Greco-Roman titles in the world championships. The only American champion was Chris Campbell of Ames, Iowa, in the 180.5-pound class of free-style. Greg Gibson of Redding, Calif., took the World Cup heavyweight title in sambo, a variation of wrestling.

Other Champions. *Archery,* world champions: men, Kyoti Laasonen, Finland; women, Natalia Boutousova, Russia. *Badminton,* All-England champions: men, Liem Swei King, Indonesia; women, Sun Ai Hwang, South Korea. *Biathlon,* world champions: 10-kilometer, Heikki Ikola, Finland; 20-kilometer, Frank Ullrich, East Germany. *Billiards,* world pocket champions: men, Mike Sigel, Towson, Md.; women, Loree-Jon Ogonowski, Garwood, N.J. *Bobsledding,* world champions: four-man and two-man, Bernhard Germeshausen, East Germany. *Canoeing,* U.S. 500-meter champions: canoe, Roland Muhlen, Cincinnati, Ohio; men's kayak, Terry White, Peru, Vt.; women's kayak, Theresa DiMarino, Washington, D.C. *Casting,* U.S. all-around champion: Steve Rajeff, San Francisco. *Court tennis,* U.S. Open champion: Graham Hyland, Australia. *Croquet,* U.S. champion: Richard Pearman, Bermuda. *Cross-country,* world champions: men, Craig Virgin, St. Louis; women, Grete Waitz, Norway. *Curling,* world champions: men, Switzerland; women, Sweden. *Cycling,* world women's sprint: Sheila Young Ochowitz, Milwaukee; Tour de France, Bernard Hinault, France. *Darts,* U.S. champion: Cam Melchiore, Berwick, Pa. *Equestrian events,* World Cup jumping champion: Michael Matz, Lafayette Hills, Pa. *Field hockey,* Women's American Cup: Australia. *Frisbee,* world champions: men, Scott Zimmerman, Sierra Madre, Calif.; women, Judy Horowitz, Poughkeepsie, N.Y. *Handball,* U.S. four-wall champion: Fred Lewis, Tucson, Ariz. *Hang gliding,* U.S. champion: Rick Pfeiffer, Lake Elsinore, Calif. *Horseshoe pitching,* world champions: men, Walter Ray Williams, Chino, Calif.; women, Vicki Winston, LaMonte, Mo. *Iceboating,* DN Class world champion: Henry Bossett, Point Pleasant, N.J. *Judo,* U.S. open champions: men, Mitch Santa Maria, Roselle Park, N.J.; women, Karen Mackey, Sioux City, Iowa. *Karate,* U.S. form champions: men, Domingo Llanos, Haverstraw, N.Y.; women, Pam Glasser, Hartford, Conn. *Lacrosse,* U.S. champions: club, Long Island Athletic Club; college, North Carolina. *Lawn bowling,* U.S. champions: men, Skip Arculli, Nutley, N.J.; women, Ann Sisson, Berkeley, Calif. *Luge,* world champions: men, Sergei Damilin, Russia; women, Melitta Sollman, East Germany. *Modern pentathlon,* world champions: men, Janusz Peciak, Poland; women, Ann Ahlgren, Sweden. *Motorcycling,* world speedway champion: Bruce Penhall, Huntington Beach, Calif. *Paddle tennis,* U.S. champion: Mark Rifenback, Los Angeles. *Paddleball,* U.S. champion: Steve Wilson, Flint, Mich. *Parachute jumping,* U.S. champions: men, Gene Koehler, Fort Bragg, N.C.;

women, Cheryl Stearns, Fort Bragg. *Polo,* Gold Cup: Boca Raton, Fla. *Racquetball,* U.S. pro champions: men, Marty Hogan, San Diego; women, Heather McKay, Toronto, Canada. *Racquets,* U.S. open champion: Doug McLernon, Montreal, Canada. *Rodeo,* U.S. all-around champion: Jimmie Cooper, Monument, N. Mex. *Roller skating,* world artistic champions: men, Tim McGuire, Flint, Mich.; women, Tina Kneisley, Marion, Ohio. *Roque,* U.S. champion: Wayne Stephens, Lubbock, Tex. *Rugby,* U.S. champion: Old Blues, Berkeley, Calif. *Shuffleboard,* U.S. champions: men, Tom Brown, Huntington, Ind.; women, Lois Upderapf, Brownsville, Tex. *Sled-dog racing,* world champion: George Attala, Fairbanks, Alaska. *Snowmobile racing,* world champion: Brad Hulings, Edinboro, Pa. *Softball,* U.S. fast-pitch champions: men, ADM, Decatur, Ill.; women, Orlando (Fla.) Rebels. *Sports acrobatics,* U.S. tumbling champions: men, Steve Elliott, Amarillo, Tex.; women, Julie Beaty, Roy, Utah. *Squash racquets,* U.S. champions: men, Michael Desaulniers, Montreal, Canada; women, Barbara Maltby, Philadelphia. *Squash tennis,* U.S. champion: Dave Stafford, Bronxville, N.Y. *Surfing,* U.S. pro champions: men, Mark Richards, Australia; women, Margo Obert, Kauai, Hawaii. *Synchronized swimming,* U.S. figure and solo champion: Tracie Ruiz, Seattle. *Table tennis,* world champions: men, Guo Yuehua, China; women, Tong Ling, China. *Tae kwon do,* U.S. heavyweight champions: men, Kim Royce, Berkeley, Calif.; women, Lynnette Love, Detroit. *Team handball,* U.S. champions: men, Jersey Jets; women, New England. *Volleyball,* U.S. champions: men, Nautilus/Nike, Long Beach, Calif.; women, Utah State University. *Water polo,* World Cup: Russia. *Water skiing,* world overall champions: men, Sammy Duvall, Greenville, S.C.; women, Karin Roberge, Orlando, Fla. Frank Litsky

See also articles on the various sports. In WORLD BOOK, see articles on the various sports.

SRI LANKA during 1981 suffered more outbursts of ethnic conflict between its Sinhalese majority and its Tamil minority. The Sinhalese, who make up 71 per cent of Sri Lanka's people, speak a language called Sinhala and are mostly Buddhists. Eleven per cent of the population belong to a group known as the Sri Lankan Tamils, Tamil-speaking Hindus whose families have lived on the island of Sri Lanka for centuries. Another group, which takes little part in the conflict, is the 9 per cent of the population who are Tamil immigrants from India.

The Sri Lankan Tamils accuse the government of discriminating politically and economically in favor of the Sinhalese. The Tamils demand an autonomous Tamil state, and some call for a totally separate nation. A few have turned to violence to try to enforce their demands.

Two policemen were killed in Jaffna, a city with a large Tamil population, on May 31. The police reacted with what a government leader called a police mutiny. Appapillai Amirthalingam, the leader of the Tamil United Liberation Front (TULF), charged that police burned the Jaffna library, the offices of a leading Tamil newspaper, and other buildings. During the summer, more than 20 police officers were reported gunned down by terrorists called the Tamil Liberation Tigers.

A riot broke out in early August, leading to 12 days of widespread fighting between Sinhalese and

Tamils. Police said there were at least 7 deaths, 35 incidents of looting, and 196 cases of arson. Some victims were Tamil immigrants, whose leaders complained that they had done nothing to provoke Sinhalese attacks.

President J. R. Jayewardene declared a nationwide state of emergency on August 17 and restored order. A team of Cabinet ministers then negotiated with the TULF. On August 31, they announced a plan "to ease racial tension." Amirthalingam agreed to a six-month halt on demands for a separate Tamil nation while seeing how a scheme to decentralize governmental authority worked.

Economic News was mixed. Unemployment, which was 1.5 million in 1977, fell to 875,000 in 1981 as a result of more liberal economic policies. But the economic growth in 1978 and 1979 slowed down, and inflation still raged. Tourism boomed, and some new industries were lured to Sri Lanka, which has long had free, compulsory education, by the availability of educated workers at low wages. On the other hand, such traditional exports as tea and rubber were in a slump. Under the prodding of international aid givers, who pledged a record $834-million at a 1981 meeting, Sri Lanka devalued the rupee, its national currency, and reduced government spending.   Henry S. Bradsher

See also ASIA (Facts in Brief Table). In WORLD BOOK, see SRI LANKA.

STAMP COLLECTING. The United States Postal Service on March 15, 1981, issued purple "B" stamps in an eagle design last used for "A" stamps in 1978. The "B" stamps were to be used to mail first-class letters after the postage rate was raised from 15 cents to 18 cents per ounce on March 22. On October 11, the Postal Service issued a brown "C" stamp because of a postage rate raise from 18 cents to 20 cents on November 1. See POSTAL SERVICE, UNITED STATES.

A block of eight 18-cent stamps commemorating United States achievements in space was issued on May 21. The format of the block is most unusual. The center design consists of a block of four stamps showing the space shuttle *Columbia* taking off, being boosted into orbit, circling the earth, and landing. On the left side of the block of four is a vertical pair of smaller stamps commemorating the *Apollo* moon missions and the *Pioneer 2* planetary probe. On the right side, a similar pair show the projected Spacelab workshop and space telescope to be carried by the shuttle.

The U.S. Postal Service issued 15-cent commemoratives in 1981 to honor black civil rights leader Whitney M. Young and Everett M. Dirksen, longtime senator from Illinois. Eighteen-cent issues honored poet Edna St. Vincent Millay, Western painter and sculptor Frederic Remington, and athlete Babe Didrikson Zaharias. The Irish Post Of-

fice and the U.S. Postal Service jointly issued stamps honoring James Hoban, the Irish-born architect of the White House. The stamps are identical except for country name and denomination.

Readers who responded to polls conducted by *Linn's Stamp News* and *Stamp Collector* chose the 15-cent coral reefs commemorative block of four as the most popular and best designed stamps issued by the United States during 1980. The 19-cent postal card featuring Sir Francis Drake's ship, the *Golden Hind,* won in *Stamp Collector's* stationery category.

Major Sales. A world-record price for a philatelic item was set at the auction house of David Feldman SA in Geneva, Switzerland, on May 9, 1981. A cover bearing an 1846 Alexandria, Va., postmaster's provisional 5-cent blue stamp was sold for $1-million to a European collector in a closed-bid auction sale. Postmaster's stamps were issued briefly in several cities before the federal government began issuing stamps in 1847. The cover, known as the "Blue Alexandria" or "Blue Boy," is a folded love letter containing a marriage proposal from a man named Hough to a Miss Jannett Brown in Richmond, Va. The provisional stamp, on bluish paper, has a circular design in black consisting of the words "Alexandria Post Office" with "Paid 5" in the center and framed by a rosette. The cover

This letter, posted with a rare 5-cent 1846 "Blue Boy" stamp, sold for $1 million at a Geneva, Switzerland, auction in May.

was discovered in 1907 among the belongings of Mrs. Hough and was sold soon afterward for $3,000. It was resold in 1975 for $200,000.

A copy of the popular 1918 U.S. 24-cent inverted-center airmail stamp sold for $160,000 on April 29 at the Robert A. Siegel Auction Galleries' Rarities of the World sale in New York City. At the same sale, a U.S. 1893 4-cent blue Columbian error of color sold for $16,000; a block of four 1959 5-cent Canadian Seaway inverted-center stamps sold for $57,500; and a copy of the 1962 4-cent Canal Zone Thatcher Ferry Bridge stamp with the bridge missing brought $16,500.

New Stamps. Great Britain commemorated the wedding of Prince Charles and Lady Diana Spencer on July 29 with a pair of stamps featuring a pleasing photographic design of the smiling royal couple. Countries associated with the Commonwealth of Nations also issued stamps to honor the event. Twenty-two of these each released an omnibus issue of three designs: a wedding bouquet of local flowers, Prince Charles alone, and the couple.

On September 25, the United Nations released the second set of 16 stamps in its projected 10-year series depicting flags of its member nations. Like the set released in 1980, the 20-cent stamps were issued in four minisheets, which encourages collectors to purchase entire sheets.   Paul A. Larsen

In WORLD BOOK, see STAMP COLLECTING.

STATE GOVERNMENT. State leaders welcomed President Ronald Reagan's inaugural call on Jan. 20, 1981, for a new federalism, but doubts set in by year's end. State and local governments were expected to absorb $13 billion in federal budget cuts, with more cuts to come. Furthermore, the states were disappointed by funding cuts of 25 per cent in federal block grants – funds that local authorities could administer as they wished.

Money Problems prevented many states from providing domestic programs slashed by the federal government. Some states had passed tax reductions recently, leaving them with little cushion for hard times. Many states froze hiring, laid off government workers, reduced spending, or raised taxes. Few imposed general tax hikes, however.

Michigan made massive budget cuts and laid off thousands of workers. Washington's Governor John Spellman urged a 10 per cent cutback in state spending, and a special legislative session late in 1981 raised the sales tax. Oregon reduced spending, raised taxes, and delayed indexing its income tax to inflation to forestall a deficit. Ohio hiked sales taxes and other levies. Massachusetts cut state programs to provide $265 million to localities hurt by Proposition 2½, a measure that limited property taxes. However, the bailout plan was struck down by the state Supreme Court.

Kentucky's Governor John Y. Brown, Jr., or-

dered spending cuts that brought the state's total savings to $676 million for two years. Wisconsin, which had returned a surplus to taxpayers two years ago, raised taxes. Connecticut's legislature held a special session in late 1981 to consider additional tax hikes and layoffs to supplement those enacted during the regular session. California exhausted its surplus by cushioning the effect of Proposition 13, a measure that voters adopted in 1978 to limit property taxes. Idaho, Illinois, Iowa, Kansas, Mississippi, Missouri, Nebraska, and South Carolina also dealt with budget problems.

By contrast, energy taxes provided large revenues in Alaska, Louisiana, Oklahoma, New Mexico, Montana, North Dakota, Texas, and Wyoming. A survey conducted by the National Governors' Association and the National Association of State Budget Officers in the spring projected a drop in state general-fund balances from $11.3 billion in fiscal year 1980 to $4.7 billion in 1981 and $2.3-billion in 1982. States are required to maintain balances to avoid illegal deficits.

Tax Legislation. All state legislatures, except Kentucky's, held regular or special sessions in 1981. Legislatures in 30 states increased revenues by a net of $2.5 billion per year, the largest annual statutory increase in 10 years, according to the Tax Foundation, a private organization. By comparison, taxes increased only $420 million in 1980.

Higher gasoline taxes were enacted by legislatures in 22 states and the District of Columbia, while administrative action increased them in Kentucky, Massachusetts, and New Mexico. Some 18 states hiked truck fees, and 11 states increased automobile registration fees. New York passed the largest tax package, $793 million, to help fund the Metropolitan Transportation Authority, which serves the New York City area.

New or higher *severance taxes* (taxes that states levy on minerals or other natural resources) were imposed on oil or gas production in Alaska, Idaho, Montana, Nebraska, Oregon, and Wyoming; on timber in Mississippi, Oregon, and Virginia; on precious metal in South Dakota; on uranium in New Mexico; and on minerals in Florida.

State and local taxes rose by $53 to $987 per person in fiscal year 1980, according to the United States Bureau of the Census. Total state and local tax collections amounted to $223.5 billion, up 8.8 per cent over fiscal year 1979.

Education. Arkansas and Louisiana passed laws that would require schools to provide balanced treatment of creationist theory along with Darwinian evolutionary theory in classroom discussions of the origins of the universe, the earth, and the inhabitants of the earth. For example, a biology teacher would have to present the idea that humanity was created spontaneously in its present form as well as the view that human beings developed out

Selected Statistics on State Governments

State	Resident population (a)	Governor	House (D)	(R)	Senate (D)	(R)	State tax revenue (c)	Tax revenue per capita (d)	Public school enrollment 1980-81 (e)	Public school expenditures per pupil in average daily attendance 1980-81 (f)
Alabama	3,890	Forrest H. James, Jr. (D)	101	4	35	0	$ 1,857	$ 493	767	$ n/a
Alaska	400	Jay S. Hammond (R)	22	16(k)	10	10	1,438	3,541	87	5,010
Arizona	2,718	Bruce E. Babbitt (D)	17	43	14	16	1,684	688	513	n/a
Arkansas	2,286	Frank White (R)	93	7	34	1	1,161	532	448	1,571
California	23,669	Edmund G. Brown, Jr. (D)	48	32	23	17	19,367	853	4,061	2,594
Colorado	2,889	Richard D. Lamm (D)	25	40	13	22	1,491	538	546	2,656
Connecticut	3,108	William A. O'Neill (D)	83	68	23	13	1,840	591	531	2,697
Delaware	595	Pierre S. du Pont IV (R)	16	25	12	9	516	886	99	2,781
Florida	9,740	D. Robert Graham (D)	81	39	27	13	4,804	542	1,510	2,262
Georgia	5,464	George D. Busbee (D)	157	23	51	5	2,729	533	1,069	1,652
Hawaii	965	George R. Ariyoshi (D)	39	12	17	8	998	1,091	165	2,121
Idaho	944	John V. Evans (D)	14	56	13	22	490	542	203	1,780
Illinois	11,418	James R. Thompson (R)	86	91	30	29	7,073	630	1,983	2,441
Indiana	5,490	Robert D. Orr (R)	37	63	15	35	2,696	499	1,056	1,793
Iowa	2,913	Robert D. Ray (R)	42	58	21	29	1,747	602	534	2,560
Kansas	2,363	John W. Carlin (D)	53	72	16	24	1,270	536	415	2,714
Kentucky	3,661	John Y. Brown, Jr. (D)	76	24(j)	29	9	2,145	608	670	1,865
Louisiana	4,204	David C. Treen (R)	94	10(g)	39	0	2,397	595	778	1,972
Maine	1,125	Joseph E. Brennan (D)	84	67	16	17	619	564	222	2,055
Maryland	4,216	Harry R. Hughes (D)	125	15(g)	40	7	2,761	665	751	2,541
Massachusetts	5,737	Edward J. King (D)	127	32(g)	32	7(g)	3,927	681	1,022	3,174
Michigan	9,258	William G. Milliken (R)	64	46	24	14	5,948	646	1,863	2,461
Minnesota	4,077	Albert H. Quie (I)	70	64	45	22	3,203	789	756	2,464
Mississippi	2,521	William F. Winter (D)	116	4	48	4	1.258	518	477	1,536
Missouri	4,917	Christopher S. Bond (R)	111	52	23	11	2,095	430	845	2,079
Montana	787	Ted Schwinden (D)	43	57	22	28	436	554	157	2,950
Nebraska	1,570	Charles Thone (R)	49(i)	(unicameral)			817	519	280	2,105
Nevada	799	Robert F. List (R)	26	14	15	5	477	679	149	2,179
New Hampshire	921	Hugh J. Gallen (D)	160	240	10	14	267	302	172	n/a
New Jersey	7,364	Thomas H. Kean (R)	43	37	22	18	4,104	560	1,249	2,791
New Mexico	1,300	Bruce King (D)	41	29	22	20	926	746	276	n/a
New York	17,557	Hugh L. Carey (D)	86	64	25	35	12,717	721	2,871	3,358
North Carolina	5,874	James B. Hunt, Jr. (D)	96	24	40	10	3,215	574	1,129	1,992
North Dakota	653	Allen I. Olson (R)	26	74	10	40	372	566	117	2,062
Ohio	10,797	James A. Rhodes (R)	56	43	15	18	4,767	444	1,957	2,143
Oklahoma	3,025	George P. Nigh (D)	73	28	37	11	1,776	614	578	2,007
Oregon	2,633	Victor G. Atiyeh (R)	33	27	22	8	1,455	576	465	3,049
Pennsylvania	11,867	Richard L. Thornburgh (R)	100	103	24	26	7,241	617	1,910	2,798
Rhode Island	947	J. Joseph Garrahy (D)	82	18	43	7	551	593	148	2,559
South Carolina	3,119	Richard W. Riley (D)	107	17	41	5	1,678	572	619	1,560
South Dakota	690	William J. Janklow (R)	21	49	10	25	271	393	129	1,995
Tennessee	4,591	Lamar Alexander (R)	58	39(h)	20	12(g)	1,887	431	854	1,458
Texas	14,228	William P. Clements, Jr. (R)	114	36	24	7	6,759	505	2,900	1,922
Utah	1,461	Scott M. Matheson (D)	18	57	7	22	786	575	344	1,742
Vermont	511	Richard A. Snelling (R)	65	85	14	16	266	540	96	2,017
Virginia	5,346	Charles S. Robb (D)	66	33(g)	31	9	2,743	528	1,010	2,223
Washington	4,130	John Spellman (R)	42	56	24	25	2,917	743	757	2,653
West Virginia	1,950	John D. Rockefeller IV (D)	79	21	27	7	1,219	649	384	1,816
Wisconsin	4,705	Lee S. Dreyfus (R)	60	39	19	14(j)	3,366	713	830	2,769
Wyoming	471	Ed Herschler (D)	23	39	11	19	388	863	98	2,596

(a) Number in thousands, 1980 census (Bureau of the Census).
(b) As of Dec. 18, 1981.
(c) 1980 preliminary figures in millions (Bureau of the Census).
(d) 1980 preliminary figures (Bureau of the Census).
(e) Numbers in thousands, fall, 1980 (National Center for Education Statistics).
(f) 1980-81 (National Center for Education Statistics).

(g) 1 independent.
(h) 2 independents.
(i) Nonpartisan.
(j) 1 vacancy.
(k) 2 Libertarians.

Massachusetts citizens rally in Boston against Proposition 2½, a tax-cutting measure that caused massive reductions in school budgets.

of other types of creatures. A court trial in December placed the Arkansas law in jeopardy. Alabama and Maine passed laws requiring that schools set aside time for pupils to meditate silently.

Environment. California spent some $56 million fighting the Mediterranean fruit fly (Medfly), which threatened fruit crops. On July 8, Governor Edmund G. Brown, Jr., refused to treat infested areas by spraying the pesticide malathion from aircraft. United States Secretary of Agriculture John R. Block warned that if California did not control the Medfly, the federal government would quarantine California produce. Brown ordered extensive aerial spraying of malathion on July 10. See FARM AND FARMING.

At least 20 states passed laws restricting the disposal of hazardous waste, while 11 states passed bills on controlling or disposing of radioactive waste. Nuclear emergencies were the subject of new laws in Arizona and Maine.

Federal charges against highway contractors for bid-rigging led to new laws in North Carolina and Tennessee. Oklahoma passed laws in a special session after the eruption of a kickback scandal among county commissioners. By year-end, 105 commissioners or former commissioners had pleaded guilty to or been convicted of fraud.

On August 14, a federal judge sentenced former Tennessee Governor Ray Blanton to three years in prison and fined him $11,000 for selling state liquor licenses while in public office. Lieutenant Governor David O'Neal of Illinois resigned on August 1, saying that the job was not challenging and lacked authority. O'Neal said that "any halfway intelligent person can understand and function in the office in a week."

Minnesota state employees struck for 22 days in July and August. The settlement provided for wage hikes of 9 to 13 per cent in the first year and a cost-of-living increase in the second.

A Ballot Issue calling for a $750-million road bond failed in West Virginia. New York state voters turned down a $500-million corrections bond, while Texas rejected $500 million in water bonds. Voters approved a $500-million bond issue for water supplies, toxic waste cleanup, and farmland preservation in New Jersey; $315-million issues for water projects and volunteer emergency services in Pennsylvania; $250 million for land for Texas veterans; and $47.6 million to be spent on economic development, highways, energy conservation, and recycling in Maine. See ELECTIONS.

Health and Welfare. California, Nebraska, Pennsylvania, and Rhode Island passed laws that prohibit spending public funds for abortions. New laws in Illinois, Louisiana, North Dakota, and Utah require that the parents or spouses of women who seek abortions give their consent to the procedure. Similar laws in Minnesota, Nevada, and Rhode Island require that the parents or husband be notified of the intent to abort. Maryland and Missouri cut their Medicaid budgets. Florida, Maine, Montana, Oregon, and Washington permitted the controversial substance dimethyl sulfoxide (DMSO) to be used as a painkiller. Four states passed laws regulating so-called Medigap insurance for costs not covered by Medicare.

Law Enforcement. Thirteen states enacted laws aimed at "head shops" and other sellers of drug paraphernalia, and 11 states cracked down on look-alike drugs — legal substances that look like illegal drugs. Illicit drug dealers often sell look-alike drugs to people who believe that they are buying unlawful substances. Connecticut and New Hampshire made spousal rape a crime.

Numerous thefts of household silver items led to controls on the sale of such goods in five states. At least 10 states cracked down on drunk driving. Alabama and Ohio restored capital punishment. Connecticut made a one-year sentence for carrying a handgun mandatory, and, with four other states, increased penalties for crimes with guns.

At least six states provided more funds for new or expanded prisons, and eight states passed legislation allowing early release and other programs to prevent prison overcrowding. Elaine Knapp

In WORLD BOOK, see STATE GOVERNMENT and articles on the individual states.

STEEL INDUSTRY. The United States steel industry, long beleaguered by aging factories and low productivity, moved ahead on a massive modernization program in 1981. It was designed to make domestic steel more competitive with imported steel from the ultramodern mills of Japan and other countries.

On June 26, the American Iron and Steel Institute, the chief association of U.S. steel producers, said that progress in modernizing factories and equipment was "substantial." William J. De Lancey, chairman of the institute, reported that domestic steel companies had announced modernization programs totaling $3.3 billion. The plans called for at least 13 new continuous-casting units, which eliminate several steps in the shaping of steel. Steelmakers also planned to install batteries of new coke ovens with a capacity of more than 1 million short tons (910,000 metric tons) per year. In addition, old open-hearth furnaces would be replaced by basic oxygen furnaces that can make up to 300 short tons (270 metric tons) of steel in 45 minutes. Open-hearth furnaces require from five to eight hours to produce an equal amount of steel. The modernization plans also called for installation of computer-controlled blast furnaces and new facilities to make finished steel products.

Imported Steel continued to claim a bigger share of the market in the United States. During the first eight months of 1981, imports were 20.6 per cent higher than during the same period in 1980. The United States imported 12.7 million short tons (11.5 million metric tons) of steel during the 1981 period compared with 10.6 million short tons (9.6 million metric tons) a year earlier. By August, imports accounted for fully 25 per cent of the domestic steel supply, the highest level in history. Most of the imports came from Japan and the European Community (EC or Common Market).

Domestic steel production for the first eight months of 1981 totaled 85.7 million short tons (77.7 million metric tons). Production was 73.7 million short tons (66.8 million metric tons) during the same period in 1980, the year of a steel slump.

An Extension of the Clean Air Act signed by President Ronald Reagan on July 17 gave the steel industry an extra three years to comply with federal clean-air standards. The act originally required steelmakers to install pollution-control equipment by Dec. 31, 1982. The 1981 law allowed the Environmental Protection Agency to grant extensions case by case. However, steel companies must use the money they save by delaying antipollution measures to modernize their aging plants.

Development of a new steel super alloy with greatly improved strength at high temperatures was announced on June 2 by the Oak Ridge National Laboratory in Tennessee.   Michael Woods

In WORLD BOOK, see IRON AND STEEL.

STOCKMAN, DAVID ALAN (1946-   ), was sworn in as director of the United States Office of Management and Budget (OMB) on Jan. 20, 1981. As architect of President Ronald Reagan's economic program, he engineered massive cuts in the 1982 federal budget. However, in an apparent about-face, he expressed a lack of confidence in Administration economic theory in interviews published in *The Atlantic* magazine in November. Stockman offered his resignation, but the President refused it.

Stockman was born in Fort Hood, Tex., on Nov. 10, 1946, but moved with his family to St. Joseph, Mich. He graduated from Michigan State University in East Lansing in 1968, and studied theology at Harvard University in Cambridge, Mass.

Stockman developed an early interest in politics. As a high school senior he campaigned for the Republican candidate, Senator Barry Goldwater, in the presidential election of 1964. He deviated from the Republican Party in college, where he was a campus spokesman against the Vietnam War, but returned to the fold in 1970 as an administrative assistant to Congressman John B. Anderson (R., Ill.). In 1972, he was appointed executive director of the House Republican Conference.

In 1976, Stockman was elected to the House of Representatives from Michigan. He was chairman of the Republican Economic Policy Task Force until his OMB appointment.   Beverly Merz

STOCKS AND BONDS. Despite several dramatic incidents and growing evidence of a recession in the United States, the stock market in 1981 overall had a rather uninteresting year. The Standard & Poor's (S&P) index of 500 common stocks began the year at 136.34 and peaked early. On January 6, it hit a high of 140.32. It slid below 130 later in January, remained within a few points of 130 until the end of July, and then began a two-month slide to a low of 112.77 on September 25. It fluctuated for the rest of the year, finishing at 122.50. The S&P index covers only stocks traded on the New York Stock Exchange (NYSE).

The Media General Composite Stock Index, which tracks a broad range of stocks traded on the NYSE, the American Stock Exchange (AMEX), and many over-the-counter (OTC) stocks, began the year at 159.72. It ended 1981 at 144.50.

Granville's Guesses. Stock-market guru Joseph Granville touched off two dramatic but short-lived incidents in the market during the year. On January 6, his investors' service telephoned customers to say that now was the time to sell, even though the Dow Jones average of 30 blue-chip industrial stocks (the Dow) had soared to a four-year high of 1,004.69 that day. January 7 saw a record volume of 92,890,000 shares traded on the NYSE and more than 15 million shares, another record, traded on the AMEX. The Dow plunged 23.8 points, and the

AMEX index skidded 14.5. But the market took it back the next week as the Dow rose 4.6 points, making up for the 4.09-point loss from the week of the slide. The Dow peaked at 1,024.05 on April 27. It ended the year at 875.00.

On Friday, September 25, Granville predicted that September 28 would be a "blue Monday" on the NYSE. Markets around the world opened Monday to a trading frenzy. The wave of selling followed the sun, starting in Tokyo, where the Nikkei-Dow index dropped 4.1 per cent. Exchanges in London; Paris; Zurich, Switzerland; Milan, Italy; and other cities also posted declines. In New York City, the Dow, which had hit a low for the year of 824.01 on Friday, lost 14 points in the first half-hour of Monday trading. By the end of the afternoon, however, the Dow had risen more than 32 points.

Winners and Losers. In the United States, only recreation-industry stocks climbed more than 20 per cent. Retailing, banking, and communications stocks rose more than 15 per cent. The big losers were rare metal producers, savings and loan associations, heavy construction companies, and business equipment manufacturers, whose stocks tumbled more than 30 per cent. Abroad, only exchanges in Italy, Japan, South Africa, and Sweden posted gains for the year.

Stocks Ups and Downs in 1981

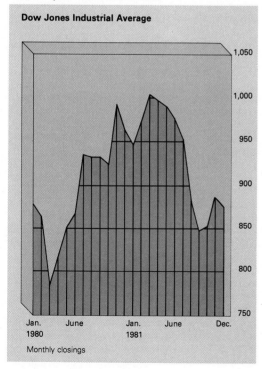

Dow Jones Industrial Average

Jan. 1980 — June — Jan. 1981 — June — Dec.

Monthly closings

The volume of trading on U.S. exchanges remained high during 1981. In 1980, the number of investors reached 29.8 million, close to the 1970 peak of 30.8 million. Most of these investors stayed in the market through 1981, as the NYSE averaged more than 45 million shares traded daily.

A Gloomy Bond Market throughout most of the year may have enhanced the appeal of stock financing. Yields on corporate Aaa-rated bonds rose steadily from 12.9 per cent in January to almost 16 per cent in October, before beginning to fall in November. Prices for existing bonds must fall when interest rates rise or else investors would buy new bonds with higher promised rates. During November, bond rates fell more than 15 per cent, and this caused bond prices to rise by 10 to 15 per cent.

The bond market reacted by shifting to shorter maturities, which are less vulnerable to rate rises. Before 1979, a 30- to 40-year maturity was standard. But big institutional bond buyers began demanding — and some corporate treasurers began issuing — 10- to 20-year bonds. Companies turned to commercial paper with its three- to nine-month maturity early in the year while waiting for rates to drop before floating new, longer-maturity bonds in November and December.   Donald W. Swanton

In WORLD BOOK, see BOND; INVESTMENT; STOCK, CAPITAL.

SUDAN. President and Prime Minister Gaafar Mohamed Nimeiri survived an attempted coup d'état in March 1981, reportedly the 15th since he seized power in 1969. The attempt was led by a retired Sudanese army general and a few army dissidents, but it was easily crushed.

Sudan's relations with Libya deteriorated after Libyan troops intervened in Chad's civil war in 1980. While in Cairo, Egypt, for the funeral of his close ally, President Anwar el-Sadat, Nimeiri said on October 12 that he expected Libya to invade the Sudan to overthrow his government. The United States pledged prompt arms deliveries to emphasize Sudan's strategic importance.

Survival Strategy. Nimeiri's continued ability to survive in office resulted from bringing political opponents into his administration and decentralizing power. On October 5, Nimeiri dissolved both parliaments — one in the north of the country and one in the south, which has been autonomous since 1972. Elections were to be held within 60 days for a new National People's Assembly, which would be reduced from 366 members to 155 and would delegate responsibility for education, health, and welfare to the provinces. The other parliament, the Southern Region People's Assembly, was given six months to call an election.   William Spencer

See also AFRICA (Facts in Brief Table). In WORLD BOOK, see SUDAN.

SUPREME COURT OF THE UNITED STATES acquired its first woman justice in 1981. President Ronald Reagan on July 7 nominated Sandra Day O'Connor, 51, an Arizona state appellate court judge, to fill a vacancy created by the retirement of Potter Stewart, 66, who had served on the court since 1958. O'Connor won a 99 to 0 confirmation vote from the United States Senate on September 21 and was sworn in four days later as the 102nd justice in the high court's history. See Close-Up; O'CONNOR, SANDRA DAY.

The Supreme Court's 1980-1981 term, which ended in July, was devoid of major landmark decisions and marked by deference to Congress on policy decisions. For the first time in years, there were no significant rulings on racial discrimination. However, sexual-equality questions received increasing attention.

The most controversial ruling was a 6 to 3 decision on June 25 upholding the constitutionality of a law requiring only men to register for a possible future military draft. Justice William H. Rehnquist argued in the majority opinion that Congress, not the courts, should make important decisions about national defense. "Not only is the scope of Congress's constitutional power in this area broad, but the lack of competence on the part of the courts is marked," he wrote.

Two other sex-discrimination cases involved criminal law and "comparable pay." The court approved, by 5 to 4 on March 23, state laws that punish men for having sexual relations with underage women but do not outlaw similar conduct by women with underage men. Women's rights advocates cheered a 5 to 4 decision on June 8 that women could bring a civil rights suit alleging discrimination through low pay even if higher-paid men were not doing precisely the same work.

Iran Resolution. The high court on July 2 unanimously approved the agreement President Jimmy Carter executed with Iran on January 19 to resolve the U.S. Embassy hostage issue. Although the arrangement nullified attachments of some $8 billion of Iranian assets by U.S. courts and turned claims against Iran over to an international claims tribunal to be set up by the United States and Iran, the justices explained that the President enjoys emergency powers in handling foreign affairs that Congress has ratified.

Worker Safety. The most important regulatory ruling of the term involved standards for worker exposure to cotton dust promulgated by the Occupational Safety and Health Administration. Shortly after taking office, President Ronald Reagan's Administration reversed the Justice Department's support of the regulations, and asked that industry

A "sister" joins "the brethren" on September 25 as Sandra Day O'Connor becomes the first woman to serve on the United States Supreme Court.

Another Barrier Falls

When Sandra Day O'Connor took her seat on the Supreme Court of the United States on Sept. 25, 1981, she set the latest in a series of historic precedents. Although the Constitution of the United States sets forth no specific qualifications for justices, a place on the nation's highest court was long considered the prerogative of white Protestant males. Those who broke the mold faced strong and sometimes vicious opposition, which was directed—on the surface—at their political persuasions.

Roger Brooke Taney, a member of a prominent Maryland family, was the first Roman Catholic to become one of "the brethren." President Andrew Jackson appointed him an associate justice in 1835, but the Senate refused to confirm the appointment. Conservative Whig senators publicly stated their dismay at Taney's "radical" Jacksonian Democrat opinions while privately sniffing because he was simply not "a member of the club." A year later, Jackson again proposed his name, this time for the position of chief justice. Taney's qualifications outweighed objections and, to the Whigs' horror, a 29-15 vote confirmed him on March 15, 1836. Taney served with distinction until 1864.

Louis Dembitz Brandeis, the first Jewish justice, faced even fiercer opposition 80 years later. President Woodrow Wilson greatly esteemed Boston's "people's lawyer," who was an outstanding progressive and a critic of big business, and often sought his opinion. For those very reasons, Brandeis was hated by most conservatives as well as despised on principle by anti-Semites. For four months, he suffered vicious attacks in the press and Senate, but Wilson wanted him and he was confirmed by a 47-22 vote on June 1, 1916. Brandeis had a brilliant Supreme Court career until he retired in 1939. Boston's federal district attorney told Wilson that the Brandeis appointment was a victory for "freedom from the trammels of race prejudice . . . freedom to think and to act and to speak as men ought to think and act and speak in a real democracy."

More than 50 years passed before another member of a group that was pressing for real guarantees of those freedoms joined the court. President Lyndon B. Johnson nominated Thurgood Marshall, the first black to be so considered, in June 1967. As a lawyer and as the first black solicitor general in the United States from 1965 to 1967, Marshall had won notable cases involving civil and constitutional rights. These victories did not endear him to every Southern senator, but in 1967 many other people believed that high-level participation in government by black Americans was long overdue. Therefore, the Senate confirmed Marshall's appointment by a 69-11 vote on Aug. 30, 1967. In 1981, he was still actively at work.

A similar feeling that-"the time is ripe" paved the way for Sandra Day O'Connor's elevation to the Supreme Court. President Ronald Reagan promised during his election campaign that a woman would fill one of the court's first vacancies in his Administration. Justice Potter Stewart announced his retirement on June 18, 1981, and Reagan announced O'Connor's appointment on July 7. Unexpected opposition arose from people and organizations who said she cast several pro-abortion votes while a member of the Arizona state Senate. But most other people, ranging from liberals and women's rights advocates to Arizona's conservative Republican Senator Barry M. Goldwater, expressed total approval. The Senate unanimously confirmed O'Connor's appointment, 99-0, on September 21.

While confirmation of the first female justice was under consideration, no one, of course, said a word about "a woman's place." Neither had much been said earlier about a Catholic's place, a Jew's place, or a black's place. But despite the diehard old guard's apparent concentration on "the issues," the real issue was always exclusivity. The fact that people who belonged to once-disdained groups finally achieved a well-deserved place on the nation's Supreme Court is eloquent proof that in America, justice eventually triumphs.

Marsha F. Goldsmith

Justice O'Connor

be required to clean up workplace pollutants only when the benefits of such efforts clearly outweighed their costs. However, the Supreme Court ruled 5 to 3 on June 17 that textile industries had to protect their employees' health regardless of the costs involved. See SAFETY.

First Amendment Rights of free expression figured in several decisions. On June 29, in a 6 to 3 ruling, the court upheld revocation of former Central Intelligence Agency agent Philip Agee's passport. The court stated that Agee's activities, including publicizing names of undercover agents abroad, were a "serious danger to the national security." However, other forms of free expression received high court protection. The justices struck down a San Diego ordinance that virtually banned billboard advertising, voided a New Jersey town's flat prohibition against topless dancing, and overturned a Washington state statute that declared adult theaters and bookstores to be "moral nuisances" subject to extralegal censorship. The court also supported TV in courtrooms, refusing to cancel the murder conviction of a defendant whose trial was televised against his wishes.

Criminal Law Decisions. The court ruled on July 1 that police officers could lawfully search the passenger compartment of the automobile of a motorist being arrested – but not the trunk area. It also said police armed with a search warrant can temporarily detain the occupant of a house being examined, but they cannot search the home of a third party if they have obtained only an arrest warrant for a suspect. Two decisions strengthened court-ordered warnings about possible self-incrimination. One stated that suspects who ask to see a lawyer cannot be subsequently talked with unless they initiate the conversation. The other declared that the warning about possible court use of incriminating statements must be read to suspects before they are examined by a psychiatrist.

Other Important Rulings included:
- An 8 to 1 ruling, on June 15, that "double celling," housing of more than one prisoner in a small cell intended for one, does not violate constitutional prohibitions against cruel and unusual punishment.
- A 6 to 3 ruling, on March 23, that upheld a Utah law requiring physicians to notify parents of minors seeking abortions.
- A 4 to 4 decision, on June 22, that affirmed a ruling requiring former President Richard M. Nixon and others to stand trial for illegal wiretapping in a civil suit brought by a former national security official. David C. Beckwith

See also COURTS AND LAWS. In WORLD BOOK, see SUPREME COURT OF THE UNITED STATES.

SURGERY. See MEDICINE.

SURINAM. See LATIN AMERICA.

SWAZILAND. See AFRICA.

SWEDEN. Prime Minister Thorbjorn Falldin's government of Conservatives, Liberals, and Centrists fell apart on May 4, 1981, when the Conservative ministers withdrew because of a disagreement over income tax reform. The coalition had wanted to cut the taxes on the highest incomes from 85 to 50 per cent. The opposition Social Democrats wished to link the income tax cut to tax deductions for interest payments. The Centrists and Liberals yielded and also agreed to a one-year delay in putting the tax plan into effect. But the Conservatives said that the two parties had given away too much.

Falldin put together a coalition of Centrists and Liberals on May 22. He said that he still planned to reform the tax system, cut public spending, and encourage industrial competition. However, he also announced that he would not introduce the income tax proposal until after national elections in September 1982. Falldin needed Conservative support to counter the strong opposition of the Social Democrats and the Communists.

Krona Devalued. On September 14, Sweden devalued the krona, its unit of currency, by 10 per cent and froze prices until the end of 1981. At the same time, Falldin announced a cut in the value-added tax (VAT), a kind of sales tax, from 23.46 per cent to 20 per cent, effective November 1. Sweden's inflation rate remained one of the highest

Swedish ships escort a Russian submarine to the open sea in November. The sub had run aground in a restricted area of Sweden.

among industrial countries, reaching 13 per cent in August. Employers and labor unions had agreed in 1980 on a plan that called for wage hikes if the Consumer Price Index increased by 9.4 per cent before the end of 1981, after deducting increases in the cost of energy. As 1981 drew to a close, the government saw little hope of avoiding these pay increases, despite the cut in VAT.

The 24-nation Organization for Economic Cooperation and Development (OECD) forecast in June that Sweden's foreign debt would remain at $4.5-billion in 1981 and 1982. The OECD urged Sweden to cut public spending, conserve energy, and increase its use of energy sources other than oil.

Russian Submarine. Sweden protested vigorously to Russia on October 28 after a Russian submarine ran aground near a Swedish naval base at Karlskrona. Radiation coming from the submarine indicated that it carried nuclear weapons.

Russia agreed to apologize and pay for towing the submarine. Sweden finally released the submarine on November 6, even though its officers and their superiors in Moscow had not explained satisfactorily what it had been doing in a restricted area. Sweden, Norway, and Denmark protested the incident by boycotting Russia's military parade in Moscow on November 7.   Kenneth Brown

See also EUROPE (Facts in Brief Table). In WORLD BOOK, see SWEDEN.

SWIMMING. Most world records in swimming remained intact in 1981, an unusual·happening in recent years. Records were broken in only four of the 16 events for men and four of the 15 for women.

Record Breakers. The most successful record breakers were two women – Mary T. Meagher of Louisville, Ky., and Ute Geweniger of East Germany. Meagher broke both of her own world butterfly records in the United States long-course championships held from August 13 to 16 in Brown Deer, Wis. Her times were 57.93 seconds for 100 meters and 2 minutes 5.96 seconds for 200 meters. She ended the year with four of the five fastest times ever for a woman in the 100 meters and 10 of the 11 fastest in the 200 meters.

Geweniger set world records for the 200-meter individual medley (2:11.73) and the 100-meter breaststroke (1:08.60). In 1978, Geweniger was not even ranked among the 100 fastest women in the world in the breaststroke.

The men who broke world records were Ambrose (Rowdy) Gaines IV of Winter Haven, Fla., in the 100-meter free-style (49.36 seconds); William Paulus of Austin, Tex., in the 100-meter butterfly (53.81 seconds); Craig Beardsley of Harrington Park, N.J., in the 200-meter butterfly (1:58.01); and Alex Baumann of Sudbury, Canada, in the 200-meter individual medley (2:02.78).

Gaines retained his 100-yard and 200-yard free-style titles in the college championships held from March 26 to 28 in Austin. On April 3, in the same pool, he broke Jonty Skinner's 1976 world record of 49.44 seconds for the 100-meter free-style.

Eighteen-year-old Tracy Caulkins of Nashville, Tenn., had another outstanding year. She won four titles in the United States short-course championships in April in Boston and four in the national long-course meet. Her victories gave her 35 titles and 6 second-place finishes in 42 national events since 1977, with championships in all strokes. She broke Ann Curtis' women's record of 31 titles.

In the United States-Russia meet held in August in Kiev, the Americans took 20 of the 29 events and won the team title. Three weeks later, the Russian men and the East German women dominated the European championships at Split, Yugoslavia.

Diving. Three divers won two or more titles in the national indoor and outdoor championships. Greg Louganis of Mission Viejo, Calif., swept the four springboard titles for men; Bruce Kimball of Ann Arbor, Mich., the two platform titles for men; and Megan Neyer of Mission Viejo, the two 3-meter springboard titles for women. In the World Cup meet held in June in Mexico City, Mexico, Louganis and Neyer took silver medals, and Kimball and Wendy Wyland of Mission Viejo won bronze medals.   Frank Litsky

In WORLD BOOK, see SWIMMING; DIVING.

SWITZERLAND approved a constitutional amendment in 1981 that guaranteed the equal rights of women. The Swiss supported the measure by 797,679 votes to 525,950 in a national referendum on June 14. The amendment states, "Men and women have equal rights. The law provides for equality, particularly within the family, in education, and in work. Men and women have the right to equal pay for equal work." Before the referendum, women's pay was generally 30 per cent lower than men's, and women were not allowed to vote in local elections in two half-cantons and 29 mountain communities. In a referendum on April 5, voters overwhelmingly rejected proposals that would have improved the living conditions of foreign workers hired on seasonal contracts.

Young Swiss demonstrators clashed with police in Zurich and Basel on February 1. The youths were rebelling against what they saw as Switzerland's rigid society. They claimed that local governments did not provide for social and housing needs.

The Swiss voted in a November 29 referendum to raise wholesale sales taxes from 8.4 to 9.3 per cent and retail sales taxes from 5.6 to 6.2 per cent. The measure was expected to increase revenues by $452 million per year.   Kenneth Brown

See also EUROPE (Facts in Brief Table). In WORLD BOOK, see SWITZERLAND.

SYRIA challenged Israel in April 1981 over Israeli support of the Christian Falange militia in Lebanon. The result was a Middle East scare that threatened to develop into a fifth Arab-Israeli war before it was defused.

After a series of Falangist attacks on Syrian troops—members of the Arab peacekeeping force stationed in Lebanon—Syrian artillery bombarded Christian cities in Lebanon and besieged the Falangist stronghold of Zahlah, east of Beirut. On April 28, Israeli jet fighters shot down two Syrian helicopters over Lebanese territory as a warning that Israel would not allow the Lebanese Christians to be defeated. The next day, Syria moved Russian-made surface-to-air missiles into Lebanon's Al Biqa—or Bekaa—Valley. Arab League mediation brought about a cease-fire in the Falange-Syrian conflict in early May and tensions eased, but Syria refused to withdraw the missiles.

Merger with Libya. President Hafiz al-Assad met with Libya's Leader of the Revolution Muammar Muhammad al-Qadhafi in January, and the two agreed that joint committees would be formed to implement details of a 1980 agreement that would merge Libya and Syria into one Arab country. But their geographic separation as well as differences in political and economic outlook prevented any early moves toward full unity. Syria has a free enterprise mercantile tradition and a history of political activity. On the other hand, political parties never developed in Libya, and the economic direction there is toward state control.

Internal Opposition to the Assad regime lessened, compared with the violence of previous years, as tough security measures took effect. In April, several local leaders of the minority Alawi Muslim sect, to which the president belongs, were assassinated in the Hama area, a center of antigovernment activity. Security forces killed or arrested about 300 people in retaliation.

The Economy. The relative internal tranquility was a boon to the economy. The 18th anniversary of rule by the Syrian Baath Party was marked in March by the completion of a number of projects. They included water-pumping generating stations for 118 villages in Euphrates province; electricity for all municipalities in Damascus, Dara, and al-Suwayda provinces; and a standard-gauge rail line from Damascus to Homs.

The People's Council approved the 1981 budget and the 1981-1985 five-year plan in August, then dissolved itself to prepare for parliamentary elections. In the election, held on November 9, the Communist Party lost all its seats, the Baath Party won at least 60 per cent of the seats, and the rest were distributed among Baath's partners in the ruling coalition.   William Spencer

See also MIDDLE EAST (Facts in Brief Table). In WORLD BOOK, see SYRIA.

TAIWAN in 1981 rejected the most specific proposal for reunification made by the People's Republic of China since the 1949 split between Communists on the mainland and the Nationalist regime on the island of Taiwan. The proposal was made on September 30 by Ye Jianying, China's equivalent of a chief of state. He suggested that representatives meet for "an exhaustive exchange of views." While talks went on, exchanges could begin of mail, tourists, cultural delegations, and sports teams. "After the country is unified," Ye said, "Taiwan can enjoy a high degree of autonomy . . . and it can retain its armed forces. The central government will not interfere with local affairs on Taiwan." Taiwan's president, Chiang Ching-kuo, denounced the proposal.

Nevertheless, Taiwan's unofficial contacts with China flourished. Indirect trade, valued at $240-million in 1980, boomed. Taiwan supplied electronic and other technical products in exchange for food, herbal medicines, and traditional goods.

Relations with the United States. The new Administration of United States President Ronald Reagan hinted at stronger U.S. support for Taiwan. But China issued a series of warnings against equal treatment for the Taiwan government and protested the sale of weapons to the island nation.

The question of arms sales to Taiwan was complicated by reaction in the U.S. Congress to the mysterious death on July 3 of Chen Wen-cheng, a Taiwan-born professor at Carnegie-Mellon University in Pittsburgh, Pa. Chen was questioned in Taipei, Taiwan's capital, by the Taiwanese security police about his possible involvement in the Taiwanese independence movement. The movement opposes the view of both Taiwan's ruling Kuomintang Party and the mainland Chinese government that the island is part of China and should some day be reunited with it. Hours later, he was found dead on the campus of the National Taiwan University. An autopsy showed that he had apparently fallen from a high place.

The district prosecutor's office in Taipei reported that there was no evidence the security police had murdered Chen, but Chen's friends disagreed.

Taiwan's Economy grew at a rate of about 6 per cent per year in mid-1981. The government devalued the currency 4.86 per cent in August.

Taiwan and China reached a compromise on March 24 enabling both nations to compete in the Olympic Games under different emblems. China had demanded that Taiwan remove the words *Republic of China* from its name, flag, and emblem for Olympic activities, and Taiwan agreed to use the name *Taipei* instead.   Henry S. Bradsher

See also ASIA (Facts in Brief Table); CHINA. In WORLD BOOK, see TAIWAN.

TANZANIA. See AFRICA.

TAPE RECORDER. See RECORDINGS.

TAXATION

TAXATION. The Economic Recovery Tax Act of 1981 was described by President Ronald Reagan as "the first real tax cut for everyone in almost 20 years." It provided a 25 per cent reduction in personal income taxes over a three-year period, significant tax relief for American business, and incentives for investment and savings. The Senate approved the bill on August 3; the House of Representatives approved it on August 4; and the President signed it on August 13.

The Tax Act was to become effective in stages. Withholding taxes on individual income were cut 5 per cent on October 1, with additional 10 per cent cuts scheduled for July 1, 1982, and July 1, 1983. On Jan. 1, 1982, the tax rate on the highest personal income was to be reduced from 70 to 50 per cent. Beginning in 1985, personal exemptions and tax bracket boundaries will be adjusted annually to offset the effects of inflation.

The law provided that new savings certificates — the all-savers certificates – could be issued by banks and savings institutions from Oct. 1, 1981, to Jan. 1, 1983. The certificates offer tax-free interest of up to $1,000 for an individual and $2,000 for a married couple filing jointly.

In 1982, maximum limits on contributions to Keogh plan retirement accounts for self-employed people were raised, and provisions for individual retirement accounts (IRA's) were liberalized. Deductible contributions to IRA's were raised from $1,500 to $2,000 annually, and workers covered by other pension plans could establish IRA's.

The tax rate on estates and gifts was lowered, and rules governing charitable deductions were relaxed. Tax rates on capital gains were lowered. Beginning in 1982, many working couples would benefit from increased credits for child care and obtain relief from the "marriage penalty."

Business Tax Relief was scheduled to begin in 1982 with a revised system of calculating business depreciation that would allow businesses to write off the cost of capital investments more rapidly. Tax rates on corporate income in the two lowest brackets were to be reduced by one percentage point in 1982 and 1983. Windfall profits on newly discovered oil would be reduced in stages by 1986 from 30 to 15 per cent.

Social Security Taxes were scheduled to rise. The tax rate was to increase to 6.7 per cent from 6.65 per cent of the first $29,700 in annual income in January 1982. By 1986, the Social Security tax is scheduled to rise to 7.15 per cent. By 1990, according to some estimates, the ceiling on taxable earnings may reach $66,900, and the maximum tax may reach $5,117.85. For 1982, the maximum Social Security tax paid was to be $2,170.80, compared with $144 in 1962. See SOCIAL SECURITY.

Federal Tax Receipts totaled $606.8 billion in the fiscal year ending on Sept. 30, 1981. Individual income and employment tax receipts totaled $485.8 billion; corporation taxes, $73.7 billion; estate and gift taxes, $6.9 billion; and excise taxes, $40.4 billion.

Cheating and Audits. The IRS issued its annual report for fiscal 1980 on Feb. 5, 1981. The report noted that in 1980 only 2 per cent of all individual tax returns were audited, compared with 2.3 per cent in 1975. According to IRS records, the number of delinquent tax accounts rose 83 per cent between 1976 and 1979, and overdue taxes totaled $2.9 billion. The IRS attributed the decline in the number of audits and the increase in delinquent accounts to a 7 per cent decrease in the number of IRS auditors between 1975 and 1980. The growing underground barter economy, in which individuals or corporations trade goods or services rather than make monetary payments, also accounts for some lost tax revenue. Although barter transactions are taxable under the law, they are harder to trace than cash transactions. In November, the IRS announced that it was auditing more than 2,600 tax returns involving barter.

State and Local Taxes. A study released by the Tax Foundation Incorporated in September revealed that 30 state legislatures in fiscal 1981 had raised taxes some $2.5 billion — the largest increase in a single year since 1971. Of that amount, 33 per

Dressed casually and sitting outside his ranch house in California, President Reagan signs tax- and budget-cutting measures on August 13.

482

The International Tax Bite

Tax revenue as a percentage of the total output of goods and services

	1965	1975	1979
Sweden	35.6	44.2	50.3
Netherlands	35.5	45.8	47.4
Norway	33.2	44.8	46.1
Belgium	31.2	41.0	44.7
Denmark	30.0	41.0	44.1
Austria	34.6	38.5	41.4
France	35.0	37.4	41.2
West Germany	31.6	35.7	37.3
Finland	30.1	36.1	35.0
Great Britain	30.8	36.1	34.0
Ireland	26.0	32.5	31.8
United States	26.5	30.2	31.3
New Zealand	24.3	30.0	31.2
Switzerland	20.7	29.6	31.1
Canada	25.9	32.9	31.0
Italy	27.2	29.0	30.1
Australia	23.8	29.1	29.8
Portugal	18.6	24.8	25.8
Japan	18.0	21.1	24.8
Spain	14.7	19.6	23.3

Source: Organization for Economic Cooperation and Development

TELEVISION. The most significant television events of 1981 occurred off camera in the United States. On screen, viewers found retreads of old series, tired themes, and generally lackluster network programming. Meanwhile, behind the scenes, the television industry was being transformed by several forces — governmental deregulation, consumer activism, labor unrest, and the emergence of pay-TV.

Deregulation. The Federal Communications Commission (FCC) in 1981 asked Congress to repeal several regulations — among them, the fairness doctrine, which requires broadcasters to give balanced coverage to issues of public importance. The commission also asked Congress to repeal the equal-time regulation, which requires broadcasters to provide equal access to the airwaves to all major candidates for political office.

The FCC on August 4 also granted CBS Inc., owner of the CBS television network, permission to own cable-television systems to experiment with new technologies. An FCC staff proposal, not put to a vote in 1981, would repeal the regulation barring individuals and companies from owning television stations and cable-TV franchises in the same market.

Consumer Pressure. While the federal government was pulling back from television, crusading consumers were plunging in. Donald E. Wildmon,

cent was attributed to an increase in general sales taxes. An increase in gasoline taxes in 24 states and the District of Columbia accounted for $750 million. At least 12 states levied new or higher taxes on minerals mined within their boundaries; 8 states raised taxes on alcoholic beverages; and 6 states raised taxes on cigarettes.

The increased state tax rates were attributed to repercussions from the taxpayers' revolts of 1978 and 1979, the prospect of declining revenue from the federal government, and higher interest rates. In California, three years after Proposition 13 cut property taxes by almost 60 per cent, the state's budget surplus had been spent. At year-end, Governor Edmund G. Brown, Jr., was thinking of calling a special session of the legislature to consider the state's precarious financial condition.

In fiscal 1981, state tax revenues totaled $149.7-billion. Preliminary figures indicated that the 10 states leading in state tax collections in fiscal 1981 were, in order: California, New York, Texas, Pennsylvania, Illinois, Michigan, Florida, Ohio, New Jersey, and Massachusetts. California's collections totaled $20.5 billion; and New York's, $13.9 billion. The largest sources of state tax revenue were taxes on sales and gross receipts at $72.7 billion. Forty-four states collected $40.9 billion in personal income taxes.   Carol L. Thompson

In WORLD BOOK, see TAXATION.

Videodiscs – "records" of programs that can be played on TV sets – were advertised in 1981 as an alternative to video cassettes.

Daniel J. Travanti, right, and Michael Conrad head the cast of "Hill Street Blues," NBC's popular comedy-infused weekly police series.

a Methodist minister from Tupelo, Miss., announced in February that he had founded a new interest group called the Coalition for Better Television to rid programs of what its members considered to be excessive sex, violence, and profanity. Wildmon said that the coalition would monitor programs and urge consumers to boycott sponsors of the programs it found objectionable. The coalition called off a proposed boycott on June 29 because advertisers had promised to "clean up" television.

Writers' Strike. For the second consecutive year, the start of the television season was delayed by a strike. The Writers Guild of America staged a 13-week strike to win a larger share of revenues from pay-television, pushing back the beginning of the commercial networks' 1981-1982 season from mid-September to October 5. The 1980-1981 season had been postponed by actors striking for the same reason.

The strike was settled on July 11. Under the terms of the agreement, writers will get an increased base salary plus 2 per cent of the net revenue above a certain sum.

The New Series reflected the shift to more conservative attitudes throughout the United States. There was less emphasis on sex than in recent years, but some observers detected a marked increase in violence. Many of the new shows featured stars from past seasons, and police shows, which had virtually disappeared from the airwaves in the mid-1970s, reappeared in force.

James Arness, who starred in the long-running CBS Western "Gunsmoke," returned to network television in a contemporary NBC police drama, "McClain's Law." Robert Stack, who played a crime fighter on "The Untouchables," returned to ABC as a police officer in "Strike Force." ABC also added an updated version of its old "FBI" series, called "Today's FBI," starring Mike Connors, formerly the star of "Mannix." Rock Hudson, who played a police commissioner in "McMillan and Wife," was cast as a private detective in a new NBC series, "The Devlin Connection." James Garner starred in "Bret Maverick," an updated version of his old "Maverick" series.

The Stories and the Situations, like the casting choices, suggested that the networks were stepping back to embrace slightly more traditional values. Families continued to be in disarray, but in 1981 they were disrupted by death, not divorce. Widowers starred in CBS's "Shannon," NBC's "Gimme a Break," and ABC's "Best of the West." Another new NBC series, "Father Murphy," featured several orphans.

The most controversial new series of the season – NBC's "Love, Sidney" – starred another veteran television actor, Tony Randall, as a homosexual artist. Although some consumer activists, including Wildmon, eventually voiced support for the series, NBC executives, concerned about adverse public reaction, disavowed any intention of dwelling on the character's sexual preferences.

The most ambitious special program of the year was *Masada,* an eight-hour ABC miniseries produced at a cost of $22 million and broadcast on April 5, 6, 7, and 8. *Masada,* the story of 960 Judeans defending their rugged mountain fortress against 5,000 Roman soldiers nearly 2,000 years ago, starred Peter O'Toole and Peter Strauss.

The Ratings Race. None of the new series drew large ratings during the first quarter of the season. Instead, old favorites, including "Dallas," "60 Minutes," and "The Jeffersons," continued to be more popular. Likewise, overall prime-time ratings mirrored those of the previous season with CBS ranked first; ABC, second; and NBC, third.

The news divisions of the three networks were locked in an unusually competitive ratings race, due primarily to the increasing popularity of ABC's evening newscast. On March 9, Dan Rather replaced popular Walter Cronkite as anchorman and managing editor of the top-rated "The CBS Evening News." In June, NBC announced plans to replace its veteran anchorman, John Chancellor, with Washington correspondent Roger Mudd and "Today Show" host Tom Brokaw. In September,

ABC hired veteran NBC anchorman and commentator David Brinkley as host of a new Sunday news program, "This Week." After Cronkite's departure, "The CBS Evening News" was occasionally bumped from first place in the weekly ratings.

Sports Story. The major television sports story of 1981 was also played out off camera. NBC attempted to purchase rights to televise college football games, circumventing the National Collegiate Athletic Association (NCAA), which controls the rights. The NCAA agreed on July 30 to sell the rights for telecasts from 1982 through 1985 to CBS and ABC. However, on August 22 NBC offered $180 million to the College Football Association (CFA) — an organization of 61 colleges that also belong to the NCAA — for the rights to televise their games exclusively during that four-year period. The NCAA retaliated by giving the CFA schools a larger share of the NCAA's television revenues to refuse the NBC offer. On December 14, the CFA said it was unable to get enough colleges to accept the offer.

Pay-TV. The three major networks faced growing competition from new forms of television. The number of homes wired to receive cable-television service grew from 15.5 million — or 20 per cent of the nation — in 1980, to 22 million — or 27 per cent — in 1981. An estimated 250,000 homes were being

Peter Strauss, center, leads the Judean defense against Roman soldiers in *Masada,* an eight-hour miniseries that was one of 1981's most popular shows.

added to cable systems each month, and 46 networks had sprung up to supply cable channels.

ABC, CBS, and NBC moved to become suppliers of cable programming. ABC joined Westinghouse Broadcasting System to start a 24-hour satellite news service, and teamed with the Entertainment and Sports Programming Network to produce sports programs for cable subscribers. All three networks announced plans to establish cable offshoots to carry fine arts programming to an audience of paying subscribers that was too small to support regular commercial programming. Plans for such programming, known as "narrowcasting," posed a particular threat to public television. Public TV has provided the bulk of cultural television programming but, in an era of government cutbacks, was finding federal funding increasingly difficult to obtain.

Another form of pay-television, the over-the-air subscription television service (STV), grew appreciably in 1981. In this system, programs are transmitted through a scrambled signal that is decoded by devices attached to subscribers' TV sets. Eight new stations began offering STV service in 1981, bringing the total to 22, and plans were announced for 85 additional stations.   Ron Alridge

See also AWARDS AND PRIZES. In WORLD BOOK, see TELEVISION.

TENNESSEE. See STATE GOVERNMENT.

TENNIS. John McEnroe, a tempestuous 22-year-old from New York City, won the world's two major championships for men in 1981, the Wimbledon and the United States Open. Chris Evert Lloyd of Fort Lauderdale, Fla., and Tracy Austin of Rolling Hills Estates, Calif., took the major women's titles, though the leading money winner among women was Martina Navratilova of Dallas.

McEnroe's frequent run-ins with Wimbledon officials in England overshadowed his victory there. In his opening-round triumph over Tom Gullikson of Boca Raton, Fla., he was cited once for using an obscene word in an argument with the referee and again for calling the umpire "an incompetent fool."

McEnroe was fined $750 for each incident. Later, he was accused of verbally abusing a linesman during a doubles match and was fined an additional $750. In his semifinal against Rod Frawley of Australia, he was assessed a penalty point for arguing excessively with the umpire.

After the Gullikson match, British newspapers castigated McEnroe with such front-page headlines as "The Shame of John McEnroe" and "The Disgrace of Super Brat." A psychologist interviewed by one newspaper called McEnroe a classic example of a "hysterical extrovert."

McEnroe had been threatened with an additional $10,000 fine and suspension. Instead, the Men's

International Professional Tennis Council fined him $5,000 for "aggravated behavior." In November, after later fines had raised McEnroe's 12-month total to more than $5,000, he incurred an automatic 21-day suspension from Grand Prix tournaments.

The Men. Despite frequent arguments with umpires and linesmen, McEnroe consistently played winning tennis. On July 4, he defeated Bjorn Borg of Sweden in the Wimbledon final, 4-6, 7-6, 7-6, 6-4, breaking Borg's streak of five Wimbledon titles and 41 winning matches there.

On September 13, McEnroe won his third straight United States Open by beating Borg 4-6, 6-2, 6-4, 6-3, in the final. He thus became the first man to win three Open titles in a row since Bill Tilden took six straight from 1920 to 1925. In December, McEnroe starred for the United States in its victory over Argentina in the 1981 Davis Cup finals, held in Cincinnati, Ohio.

McEnroe's earnings included $150,000 for winning the Pepsi Grand Slam, $100,000 for winning the World Championship Tennis final, and $100,000 for second place in the Molson Challenge. For the year, he earned almost $700,000 in tournaments, making him the biggest money winner among the men.

The 25-year-old Borg won his sixth French Open title and his second straight Volvo Masters, but he was frustrated in the two major championships. He had never won the United States Open in 10 attempts, and he was beaten in the final for the fourth time. In December, Borg started what he said would be a five-month layoff from tennis.

The Women. The 26-year-old Lloyd, whose game had slipped in 1979 after her marriage to British tennis player John Lloyd, regained her number-one ranking in 1980. In 1981, she won her third Wimbledon title with a 6-2, 6-2 victory over Hana Mandlikova of Czechoslovakia and did not lose a set in seven Wimbledon matches. She also won her sixth Family Circle Cup and her second Clairol Crown. She lost to Mandlikova in the French Open semifinals and to Navratilova in the United States Open semifinals.

The year started badly for the 18-year-old Austin, who was sidelined for four months with sciatica. But she regained her health, improved her serve, and won her second United States Open title in three years by beating Navratilova, 1-6, 7-6, 7-6. Austin also won the Colgate series final and the Canadian Open.

Navratilova won more than $900,000 in prize money, but she lost to Austin in the United States Open final and to Mandlikova in the Wimbledon semifinals. Mandlikova won the French Open and reached the Wimbledon final.   Frank Litsky

In WORLD BOOK, see TENNIS.

TEXAS. See HOUSTON; STATE GOVERNMENT.

THAILAND was shaken by an attempted military coup in April 1981. The deputy commander in chief of the army, General Sant Chitpatima, headed a group of military officers who tried to seize power, the 15th such attempt in Thailand since 1932. However, Prime Minister Prem Tinsulanonda, who was commander in chief of the army, thwarted the attempt.

The rebels took over Bangkok, Thailand's capital, before dawn on April 1. Prem escaped to the headquarters of the Second Army, which he had formerly commanded, at Nakhon Ratchasima. The rebels then asked to see King Bhumibol Adulyadej. In the past, the king had accepted as head of government any military leader who seized control of the capital. But this time he refused to see the rebels. Instead, he joined Prem.

With royal backing, Prem rallied enough army units loyal to himself to regain control of Bangkok. By April 3, the coup attempt had collapsed. Sant fled to Burma, but Prem pardoned him and he returned on June 22. Prem relinquished the army command on August 26, his 61st birthday, to General Prayuth Charumanee. Prem had caused controversy in 1980 by changing a law that would have required him to retire from command when he became 60.

Other Political Events. Prem's three-party coalition government collapsed on March 3 in disagreement over economic policy. Prem assembled a new government, sworn in on March 12, with many of the same leaders. However, the top economic policymaker, Deputy Prime Minister and Economics Minister Boonchu Rojanasathien, stayed out of the new government.

On a visit to Washington, D.C., Prem was promised by United States President Ronald Reagan on October 6 that the United States would continue to support Thailand against "aggressive actions of the Vietnamese Communists" along Thailand's Cambodian border. Tension there, and the continuing struggle with Thai Communist guerrillas, kept the army active. The guerrillas, who had waged war against the government since the 1960s, proposed a truce, but the talks broke down.

Economic Plans. After long stressing economic growth, the government shifted to emphasis on better distribution of wealth. The five-year development plan for 1982-1986 announced on October 1 included plans to alleviate poverty among the rural population, reduce subsidies for Bangkok residents, and cut foreign-trade deficits.

The discovery of vast natural gas reserves in the Gulf of Thailand helped open "a new economic era," Prem said. Gas began to flow ashore in September through the world's longest underwater gas pipeline.   Henry S. Bradsher

See also ASIA (Facts in Brief Table). In WORLD BOOK, see THAILAND.

A Thai army tank stands near a Bangkok temple on April 1, the beginning of an attempted military take-over of Thailand's government.

THEATER

Despite sharply higher ticket prices and a recession in the United States, business on Broadway during the 1980-1981 season was as bright as the lights along the Great White Way. After stagnating for the two previous seasons, attendance at Broadway productions nearly equaled the record set more than 50 years ago. Broadway and off-Broadway theaters also set a record of a different sort. More works by women playwrights were produced in 1981 than in any previous year in American theater history. In addition, women playwrights won a number of the theater's most prestigious awards.

Broadway Boom. Attendance at Broadway shows during the season that ran from June 1980 to May 1981 climbed to 11 million, close to the record of 12 million set during the 1927-1928 season and a 15 per cent increase over the previous season's total of 9.6 million.

Ticket prices climbed with attendance. For example, the musical *42nd Street* charged $35 for orchestra seats at evening performances. However, *Nicholas Nickleby,* a two-part, 8½-hour adaptation of Charles Dickens' novel imported from England, offered the most expensive tickets in Broadway history. Theatergoers paid $100 each to see the lavish production, which featured 39 actors.

Works by Women. British women wrote two of the season's most controversial plays. Pam Gems's *Piaf* presents an earthy chronicle of the career of the legendary French singer. Jane Lapotaire won the 1981 Antoinette Perry (Tony) Award for best actress for her electrifying performance as Edith Piaf. Caryl Churchill's *Cloud 9* is an outrageous farce that contrasts sexual mores in Victorian times with those of today.

Crimes of the Heart by Beth Henley won a New York Drama Critics Circle Award for best new American play. Henley also became the first woman in 23 years to win the Pulitzer Prize for drama. A poetic work, *Crimes of the Heart* follows the tribulations of three sisters in a small Mississippi town. Babe (Mia Dillon), the youngest sister, is out on bail after shooting her husband. Meg (Mary Beth Hurt) is a would-be singer and a recent patient in a psychiatric ward. Lenny (Lizbeth Mackay), the oldest, sees her prospects for romance waning as her 30th birthday approaches. But the sisters are undaunted, convinced that they will "figure out a way to get through these bad days here."

A giant blowup of jazz great Duke Ellington looks out over dancers in the Broadway show *Sophisticated Ladies,* a glittery celebration of his music.

Other notable women playwrights included Emily Mann, who shared an Obie (off-Broadway) Award for best new play for *Still Life;* Barbara Schottenfeld, who wrote the book, lyrics, and music for *I Can't Keep Running in Place;* and Joanna Glass, author of *To Grandmother's House We Go.*

The Little Foxes by Lillian Hellman was revived on Broadway in May with movie star Elizabeth Taylor creating a sensation in her stage debut. Under the sensitive direction of Austin Pendleton, Taylor's Regina blended coquetry with ruthlessness and presented an effective contrast to Maureen Stapleton's pathetic Birdie. The American Conservatory Theatre in Los Angeles held a Lillian Hellman Festival, offering both *The Little Foxes* and *Another Part of the Forest.*

Women directors in the spotlight included Geraldine Fitzgerald, praised for *Mass Appeal,* Bill C. Davis' drama about the conflict between a conservative, popular, older priest (Milo O'Shea) and his young, liberal deacon. Teresa Massaro directed the première of German playwright Peter Weiss's *Night with Guests* at the new $50-million Herbert H. Lehman College Center for the Performing Arts in New York City.

British Imports, in addition to *Nicholas Nickleby,* included *The Dresser* by Ronald Harwood and *Amadeus* by Peter Shaffer. With Tom Courtenay in the title role, *The Dresser* pitted an egotistical, aging actor (Paul Rogers) and his dresser against each other and the world. Shaffer, whose earlier play *Equus* became a Broadway sensation, repeated his success with *Amadeus,* which opened late in 1980. The play, based on the rivalry between Wolfgang Amadeus Mozart (Tim Curry) and Antonio Salieri (Ian McKellen), a mediocre court composer, won three Tony awards.

Among Musicals, *Sophisticated Ladies* sparkled. It combined a talented cast headed by Gregory Hines and Judith Jamison, stylish costumes by Willa Kim, art deco neon sets by Tony Walton, and 36 of Duke Ellington's best songs.

Who but Joseph Papp would have believed that Gilbert and Sullivan's operetta *The Pirates of Penzance* could outdo Broadway musicals? Papp's New York Shakespeare Festival production, directed as a zany farce by Wilford Leach, starred pop singers Linda Ronstadt and Rex Smith. But comics George Rose as the Major General and Kevin Kline as the Pirate King stole the show.

Off-Broadway Productions included Brian Friel's *Translations.* Set in Ireland in 1833, the play presents a humorous and thoughtful perspective on Anglo-Irish conflicts. *A Tale Told,* Lanford Wilson's latest installment in the Talley family saga, was staged by the Circle Repertory Company in New

Movie actress Elizabeth Taylor won rave reviews for her stage debut in Lillian Hellman's *The Little Foxes,* which opened on Broadway in May.

Charles Dickens' novel *Nicholas Nickleby* comes alive as a two-part, 8½-hour Broadway play with 39 actors in 150 roles and a ticket price of $100.

York City and the Mark Taper Forum in Los Angeles. Satirist Christopher Durang presented two one-act plays – *Sister Mary Ignatius Explains It All for You*, a lampoon of Roman Catholic education, and *The Actor's Nightmare*.

An Outstanding *Othello* was staged at the American Shakespeare Theater in Stratford, Conn. James Earl Jones effectively played the trusting general transformed into an enraged barbarian by Iago's insinuations. Christopher Plummer's Iago was a witty, deadly villain. After a tour that included Washington, D.C., and Chicago, the play was to open on Broadway in February 1982.

All's Well. After weeks of crisis, the board of Canada's Stratford (Ont.) Shakespeare Festival in January named a Canadian, John Hirsch, as its artistic director. The board's decision in November 1980 to hire British director John Dexter had ignited a furor. The Canadian Actors Equity Association declared a boycott of the annual festival. In addition, the Canadian government denied Dexter a work permit, contending that the board had not searched thoroughly enough for a Canadian to fill the position. Alice Griffin

See also AWARDS AND PRIZES (Arts Awards). In WORLD BOOK, see DRAMA; THEATER.

TIMOR. See ASIA.

TOGO. See AFRICA.

TOYS. See GAMES AND TOYS.

TRACK AND FIELD. The mile run, always a popular event, was never more prominent than in 1981, when the world record was broken three times in 10 days. The record breakers were 24-year-old Sebastian Coe and 25-year-old Steve Ovett, two Englishmen who disliked racing against each other. They did not meet on the track all year.

When the year began, Coe held two world records, and he broke both. On June 10, he ran 800 meters in 1 minute 41.72 seconds in Florence, Italy. On July 11, at Oslo, Norway, he won the 1,000 meters in 2:12.18. But those marks were only preliminaries to the assault on Ovett's 1980 record mile of 3:48.8.

On July 11, only hours after Coe had set his new 1,000-meter record, Ovett ran a 3:49.25 mile on the same Oslo track. The record fell on August 19 in Zurich, Switzerland, when Coe ran the mile in 3:48.53. On August 26, at Koblenz, West Germany, Ovett lowered the record to 3:48.40.

Coe and Ovett were supposed to meet in the Golden Mile on August 28 in Brussels, Belgium, but Ovett withdrew. Two days before the race, Coe telephoned the meet director and asked if Ovett would run. Told that Ovett had withdrawn, Coe said, "In that case, I'll break the world record." He did, running 3:47.33.

At the start of 1981, the mile had been run faster than 3:50 only four times. By year's end, the number had climbed to 17 times – including five by Ovett and three by Coe.

Jim Ryun's 1967 U.S. records for 1,500 meters and the mile also fell in 1981. Steve Scott of Tempe, Ariz., a four-time American champion, broke those records by running 3:31.96 in the 1,500 meters and 3:49.68 in the mile. Sydney Maree of Philadelphia, who beat Scott for the American 1,500-meter title in June, bettered Scott's record mile by beating Ovett in 3:48.83 on September 9 in Rieti, Italy.

World Cup. Maree, a black South African who had been banned from international competition because of South Africa's discrimination against blacks, became a permanent resident of the United States in 1981. He ran for the United States in the World Cup competition held in September in Rome, finishing fifth in the 1,500 meters in 3:36.56. Ovett won that race in 3:34.95, and Coe took the 800 meters in 1:46.16. Ovett and Coe competed as members of the European all-star team.

The European team won the men's title, and the United States placed third. East Germany took the women's championship, with the United States fourth. The only double winner was Evelyn Ashford of Los Angeles. She took the women's 100-meter dash in 11.02 seconds and the 200-meter dash in 22.18 seconds.

Other Events. Renaldo Nehemiah of Scotch Plains, N.J., lowered his world record of 13.0 seconds in the 110-meter high hurdles to 12.93 sec-

World Track and Field Records Established in 1981

Men

Event	Holder	Country	Where set	Date	Record
800 meters	Sebastian Coe	Great Britain	Florence, Italy	June 10	1:41.72
1,000 meters	Sebastian Coe	Great Britain	Oslo, Norway	July 11	2:12.18
1 mile	Sebastian Coe	Great Britain	Brussels, Belgium	August 28	3:47.33
5,000 meters	Henry Rono	Kenya	Narvik, Norway	September 13	13:06.20
25,000 meters	Toshihiko Seko	Japan	Christchurch, New Zealand	March 22	1:13:55.8
30,000 meters	Toshihiko Seko	Japan	Christchurch, New Zealand	March 22	1:29:18.8
110-meter hurdles	Renaldo Nehemiah	U.S.A.	Zurich, Switzerland	August 19	:12.93
*Pole vault	Konstantin Volkov	Russia	Irkutsk, Russia	August 2	19 ft. 2 in. (5.84 m.)
*Marathon	Alberto Salazar	U.S.A.	New York City	October 25	2.08:13

Women

Event	Holder	Country	Where set	Date	Record
1 mile	Ludmilla Veselkova	Russia	Bologna, Italy	September 12	4:20.89
5,000 meters	Paula Fudge	Great Britain	Narvik, Norway	September 13	15:14.51
10,000 meters	Olga Krentser	Russia	Moscow	August 7	32:42.3
Javelin throw	Antoaneta Todorova	Bulgaria	Zagreb, Yugoslavia	August 17	235 ft. 10 in. (71.88 m.)
Heptathlon	Ramona Neubert	East Germany	Kiev, Russia	June 27-28	6,716 points
*Marathon	Allison Roe	New Zealand	New York City	October 25	2:25:28

m. = meters; *unofficial record

Sebastian Coe of England streaks to the finish line as he sets a new mile record of 3 minutes 47.33 seconds on August 28 in Brussels, Belgium.

onds. Carl Lewis, of Willingboro, N.J., made the second-longest long jump in history (28 feet 3½ inches or 8.62 meters), and Willie Banks of Los Angeles made the second-longest triple jump (57 feet 7½ inches or 17.56 meters).

Edwin Moses of Mission Viejo, Calif., ran 13 races in the 400-meter hurdles in 1981 and won them all. He had not lost in the event since 1977.

History's first 19-foot pole vaults were achieved by Thierry Vigneron of France (19 feet ¼ inch or 5.80 meters) and Vladimir Polyakov of Russia (19 feet ¾ inch or 5.81 meters) in June and Konstantin Volkov of Russia (19 feet 2 inches or 5.84 meters) in August.

Ben Plucknett's two world records in the discus throw — 233 feet 7 inches (71.20 meters) in May and 237 feet 4 inches (72.34 meters) in July — were thrown out by the International Amateur Athletic Federation (IAAF), the governing body of track and field. Drug tests during a New Zealand meet showed that Plucknett's blood had traces of banned hormones. Plucknett, of San Jose, Calif., was suspended indefinitely.

Alberto Salazar of Eugene, Ore., set a new men's marathon record of 2 hours 8 minutes 13 seconds on October 25 in New York City. In the same race, Allison Roe of New Zealand broke the women's record with 2:25:28.　　　　Frank Litsky

In WORLD BOOK, see TRACK AND FIELD.

TRANSIT systems in United States urban areas ran into trouble in 1981 as federal and local authorities trimmed financing. Service reductions were common, and some large systems even closed down temporarily. Fare increases picked up speed, discouraging ridership.

The American Public Transit Association (APTA) said that ridership on city mass-transit systems declined for the first time since 1972. The systems carried 6.65 billion passengers in the first 10 months of 1981, down 3.4 per cent from the same period in 1980. The APTA estimated that the nationwide operating deficit of transit systems was about $4 billion, up from $3.6 billion in 1980.

Through October 1981, New York City ridership declined 10.0 per cent from the first 10 months of 1980. Ridership in Philadelphia decreased 15.9 per cent, pulled down by a 19-day transit strike. Patronage fell 1.2 per cent in Atlanta, Ga.; 6.3 per cent in Cincinnati, Ohio; and 10.5 per cent in San Diego. But ridership rose 4.9 per cent in Detroit; 3.4 per cent in Charleston, S.C.; and 36.4 per cent in Ann Arbor, Mich.

Fares Head Upward. The price of urban transit skyrocketed as systems came under pressure to cover more of their costs from the farebox. The General Accounting Office said in a February report that most transit fares were "unrealistically low." However, fares had risen an average of 11 per cent in 1980, after increases averaging 4 per cent per year from 1975 through 1979.

The nation's first $1 basic transit fare appeared to be on its way, as the Chicago area's Regional Transportation Authority (RTA) approved a rise from 80 cents to 90 cents in July. Fares rose from 60 cents to 75 cents in New York City; from 35 cents to 50 cents in Santa Clara County, Calif.; from 65 cents to 85 cents in Los Angeles; and from 65 cents to 70 cents in Dallas. Some fares for commuter railroads soared by well over 50 per cent.

Funding Sources Shrink. Federal, state, and local budgets grew tighter, cutting transit assistance. The Administration of President Ronald Reagan planned to phase out by 1985 operating subsidies that covered about 15 per cent of cities' transit deficits. The Administration slashed funding for new subways and other new rapid-transit projects in the budget for fiscal 1982.

Most transit projects faced slowdowns or cancellation. These included systems under construction in Atlanta and Washington, D.C., and projects planned for Detroit, Houston, and Los Angeles. But Baltimore neared completion of the first stage of its new subway system; the Metropolitan Atlanta Rapid Transit Authority opened a 1.9-mile (3-kilometer) subway segment on December 4; and the Washington Metropolitan Area Transit Authority opened a 2.5-mile (4-kilometer) stretch on December 6. A 16-mile (26-kilometer) *light-rail*

(trolley) line from San Diego to Tijuana, Mexico, began running on July 26.

Service Deterioration. Financial distress worsened service offered by many transit systems. The Chicago area's RTA was on the brink of bankruptcy, and the city's Chicago Transit Authority seemed on the verge of collapse. A city plan to bail out the transit system with a 1 per cent tax on the services of physicians, lawyers, and other professionals failed in November, when the Illinois Supreme Court ruled the tax unconstitutional.

The Birmingham, Ala., bus system ran out of cash and closed down on March 1 but resumed service on a reduced scale on June 1. The Youngstown, Ohio, system stopped running on November 7 but started running again a month later. The Tucson, Ariz., system reduced weekday service hours on most routes on June 7.

On July 17, the U.S. Department of Transportation revoked rules that required transit systems to make buses and subways accessible to the handicapped. Instead, the department permitted operators to offer such special services as door-to-door van transportation. A federal court had ruled in May that the accessibility requirement laid too costly a burden on transit systems.   Albert R. Karr

See also TRANSPORTATION. In WORLD BOOK, see TRANSPORTATION.

TRANSKEI. See AFRICA.

TRANSPORTATION. Most United States transportation industries registered financial gains in 1981, but they had problems. Airlines' earnings improved only slightly. High increases in basic fares caused a decline in air travel, while fare bargains offered on highly competitive routes cut into profits. In addition, an illegal strike by air-traffic controllers and President Ronald Reagan's decision to fire the 11,500 strikers disrupted flight patterns severely.

Although some trucking companies showed losses, many managed to boost revenues and profits as they began learning to cope with deregulation. Railroads benefited from heavy traffic in coal and a greater freedom to raise and lower freight rates. Ocean shipping continued to be plagued by overcapacity and depressed tanker rates. Shipbuilding increased worldwide but slumped further in the United States.

Frank Smith, senior vice-president of the Transportation Association of America (TAA), estimated U.S. transportation revenues at $634 billion for 1981, up 13 per cent from 1980. Mainland intercity freight, measured in ton-miles, decreased 1.2 per cent, with truck freight down 1.0 per cent; pipelines, 4.8 per cent; air freight, 2 per cent; and Great Lakes traffic, 4 per cent. However, railroad freight rose 0.3 per cent and rivers and canals 1 per cent.

Intercity passenger traffic increased 2.5 per cent,

spurred by a 4 per cent rise in automobile travel. Motorists took to the road more frequently than in recent years, though they continued to use less gasoline in more fuel-efficient cars. Railroad passenger traffic was up about 3.0 per cent. However, air travel fell 5.6 per cent, and bus traffic edged downward about 0.7 per cent.

The Deregulation Trend took a tighter hold on transportation in 1981. Truck firms responded to a 1980 decontrol law and Interstate Commerce Commission generosity by expanding service and trimming rates considerably. Railroads took advantage of a similar 1980 deregulation law, raising or trimming various freight rates frequently. In their third year of deregulation, airlines added more routes, cut more flights that served smaller communities, and changed fares frequently. But the air-traffic control squeeze caused the Federal Aviation Administration to limit peak-hour flights at major airports. Legislation to deregulate intercity bus firms began to move through Congress with the support of the Reagan Administration and the bus industry.

Transportation Secretary Andrew L. (Drew) Lewis, Jr., led government efforts to help the U.S. automobile industry by removing federal regulations and by urging Japan's carmakers to hold down shipments to the United States. He also maintained a tough position against the striking air-traffic controllers and worked to rebuild the system during the controller pinch that followed. In addition, Lewis pushed successfully for congressional approval of a plan for selling the Consolidated Rail Corporation (Conrail).

Auto Safety. On October 23, Raymond A. Peck, the National Highway Traffic Safety Administrator, decided to cancel the requirement that new cars be equipped with airbags or automatic safety belts. Peck said that automakers did not plan to sell airbags and that there was little evidence that more motorists would use the automatic belts than the small number who use ordinary seat belts and shoulder belts. On October 21, a federal judge upheld the December 1980 decision of the Department of Transportation to allow Ford Motor Company to forgo a recall of millions of cars and light trucks with transmissions that allegedly jumped easily from parking gear to reverse gear.

Canada's transport minister, Jean-Luc Pepin, announced on July 27 that VIA Rail, Canada's national rail-passenger system, would trim service by 19.5 per cent on November 15 and use the money saved to buy new equipment. Calgary, Alta., opened a $167-million *light rail* (trolley) transit system on May 25.   Albert R. Karr

See also AUTOMOBILE; AVIATION; LEWIS, ANDREW L. (DREW), JR.; RAILROAD; SHIP AND SHIPPING; TRANSIT; TRUCK AND TRUCKING. In WORLD BOOK, see TRANSPORTATION.

TRAVEL. Inflation, a lagging economy, the uncertainties resulting from airline deregulation, and a strike by the Professional Air Traffic Controllers Organization (PATCO) made 1981 a shaky and volatile year for the United States travel industry. The International Air Transport Association reported "the worst year ever," with losses of $2.5-billion by its members, who cover 70 per cent of all worldwide air routes. Widespread tightening of travel budgets by industry cut into the revenues of carriers, hotels, restaurants, and other businesses that benefit from convention and business trade. United States airlines suffered a loss in passenger-miles of about 6 per cent, most of it in domestic travel (see AVIATION).

For the second year since records have been kept, overseas travel to the United States outpaced U.S. travel abroad. The strengthening of the U.S. dollar in world markets might reverse this trend, but the rebound occurred too late in the year to have a significant effect on vacation planning for 1981. Also, continued galloping inflation in many countries had a dampening effect on travel.

The PATCO Walkout began on August 3. President Ronald Reagan responded by firing some 11,500 strikers.

As a result of the strike, airlines reduced the number of trips per day between major cities and shifted routes around hub cities, in some cases improving service to smaller cities. The *load factor* (percentage of seats sold on any one flight) increased substantially. The Federal Aviation Administration ordered airlines to cut service to about 75 per cent of prestrike capacity. Airlines increased the use of wide-bodied aircraft on heavily traveled routes. Many lines laid off employees and reduced some executive salaries.

The Department of Commerce predicted that, in the long run, the airline industry would earn increased profits from running a leaner, tighter operation. During 1981, however, most carriers suffered huge losses.

An All-Out Fare War resulted from the deregulation of airline fares. To attract customers, airlines used such marketing devices as two-for-one tickets, "super saver" fares, "frequent flyer" discounts, merchandise giveaways, and free upgrading to first-class seats.

The effect of these tactics on the airline industry remained to be seen, but individual travelers enjoyed substantial savings. During August, 74 per cent of all passenger-miles flown in coach on all domestic airlines were paid for with fares discounted by an average of 46 per cent.

Travel Agents found the PATCO strike a staggering blow after a very bad beginning to the year. Continual changes in schedules, routes, and fares made it almost impossible for small agencies to provide good service to their customers. Since the late 1970s, about 60 per cent of all U.S. travel agencies have installed computers with direct tie-ins to the airlines. Agencies without computers, as well as individuals, experienced long, frustrating delays in attempts to book travel by telephone during the first few weeks of the strike.

Automobile Travel suffered less than other segments of the travel industry because gasoline prices did not increase greatly during 1981. Pump prices varied widely from one location to another and fluctuated during the year, but they rose little overall. However, inflation made the total cost of an automobile vacation, including food and lodging, about 10 per cent higher than in 1980.

Other Developments. The National Railroad Passenger Corporation (Amtrak) made further cuts in service. Package-tour operators, on the other hand, competed vigorously for the vacation traveler's business. They offered many attractive, inexpensive packages.

Cruise travel was not hit as hard as other parts of the industry, largely because all-inclusive prices for most cruises were set well in advance, and customers could be certain about what a vacation would cost. Sylvia McNair

See also TRANSPORTATION. In WORLD BOOK, see AIRLINE; TRANSPORTATION.

TRINIDAD AND TOBAGO. See LATIN AMERICA.

TRUCK AND TRUCKING. A major deregulation law enacted in 1980 meant both opportunities and difficulties for United States trucking firms in 1981. The law made it easier to enter the trucking business and gave truckers greater freedom to change rates. Increased competition, spurred by the 1980 decontrol law, led to freight-rate reductions in 1981, as truckers jockeyed for hauls. Reese H. Taylor, Jr., the new chairman of the Interstate Commerce Commission (ICC), tried to slow down the deregulation effort, which many companies still opposed.

The American Trucking Associations, Incorporated (ATA), estimated that freight hauled increased about 1.5 per cent, to 840 million short tons (760 million metric tons), and revenues increased 12 per cent, to approximately $48 billion. Operating profit rose 9 per cent, to $1.7 billion. However, net income soared 64 per cent, to an estimated $1.2 billion.

Most of the increase in net income came from effects of 1980 write-offs of operating-rights certificates. The deregulation law allowed companies to enter or expand in the trucking business by easily obtaining an operating-rights certificate, and so the certificates became worthless. Therefore, a firm that already held a certificate could write off the certificate's old value.

"Must we always take advantage of the low off-season rates?"

TRUCK AND TRUCKING

Higher freight rates also helped earnings. The ICC approved general rate increases ranging from 1.3 per cent to 8.4 per cent in a patchwork pattern throughout the year.

Tussling with Deregulation. With entry into trucking made easier, the new and expanded service produced sharp rate cuts and discounts. Shippers gained from improved and lower-priced service, but many truck companies complained.

After taking office on July 1, Taylor sought to slow down trucking decontrol. He said that previous chairmen had gone beyond the requirements of the 1980 law.

New ICC Rules. On March 11, the ICC gave movers of household goods more leeway in making estimates and encouraged competitive pricing and service alternatives. Other new rules would also give consumers a better break. On October 8, the ICC said that it would abolish a controversial surcharge paid by shippers to regulated carriers who hired independent truckers. The surcharge was intended to cover the independents' increased fuel costs. Instead, the ICC would allow the regulated carriers to cover fuel expenses in their usual freight rates and to pay the owner-operators by the mile.   Albert R. Karr

See also TRANSPORTATION. In WORLD BOOK, see TRUCK.

TRUDEAU, PIERRE ELLIOTT (1919-   ), in his 13th year as Canada's prime minister, committed himself strongly to two main objectives in 1981. Trudeau had long looked forward to transferring Canada's constitution from Great Britain, making it amendable by a purely Canadian process. He also wanted to build into the constitution a charter of civil and language rights applicable across Canada.

A federal parliamentary resolution to achieve these ends was declared legally correct by Canada's Supreme Court on September 28, but the court said Canadian usage required consent of the provinces before undertaking such change. On November 5, Trudeau gained the consent of nine of the 10 provincial premiers and on December 9, his proposals were given to the British Parliament.

Trudeau's other objective was the renewal of dialogue between rich and poor nations on how to improve the functioning of the world's economy. He forced Western leaders to discuss the issue at the economic conference held at Montebello, near Ottawa, Ont., in July which he chaired as head of the host country. Again, as co-chairman of the Cancún, Mexico, conference in October, he tried to move the group toward beginning global negotiations, but had little success.   David M. L. Farr

See also CANADA. In WORLD BOOK, see TRUDEAU, PIERRE ELLIOTT.

Prime Minister Pierre Trudeau demonstrates his acrobatic abilities on a trampoline during Canada Day celebrations in Ottawa on July 1.

TUNISIA. The gradual liberalization of Tunisia's political life passed a historic milestone in April 1981. President Habib Bourguiba announced at a special session of the ruling Socialist Destour Party (SDP), the country's only legal political party, that he was ready to approve a multiparty system. Bourguiba also said labor unions, particularly the General Union of Tunisian Workers (UGTT), would be politically autonomous. New parties would be allowed to organize and participate in elections provided they upheld a national charter that required rejection of the use of violence, freedom from foreign control, acceptance of Bourguiba's historical legitimacy as founder of the state, and neither religious nor regional affiliation.

To demonstrate his commitment to the liberalization process, Bourguiba pardoned five UGTT leaders jailed in 1978. He also restored the civil liberties of 22 members of the opposition United People's Movement.

The Transfer to a multiparty system did not come easily. In July, the National Assembly was dissolved at the end of its five-year session, and new elections were set for November 1. But a government ruling that only parties receiving more than 5 per cent of the vote would be legalized drew angry criticism from opposition groups. Three groups said they would boycott the elections; only the moderate Movement for Peoples' Unity supported the ruling. The Tunisian Communist Party — illegal since 1963 — was legally recognized on July 18, but its leaders said they would also boycott the elections. In the elections, the SDP won 109 seats, and its ally, the UGTT, won the remaining 27.

In late July, a government decision to allow shops and restaurants to remain open during the fasting hours of the Muslims' holy month of Ramadan led to a wave of violence. Seventy-six members of groups advocating a revival of Islamic practices were given prison sentences of up to 11 years.

The Economy. In an effort to spur the lagging economy, the government approved a new foreign-investment law in January. Five decentralized investment zones are to be established, with special incentives for companies to locate plants inland, free site preparation, and exemption of foreign companies from wage limits for Tunisian labor.

Citrus production for the year increased 20 per cent, and a 400 per cent increase in the production of processed tomatoes made them an important item in Tunisian agricultural exports. The improvement in agriculture was counterbalanced, however, by an anticipated 35 per cent foreign trade deficit and heavy defense spending of $262-million because of tensions with neighboring Libya. William Spencer

See also AFRICA (Facts in Brief Table). In WORLD BOOK, see TUNISIA.

TUNNEL. See BUILDING AND CONSTRUCTION.

TURKEY experienced its first full "year of the generals" in 1981 following the bloodless coup of Sept. 12, 1980, when the armed forces seized power to avert civil war. During the year, the ruling National Security Council (NSC) had considerable success in restoring order to the country. By coincidence, 1981 also marked the 100th anniversary of the birth of Kemal Atatürk, founder of the Turkish republic. As other generals had done after a 1960 coup, the generals of the 1980 seizure of power insisted they had acted in accordance with Atatürk's principles to preserve the republic. They said they would restore parliamentary government after the country had returned to law and order.

Antiterrorism Actions. The military regime indeed reduced terrorism sharply. By March, some 25,000 persons had been arrested, 17,000 held for trial, and 886 given jail sentences. A large number of weapons had been seized. The majority of those arrested were leftists, but about 2,000 belonged to the extreme right wing Nationalist Action Party (NAP) or to the Kurdish separatist movement. There were a number of trials by military tribunals during the year. On August 19, former Deputy Prime Minister Alpaslan Turkes, head of the NAP, went on trial along with 673 members of the party on charges of plotting to establish an ultranationalist right wing government.

Altogether, about 40 terrorist groups were broken up, with 16 death sentences imposed and six executions carried out. Although criticized by Amnesty International for the executions and the long detention of political leaders, the regime was given fair marks by many observers for its treatment of both left and right wing groups.

On May 13, a right wing Turkish terrorist, Mehmet Ali Agca, shot Pope John Paul II in Rome (see ROMAN CATHOLIC CHURCH). Agca, a convicted murderer, had escaped from a Turkish prison in November 1979.

The Restoration of democratic civilian government moved slowly, however. On Oct. 15, 1981, a 160-member Consultative Assembly began work on a new constitution and election law to replace the suspended 1961 Constitution.

Lack of more definite guarantees of a return to democracy caused the European Community (EC or Common Market) to delay a $650-million, five-year aid package. The EC had agreed to provide the money to help Turkey get back on its feet.

Although the EC balked, about $940 million in aid was promised for the hard-pressed Turkish economy by members of the Organization for Economic Cooperation and Development. But with the country almost totally dependent on imported oil, prospects for an economic breakthrough remained poor. William Spencer

See also MIDDLE EAST (Facts in Brief Table). In WORLD BOOK, see ATATÜRK, KEMAL; TURKEY.

UGANDA experienced serious political instability in 1981. Opposition groups waged guerrilla warfare against the government of President Milton Obote, and undisciplined army troops killed civilians and looted in several parts of the country.

Rebel Movements. A month-long episode of violence broke out in Uganda's capital, Kampala, on February 4. Ugandan soldiers ransacked homes in the suburb of Rubaga, killing one person and injuring several others. In an attack on another suburb on February 9, men in army uniforms killed three civilians and wounded three others.

A faction of the Democratic Party (DP), which charged that it had been cheated out of winning the December 1980 parliamentary elections by the Uganda People's Congress (UPC), formed the underground Uganda Freedom Movement (UFM). The UFM also participated in the February violence and mounted several other attacks in April.

Another guerrilla group, the People's Revolutionary Army (PRA), was established by Yoweri Museveni, a defense minister during the 1979-1980 military government. Forces of the PRA killed about 200 regular army troops in a clash on April 7, 18 miles (28 kilometers) northwest of Kampala. By November, the PRA reportedly controlled a considerable amount of territory in that region.

Obote's government began detaining opposition politicians in March following the March 24 guerrilla bombings of power stations and a machine-gun attack on UPC headquarters. The DP leader, Paul Ssemogerere, charged in July that about 300 supporters of his party were then illegally jailed.

In addition to coping with strong political opposition, Obote's government had to face serious lack of discipline within its regular army and a general deterioration in public order. On June 24, more than 100 soldiers invaded a Roman Catholic mission at Ombachi in the West Nile district. They killed 86 civilians and wounded at least 70 others.

Famine and Poverty. The breakdown of law and order in the drought-stricken Karamoja region contributed to the failure of relief supplies to reach the region's starving nomads. As many as 30,000 people may have died in an 18-month period ending in March 1981.

The World Bank agreed to loan Uganda $95-million to revitalize industries on condition that the government stop using its holdings of foreign currency to buy Ugandan money in an effort to keep the exchange rate high. As a result, the Ugandan shilling was devalued from 7.7 = U.S. $1 to 80 = U.S. $1.   J. Dixon Esseks

See also AFRICA (Facts in Brief Table). In WORLD BOOK, see UGANDA.

UNEMPLOYMENT. See ECONOMICS; LABOR.

UNION OF SOVIET SOCIALIST REPUBLICS (U.S.S.R.). See RUSSIA.

UNITED ARAB EMIRATES (UAE). See MIDDLE EAST.

UNITED NATIONS (UN). The UN Security Council nominated Javier Pérez de Cuéllar of Peru for secretary-general on Dec. 11, 1981, breaking a six-week deadlock. Secretary-General Kurt Waldheim of Austria was seeking a third 5-year term, which would begin in 1982. No one had held the post for more than two terms. Waldheim's chief opponent was Tanzania's Foreign Minister Salim Ahmed Salim, candidate of the 93-nation Nonaligned Movement and of the Organization of African Unity, which has 50 members.

The Security Council held four private meetings between October 27 and November 17, voting first on one candidate and then on the other. The Council cast 16 pairs of ballots at these meetings without nominating either man. Waldheim always reached or exceeded the required nine votes but was vetoed by China, which said that it wanted a secretary-general from the Third World. Salim got nine votes or more on five ballots but was also vetoed, evidently by the United States.

On December 3, Waldheim withdrew from the race. Salim dropped out on December 8. On December 11, the Security Council announced that it had selected Pérez de Cuéllar. The UN General Assembly elected him on December 15. See PÉREZ DE CUÉLLAR, JAVIER.

United States President Ronald Reagan appointed Jeane J. Kirkpatrick as U.S. ambassador to the UN. On January 29, she became the first woman to hold that post. Kirkpatrick had been a professor of political science at Georgetown University in Washington, D.C. See KIRKPATRICK, JEANE J.

Middle East. In Security Council negotiations on March 19, Kirkpatrick at first agreed to a Council statement that condemned Major Saad Haddad's pro-Israeli Lebanese irregulars for attacking UN troops in southern Lebanon. But she then reexamined the text and withdrew her agreement because it singled out Israel for condemnation. She kept the Council negotiating until after midnight before it produced a statement she could accept.

On June 7, Israeli planes bombed the partly built Osirak nuclear reactor near Baghdad, Iraq. On June 8, Iraq complained to the Council, calling the raid a "grave act of aggression." Israel sent a note to the Council on the same day, saying that Iraq meant to use the reactor to make material for atomic bombs for possible use against Israel. Kirkpatrick, Iraq's Foreign Minister Saadun Hamadi, and others drafted a resolution that strongly condemned the attack, recognized Iraq's right to nuclear energy, and called on Israel to put its nuclear facilities under the same international safeguards against military use already applied in Iraq. The Council adopted the resolution unanimously on June 19.

Syrian Peacekeeping Troops in Lebanon installed Russian-made surface-to-air missiles on

Lebanese soil on April 29 in an apparent response to Israeli attacks. Israel said it would bomb the missiles if Syria left them there, but Syria refused to remove them. President Reagan announced on May 5 that Philip C. Habib, former undersecretary of state, would try to settle the dispute.

While Habib made repeated visits to the Middle East, Israeli air raids on Palestinian guerrilla locations in Lebanon increased in intensity. A July 17 attack on Beirut killed about 300 people, including many Lebanese civilians. At Lebanon's request, the Security Council met on that day and issued a statement expressing deep concern at "the deplorable events" and appealing for an immediate end to all armed attacks. On July 21, the Council unanimously adopted a resolution sponsored by Ireland, Japan, and Spain repeating the appeal and asking Waldheim to report on its effect in 48 hours. Waldheim reported on July 24 that Habib had arranged for "all hostile military activity between Lebanese and Israeli territory in either direction" to cease at 1:30 P.M. Greenwich Mean Time that day.

Israel annexed the Golan Heights, a narrow strip of land northeast of Israel, on December 14. Israel had seized the territory from Syria during the Six-Day War in 1967. On December 17, the Security Council unanimously approved a resolution declaring the annexation "null and void."

Hostages Released. On January 20, Iran released 52 United States citizens who had been held hostage in Teheran since Nov. 4, 1979. Their release closed a case for the UN Security Council and the International Court of Justice in The Hague, the Netherlands. Both of these bodies had called on Iran to free the hostages.

Sea Law. Delegates to the seven-year-old UN Law of the Sea Conference had agreed in 1980 to complete a general treaty at its 10th session, which was scheduled to begin in New York City on March 9. But on March 3, the Reagan Administration said that it wanted time to review the treaty text. Third World countries said at the beginning of the session that they would wait until the United States finished its review before considering what to do about seabed mining investments made before the treaty took effect.

Third World countries rejected a U.S. demand to delay the next session until 1982. Instead, the delegates agreed to meet in Geneva, Switzerland, on Aug. 3, 1981, and then adjourned on April 17.

In Geneva, they agreed to make the final decisions at an eight-week session scheduled to begin in New York City on March 8, 1982. The Geneva session ended on August 28. The delegates hope to sign the treaty in September 1982.

Cambodia. Under a 1980 Assembly resolution, an international conference on Cambodia was held at UN headquarters from July 13 to 17. Ninety-

Jeane J. Kirkpatrick, the first woman to be named U.S. ambassador to the United Nations, chats with Yehuda Blum, the Israeli delegate.

three states attended, including the former Cambodian government of Pol Pot, who had been Communist Party secretary and prime minister. Vietnamese troops had ousted the Pol Pot government from Phnom Penh, the capital, in January 1979. Other anti-Vietnamese Cambodian parties observed the conference, but Vietnam and Russia, along with 49 other nations, stayed away. The conference adopted a declaration calling for a cease-fire in Cambodia, withdrawal of foreign troops, and a UN-supervised election.

Namibia. Waldheim convened a conference on Namibia in Geneva from January 7 to 14. The delegates were to set dates for a cease-fire and the deployment of UN troops and civilian observers to monitor elections. The Namibians were to vote for an assembly that would draft a constitution under which Namibia would become independent of South Africa. The plan was the work of the so-called Western Five – also known as the "contact group" – the United States, Great Britain, France, West Germany, and Canada. The Security Council had approved the plan in 1978.

Present at the January meeting were the Western Five; South Africa; Namibian political parties, including the South West Africa People's Organization (SWAPO); and the so-called front-line states – Angola, Botswana, Mozambique, Tanzania, and Zambia. UN officials suggested a cease-fire date of March 30. However, South Africa rejected this date on the grounds that the UN was biased in favor of SWAPO.

The General Assembly resumed its 1980 regular session on March 2 to debate the question of Namibia. South Africa, which had been expelled from the UN in 1974 and 1979, took its General Assembly seat and was expelled a third time. The vote was 112 to 22, with 6 abstentions.

On March 6, the Assembly adopted 10 resolutions sponsored by Third World and Communist countries. Two resolutions called for Security Council sanctions to force South Africa out of Namibia. One, taking into account the likelihood of Western vetoes, said if the Council could not adopt "concrete measures" to that end, the Assembly would "urgently consider necessary action." Votes for the resolutions ranged from 108 to 0, with 26 abstentions, to 133 to 0, with 5 abstentions. The Western Five abstained.

On an African request, the Security Council held 11 meetings on Namibia between April 21 and 30. Uganda, Niger, Tunisia, Mexico, and Panama proposed a resolution declaring South Africa's "continued illegal occupation" of Namibia to be a breach of peace. The resolution also proposed imposing an oil embargo, an arms embargo, and a diplomatic and economic boycott on South Africa. Niger, Tunisia, and Uganda also submitted three separate resolutions for the three kinds of sanc-

tions. The United States, Great Britain, and France vetoed all four resolutions on April 30.

The vetoes triggered an emergency special session of the General Assembly, beginning on September 3. South Africa turned up again and was expelled a fourth time on September 4. The session ended on the morning of September 14 with the adoption of a Third World resolution demanding "immediate commencement" of an independence plan, declaring that South Africa threatened the peace, and calling for worldwide "comprehensive, mandatory sanctions" against the country. The vote was 117 to 0, with 25 abstentions, including the Western Five.

The 36th Session of the General Assembly began on September 15. Its retiring president, Rüdiger von Wechmar of West Germany, conducted the election of a new president. On the first ballot, Ismat T. Kittani of Iraq got 64 votes; Khwaja Mohammed Kaiser of Bangladesh, 46; and Tommy Koh of Singapore, 40. Kittani was short of a majority of those voting. Von Wechmar therefore conducted a second ballot, limited under the rules to the top two candidates. On this ballot, Kittani and Kaiser each got 73 votes. Following the rule for breaking a tie, Von Wechmar drew lots and Kittani won.

The new session dealt with a record 137 items. The Assembly raised UN membership to 157 by admitting Vanuatu on September 15, Belize on September 25, and Antigua and Barbuda on November 11. The Security Council was made up of the five permanent members – China, France, Great Britain, Russia, and the United States – and East Germany, Ireland, Japan, Mexico, Niger, Panama, the Philippines, Spain, Tunisia, and Uganda. In October, the Assembly elected Guyana, Jordan, Poland, Togo, and Zaire to succeed Mexico, the Philippines, East Germany, Niger, and Tunisia for two-year terms beginning in 1982.

On October 21, the Assembly voted 100 to 25, with 19 abstentions, to urge withdrawal of foreign troops from Cambodia. On November 11, a 109 to 2 vote, with 34 abstentions, strongly condemned Israel's raid on Iraq's reactor. Israel and the United States voted against the resolution. On November 18, the General Assembly voted 116 to 23, with 12 abstentions, to call for the withdrawal of foreign troops from Afghanistan.

Canadian Ambassador Gerard Pelletier told the Assembly on November 20 that the Western Five hoped to see the plan for Namibia's independence put into effect in 1982. Pelletier said that the Western Five wanted the African nations to accept confidence-building measures – aimed at reassuring Namibia's white minority – to be incorporated in Namibia's constitution. He said that the Western Five would suggest ways to guarantee a fair changeover to independence. Pelletier warned the

Year of Disabled Persons

Governments and private organizations redoubled their efforts during 1981 to rehabilitate the world's millions of physically or mentally disabled persons. The United Nations (UN) proclaimed 1981 the International Year of Disabled Persons (IYDP) and recommended that individual countries carry out rehabilitation programs in an effort to reach the 75 per cent of the world's disabled who have received no aid from trained specialists.

The UN called for a special effort in the developing countries. Eighty per cent of the world's disabled persons live in these nations, and fewer than 1 per cent of them have been helped by specialists.

The UN said disabled persons should have access to the world around them, including social and economic activities. IYDP programs should focus on preventing disabilities, helping the disabled to adjust psychologically to society, encouraging them to participate in everyday life, training them for work, and providing jobs and employment counseling. The programs should also educate the public about the rights and capabilities of the disabled.

Infectious diseases, accidents, malnutrition, genetic abnormalities, and the stresses of living exact a heavy toll from humanity. The UN estimates that 70 million people throughout the world have a hearing impairment, 42 million are blind or visually disabled, 20 million have leprosy, 15 million are victims of cerebral palsy, and 15 million suffer from epilepsy.

Home accidents have disabled 30 million people; traffic accidents, 30 million; and accidents on the job, 15 million. Wars, natural disasters, and sports activities have disabled an additional 3 million. About 40 million people are mentally retarded, and 40 million are mentally ill.

Many disabled persons cannot get jobs because some employers have false ideas about their injury rates, their needs for special treatment, and their productivity. A study conducted by E. I. du Pont de Nemours & Company, a giant United States chemical firm that employs 1,000 disabled persons, showed that hiring the disabled does not lead to increased workers' compensation costs or lost-time injuries and that 96 per cent of disabled employees rate average or better in safety both on and off the job. The report also indicated that most disabled workers need no special work arrangement.

Hundreds of meetings throughout the world in 1981 laid the groundwork for programs that eventually will reach the disabled. In April, about 1,100 disability specialists from 48 nations attended a conference on the disabled in Vienna, Austria, and representatives of 22 Arab countries and delegates from international agencies met for four days in Kuwait. In August, about 200 people gathered in Toronto, Canada, to attend the 1981 conference of Mobility International, an organization that promotes travel as a means of enriching the lives of disabled persons. Libya held a symposium on the disabled in Tripoli in September, and the Latin American Medical Congress dealt with the subject in Quito, Ecuador, in November.

Exhibits and demonstrations throughout the world showed what the disabled can do. Spectators at Japan's International Abilympic watched disabled persons compete in such vocational skills as typing, tailoring, and watch repairing. Venezuelans who attended their country's First National Sports Contests for the Blind and Visually Impaired learned that poor vision and even blindness cannot stop a determined competitor.

In the United States, champion wheelchair racers George Murray of Tampa, Fla., and Phil Carpenter of Holiday, Fla., showed that even the breadth of a continent is no match for disabled persons who develop their remaining capabilities. The two men proved the point by traveling by wheelchair from Los Angeles to New York City. Perhaps programs begun during the International Year of Disabled Persons will help millions of others to develop their capabilities so that they can take their rightful places among their more fortunate brothers and sisters.　Jay Myers

INTERNATIONAL YEAR
OF DISABLED PERSONS
(IYDP) – 1981

IYDP symbol

Actress Liv Ullmann, the first woman good-will ambassador for the United Nations Children's Fund (UNICEF), visits a refugee camp in Ethiopia.

Assembly against adopting "unhelpful" resolutions on Namibia.

At a meeting in Geneva on May 20, the World Health Organization, a UN-affiliated agency, endorsed an international code promoting the breast-feeding of babies and regulating the marketing of infant formulas. The vote was 118 to 1, with the United States opposed and Argentina, Japan, and South Korea abstaining.

New Leaders. On July 1, Alden W. Clausen of the United States became president of the World Bank, a UN affiliate in Washington, D.C. Clausen replaced Robert S. McNamara, who retired. Clausen had been president and chief executive officer of the Bank of America in San Francisco.

The members of the International Atomic Energy Agency named Hans Blix of Sweden director general on September 26. Blix succeeded Sigvard Eklund of Sweden, who retired on November 30 after holding the post for 20 years.

The Office of the UN High Commissioner for Refugees in Geneva won the 1981 Nobel Prize for Peace. Norway's Nobel Committee, announcing the award in Oslo on October 14, said the office gave important help to refugees despite "political difficulties." In Geneva, High Commissioner Poul Hartling of Denmark accepted the honor "in the name of refugees everywhere."   William N. Oatis

In WORLD BOOK, see UNITED NATIONS.

UNITED STATES, GOVERNMENT OF THE. The American government seemed infused with new energy in 1981 as the 52 Americans held hostage for more than a year in Iran were freed; the space shuttle *Columbia* made two spectacular trips into orbit and returned safely; and President Ronald Reagan survived an assassination attempt to wield greater authority over Congress than any President since Lyndon B. Johnson. See IRAN; SPACE EXPLORATION; REAGAN, RONALD WILSON.

The economic outlook was sobering, however. High interest rates and growing unemployment indicated that the United States was indeed in the midst of a recession – and many projections indicated that the economic decline would last at least through 1982. Because the President's proposed remedy – a package of tax cuts and federal budget slashes known as Reaganomics – did not go into effect until the 1982 fiscal year, which began on Oct. 1, 1981, its influence on the economy had yet to be measured.

Pruning the Bureaucracy. In the early days of his Administration, Reagan set to work paring the federal government. Regulations proposed during the Administration of President Jimmy Carter were scrapped; federal payrolls were cut; and oil price decontrol and industry deregulation were accelerated. On January 22, Reagan appointed Vice-President George H. W. Bush as head of the Task

Federal Spending

Estimated U.S. Budget for Fiscal 1982*

	Billions of dollars
National defense	184.4
International affairs†	12.2
Science and space research	7.6
Natural resources, environment, energy	26.0
Agriculture	4.8
Commerce, transportation, housing credit	29.7
Community and regional development	9.1
Education, employment, social services	34.5
Health	74.6
Income security	255.0
Veterans benefits and services	24.5
Law enforcement and justice	4.9
General government	5.2
Revenue sharing and federal aid	6.9
Interest	89.9
Allowances	1.9
Undistributed funds	−31.9
Total	739.3

*Preliminary budget submitted by
President Jimmy Carter on Jan. 15, 1981,
subject to later revision
†Includes foreign aid

U.S. Income and Outlays

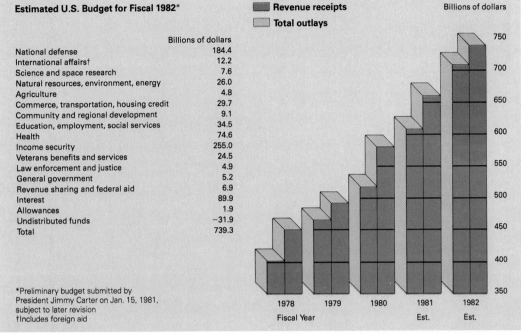

Revenue receipts
Total outlays
Billions of dollars

Fiscal Year   1978   1979   1980   1981 Est.   1982 Est.

Source: U.S. Office of Management and Budget

Force on Regulatory Relief. By March 5, the task force had thrown out most of the regulations set forth in the last weeks of the Carter Administration. On February 17, Reagan signed an executive order providing for the review of all new regulations to ensure that the potential benefits of such rulings outweigh the potential costs.

In response to a general request by the President, department heads began to trim their agencies. On June 12, Anne M. Gorsuch, administrator of the Environmental Protection Agency (EPA), announced that the EPA office of enforcement would be eliminated, making each division within the EPA responsible for enforcing its own regulations. In mid-November, the EPA and the National Highway Traffic Safety Administration proposed the delay or elimination of 34 safety and antipollution requirements for cars and trucks.

The Department of the Interior also provided cuts. On May 7, Interior Secretary James G. Watt said that federal funds would not be used to buy more parkland, but only to restore and improve existing national parks. See ENVIRONMENT.

Secretary of Labor Raymond J. Donovan announced on May 1 that his department would lift the ban on working at home in industries where "industrial homework" had been prohibited. On August 24, Donovan proposed new regulations relaxing antidiscrimination requirements and re-ducing affirmative-action procedures for most federal contractors.

On December 16, President Reagan approved a proposal to dismantle the Department of Energy (DOE) and transfer many of its functions to the Department of Commerce.

Cutting Services. Perhaps the sharpest cuts in services were made by the Department of Health and Human Services (HHS) after Congress cut funds for many of its programs. On September 21, HHS Secretary Richard S. Schweiker issued new regulations ending federal benefits for 10 per cent of all welfare recipients, projecting an estimated saving of $1.1 billion in fiscal year 1982 (see WELFARE). On October 1, the HHS eliminated the Community Services Administration (CSA), formerly the Office of Economic Opportunity. Funds budgeted to the CSA were added to block grants — grants for dozens of health, education, and social services — for the states in the budget-cutting bill passed by Congress on July 31.

In mid-December, however, President Reagan rejected one cost-cutting proposal. He decided to keep the Community Development Block Grants and the Urban Development Action Grants operating at least through 1984 at an annual budget of $3.8 billion.

The Government Printing Office announced in November that more than 900 periodicals and

Major Agencies and Bureaus of the U.S. Government*

Executive Office of the President
President, Ronald Reagan

Vice-President, George H. W. Bush
White House Chief of Staff, James A. Baker III
Presidential Press Secretary, James S. Brady
Central Intelligence Agency – William J. Casey, Director
Council of Economic Advisers – Murray L. Weidenbaum, Chairman
Council on Environmental Quality – A. Alan Hill, Chairman
Office of Management and Budget – David A. Stockman, Director
Office of Science and Technology Policy – George A. Keyworth II, Director

The Supreme Court of the United States
Chief Justice of the United States, Warren E. Burger

Associate Justices:
William J. Brennan, Jr.	Lewis F. Powell, Jr.
Byron R. White	William H. Rehnquist
Thurgood Marshall	John Paul Stevens
Harry A. Blackmun	Sandra Day O'Connor

State Department
Secretary of State, Alexander M. Haig, Jr.

U.S. Representative to the United Nations – Jeane J. Kirkpatrick

Department of the Treasury
Secretary of the Treasury, Donald T. Regan

Bureau of Alcohol, Tobacco, and Firearms – G. R. Dickerson, Director
Bureau of Engraving and Printing – Harry R. Clements, Director
Bureau of the Mint – Donna Pope, Director
Comptroller of the Currency – C. T. Conover
Internal Revenue Service – Roscoe L. Egger, Jr., Commissioner
Treasurer of the United States – Angela M. Buchanan
U.S. Customs Service – William von Raab, Commissioner
U.S. Secret Service – John R. Simpson, Director

Department of Defense
Secretary of Defense, Caspar W. Weinberger

Joint Chiefs of Staff – General David C. Jones, Chairman
Secretary of the Air Force – Verne L. Orr
Secretary of the Army – John O. Marsh, Jr.
Secretary of the Navy – John F. Lehman, Jr.

Department of Justice
Attorney General, William French Smith

Bureau of Prisons – Norman A. Carlson, Director
Drug Enforcement Administration – Francis Mullen, Acting Administrator
Federal Bureau of Investigation – William H. Webster, Director
Immigration and Naturalization Service – Alan C. Nelson†, Commissioner
Office of Justice Assistance, Research, and Statistics – Robert F. Diegelman, Acting Director
Solicitor General – Rex E. Lee

Department of the Interior
Secretary of the Interior, James G. Watt

Assistant Secretary for Indian Affairs – Kenneth L. Smith
Bureau of Land Management – Robert F. Burford, Director
Bureau of Mines – Robert Carlton Horton, Director
Bureau of Reclamation – Robert N. Broadbent, Commissioner
Geological Survey – Dallas L. Peck, Director
National Park Service – Russell E. Dickenson, Director
Office of Territorial Affairs – Pedro A. Sanjuan, Director
U.S. Fish and Wildlife Service – Robert A. Jantzen, Director

Department of Agriculture
Secretary of Agriculture, John R. Block

Agricultural Economics – William Gene Lesher, Director
Agricultural Marketing Service – Mildred Thymian, Administrator
Agricultural Stabilization and Conservation Service – Everett G. Rank, Jr., Acting Administrator
Farmers Home Administration – Charles Wilson Shuman, Administrator
Federal Crop Insurance Corporation – Melvin Sims, Chairman
Food and Consumer Services – Mary C. Jarratt, Administrator
Forest Service – R. Max Peterson, Chief
Rural Electrification Administration – Harold V. Hunter, Administrator
Soil Conservation Service – Norman A. Berg, Chief

Department of Commerce
Secretary of Commerce, Malcolm Baldrige

Bureau of the Census – Bruce K. Chapman, Director
Economic Development Administration – Carlos C. Campbell, Administrator
National Bureau of Standards – Ernest Ambler, Director
National Oceanic and Atmospheric Administration – John V. Byrne, Administrator
Minority Business Development Agency – Victor Rivera, Director
Patent and Trademark Office – Gerald J. Mossinghoff, Commissioner

Department of Labor
Secretary of Labor, Raymond J. Donovan

Bureau of Labor Statistics – Janet L. Norwood, Commissioner
Employment and Training Administration – Albert Angrisani, Administrator
Employment Standards Administration – Robert B. Collyer, Administrator
Labor-Management Services Administration – Donald L. Dotson, Administrator
Mine Safety and Health Administration – Ford Barney Ford, Administrator
Occupational Safety and Health Administration – Thorne G. Auchter, Administrator
Women's Bureau – Lenora Cole-Alexander, Director

Department of Health and Human Services
Secretary of Health and Human Services, Richard S. Schweiker

Administration for Children, Youth and Families – (vacant)
Administration on Aging – Marie P. Tolliver, Commissioner
Alcohol, Drug Abuse, and Mental Health Administration – William E. Mayer, Administrator
Centers for Disease Control – William H. Foege, Director
Food and Drug Administration – Arthur Hull Hayes, Jr., Commissioner
Health Care Financing Administration – Carolyne K. Davis, Administrator
Health Resources Administration – Robert Graham, Acting Administrator
Health Services Administration – John H. Kelso, Acting Administrator
National Institutes of Health – Donald S. Fredrickson, Director
Office of Consumer Affairs – Virginia Knauer, Director
Public Health Service – C. Everett Koop, Director
Social Security Administration – John A. Svahn, Commissioner

Department of Housing and Urban Development
Secretary of Housing and Urban Development, Samuel R. Pierce, Jr.

Community Planning and Development – Stephen J. Bollinger, Administrator
Federal Housing Commissioner – Philip B. Winn
Government National Mortgage Association – Robert W. Karpe, President
New Community Development Corporation – Warren T. Lindquist, General Manager

Department of Transportation
Secretary of Transportation, Andrew L. Lewis, Jr.

Federal Aviation Administration – J. Lynn Helms, Administrator
Federal Highway Administration – Ray A. Barnhart, Administrator
Federal Railroad Administration – Robert W. Blanchette, Administrator
National Highway Traffic Safety Administration – Raymond A. Peck, Jr., Administrator
U.S. Coast Guard – Admiral John B. Hayes, Commandant
Urban Mass Transportation Administration – Arthur E. Teele, Jr., Administrator

Department of Energy
Secretary of Energy, James B. Edwards

Economic Regulatory Administration – Rayburn D. Hanzlik, Administrator
Energy Information Administration – J. Erich Evered, Administrator
Federal Energy Regulatory Commission – Charles M. Butler III, Chairman
Office of Energy Research – Alvin W. Trivelpiece, Director

Department of Education
Secretary of Education, Terrel H. Bell

National Institute of Education – Edward A. Curran, Director
Rehabilitation Services Administration – George A. Conn, Commissioner

Congressional Officials
President of the Senate pro tempore – Strom Thurmond

Speaker of the House – Thomas P. O'Neill, Jr.
Architect of the Capitol – George M. White
Comptroller General of the U.S. – Charles A. Bowsher
Congressional Budget Office – Alice M. Rivlin, Director
Librarian of Congress – Daniel J. Boorstin
Office of Technology Assessment – John H. Gibbons, Director
Public Printer of the U.S. – Danford L. Sawyer

Independent Agencies
ACTION – Thomas W. Pauken, Director
Civil Aeronautics Board – C. Dan McKinnon, Chairman
Commodity Futures Trading Commission – Philip J. Johnson, Chairman
Consumer Product Safety Commission – Nancy Harvey Steorts, Chairman
Environmental Protection Agency – Ann McGill Gorsuch, Administrator
Equal Employment Opportunity Commission – William M. Bell†, Chairman
Export-Import Bank – William H. Draper III, President
Farm Credit Administration – Donald E. Wilkinson, Governor
Federal Communications Commission – Mark S. Fowler, Chairman
Federal Deposit Insurance Corporation – William Isaac, Chairman
Federal Election Commission – John W. McGarry, Chairman
Federal Emergency Management Agency – Louis O. Giuffrida, Director
Federal Home Loan Bank Board – Richard Pratt, Chairman
Federal Maritime Commission – Alan Green, Jr., Chairman
Federal Mediation and Conciliation Service – Kenneth E. Moffett†, Acting Director
Federal Reserve System – Paul A. Volcker, Board of Governors Chairman
Federal Trade Commission – James C. Miller III, Chairman
General Services Administration – Gerald P. Carmen, Administrator
Interstate Commerce Commission – Reese H. Taylor, Jr., Director
National Aeronautics and Space Administration – James M. Beggs, Administrator
National Credit Union Administration – Edgar F. Callahan, Chairman
National Endowment for the Arts – Francis S. M. Hodsoll, Chairman
National Endowment for the Humanities – William J. Bennett†, Chairman
National Labor Relations Board – John R. Van de Water†, Chairman
National Mediation Board – George S. Ives, Chairman
National Railroad Passenger Corporation (AMTRAK) – Alan S. Boyd, President
National Science Foundation – John Brooks Slaughter, Director
National Transportation Safety Board – James E. Burnett, Jr., Chairman
Nuclear Regulatory Commission – Nunzio J. Palladino, Chairman
Occupational Safety and Health Review Commission – Timothy F. Cleary, Chairman
Office of Personnel Management – Donald J. Devine, Director
Panama Canal Commission – Dennis P. McAuliffe, Administrator
Securities and Exchange Commission – John S. R. Shad, Chairman
Small Business Administration – Michael Cardenas, Administrator
Smithsonian Institution – S. Dillon Ripley, Secretary
Synthetic Fuels Corporation – Edward E. Noble, Chairman
Tennessee Valley Authority – Charles H. Dean, Jr., Chairman
U.S. Arms Control and Disarmament Agency – Eugene V. Rostow, Director
U.S. Commission on Civil Rights – Clarence M. Pendleton, Jr., Chairman
U.S. Information Agency – Charles Z. Wick, Director
U.S. International Development Cooperation Agency – M. Peter McPherson, Director
U.S. International Trade Commission – Bill Alberger, Chairman
U.S. Metric Board – Louis F. Polk, Chairman
U.S. Postal Service – William F. Bolger, Postmaster General
Veterans Administration – Robert P. Nimmo, Administrator

*As of Jan. 1, 1982. † Nominated but not yet confirmed.

pamphlets published by the federal government had been canceled. Moreover, no new federal publications were to be initiated.

Other cuts in federal regulations and services included reduced requirements for special facilities for the handicapped and provisions for bilingual education. See EDUCATION; HANDICAPPED.

Labor Negotiations. The United States Postal Service, in an effort to overcome a mounting deficit, raised its rates for first-class postage twice in 1981. On March 22, the cost of a first-class stamp rose from 15 cents to 18 cents; on November 1, it increased to 20 cents. On July 21, a postal strike was averted when the service and two workers unions agreed on a new three-year contract. See POSTAL SERVICE, UNITED STATES.

On August 5, upon the President's orders, the Federal Aviation Administration (FAA) fired striking air-traffic controllers – all government employees – for an illegal walkout. The Professional Air Traffic Controllers Organization (PATCO) was decertified on October 22. On December 9, President Reagan announced that PATCO members could be rehired by the federal government, but not as air-traffic controllers. See AVIATION.

The Legislative Branch. A coalition in the 97th Congress worked to give the President almost unprecedented support for his programs. A major triumph of the Reagan Administration was the passage of the Omnibus Budget Reconciliation Act of 1981, passed by Congress on July 31, which specified $35.2 billion in budget cuts affecting 83 major federal programs for fiscal 1982.

Another keystone of Reagan's economic program, the Economic Recovery Tax Act of 1981, providing for a 25 per cent reduction in individual income taxes over a three-year period, also passed by wide margins in both houses in August. But Administration efforts to reform the Social Security system were abandoned (see SOCIAL SECURITY).

Congress approved the President's policies in other actions, including the sale of five Airborne Warning and Control System (AWACS) aircraft to Saudi Arabia; an increase in military spending to $200 billion – the largest peacetime increase in history; an $11-billion farm bill that set subsidy levels for the next four years; and the Alaska pipeline bill, shifting some of the construction costs to taxpayers. See ARMED FORCES; FARM AND FARMING; PETROLEUM AND GAS.

In late 1981, however, Congress became increasingly reluctant to support further slashes in federal programs, despite the President's urging. Instead, Congress approved continuing resolutions to fund government operations. On December 15, the President signed a $413-billion federal-funding bill to keep the government running through March 31, 1982. The bill was necessary because by mid-December Congress had not completed its work on the 13 appropriations bills needed to fund all government operations in fiscal 1982.

The first session of the 97th Congress twice raised the temporary federal debt ceiling – to $985-billion on February 6 and to $1.079 trillion on September 29. See CONGRESS OF THE U.S.

The Supreme Court. In 1981, the Supreme Court of the United States ruled on the controversial issues of rape and abortion. On March 23, it ruled 5 to 4 to uphold a lower court ruling in California that penalizes males but not females for having sexual relations with an underage partner. That same day, the high court ruled 6 to 3 to uphold a lower court ruling that a Utah law requiring physicians to notify the parents of a dependent teen-age girl if possible before performing an abortion was constitutional.

The court also ruled on citizens' rights. On April 20, the court ruled 6 to 3 that states are not required to provide a specific level of care or training for retarded people in state institutions. On June 1, it ruled 5 to 4 that indigent parents have no right to free legal assistance in custody cases. See SUPREME COURT OF THE U.S.   Carol L. Thompson

In WORLD BOOK, see UNITED STATES, GOVERNMENT OF THE.

UNITED STATES CONSTITUTION. See CONSTITUTION OF THE UNITED STATES.

UPPER VOLTA. See AFRICA.

URUGUAY. General Gregorio Alvarez, retired commander in chief of the army, became president of Uruguay on Sept. 1, 1981. Alvarez was chosen by leaders of the armed forces to replace President Aparicio Mendez Manfredini, whose term had expired. The armed forces promised that the country would choose Alvarez' successor through elections. Alvarez announced the expansion of Uruguay's Council of State, largely a rubber-stamp assembly, to include 35 members.

The Council of State was charged with developing a framework for elections that will reconcile the interests of the armed forces with those of the reactivated political parties. Two leaders of the traditional parties – Carlos Julio Pereira of the Blanco Party and Jorge Battle of the Colorado Party – faulted the council because of its lack of elected representatives.

The council's powers include calling a constitutional assembly to modify the 1967 constitution, which was set aside in 1973. The council is also responsible for calling a plebiscite on the modified constitution and for arranging general elections in November 1984 to pick a successor to Alvarez.

In April, Uruguay's military government was shaken by a scandal involving corruption and gambling. Several senior military officers, the minister of the interior, the Montevideo police chief, and other officials were forced to resign.

The Economy. Uruguay withstood the recessionary factors in the global economy in 1981 better than most other Latin American countries. Uruguay's exports, mainly agricultural products, were worth about $1.3 billion in 1981, an increase of more than 25 per cent over 1980. In April, the nation reported financial reserves of $1.6 billion, a 10 per cent annual rate of inflation, and 5.6 per cent unemployment.

In the last half of 1981, Uruguay was hurt by an economic crisis in neighboring Argentina, which buys 20 per cent of Uruguay's manufactured goods. There was a slowdown in Argentine tourism to Uruguay's vacation resorts, and Argentine investment in Uruguayan construction declined.

The military leadership of Uruguay came under increasing criticism for its economic policies in 1981. Critics charged that the overvalued Uruguayan peso, which has been supported by the military to combat domestic inflation, was slowing down foreign investment.   Nathan A. Haverstock

See also LATIN AMERICA (Facts in Brief Table). In WORLD BOOK, see URUGUAY.

UTAH. See STATE GOVERNMENT.

UTILITIES. See COMMUNICATIONS; ENERGY; PETROLEUM AND GAS.

VANUATU. See PACIFIC ISLANDS; WORLD BOOK SUPPLEMENT section.

VENDA. See AFRICA.

VENEZUELA. Despite its oil wealth, Venezuela suffered an economic slump in 1981. Critics blamed the Administration of President Luis Herrera Campins, who came to power in March 1979. Herrera has tried to cool off the Venezuelan economy, overheated by years of rapid growth following a quadrupling of oil earnings in 1973. His program included restraints on government spending, elimination of price controls, cutting government subsidies, and lowering duties on imports to force local manufacturers to become more competitive.

Economic Troubles. Critics claimed that the government has failed to put its own house in order. The government is dominant in the economy through its control of many state-run corporations. The number of government employees increased from 300,000 in 1974 to 827,000 in 1980, and an additional 120,000 workers were added in the first two years of the Herrera Administration. The state-run steel company was reported to be losing $1 million a day, and the state-run airline, which lost $20 million in 1980, continued to post losses in 1981. A cutoff of electric power at the government's aluminum plant at Ciudad Guayana, due to carelessness or incompetence, caused from $30 million to $75 million in damage.

Such widely publicized fumbles by the government resulted in a lack of confidence among the business community and a flight of capital to United States financial markets for higher interest rates. In an attempt to stem this flow, the Venezuelan government in September eliminated the fixed interest rates administered by the Central Bank.

More and more Venezuelans came to view their country's oil wealth as a curse. It has stimulated inflation, which ran at 20 per cent in 1981, and spawned a massive migration to the cities, which have become choked with pollution. In Caracas, people paid more for drinking water in 1981 than for gasoline.

A Long-Standing Territorial Dispute between Venezuela and neighboring Guyana flared up during 1981. Venezuelan interest in its claim was heightened by rumors of oil and Guyana's plans to build a hydroelectric plant in the disputed area.

The dispute with Guyana plus the perceived threat from Cuban Communist agitation in the Caribbean provided the rationale for a military build-up. The Venezuelan government ordered six Italian-built missile-firing frigates and reportedly placed orders for advanced fighter planes from the United States. Nathan A. Haverstock

See also LATIN AMERICA (Facts in Brief Table). In WORLD BOOK, see VENEZUELA.

VERMONT. See STATE GOVERNMENT.

VETERANS. See COMMUNITY ORGANIZATIONS.

VICE-PRESIDENT OF THE UNITED STATES. See BUSH, GEORGE H. W.

Vietnam's Prime Minister Pham Van Dong, left, and Palestine Liberation Organization Chairman Yasir Arafat, right, tour Hanoi in October.

VIETNAM in 1981 held its first nationwide election since North and South Vietnam were united in 1976, after the Vietnam War had ended. On April 26, 1981, Vietnamese voters chose 496 members of the National Assembly from a list of 613 candidates drawn up by the Vietnam Fatherland Front, an organization controlled by the Communist Party.

Opening the new Assembly on June 25, Communist Party Secretary General Le Duan praised Vietnam's close ties with Russia. The two nations' friendship and cooperation treaty, he said, was "the foundation of the international line and foreign policy of our party and state . . . ."

Pham Van Dong remained as prime minister despite his reported desire to retire. To Huu became deputy prime minister. Huu delivered the official speech for the holiday of National Day on September 2, an event that caused many experts to think he might become Dong's successor.

Huu's speech admitted many failures in the economy and in governmental management. He promised that government would be reorganized to make it "less cumbersome and more dynamic." Although land would be collectivized, more material incentives would be used to increase production, Huu said.

Grave Economic Problems continued throughout the year. The 1976-1980 economic plan had failed to achieve its goals, and in 1981 the country was unable even to feed itself. In Ho Chi Minh City, Vietnam's largest urban center, a pediatrician reported that 38 per cent of the children were suffering from malnutrition. Living standards continued to decline in most areas, and thousands fled or tried to flee abroad.

The Soviet Union, the main contributor of economic aid to Vietnam as well as its major supplier of arms, criticized Vietnam for waste and inefficient use of its aid. Nevertheless, Moscow Radio announced on July 24 a new agreement on economic and technical cooperation. The agreement provided for more than 100 industrial projects to be undertaken in Vietnam by 1985 and for the Soviet Union to furnish help in technical and vocational training. A July 30 agreement called for a 90 per cent increase in Soviet supplies.

Foreign Relations. Despite the economic strain, Vietnam refused to withdraw its 200,000 troops from Cambodia. Vietnam had invaded Cambodia in 1979 and installed a Vietnamese-controlled Communist government there.

Relations with China remained bad. Talks between the two countries intended to make peace after their 1979 war were stalemated. Occasional clashes occurred on the border, with each side accusing the other of attacking. Henry S. Bradsher

See also ASIA (Facts in Brief Table). In WORLD BOOK, see VIETNAM.

VIOLA, ROBERTO EDUARDO (1924-), former commander in chief of Argentina's army, served as that nation's president from March 29 to December 11, 1981. A skilled politician elevated to office by the ruling military junta, Viola appealed to all Argentines to participate in national affairs and thus prepare the country for democracy. The junta, however, removed him from office after only 8½ months. See ARGENTINA.

Viola was born in Buenos Aires on Oct. 13, 1924. He was trained at the Argentine Military Academy, graduating as a second lieutenant in 1944. He was assigned to the infantry and served in that division until 1951, when he entered the war college. He graduated as a staff officer in 1954.

A specialist in military intelligence, Viola rose steadily through army ranks, becoming a colonel in 1965 and a brigadier general in 1971. He retired from the army as a lieutenant general in 1979.

Viola's appeal seemed broader than that of his predecessor, Jorge Rafael Videla, who engineered the 1976 coup d'état against Isabel Perón. In an effort to mend political fences both in Argentina and abroad, Viola released some 1,200 political prisoners, including Perón. He traveled to the United States in March to discuss with President Ronald Reagan the possibility of obtaining weapons from the United States.   Beverly Merz

VIRGINIA. See STATE GOVERNMENT.

VISUAL ARTS, like so much else in the United States in 1981, were affected by budgetary cuts announced by the Administration of President Ronald Reagan. The art world, led by museums and arts organizations, pressed vigorous campaigns for continued grants from the National Foundation on the Arts and the Humanities to ensure the survival of an enthusiastic cultural atmosphere in the United States.

Public sculpture, largely dependent on government funding, may have become so vital an American adornment for outdoor spaces that its production will continue unabated. Recent public monuments showed a wide range of style. Primitive was the word for Spanish artist Joan Miró's enigmatic 40-foot (12-meter) female *Chicago.* The work, installed in a downtown plaza in that city, helped celebrate Miró's 88th birthday. Richard Serra's large construction of steel plates in St. Louis was minimalist, while Claes Oldenburg worked in his usual pop art mode to produce a colossal *Flashlight* for the University of Nevada in Reno. The massive piece is 38 feet (12 meters) high and weighs 37 short tons (34 metric tons).

New Museum Facilities opened at the Boston Museum of Fine Arts, where the West Wing, designed by architect I. M. Pei, added new galleries and educational areas as part of the museum's $22-million revitalization. The San Antonio Museum of Art, after a $7.2-million renovation, moved into the former Lone Star Brewery Building, which dates from 1883. A 164-acre (66-hectare) park in Raleigh is the site of a $15.7-million building being constructed for the North Carolina Museum of Art. Plans proceeded in Washington, D.C., for a new $50-million underground complex of two museums – the Museum of African Art and an extension of the Freer Gallery of Art. Plans were announced to build a permanent structure in Houston to house the almost 10,000 items that make up the private art collection of Domenique and John de Menil, one of the largest private collections in the United States. In New York City, the Asia Society opened a new $16.6-million building. In Canada, the Vancouver Art Gallery in Edmonton, Alta., will move into a downtown courthouse after a $16.1-million renovation.

Museum-Sharing, still unusual among United States institutions, operated on a grand scale in 1981. The Peabody Museum at Harvard University in Cambridge, Mass., agreed to send portions of its undisplayed ethnographic and archaeological collection to nine other museums as the start of a long-term collection-sharing program. *The Holy Family with Saint John and Saint Elizabeth,* painted in 1651 by French artist Nicolas Poussin, was acquired jointly by two California museums, the Norton Simon Foundation in Pasadena and the J. Paul Getty Museum in Malibu, for $3.6 million. Each museum will display the painting six months every year.

Other acquisitions included a "promised gift" of 70 important modern works and 30 examples of primitive art from Oceania, the Americas, and Africa to New York City's Metropolitan Museum of Art. The donor is Muriel K. S. Newman, a Chicago collector. The Art Institute of Chicago purchased a mural-sized painting done by French artist Edouard Vuillard in 1899 titled *Landscape: Window Overlooking the Woods.*

Guernica, Spanish artist Pablo Picasso's huge and powerful protest against the horrors of the Spanish Civil War, left its 42-year abode at New York City's Museum of Modern Art for a permanent home in the Prado museum in Madrid, Spain. Picasso painted *Guernica* in Paris in 1937, sent it to New York City in 1939, and said he wanted it to go to his homeland only with "the re-establishment of public liberties" in that country. His heirs decided the conditions were finally met in September 1981.

Recent American Works were shown around the country. The Albright-Knox Gallery in Buffalo, N.Y., organized a retrospective for sculptor Kenneth Snelson. Large exhibitions documented the return to realism. "Real, Really Real, SuperReal" was the insistent name of a show at the San Antonio Museum of Art. Philadelphia's more staid Pennsylvania Academy of Fine Art mounted "Con-

Guernica, perhaps Pablo Picasso's most famous painting, is installed in the Prado museum in Madrid, Spain, in October after 42 years in America.

temporary American Realism Since 1960." The Guggenheim Museum of Art in New York City presented a pioneer abstract artist in "Arshile Gorky, 1904-1948: A Retrospective."

Artists of the 1800s received new appreciation. The National Gallery of Art in Washington, D.C., held "Rodin Rediscovered," featuring nearly 400 of French sculptor Auguste Rodin's sculptures, drawings, portraits, and photographs. The Philadelphia Museum of Art held the first museum show in the United States to concentrate on the works of British painter Sir Edwin Landseer, the highly popular Victorian artist known especially for his paintings of dogs. Paintings of French artist Camille Pissarro appeared in "Camille Pissarro: The Unexplored Impressionist" at the Boston Museum of Fine Arts. And in Toronto, Canada, the Art Gallery of Ontario organized "Vincent van Gogh and the Birth of Cloisonism."

Exotic Exhibitions of 1981 included a rare presentation of medieval art. The Metropolitan Museum of Art gathered religious works dispersed during the French Revolution and organized "The Royal Abbey of St. Denis in the Time of Abbot Suger, 1122-1151." The Philadelphia Museum of Art displayed 2,000 years of Indian art in "Manifestations of Shiva."

The National Gallery of Art featured "Between Continents; Between Seas: Precolumbian Art of Costa Rica," the first exhibition outside of Central America to focus on that culture.

Two museums honored United States popular art. "Center Ring: The Artist" at the Milwaukee Art Museum was the first scholarly exhibition of actual circus art, such as carved wagons and banners. New York City's Whitney Museum of American Art organized "Disney Animations and Animators," the first museum show of cartoonist Walt Disney's characters from the classic period of 1932 to 1942.

Other American Shows. The National Museum of American Art in Washington, D.C., presented the works of a famous painter of the American Indian in "George Caitlin, 1796-1872." Formal portraits had their first important U.S. exhibition in "Portraiture in the Grand Manner, 1720-1920" at the Los Angeles County Museum of Art. Craft was viewed as an art form in "A Century of Ceramics: 1878-1978," produced by the Everson Museum of Art in Syracuse, N.Y., and exhibited across the country.

Older European art was shown in an exhibition organized jointly by the Detroit Institute of Arts and the Art Institute of Chicago. "The Golden Age of Naples, 1734-1805" displayed art from the reign of the Bourbon kings. Two Italian Renaissance masters, the architect Andrea Palladio and the multifaceted genius Gian Lorenzo Bernini, became

Joan Miró's *Chicago,* an abstract sculpture of a woman with outstretched arms, is unveiled in a downtown plaza in Chicago on April 21.

better known through their drawings seen in traveling exhibitions across the United States.

Italy's art conservation efforts also made news. A 12-year, $3-million renovation project was begun on the ceiling frescoes painted by Michelangelo in the Vatican City's Sistine Chapel. Restorers hoped to remove centuries of grime as well as colors applied by earlier practitioners of their art. The Archaeological Museum in Florence unveiled a triumph of the restorer's art: two 5th-century B.C. Greek bronze sculptures found in 1973 and important for their quality and rarity.

Auction Sales provided one means of celebrating the 100th anniversary of Picasso's birth. His 1901 *Self-Portrait: Yo* sold for $5.3 million at Sotheby Parke Bernet in New York City on May 21. It was the highest price ever paid for any 20th-century work of art. Other record sale prices were the $420,000 paid for French lithographer Honoré Daumier's *Outside the Printshop;* the $380,000 for Belgian surrealist René Magritte's 1937 painting *The Threshold of Liberty;* and the $820,000 paid for *Gravesend Bay* by American impressionist William Merritt Chase.   Joshua B. Kind

In WORLD BOOK, see ART AND THE ARTS; PAINTING; SCULPTURE.

VITAL STATISTICS. See CENSUS; POPULATION.

WALES. See GREAT BRITAIN.

WASHINGTON. See STATE GOVERNMENT.

WASHINGTON, D.C., voters, in a referendum held on Nov. 3, 1981, rejected a school-tuition tax credit that could have reduced city income taxes by as much as $1,200 for each of a taxpayer's children who attended a private school or a public school outside the city. The measure also would have allowed nonparents to claim a tax credit if they paid the tuition of a low-income child. This provision would have enabled corporations that grant scholarships to claim a tax credit for up to 50 per cent of funds spent on tuition. The initiative was sponsored by the National Taxpayers Union and the District of Columbia Committee for Improved Education.

Mayor Marion S. Barry, Jr.; the District of Columbia City Council; the Washington, D.C., Board of Education; teachers' unions; and the superintendent of schools opposed the measure. Opponents claimed that the city would lose $24 million to $38 million in school taxes, which, Mayor Barry warned, would result in increased property taxes and layoffs of 3,000 to 4,000 city workers. The opponents of the measure also contended that the school system would be destroyed because the tax credit would make private school tuition more affordable, and would thus enable more parents to withdraw their children from Washington public schools.

Proponents countered that, even if large numbers of pupils were withdrawn, the school system would save money. They reasoned that the maximum $1,200 credit was less than the average annual cost of educating one pupil — about $3,000.

The vote marked the first time that the issue of tuition tax credits had been put to a referendum. The measure was defeated by a vote of 73,829 to 8,904 — an 8- to- 1 margin.

Budget Surplus. Reductions in the number of city workers, program cuts, and a windfall in tax revenue turned the city's anticipated $60-million deficit for fiscal 1981 into a $7-million surplus. Philip M. Dearborn, financial counselor to Mayor Barry, announced on July 10 that increases in licenses and user fees contributed to an unexpected $29 million in revenues. Although some city agencies continued to spend more than was budgeted, such overruns were expected to be offset by rising tax revenues and further personnel and program cuts. The city expected to spend $1.462 billion and to take in $1.469 billion.

However, Washington still must eliminate an accumulated deficit of $388 million dating back to the 1970s, as well as a $195-million deficit from fiscal 1980. On November 12, the Congress of the United States increased the federal payment to the city — funds paid in lieu of property taxes on federal buildings — from $300 million to $336 million. The 1975 Home Rule Charter had placed a $300-million floor on the federal payment.

The School Board budget was still in the red, however. At Mayor Barry's request on June 22, the City Council transferred $4.5 million to the school board account. However, the deficit stood at $4.8-million in August, and the school board planned a six-day layoff of 8,800 employees. On August 20, District of Columbia Budget Director Gladys Mack announced that $2.8 million in surplus city funds was being added to the Board of Education's $256-million budget. The school board planned to postpone capital improvements, delay purchases, and take other economic measures to wipe out the remainder of the deficit.

On February 16, Acting Superintendent of Schools James T. Guines announced the start of Operation Rescue, a large-scale tutoring program. The program was expanded when schools opened on September 8.

Appointments. The Board of Education hired Floretta D. McKenzie, a deputy assistant secretary of the United States Department of Education, as superintendent of schools on June 17.

On April 30, Mayor Barry appointed Maurice T. Turner as chief of Washington's 3,628-member police force. Turner promised a crackdown on drug traffic, and on May 13 announced a 13-point plan to fight crime. Lynn Dunson

In WORLD BOOK, see WASHINGTON, D.C.

WATER. Rain fell heavily in most sections of the United States in June 1981, ending what had threatened to be a severe nationwide drought. January had been the fourth driest month in the 87 years since the government started recording national averages, and the period from December 1980 through February 1981 had been the second driest in record-keeping history.

South Florida had faced the most severe drought in its history. Despite daily cloud seeding, Lake Okeechobee, which supplies water to a $1-billion farming industry, dropped to an all-time low on July 29 after a 14-month decline. The United States Geological Survey reported that in the year ending on September 30, waterflow in five North American rivers – the Mississippi, St. Lawrence, Ohio, Columbia, and Missouri – was 12 per cent below normal. See WEATHER.

The Water Resources Council declared in June that a potential water shortage is the most serious long-range problem confronting the United States. In the Special Reports section, see THE THREATS TO OUR WATER SUPPLY.

Federal Policy. United States Secretary of the Interior James G. Watt announced on September 11 a reversal of a policy that had allowed the federal government to pre-empt state water rights. A controversial 1979 legal opinion had maintained

The ground collapsed in Winter Park, Fla., in May after too much water was pumped from natural underground caverns during a drought.

that a "federal nonreserved water right" gave the Department of the Interior authority to pre-empt water for its own use in national parks and wildlife refuges. Watt said the new approach to water policy reasserts "the historic primacy of state water management."

The cuts in federal spending imposed by President Ronald Reagan's Administration aroused fears in the arid West. The area has depended upon billions of dollars in federal funds for the vast water projects needed to make it one of the most prosperous and rapidly growing sections of the United States.

Subsidies. The General Accounting Office (GAO) reported on March 17 that taxpayers are paying much more than they should to build and operate federal irrigation projects that provide water to farmers in the West. The GAO said that, in one California project area, farmers pay only $7.79 for 1 acre-foot (about 325,000 gallons or 1,230,000 liters) of water. The full cost is $86.54 per acre-foot, with taxpayers picking up the balance. On March 18, Representative George Miller (D., Calif.) introduced a bill that would reduce subsidies paid to users of water from federal irrigation projects.

Miller's action was part of the continuing controversy over whether federally irrigated farmland should be reserved for family farms limited to 160 acres (65 hectares) for each family member. Congress set this limit in 1902 to encourage settlers.

In 1977, large landowners won a delay of a court order that would have required the Interior Department to enforce the 160-acre limitation. Watt announced on February 18 that he was suspending indefinitely the comment period on proposed regulations to administer the acreage limitation.

Conflicting Interests. The nation's drive to develop new sources of domestic energy emphasizes using the resources of the arid West. This emphasis has forced Westerners to decide whether to use precious water to irrigate farmland or to develop energy. Farmers consume by far the largest percentage of water among all water users in the West. Agriculture's share ranges from 68 per cent in Texas to 90 per cent in New Mexico. However, water is worth much more to energy developers than to even the most prosperous farmer, so energy companies have offered farmers huge profits for their water rights. For example, the Intermountain Power Project (IPP) in Utah has offered farmers $1,750 per acre-foot—more than five times the price of water before the IPP entered the picture.

South Dakota agreed on September 24 to sell 50,000 acre-feet of water per year to an energy firm to move a mixture of water and coal through a pipeline from Wyoming to ports on the Gulf of Mexico.

Andrew L. Newman

In WORLD BOOK, see WATER.

WATT, JAMES GAIUS (1938-   ), became United States secretary of the interior on Jan. 23, 1981. A member of the "sagebrush rebellion"—a coalition of Western business executives and politicians who favor private development of federal lands—he was poorly received by environmentalists who felt that he would allow exploitation of public lands.

Watt was born in Lusk, Wyo., on Jan. 31, 1938. He received a bachelor's degree from the University of Wyoming in 1960 and a law degree from that institution in 1962.

After graduating from law school, Watt served as legislative assistant and political adviser to Senator Milward L. Simpson (R., Wyo.). In 1966, Watt left that post to spearhead the U.S. Chamber of Commerce's campaign against the establishment of federal water-pollution standards and strip-mining regulations. Such activities made him a controversial choice for two positions within the Department of the Interior—deputy assistant secretary for water and power development in 1969 and director of the Bureau of Outdoor Recreation in 1975.

Watt was appointed a federal power commissioner in 1975. In 1977, he became president of the Mountain States Legal Foundation in Denver, a nonprofit conservative interest group. He held that position until joining the Cabinet.

Watt married Leilani Bomgardner in 1957. They have a daughter and a son.

Beverly Merz

WEATHER. A severe drought withered the United States as 1981 began, drastically lowering river levels and threatening water supplies in the Eastern half of the country. In January, the level of the Mississippi River fell to a record low, snarling barge traffic and interrupting shipments of grain and fuel. Fresh water flow into Chesapeake Bay—reflecting river conditions over a 65,000-square-mile (170,000-square-kilometer) area of the Middle Atlantic States—was 79 per cent below average. Reservoirs serving the New York City area sank to 30 per cent of their capacity.

Heavy spring and summer rains brought relief throughout the nation. Parts of the Midwest were so rain-soaked in June that many farmers had to delay planting corn.

The effects of the winter drought lingered, however. Ground-water levels in New England remained low throughout the year. In October, the U.S. Geological Survey reported that the flows of such major rivers as the Columbia, the Mississippi, the Missouri, and the Ohio were considerably lower than normal in the period from Oct. 1, 1980, to Sept. 30, 1981. The Geological Survey also said that more than three-fourths of the nation's rivers had below-normal flows during that same period.

In December 1981, a surprise blizzard battered parts of New England, blocking highways and causing power failures. Boston recorded up to 16 inches (41 centimeters) of snow, its heaviest December snowfall in more than 50 years.

Record Drought. According to the National Oceanic and Atmospheric Administration (NOAA), January 1981 was the driest January and the fourth driest month ever recorded in the United States. Eight states – Delaware, Illinois, Indiana, Iowa, Kentucky, Maryland, West Virginia, and Wisconsin – had their driest January on record.

Meteorologists blamed the drought on northwesterly winds that prevented moist air from the Gulf of Mexico and the Atlantic Ocean from moving inland. A high-pressure ridge near the West Coast blocked the advance of moist air from the Pacific Ocean. The drought maintained its grip on the East and the Midwest until May, when a southerly shift of the *jet stream* (high altitude winds) brought moisture from the Gulf of Mexico.

Atmospheric Warming Trend. An analysis of global temperature records dating from 1880 to 1980 indicated an overall warming trend in the earth's atmosphere. The study, made by a team of seven atmospheric physicists at the Institute for Space Studies of the National Aeronautics and Space Administration (NASA) in New York City, showed a 100-year temperature increase of 0.2 Celsius degree (0.36 Fahrenheit degree). The scientists saw this warming as evidence of the *greenhouse effect*, in which a build-up of carbon dioxide in the atmosphere causes a rise in air temperatures. Coal, oil, and other fuels produce carbon dioxide when they burn. During the 1900s, the amount of carbon dioxide in the atmosphere has grown markedly because people have burned large amounts of fuel in their homes and in factories.

Because of estimates that the amount of carbon dioxide in the atmosphere will almost double during the 21st century, the NASA scientists predicted a worldwide warming of "almost unprecedented magnitude" in the next century. They said that the warming trend could melt part of the Antarctic icecap and eventually raise sea levels as much as 20 feet (6 meters). Such a rise would flood many of the world's lowlands, including much of Florida, Louisiana, and New Jersey.

A "Benign" Volcano. The massive eruption of the Mount St. Helens volcano in Washington in May 1980 affected the world's weather far less than climatologists had originally predicted. For example, scientists had expected ash from the volcano to form a thick haze in the atmosphere that would screen out sunlight and thus cause slightly cooler weather around the world. Such cooling had occurred after other volcanic eruptions of comparable size. But in January 1981, climatologist J. Murray Mitchell of NOAA in Silver Spring, Md., said a global cooling had failed to materialize. He attributed this failure to the volcano's relatively low production of sulfurous gases, which convert into droplets of sulfuric acid in the *stratosphere* (upper atmosphere) and block sunlight.

Scientists had also expected increased precipitation in the Pacific Northwest in the months following the Mount St. Helens eruption. They thought that particles of volcanic ash in the atmosphere would act as seeds around which water vapor would collect and form precipitation. No noticeable increase in precipitation took place, however. A team of NOAA scientists led by atmospheric physicist Rudolf Pueschel reported in March that chemical analysis of the ash showed it to be low in water-soluble nitrates and therefore a poor conductor of water vapor. Summing up the climatic impact of the Mount St. Helens eruption, Pueschel remarked, "As far as local weather is concerned, the volcano is relatively benign."

Measuring Soil Moisture. In September, the U.S. Department of Agriculture announced the development of a device that can measure moisture in soil as deep as 6 inches (15 centimeters) below the earth's surface. The device "sees" moisture by means of a microwave detector similar to a radar dish. Data provided by the device could enable farmers to manage irrigation better. William T. Graham

In the Special Reports section, see THE THREATS TO OUR WATER SUPPLY. In WORLD BOOK, see METEOROLOGY; WEATHER.
WEIGHT LIFTING. See SPORTS.

WEINBERGER, CASPAR WILLARD (1917-), was sworn in as United States secretary of defense on Jan. 21, 1981. He had been vice-president and general counsel of the Bechtel Group of companies. In his Cabinet post, Weinberger was expected to oversee the United States biggest peacetime military build-up (see ARMED FORCES).

Weinberger was born in San Francisco on Aug. 18, 1917. He graduated from Harvard University in 1938 and from Harvard Law School in 1941. He served in the U.S. Army during World War II as an infantryman and, later, as a member of General Douglas MacArthur's intelligence staff.

In 1947, Weinberger entered private law practice. He was a member of the California state legislature from 1952 to 1958. In 1968, then-Governor Ronald Reagan named him California state finance director. Weinberger served in that post until January 1970, when President Richard M. Nixon appointed him chairman of the Federal Trade Commission. Six months later, Nixon named him deputy director of the Office of Management and Budget (OMB). He became OMB director in June 1972 and held that post until February 1973, when Nixon named him secretary of health, education, and welfare. Weinberger continued to head that agency under President Gerald R. Ford until he resigned to enter private business in 1975. Wayne Wille

WELFARE programs in the United States underwent sweeping cuts in 1981 under President Ronald Reagan's Administration. Declaring that government generosity and good intentions were out of control, the President called for a "new federalism," returning to states and communities many federal programs.

Welfare Cuts. Reagan turned to budget-cutting as the most effective tool for achieving his goal of a new federalism. The welfare reductions were included in a package of budget cuts, the Omnibus Budget Reconciliation Act of 1981, which he signed into law on August 13.

The legislation consolidated dozens of specific federal grant programs into nine block grants to the states. The total amount of money for the grants was cut by 25 per cent.

On September 21, Secretary of Health and Human Services Richard S. Schweiker announced new welfare rules resulting from the cuts. The changes went into effect on Oct. 1, 1981, the beginning of the government's 1982 fiscal year. Benefits for approximately 10 per cent of the 3.9 million families receiving welfare were cut, saving the federal government $1.1 billion in fiscal 1982. Savings for states, which share the cost of most programs, were estimated at $900 million. The rules were intended to ensure that only the neediest families would receive assistance and to encourage adult welfare recipients to take jobs.

Under the new rules, a family may not receive welfare if it has assets of more than $1,000, not counting a home and an automobile. The rules also say that states may require welfare recipients to take public-service jobs under "community work experience programs." In determining benefits, states subtract certain expenses from the income earned by a welfare recipient. Under the new rules, the deduction for child-care expenses is limited to $160 a month for each child.

The food-stamp program also suffered substantial cuts. Of the 22.6 million food-stamp recipients, an estimated 875,000 became ineligible, and benefits were reduced for most of the remaining recipients. The cutbacks came as a result of a new law that families whose gross income is 130 per cent of the official poverty level set by the federal government would no longer qualify. In 1981, the poverty level for a family of four was about $9,000.

Action Against Fraud. The Department of Justice set up a special unit to coordinate investigations of charges of fraud in the food-stamp program. The unit is made up of officials from the Justice Department, the Department of Agriculture, and the United States Postal Service. In a further move to combat fraud, recipients of food

About 260,000 demonstrators gather in a Solidarity Day rally in Washington, D.C., on September 19 to protest welfare cutbacks.

stamps in 17 large cities were required to have photographic identification cards.

Proposed School-Lunch Cuts, another of the President's recommendations, met with defeat. The Department of Agriculture drafted a plan to reduce the nutritional requirements for school lunches, abandoning its 35-year-old goal of requiring lunches that give children one-third of the recommended daily allowances of essential nutrients. The amount of milk in a lunch was reduced from 6 ounces (180 milliliters) to 4 ounces (120 milliliters). In some instances, catchup and pickle relish could be counted as vegetables. Members of Congress ridiculed the idea, and the plan was dropped.

Other Developments. On September 24, Reagan called for further budget cuts of $13 billion, which he said were necessary to avoid a larger-than-anticipated deficit for 1982. The proposed spending cuts included deeper reductions in so-called "entitlement" programs, such as food stamps, where benefits are guaranteed by law to all who meet specific qualifications. This time, the response from Congress was cool.

In October, President Reagan announced his plan to appoint a panel to study ways in which private volunteer efforts could take care of the poor. He set an example by personally giving $1,000 to charity and the arts.   Virginia E. Anderson

In WORLD BOOK, see WELFARE.

WEST INDIES. The countries of the West Indies received increased attention from the United States during 1981, mainly because President Ronald Reagan expressed alarm over alleged subversive efforts in the region by Cuba, Nicaragua, and Russia. The United States took steps to heighten its involvement in promoting Caribbean development as a security measure against Communist encroachment in the region.

In July, Secretary of State Alexander M. Haig, Jr., met with the foreign ministers of Canada, Mexico, and Venezuela in Nassau, the Bahamas, to discuss coordination of their countries' aid programs for the Caribbean. These talks led to a vague agreement to promote the region's welfare that stops short of compromising any nation's freedom of action.

United States priorities for the Caribbean were challenged in October by leaders of the Dominican Republic. U.S. Vice-President George H. W. Bush delivered a speech to the Dominican legislature stressing the need to contain Cuban-Soviet expansionism in the Caribbean. Before Bush addressed the legislature, however, he was himself lectured by some of his hosts, including Senator Helvio A. Rodriguez, president of the Dominican Senate. Rodriguez stressed the primacy of economic issues in the Caribbean, in particular the serious menace to the "hard-won advances we have made toward

the exercise of democracy in the past 15 years" posed by the possible bankruptcy of his country's sugar industry.

Jamaica. The United States focused attention on Jamaica in 1981, where a pro-United States administration had replaced a Socialist administration in 1980. The first foreign head of state Reagan received after taking office in January 1981 was Jamaican Prime Minister Edward Seaga. Reagan later asked David Rockefeller, who retired as chairman of the Chase Manhattan Bank in April, to head a group of business executives to promote foreign investment and provide advice to Jamaica.

During 1981, Jamaica borrowed $650 million from the International Monetary Fund, renegotiated its outstanding debts to 25 commercial banks, and obtained an additional $70 million in new financing. Despite the infusion of money, the Jamaican economy remained sluggish. Some Jamaicans complained that the United States was hurting the Jamaican economy by its insistence on a crackdown on the cultivation of marijuana. Although illegal, the raising of marijuana has become the island's top money earner. This source of income was especially important in 1981, when there were cutbacks in bauxite production, which provides three-fourths of Jamaica's legitimate foreign-exchange earnings. In addition, the tourist industry, an important money-maker, was hurt by the air controllers' strike in the United States.

Antigua and Barbuda. On Nov. 1, 1981, two small islands in the West Indies joined to become the independent nation of Antigua and Barbuda. The newly independent nation has a land area of about 171 square miles (442 square kilometers) and a population of about 79,000, most of whom live on Antigua, the larger of the islands. Antigua and Barbuda had been self-governing territories of Great Britain since 1967.

Dominican Intrigue. A plot to overthrow the Dominican government headed by Prime Minister Mary Eugenia Charles was foiled in April when U.S. federal agents arrested 10 mercenaries near New Orleans as they prepared to set sail for Dominica. The mercenaries were seized with firearms, dynamite, a rubber raft, and a document described as a "contract" with Patrick R. John, a former prime minister of Dominica who had been ousted in 1979. In Dominica, 11 people, including John, were jailed in connection with the plot.

Trinidad and Tobago mourned the death of Prime Minister Eric E. Williams on March 29, 1981. Williams had served as prime minister since the country gained its independence in 1962. Williams was praised as a leader of vision who led his nation on a progressive track.   Nathan A. Haverstock

See also LATIN AMERICA (Facts in Brief Table). In WORLD BOOK, see WEST INDIES.

WEST VIRGINIA. See STATE GOVERNMENT.

WILLIAMS, ROY LEE (1915-   ), was elected president of the International Brotherhood of Teamsters on June 4, 1981. He had served as interim president of the union since the death of long-time Teamster President Frank E. Fitzsimmons on May 15. Williams was indicted by a federal grand jury on May 22 on charges of conspiring to bribe Senator Howard W. Cannon (D., Nev.) to stall legislation that would deregulate the trucking industry.

Williams was born in Ottumwa, Iowa, on March 22, 1915. One of 12 children, he grew up in an impoverished region of the Ozark Mountains.

In 1935, Williams entered the trucking industry as a livestock hauler. He joined the Teamsters Union in Kansas City in 1938. From 1942 to 1946, he served in the United States armed forces.

Williams' career as a union official began in 1948 when he became a business agent for the Teamsters in Wichita, Kans. He was elected to the presidencies of Teamster locals in Wichita and Kansas City and became trustee of the Central States, Southeast, and Southwest Areas Pension Fund. He was forced to resign the last position in 1977 when he became a subject of a federal investigation of the mismanagement of the $1.4-billion fund.

In 1976, Williams became director of the Central Conference of Teamsters and served until he assumed the national presidency.   Beverly Merz

WILLOCH, KAARE (1928-   ), became prime minister of Norway on Oct. 14, 1981, heading a Conservative government. National elections in September had given a coalition of Conservatives and two other nonsocialist parties a majority in the *Storting* (parliament), rejecting the Labor Party government of Gro Harlem Brundtland. See BRUNDTLAND, GRO HARLEM; NORWAY.

Kaare Isaachsen Willoch was born in Oslo on Oct. 3, 1928. He received a degree in economics from the University of Oslo in 1953.

The new prime minister has been in the Storting since 1957. The Conservative members of the Storting elected him their chairman in 1970. Willoch was national chairman of the party from 1970 until 1974. He served as minister of trade and shipping in 1963 and from 1965 until 1970.

Since 1970, Willoch has been a member of the Nordic Council, which oversees relationships among Denmark, Finland, Iceland, Norway, and Sweden.   Jay Myers

WISCONSIN. See STATE GOVERNMENT.

WYOMING. See STATE GOVERNMENT.

YEMEN (ADEN). See MIDDLE EAST.

YEMEN (SANA). See MIDDLE EAST.

YOUNG MEN'S CHRISTIAN ASSOCIATION (YMCA). See COMMUNITY ORGANIZATIONS.

YOUNG WOMEN'S CHRISTIAN ASSOCIATION (YWCA). See COMMUNITY ORGANIZATIONS.

YOUTH ORGANIZATIONS. The Boy Scouts of America (BSA) introduced on Sept. 22, 1981, a package of 14 new or modified programs called "Foundations for Growth." These programs focus on such contemporary subjects as computers, conservation, and family life. Scout leaders hope the programs will attract new members to the organization, whose youth membership dropped from 4.9 million in 1972 to 3.2 million at the end of 1980. The BSA also announced the formation of a program called Tiger Cubs for 7-year-olds. Boys must be at least 8 years old to join the Cub Scouts.

The 1981 National Boy Scout Jamboree drew more than 30,000 Scouts and adult leaders to Fort AP Hill, Virginia, from July 29 through August 4.

Chuck Wolfe, 19, of Lake Park, Fla., was elected president of America's 447,000 Explorers – young adults aged 14 through 20 – at the 11th annual National Explorer Congress in Indianapolis in May.

Boys Clubs of America (BCA) in 1981 conducted programs on learning skills and job skills for 40,000 youngsters in 30 cities. The United States Department of Justice reported that the juvenile arrest rate in nine urban communities served by BCA programs dropped an average of 31 per cent from 1977 to 1979, despite a national increase of 9 per cent for the same period. BCA estimated that

Boy Scouts swap badges at the National Boy Scout Jamboree at Fort AP Hill, Virginia. Some 30,000 Scouts and leaders attended the weeklong jamboree.

the project may have prevented as many as 1,650 arrests per year.

Boys Clubs from coast to coast celebrated the organization's Diamond Jubilee (75th anniversary) with activities ranging from parties to marathons. In a special White House ceremony on September 16, John Magee, 17, a member of the North Little Rock, Ark., Boys Club, was named 1981-1982 National Boy of the Year by President Ronald Reagan, honorary chairman of the BCA.

Camp Fire, during the second year of its Youth Employment and Training Program, provided vocational guidance to 64,000 members in eight areas around the United States. About 1,000 delegates attended the biennial National Congress held in Dallas from November 4 to 7. The winner of the National Speech Competition, 14-year-old Stacey Savage of the Greater Boston Council, gave the keynote address.

Girl Scouts of the United States of America (GSUSA), as a participant in the U.S. Council for the International Year of Disabled Persons, intensified its efforts to serve disabled girls. During 1981, Girl Scouts participated in Project MAY (Mainstreaming Activities for Youth), a collaborative effort to integrate disabled young people into programs and activities that appealed to them.

In an effort to eliminate language and cultural barriers to full participation in Scouting by Spanish-speaking girls and volunteers, GSUSA released *Mundos a Explorar*, a Spanish-language and cultural adaptation of the Brownie and Junior Girl Scout handbook, *Worlds to Explore*.

Girls Clubs of America (GCA) opened its National Resource Center in Indianapolis in June. Dedication ceremonies were held in October. Data banks, a library, and other resources at the facility provide information to youth service professionals and others seeking to develop programs for girls. The center also plans to sponsor research on issues facing today's girls and young women.

Future Farmers of America (FFA). Membership in FFA in 1981 increased by 935 to 482,611, reversing a three-year decline. In July, state and national officers attended the dedication of the remodeled lobby of the National FFA Center in Alexandria, Va. In November, FFA opened a National Hall of Achievement, also at organization headquarters. Visitors to the hall can view audio-visual displays on FFA programs, agricultural and FFA history, and agricultural education.

More than 23,000 FFA members attended the 54th annual national convention in Kansas City, Mo., from November 12 to 14. Chuck Berry, 21, of Elma, Wash., was named Star Farmer of America, and Dale Wolfe, Jr., of Baldwin, Wis., was designated Star Agribusinessman of America.

4-H Clubs in 1981 made a number of special efforts to attract young people from all socioeco-

nomic, cultural, and ethnic groups as well as the handicapped. They also worked during the year to increase the number of volunteers and strengthen staff development and training programs. "4-H — Pathways to the Future" was designated the national 4-H theme for 1981 and 1982. In his message to 4-H clubs during National 4-H Week in October, President Reagan noted that the organization "has served and continues to be a pathway to achievement for many individuals, not only in their careers, but in their overall pursuit of more productive, meaningful lives."

Junior Achievement (JA) set new records during the 1980-1981 academic year. More than 210,000 high school students, a 9 per cent increase over the previous year, established and ran their own business with the aid of more than 30,000 volunteer advisers.

JA's seventh annual National Business Leadership Conference and Business Hall of Fame induction ceremony attracted about 2,000 JA students and adult volunteers to Washington, D.C., in March. Among those honored were engineer Willis H. Carrier, the designer of the first scientific air-conditioning system; Edwin H. Land, inventor of the Polaroid-Land camera; and Secretary of the Treasury Donald T. Regan.   Virginia E. Anderson

In WORLD BOOK, see entries on the individual organizations.

YUGOSLAVIA suffered internal unrest and economic difficulties in 1981. Virtually the entire government and Communist Party leadership of Kosovo, a province of the Republic of Serbia, was replaced after riots broke out on March 11. The riots began as student demonstrations against university policies in Priština, the provincial capital, and against the province's poor economy. However, the rioting soon spread to the general public and was compounded by nationalist tensions.

About 80 per cent of Kosovo's people are ethnic Albanians. Many of these people want Yugoslavia to elevate Kosovo to the status of a republic.

Police officers and military troops, armed with tanks, armored cars, and helicopters, finally put down the riots in May. The government said that eight people died and 257 were injured.

On May 5, Meli Deva replaced Mahmut Bakalli as party president in Kosovo. Deva had held the post from 1965 to 1971. On August 5, Ali Sukrija, another party veteran, replaced Dzavid Nimania as president of the Kosovo government. Nearly 300 Kosovo Albanians received sentences of up to 15 years for their part in the riots.

Yugoslavia said that Albania had incited and organized the Kosovo disturbances, but Albania denied the charge. Yugoslavia canceled all agreements on cultural and economic cooperation between the two countries.

New Presidents. Under Yugoslavia's system of annual rotation of top state and party offices, Cvijetin Mijatovic, a Serb from Bosnia, retired as president of the eight-member state Presidency on May 15. His replacement was Sergej Kraigher, a Slovene. On October 20, Lazar Mojsov, a Macedonian, retired as president of the country's Communist Party. He was succeeded by Dusan Dragosavac, a Serb from Croatia.

The Crackdown on the Dissidents in Croatia continued. On February 20, in Zagreb, General Franjo Tudjman, who fought with the partisan guerrillas of Josip Broz Tito during World War II, received a prison sentence of three years. On May 20, Dobroslav Paraga, a student who circulated a petition demanding the release of political prisoners in 1980, was sentenced to three years. On June 6, Vlado Gotoovac, a poet and former editor, was sentenced to two years in prison and an additional four-year ban on publishing. And on September 9, Marko Veselica, a former Central Committee member, received a prison sentence of 11 years.

Exports were 19 per cent higher in the period from January through September 1981 than in the first nine months of 1980. Imports were up 10 per cent. Exports to non-Communist countries were 3 per cent lower. Chris Cviic

See also EUROPE (Facts in Brief Table). In WORLD BOOK, see YUGOSLAVIA.

YUKON TERRITORY advanced its claim for provincial status by establishing an office in Ottawa, Ont., in August 1981. The office, to be headed by a deputy minister of the territorial government, will have an administrative and a political role – to lobby for political autonomy. The territory previously did business with Canada's federal government in Ottawa through the Department of Indian and Northern Affairs.

The territorial budget, presented on March 26, called for increases in health-care premiums and in gasoline and cigarette taxes. The extra revenue would bring in $33 million (Canadian dollars; $1=U.S. 84 cents as of Dec. 31, 1981), about the same amount as the government's expected deficit in the 1980-1981 fiscal year. Total spending for 1981-1982 was expected to be $104 million.

The Progressive Conservative Party under Christopher Pearson, government leader and minister of finance, held 10 of the 16 seats in the territorial legislature. The New Democratic Party became the official opposition when it won a by-election in Whitehorse on October 14, earning three seats. The Liberal Party held two seats, and there was one independent. David M. L. Farr

See also CANADA. In WORLD BOOK, see YUKON TERRITORY.

ZAIRE. See AFRICA.

ZAMBIA. See AFRICA.

ZIMBABWE. Conflict between Zimbabwe's two largest black ethnic groups in 1981 threatened the stability of the nation, which became independent in 1980. The Mashona people, comprising about 80 per cent of the population, are primarily followers of Prime Minister Robert Mugabe and his party, the Zimbabwe African National Union-Patriotic Front (ZANU). The Matabele people, who represent less than 20 per cent of the population, have tended to support the Zimbabwe African People's Union (ZAPU), led by Joshua Nkomo. Each party had its own army during the guerrilla war waged from 1972 to 1979 against white rule.

Military Strife. Mugabe integrated the two guerrilla groups into a national army. However, on February 7 fighting broke out near Bulawayo, the nation's second largest city, between ZANU and ZAPU soldiers serving in the newly formed 12th Army Battalion. Similar clashes erupted in the 13th and 41st battalions and spread to camps of former guerrillas waiting to be inducted into the Zimbabwean army. On February 12, Mugabe ordered white-led units to separate the rival factions. By the time the fighting ended on February 13, at least 150 people were reported dead. Following this violence, the Mugabe government undertook to disarm about 18,000 former guerrillas who remained in assembly camps around the country.

Political Disputes. Mugabe and Nkomo followers also clashed in elections. Mugabe's party swept the municipal elections on March 28 and 29 in Salisbury, but Nkomo's party won all 15 black council seats in Bulawayo on June 7.

The alliance between Mugabe and Nkomo seemed even more uneasy after Mugabe demoted Nkomo from minister in charge of police to minister without portfolio during a Cabinet shuffle on January 10. However, Nkomo resisted requests from some of his followers to walk out of Parliament. In July, Mugabe appointed a Nkomo man to a high military position as a conciliatory measure.

Economic Concerns. Mugabe's government wanted whites to remain in the country so that they could contribute their skills to Zimbabwe's economic development. White farmers, who produce most of Zimbabwe's commercial food crops, were encouraged by increases in government-set crop prices. To reassure the country's white population – about 3 per cent of the total – Mugabe appointed a white as supreme commander of Zimbabwe's military forces. In another step to mollify the country's white minority, Mugabe fired Edgar Z. Tekere, manpower and planning minister, on January 10. Tekere had been accused of killing a white farmer in 1980, but was acquitted on a technicality. Mugabe removed him from his post as secretary general of ZANU on August 6. J. Dixon Esseks

See also AFRICA (Facts in Brief Table). In WORLD BOOK, see ZIMBABWE.

ZOOLOGY. On Sept. 17, 1981, paleontologist Farish A. Jenkins, Jr., of Harvard University's Museum of Comparative Zoology in Cambridge, Mass., announced the discovery of the fossil jaw of a previously unknown mammal. The jaw, found in Arizona, belonged to a tiny, shrewlike animal. It dates from more than 180 million years ago.

The newly found fossil may force zoologists to revise their ideas about the early stages of mammalian evolution. Previously, most scientists believed that all mammals were descended from two varieties of ancient mammals. One variety was thought to be the ancestor of the platypus and other egg-laying mammals; the other, that of all other mammals. The recently discovered fossil differs from both previously known varieties and is older than either of them.

A New Sting Ray, so strikingly different from other fish that it has been placed in a new suborder and family, was found in South Africa. The new sting ray belongs to the suborder *Hexatrygonoidei* and the family *Hexatrygonidae*. Its scientific name is *Hexatrygon bickelli*.

P. C. Heemstra and Margaret M. Smith, two South African ichthyologists, studied the differences that make *H. bickelli* unique. It has six pairs of gill slits, the openings through which water leaves the gills, instead of the usual five. *H. bickelli* also possesses a long snout equipped with organs that are sensitive to changes in the electrical field in the surrounding water. These organs may help the fish find food in deep water. Unlike other sting rays, which inhabit shallow coastal waters, the new ray probably lives at depths of from 1,300 to 3,300 feet (400 to 1,000 meters).

Sibling Recognition in Frogs. Zoologists Andrew R. Blaustein and Richard K. O'Hara of Oregon State University in Corvallis studied the ability of frogs to recognize their close relatives. The study was inspired by the work of British sociobiologist William D. Hamilton. Hamilton predicted that the more closely related individuals were, the more likely they would be to behave unselfishly toward one another. Sociobiologists believe that an animal inherits behavior patterns that increase the chances of its genes being passed on to the next generation. Because relatives share many of the same genes, an animal can pass on its genes not only by reproducing, but also by helping related animals to survive. To do so, animals need to recognize their kin.

Blaustein and O'Hara divided batches of frog eggs and reared the tadpoles in isolated conditions. They found that even tadpoles raised in isolation preferred to associate with their siblings rather than with nonsiblings. The experiment suggests that frogs have an inborn ability to recognize their relatives.   Barbara N. Benson

See also BIOLOGY; ZOOS AND AQUARIUMS. In WORLD BOOK, see ZOOLOGY.

From *The Wall Street Journal*, by permission of Cartoon Features Syndicate

". . . And, so, we see that a woodchuck could chuck approximately .56 cords of wood per day."

ZOOS AND AQUARIUMS around the world continued to devote increasing attention to the preservation of endangered species in 1981. The American Association of Zoological Parks and Aquariums promoted cooperative management among zoos in its "species survival plans." The animals on the association's endangered list include Przewalski's horse, the golden lion tamarin, the Siberian tiger, the okapi, the Bali mynah, and the Chinese alligator. Immediate goals are the reduction of the inbreeding of endangered species at some zoos and the maintenance of genetically diverse populations.

Breeding Efforts. Zoologists also developed techniques to enhance the reproductive potential of various species. They hope to minimize the risk and expense of long-distance loans of animals for breeding by using artificial insemination and embryo transplants. Zookeepers determine the reproductive status of animals for these procedures by monitoring hormone levels in the animals' urine.

On August 11, at New York City's Bronx Zoo, a Holstein cow gave birth to a *gaur* (a type of wild ox from southeastern Asia) after a gaur embryo was transplanted into the cow's womb. Similar embryo-transplant efforts are underway at the Cincinnati (Ohio) Zoo using cows as surrogate mothers for elands, a type of African antelope. At the International Crane Foundation in Baraboo, Wis., the first captive-bred Siberian crane was hatched. The mother had been artificially inseminated.

Increasing the reproductive capacity of the giant panda is the object of a cooperative program in the Wolong Reserve in Szechwan (Sichuan) Province in China by U.S. and Chinese researchers and veterinarians. At the National Zoo in Washington, D.C., there was an unsuccessful attempt in 1981 to mate a female giant panda, Ling-Ling, with Chia-Chia, a male panda from the London Zoo. Subsequent artificial insemination attempts with Ling-Ling also failed. In Mexico City, Mexico, zookeepers gave rigorous privacy to giant panda Ying-Ying, and she successfully raised the cub she gave birth to in July. In the Special Reports section, see THE PLIGHT OF THE PANDA.

The Jersey Wildlife Preservation Trust on Jersey, the largest of Great Britain's Channel Islands, acquired additional property in 1981 to house its International Center. The center will be devoted to training zoologists in the techniques of captive reproduction of endangered species.

New Exhibits. The new National Aquarium in Baltimore opened to long lines of visitors in August 1981. The $21.3-million aquarium includes a two-story reef tank, a dolphin pool, and a rooftop rain forest among its exhibits. Exhibit improvements were underway in 1981 for hoofed animals at the Cleveland Zoo; for birds of prey at the zoo in Albuquerque, N. Mex.; and for large mammals at the Lincoln Park Zoo in Chicago.

A new exhibit of koalas was scheduled to open in 1982 at the Los Angeles Zoo. Since native Australian koalas eat only the leaves of eucalyptus trees, the Los Angeles Zoo first sent leaves from trees in the Los Angeles area to be tested with koalas in the Melbourne Zoo in Australia.

The Metrozoo in Miami, Fla., officially opened on a regular basis on Dec. 12, 1981. It houses 53 exhibits on 160 acres (65 hectares) of land. New education facilities include a science center at Vancouver Aquarium in Canada and a nature center at Washington Park Zoo in Portland, Ore. At the Bronx Zoo, a new children's zoo was opened in May. It features natural exhibits and devices for children to play with that relate to aspects of animal behavior or ecology.

Closings. A lack of federal funds may affect future improvements and programs at zoos and aquariums throughout the United States in the next few years. The federal budget cuts enacted by Congress in 1981 have already hurt several zoos and aquariums. The federally supported Northeast Fisheries Center Aquarium at Woods Hole, Mass., was closed in September.   George B. Rabb

In WORLD BOOK, see AQUARIUM; ZOO.

Mukluk the polar bear greets visiting children through a viewing window of the new polar bear habitat in the Point Defiance Zoo in Tacoma, Wash.

Census
Supplement

1976
1977
1978
1979
1980
1981

This section lists official population figures according to the 1980 census of the United States conducted by the U.S. Bureau of the Census. The following pages give population totals for states, metropolitan areas, counties, and cities. The states are arranged in alphabetical order, and each community is listed alphabetically under the state in which it is located. The supplement is presented as a service to owners of THE WORLD BOOK ENCYCLOPEDIA.

ALABAMA

Population 3,890,061

METROPOLITAN AREAS

Anniston 116,936
Birmingham 847,360
Columbus (Ga.) 239,196
(191,840 in Ga.; 47,356 in Ala.)
Florence 135,023
Gadsden 103,057
Huntsville 308,593
Mobile 442,819
Montgomery 272,687
Tuscaloosa 137,473

COUNTIES

Autauga 32,259
Baldwin 78,440
Barbour 24,756
Bibb 15,723
Blount 36,459
Bullock 10,596
Butler 21,680
Calhoun 116,936
Chambers 39,191
Cherokee 18,760
Chilton 30,612
Choctaw 16,839
Clarke 27,702
Clay 13,703
Cleburne 12,595
Coffee 38,533
Colbert 54,519
Conecuh 15,884
Coosa 11,377
Covington 36,850
Crenshaw 14,110
Cullman 61,642
Dale 47,821
Dallas 53,981
De Kalb 53,658
Elmore 43,390
Escambia 38,392
Etowah 103,057
Fayette 18,809
Franklin 28,350
Geneva 24,253
Greene 11,021
Hale 15,604
Henry 15,302
Houston 74,632
Jackson 51,407
Jefferson 671,197
Lamar 16,453
Lauderdale 80,504
Lawrence 30,170
Lee 76,283
Limestone 46,005
Lowndes 13,253
Macon 26,829
Madison 196,966
Marengo 25,047
Marion 30,041
Marshall 65,622
Mobile 364,379
Monroe 22,651
Montgomery 197,038
Morgan 90,231
Perry 15,012
Pickens 21,481
Pike 28,050
Randolph 20,075
Russell 47,356
St. Clair 41,205
Shelby 66,298
Sumter 16,908
Talladega 73,826
Tallapoosa 38,676
Tuscaloosa 137,473
Walker 68,660
Washington 16,821
Wilcox 14,755
Winston 21,953

CITIES AND TOWNS

Abbeville 3,155
Adamsville 2,498
Addison 746
Akron 604
Alabaster 7,079
Albertville 12,039
Alexander City 13,807
Aliceville 3,207
Allgood 387
Altoona 928
Andalusia 10,415
Anderson 405
Anniston 29,523
Arab 5,967
Ardmore 1,096
Ariton 844
Arley 276
Ashford 2,165
Ashland 2,052
Ashville 1,489
Athens 14,558
Atmore 8,789
Attalla 7,737
Auburn 28,471
Autaugaville 843
Avon 433
Babbie 553
Baileyton 396
Banks 160
Bay Minette 7,455
Bayou La Batre 2,005
Bear Creek 353
Beatrice 558
Beaverton 360
Belk 308
Benton 74
Berry 916
Bessemer 31,729
Billingsley 106
Birmingham 284,413
Black 156
Blountsville 1,509
Blue Mountain 284
Blue Springs 112
Boaz 7,151
Boligee 164
Bon Air 118
Branchville 365
Brantley 1,151
Brent 2,862
Brewton 6,680
Bridgeport 2,974
Brighton 5,308
Brilliant 871
Brookside 1,409
Brookwood 492
Brownville 2,386
Brundidge 3,213
Butler 1,882
Calera 2,035
Camden 2,406
Camp Hill 1,628
Carbon Hill 2,452
Cardiff 140
Carolina 203
Carrollton 1,104
Carrville 820
Castleberry 847
Cedar Bluff 1,129
Centre 2,351
Centreville 2,504
Chatom 1,122
Cherokee 1,589
Chickasaw 7,402
Childersburg 5,084
Citronelle 2,841
Clanton 5,832
Clayhatchee 560
Clayton 1,589
Cleveland 487
Clio 1,224
Coffee Springs 339
Coffeeville 448
Collinsville 1,383
Columbia 881
Columbiana 2,655
Coosada 980
Cordova 3,123
Cottonwood 1,352
County Line 199
County Line 124
Courtland 456
Cowarts 418
Creola 673
Crossville 1,222
Cuba 486
Cullman 13,084
Dadeville 3,263
Daleville 4,250
Daphne 3,406
Daviston 334
Dayton 911
Decatur 42,002
Demopolis 7,678
Detroit 326
Dora 2,327
Dothan 48,750
Double Springs 1,057
Douglas 116
Dozier 494
Dutton 276
East Brewton 2,964
Eclectic 1,124
Edwardsville 207
Elba 4,365
Elberta 491
Eldridge 230
Elkmont 429
Enterprise 18,033
Epes 399
Ethelsville 95
Eufaula 12,097
Eunola 169
Eutaw 2,444
Eva 185
Evergreen 4,171
Excel 385
Fairfield 13,040
Fairhope 7,286
Fairview 450
Falkville 1,310
Faunsdale 174
Fayette 5,287
Five Points 197
Flint City 673
Flomaton 1,882
Florala 2,165
Florence 37,029
Foley 4,003
Forkland 429
Fort Deposit 1,519
Fort Payne 11,485
Franklin 133
Frisco City 1,424
Fruithurst 239
Fulton 606
Fultondale 6,217
Fyffe 1,305
Gadsden 47,565
Gainesville 207
Gantt 314
Gantts Quarry 71
Garden City 655
Gardendale 7,928
Gaylesville 192
Geiger 200
Geneva 4,866
Georgiana 1,993
Geraldine 911
Gilbertown 218
Glen Allen 312
Glencoe 4,648
Glenwood 341
Goldville 89
Good Hope 1,442
Goodwater 1,895
Gordo 2,112
Gordon 362
Goshen 365
Grant 632
Graysville 2,642
Greensboro 3,248
Greenville 7,807
Grimes 298
Grove Hill 1,912
Guin 2,418
Gulf Shores 1,233
Guntersville 7,041
Gurley 735
Gu-Win 266
Hackleburg 883
Haleburg 106
Haleyville 5,306
Hamilton 4,792
Hammondville 369
Hanceville 2,220
Harpersville 934
Hartford 2,647
Hartselle 8,858
Hayden 268
Hayneville 592
Headland 3,327
Heath 354
Heflin 3,014
Helena 2,130
Henagar 1,188
Highland Lake 210
Hillsboro 278
Hobson City 1,268
Hodges 250
Hokes Bluff 3,216
Holly Pond 493
Hollywood 1,110
Homewood 21,271
Hoover 15,064
Horn Hill 186
Hueytown 13,309
Huntsville 142,513
Hurtsboro 752
Ider 698
Irondale 6,521
Jackson 6,073
Jacksonville 9,735
Jasper 11,894
Jemison 1,828
Kansas 267
Kennedy 604
Killen 747
Kimberly 1,043
Kinsey 1,239
Kinston 604
Lafayette 3,647
Lakeview 441
Lanett 6,897
Leeds 8,638
Leesburg 116
Leighton 1,218
Lester 117
Level Plains 867
Lexington 884
Libertyville 141
Lincoln 2,081
Linden 2,773
Lineville 2,257
Lipscomb 3,741
Lisman 401
Littleville 1,262
Livingston 3,187
Loachapoka 335
Lockhart 547
Locust Fork 488
Louisville 791
Lowndesboro 207
Loxley 804
Luverne 2,639
Lynn 554
Madison 4,057
Madrid 172
Malvern 558
Maplesville 754
Margaret 757
Marion 4,467
Maytown 538
McIntosh 319
McKenzie 605
McMullen 164
Memphis 95
Mentone 476
Midfield 6,536
Midland City 1,903
Midway 593
Millbrook 3,101
Millport 1,287
Millry 956
Mobile 200,452
Monroeville 5,674
Montevallo 3,965
Montgomery 178,157
Moody 1,840
Mooresville 58
Morris 623
Mosses 649
Moulton 3,197
Moundville 1,310
Mount Vernon 1,038
Mountain Brook 17,400
Mountainboro 266
Mulga 405
Muscle Shoals 8,911
Myrtlewood 252
Napier Field 493
Nauvoo 259
Nectar 367
New Brockton 1,392
New Hope 1,546
New Site 340
Newbern 307
Newton 1,540
Newville 814
North Johns 243
Northport 14,291
Notasulga 876
Oak Grove 638
Oak Hill 63
Oakman 770
Odenville 724
Ohatchee 860
Oneonta 4,824
Onycha 147
Opelika 21,896
Opp 7,204
Orrville 349
Owens Cross Roads 804
Oxford 8,939
Ozark 13,188
Paint Rock 221
Parrish 1,583
Pelham 6,759
Pell City 6,616
Pennington 355
Petrey 93
Phenix City 26,928
Phil Campbell 1,549
Pickensville 132
Piedmont 5,544
Pinckard 771
Pine Apple 298
Pine Hill 510
Pisgah 699
Pleasant Grove 7,102
Pollard 144
Powell's Crossroads 636
Prattville 18,647
Priceville 966
Prichard 39,541
Providence 363
Ragland 1,860
Rainbow City 6,299
Rainsville 3,907
Ranburne 417
Red Bay 3,232
Red Level 504
Reece City 718
Reform 2,245
Repton 313
Ridgeville 182
River Falls 669
Riverside 849
Riverview 132
Roanoke 5,896
Robertsdale 2,306
Rockford 494
Rogersville 1,224
Roosevelt City 3,352
Rosa 204
Russellville 8,195
Rutledge 496
St. Florian 263
Samson 2,402
Sanford 250
Saraland 9,833
Sardis 883
Satsuma 3,791
Scottsboro 14,758
Section 821
Selma 26,684
Sheffield 11,903
Shiloh 297
Silas 343
Silverhill 624
Sipsey 678
Slocomb 2,153
Snead 667
Somerville 140
South Vinemont 615
Southside 4,848
Springville 1,476
Steele 795
Stevenson 2,568
Sulligent 2,130
Sumiton 2,815
Summerdale 546
Sweet Water 253
Sylacauga 12,708
Sylvan Springs 450
Sylvania 1,156
Talladega 19,128
Talladega Springs 196
Tallassee 4,763
Tarrant 8,148
Taylor 1,003
Thomaston 679
Thomasville 4,387
Thorsby 1,422
Town Creek 1,201
Toxey 265
Trafford 673
Triana 285
Trinity 1,328
Troy 12,587
Trussville 3,507
Tuscaloosa 75,143
Tuscumbia 9,137
Tuskegee 12,716
Union 358
Union Grove 127
Union Springs 4,431
Uniontown 2,112
Valley Head 609
Vance 254
Vernon 2,609
Vestavia Hills 15,733
Vina 346
Vincent 1,652
Vredenburgh 433
Wadley 532
Waldo 231
Walnut Grove 510
Warrior 3,260
Waterloo 260
Waverly 228
Weaver 2,765
Webb 448
Wedowee 908
West Blocton 1,147
West Jefferson 357
West Point 248
Weston 645
Wetumpka 4,341
Whites Chapel 336
Wilmer 581
Wilsonville 914
Wilton 642
Winfield 3,781
Woodland 192
Woodville 609
York 3,392

ALASKA

Population 400,481

METROPOLITAN AREA

Anchorage† 173,017

BOROUGHS

Anchorage 173,017
Bristol Bay 1,094
Fairbanks North Star 53,983
Haines 1,680
Juneau 19,528
Kenai Peninsula 25,282
Ketchikan Gateway 11,316
Kodiak Island 9,939
Matanuska-Susitna 17,766
North Slope 4,199
Sitka 7,803

CENSUS AREAS

Aleutian Islands 7,768
Bethel 10,999
Dillingham 4,616
Kobuk 4,831
Nome 6,537
Prince of Wales-Outer Ketchikan 3,822
Skagway-Yakutat-Angoon 3,478
Southeast Fairbanks 5,770
Valdez-Cordova 8,348
Wade Hampton 4,665
Wrangell-Petersburg 6,167
Yukon-Koyukuk 7,873

CITIES AND TOWNS

Akhiok 105
Akiachak 438
Akiak 198
Akolmiut 641
Akutan 169
Alakanuk 522
Aleknagik 154
Allakaket 163
Ambler 192
Anaktuvuk Pass 203
Anchorage 173,017
Anderson 517
Angoon 465
Aniak 341
Anvik 114
Atamautluak 219
Barrow 2,207
Bethel 3,576
Buckland 177
Chefornak 230
Chevak 466
Chuathbaluk 105
Clarks Point 79
Cordova 1,879
Craig 527
Deering 150
Delta Junction 945
Dillingham 1,563
Diomede 139
Eagle 110
Eek 228
Ekwok 77
Elim 211
Emmonak 567
Fairbanks 22,645
Fort Yukon 619
Fortuna Ledge 262
Galena 765
Gambell 445
Golovin 87
Goodnews Bay 168
Grayling 209
Haines 993
Holy Cross 241
Homer 2,209
Hoonah 680
Hooper Bay 627
Houston 370
Hughes 73
Huslia 188
Hydaburg 298
Juneau 19,528
Kachemak 403
Kake 555
Kaktovik 165
Kaltag 247
Kasaan 25
Kenai 4,324
Ketchikan 7,198
Kiana 345
King Cove 460
Kivalina 241
Klawock 318
Kobuk 62
Kodiak 4,756
Kotlik 293
Kotzebue 2,054
Koyuk 188
Koyukuk 98
Kupreanof 47
Kwethluk 454
Larsen Bay 168
Lower Kalskag 246
Manokotak 294
McGrath 355
Mekoryuk 160
Mountain Village 583
Napakiak 262
Napaskiak 244
Nenana 470
New Stuyahok 331
Newhalen 87
Newtok 131
Nightmute 119
Nikolai 91
Nome 2,301
Nondalton 173
Noorvik 492
North Pole 724
Nuiqsut 208
Nulato 350
Old Harbor 340
Ouzinkie 173
Palmer 2,141
Pelican 180
Petersburg 2,821
Pilot Station 325
Platinum 55
Point Hope 464
Port Alexander 86
Port Heiden 92
Port Lions 215
Quinhagak 412
Ruby 197
Russian Mission 169
St. Marys 382
St. Michael 239
St. Paul 551
Sand Point 625
Savoonga 491
Saxman 273
Scammon Bay 250
Selawik 361
Seldovia 479
Seward 1,843
Shageluk 131
Shaktoolik 164

Sheldon Point . . . 103
Shishmaref . . . 394
Shungnak . . . 202
Sitka . . . 7,803
Skagway . . . 768
Soldotna . . . 2,320
Stebbins . . . 331
Tanana . . . 388
Teller . . . 212
Teller Mission [Brevig Mission] . . . 138
Tenakee Springs . . . 138
Togiak . . . 470
Toksook Bay . . . 333
Tuluksak . . . 236
Tununak . . . 298
Unalakleet . . . 623
Unalaska . . . 1,322
Upper Kalskag . . . 129
Valdez . . . 3,079
Wainwright . . . 405
Wales . . . 133
Wasilla . . . 1,559
White Mountain . . . 125
Whittier . . . 198
Wrangell . . . 2,184
Yakutat . . . 449

†City and metropolitan area have same boundary and population.

ARIZONA

Population 2,717,866

METROPOLITAN AREAS

Phoenix . . . 1,508,030
Tucson . . . 531,263

COUNTIES

Apache . . . 52,083
Cochise . . . 86,717
Coconino . . . 74,947
Gila . . . 37,080
Graham . . . 22,862
Greenlee . . . 11,406
Maricopa . . . 1,508,030
Mohave . . . 55,693
Navajo . . . 67,709
Pima . . . 531,263
Pinal . . . 90,918
Santa Cruz . . . 20,459
Yavapai . . . 68,145
Yuma . . . 90,554

CITIES AND TOWNS

Apache Junction . . . 9,935
Avondale . . . 8,134
Benson . . . 4,190
Bisbee . . . 7,154
Buckeye . . . 3,434
Casa Grande . . . 14,971
Chandler . . . 29,673
Chino Valley . . . 2,858
Clarkdale . . . 1,512
Clifton . . . 4,245
Coolidge . . . 6,851
Cottonwood . . . 4,550
Douglas . . . 13,058
Duncan . . . 603
Eagar . . . 2,791
El Mirage . . . 4,307
Eloy . . . 6,240
Flagstaff . . . 34,641
Florence . . . 3,391
Fredonia . . . 1,040
Gila Bend . . . 1,585
Gilbert . . . 5,717
Glendale . . . 96,988
Globe . . . 6,708
Goodyear . . . 2,747
Guadalupe . . . 4,506
Hayden . . . 1,205
Holbrook . . . 5,785
Huachuca City . . . 1,661
Jerome . . . 420
Kearny . . . 2,646
Kingman . . . 9,257
Lake Havasu City . . . 15,737
Mammoth . . . 1,906
Marana . . . 1,674
Mesa . . . 152,453
Miami . . . 2,716
Nogales . . . 15,683
Oro Valley . . . 1,489
Page . . . 4,907
Paradise Valley . . . 10,832
Parker . . . 2,542
Patagonia . . . 980
Payson . . . 5,068
Peoria . . . 12,251
Phoenix . . . 764,911
Pima . . . 1,599
Prescott . . . 20,055
Prescott Valley . . . 2,284
Safford . . . 7,010
St. Johns . . . 3,343
San Luis . . . 1,946
Scottsdale . . . 88,364
Show Low . . . 4,298
Sierra Vista . . . 25,968
Snowflake . . . 3,510
Somerton . . . 5,761
South Tucson . . . 6,554
Springerville . . . 1,452
Superior . . . 4,600
Surprise . . . 3,723
Taylor . . . 1,915
Tempe . . . 106,743
Thatcher . . . 3,374
Tolleson . . . 4,433
Tombstone . . . 1,632
Tucson . . . 330,537
Wellton . . . 911
Wickenburg . . . 3,535
Willcox . . . 3,243
Williams . . . 2,266
Winkelman . . . 1,060
Winslow . . . 7,921
Youngtown . . . 2,254
Yuma . . . 42,433

ARKANSAS

Population 2,285,513

METROPOLITAN AREAS

Fayetteville-Springdale . . . 177,850
Fort Smith . . . 203,269 (131,822 in Ark.; 71,447 in Okla.)
Little Rock-North Little Rock . . . 393,494
Memphis (Tenn.) . . . 912,887 (809,860 in Tenn.; 49,097 in Ark.; 53,930 in Miss.)
Pine Bluff . . . 90,718
Texarkana-Texarkana (Tex.) . . . 127,019 (75,301 in Tex.; 51,718 in Ark.)

COUNTIES

Arkansas . . . 24,175
Ashley . . . 26,538
Baxter . . . 27,409
Benton . . . 78,115
Boone . . . 26,067
Bradley . . . 13,803
Calhoun . . . 6,079
Carroll . . . 16,203
Chicot . . . 17,793
Clark . . . 23,326
Clay . . . 20,616
Cleburne . . . 16,909
Cleveland . . . 7,868
Columbia . . . 26,644
Conway . . . 19,505
Craighead . . . 63,218
Crawford . . . 36,892
Crittenden . . . 49,097
Cross . . . 20,434
Dallas . . . 10,515
Desha . . . 19,760
Drew . . . 17,910
Faulkner . . . 46,192
Franklin . . . 14,705
Fulton . . . 9,975
Garland . . . 69,916
Grant . . . 13,008
Greene . . . 30,744
Hempstead . . . 23,635
Hot Spring . . . 26,819
Howard . . . 13,459
Independence . . . 30,147
Izard . . . 10,768
Jackson . . . 21,646
Jefferson . . . 90,718
Johnson . . . 17,423
Lafayette . . . 10,213
Lawrence . . . 18,447
Lee . . . 15,539
Lincoln . . . 13,369
Little River . . . 13,952
Logan . . . 20,144
Lonoke . . . 34,518
Madison . . . 11,373
Marion . . . 11,334
Miller . . . 37,766
Mississippi . . . 59,517
Monroe . . . 14,052
Montgomery . . . 7,771
Nevada . . . 11,097
Newton . . . 7,756
Ouachita . . . 30,541
Perry . . . 7,266
Phillips . . . 34,772
Pike . . . 10,373
Poinsett . . . 27,032
Polk . . . 17,007
Pope . . . 39,003
Prairie . . . 10,140
Pulaski . . . 340,613
Randolph . . . 16,834
St. Francis . . . 30,858
Saline . . . 52,881
Scott . . . 9,685
Searcy . . . 8,847
Sebastian . . . 94,930
Sevier . . . 14,060
Sharp . . . 14,607
Stone . . . 9,022
Union . . . 49,988
Van Buren . . . 13,357
Washington . . . 99,735
White . . . 50,835
Woodruff . . . 11,222
Yell . . . 17,026

CITIES AND TOWNS

Adona . . . 230
Alexander . . . 223
Alicia . . . 246
Allport . . . 295
Alma . . . 2,755
Almyra . . . 294
Alpena . . . 344
Altheimer . . . 1,231
Altus . . . 441
Amagon . . . 126
Amity . . . 859
Antoine . . . 194
Arkadelphia . . . 10,005
Arkansas City . . . 668
Ash Flat . . . 524
Ashdown . . . 4,218
Atkins . . . 3,002
Aubrey . . . 267
Augusta . . . 3,496
Austin . . . 269
Avoca . . . 256
Bald Knob . . . 2,756
Banks . . . 216
Barling . . . 3,761
Bassett . . . 243
Batesville . . . 8,263
Bauxite . . . 433
Bay . . . 1,605
Bearden . . . 1,191
Beebe . . . 3,599
Beedeville . . . 183
Bellefonte . . . 393
Belleville . . . 571
Ben Lomond . . . 155
Benton . . . 17,437
Bentonville . . . 8,756
Bergman . . . 320
Berryville . . . 2,966
Bethel Heights . . . 296
Big Flat . . . 150
Bigelow . . . 373
Biggers . . . 363
Black Oak . . . 309
Black Rock . . . 848
Black Springs . . . 92
Blevins . . . 314
Blue Mountain . . . 112
Bluff City . . . 292
Blytheville . . . 24,314
Bodcaw . . . 197
Bonanza . . . 553
Bono . . . 967
Booneville . . . 3,718
Bradford . . . 950
Bradley . . . 790
Branch . . . 353
Brinkley . . . 4,909
Brookland . . . 840
Bryant . . . 2,682
Buckner . . . 436
Bull Shoals . . . 1,312
Burdette . . . 328
Cabot . . . 4,806
Caddo Valley . . . 388
Caldwell . . . 283
Cale . . . 110
Calico Rock . . . 1,046
Calion . . . 638
Camden . . . 15,356
Cammack Village . . . 920
Campbell Station . . . 297
Caraway . . . 1,165
Carlisle . . . 2,567
Carthage . . . 568
Casa . . . 179
Cash . . . 285
Caulksville . . . 234
Cave City . . . 1,634
Cave Springs . . . 429
Centerton . . . 425
Central City . . . 339
Charleston . . . 1,748
Cherry Valley . . . 729
Chester . . . 139
Chidester . . . 342
Clarendon . . . 2,361
Clarksville . . . 5,237
Clinton . . . 1,284
Coal Hill . . . 859
College City . . . 432
Colt . . . 378
Concord . . . 234
Conway . . . 20,375
Corning . . . 3,650
Cotter . . . 920
Cotton Plant . . . 1,323
Cove . . . 391
Coy . . . 183
Crawfordsville . . . 685
Crossett . . . 6,706
Cushman . . . 556
Daisy . . . 177
Damascus . . . 307
Danville . . . 1,698
Dardanelle . . . 3,621
Datto . . . 112
Decatur . . . 1,013
Delaplaine . . . 161
Delight . . . 431
Dell . . . 310
Denning . . . 238
De Queen . . . 4,594
Dermott . . . 4,731
Des Arc . . . 2,001
De Valls Bluff . . . 738
De Witt . . . 3,928
Diamond City . . . 650
Diaz . . . 1,192
Dierks . . . 1,249
Dover . . . 948
Dumas . . . 6,091
Dyer . . . 608
Dyess . . . 446
Earle . . . 3,517
East Camden . . . 632
Edmondson . . . 344
Elaine . . . 991
El Dorado . . . 26,685
Elkins . . . 579
Elm Springs . . . 781
Emerson . . . 444
Emmet . . . 475
England . . . 3,081
Enola . . . 186
Eudora . . . 3,840
Eureka Springs . . . 1,989
Evening Shade . . . 397
Everton . . . 134
Farmington . . . 1,283
Fayetteville . . . 36,604
Felsenthal . . . 220
Fiftysix . . . 157
Fisher . . . 302
Flippin . . . 1,072
Fordyce . . . 5,175
Foreman . . . 1,377
Forrest City . . . 13,803
Fort Smith . . . 71,384
Fouke . . . 614
Fountain Hill . . . 352
Franklin . . . 253
Fredonia . . . 486
Friendship . . . 163
Fulton . . . 326
Garfield . . . 187
Garland . . . 660
Garner . . . 216
Gassville . . . 859
Gateway . . . 75
Gentry . . . 1,468
Gillett . . . 927
Gillham . . . 252
Gilmore . . . 503
Glenwood . . . 1,402
Gosnell . . . 2,745
Gould . . . 1,671
Grady . . . 488
Grannis . . . 349
Gravette . . . 1,218
Green Forest . . . 1,609
Greenbrier . . . 1,423
Greenland . . . 622
Greenway . . . 317
Greenwood . . . 3,317
Greers Ferry . . . 558
Griffithville . . . 254
Grubbs . . . 546
Guion . . . 177
Gum Springs . . . 255
Gurdon . . . 2,707
Guy . . . 209
Hackett . . . 505
Hamburg . . . 3,394
Hampton . . . 1,627
Hardy . . . 643
Harrell . . . 302
Harrisburg . . . 1,921
Harrison . . . 9,567
Hartford . . . 613
Hartman . . . 517
Haskell . . . 1,074
Hatfield . . . 410
Havana . . . 352
Haynes . . . 359
Hazen . . . 1,636
Heber Springs . . . 4,589
Hector . . . 449
Helena . . . 9,598
Hermitage . . . 378
Hickory Ridge . . . 478
Higden . . . 45
Higginson . . . 333
Highfill . . . 92
Holly Grove . . . 754
Hope . . . 10,290
Horatio . . . 989
Horseshoe Bend . . . 1,909
Hot Springs . . . 35,166
Houston . . . 183
Hoxie . . . 2,961
Hughes . . . 1,919
Humnoke . . . 442
Humphrey . . . 872
Hunter . . . 170
Huntington . . . 662
Huntsville . . . 1,394
Huttig . . . 976
Imboden . . . 661
Jacksonport . . . 288
Jacksonville . . . 27,589
Jasper . . . 519
Johnson . . . 519
Joiner . . . 725
Jonesboro . . . 31,530
Judsonia . . . 2,025
Junction City . . . 813
Keiser . . . 962
Kensett . . . 1,751
Keo . . . 208
Kibler . . . 798
Kingsland . . . 320
Knobel . . . 503
Knoxville . . . 264
Lafe . . . 215
Lake City . . . 1,842
Lake View . . . 609
Lake Village . . . 3,088
Lakeview . . . 512
Lamar . . . 708
Lavaca . . . 1,092
Leachville . . . 1,882
Lead Hill . . . 247
Leola . . . 481
Lepanto . . . 1,964
Leslie . . . 501
Letona . . . 231
Lewisville . . . 1,476
Lincoln . . . 1,422
Little Flock . . . 663
Little Rock . . . 158,461
Lockesburg . . . 616
London . . . 859
Lonoke . . . 4,128
Lonsdale . . . 117
Louann . . . 282
Lowell . . . 1,078
Luxora . . . 1,739
Lynn . . . 345
Madison . . . 1,227
Magazine . . . 799
Magness . . . 196
Magnolia . . . 11,909
Malvern . . . 10,163
Mammoth Spring . . . 1,158
Manila . . . 2,553
Mansfield . . . 1,000
Marianna . . . 6,220
Marie . . . 287
Marion . . . 2,996
Marked Tree . . . 3,201
Marmaduke . . . 1,168
Marshall . . . 1,595
Marvell . . . 1,724
Mayflower . . . 1,381
Maynard . . . 381
McCaskill . . . 87
McCrory . . . 1,942
McDougal . . . 239
McGehee . . . 5,671
McNeil . . . 725
McRae . . . 641
Melbourne . . . 1,619
Mena . . . 5,154
Menifee . . . 368
Midland . . . 286
Mineral Springs . . . 936
Minturn . . . 169
Mitchellville . . . 618
Monette . . . 1,165
Monticello . . . 8,259
Montrose . . . 641
Moorefield . . . 129
Moro . . . 327
Morrilton . . . 7,355
Morrison Bluff . . . 69
Mount Ida . . . 1,023
Mount Pleasant . . . 438
Mount Vernon . . . 157
Mountain Home . . . 7,447
Mountain Pine . . . 1,068
Mountain View . . . 2,147
Mountainburg . . . 595
Mulberry . . . 1,444
Murfreesboro . . . 1,883
Nashville . . . 4,554
Newark . . . 1,109
Newport . . . 8,339
Nimmons . . . 112
Norfork . . . 399
Norman . . . 539
Norphlet . . . 756
Norristown . . . 625
North Little Rock . . . 64,419
Oak Grove . . . 265
Oak Grove Heights . . . 486
Oakhaven . . . 72
Oden . . . 186
Ogden . . . 334
Oil Trough . . . 280
O'Kean . . . 291
Okolona . . . 200
Ola . . . 1,121
Omaha . . . 191
Oppelo . . . 486
Osceola . . . 8,881
Oxford . . . 520
Ozan . . . 111
Ozark . . . 3,597
Palestine . . . 976
Pangburn . . . 673
Paragould . . . 15,214
Paris . . . 3,991
Parkdale . . . 471
Parkin . . . 2,035
Patmos . . . 88
Patterson . . . 567
Pea Ridge . . . 1,488
Peach Orchard . . . 243
Perla . . . 149
Perry . . . 254
Perrytown . . . 282
Perryville . . . 1,058
Piggott . . . 3,762
Pine Bluff . . . 56,576
Pineville . . . 163
Plainview . . . 752
Pleasant Plains . . . 267
Plumerville . . . 785
Pocahontas . . . 5,995
Pollard . . . 298
Portia . . . 480
Portland . . . 701
Pottsville . . . 564
Powhatan . . . 49
Poyen . . . 329
Prairie Grove . . . 1,708
Prattsville . . . 317
Prescott . . . 4,103
Pyatt . . . 217
Quitman . . . 556
Ratcliff . . . 197
Ravenden . . . 338
Ravenden Springs . . . 230
Reader . . . 127
Rector . . . 2,336
Redfield . . . 745
Reed . . . 395
Reyno . . . 521
Rison . . . 1,325
Rockport . . . 231
Roe . . . 136
Rogers . . . 17,429
Rondo . . . 330
Rose Bud . . . 202
Rosston . . . 274
Rudy . . . 79
Russell . . . 232
Russellville . . . 14,000
St. Charles . . . 199
St. Francis . . . 266
St. Paul . . . 198
Salem . . . 1,424
Salesville . . . 406
Scranton . . . 244
Searcy . . . 13,612
Sedgwick . . . 205
Shannon Hills . . . 1,656
Sheridan . . . 3,042
Sherrill . . . 161
Sherwood . . . 10,586
Shirley . . . 354
Sidney . . . 270
Siloam Springs . . . 7,940
Smackover . . . 2,453
Smithville . . . 113
South Lead Hill . . . 85
Sparkman . . . 622
Springdale . . . 23,458
Stamps . . . 2,859
Star City . . . 2,066
Stephens . . . 1,366
Strawberry . . . 280
Strong . . . 785
Stuttgart . . . 10,941
Subiaco . . . 744
Success . . . 223
Sulphur Rock . . . 316
Sulphur Springs . . . 496
Summit . . . 506
Sunset . . . 582
Swifton . . . 859
Taylor . . . 657
Texarkana . . . 21,459

ARKANSAS (continued)

Thornton ... 711
Tillar ... 280
Tinsman ... 112
Tollette ... 407
Tontitown ... 571
Traskwood ... 459
Trumann ... 6,044
Tuckerman ... 2,078
Tull ... 281
Tupelo ... 248
Turrell ... 1,041
Tyronza ... 777
Ulm ... 201
Valley Springs ... 190
Van Buren ... 12,020
Vandervoort ... 98
Victoria ... 175
Vilonia ... 736
Viola ... 362
Wabbaseka ... 428
Waldenburg ... 124
Waldo ... 1,685
Waldron ... 2,642
Walnut Ridge ... 4,152
Ward ... 981
Warren ... 7,646
Washington ... 265
Watson ... 433
Weiner ... 750
Weldon ... 161
West Fork ... 1,526
West Helena ... 11,367
West Memphis ... 28,138
West Point ... 226
Western Grove ... 378
Wheatley ... 523
Whelen Springs ... 156
White Hall ... 2,214
Wickes ... 464
Widener ... 316
Wiederkehr Village ... 71
Williford ... 169
Willisville ... 209
Wilmar ... 747
Wilmot ... 1,227
Wilson ... 1,115
Wilton ... 495
Winchester ... 279
Winslow ... 247
Winthrop ... 238
Wooster ... 398
Wynne ... 7,805
Yellville ... 1,044
Zinc ... 113

CALIFORNIA Population 23,668,562

METROPOLITAN AREAS

Anaheim-Santa Ana-Garden Grove ... 1,931,570
Bakersfield ... 403,089
Fresno ... 515,013
Los Angeles-Long Beach ... 7,477,657
Modesto ... 265,902
Oxnard-Simi Valley-Ventura ... 529,899
Riverside-San Bernardino-Ontario ... 1,557,080
Sacramento ... 1,014,002
Salinas-Seaside-Monterey ... 290,444
San Diego ... 1,861,846
San Francisco-Oakland ... 3,252,721
San Jose ... 1,295,071
Santa Barbara-Santa Maria-Lompoc ... 298,660
Santa Cruz ... 188,141
Santa Rosa ... 299,827
Stockton ... 347,342
Vallejo-Fairfield-Napa ... 334,402

COUNTIES

Alameda ... 1,105,379
Alpine ... 1,097
Amador ... 19,314
Butte ... 143,851
Calaveras ... 20,710
Colusa ... 12,791
Contra Costa ... 657,252
Del Norte ... 18,217
El Dorado ... 85,812
Fresno ... 515,013
Glenn ... 21,350
Humboldt ... 108,024
Imperial ... 92,110
Inyo ... 17,895
Kern ... 403,089
Kings ... 73,738
Lake ... 36,366
Lassen ... 21,661
Los Angeles ... 7,477,657
Madera ... 63,116
Marin ... 222,952
Mariposa ... 11,108
Mendocino ... 66,738
Merced ... 134,560
Modoc ... 8,610
Mono ... 8,577
Monterey ... 290,444
Napa ... 99,199
Nevada ... 51,645
Orange ... 1,931,570
Placer ... 117,247
Plumas ... 17,340
Riverside ... 663,923
Sacramento ... 783,381
San Benito ... 25,005
San Bernardino ... 893,157
San Diego ... 1,861,846
San Francisco ... 678,974
San Joaquin ... 347,342
San Luis Obispo ... 115,345
San Mateo ... 588,164
Santa Barbara ... 298,660
Santa Clara ... 1,295,071
Santa Cruz ... 188,141
Shasta ... 115,715
Sierra ... 3,073
Siskiyou ... 39,732
Solano ... 235,203
Sonoma ... 299,827
Stanislaus ... 265,902
Sutter ... 52,246
Tehama ... 38,888
Trinity ... 11,858
Tulare ... 245,751
Tuolumne ... 33,920
Ventura ... 529,899
Yolo ... 113,374
Yuba ... 49,733

CITIES AND TOWNS

Adelanto ... 2,164
Alameda ... 63,852
Albany ... 15,130
Alhambra ... 64,615
Alturas ... 3,025
Amador City ... 136
Anaheim ... 221,847
Anderson ... 7,381
Angels ... 2,302
Antioch ... 43,559
Arcadia ... 45,994
Arcata ... 12,338
Arroyo Grande ... 11,290
Artesia ... 14,301
Arvin ... 6,863
Atascadero ... 15,930
Atherton ... 7,797
Atwater ... 17,530
Auburn ... 7,540
Avalon ... 2,010
Avenal ... 4,137
Azusa ... 29,380
Bakersfield ... 105,611
Baldwin Park ... 50,554
Banning ... 14,020
Barstow ... 17,690
Beaumont ... 6,818
Bell ... 25,450
Bell Gardens ... 34,117
Bellflower ... 53,441
Belmont ... 24,505
Belvedere ... 2,401
Benicia ... 15,376
Berkeley ... 103,328
Beverly Hills ... 32,367
Biggs ... 1,413
Bishop ... 3,333
Blue Lake ... 1,201
Blythe ... 6,805
Bradbury ... 846
Brawley ... 14,946
Brea ... 27,913
Brentwood ... 4,434
Brisbane ... 2,969
Buena Park ... 64,165
Burbank ... 84,625
Burlingame ... 26,173
Calexico ... 14,412
California City ... 2,743
Calipatria ... 2,636
Calistoga ... 3,879
Camarillo ... 37,732
Campbell ... 27,067
Capitola ... 9,095
Carlsbad ... 35,490
Carmel-by-the-Sea ... 4,707
Carpinteria ... 10,835
Carson ... 81,221
Ceres ... 13,281
Cerritos ... 52,756
Chico ... 26,601
Chino ... 40,165
Chowchilla ... 5,122
Chula Vista ... 83,927
Claremont ... 30,950
Clayton ... 4,325
Cloverdale ... 3,989
Clovis ... 33,021
Coachella ... 9,129
Coalinga ... 6,593
Colfax ... 981
Colma ... 395
Colton ... 27,419
Colusa ... 4,075
Commerce ... 10,509
Compton ... 81,286
Concord ... 103,251
Corcoran ... 6,454
Corning ... 4,745
Corona ... 37,791
Coronado ... 16,859
Corte Madera ... 8,074
Costa Mesa ... 82,291
Cotati ... 3,475
Covina ... 33,751
Crescent City ... 3,099
Cucamonga ... 55,250
Cudahy ... 17,984
Culver City ... 38,139
Cupertino ... 25,770
Cypress ... 40,391
Daly City ... 78,519
Davis ... 36,640
Delano ... 16,491
Del Mar ... 5,017
Del Rey Oaks ... 1,557
Desert Hot Springs ... 5,941
Dinuba ... 9,907
Dixon ... 7,541
Dorris ... 836
Dos Palos ... 3,123
Downey ... 82,602
Duarte ... 16,766
Dunsmuir ... 2,253
El Cajon ... 73,892
El Centro ... 23,996
El Cerrito ... 22,731
El Monte ... 79,494
El Segundo ... 13,752
Emeryville ... 3,763
Escalon ... 3,127
Escondido ... 62,480
Etna ... 754
Eureka ... 24,153
Exeter ... 5,619
Fairfax ... 7,391
Fairfield ... 58,099
Farmersville ... 5,544
Ferndale ... 1,367
Fillmore ... 9,602
Firebaugh ... 3,740
Folsom ... 11,003
Fontana ... 37,109
Fort Bragg ... 5,019
Fort Jones ... 544
Fortuna ... 7,591
Foster City ... 23,287
Fountain Valley ... 55,080
Fowler ... 2,496
Fremont ... 131,945
Fresno ... 218,202
Fullerton ... 102,034
Galt ... 5,514
Garden Grove ... 123,351
Gardena ... 45,165
Gilroy ... 21,641
Glendale ... 139,060
Glendora ... 38,654
Gonzales ... 2,891
Grand Terrace ... 8,498
Grass Valley ... 6,697
Greenfield ... 4,181
Gridley ... 3,982
Grover City ... 8,827
Guadalupe ... 3,629
Gustine ... 3,142
Half Moon Bay ... 7,282
Hanford ... 20,958
Hawaiian Gardens ... 10,548
Hawthorne ... 56,447
Hayward ... 94,167
Healdsburg ... 7,217
Hemet ... 23,211
Hercules ... 5,963
Hermosa Beach ... 18,070
Hidden Hills ... 1,760
Hillsborough ... 10,451
Hollister ... 11,488
Holtville ... 4,399
Hughson ... 2,943
Huntington Beach ... 170,505
Huntington Park ... 46,223
Huron ... 2,768
Imperial ... 3,451
Imperial Beach ... 22,689
Indian Wells ... 1,394
Indio ... 21,611
Industry ... 664
Inglewood ... 94,245
Ione ... 2,207
Irvine ... 62,134
Irwindale ... 1,030
Isleton ... 914
Jackson ... 2,331
Kerman ... 4,002
King City ... 5,495
Kingsburg ... 5,115
La Canada-Flintridge ... 20,153
Lafayette ... 20,879
Laguna Beach ... 17,860
La Habra ... 45,232
La Habra Heights ... 4,874
Lake Elsinore ... 5,982
Lakeport ... 3,675
Lakewood ... 74,654
La Mesa ... 50,342
La Mirada ... 40,986
Lancaster ... 48,027
La Palma ... 15,663
La Puente ... 30,882
Larkspur ... 11,064
La Verne ... 23,508
Lawndale ... 23,460
Lemon Grove ... 20,780
Lemoore ... 8,832
Lincoln ... 4,132
Lindsay ... 6,924
Live Oak ... 3,103
Livermore ... 48,349
Livingston ... 5,326
Lodi ... 35,221
Loma Linda ... 10,694
Lomita ... 17,191
Lompoc ... 26,267
Long Beach ... 361,334
Los Alamitos ... 11,529
Los Altos ... 25,769
Los Altos Hills ... 7,421
Los Angeles ... 2,966,763
Los Banos ... 10,341
Los Gatos ... 26,593
Loyalton ... 1,030
Lynwood ... 48,548
Madera ... 21,732
Manhattan Beach ... 31,542
Manteca ... 24,925
Maricopa ... 946
Marina ... 20,647
Martinez ... 22,582
Marysville ... 9,898
Maywood ... 21,810
McFarland ... 5,151
Mendota ... 5,038
Menlo Park ... 25,673
Merced ... 36,499
Mill Valley ... 12,967
Millbrae ... 20,058
Milpitas ... 37,820
Modesto ... 106,105
Monrovia ... 30,531
Montague ... 1,285
Montclair ... 22,628
Monte Sereno ... 3,434
Montebello ... 52,929
Monterey ... 27,558
Monterey Park ... 54,338
Moraga ... 15,014
Morgan Hill ... 17,060
Morro Bay ... 9,064
Mount Shasta ... 2,837
Mountain View ... 58,655
Napa ... 50,879
National City ... 48,772
Needles ... 4,120
Nevada City ... 2,431
Newark ... 32,126
Newman ... 2,785
Newport Beach ... 63,475
Norco ... 21,126
Norwalk ... 85,232
Novato ... 43,916
Oakdale ... 8,474
Oakland ... 339,288
Oceanside ... 76,698
Ojai ... 6,816
Ontario ... 88,820
Orange ... 91,788
Orange Cove ... 4,026
Orland ... 3,976
Oroville ... 8,683
Oxnard ... 108,195
Pacific Grove ... 15,755
Pacifica ... 36,866
Palm Desert ... 11,801
Palm Springs ... 32,271
Palmdale ... 12,277
Palo Alto ... 55,225
Palos Verdes Estates ... 14,376
Paradise ... 22,571
Paramount ... 36,407
Parlier ... 2,680
Pasadena ... 119,374
Paso Robles ... 9,163
Patterson ... 3,866
Perris ... 6,740
Petaluma ... 33,834
Pico Rivera ... 53,459
Piedmont ... 10,498
Pinole ... 14,253
Pismo Beach ... 5,364
Pittsburg ... 33,034
Placentia ... 35,041
Placerville ... 6,739
Pleasant Hill ... 25,124
Pleasanton ... 35,160
Plymouth ... 699
Point Arena ... 425
Pomona ... 92,742
Port Hueneme ... 17,803
Porterville ... 19,707
Portola ... 1,885
Portola Valley ... 3,939
Rancho Mirage ... 6,281
Rancho Palos Verdes ... 35,227
Red Bluff ... 9,490
Redding ... 41,995
Redlands ... 43,619
Redondo Beach ... 57,102
Redwood City ... 54,965
Reedley ... 11,071
Rialto ... 35,615
Richmond ... 74,676
Ridgecrest ... 15,929
Rio Dell ... 2,687
Rio Vista ... 3,142
Ripon ... 3,509
Riverbank ... 5,695
Riverside ... 170,876
Rocklin ... 7,344
Rohnert Park ... 22,965
Rolling Hills ... 2,049
Rolling Hills Estates ... 9,412
Rosemead ... 42,604
Roseville ... 24,347
Ross ... 2,682
Sacramento ... 275,741
St. Helena ... 4,898
Salinas ... 80,479
San Anselmo ... 11,927
San Bernardino ... 118,057
San Bruno ... 35,417
San Carlos ... 24,710
San Clemente ... 27,325
Sand City ... 182
San Diego ... 875,504
San Dimas ... 24,014
San Fernando ... 17,731
San Francisco ... 678,974
San Gabriel ... 30,072
San Jacinto ... 7,098
San Joaquin ... 1,930
San Jose ... 636,550
San Juan Bautista ... 1,276
San Juan Capistrano ... 18,959
San Leandro ... 63,952
San Luis Obispo ... 34,252
San Marcos ... 17,479
San Marino ... 13,307
San Mateo ... 77,561
San Pablo ... 19,750
San Rafael ... 44,700
Sanger ... 12,558
Santa Ana ... 203,713
Santa Barbara ... 74,542
Santa Clara ... 87,746
Santa Cruz ... 41,483
Santa Fe Springs ... 14,559
Santa Maria ... 39,685
Santa Monica ... 88,314
Santa Paula ... 20,552
Santa Rosa ... 83,205
Saratoga ... 29,261
Sausalito ... 7,090
Scotts Valley ... 6,891
Seal Beach ... 25,975
Seaside ... 36,567
Sebastopol ... 5,500
Selma ... 10,942
Shafter ... 7,010
Sierra Madre ... 10,837
Signal Hill ... 5,734
Simi Valley ... 77,500
Soledad ... 5,928
Sonoma ... 6,054
Sonora ... 3,239
South El Monte ... 16,623
South Gate ... 66,784
South Lake Tahoe ... 20,681
South Pasadena ... 22,681
South San Francisco ... 49,393
Stanton ... 21,144
Stockton ... 149,779
Suisun City ... 11,087
Sunnyvale ... 106,618
Susanville ... 6,520
Sutter Creek ... 1,705
Taft ... 5,316
Tehachapi ... 4,126
Tehama ... 365
Temple City ... 28,972
Thousand Oaks ... 77,797
Tiburon ... 6,685
Torrance ... 131,497
Tracy ... 18,428
Trinidad ... 379
Tulare ... 22,475
Tulelake ... 783
Turlock ... 26,291
Tustin ... 32,073
Ukiah ... 12,035
Union City ... 39,406
Upland ... 47,647
Vacaville ... 43,367
Vallejo ... 80,188
Ventura ... 74,474
Vernon ... 90
Victorville ... 14,220
Villa Park ... 7,137
Visalia ... 49,729
Vista ... 35,834
Walnut ... 9,978
Walnut Creek ... 53,643
Wasco ... 9,613
Waterford ... 2,683
Watsonville ... 23,543
Weed ... 2,879
West Covina ... 80,094
Westminster ... 71,133
Westmorland ... 1,590
Wheatland ... 1,474
Whittier ... 68,872
Williams ... 1,655
Willits ... 4,008
Willows ... 4,777
Winters ... 2,652
Woodlake ... 5,375
Woodland ... 30,235
Woodside ... 5,291
Yorba Linda ... 28,254
Yountville ... 2,893
Yreka ... 5,916
Yuba City ... 18,736

COLORADO Population 2,888,834

METROPOLITAN AREAS

Colorado Springs ... 317,458
Denver-Boulder ... 1,619,921
Fort Collins ... 149,184
Greeley ... 123,438
Pueblo ... 125,972

COUNTIES

Adams ... 245,944
Alamosa ... 11,799
Arapahoe ... 293,621
Archuleta ... 3,664
Baca ... 5,419
Bent ... 5,945
Boulder ... 189,625
Chaffee ... 13,227
Cheyenne ... 2,153
Clear Creek ... 7,308
Conejos ... 7,794
Costilla ... 3,071
Crowley ... 2,988
Custer ... 1,528
Delta ... 21,225
Denver ... 491,396
Dolores ... 1,658
Douglas ... 25,153
Eagle ... 13,171
Elbert ... 6,850
El Paso ... 309,424
Fremont ... 28,676
Garfield ... 22,514
Gilpin ... 2,441
Grand ... 7,475
Gunnison ... 10,689
Hinsdale ... 408
Huerfano ... 6,440
Jackson ... 1,863
Jefferson ... 371,741
Kiowa ... 1,936
Kit Carson ... 7,599
Lake ... 8,830
La Plata ... 27,424
Larimer ... 149,184
Las Animas ... 14,897
Lincoln ... 4,663
Logan ... 19,800
Mesa ... 81,530
Mineral ... 804
Moffat ... 13,133
Montezuma ... 16,510
Montrose ... 24,352
Morgan ... 22,513
Otero ... 22,567
Ouray ... 1,925
Park ... 5,333
Phillips ... 4,542
Pitkin ... 10,338
Prowers ... 13,070
Pueblo ... 125,972

Rio Blanco 6,255
Rio Grande 10,511
Routt 13,404
Saguache 3,935
San Juan 833
San Miguel 3,192
Sedgwick 3,266
Summit 8,848
Teller 8,034
Washington 5,304
Weld 123,438
Yuma 9,682

CITIES AND TOWNS

Aguilar 624
Akron 1,716
Alamosa 6,830
Alma 132
Antonito 1,103
Arriba 236
Arvada 84,576
Aspen 3,678
Ault 1,056
Aurora 158,588
Avon 640
Basalt 529
Bayfield 724
Bennett 942
Berthoud 2,362
Bethune 149
Black Hawk 232
Blanca 252
Blue River 230
Bonanza 8
Boone 431
Boulder 76,685
Bow Mar 930
Branson 73
Breckenridge 818
Brighton 12,773
Brookside 178
Broomfield 20,730
Brush 4,082
Buena Vista 2,075
Burlington 3,107
Calhan 541
Campo 185
Canon City 13,037
Carbondale 2,084
Castle Rock 3,921
Cedaredge 1,184
Center 1,630
Central City 329
Cheraw 233
Cherry Hills Village 5,127
Cheyenne Wells 950
Coal Creek 190
Cokedale 90
Collbran 344
Colorado Springs 215,150
Columbine Valley 923
Commerce City 16,234
Cortez 7,095
Craig 8,133
Crawford 268
Creede 610
Crested Butte 959
Crestone 54
Cripple Creek 655
Crook 177
Crowley 192
Dacono 2,321
De Beque 279
Deer Trail 463
Del Norte 1,709
Delta 3,931
Denver 491,396
Dillon 337
Dinosaur 313
Dolores 802
Dove Creek 826
Durango 11,426
Eads 878
Eagle 801
Eaton 1,932
Eckley 262
Edgewater 5,714
Elizabeth 789
Empire 423
Englewood 30,021
Erie 1,254
Estes Park 2,703
Evans 5,063
Fairplay 421
Federal Heights 7,846
Firestone 1,204
Flagler 550
Fleming 388
Florence 2,987
Fort Collins 64,632
Fort Lupton 4,251
Fort Morgan 8,768
Fountain 8,324
Fowler 1,227
Fraser 470
Frederick 855
Frisco 1,221
Fruita 2,810
Garden City 85
Genoa 165
Georgetown 830
Gilcrest 1,025
Glendale 2,496
Glenwood Springs 4,637
Golden 12,237
Granada 557
Granby 963
Grand Junction 28,144
Grand Lake 382
Grand Valley 338
Greeley 53,006
Green Mountain Falls 607
Greenwood Village 5,729
Grover 158
Gunnison 5,785
Gypsum 743
Hartman 122
Haswell 126
Haxtun 1,014
Hayden 1,720
Hillrose 213
Holly 969
Holyoke 2,092
Hooper 71
Hot Sulphur Springs 405
Hotchkiss 849
Hudson 698
Hugo 776
Idaho Springs 2,077
Ignacio 667
Iliff 218
Jamestown 223
Johnstown 1,535
Julesburg 1,528
Keenesburg 541
Kersey 913
Kim 100
Kiowa 206
Kit Carson 278
Kremmling 1,296
Lafayette 8,985
La Jara 858
La Junta 8,338
Lake City 206
Lakeside 19
Lakewood 112,848
Lamar 7,713
Larkspur 141
La Salle 1,929
Las Animas 2,818
La Veta 611
Leadville 3,879
Limon 1,805
Littleton 28,631
Lochbuie 895
Log Lane Village 709
Longmont 42,942
Louisville 5,593
Loveland 30,244
Lyons 1,137
Manassa 945
Mancos 870
Manitou Springs 4,475
Manzanola 459
Marble 30
Mead 356
Meeker 2,356
Merino 255
Milliken 1,506
Minturn 1,060
Moffat 105
Monte Vista 3,902
Montrose 8,722
Monument 690
Morrison 478
Mount Crested Butte 272
Mountain View 584
Naturita 819
Nederland 1,212
New Castle 563
Northglenn 29,847
Norwood 478
Nucla 1,027
Nunn 295
Oak Creek 929
Olathe 1,262
Olney Springs 253
Ophir 38
Orchard City 1,914
Ordway 1,135
Otis 534
Ouray 684
Ovid 439
Pagosa Springs 1,331
Palisade 1,551
Palmer Lake 1,130
Paoli 81
Paonia 1,425
Peetz 220
Pierce 878
Pitkin 59
Platteville 1,662
Poncha Springs 321
Pritchett 183
Prospect Heights 34
Pueblo 101,686
Ramah 119
Rangely 2,113
Raymer 80
Red Cliff 409
Rico 76
Ridgway 369
Rifle 3,215
Rockvale 338
Rocky Ford 4,804
Romeo 308
Rosedale 38
Rye 232
Saguache 656
Salida 4,870
San Luis 842
Sanford 687
Sedgwick 258
Seibert 180
Severance 102
Sheridan 5,377
Sheridan Lake 87
Silt 923
Silver Cliff 280
Silver Plume 140
Silverthorne 989
Silverton 794
Simla 494
Snowmass Village 999
Springfield 1,657
Starkville 127
Steamboat Springs 5,098
Sterling 11,385
Stratton 705
Sugar City 306
Superior 208
Swink 668
Telluride 1,047
Thornton 40,343
Timnath 185
Trinidad 9,663
Two Buttes 84
Vail 2,261
Victor 265
Vilas 118
Vona 94
Walden 947
Walsenburg 3,945
Walsh 884
Ward 129
Wellington 1,215
Westcliffe 324
Westminster 50,211
Wheat Ridge 30,293
Wiggins 531
Wiley 425
Williamsburg 72
Windsor 4,277
Winter Park 480
Woodland Park 2,634
Wray 2,131
Yampa 472
Yuma 2,824

CONNECTICUT Population 3,107,576

METROPOLITAN AREAS

Bridgeport 395,455
Bristol 73,762
Danbury 146,405
Hartford 726,114
Meriden 57,118
New Britain 142,241
New Haven-West Haven 417,592
New London-Norwich 248,554 (223,568 in Conn.; 24,986 in R.I.)
Norwalk 126,692
Springfield-Chicopee-Holyoke (Mass.) 528,668 (520,195 in Mass.; 8,473 in Conn.)
Stamford 198,854
Waterbury 228,178

COUNTIES

Fairfield 807,143
Hartford 807,766
Litchfield 156,769
Middlesex 129,017
New Haven 761,337
New London 238,409
Tolland 114,823
Windham 92,312

CITIES, TOWNS, AND BOROUGHS

Andover 2,144▲
Ansonia 19,039
Ashford 3,221▲
Avon 11,201▲
Bantam 860
Barkhamsted 2,935▲
Beacon Falls 3,995▲
Berlin 15,121▲
Bethany 4,330▲
Bethel 16,004▲
Bethlehem 2,573▲
Bloomfield 18,608▲
Bolton 3,951▲
Bozrah 2,135▲
Branford 23,363▲
Bridgeport 142,546
Bridgewater 1,563▲
Bristol 57,370
Brookfield 12,872▲
Brooklyn 5,691▲
Burlington 5,660▲
Canaan 1,002▲
Canterbury 3,426▲
Canton 7,635▲
Chaplin 1,793▲
Cheshire 21,788▲
Chester 3,068▲
Clinton 11,195▲
Colchester 3,190 (7,761▲)
Colebrook 1,221▲
Columbia 3,386▲
Cornwall 1,288▲
Coventry 8,895▲
Cromwell 10,265▲
Danbury 60,470
Danielson 4,553
Darien 18,892▲
Deep River 3,994▲
Derby 12,346
Durham 5,143▲
East Granby 4,102▲
East Haddam 5,621▲
East Hampton 8,572▲
East Hartford 52,563▲
East Haven 25,028▲
East Lyme 13,870▲
East Windsor 8,925▲
Eastford 1,028▲
Easton 5,962▲
Ellington 9,711▲
Enfield 42,695▲
Essex 5,078▲
Fairfield 54,849▲
Farmington 16,407▲
Franklin 1,592▲
Glastonbury 24,327▲
Goshen 1,706▲
Granby 7,956▲
Greenwich 59,578▲
Griswold 8,967▲
Groton 10,086 (41,062▲)
Guilford 17,375▲
Haddam 6,383▲
Hamden 51,071▲
Hampton 1,322▲
Hartford 136,392
Hartland 1,416▲
Harwinton 4,889▲
Hebron 5,453▲
Jewett City 3,294
Kent 2,505▲
Killingly 14,519▲
Killingworth 3,976▲
Lebanon 4,762▲
Ledyard 13,735▲
Lisbon 3,279▲
Litchfield 1,489 (7,605▲)
Lyme 1,822▲
Madison 14,031▲
Manchester 49,761▲
Mansfield 20,634▲
Marlborough 4,746▲
Meriden 57,118
Middlebury 5,995▲
Middlefield 3,796▲
Middletown 39,040
Milford 49,101 (50,898▲)
Monroe 14,010▲
Montville 16,455▲
Morris 1,899▲
Naugatuck 26,456
New Britain 73,840
New Canaan 17,931▲
New Fairfield 11,260▲
New Hartford 4,884▲
New Haven 126,109
New London 28,842
New Milford 19,420▲
Newington 28,841▲
Newtown 2,022 (19,107▲)
Norfolk 2,156▲
North Branford 11,554▲
North Canaan 3,185▲
North Haven 22,080▲
North Stonington 4,219▲
Norwalk 77,767
Norwich 38,074
Old Lyme 6,159▲
Old Saybrook 9,287▲
Orange 13,237▲
Oxford 6,634▲
Plainfield 12,774▲
Plainville 16,401▲
Plymouth 10,732▲
Pomfret 2,775▲
Portland 8,383▲
Preston 4,644▲
Prospect 6,807▲
Putnam 6,855 (8,580▲)
Redding 7,272▲
Ridgefield 20,120▲
Rocky Hill 14,559▲
Roxbury 1,468▲
Salem 2,335▲
Salisbury 3,896▲
Scotland 1,072▲
Seymour 13,434▲
Sharon 2,623▲
Shelton 31,314
Sherman 2,281▲
Simsbury 21,161▲
Somers 8,473▲
South Windsor 17,198▲
Southbury 14,156▲
Southington 36,879▲
Sprague 2,996▲
Stafford 9,268▲
Stafford Springs 3,392
Stamford 102,453
Sterling 1,791▲
Stonington 1,228 (16,220▲)
Stratford 50,541▲
Suffield 9,294▲
Thomaston 6,276▲
Thompson 8,141▲
Tolland 9,694▲
Torrington 30,987
Trumbull 32,989▲
Union 546▲
Vernon 27,974▲
Voluntown 1,637▲
Wallingford 37,274▲
Warren 1,027▲
Washington 3,657▲
Waterbury 103,266
Waterford 17,843▲
Watertown 19,489▲
West Hartford 61,301▲
West Haven 53,184
Westbrook 5,216▲
Weston 8,284▲
Westport 25,290▲
Wethersfield 26,013▲
Willimantic 14,652
Willington 4,694▲
Wilton 15,351▲
Winchester 10,841▲
Windham 21,062▲
Windsor 25,204▲
Windsor Locks 12,190▲
Wolcott 13,008▲
Woodbridge 7,761▲
Woodbury 6,942▲
Woodmont 1,797
Woodstock 5,117▲

▲Entire town (township), including rural area.

DELAWARE Population 595,225

METROPOLITAN AREA

Wilmington 524,108 (399,002 in Del.; 64,676 in N.J.; 60,430 in Md.)

COUNTIES

Kent 98,219
New Castle 399,002
Sussex 98,004

CITIES AND TOWNS

Arden 516
Ardencroft 267
Ardentown 1,194
Bellefonte 1,279
Bethany Beach 330
Bethel 197
Blades 664
Bowers 198
Bridgeville 1,238
Camden 1,757
Cheswold 269
Clayton 1,216
Dagsboro 344
Delaware City 1,858
Delmar 948
Dover 23,512
Ellendale 361
Elsmere 6,493
Farmington 141
Felton 547
Fenwick Island 114
Frankford 686
Frederica 864
Georgetown 1,710
Greenwood 578
Harrington 2,405
Henlopen Acres 176
Houston 357
Kenton 243
Laurel 3,052
Leipsic 228
Lewes 2,197
Little Creek 230
Magnolia 197
Middletown 2,946
Milford 5,356
Millsboro 1,233
Millville 178
Milton 1,359
New Castle 4,907
Newark 25,247
Newport 1,167
Ocean View 495
Odessa 384
Rehoboth Beach 1,730
Seaford 5,256
Selbyville 1,251
Slaughter Beach 121
Smyrna 4,750
South Bethany 115
Townsend 386
Viola 167
Wilmington 70,195
Woodside 248
Wyoming 960

FLORIDA Population 9,739,992

METROPOLITAN AREAS

Bradenton 148,442
Daytona Beach 258,762
Fort Lauderdale-Hollywood 1,014,043
Fort Myers-Cape Coral 205,266
Gainesville 151,348
Jacksonville 737,519
Lakeland-Winter Haven 321,652
Melbourne-Titusville-Cocoa 272,959
Miami 1,625,979
Orlando 700,699
Panama City 97,740
Pensacola 289,782
Sarasota 202,251
Tallahassee 159,542
Tampa-St. Petersburg 1,569,492
West Palm Beach-Boca Raton 573,125

COUNTIES

Alachua 151,348
Baker 15,289
Bay 97,740
Bradford 20,023
Brevard 272,959
Broward 1,014,043
Calhoun 9,294
Charlotte 59,115
Citrus 54,703
Clay 67,052
Collier 85,791
Columbia 35,399
Dade 1,625,979
De Soto 19,039
Dixie 7,751
Duval 570,981
Escambia 233,794
Flagler 10,913
Franklin 7,661
Gadsden 41,565
Gilchrist 5,767
Glades 5,992
Gulf 10,658
Hamilton 8,761

FLORIDA (continued)

Hardee 19,379
Hendry 18,599
Hernando 44,469
Highlands 47,526
Hillsborough 646,960
Holmes 14,723
Indian River 59,896
Jackson 39,154
Jefferson 10,703
Lafayette 4,035
Lake 104,870
Lee 205,266
Leon 148,655
Levy 19,870
Liberty 4,260
Madison 14,894
Manatee 148,442
Marion 122,488
Martin 64,014
Monroe 63,098
Nassau 32,894
Okaloosa 109,920
Okeechobee 20,264
Orange 471,660
Osceola 49,287
Palm Beach 573,125
Pasco 194,123
Pinellas 728,409
Polk 321,652
Putnam 50,549
St. Johns 51,303
St. Lucie 87,182
Santa Rosa 55,988
Sarasota 202,251
Seminole 179,752
Sumter 24,272
Suwannee 22,287
Taylor 16,532
Union 10,166
Volusia 258,762
Wakulla 10,887
Walton 21,300
Washington 14,509

CITIES, TOWNS, AND VILLAGES

Alachua 3,561
Alford 548
Altamonte Springs 22,028
Altha 478
Anna Maria 1,537
Apalachicola 2,565
Apopka 6,019
Arcadia 6,002
Archer 1,230
Astatula 755
Atlantic Beach 7,847
Atlantis 1,325
Auburndale 6,501
Avon Park 8,026
Bal Harbour 2,575
Baldwin 1,526
Bartow 14,780
Bascom 134
Bay Harbor Islands 4,869
Bay Lake 74
Bell 227
Belle Glade 16,535
Belle Isle 2,848
Belleair 3,673
Belleair Beach 1,643
Belleair Bluffs 2,522
Belleair Shore 80
Belleview 1,913
Beverly Beach 217
Biscayne Park 3,088
Blountstown 2,632
Boca Raton 49,505
Bonifay 2,534
Bowling Green 2,310
Boynton Beach 35,624
Bradenton 30,170
Bradenton Beach 1,595
Branford 622
Briny Breezes 387
Bristol 1,044
Bronson 853
Brooker 429
Brooksville 5,582
Bunnell 1,816
Bushnell 983
Callahan 869
Callaway 7,154
Campbellton 336
Cape Canaveral 5,733
Cape Coral 32,103
Carrabelle 1,304
Caryville 633
Casselberry 15,247
Cedar Grove 1,104
Cedar Key 700
Center Hill 751
Century 495
Chattahoochee 5,332
Chiefland 1,986
Chipley 3,330
Cinco Bayou 202
Clearwater 85,450
Clermont 5,461
Clewiston 5,219
Cloud Lake 160
Cocoa 16,096
Cocoa Beach 10,926
Coconut Creek 6,288
Coleman 1,022
Cooper City 10,140
Coral Gables 43,241
Coral Springs 37,349
Cottondale 1,056
Crescent City 1,722
Crestview 7,617
Cross City 2,154
Crystal River 2,778
Dade City 4,923
Dania 11,811
Davenport 1,509
Davie 20,877
Daytona Beach 54,176
Daytona Beach Shores 1,324
Deerfield Beach 39,193
De Funiak Springs 5,563
De Land 15,354
Delray Beach 34,325
Dundee 2,227
Dunedin 30,203
Dunnellon 1,427
Eagle Lake 1,678
Eatonville 2,185
Ebro 233
Edgewater 6,726
Edgewood 1,034
El Portal 1,819
Esto 304
Eustis 9,453
Everglades 344
Fanning Springs 314
Fellsmere 1,161
Fernandina Beach 7,224
Flagler Beach 1,951
Florida City 6,174
Fort Lauderdale 153,256
Fort Meade 5,546
Fort Myers 36,638
Fort Pierce 33,802
Fort Walton Beach 20,829
Fort White 386
Freeport 669
Frostproof 2,995
Fruitland Park 2,259
Gainesville 81,371
Glen Ridge 235
Glen St. Mary 462
Golden Beach 612
Golf 110
Golfview 210
Graceville 2,918
Grand Ridge 591
Green Cove Springs 4,154
Greenacres City 8,843
Greensboro 562
Greenville 1,096
Greenwood 577
Gretna 1,448
Groveland 1,992
Gulf Breeze 5,478
Gulf Stream 475
Gulfport 11,180
Hacienda 126
Haines City 10,799
Hallandale 36,517
Hampton 466
Hastings 636
Havana 2,782
Haverhill 1,249
Hawthorne 1,303
Hialeah 145,254
Hialeah Gardens 2,700
High Springs 2,491
Highland Beach 2,030
Highland Park 184
Hillcrest Heights 177
Hilliard 1,869
Hillsboro Beach 1,554
Holly Hill 9,953
Hollywood 117,188
Holmes Beach 4,023
Homestead 20,668
Horseshoe Beach 304
Howey-in-the-Hills 626
Hypoluxo 573
Indialantic 2,883
Indian Creek 103
Indian Harbor Beach 5,967
Indian River Shores 1,254
Indian Rocks Beach 3,717
Indian Shores 1,012
Inglis 1,173
Interlachen 848
Inverness 4,095
Jacksonville 540,898
Jacksonville Beach 15,462
Jasper 2,093
Jay 633
Jennings 749
Juno Beach 1,142
Jupiter 9,868
Jupiter Inlet Beach Colony 378
Jupiter Island 364
Kenneth City 4,344
Key Colony Beach 977
Key West 24,292
Keystone Heights 1,056
Kissimmee 15,487
La Belle 2,287
La Crosse 170
Lady Lake 1,193
Lake Alfred 3,134
Lake Buena Vista 1,290
Lake Butler 1,830
Lake City 9,257
Lake Clarke Shores 3,174
Lake Hamilton 1,552
Lake Helen 2,047
Lake Mary 2,853
Lake Park 6,909
Lake Placid 963
Lake Wales 8,466
Lake Worth 27,048
Lakeland 47,406
Lantana 8,048
Largo 58,977
Lauderdale-by-the-Sea 2,639
Lauderdale Lakes 25,426
Lauderhill 37,271
Laurel Hill 610
Lawtey 692
Lazy Lake 31
Lee 297
Leesburg 13,191
Lighthouse Point 11,488
Live Oak 6,732
Long Key (Layton) 88
Longboat Key 4,843
Longwood 10,029
Lynn Haven 6,239
Macclenny 3,851
Madeira Beach 4,520
Madison 3,487
Maitland 8,763
Malabar 1,118
Malone 897
Manalapan 329
Mangonia Park 1,419
Margate 36,044
Marianna 7,074
Marineland 31
Mary Esther 3,530
Mascotte 1,112
Mayo 891
McIntosh 404
Medley 537
Melbourne 46,536
Melbourne Beach 2,713
Melbourne Village 1,004
Mexico Beach 632
Miami 346,931
Miami Beach 96,298
Miami Shores 9,244
Miami Springs 12,350
Micanopy 737
Milton 7,206
Minneola 851
Miramar 32,813
Monticello 2,994
Montverde 397
Moore Haven 1,250
Mount Dora 5,883
Mulberry 2,932
Naples 17,581
Neptune Beach 5,248
New Port Richey 11,196
New Smyrna Beach 13,557
Newberry 1,826
Niceville 8,543
Noma 113
North Bay Village 4,920
North Lauderdale 18,479
North Miami 42,566
North Miami Beach 36,481
North Palm Beach 11,344
North Port 6,205
North Redington Beach 1,156
Oak Hill 938
Oakland 658
Oakland Park 21,939
Ocala 37,170
Ocean Breeze Park 469
Ocean Ridge 1,355
Ocoee 7,803
Okeechobee 4,225
Oldsmar 2,608
Opa-locka 14,460
Orange City 2,795
Orange Park 8,766
Orchid 42
Orlando 128,394
Ormond Beach 21,378
Otter Creek 167
Oviedo 3,074
Pahokee 6,346
Painters Hill 40
Palatka 10,175
Palm Bay 18,560
Palm Beach 9,729
Palm Beach Gardens 14,407
Palm Beach Shores 1,232
Palm Shores 77
Palm Springs 8,166
Palmetto 8,637
Panama City 33,346
Panama City Beach 2,148
Parker 4,298
Parkland 545
Paxton 659
Pembroke Park 4,783
Pembroke Pines 35,776
Penney Farms 630
Pensacola 57,619
Perry 8,254
Pierson 1,085
Pinellas Park 32,811
Plant City 19,270
Plantation 48,501
Polk City 576
Pomona Park 791
Pompano Beach 52,618
Ponce de Leon 454
Ponce Inlet 1,003
Port Orange 18,756
Port Richey 2,165
Port St. Joe 4,027
Port St. Lucie 14,690
Punta Gorda 6,797
Quincy 8,591
Raiford 259
Reddick 657
Redington Beach 1,708
Redington Shores 2,114
Riviera Beach 26,596
Rockledge 11,877
Royal Palm Beach 3,423
Safety Harbor 6,461
St. Augustine 11,985
St. Augustine Beach 1,289
St. Cloud 7,840
St. Leo 899
St. Lucie 593
St. Marks 286
St. Petersburg 236,893
St. Petersburg Beach 9,354
San Antonio 529
Sanford 23,176
Sanibel 3,363
Sarasota 48,868
Satellite Beach 9,163
Sea Ranch Lakes 584
Sebastian 2,831
Sebring 8,736
Seminole 4,586
Sewalls Point 1,187
Shalimar 390
Sneads 1,690
Sopchoppy 444
South Bay 3,886
South Daytona 9,608
South Miami 10,884
South Palm Beach 1,304
South Pasadena 4,188
Springfield 7,220
Starke 5,306
Stuart 9,467
Sunrise 39,681
Surfside 3,763
Sweetwater 8,251
Tallahassee 81,548
Tamarac 29,142
Tampa 271,523
Tarpon Springs 13,251
Tavares 4,103
Temple Terrace 11,097
Tequesta 3,685
Titusville 31,910
Treasure Island 6,316
Trenton 1,131
Umatilla 1,872
Valparaiso 6,142
Venice 12,153
Vernon 885
Vero Beach 16,176
Virginia Gardens 1,742
Waldo 993
Ward Ridge 104
Wauchula 2,986
Wausau 347
Webster 856
Welaka 492
West Melbourne 5,078
West Miami 6,076
West Palm Beach 62,530
Westville 343
Wewahitchka 1,742
White Springs 781
Wildwood 2,665
Williston 2,240
Wilton Manors 12,742
Windermere 1,302
Winter Garden 6,789
Winter Haven 21,119
Winter Park 22,314
Winter Springs 10,475
Worthington Springs 220
Yankeetown 600
Zephyrhills 5,742
Zolfo Springs 1,495

GEORGIA

Population 5,464,265

METROPOLITAN AREAS

Albany 112,662
Atlanta 2,029,618
Augusta 327,372 (221,747 in Ga.; 105,625 in S.C.)
Chattanooga (Tenn.) 426,540 (320,761 in Tenn.; 105,779 in Ga.)
Columbus 239,196 (191,840 in Ga.; 47,356 in Ala.)
Macon 254,623
Savannah 230,728

COUNTIES

Appling 15,565
Atkinson 6,141
Bacon 9,379
Baker 3,808
Baldwin 34,686
Banks 8,702
Barrow 21,293
Bartow 40,760
Ben Hill 16,000
Berrien 13,525
Bibb 151,085
Bleckley 10,767
Brantley 8,701
Brooks 15,255
Bryan 10,175
Bulloch 35,785
Burke 19,349
Butts 13,665
Calhoun 5,717
Camden 13,371
Candler 7,518
Carroll 56,346
Catoosa 36,991
Charlton 7,343
Chatham 202,226
Chattahoochee 21,732
Chattooga 21,856
Cherokee 51,699
Clarke 74,498
Clay 3,553
Clayton 150,357
Clinch 6,660
Cobb 297,694
Coffee 26,894
Colquitt 35,376
Columbia 40,118
Cook 13,490
Coweta 39,268
Crawford 7,684
Crisp 19,489
Dade 12,318
Dawson 4,774
Decatur 25,495
DeKalb 483,024
Dodge 16,955
Dooly 10,826
Dougherty 100,978
Douglas 54,573
Early 13,158
Echols 2,297
Effingham 18,327
Elbert 18,758
Emanuel 20,795
Evans 8,428
Fannin 14,748
Fayette 29,043
Floyd 79,800
Forsyth 27,958
Franklin 15,185
Fulton 589,904
Gilmer 11,110
Glascock 2,382
Glynn 54,981
Gordon 30,070
Grady 19,845
Greene 11,391
Gum Branch 272
Gwinnett 166,903
Habersham 25,020
Hall 75,649
Hancock 9,466
Haralson 18,422
Harris 15,464
Hart 18,585
Heard 6,520
Henry 36,309
Houston 77,605
Industrial City 1,054
Irwin 8,988
Jackson 25,343
Jasper 7,553
Jeff Davis 11,473
Jefferson 18,403
Jenkins 8,841
Johnson 8,660
Jones 16,579
Lamar 12,215
Lanier 5,654
Laurens 36,990
Lee 11,684
Liberty 37,583
Lincoln 6,949
Long 4,524
Lowndes 67,972
Lumpkin 10,762
Macon 14,003
Madison 17,747
Marion 5,297
McDuffie 18,546
McIntosh 8,046
Meriwether 21,229
Miller 7,038
Mitchell 21,114
Monroe 14,610
Montgomery 7,011
Morgan 11,572
Murray 19,685
Muscogee 170,108
Newton 34,489
Oconee 12,427
Oglethorpe 8,929
Paulding 26,042
Peach 19,151
Pickens 11,652
Pierce 11,897
Pike 8,937
Polk 32,386
Pulaski 8,950
Putnam 10,295
Quitman 2,357
Rabun 10,466
Randolph 9,599
Richmond 181,629
Rockdale 36,747
Schley 3,433
Screven 14,043
Seminole 9,057
Spalding 47,899
Stephens 21,763
Stewart 5,896
Sumter 29,360
Talbot 6,536
Taliaferro 2,032
Tattnall 18,134
Taylor 7,902
Telfair 11,445
Terrell 12,017
Thomas 38,098
Tift 32,862
Toombs 22,592
Towns 5,638
Treutlen 6,087
Troup 50,003
Turner 9,510
Twiggs 9,354
Union 9,390
Upson 25,998
Walker 56,470
Walton 31,211
Ware 37,180
Warren 6,583
Washington 18,842
Wayne 20,750
Webster 2,341
Wheeler 5,155
White 10,120
Whitfield 65,780
Wilcox 7,682
Wilkes 10,951
Wilkinson 10,368
Worth 18,064

CITIES, TOWNS, AND VILLAGES

Abbeville 985
Acworth 3,648
Adairsville 1,739
Adel 5,592
Adrian 756
Ailey 579
Alamo 993
Alapaha 771
Albany 73,934
Aldora 139
Allenhurst 606
Allentown 321
Alma 3,819
Alpharetta 3,128
Alston 111
Alto 618
Alvaton 91
Ambrose 360
Americus 16,120
Andersonville 267
Arabi 376
Aragon 855
Arcade 223
Argyle 206
Arlington 1,572
Arnoldsville 187
Ashburn 4,766

Athens 42,549
Atlanta 425,022
Attapulgus 623
Auburn 692
Augusta 47,532
Austell 3,939
Avalon 200
Avera 248
Avondale Estates 1,313
Baconton 763
Bainbridge 10,553
Baldwin 1,080
Ball Ground 640
Barnesville 4,887
Barney 146
Bartow 357
Barwick 413
Baxley 3,586
Bellville 173
Benevolence 138
Berkeley Lake 503
Berlin 538
Bethlehem 281
Between 87
Bibb City 667
Bishop 172
Blackshear 3,222
Blairsville 530
Blakely 5,880
Bloomingdale 1,855
Blue Ridge 1,376
Bluffton 132
Blythe 367
Bogart 819
Boston 1,424
Bostwick 357
Bowdon 1,743
Bowersville 318
Bowman 890
Braselton 308
Braswell 282
Bremen 3,966
Brinson 274
Bronwood 524
Brooklet 1,035
Brooks 199
Broxton 1,117
Brunswick 17,605
Buchanan 1,019
Buckhead 219
Buena Vista 1,544
Buford 6,697
Butler 1,959
Byromville 567
Byron 1,661
Cadwell 353
Cairo 8,777
Calhoun 5,335
Camak 283
Camilla 5,414
Canon 704
Canton 3,601
Carl 239
Carlton 291
Carnesville 465
Carrollton 14,078
Cartersville 9,508
Cave Springs 883
Cecil 280
Cedartown 8,619
Center 330
Centerville 2,622
Centralhatchee 240
Chalybeate Springs 265
Chamblee 7,137
Chatsworth 2,493
Chauncey 350
Chester 409
Chickamauga 2,232
Clarkesville 1,348
Clarkston 4,539
Claxton 2,694
Clayton 1,838
Clermont 300
Cleveland 1,578
Climax 407
Cobbtown 494
Cochran 5,121
Cohutta 407
Colbert 498
Coleman 164
College Park 24,632
Collins 639
Colquitt 2,065
Columbus 169,441
Comer 930
Commerce 4,092
Concord 317
Conyers 6,567
Coolidge 736
Cordele 10,914
Corinth 75
Cornelia 3,203
Cotton 122
Covington 10,586
Crawford 498
Crawfordville 594
Culloden 281
Cumming 2,094
Cusseta 1,218
Cuthbert 4,340
Dacula 1,577
Dahlonega 2,844
Daisy 174
Dallas 2,440
Dalton 20,743
Damascus 403
Danielsville 354
Danville 529
Darien 1,731
Dasher 659
Davisboro 433
Dawson 5,699
Dawsonville 342
Dearing 539
Decatur 18,404
Deepstep 120
Demorest 1,130
Denton 286
De Soto 248
Dexter 527
Dillard 238
Dixie 259
Doerun 1,062
Donalsonville 3,320
Doraville 7,414
Douglas 10,980
Douglasville 7,641
Dublin 16,083
Dudley 425
Duluth 2,956
Du Pont 267
Durand 206
East Dublin 2,916
East Ellijay 469
East Point 37,486
Eastman 5,330
Eatonton 4,833
Edge Hill 53
Edison 1,128
Elberton 5,686
Ellaville 1,684
Ellenton 277
Ellijay 1,507
Emerson 1,110
Enigma 574
Ephesus 184
Eton 301
Euharlee 477
Fairburn 3,466
Fairmount 842
Fayetteville 2,715
Finleyson 101
Fitzgerald 10,187
Flemington 440
Flovilla 458
Flowery Branch 755
Folkston 2,243
Forest Park 18,782
Forsyth 4,624
Fort Gaines 1,260
Fort Oglethorpe 5,443
Fort Valley 9,000
Franklin 711
Franklin Springs 797
Funston 337
Gainesville 15,280
Garden City 6,895
Garfield 222
Gay 175
Geneva 232
Georgetown 935
Gibson 730
Gillsville 142
Girard 225
Glennville 4,144
Glenwood 824
Good Hope 200
Gordon 2,768
Grantville 1,110
Gray 2,145
Grayson 464
Graysville 193
Greensboro 2,985
Greenville 1,213
Griffin 20,728
Grovetown 3,491
Guyton 749
Hagan 880
Hahira 1,534
Hamilton 506
Hampton 2,059
Hapeville 6,166
Haralson 123
Harlem 1,485
Harrison 456
Hartwell 4,855
Hawkinsville 4,372
Hazlehurst 4,249
Helen 265
Helena 1,390
Hephzibah 1,452
Hiawassee 491
Higgston 152
Hiltonia 515
Hinesville 11,309
Hiram 711
Hoboken 514
Hogansville 3,362
Holly Springs 687
Homeland 683
Homer 734
Homerville 3,112
Hoschton 490
Hull 188
Ideal 619
Ila 287
Iron City 367
Irwinton 841
Ivey 455
Jackson 4,133
Jacksonville 206
Jakin 194
Jasper 1,556
Jefferson 1,820
Jeffersonville 1,473
Jenkinsburg 360
Jersey 201
Jesup 9,418
Jonesboro 4,132
Junction City 254
Kennesaw 5,095
Kingsland 2,008
Kingston 733
Kite 328
La Fayette 6,517
La Grange 24,204
Lake City 2,963
Lake Park 448
Lakeland 2,647
Lavonia 2,024
Lawrenceville 8,928
Leary 783
Leesburg 1,301
Lenox 965
Leslie 470
Lexington 278
Lilburn 3,765
Lilly 202
Lincolnton 1,406
Linwood 417
Lithonia 2,637
Locust Grove 1,479
Loganville 1,841
Lone Oak 119
Lookout Mountain 1,505
Louisville 2,823
Lovejoy 205
Ludowici 1,286
Lula 857
Lumber City 1,426
Lumpkin 1,335
Luthersville 597
Lyerly 482
Lyons 4,203
Macon 116,860
Madison 2,954
Manassas 116
Manchester 4,796
Mansfield 435
Marietta 30,805
Marshallville 1,540
Martin 305
Maxeys 205
Maysville 619
McCaysville 1,219
McDonough 2,778
McIntyre 386
McRae 3,409
Meansville 303
Meigs 1,231
Menlo 611
Metter 3,531
Midville 670
Midway 457
Milan 1,115
Milledgeville 12,176
Millen 3,988
Milner 320
Mineral Bluff 130
Mitchell 214
Molena 379
Monroe 8,854
Montezuma 4,830
Monticello 2,382
Montrose 170
Moreland 358
Morgan 364
Morganton 263
Morrow 3,791
Morven 471
Moultrie 15,708
Mount Airy 670
Mount Vernon 1,737
Mount Zion 445
Mountain City 701
Mountain Park 378
Mountville 168
Nahunta 951
Nashville 4,831
Naylor 228
Nelson 562
Newborn 391
Newington 402
Newnan 11,449
Newton 711
Nicholls 1,114
Nicholson 491
Norcross 3,317
Norman Park 757
North High Shoals 256
Norwood 306
Nunez 168
Oak Park 256
Oakfield 113
Oakman 150
Oakwood 723
Ochlocknee 627
Ocilla 3,436
Oconee 306
Odessadale 142
Odum 401
Oglethorpe 1,305
Oliver 239
Omaha 169
Omega 996
Orchard Hill 162
Oxford 1,750
Palmetto 2,086
Parrott 222
Patterson 763
Pavo 830
Payne 196
Peachtree City 6,429
Pearson 1,827
Pelham 4,306
Pembroke 1,400
Pendergrass 302
Perry 9,453
Pine Lake 901
Pine Mountain 984
Pinehurst 431
Pineora 387
Pineview 564
Pitts 384
Plainfield 128
Plains 651
Plainville 281
Pooler 2,543
Port Wentworth 3,947
Portal 694
Porterdale 1,451
Poulan 818
Powder Springs 3,381
Preston 429
Primrose 30
Pulaski 257
Quitman 5,188
Ranger 171
Ray City 658
Rayle 177
Rebecca 272
Reidsville 2,296
Remerton 443
Rentz 337
Rest Haven 231
Reynolds 1,298
Rhine 590
Riceboro 216
Richland 1,802
Richmond Hill 1,177
Riddleville 154
Rincon 1,988
Ringgold 1,821
Riverdale 7,121
Riverside 99
Roberta 859
Rochelle 1,626
Rock, The 78
Rockmart 3,645
Rocky Ford 223
Rocky Mount 56
Rome 29,654
Roopville 229
Rossville 3,749
Roswell 23,337
Royston 2,404
Russell 378
Rutledge 694
St. Marks 36
St. Marys 3,596
Sale City 336
Sandersville 6,137
Santa Claus 167
Sardis 1,180
Sasser 407
Savannah 141,634
Scotland 222
Scott 139
Screven 872
Senoia 900
Seville 209
Shady Dale 155
Sharon 140
Sharpsburg 194
Shellman 1,254
Shiloh 392
Siloam 446
Sky Valley 65
Smithville 867
Smyrna 20,312
Snellville 8,514
Social Circle 2,591
Soperton 2,981
Sparks 1,353
Sparta 1,754
Spring Place 246
Springfield 1,075
Stapleton 388
Statesboro 14,866
Statham 1,101
Stillmore 527
Stockbridge 2,103
Stone Mountain 4,867
Sugar Hill 2,340
Summertown 215
Summerville 4,878
Sumner 213
Sunny Side 338
Surrency 368
Suwanee 1,026
Swainsboro 7,602
Sycamore 474
Sylvania 3,352
Sylvester 5,860
Talbotton 1,140
Talking Rock 72
Tallapoosa 2,647
Tallulah Falls 162
Tarrytown 145
Taylorsville 266
Temple 1,520
Tennille 1,709
Thomaston 9,682
Thomasville 18,463
Thomson 7,001
Thunderbolt 2,165
Tifton 13,749
Tiger 299
Tignall 733
Toccoa 9,104
Toomsboro 673
Trenton 1,636
Trion 1,732
Tunnel Hill 867
Turin 260
Twin City 1,402
Ty Ty 618
Tybee Island 2,240
Tyrone 1,038
Unadilla 1,566
Union City 4,780
Union Point 1,750
Uvalda 646
Valdosta 37,596
Van Wert 303
Varnell 288
Vernonburg 178
Vidalia 10,393
Vienna 2,886
Villa Rica 3,420
Waco 471
Wadley 2,438
Waleska 450
Walnut Grove 387
Walthourville 905
Warm Springs 425
Warner Robins 39,893
Warrenton 2,172
Warwick 488
Washington 4,662
Watkinsville 1,240
Waverly Hall 913
Waycross 19,371
Waynesboro 5,760
West Point 4,294
Weston 109
Whigham 507
White 501
White Plains 231
White Sulphur Springs 118
Whitesburg 775
Willacoochee 1,166
Williamson 250
Winder 6,705
Winterville 621
Woodbine 910
Woodbury 1,738
Woodland 664
Woodstock 2,699
Woodville 455
Woolsey 99
Wrens 2,415
Wrightsville 2,526
Yatesville 390
Young Harris 687
Zebulon 995

HAWAII

Population 965,000

METROPOLITAN AREA

Honolulu 762,874

COUNTIES

Hawaii 92,053
Honolulu 762,874
Kalawao 144
Kauai 39,082
Maui 70,847

ISLANDS

Hawaii 92,053
Kauai 38,856
Lanai 2,119
Maui 62,823
Molokai 6,049
Niihau 226

Oahu (including outlying islands) 762,874

CITIES, TOWNS, AND VILLAGES

Ahuimanu 6,238
Aiea 32,879
Anahola 915
Barbers Point Housing 1,373
Captain Cook 2,008
Eleele 580
Ewa 2,637
Ewa Beach 14,369
Haiku 619
Hakalau 249
Haleiwa 2,412
Haliimaile 741
Hana 643
Hanalei 483
Hanamaulu 3,227
Hanapepe 1,417
Hauula 2,997
Hawi 795
Heeia 5,432
Hickam Housing 4,425
Hilo 35,269
Holualoa 1,243
Honokaa 1,936
Honokahua 309
Honolulu 365,048
Honomu 559
Iroquois Point 3,915
Kaaawa 959
Kaanapali 541
Kahaluu 2,925
Kahuku 935
Kahului 12,978
Kailua 4,751
Kailua 35,812
Kainaliu 512
Kalaheo 2,500
Kaneohe 29,919
Kapaa 4,467
Kapaau 612
Kaumakani 888
Kaunakakai 2,231
Keaau 775
Kealakekua 1,033
Kekaha 3,260
Kihei 5,644
Kilauea 895
Koloa 1,457
Kualapuu 502
Kukuihaele 332
Lahaina 6,095
Laie 4,643
Lanai City 2,092
Laupahoehoe 500
Lihue 4,000
Lower Paia 1,500
Maili 5,026
Makaha 7,905
Makakilo City 7,691
Makapala 191
Makawao 2,900
Maunaloa 633
Maunawili 5,276
Mililani Town 20,351
Mokapu 11,578
Mountain View 540
Naalehu 1,168
Nanakuli 8,185
Napili-Honokowai 2,446
Ookala 401
Paauilo 755
Pahala 1,619
Pahoa 923
Paia 193
Papaaloa 267
Papaikou 1,567
Paukaa 544
Pauwela 468
Pearl City 42,575
Poipu 685
Princeville 500
Puhi 991
Pukalani 3,950
Puunene 572
Schofield Barracks 18,851
Wahiawa 15,137
Waialua 4,051
Waianae 7,941
Waihee 413
Waikapu 698
Wailea 1,124
Wailua 1,587
Wailuku 10,260
Waimanalo 3,562
Waimanalo Beach 4,161
Waimea 1,179
Waimea 1,569
Wainaku 1,045
Waipahu 29,139
Waipio Acres 4,091
Whitmore Village 2,318

IDAHO

Population 943,935

METROPOLITAN AREA

Boise 173,036

COUNTIES

Ada 173,036
Adams 3,347
Bannock 65,421
Bear Lake 6,931
Benewah 8,292
Bingham 36,489
Blaine 9,841
Boise 2,999
Bonner 24,163
Bonneville 65,980
Boundary 7,289
Butte 3,342
Camas 818

IDAHO (continued)

Canyon 83,756
Caribou 8,695
Cassia 19,427
Clark 798
Clearwater 10,390
Custer 3,385
Elmore 21,565
Franklin 8,895
Fremont 10,813
Gem 11,972
Gooding 11,874
Idaho 14,769
Jefferson 15,304
Jerome 14,840
Kootenai 59,770
Latah 28,749
Lemhi 7,460
Lewis 4,118
Lincoln 3,436
Madison 19,480
Minidoka 19,718
Nez Perce 33,220
Oneida 3,258
Owyhee 8,272
Payette 15,722
Power 6,844
Shoshone 19,226
Teton 2,897
Twin Falls 52,927
Valley 5,604
Washington 8,803

CITIES AND TOWNS

Aberdeen 1,528
Acequia 100
Albion 286
American Falls 3,626
Ammon 4,669
Arco 1,241
Arimo 338
Ashton 1,219
Athol 312
Atomic City 34
Bancroft 505
Basalt 414
Bellevue 1,016
Blackfoot 10,065
Bliss 208
Bloomington 212
Boise 102,451
Bonners Ferry 1,906
Bovill 289
Buhl 3,629
Burley 8,761
Butte City 93
Caldwell 17,699
Cambridge 428
Cascade 945
Castleford 191
Challis 758
Chatcolet 181
Chubbuck 7,052
Clark Fork 449
Clayton 43
Clifton 208
Coeur d'Alene 20,054
Cottonwood 941
Council 917
Craigmont 617
Crouch 69
Culdesac 261
Dalton Gardens 1,795
Dayton 368
Deary 539
Declo 276
Dietrich 101
Donnelly 139
Downey 645
Driggs 727
Drummond 25
Dubois 413
Eagle 2,620
East Hope 258
Eden 355
Elk River 265
Emmett 4,605
Fairfield 404
Ferdinand 144
Fernan Lake 178
Filer 1,645
Firth 460
Franklin 423
Fruitland 2,456
Garden City 4,571
Genesee 791
Georgetown 544
Glenns Ferry 1,374
Gooding 2,949
Grace 1,216
Grand View 366
Grangeville 3,666
Greenleaf 663
Hagerman 602
Hailey 2,109
Hamer 93
Hansen 1,078
Harrison 260
Hauser 305
Hayden 2,586
Hayden Lake 273
Hazelton 496
Heyburn 2,889
Hollister 167
Homedale 2,078
Hope 106
Horseshoe Bend 700
Huetter 65
Idaho City 300
Idaho Falls 39,590
Inkom 830
Iona 1,072
Irwin 113
Island Park 154
Jerome 6,891
Juliaetta 522
Kamiah 1,478
Kellogg 3,417
Kendrick 395
Ketchum 2,200
Kimberly 2,307
Kooskia 784
Kootenai 280
Kuna 1,767
Lapwai 1,043
Lava Hot Springs 467
Leadore 114
Lewiston 27,986
Lewisville 502
Lost River 28
Mackay 541
Malad City 1,915
Malta 196
Marsing 786
McCall 2,188
McCammon 770
Melba 276
Menan 605
Meridian 6,658
Middleton 1,901
Midvale 205
Minidoka 101
Montpelier 3,107
Moore 210
Moscow 16,513
Mountain Home 7,540
Moyie Springs 386
Mud Lake 243
Mullan 1,269
Murtaugh 114
Nampa 25,112
New Meadows 576
New Plymouth 1,186
Newdale 329
Nezperce 517
Notus 437
Oakley 663
Oldtown 257
Onaway 254
Orofino 3,711
Osburn 2,220
Oxford 66
Paris 707
Parker 262
Parma 1,820
Paul 940
Payette 5,448
Peck 209
Pierce 1,060
Pinehurst 2,183
Placerville 20
Plummer 634
Pocatello 46,340
Ponderay 399
Post Falls 5,736
Potlatch 819
Preston 3,759
Priest River 1,639
Rathdrum 1,369
Reubens 87
Rexburg 11,559
Richfield 357
Rigby 2,624
Riggins 527
Ririe 555
Roberts 466
Rockland 283
Rupert 5,476
St. Anthony 3,212
St. Charles 211
St. Maries 2,794
Salmon 3,308
Sandpoint 4,460
Shelley 3,300
Shoshone 1,242
Smelterville 776
Soda Springs 4,051
Spencer 29
Spirit Lake 834
Stanley 99
State Line 26
Stites 253
Sugar City 1,022
Sun Valley 545
Swan Valley 135
Tensed 113
Teton 559
Tetonia 191
Troy 820
Twin Falls 26,209
Ucon 833
Victor 323
Wallace 1,736
Wardner 423
Weippe 828
Weiser 4,771
Wendell 1,974
Weston 310
White Bird 154
Wilder 1,260
Winchester 343
Worley 206

ILLINOIS

Population 11,418,461

METROPOLITAN AREAS

Bloomington-Normal 119,149
Champaign-Urbana-Rantoul 168,392
Chicago 7,102,328
Davenport (Ia.)-Rock Island-Moline 383,958 (223,936 in Ill.; 160,022 in Ia.)
Decatur 131,375
Kankakee 102,926
Peoria 365,864
Rockford 279,514
St. Louis (Mo.) 2,355,276 (1,789,402 in Mo.; 565,874 in Ill.)
Springfield 187,789

COUNTIES

Adams 71,622
Alexander 12,264
Bond 16,224
Boone 28,630
Brown 5,411
Bureau 39,114
Calhoun 5,867
Carroll 18,779
Cass 15,084
Champaign 168,392
Christian 36,446
Clark 16,913
Clay 15,283
Clinton 32,617
Coles 52,992
Cook 5,253,190
Crawford 20,818
Cumberland 11,062
De Kalb 74,624
De Witt 18,108
Douglas 19,774
Du Page 658,177
Edgar 21,725
Edwards 7,961
Effingham 30,944
Fayette 22,167
Ford 15,265
Franklin 43,201
Fulton 43,687
Gallatin 7,590
Greene 16,661
Grundy 30,582
Hamilton 9,172
Hancock 23,877
Hardin 5,383
Henderson 9,114
Henry 57,968
Iroquois 32,976
Jackson 61,522
Jasper 11,318
Jefferson 36,354
Jersey 20,538
Jo Daviess 23,520
Johnson 9,624
Kane 278,405
Kankakee 102,926
Kendall 37,202
Knox 61,607
Lake 440,372
La Salle 109,139
Lawrence 17,807
Lee 36,328
Livingston 41,381
Logan 31,802
Macon 131,375
Macoupin 49,384
Madison 247,671
Marion 43,523
Marshall 14,479
Mason 19,492
Massac 14,990
McDonough 37,236
McHenry 147,724
McLean 119,149
Menard 11,700
Mercer 19,286
Monroe 20,117
Montgomery 31,686
Morgan 37,502
Moultrie 14,546
Ogle 46,338
Peoria 200,466
Perry 21,714
Piatt 16,581
Pike 18,896
Pope 4,404
Pulaski 8,840
Putnam 6,085
Randolph 35,566
Richland 17,587
Rock Island 165,968
St. Clair 265,469
Saline 27,360
Sangamon 176,089
Schuyler 8,365
Scott 6,142
Shelby 23,923
Stark 7,389
Stephenson 49,536
Tazewell 132,078
Union 16,851
Vermilion 95,222
Wabash 13,713
Warren 21,943
Washington 15,472
Wayne 18,059
White 17,864
Whiteside 65,970
Will 324,460
Williamson 56,538
Winnebago 250,884
Woodford 33,320

CITIES, TOWNS, AND VILLAGES

Abingdon 4,210
Addison 28,836
Albany 1,014
Albers 663
Albion 2,285
Aledo 3,881
Alexis 1,076
Algonquin 5,834
Alhambra 643
Allendale 613
Alorton 2,237
Alpha 815
Alsip 17,134
Altamont 2,389
Alton 34,171
Altona 610
Amboy 2,377
Andalusia 1,238
Andover 612
Anna 5,408
Annawan 908
Antioch 4,419
Arcola 2,714
Argenta 994
Arlington Heights 66,116
Aroma Park 673
Arthur 2,122
Ashkum 735
Ashland 1,351
Ashley 658
Ashmore 883
Ashton 1,140
Assumption 1,283
Astoria 1,370
Athens 1,371
Atkinson 1,138
Atlanta 1,807
Atwood 1,464
Auburn 3,616
Augusta 764
Aurora 81,293
Ava 811
Aviston 846
Avon 1,019
Bannockburn 1,316
Barrington 9,029
Barrington Hills 3,631
Barry 1,487
Bartlett 13,254
Bartonville 6,110
Batavia 12,574
Beardstown 6,338
Beckemeyer 1,119
Bedford Park 988
Beecher 2,024
Belgium 568
Belleville 42,150
Bellevue 2,045
Bellwood 19,811
Belvidere 15,176
Bement 1,770
Benld 1,638
Bensenville 16,124
Benton 7,778
Berkeley 5,467
Berwyn 46,849
Bethalto 8,630
Bethany 1,550
Blandinsville 886
Bloomingdale 12,659
Bloomington 44,189
Blue Island 21,855
Blue Mound 1,338
Bluffs 821
Bluford 728
Bolingbrook 37,261
Bourbonnais 13,280
Braceville 721
Bradford 924
Bradley 11,008
Braidwood 3,429
Breese 3,516
Bridgeport 2,281
Bridgeview 14,155
Brighton 2,364
Brimfield 890
Broadview 8,618
Brookfield 19,395
Brooklyn 1,233
Brookport 1,128
Brownstown 708
Buckley 604
Buda 668
Buffalo Grove 22,230
Bunker Hill 1,700
Burbank 28,462
Burnham 4,030
Burr Ridge 3,833
Bushnell 3,811
Byron 2,035
Cahokia 18,904
Cairo 5,931
Calumet City 39,673
Calumet Park 8,788
Cambria 1,090
Cambridge 2,217
Camp Point 1,285
Canton 14,626
Capron 678
Carbon Cliff 1,578
Carbondale 27,194
Carlinville 5,439
Carlyle 3,388
Carmi 6,264
Carol Stream 15,472
Carpentersville 23,272
Carrier Mills 2,268
Carrollton 2,816
Carterville 3,445
Carthage 2,978
Cary 6,640
Casey 3,026
Caseyville 4,308
Catlin 2,226
Cedarville 766
Central City 1,505
Centralia 15,126
Centreville 9,747
Cerro Gordo 1,553
Chadwick 631
Champaign 58,133
Chandlerville 842
Channahon 3,734
Chapin 648
Charleston 19,355
Chatham 5,597
Chatsworth 1,187
Chebanse 1,191
Chenoa 1,847
Cherry 541
Cherry Valley 946
Chester 8,027
Chicago 3,005,072
Chicago Heights 37,026
Chicago Ridge 13,473
Chillicothe 6,176
Chrisman 1,413
Christopher 3,086
Cicero 61,232
Cisne 705
Cissna Park 825
Clarendon Hills 6,857
Clay City 1,038
Clayton 889
Clifton 1,390
Clinton 8,014
Coal City 3,028
Coal Valley 3,800
Cobden 571
Coffeen 842
Colchester 1,729
Colfax 920
Collinsville 19,613
Colona 2,172
Columbia 4,269
Cordova 697
Cornell 603
Cortland 1,019
Coulterville 1,118
Country Club Hills 14,676
Countryside 6,538
Cowden 623
Crainville 910
Creal Springs 845
Crescent City 641
Crest Hill 9,252
Crestwood 10,712
Crete 5,417
Creve Coeur 6,851
Crossville 944
Crystal Lake 18,590
Cuba 1,648
Cullom 608
Dakota 571
Dallas City 1,408
Dalton City 574
Dalzell 824
Danforth 554
Danvers 921
Danville 38,985
Darien 14,968
Davis 560
Decatur 94,081
Deer Creek 688
Deer Park 1,368
Deerfield 17,430
De Kalb 33,099
Delavan 1,973
Depue 1,873
De Soto 1,589
Des Plaines 53,568
Diamond 1,170
Dieterich 633
Divernon 1,081
Dixmoor 4,175
Dixon 15,659
Dolton 24,766
Dongola 611
Downers Grove 39,274
Downs 561
Dunlap 824
Dupo 3,039
Du Quoin 6,594
Durand 1,073
Dwight 4,146
Earlville 1,382
East Alton 7,123
East Cape Girardeau 539
East Carondelet 628
East Chicago Heights 5,347
East Dubuque 2,194
East Dundee 2,618
East Galesburg 928
East Hazel Crest 1,362
East Moline 20,907
East Peoria 22,385
East St. Louis 55,200
Edgewood 574
Edinburg 1,231
Edwardsville 12,460
Effingham 11,270
Eileen 569
Elburn 1,224
Eldorado 5,198
Elgin 63,798
Elizabeth 772
Elizabethtown 478
Elk Grove Village 28,907
Elkville 973
Elmhurst 44,251
Elmwood 2,117
Elmwood Park 24,016
El Paso 2,676
Elsah 990
Elwood 814
Energy 1,138
Enfield 890
Equality 831
Erie 1,725
Eureka 4,306
Evanston 73,706
Evansville 863
Evergreen Park 22,260
Fairbury 3,544
Fairfield 5,954
Fairmont City 2,313
Fairmount 851
Fairview 594
Fairview Heights 12,414
Farina 594
Farmer City 2,252
Farmersville 686
Farmington 3,118
Findlay 868
Fisher 1,572
Fithian 540
Flanagan 978
Flora 5,379
Flossmoor 8,423
Forest Park 15,177
Forest View 764
Forrest 1,246
Forreston 1,384
Forsyth 1,072
Fox Lake 6,831
Fox River Grove 2,515
Fox River Valley Gardens 541
Frankfort 4,357
Franklin 645
Franklin Grove 965
Franklin Park 17,507
Freeburg 2,989
Freeport 26,406
Fulton 3,936
Galatia 1,042
Galena 3,876
Galesburg 35,305
Galva 3,185
Gardner 1,322
Geneseo 6,373
Geneva 9,881
Genoa 3,276
Georgetown 4,220
Germantown 1,191
Gibson City 3,498
Gifford 848
Gillespie 3,740
Gilman 1,913
Girard 2,246
Glasford 1,201
Glen Carbon 5,197
Glen Ellyn 23,649
Glencoe 9,200
Glendale Heights 23,163
Glenview 30,842
Glenwood 10,538
Golconda 960
Golden 558
Goreville 978
Grafton 1,024
Grand Ridge 684
Grand Tower 748
Grandview 1,794
Granite City 36,815
Grant Park 1,038
Granville 1,537
Grayslake 5,260
Grayville 2,313
Green Oaks 1,415
Green Rock 3,324
Green Valley 768
Greenfield 1,090
Greenup 1,655
Greenview 830
Greenville 5,271
Gridley 1,246
Griggsville 1,301
Gurnee 7,179
Hamilton 3,509
Hammond 556
Hampshire 1,735
Hampton 1,873
Hanna City 1,361
Hanover 1,069
Hanover Park 28,850
Hardin 1,107
Harrisburg 9,322
Harristown 1,456
Hartford 1,887
Harvard 5,126
Harvey 35,810
Harwood Heights 8,228
Havana 2,682
Hawthorn Woods 1,658
Hazel Crest 13,973
Hebron 786
Hennepin 716

Henry 2,740
Herrin 10,040
Herscher 1,214
Heyworth 1,598
Hickory Hills 13,778
Highland 7,122
Highland Park 30,611
Highwood 5,452
Hillcrest 818
Hillsboro 4,408
Hillsdale 731
Hillside 8,279
Hinckley 1,447
Hinsdale 16,726
Hodgkins 2,005
Hoffman Estates 38,258
Holiday Hills 802
Homer 1,279
Hometown 5,324
Homewood 19,724
Hoopeston 6,411
Hopedale 913
Hoyleton 542
Hudson 929
Huntley 1,646
Hurst 938
Hutsonville 705
Illiopolis 1,118
Indian Head Park 2,915
Industry 600
Inverness 4,046
Ipava 661
Irving 612
Irvington 789
Island Lake 2,293
Itasca 7,948
Jacksonville 20,284
Jerome 1,374
Jerseyville 7,506
Johnston City 3,873
Joliet 77,956
Jonesboro 1,842
Justice 10,552
Kankakee 30,141
Kansas 791
Karnak 646
Keithsburg 936
Kenilworth 2,708
Kewanee 14,508
Kildeer 1,609
Kincaid 1,591
Kingston 618
Kinmundy 945
Kirkland 1,155
Kirkwood 1,008
Knoxville 3,432
Lacon 2,135
Ladd 1,337
La Grange 15,681
La Grange Park 13,359
La Harpe 1,471
Lake Barrington 2,320
Lake Bluff 4,434
Lake Forest 15,245
Lake in the Hills 5,651
Lake Villa 1,462
Lake Zurich 8,225
Lakemoor 723
Lakewood 1,254
La Moille 734
Lanark 1,483
Lansing 29,039
La Salle 10,347
Latham 564
Lawrenceville 5,652
Leaf River 637
Lebanon 3,245
Leland 775
Leland Grove 1,692
Lemont 5,640
Lena 2,295
Le Roy 2,870
Lewistown 2,758
Lexington 1,806
Liberty 587
Libertyville 16,520
Lincoln 16,327
Lincolnshire 4,151
Lincolnwood 11,921
Lindenhurst 6,220
Lisle 13,625
Litchfield 7,204
Livingston 949
Loami 770
Lockport 9,017
Lomax 601
Lombard 37,295
London Mills 587
Long Grove 2,013
Lostant 539
Louisville 1,166
Loves Park 13,192
Lovington 1,313
Lyndon 777
Lynwood 4,195
Lyons 9,925
Mackinaw 1,354
Macomb 19,632
Macon 1,300
Madison 5,915
Mahomet 1,986
Malta 995
Manhattan 1,944
Manito 1,869
Mansfield 921
Manteno 3,155
Maple Park 637
Marengo 4,361
Marine 957
Marion 14,031
Marissa 2,568
Markham 15,172
Maroa 1,760
Marquette Heights 3,386
Marseilles 4,766
Marshall 3,655
Martinsville 1,298
Maryville 1,937
Mascoutah 4,962
Mason City 2,719
Matherville 793
Matteson 10,223
Mattoon 19,787
Maywood 27,998
Mazon 828
McCullom Lake 947
McHenry 10,908
McHenry Shores 1,041
McLean 836
McLeansboro 2,960
Melrose Park 20,735
Mendon 979
Mendota 7,134
Meredosia 1,272
Merrionette Park 2,054
Metamora 2,482
Metropolis 7,171
Midlothian 14,274
Milan 6,264
Milford 1,716
Milledgeville 1,209
Millstadt 2,736
Minier 1,261
Minonk 2,039
Minooka 1,565
Mokena 4,578
Moline 45,709
Momence 3,297
Monee 993
Monmouth 10,706
Montgomery 3,363
Monticello 4,753
Morris 8,833
Morrison 4,605
Morrisonville 1,208
Morristown 687
Morton 14,178
Morton Grove 23,747
Mound City 1,102
Mounds 1,669
Mount Auburn 598
Mount Carmel 8,908
Mount Carroll 1,936
Mount Morris 2,989
Mount Olive 2,357
Mount Prospect 52,634
Mount Pulaski 1,783
Mount Sterling 2,186
Mount Vernon 16,995
Mount Zion 4,563
Moweaqua 1,922
Mulberry Grove 707
Mundelein 17,053
Murphysboro 9,866
Murrayville 712
Naperville 42,330
Naplate 581
Nashville 3,186
Nauvoo 1,133
Neoga 1,736
Neponset 575
New Athens 1,937
New Baden 2,476
New Berlin 834
New Boston 731
New Haven 559
New Lenox 5,792
Newark 798
Newman 1,079
Newton 3,186
Niantic 761
Niles 30,363
Noble 832
Nokomis 2,656
Normal 35,672
Norridge 16,483
Norris City 1,515
North Aurora 5,205
North Barrington 1,475
North Chicago 38,774
North Pekin 1,824
North Riverside 6,764
North Utica 1,067
Northbrook 30,735
Northfield 5,807
Northlake 12,166
Norwood 612
Oak Brook 6,641
Oak Forest 26,096
Oak Grove 695
Oak Lawn 60,590
Oak Park 54,887
Oakbrook Terrace 2,285
Oakland 1,035
Oakwood 1,627
Oakwood Hills 1,255
Oblong 1,840
Odell 1,083
Odin 1,285
O'Fallon 10,217
Ogden 818
Oglesby 3,979
Ohio 544
Okawville 1,337
Olney 9,026
Olympia Fields 4,146
Onarga 1,269
Oneida 765
Oquawka 1,533
Orangeville 598
Oreana 999
Oregon 3,559
Orion 2,013
Orland Park 23,045
Oswego 3,021
Ottawa 18,166
Palatine 32,166
Palestine 1,718
Palmyra 864
Palos Heights 11,096
Palos Hills 16,654
Palos Park 3,150
Pana 6,040
Panama 637
Paris 9,885
Park City 3,673
Park Forest 26,222
Park Forest South 6,245
Park Ridge 38,704
Patoka 662
Paw Paw 839
Pawnee 2,577
Paxton 4,258
Payson 1,065
Pearl City 661
Pecatonica 1,732
Pekin 33,967
Pembroke 662
Peoria 124,160
Peoria Heights 7,453
Peotone 2,832
Percy 1,053
Peru 10,886
Pesotum 651
Petersburg 2,419
Philo 973
Phoenix 2,850
Pierron 577
Pinckneyville 3,319
Piper City 905
Pittsburg 605
Pittsfield 4,170
Plainfield 4,485
Plano 4,875
Pleasant Hill 1,112
Pleasant Plains 688
Plymouth 649
Pocahontas 866
Polo 2,643
Pontiac 11,227
Pontoon Beach 3,336
Poplar Grove 818
Port Byron 1,289
Posen 4,642
Potomac 874
Prairie City 580
Prairie du Rocher 701
Prairie Grove 680
Princeton 7,342
Princeville 1,712
Prophetstown 2,141
Prospect Heights 11,808
Quincy 42,352
Ramsey 1,058
Rankin 727
Rantoul 20,161
Rapids City 1,058
Raymond 957
Red Bud 2,850
Reynolds 701
Richmond 1,068
Richton Park 9,403
Ridge Farm 1,096
Ridgway 1,245
River Forest 12,392
River Grove 10,368
Riverdale 13,233
Riverside 9,236
Riverton 2,783
Riverwoods 2,804
Roanoke 2,001
Robbins 8,119
Robinson 7,285
Rochelle 8,982
Rochester 2,488
Rock Falls 10,624
Rock Island 47,036
Rockdale 1,913
Rockford 139,712
Rockton 2,313
Rolling Meadows 20,167
Romeoville 15,519
Roodhouse 2,364
Roscoe 1,388
Roselle 16,948
Rosemont 4,137
Roseville 1,254
Rosiclare 1,441
Rossville 1,363
Round Lake 2,644
Round Lake Beach 12,921
Round Lake Heights 1,192
Round Lake Park 4,032
Roxana 1,587
Royalton 1,320
Rushville 3,348
St. Anne 1,421
St. Charles 17,492
St. David 786
St. Elmo 1,611
St. Francisville 1,040
St. Jacob 792
St. Joseph 1,900
St. Libory 549
Salem 7,813
San Jose 784
Sandoval 1,734
Sandwich 3,675
Sauk Village 10,906
Savanna 4,529
Savoy 2,126
Saybrook 882
Schaumburg 52,319
Schiller Park 11,458
Schram City 708
Seneca 2,098
Sesser 2,238
Shabbona 851
Shannon 938
Shawneetown 1,841
Sheffield 1,130
Shelbyville 5,259
Sheldon 1,215
Sheridan 719
Sherman 1,501
Sherrard 811
Shiloh 1,045
Shipman 581
Shorewood 4,714
Sidell 625
Sidney 886
Silvis 7,130
Skokie 60,278
Sleepy Hollow 2,000
Smithton 1,447
Somonauk 1,344
Sorento 677
South Barrington 1,168
South Beloit 4,088
South Chicago Heights 3,932
South Elgin 6,218
South Holland 24,977
South Jacksonville 3,382
South Pekin 1,243
South Roxana 2,286
South Wilmington 747
Southern View 1,306
Sparland 624
Sparta 4,957
Spring Grove 571
Spring Valley 5,822
Springfield 99,637
Stanford 720
Staunton 4,744
Steeleville 2,240
Steger 9,269
Sterling 16,273
Stewardson 745
Stickney 5,893
Stillman Valley 961
Stockton 1,872
Stone Park 4,273
Stonington 1,184
Streamwood 23,456
Streator 14,769
Stronghurst 865
Sugar Grove 1,366
Sullivan 4,526
Summit 10,110
Sumner 1,238
Sunnyside 1,432
Sunrise Ridge 752
Swansea 5,347
Sycamore 9,219
Tallula 681
Tamaroa 885
Tamms 826
Tampico 966
Taylor Springs 671
Taylorville 11,386
Teutopolis 1,414
Thayer 759
Thomasboro 1,242
Thompsonville 610
Thomson 911
Thornton 3,022
Tilden 1,025
Tilton 2,405
Tinley Park 26,171
Tiskilwa 990
Toledo 1,284
Tolono 2,434
Toluca 1,471
Tonica 695
Toulon 1,390
Tovey 598
Towanda 630
Tower Hill 715
Tower Lakes 1,177
Tremont 2,096
Trenton 2,504
Troy 3,772
Tuscola 3,839
Ullin 550
Union 622
Urbana 35,978
Valier 729
Valley View 2,112
Valmeyer 898
Vandalia 5,338
Venice 3,480
Vermont 885
Vernon Hills 9,827
Vienna 1,420
Villa Grove 2,707
Villa Park 23,185
Viola 1,144
Virden 3,899
Virginia 1,825
Wadsworth 1,104
Walnut 1,513
Wamac 1,665
Wapella 768
Warren 1,595
Warrensburg 1,372
Warrenville 7,519
Warsaw 1,842
Washburn 1,206
Washington 10,364
Washington Park 8,223
Wataga 996
Waterloo 4,646
Waterman 943
Watseka 5,543
Watson 551
Wauconda 5,688
Waukegan 67,653
Waverly 1,537
Wayne 940
Wayne City 1,132
Waynesville 569
Wenona 1,025
West Chicago 12,550
West City 886
West Dundee 3,502
West Frankfort 9,437
West Salem 1,145
Westchester 17,730
Western Springs 12,876
Westfield 733
Westhaven 2,784
Westmont 16,718
Westville 3,573
Wheaton 43,043
Wheeling 23,266
White Hall 2,935
Williamsfield 585
Williamsville 996
Willisville 628
Willow Springs 4,147
Willowbrook 4,953
Wilmette 28,229
Wilmington 4,424
Wilsonville 608
Winchester 1,716
Windsor 1,228
Windsor 863
Winfield 4,422
Winnebago 1,644
Winnetka 12,772
Winthrop Harbor 5,438
Witt 1,205
Wood Dale 11,251
Wood River 12,449
Woodhull 811
Woodridge 22,322
Woodstock 11,725
Worden 953
Worth 11,592
Wyanet 1,069
Wyoming 1,614
Yates City 860
Yorkville 3,422
Zeigler 1,858
Zion 17,861

INDIANA

Population 5,490,179

METROPOLITAN AREAS

Anderson 139,336
Bloomington 98,387
Cincinnati (O.) 1,401,403 (1,100,895 in O.; 266,217 in Ky.; 34,291 in Ind.)
Evansville 309,408 (268,559 in Ind.; 40,849 in Ky.)
Fort Wayne 382,961
Gary-Hammond-East Chicago 642,781
Indianapolis 1,166,929
Kokomo 103,715
Lafayette-West Lafayette 121,702
Louisville (Ky.) 906,240 (756,233 in Ky.; 150,007 in Ind.)
Muncie 128,587
South Bend 280,772
Terre Haute 176,583

COUNTIES

Adams 29,619
Allen 294,335
Bartholomew 65,088
Benton 10,218
Blackford 15,570
Boone 36,446
Brown 12,377
Carroll 19,722
Cass 40,936
Clark 88,838
Clay 24,862
Clinton 31,545
Crawford 9,820
Daviess 27,836
Dearborn 34,291
Decatur 23,841
DeKalb 33,606
Delaware 128,587
Dubois 34,238
Elkhart 137,330
Fayette 28,272
Floyd 61,169
Fountain 19,033
Franklin 19,612
Fulton 19,335
Gibson 33,156
Grant 80,934
Greene 30,416
Hamilton 82,381
Hancock 43,939
Harrison 27,276
Hendricks 69,804
Henry 53,336
Howard 86,896
Huntington 35,596
Jackson 36,523
Jasper 26,138
Jay 23,239
Jefferson 30,419
Jennings 22,854
Johnson 77,240
Knox 41,838
Kosciusko 59,555
Lagrange 25,550
Lake 522,965
La Porte 108,632
Lawrence 42,472
Madison 139,336
Marion 765,233
Marshall 39,155
Martin 11,001
Miami 39,820
Monroe 98,387
Montgomery 35,501
Morgan 51,999
Newton 14,844
Noble 35,443
Ohio 5,114
Orange 18,677
Owen 15,840
Parke 16,372
Perry 19,346
Pike 13,465
Porter 119,816
Posey 26,414
Pulaski 13,258
Putnam 29,163
Randolph 29,997
Ripley 24,398
Rush 19,604
St. Joseph 241,617
Scott 20,422
Shelby 39,887
Spencer 19,361
Starke 21,997
Steuben 24,694
Sullivan 21,107
Switzerland 7,153
Tippecanoe 121,702
Tipton 16,819
Union 6,860
Vanderburgh 167,515
Vermillion 18,229
Vigo 112,385
Wabash 36,640
Warren 8,976
Warrick 41,474
Washington 21,932
Wayne 76,058
Wells 25,401
White 23,867
Whitley 26,215

CITIES AND TOWNS

Advance 559
Akron 1,045
Alamo 178
Albany 2,625
Albion 1,637
Alexandria 6,028
Alfordsville 132
Alton 64
Altona 263
Ambia 274
Amboy 450
Amo 444
Anderson 64,695
Andrews 1,243
Angola 5,486
Arcadia 1,801
Argos 1,547
Ashley 841
Atlanta 657
Attica 3,841
Auburn 8,122
Aurora 3,816
Austin 4,857
Avilla 1,272
Bainbridge 644
Bargersville 1,647
Batesville 4,152
Battle Ground 812
Bedford 14,410
Beech Grove 13,196
Berne 3,300
Bethany 127
Beverly Shores 864
Bicknell 4,713
Birdseye 533
Bloomfield 2,705
Bloomingdale 409
Bloomington 51,646
Blountsville 213

INDIANA (continued)

Bluffton 8,705
Boonville 6,300
Borden
(New Providence) 384
Boston 189
Boswell 810
Bourbon 1,522
Brazil 7,852
Bremen 3,565
Bristol 1,203
Brook 926
Brooklyn 889
Brooksburg 132
Brookston 1,701
Brookville 2,874
Brownsburg 6,242
Brownstown 2,704
Bruceville 646
Bryant 277
Bunker Hill 984
Burket 260
Burlington 680
Burnettsville 496
Burns Harbor 920
Butler 2,509
Cadiz 180
Cambridge City 2,407
Camden 618
Campbellsburg 695
Cannelburg 152
Cannelton 2,373
Carbon 307
Carlisle 717
Carmel 18,272
Carthage 886
Castleton 80
Cayuga 1,258
Cedar Grove 217
Cedar Lake 8,754
Center Point 242
Centerville 2,284
Chalmers 554
Chandler 3,043
Charlestown 5,596
Chesterfield 2,701
Chesterton 8,531
Chrisney 537
Churubusco 1,638
Cicero 2,557
Clarks Hill 653
Clarksville 15,164
Clay City 883
Claypool 464
Clayton 703
Clear Lake 301
Clermont 1,671
Clifford 310
Clinton 5,267
Cloverdale 1,357
Coatesville 474
Colfax 823
Columbia City 5,091
Columbus 30,292
Connersville 17,023
Converse 1,190
Corunna 304
Corydon 2,724
Country Club Heights 97
Covington 2,883
Crandall 176
Crane 297
Crawfordsville 13,325
Cromwell 458
Crothersville 1,747
Crown Point 16,455
Crows Nest 106
Culver 1,601
Cumberland 3,375
Cynthiana 874
Dale 1,693
Dana 803
Danville 4,220
Darlington 811
Darmstadt 1,280
Dayton 781
Decatur 8,649
Decker 256
Delphi 3,042
DeMotte 2,559
Denver 589
Dillsboro 1,038
Dublin 979
Dugger 1,118
Dune Acres 291
Dunkirk 3,180
Dunreith 184
Dupont 392
Dyer 9,555
Earl Park 469
East Chicago 39,786
East Germantown 438
Eaton 1,804
Economy 237
Edgewood 2,215
Edinburg 4,856
Edwardsport 459
Elberfeld 640
Elizabeth 178
Elizabethtown 603
Elkhart 41,305
Ellettsville 3,328
Elnora 756
Elwood 10,867
English 633
Etna Green 522
Evansville 130,496
Fairmount 3,286
Fairview Park 1,545
Farmersburg 1,240
Farmland 1,560
Ferdinand 2,192
Fishers Station 2,008
Flora 2,303
Fort Branch 2,504
Fort Wayne 172,196
Fortville 2,787
Fountain City 839
Fowler 2,319
Fowlerton 300
Francesville 944
Francisco 612
Frankfort 15,168
Franklin 11,563
Frankton 2,080
Fredericksburg 233
Fremont 1,180
French Lick 2,265
Fulton 393
Galveston 1,822
Garrett 4,874
Gary 151,953
Gas City 6,370
Gaston 1,150
Geneva 1,430
Gentryville 299
Georgetown 1,494
Glenwood 370
Goodland 1,200
Goshen 19,665
Gosport 1,341
Grabill 658
Grandview 670
Greencastle 8,403
Greendale 3,795
Greenfield 11,439
Greensboro 175
Greensburg 9,254
Greensfork 426
Greentown 2,265
Greenville 537
Greenwood 19,327
Griffin 192
Griffith 17,026
Hagerstown 1,950
Hamilton 587
Hamlet 738
Hammond 93,714
Hanover 4,054
Hardinsburg 298
Harmony 613
Hartford City 7,622
Hartsville 379
Haubstadt 1,389
Hazleton 368
Hebron 2,696
Highland 25,935
Hillsboro 561
Hobart 22,987
Holland 683
Holton 487
Homecroft 831
Hope 2,185
Hudson 447
Huntertown 1,265
Huntingburg 5,376
Huntington 16,202
Hymera 1,054
Indian Village 151
Indianapolis 700,807
Ingalls 909
Jamestown 924
Jasonville 2,497
Jasper 9,097
Jeffersonville 21,220
Jonesboro 2,279
Jonesville 213
Judson 80
Kempton 410
Kendallville 7,299
Kennard 441
Kentland 1,936
Kewanna 711
Kingman 566
Kingsbury 329
Kingsford Heights 1,618
Kirklin 662
Knightstown 2,325
Knightsville 763
Knox 3,674
Kokomo 47,808
Kouts 1,619
Laconia 58
La Crosse 713
Ladoga 1,151
Lafayette 43,011
La Fontaine 946
Lagrange 2,164
Lagro 549
Lake Hart 231
Lake Station 14,294
Lakeville 629
Lanesville 570
La Paz 651
Lapel 1,881
La Porte 21,796
Larwill 286
Laurel 819
Lawrence 25,591
Lawrenceburg 4,403
Leavenworth 356
Lebanon 11,456
Leesburg 629
Lewisville 577
Liberty 1,844
Ligonier 3,134
Linden 700
Linton 6,315
Little York 150
Livonia 120
Lizton 456
Logansport 17,899
Long Beach 2,262
Loogootee 3,100
Losantville 306
Lowell 5,827
Lynhurst 167
Lynn 1,250
Lynnville 566
Lyons 782
Mackey 165
Macy 282
Madison 12,472
Marengo 892
Marion 35,874
Markle 975
Markleville 427
Marshall 413
Martinsville 11,311
Matthews 745
Mauckport 109
Mecca 482
Medaryville 731
Medora 853
Mellott 294
Mentone 973
Meridian Hills 1,801
Merom 360
Merrillville 27,677
Michiana
Shores 464
Michigan City 36,850
Michigantown 453
Middlebury 1,665
Middletown 2,978
Milan 1,566
Milford 177
Milford 1,153
Millersburg 809
Millhousen 214
Milltown 1,006
Milton 729
Mishawaka 40,224
Mitchell 4,641
Modoc 243
Monon 1,540
Monroe 739
Monroe City 569
Monroeville 1,372
Monterey 236
Montezuma 1,352
Montgomery 390
Monticello 5,162
Montpelier 1,995
Mooreland 479
Moores Hill 566
Mooresville 5,349
Morgantown 897
Morocco 1,348
Morristown 989
Mount Auburn 192
Mount Ayr 207
Mount Carmel 151
Mount Etna 122
Mount Summit 357
Mount Vernon 7,656
Mulberry 1,225
Muncie 77,216
Munster 20,671
Napoleon 246
Nappanee 4,694
Nashville 705
New Albany 37,103
New Carlisle 1,439
New Castle 20,056
New Chicago 3,284
New Harmony 945
New Haven 6,714
New Market 608
New Middletown 115
New Palestine 749
New Pekin 1,125
New Richmond 403
New Ross 306
New Whiteland 4,502
Newberry 246
Newburgh 2,906
Newpoint 296
Newport 704
Newtown 277
Noblesville 12,056
North Crows Nest 82
North Grove 91
North Judson 1,653
North Liberty 1,211
North Manchester 5,998
North Salem 581
North Vernon 5,768
North Webster 709
Oakland City 3,301
Oaktown 776
Odon 1,463
Ogden Dunes 1,489
Oldenburg 770
Onward 121
Oolitic 1,495
Orestes 539
Orland 424
Orleans 2,161
Osceola 1,987
Osgood 1,554
Ossian 1,945
Otterbein 1,118
Owensville 1,261
Oxford 1,327
Palmyra 692
Paoli 3,637
Paragon 538
Parker City 1,414
Patoka 832
Patriot 265
Pendleton 2,130
Pennville 805
Perrysville 532
Peru 13,764
Petersburg 2,987
Pierceton 1,086
Pine Village 257
Pittsboro 891
Plainfield 9,191
Plainville 556
Plymouth 7,693
Poneto 250
Portage 27,409
Porter 2,988
Portland 7,074
Poseyville 1,247
Pottawattomie Park 284
Princes Lakes 937
Princeton 8,976
Ravenswood 424
Redkey 1,537
Remington 1,268
Rensselaer 4,944
Reynolds 632
Richmond 41,349
Ridgeville 933
Riley 269
Rising Sun 2,478
Roachdale 958
Roann 548
Roanoke 891
Rochester 5,050
Rockport 2,590
Rockville 2,785
Rocky Ripple 778
Rome City 1,319
Rosedale 744
Roseland 832
Rossville 1,148
Royal Center 908
Rushville 6,113
Russellville 376
Russiaville 973
St. Joe 546
St. John 3,974
St. Leon 515
St. Paul 976
Salamonia 147
Salem 5,290
Saltillo 134
Sandborn 576
Santa Claus 514
Saratoga 338
Schererville 13,209
Schneider 364
Scottsburg 5,068
Seelyville 1,374
Sellersburg 3,211
Selma 1,056
Seymour 15,050
Shamrock Lakes 206
Sharpsville 617
Shelburn 1,259
Shelbyville 14,989
Sheridan 2,200
Shipshewana 466
Shirley 919
Shoals 967
Sidney 194
Silver Lake 576
Somerville 340
South Bend 109,727
South Whitley 1,575
Southport 2,266
Speedway 12,641
Spencer 2,732
Spiceland 940
Spring Grove 469
Spring Lake 236
Springport 221
Spurgeon 250
State Line City 233
Staunton 607
Stilesville 350
Stinesville 227
Straughn 331
Sullivan 4,774
Sulphur Springs 345
Summitville 1,085
Sunman 924
Swayzee 1,127
Sweetser 944
Switz City 300
Syracuse 2,579
Tell City 8,704
Tennyson 331
Terre Haute 61,125
Thorntown 1,468
Tipton 5,004
Topeka 876
Town of Pines 962
Trafalgar 466
Trail Creek 2,581
Troy 550
Ulen 193
Union City 3,908
Uniondale 303
Universal 428
Upland 3,335
Utica 501
Valparaiso 22,247
Van Buren 935
Veedersburg 2,261
Vera Cruz 117
Vernon 329
Versailles 1,560
Vevay 1,343
Vincennes 20,857
Wabash 12,985
Wakarusa 1,281
Walkerton 2,051
Wallace 88
Walton 1,202
Wanatah 879
Warren 1,254
Warren Park 1,803
Warsaw 10,647
Washington 11,325
Waterloo 1,951
Waveland 559
Waynetown 915
West Baden
Springs 796
West College
Corner 614
West Harrison 328
West Lafayette 21,247
West Lebanon 946
West Terre Haute 2,806
Westfield 2,783
Westport 1,450
Westville 2,887
Wheatfield 755
Wheatland 532
Whiteland 1,956
Whitestown 497
Whitewater 107
Whiting 5,630
Wilkinson 493
Williams Creek 427
Williamsport 1,747
Winamac 2,370
Winchester 5,659
Windfall City 911
Wingate 373
Winona Lake 2,827
Winslow 1,017
Wolcott 923
Wolcottville 890
Woodburn 1,002
Woodlawn Heights 109
Worthington 1,574
Wynnedale 289
Yeoman 154
Yorktown 3,945
Zionsville 3,948

IOWA

Population 2,913,387

METROPOLITAN AREAS

Cedar Rapids 169,775
Davenport-Rock
Island (Ill.)-
Moline (Ill.) 383,958
(223,936 in Ill.;
160,022 in Ia.)
Des Moines 338,048
Dubuque 93,745
Iowa City 81,717
Omaha (Nebr.) 570,399
(483,899 in Nebr.;
86,500 in Ia.)
Sioux City 117,457
(100,884 in Ia.;
16,573 in Nebr.)
Waterloo-
Cedar Falls 137,961

COUNTIES

Adair 9,509
Adams 5,731
Allamakee 15,108
Appanoose 15,511
Audubon 8,559
Benton 23,649
Black Hawk 137,961
Boone 26,184
Bremer 24,820
Buchanan 22,900
Buena Vista 20,774
Butler 17,668
Calhoun 13,542
Carroll 22,951
Cass 16,932
Cedar 18,635
Cerro Gordo 48,458
Cherokee 16,238
Chickasaw 15,437
Clarke 8,612
Clay 19,576
Clayton 21,098
Clinton 57,122
Crawford 18,935
Dallas 29,513
Davis 9,104
Decatur 9,794
Delaware 18,933
Des Moines 46,203
Dickinson 15,629
Dubuque 93,745
Emmet 13,336
Fayette 25,488
Floyd 19,597
Franklin 13,036
Fremont 9,401
Greene 12,119
Grundy 14,366
Guthrie 11,983
Hamilton 17,862
Hancock 13,833
Hardin 21,776
Harrison 16,348
Henry 18,890
Howard 11,114
Humboldt 12,246
Ida 8,908
Iowa 15,429
Jackson 22,503
Jasper 36,425
Jefferson 16,316
Johnson 81,717
Jones 20,401
Keokuk 12,921
Kossuth 21,891
Lee 43,106
Linn 169,775
Louisa 12,055
Lucas 10,313
Lyon 12,896
Madison 12,597
Mahaska 22,507
Marion 29,669
Marshall 41,652
Mills 13,406
Mitchell 12,329
Monona 11,692
Monroe 9,209
Montgomery 13,413
Muscatine 40,436
O'Brien 16,972
Osceola 8,371
Page 19,063
Palo Alto 12,721
Plymouth 24,743
Pocahontas 11,369
Polk 303,170
Pottawattamie 86,500
Poweshiek 19,306
Ringgold 6,112
Sac 14,118
Scott 160,022
Shelby 15,043
Sioux 30,813
Story 72,326
Tama 19,533
Taylor 8,353
Union 13,858
Van Buren 8,626
Wapello 40,241
Warren 34,878
Washington 20,141
Wayne 8,199
Webster 45,953
Winnebago 13,010
Winneshiek 21,876
Woodbury 100,884
Worth 9,075
Wright 16,319

CITIES AND TOWNS

Ackley 1,900
Ackworth 83
Adair 883
Adel 2,846
Afton 985
Agency 657
Ainsworth 547
Akron 1,517
Albert City 818
Albia 4,184
Albion 739
Alburnett 411
Alden 953
Alexander 190
Algona 6,289
Alleman 307
Allerton 670
Allison 1,132
Alta 1,720
Alta Vista 314
Alton 986
Altoona 5,764
Alvord 246
Ames 45,775
Anamosa 4,958
Andover 107
Andrew 349
Anita 1,153
Ankeny 15,429
Anthon 687
Aplington 1,027
Arcadia 454
Archer 134
Aredale 88
Arion 207
Arispe 89
Arlington 498
Armstrong 1,153
Arnolds Park 1,051
Arthur 288
Asbury 2,017
Ashton 441
Aspinwall 65

Atalissa 360
Athelstan 45
Atkins 678
Atlantic 7,789
Auburn 320
Audubon 2,841
Aurelia 1,143
Aurora 248
Avoca 1,650
Ayrshire 243
Badger 653
Bagley 370
Baldwin 198
Balltown 106
Bancroft 1,082
Bankston 40
Barnes City 266
Barnum 198
Bassett 128
Batavia 525
Battle Creek 919
Baxter 951
Bayard 637
Beacon 530
Beaman 219
Beaver 85
Bedford 1,692
Belle Plaine 2,903
Bellevue 2,450
Belmond 2,505
Bennett 458
Berkley 49
Bernard 130
Bertram 216
Bettendorf 27,381
Bevington 60
Birmingham 410
Blairsburg 288
Blairstown 695
Blakesburg 404
Blanchard 101
Blencoe 247
Blockton 280
Bloomfield 2,849
Blue Grass 1,377
Bode 406
Bonaparte 489
Bondurant 1,283
Boone 12,602
Bouton 139
Boxholm 267
Boyden 708
Braddyville 199
Bradgate 151
Brandon 337
Brayton 170
Breda 502
Bridgewater 233
Brighton 804
Bristow 252
Britt 2,185
Bronson 289
Brooklyn 1,509
Brunsville 140
Buck Grove 84
Buckeye 154
Buffalo 1,441
Buffalo Center 1,233
Burlington 29,529
Burt 689
Bussey 579
Calamus 452
Callender 446
Calmar 1,053
Calumet 212
Camanche 4,725
Cambridge 732
Cantril 299
Carbon 110
Carlisle 3,073
Carpenter 109
Carroll 9,705
Carson 716
Carter Lake 3,438
Cascade 1,912
Casey 473
Castalia 188
Castana 228
Cedar Falls 36,322
Cedar Rapids 110,243
Center Junction 182
Center Point 1,591
Centerville 6,558
Central City 1,067
Centralia 106
Chariton 4,987
Charles City 8,778
Charlotte 442
Charter Oak 615
Chatsworth 110
Chelsea 376
Cherokee 7,004
Chester 175
Chillicothe 131
Churdan 540
Cincinnati 598
Clare 229
Clarence 1,001
Clarinda 5,458
Clarion 3,060
Clarksville 1,424
Clayton 68
Clear Lake 7,458
Clearfield 433
Cleghorn 275
Clemons 175
Clermont 602
Clinton 32,828
Clio 106
Clive 5,906
Clutier 249
Coburg 52
Coggon 639
Coin 316
Colesburg 463

Colfax 2,211
College Springs 307
Collins 451
Colo 808
Columbus City 367
Columbus
Junction 1,429
Colwell 91
Conesville 301
Conrad 1,133
Conway 93
Coon Rapids 1,448
Coppock 47
Coralville 7,687
Corning 1,939
Correctionville 935
Corwith 480
Corydon 1,818
Cotter 60
Coulter 264
Council Bluffs 56,449
Craig 105
Crawfordsville 290
Crescent 547
Cresco 3,860
Creston 8,429
Cromwell 157
Crystal Lake 314
Cumberland 351
Cumming 151
Curlew 85
Cushing 270
Cylinder 119
Dakota City 1,072
Dallas 451
Dallas Center 1,360
Dana 110
Danbury 492
Danville 994
Davenport 103,264
Davis City 327
Dawson 229
Dayton 941
Decatur City 199
Decorah 7,991
Dedham 321
Deep River 323
Defiance 383
Delaware 170
Delhi 511
Delmar 633
Deloit 345
Delphos 45
Delta 482
Denison 6,675
Denver 1,647
Derby 171
Des Moines 191,003
De Soto 1,035
De Witt 4,512
Dexter 678
Diagonal 362
Dickens 289
Dike 987
Dixon 312
Dolliver 125
Donahue 289
Donnan 10
Donnellson 972
Doon 537
Dougherty 128
Dow City 616
Dows 771
Drakesville 212
Dubuque 62,321
Dumont 815
Duncombe 504
Dundee 164
Dunkerton 718
Dunlap 1,374
Durango 41
Durant 1,583
Dyersville 3,825
Dysart 1,355
Eagle Grove 4,324
Earlham 1,140
Earling 520
Earlville 844
Early 670
East Peru 124
Eddyville 1,116
Edgewood 900
Elberon 194
Eldon 1,255
Eldora 3,063
Eldridge 3,279
Elgin 702
Elk Horn 746
Elk Run Heights 1,186
Elkader 1,688
Elkhart 256
Elkport 98
Elliott 493
Ellston 60
Ellsworth 480
Elma 714
Ely 425
Emerson 502
Emmetsburg 4,621
Epworth 1,380
Essex 1,001
Estherville 7,518
Evansdale 4,798
Everly 348
Exira 978
Exline 217
Fairbank 980
Fairfax 683
Fairfield 9,428
Farley 1,287
Farmersburg 276
Farmington 869
Farnhamville 461
Farragut 603
Fayette 1,515

Fenton 394
Ferguson 173
Fertile 372
Floris 187
Floyd 408
Fonda 863
Fontanelle 805
Forest City 4,270
Fort Atkinson 374
Fort Dodge 29,423
Fort Madison 13,520
Fostoria 261
Franklin 142
Fraser 139
Fredericksburg 1,075
Frederika 223
Fredonia 224
Fremont 730
Fruitland 461
Galt 60
Galva 420
Garber 140
Garden Grove 297
Garnavillo 723
Garner 2,908
Garrison 411
Garwin 626
Geneva 218
George 1,241
Gibson 75
Gilbert 805
Gilbertville 740
Gillett Grove 93
Gilman 642
Gilmore City 626
Gladbrook 970
Glenwood 5,280
Glidden 1,076
Goldfield 789
Goodell 220
Goose Lake 274
Gowrie 1,089
Graettinger 923
Graf 57
Grafton 255
Grand Junction 970
Grand Mound 674
Grand River 188
Grandview 473
Granger 619
Grant 143
Granville 336
Gravity 245
Gray 108
Greeley 313
Green Island 103
Greene 1,332
Greenfield 2,243
Greenville 122
Grimes 1,973
Grinnell 8,868
Griswold 1,176
Grundy Center 2,880
Gruver 145
Guernsey 83
Guthrie Center 1,713
Guttenberg 2,428
Halbur 229
Hamburg 1,597
Hamilton 163
Hampton 4,630
Hancock 254
Hanlontown 213
Hansell 138
Harcourt 347
Hardy 72
Harlan 5,357
Harper 138
Harpers Ferry 258
Harris 228
Hartford 761
Hartley 1,700
Hartwick 92
Harvey 275
Hastings 215
Havelock 279
Haverill 173
Hawarden 2,722
Hawkeye 512
Hayesville 93
Hazleton 877
Hedrick 847
Henderson 236
Hepburn 42
Hiawatha 4,825
Hills 547
Hillsboro 208
Hinton 659
Holland 278
Holstein 1,477
Holy Cross 310
Hopkinton 774
Hornick 239
Hospers 655
Houghton 124
Hubbard 852
Hudson 2,267
Hull 1,714
Humboldt 4,794
Humeston 671
Hurstville 57
Huxley 1,884
Ida Grove 2,285
Imogene 188
Independence 6,392
Indianola 10,843
Inwood 755
Ionia 350
Iowa City 50,508
Iowa Falls 6,174
Ireton 588
Irwin 427
Jackson Junction 94
Jamaica 275
Janesville 840

Jefferson 4,854
Jesup 2,343
Jewell 1,145
Johnston 2,617
Joice 233
Jolley 91
Kalona 1,862
Kamrar 225
Kanawha 756
Kellerton 278
Kelley 237
Kellogg 654
Kensett 360
Kent 70
Keokuk 13,536
Keomah 99
Keosauqua 1,003
Keota 1,034
Keswick 300
Keystone 618
Kimballton 362
Kingsley 1,209
Kinross 79
Kirkman 95
Kirkville 220
Kiron 317
Klemme 620
Knierim 125
Knoxville 8,143
Lacona 376
Ladora 289
Lake City 2,006
Lake Mills 2,281
Lake Park 1,123
Lake View 1,291
Lakeside 589
Lakota 330
Lambs Grove 228
Lamoni 2,705
Lamont 554
La Motte 322
Lanesboro 196
Lansing 1,181
La Porte City 2,324
Larchwood 701
Larrabee 169
Latimer 441
Laurel 278
Laurens 1,606
Lawler 534
Lawton 447
Le Claire 2,899
Ledyard 215
Le Grand 921
Lehigh 654
Leighton 137
Leland 274
Le Mars 8,276
Lenox 1,338
Leon 2,094
Lester 274
Letts 473
Lewis 497
Libertyville 281
Lidderdale 197
Lime Springs 476
Lincoln 202
Linden 264
Lineville 319
Linn Grove 205
Lisbon 1,458
Liscomb 296
Little Rock 490
Little Sioux 251
Littleport 106
Livermore 490
Lockridge 271
Logan 1,540
Lohrville 521
Lone Rock 169
Lone Tree 1,014
Long Grove 596
Lorimor 405
Lost Nation 524
Lovilia 637
Low Moor 346
Lowden 717
Luana 246
Lucas 292
Luther 155
Lu Verne 418
Luxemburg 271
Luzerne 114
Lynnville 406
Lytton 377
Macedonia 279
Macksburg 132
Madrid 2,281
Magnolia 207
Malcom 418
Mallard 407
Maloy 38
Malvern 1,244
Manchester 4,942
Manilla 1,020
Manly 1,496
Manning 1,609
Manson 1,924
Mapleton 1,495
Maquoketa 6,313
Marathon 442
Marble Rock 419
Marcus 1,206
Marengo 2,308
Marion 19,474
Marne 162
Marquette 528
Marshalltown 26,938
Martelle 316
Martensdale 438
Martinsburg 174
Marysville 84
Mason City 30,144
Masonville 150
Massena 518

Matlock 109
Maurice 288
Maxwell 783
Maynard 561
Maysville 151
McCallsburg 304
McCausland 381
McClelland 177
McGregor 945
McIntire 197
Mechanicsville 1,166
Mediapolis 1,685
Melbourne 732
Melcher 953
Melrose 218
Melvin 277
Menlo 410
Meriden 233
Merrill 737
Meservey 324
Middletown 487
Miles 398
Milford 2,076
Millersburg 184
Millerton 72
Millville 50
Milo 778
Milton 567
Minburn 390
Minden 419
Mingo 303
Missouri Valley 3,107
Mitchell 193
Mitchellville 1,530
Modale 373
Mondamin 423
Moneta 43
Monmouth 210
Monona 1,530
Monroe 1,875
Montezuma 1,485
Monticello 3,641
Montour 387
Montrose 1,038
Moorhead 264
Moorland 257
Moravia 706
Morley 94
Morning Sun 959
Morrison 146
Moulton 762
Mount Auburn 188
Mount Ayr 1,938
Mount Pleasant 7,322
Mount Sterling 96
Mount Union 145
Mount Vernon 3,325
Moville 1,273
Murray 703
Muscatine 23,467
Mystic 665
Nashua 1,846
Nemaha 120
Neola 839
Nevada 5,912
New Albin 609
New Hampton 3,940
New Hartford 764
New Liberty 136
New London 2,043
New Market 554
New Providence 249
New Sharon 1,225
New Vienna 430
New Virginia 512
Newell 913
Newhall 899
Newton 15,292
Nichols 375
Nodaway 185
Nora Springs 1,572
North Buena Vista 155
North English 990
North Liberty 2,046
North Washington 142
Northboro 115
Northwood 2,193
Norwalk 2,676
Norway 633
Numa 205
Oakland 1,552
Oakland Acres 139
Oakville 470
Ocheyedan 599
Odebolt 1,299
Oelwein 7,564
Ogden 1,953
Okoboji 559
Olds 225
Olin 735
Ollie 232
Onawa 3,283
Oneida 61
Onslow 218
Orange City 4,588
Orchard 95
Orient 416
Orleans 546
Osage 3,718
Osceola 3,750
Oskaloosa 10,629
Ossian 829
Osterdock 35
Otho 692
Oto 172
Ottosen 92
Ottumwa 27,381
Owasa 65
Oxford 676
Oxford Junction 600
Oyens 146
Pacific Junction 511
Packwood 210
Palmer 288
Palo 529

Panama 229
Panora 1,211
Panorama Park 145
Parkersburg 1,968
Parnell 234
Paton 291
Patterson 138
Paullina 1,224
Pella 8,349
Peosta 120
Perry 7,053
Persia 355
Peterson 470
Pierson 408
Pilot Mound 223
Pioneer 40
Pisgah 307
Plain View 45
Plainfield 469
Plano 111
Pleasant Hill 3,493
Pleasant Plain 144
Pleasanton 75
Pleasantville 1,531
Plover 135
Plymouth 463
Pocahontas 2,352
Polk City 1,658
Pomeroy 895
Popejoy 112
Portsmouth 240
Postville 1,475
Prairie City 1,278
Prairieburg 197
Prescott 349
Preston 1,120
Primghar 1,050
Princeton 965
Promise City 149
Protivin 368
Pulaski 267
Quasqueton 599
Quimby 424
Radcliffe 593
Rake 283
Ralston 108
Randalia 101
Randall 171
Randolph 223
Rathbun 93
Raymond 655
Readlyn 858
Reasnor 277
Red Oak 6,810
Redding 91
Redfield 959
Reinbeck 1,808
Rembrandt 291
Remsen 1,592
Renwick 410
Rhodes 367
Riceville 919
Richland 600
Rickardsville 215
Ricketts 143
Ridgeway 308
Rinard 97
Ringsted 557
Rippey 304
Riverdale 462
Riverside 826
Riverton 342
Robins 726
Rock Falls 148
Rock Rapids 2,693
Rock Valley 2,706
Rockford 1,012
Rockwell 1,039
Rockwell City 2,276
Rodman 86
Rodney 82
Roland 1,005
Rolfe 796
Rome 113
Rose Hill 214
Rossie 72
Rowan 259
Rowley 275
Royal 522
Rudd 460
Runnells 295
Russell 593
Ruthven 769
Rutland 163
Ryan 390
Sabula 824
Sac City 3,000
Sageville 291
St. Ansgar 1,100
St. Anthony 140
St. Charles 507
St. Donatus 197
St. Lucas 194
St. Marys 111
St. Olaf 138
St. Paul 141
Salem 463
Salix 429
Sanborn 1,398
Sandyville 86
Scarville 82
Schaller 832
Schleswig 868
Scranton 748
Searsboro 134
Sergeant Bluff 2,416
Seymour 1,036
Shambaugh 197
Shannon City 93
Sharpsburg 114
Sheffield 1,224
Shelby 665
Sheldahl 315
Sheldon 5,003
Shell Rock 1,478

IOWA (continued)

Shellsburg 771
Shenandoah 6,274
Sherrill 208
Shueyville 287
Sibley 3,051
Sidney 1,308
Sigourney 2,330
Silver City 291
Sioux Center 4,588
Sioux City 82,003
Sioux Rapids 897
Slater 1,312
Sloan 978
Smithland 282
Soldier 257
Solon 969
Somers 220
South English 211
Spencer 11,726
Spillville 415
Spirit Lake 3,976
Spragueville 149
Spring Hill 95
Springbrook 209
Springville 1,165
Stacyville 538
Stanhope 492

Stanley 154
Stanton 747
Stanwood 705
State Center 1,292
Steamboat Rock 387
Stockport 272
Stockton 240
Storm Lake 8,814
Story City 2,762
Stout 190
Stratford 806
Strawberry Point 1,463
Struble 70
Stuart 1,650
Sully 828
Sumner 2,335
Superior 188
Sutherland 897
Swaledale 186
Swan 102
Swea City 813
Swisher 654
Tabor 1,088
Tama 2,968
Templeton 319
Tennant 77
Terril 420

Thayer 87
Thompson 668
Thor 200
Thornburg 103
Thornton 442
Thurman 221
Tiffin 413
Tingley 210
Tipton 3,055
Titonka 607
Toledo 2,445
Toronto 172
Traer 1,703
Treynor 920
Tripoli 1,280
Truesdale 128
Truro 407
Turin 103
Udell 75
Underwood 448
Union 515
Unionville 150
University Heights 1,069
University Park 645
Urbana 574
Urbandale 17,869
Ute 479

Vail 490
Valeria 80
Van Horne 682
Van Meter 747
Van Wert 245
Varina 122
Ventura 614
Victor 1,046
Villisca 1,434
Vincent 207
Vining 96
Vinton 5,040
Volga City 310
Wadena 230
Wahpeton 372
Walcott 1,425
Walford 285
Walker 733
Wall Lake 892
Wallingford 256
Walnut 897
Wapello 2,011
Washington 6,584
Washta 230
Waterloo 75,985
Waterville 157
Waucoma 308

Waukee 2,227
Waukon 3,983
Waverly 8,444
Wayland 720
Webb 222
Webster 124
Webster City 8,572
Weldon 187
Wellman 1,125
Wellsburg 761
Welton 119
Wesley 598
West Bend 941
West Branch 1,867
West Burlington 3,371
West Chester 191
West Des Moines 21,894
West Liberty 2,723
West Okoboji 435
West Point 1,133
West Union 2,783
Westfield 199
Westgate 263
Westphalia 169
Westside 387
What Cheer 803

Wheatland 840
Whiting 734
Whittemore 647
Whitten 168
Willey 94
Williams 410
Williamsburg 2,033
Williamson 210
Wilton 2,502
Windsor Heights 5,632
Winfield 1,042
Winterset 4,021
Winthrop 767
Wiota 181
Woden 287
Woodbine 1,463
Woodburn 207
Woodward 1,212
Woolstock 235
Worthington 432
Wyoming 702
Yale 299
Yetter 52
Yorktown 123
Zearing 630
Zwingle 119

KANSAS

Population 2,363,208

METROPOLITAN AREAS

Kansas City 1,327,020
(884,416 in Mo.; 442,604 in Kans.)
Lawrence 67,640
Topeka 185,442
Wichita 411,313

COUNTIES

Allen 15,654
Anderson 8,749
Atchison 18,397
Barber 6,548
Barton 31,343
Bourbon 15,969
Brown 11,955
Butler 44,782
Chase 3,309
Chautauqua 5,016
Cherokee 22,304
Cheyenne 3,678
Clark 2,599
Clay 9,802
Cloud 12,494
Coffey 9,370
Comanche 2,554
Cowley 36,824
Crawford 37,916
Decatur 4,509
Dickinson 20,175
Doniphan 9,268
Douglas 67,640
Edwards 4,271
Elk 3,918
Ellis 26,098
Ellsworth 6,640
Finney 23,825
Ford 24,315
Franklin 21,813
Geary 29,852
Gove 3,726
Graham 3,995
Grant 6,977
Gray 5,138
Greeley 1,845
Greenwood 8,764
Hamilton 2,514
Harper 7,778
Harvey 30,531
Haskell 3,814
Hodgeman 2,269
Jackson 11,644
Jefferson 15,207
Jewell 5,241
Johnson 270,269
Kearny 3,435
Kingman 8,960
Kiowa 4,046
Labette 25,682
Lane 2,472
Leavenworth 54,809
Lincoln 4,145
Linn 8,234
Logan 3,478
Lyon 35,108
Marion 13,522
Marshall 12,720
McPherson 26,855
Meade 4,788
Miami 21,618
Mitchell 8,117
Montgomery 42,281
Morris 6,419
Morton 3,454
Nemaha 11,211
Neosho 18,967
Ness 4,498
Norton 5,959
Osage 15,319
Osborne 5,959
Ottawa 5,971
Pawnee 8,065
Phillips 7,406
Pottawatomie 14,782
Pratt 10,275
Rawlins 4,105

Reno 64,983
Republic 7,569
Rice 11,900
Riley 63,505
Rooks 7,006
Rush 4,516
Russell 8,868
Saline 48,905
Scott 5,782
Sedgwick 366,531
Seward 17,071
Shawnee 154,916
Sheridan 3,544
Sherman 7,759
Smith 5,947
Stafford 5,539
Stanton 2,339
Stevens 4,736
Sumner 24,928
Thomas 8,451
Trego 4,165
Wabaunsee 6,867
Wallace 2,045
Washington 8,543
Wichita 3,041
Wilson 12,128
Woodson 4,600
Wyandotte 172,335

CITIES

Abbyville 123
Abilene 6,572
Admire 158
Agenda 106
Agra 321
Albert 236
Alden 205
Alexander 116
Allen 205
Alma 925
Almena 517
Alta Vista 430
Altamont 1,054
Alton 135
Altoona 564
Americus 915
Andale 538
Andover 2,801
Anthony 2,661
Arcadia 460
Argonia 587
Arkansas City 13,201
Arlington 631
Arma 1,676
Ashland 1,096
Assaria 414
Atchison 11,407
Athol 90
Atlanta 256
Attica 730
Atwood 1,665
Auburn 890
Augusta 6,968
Aurora 130
Axtell 470
Baldwin City 2,829
Barnard 163
Barnes 257
Bartlett 163
Basehor 1,483
Bassett 31
Baxter Springs 4,773
Bazine 333
Beattie 316
Belle Plaine 1,706
Belleville 2,805
Beloit 4,367
Belpre 154
Belvue 212
Benedict 111
Bennington 579
Bentley 311
Benton 609
Bern 220
Beverly 171
Bird City 546
Bison 279
Blue Mound 319
Blue Rapids 1,280

Bluff City 95
Bogue 197
Bonner Springs 6,266
Brewster 327
Bronson 414
Brookville 259
Brownell 92
Bucklin 786
Buffalo 386
Buhler 1,188
Bunker Hill 124
Burden 518
Burdett 275
Burlingame 1,239
Burlington 2,901
Burns 224
Burr Oak 366
Burrton 976
Bushong 82
Bushton 388
Byers 47
Caldwell 1,401
Cambridge 113
Caney 2,284
Canton 926
Carbondale 1,518
Carlton 49
Cassoday 122
Cawker City 640
Cedar 53
Cedar Point 66
Cedar Vale 848
Centralia 486
Chanute 10,506
Chapman 1,255
Chase 753
Chautauqua 156
Cheney 1,404
Cherokee 775
Cherryvale 2,769
Chetopa 1,751
Cimarron 1,491
Circleville 164
Claflin 764
Clay Center 4,948
Clayton 102
Clearwater 1,684
Clifton 695
Climax 81
Clyde 909
Coats 153
Coffeyville 15,185
Colby 5,544
Coldwater 989
Collyer 151
Colony 474
Columbus 3,426
Colwich 935
Concordia 6,847
Conway Springs 1,313
Coolidge 82
Copeland 323
Corning 158
Cottonwood Falls 954
Council Grove 2,381
Countryside 346
Courtland 377
Coyville 98
Cuba 286
Cullison 154
Culver 167
Cunningham 540
Damar 204
Danville 71
Dearing 475
Deerfield 538
Delia 181
Delphos 570
Denison 231
Denton 156
Derby 9,786
De Soto 2,061
Dexter 366
Dighton 1,390
Dodge City 18,001
Dorrance 220
Douglass 1,450
Downs 1,324
Dresden 84
Dunlap 82

Durham 130
Dwight 320
Earlton 79
Eastborough 854
Easton 460
Edgerton 1,214
Edmond 56
Edna 537
Edwardsville 3,364
Effingham 634
Elbing 175
El Dorado 10,510
Elgin 139
Elk City 404
Elk Falls 151
Elkhart 2,243
Ellinwood 2,508
Ellis 2,062
Ellsworth 2,465
Elmdale 104
Elsmore 104
Elwood 1,275
Emmett 203
Emporia 25,287
Englewood 111
Ensign 209
Enterprise 839
Erie 1,415
Esbon 234
Eskridge 603
Eudora 2,934
Eureka 3,425
Everest 331
Fairview 258
Fairway 4,619
Fall River 173
Florence 729
Fontana 173
Ford 272
Formoso 166
Fort Scott 8,893
Fowler 592
Frankfort 1,038
Fredonia 3,047
Frontenac 2,586
Fulton 194
Galatia 69
Galena 3,587
Galesburg 181
Galva 651
Garden City 18,256
Garden Plain 775
Gardner 2,392
Garfield 252
Garnett 3,310
Gas 543
Gaylord 203
Gem 101
Geneseo 496
Geuda Springs 217
Girard 2,888
Glade 131
Glasco 710
Glen Elder 491
Goddard 1,427
Goessel 421
Goff 196
Goodland 5,708
Gorham 355
Gove 148
Grainfield 417
Grandview Plaza 1,189
Great Bend 16,608
Greeley 405
Green 155
Greenleaf 462
Greensburg 1,885
Grenola 335
Gridley 404
Grinnell 410
Gypsum 423
Haddam 239
Halstead 1,994
Hamilton 363
Hamlin 80
Hanover 802
Hanston 257
Hardtner 336
Harper 1,823
Harris 80

Hartford 551
Harveyville 280
Havana 169
Haven 1,125
Havensville 183
Haviland 770
Hays 16,301
Haysville 8,006
Hazelton 143
Hepler 165
Herington 2,930
Herndon 220
Hesston 3,013
Hiawatha 3,702
Highland 954
Hill City 2,028
Hillsboro 2,717
Hoisington 3,678
Holcomb 816
Hollenberg 57
Holton 3,132
Holyrood 567
Hope 468
Horace 137
Horton 2,130
Howard 965
Hoxie 1,462
Hoyt 536
Hudson 157
Hugoton 3,165
Humboldt 2,230
Hunnewell 86
Hunter 135
Huron 107
Hutchinson 40,284
Independence 10,598
Ingalls 274
Inman 947
Iola 6,938
Isabel 137
Iuka 235
Jamestown 440
Jennings 194
Jetmore 862
Jewell 589
Johnson 1,244
Junction City 19,305
Kanopolis 729
Kanorado 217
Kansas City 161,087
Kechi 288
Kensington 681
Kincaid 192
Kingman 3,563
Kinsley 2,074
Kiowa 1,409
Kirwin 249
Kismet 368
Labette 123
La Crosse 1,618
La Cygne 1,025
La Harpe 687
Lake Quivira 1,087
Lakin 1,823
Lancaster 274
Lane 249
Langdon 84
Lansing 5,307
Larned 4,811
Latham 148
Latimer 31
Lawrence 52,738
Leavenworth 33,656
Leawood 13,360
Lebanon 440
Lebo 966
Lecompton 576
Lehigh 173
Lenexa 18,639
Lenora 444
Leon 667
Leona 73
Leonardville 437
Leoti 1,869
Le Roy 701
Lewis 551
Liberal 14,911
Liberty 174
Liebenthal 163
Lincoln 1,599

Lincolnville 235
Lindsborg 3,155
Linn 483
Linwood 343
Little River 529
Logan 720
Lone Elm 55
Long Island 187
Longford 109
Longton 396
Lorraine 157
Lost Springs 94
Louisburg 1,744
Louisville 207
Lucas 524
Luray 295
Lyndon 1,132
Lyons 4,152
Macksville 546
Madison 1,099
Mahaska 119
Maize 1,294
Manchester 98
Manhattan 32,644
Mankato 1,205
Manter 205
Maple Hill 381
Mapleton 121
Marion 1,951
Marquette 639
Marysville 3,670
Matfield Green 71
Mayetta 287
Mayfield 128
McCracken 292
McCune 528
McDonald 239
McFarland 242
McLouth 700
McPherson 11,753
Meade 1,777
Medicine Lodge 2,384
Melvern 481
Menlo 42
Meriden 707
Merriam 10,794
Milan 135
Mildred 64
Milford 465
Miltonvale 588
Minneapolis 2,075
Minneola 712
Mission 8,643
Mission Hills 3,904
Mission Woods 213
Moline 553
Montezuma 730
Moran 643
Morganville 261
Morland 223
Morrill 336
Morrowville 180
Moscow 228
Mound City 755
Mound Valley 381
Moundridge 1,453
Mount Hope 791
Mulberry 647
Mullinville 339
Mulvane 4,254
Munden 152
Muscotah 248
Narka 120
Nashville 127
Natoma 515
Neodesha 3,414
Neosho Falls 157
Neosho Rapids 289
Ness City 1,769
Netawaka 218
New Albany 78
New Cambria 175
New Strawn 457
Newton 16,332
Nickerson 1,292
Niotaze 104
Norcatur 226
North Newton 1,222
Norton 3,400
Nortonville 692

Norwich 476
Oak Hill 35
Oakley 2,343
Oberlin 2,387
Offerle 244
Ogden 1,804
Oketo 130
Olathe 37,258
Olivet 65
Olmitz 140
Olpe 477
Olsburg 166
Onaga 752
Oneida 120
Osage City 2,667
Osawatomie 4,459
Osborne 2,120
Oskaloosa 1,092
Oswego 2,218
Otis 410
Ottawa 11,016
Overbrook 930
Overland Park 81,784
Oxford 1,125
Ozawkie 472
Palco 329
Palmer 149
Paola 4,557
Paradise 89
Park 183
Parker 270
Parkerville 42
Parsons 12,898
Partridge 268
Pawnee Rock 409
Paxico 168
Peabody 1,474
Penalosa 31
Perry 907
Peru 286
Phillipsburg 3,229
Pittsburg 18,770
Plains 1,044
Plainville 2,458
Pleasanton 1,303
Plevna 115
Pomona 868
Portis 172
Potwin 563
Powhattan 95
Prairie View 145
Prairie Village 24,657
Pratt 6,885
Prescott 319
Preston 227
Pretty Prairie 655
Princeton 244
Protection 684
Quenemo 413
Quinter 951
Radium 47
Ramona 116
Randall 154
Randolph 131
Ransom 448
Rantoul 212
Raymond 132
Reading 244
Redfield 185
Republic 223
Reserve 105
Rexford 204
Richfield 81
Richmond 510
Riley 779
Robinson 324
Roeland Park 7,962
Rolla 417
Rose Hill 1,557
Roseland 119
Rossville 1,045
Rozel 219
Rush Center 207
Russell 5,427
Russell Springs 56
Sabetha 2,286
St. Francis 1,610
St. George 309
St. John 1,346
St. Marys 1,598
St. Paul 746
Salina 41,843
Satanta 1,117
Savonburg 113
Sawyer 213
Scammon 501
Scandia 480
Schoenchen 209
Scott City 4,154
Scottsville 56
Scranton 664
Sedan 1,579
Sedgwick 1,471
Selden 266
Seneca 2,389
Severance 134
Severy 447
Seward 88
Sharon 283
Sharon Springs 982
Shawnee 29,653
Silver Lake 1,350
Simpson 123
Smith Center 2,240
Smolan 169
Soldier 165
Solomon 1,018
South Haven 439
South Hutchinson 2,226
Spearville 693
Speed 41
Spivey 83
Spring Hill 2,005
Stafford 1,425
Stark 143
Sterling 2,312
Stockton 1,825
Strong City 675
Sublette 1,293
Summerfield 158
Sun City 85
Susank 52
Sylvan Grove 376
Sylvia 353
Sycracuse 1,654
Tampa 113
Tescott 331
Thayer 517
Timken 99
Tipton 321
Tonganoxie 1,864
Topeka 115,266
Toronto 466
Towanda 1,332
Treece 194
Tribune 955
Troy 1,240
Turon 481
Tyro 289
Udall 891
Ulysses 4,653
Uniontown 371
Utica 275
Valley Center 3,300
Valley Falls 1,189
Vermillion 191
Victoria 1,328
Vining 85
Viola 199
Virgil 169
WaKeeney 2,388
Wakefield 803
Waldo 75
Waldron 29
Wallace 86
Walnut 308
Walton 269
Wamego 3,159
Washington 1,488
Waterville 694
Wathena 1,418
Waverly 671
Webber 53
Weir 705
Wellington 8,212
Wellsville 1,363
West Mineral 229
Westmoreland 598
Westphalia 204
Westwood 1,783
Westwood Hills 437
Wetmore 376
Wheaton 90
White City 534
White Cloud 234
Whitewater 751
Whiting 270
Wichita 279,272
Willard 128
Williamsburg 362
Willis 85
Willowbrook 109
Wilmore 97
Wilsey 179
Wilson 978
Winchester 570
Windom 160
Winfield 10,736
Winona 258
Woodbine 172
Woodston 157
Yates Center 1,998
Zenda 146
Zurich 185

KENTUCKY

Population 3,661,433

METROPOLITAN AREAS

Ashland-Huntington (W. Va.) 311,350 (152,856 in W. Va.; 63,849 in O.; 94,645 in Ky.)
Cincinnati (O.) 1,401,403 (1,100,895 in O.; 266,217 in Ky.; 34,291 in Ind.)
Evansville (Ind.) 309,408 (268,559 in Ind.; 40,849 in Ky.)
Hopkinsville-Clarksville (Tenn.) 150,220 (83,342 in Tenn.; 66,878 in Ky.)
Lexington-Fayette 318,136
Louisville 906,240 (756,233 in Ky.; 150,007 in Ind.)
Owensboro 85,949

COUNTIES

Adair 15,233
Allen 14,128
Anderson 12,567
Ballard 8,798
Barren 34,009
Bath 10,025
Bell 34,330
Boone 45,842
Bourbon 19,405
Boyd 55,513
Boyle 25,066
Bracken 7,738
Breathitt 17,004
Breckinridge 16,861
Bullitt 43,346
Butler 11,064
Caldwell 13,473
Calloway 30,031
Campbell 83,317
Carlisle 5,487
Carroll 9,270
Carter 25,060
Casey 14,818
Christian 66,878
Clark 28,322
Clay 22,752
Clinton 9,321
Crittenden 9,207
Cumberland 7,289
Daviess 85,949
Edmonson 9,962
Elliott 6,908
Estill 14,495
Fayette† 204,165
Fleming 12,323
Floyd 48,764
Franklin 41,830
Fulton 8,971
Gallatin 4,842
Garrard 10,853
Grant 13,308
Graves 34,049
Grayson 20,854
Green 11,043
Greenup 39,132
Hancock 7,742
Hardin 88,917
Harlan 41,889
Harrison 15,166
Hart 15,402
Henderson 40,849
Henry 12,740
Hickman 6,065
Hopkins 46,174
Jackson 11,996
Jefferson 684,793
Jessamine 26,653
Johnson 24,432
Kenton 137,058
Knott 17,940
Knox 30,239
Larue 11,983
Laurel 38,982
Lawrence 14,121
Lee 7,754
Leslie 14,882
Letcher 30,687
Lewis 14,545
Lincoln 19,053
Livingston 9,219
Logan 24,138
Lyon 6,490
Madison 53,352
Magoffin 13,515
Marion 17,910
Marshall 25,637
Martin 13,925
Mason 17,760
McCracken 61,310
McCreary 15,634
McLean 10,090
Meade 22,854
Menifee 5,117
Mercer 19,011
Metcalfe 9,484
Monroe 12,353
Montgomery 20,046
Morgan 12,103
Muhlenberg 32,238
Nelson 27,584
Nicholas 7,157
Ohio 21,765
Oldham 28,094
Owen 8,924
Owsley 5,709
Pendleton 10,989
Perry 33,763
Pike 81,123
Powell 11,101
Pulaski 45,803
Robertson 2,270
Rockcastle 13,973
Rowan 19,049
Russell 13,708
Scott 21,813
Shelby 23,328
Simpson 14,673
Spencer 5,929
Taylor 21,178
Todd 11,874
Trigg 9,384
Trimble 6,253
Union 17,821
Warren 71,828
Washington 10,764
Wayne 17,022
Webster 14,832
Whitley 33,396
Wolfe 6,698
Woodford 17,778

CITIES

Adairville 1,105
Albany 2,083
Alexandria 4,735
Allen 338
Allensville 170
Anchorage 1,726
Arlington 511
Ashland 27,064
Auburn 1,467
Audubon Park 1,571
Augusta 1,455
Bancroft 725
Barbourmeade 1,038
Barbourville 3,333
Bardstown 6,155
Bardwell 988
Barlow 746
Beattyville 1,068
Beaver Dam 3,185
Bedford 835
Beechwood Village 1,462
Bellefonte 908
Bellemeade 918
Bellevue 7,678
Bellewood 307
Benham 936
Benton 3,700
Berea 8,226
Berry 287
Blaine 358
Bloomfield 954
Blue Ridge Manor 465
Bonnieville 372
Booneville 191
Bowling Green 40,450
Bradfordsville 331
Brandenburg 1,831
Bremen 179
Briarwood 374
Broadfields 295
Brodhead 686
Bromley 844
Brooksville 680
Brownsboro Farm 790
Brownsboro Village 410
Brownsville 674
Burgin 1,008
Burkesville 2,051
Burnside 775
Butler 663
Cadiz 1,661
Calhoun 1,080
California 135
Calvert City 2,388
Camargo 1,301
Cambridge 193
Campbellsburg 714
Campbellsville 8,715
Campton 486
Caneyville 642
Carlisle 1,757
Carrollton 3,967
Carrsville 99
Catlettsburg 3,005
Cave City 2,098
Centertown 462
Central City 5,214
Cherrywood Village 362
Clarkson 666
Clay 1,356
Clay City 1,276
Clinton 1,720
Cloverport 1,585
Coal Run 348
Cold Spring 2,117
Columbia 3,710
Columbus 296
Corbin 8,075
Corinth 258
Corydon 874
Covington 49,013
Crab Orchard 843
Creekside 419
Crescent Park 351
Crescent Springs 1,951
Crestview 528
Crestview Hills 1,408
Crestwood 531
Crittenden 597
Crofton 823
Crossgate 262
Cumberland 3,712
Cynthiana 5,881
Danville 12,942
Dawson Springs 3,275
Dayton 6,979
Devondale 1,466
Dixon 533
Douglass Hills 4,384
Dover 305
Drakesboro 798
Druid Hills 338
Dry Ridge 1,250
Earlington 2,011
Eddyville 1,949
Edgewood 7,230
Edmonton 1,401
Ekron 239
Elizabethtown 15,380
Elkhorn City 1,446
Elkton 1,815
Elsmere 7,203
Eminence 2,260
Erlanger 14,433
Eubank 207
Evarts 1,234
Fairfield 169
Fairmeade 272
Fairview 198
Falmouth 2,482
Ferguson 1,009
Fincastle 804
Flatwoods 8,354
Fleming [-Neon] 1,195
Flemingsburg 2,835
Florence 15,586
Fordsville 561
Forest Hills 502
Fort Mitchell 7,297
Fort Thomas 16,012
Fort Wright 4,481
Fountain Run 340
Frankfort 25,973
Franklin 7,738
Fredonia 535
Frenchburg 550
Fulton 3,137
Gamaliel 456
Georgetown 10,972
Germantown 347
Ghent 439
Glasgow 12,958
Glencoe 354
Glenview Hills 433
Glenview Manor 212
Goose Creek 394
Grand Rivers 428
Gratz 124
Graymoor 1,194
Grayson 3,423
Greensburg 2,377
Green Spring 634
Greenup 1,386
Greenville 4,631
Guthrie 1,361
Hanson 485
Hardin 545
Hardinsburg 2,211
Harlan 3,024
Harrodsburg 7,265
Hartford 2,512
Hawesville 1,036
Hazard 5,429
Hazel 465
Henderson 24,834
Hickman 2,894
Hickory Hill 171
Highland Heights 4,435
Hills and Dales 151
Hillview 5,196
Hindman 876
Hiseville 349
Hodgenville 2,459
Hollow Creek 1,023
Hollyvilla 476
Hopkinsville 27,318
Horse Cave 2,045
Houston Acres 608
Hurstbourne Acres 386
Hustonville 339
Hyden 488
Independence 7,998
Indian Hills 787
Indian Hills Cherokee Section 585
Irvine 2,889
Irvington 1,409
Island 532
Jackson 2,651
Jamestown 1,441
Jeffersontown 15,795
Jeffersonville 1,528
Jenkins 3,271
Junction City 2,045
Keeneland 432
Kenton Vale 145
Kevil 382
Kingsley 464
Kuttawa 560
La Center 1,044
La Fayette 160
La Grange 2,971
Lakeside Park 3,038
Lakeview Heights 478
Lancaster 3,365
Langdon Place 308
Latonia Lakes 396
Lawrenceburg 5,167
Lebanon 6,590
Lebanon Junction 1,581
Leitchfield 4,533
Lewisburg 972
Lewisport 1,832
Lexington† 204,165
Liberty 2,206
Lincolnshire 139
Livermore 1,672
Livingston 334
London 4,002
Lone Oak 443
Loretto 954
Louisa 1,832
Louisville 298,451
Loyall 1,210
Ludlow 4,959
Lynch 1,614
Lyndon 1,553
Lynnview 1,157
Mackville 229
Madisonville 16,979
Manchester 1,838
Manor Creek 241
Marion 3,392
Martin 827
Maryhill Estates 225
Mayfield 10,705
Maysville 7,983
McHenry 582
McKee 759
Meadow Vale 1,008
Meadowbrook Farm 683
Meadowview Estates 212
Melbourne 628
Mentor 169
Middlesboro 12,251
Middletown 414
Midway 1,445
Millersburg 987
Milton 718
Minor Lane Heights 1,882
Mockingbird Valley 205
Monterey 186
Monticello 5,677
Moorland 513
Morehead 7,789
Morganfield 3,781
Morgantown 2,000
Mortons Gap 1,201
Mount Olivet 346
Mount Sterling 5,820
Mount Vernon 2,334
Mount Washington 3,997
Muldraugh 1,752
Munfordville 1,783
Murray 14,248
Nebo 269
New Castle 832
New Haven 926
Newport 21,587
Nicholasville 10,400
Norbourne Estates 446
North Middletown 637
Northfield 906
Nortonville 1,336
Norwood 254
Oak Grove 2,088
Oakland 264
Old Brownsboro Place 358
Olive Hill 2,539
Orchard Grass Hills 1,047
Owensboro 54,450
Owenton 1,341
Owingsville 1,419
Paducah 29,315
Paintsville 3,815
Paris 7,935
Park City 614
Park Hills 3,500
Parkway Village 754
Pembroke 636
Perryville 841
Pewee Valley 982
Phelps 1,126
Pikeville 4,756
Pineville 2,599
Pioneer Village 390
Plantation 969
Pleasant Valley 342
Pleasureville 837
Plum Springs 393
Plymouth Village 231
Powderly 848
Prestonsburg 4,011
Prestonville 205
Princeton 7,073
Prospect 1,981
Providence 4,434
Raceland 1,970
Radcliff 14,519
Ravenna 793
Richlawn 485
Richmond 21,705
Ridgeview Heights 729
Riverwood 435
Robinswood 273
Rochester 289
Rockport 511
Rolling Fields 731
Rolling Hills 1,067
Russell 3,824
Russell Springs 1,831
Russellville 7,520
Ryland Heights 252
Sacramento 538
Sadieville 253
St. Charles 405
St. Matthews 13,354
St. Regis Park 1,735
Salem 833
Salt Lick 347
Salyersville 1,352
Sanders 332
Sandy Hook 627
Sardis 203
Science Hill 655
Scottsville 4,278
Sebree 1,516
Seneca Gardens 748
Sharpsburg 339
Shelbyville 5,308
Shepherdsville 4,454
Shively 16,819
Silver Grove 1,260
Simpsonville 642
Slaughters 269
Smithfield 137
Smithland 512
Smiths Grove 767
Somerset 10,649
Sonora 416

South Carrollton ... 262
South Park View ... 248
South Shore ... 1,525
Southgate ... 2,833
Sparta ... 192
Springfield ... 3,179
Springlee ... 498
Stamping Ground ... 562
Stanford ... 2,764
Stanton ... 2,691
Strathmoor Gardens ... 292
Strathmoor Manor ... 368
Strathmoor Village ... 466
Sturgis ... 2,293
Taylor Mill ... 4,509
Taylorsville ... 801
Thornhill ... 367
Tollesboro ... 808
Tompkinsville ... 4,366
Trenton ... 465
Union ... 601
Uniontown ... 1,169
Upton ... 731
Vanceburg ... 1,939
Versailles ... 6,427
Vicco ... 456
Villa Hills ... 4,402
Vine Grove ... 3,583
Visalia ... 198
Wallins Creek ... 459
Walton ... 1,651
Warsaw ... 1,328
Washington ... 624
Water Valley ... 395
Waverly ... 434
Wayland ... 601
Wellington ... 653
West Buechel ... 1,205
West Liberty ... 1,381
West Point ... 1,339
Westwood ... 826
Wheatcroft ... 325
Wheelwright ... 865
Whipps Millgate ... 227
White Plains ... 859
Whitesburg ... 1,525
Whitesville ... 788
Wickliffe ... 1,044
Wilder ... 633
Wildwood ... 309
Williamsburg ... 5,560
Williamstown ... 2,502
Willisburg ... 235
Wilmore ... 3,787
Winchester ... 15,216
Winding Falls ... 454
Windy Hills ... 2,214
Wingo ... 606
Woodburn ... 330
Woodland Hills ... 839
Woodlawn ... 331
Woodlawn Park ... 1,052
Worthington ... 1,948
Worthville ... 272
Wurtland ... 1,301
Yorktown ... 155

†Lexington and Fayette County were consolidated as Lexington-Fayette Urban County on Jan. 1, 1974.

LOUISIANA

Population 4,203,972

METROPOLITAN AREAS

Alexandria ... 151,985
Baton Rouge ... 493,973
Lafayette ... 150,017
Lake Charles ... 167,048
Monroe ... 139,241
New Orleans ... 1,186,725
Shreveport ... 376,646

PARISHES (COUNTIES)

Acadia ... 56,427
Allen ... 21,390
Ascension ... 50,068
Assumption ... 22,084
Avoyelles ... 41,393
Beauregard ... 29,692
Bienville ... 16,387
Bossier ... 80,721
Caddo ... 252,294
Calcasieu ... 167,048
Caldwell ... 10,761
Cameron ... 9,336
Catahoula ... 12,287
Claiborne ... 17,095
Concordia ... 22,981
De Soto ... 25,664
East Baton Rouge ... 366,164
East Carroll ... 11,772
East Feliciana ... 19,015
Evangeline ... 33,343
Franklin ... 24,141
Grant ... 16,703
Iberia ... 63,752
Iberville ... 32,159
Jackson ... 17,321
Jefferson ... 454,592
Jefferson Davis ... 32,168
Lafayette ... 150,017
Lafourche ... 82,483
La Salle ... 17,004
Lincoln ... 39,763
Livingston ... 58,655
Madison ... 14,733
Morehouse ... 34,803
Natchitoches ... 39,863
Orleans ... 557,482
Ouachita ... 139,241
Plaquemines ... 26,049
Pointe Coupee ... 24,045
Rapides ... 135,282
Red River ... 10,433
Richland ... 22,187
Sabine ... 25,280
St. Bernard ... 64,097
St. Charles ... 37,259
St. Helena ... 9,827
St. James ... 21,495
St. John the Baptist ... 31,924
St. Landry ... 84,128
St. Martin ... 40,214
St. Mary ... 64,395
St. Tammany ... 110,554
Tangipahoa ... 80,698
Tensas ... 8,525
Terrebonne ... 94,393
Union ... 21,167
Vermilion ... 48,458
Vernon ... 53,475
Washington ... 44,207
Webster ... 43,631
West Baton Rouge ... 19,086
West Carroll ... 12,922
West Feliciana ... 12,186
Winn ... 17,253

CITIES, TOWNS, AND VILLAGES

Abbeville ... 12,391
Abita Springs ... 1,072
Addis ... 1,320
Albany ... 857
Alexandria ... 51,565
Amite ... 4,301
Anacoco ... 90
Angie ... 311
Arcadia ... 3,403
Arnaudville ... 1,679
Ashland ... 307
Athens ... 419
Atlanta ... 127
Baker ... 12,865
Baldwin ... 2,644
Ball ... 3,405
Basile ... 2,635
Baskin ... 286
Bastrop ... 15,527
Baton Rouge ... 219,486
Belcher ... 436
Benton ... 1,864
Bernice ... 1,956
Berwick ... 4,466
Bienville ... 249
Blanchard ... 1,128
Bogalusa ... 16,976
Bonita ... 503
Bossier City ... 49,969
Boyce ... 1,198
Breaux Bridge ... 5,922
Broussard ... 2,923
Brusly Landing ... 1,762
Bryceland ... 94
Bunkie ... 5,364
Calvin ... 263
Campti ... 1,069
Cankton ... 303
Carencro ... 3,712
Castor ... 195
Chataignier ... 431
Chatham ... 714
Cheneyville ... 865
Choudrant ... 809
Church Point ... 4,599
Clarence ... 612
Clarks ... 931
Clayton ... 1,204
Clinton ... 1,919
Colfax ... 1,680
Collinston ... 439
Columbia ... 687
Converse ... 449
Cotton Valley ... 1,445
Cottonport ... 1,911
Coushatta ... 2,084
Covington ... 7,892
Crowley ... 16,036
Cullen ... 1,869
Delcambre ... 2,216
Delhi ... 3,290
Delta ... 295
Denham Springs ... 8,412
De Quincy ... 3,966
De Ridder ... 11,057
Dixie Inn ... 453
Dodson ... 469
Donaldsonville ... 7,901
Downsville ... 213
Doyline ... 801
Dry Prong ... 526
Dubach ... 1,161
Dubberly ... 421
Duson ... 1,253
East Hodge ... 439
Edgefield ... 312
Elizabeth ... 454
Elton ... 1,450
Epps ... 672
Erath ... 2,133
Eros ... 158
Estherwood ... 691
Eunice ... 12,479
Evergreen ... 272
Farmerville ... 3,768
Fenton ... 491
Ferriday ... 4,472
Fisher ... 325
Florien ... 964
Folsom ... 319
Fordoche ... 676
Forest ... 299
Forest Hill ... 494
Franklin ... 9,584
Franklinton ... 4,119
French Settlement ... 761
Georgetown ... 381
Gibsland ... 1,354
Gilbert ... 800
Gilliam ... 244
Glenmora ... 1,479
Golden Meadow ... 2,282
Goldonna ... 526
Gonzales ... 7,287
Grambling ... 4,226
Gramercy ... 3,211
Grand Cane ... 252
Grand Coteau ... 1,165
Grand Isle ... 1,982
Grayson ... 564
Greensburg ... 662
Greenwood ... 1,043
Gretna ... 20,615
Grosse Tete ... 749
Gueydan ... 1,695
Hall Summit ... 276
Hammond ... 15,043
Harahan ... 11,384
Harrisonburg ... 610
Haughton ... 1,510
Haynesville ... 3,454
Heflin ... 279
Henderson ... 1,560
Hessmer ... 743
Hodge ... 708
Homer ... 4,307
Hornbeck ... 470
Hosston ... 480
Houma ... 32,602
Ida ... 306
Independence ... 1,684
Iota ... 1,326
Iowa ... 2,437
Jackson ... 3,133
Jamestown ... 131
Jean Lafitte ... 541
Jeanerette ... 6,511
Jena ... 4,332
Jennings ... 12,401
Jonesboro ... 5,061
Jonesville ... 2,828
Junction City ... 727
Kaplan ... 5,016
Keatchie ... 342
Kenner ... 66,382
Kentwood ... 2,667
Kilbourne ... 286
Killian ... 611
Kinder ... 2,603
Krotz Springs ... 1,374
Lafayette ... 81,961
Lake Arthur ... 3,615
Lake Charles ... 75,051
Lake Providence ... 6,361
Lecompte ... 1,661
Leesville ... 9,054
Leonville ... 1,143
Lillie ... 172
Lisbon ... 138
Livingston ... 1,260
Livonia ... 980
Lockport ... 2,424
Logansport ... 1,565
Longstreet ... 281
Loreauville ... 860
Lucky ... 370
Lutcher ... 4,730
Madisonville ... 799
Mamou ... 3,194
Mandeville ... 6,076
Mangham ... 867
Mansfield ... 6,485
Mansura ... 2,074
Many ... 3,988
Maringouin ... 1,291
Marion ... 989
Marksville ... 5,113
Martin ... 584
Maurice ... 478
McNary ... 240
Melville ... 1,764
Mer Rouge ... 802
Mermentau ... 771
Merryville ... 1,286
Minden ... 15,074
Monroe ... 57,597
Montgomery ... 843
Montpelier ... 219
Mooringsport ... 911
Moreauville ... 853
Morgan City ... 16,114
Morganza ... 846
Morse ... 835
Mount Lebanon ... 105
Napoleonville ... 829
Natchez ... 527
Natchitoches ... 16,664
New Iberia ... 32,766
New Orleans ... 557,482
New Roads ... 3,924
Newellton ... 1,726
Newllano ... 2,213
Noble ... 194
North Hodge ... 573
Norwood ... 421
Oak Grove ... 2,214
Oak Ridge ... 257
Oakdale ... 7,155
Oberlin ... 1,764
Oil City ... 1,323
Olla ... 1,603
Opelousas ... 18,903
Palmetto ... 327
Parks ... 545
Patterson ... 4,584
Pearl River ... 1,693
Pine Prairie ... 734
Pineville ... 12,034
Pioneer ... 221
Plain Dealing ... 1,213
Plaquemine ... 7,521
Plaucheville ... 196
Pleasant Hill ... 776
Pollock ... 399
Ponchatoula ... 5,469
Port Allen ... 6,114
Port Barre ... 2,625
Port Vincent ... 450
Powhatan ... 279
Provencal ... 695
Quitman ... 231
Rayne ... 9,066
Rayville ... 4,610
Reeves ... 199
Richmond ... 505
Richwood ... 1,223
Ridgecrest ... 895
Ringgold ... 1,655
Robeline ... 238
Rodessa ... 337
Rosedale ... 658
Roseland ... 1,346
Rosepine ... 953
Ruston ... 20,585
St. Francisville ... 1,471
St. Joseph ... 1,687
St. Martinville ... 7,965
Saline ... 293
Sarepta ... 831
Scott ... 2,239
Shongaloo ... 163
Shreveport ... 205,815
Sibley ... 1,211
Sicily Island ... 691
Sikes ... 226
Simmesport ... 2,293
Simpson ... 534
Simsboro ... 553
Slaughter ... 729
Slidell ... 26,718
Sorrento ... 1,197
South Mansfield ... 419
Spearsville ... 181
Springfield ... 424
Springhill ... 6,516
Stanley ... 151
Sterlington ... 1,400
Stonewall ... 1,175
Sulphur ... 19,709
Sun ... 338
Sunset ... 2,300
Tallulah ... 10,392
Tangipahoa ... 493
Thibodaux ... 15,810
Tickfaw ... 571
Tullos ... 772
Turkey Creek ... 366
Urania ... 849
Varnado ... 249
Vidalia ... 5,936
Vienna ... 519
Ville Platte ... 9,201
Vinton ... 3,631
Vivian ... 4,146
Walker ... 2,957
Washington ... 1,266
Waterproof ... 1,339
Welsh ... 3,515
West Monroe ... 14,993
Westlake ... 5,246
Westwego ... 12,663
White Castle ... 2,160
Wilson ... 656
Winnfield ... 7,311
Winnsboro ... 5,921
Wisner ... 1,424
Woodworth ... 412
Youngsville ... 1,053
Zachary ... 7,297
Zwolle ... 2,602

MAINE

Population 1,124,660

METROPOLITAN AREAS

Lewiston-Auburn ... 72,378
Portland ... 183,625

COUNTIES

Androscoggin ... 99,657
Aroostook ... 91,331
Cumberland ... 215,789
Franklin ... 27,098
Hancock ... 41,781
Kennebec ... 109,889
Knox ... 32,941
Lincoln ... 25,691
Oxford ... 48,968
Penobscot ... 137,015
Piscataquis ... 17,634
Sagadahoc ... 28,795
Somerset ... 45,028
Waldo ... 28,414
Washington ... 34,963
York ... 139,666

CITIES AND TOWNS

Abbot ... 576▲
Acton ... 1,228▲
Addison ... 1,061▲
Albion ... 1,551▲
Alexander ... 385▲
Alfred ... 1,890▲
Allagash ... 448▲
Alna ... 425▲
Alton ... 468▲
Amherst ... 203▲
Amity ... 168▲
Andover ... 850▲
Anson ... 2,226▲
Appleton ... 818▲
Argyle ... 225
Arrowsic ... 305▲
Arundel ... 2,150▲
Ashland ... 1,865▲
Athens ... 802▲
Atkinson ... 306▲
Auburn ... 23,128
Augusta ... 21,819
Aurora ... 110▲
Avon ... 475▲
Baileyville ... 2,188▲
Baldwin ... 1,140▲
Bancroft ... 61▲
Bangor ... 31,643
Bar Harbor ... 4,124▲
Baring ... 308
Barnard ... 48
Bath ... 10,246
Beals ... 695▲
Beaver Cove ... 56
Beddington ... 36▲
Belfast ... 6,243
Belgrade ... 2,043▲
Belmont ... 520▲
Benedicta ... 225▲
Benton ... 2,188▲
Berwick ... 4,149▲
Bethel ... 2,340▲
Biddeford ... 19,638
Bingham ... 1,184▲
Blaine ... 922▲
Blanchard ... 64
Blue Hill ... 1,644▲
Boothbay ... 2,308▲
Boothbay Harbor ... 2,207▲
Bowdoin ... 1,629▲
Bowdoinham ... 1,828▲
Bowerbank ... 27▲
Bradford ... 888▲
Bradley ... 1,149▲
Bremen ... 598▲
Brewer ... 9,017
Bridgewater ... 742▲
Bridgton ... 3,528▲
Brighton ... 74▲
Bristol ... 2,095▲
Brooklin ... 619▲
Brooks ... 804▲
Brooksville ... 753▲
Brownfield ... 767▲
Brownville ... 1,545▲
Brunswick ... 17,366▲
Buckfield ... 1,333▲
Bucksport ... 4,345▲
Burlington ... 322▲
Burnham ... 951▲
Buxton ... 5,775▲
Byron ... 114▲
Calais ... 4,262
Cambridge ... 445▲
Camden ... 4,584▲
Canaan ... 1,189▲
Canton ... 831▲
Cape Elizabeth ... 7,838▲
Caratunk ... 84
Caribou ... 9,916
Carmel ... 1,695▲
Carrabassett Valley ... 107
Carroll ... 175
Carthage ... 438▲
Cary ... 229
Casco ... 2,243▲
Castine ... 1,304▲
Castle Hill ... 509▲
Caswell ... 586
Centerville ... 28▲
Central Aroostook ... 16
Central Hancock ... 124
Central Somerset ... 278
Chapman ... 406▲
Charleston ... 1,037▲
Charlotte ... 300▲
Chelsea ... 2,522▲
Cherryfield ... 983▲
Chester ... 434▲
Chesterville ... 869▲
China ... 2,918▲
Clifton ... 462▲
Clinton ... 2,696▲
Codyville ... 43
Columbia ... 275▲
Columbia Falls ... 517▲
Connor ... 574
Cooper ... 105▲
Coplin ... 111
Corinna ... 1,887▲
Corinth ... 1,711▲
Cornish ... 1,047▲
Cornville ... 838▲
Cranberry Isles ... 198▲
Crawford ... 86▲
Criehaven ... 5
Crystal ... 349▲
Cumberland ... 5,284▲
Cushing ... 795▲
Cutler ... 726▲
Cyr ... 147
Dallas ... 146
Damariscotta ... 1,493▲
Danforth ... 826▲
Dayton ... 882▲
Deblois ... 44▲
Dedham ... 841▲
Deer Isle ... 1,492▲
Denmark ... 672▲
Dennistown ... 30
Dennysville ... 296▲
Detroit ... 744▲
Dexter ... 4,286▲
Dixfield ... 2,389▲
Dixmont ... 812▲
Dover-Foxcroft ... 4,323▲
Dresden ... 998▲
Drew ... 57
Durham ... 2,074▲
Dyer Brook ... 275▲
E ... 55
Eagle Lake ... 1,019▲
East Central Washington ... 625
East Franklin ... 2
East Hancock ... 44
East Machias ... 1,233▲
East Millinocket ... 2,372▲
Eastbrook ... 262▲
Easton ... 1,305▲
Eastport ... 1,982
Eddington ... 1,769▲
Edgecomb ... 841▲
Edinburg ... 126▲
Eliot ... 4,948▲
Elliottsville ... 26
Ellsworth ... 5,179
Embden ... 536▲
Enfield ... 1,397▲
Etna ... 758▲
Eustis ... 582▲
Exeter ... 823▲
Fairfield ... 6,113▲
Falmouth ... 6,853▲
Farmingdale ... 2,535▲
Farmington ... 6,730▲
Fayette ... 812▲
Fort Fairfield ... 4,376▲
Fort Kent ... 4,826▲
Frankfort ... 783▲
Franklin ... 979▲
Freedom ... 458▲
Freeport ... 5,863▲
Frenchboro ... 43▲
Frenchville ... 1,450▲
Friendship ... 1,000▲
Fryeburg ... 2,715▲
Gardiner ... 6,485
Garfield ... 107
Garland ... 718▲
Georgetown ... 735▲
Gilead ... 191▲
Glenburn ... 2,319▲
Glenwood ... 7
Gorham ... 10,101▲
Gouldsboro ... 1,574▲
Grand Falls ... 1
Grand Isle ... 719▲
Grand Lake Stream ... 198
Gray ... 4,344▲
Great Pond ... 45
Greenbush ... 1,064▲
Greene ... 3,037▲
Greenfield ... 194▲
Greenville ... 1,839▲

Greenwood 653▲
Guilford 1,793▲
Hallowell 2,502
Hamlin 340
Hammond 73
Hampden 5,250▲
Hancock 1,409▲
Hanover 256▲
Harmony 755▲
Harpswell 3,796▲
Harrington 859▲
Harrison 1,667▲
Hartford 480▲
Hartland 1,669▲
Haynesville 169▲
Hebron 665▲
Hermon 3,170▲
Hersey 67▲
Hibberts 2
Highland 60
Hiram 1,067▲
Hodgdon 1,084▲
Holden 2,554▲
Hollis 2,892▲
Hope 730▲
Houlton 6,766▲
Howland 1,602▲
Hudson 797▲
Industry 563▲
Island Falls 981▲
Isle au Haut 57▲
Islesboro 521▲
Jackman 1,003▲
Jackson 346▲
Jay 5,080▲
Jefferson 1,616▲
Jonesboro 553▲
Jonesport 1,512▲
Kenduskeag 1,210▲
Kennebunk 6,621▲
Kennebunkport 2,952▲
Kingfield 1,083▲
Kingman 281
Kingsbury 4
Kittery 9,314▲
Knox 558▲
Lagrange 509▲
Lake View 20
Lakeville 32
Lamoine 953▲
Lebanon 3,234▲
Lee 688▲
Leeds 1,463▲
Levant 1,117▲
Lewiston 40,481
Liberty 694▲
Limerick 1,356▲
Limestone 8,719▲
Limington 2,203▲
Lincoln 5,066▲
Lincoln 50
Lincolnville 1,414▲
Linneus 752▲
Lisbon 8,769▲
Litchfield 1,954▲
Littleton 1,009▲
Livermore 1,826▲
Livermore Falls 3,572▲
Lovell 767▲
Lowell 194▲
Lubec 2,045
Ludlow 403▲
Lyman 2,509▲
Machias 2,458▲
Machiasport 1,108▲
Macwahoc 126
Madawaska 5,282▲
Madison 4,367▲
Madrid 178▲
Magalloway 79
Manchester 1,949▲
Mapleton 1,895▲
Mariaville 168▲
Mars Hill 1,892▲
Marshfield 416▲
Masardis 328▲
Matinicus Isle 66
Mattawamkeag 1,000▲
Maxfield 64▲
Mechanic Falls 2,616▲
Meddybemps 110▲
Medford 163▲
Medway 1,871▲
Mercer 448▲
Merrill 285▲
Mexico 3,698▲
Milbridge 1,306▲
Milford 2,160▲
Millinocket 7,567▲
Milo 2,624▲
Milton 123
Minot 1,631▲
Monhegan 109
Monmouth 2,888▲
Monroe 657▲
Monson 804▲
Monticello 950▲
Montville 631▲
Moose River 252▲
Moro 30
Morrill 506▲
Moscow 570▲
Mount Chase 233
Mount Desert 2,063▲
Mount Vernon 1,021▲
Naples 1,833▲
Nashville 48
New Canada 269
New Gloucester 3,180▲
New Limerick 513▲
New Portland 651▲
New Sharon 969▲
New Sweden 737▲
New Vineyard 607▲
Newburgh 1,228▲
Newcastle 1,227▲
Newfield 644▲
Newport 2,755▲
Newry 235▲
Nobleboro 1,154▲
Norridgewock 2,552▲
North Berwick 2,878▲
North Franklin 28
North Haven 373▲
North Oxford 37
North Penobscot 246
North Washington 393
North Yarmouth 1,919▲
Northeast Piscataquis 132
Northeast Somerset 301
Northfield 88
Northport 958▲
Northwest Aroostook 101
Northwest Piscataquis 99
Northwest Somerset 15
Norway 4,042▲
Oakfield 847▲
Oakland 5,162▲
Ogunquit 1,492
Old Orchard Beach 6,291▲
Old Town 8,422
Orient 97▲
Orland 1,645▲
Orono 10,578▲
Orrington 3,244▲
Osborn 47
Otis 307▲
Otisfield 897▲
Owls Head 1,633▲
Oxbow 84
Oxford 3,143▲
Palermo 760▲
Palmyra 1,485▲
Paris 4,168▲
Parkman 621▲
Parsonfield 1,089▲
Passadumkeag 430▲
Passamaquoddy Indian Township Indian Reservation 423
Passamaquoddy Pleasant Point Indian Reservation 549
Patten 1,368▲
Pembroke 920▲
Penobscot 1,104▲
Penobscot Indian Island Indian Reservation 458
Perham 437▲
Perkins 2
Perry 737▲
Peru 1,564▲
Phillips 1,092▲
Phippsburg 1,527▲
Pittsfield 4,125▲
Pittston 2,267▲
Plantation Number 14 52
Plantation Number 21 127
Pleasant Ridge 99
Plymouth 811▲
Poland 3,578▲
Portage Lake 562▲
Porter 1,222▲
Portland 61,572
Pownal 1,189▲
Prentiss 205
Presque Isle 11,172
Princeton 994▲
Prospect 511▲
Randolph 1,834▲
Rangeley 1,023▲
Rangeley 69
Raymond 2,251▲
Readfield 1,943▲
Reed 274
Richmond 2,627▲
Ripley 439▲
Robbinston 492▲
Rockland 7,919
Rockport 2,749▲
Rome 627▲
Roque Bluffs 244▲
Roxbury 373▲
Rumford 8,240▲
Sabattus 3,081▲
Saco 12,921
St. Agatha 1,035▲
St. Albans 1,400▲
St. Francis 839▲
St. George 1,948▲
St. John 322
Sandy River 50
Sanford 18,020▲
Sangerville 1,219▲
Scarborough 11,347▲
Searsmont 782▲
Searsport 2,309▲
Sebago 974▲
Sebec 469▲
Seboeis 53
Seboomook Lake 37
Sedgwick 795▲
Shapleigh 1,370▲
Sherman 1,021▲
Shirley 242▲
Sidney 2,052▲
Skowhegan 8,098▲
Smithfield 748▲
Smyrna 354▲
Solon 827▲
Somerville 377
Sorrento 276▲
South Aroostook 261
South Berwick 4,046▲
South Bristol 800▲
South Franklin 48
South Oxford 348
South Portland 22,712
South Thomaston 1,064▲
Southeast Piscataquis 183
Southport 598
Southwest Harbor 1,855▲
Springfield 443▲
Square Lake 604
Stacyville 554▲
Standish 5,946▲
Starks 440▲
Stetson 618▲
Steuben 970▲
Stockholm 319▲
Stockton Springs 1,230▲
Stoneham 204▲
Stonington 1,273▲
Stow 186▲
Strong 1,506▲
Sullivan 967▲
Summit 7
Sumner 613▲
Surry 894▲
Swans Island 337▲
Swanville 873▲
Sweden 163▲
Talmadge 40▲
Temple 518▲
The Forks 72
Thomaston 2,900▲
Thorndike 603▲
Topsfield 240
Topsham 6,431▲
Tremont 1,222▲
Trenton 718▲
Troy 701▲
Turner 3,539▲
Union 1,569▲
Unity 1,431▲
Unity 37
Upton 65▲
Van Buren 3,557▲
Vanceboro 256▲
Vassalboro 3,410▲
Veazie 1,610▲
Verona 559▲
Vienna 454▲
Vinalhaven 1,211▲
Wade 285▲
Waite 130▲
Waldo 495▲
Waldoboro 3,985▲
Wales 862▲
Wallagrass 653
Waltham 186▲
Warren 2,566▲
Washburn 2,028▲
Washington 954▲
Waterboro 2,943▲
Waterford 951▲
Waterville 17,779
Wayne 680▲
Webster 82
Weld 435▲
Wellington 287▲
Wells 8,211▲
Wesley 140▲
West Bath 1,309▲
West Forks 72
West Gardiner 2,113▲
West Paris 1,390▲
Westbrook 14,976
Westfield 647▲
Westmanland 53
Weston 155▲
Westport 420▲
Whitefield 1,606▲
Whiting 335▲
Whitneyville 264▲
Willimantic 164▲
Wilton 4,382▲
Windham 11,282▲
Windsor 1,702▲
Winn 503▲
Winslow 8,057▲
Winter Harbor 1,120▲
Winterport 2,675▲
Winterville 235
Winthrop 5,889▲
Wiscasset 2,832▲
Woodland 1,369▲
Woodstock 1,087▲
Woodville 226▲
Woolwich 2,156▲
Wyman 7
Yarmouth 6,585▲
York 8,465▲

▲Entire town (township), including rural area.

MARYLAND

Population 4,216,446

METROPOLITAN AREAS

Baltimore 2,174,023
Washington, D.C. 3,060,240 (1,316,875 in Md.; 1,105,714 in Va.; 637,651 in D.C.)
Wilmington (Del.) 524,108 (399,002 in Del.; 64,676 in N.J.; 60,430 in Md.)

COUNTIES

Allegany 80,548
Anne Arundel 370,775
Baltimore 655,615
Calvert 34,638
Caroline 23,143
Carroll 96,356
Cecil 60,430
Charles 72,751
Dorchester 30,623
Frederick 114,263
Garrett 26,498
Harford 145,930
Howard 118,572
Kent 16,695
Montgomery 579,053
Prince Georges 665,071
Queen Annes 25,508
St. Marys 59,895
Somerset 19,188
Talbot 25,604
Washington 113,086
Wicomico 64,540
Worcester 30,889

CITIES, TOWNS, AND VILLAGES

Aberdeen 11,533
Accident 246
Annapolis 31,740
Baltimore 786,775†
Barclay 132
Barnesville 141
Barton 617
Bel Air 7,814
Berlin 2,162
Berwyn Heights 3,135
Betterton 356
Bladensburg 7,691
Boonsboro 1,908
Bowie 33,695
Brentwood 2,988
Brookeville 120
Brookview 78
Brunswick 4,572
Burkittsville 202
Cambridge 11,703
Capitol Heights 3,271
Cecilton 508
Centreville 2,018
Charlestown 720
Chesapeake Beach 1,408
Chesapeake City 899
Chestertown 3,300
Cheverly 5,751
Chevy Chase 2,118
Chevy Chase Section Four 2,903
Church Creek 124
Church Hill 319
Clear Spring 477
College Park 23,614
Colmar Manor 1,286
Cottage City 1,122
Crisfield 2,924
Cumberland 25,933
Deer Park 486
Delmar 1,232
Denton 1,927
District Heights 6,799
Eagle Harbor 45
East New Market 230
Easton 7,536
Edmonston 1,109
Eldorado 93
Elkton 6,468
Emmitsburg 1,552
Fairmount Heights 1,616
Federalsburg 1,952
Forest Heights 2,999
Frederick 27,557
Friendsville 511
Frostburg 7,715
Fruitland 2,694
Funkstown 1,103
Gaithersburg 26,424
Galena 374
Galestown 142
Garrett Park 1,178
Glen Echo 229
Glenarden 4,993
Goldsboro 188
Grantsville 498
Greenbelt 16,000
Greensboro 1,253
Hagerstown 34,132
Hampstead 1,293
Hancock 1,887
Havre de Grace 8,763
Hebron 714
Henderson 156
Highland Beach 8
Hillsboro 180
Hurlock 1,690
Hyattsville 12,709
Indian Head 1,381
Keedysville 476
Kensington 1,822
Kitzmiller 387
Landover Hills 1,428
La Plata 2,484
Laurel 12,103
Laytonsville 195
Leonardtown 1,448
Loch Lynn Heights 503
Lonaconing 1,420
Luke 329
Manchester 1,830
Mardela Springs 320
Marydel 152
Middletown 1,748
Midland 601
Millington 546
Morningside 1,395
Mount Airy 2,450
Mount Rainier 7,361
Mountain Lake Park 1,597
Myersville 432
New Carrollton 12,632
New Market 306
New Windsor 799
North Beach 1,504
North Brentwood 580
North East 1,469
Oakland 1,994
Ocean City 4,946
Oxford 754
Perryville 2,018
Pittsville 519
Pocomoke City 3,558
Poolesville 3,428
Port Deposit 664
Port Tobacco 40
Preston 498
Princess Anne 1,499
Queen Anne 181
Queenstown 491
Ridgely 933
Rising Sun 1,160
Riverdale 4,748
Rock Hall 1,511
Rockville 43,811
Rosemont 305
St. Michaels 1,301
Salisbury 16,429
Seat Pleasant 5,217
Secretary 487
Sharpsburg 721
Sharptown 654
Smithsburg 833
Snow Hill 2,192
Somerset 1,101
Sudlersville 443
Sykesville 1,712
Takoma Park 16,231
Taneytown 2,618
Templeville 96
Thurmont 2,934
Trappe 739
Union Bridge 927
University Park 2,536
Upper Marlboro 828
Vienna 300
Walkersville 2,212
Washington Grove 527
Westernport 2,706
Westminster 8,808
Willards 540
Williamsport 1,867
Woodsboro 506

†Independent city.

MASSACHUSETTS

Population 5,737,037

METROPOLITAN AREAS

Boston 2,763,357
Brockton 169,374
Fall River 176,831 (145,963 in Mass.; 30,868 in R.I.)
Fitchburg-Leominster 99,777
Lawrence-Haverhill 281,981 (231,223 in Mass.; 50,758 in N.H.)
Lowell 233,410 (225,320 in Mass.; 8,090 in N.H.)
New Bedford 169,425
Pittsfield 90,505
Providence-Warwick-Pawtucket (R.I.) 919,216 (817,276 in R.I.; 101,940 in Mass.)
Springfield-Chicopee-Holyoke 528,668 (520,195 in Mass.; 8,473 in Conn.)
Worcester 372,940

COUNTIES

Barnstable 147,925
Berkshire 145,110
Bristol 474,641
Dukes 8,942
Essex 633,632
Franklin 64,317
Hampden 443,018
Hampshire 138,813
Middlesex 1,367,034
Nantucket 5,087
Norfolk 606,587
Plymouth 405,437
Suffolk 650,142
Worcester 646,352

CITIES AND TOWNS

Abington 13,517▲
Acton 17,544▲
Acushnet 8,704▲
Adams 10,381▲
Agawam 26,271▲
Alford 394▲
Amesbury 13,971▲
Amherst 33,229▲
Andover 26,370▲
Arlington 48,219▲
Ashburnham 4,075▲
Ashby 2,311▲
Ashfield 1,458▲
Ashland 9,165▲
Athol 10,634▲
Attleboro 34,196
Auburn 14,845▲
Avon 5,026▲
Ayer 6,993▲
Barnstable 30,898▲
Barre 4,102▲
Becket 1,339▲
Bedford 13,067▲
Belchertown 8,339▲
Bellingham 14,300▲
Belmont 26,100▲
Berkley 2,731▲
Berlin 2,215▲
Bernardston 1,750▲
Beverly 37,655
Billerica 36,727▲
Blackstone 6,570▲
Blandford 1,038▲
Bolton 2,530▲
Boston 562,994
Bourne 13,874▲
Boxborough 3,126▲
Boxford 5,374▲
Boylston 3,470▲
Braintree 36,337▲
Brewster 5,226▲
Bridgewater 17,202▲
Brimfield 2,318▲
Brockton 95,172
Brookfield 2,397▲
Brookline 55,062▲
Buckland 1,864▲
Burlington 23,486▲
Cambridge 95,322
Canton 18,182▲
Carlisle 3,306▲
Carver 6,988▲
Charlemont 1,149▲
Charlton 6,719▲
Chatham 6,071▲

MASSACHUSETTS (continued)

Chelmsford 31,174▲
Chelsea 25,431
Cheshire 3,124▲
Chester 1,123▲
Chesterfield 1,000▲
Chicopee 55,112
Chilmark 489▲
Clarksburg 1,871▲
Clinton 12,771▲
Cohasset 7,174▲
Colrain 1,552▲
Concord 16,293▲
Conway 1,213▲
Cummington 657▲
Dalton 6,797▲
Danvers 24,100▲
Dartmouth 23,966▲
Dedham 25,298▲
Deerfield 4,517▲
Dennis 12,360▲
Dighton 5,352▲
Douglas 3,730▲
Dover 4,703▲
Dracut 21,249▲
Dudley 8,717▲
Dunstable 1,671▲
Duxbury 11,807▲
East Bridgewater 9,945▲
East Brookfield 1,955▲
East Longmeadow 12,905▲
Eastham 3,472▲
Easthampton 15,580▲
Easton 16,623▲
Edgartown 2,204▲
Egremont 1,311▲
Erving 1,326▲
Essex 2,998▲
Everett 37,195
Fairhaven 15,759▲
Fall River 92,574
Falmouth 23,640▲
Fitchburg 39,580
Florida 730▲
Foxborough 14,148▲
Framingham 65,113▲
Franklin 18,217▲
Freetown 7,058▲
Gardner 17,900
Gay Head 220▲
Georgetown 5,687▲
Gill 1,259▲
Gloucester 27,768
Goshen 651▲
Gosnold 63▲
Grafton 11,238▲
Granby 5,380▲
Granville 1,204▲
Great Barrington 7,405▲
Greenfield 18,436▲
Groton 6,154▲
Groveland 5,040▲
Hadley 4,125▲
Halifax 5,513▲
Hamilton 6,960▲
Hampden 4,745▲
Hancock 643▲
Hanover 11,358▲
Hanson 8,617▲
Hardwick 2,272▲
Harvard 12,170▲
Harwich 8,971▲
Hatfield 3,045▲
Haverhill 46,865
Hawley 280▲
Heath 482▲
Hingham 20,339▲
Hinsdale 1,707▲
Holbrook 11,140▲
Holden 13,336▲
Holland 1,589▲
Holliston 12,622▲
Holyoke 44,678
Hopedale 3,905▲
Hopkinton 7,114▲
Hubbardston 1,797▲
Hudson 16,408▲
Hull 9,714▲
Huntington 1,804▲
Ipswich 11,158▲
Kingston 7,362▲
Lakeville 5,931▲
Lancaster 6,334▲
Lanesborough 3,131▲
Lawrence 63,175
Lee 6,247▲
Leicester 9,446▲
Lenox 6,523▲
Leominster 34,508
Leverett 1,471▲
Lexington 29,479▲
Leyden 498▲
Lincoln 7,098▲
Littleton 6,970▲
Longmeadow 16,301▲
Lowell 92,418
Ludlow 18,150▲
Lunenburg 8,405▲
Lynn 78,471
Lynnfield 11,267▲
Malden 53,386
Manchester 5,424▲
Mansfield 13,453▲
Marblehead 20,126▲
Marion 3,932▲
Marlborough 30,617
Marshfield 20,916▲
Mashpee 3,700▲
Mattapoisett 5,597▲
Maynard 9,590▲
Medfield 10,220▲
Medford 58,076
Medway 8,447▲
Melrose 30,055
Mendon 3,108▲
Merrimac 4,451▲
Methuen 36,701▲
Middleborough 16,404▲
Middlefield 385▲
Middleton 4,135▲
Milford 23,390▲
Millbury 11,808▲
Millis 6,908▲
Millville 1,693▲
Milton 25,860▲
Monroe 179▲
Monson 7,315▲
Montague 8,011▲
Monterey 818▲
Montgomery 637▲
Mount Washington 93▲
Nahant 3,947▲
Nantucket 5,087▲
Natick 29,461▲
Needham 27,901▲
New Ashford 159▲
New Bedford 98,478
New Braintree 671▲
New Marlborough 1,160▲
New Salem 688▲
Newbury 4,529▲
Newburyport 15,900
Newton 83,622
Norfolk 6,363▲
North Adams 18,063
North Andover 20,129▲
North Attleborough 21,095▲
North Brookfield 4,150▲
North Reading 11,455▲
Northampton 29,286
Northborough 10,568▲
Northbridge 12,246▲
Northfield 2,386▲
Norton 12,690▲
Norwell 9,182▲
Norwood 29,711▲
Oak Bluffs 1,984▲
Oakham 994▲
Orange 6,844▲
Orleans 5,306▲
Otis 963▲
Oxford 11,680▲
Palmer 11,389▲
Paxton 3,762▲
Peabody 45,976
Pelham 1,112▲
Pembroke 13,487▲
Pepperell 8,061▲
Peru 633▲
Petersham 1,024▲
Phillipston 953▲
Pittsfield 51,974
Plainfield 425▲
Plainville 5,857▲
Plymouth 35,913▲
Plympton 1,974▲
Princeton 2,425▲
Provincetown 3,536▲
Quincy 84,743
Randolph 28,218▲
Raynham 9,085▲
Reading 22,678▲
Rehoboth 7,570▲
Revere 42,423
Richmond 1,659▲
Rochester 3,205▲
Rockland 15,695▲
Rockport 6,345▲
Rowe 336▲
Rowley 3,867▲
Royalston 955▲
Russell 1,570▲
Rutland 4,334▲
Salem 38,220
Salisbury 5,973▲
Sandisfield 720▲
Sandwich 8,727▲
Saugus 24,746▲
Savoy 644▲
Scituate 17,317▲
Seekonk 12,269▲
Sharon 13,601▲
Sheffield 2,743▲
Shelburne 2,002▲
Sherborn 4,049▲
Shirley 5,124▲
Shrewsbury 22,674▲
Shutesbury 1,049▲
Somerset 18,813▲
Somerville 77,372
South Hadley 16,399▲
Southampton 4,137▲
Southborough 6,193▲
Southbridge 16,665▲
Southwick 7,382▲
Spencer 10,774▲
Springfield 152,319
Sterling 5,440▲
Stockbridge 2,328▲
Stoneham 21,424▲
Stoughton 26,710▲
Stow 5,144▲
Sturbridge 5,976▲
Sudbury 14,027▲
Sunderland 2,929▲
Sutton 5,855▲
Swampscott 13,837▲
Swansea 15,461▲
Taunton 45,001
Templeton 6,070▲
Tewksbury 24,635▲
Tisbury 2,972▲
Tolland 235▲
Topsfield 5,709▲
Townsend 7,201▲
Truro 1,486▲
Tyngsborough 5,683▲
Tyringham 344▲
Upton 3,886▲
Uxbridge 8,374▲
Wakefield 24,895▲
Wales 1,177▲
Walpole 18,859▲
Waltham 58,200
Ware 8,953▲
Wareham 18,457▲
Warren 3,777▲
Warwick 603▲
Washington 587▲
Watertown 34,384▲
Wayland 12,170▲
Webster 14,480▲
Wellesley 27,209▲
Wellfleet 2,209▲
Wendell 694▲
Wenham 3,897▲
West Boylston 6,204▲
West Bridgewater 6,359▲
West Brookfield 3,026▲
West Newbury 2,861▲
West Springfield 27,042▲
West Stockbridge 1,280▲
West Tisbury 1,010▲
Westborough 13,619▲
Westfield 36,465
Westford 13,434▲
Westhampton 1,137▲
Westminster 5,139▲
Weston 11,169▲
Westport 13,763▲
Westwood 13,212▲
Weymouth 55,601▲
Whately 1,341▲
Whitman 13,534▲
Wilbraham 12,053▲
Williamsburg 2,237▲
Williamstown 8,741▲
Wilmington 17,471▲
Winchendon 7,019▲
Winchester 20,701▲
Windsor 598▲
Winthrop 19,294▲
Woburn 36,626
Worcester 161,799
Worthington 932▲
Wrentham 7,580▲
Yarmouth 18,449▲

▲Entire town (township), including rural area.

MICHIGAN

Population 9,258,344

METROPOLITAN AREAS

Ann Arbor 264,748
Battle Creek 187,338
Bay City 119,881
Detroit 4,352,762
Flint 521,589
Grand Rapids 601,680
Jackson 151,495
Kalamazoo-Portage 279,192
Lansing-East Lansing 468,482
Muskegon-Norton Shores-Muskegon Heights 179,591
Saginaw 228,059
Toledo (O.) 791,599 (656,940 in O.; 134,659 in Mich.)

COUNTIES

Alcona 9,740
Alger 9,225
Allegan 81,555
Alpena 32,315
Antrim 16,194
Arenac 14,706
Baraga 8,484
Barry 45,781
Bay 119,881
Benzie 11,205
Berrien 171,276
Branch 40,188
Calhoun 141,557
Cass 49,499
Charlevoix 19,907
Cheboygan 20,649
Chippewa 29,029
Clare 23,822
Clinton 55,893
Crawford 9,465
Delta 38,947
Dickinson 25,341
Eaton 88,337
Emmet 22,992
Genesee 450,449
Gladwin 19,957
Gogebic 19,686
Grand Traverse 54,899
Gratiot 40,448
Hillsdale 42,071
Houghton 37,872
Huron 36,459
Ingham 272,437
Ionia 51,815
Iosco 28,349
Iron 13,635
Isabella 54,110
Jackson 151,495
Kalamazoo 212,378
Kalkaska 10,952
Kent 444,506
Keweenaw 1,963
Lake 7,711
Lapeer 70,038
Leelanau 14,007
Lenawee 89,948
Livingston 100,289
Luce 6,659
Mackinac 10,178
Macomb 694,600
Manistee 23,019
Marquette 74,101
Mason 26,365
Mecosta 36,961
Menominee 26,201
Midland 73,578
Missaukee 10,009
Monroe 134,659
Montcalm 47,555
Montmorency 7,492
Muskegon 157,589
Newaygo 34,917
Oakland 1,011,793
Oceana 22,002
Ogemaw 16,436
Ontonagon 9,861
Osceola 18,928
Oscoda 6,858
Otsego 14,993
Ottawa 157,174
Presque Isle 14,267
Roscommon 16,374
Saginaw 228,059
St. Clair 138,802
St. Joseph 56,083
Sanilac 40,789
Schoolcraft 8,575
Shiawassee 71,140
Tuscola 56,961
Van Buren 66,814
Washtenaw 264,748
Wayne 2,337,240
Wexford 25,102

CITIES, TOWNS, AND VILLAGES

Addison 655
Adrian 21,186
Ahmeek 210
Akron 538
Alanson 508
Albion 11,059
Algonac 4,412
Allegan 4,576
Allen 266
Allen Park 34,196
Alma 9,652
Almont 1,857
Alpena 12,214
Alpha 229
Ann Arbor 107,316
Applegate 257
Armada 1,392
Ashley 570
Athens 960
Auburn 1,921
Au Gres 768
Augusta 913
Bad Axe 3,184
Baldwin 674
Bancroft 618
Bangor 2,001
Baraga 1,055
Baroda 627
Barryton 422
Barton Hills 357
Battle Creek 35,724
Bay City 41,593
Bear Lake 388
Beaverton 1,025
Belding 5,634
Bellaire 1,063
Belleville 3,366
Bellevue 1,289
Benton Harbor 14,707
Benzonia 466
Berkley 18,637
Berrien Springs 2,042
Bessemer 2,553
Beulah 454
Beverly Hills 11,598
Big Rapids 14,361
Bingham Farms 529
Birch Run 1,196
Birmingham 21,689
Blissfield 3,107
Bloomfield Hills 3,985
Bloomingdale 537
Boyne City 3,348
Boyne Falls 378
Breckenridge 1,495
Breedsville 244
Bridgman 2,235
Brighton 4,268
Britton 693
Bronson 2,271
Brooklyn 1,110
Brown City 1,163
Buchanan 5,142
Buckley 357
Burlington 367
Burr Oak 853
Burton 29,976
Byron 689
Cadillac 10,199
Caledonia 722
Calumet 1,013
Camden 420
Capac 1,377
Carleton 2,786
Caro 4,317
Carson City 1,229
Carsonville 622
Caseville 851
Casnovia 348
Caspian 1,038
Cass City 2,258
Cassopolis 1,933
Cedar Springs 2,615
Cement City 539
Center Line 9,293
Central Lake 895
Centreville 1,202
Charlevoix 3,296
Charlotte 8,251
Chatham 315
Cheboygan 5,106
Chelsea 3,816
Chesaning 2,656
Clare 3,300
Clarkston 968
Clarksville 348
Clawson 15,103
Clayton 396
Clifford 406
Climax 619
Clinton 2,342
Clio 2,669
Coldwater 9,461
Coleman 1,429
Coloma 1,833
Colon 1,190
Columbiaville 953
Concord 900
Constantine 1,680
Coopersville 2,889
Copemish 287
Copper City 244
Corunna 3,206
Croswell 2,073
Crystal Falls 1,965
Custer 341
Daggett 274
Dansville 479
Davison 6,087
Dearborn 90,660
Dearborn Heights 67,706
Decatur 1,915
Deckerville 887
Deerfield 957
De Tour Village 466
Detroit 1,203,339
DeWitt 3,165
Dexter 1,524
Dimondale 1,008
Douglas 948
Dowagiac 6,307
Dryden 650
Dundee 2,575
Durand 4,238
Eagle 155
East Detroit 38,280
East Grand Rapids 10,914
East Jordan 2,185
East Lake 514
East Lansing 48,309
East Tawas 2,584
Eaton Rapids 4,510
Eau Claire 573
Ecorse 14,447
Edmore 1,176
Edwardsburg 1,135
Elberta 556
Elk Rapids 1,504
Elkton 953
Ellsworth 436
Elsie 1,022
Emmett 285
Empire 340
Escanaba 14,355
Essexville 4,378
Estral Beach 463
Evart 1,945
Fairgrove 691
Farmington 11,022
Farmington Hills 58,056
Farwell 804
Fennville 934
Fenton 8,098
Ferndale 26,227
Ferrysburg 2,440
Fife Lake 402
Flat Rock 6,853
Flint 159,611
Flushing 8,624
Forestville 159
Fountain 195
Fowler 1,021
Fowlerville 2,289
Frankenmuth 3,753
Frankfort 1,603
Franklin 2,864
Fraser 14,560
Free Soil 212
Freeport 479
Fremont 3,672
Fruitport 1,143
Gaastra 404
Gagetown 428
Gaines 440
Galesburg 1,822
Galien 692
Garden 296
Garden City 35,640
Gaylord 3,011
Gibraltar 4,458
Gladstone 4,533
Gladwin 2,479
Gobles 816
Goodrich 795
Grand Beach 227
Grand Blanc 6,848
Grand Haven 11,763
Grand Ledge 6,920
Grand Rapids 181,843
Grandville 12,412
Grant 683
Grass Lake 962
Grayling 1,792
Greenville 8,019
Grosse Pointe 5,901
Grosse Pointe Farms 10,551
Grosse Pointe Park 13,639
Grosse Pointe Shores 3,122
Grosse Pointe Woods 18,886
Hamtramck 21,300
Hancock 5,122
Hanover 490
Harbor Beach 2,000
Harbor Springs 1,567
Harper Woods 16,361
Harrietta 139
Harrison 1,700
Harrisville 559
Hart 1,888
Hartford 2,493
Hastings 6,418
Hazel Park 20,914
Hersey 364
Hesperia 876
Highland Park 27,909
Hillman 373
Hillsdale 7,432
Holland 26,281
Holly 4,874
Homer 1,791
Honor 281
Hopkins 536
Houghton 7,512
Howard City 1,118
Howell 6,976
Hubbardston 421
Hudson 2,545
Hudsonville 4,844
Huntington Woods 6,937
Imlay City 2,495
Inkster 35,190
Ionia 5,920
Iron Mountain 8,341
Iron River 2,426
Ironwood 7,741
Ishpeming 7,538
Ithaca 2,950
Jackson 39,739
Jonesville 2,172
Kalamazoo 79,722
Kaleva 445
Kalkaska 1,654
Keego Harbor 3,083
Kent City 860
Kentwood 30,438
Kinde 600
Kingsford 5,290
Kingsley 664
Kingston 417
Laingsburg 1,145
Lake Angelus 397
Lake Ann 235
Lake City 843
Lake Linden 1,181
Lake Odessa 2,171
Lake Orion 2,907
Lakeview 1,139
Lakewood Club 695
L'Anse 2,500
Lansing 130,414
Lapeer 6,225
Lathrup Village 4,639
Laurium 2,678
Lawrence 903
Lawton 1,558

Lennon 600
Leonard 423
LeRoy 293
Leslie 2,110
Lexington 765
Lincoln 361
Lincoln Park 45,105
Linden 2,174
Litchfield 1,353
Livonia 104,814
Lowell 3,707
Ludington 8,937
Luna Pier 1,443
Luther 414
Lyons 708
Mackinac Island 479
Mackinaw City 820
Madison Heights 35,375
Mancelona 1,432
Manchester 1,686
Manistee 7,566
Manistique 3,962
Manton 1,212
Maple Rapids 683
Marcellus 1,134
Marine City 4,414
Marion 816
Marlette 1,761
Marquette 23,288
Marshall 7,201
Martin 447
Marysville 7,345
Mason 6,019
Mattawan 2,143
Maybee 490
Mayville 958
McBain 519
McBrides 252
Mecosta 428
Melvin 171
Melvindale 12,322
Memphis 1,171
Mendon 951
Menominee 10,099
Merrill 851
Mesick 374
Metamora 552
Michiana 333
Middleville 1,797
Midland 37,250
Milan 4,182
Milford 5,041
Millersburg 231
Millington 1,237
Minden City 284
Mineral Hills 257
Monroe 23,531
Montague 2,332
Montgomery 408
Montrose 1,706
Morenci 2,110
Morley 507
Morrice 733
Mount Clemens 18,806
Mount Morris 3,246
Mount Pleasant 23,746
Muir 698
Mulliken 550
Munising 3,083
Muskegon 40,823
Muskegon Heights 14,611
Nashville 1,628
Negaunee 5,189
New Baltimore 5,439
New Buffalo 2,821
New Era 534
New Haven 1,871
New Lothrop 646
Newaygo 1,271
Newberry 2,120
Niles 13,115
North Adams 565
North Branch 896
North Muskegon 4,024
Northport 611
Northville 5,698
Norton Shores 22,025
Norway 2,919
Novi 22,525
Oak Park 31,537
Oakley 412
Olivet 1,604
Omer 403
Onaway 1,084
Onekama 582
Onsted 670
Ontonagon 2,182
Orchard Lake Village 1,798
Ortonville 1,190
Otisville 682
Otsego 3,802
Otter Lake 456
Ovid 1,712
Owendale 308
Owosso 16,455
Oxford 2,746
Parchment 1,817
Parma 873
Paw Paw 3,211
Peck 606
Pellston 565
Pentwater 1,165
Perrinton 448
Perry 2,051
Petersburg 1,222
Petoskey 6,097
Pewamo 488
Pierson 216
Pigeon 1,247
Pinckney 1,390
Pinconning 1,430
Plainwell 3,751
Pleasant Ridge 3,217
Plymouth 9,986
Pontiac 76,715
Port Austin 839
Port Hope 369
Port Huron 33,981
Port Sanilac 598
Portage 38,157
Portland 3,963
Posen 270
Potterville 1,502
Powers 490
Prescott 332
Quincy 1,569
Ravenna 951
Reading 1,203
Reed City 2,221
Reese 1,645
Richland 486
Richmond 3,536
River Rouge 12,912
Riverview 14,569
Rochester 7,203
Rockford 3,324
Rockwood 3,346
Rogers City 3,923
Romeo 3,509
Romulus 24,857
Roosevelt Park 4,015
Roscommon 834
Rose City 661
Rosebush 336
Roseville 54,311
Rothbury 522
Royal Oak 70,893
Saginaw 77,508
St. Charles 2,276
St. Clair 4,780
St. Clair Shores 76,210
St. Ignace 2,632
St. Johns 7,376
St. Joseph 9,622
St. Louis 4,107
Saline 6,483
Sand Lake 388
Sandusky 2,216
Sanford 864
Saranac 1,421
Saugatuck 1,079
Sault Ste. Marie 14,448
Schoolcraft 1,359
Scottville 1,241
Sebewaing 2,046
Shelby 1,624
Shepherd 1,534
Sheridan 664
Sherwood 353
Shoreham 742
South Haven 5,943
South Lyon 5,214
South Range 861
South Rockwood 1,353
Southfield 75,568
Southgate 32,058
Sparta 3,373
Spring Lake 2,731
Springfield 5,917
Springport 675
Stambaugh 1,442
Standish 1,264
Stanton 1,315
Stanwood 209
Stephenson 967
Sterling 457
Sterling Heights 108,999
Stevensville 1,268
Stockbridge 1,213
Sturgis 9,468
Sunfield 591
Suttons Bay 504
Swartz Creek 5,013
Sylvan Lake 1,949
Tawas City 1,967
Taylor 77,568
Tecumseh 7,320
Tekonsha 755
Thompsonville 331
Three Oaks 1,774
Three Rivers 7,015
Traverse City 15,516
Trenton 22,762
Troy 67,102
Turner 187
Tustin 264
Twining 196
Ubly 862
Union City 1,667
Unionville 578
Utica 5,282
Vandalia 447
Vanderbilt 525
Vassar 2,727
Vermontville 832
Vernon 1,008
Vicksburg 2,224
Wakefield 2,591
Waldron 570
Walker 15,088
Walkerville 296
Walled Lake 4,748
Warren 161,134
Watervliet 1,867
Wayland 2,023
Wayne 21,159
Webberville 1,535
West Branch 1,785
Westland 84,603
Westphalia 896
White Cloud 1,101
White Pigeon 1,478
Whitehall 2,856
Whittemore 438
Williamston 2,981
Wixom 6,705
Wolverine 364
Wolverine Lake 4,968
Woodhaven 10,902
Woodland 431
Wyandotte 34,006
Wyoming 59,616
Yale 1,814
Ypsilanti 24,031
Zeeland 4,764
Zilwaukee 2,201

MINNESOTA

Population 4,077,148

METROPOLITAN AREAS

Duluth-Superior (Wis.) 266,650 (222,229 in Minn.; 44,421 in Wis.)
Fargo (N. Dak.)-Moorhead 137,574 (88,247 in N. Dak.; 49,327 in Minn.)
Grand Forks (N. Dak.) 100,944 (66,100 in N. Dak.; 34,844 in Minn.)
Minneapolis-St. Paul 2,114,256 (2,070,384 in Minn.; 43,872 in Wis.)
Rochester 91,971
St. Cloud 163,256

COUNTIES

Aitkin 13,404
Anoka 195,998
Becker 29,336
Beltrami 30,982
Benton 25,187
Big Stone 7,716
Blue Earth 52,314
Brown 28,645
Carlton 29,936
Carver 37,046
Cass 21,050
Chippewa 14,941
Chisago 25,717
Clay 49,327
Clearwater 8,761
Cook 4,092
Cottonwood 14,854
Crow Wing 41,722
Dakota 194,111
Dodge 14,773
Douglas 27,839
Faribault 19,714
Fillmore 21,930
Freeborn 36,329
Goodhue 38,749
Grant 7,171
Hennepin 941,411
Houston 19,617
Hubbard 14,098
Isanti 23,600
Itasca 43,006
Jackson 13,690
Kanabec 12,161
Kandiyohi 36,763
Kittson 6,672
Koochiching 17,571
Lac qui Parle 10,592
Lake 13,043
Lake of the Woods 3,764
Le Sueur 23,434
Lincoln 8,207
Lyon 25,207
Mahnomen 5,535
Marshall 13,027
Martin 24,687
McLeod 29,657
Meeker 20,594
Mille Lacs 18,430
Morrison 29,311
Mower 40,390
Murray 11,507
Nicollet 26,929
Nobles 21,840
Norman 9,379
Olmsted 91,971
Otter Tail 51,937
Pennington 15,258
Pine 19,871
Pipestone 11,690
Polk 34,844
Pope 11,657
Ramsey 459,784
Red Lake 5,471
Redwood 19,341
Renville 20,401
Rice 46,087
Rock 10,703
Roseau 12,574
St. Louis 222,229
Scott 43,784
Sherburne 29,908
Sibley 15,448
Stearns 108,161
Steele 30,328
Stevens 11,322
Swift 12,920
Todd 24,991
Traverse 5,542
Wabasha 19,335
Wadena 14,192
Waseca 18,448
Washington 113,571
Watonwan 12,361
Wilkin 8,382
Winona 46,256
Wright 58,962
Yellow Medicine 13,653

CITIES

Ada 1,971
Adams 797
Adrian 1,336
Afton 2,550
Aitkin 1,770
Akeley 486
Albany 1,569
Albert Lea 19,190
Alberta 145
Albertville 564
Alden 687
Aldrich 88
Alexandria 7,608
Alpha 180
Altura 354
Alvarado 385
Amboy 606
Andover 9,387
Annandale 1,568
Anoka 15,634
Apple Valley 21,818
Appleton 1,842
Arco 96
Arden Hills 8,012
Argyle 741
Arlington 1,779
Ashby 486
Askov 350
Atwater 1,128
Audubon 383
Aurora 2,670
Austin 23,020
Avoca 201
Avon 804
Babbitt 2,435
Backus 255
Badger 320
Bagley 1,321
Balaton 752
Barnesville 2,207
Barnum 464
Barrett 388
Battle Lake 708
Baudette 1,170
Baxter 2,625
Bayport 2,932
Beardsley 344
Beaver Bay 283
Beaver Creek 260
Becker 601
Bejou 109
Belgrade 805
Belle Plaine 2,754
Bellechester 220
Bellingham 290
Beltrami 134
Belview 438
Bemidji 10,949
Bena 153
Benson 3,656
Bertha 510
Bethel 272
Big Falls 490
Big Lake 2,210
Bigelow 249
Bigfork 457
Bingham Lake 222
Birchwood 1,059
Bird Island 1,372
Biscay 114
Biwabik 1,428
Blackduck 653
Blaine 28,558
Blomkest 200
Blooming Prairie 1,969
Bloomington 81,831
Blue Earth 4,132
Bluffton 206
Bock 105
Borup 160
Bovey 813
Bowlus 276
Boyd 329
Braham 1,015
Brainerd 11,489
Branch 1,866
Brandon 473
Breckenridge 3,909
Breezy Point 384
Brewster 559
Bricelyn 487
Brook Park 93
Brooklyn Center 31,230
Brooklyn Park 43,332
Brooks 173
Brookston 124
Brooten 647
Browerville 693
Browns Valley 887
Brownsdale 691
Brownsville 418
Browton 697
Bruno 130
Buckman 171
Buffalo 4,560
Buffalo Lake 782
Buhl 1,284
Burnsville 35,674
Burtrum 177
Butterfield 634
Byron 1,715
Caledonia 2,691
Callaway 238
Calumet 469
Cambridge 3,170
Campbell 286
Canby 2,143
Cannon Falls 2,653
Canton 386
Carlos 364
Carlton 862
Carver 642
Cass Lake 1,001
Cedar Mills 73
Center City 458
Centerville 734
Ceylon 543
Champlin 9,006
Chandler 344
Chanhassen 6,359
Chaska 8,346
Chatfield 2,055
Chickamaw Beach 124
Chisago City 1,634
Chisholm 5,930
Chokio 559
Circle Pines 3,321
Clara City 1,574
Claremont 591
Clarissa 663
Clarkfield 1,171
Clarks Grove 620
Clear Lake 266
Clearbrook 579
Clearwater 379
Clements 227
Cleveland 699
Climax 273
Clinton 622
Clitherall 121
Clontarf 196
Cloquet 11,142
Coates 207
Cobden 72
Cokato 2,056
Cold Spring 2,294
Coleraine 1,116
Cologne 545
Columbia Heights 20,029
Comfrey 548
Comstock 110
Conger 183
Cook 800
Coon Rapids 35,826
Corcoran 4,252
Correll 83
Cosmos 571
Cottage Grove 18,994
Cottonwood 924
Courtland 399
Cromwell 229
Crookston 8,628
Crosby 2,218
Cross Lake 1,064
Crystal 25,543
Currie 359
Cuyuna 157
Cyrus 334
Dakota 350
Dalton 248
Danube 590
Danvers 152
Darfur 139
Darwin 282
Dassel 1,066
Dawson 1,901
Dayton 4,070
Deephaven 3,716
Deer Creek 392
Deer River 907
Deerwood 580
De Graff 179
Delano 2,480
Delavan 262
Delhi 96
Dellwood 751
Denham 48
Dennison 176
Dent 167
Detroit Lakes 7,106
Dexter 279
Dilworth 2,585
Dodge Center 1,816
Donaldson 84
Donnelly 317
Doran 77
Dover 312
Dovray 87
Duluth 92,811
Dumont 173
Dundas 422
Dundee 129
Dunnell 216
Eagan 20,532
Eagle Bend 593
Eagle Lake 1,470
East Bethel 6,626
East Grand Forks 8,537
East Gull Lake 586
Easton 283
Echo 334
Eden Prairie 16,263
Eden Valley 763
Edgerton 1,123
Edina 46,073
Effie 141
Eitzen 226
Elba 198
Elbow Lake 1,358
Elgin 667
Elizabeth 195
Elk River 6,785
Elko 274
Elkton 139
Ellendale 555
Ellsworth 629
Elmdale 126
Elmore 882
Elrosa 214
Ely 4,820
Elysian 454
Emily 588
Emmons 465
Erhard 194
Erskine 585
Evan 90
Evansville 571
Eveleth 5,042
Excelsior 2,523
Eyota 1,244
Fairfax 1,405
Fairmont 11,506
Falcon Heights 5,291
Faribault 16,241
Farmington 4,370
Farwell 77
Federal Dam 192
Felton 264
Fergus Falls 12,519
Fertile 869
Fifty Lakes 263
Finlayson 202
Fisher 453
Flensburg 256
Floodwood 648
Foley 1,606
Forada 191
Forest Lake 4,596
Foreston 283
Fort Ripley 83
Fosston 1,599
Fountain 327
Foxhome 161
Franklin 512
Frazee 1,284
Freeborn 323
Freeport 563
Fridley 30,228
Frost 293
Fulda 1,308
Garfield 284
Garrison 174
Garvin 172
Gary 241
Gaylord 1,933
Gem Lake 394
Geneva 417
Genola 83
Georgetown 124
Ghent 356
Gibbon 787
Gilbert 2,721
Gilman 156
Glencoe 4,396
Glenville 851
Glenwood 2,523
Glyndon 882
Golden Valley 22,775
Gonvick 362
Good Thunder 560
Goodhue 657
Goodridge 191
Goodview 2,567
Graceville 780
Granada 377
Grand Marais 1,289
Grand Meadow 965
Grand Rapids 7,934
Granite Falls 3,451
Grasston 123
Green Isle 357
Greenbush 817
Greenfield 1,391
Greenwald 259
Greenwood 653
Grey Eagle 338
Grove City 596
Grygla 216
Gully 116
Hackensack 285
Hadley 137
Hallock 1,405
Halma 97
Halstad 690
Ham Lake 7,832
Hamburg 475
Hammond 178

Hampton 299
Hancock 877
Hanley Falls 265
Hanover 647
Hanska 429
Harding 93
Hardwick 279
Harmony 1,133
Harris 678
Hartland 322
Hastings 12,827
Hatfield 87
Hawley 1,634
Hayfield 1,243
Hayward 294
Hazel Run 93
Hector 1,252
Heidelberg 102
Henderson 739
Hendricks 737
Hendrum 336
Henning 832
Henriette 61
Herman 600
Hermantown 6,759
Heron Lake 783
Hewitt 299
Hibbing 21,193
Hill City 533
Hillman 51
Hills 598
Hilltop 817
Hinckley 963
Hitterdal 253
Hoffman 631
Hokah 686
Holdingford 635
Holland 234
Hollandale 290
Holloway 142
Holt 119
Hopkins 15,336
Houston 1,057
Howard Lake 1,240
Hoyt Lakes 3,186
Hugo 3,771
Humboldt 111
Hutchinson 9,244
Ihlen 129
Independence 2,640
International Falls 5,611
Inver Grove Heights 17,171
Iona 248
Iron Junction 134
Ironton 537
Isanti 858
Island View 101
Isle 573
Ivanhoe 761
Jackson 3,797
Janesville 1,897
Jasper 731
Jeffers 437
Jenkins 219
Johnson 57
Jordan 2,663
Kandiyohi 447
Karlstad 934
Kasota 739
Kasson 2,827
Keewatin 1,443
Kelliher 324
Kellogg 440
Kennedy 405
Kenneth 95
Kensington 331
Kent 121
Kenyon 1,529
Kerkhoven 761
Kerrick 79
Kettle River 174
Kiester 670
Kilkenny 177
Kimball Prairie 651
Kingston 141
Kinney 447
La Crescent 3,674
Lafayette 507
Lake Benton 869
Lake Bronson 298
Lake City 4,505
Lake Crystal 2,078
Lake Elmo 5,296
Lake Henry 90
Lake Lillian 329
Lake Park 716
Lake St. Croix Beach 1,176
Lake Shore 583
Lake Wilson 380
Lakefield 1,845
Lakeland 1,812
Lakeland Shores 171
Lakeville 14,790
Lamberton 1,032
Lancaster 368
Landfall 679
Lanesboro 923
Laporte 160
La Prairie 536
La Salle 115
Lastrup 150
Lauderdale 1,985
Le Center 1,967
Lengby 123
Leonidas 95
Le Roy 930
Lester Prairie 1,229
Le Sueur 3,763
Lewiston 1,226
Lewisville 273
Lexington 2,150
Lilydale 417
Lindstrom 1,972
Lino Lakes 4,966
Lismore 276
Litchfield 5,904
Little Canada 7,102
Little Falls 7,250
Littlefork 918
Long Beach 263
Long Lake 1,747
Long Prairie 2,859
Longville 191
Lonsdale 1,160
Loretto 297
Louisburg 52
Lowry 283
Lucan 262
Luverne 4,568
Lyle 576
Lynd 304
Mabel 861
Madelia 2,130
Madison 2,212
Madison Lake 592
Magnolia 234
Mahnomen 1,283
Mahtomedi 3,851
Manchester 96
Manhattan Beach 60
Mankato 28,651
Mantorville 705
Maple Grove 20,525
Maple Lake 1,132
Maple Plain 1,421
Mapleton 1,516
Mapleview 253
Maplewood 26,990
Marble 757
Marietta 279
Marine-on-St. Croix 543
Marshall 11,161
Mayer 388
Maynard 428
Mazeppa 680
McGrath 81
McGregor 447
McIntosh 681
McKinley 230
Meadowlands 135
Medford 775
Medicine Lake 419
Medina 2,623
Meire Grove 174
Melrose 2,409
Menahga 980
Mendota 219
Mendota Heights 7,288
Mentor 219
Middle River 349
Miesville 179
Milaca 2,104
Milan 417
Millerville 124
Millville 186
Milroy 242
Miltona 187
Minneapolis 370,951
Minneiska 132
Minneota 1,470
Minnesota City 265
Minnesota Lake 744
Minnetonka 38,683
Minnetonka Beach 575
Minnetrista 3,236
Mizpah 129
Montevideo 5,845
Montgomery 2,349
Monticello 3,111
Montrose 762
Moorhead 29,998
Moose Lake 1,408
Mora 2,890
Morgan 975
Morris 5,367
Morristown 639
Morton 549
Motley 444
Mound 9,280
Mounds View 12,593
Mountain Iron 4,134
Mountain Lake 2,277
Murdock 343
Myrtle 86
Nashua 89
Nashwauk 1,419
Nassau 115
Nelson 209
Nerstrand 255
Nevis 332
New Auburn 331
New Brighton 23,269
New Germany 347
New Hope 23,087
New London 812
New Market 286
New Munich 302
New Prague 2,952
New Richland 1,263
New Trier 115
New Ulm 13,755
New York Mills 972
Newfolden 384
Newport 3,323
Nicollet 709
Nielsville 145
Nimrod 69
Nisswa 1,407
Norcross 124
North Branch 1,597
North Mankato 9,145
North Oaks 2,846
North Redwood 206
North St. Paul 11,921
Northfield 12,562
Northome 312
Northrop 269
Norwood 1,219
Oak Park Heights 2,591
Oakdale 12,123
Odessa 177
Odin 134
Ogema 215
Ogilvie 423
Okabena 263
Oklee 536
Olivia 2,802
Onamia 691
Ormsby 181
Orono 6,845
Oronoco 574
Orr 294
Ortonville 2,550
Osakis 1,355
Oslo 379
Osseo 2,974
Ostrander 293
Ottertail 239
Owatonna 18,632
Palisade 155
Park Rapids 2,976
Parkers Prairie 917
Paynesville 2,140
Pease 174
Pelican Rapids 1,867
Pemberton 208
Pennock 410
Pequot Lakes 681
Perham 2,086
Perley 134
Peterson 291
Pierz 1,018
Pillager 341
Pine City 2,489
Pine Island 1,986
Pine River 881
Pine Springs 267
Pipestone 4,887
Plainview 2,416
Plato 390
Pleasant Lake 120
Plummer 353
Plymouth 31,615
Porter 211
Preston 1,478
Princeton 3,146
Prinsburg 557
Prior Lake 7,284
Proctor 3,180
Quamba 122
Racine 285
Ramsey 10,093
Randall 527
Randolph 351
Ranier 237
Raymond 723
Red Lake Falls 1,732
Red Wing 13,736
Redwood Falls 5,210
Regal 70
Remer 396
Renville 1,493
Revere 158
Rice 499
Richfield 37,851
Richmond 867
Richville 132
Riverton 112
Robbinsdale 14,422
Rochester 57,855
Rock Creek 890
Rockford 2,408
Rockville 597
Rogers 652
Rollingstone 528
Ronneby 56
Roosevelt 124
Roscoe 154
Rose Creek 371
Roseau 2,272
Rosemount 5,083
Roseville 35,820
Rothsay 476
Round Lake 480
Royalton 660
Rush City 1,198
Rushford 1,478
Rushford Village 688
Rushmore 387
Russell 412
Ruthton 328
Rutledge 185
Sabin 446
Sacred Heart 666
St. Anthony 78
St. Anthony 7,981
St. Bonifacius 857
St. Charles 2,184
St. Clair 655
St. Cloud 42,566
St. Francis 1,184
St. Hilaire 388
St. James 4,346
St. Joseph 2,994
St. Leo 147
St. Louis Park 42,931
St. Martin 220
St. Marys Point 348
St. Michael 1,519
St. Paul 270,230
St. Paul Park 4,864
St. Peter 9,056
St. Rosa 77
St. Stephen 453
St. Vincent 141
Sanborn 518
Sandstone 1,594
Sargeant 95
Sartell 3,427
Sauk Centre 3,709
Sauk Rapids 5,793
Savage 3,954
Scanlon 1,050
Seaforth 90
Sebeka 774
Sedan 62
Shafer 180
Shakopee 9,941
Shelly 276
Sherburn 1,275
Shevlin 193
Shoreview 17,300
Shorewood 4,646
Silver Bay 2,917
Silver Lake 698
Skyline 399
Slayton 2,420
Sleepy Eye 3,581
Sobieski 219
Solway 89
South Haven 205
South International Falls 2,806
South St. Paul 21,235
Spicer 909
Spring Grove 1,275
Spring Hill 94
Spring Lake Park 6,477
Spring Park 1,465
Spring Valley 2,616
Springfield 2,303
Squaw Lake 162
Stacy 996
Staples 2,887
Starbuck 1,224
Steen 153
Stephen 898
Stewart 616
Stewartville 3,925
Stillwater 12,290
Stockton 517
Storden 341
Strandquist 136
Sturgeon Lake 222
Sunburg 130
Sunfish Lake 344
Swanville 295
Taconite 331
Tamarack 83
Taopi 96
Taunton 177
Taylors Falls 623
Tenstrike 159
Thief River Falls 9,105
Thomson 152
Tintah 119
Tonka Bay 1,354
Tower 640
Tracy 2,478
Trail 97
Trimont 805
Trommald 84
Trosky 113
Truman 1,392
Turtle River 60
Twin Lakes 210
Twin Valley 907
Two Harbors 4,039
Tyler 1,353
Ulen 514
Underwood 332
Upsala 400
Urbank 95
Utica 249
Vadnais Heights 5,111
Vergas 287
Vermillion 438
Verndale 504
Vernon Center 365
Vesta 360
Victoria 1,425
Viking 129
Villard 275
Vining 87
Virginia 11,056
Wabasha 2,372
Wabasso 745
Waconia 2,638
Wadena 4,699
Wahkon 271
Waite Park 3,496
Waldorf 249
Walker 970
Walnut Grove 753
Walters 118
Waltham 176
Wanamingo 717
Wanda 118
Warba 150
Warren 2,105
Warroad 1,216
Waseca 8,219
Watertown 1,818
Waterville 1,717
Watkins 757
Watson 238
Waubun 390
Waverly 470
Wayzata 3,621
Welcome 855
Wells 2,777
Wendell 216
West Concord 762
West St. Paul 18,527
West Union 74
Westbrook 978
Whalan 119
Wheaton 1,969
White Bear Lake 22,538
Wilder 120
Willernie 654
Williams 217
Willmar 15,895
Willow River 303
Wilmont 380
Wilton 176
Windom 4,666
Winger 200
Winnebago 1,869
Winona 25,075
Winsted 1,522
Winthrop 1,376
Winton 276
Wolf Lake 67
Wolverton 126
Wood Lake 420
Woodbury 10,297
Woodland 526
Woodstock 180
Worthington 10,243
Wrenshall 333
Wright 162
Wykoff 482
Wyoming 1,559
Young America 1,237
Zemple 62
Zimmerman 1,074
Zumbro Falls 208
Zumbrota 2,129

MISSISSIPPI

Population 2,520,638

METROPOLITAN AREAS

Biloxi-Gulfport 191,918
Jackson 320,425
Memphis (Tenn.) 912,887 (809,860 in Tenn.; 49,097 in Ark.; 53,930 in Miss.)
Pascagoula-Moss Point 118,015

COUNTIES

Adams 38,035
Alcorn 33,036
Amite 13,369
Attala 19,865
Benton 8,153
Bolivar 45,965
Calhoun 15,664
Carroll 9,776
Chickasaw 17,853
Choctaw 8,996
Claiborne 12,279
Clarke 16,945
Clay 21,082
Coahoma 36,918
Copiah 26,503
Covington 15,927
De Soto 53,930
Forrest 66,018
Franklin 8,208
George 15,297
Greene 9,827
Grenada 21,043
Hancock 24,537
Harrison 157,665
Hinds 250,998
Holmes 22,970
Humphreys 13,931
Issaquena 2,513
Itawamba 20,518
Jackson 118,015
Jasper 17,265
Jefferson 9,181
Jefferson Davis 13,846
Jones 61,912
Kemper 10,148
Lafayette 31,030
Lamar 23,821
Lauderdale 77,285
Lawrence 12,518
Leake 18,790
Lee 57,061
Leflore 41,525
Lincoln 30,174
Lowndes 57,304
Madison 41,613
Marion 25,708
Marshall 29,296
Monroe 36,404
Montgomery 13,366
Neshoba 23,789
Newton 19,944
Noxubee 13,212
Oktibbeha 36,018
Panola 28,164
Pearl River 33,795
Perry 9,864
Pike 36,173
Pontotoc 20,918
Prentiss 24,025
Quitman 12,636
Rankin 69,427
Scott 24,556
Sharkey 7,964
Simpson 23,441
Smith 15,077
Stone 9,716
Sunflower 34,844
Tallahatchie 17,157
Tate 20,119
Tippah 18,739
Tishomingo 18,434
Tunica 9,652
Union 21,741
Walthall 13,761
Warren 51,627
Washington 72,344
Wayne 19,135
Webster 10,300
Wilkinson 10,021
Winston 19,474
Yalobusha 13,139
Yazoo 27,349

CITIES, TOWNS, AND VILLAGES

Abbeville 448
Aberdeen 7,184
Ackerman 1,567
Alligator 256
Amory 7,307
Anguilla 950
Arcola 588
Artesia 526
Ashland 532
Baldwyn 3,427
Bassfield 325
Batesville 4,692
Bay St. Louis 7,891
Bay Springs 1,884
Beaumont 1,112
Beauregard 185
Belmont 1,420
Belzoni 2,982
Benoit 499
Bentonia 518
Beulah 431
Big Creek 146
Biloxi 49,311
Blue Mountain 867
Blue Springs 131
Bolton 664
Booneville 6,199
Boyle 888
Brandon 9,626
Braxton 172
Brookhaven 10,800
Brooksville 1,038
Bruce 2,208
Bude 1,092
Burnsville 889
Byhalia 757
Caledonia 497
Calhoun City 2,033
Canton 11,116
Carrollton 338
Carthage 3,453
Cary 470
Centreville 1,844
Charleston 2,878
Chunky 277
Clarksdale 21,137
Cleveland 14,524
Clinton 14,660
Coffeeville 1,129
Coldwater 1,505
Collins 2,131
Columbia 7,733
Columbus 27,383
Como 1,378
Corinth 13,839
Courtland 381
Crawford 495
Crenshaw 1,019
Crosby 349
Crowder 789
Cruger 540
Crystal Springs 4,902
Decatur 1,148
De Kalb 1,159
Derma 793
D'Lo 463
Doddsville 232
Drew 2,528
Duck Hill 706
Dumas 312
Duncan 501
Durant 2,889
Ecru 687
Eden 150

Edwards 1,515	Holly Springs 7,285	Magee 3,497	Oakland 540	Rienzi 423	Taylor 301
Ellisville 4,652	Horn Lake 4,326	Magnolia 2,461	Ocean Springs 14,504	Ripley 4,271	Taylorsville 1,387
Enterprise 607	Houlka 710	Mantachie 732	Okolona 3,409	Rolling Fork 2,590	Tchula 1,931
Ethel 486	Houston 3,747	Mantee 158	Olive Branch 2,067	Rosedale 2,793	Terry 655
Eupora 2,048	Indianola 8,221	Marietta 298	Osyka 581	Roxie 591	Thaxton 404
Falcon 260	Inverness 1,034	Marion 771	Oxford 9,882	Ruleville 3,332	Tishomingo 387
Falkner 251	Isola 834	Marks 2,260	Pace 519	Sallis 211	Toccopola 184
Fayette 2,033	Itta Bena 2,904	Mathiston 632	Pachuta 256	Saltillo 1,271	Tremont 379
Flora 1,507	Iuka 2,846	Mayersville 378	Paden 119	Sandersville 800	Tunica 1,361
Florence 1,111	Jackson 202,895	McComb 12,331	Pascagoula 29,318	Sardis 2,278	Tupelo 23,905
Flowood 943	Jonestown 1,231	McCool 203	Pass Christian 5,014	Schlater 429	Tutwiler 1,174
Forest 5,229	Jumpertown 472	McLain 688	Pearl 20,778	Scooba 511	Tylertown 1,976
French Camp 306	Kilmichael 906	Meadville 575	Pelahatchie 1,445	Sebastopol 314	Union 1,931
Friars Point 1,400	Kosciusko 7,415	Mendenhall 2,533	Petal 8,476	Seminary 327	Utica 865
Fulton 3,238	Kossuth 190	Meridian 46,577	Philadelphia 6,434	Senatobia 5,013	Vaiden 924
Gattman 151	Lake 524	Merigold 574	Picayune 10,361	Shannon 680	Vardaman 1,009
Georgetown 343	Lambert 1,624	Metcalfe 952	Pickens 1,386	Shaw 2,461	Verona 2,497
Glendora 220	Laurel 21,897	Mize 363	Pittsboro 269	Shelby 2,540	Vicksburg 25,434
Gloster 1,726	Leakesville 1,120	Monticello 1,834	Plantersville 920	Sherman 499	Walnut 513
Golden 292	Learned 113	Montrose 120	Polkville 129	Shubuta 626	Walnut Grove 439
Goodman 1,285	Leland 6,667	Moorhead 2,358	Pontotoc 4,723	Shuqualak 554	Walthall 206
Greenville 40,613	Lena 231	Morgan City 319	Pope 208	Sidon 450	Water Valley 4,147
Greenwood 20,115	Lexington 2,628	Morton 3,303	Poplarville 2,562	Silver City 378	Waveland 4,186
Grenada 12,641	Liberty 669	Moss Point 18,998	Port Gibson 2,371	Silver Creek 272	Waynesboro 5,349
Gulfport 39,676	Long Beach 7,967	Mound Bayou 2,917	Potts Camp 525	Sledge 699	Webb 782
Gunnison 708	Louin 338	Mount Olive 993	Prentiss 1,465	Smithville 866	Weir 553
Guntown 359	Louise 400	Myrtle 402	Puckett 279	Soso 434	Wesson 1,313
Hatley 497	Louisville 7,323	Natchez 22,015	Purvis 2,256	Starkville 15,169	West 253
Hattiesburg 40,829	Lucedale 2,429	Nettleton 1,911	Quitman 2,632	State Line 484	West Point 8,811
Hazlehurst 4,437	Lula 394	New Albany 7,072	Raleigh 998	Stonewall 1,345	Wiggins 3,205
Heidelberg 1,098	Lumberton 2,217	New Augusta 589	Raymond 1,967	Sturgis 269	Winona 6,177
Hernando 2,969	Lyon 531	Newhebron 470	Renova 659	Summit 1,753	Winstonville 486
Hickory 670	Maben 855	Newton 3,708	Richland 3,955	Sumner 452	Woodland 135
Hickory Flat 458	Macon 2,396	North Carrollton 859	Richton 1,205	Sumrall 1,197	Woodville 1,512
Hollandale 4,336	Madison 2,241	Noxapater 516	Ridgeland 5,461	Sunflower 1,027	Yazoo City 12,426

MISSOURI — Population 4,917,444

METROPOLITAN AREAS

Columbia 100,376
Kansas City 1,327,020
(884,416 in Mo.;
442,604 in Kans.)
St. Joseph 101,868
St. Louis 2,355,276
(1,789,402 in Mo.;
565,874 in Ill.)
Springfield 207,704

COUNTIES

Adair 24,870	McDonald 14,917
Andrew 13,980	Mercer 4,685
Atchison 8,605	Miller 18,532
Audrain 26,458	Mississippi 15,726
Barry 24,408	Moniteau 12,068
Barton 11,292	Monroe 9,716
Bates 15,873	Montgomery 11,537
Benton 12,183	Morgan 13,807
Bollinger 10,301	New Madrid 22,945
Boone 100,376	Newton 40,555
Buchanan 87,888	Nodaway 21,996
Butler 37,693	Oregon 10,238
Caldwell 8,660	Osage 12,014
Callaway 32,252	Ozark 7,961
Camden 19,963	Pemiscot 24,987
Cape Girardeau 58,837	Perry 16,784
Carroll 12,131	Pettis 36,378
Carter 5,428	Phelps 33,633
Cass 51,029	Pike 17,568
Cedar 11,894	Platte 46,341
Chariton 10,489	Polk 18,822
Christian 22,402	Pulaski 42,011
Clark 8,493	Putnam 6,092
Clay 136,488	Ralls 8,911
Clinton 15,916	Randolph 25,460
Cole 56,663	Ray 21,378
Cooper 14,643	Reynolds 7,230
Crawford 18,300	Ripley 12,458
Dade 7,383	St. Charles 143,455
Dallas 12,096	St. Clair 8,622
Daviess 8,905	St. Francois 42,600
De Kalb 8,222	St. Louis 974,815
Dent 14,517	Ste. Genevieve 15,180
Douglas 11,594	Saline 24,919
Dunklin 36,324	Schuyler 4,979
Franklin 71,233	Scotland 5,415
Gasconade 13,181	Scott 39,647
Gentry 7,887	Shannon 7,885
Greene 185,302	Shelby 7,826
Grundy 11,959	Stoddard 29,009
Harrison 9,890	Stone 15,587
Henry 19,672	Sullivan 7,434
Hickory 6,367	Taney 20,467
Holt 6,882	Texas 21,070
Howard 10,008	Vernon 19,806
Howell 28,807	Warren 14,900
Iron 11,084	Washington 17,983
Jackson 629,180	Wayne 11,277
Jasper 86,958	Webster 20,414
Jefferson 146,814	Worth 3,008
Johnson 39,059	Wright 16,188
Knox 5,508	
Laclede 24,323	
Lafayette 29,925	
Lawrence 28,973	
Lewis 10,901	
Lincoln 22,193	
Linn 15,495	
Livingston 15,739	
Macon 16,313	
Madison 10,725	
Maries 7,551	
Marion 28,638	

CITIES, TOWNS, AND VILLAGES

Adrian 1,484	Archie 753	Bridgeton 18,445	Cole Camp 1,022	Ethel 145
Advance 1,054	Arcola 136	Bridgeton Terrace 334	Collins 145	Eugene 220
Agency 419	Argyle 216	Brimson 104	Columbia 62,061	Eureka 3,862
Airport Drive 702	Arkoe 63	Bronaugh 209	Commerce 199	Everton 317
Alba 474	Armstrong 360	Brookfield 5,555	Conception Junction 252	Ewing 400
Albany 2,152	Arnold 19,141	Brookline 211	Concordia 2,129	Excelsior Springs 10,424
Aldrich 53	Arrow Rock 82	Brooklyn Heights 125	Conway 601	Exeter 588
Alexandria 417	Asbury 210	Browning 368	Cool Valley 2,084	Fair Grove 863
Allendale 95	Ash Grove 1,157	Brownington 112	Cooter 479	Fair Play 384
Alma 445	Ashburn 89	Brumley 109	Corder 483	Fairfax 835
Altamont 192	Ashland 1,021	Brunswick 1,272	Corning 126	Fairview 282
Altenburg 280	Atlanta 441	Bucklin 713	Cosby 148	Fairview Acres 31
Alton 721	Augusta 308	Buckner 2,848	Cottleville 184	Farber 503
Amazonia 314	Aullville 92	Buffalo 2,217	Country Club Hills 1,315	Farley 184
Amity 74	Aurora 6,437	Bunceton 419	Country Club 1,234	Farmington 8,270
Amoret 238	Auxvasse 858	Bunker 673	Country Life Acres 77	Fayette 2,983
Amsterdam 231	Ava 2,761	Burgess 98	Cowgill 267	Fenton 2,417
Anderson 1,237	Avilla 151	Burlington Junction 657	Craig 379	Ferguson 24,740
Annada 70	Avondale 612	Butler 4,107	Crane 1,185	Ferrelview 447
Annapolis 370	Bagnell 71	Butterfield 234	Creighton 301	Festus 7,574
Anniston 320	Baker 31	Cabool 2,090	Crestwood 12,815	Fidelity 274
Appleton City 1,257	Bakersfield 221	Cainesville 496	Creve Coeur 12,694	Fillmore 265
Arbela 67	Baldwin Park 126	Cairo 315	Crocker 979	Fisk 450
Arbyrd 704	Ballwin 12,750	Caledonia 162	Cross Timbers 217	Flat River 4,443
Arcadia 683	Baring 206	Calhoun 427	Crystal City 3,573	Fleming 144
	Barnard 234	California 3,381	Crystal Lake Park 496	Flemington 140
	Barnett 203	Callao 326	Cuba 2,120	Flinthill 219
	Bates City 199	Calverton Park 1,717	Curryville 323	Flordell Hills 919
	Battlefield 1,227	Camden 219	Dadeville 216	Florissant 55,372
	Bell City 539	Camden Point 263	Dalton 76	Foley 216
	Bella Villa 758	Camdenton 2,303	Darlington 131	Ford City 30
	Belle 1,233	Cameron 4,519	Dearborn 547	Fordland 569
	Bellefontaine Neighbors 12,082	Campbell 2,134	Deepwater 475	Forest City 387
	Bellerive 255	Canalou 369	Deerfield 95	Foristell 119
	Bellflower 403	Canton 2,435	De Kalb 245	Forsyth 1,010
	Bel-Nor 2,047	Cape Girardeau 34,361	Dellwood 6,200	Fortescue 51
	Bel-Ridge 3,682	Cardwell 831	Delta 524	Foster 175
	Belton 12,708	Carl Junction 3,937	Dennis Acres 56	Frankford 443
	Benton 674	Carrollton 4,700	Denver 74	Franklin 196
	Benton City 155	Carterville 1,973	Des Arc 237	Fredericktown 4,036
	Berger 214	Carthage 11,104	Desloge 3,481	Freeburg 554
	Berkeley 16,146	Caruthersville 7,958	De Soto 5,993	Freeman 485
	Bernie 1,975	Carytown 180	Des Peres 8,254	Freistatt 139
	Bertrand 688	Cassville 2,091	Dewitt 132	Frohna 265
	Bethany 3,095	Catron 132	Dexter 7,043	Frontenac 3,654
	Bethel 132	Cedar City 665	Diamond 766	Fulton 11,046
	Beverly Hills 712	Cedar Hill Lakes 200	Diehlstadt 170	Gainesville 707
	Bevier 733	Center 596	Diggins 245	Galena 423
	Bigelow 67	Centertown 304	Dixon 1,402	Gallatin 2,063
	Billings 911	Centerview 223	Doniphan 1,921	Galt 323
	Birch Tree 622	Centerville 241	Doolittle 701	Garden City 1,021
	Birmingham 240	Centralia 3,537	Dover 126	Gasconade 250
	Bismarck 1,625	Chaffee 3,241	Downing 462	Gentry 126
	Black Jack 5,293	Chain-O-Lakes 76	Drexel 908	Gerald 921
	Blackburn 314	Chamois 546	Dudley 287	Gerster 45
	Blackwater 290	Champ 28	Duenweg 703	Gibbs 107
	Blairstown 144	Charlack 1,537	Duquesne 1,252	Gideon 1,240
	Bland 662	Charleston 5,230	Eagleville 364	Gilliam 227
	Blodgett 255	Chilhowee 349	East Lynne 286	Gilman City 414
	Bloomfield 1,795	Chillicothe 9,089	East Prairie 3,713	Gladstone 24,990
	Bloomsdale 397	Chula 244	Easton 313	Glasgow 1,336
	Blue Eye 94	Circle City 154	Edgar Springs 271	Glen Echo Park 249
	Blue Springs 25,927	Clarence 1,147	Edgerton 584	Glenaire 541
	Blythedale 219	Clark 304	Edina 1,520	Glenallen 125
	Bogard 285	Clarksburg 352	Edmundson 1,374	Glendale 6,035
	Bolckow 245	Clarksdale 278	Eldon 4,342	Glenwood 218
	Bolivar 5,919	Clarkson Valley 1,435	El Dorado Springs 3,868	Golden City 900
	Bonne Terre 3,797	Clarksville 585	Ellington 1,215	Goodman 1,030
	Boonville 6,959	Clarkton 1,228	Ellisville 6,233	Gordonville 267
	Bosworth 394	Claycomo 1,671	Ellsinore 362	Gower 1,276
	Bourbon 1,259	Clayton 14,219	Elmer 180	Graham 253
	Bowling Green 3,022	Clearmont 261	Elmira 109	Grain Valley 1,327
	Bragg City 200	Cleveland 485	Elmo 215	Granby 1,908
	Brandsville 133	Clever 551	Elsberry 1,272	Grand Pass 71
	Branson 2,550	Cliff Village 24	Elvins 1,548	Grandin 265
	Brashear 332	Clifton Hill 152	Eminence 614	Grandview 24,502
	Braymer 986	Climax Springs 87	Emma 267	Granger 91
	Breckenridge 523	Clinton 8,366	Eolia 401	Grant City 1,068
	Breckenridge Hills 5,666	Clyde 61	Essex 545	Grantwood 1,002
	Brentwood 8,209	Cobalt City 272	Esther 1,038	Green City 719
		Coffey 165		Green Ridge 488

MISSOURI (continued)

Greencastle	285
Greendale	853
Greenfield	1,394
Greentop	538
Greenville	393
Greenwood	1,315
Guilford	87
Gunn City	58
Hale	529
Halfway	157
Hallsville	457
Halltown	149
Hamilton	1,582
Hanley Hills	2,439
Hannibal	18,811
Hardin	688
Harris	116
Harrisburg	283
Harrisonville	6,372
Hartsburg	118
Hartville	576
Harwood	104
Hawk Point	386
Hayti	3,964
Hayti Heights	1,023
Hayward	56
Haywood City	425
Hazelwood	12,935
Henrietta	424
Herculaneum	2,293
Hermann	2,695
Hermitage	384
Higbee	817
Higginsville	4,595
High Hill	254
Highley Heights	100
Hillsboro	1,508
Hillsdale	2,247
Hoberg	77
Holcomb	632
Holden	2,195
Holland	295
Holliday	168
Hollister	1,439
Holt	276
Holts Summit	2,540
Homestead	138
Homestown	306
Hopkins	634
Hornersville	704
Houston	2,157
Houston Lake	280
Houstonia	327
Howardville	536
Hughesville	152
Humansville	907
Hume	315
Humphreys	133
Hunnewell	235
Huntleigh	428
Huntsville	1,657
Hurdland	227
Hurley	125
Hurricane Deck	210
Iatan	64
Iberia	852
Illmo	1,368
Independence	111,806
Ionia	131
Iron Gates	314
Irondale	349
Ironton	1,743
Jackson	7,827
Jacksonville	130
Jameson	172
Jamesport	651
Jamestown	317
Jasper	1,012
Jefferson City	33,619
Jennings	17,026
Jerico Springs	208
Jonesburg	614
Joplin	38,893
Josephville	58
Junction City	238
Kahoka	2,101
Kansas City	448,159
Kearney	1,433
Kelso	455
Kennett	10,145
Keytesville	689
Kidder	265
Kimberling City	1,285
Kimmswick	207
King City	1,063
Kingdom City	146
Kingston	280
Kingsville	365
Kinloch	4,455
Kirksville	17,167
Kirkwood	27,987
Knob Noster	2,040
Knox City	281
Koshkonong	245
La Belle	845
Laclede	445
Laddonia	726
Ladue	9,376
La Grange	1,217
Lake Lotawana	1,875
Lake Mykee Town	188
Lake Ozark	427
Lake St. Louis	3,843
Lake Tapawingo	892
Lake Waukomis	1,050
Lake Winnebago	681
Lakeland	197
Lakeshire	1,593
Lakeside	215
Lakeview	119
Lakeview	58
Lamar	4,053
Lamar Heights	171
Lambert	34
La Monte	1,054
Lanagan	440
Lancaster	855
La Plata	1,423
Laredo	340
Larussell	126
Lathrop	1,732
La Tour	84
Lawson	1,688
Leadington	238
Leadwood	1,371
Leasburg	304
Leawood	631
Lebanon	9,507
Lees Summit	28,741
Leeton	604
Leonard	109
Leslie	108
Levasy	235
Lewis and Clark Village	131
Lewistown	502
Lexington	5,063
Liberal	701
Liberty	16,251
Licking	1,272
Lilbourn	1,463
Lincoln	819
Linn	1,211
Linn Creek	242
Linneus	421
Lithium	81
Livonia	162
Lock Springs	85
Lockwood	971
Lohman	168
Lone Jack	420
Longtown	121
Louisburg	140
Louisiana	4,261
Lowry City	676
Lucerne	130
Ludlow	178
Lupus	50
Luray	175
Lutesville	865
Mackenzie	186
Macks Creek	171
Macon	5,680
Madison	656
Maitland	415
Malden	6,096
Malta Bend	292
Manchester	6,191
Mansfield	1,423
Maplewood	10,960
Marble Hill	601
Marceline	2,938
Marionville	1,920
Marlborough	2,012
Marquand	397
Marshall	12,781
Marshfield	3,871
Marston	742
Marthasville	543
Martinsburg	309
Martinsville	44
Maryville	9,558
Matthews	547
Maysville	1,187
Mayview	291
McFall	139
McKittrick	87
Meadville	416
Memphis	2,105
Mendon	252
Mercer	442
Merwin	85
Meta	336
Metz	136
Mexico	12,276
Miami	177
Middletown	268
Midway	223
Milan	1,947
Milford	67
Mill Spring	257
Millard	92
Miller	795
Milo	78
Mindenmines	318
Miner	1,182
Mineral Point	358
Missouri City	343
Moberly	13,418
Mokane	293
Moline Acres	2,774
Monett	6,148
Monroe City	2,557
Montgomery City	2,101
Monticello	134
Montrose	498
Mooresville	129
Morehouse	1,220
Morley	745
Morrison	169
Morrisville	331
Mosby	284
Moscow Mills	484
Mound City	1,447
Moundville	149
Mount Leonard	131
Mount Moriah	162
Mount Vernon	3,341
Mountain Grove	3,974
Mountain View	1,664
Napoleon	271
Naylor	602
Neck City	151
Neelyville	474
Nelson	248
Neosho	9,493
Nevada	9,044
New Bloomfield	519
New Cambria	246
New Florence	731
New Franklin	1,228
New Hampton	358
New Haven	1,581
New London	1,161
New Madrid	3,204
New Melle	168
Newark	105
Newburg	743
Newtonia	224
Newtown	170
Niangua	376
Nixa	2,662
Noel	1,161
Norborne	931
Normandy	5,174
North Kansas City	4,507
North Lilbourn	237
North Wardell	184
Northmoor	506
Northwoods	5,831
Northwye	135
Norwood	391
Norwood Court	881
Novelty	187
Novinger	626
Oak Grove	386
Oak Grove	4,067
Oak Ridge	252
Oakland	1,728
Oakland Park	143
Oaks	126
Oakview	497
Oakwood	227
Oakwood Manor	137
Oakwood Park	231
Odessa	3,088
O'Fallon	8,654
Old Monroe	272
Olean	128
Olivette	8,039
Olympian Village	774
Oran	1,266
Oregon	901
Oronogo	525
Orrick	922
Osage Beach	1,992
Osborn	381
Osceola	841
Osgood	93
Otterville	472
Overland	19,620
Owensville	2,241
Ozark	2,980
Pacific	4,410
Pagedale	4,542
Palmyra	3,469
Paris	1,598
Parkdale	270
Parkville	1,997
Parkway	254
Parma	1,081
Parnell	223
Pasadena Hills	1,221
Pasadena Park	531
Pascola	211
Passaic	53
Pattonsburg	502
Paynesville	85
Peculiar	1,571
Peerless Park	79
Penermon	136
Perry	836
Perryville	7,343
Pevely	2,732
Phelps City	39
Phillipsburg	134
Pickering	215
Piedmont	2,359
Pierce City	1,391
Pilot Grove	745
Pilot Knob	722
Pine Lawn	6,662
Pineville	504
Platte City	2,114
Platte Woods	467
Plattsburg	2,095
Pleasant Hill	3,301
Pleasant Hope	354
Pleasant Valley	1,545
Pocahontas	130
Pollock	102
Polo	583
Poplar Bluff	17,139
Portage Des Sioux	488
Portageville	3,470
Potosi	2,528
Powersville	116
Prairie Home	279
Prathersville	141
Preston	149
Princeton	1,264
Purcell	322
Purdin	243
Purdy	928
Puxico	833
Queen City	783
Quitman	66
Qulin	545
Randolph	91
Ravenwood	436
Raymondville	388
Raymore	3,154
Raytown	31,759
Rayville	197
Rea	78
Redings Mill	222
Reeds	105
Reeds Spring	461
Renick	195
Republic	4,485
Revere	191
Rhineland	172
Rich Hill	1,471
Richards	117
Richland	1,922
Richmond	5,499
Richmond Heights	11,516
Ridgely	78
Ridgeway	516
Risco	446
Ritchey	126
Rivermines	414
Riverside	3,206
Riverview	3,367
Rocheport	272
Rock Hill	5,702
Rockaway Beach	292
Rock Port	1,511
Rockville	281
Rogersville	741
Rolla	13,303
Roscoe	91
Rosebud	326
Rosendale	223
Rothville	118
Rush Hill	140
Rushville	271
Russellville	667
Rutledge	128
Saginaw	293
St. Ann	15,523
St. Charles	37,379
St. Clair	3,485
St. Cloud	40
St. Elizabeth	312
St. George	1,545
St. James	3,328
St. John	7,854
St. Joseph	76,691
St. Louis	453,085†
St. Martins	739
St. Marys	565
St. Paul	607
St. Peters	15,700
St. Robert	1,735
St. Thomas	337
Ste. Genevieve	4,481
Salem	4,454
Salisbury	1,975
Sarcoxie	1,381
Savannah	4,184
Schell City	327
Schuermann Heights	234
Scott City	3,262
Sedalia	20,927
Sedgewickville	115
Seligman	508
Senath	1,728
Seneca	1,853
Seymour	1,535
Shelbina	2,169
Shelbyville	645
Sheldon	491
Sheridan	220
Shoal Creek Drive	374
Shoal Creek Estates	89
Shrewsbury	5,077
Sibley	382
Sikeston	17,431
Silex	287
Silver Creek	519
Skidmore	437
Slater	2,492
Smithton	559
Smithville	1,873
South Gifford	98
South Gorin	212
South Greenfield	110
South Lineville	55
South West City	516
Sparta	743
Spickardsville	389
Springfield	133,116
Spring Valley	67
Stanberry	1,387
Stark City	132
Steele	2,419
Steelville	1,470
Stella	230
Stewartsville	832
Stockton	1,432
Stotesbury	48
Stotts City	232
Stoutland	232
Stoutsville	34
Stover	1,041
Strafford	1,121
Strasburg	170
Sturgeon	901
Sugar Creek	4,305
Sullivan	5,461
Summersville	551
Sumner	182
Sundown	39
Sunnyvale	353
Sunrise Beach	148
Sunset Hills	4,363
Sweet Springs	1,694
Sycamore Hills	741
Syracuse	222
Table Rock Townsite	58
Tallapoosa	197
Taneyville	300
Taos	759
Tarkio	2,375
Tarrants	50
Tarsney Lakes	329
Thayer	2,211
Theodosia	204
Times Beach	2,041
Tina	202
Tindall	104
Tipton	2,155
Town and Country	3,187
Tracy	310
Trenton	6,811
Trimble	262
Triplett	137
Troy	2,624
Truesdale	297
Turney	379
Tuscumbia	241
Twin Oaks	426
Umber View Heights	41
Union	5,506
Union Star	423
Unionville	2,178
Unity Village	202
University City	42,738
Uplands Park	544
Urbana	329
Urich	509
Valley Park	3,232
Van Buren	850
Vandalia	3,170
Vandiver	88
Vanduser	320
Velda	1,988
Velda Village Hills	1,393
Verona	592
Versailles	2,406
Viburnum	836
Vienna	514
Vinita Park	2,283
Vinita Terrace	349
Vista	73
Waco	129
Wakenda	98
Walker	325
Walnut Grove	504
Wardell	299
Wardsville	535
Warrensburg	13,807
Warrenton	3,219
Warsaw	1,494
Warson Woods	2,127
Washburn	289
Washington	9,251
Watson	171
Waverly	941
Wayland	498
Waynesville	2,879
Weatherby	121
Weatherby Lake	1,446
Weaubleau	464
Webb City	7,309
Webster Groves	23,097
Weldon Spring Heights	144
Wellington	780
Wellston	4,495
Wellsville	1,546
Wentworth	138
Wentzville	3,193
West Line	91
West Plains	7,741
Westboro	188
Weston	1,440
Westphalia	285
Westwood	319
Wheatland	364
Wheaton	548
Wheeling	379
Whiteside	97
Whitewater	161
Wilbur Park	546
Willard	1,799
Williamsville	418
Willow Springs	2,215
Wilson City	309
Winchester	2,237
Windsor	3,058
Winfield	592
Winona	1,050
Winston	246
Woods Heights	747
Woodson Terrace	4,564
Wooldridge	79
Worth	137
Worthington	105
Wright City	1,179
Wyaconda	359
Wyatt	441
Zalma	121

†Independent city, not part of any county.

MONTANA

Population 786,690

METROPOLITAN AREAS

Billings	87,367
Great Falls	81,804

COUNTIES

Beaverhead	8,186
Big Horn	11,096
Blaine	6,999
Broadwater	3,267
Carbon	8,099
Carter	1,799
Cascade	80,696
Chouteau	6,092
Custer	13,109
Daniels	2,835
Dawson	11,805
Deer Lodge	12,518
Fallon	3,763
Fergus	13,076
Flathead	51,966
Gallatin	42,865
Garfield	1,656
Glacier	10,628
Golden Valley	1,026
Granite	2,700
Hill	17,985
Jefferson	7,029
Judith Basin	2,646
Lake	19,056
Lewis and Clark	43,039
Liberty	2,329
Lincoln	17,752
Madison	5,448
McCone	2,702
Meagher	2,154
Mineral	3,675
Missoula	76,016
Musselshell	4,428
Park	12,660
Petroleum	655
Phillips	5,367
Pondera	6,731
Powder River	2,520
Powell	6,958
Prairie	1,836
Ravalli	22,493
Richland	12,243
Roosevelt	10,467
Rosebud	9,899
Sanders	8,675
Sheridan	5,414
Silver Bow	38,092
Stillwater	5,598
Sweet Grass	3,216
Teton	6,491
Toole	5,559
Treasure	981
Valley	10,250
Wheatland	2,359
Wibaux	1,476
Yellowstone	108,035
Yellowstone National Park	275

CITIES AND TOWNS

Alberton	368
Anaconda†	12,518
Bainville	245
Baker	2,354
Belgrade	2,336
Belt	825
Big Sandy	835
Big Timber	1,690
Billings	66,798
Boulder	1,441
Bozeman	21,645
Bridger	724
Broadus	712
Brockton	374
Browning	1,226
Butte	37,205
Cascade	773
Chester	963
Chinook	1,660
Choteau	1,798
Circle	931
Clyde Park	283
Columbia Falls	3,112
Columbus	1,439
Conrad	3,074
Culbertson	887
Cut Bank	3,688
Darby	581
Deer Lodge	4,023
Denton	356
Dillon	3,976
Dodson	158
Drummond	414
Dutton	359
East Helena	1,647
Ekalaka	620
Ennis	660
Eureka	1,119
Fairfield	650
Fairview	1,366

Montana (continued)

Flaxville 142
Forsyth 2,553
Fort Benton 1,693
Froid 323
Fromberg 469
Geraldine 305
Glasgow 4,455
Glendive 5,978
Great Falls 56,725
Hamilton 2,661
Hardin 3,300
Harlem 1,023
Harlowton 1,181
Havre 10,891

Helena 23,938
Hingham 186
Hobson 261
Hot Springs 601
Hysham 449
Joliet 580
Jordan 485
Judith Gap 213
Kalispell 10,648
Kevin 208
Laurel 5,481
Lewistown 7,104
Libby 2,748
Lima 272

Livingston 6,994
Lodge Grass 771
Malta 2,367
Manhattan 988
Medicine Lake 408
Melstone 238
Miles City 9,602
Missoula 33,388
Moore 229
Nashua 495
Opheim 210
Outlook 122
Philipsburg 1,138
Plains 1,116

Plentywood 2,476
Plevna 191
Polson 2,798
Poplar 995
Red Lodge 1,896
Richey 417
Ronan 1,530
Roundup 2,119
Ryegate 273
Saco 252
St. Ignatius 877
Scobey 1,382
Shelby 3,142
Sheridan 646

Sidney 5,726
Stanford 595
Stevensville 1,207
Sunburst 476
Superior 1,054
Terry 929
Thompson Falls 1,478
Three Forks 1,247
Townsend 1,587
Troy 1,088
Twin Bridges 437
Valier 640
Virginia City 192
Walkerville 887

West Yellowstone 735
Westby 291
White Sulphur Springs 1,302
Whitefish 3,703
Whitehall 1,030
Wibaux 782
Winnett 207
Wolf Point 3,074

†City of Anaconda and Deer Lodge County were consolidated as Anaconda-Deer Lodge County on May 2, 1977.

NEBRASKA

Population   1,570,006

METROPOLITAN AREAS

Lincoln 192,884
Omaha ....570,399 (483,899 in Nebr.; 86,500 in Ia.)
Sioux City (Ia.) ....117,457 (100,884 in Ia.; 16,573 in Nebr.)

COUNTIES

Adams 30,656
Antelope 8,675
Arthur 513
Banner 918
Blaine 867
Boone 7,391
Box Butte 13,696
Boyd 3,331
Brown 4,377
Buffalo 34,797
Burt 8,813
Butler 9,330
Cass 20,297
Cedar 10,852
Chase 4,758
Cherry 6,758
Cheyenne 10,057
Clay 8,106
Colfax 9,890
Cuming 11,664
Custer 13,877
Dakota 16,573
Dawes 9,609
Dawson 22,162
Deuel 2,462
Dixon 7,137
Dodge 35,847
Douglas 397,884
Dundy 2,861
Fillmore 7,920
Franklin 4,377
Frontier 3,647
Furnas 6,486
Gage 24,456
Garden 2,802
Garfield 2,363
Gosper 2,140
Grant 877
Greeley 3,462
Hall 47,690
Hamilton 9,301
Harlan 4,292
Hayes 1,356
Hitchcock 4,079
Holt 13,552
Hooker 990
Howard 6,773
Jefferson 9,817
Johnson 5,285
Kearney 7,053
Keith 9,364
Keya Paha 1,301
Kimball 4,882
Knox 11,457
Lancaster 192,884
Lincoln 36,455
Logan 983
Loup 859
Madison 31,382
McPherson 593
Merrick 8,945
Morrill 6,085
Nance 4,740
Nemaha 8,367
Nuckolls 6,726
Otoe 15,183
Pawnee 3,937
Perkins 3,637
Phelps 9,769
Pierce 8,481
Platte 28,852
Polk 6,320
Red Willow 12,615
Richardson 11,315
Rock 2,383
Saline 13,131
Sarpy 86,015
Saunders 18,716
Scotts Bluff 38,344
Seward 15,789
Sheridan 7,544
Sherman 4,226
Sioux 1,845
Stanton 6,549
Thayer 7,582
Thomas 973
Thurston 7,186
Valley 5,633
Washington 15,508
Wayne 9,858
Webster 4,858
Wheeler 1,060
York 14,798

CITIES AND VILLAGES

Abie 107
Adams 395
Ainsworth 2,256
Albion 1,997
Alda 601
Alexandria 255
Allen 390
Alliance 9,869
Alma 1,369
Alvo 144
Amherst 269
Anoka 24
Anselmo 187
Ansley 644
Arapahoe 1,107
Arcadia 412
Arlington 1,117
Arnold 813
Arthur 124
Ashland 2,274
Ashton 273
Atkinson 1,521
Atlanta 102
Auburn 3,482
Aurora 3,717
Avoca 242
Axtell 602
Ayr 112
Bancroft 552
Barada 36
Barneston 155
Bartlett 144
Bartley 342
Bassett 1,009
Battle Creek 948
Bayard 1,435
Bazile Mills 54
Beatrice 12,891
Beaver City 775
Beaver Crossing 458
Bee 192
Beemer 853
Belden 151
Belgrade 195
Bellevue 21,813
Bellwood 407
Belvidere 158
Benedict 228
Benkelman 1,235
Bennet 523
Bennington 631
Bertrand 775
Berwyn 104
Big Springs 505
Bladen 298
Blair 6,418
Bloomfield 1,393
Bloomington 138
Blue Hill 883
Blue Springs 521
Boys Town 622
Bradshaw 373
Brady 377
Brainard 275
Brewster 46
Bridgeport 1,668
Bristow 123
Broadwater 161
Brock 189
Broken Bow 3,979
Brownville 203
Brule 438
Bruning 330
Bruno 154
Brunswick 190
Burchard 122
Burr 101
Burton 12
Burwell 1,383
Bushnell 187
Butte 529
Byron 154
Cairo 737
Callaway 579
Cambridge 1,206
Campbell 441
Carleton 160
Carroll 246
Cedar Bluffs 632
Cedar Creek 311
Cedar Rapids 447
Center 123
Central City 3,083

Ceresco 836
Chadron 5,933
Chambers 390
Chapman 349
Chappell 1,095
Chester 435
Clarks 445
Clarkson 817
Clatonia 273
Clay Center 962
Clearwater 409
Cody 177
Coleridge 673
Colon 148
Columbus 17,328
Comstock 168
Concord 145
Cook 341
Cordova 129
Cornlea 40
Cortland 403
Cotesfield 82
Cowles 48
Cozad 4,453
Crab Orchard 82
Craig 237
Crawford 1,315
Creighton 1,341
Creston 210
Crete 4,872
Crofton 948
Crookston 86
Culbertson 767
Curtis 1,014
Cushing 48
Dakota City 1,440
Dalton 345
Danbury 143
Dannebrog 356
Davenport 445
Davey 190
David City 2,514
Dawson 215
Daykin 207
Decatur 723
Denton 164
Deshler 997
Deweese 69
De Witt 642
Dickens 24
Diller 311
Dix 275
Dixon 127
Dodge 815
Doniphan 696
Dorchester 611
Douglas 207
Du Bois 178
Dunbar 216
Duncan 410
Dunning 182
Dwight 221
Eagle 832
Eddyville 121
Edgar 705
Edison 210
Elba 218
Elgin 807
Elk Creek 144
Elkhorn 1,344
Elm Creek 862
Elmwood 598
Elsie 133
Elwood 716
Elyria 82
Emerson 874
Emmet 73
Endicott 198
Ericson 132
Eustis 460
Ewing 520
Exeter 807
Fairbury 4,885
Fairfield 543
Fairmont 767
Falls City 5,374
Farnam 268
Farwell 165
Filley 172
Firth 384
Fordyce 148
Fort Calhoun 641
Foster 81
Franklin 1,167
Fremont 23,979
Friend 1,079
Fullerton 1,506
Funk 189
Gandy 53
Garland 257
Garrison 68
Geneva 2,400
Genoa 1,090

Gering 7,760
Gibbon 1,531
Gilead 69
Giltner 400
Glenvile (Glenvil) 363
Goehner 165
Gordon 2,167
Gothenburg 3,479
Grafton 185
Grainton 20
Grand Island 33,180
Grant 1,270
Greeley 597
Greenwood 587
Gresham 320
Gretna 1,609
Gross 2
Guide Rock 344
Gurley 212
Hadar 286
Haigler 225
Hallam 290
Halsey 144
Hamlet 74
Hampton 419
Harbine 50
Hardy 232
Harrison 361
Hartington 1,730
Harvard 1,217
Hastings 23,045
Hay Springs 794
Hayes Center 231
Hazard 75
Heartwell 87
Hebron 1,906
Hemingford 1,023
Henderson 1,072
Hendley 39
Henry 155
Herman 340
Hershey 633
Hickman 687
Hildreth 394
Holbrook 297
Holdrege 5,624
Holstein 241
Homer 564
Hooper 932
Hordville 155
Hoskins 306
Howard City 228
Howells 677
Hubbard 234
Hubbell 71
Humboldt 1,176
Humphrey 799
Huntley 64
Hyannis 336
Imperial 1,941
Indianola 856
Inglewood 257
Inman 181
Ithaca 156
Jackson 287
Jansen 204
Johnson 341
Johnstown 78
Julian 87
Juniata 703
Kearney 21,158
Kenesaw 854
Kennard 372
Kilgore 76
Kimball 3,120
Lamar 60
Laurel 508
La Vista 9,588
Lawrence 350
Lebanon 102
Leigh 509
Leshara 133
Lewellen 368
Lewiston 102
Lexington 6,898
Liberty 105
Lincoln 171,932
Lindsay 383
Linwood 119
Litchfield 256
Lodgepole 413
Long Pine 521
Loomis 447
Lorton 47
Louisville 1,022
Loup City 1,368
Lushton 33
Lyman 551
Lynch 357
Lyons 1,214
Madison 1,950
Madrid 284
Magnet 59

Malcolm 355
Malmo 100
Manley 124
Marquette 303
Marsland 27
Martinsburg 100
Maskell 76
Mason City 196
Maxwell 410
Maywood 332
McCook 8,404
McCool Junction 404
McGrew 110
McLean 46
Mead 506
Meadow Grove 400
Melbeta 151
Memphis 89
Merna 389
Merriman 159
Milford 2,108
Miller 147
Milligan 332
Minatare 969
Minden 2,939
Mitchell 1,956
Monowi 18
Monroe 294
Moorefield 36
Morrill 1,097
Morse Bluff 132
Mullen 720
Murdock 242
Murray 465
Naper 136
Naponee 160
Nebraska City 7,127
Nehawka 270
Neligh 1,893
Nelson 733
Nemaha 209
Nenzel 28
Newcastle 348
Newman Grove 930
Newport 141
Nickerson 254
Niobrara 419
Nora 24
Norfolk 19,449
Norman 58
North Bend 1,368
North Loup 405
North Platte 24,479
Oak 79
Oakdale 410
Oakland 1,393
Obert 44
Oconto 176
Octavia 127
Odell 322
Ogallala 5,638
Ohiowa 143
Omaha 311,681
O'Neill 4,049
Ong 104
Orchard 482
Ord 2,658
Orleans 527
Osceola 975
Oshkosh 1,057
Osmond 871
Otoe 197
Overton 633
Oxford 1,109
Page 172
Palisade 401
Palmer 487
Palmyra 512
Panama 160
Papillion 6,399
Pawnee City 1,156
Paxton 568
Pender 1,318
Peru 998
Petersburg 381
Phillips 405
Pickrell 184
Pierce 1,535
Pilger 400
Plainview 1,456
Platte Center 367
Plattsmouth 6,295
Pleasant Dale 259
Pleasanton 349
Plymouth 506
Polk 440
Ponca 1,057
Potter 369
Prague 285
Preston 45
Primrose 102
Prosser 98
Ragan 71

Ralston 5,143
Randolph 1,106
Ravenna 1,296
Raymond 179
Red Cloud 1,300
Republican City 231
Reynolds 125
Richland 114
Rising City 392
Riverdale 204
Riverton 212
Roca 130
Rockville 116
Rogers 89
Rosalie 224
Roseland 254
Royal 86
Rulo 261
Rushville 1,217
Ruskin 224
St. Edward 891
St. Helena 111
St. Paul 2,094
Salem 221
Santee 388
Sargent 828
Saronville 63
Schuyler 1,940
Scotia 349
Scottsbluff 14,156
Scribner 1,011
Seneca 90
Seward 5,713
Shelby 724
Shelton 1,046
Shickley 413
Sholes 27
Shubert 267
Sidney 6,010
Silver Creek 496
Smithfield 68
Snyder 387
South Bend 107
South Sioux City 9,339
Spalding 645
Spencer 596
Sprague 168
Springfield 782
Springview 326
Stamford 214
Stanton 1,603
Staplehurst 306
Stapleton 340
Steele City 137
Steinauer 108
Stella 289
Sterling 526
Stockham 68
Stockville 45
Strang 59
Stratton 499
Stromsburg 1,290
Stuart 641
Sumner 254
Superior 2,502
Surprise 60
Sutherland 1,238
Sutton 1,416
Swanton 131
Syracuse 1,638
Table Rock 393
Talmage 246
Tamora 50
Tarnov 63
Taylor 278
Tecumseh 1,926
Tekamah 1,886
Terrytown 727
Thayer 70
Thedford 313
Thurston 139
Tilden 1,012
Tobias 138
Trenton 796
Trumbull 216
Uehling 273
Ulysses 270
Unadilla 291
Union 307
Upland 192
Utica 689
Valentine 2,829
Valley 1,716
Valparaiso 484
Venango 230
Verdel 72
Verdigre 617
Verdon 278
Virginia 90
Waco 259
Wahoo 3,555
Wakefield 1,125
Wallace 349

NEBRASKA (continued)

Walthill 847
Washington 113
Waterbury 92
Waterloo 450
Wauneta 746
Wausa 647
Waverly 1,726
Wayne 5,240
Weeping Water 1,109
Wellfleet 83
West Point 3,609
Western 336
Weston 286
Whitney 72
Wilber 1,624
Wilcox 379
Wilsonville 189
Winnebago 902
Winnetoon 82
Winside 439
Winslow 143
Wisner 1,335
Wolbach 301
Wood Lake 89
Wood River 1,334
Wymore 1,841
Wynot 222
York 7,723
Yutan 631

NEVADA

Population 799,184

METROPOLITAN AREAS

Las Vegas 461,816
Reno 193,623

COUNTIES

Churchill 13,917
Clark 461,816
Douglas 19,421
Elko 17,269
Esmeralda 777
Eureka 1,198
Humboldt 9,434
Lander 4,082
Lincoln 3,732
Lyon 13,594
Mineral 6,217
Nye 9,048
Pershing 3,408
Storey 1,459
Washoe 193,623
White Pine 8,167

CITIES AND TOWNS

Boulder City 9,590
Caliente 982
Carlin 1,232
Carson City 32,022†
Elko 8,758
Ely 4,882
Fallon 4,262
Gabbs 811
Henderson 24,363
Las Vegas 164,674
Lovelock 1,680
North Las Vegas 42,739
Reno 100,756
Sparks 40,780
Wells 1,218
Winnemucca 4,140
Yerington 2,021

†Independent city, not part of any county.

NEW HAMPSHIRE

Population 920,610

METROPOLITAN AREAS

Lawrence-Haverhill (Mass.) 281,981 (231,223 in Mass.; 50,758 in N.H.)
Lowell (Mass.) 233,410 (225,320 in Mass.; 8,090 in N.H.)
Manchester 160,767
Nashua 114,221

COUNTIES

Belknap 42,884
Carroll 27,931
Cheshire 62,116
Coos 35,147
Grafton 65,806
Hillsborough 276,608
Merrimack 98,302
Rockingham 190,345
Strafford 85,408
Sullivan 36,063

CITIES AND TOWNS

Acworth 590▲
Albany 383▲
Alexandria 706▲
Allenstown 4,398▲
Alstead 1,461▲
Alton 2,440▲
Amherst 8,243▲
Andover 1,587▲
Antrim 2,208▲
Ashland 1,807▲
Atkinson 4,397▲
Auburn 2,883▲
Barnstead 2,292▲
Barrington 4,404▲
Bartlett 1,566▲
Bath 761▲
Bedford 9,481▲
Belmont 4,026▲
Bennington 890▲
Benton 333▲
Berlin 13,084
Bethlehem 1,784▲
Boscawen 3,435▲
Bow 4,015▲
Bradford 1,115▲
Brentwood 2,004▲
Bridgewater 606▲
Bristol 2,198▲
Brookfield 385▲
Brookline 1,766▲
Campton 1,694▲
Canaan 2,456▲
Candia 2,989▲
Canterbury 1,410▲
Carroll 647▲
Center Harbor 808▲
Charlestown 4,417▲
Chatham 189▲
Chester 2,006▲
Chesterfield 2,561▲
Chichester 1,492▲
Claremont 14,557
Clarksville 262▲
Colebrook 2,459▲
Columbia 673▲
Concord 30,400
Conway 7,158▲
Cornish 1,390▲
Croydon 457▲
Dalton 672▲
Danbury 680▲
Danville 1,318▲
Deerfield 1,979▲
Deering 1,041▲
Derry 18,875▲
Dorchester 244▲
Dover 22,377
Dublin 1,303▲
Dummer 390▲
Dunbarton 1,174▲
Durham 10,652▲
East Kingston 1,135▲
Easton 124▲
Eaton 256▲
Effingham 599▲
Ellsworth 53▲
Enfield 3,175▲
Epping 3,460▲
Epsom 2,743▲
Errol 313▲
Exeter 11,024▲
Farmington 4,630▲
Fitzwilliam 1,795▲
Francestown 830▲
Franconia 743▲
Franklin 7,901
Freedom 720▲
Fremont 1,333▲
Gilford 4,841▲
Gilmanton 1,941▲
Gilsum 652▲
Goffstown 11,315▲
Gorham 3,322▲
Goshen 549▲
Grafton 739▲
Grantham 704▲
Greenfield 972▲
Greenland 2,129▲
Greenville 1,988▲
Groton 255▲
Hampstead 3,785▲
Hampton 10,493▲
Hampton Falls 1,372▲
Hancock 1,193▲
Hanover 9,119▲
Harrisville 860▲
Haverhill 3,445▲
Hebron 349▲
Henniker 3,246▲
Hill 736▲
Hillsborough 3,437▲
Hinsdale 3,631▲
Holderness 1,586▲
Hollis 4,679▲
Hooksett 7,303▲
Hopkinton 3,861▲
Hudson 14,022▲
Jackson 642▲
Jaffrey 4,349▲
Jefferson 803▲
Keene 21,449
Kensington 1,322▲
Kingston 4,111▲
Laconia 15,575
Lancaster 3,401▲
Landaff 266▲
Langdon 437▲
Lebanon 11,134
Lee 2,111▲
Lempster 637▲
Lincoln 1,313▲
Lisbon 1,517▲
Litchfield 4,150▲
Littleton 5,558▲
Londonderry 13,598▲
Loudon 2,454▲
Lyman 281▲
Lyme 1,289▲
Lyndeborough 1,070▲
Madbury 987▲
Madison 1,051▲
Manchester 90,936
Marlborough 1,846▲
Marlow 542▲
Mason 792▲
Meredith 4,646▲
Merrimack 15,406▲
Middleton 734▲
Milan 1,013▲
Milford 8,685▲
Milton 2,438▲
Monroe 619▲
Mont Vernon 1,444▲
Moultonborough 2,206▲
Nashua 67,865
Nelson 442▲
New Boston 1,928▲
New Castle 936▲
New Durham 1,183▲
New Hampton 1,249▲
New Ipswich 2,433▲
New London 2,935▲
Newbury 961▲
Newfields 817▲
Newington 716▲
Newmarket 4,290▲
Newport 6,229▲
Newton 3,068▲
North Hampton 3,425▲
Northfield 3,051▲
Northumberland 2,520▲
Northwood 2,175▲
Nottingham 1,952▲
Orange 197▲
Orford 928▲
Ossipee 2,465▲
Pelham 8,090▲
Pembroke 4,861▲
Peterborough 4,895▲
Piermont 507▲
Pittsburg 780▲
Pittsfield 2,889▲
Plainfield 1,749▲
Plaistow 5,609▲
Plymouth 5,094▲
Portsmouth 26,254
Randolph 274▲
Raymond 5,453▲
Richmond 518▲
Rindge 3,375▲
Rochester 21,560
Rollinsford 2,319▲
Roxbury 190▲
Rumney 1,212▲
Rye 4,508▲
Salem 24,124▲
Salisbury 781▲
Sanbornton 1,679▲
Sandown 2,057▲
Sandwich 905▲
Seabrook 5,917▲
Sharon 184▲
Shelburne 318▲
Somersworth 10,350
South Hampton 660▲
Springfield 532▲
Stark 470▲
Stewartstown 943▲
Stoddard 482▲
Strafford 1,663▲
Stratford 989▲
Stratham 2,507▲
Sugar Hill 397▲
Sullivan 585▲
Sunapee 2,312▲
Surry 656▲
Sutton 1,091▲
Swanzey 5,183▲
Tamworth 1,672▲
Temple 692▲
Thornton 952▲
Tilton 3,387▲
Troy 2,131▲
Tuftonboro 1,500▲
Unity 1,092▲
Wakefield 2,237▲
Walpole 3,188▲
Warner 1,963▲
Warren 650▲
Washington 411▲
Waterville Valley 180▲
Weare 3,232▲
Webster 1,095▲
Wentworth 527▲
Wentworth 49▲
Westmoreland 1,452▲
Whitefield 1,681▲
Wilmot 725▲
Wilton 2,669▲
Winchester 3,465▲
Windham 5,664▲
Windsor 72▲
Wolfeboro 3,968▲
Woodstock 1,008▲

▲Entire town (township), including rural area.

NEW JERSEY

Population 7,364,158

METROPOLITAN AREAS

Allentown-Bethlehem-Easton, Pa. 636,714 (552,285 in Pa.; 84,429 in N.J.)
Atlantic City 194,119
Jersey City 556,972
Long Branch-Asbury Park 503,173
New Brunswick-Perth Amboy-Sayreville 595,893
New York City 9,119,737 (8,274,352 in N.Y.; 845,385 in N.J.)
Newark 1,965,304
Paterson-Clifton-Passaic 447,585
Philadelphia, Pa. 4,716,818 (3,682,709 in Pa.; 1,034,109 in N.J.)
Trenton 307,863
Vineland-Millville-Bridgeton 132,866
Wilmington, Del. 524,108 (399,002 in Del.; 64,676 in N.J.; 60,430 in Md.)

COUNTIES

Atlantic 194,119
Bergen 845,385
Burlington 362,542
Camden 471,650
Cape May 82,266
Cumberland 132,866
Essex 850,451
Gloucester 199,917
Hudson 556,972
Hunterdon 87,361
Mercer 307,863
Middlesex 595,893
Monmouth 503,173
Morris 407,630
Ocean 346,038
Passaic 447,585
Salem 64,676
Somerset 203,129
Sussex 116,119
Union 504,094
Warren 84,429

CITIES, TOWNS, TOWNSHIPS, BOROUGHS, AND VILLAGES

Aberdeen 17,235▲
Absecon 6,859
Alexandria 2,798▲
Allamuchy 2,560▲
Allendale 5,901
Allenhurst 912
Allentown 1,962
Alloway 2,680▲
Alpha 2,644
Alpine 1,549
Andover 4,506▲
Andover 892
Asbury Park 17,015
Atlantic City 40,199
Atlantic Highlands 4,950
Audubon 9,533
Audubon Park 1,274
Avalon 2,162
Avon-by-the-Sea 2,337
Barnegat 8,702▲
Barnegat Light 619
Barrington 7,418
Bass River 1,344▲
Bay Head 1,340
Bayonne 65,047
Beach Haven 1,714
Beachwood 7,687
Bedminster 2,469▲
Belleville 35,367
Bellmawr 13,721
Belmar 6,771
Belvidere 2,475
Bergenfield 25,568
Berkeley 23,151▲
Berkeley Heights 12,549▲
Berlin 5,348▲
Berlin 5,786
Bernards 12,920▲
Bernardsville 6,715
Bethlehem 3,045▲
Beverly 2,919
Blairstown 4,360▲
Bloomfield 47,792
Bloomingdale 7,867
Bloomsbury 864
Bogota 8,344
Boonton 8,620▲
Boonton 3,273
Bordentown 7,170▲
Bordentown 4,441
Bound Brook 9,710
Bradley Beach 4,772
Branchburg Park 7,846
Branchville 870
Brick 53,629▲
Bridgeton 18,795
Bridgewater 29,175▲
Brielle 4,068
Brigantine 8,318
Brooklawn 2,133
Buena 3,642
Buena Vista 6,959▲
Burlington 11,527▲
Burlington 10,246
Butler 7,616
Byram 7,502▲
Caldwell 7,624
Califon 1,023
Camden 84,910
Cape May 4,853
Cape May Point 255
Carlstadt 6,166
Carneys Point 8,396
Carteret 20,598
Cedar Grove 12,600▲
Chatham 8,883▲
Chatham 8,537
Cherry Hill 68,785▲
Chesilhurst 1,590
Chester 5,198▲
Chester 1,433
Chesterfield 3,867▲
Cinnaminson 16,072▲
Clark 24,573▲
Clayton 6,013
Clementon 5,764
Cliffside Park 21,464
Clifton 74,388
Clinton 7,345▲
Clinton 1,910
Closter 8,164
Collingswood 15,838
Colts Neck 7,888▲
Commercial 4,674▲
Corbin City 254
Cranbury 1,927▲
Cresskill 7,609
Deal 1,952
Deerfield 2,523▲
Delanco 3,730▲
Delaware 3,816▲
Delran 14,811▲
Demarest 4,963
Dennis 3,989▲
Denville 14,380▲
Deptford 23,473▲
Dover 64,455▲
Dover 14,681
Downe 1,803▲
Dumont 18,334
Dunellen 6,593
Eagleswood 1,009▲
East Amwell 3,468▲
East Brunswick 37,711▲
East Greenwich 4,144▲
East Hanover 9,319▲
East Newark 1,923
East Orange 77,025
East Rutherford 7,849
East Windsor 21,041▲
Eastampton 3,814▲
Eatontown 12,703
Edgewater 4,628
Edgewater Park 9,273▲
Edison 70,193▲
Egg Harbor 19,381▲
Egg Harbor City 4,618
Elizabeth 106,201
Elk 3,187▲
Elmer 1,569
Elmwood Park 18,377
Elsinboro 1,290▲
Emerson 7,793
Englewood 23,701
Englewood Cliffs 5,698
Englishtown 976
Essex Fells 2,363
Estell Manor 848
Evesham 21,659▲
Ewing 34,842▲
Fair Haven 5,679
Fair Lawn 32,229
Fairfield 5,693▲
Fairfield 7,987
Fairview 10,519
Fanwood 7,767
Far Hills 677
Farmingdale 1,348
Fieldsboro 597
Flemington 4,132
Florence 9,084▲
Florham Park 9,359
Folsom 1,892
Fort Lee 32,449
Frankford 4,654▲
Franklin 2,341▲
Franklin 2,294▲
Franklin 31,358▲
Franklin 12,396▲
Franklin 4,486
Franklin Lakes 8,769
Fredon 2,281▲
Freehold 19,202▲
Freehold 10,020
Frelinghuysen 1,435▲
Frenchtown 1,573
Galloway 12,176▲
Garfield 26,803
Garwood 4,752
Gibbsboro 2,510
Glassboro 14,574
Glen Gardner 834
Glen Ridge 7,855
Glen Rock 11,497
Gloucester 45,156▲
Gloucester City 13,121
Green 2,450▲
Green Brook 4,640▲
Greenwich 1,738▲
Greenwich 5,404▲
Greenwich 973▲
Guttenberg 7,340
Hackensack 36,039
Hackettstown 8,850
Haddon 15,875▲
Haddon Heights 8,361
Haddonfield 12,337
Hainesport 3,236▲
Haledon 6,607
Hamburg 1,832
Hamilton 82,801▲

Hamilton 9,499▲
Hammonton 12,298
Hampton 3,916▲
Hampton 1,614
Hanover 11,846▲
Harding 3,236▲
Hardwick 947▲
Hardyston 4,553▲
Harmony 2,592▲
Harrington Park 4,532
Harrison 3,585▲
Harrison 12,242
Harvey Cedars 363
Hasbrouck Heights 12,166
Haworth 3,509
Hawthorne 18,200
Hazlet 23,013▲
Helmetta 955
High Bridge 3,435
Highland Park 13,396
Highlands 5,187
Hightstown 4,581
Hillsborough 19,061▲
Hillsdale 10,495
Hillside 21,440▲
Hi-Nella 1,250
Hoboken 42,460
Ho-Ho-Kus 4,129
Holland 4,593▲
Holmdel 8,447▲
Hopatcong 15,531
Hope 1,468▲
Hopewell 10,893▲
Hopewell 4,365▲
Hopewell 2,001
Howell 25,065▲
Independence 2,829▲
Interlaken 1,037
Irvington 61,493
Island Heights 1,575
Jackson 25,644▲
Jamesburg 4,114
Jefferson 16,413▲
Jersey City 223,532
Keansburg 10,613
Kearny 35,735
Kenilworth 8,221
Keyport 7,413
Kingwood 2,772▲
Kinnelon 7,770
Knowlton 2,074▲
Lacey 14,161▲
Lafayette 1,614▲
Lakehurst 2,908
Lakewood 38,464▲
Lambertville 4,044
Laurel Springs 2,249
Lavallette 2,072
Lawnside 3,042
Lawrence 19,724▲
Lawrence 2,116▲
Lebanon 5,459▲
Lebanon 820
Leonia 8,027
Liberty 1,730▲
Lincoln Park 8,806
Linden 37,836
Lindenwold 18,196
Linwood 6,144
Little Egg Harbor 8,483▲
Little Falls 11,496▲
Little Ferry 9,399
Little Silver 5,548
Livingston 28,040▲
Loch Arbour 369
Lodi 23,956
Logan 3,078▲
Long Beach 3,488▲
Long Branch 29,819
Longport 1,249
Lopatcong 4,998▲
Lower 17,105▲
Lower Alloways Creek 1,547▲
Lumberton 5,236▲
Lyndhurst 20,326▲
Madison 15,357
Magnolia 4,881
Mahwah 12,127▲
Manalapan 18,914▲
Manasquan 5,354
Manchester 27,987▲
Mannington 1,740▲
Mansfield 5,780▲
Mansfield 2,523▲
Mantoloking 433
Mantua 9,193▲
Manville 11,278
Maple Shade 20,525▲
Maplewood 22,950▲
Margate City 9,179
Marlboro 17,560▲
Matawan 8,837
Maurice River 4,577▲
Maywood 9,895
Medford 17,471▲
Medford Lakes 4,958
Mendham 4,488▲
Mendham 4,899
Merchantville 3,972
Metuchen 13,762
Middle 11,373▲
Middlesex 13,480
Middletown 62,574▲
Midland Park 7,381
Milford 1,368
Millburn 19,543▲
Millstone 3,926▲
Millstone 530
Milltown 7,136
Millville 24,815
Mine Hill 3,325▲
Monmouth Beach 3,318
Monroe 15,858▲
Monroe 21,639▲
Montague 2,066▲
Montclair 38,321
Montgomery 7,360▲
Montvale 7,318
Montville 14,290▲
Moonachie 2,706
Moorestown 15,596▲
Morris 18,486▲
Morris Plains 5,305
Morristown 16,614
Mount Arlington 4,251
Mount Ephraim 4,863
Mount Holly 10,818▲
Mount Laurel 17,614▲
Mount Olive 18,748▲
Mountain Lakes 4,153
Mountainside 7,118
Mullica 5,243▲
National Park 3,552
Neptune 28,366▲
Neptune City 5,276
Netcong 3,557
New Brunswick 41,442
New Hanover 14,258▲
New Milford 16,876
New Providence 12,426
Newark 329,248
Newfield 1,563
Newton 7,748
North Arlington 16,587
North Bergen 47,019▲
North Brunswick 22,220▲
North Caldwell 5,832
North Haledon 8,177
North Hanover 9,050▲
North Plainfield 19,108
North Wildwood 4,714
Northfield 7,795
Northvale 5,046
Norwood 4,413
Nutley 28,998
Oakland 13,443
Oaklyn 4,223
Ocean 23,570▲
Ocean 3,731▲
Ocean City 13,949
Ocean Gate 1,385
Oceanport 5,888
Ogdensburg 2,737
Old Bridge 51,515
Old Tappan 4,168
Oldmans 1,847▲
Oradell 8,658
Orange 31,136
Oxford 1,659▲
Pahaquarry 26▲
Palisades Park 13,732
Palmyra 7,085
Paramus 26,474
Park Ridge 8,515
Parsippany-Troy Hills 49,868▲
Passaic 7,275▲
Passaic 52,463
Paterson 137,970
Paulsboro 6,944
Peapack [and Gladstone] 2,038
Pemberton 29,720▲
Pemberton 1,198
Pennington 2,109
Penns Grove 5,760
Pennsauken 33,775▲
Pennsville 13,848▲
Pequannock 13,776▲
Perth Amboy 38,951
Phillipsburg 16,647
Pilesgrove 2,810▲
Pine Beach 1,796
Pine Hill 8,684
Pine Valley 23
Piscataway 42,223▲
Pitman 9,744
Pittsgrove 6,954▲
Plainfield 45,555
Plainsboro 5,605▲
Pleasantville 13,435
Plumsted 4,674▲
Pohatcong 3,856▲
Point Pleasant 17,747
Point Pleasant Beach 5,415
Pompton Lakes 10,660
Port Republic 837
Princeton 13,683▲
Princeton 12,035
Prospect Park 5,142
Quinton 2,887▲
Rahway 26,723
Ramsey 12,899
Randolph 17,828▲
Raritan 8,292▲
Raritan 6,128
Readington 10,855▲
Red Bank 12,031
Ridgefield 10,294
Ridgefield Park 12,738
Ridgewood 25,208
Ringwood 12,625
River Edge 11,111
River Vale 9,489▲
Riverdale 2,530
Riverside 7,941▲
Riverton 3,068
Rochelle Park 5,603▲
Rockaway 19,850▲
Rockaway 6,852
Rockleigh 192
Rocky Hill 717
Roosevelt 835
Roseland 5,330
Roselle 20,641
Roselle Park 13,377
Roxbury 18,878▲
Rumson 7,623
Runnemede 9,461
Rutherford 19,068
Saddle Brook 14,084▲
Saddle River 2,763
Salem 6,959
Sandyston 1,485▲
Sayreville 29,969
Scotch Plains 20,774▲
Sea Bright 1,812
Sea Girt 2,650
Sea Isle City 2,644
Seaside Heights 1,802
Seaside Park 1,795
Secaucus 13,719
Shamong 4,537▲
Shiloh 604
Ship Bottom 1,427
Shrewsbury 995▲
Shrewsbury 2,962
Somerdale 5,900
Somers Point 10,330
Somerville 11,973
South Amboy 8,322
South Belmar 1,566
South Bound Brook 4,331
South Brunswick 17,127▲
South Hackensack 2,229▲
South Harrison 1,486▲
South Orange 15,864
South Plainfield 20,521
South River 14,361
South Toms River 3,954
Southampton 8,808▲
Sparta 13,333▲
Spotswood 7,840
Spring Lake 4,215
Spring Lake Heights 5,424
Springfield 2,691▲
Springfield 13,955▲
Stafford 3,954▲
Stanhope 3,638
Stillwater 3,887▲
Stockton 643
Stone Harbor 1,187
Stow Creek 1,365▲
Stratford 8,005
Summit 21,071
Surf City 1,571
Sussex 2,418
Swedesboro 2,031
Tabernacle 6,236▲
Teaneck 39,007▲
Tenafly 13,552
Tewksbury 4,094▲
Tinton Falls 7,740▲
Totowa 11,448
Trenton 92,124
Tuckerton 2,472
Union 3,971▲
Union 50,184▲
Union Beach 6,354
Union City 55,593
Upper 6,713▲
Upper Deerfield 6,810▲
Upper Freehold 2,750▲
Upper Pittsgrove 3,139▲
Upper Saddle River 7,958
Ventnor City 11,704
Vernon 16,302▲
Verona 14,166
Victory Gardens 1,043
Vineland 53,753
Voorhees 12,919▲
Waldwick 10,802
Wall 18,952▲
Wallington 10,741
Walpack 150▲
Wanaque 10,025
Wantage 7,268▲
Warren 9,805▲
Washington 9,550▲
Washington 4,243▲
Washington 11,402▲
Washington 3,487▲
Washington 27,878▲
Washington 808▲
Washington 6,429
Watchung 5,290
Waterford 8,126▲
Wayne 46,474▲
Weehawken 13,168▲
Wenonah 2,303
West Amwell 2,299▲
West Caldwell 11,407
West Cape May 1,091
West Deptford 18,002▲
West Long Branch 7,380
West Milford 22,750▲
West New York 39,194
West Orange 39,510
West Paterson 11,293
West Wildwood 360
West Windsor 8,542▲
Westampton 3,383▲
Westfield 30,447
Westville 4,786
Westwood 10,714
Weymouth 1,260▲
Wharton 5,485
White 2,748▲
Wildwood 4,913
Wildwood Crest 4,149
Willingboro 39,912▲
Winfield 1,785▲
Winslow 20,034▲
Wood-Ridge 7,929
Woodbine 2,809
Woodbridge 90,074▲
Woodbury 10,353
Woodbury Heights 3,460
Woodcliff Lake 5,644
Woodland 2,285▲
Woodlynne 2,578
Woodstown 3,250
Woolwich 1,129▲
Wrightstown 3,031
Wyckoff 15,500▲

▲Entire township, including rural area.

NEW MEXICO

Population 1,299,968

METROPOLITAN AREAS

Albuquerque 454,499
Las Cruces 96,340

COUNTIES

Bernalillo 419,700
Catron 2,720
Chaves 51,103
Colfax 13,706
Curry 42,019
De Baca 2,454
Doña Ana 96,340
Eddy 47,855
Grant 26,204
Guadalupe 4,496
Harding 1,090
Hidalgo 6,049
Lea 55,634
Lincoln 10,997
Los Alamos 17,599
Luna 15,585
McKinley 54,950
Mora 4,205
Otero 44,665
Quay 10,577
Rio Arriba 29,282
Roosevelt 15,695
San Juan 80,833
San Miguel 22,751
Sandoval 34,799
Santa Fe 75,306
Sierra 8,454
Socorro 12,969
Taos 18,862
Torrance 7,491
Union 4,725
Valencia 60,853

CITIES, TOWNS, AND VILLAGES

Alamogordo 24,024
Albuquerque 331,767
Artesia 10,385
Aztec 5,512
Bayard 3,036
Belen 5,617
Bernalillo 2,763
Bloomfield 4,881
Bosque Farms 3,353
Capitan 762
Carlsbad 25,496
Carrizozo 1,222
Causey 81
Central 1,968
Chama 1,090
Cimarron 888
Clayton 2,968
Cloudcroft 521
Clovis 31,194
Columbus 414
Corona 236
Corrales 2,791
Cuba 609
Deming 9,964
Des Moines 178
Dexter 882
Dora 168
Eagle Nest 202
Elida 202
Encino 155
Española 6,803
Estancia 830
Eunice 2,970
Farmington 30,729
Floyd 146
Folsom 73
Fort Sumner 1,421
Gallup 18,161
Grady 122
Grants 11,451
Grenville 39
Hagerman 936
Hatch 1,028
Hobbs 28,794
Hope 111
House 117
Hurley 1,616
Jal 2,675
Jemez Springs 316
Lake Arthur 327
Las Cruces 45,086
Las Vegas 14,322
Logan 735
Lordsburg 3,195
Los Lunas 3,525
Los Ranchos de Albuquerque 2,702
Loving 1,355
Lovington 9,727
Magdalena 1,022
Maxwell 316
Melrose 649
Mesilla 2,029
Milan 3,747
Moriarty 1,276
Mosquero 197
Mountainair 1,170
Pecos 885
Portales 9,940
Questa 608
Raton 8,225
Red River 332
Reserve 439
Roswell 39,676
Roy 381
Ruidoso 4,260
Ruidoso Downs 949
San Jon 341
San Ysidro 199
Santa Fe 48,899
Santa Rosa 2,469
Silver City 9,887
Socorro 7,576
Springer 1,696
Taos 3,369
Tatum 896
Texico 958
Tijeras 311
Truth or Consequences 5,219
Tucumcari 6,765
Tularosa 2,536
Vaughn 737
Virden 246
Wagon Mound 416
Willard 166
Williamsburg 433

NEW YORK

Population 17,557,288

METROPOLITAN AREAS

Albany-Schenectady-Troy 795,019
Binghamton 301,336 (263,460 in N.Y.; 37,876 in Pa.)
Buffalo 1,242,573
Elmira 279,780
Nassau-Suffolk 2,605,813
New York City 9,119,737 (8,274,352 in N.Y.; 845,385 in N.J.)
Poughkeepsie 245,055
Rochester 971,879
Syracuse 642,375
Utica-Rome 320,180

COUNTIES

Albany 285,909
Allegany 51,742
Bronx 1,169,115
Broome 213,648
Cattaraugus 85,697
Cayuga 79,894
Chautauqua 146,925
Chemung 97,656
Chenango 49,344
Clinton 80,750
Columbia 59,487
Cortland 48,820
Delaware 46,931
Dutchess 245,055
Erie 1,015,472
Essex 36,176
Franklin 44,929
Fulton 55,153
Genesee 59,400
Greene 40,861
Hamilton 5,034
Herkimer 66,714
Jefferson 88,151
Kings 2,230,936
Lewis 25,035
Livingston 57,006
Madison 65,150
Monroe 702,238
Montgomery 53,439
Nassau 1,321,582
New York 1,427,533
Niagara 227,101
Oneida 253,466
Onondaga 463,324
Ontario 88,909
Orange 259,603
Orleans 38,496
Oswego 113,901
Otsego 59,075
Putnam 77,193
Queens 1,891,325
Rensselaer 151,966
Richmond 352,121
Rockland 259,530
St. Lawrence 114,254
Saratoga 153,759
Schenectady 149,946
Schoharie 29,710
Schuyler 17,686
Seneca 33,733
Steuben 99,135
Suffolk 1,284,231
Sullivan 65,155
Tioga 49,812
Tompkins 87,085
Ulster 158,158
Warren 54,854
Washington 54,795
Wayne 85,230
Westchester 866,599
Wyoming 39,895
Yates 21,459

CITIES AND VILLAGES

Adams 1,701
Addison 2,028
Afton 982
Akron 2,971
Albany 101,727
Albion 4,897
Alden 2,488
Alexander 483
Alexandria Bay 1,265
Alfred 4,967
Allegany 2,078
Almond 568
Altamont 1,292
Altmar 347
Ames 224
Amityville 9,076
Amsterdam 21,872
Andes 372
Andover 1,120
Angelica 982
Angola 2,292
Antwerp 749
Arcade 2,052
Ardsley 4,183
Argyle 320
Arkport 811
Asharoken 635
Athens 1,738
Atlantic Beach 1,775
Attica 2,659
Auburn 32,548
Aurora 926
Avoca 1,144
Avon 3,006

Babylon 12,388	Croghan 703	Hammond 271	Margaretville 755	Panama 511	Sloatsburg 3,154
Bainbridge 1,603	Croton-on-Hudson 6,889	Hammondsport 1,065	Massapequa Park 19,779	Parish 535	Smyrna 225
Baldwinsville 6,446	Cuba 1,739	Hancock 1,526	Massena 12,851	Patchogue 11,291	Sodus 1,790
Ballston Spa 4,711	Dannemora 3,770	Hannibal 680	Matinecock 985	Pawling 1,996	Sodus Point 1,334
Barker 535	Dansville 4,979	Harriman 796	Maybrook 2,007	Peekskill 18,236	Solvay 7,140
Barneveld 396	Deferiet 326	Harrison 23,046	Mayfield 944	Pelham 6,848	South Corning 1,195
Batavia 16,703	Delanson 448	Harrisville 937	Mayville 1,626	Pelham Manor 6,130	South Dayton 661
Bath 6,042	Delevan 1,113	Hastings-on-Hudson 8,573	McGraw 1,188	Penn Yan 5,242	South Floral Park . . .1,490
Baxter Estates 911	Delhi 3,374	Haverstraw 8,800	Mechanicville 5,500	Perry 4,198	South Glens Falls . . .3,714
Bayville 7,034	Depew 19,819	Head of the Harbor 1,023	Medina 6,392	Perrysburg 405	South Nyack 3,602
Beacon 12,937	Deposit 1,897	Hempstead 40,404	Menands 4,012	Phelps 2,004	Southampton 4,000
Belle Terre 826	Dering Harbor 16	Herkimer 8,383	Meridian 344	Philadelphia 855	Speculator 408
Bellerose 1,187	DeRuyter 542	Hermon 490	Mexico 1,621	Philmont 1,539	Spencer 863
Bellport 2,809	Dexter 1,053	Herrings 170	Middleburgh 1,358	Phoenix 2,357	Spencerport 3,424
Belmont 1,024	Dobbs Ferry 10,053	Heuvelton 777	Middleport 1,995	Piermont 2,269	Spring Valley 20,537
Bemus Point 444	Dolgeville 2,602	Hewlett Bay Park 489	Middletown 21,454	Pike 367	Springville 4,285
Bergen 976	Dresden 378	Hewlett Harbor 1,331	Middleville 647	Pine Hill 216	Stamford 1,240
Binghamton 55,860	Dryden 1,761	Hewlett Neck 472	Milford 514	Pittsford 1,568	Staten Island 352,121
Black River 1,384	Dundee 1,556	Highland Falls 4,187	Mill Neck 959	Plandome 1,503	Stewart Manor 2,373
Blasdell 3,288	Dunkirk 15,310	Hillburn 926	Millbrook 1,343	Plandome Heights 963	Stillwater 1,572
Bloomingburg 338	Earlville 985	Hilton 4,151	Millerton 1,013	Plandome Manor 883	Suffern 10,794
Bloomingdale 608	East Aurora 6,803	Hobart 473	Millport 440	Plattsburgh 21,057	Sylvan Beach 1,243
Bolivar 1,345	East Bloomfield 587	Holcomb 952	Mineola 20,757	Pleasantville 6,749	Syracuse 170,105
Boonville 2,344	East Hampton 1,886	Holland Patent 534	Minoa 3,640	Poland 553	Tannersville 685
Brewster 1,650	East Hills 7,160	Holley 1,882	Mohawk 2,956	Pomona 2,421	Tarrytown 10,648
Briarcliff Manor . . . 7,115	East Randolph 655	Homer 3,635	Monroe 5,996	Poquott 588	Theresa 827
Bridgewater 578	East Rochester 7,596	Honeoye Falls 2,410	Montgomery 2,316	Port Byron 1,400	Thomaston 2,684
Brightwaters 3,286	East Rockaway 10,917	Hoosick Falls 3,609	Monticello 6,306	Port Chester 23,565	Ticonderoga 2,938
Broadalbin 1,415	East Syracuse 3,412	Hornell 10,234	Montour Falls 1,791	Port Dickinson 1,974	Tivoli 711
Brockport 9,776	East Williston 2,708	Horseheads 7,348	Mooers 549	Port Henry 1,450	Tonawanda 18,693
Brocton 1,416	Edwards 561	Hudson 7,986	Moravia 1,582	Port Jefferson 6,731	Troy 56,638
Bronx 1,169,115	Elba 750	Hudson Falls 7,419	Morris 681	Port Jervis 8,699	Trumansburg 1,722
Bronxville 6,267	Elbridge 1,099	Hunter 511	Morristown 461	Port Leyden 740	Tuckahoe 6,076
Brooklyn 2,230,936	Elizabethtown 659	Huntington Bay 3,943	Morrisville 2,707	Port Washington North 3,147	Tully 1,049
Brookville 3,290	Ellenville 4,405	Ilion 9,190	Mount Kisco 8,025	Portville 1,136	Tupper Lake 4,478
Brownville 1,099	Ellicottville 713	Interlaken 685	Mount Morris 3,039	Potsdam 10,635	Turin 284
Brushton 577	Ellisburg 307	Irvington 5,774	Mount Vernon 66,713	Poughkeepsie 29,757	Tuxedo Park 809
Buchanan 2,041	Elmira 35,327	Island Park 4,847	Munnsville 499	Prospect 368	Unadilla 1,367
Buffalo 357,870	Elmira Heights 4,279	Ithaca 28,732	Munsey Park 2,806	Pulaski 2,415	Union Springs 1,201
Burdett 410	Elmsford 3,361	Jamestown 35,775	Muttontown 2,725	Queens 1,891,325	Unionville 574
Burke 226	Endicott 14,457	Jeffersonville 554	Naples 1,225	Quogue 966	Upper Brookville 1,245
Caledonia 2,188	Esperance 374	Johnson City 17,126	Nassau 1,285	Randolph 1,398	Upper Nyack 1,906
Cambridge 1,820	Evans Mills 651	Johnstown 9,360	Nelliston 691	Ravena 3,091	Utica 75,632
Camden 2,667	Fabius 367	Jordan 1,371	Nelsonville 567	Red Creek 645	Valatie 1,492
Camillus 1,298	Fair Haven 976	Keeseville 2,025	New Berlin 1,392	Red Hook 1,692	Valley Falls 554
Canajoharie 2,412	Fairport 5,970	Kenmore 18,474	New Hartford 2,313	Remsen 621	Valley Stream 35,769
Canandaigua 10,419	Falconer 2,778	Kensington 1,132	New Hyde Park 9,801	Rensaleer Falls 360	Van Etten 559
Canaseraga 700	Farmingdale 7,946	Kinderhook 1,377	New Paltz 4,941	Rensselaer 9,047	Vernon 1,373
Canastota 4,773	Farnham 404	Kings Point 5,234	New Rochelle 70,794	Rhinebeck 2,542	Victor 2,370
Candor 901	Fayetteville 4,709	Kingston 24,481	New Square 1,750	Richburg 494	Victory 571
Canisteo 2,679	Fillmore 563	Kiryas Joel 2,088	New York City 7,071,030	Richfield Springs . . .1,561	Village of the Branch 1,707
Canton 7,055	Fishkill 1,555	Lackawanna 22,701	New York Mills 3,549	Richmondville 792	Voorheesville 3,320
Cape Vincent 785	Fleischmanns 346	Lacona 582	Newark 10,017	Riverside 684	Waddington 980
Carthage 3,643	Floral Park 16,805	Lake George 1,047	Newark Valley 1,190	Rochester 241,741	Walden 5,659
Cassadaga 821	Florida 1,947	Lake Grove 9,692	Newburgh 23,438	Rockville Centre . . .25,405	Walton 3,329
Castile 1,135	Flower Hill 4,558	Lake Placid 2,490	Newport 746	Rome 43,826	Wampsville 569
Castleton-on-Hudson 1,627	Fonda 1,006	Lake Success 2,396	Niagara Falls 71,384	Roslyn 2,134	Wappingers Falls . . .5,110
Castorland 277	Forestville 804	Lakewood 3,941	Nichols 613	Roslyn Estates 1,292	Warsaw 3,619
Cato 475	Fort Ann 509	Lancaster 13,056	Nissequogue 1,462	Roslyn Harbor 1,129	Warwick 4,320
Catskill 4,718	Fort Edward 3,561	Lansing 3,039	North Collins 1,496	Round Lake 791	Washingtonville 2,380
Cattaraugus 1,200	Fort Johnson 646	Larchmont 6,308	North Haven 738	Rouses Point 2,266	Waterford 2,405
Cayuga 604	Fort Plain 2,555	Lattingtown 1,749	North Hills 1,587	Rushville 548	Waterloo 5,303
Cayuga Heights . . . 3,170	Frankfort 2,995	Laurel Hollow 1,527	North Hornell 813	Russell Gardens . . .1,263	Watertown 27,861
Cazenovia 2,599	Franklin 440	Laurens 276	North Syracuse 7,970	Rye 15,083	Waterville 1,672
Cedarhurst 6,162	Franklinville 1,887	Lawrence 6,175	North Tarrytown 7,994	Sackets Harbor 1,017	Watervliet 11,354
Celoron 1,405	Fredonia 11,126	Le Roy 4,900	North Tonawanda 35,760	Saddle Rock 921	Watkins Glen 2,440
Central Square 1,418	Freeport 38,272	Leicester 462	Northport 7,651	Sag Harbor 2,581	Waverly 4,738
Centre Island 378	Freeville 449	Lewiston 3,326	Northville 1,304	St. Johnsville 2,019	Wayland 1,846
Champlain 1,410	Fulton 13,312	Liberty 4,293	Norwich 8,082	Salamanca 6,890	Webster 5,499
Chateaugay 869	Fultonville 777	Lima 2,025	Norwood 1,902	Salem 959	Weedsport 1,952
Chatham 2,001	Gainesville 334	Limestone 466	Nunda 1,169	Saltaire 35	Wellsburg 647
Chaumont 620	Galway 245	Lindenhurst 26,919	Nyack 6,428	Sands Point 2,742	Wellsville 5,769
Cherry Creek 677	Garden City Park . . 22,927	Lisle 357	Oakfield 1,791	Sandy Creek 765	West Carthage 1,824
Cherry Valley 684	Geneseo 6,746	Little Falls 6,156	Ocean Beach 155	Saranac Lake 5,578	West Haverstraw . . .9,181
Chester 1,910	Geneva 15,133	Little Valley 1,203	Odessa 613	Saratoga Springs . . .23,906	West Winfield 979
Chittenango 4,290	Gilbertsville 455	Liverpool 2,849	Ogdensburg 12,375	Saugerties 3,882	Westbury 13,871
Churchville 1,399	Glen Cove 24,618	Livonia 1,238	Old Brookville 1,574	Savona 932	Westfield 3,446
Clayton 1,816	Glen Park 504	Lloyd Harbor 3,405	Old Field 829	Scarsdale 17,650	Westhampton Beach 1,629
Clayville 478	Glens Falls 15,897	Lockport 24,844	Old Westbury 3,277	Schaghticoke 677	Westport 613
Cleveland 855	Gloversville 17,836	Lodi 334	Olean 18,207	Schenectady 67,972	White Plains 46,999
Clifton Springs 2,039	Goshen 4,874	Long Beach 34,073	Oneida 10,810	Schenevus 625	Whitehall 3,241
Clinton 2,107	Gouverneur 4,285	Lowville 3,364	Oneida Castle 751	Schoharie 1,016	Whitesboro 4,460
Clyde 2,491	Gowanda 2,713	Lynbrook 20,431	Oneonta 14,933	Schuylerville 1,256	Whitney Point 1,093
Cobleskill 5,272	Grand View-on-Hudson 312	Lyndonville 916	Orchard Park 3,671	Scotia 7,280	Williamsville 6,017
Cohocton 902	Granville 2,696	Lyons 4,160	Oriskany 1,680	Scottsville 1,789	Williston Park 8,216
Cohoes 18,144	Great Neck 9,168	Lyons Falls 755	Oriskany Falls 802	Sea Cliff 5,364	Wilson 1,259
Cold Brook 402	Great Neck Estates 2,936	Macedon 1,400	Ossining 20,196	Seneca Falls 7,466	Windsor 1,155
Cold Spring 2,161	Great Neck Plaza . . .5,604	Madison 396	Oswego 19,793	Sharon Springs 514	Wolcott 1,496
Colonie 8,869	Green Island 2,696	Malone 7,668	Otego 1,089	Sherburne 1,561	Woodhull 315
Constableville 330	Greene 1,747	Malverne 9,262	Otisville 953	Sherman 775	Woodridge 809
Cooperstown 2,342	Greenport 2,273	Mamaroneck 17,616	Ovid 666	Sherrill 2,830	Woodsburgh 847
Copenhagen 656	Greenwich 1,955	Manchester 1,698	Owego 4,364	Shoreham 555	Wurtsboro 1,128
Corfu 689	Greenwood Lake . . .2,809	Manhattan 1,427,533	Oxford 1,765	Shortsville 1,669	Wyoming 507
Corinth 2,702	Groton 2,313	Manlius 5,241	Oyster Bay Cove . . .1,799	Sidney 4,861	Yonkers 195,351
Corning 12,953	Hagaman 1,331	Manorhaven 5,384	Painted Post 2,196	Silver Creek 3,088	Yorkville 3,115
Cornwall 3,164	Hamburg 10,582	Mannsville 431	Palatine Bridge 604	Silver Springs 801	Youngstown 2,191
Cortland 20,138	Hamilton 3,725	Marathon 1,046	Palmyra 3,729	Sinclairville 772	
Cove Neck 331		Marcellus 1,870		Skaneateles 2,789	
Coxsackie 2,786				Sloan 4,529	

NORTH CAROLINA

Population 5,874,429

METROPOLITAN AREAS

Asheville 177,761	
Burlington 99,136	
Charlotte-Gastonia 637,218	
Fayetteville 247,160	
Greensboro-Winston-Salem-High Point 827,385	
Norfolk-Virginia Beach-Portsmouth (Va.) . . . . . . .806,691 (795,602 in Va.; 11,089 in N.C.)	
Raleigh-Durham . 530,673	
Wilmington 139,238	

COUNTIES

Alamance 99,136	Catawba 105,208	Gates 8,875	Macon 20,178	Polk 12,984
Alexander 24,999	Chatham 33,415	Graham 7,217	Madison 16,827	Randolph 91,861
Alleghany 9,587	Cherokee 18,933	Granville 33,995	Martin 25,948	Richmond 45,481
Anson 25,562	Chowan 12,558	Greene 16,117	McDowell 35,135	Robeson 101,577
Ashe 22,325	Clay 6,619	Guilford 317,154	Mecklenburg 404,270	Rockingham 83,426
Avery 14,409	Cleveland 83,435	Halifax 55,286	Mitchell 14,428	Rowan 99,186
Beaufort 40,266	Columbus 51,037	Harnett 59,570	Montgomery 22,469	Rutherford 53,787
Bertie 21,024	Craven 71,043	Haywood 46,495	Moore 50,505	Sampson 49,687
Bladen 30,448	Cumberland 247,160	Henderson 58,580	Nash 67,153	Scotland 32,273
Brunswick 35,767	Currituck 11,089	Hertford 23,368	New Hanover 103,471	Stanly 48,517
Buncombe 160,934	Dare 13,377	Hoke 20,383	Northampton 22,584	Stokes 33,086
Burke 72,504	Davidson 113,162	Hyde 5,873	Onslow 112,784	Surry 59,449
Cabarrus 85,895	Davie 24,599	Iredell 82,538	Orange 77,055	Swain 10,283
Caldwell 67,746	Duplin 40,952	Jackson 25,811	Pamlico 10,398	Transylvania 23,417
Camden 5,829	Durham 152,785	Johnston 70,599	Pasquotank 28,462	Tyrrell 3,975
Carteret 41,092	Edgecombe 55,988	Jones 9,705	Pender 22,215	Union 70,380
Caswell 20,705	Forsyth 243,683	Lee 36,718	Perquimans 9,486	Vance 36,748
	Franklin 30,055	Lenoir 59,819	Person 29,164	Wake 300,833
	Gaston 162,568	Lincoln 42,372	Pitt 83,651	Warren 16,232

Washington 14,801
Watauga 31,678
Wayne 97,054
Wilkes 58,657
Wilson 63,132
Yadkin 28,439
Yancey 14,934

CITIES, TOWNS, AND VILLAGES

Aberdeen 1,945
Ahoskie 4,887
Alamance 320
Albemarle 15,110
Alexander Mills 643
Alliance 616
Andrews 1,621
Angier 1,709
Ansonville 794
Apex 2,847
Arapahoe 467
Archdale 5,305
Arlington 872
Asheboro 15,252
Asheville 53,281
Askewville 227
Atkinson 298
Atlantic Beach 941
Aulander 1,214
Aurora 698
Autryville 228
Ayden 184
Bailey 685
Bakersville 373
Banner Elk 1,087
Bath 207
Battleboro 632
Bayboro 759
Beargrass 82
Beaufort 3,826
Belhaven 2,430
Belmont 4,607
Belville 102
Belwood 613
Benson 2,792
Bessemer City 4,787
Bethel 1,825
Beulaville 1,060
Biltmore Forest 1,499
Biscoe 1,334
Black Creek 523
Black Mountain 4,083
Bladenboro 1,385
Blowing Rock 1,337
Boiling Springs 2,381
Boiling Spring Lakes 998
Bolivia 252
Bolton 563
Boone 10,191
Boonville 1,028
Bostic 476
Brevard 5,323
Bridgeton 461
Broadway 908
Brookford 467
Brunswick 223
Bryson City 1,556
Bunn 505
Burgaw 1,586
Burlington 37,266
Burnsville 1,452
Calabash 128
Calypso 689
Cameron 225
Candor 868
Canton 4,631
Cape Carteret 944
Carolina Beach 2,000
Carrboro 7,517
Carthage 925
Cary 21,612
Casar 346
Cashiers 553
Castalia 358
Caswell Beach 110
Catawba 509
Centerville 135
Cerro Gordo 295
Chadbourn 1,975
Chadwick Acres 15
Chapel Hill 32,421
Charlotte 314,447
Cherryville 4,844
China Grove 2,081
Chocowinity 644
Claremont 880
Clarkton 664
Clayton 4,091
Cleveland 595
Clinton 7,552
Clyde 1,008
Coats 1,385
Cofield 465
Colerain 284
Columbia 758
Columbus 727
Como 89
Concord 16,942
Conetoe 215
Conover 4,245
Conway 678
Cornelius 1,460
Cove City 500
Cramerton 1,869
Creedmoor 1,641
Creswell 426
Crossnore 297
Dallas 3,340
Danbury 140
Davidson 3,241
Denton 949
Dillsboro 179
Dobson 1,222
Dortches 885
Dover 600
Drexel 1,392
Dublin 477
Dunn 8,962
Durham 100,831
Earl 206
East Arcadia 461
East Bend 602
East Laurinburg 536
East Spencer 2,150
Eden 15,672
Edenton 5,264
Elizabeth City 13,784
Elizabethtown 3,551
Elk Park 535
Elkin 2,858
Ellenboro 560
Ellerbe 1,415
Elm City 1,561
Elon College 2,873
Emerald Isle 865
Enfield 2,995
Erwin 2,828
Eureka 303
Everetts 213
Fair Bluff 1,095
Fairmont 2,658
Faison 636
Faith 552
Falcon 339
Falkland 118
Fallston 614
Farmville 4,707
Fayetteville 59,507
Forest City 7,688
Fountain 424
Four Oaks 1,049
Foxfire Village 153
Franklin 2,640
Franklinton 1,394
Franklinville 607
Fremont 1,736
Fuquay-Varina 3,110
Garland 885
Garner 9,556
Garysburg 1,434
Gaston 883
Gastonia 47,333
Gatesville 363
Gibson 533
Gibsonville 2,865
Glen Alpine 645
Godwin 340
Goldsboro 31,871
Goldston 353
Graham 8,415
Granite Falls 2,580
Granite Quarry 1,294
Greenevers 477
Greensboro 155,642
Greenville 35,740
Grifton 2,179
Grimesland 453
Grover 597
Halifax 253
Hamilton 638
Hamlet 4,720
Harmony 470
Harrells 255
Harrellsville 151
Harrisburg 1,433
Hassell 109
Havelock 17,718
Haw River 2,117
Hayesville 376
Haywood 190
Hazelwood 1,811
Henderson 13,522
Hendersonville 6,862
Hertford 1,941
Hickory 20,757
High Point 64,107
High Shoals 586
Highlands 653
Hildebran 628
Hillsborough 3,019
Hobgood 483
Hoffman 389
Holden Beach 232
Holly Ridge 465
Holly Springs 688
Hollyville (Cash Corner) 100
Hookerton 460
Hope Mills 5,412
Hot Springs 678
Hudson 2,888
Huntersville 1,294
Indian Beach 54
Indian Trail 811
Jackson 720
Jacksonville 17,056
Jamestown 2,148
Jamesville 604
Jefferson 1,086
Jonesville 1,752
Kelford 254
Kenansville 931
Kenly 1,433
Kernersville 6,802
Kill Devil Hills 1,796
Kings Mountain 9,080
Kinston 25,234
Kittrell 225
Knightdale 985
Kure Beach 611
La Grange 3,147
Lake Lure 488
Lake Waccamaw 1,133
Landis 2,092
Lansing 194
Lasker 96
Lattimore 237
Laurel Park 764
Laurinburg 11,480
Lawndale 469
Leggett 99
Lenoir 13,748
Lewiston 459
Lexington 15,711
Liberty 1,997
Lilesville 588
Lillington 1,948
Lincolnton 4,879
Linden 365
Linville 244
Littleton 820
Locust 1,590
Long Beach 1,834
Longview 3,587
Louisburg 3,238
Love Valley 55
Lowell 2,917
Lucama 1,070
Lumber Bridge 171
Lumberton 18,340
MacClesfield 504
Macon 153
Madison 2,806
Maggie Valley 202
Magnolia 592
Maiden 2,574
Manteo 902
Marion 3,684
Mars Hill 2,126
Marshall 809
Marshville 2,011
Matthews 1,648
Maxton 2,711
Mayodan 2,627
Maysville 877
McAdenville 947
McDonald 117
McFarlan 133
Mebane 2,782
Mesic 390
Micro 438
Middleburg 185
Middlesex 837
Milton 235
Minnesott Beach 171
Mint Hill 9,830
Mocksville 2,637
Monroe 12,639
Montreat 741
Mooresboro 405
Mooresville 8,575
Morehead City 4,359
Morganton 13,763
Morrisville 251
Morven 765
Mount Airy 6,862
Mount Gilead 1,423
Mount Holly 4,530
Mount Olive 4,876
Mount Pleasant 1,210
Murfreesboro 3,007
Murphy 2,070
Nags Head 1,020
Nashville 2,678
Navassa 439
New Bern 14,557
New London 454
New Topsail Beach (Topsail Beach) 264
Newland 722
Newport 1,883
Newton 7,624
Newton Grove 564
Norlina 901
Norman 252
North Wilkesboro 3,260
Norwood 1,818
Oak City 475
Oakboro 587
Ocean Isle Beach 143
Old Fort 752
Oriental 536
Orrum 167
Oxford 7,580
Pantego 185
Parkton 564
Parmele 484
Patterson Springs 731
Peachland 506
Pembroke 2,698
Pikeville 662
Pilot Mountain 1,090
Pine Knoll Shores 646
Pine Level 953
Pinebluff 935
Pinetops 1,465
Pineville 1,525
Pink Hill 644
Pittsboro 1,332
Plymouth 4,571
Polkton 762
Polkville 528
Pollocksville 318
Powellsville 320
Princeton 1,034
Princeville 1,508
Proctorville 205
Raeford 3,630
Raleigh 149,771
Ramseur 1,162
Randleman 2,156
Ranlo 1,774
Raynham 83
Red Oak 314
Red Springs 3,607
Reidsville 12,492
Rennert 178
Rhodhiss 727
Rich Square 1,057
Richfield 373
Richlands 825
Roanoke Rapids 14,702
Robbins 1,256
Robbinsville 1,370
Robersonville 1,981
Rockingham 8,300
Rockwell 1,339
Rocky Mount 41,283
Rolesville 381
Ronda 457
Roper 795
Rose Hill 1,508
Roseboro 1,227
Rosman 512
Rowland 1,841
Roxboro 7,532
Roxobel 278
Rural Hall 1,336
Ruth 381
Rutherford College 1,108
Rutherfordton 3,434
St. Pauls 1,639
Salemburg 742
Salisbury 22,677
Saluda 607
Sanford 14,773
Saratoga 381
Scotland Neck 2,834
Seaboard 687
Seagrove 294
Selma 4,762
Seven Devils 21
Seven Springs 166
Severn 309
Shady Forest 43
Shallotte 680
Sharpsburg 997
Shelby 15,310
Siler City 4,446
Simpson 407
Sims 192
Smithfield 7,288
Snow Hill 1,374
Southern Pines 8,620
Southern Shores 395
Southport 2,824
Sparta 1,687
Speed 95
Spencer 2,938
Spencer Mountain 169
Spindale 4,246
Spring Hope 1,254
Spring Lake 6,273
Spruce Pine 2,282
Staley 204
Stallings 1,826
Stanfield 463
Stanley 2,341
Stantonsburg 920
Star 816
Statesville 18,622
Stedman 723
Stem 222
Stoneville 1,054
Stonewall 360
Stovall 417
Sunset Beach 304
Surf City 391
Swansboro 976
Sylva 1,699
Tabor City 2,710
Tar Heel 118
Tarboro 8,634
Taylorsville 1,103
Teachey 373
Thomasville 14,144
Trent Woods 1,177
Trenton 407
Troutman 1,360
Troy 2,702
Tryon 1,796
Turkey 417
Valdese 3,364
Vanceboro 833
Vandemere 335
Vass 828
Waco 322
Wade 474
Wadesboro 4,119
Wagram 617
Wake Forest 3,780
Wallace 2,903
Walnut Cove 1,147
Walnut Creek 343
Walstonburg 181
Warrenton 908
Warsaw 2,910
Washington 8,418
Washington Park 514
Watha 196
Waxhaw 1,208
Waynesville 6,765
Weaverville 1,495
Webster 200
Weldon 1,844
Wendell 2,222
West Jefferson 822
Whispering Pines 1,160
Whitakers 924
White Lake 968
Whiteville 5,565
Wilkesboro 2,335
Williamsboro 59
Williamston 6,159
Wilmington 44,000
Wilson 34,424
Windsor 2,126
Winfall 634
Wingate 2,615
Winston-Salem 131,885
Winterville 2,052
Winton 825
Woodfin 3,260
Woodland 861
Woodville 212
Wrightsville Beach 2,910
Yadkinville 2,216
Yaupon Beach 569
Youngsville 486
Zebulon 2,055

NORTH DAKOTA

Population 652,695

METROPOLITAN AREAS

Bismarck 79,988
Fargo-Moorhead (Minn.) 137,574 (88,247 in N. Dak.; 49,327 in Minn.)
Grand Forks 100,944 (66,100 in N. Dak.; 34,844 in Minn.)

COUNTIES

Adams 3,584
Barnes 13,960
Benson 7,944
Billings 1,138
Bottineau 9,338
Bowman 4,229
Burke 3,822
Burleigh 54,811
Cass 88,247
Cavalier 7,636
Dickey 7,207
Divide 3,494
Dunn 4,627
Eddy 3,554
Emmons 5,877
Foster 4,611
Golden Valley 2,391
Grand Forks 66,100
Grant 4,274
Griggs 3,714
Hettinger 4,275
Kidder 3,833
La Moure 6,473
Logan 3,493
McHenry 7,858
McIntosh 4,800
McKenzie 7,132
McLean 12,288
Mercer 9,378
Morton 25,177
Mountrail 7,679
Nelson 5,233
Oliver 2,495
Pembina 10,399
Pierce 6,166
Ramsey 13,048
Ransom 6,698
Renville 3,608
Richland 19,207
Rolette 12,177
Sargent 5,512
Sheridan 2,819
Sioux 3,620
Slope 1,157
Stark 23,697
Steele 3,106
Stutsman 24,154
Towner 4,052
Traill 9,624
Walsh 15,371
Ward 58,392
Wells 6,979
Williams 22,237

CITIES

Abercrombie 260
Adams 303
Alamo 122
Alexander 358
Alice 62
Almont 146
Alsen 169
Ambrose 60
Amenia 93
Amidon 43
Anamoose 355
Aneta 341
Antler 101
Ardoch 78
Argusville 147
Arnegard 193
Arthur 445
Ashley 1,192
Ayr 42
Balfour 51
Balta 139
Bantry 28
Barney 70
Barton 38
Bathgate 67
Beach 1,381
Belfield 1,274
Benedict 68
Bergen 24
Berlin 57
Berthold 485
Berwick 22
Beulah 2,878
Binford 293
Bisbee 257
Bismarck 44,485
Bottineau 2,829
Bowbells 587
Bowdon 220
Bowman 2,071
Braddock 86
Briarwood 47
Brinsmade 54
Brocket 74
Bucyrus 32
Buffalo 226
Burlington 762
Butte 157
Buxton 336
Calio 60
Calvin 61
Cando 1,496
Canton City (Hensel) 68
Carpio 244
Carrington 2,641
Carson 469
Casselton 1,661
Cathay 66
Cavalier 1,505
Cayuga 75
Center 900
Christine 147
Churchs Ferry 139
Cleveland 130
Clifford 51
Cogswell 227
Coleharbor 150
Colfax 101
Columbus 325
Conway 33
Cooperstown 1,308
Courtenay 110
Crary 139
Crosby 1,469
Crystal 256
Davenport 195
Dawson 144
Dazey 143
Deering 85
Des Lacs 212
Devils Lake 7,442
Dickey 74
Dickinson 15,924
Dodge 199
Donnybrook 139
Douglas 112
Drake 479
Drayton 1,082
Dunn Center 170
Dunseith 625
Dwight 72
Edgeley 843
Edinburg 300
Edmore 416
Egeland 112
Elgin 930
Ellendale 1,967
Elliott 44
Emerado 596
Enderlin 1,151
Epping 104
Esmond 337
Fairdale 97
Fairmount 480
Fargo 61,308
Fessenden 761
Fingal 151
Finley 718
Flasher 410
Flaxton 182
Forbes 84
Fordville 326
Forest River 152
Forman 629
Fort Ransom 99
Fort Yates 771
Fortuna 98
Fredonia 82
Frontier 160
Fullerton 107
Gackle 456
Galesburg 165
Gardena 66
Gardner 94
Garrison 1,830
Gascoyne 23
Gilby 283
Gladstone 317
Glen Ullin 1,125
Glenburn 454
Glenfield 164
Golden Valley 287
Golva 101
Goodrich 288
Grafton 5,293
Grand Forks 43,765
Grandin 210

NORTH DAKOTA (continued)

Grano .6
Granville .281
Great Bend .113
Grenora .362
Gwinner .725
Hague .127
Halliday .355
Hamberg .41
Hamilton .109
Hampden .126
Hankinson .1,158
Hanks .10
Hannaford .201
Hannah .90
Hansboro .43
Harvey .2,527
Harwood .326
Hatton .787
Havana .148
Haynes .268
Hazelton .266
Hazen .2,365
Hebron .1,078
Hettinger .1,739
Hillsboro .1,600
Hoople .350
Hope .406
Horace .494
Hovey Mobile Park .3
Hunter .369
Hurdsfield .113
Inkster .135
Jamestown .16,280
Jud .118
Karlsruhe .164
Kathryn .95
Kenmare .1,456
Kensal .210

Kief .36
Killdeer .790
Kindred .568
Knox .69
Kramer .84
Kulm .570
Lakota .963
LaMoure .1,077
Landa .62
Langdon .2,335
Lankin .175
Lansford .294
Larimore .1,524
Larson .21
Lawton .101
Leal .45
Leeds .678
Lehr .254
Leith .59
Leonard .289
Lidgerwood .971
Lignite .332
Lincoln .656
Linton .1,561
Lisbon .2,283
Litchville .251
Loma .39
Loraine .21
Ludden .47
Luverne .65
Maddock .677
Makoti .199
Mandan .15,513
Mantador .76
Manvel .308
Mapleton .306
Marion .214
Marmarth .190

Martin .114
Max .317
Maxbass .141
Mayville .2,255
Maza .21
McClusky .658
McHenry .113
McVille .626
Medina .521
Medora .94
Mercer .134
Merricourt .17
Michigan .502
Milnor .716
Milton .195
Minnewaukan .461
Minot .32,843
Minto .592
Mohall .1,049
Monango .59
Montpelier .96
Mooreton .216
Mott .1,315
Mountain .156
Munich .300
Mylo .31
Napoleon .1,103
Neche .471
Nekoma .102
New England .825
New Leipzig .352
New Rockford .1,791
New Salem .1,081
New Town .1,335
Newburg .151
Niagara .76
Nome .67
Noonan .283

North River .65
Northwood .1,240
Oakes .2,112
Oberon .150
Omemee .10
Oriska .125
Osnabrock .222
Overly .25
Page .329
Palermo .97
Park River .1,844
Parshall .1,059
Pekin .101
Pembina .673
Perth .20
Petersburg .230
Pettibone .127
Pick City .182
Pillsbury .46
Pingree .88
Pisek .156
Plaza .222
Portal .238
Portland .627
Powers Lake .466
Prairie Rose .76
Rawson .12
Ray .766
Reeder .355
Regan .71
Regent .297
Reile's Acres .191
Reynolds .309
Rhame .222
Richardton .699
Riverside .465
Robinson .129
Rock Lake .287

Rogers .68
Rolette .667
Rolla .1,538
Ross .104
Rugby .3,335
Ruso .12
Russell .18
Rutland .250
Ryder .158
St. John .401
St. Thomas .528
Sanborn .237
Sarles .111
Sawyer .417
Scranton .415
Selfridge .273
Sentinel Butte .86
Sharon .166
Sheldon .173
Sherwood .294
Sheyenne .307
Sibley .21
Solen .138
Souris .122
South Heart .294
Spiritwood Lake .50
Spring Brook .52
Stanley .1,631
Stanton .623
Starkweather .210
Steele .796
Strasburg .623
Streeter .264
Surrey .999
Sykeston .193
Tappen .271
Taylor .239
Thompson .785

Tioga .1,597
Tolley .103
Tolna .241
Tower City .293
Towner .867
Turtle Lake .707
Tuttle .202
Underwood .1,329
Upham .227
Valley City .7,774
Velva .1,101
Venturia .40
Verona .126
Voltaire .65
Wahpeton .9,064
Walcott .186
Wales .74
Walhalla .1,429
Warwick .108
Washburn .1,767
Watford City .2,119
West Fargo .10,099
Westhope .741
Wheelock .34
White Earth .98
Wildrose .214
Williston .13,336
Willow City .329
Wilton .950
Wimbledon .330
Wing .220
Wishek .1,345
Wolford .76
Woodworth .137
Wyndmere .550
York .69
Zap .511
Zeeland .253

OHIO   Population 10,797,419

METROPOLITAN AREAS

Akron .660,328
Canton .404,421
Cincinnati .1,401,403
(1,100,895 in O.;
266,217 in Ky.;
34,291 in Ind.)
Cleveland .1,898,720
Columbus .1,093,293
Dayton .830,070
Hamilton-
Middletown .258,787
Huntington (W. Va.)-
Ashland (Ky.) .311,350
(152,856 in W. Va.;
94,645 in Ky.;
63,849 in O.)
Lima .218,244
Lorain-Elyria .274,909
Mansfield .131,205
Marietta-Parkersburg
(W. Va.) .162,836
(98,570 in W. Va.;
64,266 in O.)
Springfield .183,885
Steubenville-Weirton
(W. Va.) .163,099
(91,564 in O.;
71,535 in W. Va.)
Toledo .791,599
(656,940 in O.;
134,659 in Mich.)
Wheeling
(W. Va.) .185,566
(102,997 in W. Va.;
82,569 in O.)
Youngstown-
Warren .531,350

COUNTIES

Adams .24,328
Allen .112,241
Ashland .46,178
Ashtabula .104,215
Athens .56,399
Auglaize .42,554
Belmont .82,569
Brown .31,920
Butler .258,787
Carroll .25,598
Champaign .33,649
Clark .150,236
Clermont .128,483
Clinton .34,603
Columbiana .113,572
Coshocton .36,024
Crawford .50,075
Cuyahoga .1,498,295
Darke .55,096
Defiance .39,987
Delaware .53,840
Erie .79,655
Fairfield .93,678
Fayette .27,467
Franklin .869,109
Fulton .37,751
Gallia .30,098
Geauga .74,474
Greene .129,769
Guernsey .42,024
Hamilton .873,136
Hancock .64,581
Hardin .32,719

Harrison .18,152
Henry .28,383
Highland .33,477
Hocking .24,304
Holmes .29,416
Huron .54,608
Jackson .30,592
Jefferson .91,564
Knox .46,309
Lake .212,801
Lawrence .63,849
Licking .120,981
Logan .39,155
Lorain .274,909
Lucas .471,741
Madison .33,004
Mahoning .289,487
Marion .67,974
Medina .113,150
Meigs .23,641
Mercer .38,334
Miami .90,381
Monroe .17,382
Montgomery .571,697
Morgan .14,241
Morrow .26,480
Muskingum .83,340
Noble .11,310
Ottawa .40,076
Paulding .21,302
Perry .31,032
Pickaway .43,662
Pike .22,802
Portage .135,856
Preble .38,223
Putnam .32,991
Richland .131,205
Ross .65,004
Sandusky .63,267
Scioto .84,545
Seneca .61,901
Shelby .43,089
Stark .378,823
Summit .524,472
Trumbull .241,863
Tuscarawas .84,614
Union .29,536
Van Wert .30,458
Vinton .11,584
Warren .99,276
Washington .64,266
Wayne .97,408
Williams .36,369
Wood .107,372
Wyandot .22,651

CITIES AND VILLAGES

Aberdeen .1,566
Ada .5,669
Adamsville .229
Addyston .1,195
Adelphi .472
Adena .1,062
Akron .237,177
Albany .905
Alexandria .489
Alger .992
Alliance .24,315
Alvordton .362
Amanda .720
Amberly .3,442
Amelia .1,108
Amesville .247
Amherst .10,638
Amsterdam .783
Andover .1,205

Anna .1,038
Ansonia .1,267
Antwerp .1,765
Apple Creek .741
Aquilla .355
Arcadia .580
Arcanum .2,002
Archbold .3,318
Arlington .1,187
Arlington Heights .1,082
Ashland .20,326
Ashley .1,057
Ashtabula .23,449
Ashville .2,046
Athalia .367
Athens .19,743
Attica .865
Aurora .8,177
Avon .7,241
Avon Lake .13,222
Bailey Lakes .397
Bainbridge .1,042
Baltic .563
Baltimore .2,689
Barberton .29,751
Barnesville .4,633
Barnhill .327
Batavia .1,896
Bay Village .17,846
Bay View .804
Beach City .1,083
Beachwood .9,983
Beallsville .601
Beaver .330
Beavercreek .31,589
Beaverdam .492
Bedford .15,056
Bedford Heights .13,214
Bellaire .8,241
Bellbrook .5,174
Belle Center .930
Belle Valley .262
Bellefontaine .11,888
Bellevue .8,187
Bellville .1,714
Belmont .714
Belmore .205
Beloit .1,093
Belpre .7,193
Bentleyville .381
Benton Ridge .343
Berea .19,567
Bergholz .914
Berkey .306
Berlin Heights .756
Bethel .2,231
Bethesda .1,429
Bettsville .752
Beverly .1,471
Bexley .13,405
Blanchester .3,202
Bloomdale .744
Bloomingburg .869
Bloomingdale .254
Bloomville .1,019
Blue Ash .9,506
Bluffton .3,310
Bolivar .989
Boston Heights .781
Botkins .1,372
Bowerston .487
Bowersville .329
Bowling Green .25,728
Bradford .2,166
Bradner .1,175
Brady Lake .470
Bratenahl .1,485
Brecksville .10,132
Bremen .1,432

Brewster .2,321
Briarwood Beach .628
Bridgeport .2,642
Brilliant .1,751
Broadview
  Heights .10,920
Brook Park .26,195
Brooklyn .12,342
Brooklyn Heights .1,653
Brookside .887
Brookville .4,322
Broughton .271
Brunswick .27,689
Bryan .7,879
Buchtel .585
Buckland .271
Bucyrus .13,433
Burbank .365
Burgoon .244
Burkettsville .295
Burton .1,401
Butler .955
Butlerville .223
Byesville .2,572
Cadiz .4,058
Cairo .596
Caldwell .1,935
Caledonia .759
Cambridge .13,573
Camden .1,971
Campbell .11,619
Canal Fulton .3,481
Canal Winchester .2,749
Canfield .5,535
Canton .94,730
Cardington .1,665
Carey .3,674
Carlisle .4,276
Carroll .641
Carrollton .3,065
Casstown .331
Castalia .973
Catawba .317
Cecil .267
Cedarville .2,799
Celina .9,137
Centerburg .1,275
Centerville .18,886
Chagrin Falls .4,335
Chardon .4,434
Chatfield .228
Chauncey .1,050
Cherry Fork .210
Chesapeake .1,370
Cheshire .297
Chesterhill .395
Chesterville .242
Cheviot .9,888
Chickasaw .381
Chillicothe .23,420
Chilo .173
Chippewa-on-
  the-Lake .245
Christiansburg .593
Cincinnati .385,457
Circleville .11,700
Clarington .558
Clarksburg .483
Clarksville .525
Clay Center .327
Clayton .752
Cleveland .573,822
Cleveland
  Heights .56,438
Cleves .2,094
Clifton .182
Clinton .1,277
Cloverdale .304
Clyde .5,489

Coal Grove .2,630
Coalton .639
Coldwater .4,220
College Corner .364
Columbiana .4,987
Columbus .564,871
Columbus Grove .2,313
Commercial Point .316
Conesville .451
Congress .178
Conneaut .13,835
Continental .1,179
Convoy .1,140
Coolville .649
Corning .789
Cortland .5,011
Corwin .276
Coshocton .13,405
Covington .2,610
Craig Beach .1,657
Crestline .5,406
Creston .1,828
Cridersville .1,843
Crooksville .2,766
Crown City .513
Cumberland .461
Custar .254
Cuyahoga Falls .43,710
Cuyahoga Heights .739
Cygnet .646
Dalton .1,357
Danville .1,132
Darbydale .825
Darbyville .282
Dayton .203,588
De Graff .1,358
Deer Park .6,745
Defiance .16,810
Delaware .18,780
Dellroy .346
Delphos .7,314
Delta .2,886
Dennison .3,398
Deshler .1,870
Dexter City .173
Dillonvale .912
Donnelsville .219
Dover .11,526
Doylestown .2,493
Dresden .1,646
Dublin .3,855
Dunkirk .954
Dupont .308
East Canton .1,721
East Cleveland .36,957
East Liverpool .16,687
East Palestine .5,306
East Sparta .868
Eastlake .22,104
Eaton .6,839
Edgerton .1,813
Edison .504
Edon .947
Eldorado .509
Elida .1,349
Elmore .1,271
Elmwood Place .2,840
Elyria .57,504
Empire .308
Englewood .11,329
Enon .2,597
Euclid .59,999
Evendale .1,954
Fairborn .29,702
Fairfax .2,222
Fairfield .30,777
Fairlawn .6,100
Fairport Harbor .3,357
Fairview Park .19,311

Farmersville .950
Fayette .1,222
Fayetteville .478
Felicity .929
Findlay .35,594
Fletcher .498
Florida .294
Flushing .1,266
Forest .1,633
Forest Park .18,675
Fort Jennings .538
Fort Loramie .977
Fort Recovery .1,370
Fort Shawnee .4,541
Fostoria .15,743
Frankfort .1,008
Franklin .10,711
Frazeysburg .1,025
Fredericksburg .511
Fredericktown .2,299
Freeport .525
Fremont .17,834
Fulton .378
Fultonham .281
Gahanna .18,001
Galena .358
Galion .12,391
Gallipolis .5,576
Gambier .2,056
Gann .173
Garfield Heights .33,380
Garrettsville .1,769
Gates Mills .2,236
Geneva .6,655
Geneva-on-the-
  Lake .1,634
Genoa .2,213
Georgetown .3,467
Germantown .5,015
Gettysburg .545
Gibsonburg .2,479
Gilboa .220
Girard .12,517
Glandorf .746
Glendale .2,368
Glenford .173
Glenmont .270
Glenwillow .492
Gloria Glens Park .435
Glouster .2,211
Gnadenhutten .1,320
Golf Manor .4,317
Gordon .230
Grafton .2,231
Grand Rapids .962
Grand River .412
Grandview Heights .7,420
Granville .3,851
Gratiot .227
Gratis .809
Green Camp .475
Green Springs .1,568
Greenfield .5,034
Greenhills .4,927
Greenville .12,999
Greenwich .1,458
Grove City .16,793
Groveport .3,286
Grover Hill .486
Hamden .1,010
Hamersville .688
Hamilton .63,189
Hamler .625
Hanging Rock .353
Hanover .926
Hanoverton .490
Harbor View .164

Harpster 239
Harrisburg 363
Harrison 5,855
Harrisville 324
Harrod 506
Hartford 444
Hartville 1,772
Harveysburg 425
Haskins 568
Haviland 219
Hayesville 518
Heath 6,969
Hebron 2,035
Helena 307
Hemlock 197
Hicksville 3,742
Higginsport 343
Highland 284
Highland Heights 5,739
Hilliard 8,008
Hills and Dales 281
Hillsboro 6,356
Hiram 1,360
Holgate 1,315
Holland 1,048
Hollansburg 339
Holloway 459
Holmesville 436
Hopedale 857
Hoytville 315
Hubbard 9,245
Hudson 4,615
Hunting Valley 786
Huntsville 489
Huron 7,123
Independence 8,165
Indian Hill 5,521
Irondale 535
Ironton 14,290
Jackson 6,675
Jackson Center 1,310
Jacksonville 651
Jamestown 1,702
Jefferson 2,952
Jefferson 4,448
Jeffersonville 1,252
Jenera 302
Jeromesville 582
Jerry City 512
Jerusalem 237
Jewett 972
Johnstown 3,158
Junction City 754
Kalida 1,019
Kent 26,164
Kenton 8,605
Kettering 61,186
Kettlersville 199
Killbuck 937
Kimbolton 255
Kingston 1,208
Kipton 352
Kirkersville 626
Kirtland 5,969
Kirtland Hills 506
Lafayette 488
Lagrange 1,258
Lakeline 258
Lakemore 2,744
Lakeview 1,089
Lakewood 61,963
Lancaster 34,953
La Rue 861
Latty 261
Laura 501
Laurelville 591
Lawrenceville 307
Lebanon 9,636
Leesburg 1,019
Leesville 233
Leetonia 2,121
Leipsic 2,171
Lewisburg 1,450
Lewisville 285
Lexington 3,823
Liberty Center 1,111
Lima 47,381
Limaville 164
Lincoln Heights 5,259
Lindsey 571
Lisbon 3,159
Lithopolis 652
Lockbourne 373
Lockington 203
Lockland 4,292
Lodi 2,942
Logan 6,557
London 6,958
Lorain 75,416
Lordstown 3,280
Lore City 443
Loudonville 2,945
Louisville 7,873
Loveland 9,106
Lowell 729
Lowellville 1,558
Lucas 753
Luckey 895
Ludlow Falls 248
Lynchburg 1,205
Lyndhurst 18,092
Lyons 596
Macedonia 6,571
Macksburg 295
Madeira 9,341
Madison 2,291
Magnetic Springs 314
Magnolia 986
Maineville 307
Malinta 327
Malta 956
Malvern 1,032
Manchester 2,313
Mansfield 53,927
Mantua 1,041
Maple Heights 29,735
Marble Cliff 630
Marblehead 679
Marengo 329
Mariemont 3,295
Marietta 16,467
Marion 37,040
Marseilles 164
Marshallville 788
Martins Ferry 9,331
Martinsburg 240
Martinsville 539
Marysville 7,414
Mason 8,692
Massillon 30,557
Maumee 15,747
Mayfield 3,577
Mayfield Heights 21,550
McArthur 1,912
McClure 694
McComb 1,608
McConnelsville 2,018
McDonald 3,744
McGuffey 646
Mechanicsburg 1,792
Medina 15,268
Melrose 315
Mendon 749
Mentor 42,065
Mentor-on-the-Lake 7,919
Metamora 556
Meyers Lake 222
Miamisburg 15,304
Middleburg Heights 16,218
Middlefield 1,997
Middle Point 709
Middleport 2,971
Middletown 43,719
Midland 365
Midvale 654
Midway 339
Mifflin 203
Milan 1,569
Milford 5,232
Milford Center 764
Millbury 955
Milledgeville 162
Miller City 168
Millersburg 3,247
Millersport 844
Millville 809
Milton Center 181
Mineral City 884
Minerva 4,549
Minerva Park 1,618
Mingo Junction 4,834
Minster 2,557
Mogadore 4,190
Monroe 4,256
Monroeville 1,329
Montezuma 200
Montgomery 10,088
Montpelier 4,431
Moraine 5,325
Moreland Hills 3,083
Morral 454
Morristown 463
Morrow 1,254
Moscow 324
Mount Blanchard 492
Mount Cory 276
Mount Eaton 289
Mount Gilead 2,911
Mount Healthy 7,562
Mount Orab 1,573
Mount Pleasant 616
Mount Sterling 1,623
Mount Vernon 14,380
Mount Victory 667
Mowrystown 475
Munroe Falls 4,731
Murray City 579
Mutual 159
Napoleon 8,614
Nashville 211
Navarre 1,343
Nelsonville 4,567
Nevada 945
New Albany 409
New Alexandria 410
New Athens 440
New Bloomington 303
New Boston 3,188
New Bremen 2,393
New Carlisle 6,498
New Concord 1,860
New Holland 783
New Knoxville 760
New Lebanon 4,501
New Lexington 5,179
New London 2,449
New Madison 1,008
New Matamoras 1,172
New Miami 2,980
New Middletown 2,195
New Paris 1,709
New Philadelphia 16,883
New Richmond 2,769
New Riegel 329
New Straitsville 937
New Vienna 1,133
New Washington 1,213
New Waterford 1,314
New Weston 184
Newark 41,200
Newburgh Heights 2,678
Newcomerstown 3,986
Newton Falls 4,960
Newtonsville 434
Newtown 1,817
Ney 379
Niles 23,088
North Baltimore 3,127
North Bend 546
North Canton 14,228
North College Hill 10,990
North Fairfield 525
North Hampton 421
North Kingsville 2,939
North Lewisburg 1,072
North Olmsted 36,486
North Perry 897
North Randall 1,054
North Ridgeville 21,522
North Robinson 302
North Royalton 17,671
North Star 254
Northfield 3,913
Northwood 5,495
Norton 12,242
Norwalk 14,358
Norwich 170
Norwood 26,342
Oak Harbor 2,678
Oak Hill 1,713
Oakwood 3,786
Oakwood 886
Oakwood 9,372
Oberlin 8,660
Obetz 3,095
Ohio City 881
Olmsted Falls 5,868
Ontario 4,123
Orange 2,376
Orangeville 223
Oregon 18,675
Orient 283
Orrville 7,511
Orwell 1,067
Osgood 306
Ostrander 397
Ottawa 3,874
Ottawa Hills 4,065
Ottoville 833
Otway 161
Owensville 858
Oxford 17,655
Painesville 16,391
Palestine 213
Pandora 977
Parma 92,548
Parma Heights 23,112
Parral 259
Pataskala 2,284
Paulding 2,754
Payne 1,399
Peebles 1,790
Pemberville 1,321
Peninsula 604
Pepper Pike 6,177
Perry 961
Perrysburg 10,215
Perrysville 836
Phillipsburg 705
Philo 799
Pickerington 3,917
Piketon 1,726
Pioneer 1,133
Piqua 20,480
Pitsburg 460
Plain City 2,102
Plainfield 221
Pleasant City 481
Pleasant Hill 1,051
Pleasant Plain 210
Pleasantville 780
Plymouth 1,939
Poland 3,084
Polk 351
Pomeroy 2,728
Port Clinton 7,223
Port Jefferson 482
Port Washington 622
Port William 300
Portage 479
Portsmouth 25,943
Potsdam 289
Powell 387
Powhatan Point 2,181
Proctorville 975
Prospect 1,159
Quaker City 698
Quincy 633
Racine 908
Rarden 199
Ravenna 11,987
Rawson 477
Rayland 566
Reading 12,879
Reminderville 1,960
Republic 656
Reynoldsburg 20,661
Richfield 3,437
Richmond 624
Richmond Heights 10,095
Richwood 2,181
Ridgeway 388
Rio Grande 864
Ripley 2,174
Risingsun 698
Rittman 6,063
Riverlea 528
Riverside 1,475
Roaming Shores 581
Rochester 207
Rock Creek 652
Rockford 1,245
Rocky Ridge 457
Rocky River 21,084
Rogers 298
Roseville 1,915
Rossburg 260
Rossford 5,978
Roswell 264
Rushsylvania 610
Rushville 299
Russells Point 1,156
Russellville 445
Russia 438
Rutland 635
Sabina 2,799
St. Bernard 5,396
St. Clairsville 5,452
St. Henry 1,596
St. Louisville 375
St. Marys 8,414
St. Paris 1,742
Salem 12,869
Salineville 1,629
Sandusky 31,360
Sarahsville 226
Sardinia 826
Savannah 351
Scio 1,003
Scott 340
Seaman 1,039
Sebring 5,078
Senecaville 458
Seven Hills 13,650
Seven Mile 841
Seville 1,568
Shadyside 4,315
Shaker Heights 32,487
Sharonville 10,108
Shawnee 924
Shawnee Hills 430
Sheffield 1,886
Sheffield Lake 10,484
Shelby 9,645
Sherrodsville 396
Sherwood 915
Shiloh 857
Shreve 1,608
Sidney 17,657
Silver Lake 2,915
Silverton 6,172
Sinking Spring 239
Smithfield 1,308
Smithville 1,467
Solon 14,341
Somerset 1,432
Somerville 357
South Amherst 1,848
South Bloomfield 934
South Charleston 1,682
South Euclid 25,713
South Lebanon 2,700
South Point 3,918
South Russell 2,784
South Salem 252
South Solon 416
South Vienna 464
South Webster 886
South Zanesville 1,739
Sparta 219
Spencer 764
Spencerville 2,184
Spring Valley 541
Springboro 4,962
Springdale 10,111
Springfield 72,563
Steubenville 26,400
Stockport 558
Stoutsville 537
Stow 25,303
Strasburg 2,091
Stratton 356
Streetsboro 9,055
Strongsville 28,577
Struthers 13,624
Stryker 1,423
Sugar Bush Knolls 201
Sugar Grove 407
Sugarcreek 1,966
Summerfield 299
Sunbury 1,911
Swanton 3,424
Sycamore 1,059
Sylvania 15,527
Syracuse 946
Tallmadge 15,269
Tarlton 394
Terrace Park 2,044
Thornville 838
Thurston 527
Tiffin 19,549
Tiltonsville 1,750
Timberlake 885
Tipp City 5,595
Tiro 279
Toledo 354,635
Tontogany 367
Toronto 6,934
Tremont City 374
Trenton 6,401
Trimble 579
Trotwood 7,802
Troy 19,086
Tuscarawas 917
Twinsburg 7,632
Uhrichsville 6,130
Union 5,219
Union City 1,716
Unionville 272
Uniopolis 259
University Heights 15,401
Upper Arlington 35,648
Upper Sandusky 5,967
Urbana 10,762
Urbancrest 880
Utica 2,238
Valley View 1,576
Valley View 730
Van Buren 342
Van Wert 11,035
Vandalia 13,161
Vanlue 390
Venedocia 161
Vermilion 11,012
Verona 571
Versailles 2,384
Vinton 375
Wadsworth 15,166
Waite Hill 529
Wakeman 906
Walbridge 2,900
Waldo 347
Walton Hills 2,199
Wapakoneta 8,402
Warren 56,629
Warrensville Heights 16,565
Warsaw 765
Washington 279
Washington Court House 12,682
Washingtonville 865
Waterville 3,884
Wauseon 6,173
Waverly 4,603
Wayne 894
Waynesburg 1,160
Waynesfield 826
Waynesville 1,796
Wellington 4,146
Wellston 6,016
Wellsville 5,095
West Alexandria 1,313
West Carrollton 13,148
West Elkton 277
West Farmington 563
West Lafayette 2,225
West Leipsic 298
West Liberty 1,653
West Manchester 448
West Mansfield 716
West Millgrove 205
West Milton 4,119
West Rushville 159
West Salem 1,357
West Union 2,791
West Unity 1,639
Westerville 23,414
Westfield Center 791
Westlake 19,483
Weston 1,708
Wharton 432
Whitehall 21,299
Whitehouse 2,137
Wickliffe 16,790
Wilkesville 189
Willard 5,674
Williamsburg 1,952
Williamsport 792
Willoughby 19,329
Willoughby Hills 8,612
Willowick 17,834
Willshire 564
Wilmington 10,431
Wilmot 329
Winchester 1,080
Windham 3,721
Wintersville 4,724
Woodlawn 2,715
Woodmere 772
Woodsfield 3,145
Woodstock 292
Woodville 2,050
Wooster 19,289
Worthington 15,016
Wren 282
Wyoming 8,282
Xenia 24,653
Yellow Springs 4,077
Yorkville 1,447
Youngstown 115,436
Zaleski 347
Zanesfield 269
Zanesville 145
Zanesville 28,655
Zoar 264

OKLAHOMA

Population 3,025,266

METROPOLITAN AREAS

Enid 62,820
Fort Smith (Ark.) 203,269 (131,822 in Ark.; 71,447 in Okla.)
Lawton 112,456
Oklahoma City 834,088
Tulsa 689,628

COUNTIES

Adair 18,575
Alfalfa 7,077
Atoka 12,748
Beaver 6,806
Beckham 19,243
Blaine 13,443
Bryan 30,535
Caddo 30,905
Canadian 56,452
Carter 43,610
Cherokee 30,684
Choctaw 17,203
Cimarron 3,648
Cleveland 133,173
Coal 6,041
Comanche 112,456
Cotton 7,338
Craig 15,014
Creek 59,210
Custer 25,995
Delaware 23,946
Dewey 5,922
Ellis 5,596
Garfield 62,820
Garvin 27,856
Grady 39,490
Grant 6,518
Greer 6,877
Harmon 4,519
Harper 4,715
Haskell 11,010
Hughes 14,338
Jackson 30,356
Jefferson 8,183
Johnston 10,356
Kay 49,852
Kingfisher 14,187
Kiowa 12,711
Latimer 9,840
Le Flore 40,698
Lincoln 26,601
Logan 26,881
Love 7,469
Major 8,772
Marshall 10,550
Mayes 32,261
McClain 20,291
McCurtain 36,151
McIntosh 15,495
Murray 12,147
Muskogee 66,939
Noble 11,573
Nowata 11,486
Okfuskee 11,125
Oklahoma 568,933
Okmulgee 39,169
Osage 39,327
Ottawa 32,870
Pawnee 15,310
Payne 62,435
Pittsburg 40,524
Pontotoc 32,598
Pottawatomie 55,239
Pushmataha 11,773
Roger Mills 4,799
Rogers 46,436
Seminole 27,473
Sequoyah 30,749
Stephens 43,419
Texas 17,727
Tillman 12,398
Tulsa 470,593
Wagoner 41,801
Washington 48,113
Washita 13,798
Woods 10,923
Woodward 21,172

CITIES AND TOWNS

Achille 480
Ada 15,902
Adair 508
Addington 141
Afton 1,174
Agra 354
Albion 165
Alderson 366
Alex 769
Aline 313

OKLAHOMA (continued)

Allen ...998
Alluwe ...129
Altus ...23,101
Alva ...6,416
Amber ...416
Ames ...314
Amorita ...66
Anadarko ...6,378
Antlers ...2,989
Apache ...1,560
Arapaho ...851
Ardmore ...23,689
Arkoma ...2,175
Arnett ...714
Asher ...659
Ashland ...72
Atoka ...3,409
Avant ...461
Avard ...51
Barnsdall ...1,501
Bartlesville ...34,568
Beaver ...1,939
Beggs ...1,428
Bennington ...302
Bernice ...318
Bessie ...245
Bethany ...22,130
Bethel Acres ...2,314
Big Cabin ...252
Billings ...632
Binger ...791
Bixby ...6,969
Blackburn ...114
Blackwell ...8,400
Blair ...1,092
Blanchard ...1,616
Bluejacket ...247
Boise City ...1,761
Bokchito ...628
Bokoshe ...556
Boley ...423
Boswell ...702
Bowlegs ...522
Boynton ...518
Bradley ...284
Braggs ...351
Braman ...355
Bray ...591
Breckenridge ...261
Bridgeport ...115
Bristow ...4,702
Broken Arrow ...35,761
Broken Bow ...3,965
Bromide ...180
Brooksville ...46
Bryant ...74
Buffalo ...1,381
Burbank ...161
Burlington ...206
Burns Flat ...2,431
Butler ...388
Byars ...353
Byng ...833
Byron ...67
Cache ...1,681
Caddo ...923
Calera ...1,390
Calida ...19
Calumet ...469
Calvin ...315
Camargo ...264
Cameron ...365
Canadian ...279
Caney ...147
Canton ...854
Canute ...676
Capron ...54
Carmen ...516
Carnegie ...2,016
Carney ...622
Carrier ...259
Carter ...367
Cashion ...547
Castle ...130
Catoosa ...1,772
Cement ...884
Centrahoma ...166
Chandler ...2,926
Chattanooga ...403
Checotah ...3,454
Chelsea ...1,754
Cherokee ...2,105
Cheyenne ...1,207
Chickasha ...15,828
Choctaw ...7,520

Chouteau ...1,559
Claremore ...12,085
Clayton ...833
Cleo Springs ...514
Cleveland ...2,972
Clinton ...8,796
Coalgate ...2,001
Colbert ...1,122
Colcord ...530
Cole ...309
Collinsville ...3,556
Colony ...185
Comanche ...1,937
Commerce ...2,556
Cooperton ...31
Copan ...960
Cordell ...3,301
Corn ...542
Cornish ...115
Council Hill ...141
Covington ...715
Coweta ...4,554
Cowlington ...546
Coyle ...345
Crescent ...1,651
Cromwell ...337
Crowder ...431
Cushing ...7,720
Custer City ...530
Cyril ...1,220
Dacoma ...226
Davenport ...974
Davidson ...501
Davis ...2,782
Deer Creek ...174
Del City ...28,424
Delaware ...544
Depew ...682
Devol ...186
Dewar ...1,048
Dewey ...3,545
Dibble ...348
Dickson ...996
Dill City ...649
Disney ...464
Dougherty ...210
Douglas ...89
Dover ...570
Drummond ...482
Drumright ...3,162
Duke ...484
Duncan ...22,517
Durant ...11,972
Dustin ...498
Eakly ...452
Earlsboro ...266
East Ninnekah ...1,085
Edmond ...34,637
Eldorado ...688
Elgin ...1,003
Elk City ...9,579
Elmer ...131
Elmore City ...582
El Reno ...15,486
Enid ...50,363
Erick ...1,375
Eufaula ...3,092
Fair Oaks ...324
Fairfax ...1,949
Fairland ...1,073
Fairmont ...419
Fairview ...3,370
Fallis ...22
Fanshawe ...416
Fargo ...409
Faxon ...140
Fletcher ...1,074
Foraker ...34
Forest Park ...1,148
Forgan ...611
Fort Cobb ...760
Fort Gibson ...2,483
Fort Supply ...559
Fort Towson ...789
Foss ...188
Foyil ...191
Francis ...365
Frederick ...6,153
Freedom ...339
Gage ...667
Gans ...346
Garber ...1,215
Garvin ...162
Gate ...146
Geary ...1,700

Gene Autry ...178
Geronimo ...726
Gerty ...149
Glencoe ...490
Glenpool ...2,706
Goldsby ...603
Goltry ...305
Goodwell ...1,186
Gore ...445
Gotebo ...457
Gould ...318
Gracemont ...503
Grainola ...67
Grand Lake Towne ...36
Grandfield ...1,445
Granite ...1,617
Grayson ...150
Greenfield ...233
Grove ...3,378
Guthrie ...10,312
Guymon ...8,492
Haileyville ...832
Hall Park ...577
Hallett ...186
Hammon ...866
Hanna ...157
Hardesty ...243
Harrah ...2,897
Harris ...192
Hartshorne ...2,380
Haskell ...1,953
Hastings ...246
Haworth ...341
Headrick ...223
Healdton ...3,769
Heavener ...2,776
Helena ...710
Hennessey ...2,287
Henryetta ...6,432
Hickory ...95
Hillsdale ...110
Hinton ...1,432
Hitchcock ...172
Hitchita ...126
Hobart ...4,735
Hoffman ...407
Holdenville ...5,469
Hollis ...2,958
Hollister ...82
Hominy ...3,130
Hooker ...1,788
Howe ...562
Hugo ...7,172
Hulbert ...633
Hunter ...276
Hydro ...938
Idabel ...7,622
Indiahoma ...364
Indianola ...254
Inola ...1,550
Jay ...2,100
Jefferson ...92
Jenks ...5,876
Jennings ...395
Jet ...352
Jones ...2,270
Kansas ...491
Kaw City ...283
Kellyville ...960
Kemp ...178
Kemp City (Hendrix) ...106
Kendrick ...132
Kenefic ...140
Keota ...661
Ketchum ...326
Keyes ...557
Kiefer ...912
Kildare ...112
Kingfisher ...4,245
Kingston ...1,171
Kinta ...303
Kiowa ...866
Knowles ...44
Konawa ...1,711
Krebs ...1,754
Kremlin ...301
Lahoma ...537
Lake Aluma ...101
Lamar ...121
Lambert ...20
Lamont ...571
Langley ...582
Langston ...443
Laverne ...1,563
Lawton ...80,054

Leedey ...499
Leflore ...322
Lehigh ...284
Lenapah ...350
Leon ...120
Lexington ...1,731
Liberty ...19
Lima ...256
Lindsay ...3,454
Loco ...215
Locust Grove ...1,179
Lone Grove ...3,369
Lone Wolf ...613
Longdale ...405
Lookeba ...221
Loveland ...21
Loyal ...112
Luther ...1,159
Macomb ...58
Madill ...3,173
Manchester ...146
Mangum ...3,833
Manitou ...322
Mannford ...1,610
Mannsville ...568
Maramec ...101
Marble City ...294
Marietta ...2,494
Marland ...340
Marlow ...5,017
Marshall ...372
Martha ...219
Maud ...1,444
May ...89
Maysville ...1,396
McAlester ...17,255
McBride ...91
McCurtain ...566
McLoud ...4,061
Mead ...143
Medford ...1,419
Medicine Park ...437
Meeker ...1,032
Meno ...171
Meridian ...78
Miami ...14,237
Midwest City ...49,559
Milburn ...376
Mill Creek ...431
Millerton ...262
Minco ...1,489
Moffett ...269
Moore ...35,063
Mooreland ...1,383
Morris ...1,288
Morrison ...671
Mounds ...1,086
Mountain Park ...557
Mountain View ...1,189
Muldrow ...2,538
Mulhall ...301
Muskogee ...40,011
Mustang ...7,496
Mutual ...135
Nardin ...98
Nash ...301
New Tulsa ...252
New Woodville ...94
Newcastle ...3,076
Newkirk ...2,413
Nichols Hills ...4,171
Nicoma Park ...2,588
Noble ...3,497
Norge ...87
Norman ...68,020
North Enid ...992
North Miami ...544
Nowata ...4,270
Oak Grove ...660
Oakland ...485
Oaks ...591
Oakwood ...140
Ochelata ...480
Oilton ...1,244
Okarche ...1,064
Okay ...554
Okeene ...1,601
Okemah ...3,381
Oklahoma City ...403,213
Okmulgee ...16,263
Oktaha ...376
Olustee ...721
Oologah ...798
Optima ...133
Orlando ...218

Osage ...243
Owasso ...6,149
Paden ...448
Panama ...1,164
Paoli ...573
Paradise Hill ...154
Pauls Valley ...5,664
Pawhuska ...4,771
Pawnee ...1,688
Pensacola ...82
Peoria ...165
Perkins ...1,762
Perry ...5,796
Peterman Ridge ...14
Phillips ...178
Picher ...2,180
Piedmont ...2,016
Pink ...911
Pittsburg ...305
Pocola ...3,268
Ponca City ...26,238
Pond Creek ...949
Porter ...642
Porum ...668
Poteau ...7,089
Prague ...2,208
Prue ...554
Pryor Creek ...8,483
Purcell ...4,638
Putnam ...74
Quapaw ...1,097
Quay ...50
Quinlan ...64
Quinton ...1,228
Ralston ...495
Ramona ...567
Ranchwood Manor ...296
Randlett ...461
Ratliff City ...350
Ratan ...332
Ravia ...487
Red Bird ...199
Red Oak ...676
Red Rock ...376
Renfrow ...27
Rentiesville ...78
Reydon ...252
Rigsby ...21
Ringling ...1,561
Ringwood ...389
Ripley ...451
Rocky ...242
Roff ...729
Roland ...1,472
Roosevelt ...396
Rosedale ...97
Rosston ...66
Rush Springs ...1,451
Ryan ...1,083
St. Louis ...109
Salina ...1,115
Sallisaw ...6,403
Sand Point ...179
Sand Springs ...13,246
Sapulpa ...15,853
Sasakwa ...335
Savanna ...828
Sayre ...3,177
Seiling ...1,103
Seminole ...8,590
Sentinel ...1,016
Shady Point ...235
Shamrock ...218
Sharon ...171
Shattuck ...1,759
Shawnee ...26,506
Shidler ...708
Silo ...43
Skedee ...117
Skiatook ...3,596
Slaughterville ...1,953
Slick ...187
Smith Village ...82
Smithville ...133
Snyder ...1,848
Soper ...465
South Coffeyville ...873
Sparks ...772
Spavinaw ...623
Spencer ...4,064
Sperry ...1,276
Spiro ...2,221
Sportsmen Acres ...218
Springer ...679
Sterling ...702

Stidham ...60
Stigler ...2,630
Stillwater ...38,268
Stilwell ...2,369
Stonewall ...672
Strang ...126
Stratford ...1,459
Stringtown ...1,047
Strong City ...56
Stroud ...3,148
Stuart ...235
Sugden ...76
Sulphur ...5,516
Taft ...489
Tahlequah ...9,708
Talala ...191
Talihina ...1,387
Taloga ...446
Tamaha ...145
Tecumseh ...5,123
Temple ...1,339
Terlton ...155
Terral ...604
Texhoma ...785
Texola ...106
Thackerville ...431
Thomas ...1,515
Timberlane ...21
Tipton ...1,475
Tishomingo ...3,212
Tonkawa ...3,524
Tribbey ...215
Tryon ...435
Tullahassee ...145
Tulsa ...360,919
Tupelo ...542
Tushka ...358
Tuttle ...3,051
Tyrone ...928
Union City ...558
Valley Brook ...921
Valley Park ...16
Valliant ...927
Velma ...831
Vera ...182
Verden ...625
Vian ...1,521
Vici ...845
Village, The ...11,049
Vinita ...6,740
Wagoner ...6,191
Wainwright ...182
Wakita ...526
Walters ...2,778
Wanette ...473
Wann ...156
Wapanucka ...472
Warner ...1,310
Warr Acres ...9,940
Warwick ...167
Washington ...477
Watonga ...4,139
Watts ...316
Waukomis ...1,551
Waurika ...2,258
Wayne ...621
Waynoka ...1,377
Weatherford ...9,640
Webb City ...157
Webbers Falls ...461
Welch ...697
Weleetka ...1,195
Wellston ...802
Wes ...31
West Siloam Springs ...431
Westport ...265
Westville ...1,049
Wetumka ...1,725
Wewoka ...5,480
Whitefield ...240
Wilburton ...2,996
Willow ...11
Wilson ...1,585
Winchester ...150
Wister ...444
Woodlawn Park ...167
Woodward ...13,610
Wright City ...1,168
Wyandotte ...336
Wynnewood ...2,615
Wynona ...780
Yale ...1,652
Yeager ...138
Yukon ...17,112

OREGON   Population 2,632,663

METROPOLITAN AREAS

Eugene-Springfield ...275,226
Portland ...1,242,187
(1,049,960 in Ore.;192,227 in Wash.)
Salem ...249,895

COUNTIES

Baker ...16,134
Benton ...68,211
Clackamas ...241,919
Clatsop ...32,489
Columbia ...35,646
Coos ...64,047
Crook ...13,091
Curry ...16,992
Deschutes ...62,142
Douglas ...93,748
Gilliam ...2,057
Grant ...8,210
Harney ...8,314
Hood River ...15,835
Jackson ...132,456
Jefferson ...11,599
Josephine ...58,820
Klamath ...59,117
Lake ...7,532
Lane ...275,226
Lincoln ...35,264
Linn ...89,495
Malheur ...26,896
Marion ...204,692
Morrow ...7,519
Multnomah ...562,640
Polk ...45,203
Sherman ...2,172
Tillamook ...21,164
Umatilla ...58,861
Union ...23,921
Wallowa ...7,273
Wasco ...21,732
Washington ...245,401
Wheeler ...1,513
Yamhill ...55,332

CITIES AND TOWNS

Adair Village ...589
Adams ...240
Adrian ...162
Albany ...26,546
Amity ...1,092
Antelope ...39
Arlington ...521
Ashland ...14,943
Astoria ...9,998
Athena ...965
Aumsville ...1,432
Aurora ...523
Baker ...9,471
Bandon ...2,311
Banks ...489
Barlow ...105
Barview ...1,338
Bay City ...986
Beaverton ...30,582
Bend ...17,263
Boardman ...1,261
Bonanza ...270
Brookings ...3,384
Brownsville ...1,261
Bunker Hill ...1,549
Burns ...3,579
Butte Falls ...428
Canby ...7,659
Cannon Beach ...1,187
Canyon City ...639
Canyonville ...1,288
Carlton ...1,302
Cascade Locks ...838
Cave Junction ...1,023
Central Point ...6,357
Chenoweth ...2,329
Chiloquin ...778
Clatskanie ...1,648
Coburg ...699
Columbia City ...678
Condon ...783
Coos Bay ...14,424
Coquille ...4,481
Cornelius ...4,055
Corvallis ...40,960
Cottage Grove ...7,148
Cove ...451
Creswell ...1,770
Culver ...514
Dallas ...8,530
Dalles, The ...10,820
Dayton ...1,409
Dayville ...199
Depoe Bay ...723
Detroit ...367
Donald ...267
Drain ...1,148
Drewsey ...22
Dufur ...560
Dundee ...1,223
Dunes City ...1,124
Durham ...707
Eagle Point ...2,764
Eastside ...1,601
Echo ...624
Elgin ...1,701
Elkton ...155
Enterprise ...2,003
Estacada ...1,419
Eugene ...105,624
Fairview ...1,749
Falcon Heights ...1,389
Falls City ...804
Florence ...4,411
Forest Grove ...11,499
Fossil ...535
Garibaldi ...999
Gaston ...471

Gates 455
Gearhart 967
Gervais 1,144
Gladstone 9,500
Glendale 712
Gold Beach 1,515
Gold Hill 904
Granite 17
Grants Pass 14,997
Grass Valley 164
Gresham 33,005
Haines 341
Halfway 380
Halsey 693
Hammond 516
Happy Valley 1,499
Harrisburg 1,881
Helix 155
Heppner 1,498
Hermiston 9,408
Hillsboro 27,664
Hines 1,632
Hood River 4,329
Hubbard 1,640
Huntington 539
Idanha 319
Imbler 292
Independence 4,024
Ione 345
Irrigon 700
Island City 477
Jacksonville 2,030
Jefferson 1,702
John Day 2,012
Johnson City 378
Jordan Valley 473
Joseph 999
Junction City 3,320
King City 1,853
Klamath Falls 16,661
Lafayette 1,215
La Grande 11,354
Lake Oswego 22,868
Lakeside 1,453
Lakeview 2,770
Lebanon 10,413
Lexington 307
Lincoln City 5,469
Lonerock 26
Long Creek 252
Lostine 250
Lowell 661
Lyons 877
Madras 2,235
Malin 539
Manzanita 443
Maupin 495
Maywood Park 1,083
McMinnville 14,080
Medford 39,603
Merrill 809
Metolius 451
Mill City 1,565
Millersburg 562
Milton-Freewater 5,086
Milwaukie 17,931
Mitchell 183
Molalla 2,992
Monmouth 5,594
Monroe 412
Monument 192
Moro 336
Mosier 340
Mount Angel 2,876
Mount Vernon 569
Myrtle Creek 3,365
Myrtle Point 2,859
Nehalem 258
Newberg 10,394
Newport 7,519
North Bend 9,779
North Plains 715
North Powder 430
Nyssa 2,862
Oakland 886
Oakridge 3,729
Ontario 8,814
Oregon City 14,673
Paisley 343
Pendleton 14,521
Philomath 2,673
Phoenix 2,309
Pilot Rock 1,630
Port Orford 1,061
Portland 366,383
Powers 819
Prairie City 1,106
Prescott 73
Prineville 5,276
Rainier 1,655
Redmond 6,452
Reedsport 4,984
Richland 181
Riddle 1,265
Rivergrove 314
Rockaway 906
Rogue River 1,308
Roseburg 16,644
Rufus 352
St. Helens 7,064
St. Paul 312
Salem 89,233
Sandy 2,905
Scappoose 3,213
Scio 579
Scotts Mills 249
Seaside 5,193
Seneca 285
Shady Cove 1,097
Shaniko 30
Sheridan 2,249
Sherwood 2,386
Siletz 1,001
Silverton 5,168
Sisters 696
Sodaville 171
Spray 155
Springfield 41,621
Stanfield 1,568
Stayton 4,396
Sublimity 1,077
Summerville 132
Sumpter 133
Sutherlin 4,560
Sweet Home 6,921
Talent 2,577
Tangent 478
Tigard 14,286
Tillamook 3,981
Toledo 3,151
Troutdale 5,908
Tualatin 7,348
Turner 1,116
Ukiah 249
Umatilla 3,199
Union 2,062
Unity 115
Vale 1,558
Veneta 2,449
Vernonia 1,785
Waldport 1,274
Wallowa 847
Warrenton 2,493
Wasco 415
Waterloo 221
West Linn 12,956
Westfir 312
Weston 719
Wheeler 319
Willamina 1,749
Wilsonville 2,920
Winston 3,359
Wood Village 2,253
Woodburn 11,196
Yachats 482
Yamhill 690
Yoncalla 805

PENNSYLVANIA

Population 11,866,728

METROPOLITAN AREAS

Allentown-Bethlehem-Easton 636,714 (552,285 in Pa.; 84,429 in N.J.)
Altoona 136,621
Binghamton, N.Y. 301,336 (263,460 in N.Y.; 37,876 in Pa.)
Erie 279,780
Harrisburg 446,072
Johnstown 264,506
Lancaster 362,346
Northeast Pennsylvania 640,396
Philadelphia 4,716,818 (3,682,709 in Pa.; 1,034,109 in N.J.)
Pittsburgh 2,263,894
Reading 312,509
Williamsport 118,416
York 381,255

COUNTIES

Adams 68,292
Allegheny 1,450,085
Armstrong 77,768
Beaver 204,441
Bedford 46,784
Berks 312,509
Blair 136,621
Bradford 62,919
Bucks 479,211
Butler 147,912
Cambria 183,263
Cameron 6,674
Carbon 53,285
Centre 112,760
Chester 316,660
Clarion 43,362
Clearfield 83,578
Clinton 38,971
Columbia 61,967
Crawford 88,869
Cumberland 178,037
Dauphin 232,317
Delaware 555,007
Elk 38,338
Erie 279,780
Fayette 160,395
Forest 5,072
Franklin 113,629
Fulton 12,842
Greene 40,355
Huntingdon 42,253
Indiana 92,281
Jefferson 48,303
Juniata 19,188
Lackawanna 227,908
Lancaster 362,346
Lawrence 107,150
Lebanon 109,829
Lehigh 273,582
Luzerne 343,079
Lycoming 118,416
McKean 50,635
Mercer 128,299
Mifflin 46,908
Monroe 69,409
Montgomery 643,621
Montour 16,675
Northampton 225,418
Northumberland 100,381
Perry 35,718
Philadelphia 1,688,210
Pike 18,271
Potter 17,726
Schuylkill 160,630
Snyder 33,584
Somerset 81,243
Sullivan 6,349
Susquehanna 37,876
Tioga 40,973
Union 32,870
Venango 64,444
Warren 47,449
Washington 217,074
Wayne 35,237
Westmoreland 392,294
Wyoming 26,433
York 312,963

CITIES AND BOROUGHS

Abbottstown 689
Adamstown 1,119
Akron 3,471
Albion 1,818
Alburtis 1,428
Aldan 4,671
Alexandria 435
Aliquippa 17,094
Allenport 735
Allentown 103,758
Altoona 57,078
Ambler 6,628
Ambridge 9,575
Apollo 2,212
Applewood 395
Archbald 6,295
Arendtsville 600
Arnold 6,853
Arona 446
Ashland 4,235
Ashley 3,512
Ashville 383
Aspinwall 3,284
Atglen 669
Athens 3,622
Auburn 999
Austin 740
Avalon 6,240
Avis 1,718
Avoca 3,536
Avondale 891
Avonmore 1,234
Baden 5,318
Baldwin 24,598
Bally 1,051
Bangor 5,006
Barnesboro 2,741
Bath 1,953
Beallsville 588
Beaver 5,441
Beaver Falls 12,525
Beaver Meadows 1,078
Beavertown 853
Bechtelsville 832
Bedford 3,326
Beech Creek 760
Bell Acres 1,307
Belle Vernon 1,489
Bellefonte 6,300
Bellevue 10,128
Bellwood 2,114
Ben Avon 2,314
Ben Avon Heights 398
Bendersville 533
Bentleyville 2,525
Benton 981
Berlin 1,999
Bernville 798
Berrysburg 447
Berwick 12,189
Bessemer 1,293
Bethel Park 34,755
Bethlehem 70,419
Big Beaver 2,815
Big Run 822
Biglerville 991
Birdsboro 3,481
Blairsville 4,166
Blakely 7,438
Blawnox 1,653
Blooming Valley 374
Bloomsburg 11,717
Blossburg 1,757
Bolivar 706
Bonneauville 920
Boswell 1,480
Bowmanstown 1,078
Boyertown 3,979
Brackenridge 4,297
Braddock 5,634
Braddock Hills 2,556
Bradford 11,211
Bradford Woods 1,264
Brentwood 11,907
Briar Creek 637
Bridgeport 4,843
Bridgeville 6,154
Bridgewater 879
Brisbin 387
Bristol 10,867
Broad Top City 340
Brockway 2,376
Brookhaven 7,912
Brookville 4,568
Brownstown 649
Brownsville 4,043
Bruin 722
Bryn Athyn 947
Burgettstown 1,867
Burnham 2,457
Burnside 347
Butler 17,026
California 5,703
Callery 415
Cambridge Springs 2,102
Camp Hill 8,422
Canonsburg 10,459
Canton 1,959
Carbondale 11,255
Carlisle 18,314
Carmichaels 630
Carnegie 10,099
Carroll Valley 817
Carrolltown 1,395
Castle Shannon 10,164
Catasauqua 7,944
Catawissa 1,568
Centerville 4,207
Central City 1,496
Centralia 1,017
Centre Hall 1,233
Chalfant 1,119
Chalfont 2,802
Chambersburg 16,174
Charleroi 5,717
Cherry Tree 520
Chester 45,794
Chester Heights 1,302
Chester Hill 1,054
Cheswick 2,336
Chicora 1,192
Christiana 1,183
Churchill 4,285
Clarendon 776
Clairton 12,188
Clarion 6,664
Clark 667
Clarks Green 1,862
Clarks Summit 5,272
Claysville 1,029
Clearfield 7,580
Cleona 2,003
Clifton Heights 7,320
Clintonville 512
Clymer 1,761
Coaldale 2,762
Coalport 739
Coatesville 10,698
Cochranton 1,240
Cokeburg 796
Collegeville 3,406
Collingdale 9,539
Columbia 10,466
Colwyn 2,851
Confluence 968
Conneaut Lake 767
Conneautville 971
Connellsville 10,319
Connoquenessing 539
Conshohocken 8,475
Conway 2,747
Conyngham 2,242
Coopersburg 2,595
Cooperstown 644
Coplay 3,130
Coraopolis 7,308
Cornwall 2,653
Corsica 381
Corry 7,149
Coudersport 2,791
Courtdale 844
Crafton 7,623
Cranesville 703
Creekside 383
Cresson 2,184
Cressona 1,810
Curwensville 3,116
Daisytown 421
Dale 1,906
Dallas 2,679
Dallastown 3,949
Dalton 1,383
Danville 5,239
Darby 11,513
Darlington 377
Dauphin 901
Dawson 661
Dayton 648
Deemston 829
Deer Lake 515
Delaware Water Gap 597
Delmont 2,159
Delta 692
Denver 2,018
Derry 3,072
Dickson City 6,699
Dillsburg 1,733
Donora 7,524
Dormont 11,275
Dover 1,910
Downingtown 7,650
Doylestown 8,717
Dravosburg 2,511
Du Bois 9,290
Dublin 1,565
Duboistown 1,218
Dunbar 1,369
Duncannon 1,645
Duncansville 1,355
Dunlevy 463
Dunmore 16,781
Dupont 3,460
Duquesne 10,094
Duryea 5,415
Dushore 692
East Berlin 1,054
East Bangor 955
East Brady 1,153
East Butler 799
East Conemaugh 2,128
East Greenville 2,456
East Lansdowne 2,806
East McKeesport 2,940
East Petersburg 3,600
East Pittsburgh 2,493
East Prospect 529
East Rochester 789
East Stroudsburg 8,039
East Vandergrift 955
East Washington 2,241
Easton 26,027
Eastvale 379
Eau Claire 420
Ebensburg 4,096
Economy 9,538
Eddystone 2,555
Edgewood 4,382
Edgeworth 1,738
Edinboro 6,324
Edwardsville 5,729
Ehrenfeld 360
Elco 417
Elderton 420
Eldred 965
Elizabeth 1,892
Elizabethtown 8,233
Elizabethville 1,531
Elkland 1,974
Ellport 1,290
Ellsworth 1,228
Ellwood City 9,998
Elverson 530
Emlenton 807
Emmaus 11,001
Emporium 2,837
Emsworth 3,074
Enon Valley 408
Ephrata 11,095
Erie 119,123
Ernest 584
Etna 4,534
Evans City 2,299
Everett 1,828
Everson 1,032
Exeter 5,493
Export 1,143
Factoryville 924
Fairchance 2,106
Fairfield 591
Fairview 1,855
Falls Creek 1,208
Farrell 8,645
Fawn Grove 516
Fayette City 788
Felton 483
Ferndale 2,204
Finleyville 402
Fleetwood 3,422
Flemington 1,416
Folcroft 8,231
Ford City 3,923
Ford Cliff 516
Forest City 1,924
Forest Hills 8,198
Forty Fort 5,590
Fountain Hill 4,805
Fox Chapel 5,049
Frackville 5,308
Franklin 559
Franklin 8,146
Franklin Park 6,135
Fredonia 712
Freeburg 643
Freedom 2,272
Freeland 4,285
Freemansburg 1,879
Freeport 2,381
Galeton 1,462
Gallitzin 2,315
Garrett 563
Geistown 3,304
Gettysburg 7,194
Gilberton 1,096
Girard 2,615
Girardville 2,268
Glassport 6,242
Glen Campbell 352
Glen Rock 1,662
Glendon 354
Glenolden 7,633
Goldsboro 477
Gordon 892
Grampion 464
Gratz 678
Great Bend 740
Green Lane 542
Green Tree 5,722
Greencastle 3,679
Greensboro 377
Greensburg 17,558
Greenville 7,730
Grove City 8,162
Halifax 909
Hallam 1,428
Hallstead 1,280
Hamburg 4,011
Hanover 14,890
Harmony 1,334
Harrisburg 53,264
Harrisville 1,033
Harveys Lake 2,318
Hastings 1,574
Hatboro 7,579
Hatfield 2,533
Hawley 1,181
Hawthorn 547
Hazleton 27,318
Heidelberg 1,606
Hellertown 6,025
Herndon 483
Highspire 2,959
Hollidaysburg 5,892
Homer City 2,248
Homestead 5,092
Honesdale 5,128
Honey Brook 1,164
Hooversville 863
Hop Bottom 405
Houston 1,568
Houtzdale 1,222
Howard 838
Hughestown 1,783
Hughesville 2,174
Hulmville 1,014
Hummelstown 4,267
Hunker 359
Hyde Park 633
Hydetown 760
Huntingdon 7,042
Hyndman 1,106
Indiana 16,051
Industry 2,417
Ingram 4,346
Irvona 644
Irwin 4,995
Ivyland 581
Jacobus 1,396
Jamestown 854
Jeannette 13,106
Jefferson 8,643
Jefferson 685
Jefferson 413
Jenkintown 4,942
Jennerstown 656
Jermyn 2,411
Jersey Shore 4,631
Jessup 4,974
Jim Thorpe 5,263
Johnsonburg 3,938
Johnstown 35,496
Jonestown 814
Juniata Terrace 631
Kane 4,916
Karns City 354
Kenhorst 3,187
Kennett Square 4,715
Kingston 15,681
Kistler 364
Kittanning 5,432
Knox 1,364
Knoxville 650
Koppel 1,146
Kulpmont 3,675
Kutztown 4,040
Laceyville 498
Laflin 1,650
Lake City 2,384
Lancaster 54,725
Lanesboro 465
Langhorne 1,697
Langhorne Manor 1,103
Lansdale 16,526
Lansdowne 11,891
Lansford 4,466
Laporte 230
Larksville 4,410
Latrobe 10,799
Laurel Run 725
Laureldale 4,047
Le Raysville 356
Lebanon 25,711
Leechburg 2,682
Leesport 1,258
Leetsdale 1,604
Lehighton 5,826
Lemoyne 4,178
Lewis Run 677
Lewisburg 5,407
Lewistown 9,830
Liberty 3,112
Ligonier 1,917
Lilly 1,462
Lincoln 1,428
Linesville 1,198
Lititz 7,590
Little Meadows 375
Littlestown 2,870
Liverpool 809
Lock Haven 9,617

PENNSYLVANIA (continued)

Loganton 474
Loganville 1,020
Long Branch 610
Lorain 989
Loretto 1,395
Lower Burrell 13,200
Luzerne 3,703
Lykens 2,181
Lyons 579
Macungie 1,899
Madison 531
Mahaffey 513
Mahanoy City 6,167
Malvern 2,999
Manchester 2,027
Manheim 5,015
Manor 2,235
Manorville 409
Mansfield 3,322
Mapleton 591
Marcus Hook 2,638
Marianna 907
Marietta 2,740
Marion Center 494
Marion Heights 921
Markleysburg 356
Mars 1,803
Martinsburg 2,231
Marysville 2,452
Masontown 4,909
Matamoras 2,111
Mayfield 1,812
McAdoo 2,940
McClure 1,024
McConnellsburg 1,178
McDonald 2,772
McKean 465
McKees Rocks 8,742
McKeesport 31,012
McSherrystown 2,764
McVeytown 447
Meadville 15,544
Mechanicsburg 9,487
Mechanicsville 519
Media 6,119
Mercer 2,532
Mercersburg 1,617
Meshoppen 571
Meyersdale 2,581
Middleburg 1,357
Middleport 577
Middletown 10,122
Midland 4,310
Mifflin 648
Mifflinburg 3,151
Mifflintown 783
Milesburg 1,309
Milford 1,143
Mill Creek 367
Mill Hall 1,744
Mill Village 427
Millbourne 652
Millersburg 2,770
Millerstown 550
Millersville 7,668
Millheim 800
Millvale 4,754
Millville 975
Milton 6,730
Minersville 5,635
Modena 672
Mohnton 2,156
Monaca 7,661
Monessen 11,928
Monongahela 5,950
Monroe 627
Monroeville 30,977
Mont Alto 1,197
Montgomery 1,653
Montoursville 5,403
Montrose 1,980
Moosic 6,068
Morrisville 9,845
Morton 2,412
Moscow 1,536
Mount Carmel 8,190
Mount Holly Springs 2,068
Mount Jewett 1,053
Mount Joy 5,680
Mount Oliver 4,576
Mount Penn 3,025
Mount Pleasant 5,354
Mount Pocono 1,237
Mount Union 3,101
Mount Wolf 1,517
Mountville 1,505
Muncy 2,700
Munhall 14,532
Murrysville 16,036
Myerstown 3,131
Nanticoke 13,044
Nanty-Glo 3,936
Narberth 4,496
Nazareth 5,443
Nescopeck 1,768
Nesquehoning 3,346
New Alexandria 697
New Beaver 1,885
New Berlinville 783
New Bethlehem 1,441
New Bloomfield 1,109
New Brighton 7,364
New Britain 2,519
New Castle 33,621
New Cumberland 8,051
New Eagle 2,617
New Florence 855
New Freedom 2,205
New Galilee 596
New Holland 4,147
New Hope 1,473
New Kensington 17,660
New Milford 1,040
New Oxford 1,921
New Philadelphia 1,341
New Salem 832
New Stanton 2,600
New Wilmington 2,774
Newell 629
Newport 1,600
Newry 353
Newtown 2,519
Newville 1,370
Nicholson 945
Norristown 34,684
North Apollo 1,487
North Belle Vernon 2,425
North Braddock 8,711
North Catasauqua 2,554
North Charleroi 1,760
North East 4,568
North Irwin 1,016
North Wales 3,391
North York 1,755
Northampton 8,240
Northumberland 3,636
Norwood 6,647
Nuangola 726
Oakdale 1,955
Oakland 734
Oakmont 7,039
Ohioville 4,217
Oil City 13,881
Oklahoma 1,078
Old Forge 9,304
Olyphant 5,204
Orangeville 507
Orbisonia 506
Orwigsburg 2,700
Osborne 529
Osceola 1,466
Oxford 3,633
Paint 1,177
Palmerton 5,455
Palmyra 7,228
Palo Alto 1,321
Parker 808
Parkesburg 2,578
Parkside 2,464
Parryville 481
Patterson Heights 797
Patton 2,441
Paxtang 1,649
Pen Argyl 3,388
Penbrook 3,006
Penn 619
Penndel 2,703
Pennsburg 2,339
Pennsbury Village 798
Perkasie 5,241
Perryopolis 2,139
Petersburg 543
Petrolia 472
Philadelphia 1,688,210
Philipsburg 3,464
Phoenixville 14,165
Picture Rocks 615
Pillow 359
Pine Grove 2,244
Pitcairn 4,175
Pittsburgh 423,938
Pittston 9,930
Platea 492
Pleasant Gap 9,676
Pleasantville 1,099
Plum 25,390
Plumville 431
Plymouth 7,605
Point Marion 1,642
Polk 1,884
Port Allegany 2,593
Port Carbon 2,576
Port Clinton 337
Port Matilda 647
Port Royal 835
Port Vue 5,316
Portage 3,510
Portland 540
Pottstown 22,729
Pottsville 18,195
Pringle 1,221
Prospect 1,016
Prospect Park 6,593
Punxsutawney 7,479
Quakertown 8,867
Quarryville 1,558
Ramey 568
Rankin 2,892
Reading 78,686
Red Hill 1,727
Red Lion 5,824
Renovo 1,812
Reynoldsville 3,016
Rices Landing 516
Richland 1,470
Richlandtown 1,180
Ridgway 5,604
Ridley Park 7,889
Riegelsville 993
Rimersburg 1,096
Ringtown 837
Riverside 2,266
Roaring Spring 2,962
Robesonia 1,748
Rochester 4,759
Rockhill Furnace 472
Rockledge 2,538
Rockwood 1,058
Rome 426
Roscoe 1,123
Rose Valley 1,038
Roseto 1,484
Rosslyn Farms 521
Rouseville 734
Royalton 981
Royersford 4,243
Rural Valley 1,033
Rutledge 934
Saegerstown 942
St. Clair 4,037
St. Lawrence 1,376
St. Marys 6,417
St. Petersburg 452
Salisbury 817
Saltillo 373
Saltsburg 964
Sandy Lake 779
Sankertown 804
Saxonburg 1,336
Saxton 814
Sayre 6,951
Scalp Level 1,186
Schuylkill Haven 5,977
Schwenksville 1,041
Scottdale 5,833
Scranton 88,117
Selinsgrove 5,227
Sellersville 3,143
Seven Valleys 500
Seward 675
Sewickley 4,778
Sewickley Heights 899
Sewickley Hills 419
Shamokin 10,357
Shamokin Dam 1,622
Sharon 19,057
Sharon Hill 6,221
Sharpsburg 4,351
Sharpsville 5,375
Shenandoah 7,589
Shickshinny 1,192
Shillington 5,601
Shinglehouse 1,310
Shippensburg 5,261
Shippenville 558
Shiremanstown 1,719
Shoemakersville 1,391
Shrewsbury 2,688
Silverdale 499
Sinking Spring 2,617
Slatington 4,277
Sligo 798
Slippery Rock 3,047
Smethport 1,797
Smithfield 1,084
Smithton 559
Snow Shoe 852
Snydertown 358
Somerset 6,474
Souderton 6,657
South Bethlehem 476
South Coatesville 1,359
South Connellsville 2,296
South Fork 1,401
South Greensburg 2,605
South Heights 765
South New Castle 879
South Philipsburg 523
South Renovo 663
South Waverly 1,176
South Williamsport 6,581
Southmont 2,683
Southwest Greensburg 2,898
Spangler 2,399
Spartansburg 403
Speers 1,425
Spring City 3,389
Spring Grove 1,832
Springboro 557
Springdale 4,418
State College 36,130
Steelton 6,484
Stewartstown 1,072
Stockdale 641
Stockertown 661
Stoneboro 1,177
Stoystown 432
Strasburg 1,999
Strattanville 555
Strausstown 377
Stroudsburg 5,148
Sugar Grove 630
Sugar Notch 1,191
Sugarcreek 5,954
Summerhill 725
Summerville 830
Summit Hill 3,418
Sunbury 12,292
Susquehanna Depot 1,994
Suterville 863
Swarthmore 5,950
Swissvale 11,345
Swoyersville 5,795
Sykesville 1,537
Tamaqua 8,843
Tarentum 6,419
Tatamy 910
Taylor 7,246
Telford 3,507
Temple 1,486
Terre Hill 1,217
Thompsontown 593
Thornburg 526
Three Springs 501
Throop 4,166
Tidioute 844
Tioga 613
Tionesta 659
Titusville 6,884
Topton 1,818
Towanda 3,526
Townville 364
Trafford 3,662
Trainer 2,056
Trappe 1,800
Tremont 1,796
Troy 1,381
Trumbauersville 781
Tullytown 2,277
Tunkhannock 2,144
Tunnelhill 513
Turbotville 675
Turtle Creek 6,959
Tyrone 6,346
Ulysses 654
Union City 3,623
Uniontown 14,510
Unionville 361
Upland 3,458
Valencia 340
Vanderbilt 689
Vandergrift 6,823
Vandling 557
Verona 3,179
Versailles 2,150
Vintondale 697
Wall 989
Wallaceton 393
Walnutport 2,007
Wampum 851
Warren 12,146
Warrior Run 784
Washington 18,363
Waterford 1,568
Watsontown 2,366
Wattsburg 513
Waymart 1,248
Waynesboro 9,726
Waynesburg 4,482
Weatherly 2,891
Weissport 486
Wellsville 347
Wellsboro 3,805
Wernersville 1,811
Wesleyville 3,998
West Brownsville 1,433
West Chester 17,435
West Conshohocken 1,516
West Easton 1,033
West Elizabeth 808
West Fairview 1,426
West Grove 1,820
West Hazleton 4,871
West Homestead 3,128
West Kittanning 1,591
West Lawn 1,686
West Leechburg 1,395
West Mayfield 1,712
West Middlesex 1,064
West Mifflin 26,279
West Newton 3,387
West Pittston 5,980
West Reading 4,507
West View 7,648
West Wyoming 3,288
West York 4,526
Westfield 1,268
Westmont 6,113
Westover 517
Wheatland 1,132
Whitaker 1,615
White Haven 1,217
White Oak 9,480
Whitehall 15,206
Wilkes-Barre 51,551
Wilkinsburg 23,669
Williamsburg 1,400
Williamsport 33,401
Williamstown 1,664
Wilmerding 2,421
Wilson 7,564
Wind Gap 2,651
Windber 5,585
Windsor 1,205
Winterstown 491
Womelsdorf 1,827
Wormleysburg 2,772
Worthington 760
Wrightsville 2,365
Wyalusing 716
Wyoming 3,655
Wyomissing 6,551
Wyomissing Hills 2,150
Yardley 2,533
Yatesville 555
Yeadon 11,727
Yoe 990
York 44,619
York Haven 746
York Springs 556
Youngstown 470
Youngsville 2,006
Youngwood 3,749
Zelienople 3,502

PUERTO RICO

Population 3,187,570

METROPOLITAN AREAS

Caguas 173,929
Mayagüez 132,814
Ponce 252,420
San Juan 1,083,664

MUNICIPALITIES

Adjuntas 18,617
Aguada 31,521
Aguadilla 53,366
Aguas Buenas 22,431
Aibonito 22,230
Añasco 22,945
Arecibo 86,660
Arroyo 17,055
Barceloneta 18,869
Barranquitas 21,690
Bayamón 195,965
Cabo Rojo 33,909
Caguas 118,020
Camuy 24,886
Canóvanas 31,934
Carolina 165,207
Cataño 26,318
Cayey 40,927
Ceiba 14,781
Ciales 16,014
Cidra 28,135
Coamo 30,752
Comerío 18,212
Corozal 28,218
Culebra 1,265
Dorado 25,515
Fajardo 32,011
Florida 7,193
Guánica 18,784
Guayama 40,137
Guayanilla 21,012
Guaynabo 80,857
Gurabo 23,576
Hatillo 28,973
Hormigueros 13,983
Humacao 45,916
Isabela 37,451
Jayuya 14,720
Juana Díaz 43,464
Juncos 25,433
Lajas 21,190
Lares 26,742
Las Marías 8,606
Las Piedras 22,425
Loíza 20,902
Luquillo 14,924
Manatí 36,480
Maricao 6,617
Muanabo 11,785
Mayagüez 95,886
Moca 29,309
Morovis 21,145
Naguabo 20,633
Naranjito 23,613
Orocovis 19,304
Patillas 17,820
Peñuelas 18,993
Ponce 188,219
Quebradillas 19,775
Rincón 11,770
Río Grande 34,326
Sabana Grande 20,164
Salinas 26,494
San Germán 32,941
San Juan 432,973
San Lorenzo 32,333
San Sebastián 35,877
Santa Isabel 19,832
Toa Alta 31,946
Toa Baja 78,119
Trujillo Alto 51,389
Utuado 34,384
Vega Alta 28,225
Vega Baja 46,841
Vieques 7,628
Villalba 20,737
Yabucoa 30,589
Yauco 37,682

CITIES, TOWNS, AND VILLAGES

Adjuntas 5,184
Aguadilla 21,618
Aibonito 9,369
Arecibo 48,586
Arroyo 8,486
Bayamón 184,854
Cabo Rojo 10,254
Caguas 87,218
Canóvanas 7,263
Carolina 147,100
Cataño 26,318
Cayey 23,315
Cidra 6,065
Coamo 12,834
Comerío 5,751
Corozal 5,891
Dorado 10,204
Fajardo 26,845
Guánica 9,627
Guayama 21,044
Guayanilla 6,191
Guaynabo 65,091
Gurabo 7,646
Hormigueros 11,991
Humacao 19,135
Isabela 12,097
Juana Díaz 10,496
Juncos 7,898
Manatí 17,254
Mayagüez 82,703
Ponce 161,260
Río Grande 12,068
Sabana Grande 7,368
Salinas 6,240
San Germán 13,093
San Juan 422,701
San Lorenzo 8,886
San Sebastián 10,792
Santa Isabel 6,965
Trujillo Alto 41,097
Utuado 11,049
Vega Alta 10,584
Vega Baja 18,020
Yabucoa 6,782
Yauco 14,598

RHODE ISLAND

Population 947,154

METROPOLITAN AREAS

Fall River 176,831 (145,963 in Mass.; 30,868 in R.I.)
New London-Norwich 248,554 (223,568 in Conn.; 24,986 in R.I.)
Providence-Warwick-Pawtucket 919,216 (817,276 in R.I.; 101,940 in Mass.)

COUNTIES

Bristol 46,942
Kent 154,163
Newport 81,383
Providence 521,349
Washington 93,317

CITIES AND TOWNS

Barrington 16,174▲
Bristol 20,128▲
Burrillville 13,164▲
Central Falls 16,995
Charlestown 4,800▲
Coventry 27,065▲
Cranston 71,992
Cumberland 27,069▲
East Greenwich 10,211▲
East Providence 50,980
Exeter 4,453▲
Foster 3,370▲
Glocester 7,550▲
Hopkinton 6,406▲
Jamestown 4,040▲
Johnston 24,907▲
Lincoln 16,949▲
Little Compton 3,085▲
Middletown 17,216▲

Narragansett . . . . .12,088▲
New Shoreham . . . . .620▲
Newport 29,259
Newport East 10,285
North Kingstown . .21,938▲
North Providence . . . . .29,188▲
North Smithfield . . .9,972▲
Pawtucket 71,204
Portsmouth . . . . . .14,257▲
Providence 156,804
Richmond . . . . .4,018▲
Scituate . . . . .8,405▲
Smithfield . . . . . . .16,886▲
South Kingstown . .20,414▲
Tiverton . . . . .13,526▲
Warren . . . . .10,640▲
Warwick 87,123
West Greenwich . . .2,738▲
West Warwick . . .27,026▲
Westerly . . . . .18,580▲
Woonsocket 45,914
▲Entire town (township), including rural area.

SOUTH CAROLINA

Population 3,119,208

METROPOLITAN AREAS

Augusta (Ga.) . . .327,372 (221,747 in Ga.; 105,625 in S.C.)
Charleston-North Charleston 430,301
Columbia 408,176
Greenville-Spartanburg . . .568,758

COUNTIES

Abbeville 22,627
Aiken 105,625
Allendale 10,700
Anderson 133,235
Bamberg 18,118
Barnwell 19,868
Beaufort 65,364
Berkeley 94,727
Calhoun 12,206
Charleston 277,308
Cherokee 40,983
Chester 30,148
Chesterfield 38,161
Clarendon 27,464
Colleton 31,676
Darlington 62,717
Dillon 31,083
Dorchester 58,266
Edgefield 17,528
Fairfield 20,700
Florence 110,163
Georgetown 42,461
Greenville 287,913
Greenwood 57,847
Hampton 18,159
Horry 101,419
Jasper 14,504
Kershaw 39,015
Lancaster 53,361
Laurens 52,214
Lee 18,929
Lexington 140,353
Marion 34,179
Marlboro 31,634
McCormick 7,797
Newberry 31,111
Oconee 48,611
Orangeburg 82,276
Pickens 79,292
Richland 267,823
Saluda 16,150
Spartanburg 201,553
Sumter 88,243
Union 30,751
Williamsburg 38,226
York 106,720

CITIES AND TOWNS

Abbeville 5,863
Aiken 14,978
Allendale 4,400
Anderson 27,313
Andrews 3,129
Arcadia Lakes 611
Atlantic Beach 289
Aynor 643
Bamberg 3,672
Barnwell 5,572
Batesburg 4,023
Beaufort 8,634
Belton 5,312
Bennettsville 8,774
Bethune 481
Bishopville 3,429
Blacksburg 1,873
Blackville 2,840
Blenheim 202
Bluffton 541
Blythewood 92
Bonneau 401
Bowman 1,137
Branchville 1,769
Briarcliffe Acres 338
Brunson 590
Burnettown 359
Calhoun Falls 2,491
Camden 7,462
Cameron 536
Campobello 472
Carlisle 503
Cayce 11,701
Central 1,914
Central Pacolet 315
Chapin 311
Chappells 109
Charleston 69,510
Cheraw 5,654
Chesnee 1,069
Chester 6,820
Chesterfield 1,432
City View 1,662
Clemson 8,118
Clinton 8,596
Clio 1,031
Clover 3,451
Columbia 99,296
Conway 10,240
Cope 167
Cordova 202
Cottageville 371
Coward 428
Cowpens 2,023
Cross Hill 604
Darlington 7,989
Denmark 4,434
Dillon 7,042
Donalds 366
Due West 1,366
Duncan 1,259
Easley 14,264
Eastover 899
Edgefield 2,713
Edisto Beach 193
Ehrhardt 353
Elgin 595
Elko 329
Elloree 909
Estill 2,308
Eutawville 615
Fairfax 2,154
Florence 30,062
Folly Beach 1,478
Forest Acres 6,033
Fort Lawn 471
Fort Mill 4,162
Fountain Inn 4,226
Furman 348
Gaffney 13,453
Gaston 960
Georgetown 10,144
Gifford 385
Gilbert 211
Goose Creek 17,811
Govan 109
Gray Court 988
Great Falls 2,601
Greeleyville 593
Greenville 58,242
Greenwood 21,613
Greer 10,525
Hampton 3,143
Hanahan 13,224
Hardeeville 1,250
Harleyville 606
Hartsville 7,631
Heath Springs 979
Hemingway 853
Hickory Grove 344
Hilda 355
Hodges 154
Holly Hill 1,785
Hollywood 729
Honea Path 4,114
Inman 1,554
Irmo 3,957
Isle of Palms 3,421
Iva 1,369
Jackson 1,771
Jamestown 193
Jefferson 651
Johnsonville 1,421
Johnston 2,624
Jonesville 1,188
Kershaw 1,993
Kingstree 4,147
Kline 315
Lake City 5,636
Lake View 939
Lamar 1,333
Lancaster 9,603
Landrum 2,141
Lane 554
Latta 1,804
Laurens 10,587
Leesville 2,296
Lexington 2,131
Liberty 3,167
Lincolnville 808
Little Mountain 282
Livingston 166
Lockhart 85
Lodge 145
Loris 2,193
Lowndesville 197
Lowrys 225
Luray 149
Lyman 1,067
Lynchburg 534
Manning 4,746
Marion 7,700
Mauldin 8,245
Mayesville 663
McBee 774
McClellanville 436
McColl 2,677
McConnells 171
McCormick 1,725
Meggett 249
Moncks Corner 3,699
Monetta 108
Mount Carmel 182
Mount Croghan 146
Mount Pleasant . . .13,838
Mullins 6,068
Myrtle Beach 18,758
Neeses 557
New Ellenton 2,628
Newberry 9,866
Nichols 606
Ninety Six 2,249
Norris 903
North 1,304
North Augusta . . .13,593
North Charleston . .65,630
North Myrtle Beach 3,960
Norway 518
Olanta 699
Olar 381
Orangeburg 14,933
Pacolet 1,556
Pacolet Mills 686
Pageland 2,720
Pamplico 1,213
Parksville 157
Patrick 375
Paxville 244
Peak 82
Pelion 213
Pelzer 130
Pendleton 3,154
Perry 273
Pickens 3,199
Pineridge 1,287
Pinewood 689
Plum Branch 73
Pomaria 271
Port Royal 2,977
Prosperity 672
Quinby 952
Ravenel 1,655
Reevesville 241
Richburg 269
Ridge Spring 969
Ridgeland 1,143
Ridgeville 603
Ridgeway 343
Rock Hill 35,344
Rowesville 388
Ruby 256
St. George 2,134
St. Matthews 2,496
St. Stephen 1,316
Salem 194
Salley 584
Saluda 2,752
Santee 612
Scotia 72
Scranton 861
Sellers 388
Seneca 7,436
Sharon 323
Silverstreet 200
Simpsonville 9,037
Six Mile 470
Smoaks 165
Smyrna 47
Snelling 111
Society Hill 848
South Congaree . . .2,113
Spartanburg 43,968
Springdale 2,985
Springfield 604
Starr 241
Stuckey 222
Sullivans Island 1,867
Summerton 1,173
Summerville 6,368
Summit 172
Sumter 24,890
Surfside Beach 2,522
Swansea 888
Sycamore 261
Tatum 101
Timmonsville 2,112
Travelers Rest 3,017
Trenton 404
Troy 705
Turbeville 549
Ulmer 91
Union 10,523
Vance 89
Varnville 1,948
Wagener 903
Walhalla 3,977
Walterboro 6,036
Ward 98
Ware Shoals 2,370
Waterloo 200
Wellford 2,143
West Columbia . . .10,409
West Pelzer 944
West Union 300
Westminster 3,114
Whitmire 2,038
Williams 205
Williamston 4,310
Williston 3,173
Windsor 55
Winnsboro 2,919
Woodford 206
Woodruff 5,171
Yemassee 1,048
York 6,412

SOUTH DAKOTA

Population 690,178

METROPOLITAN AREAS

Rapid City 90,850
Sioux Falls 109,435

COUNTIES

Aurora 3,628
Beadle 19,195
Bennett 3,236
Bon Homme 8,059
Brookings 24,332
Brown 36,962
Brule 5,245
Buffalo 1,795
Butte 8,372
Campbell 2,243
Charles Mix 9,680
Clark 4,894
Clay 13,135
Codington 20,885
Corson 5,196
Custer 6,000
Davison 17,820
Day 8,133
Deuel 5,289
Dewey 5,366
Douglas 4,181
Edmunds 5,159
Fall River 8,439
Faulk 3,327
Grant 9,013
Gregory 6,015
Haakon 2,794
Hamlin 5,261
Hand 4,948
Hanson 3,415
Harding 1,700
Hughes 14,220
Hutchinson 9,350
Hyde 2,069
Jackson 3,437
Jerauld 2,929
Jones 1,463
Kingsbury 6,679
Lake 10,724
Lawrence 18,339
Lincoln 13,942
Lyman 3,864
Marshall 5,404
McCook 6,444
McPherson 4,027
Meade 20,717
Mellette 2,249
Miner 3,739
Minnehaha 109,435
Moody 6,692
Pennington 70,133
Perkins 4,700
Potter 3,674
Roberts 10,911
Sanborn 3,213
Shannon 11,323
Spink 9,201
Stanley 2,533
Sully 1,990
Todd 7,328
Tripp 7,268
Turner 9,255
Union 10,938
Walworth 7,011
Yankton 18,952
Ziebach 2,308

CITIES AND TOWNS

Aberdeen 25,956
Agar 139
Akaska 49
Albee 23
Alcester 885
Alexandria 588
Alpena 288
Altamont 58
Andover 139
Ardmore 16
Arlington 991
Armour 819
Artas 43
Artesian 227
Ashton 154
Astoria 154
Aurora 507
Avon 576
Badger 99
Baltic 679
Bancroft 41
Batesland 163
Belle Fourche 4,692
Belvidere 80
Beresford 1,865
Big Stone City 672
Bison 457
Blunt 424
Bonesteel 358
Bowdle 644
Box Elder 3,186
Bradley 135
Brandon 2,589
Brandt 129
Brentford 91
Bridgewater 653
Bristol 445
Britton 1,590
Broadland 49
Brookings 14,951
Bruce 254
Bryant 388
Buffalo 453
Buffalo Gap 186
Burke 859
Bushnell 76
Butler 22
Camp Crook 100
Canistota 626
Canova 194
Canton 2,886
Carter 7
Carthage 274
Castlewood 557
Cavour 117
Centerville 892
Central City 232
Chamberlain 2,258
Chancellor 257
Chelsea 41
Claire City 87
Claremont 180
Clark 1,351
Clear Lake 1,310
Colman 501
Colome 361
Colton 757
Columbia 161
Conde 259
Corona 126
Corsica 644
Cottonwood 4
Cresbard 221
Crooks 594
Custer 1,830
Dallas 199
Dante 83
Davis 100
Deadwood 2,035
Dell Rapids 2,389
Delmont 290
De Smet 1,237
Dimock 140
Doland 381
Dolton 47
Draper 138
Dupree 562
Eagle Butte 435
Eden 142
Edgemont 1,468
Egan 248
Elk Point 1,661
Elkton 632
Emery 399
Erwin 66
Estelline 719
Ethan 351
Eureka 1,360
Fairburn 41
Fairfax 225
Fairview 90
Faith 576
Farmer 27
Faulkton 981
Flandreau 2,114
Florence 190
Fort Pierre 1,789
Frankfort 209
Frederick 307
Freeman 1,462
Fruitdale 88
Fulton 108
Garden City 104
Garretson 963
Gary 354
Gayville 407
Geddes 303
Gettysburg 1,623
Glenham 169
Goodwin 139
Gregory 1,503
Grenville 119
Groton 1,230
Harrisburg 558
Harrold 196
Hartford 1,207
Hayti 371
Hazel 94
Hecla 435
Henry 217
Hermosa 251
Herreid 570
Herrick 115
Hetland 66
Highmore 1,055
Hill City 535
Hillsview 9
Hitchcock 132
Hosmer 385
Hot Springs 4,742
Hoven 615
Howard 1,169
Hudson 388
Humboldt 487
Hurley 419
Huron 13,000
Interior 62
Ipswich 1,153
Irene 523
Iroquois 348
Isabel 332
Java 261
Jefferson 592
Kadoka 832
Kennebec 334
Keystone 295
Kimball 752
Kranzburg 136
La Bolt 94
Lake Andes 1,029
Lake City 46
Lake Norden 417
Lake Preston 789
Lane 83
Langford 307
Lead 4,330
Lebanon 129
Lemmon 1,871
Lennox 1,827
Leola 645
Lesterville 156
Letcher 221
Lily 38
Long Lake 117
Lowry 22
Loyalton 6
Madison 6,210
Marion 830
Martin 1,018
Marvin 52
McIntosh 418
McLaughlin 754
Mellette 192
Menno 793
Midland 277
Milbank 4,120
Miller 1,931
Mission 748
Mission Hill 197
Mitchell 13,916
Mobridge 4,174
Monroe 170
Montrose 396
Morristown 127
Mound City 111
Mount Vernon 402
Murdo 723
Naples 45
New Effington 261
New Underwood 517
Newell 638
Nisland 216
North Sioux City . . .1,992
Northville 138
Nunda 60
Oacoma 289
Oelrichs 124
Oldham 222
Olivet 96
Onaka 70
Onida 851

SOUTH DAKOTA (continued)

Orient 87
Ortley 80
Parker 999
Parkston 1,545
Peever 232
Philip 1,088
Pierpont 184
Pierre 11,973
Plankinton 644
Platte 1,334
Pollock 355
Presho 760
Pringle 105
Pukwana 234
Quinn 80
Ramona 241
Rapid City 46,492
Ravinia 88
Raymond 106
Redfield 3,027
Ree Heights 88
Reliance 190
Revillo 158
Rockham 52
Roscoe 370
Rosholt 446
Roslyn 261
Roswell 19
St. Francis 766
St. Lawrence 223
Salem 1,486
Scotland 1,022
Selby 884
Seneca 103
Sherman 100
Sinai 129
Sioux Falls 81,343
Sisseton 2,789
South Shore 241
Spearfish 5,251
Spencer 380
Springfield 1,377
Stickney 409
Stockholm 95
Strandburg 79
Stratford 82
Sturgis 5,184
Summit 290
Tabor 460
Tea 729
Timber Lake 660
Tolstoy 97
Toronto 236
Trent 197
Tripp 804
Tulare 238
Turton 101
Twin Brooks 87
Tyndall 1,253
Utica 100
Valley Springs 801
Veblen 368
Verdon 7
Vermillion 9,582
Viborg 812
Vienna 90
Vilas 28
Virgil 37
Volga 1,221
Volin 156
Wagner 1,453
Wakonda 383
Wall 542
Wallace 90
Ward 43
Warner 322
Wasta 99
Watertown 15,649
Waubay 675
Webster 2,417
Wentworth 193
Wessington 327
Wessington Springs 1,203
Westport 122
Wetonka 22
White 474
White Lake 414
White River 561
White Rock 10
Whitewood 821
Willow Lake 375
Wilmot 507
Winfred 81
Winner 3,472
Witten 134
Wolsey 437
Wood 134
Woonsocket 799
Worthing 388
Yale 136
Yankton 12,011

TENNESSEE Population 4,590,750

METROPOLITAN AREAS

Chattanooga 426,540 (320,761 in Tenn.; 105,779 in Ga.)
Clarksville-Hopkinsville 150,220 (83,342 in Tenn.; 66,878 in Ky.)
Johnson City-Kingsport-Bristol (Va.) 433,638 (343,041 in Tenn.; 90,597 in Va.)
Knoxville 476,517
Memphis 912,887 (809,860 in Tenn.; 49,097 in Ark.; 53,930 in Miss.)
Nashville-Davidson 850,505

COUNTIES

Anderson 67,346
Bedford 27,916
Benton 14,901
Bledsoe 9,478
Blount 77,770
Bradley 67,547
Campbell 34,841
Cannon 10,234
Carroll 28,285
Carter 50,205
Cheatham 21,616
Chester 12,727
Claiborne 24,595
Clay 7,676
Cocke 28,792
Coffee 38,311
Crockett 14,941
Cumberland 28,676
Davidson 477,811
Decatur 10,857
De Kalb 13,589
Dickson 30,037
Dyer 34,663
Fayette 25,305
Fentress 14,826
Franklin 31,983
Gibson 49,467
Giles 24,625
Grainger 16,751
Greene 54,406
Grundy 13,787
Hamblen 49,300
Hamilton 287,740
Hancock 6,887
Hardeman 23,873
Hardin 22,280
Hawkins 43,751
Haywood 20,318
Henderson 21,390
Henry 28,656
Hickman 15,151
Houston 6,871
Humphreys 15,957
Jackson 9,398
Jefferson 31,284
Johnson 13,745
Knox 319,694
Lake 7,455
Lauderdale 24,555
Lawrence 34,110
Lewis 9,700
Lincoln 26,483
Loudon 28,553
Macon 15,700
Madison 74,546
Marion 24,416
Marshall 19,698
Maury 51,095
McMinn 41,878
McNairy 22,525
Meigs 7,431
Monroe 28,700
Montgomery 83,342
Moore 4,510
Morgan 16,604
Obion 32,781
Overton 17,575
Perry 6,111
Pickett 4,358
Polk 13,602
Putnam 47,601
Rhea 24,235
Roane 48,425
Robertson 37,021
Rutherford 84,058
Scott 19,259
Sequatchie 8,605
Sevier 41,418
Shelby 777,113
Smith 14,935
Stewart 8,665
Sullivan 143,968
Sumner 85,790
Tipton 32,747
Trousdale 6,137
Unicoi 16,362
Union 11,707
Van Buren 4,728
Warren 32,653
Washington 88,755
Wayne 13,946
Weakley 32,896
White 19,567
Williamson 58,108
Wilson 56,064

CITIES AND TOWNS

Adams 600
Adamsville 1,453
Alamo 2,615
Alcoa 6,870
Alexandria 689
Algood 2,406
Allardt 654
Altamont 679
Ardmore 835
Arlington 1,778
Ashland City 2,329
Athens 12,080
Atoka 691
Atwood 1,143
Auburntown 204
Baileyton 289
Bartlett 17,170
Baxter 1,411
Beersheba Springs 643
Bell Buckle 450
Belle Meade 3,182
Bells 1,571
Benton 1,115
Berry Hill 1,113
Bethel Springs 873
Big Sandy 650
Blaine 1,147
Bluff City 1,121
Bolivar 6,597
Braden 293
Bradford 1,146
Brentwood 9,431
Brighton 976
Bristol 23,986
Brownsville 9,307
Bruceton 1,579
Bulls Gap 821
Burlison 386
Burns 777
Byrdstown 884
Calhoun 590
Camden 3,279
Carthage 2,672
Caryville 2,039
Cedar Hill 420
Celina 1,580
Centertown 300
Centerville 2,824
Chapel Hill 861
Charleston 756
Charlotte 788
Chattanooga 169,565
Church Hill 4,110
Clarksburg 400
Clarksville 54,777
Cleveland 26,415
Clifton 773
Clinton 5,245
Coalmont 625
Collegedale 4,607
Collierville 7,839
Collinwood 1,064
Columbia 25,767
Cookeville 20,350
Copperhill 418
Cornersville 722
Cottage Grove 117
Covington 6,065
Cowan 1,790
Crab Orchard 1,065
Cross Plains 655
Crossville 6,394
Cumberland City 276
Cumberland Gap 263
Dandridge 1,383
Dayton 5,913
Decatur 1,069
Decaturville 1,004
Decherd 2,233
Denmark 51
Dickson 7,040
Dover 1,197
Dowelltown 341
Doyle 344
Dresden 2,256
Ducktown 583
Dunlap 3,681
Dyer 2,419
Dyersburg 15,856
Eagleville 444
East Ridge 21,236
Eastview 552
Elizabethton 12,431
Elkton 540
Englewood 1,840
Enville 287
Erin 1,614
Erwin 4,739
Estill Springs 1,324
Ethridge 548
Etowah 3,758
Fairview 3,648
Fayetteville 7,559
Finger 245
Forest Hills 4,516
Franklin 12,407
Friendship 763
Friendsville 694
Gadsden 683
Gainesboro 1,119
Gallatin 17,191
Gallaway 804
Garland 301
Gates 729
Gatlinburg 3,210
Germantown 20,459
Gibson 458
Gilt Edge 142
Gleason 1,335
Goodlettsville 8,327
Gordonsville 893
Grand Junction 360
Graysville 1,380
Greenback 546
Greenbrier 3,180
Greeneville 14,097
Greenfield 2,109
Halls 2,444
Harriman 8,303
Hartsville 2,674
Henderson 4,449
Hendersonville 26,561
Henning 638
Henry 295
Hickory Valley 252
Hohenwald 3,922
Hollow Rock 955
Hornbeak 452
Hornsby 401
Humboldt 10,209
Huntingdon 3,962
Huntland 983
Huntsville 519
Iron City 482
Jacksboro 1,620
Jackson 49,131
Jamestown 2,364
Jasper 2,633
Jefferson City 5,612
Jellico 2,798
Johnson City 39,753
Jonesboro 2,829
Kenton 1,551
Kimball 1,220
Kingsport 32,027
Kingston 4,441
Kingston Springs 1,017
Knoxville 183,139
Lafayette 3,808
La Follette 8,176
La Grange 185
Lake City 2,335
Lakeland 612
Lakesite 651
Lakewood 2,325
La Vergne 5,495
Lawrenceburg 10,175
Lebanon 11,872
Lenoir City 5,446
Lewisburg 8,760
Lexington 5,934
Liberty 365
Linden 1,087
Livingston 3,372
Lobelville 993
Lookout Mountain 1,886
Loretto 1,612
Loudon 3,940
Luttrell 962
Lynchburg 668
Lynnville 383
Madisonville 2,884
Manchester 7,250
Martin 8,898
Maryville 17,480
Mason 471
Maury City 989
Maynardville 924
McEwen 1,352
McKenzie 5,405
McLemoresville 311
McMinnville 10,683
Medina 687
Medon 162
Memphis 646,356
Michie 530
Middleton 596
Milan 8,083
Milledgeville 392
Millington 20,236
Minor Hill 564
Mitchellville 209
Monteagle 1,126
Monterey 2,610
Morrison 587
Morristown 19,683
Moscow 499
Mosheim 1,539
Mount Carmel 3,764
Mount Juliet 2,879
Mount Pleasant 3,375
Mountain City 2,125
Munford 1,587
Murfreesboro 32,845
Nashville 455,651
New Hope 681
New Johnsonville 1,824
New Market 1,216
New Tazewell 1 677
Newbern 2,794
Newport 7,580
Niota 765
Normandy 118
Norris 1,374
Oak Hill 4,609
Oak Ridge 27,662
Oakdale 323
Oakland 472
Obion 1,282
Oliver Springs 3,659
Oneida 3,029
Orlinda 382
Orme 181
Palmer 1,027
Paris 10,728
Parrottsville 118
Parsons 2,422
Pegram 1,081
Petersburg 681
Philadelphia 507
Pigeon Forge 1,822
Pikeville 2,085
Piperton 746
Pittman Center 488
Pleasant Hill 371
Portland 4,030
Powells Crossroads 918
Pulaski 7,184
Puryear 624
Ramer 429
Red Bank 13,297
Red Boiling Springs 1,173
Richard City 87
Ridgely 1,932
Ridgeside 417
Ridgetop 1,225
Ripley 6,366
Rives 386
Rockford 567
Rockwood 5,767
Rogersville 4,368
Rossville 379
Rutherford 1,378
Rutledge 1,058
St. Joseph 897
Saltillo 434
Samburg 465
Sardis 301
Saulsbury 156
Savannah 6,992
Scotts Hill 668
Selmer 3,979
Sevierville 4,566
Sharon 1,134
Shelbyville 13,530
Signal Mountain 5,818
Silerton 100
Slayden 69
Smithville 3,839
Smyrna 8,839
Sneedville 1,110
Soddy-Daisy 8,388
Somerville 2,264
South Carthage 1,004
South Fulton 2,735
South Pittsburg 3,636
Sparta 4,864
Spencer 1,126
Spring City 1,951
Spring Hill 989
Springfield 10,814
Stanton 540
Stantonville 271
Surgoinsville 1,536
Sweetwater 4,725
Tazewell 2,090
Tellico Plains 698
Tennessee Ridge 1,325
Tiptonville 2,438
Toone 355
Townsend 351
Tracy City 1,356
Trenton 4,601
Trezevant 921
Trimble 722
Troy 1,093
Tullahoma 15,800
Tusculum 1,242
Union City 10,436
Vanleer 401
Viola 149
Vonore 528
Walden 1,293
Wartburg 761
Wartrace 540
Watauga 376
Watertown 1,300
Waverly 4,405
Waynesboro 2,109
Westmoreland 1,754
White Bluff 2,055
White House 2,225
White Pine 1,900
Whiteville 1,270
Whitwell 1,783
Williston 395
Winchester 5,821
Woodbury 2,160
Woodland Mills 526
Yorkville 272

TEXAS Population 14,228,383

METROPOLITAN AREAS

Abilene 139,192
Amarillo 173,699
Austin 536,450
Beaumont-Port Arthur-Orange 375,497
Brownsville-Harlingen-San Benito 209,680
Bryan-College Station 93,588
Corpus Christi 326,228
Dallas-Fort Worth 2,974,878
El Paso 479,899
Galveston-Texas City 195,940
Houston 2,905,350
Killeen-Temple 214,656
Laredo 99,258
Longview-Marshall 151,752
Lubbock 211,651
McAllen-Pharr-Edinburg 283,229
Midland 82,636
Odessa 115,374
San Angelo 84,784
San Antonio 1,071,954
Sherman-Denison 89,796
Texarkana-Texarkana (Ark.) 127,019 (75,301 in Tex.; 51,718 in Ark.)
Tyler 128,366
Waco 170,755
Wichita Falls 411,313

COUNTIES

Anderson 38,381
Andrews 13,323
Angelina 64,172
Aransas 14,260
Archer 7,266
Armstrong 1,994
Atascosa 25,055
Austin 17,726
Bailey 8,168
Bandera 7,084
Bastrop 24,726
Baylor 4,919
Bee 26,030
Bell 157,889
Bexar 988,800
Blanco 4,681
Borden 859
Bosque 13,401
Bowie 75,301
Brazoria 169,587
Brazos 93,588
Brewster 7,573
Briscoe 2,579
Brooks 8,428
Brown 33,057
Burleson 12,313
Burnet 17,803
Caldwell 23,637
Calhoun 19,574
Callahan 10,992
Cameron 209,680
Camp 9,275
Carson 6,672
Cass 29,430
Castro 10,556
Chambers 18,538
Cherokee 38,127
Childress 6,950
Clay 9,582
Cochran 4,825
Coke 3,196
Coleman 10,439
Collin 144,490
Collingsworth 4,648
Colorado 18,823
Comal 36,446

Comanche 12,617
Concho 2,915
Cooke 27,656
Coryell 56,767
Cottle 2,947
Crane 4,600
Crockett 4,608
Crosby 8,859
Culberson 3,315
Dallam 6,531
Dallas 1,556,549
Dawson 16,148
Deaf Smith 21,165
Delta 4,839
Denton 143,126
De Witt 18,903
Dickens 3,539
Dimmit 11,367
Donley 4,075
Duval 12,517
Eastland 19,480
Ector 115,374
Edwards 2,033
Ellis 59,743
El Paso 479,899
Erath 22,560
Falls 17,946
Fannin 24,285
Fayette 18,832
Fisher 5,891
Floyd 9,834
Foard 2,158
Fort Bend 130,846
Franklin 6,893
Freestone 14,830
Frio 13,785
Gaines 13,150
Galveston 195,940
Garza 5,336
Gillespie 13,532
Glasscock 1,304
Goliad 5,193
Gonzales 16,883
Gray 26,386
Grayson 89,796
Gregg 99,487
Grimes 13,580
Guadalupe 46,708
Hale 37,592
Hall 5,594
Hamilton 8,297
Hansford 6,209
Hardeman 6,368
Hardin 40,721
Harris 2,409,544
Harrison 52,265
Hartley 3,987
Haskell 7,725
Hays 40,594
Hemphill 5,304
Henderson 42,606
Hidalgo 283,229
Hill 25,024
Hockley 23,230
Hood 17,714
Hopkins 25,247
Houston 22,299
Howard 33,142
Hudspeth 2,728
Hunt 55,248
Hutchinson 26,304
Irion 1,386
Jack 7,408
Jackson 13,352
Jasper 30,781
Jeff Davis 1,647
Jefferson 250,938
Jim Hogg 5,168
Jim Wells 36,498
Johnson 67,649
Jones 17,268
Karnes 13,593
Kaufman 39,015
Kendall 10,635
Kenedy 543
Kent 1,145
Kerr 28,780
Kimble 4,063
King 425
Kinney 2,279
Kleberg 33,358
Knox 5,329
Lamar 42,156
Lamb 18,669
Lampasas 12,005
La Salle 5,254
Lavaca 19,004
Lee 10,952
Leon 9,594
Liberty 47,088
Limestone 20,224
Lipscomb 3,766
Live Oak 9,606
Llano 10,144
Loving 91
Lubbock 211,651
Lynn 8,605
Madison 10,649
Marion 10,360
Martin 4,684
Mason 3,683
Matagorda 37,828
Maverick 31,398
McCulloch 8,735
McLennan 170,755
McMullen 789
Medina 23,164
Menard 2,346
Midland 82,636
Milam 22,732
Mills 4,477
Mitchell 9,088
Montague 17,410
Montgomery 128,487
Moore 16,575

Morris 14,629
Motley 1,950
Nacogdoches 46,786
Navarro 35,323
Newton 13,254
Nolan 17,359
Nueces 268,215
Ochiltree 9,588
Oldham 2,283
Orange 83,838
Palo Pinto 24,062
Panola 20,724
Parker 44,609
Parmer 11,038
Pecos 14,618
Polk 24,407
Potter 98,637
Presidio 5,188
Rains 4,839
Randall 75,062
Reagan 4,135
Real 2,469
Red River 16,101
Reeves 15,801
Refugio 9,289
Roberts 1,187
Robertson 14,653
Rockwall 14,528
Runnels 11,872
Rusk 41,382
Sabine 8,702
San Augustine 8,785
San Jacinto 11,434
San Patricio 58,013
San Saba 5,693
Schleicher 2,820
Scurry 18,192
Shackelford 3,915
Shelby 23,084
Sherman 3,174
Smith 128,366
Somervell 4,154
Starr 27,266
Stephens 9,926
Sterling 1,206
Stonewall 2,406
Sutton 5,130
Swisher 9,723
Tarrant 860,880
Taylor 110,932
Terrell 1,595
Terry 14,581
Throckmorton 2,053
Titus 21,442
Tom Green 84,784
Travis 419,335
Trinity 9,450
Tyler 16,223
Upshur 28,595
Upton 4,619
Uvalde 22,441
Val Verde 35,910
Van Zandt 31,426
Victoria 68,807
Walker 41,789
Waller 19,798
Ward 13,976
Washington 21,998
Webb 99,258
Wharton 40,242
Wheeler 7,137
Wichita 121,082
Wilbarger 15,931
Willacy 17,495
Williamson 76,521
Wilson 16,756
Winkler 9,944
Wise 26,575
Wood 24,697
Yoakum 8,299
Young 19,001
Zapata 6,628
Zavala 11,666

CITIES, TOWNS, AND VILLAGES

Abernathy 2,904
Abilene 98,315
Addison 5,553
Agua Dulce 934
Alamo 5,831
Alamo Heights 6,252
Albany 2,450
Aledo 1,027
Alice 20,961
Allen 8,314
Alpine 5,465
Alto 1,203
Alton 2,732
Alvarado 2,701
Alvin 16,515
Alvord 874
Amarillo 149,230
Ames 1,155
Amherst 971
Anahuac 1,840
Andrews 11,061
Angleton 13,929
Anna 855
Anson 2,831
Anthony 2,640
Anton 1,180
Aransas Pass 7,173
Archer City 1,862
Argyle 1,111
Arlington 160,123
Arp 939
Asherton 1,574
Aspermont 1,357
Athens 10,197
Atlanta 6,272

Aubrey 948
Austin 345,496
Azle 5,822
Baird 1,696
Balch Springs 13,746
Balcones Heights 2,853
Ballinger 4,207
Bandera 947
Bangs 1,716
Bartlett 1,567
Bastrop 3,789
Bay City 17,837
Baytown 56,923
Beach City 977
Beaumont 118,102
Beckville 945
Bedford 20,821
Beeville 14,574
Bellaire 14,950
Bellmead 7,569
Bells 846
Bellville 2,860
Belton 10,660
Benavides 1,978
Benbrook 13,579
Benjamin 257
Bertram 824
Beverly Hills 2,083
Bevil Oaks 1,306
Big Lake 3,404
Big Sandy 1,258
Big Spring 24,804
Big Wells 939
Bishop 3,706
Blanco 1,179
Blooming Grove 823
Blossom 1,487
Blue Mound 2,169
Boerne 3,229
Bogata 1,508
Bonham 7,338
Booker 1,219
Borger 15,837
Bovina 1,499
Bowie 5,610
Boyd 889
Brackettville 1,676
Brady 5,969
Brazoria 3,025
Breckenridge 6,921
Bremond 1,025
Brenham 10,966
Briar 1,810
Bridge City 7,667
Bridgeport 3,737
Bronte 983
Brookshire 2,175
Brookside 1,453
Brownfield 10,387
Brownsville 84,997
Brownwood 19,203
Bruceville-Eddy 1,038
Bryan 44,337
Buffalo 1,507
Bunker Hill 3,750
Burkburnett 10,668
Burleson 11,734
Burnet 3,410
Cactus 898
Caddo Mills 1,060
Caldwell 2,953
Calvert 1,732
Cameron 5,721
Canadian 3,491
Canton 2,845
Canyon 10,724
Carrizo Springs 6,886
Carrollton 40,591
Carthage 6,447
Castle Hills 4,773
Castroville 1,821
Cedar Hill 6,849
Cedar Park 3,474
Celina 1,520
Center 5,827
Centerville 799
Chandler 1,308
Channing 304
Charlotte 1,443
Chico 890
Childress 5,817
Chillicothe 1,052
China 1,351
Cisco 4,517
Clarendon 2,220
Clarksville 4,917
Claude 1,112
Clear Lake Shores 755
Cleburne 19,218
Cleveland 5,977
Clifton 3,063
Clint 1,314
Clute 9,577
Clyde 2,562
Coahoma 1,069
Cockrell Hill 3,262
Coldspring 569
Coleman 5,960
College Station 37,272
Colleyville 6,700
Collinsville 860
Colorado City 5,405
Columbus 3,923
Comanche 4,075
Combes 1,441
Commerce 8,136
Converse 4,907
Coolidge 810
Cooper 2,338
Coppell 3,826
Copperas Cove 19,469
Corinth 1,264
Corpus Christi 231,999
Corrigan 1,770

Corsicana 21,712
Cotulla 3,912
Crandall 831
Crane 3,622
Crockett 7,405
Crosbyton 2,289
Cross Plains 1,240
Crowell 1,509
Crowley 5,852
Crystal Beach 776
Crystal City 8,334
Cuero 7,124
Daingerfield 3,030
Daisetta 1,177
Dalhart 6,854
Dallas 904,078
Dalworthington Gardens 1,100
Danbury 1,357
Dawson 747
Decatur 4,908
Deer Park 22,648
De Kalb 2,217
De Leon 2,478
Del Rio 30,034
Denison 23,884
Denton 48,063
Denver City 4,704
De Soto 15,538
Detroit 805
Devine 3,756
Diboll 5,227
Dickens 409
Dickinson 7,505
Dilley 2,579
Dimmitt 5,019
Donna 9,952
Double Oak 836
Dublin 2,723
Dumas 12,194
Duncanville 27,781
Eagle Lake 3,921
Eagle Pass 21,407
Early 2,313
Earth 1,512
East Mountain 855
Eastland 3,747
Edcouch 3,092
Eden 1,294
Edgecliff 2,695
Edgewood 1,413
Edinburg 24,075
Edna 5,650
El Campo 10,462
Eldorado 2,061
Electra 3,755
Elgin 4,535
Elkhart 1,317
El Lago 3,129
El Paso 425,259
Elsa 5,061
Emory 813
Ennis 12,110
Euless 24,002
Everman 5,387
Fairfield 3,505
Fairview 893
Falfurrias 6,103
Farmers Branch 24,863
Farmersville 2,360
Farwell 1,354
Ferris 2,228
Flatonia 1,070
Florence 744
Floresville 4,381
Flower Mound 4,402
Floydada 4,193
Forest Hill 11,684
Forney 2,483
Fort Gates 777
Fort Stockton 8,688
Fort Worth 385,141
Franklin 1,349
Frankston 1,255
Fredericksburg 6,412
Freeport 13,444
Freer 3,213
Friendswood 10,719
Friona 3,809
Frisco 3,420
Fritch 2,299
Fuller Springs 1,470
Gainesville 14,081
Galena Park 10,033
Galveston 61,902
Ganado 1,770
Garland 138,857
Garrison 1,059
Gatesville 6,260
George West 2,627
Georgetown 9,468
Giddings 3,950
Gilmer 5,167
Gladewater 6,548
Glenn Heights 1,033
Glen Rose 2,075
Goldthwaite 1,783
Goliad 1,990
Gonzales 7,152
Gorman 1,258
Graham 9,055
Grand Prairie 71,462
Grand Saline 2,709
Grandview 1,205
Granger 1,236
Grapeland 1,634
Grapevine 11,801
Greenville 22,161
Gregory 2,739
Griffing Park 1,802
Groesbeck 3,373
Groom 736

Groves 17,090
Groveton 1,262
Grulla 1,442
Gruver 1,216
Gun Barrel City 2,118
Gunter 849
Hale Center 2,297
Hallettsville 2,865
Hallsville 1,556
Haltom City 29,014
Hamilton 3,189
Hamlin 3,248
Hardin 779
Harker Heights 7,345
Harlingen 43,543
Hart 1,008
Haskell 3,782
Hawkins 1,302
Hearne 5,418
Heath 1,459
Hedwig Village 2,506
Hemphill 1,353
Hempstead 3,456
Henderson 11,473
Henrietta 3,149
Hereford 15,853
Hewitt 5,247
Hickory Creek 1,422
Hico 1,375
Hidalgo 2,288
Highland Park 8,909
Highland Village 3,246
Hill County Village 972
Hillcrest 771
Hillsboro 7,397
Hitchcock 6,655
Holland 863
Holliday 1,349
Hollywood Park 3,231
Hondo 6,057
Honey Grove 1,973
Hooks 2,507
Houston 1,594,086
Howe 2,072
Hubbard 1,676
Hudson 1,659
Hughes Springs 2,196
Humble 6,729
Hunters Creek Village 4,215
Huntington 1,672
Huntsville 23,936
Hurst 31,420
Hutchins 2,996
Idalou 2,348
Ingleside 5,436
Iowa Park 6,184
Iraan 1,358
Irving 109,943
Italy 1,306
Itasca 1,600
Jacinto City 8,953
Jacksboro 4,000
Jacksonville 12,264
Jasper 6,959
Jayton 638
Jefferson 2,643
Jersey Village 4,084
Joaquin 917
Johnson City 872
Jones Creek 2,634
Joshua 1,470
Jourdanton 2,743
Junction 2,593
Justin 920
Karnes City 3,296
Katy 5,660
Kaufman 4,658
Keene 3,013
Keller 4,143
Kemah 1,304
Kemp 1,035
Kenedy 4,356
Kenefick 763
Kennedale 2,594
Kerens 1,582
Kermit 8,015
Kerrville 15,276
Kilgore 10,968
Killeen 46,296
Kingsville 28,808
Kirby 6,385
Kirbyville 1,972
Knox City 1,546
Kountze 2,716
Kress 783
Krum 917
Kyle 2,093
La Coste 862
Lacy-Lakeview 2,752
Ladonia 761
La Feria 3,495
La Grange 3,768
La Joya 2,018
Lake Dallas 3,177
Lake Jackson 19,102
Lake Worth Village 4,394
Lakeport 835
Lakeside 957
Lakeway 790
La Marque 15,372
Lamesa 11,790
Lampasas 6,165
Lancaster 14,807
La Porte 14,062
Laredo 91,449
La Villa 1,442
League City 16,578
Leakey 468
Leander 2,179
Lefors 656
Leon Valley 8,951
Leonard 1,421
Levelland 13,809
Lewisville 24,273

Lexington 1,065
Liberty 7,945
Liberty City 1,121
Lindale 2,180
Linden 2,443
Little Elm 926
Little River-Academy 1,155
Littlefield 7,409
Live Oak 8,183
Livingston 4,928
Llano 3,071
Lockhart 7,953
Lockney 2,334
Lomax 2,991
Lone Star 2,036
Longview 62,762
Loraine 929
Lorenzo 1,394
Los Fresnos 2,173
Lott 865
Lubbock 173,979
Lucas 1,371
Lufkin 28,562
Luling 5,039
Lumberton 2,480
Lyford 1,618
Lytle 1,920
Mabank 1,443
Madisonville 3,660
Magnolia 867
Malakoff 2,082
Manor 1,044
Mansfield 8,092
Manvel 3,549
Marble Falls 3,252
Marfa 2,466
Marlin 7,099
Marshall 24,921
Mart 2,324
Mason 2,153
Matador 1,052
Mathis 5,667
Maud 1,059
McAllen 67,042
McCamey 2,436
McGregor 4,513
McKinney 16,249
McLean 1,160
Memphis 3,352
Menard 1,697
Mercedes 11,851
Meridian 1,330
Merkel 2,493
Mertzon 687
Mesquite 67,053
Mexia 7,094
Miami 813
Midland 70,525
Midlothian 3,219
Mineola 4,346
Mineral Wells 14,468
Mission 22,589
Missouri City 24,533
Monahans 8,397
Mont Belvieu 1,730
Moody 1,385
Morgan's Point Resort 1,082
Morton 2,674
Moulton 1,009
Mount Pleasant 11,003
Mount Vernon 2,025
Muenster 1,408
Muleshoe 4,842
Munday 1,738
Murphy 1,150
Nacogdoches 27,149
Naples 1,908
Nash 2,022
Nassau Bay 4,526
Natalia 1,264
Navasota 5,971
Nederland 16,855
Needville 1,417
New Boston 4,628
New Braunfels 22,402
New London 942
New Waverly 824
Newton 1,620
Nixon 2,008
Nocona 2,992
Nolanville 1,308
North Richland Hills 30,592
Northcrest 1,944
O'Donnell 1,200
Oak Ridge North 2,504
Odem 2,363
Odessa 90,027
Old River-Winfree 1,058
Olmos Park 2,069
Olney 4,060
Olton 2,235
Omaha 960
Orange 23,628
Orange Grove 1,212
Ore City 1,050
Overton 2,430
Ovilla 1,067
Oyster Creek 1,473
Paducah 2,216
Paint Rock 256
Palacios 4,667
Palestine 15,948
Palmer 1,187
Pampa 21,396
Panhandle 2,226
Panorama Village 1,186
Pantego 2,431
Paris 25,498
Parker 1,098
Pasadena 112,560
Patton 1,050

Pearland ...13,248
Pearsall ...7,383
Pecos ...12,855
Perryton ...7,991
Petersburg ...1,633
Petrolia ...755
Pflugerville ...745
Pharr ...21,381
Pilot Point ...2,211
Pinehurst ...3,055
Pineland ...1,111
Piney Point Village ...2,958
Pittsburg ...4,245
Plains ...1,457
Plainview ...22,187
Plano ...72,331
Pleasanton ...6,346
Point Comfort ...1,125
Port Aransas ...1,968
Port Arthur ...61,195
Port Isabel ...3,769
Port Lavaca ...10,911
Port Neches ...13,944
Portland ...12,023
Post ...3,961
Post Oak Bend City ...878
Poteet ...3,086
Poth ...1,461
Pottsboro ...895
Prairie View ...3,993
Premont ...2,984
Primera ...1,380
Princeton ...3,408
Quanah ...3,890
Queen City ...1,748
Quinlan ...1,002
Quitman ...1,893
Ralls ...2,422
Ranger ...3,142
Rankin ...1,216

Raymondville ...9,493
Red Oak ...1,882
Refugio ...3,898
Reno ...1,059
Reno ...1,174
Richardson ...72,496
Richland Hills ...7,977
Richmond ...9,692
Richwood ...2,591
Rio Hondo ...1,673
Rising Star ...1,204
River Oaks ...6,890
Roanoke ...910
Robert Lee ...1,202
Robinson ...6,074
Robstown ...12,100
Roby ...814
Rockdale ...5,611
Rockport ...3,686
Rocksprings ...1,317
Rockwall ...5,939
Rogers ...1,242
Rollingwood ...1,027
Roma-Los Saenz ...3,384
Roman Forest ...929
Roscoe ...1,628
Rosebud ...2,076
Rosenberg ...17,995
Rotan ...2,284
Round Rock ...11,812
Rowlett ...7,522
Royse City ...1,566
Rule ...1,015
Runge ...1,244
Rusk ...4,681
Sabinal ...1,827
Sachse ...1,640
Saginaw ...5,736
St. Jo ...1,071
San Angelo ...73,240

San Antonio ...785,410
San Augustine ...2,930
San Benito ...17,988
San Diego ...5,255
San Juan ...7,608
San Marcos ...23,420
San Saba ...2,336
Sanger ...2,574
Sansom Park Village ...3,921
Santa Anna ...1,535
Santa Fe ...5,413
Santa Rosa ...1,889
Savoy ...855
Schertz ...7,262
Schulenburg ...2,469
Seabrook ...4,670
Seadrift ...1,277
Seagoville ...7,304
Seagraves ...2,596
Sealy ...3,875
Seguin ...17,854
Seminole ...6,080
Seymour ...3,657
Shady Shores ...813
Shallowater ...1,932
Shamrock ...2,834
Shavano Park ...1,448
Shenandoah ...1,793
Shepherd ...1,674
Sherman ...30,413
Shiner ...2,213
Shoreacres ...1,260
Silsbee ...7,684
Silverton ...918
Sinton ...6,044
Skellytown ...899
Slaton ...6,804
Smithville ...3,470
Snyder ...12,705

Somerset ...1,102
Somerville ...1,814
Sonora ...3,856
Sour Lake ...1,807
South Houston ...13,293
South Padre Island ...791
Southlake ...2,808
Southside Place ...1,366
Spearman ...3,413
Spring Valley ...3,353
Springtown ...1,658
Spur ...1,690
Stafford ...4,755
Stamford ...4,542
Stanton ...2,314
Stephenville ...11,881
Sterling City ...915
Stinnett ...2,222
Stockdale ...1,265
Stratford ...1,917
Sudan ...1,091
Sugar Land ...8,826
Sulphur Springs ...12,804
Sundown ...1,511
Sunnyvale ...1,404
Sunray ...1,952
Sunset Valley ...773
Sweeny ...3,538
Sweetwater ...12,242
Taft ...3,686
Tahoka ...3,262
Talco ...751
Tatum ...1,339
Taylor ...10,619
Taylor Lake Village ...3,669
Teague ...3,390
Temple ...42,483
Tenaha ...1,005
Terrell ...13,225
Terrell Hills ...4,644

Texarkana ...31,271
Texas City ...41,403
The Colony ...11,586
Thorndale ...1,300
Three Rivers ...2,133
Throckmorton ...1,174
Timpson ...1,164
Tom Bean ...811
Tomball ...3,996
Tool ...1,591
Trinidad ...1,130
Trinity ...2,452
Troup ...1,911
Troy ...1,353
Tulia ...5,033
Tye ...1,394
Tyler ...70,508
Universal City ...10,720
University Park ...22,254
Uvalde ...14,178
Valley Mills ...1,236
Van ...1,881
Van Alstyne ...1,860
Van Horn ...2,772
Vega ...900
Vernon ...12,695
Victoria ...50,695
Vidor ...12,117
Waco ...101,261
Waelder ...942
Wake Village ...3,865
Waller ...1,241
Wallis ...1,138
Waskom ...1,821
Watauga ...10,284
Waxahachie ...14,624
Weatherford ...12,049
Webster ...2,168
Weimar ...2,096
Wellington ...3,043

Wells ...926
Weslaco ...19,331
West ...2,485
West Columbia ...4,109
West Lake Hills ...1,927
West Orange ...4,610
West Tawakoni ...840
West University Place ...12,010
Westworth ...3,651
Wharton ...9,033
Wheeler ...1,584
White Deer ...1,210
White Oak ...4,415
White Settlement ...13,508
Whitehouse ...2,172
Whitesboro ...3,197
Whitewright ...1,760
Whitney ...1,631
Wichita Falls ...94,201
Willis ...1,674
Wills Point ...2,631
Willow Park ...1,113
Wilmer ...2,367
Windcrest ...5,332
Wink ...1,182
Winnsboro ...3,458
Winters ...3,061
Wolfe City ...1,594
Wolfforth ...1,701
Woodsboro ...1,974
Woodville ...2,821
Woodway ...7,091
Wortham ...1,187
Wylie ...3,152
Yoakum ...6,148
Yorktown ...2,498
Zavala ...762

UTAH

Population 1,461,037

METROPOLITAN AREAS

Provo-Orem ...218,106
Salt Lake City-Ogden ...936,255

COUNTIES

Beaver ...4,378
Box Elder ...33,222
Cache ...57,176
Carbon ...22,179
Daggett ...769
Davis ...146,540
Duchesne ...12,565
Emery ...11,451
Garfield ...3,673
Grand ...8,241
Iron ...17,349
Juab ...5,530
Kane ...4,024
Millard ...8,970
Morgan ...4,917
Piute ...1,329
Rich ...2,100
Salt Lake ...619,066
San Juan ...12,253
Sanpete ...14,620
Sevier ...14,727
Summit ...10,198
Tooele ...26,033
Uintah ...20,506
Utah ...218,106
Wasatch ...8,523
Washington ...26,065
Wayne ...1,911
Weber ...144,616

CITIES AND TOWNS

Alpine ...2,649

Alta ...381
Altamont ...247
Alton ...75
Amalga ...323
American Fork ...12,417
Annabella ...463
Antimony ...94
Aurora ...874
Ballard ...558
Bear River City ...540
Beaver ...1,792
Bicknell ...296
Blanding ...3,118
Bluffdale ...1,300
Boulder ...113
Bountiful ...32,877
Brian Head ...77
Brigham City ...15,596
Cannonville ...134
Castle Dale ...1,910
Cedar City ...10,972
Cedar Fort ...269
Cedar Hills ...571
Centerfield ...653
Centerville ...8,069
Charleston ...320
Circleville ...445
Clarkston ...562
Clearfield ...17,982
Cleveland ...522
Clinton ...5,777
Coalville ...1,031
Corinne ...512
Cornish ...181
Delta ...1,930
Deweyville ...311
Draper ...5,530
Duchesne ...1,677
East Carbon ...1,942
East Layton ...3,531
Elk Ridge ...381
Elmo ...300
Elsinore ...612
Elwood ...481
Emery ...372

Enoch ...678
Enterprise ...905
Ephraim ...2,810
Escalante ...652
Eureka ...670
Fairview ...916
Farmington ...4,691
Fayette ...165
Ferron ...1,718
Fielding ...325
Fillmore ...2,083
Fountain Green ...578
Francis ...371
Fruit Heights ...2,728
Garden City ...259
Garland ...1,405
Genola ...630
Glendale ...237
Glenwood ...447
Goshen ...582
Grantsville ...4,419
Green River ...1,048
Gunnison ...1,255
Harrisville ...1,371
Hatch ...121
Heber ...4,362
Helper ...2,724
Henefer ...547
Henrieville ...167
Hiawatha ...249
Highland ...2,435
Hildale ...1,009
Hinckley ...464
Holden ...364
Honeyville ...915
Howell ...176
Huntington ...2,316
Huntsville ...577
Hurricane ...2,361
Hyde Park ...1,495
Hyrum ...3,952
Ivins ...600
Joseph ...217
Junction ...151
Kamas ...1,064

Kanab ...2,148
Kanarraville ...255
Kanosh ...435
Kaysville ...9,811
Kingston ...146
Koosharem ...183
Laketown ...271
La Verkin ...1,174
Layton ...22,862
Leamington ...113
Leeds ...218
Lehi ...6,848
Levan ...453
Lewiston ...1,438
Lindon ...2,796
Loa ...364
Logan ...26,844
Lynndyl ...90
Manila ...272
Manti ...2,080
Mantua ...484
Mapleton ...2,726
Marysvale ...359
Mayfield ...379
Meadow ...265
Mendon ...663
Midvale ...10,144
Midway ...1,194
Milford ...1,293
Millville ...848
Minersville ...552
Moab ...5,333
Mona ...536
Monroe ...1,476
Monticello ...1,929
Morgan City ...1,896
Moroni ...1,086
Mount Pleasant ...2,049
Murray ...25,750
Myton ...500
Nephi ...3,285
New Harmony ...117
Newton ...623
Nibley ...1,036
North Logan ...2,258

North Ogden ...9,309
North Salt Lake ...5,548
Oak City ...389
Oakley ...470
Ogden ...64,407
Ophir ...42
Orangeville ...1,309
Orderville ...423
Orem ...52,399
Panguitch ...1,343
Paradise ...542
Paragonah ...310
Park City ...2,823
Parowan ...1,836
Payson ...8,246
Perry ...1,084
Plain City ...2,379
Pleasant Grove ...10,669
Pleasant View ...3,983
Plymouth ...238
Portage ...196
Price ...9,086
Providence ...2,675
Provo ...73,907
Randolph ...659
Redmond ...619
Richfield ...5,482
Richmond ...1,705
River Heights ...1,211
Riverdale ...3,841
Riverton ...7,293
Roosevelt ...3,842
Roy ...19,694
Rush Valley ...356
St. George ...11,350
Salem ...2,233
Salina ...1,992
Salt Lake City ...163,033
Sandy City ...51,022
Santa Clara ...1,091
Santaquin ...2,175
Scipio ...257
Scofield ...105
Sigurd ...386
Smithfield ...4,993

Snowville ...237
Soldier Summit ...12
South Jordan ...7,492
South Ogden ...11,366
South Salt Lake ...10,561
South Weber ...1,575
Spanish Fork ...9,825
Spring City ...671
Springdale ...258
Springville ...12,101
Sterling ...199
Stockton ...437
Sunnyside ...611
Sunset ...5,733
Syracuse ...3,702
Tabiona ...152
Tooele ...14,335
Toquerville ...277
Torrey ...140
Tremonton ...3,464
Trenton ...447
Tropic ...338
Uintah ...439
Vernal ...6,600
Vernon ...181
Virgin ...169
Wales ...153
Wallsburg ...239
Washington ...3,092
Washington Terrace ...8,212
Wellington ...1,406
Wellsville ...1,952
Wendover ...1,099
West Bountiful ...3,556
West Jordan ...26,794
West Point ...2,170
Willard ...1,241
Woodland Hills ...60
Woodruff ...222
Woods Cross ...4,263
Yost ...67

VERMONT

Population 511,456

COUNTIES

Addison ...29,406
Bennington ...33,345
Caledonia ...25,808
Chittenden ...115,534
Essex ...6,313
Franklin ...34,788
Grand Isle ...4,613
Lamoille ...16,767
Orange ...22,739
Orleans ...23,440
Rutland ...58,347
Washington ...52,393
Windham ...36,933
Windsor ...51,030

CITIES, TOWNS, AND VILLAGES

Addison ...889▲

Albany ...174
(705▲)
Alburg ...496
(1,352▲)
Andover ...350▲
Arlington ...2,184▲
Athens ...250▲
Averill ...15▲
Bakersfield ...852▲
Baltimore ...181▲
Barnard ...790▲
Barnet ...1,338▲
Barre ...7,090▲
Barre ...9,824
(2,990▲)
Barton ...1,062
Bellows Falls ...3,456
Belvidere ...218▲
Bennington ...15,815▲
Benson ...739▲
Berkshire ...1,116
Berlin ...2,454▲
Bethel ...1,715▲
Bloomfield ...188▲

Bolton ...715▲
Bradford ...831
(2,191▲)
Braintree ...1,065▲
Brandon ...4,194▲
Brattleboro ...11,886▲
Bridgewater ...867▲
Bridport ...997▲
Brighton ...1,557▲
Bristol ...1,793
(3,293)
Brookfield ...959▲
Brookline ...310▲
Brownington ...708▲
Brunswick ...82▲
Buel's Gore ...9
Burke ...1,385▲
Burlington ...37,712
Cabot ...259
(958▲)
Calais ...1,207▲
Cambridge ...217
(2,019▲)
Canaan ...1,196▲

Castleton ...3,637▲
Cavendish ...1,355▲
Charleston ...851▲
Charlotte ...2,561▲
Chelsea ...1,091▲
Chester ...2,791▲
Chittenden ...927▲
Clarendon ...2,372▲
Colchester ...12,629▲
Concord ...1,125▲
Corinth ...904▲
Cornwall ...993▲
Coventry ...674▲
Craftsbury ...844▲
Danby ...992▲
Danville ...1,705▲
Derby ...4,222▲
Derby Center ...598
Derby Line ...874
Dorset ...1,648▲
Dover ...666▲
Dummerston ...1,574▲
Duxbury ...877▲
East Haven ...280▲

East Montpelier ...2,205▲
Eden ...612▲
Elmore ...421▲
Enosburg ...2,070▲
Enosburg Falls ...1,207
Essex ...14,392▲
Essex Junction ...7,033
Fair Haven ...2,819▲
Fairfax ...1,805▲
Fairfield ...1,493▲
Fairlee ...770▲
Fayston ...657▲
Ferdinand ...12▲
Ferrisburg ...2,117▲
Fletcher ...626▲
Franklin ...1,006▲
Georgia ...2,818▲
Glastenbury ...3▲
Glover ...843▲
Goshen ...163▲
Grafton ...604▲
Granby ...217▲
Grand Isle ...1,238▲
Granville ...288▲

Greensboro ...677▲
Groton ...667▲
Guildhall ...202▲
Guilford ...1,532▲
Halifax ...488▲
Hancock ...334▲
Hardwick ...1,476
(2,613▲)*
Hartford ...7,963▲
Hartland ...2,396▲
Highgate ...2,493▲
Hinesburg ...2,690▲
Holland ...473▲
Hubbardton ...490▲
Huntington ...1,161▲
Hyde Park ...475
(2,021▲)
Ira ...354▲
Irasburg ...870▲
Isle La Motte ...393▲
Jacksonville ...252
Jamaica ...681▲
Jay ...302▲
Jeffersonville ...491

Jericho 1,340 (3,575▲)
Johnson 1,393 (2,581▲)
Kirby 282▲
Landgrove 121▲
Leicester 803▲
Lemington 108▲
Lincoln 870▲
Londonderry 1,510▲
Lowell 573▲
Ludlow 1,352 (2,414▲)
Lunenburg 1,138▲
Lyndon 4,924▲
Lyndonville 1,401
Maidstone 100▲
Manchester 563 (3,261▲)
Marlboro 695▲
Marshfield 301 (1,267▲)
Mendon 1,056▲
Middlebury 7,574▲
Middlesex 1,235▲
Middletown Springs 603▲
Milton 1,411 (6,829▲)
Monkton 1,201▲
Montgomery 681▲
Montpelier 8,241
Moretown 1,221▲
Morgan 460▲
Morristown 4,448▲
Morrisville 2,074
Mount Holly 938▲
Mount Tabor 211▲
New Haven 1,217▲
Newark 280▲
Newbury 425 (1,699▲)
Newfane 119 (1,129▲)
Newport 1,319▲
Newport 4,756
North Bennington 1,685
North Hero 442▲
North Troy 717
North Westminster 310
Northfield 2,033 (5,435▲)
Norton 184▲
Norwich 2,398▲
Old Bennington 353
Orange 752▲
Orleans 983
Orwell 901▲
Panton 537▲
Pawlet 1,244▲
Peacham 531▲
Perkinsville 187
Peru 312▲
Pittsfield 396▲
Pittsford 666 (2,590▲)
Plainfield 599 (1,249▲)
Plymouth 405▲
Pomfret 856▲
Poultney 1,554 (3,196▲)
Pownal 3,269▲
Proctor 1,998▲
Proctorsville 481
Putney 1,850▲
Randolph 2,217 (4,689▲)
Reading 647▲
Readsboro 402 (638▲)
Richford 1,471 (2,206▲)
Richmond 865 (3,159▲)
Ripton 327▲
Rochester 1,054▲
Rockingham 5,538▲
Roxbury 452▲
Royalton 2,100▲
Rupert 605▲
Rutland 3,300▲
Rutland 18,436
Ryegate 1,000▲
St. Albans 3,555▲
St. Albans 7,308
St. George 677▲
St. Johnsbury 7,938▲
Salisbury 881▲
Sandgate 234▲
Saxtons River 593
Searsburg 72▲
Shaftsbury 3,001▲
Sharon 828▲
Sheffield 435▲
Shelburne 5,000▲
Sheldon 1,618▲
Sherburne 891▲
Shoreham 972▲
Shrewsbury 866▲
Somerset 2▲
South Burlington 10,679▲
South Hero 1,188▲
Springfield 10,190▲
Stamford 773▲
Stannard 142▲
Starksboro 1,336▲
Stockbridge 508▲
Stowe 531 (2,991▲)
Strafford 731▲
Stratton 122▲
Sudbury 380▲
Sunderland 768▲
Sutton 667▲
Swanton 2,520 (5,141▲)
Thetford 2,188▲
Tinmouth 406▲
Topsham 767▲
Townshend 849▲
Troy 1,498▲
Tunbridge 925▲
Underhill 2,172▲
Vergennes 2,273
Vernon 1,175▲
Vershire 442▲
Victory 56▲
Waitsfield 1,300▲
Walden 575▲
Wallingford 1,893▲
Waltham 394▲
Wardsboro 505▲
Warren 956▲
Washington 855▲
Waterbury 1,892 (4,465▲)
Waterford 882▲
Waterville 470▲
Weathersfield 2,534▲
Wells 815▲
Wells River 396
West Burke 338
West Fairlee 427▲
West Haven 253▲
West Rutland 2,351▲
West Windsor 763▲
Westfield 418▲
Westford 1,413▲
Westminster 319 (2,493▲)
Westmore 257▲
Weston 627▲
Weybridge 667▲
Wheelock 444▲
Whiting 379▲
Whitingham 1,043▲
Williamstown 2,284▲
Williston 3,843▲
Wilmington 1,808
Windham 223▲
Windsor 4,084▲
Winhall 327▲
Winooski 6,318
Wolcott 986▲
Woodbury 573▲
Woodford 314▲
Woodstock 1,178 (3,214▲)
Worcester 727▲

▲Entire town (township), including rural area.

VIRGINIA

Population 5,346,279

METROPOLITAN AREAS

Johnson City-Kingsport (Tenn.)-Bristol 433,638 (343,041 in Tenn.; 90,597 in Va.)
Lynchburg 153,260
Newport News-Hampton 364,449
Norfolk-Virginia Beach-Portsmouth 806,691 (795,602 in Va.; 11,089 in N.C.)
Petersburg-Colonial Heights-Hopewell 129,296
Richmond 632,015
Roanoke 224,548
Washington, D.C. 3,060,240 (1,316,875 in Md.; 1,105,714 in Va.; 637,651 in D.C.)

COUNTIES

Accomack 31,268
Albemarle 50,689
Alleghany 14,333
Amelia 8,405
Amherst 29,122
Appomattox 11,971
Arlington 152,599
Augusta 53,732
Bath 5,860
Bedford 34,927
Bland 6,349
Botetourt 23,270
Brunswick 15,632
Buchanan 37,989
Buckingham 11,751
Campbell 45,424
Caroline 17,904
Carroll 27,270
Charles City 6,692
Charlotte 12,266
Chesterfield 141,372
Clarke 9,965
Craig 3,948
Culpeper 22,620
Cumberland 7,881
Dickenson 19,806
Dinwiddie 22,602
Essex 8,864
Fairfax 596,901
Fauquier 35,889
Floyd 11,563
Fluvanna 10,244
Franklin 35,740
Frederick 34,150
Giles 17,810
Gloucester 20,107
Goochland 11,761
Grayson 16,579
Greene 7,625
Greensville 10,903
Halifax 30,418
Hanover 50,398
Henrico 180,735
Henry 57,654
Highland 2,937
Isle of Wight 21,603
James City 22,763
King and Queen 5,968
King George 10,543
King William 9,327
Lancaster 10,129
Lee 25,956
Loudoun 57,427
Louisa 17,825
Lunenburg 12,124
Madison 10,232
Mathews 7,995
Mecklenburg 29,444
Middlesex 7,719
Montgomery 63,516
Nelson 12,204
New Kent 8,781
Northampton 14,625
Northumberland 9,828
Nottoway 14,666
Orange 17,827
Page 19,401
Patrick 17,585
Pittsylvania 66,147
Powhatan 13,062
Prince Edward 16,456
Prince George 25,733
Prince William 144,703
Pulaski 35,229
Rappahannock 6,093
Richmond 6,952
Roanoke 72,945
Rockbridge 17,911
Rockingham 57,038
Russell 31,761
Scott 25,068
Shenandoah 27,559
Smyth 33,366
Southampton 18,731
Spotsylvania 34,435
Stafford 40,470
Surry 6,046
Sussex 10,874
Tazewell 50,511
Warren 21,200
Washington 46,487
Westmoreland 14,041
Wise 43,863
Wythe 25,522
York 35,463

CITIES AND TOWNS

Abingdon 4,318
Accomac 522
Alberta 394
Alexandria 103,217†
Altavista 3,849
Amherst 1,135
Appalachia 2,418
Appomattox 1,345
Ashland 4,640
Bedford 5,991†
Belle Haven 589
Berryville 1,752
Big Stone Gap 4,748
Blacksburg 30,638
Blackstone 3,624
Bloxom 407
Bluefield 5,946
Boones Mill 303
Bowling Green 665
Boyce 401
Boydton 486
Boykins 791
Branchville 174
Bridgewater 3,289
Bristol 19,042†
Broadway 1,234
Brodnax 492
Brookneal 1,454
Buchanan 1,205
Buena Vista 6,717†
Burkeville 606
Cape Charles 1,512
Capron 238
Cedar Bluff 1,550
Charlotte Courthouse 568
Charlottesville 45,010†
Chase City 2,749
Chatham 1,390
Cheriton 695
Chesapeake 114,226†
Chilhowie 1,269
Chincoteague 1,607
Christiansburg 10,345
Claremont 380
Clarksville 1,468
Cleveland 360
Clifton 170
Clifton Forge 5,046†
Clinchport 89
Clintwood 1,369
Clover 215
Coeburn 2,625
Colonial Beach 2,474
Colonial Heights 16,509†
Columbia 111
Courtland 976
Covington 9,063†
Craigsville 845
Crewe 2,325
Culpeper 6,621
Damascus 1,330
Danville 45,642†
Dayton 1,017
Dendron 307
Dillwyn 637
Drakes Branch 617
Dublin 2,368
Duffield 148
Dumfries 3,214
Dungannon 339
Eastville 238
Edinburg 752
Elkton 1,520
Emporia 4,840†
Exmore 1,300
Fairfax 19,390†
Falls Church 9,515†
Farmville 6,067
Fincastle 282
Floyd 411
Franklin 7,308†
Fredericksburg 15,322†
Fries 758
Front Royal 11,126
Galax 6,524†
Gate City 2,494
Glade Spring 1,722
Glasgow 1,259
Glen Lyn 235
Gordonsville 1,175
Goshen 134
Gretna 1,255
Grottoes 1,369
Grundy 1,699
Halifax 772
Hallwood 243
Hamilton 598
Hampton 122,617†
Harrisonburg 19,671†
Haymarket 230
Haysi 371
Herndon 11,449
Hillsboro 94
Hillsville 2,123
Honaker 1,475
Hopewell 23,397†
Hurt 1,481
Independence 1,112
Iron Gate 620
Irvington 567
Ivor 403
Jarratt 614
Jonesville 874
Keller 236
Kenbridge 1,352
Keysville 704
Kilmarnock 945
La Crosse 734
Lawrenceville 1,484
Lebanon 3,206
Leesburg 8,357
Lexington 7,292†
Louisa 932
Lovettsville 613
Luray 3,584
Lynchburg 66,743†
Madison 267
Manassas 15,438†
Manassas Park 6,524†
Marion 7,029
Martinsville 18,149†
McKenney 473
Melfa 391
Middleburg 619
Middletown 841
Mineral 399
Monterey 247
Montross 456
Mount Crawford 315
Mount Jackson 1,419
Narrows 2,516
Nassawadox 630
New Castle 213
New Market 1,118
Newport News 144,903†
Newsoms 368
Nickelsville 464
Norfolk 266,979†
Norton 4,757†
Occoquan 512
Onancock 1,461
Onley 526
Orange 2,631
Painter 321
Pamplin 273
Parksley 979
Pearisburg 2,128
Pembroke 1,302
Pennington Gap 1,716
Petersburg 41,055†
Phenix 250
Plains, The 382
Pocahontas 708
Poquoson 8,726†
Port Royal 291
Portsmouth 104,577†
Pound 1,086
Pulaski 10,106
Purcellville 1,567
Quantico 621
Radford 13,225†
Remington 425
Rich Creek 746
Richlands 5,796
Richmond 219,214†
Ridgeway 858
Roanoke 100,427†
Rocky Mount 4,198
Round Hill 510
Rural Retreat 1,083
St. Charles 241
St. Paul 973
Salem 23,958†
Saltville 2,376
Saxis 415
Scottsburg 335
Scottsville 250
Shenandoah 1,861
Smithfield 3,649
South Boston 7,093†
South Hill 4,347
Stanardsville 284
Stanley 1,204
Staunton 21,857†
Stephens City 1,179
Stony Creek 329
Strasburg 2,311
Stuart 1,131
Suffolk 47,621†
Surry 237
Tangier 771
Tappahannock 1,821
Tazewell 4,468
Timberville 1,510
Toms Brook 226
Troutdale 248
Troutville 496
Urbanna 518
Victoria 2,004
Vienna 15,469
Vinton 8,027
Virgilina 212
Virginia Beach 262,199†
Wachapreague 404
Wakefield 1,355
Warrenton 3,907
Warsaw 771
Washington 247
Waverly 2,284
Waynesboro 15,329†
Weber City 1,543
West Point 2,726
White Stone 409
Williamsburg 9,870†
Winchester 20,217†
Windsor 985
Wise 3,894
Woodstock 2,627
Wytheville 7,135

†Independent city, not part of any county.

WASHINGTON

Population 4,130,163

METROPOLITAN AREAS

Portland (Ore.) 1,242,187 (1,049,960 in Ore.; 192,227 in Wash.)
Richland-Kennewick-Pasco 144,469
Seattle-Everett 1,606,765
Spokane 341,835
Tacoma 485,643
Yakima 172,508

COUNTIES

Adams 13,267
Asotin 16,823
Benton 109,444
Chelan 45,061
Clallam 51,648
Clark 192,227
Columbia 4,057
Cowlitz 79,548
Douglas 22,144
Ferry 5,811
Franklin 35,025
Garfield 2,468
Grant 48,522
Grays Harbor 66,314
Island 44,048
Jefferson 15,965
King 1,269,749
Kitsap 146,609
Kittitas 24,877
Klickitat 15,822
Lewis 55,279
Lincoln 9,604
Mason 31,184
Okanogan 30,639
Pacific 17,237
Pend Oreille 8,580
Pierce 485,643
San Juan 7,838
Skagit 64,138
Skamania 7,919
Snohomish 337,016
Spokane 341,835
Stevens 28,979
Thurston 124,264
Wahkiakum 3,832
Walla Walla 47,435
Whatcom 106,701
Whitman 40,103
Yakima 172,508

CITIES AND TOWNS

Aberdeen 18,739
Airway Heights 1,730
Albion 631
Algona 1,467
Almira 330
Anacortes 9,013
Arlington 3,282
Asotin 943
Auburn 26,417
Battle Ground 2,774
Beaux Arts 328
Bellevue 73,903
Bellingham 45,794
Benton City 1,980
Bingen 644
Black Diamond 1,170
Blaine 2,363
Bonney Lake 5,328
Bothell 7,943
Bremerton 36,208
Brewster 1,337
Bridgeport 1,174
Brier 2,915
Buckley 3,143
Bucoda 519
Burlington 3,894
Camas 5,681
Carbonado 456
Carnation 913
Cashmere 2,240
Castle Rock 2,162
Cathlamet 635
Centralia 10,809
Chehalis 6,100
Chelan 2,802
Cheney 7,630
Chewelah 1,888
Clarkston 6,903
Cle Elum 1,773
Clyde Hill 3,229
Colfax 2,780
College Place 5,771
Colton 307

Colville 4,510
Conconully 157
Concrete 592
Connell 1,981
Cosmopolis 1,575
Coulee City 510
Coulee Dam 1,412
Coupeville 1,006
Creston 309
Cusick 246
Darrington 1,064
Davenport 1,559
Dayton 2,565
Deer Park 2,140
Des Moines 7,378
Dupont 559
Duvall 729
East Wenatchee 1,640
Eatonville 998
Edmonds 27,526
Electric City 927
Ellensburg 11,752
Elma 2,720
Elmer City 312
Endicott 290
Entiat 445
Enumclaw 5,427
Ephrata 5,359
Everett 54,413
Everson 898
Fairfield 582
Farmington 176
Ferndale 3,855
Fife 1,823
Fircrest 5,477
Forks 3,060
Friday Harbor 1,200
Garfield 599
George 261
Gig Harbor 2,429
Gold Bar 794
Goldendale 3,414
Grand Coulee 1,180
Grandview 5,615
Granger 1,812
Granite Falls 911
Hamilton 268
Harrah 343
Harrington 507
Hartline 165
Hatton 81
Hoquiam 9,719
Hunts Point 480
Ilwaco 604
Index 147
Ione 594
Issaquah 5,536
Kahlotus 203
Kalama 1,216
Kelso 11,129
Kennewick 34,397
Kent 23,152
Kettle Falls 1,087
Kirkland 18,779
Kittitas 782
Krupp 83
La Center 439
Lacey 13,940
La Conner 633
La Crosse 373
Lake Forest Park 2,485
Lake Stevens 1,660
Lamont 101
Langley 650
Latah 155
Leavenworth 1,522
Lind 567
Long Beach 1,199
Longview 31,052
Lyman 285
Lynden 4,022
Lynnwood 21,937
Mabton 1,248
Malden 200
Mansfield 315
Marcus 174
Marysville 5,080
Mattawa 299
McCleary 1,419
Medical Lake 3,600
Medina 3,220
Mercer Island 21,522
Mesa 278
Metaline 190
Metaline Falls 296
Millwood 1,717
Milton 3,162
Monroe 2,869
Montesano 3,247
Morton 1,264
Moses Lake 10,629
Mossyrock 463
Mount Vernon 13,009
Mountlake Terrace 16,534
Moxee City 687
Mukilteo 1,426
Naches 644
Napavine 611
Nespelem 284
Newport 1,665
Nooksack 429
Normandy Park 4,268
North Bend 1,701
North Bonneville 394
Northport 368
Oak Harbor 12,271
Oakesdale 444
Oakville 537
Ocean Shores 1,692
Odessa 1,009
Okanogan 2,302
Olympia 27,447
Omak 4,007
Oroville 1,483
Orting 1,763
Othello 4,454
Pacific 2,261
Palouse 1,005
Pasco 17,944
Pateros 555
Pe Ell 617
Pomeroy 1,716
Port Angeles 17,311
Port Orchard 4,787
Port Townsend 6,067
Poulsbo 3,453
Prescott 341
Prosser 3,896
Pullman 23,579
Puyallup 18,251
Quincy 3,525
Rainier 891
Raymond 2,991
Reardan 498
Redmond 23,318
Renton 30,612
Republic 1,018
Richland 33,578
Ridgefield 1,062
Ritzville 1,800
Riverside 243
Rock Island 491
Rockford 442
Rosalia 572
Roslyn 938
Roy 417
Royal City 676
Ruston 612
St. John 529
Seattle 493,846
Sedro-Woolley 6,110
Selah 4,372
Sequim 3,013
Shelton 7,629
Skykomish 209
Snohomish 5,294
Snoqualmie 1,370
Soap Lake 1,196
South Bend 1,686
South Cle Elum 449
South Prairie 202
Spangle 276
Spokane 171,300
Sprague 473
Springdale 281
Stanwood 2,744
Starbuck 198
Steilacoom 4,886
Stevenson 1,172
Sultan 1,578
Sumas 712
Sumner 4,936
Sunnyside 9,225
Tacoma 158,501
Tekoa 854
Tenino 1,280
Tieton 528
Toledo 637
Tonasket 985
Toppenish 6,517
Tukwila 3,578
Tumwater 6,705
Twisp 911
Union Gap 3,184
Uniontown 286
Vader 406
Vancouver 42,834
Waitsburg 1,035
Walla Walla 25,618
Wapato 3,307
Warden 1,479
Washougal 3,834
Washtucna 266
Waterville 908
Waverly 99
Wenatchee 17,257
West Richland 2,938
Westport 1,954
White Salmon 1,853
Wilbur 1,122
Wilkeson 321
Wilson Creek 222
Winlock 1,052
Winslow 2,196
Winthrop 413
Woodland 2,341
Woodway 832
Yacolt 544
Yakima 49,826
Yarrow Point 1,064
Yelm 1,294
Zillah 1,599

WEST VIRGINIA

Population 1,949,644

METROPOLITAN AREAS

Charleston 269,595
Huntington-Ashland (Ky.) 311,350 (152,856 in W. Va.; 63,849 in O.; 94,645 in Ky.)
Parkersburg-Marietta (O.) 162,836 (98,570 in W. Va.; 64,266 in O.)
Weirton-Steubenville (O.) 163,099 (91,564 in O.; 71,535 in W. Va.)
Wheeling 185,566 (102,997 in W. Va.; 82,569 in O.)

COUNTIES

Barbour 16,639
Berkeley 46,775
Boone 30,447
Braxton 13,894
Brooke 31,117
Cabell 106,835
Calhoun 8,250
Clay 11,265
Doddridge 7,433
Fayette 57,863
Gilmer 8,334
Grant 10,210
Greenbrier 37,665
Hampshire 14,867
Hancock 40,418
Hardy 10,030
Harrison 77,710
Jackson 25,794
Jefferson 30,302
Kanawha 231,414
Lewis 18,813
Lincoln 23,675
Logan 50,679
Marion 65,789
Marshall 41,608
Mason 27,045
McDowell 49,899
Mercer 73,942
Mineral 27,234
Mingo 37,336
Monongalia 75,024
Monroe 12,873
Morgan 10,711
Nicholas 28,126
Ohio 61,389
Pendleton 7,910
Pleasants 8,236
Pocahontas 9,919
Preston 30,460
Putnam 38,181
Raleigh 86,821
Randolph 28,734
Ritchie 11,442
Roane 15,952
Summers 15,875
Taylor 16,584
Tucker 8,675
Tyler 11,320
Upshur 23,427
Wayne 46,021
Webster 12,245
Wetzel 21,874
Wirt 4,922
Wood 93,648
Wyoming 35,993

CITIES, TOWNS, AND VILLAGES

Albright 357
Alderson 1,375
Anawalt 652
Anmoore 865
Ansted 1,952
Athens 1,147
Auburn 116
Bancroft 528
Barboursville 2,871
Barrackville 1,815
Bayard 540
Beckley 20,492
Beech Bottom 507
Belington 2,038
Belle 1,621
Belmont 887
Benwood 1,994
Berkeley Springs 789
Bethany 1,336
Bethlehem 2,677
Beverly 475
Blacksville 248
Bluefield 16,060
Bolivar 672
Bramwell 989
Brandonville 92
Bridgeport 6,604
Bruceton Mills 296
Buckhannon 6,820
Buffalo 1,034
Burnsville 531
Cairo 428
Camden-on-Gauley 236
Cameron 1,474
Capon Bridge 191
Cass 148
Cedar Grove 1,479
Ceredo 2,255
Chapmanville 1,164
Charles Town 2,857
Charleston 63,968
Chesapeake 2,364
Chester 3,297
Clarksburg 22,371
Clay 940
Clearview 740
Clendenin 1,373
Cowen 723
Danville 727
Davis 979
Davy 882
Delbarton 981
Dunbar 9,285
Durbin 379
East Bank 1,155
Eleanor 1,282
Elizabeth 856
Elk Garden 291
Elkins 8,536
Ellenboro 357
Fairmont 23,863
Fairview 759
Falling Spring 240
Farmington 583
Fayetteville 2,366
Flatwoods 405
Flemington 452
Follansbee 3,994
Fort Gay 886
Franklin 780
Friendly 242
Gary 2,233
Gassaway 1,225
Gauley Bridge 1,177
Gilbert 757
Glasgow 1,031
Glen Dale 1,875
Glenville 2,155
Grafton 6,845
Grant Town 987
Grantsville 788
Granville 992
Hambleton 403
Hamlin 1,219
Handley 633
Harman 181
Harpers Ferry 361
Harrisville 1,673
Hartford 556
Hedgesville 217
Henderson 604
Hendricks 390
Hillsboro 276
Hinton 4,622
Hundred 485
Huntington 63,684
Hurricane 3,751
Huttonsville 242
Iaeger 833
Jane Lew 406
Junior 591
Kenova 4,454
Kermit 705
Keyser 6,569
Keystone 902
Kimball 871
Kingwood 2,877
Leon 228
Lester 626
Lewisburg 3,065
Littleton 335
Logan 3,029
Lost Creek 604
Lumberport 939
Mabscott 1,668
Madison 3,228
Man 1,333
Mannington 3,036
Marlinton 1,352
Marmet 2,196
Martinsburg 13,063
Mason 1,432
Masontown 1,052
Matewan 822
Matoaka 613
McMechen 2,402
Meadow Bridge 530
Middlebourne 941
Mill Creek 801
Milton 2,178
Mitchell Heights 342
Monongah 1,132
Montgomery 3,104
Montrose 129
Moorefield 2,257
Morgantown 27,605
Moundsville 12,419
Mount Hope 1,849
Mullens 2,919
New Cumberland 1,752
New Haven 1,723
New Martinsville 7,109
Newburg 418
Nitro 8,074
North Hills 940
Northfork 660
Nutter Fort 2,078
Oak Hill 7,120
Oakvale 208
Oceana 2,143
Osage 285
Paden City 3,671
Parkersburg 39,967
Parsons 1,937
Paw Paw 644
Pax 274
Pennsboro 1,652
Petersburg 2,084
Peterstown 648
Philippi 3,194
Piedmont 1,491
Pine Grove 767
Pineville 1,140
Poca 1,142
Point Pleasant 5,682
Pratt 821
Princeton 7,493
Pullman 196
Quinwood 460
Rainelle 1,983
Ranson 2,471
Ravenswood 4,126
Reedsville 564
Reedy 338
Rhodell 472
Richwood 3,568
Ridgeley 994
Ripley 3,464
Rivesville 1,327
Romney 2,094
Ronceverte 2,312
Rowlesburg 966
Rupert 1,276
St. Albans 12,402
St. Marys 2,219
Salem 2,706
Sand Fork 280
Shepherdstown 1,791
Shinnston 3,059
Sistersville 2,367
Smithers 1,482
Smithfield 278
Sophia 1,216
South Charleston 15,968
Spencer 2,799
Star City 1,464
Stonewood 2,058
Summersville 2,972
Sutton 1,192
Sylvester 256
Terra Alta 1,946
Thomas 747
Thurmond 67
Triadelphia 1,461
Tunnelton 510
Union 743
Valley Grove 597
Vienna 11,618
War 2,158
Wardensville 241
Wayne 1,495
Webster Springs 939
Weirton 24,736
Welch 3,885
Wellsburg 3,963
West Hamlin 643
West Liberty 744
West Logan 630
West Milford 510
West Union 1,090
Weston 6,250
Westover 4,884
Wheeling 43,070
White Sulphur Springs 3,371
Whitesville 689
Williamson 5,219
Williamstown 3,095
Winfield 329
Womelsdorf 306
Worthington 329

WISCONSIN

Population 4,705,335

METROPOLITAN AREAS

Appleton-Oshkosh 291,325
Eau Claire 130,507
Green Bay 175,280
Kenosha 123,137
La Crosse 91,056
Madison 323,545
Milwaukee 1,397,143
Minneapolis-St. Paul (Minn.) 2,114,256 (2,070,384 in Minn.; 43,872 in Wis.)
Racine 173,132
Superior-Duluth (Minn.) 266,650 (222,229 in Minn.; 44,421 in Wis.)

COUNTIES

Adams 13,457
Ashland 16,783
Barron 38,730
Bayfield 13,822
Brown 175,280
Buffalo 14,309
Burnett 12,340
Calumet 30,867
Chippewa 51,702
Clark 32,910
Columbia 43,222
Crawford 16,556
Dane 323,545
Dodge 74,747
Door 25,029
Douglas 44,421
Dunn 34,314
Eau Claire 78,805
Florence 4,172
Fond du Lac 88,952
Forest 9,044
Grant 51,736
Green 30,012
Green Lake 18,370
Iowa 19,802
Iron 6,730
Jackson 16,831
Jefferson 66,152
Juneau 21,039
Kenosha 123,137
Kewaunee 19,539
La Crosse 91,056
Lafayette 17,412
Langlade 19,978
Lincoln 26,311
Manitowoc 82,918
Marathon 111,270
Marinette 39,314
Marquette 11,672
Menominee 3,373
Milwaukee 964,988
Monroe 35,074
Oconto 28,947
Oneida 31,216
Outagamie 128,726
Ozaukee 66,981
Pepin 7,477
Pierce 31,149
Polk 32,351
Portage 57,420
Price 15,788
Racine 173,132
Richland 17,476
Rock 139,420
Rusk 15,589
St. Croix 43,872
Sauk 43,469
Sawyer 12,843
Shawano 35,928
Sheboygan 100,935
Taylor 18,817
Trempealeau 26,158
Vernon 25,642
Vilas 16,535
Walworth 71,507
Washburn 13,174
Washington 84,848
Waukesha 280,326
Waupaca 42,831
Waushara 18,526
Winnebago 131,732
Wood 72,799

CITIES AND VILLAGES

Abbotsford 1,901
Adams 1,744

Adell 545
Albany 1,051
Algoma 3,656
Alma 848
Alma Center 454
Almena 526
Almond 477
Altoona 4,393
Amery 2,404
Amherst 701
Amherst Junction 225
Aniwa 273
Antigo 8,653
Appleton 59,032
Arcadia 2,109
Arena 451
Argyle 720
Arlington 440
Arpin 361
Ashland 9,115
Ashwaubenon 14,486
Athens 988
Auburndale 641
Augusta 1,560
Avoca 505
Bagley 317
Baldwin 1,620
Balsam Lake 749
Bangor 1,012
Baraboo 8,081
Barneveld 579
Barron 2,595
Bay City 543
Bayfield 778
Bayside 4,724
Bear Creek 454
Beaver Dam 14,149
Belgium 892
Bell Center 124
Belleville 1,302
Belmont 826
Beloit 35,207
Benton 983
Berlin 5,478
Big Bend 1,345
Big Falls 107
Birchwood 437
Birnamwood 688
Biron 698
Black Creek 1,097
Black Earth 1,145
Black River Falls 3,434
Blair 1,142
Blanchardville 803
Bloomer 3,342
Bloomington 743
Blue Mounds 387
Blue River 412
Boaz 161
Bonduel 1,160
Boscobel 2,662
Bowler 339
Boyceville 862
Boyd 660
Brandon 862
Brillion 2,907
Brodhead 3,153
Brokaw 298
Brookfield 34,035
Brooklyn 627
Brown Deer 12,921
Browntown 284
Bruce 905
Buffalo 894
Burlington 8,385
Butler 2,059
Butternut 438
Cable 227
Cadott 1,247
Cambria 680
Cambridge 844
Cameron 1,115
Camp Douglas 589
Campbellsport 1,740
Cascade 615
Casco 484
Cashton 827
Cassville 1,270
Catawba 205
Cazenovia 259
Cecil 445
Cedar Grove 1,420
Cedarburg 9,005
Centuria 711
Chaseburg 279
Chenequa 532
Chetek 1,931
Chilton 2,965
Chippewa Falls 11,845
Clayton 425
Clear Lake 899
Cleveland 1,270
Clinton 1,751
Clintonville 4,567
Clyman 317
Cobb 409
Cochrane 512
Colby 1,496
Coleman 852
Colfax 1,149
Coloma 367
Columbus 4,049
Combined Locks 2,573
Conrath 86
Coon Valley 758
Cornell 1,583
Cottage Grove 888
Couderay 114
Crandon 1,969
Crivitz 1,041
Cross Plains 2,156
Cuba City 2,129
Cudahy 19,547
Cumberland 1,983
Curtiss 127
Dallas 477
Dane 518
Darien 1,152
Darlington 2,300
Deer Park 232
Deerfield 1,466
De Forest 3,367
Delafield 4,083
Delavan 5,684
Denmark 1,475
De Pere 14,892
De Soto 318
Dickeyville 1,156
Dodgeville 3,458
Dorchester 613
Dousman 1,153
Downing 242
Doylestown 294
Dresser 670
Durand 2,047
Eagle 1,008
Eagle River 1,326
East Troy 2,385
Eastman 371
Eau Claire 51,509
Eden 534
Edgar 1,194
Edgerton 4,335
Egg Harbor 238
Eland 230
Elderon 191
Eleva 593
Elk Mound 737
Elkhart Lake 1,054
Elkhorn 4,605
Ellsworth 2,143
Elm Grove 6,735
Elmwood 885
Elmwood Park 483
Elroy 1,504
Embarrass 496
Endeavor 335
Ephraim 319
Ettrick 462
Evansville 2,835
Exeland 219
Fairchild 577
Fairwater 298
Fall Creek 1,148
Fall River 850
Fennimore 2,212
Fenwood 165
Ferryville 227
Fond du Lac 35,863
Fontana on Geneva Lake 1,764
Footville 794
Forestville 455
Fort Atkinson 9,785
Fountain City 963
Fox Lake 1,373
Fox Point 7,649
Francis Creek 538
Franklin 16,871
Frederic 1,039
Fredonia 1,437
Fremont 510
Friendship 744
Friesland 267
Galesville 1,239
Gays Mills 627
Genoa 283
Genoa City 1,202
Germantown 10,729
Gillett 1,356
Gilman 436
Glen Flora 83
Glenbeulah 423
Glendale 13,882
Glenwood City 950
Grafton 8,381
Granton 399
Grantsburg 1,153
Gratiot 280
Green Bay 87,899
Green Lake 1,208
Greendale 16,928
Greenfield 31,467
Greenwood 1,124
Gresham 534
Hales Corners 7,110
Hammond 991
Hancock 419
Hartford 7,046
Hartland 5,559
Hatley 300
Haugen 251
Hawkins 407
Hayward 1,698
Hazel Green 1,282
Hewitt 470
Highland 860
Hilbert 1,176
Hillsboro 1,263
Hixton 364
Hollandale 271
Holmen 2,411
Horicon 3,584
Hortonville 2,016
Howard 8,240
Howards Grove 1,838
Hudson 5,434
Hurley 2,015
Hustisford 874
Hustler 170
Independence 1,180
Ingram 61
Iola 957
Iron Ridge 766
Ironton 206
Jackson 1,817
Janesville 51,071
Jefferson 5,647
Johnson Creek 1,136
Junction City 523
Juneau 2,045
Kaukauna 11,310
Kekoskee 224
Kellnersville 369
Kendall 486
Kennan 194
Kenosha 77,685
Kewaskum 2,381
Kewaunee 2,801
Kiel 3,083
Kimberly 5,881
Kingston 328
Knapp 419
Kohler 1,651
Lac La Belle 289
La Crosse 48,347
Ladysmith 3,826
La Farge 746
Lake Delton 1,158
Lake Geneva 5,607
Lake Mills 3,670
Lake Nebagamon 780
Lancaster 4,076
Lannon 987
La Valle 412
Lena 585
Lime Ridge 191
Linden 395
Little Chute 7,907
Livingston 642
Lodi 1,959
Loganville 239
Lohrville 336
Lomira 1,446
Lone Rock 577
Lowell 326
Loyal 1,252
Lublin 142
Luck 997
Luxemburg 1,040
Lyndon Station 375
Lynxville 174
Madison 170,616
Maiden Rock 172
Manawa 1,205
Manitowoc 32,547
Maple Bluff 1,351
Marathon City 1,552
Maribel 363
Marinette 11,965
Marion 1,348
Markesan 1,446
Marquette 204
Marshall 2,363
Marshfield 18,290
Mason 102
Mattoon 382
Mauston 3,284
Mayville 4,338
Mazomanie 1,248
McFarland 3,783
Medford 4,010
Mellen 1,046
Melrose 507
Melvina 117
Menasha 14,728
Menomonee Falls 27,845
Menomonie 12,769
Mequon 16,193
Merrill 9,578
Merrillan 587
Merrimac 365
Merton 1,045
Middleton 11,779
Milladore 250
Milltown 732
Milton 4,092
Milwaukee 636,212
Mineral Point 2,259
Minong 557
Mishicot 1,503
Mondovi 2,545
Monona 8,809
Monroe 10,027
Montello 1,273
Montfort 616
Monticello 1,021
Montreal 887
Mosinee 3,015
Mount Calvary 585
Mount Hope 197
Mount Horeb 3,251
Mount Sterling 223
Mukwonago 4,014
Muscoda 1,331
Muskego 15,277
Nashotah 513
Necedah 773
Neenah 23,272
Neillsville 2,780
Nekoosa 2,519
Nelson 389
Nelsonville 199
Neosho 575
Neshkoro 386
New Auburn 466
New Berlin 30,529
New Glarus 1,763
New Holstein 3,412
New Lisbon 1,390
New London 6,210
New Richmond 4,306
Newburg 783
Niagara 2,079
Nichols 267
North Bay 219
North Fond du Lac 3,844
North Freedom 616
North Hudson 2,218
North Prairie 938
Norwalk 517
Oak Creek 16,932
Oakfield 990
Oconomowoc 9,909
Oconomowoc Lake 524
Oconto 4,505
Oconto Falls 2,500
Ogdensburg 214
Oliver 253
Omro 2,763
Onalaska 9,249
Ontario 398
Oostburg 1,647
Oregon 3,876
Orfordville 1,143
Osceola 1,581
Oshkosh 49,678
Osseo 1,474
Owen 998
Oxford 432
Paddock Lake 2,207
Palmyra 1,515
Pardeeville 1,594
Park Falls 3,192
Park Ridge 643
Patch Grove 259
Pepin 890
Peshtigo 2,807
Pewaukee 4,637
Phillips 1,522
Pigeon Falls 338
Pittsville 810
Plain 676
Plainfield 813
Platteville 9,580
Plover 5,310
Plum City 505
Plymouth 6,027
Poplar 569
Port Edwards 2,077
Port Washington 8,612
Portage 7,896
Potosi 736
Pound 407
Poynette 1,447
Prairie du Chien 5,859
Prairie du Sac 2,145
Prairie Farm 387
Prentice 605
Prescott 2,654
Princeton 1,479
Pulaski 1,875
Racine 85,725
Radisson 280
Randolph 1,691
Random Lake 1,287
Readstown 396
Redgranite 976
Reedsburg 5,038
Reedsville 1,134
Reeseville 649
Rewey 233
Rhinelander 7,873
Rib Lake 945
Rice Lake 7,691
Richland Center 4,923
Ridgeland 300
Ridgeway 503
Rio 785
Ripon 7,111
River Falls 9,036
River Hills 1,642
Roberts 833
Rochester 746
Rock Springs 426
Rockdale 200
Rockland 383
Rosendale 725
Rosholt 520
Rothschild 3,338
Rudolph 392
St. Cloud 560
St. Croix Falls 1,497
St. Francis 10,066
St. Nazianz 738
Sauk City 2,703
Saukville 3,494
Scandinavia 292
Schofield 2,226
Seymour 2,530
Sharon 1,280
Shawano 7,013
Sheboygan 48,085
Sheboygan Falls 5,253
Sheldon 292
Shell Lake 1,135
Sherwood 372
Shiocton 805
Shorewood 14,327
Shorewood Hills 1,837
Shullsburg 1,484
Silver Lake 1,598
Siren 896
Sister Bay 564
Slinger 1,612
Soldiers Grove 622
Solon Springs 590
Somerset 860
South Milwaukee 21,069
South Wayne 495
Sparta 6,934
Spencer 1,754
Spooner 2,365
Spring Green 1,265
Spring Valley 987
Stanley 2,095
Star Prairie 420
Stetsonville 487
Steuben 175
Stevens Point 22,970
Stockbridge 567
Stockholm 104
Stoddard 762
Stoughton 7,589
Stratford 1,385
Strum 944
Sturgeon Bay 8,847
Sturtevant 4,130
Sullivan 434
Sun Prairie 12,931
Superior 29,571
Superior 580
Suring 581
Sussex 3,482
Taylor 411
Tennyson 476
Theresa 766
Thiensville 3,341
Thorp 1,635
Tigerton 865
Tomah 7,204
Tomahawk 3,527
Tony 146
Trempealeau 956
Turtle Lake 762
Twin Lakes 3,474
Two Rivers 13,354
Union Center 216
Union Grove 3,517
Unity 418
Valders 973
Verona 3,336
Vesper 554
Viola 696
Viroqua 3,716
Waldo 416
Wales 1,992
Walworth 1,607
Warrens 300
Washburn 2,080
Waterford 2,051
Waterloo 2,393
Watertown 18,113
Waukesha 50,319
Waunakee 3,866
Waupaca 4,472
Waupun 8,132
Wausau 32,426
Wausaukee 648
Wautoma 1,629
Wauwatosa 51,308
Wauzeka 580
Webster 610
West Allis 63,982
West Baraboo 846
West Bend 21,484
West Milwaukee 3,535
West Salem 3,276
Westby 1,797
Westfield 1,033
Weyauwega 1,549
Weyerhaeuser 313
Wheeler 231
White Lake 309
Whitefish Bay 14,930
Whitehall 1,530
Whitelaw 649
Whitewater 11,520
Whiting 2,050
Wild Rose 741
Williams Bay 1,763
Wilson 155
Wilton 465
Wind Point 1,695
Winneconne 1,935
Winter 376
Wisconsin Dells 2,521
Wisconsin Rapids 17,995
Withee 509
Wittenberg 997
Wonewoc 842
Woodman 116
Woodville 725
Wrightstown 1,169
Wyeville 163
Wyocena 548
Yuba 72

WYOMING

Population 470,816

COUNTIES

Albany 29,062
Big Horn 11,896
Campbell 24,367
Carbon 21,896
Converse 14,069
Crook 5,308
Fremont 40,251
Goshen 12,040
Hot Springs 5,710
Johnson 6,700
Laramie 68,649
Lincoln 12,177
Natrona 71,856
Niobrara 2,924
Park 21,639
Platte 11,975
Sheridan 25,048
Sublette 4,548
Sweetwater 41,723
Teton 9,355
Uinta 13,021
Washakie 9,496
Weston 7,106

CITIES AND TOWNS

Afton 1,481
Albin 128
Baggs 433
Basin 1,349
Big Piney 530
Buffalo 3,799
Burns 268
Byron 633
Casper 51,016
Cheyenne 47,283
Chugwater 282
Clearmont 191
Cody 6,790
Cokeville 515
Cowley 455
Dayton 701
Deaver 178
Diamondville 1,000
Dixon 82
Douglas 6,030
Dubois 1,067
East Thermopolis 359
Edgerton 510
Elk Mountain 338
Encampment 611
Evanston 6,421
Evansville 2,652
Fort Laramie 356
Frannie 138
Gillette 12,134
Glendo 367
Glenrock 2,736
Granger 177
Green River 12,807
Greybull 2,277
Guernsey 1,512
Hanna 2,288
Hartville 149
Hudson 514
Hulett 291
Jackson 4,511
Kaycee 271
Kemmerer 3,273
Kirby 129
La Barge 302
La Grange 232
Lander 9,126
Laramie 24,410
Lingle 475
Lost Springs 9
Lovell 2,447
Lusk 1,650
Lyman 2,284
Manderson 174
Manville 94
Marbleton 537
Medicine Bow 953
Meeteetse 512
Midwest 638
Mills 2,139
Moorcroft 1,014
Mountain View 628
Newcastle 3,596
Pavillion 287
Pine Bluffs 1,077
Pinedale 1,066
Powell 5,310
Ranchester 655
Rawlins 11,547
Riverside 55
Riverton 9,588
Rock River 415
Rock Springs 19,458
Saratoga 2,410
Sheridan 15,146
Shoshoni 879
Sinclair 586
South Superior 586
Sundance 1,087
Ten Sleep 407
Thayne 256
Thermopolis 3,852
Torrington 5,441
Upton 1,193
Van Tassell 10
Wamsutter 681
Wheatland 5,816
Worland 6,391
Yoder 110

World Book Supplement

1976
1977
1978
1979
1980
1981

To help WORLD BOOK owners keep their encyclopedia up to date, the following new or revised articles are reprinted from the 1982 edition of the encyclopedia.

560 **Elephant**
567 **Vanuatu**
568 **Malaysia**
572 **Kuala Lumpur**
572 **Inflation**
575 **Mental Illness**

See ''Elephant,'' page 560

Most Elephants Live in Herds that consist of a number of adults and their young. The majority of herds are led by an old female called a *matriarch*. This picture shows a herd of African elephants grazing in a grassy clearing in Kenya. The matriarch stands in the center foreground.

Cynthia Moss

ELEPHANT is the largest animal that lives on land. Among all animals, only some kinds of whales are larger. The elephant is also the second tallest member of the animal kingdom. Only the giraffe is taller. Elephants are the only animals that have a nose in the form of a long trunk, which they use as a hand. They have larger ears than any other animal, and their tusks are the largest teeth.

There are two chief kinds of elephants, *African elephants* and *Asiatic elephants*, also known as *Indian elephants*. African elephants live only in Africa south of the Sahara. Asiatic elephants live in parts of India and Southeast Asia.

Elephants are extremely strong and highly intelligent. People have tamed and trained them for thousands of years. The logging industry in some Asian countries uses elephants to carry heavy loads. People throughout the world enjoy watching elephants in circuses and zoos. Trained circus elephants stand on their heads, lie down and roll over, dance, and perform other tricks.

One of the earliest recorded uses of elephants took place in war. In 331 B.C., a Macedonian army led by Alexander the Great defeated Persian soldiers who rode elephants in battle. In 218 B.C., the famous general Hannibal of Carthage used elephants when he crossed the Alps from France and invaded Italy.

During the 1800's, an African elephant named Jumbo was featured by the London Zoo for more than 24 years. Visitors came from all parts of the world to see Jumbo, the largest animal in captivity at that time. He stood 11

G. M. O. Maloiy, the contributor of this article, is Professor of Animal Physiology at the University of Nairobi, Nairobi, Kenya.

feet (3.4 meters) tall and weighed more than $7\frac{1}{4}$ short tons (6.6 metric tons). In 1882, the American showman P. T. Barnum purchased Jumbo and made the elephant a star attraction of his circus. The word *jumbo* became a common adjective for anything extremely large.

Through the years, people have killed large numbers of elephants. They also have settled on much of the land where the animals lived. As a result, the survival of wild elephants became seriously endangered during the late 1900's. Hunters kill elephants chiefly for their tusks, which are made of ivory. The ivory is used for jewelry and other items. Many African and Asian nations have passed laws to protect elephants from hunters. Some countries, including the United States and Canada, forbid the importing of ivory and ivory products. However, hunters continue to kill thousands of elephants illegally year after year.

The Importance of Elephants

How Elephants Help the Environment. Wild elephants perform several important natural functions. For example, they help turn wooded areas into grasslands by feeding on trees and other plants. Certain animals use the grasslands for grazing. Elephants also dig up dry riverbeds to reach the water beneath the surface of the ground. Other animals then drink this water. When elephants travel through forests and other wooded areas, they create paths used by such animals as antelope and zebras.

How Elephants Serve People. Most trained elephants, whether they do heavy tasks or perform tricks, come from Asia. African elephants are fiercer and more difficult to tame.

An elephant can carry as much as 600 pounds (272 kilograms) of cargo on its back or with its trunk. In

India and some other Asian countries, elephants are used in the logging industry. The animals can work on rough ground and in thick forests. An elephant can move a log that weighs 2 short tons (1.8 metric tons). It lifts smaller logs with its tusks and holds them with its trunk.

Nearly all circuses have at least one elephant, and some have several. Circus elephants can stand on their heads, balance on one or two legs, dance, roll balls, and even ride bicycles. Females are almost always chosen for circus training because they behave better than the males. However, the famous circus elephant Jumbo was an African male that performed tricks and took children for rides on his back. See CIRCUS (pictures).

Kinds of Elephants

African Elephants are larger and fiercer than Asiatic elephants. Wild African elephants live only in Africa south of the Sahara. In the early 1980's, there were about $1\frac{1}{3}$ million of these elephants.

An African elephant is about the same height at the shoulder and the rump. Its back dips slightly in the middle. Adult African *bull* (male) elephants stand about 11 feet (3.4 meters) tall at the shoulder and weigh about 6 short tons (5.4 metric tons). The *cows* (females) are about 9 feet (2.8 meters) tall and weigh about 4 short tons (3.6 metric tons). The largest known elephant, an African bull, measured 13 feet 2 inches (4.01 meters) tall. This elephant probably weighed about 12 short tons (11 metric tons).

Most African elephants have dark-gray skin. Their forehead forms a smooth curve. Their ears measure as wide as 4 feet (1.2 meters) and cover their shoulders. Both the bulls and cows have tusks. The tusks of most African bulls grow from 6 to 8 feet (1.8 to 2.4 meters) long and weigh 50 to 100 pounds (23 to 45 kilograms) each. The tusks of most of the cows weigh from 15 to 20 pounds (7 to 9 kilograms) each. The longest tusk of an African elephant measured $11\frac{1}{2}$ feet (3.5 meters), and the heaviest weighed 293 pounds (133 kilograms).

The trunk of an African elephant has two fingerlike knobs of flesh on the tip. The skin of the trunk has deep wrinkles. African elephants have four or five toes on each forefoot and three toes on each hind foot. A loose fold of skin joins the hind legs and the sides of the body. Asiatic elephants do not have this fold.

There are two types of African elephants, *bush elephants* and *forest elephants*. Bush elephants, which live in most countries south of the Sahara, are the larger and have heavier tusks. Forest elephants live in Cameroon, Congo, Ivory Coast, Zaire, and other countries of central and western Africa. Both kinds of African elephants inhabit forests, grasslands, mountains, swamps, and shrubby areas.

Asiatic Elephants live only in southern and southeastern Asia. They are found in forests and jungles of such countries as Burma, Cambodia, China, India, Indonesia, Malaysia, Sri Lanka, Thailand, and Vietnam. There were only about 15,000 wild Asiatic elephants in the early 1980's.

Asiatic elephants have an arched back that is slightly higher than the shoulder and the rump. An adult Asiatic bull stands from 9 to $10\frac{1}{2}$ feet (2.7 to 3.2 meters) tall at the shoulder and weighs up to 4 short tons (3.6 metric tons). The largest known Asiatic bull measured 10 feet 8

Interesting Facts About Elephants

The Skin of an Elephant is gray and wrinkled. An adult elephant's skin measures up to $1\frac{1}{2}$ inches (3 centimeters) thick and weighs about 1 short ton (0.9 metric tons). However, it is surprisingly tender. Flies, mosquitoes, and other insects can bite into the skin.

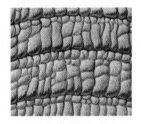

An Angry or Frightened Elephant can run at a speed of more than 25 miles (40 kilometers) an hour for a short distance. On a long journey, a herd of elephants travels at about 10 miles (16 kilometers) an hour.

An Elephant Uses Its Trunk as a Hand. The trunk can carry a 600-pound (272-kilogram) log or an object as small as a coin. Elephants also breathe and smell with their trunks.

Elephants Love Water and frequently bathe in lakes and rivers. They are excellent swimmers. An elephant gives itself a shower by shooting a stream of water from its trunk.

WORLD BOOK illustrations by James Teason

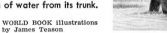

Neal Ulevich

Trained Elephants, such as the Asiatic elephant shown above, are used in the logging industry in several Asian countries. An elephant can carry heavy loads with its trunk or on its back.

The two chief kinds of elephants, African elephants and Asiatic elephants, differ in size, disposition, and body features. For example, African elephants are larger and fiercer and have bigger tusks. These drawings show various physical differences between the two species.

WORLD BOOK illustrations by John D. Dawson

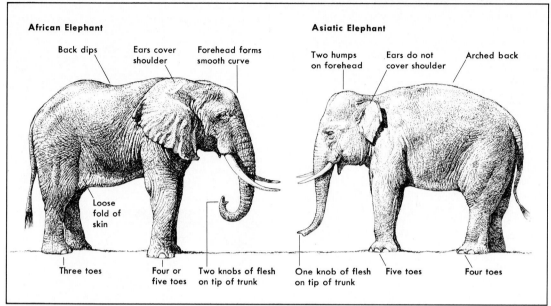

African Elephant

Back dips   Ears cover shoulder   Forehead forms smooth curve

Loose fold of skin

Three toes   Four or five toes   Two knobs of flesh on tip of trunk

Asiatic Elephant

Two humps on forehead   Ears do not cover shoulder   Arched back

One knob of flesh on tip of trunk   Five toes   Four toes

inches (3.3 meters) tall. Asiatic cows stand about 8 feet (2.4 meters) tall and weigh about 3.3 short tons (3 metric tons).

Most Asiatic elephants have light-gray skin and may have pink or white spots. An Asiatic elephant has two humps on its forehead just above the ears. The ears are about half as large as those of an African elephant and do not cover the shoulder. Most Asiatic bulls have tusks that grow from 4 to 5 feet (1.2 to 1.5 meters) long. However, some Asiatic males, called *makwahs*, have no tusks, and most Asiatic females have none. Some Asiatic females have extremely short tusks called *tushes*.

The trunk of an Asiatic elephant has smoother skin than that of an African elephant and only one fingerlike knob on the tip. Most Asiatic elephants have five toes on each forefoot and four on each hind foot.

The Body of an Elephant

The height of an adult elephant about equals the animal's length. An elephant has a short, muscular neck and an enormous head with huge, triangular ears. The trunk extends from the upper jaw, and a tusk grows from each side of the jaw at the base of the trunk. Massive legs support the body. An elephant's tail is small in relation to the rest of the animal. It measures about $3\frac{1}{3}$ feet (1 meter) long.

Skin and Hair. Elephants have gray, wrinkled skin that hangs in loose folds. The skin of an adult measures up to $1\frac{1}{2}$ inches (3 centimeters) thick. It weighs about 1 short ton (0.9 metric ton). However, an elephant's skin is surprisingly tender. Some insects, including flies and mosquitoes, can bite into the skin.

Elephants are called *pachyderms*, a term that comes from a Greek word meaning *thick-skinned*. But elephants, unlike some other mammals, do not have a layer of fat under their skin to protect them from the cold. They get

stomach cramps if the temperature drops below about 35° F. (2° C).

An elephant has no sweat glands, and so it must cool off in other ways. It may get rid of excess body heat by flapping its enormous ears or by spraying water on itself. Elephants also cool themselves off by rolling in mud. The mud dries on their skin and thus shields it from the sun.

At birth, elephants are covered with brown hair. This hair becomes black through the years, and much of it wears off. Adult elephants have so little hair that they appear almost hairless. Patches of black bristles may grow around the ears, eyes, and mouth, and the end of the tail has a bunch of long bristles.

Trunk. An elephant's trunk is a combined nose and upper lip. It consists of a strong, flexible, boneless mass of flesh. The trunk of an adult elephant measures about 5 feet (1.5 meters) long.

An elephant breathes and smells with its trunk and uses it when eating and drinking. The animal sniffs the air and the ground almost constantly with its trunk. It carries food and water to its mouth with its trunk. It also gives itself a shower by shooting a stream of water through its trunk. The trunk of an adult can hold about $1\frac{1}{2}$ gallons (6 liters) of water.

An elephant grasps objects with its trunk much as a person does with a hand. The trunk can carry a log that weighs as much as 600 pounds (272 kilograms). The tip of the trunk can pick up an object as small as a coin. An elephant also uses its trunk to stroke its mate and its young. When fighting, the animal may use its trunk to grasp an enemy. But sometimes the trunk is protected by curling it under the chin.

Tusks and Teeth. An elephant's tusks are actually long, curved upper teeth called *incisors*. They are made of ivory. About two-thirds of each tusk extends from the upper jaw. The rest is in the skull. Elephants use their tusks to dig for food and to fight. The tusks can lift and carry a load weighing as much as 1 short ton (0.9 metric ton). Most Asiatic females and some Asiatic males have no tusks.

Baby elephants grow *milk tusks,* which measure no longer than 2 inches (5 centimeters). These tusks fall out before the elephant is 2 years old. Permanent tusks replace them and continue to grow throughout the animal's life.

Elephants also have four *molars* (back teeth). The molars of an adult may measure 1 foot (30 centimeters) long and weigh about 8½ pounds (4 kilograms). These teeth have jagged edges that help grind food. One molar lies on each side of both jaws, and additional molars form in the back of the mouth. The molars in front gradually wear down and drop out, and the ones in back push forward and replace them. An elephant grows six sets of molars during its lifetime. Each set consists of four teeth. The last set of molars appears when the animal is about 40 years old.

Legs and Feet. The legs of an elephant are pillarlike structures. The feet are nearly round. Each foot has a thick pad of tissue that acts as a cushion. The foot expands under the elephant's weight and contracts when the animal lifts the leg. Elephants may sink deep into mud, but they can pull their legs out easily because the feet become smaller when lifted.

Senses. The trunk provides a keen sense of smell, and elephants depend on this sense more than on any other. They frequently wave their trunks high in the air to catch the scent of food or enemies. An elephant can smell a human being more than a mile (1.6 kilometers) away.

Elephants also have good hearing. Their huge ears pick up sounds of other animals from as far as 2 miles (3.2 kilometers) away. When an elephant is curious about a sound, its ears stand straight out.

The animal's sense of touch is in the sensitive tip of its trunk. An elephant can recognize the shape of an object and whether the object is rough or smooth and hot or cold.

Elephants have poor sight and are color blind. Their eyes are small in relation to the enormous head. An elephant cannot turn its head completely, and so it can see only in the front and to the sides. The animal must turn around to see anything behind it.

Intelligence. Elephants have one of the largest brains and rank high in intelligence among animals. An elephant can learn to perform a variety of tasks and tricks if commands and signals are repeated over and over again.

Most elephants chosen for any type of training are 15 to 20 years old. Younger elephants can be trained more easily, but they cannot do heavy work. The training process starts after an elephant has been in captivity for a number of weeks. A trainer mounts the animal and gradually teaches it to obey signals. The trainer gives signals by gently kicking the elephant behind its ears. These signals include commands to kneel, stand up, turn around, and walk forward and backward. A well-trained elephant can also learn about 30 verbal commands.

Elephants have an excellent memory and rarely forget what they learn. They can remember both pleasant and unpleasant experiences years later.

The Life of an Elephant

Elephant Herds. Most elephants live in herds. The size of an elephant herd probably depends mainly on the amount of food and water available. A herd of African elephants may have up to 1,000 members, but Asiatic elephants live in groups of only 5 to 60 animals. A herd of elephants consists of a number of families, each of which is made up of several adults and their young. Most herds of elephants are led by an old cow called a *matriarch.*

Some elephants leave the herd and live alone. Many of them are dangerous bulls called *rogues,* which may have been driven from the herd by other bulls because of their vicious behavior. Rogues usually attack immediately when they come upon another animal or a human

Internal Anatomy of a Female African Elephant

This view of a female African elephant shows the animal's skeleton and some of its internal organs. An elephant's organs resemble those of other mammals but are much larger. For example, an elephant's heart is about 5 times as large as a human heart and more than 50 times as heavy.

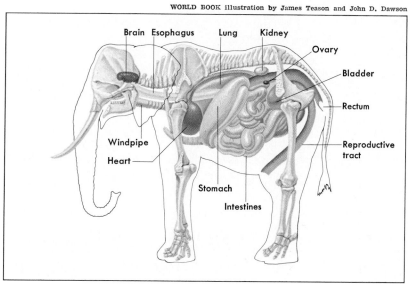

Brain Esophagus Lung Kidney Ovary Bladder Rectum Reproductive tract Windpipe Heart Stomach Intestines

being. The savageness of these elephants probably results from constant pain caused by decayed teeth, a wound, or a disease.

Elephants have no permanent homes. They roam wherever they can find enough food and water. A herd may wander over an area of about 390 square miles (1,000 square kilometers). Elephants in Kenya roam areas as large as 1,900 square miles (5,000 square kilometers). Sometimes, two or more herds gather and move to a new location. They may travel hundreds of miles together. Elephants often leave an area that has ample food and water. Zoologists believe they do so to avoid insect pests.

Wild elephants usually eat for about 16 hours every day. They bathe in lakes and rivers and like to roll in muddy water. After a mud bath, an elephant may cover itself with dirt. The dirt coating helps protect the animal's skin from the sun and insects. Elephants often play by tussling among themselves with their tusks and trunks.

Elephants communicate with one another in various ways. For example, they touch with their trunks as a greeting. A mother elephant calls to her young by slapping her ears against her head. Elephants also communicate by means of rumbling, grunting, and squealing noises.

Food. Elephants eat grass, shrubs, leaves, roots, bark, branches, fruit, and water plants. Using their heads as battering rams, they frequently knock down small trees to reach the highest leaves. An elephant can knock down a tree 30 feet (9 meters) high that has a diameter of almost 2 feet (61 centimeters). Elephants use their tusks to rip the bark off trees and to dig up roots and shrubs. They especially like bamboo, berries, coconuts, corn, dates, plums, and sugar cane. Elephants do not eat the flesh of other animals.

Wild elephants eat more than do elephants in captivity. A wild African elephant eats over 770 pounds (349 kilograms) of food a day, and a wild Asiatic elephant consumes about 650 pounds (295 kilograms). In captiv-

Peter Davey, Bruce Coleman Inc.

Elephants Touch Trunks as a Greeting. The animals also communicate among themselves by making a variety of rumbling, grunting, and squealing noises.

ity, elephants eat about 150 pounds (68 kilograms) of food daily.

Wild elephants drink up to 40 gallons (150 liters) of water daily. An elephant can live without water for about three days and may travel as far as 50 miles (80 kilometers) to find it.

Travel. The padded feet of an elephant enable the animal to walk and run with surprisingly little noise. Elephants walk at a speed of 3 to 6 miles (5 to 10 kilometers) an hour. On a long journey, a herd travels in single file at about 10 miles (16 kilometers) an hour. An angry or frightened elephant can run more than 25 miles (40 kilometers) an hour, but only for a short distance. An elephant walks and runs with shuffling steps. It cannot jump because of its great weight and the structure of its legs.

Elephants spend much of their time in water and are excellent swimmers. They hold their trunks above the water when swimming.

C. Haagner, Bruce Coleman Inc.

Elephants Cool Off by bathing. They especially like to roll in muddy water. The mud dries on the animal's skin and helps protect it from the sun. An elephant needs water and mud for cooling because its skin has no sweat glands.

Peter Davey, Bruce Coleman Inc.

A Baby Elephant stays with its mother until it reaches adulthood at the age of 10 to 14. The youngster drinks the mother's milk for two to six years and then starts to graze.

Reproduction. Male elephants reach adulthood and start to mate when they are 10 to 14 years old. Females become mature and can begin to mate at the age of 12 to 15. Elephants mate throughout the year. However, they mate most frequently when they have a plentiful supply of food. A bull elephant may mate with several cows, and the males and females do not remain together after mating.

The female carries her young inside her body for 18 to 23 months, longer than any other animal. She almost always has one baby, called a *calf*, at a time, but twins occasionally are born. African elephant calves weigh from 250 to 320 pounds (113 to 145 kilograms) at birth and stand about 3 feet (95 centimeters) tall at the shoulder. Newborn Asiatic calves weigh about 220 pounds (100 kilograms) and are about $2\frac{4}{5}$ feet (85 centimeters) tall.

A baby elephant can walk several hours after birth. Its mother stays close to the youngster and protects it for several years. At first, the calf lives chiefly on the mother's milk. The young elephant drinks the milk by curling its trunk over its head so its mouth can reach the mother's breast. When the calf is 2 to 6 years old, it starts to graze on grass and other plant life. However, an elephant calf remains with its mother until it reaches adulthood. Elephants reach full size at the age of about 20.

Musth. An elephant has a *temporal gland* on each side of its head, about midway between the eye and the ear. About once a year, the temporal glands discharge a dark, oily substance that has a strong odor. This substance stains the elephant's face. The temporal glands are active for two or three months yearly. During this period, an elephant is in a condition called *musth* or *must* (both pronounced *must*). Musth occurs chiefly in adult male elephants.

While in musth, an elephant becomes extremely dangerous if it gets excited. It attacks any nearby animals, including human beings and sometimes other elephants. It also becomes sexually aroused and more likely to mate. Elephants in captivity must be chained or caged during musth.

Zoologists do not completely understand the role of musth, which occurs when the elephant's body produces more than the normal amount of a hormone called *testosterone*. This chemical substance stimulates sexual aggressiveness in male human beings. Some zoologists believe musth is associated with the elephant's mating period. However, elephants also mate when not in musth.

Protection Against Enemies. The great size of elephants, plus the thickness of their skin, protects them from most animals. Their main enemies include lions, crocodiles, snakes, and human beings. Adult elephants are rarely attacked, but tigers and leopards frequently kill elephant calves. When a herd faces danger, the adults form a circle around the calves. Elephants may scare an enemy away by making their ears stand straight out and twitching their bodies as though trembling. If an animal attacks, an elephant may crush it to death by stepping on it. Elephants also may use their tusks to attack enemies.

Elephants are easily frightened. A sudden, strange noise, such as a gunshot, can cause a herd to panic. The animals may charge at the source of the noise or stampede away from it. When frightened or angry, elephants sometimes use their trunks to make a loud, shrill cry called *trumpeting*.

Life Span. Wild elephants live up to 60 years, and those in captivity have lived more than 65 years. Many old elephants die after they lose their teeth and can no longer chew food. Some people believe that old elephants go to certain places called "elephant graveyards" to die. This belief may have started because aged elephants tend to live in swamps and other places where the plant life is tender and easily digested. After the elephants die, most parts of their bodies rot away, but the tusks remain. People later find the ivory and believe

Norman Myers, Bruce Coleman Inc.

A Charging Elephant may make itself look especially dangerous by sticking its ears straight out. Elephants fight with their tusks and trunk or crush enemies to death by stepping on them.

ELEPHANT

they have discovered an elephant graveyard. The remains of many elephants also may be found in areas where brush fires have occurred. Such fires, some of which are set by hunters, can kill large numbers of elephants.

Protecting Elephants

Elephants are the only survivors of a group of mammals called *proboscideans*. This group of animals once consisted of more than 350 species, all of which had long snouts or trunks. The earliest known proboscidean, the *moeritherium*, was about the size of a large pig. It lived in Egypt about 40 or 50 million years ago. Other proboscideans included the *mammoth* and the *mastodon*, both of which looked much like the elephant (see MAMMOTH; MASTODON).

Today, wildlife experts classify elephants as an endangered species—that is, the animals must have human protection to survive. People have destroyed much of the elephant's natural surroundings by clearing land for settlement and farms. Fires also have ruined many areas in which elephants once lived. Many African and Asian nations have set aside land in an effort to protect the habitats of elephants and other wild animals. This land lies in national parks and in areas called *reserves*. However, some wildlife experts fear that the amount of land involved is not large enough to save many wild elephants.

Hunters, especially ivory hunters, also threaten the survival of wild elephants. Laws forbid the hunting of elephants in national parks and in reserves, and they limit the number of elephants that hunters may kill outside these areas. But such laws are difficult to enforce, and hunters illegally kill thousands of elephants yearly.

In 1976, the International Union for Conservation of Nature and Natural Resources, together with the World Wildlife Fund, established an elephant conservation organization. This organization works to end the illegal hunting of elephants and to prohibit the sale of elephant tusks and ivory products.

Scientific Classification. Elephants make up the order Proboscidea and the elephant family, Elephantidae. The African elephant is *Loxodonta africana*. The Asiatic, or Indian, elephant is *Elephas maximus*.   G. M. O. MALOIY

Related Articles in WORLD BOOK include:

Animal	Ivory
Circus	Mammoth
Comparative Psychology	Mastodon
(picture)	Republican
Ear (The Ears of Animals;	Party (picture)
picture)	Thailand (picture)
Hannibal	

Outline

I. **The Importance of Elephants**
   A. How Elephants Help the Environment
   B. How Elephants Serve People
II. **Kinds of Elephants**
   A. African Elephants
   B. Asiatic Elephants
III. **The Body of an Elephant**
   A. Skin and Hair
   B. Trunk
   C. Tusks and Teeth
   D. Legs and Feet

   E. Senses
   F. Intelligence
IV. **The Life of an Elephant**
   A. Elephant Herds
   B. Food
   C. Travel
   D. Reproduction
   E. Musth
   F. Protection Against Enemies
   G. Life Span
V. **Protecting Elephants**

Questions

What is the only animal taller than the elephant?

What have some nations done to protect elephants from hunters?

How many pounds of food does a wild elephant eat in a day? How many gallons of water does a wild elephant drink daily?

What is *musth*? How long does it usually affect an elephant?

What is the length of pregnancy for elephants? How does it compare with the pregnancy period of other animals?

Why do elephants move from place to place?

Why does an elephant cover itself with dirt after bathing?

How do elephants use their tusks?

What does an elephant do with its trunk when fighting? When swimming?

What is a *matriarch*? A *rogue*?

ELEPHANT BIRD is any one of several *species* (kinds) of giant extinct birds that once lived in Madagascar. These birds could not fly. The largest elephant bird was about 10 feet (3 meters) high and weighed about 1,000 pounds (450 kilograms). Huge eggs that could hold 2 gallons (8 liters) are found along with the birds' bones. The eggs were the largest known single cells in the animal kingdom. Some people think the legends of the giant bird called the roc were based on knowledge of elephant birds (see ROC).

Scientific Classification. Elephant birds belong to the elephant bird family, *Aepyornithidae*. They make up the genus *Aepyornis*.   R. A. PAYNTER, JR.

The Extinct Elephant Bird was huge and could not fly. It moved about swiftly on its large, powerful legs.
Field Museum of Natural History

VANUATU, *vah NOO ah too,* is an island country in the southwest Pacific Ocean. It consists of 80 islands with a total land area of about 5,700 square miles (14,763 square kilometers). For location, see PACIFIC ISLANDS (map). The largest islands are, in order of size, Espiritu Santo, Malekula, Efate, Erromango, and Tanna. Vanuatu has a population of about 113,000. Port-Vila (pop. 25,000)—on Efate—is the nation's capital and largest urban community. Vanuatu's national anthem is "Yumi, yumi, yumi" ("We, we, we").

From 1906 to 1980, Great Britain and France jointly governed the islands, which were then called the New Hebrides. In 1980, the islands became the independent nation of Vanuatu.

Government. Vanuatu is a republic. A Parliament, whose 39 members are elected by the people to four-year terms, makes the country's laws. A prime minister, who heads the majority party in Parliament, runs the government with the aid of a Council of Ministers. Village, regional, and island councils handle local government affairs. The Parliament and the regional council presidents elect a president to a five-year term. The president's role is chiefly ceremonial.

People. More than 90 per cent of Vanuatu's people are Melanesians. Asians, Europeans, and Polynesians make up the rest of the population. About three-fourths of the people live in rural villages. Many village houses are made of wood from nearby forests and of bamboo and palm leaves. Port-Vila and Santo—on Espiritu Santo—are the only urban communities. More than 100 languages are spoken in Vanuatu. Bislama, a language that combines mainly English words and Melanesian grammar, is commonly used throughout the country. Vanuatu has about 300 elementary schools and several high schools. About 85 per cent of the people are Christians and most of the rest practice local religions.

Land and Climate. The islands of Vanuatu form a Y-shaped chain that extends about 500 miles (800 kilometers) from north to south. Most of the islands have narrow coastal plains and mountainous interiors. Several islands feature active volcanoes. The northern islands have a hot, rainy climate, with a year-round temperature of about 80° F. (27° C) and annual rainfall of about 120 inches (305 centimeters). Temperatures in the southern islands range from about 67° to 88° F. (19° to 31° C), and the yearly rainfall totals about 90 inches (230 centimeters).

Economy of Vanuatu is based on agriculture. Rural families produce nearly all the food they need. They grow fruits and vegetables, raise chickens and hogs, and catch fish. Some families produce *copra* (dried coconut meat) for sale. Tourism is important to the economy.

Small ships and airplanes serve as the main means of transportation among the islands. Vanuatu has few good roads and no railroads. The government publishes a newspaper and operates a radio station.

History. Melanesians have lived in what is now Vanuatu for at least 3,000 years. In 1606, Pedro Fernandez de Queirós, a Portuguese explorer in the service of Spain, became the first European to see the islands. The British explorer James Cook mapped the region in 1774 and named the islands the New Hebrides after the Hebrides islands of Scotland.

British and French traders, missionaries, and settlers began coming to the islands during the 1820's. In 1887, Great Britain and France set up a joint naval commission to oversee the area. In 1906, the commission was replaced by a joint British and French government called a condominium (see CONDOMINIUM).

After the United States entered World War II in 1941, the New Hebrides became an important military base for the Allies. American troops built many roads, bridges, and airstrips there. A movement for independence began in the islands during the 1960's. The New Hebrides became the independent nation of Vanuatu on July 30, 1980. ROBERT LANGDON

Vanuatu Tourist Information Bureau

Vanuatu is a country that consists of 80 islands in the southwest Pacific Ocean. Boaters enjoy sailing on sparkling blue water near the sandy shore of one of the islands, *left.*

MALAYSIA

MALAYSIA, *muh LAY zhuh,* is a country in Southeast Asia. It consists of two regions about 400 miles (644 kilometers) apart, which are separated by the South China Sea. The regions are Peninsular (formerly West) Malaysia, on the southern part of the Malay Peninsula; and Sarawak and Sabah (formerly East Malaysia), on the northern part of the island of Borneo.

Malaysia is a tropical land, much of which is covered by dense rain forests. It ranks as the world's largest producer of natural rubber and tin. Malays and Chinese people make up most of the country's population. Kuala Lumpur is Malaysia's capital and largest city.

The nation of Malaysia was formed in 1963, when Malaya, Sarawak, Sabah, and Singapore united. Malaya was an independent nation that occupied what is now Peninsular Malaysia. Sarawak and Sabah were separate British colonies that covered what is now the Malaysian region of Sarawak and Sabah. Singapore was a British colony south of Malaya. Singapore withdrew from the nation in 1965.

Government

Malaysia is a constitutional monarchy. A Parliament makes the country's laws, and a prime minister and Cabinet carry out the operations of the government. The prime minister is the top government official. Local government is administered through 13 states and the federal territory of Kuala Lumpur. A king serves as head of state, but his duties are largely ceremonial.

National Government. Malaysia's Parliament is made up of a 154-member House of Representatives and a 58-member Senate. The people elect the House members to five-year terms. The head of the political party with the most seats in the House serves as prime minister. The prime minister selects the Cabinet members. Each state legislature elects two of the Senate members, and the king appoints the other senators on the advice of the prime minister. The senators serve six-year terms. Every five years, the leaders of nine of Malaysia's states elect a king from their number.

Local Government. Hereditary princes called *rulers* head nine of Malaysia's 13 state governments. Federally appointed governors head the four other states and the federal territory. Each state has a constitution and an elected legislature. The states are divided into administrative districts, each governed by a district officer.

Political Parties. The National Front, a coalition of political parties, is Malaysia's most powerful political group. Others include the Democratic Action Party and the Pan-Malayan Islamic Party.

Courts. The Federal Court is Malaysia's highest court. It has seven members, who are appointed by the king on the advice of the prime minister. The Federal Court hears appeals from High Courts—Malaysia's second level of courts. Malaysia's lower courts include local, juvenile, and religious courts.

Armed Forces of Malaysia include an army, an air force, and a navy. About 65,000 persons serve in the armed forces. All service is voluntary.

People

Population and Ethnic Groups. Malaysia has a population of 14,798,000. Slightly more people live in

Leon V. Kofod

Kuala Lumpur, Malaysia's Capital, is a bustling, crowded city. The modern National Mosque, an Islamic house of worship, *above center,* stands near an expressway.

urban areas than in rural areas. More than 80 per cent of the people live in Peninsular Malaysia. Kuala Lumpur, Malaysia's largest city, has about 1,072,000 persons.

Malaysia's largest population groups are, in order of size, the Malays, Chinese, and Asian Indians. Malays make up about 50 per cent of the population, Chinese about 35 per cent, and Indians about 10 per cent. A number of other ethnic groups who live chiefly in Sarawak and Sabah make up the rest of the population. The largest groups in Sarawak and Sabah are the Dyaks and the Kadazans (see DYAKS).

Malaysia's ethnic groups speak separate languages or dialects, and, in many areas, have different ways of life. Malays make up the most powerful group in politics, but the Chinese control much of the economy. Social, economic, and political differences between the Chinese and Malays have led to friction and—sometimes—violence between members of the two groups.

Languages. Bahasa Malaysia, a form of the Malay language, is used by most of the Malay people and

---

———————— FACTS IN BRIEF ————————

Capital: Kuala Lumpur.
Official Language: Bahasa Malaysia.
Form of Government: Constitutional monarchy.
Area: 127,317 sq. mi. (329,749 km²).
Elevation: *Highest*—Mount Kinabalu, 13,431 ft. (4,094 m) above sea level. *Lowest*—sea level, along the coast.
Population: *Estimated 1982 Population*—14,798,000; distribution, 51 per cent urban, 49 per cent rural; density, 117 persons per sq. mi. (45 per km²). *1970 Census*—10,452,309. *Estimated 1987 Population*—17,133,000.
Chief Products: *Agriculture*—rubber, rice, cacao seeds, coconuts, palm oil, pepper, pineapples, timber. *Manufacturing*—cement, chemicals, textiles, rubber goods, processed foods. *Mining*—tin, bauxite, copper, gold, iron, oil.
National Anthem: "Negara Ku" ("My Country, My Native Land").
Money: *Basic Unit*—ringgit (sometimes called Malaysian dollar). See MONEY (table: Exchange Rates).

is the country's official language. Most Chinese use the Chinese language, and most Indians use Tamil. Many Malaysians also know English, which is widely used in business and everyday life.

Way of Life. Peninsular Malaysia includes many crowded cities as well as large rural regions. Sarawak and Sabah is chiefly a rural area.

The majority of the country's Malays live in rural areas on the peninsula. Most of them work as farmers and live in settlements called *kampongs*. Many houses in rural areas are made of wood. Most have thatched roofs, but some have roofs made of tile. Some houses are raised above the ground on stilts. Most Malays who live in cities work in industry or in government jobs.

Most of Malaysia's Chinese people live in cities. Large numbers of them work in stores, banks, or business offices. Chinese people own a large proportion of Malaysia's businesses. Wealthy and middle-class Chinese live in high-rise apartments in downtown areas or in suburban homes. In the cities, some low-income Chinese—as well as Malays and Indians—live in crowded, run-down areas.

Large numbers of Malaysia's Indians work on rubber plantations. Many others hold city jobs.

Most people of Sarawak and Sabah live in small settlements in rural areas. Several families often live together in *long houses* along rivers. Many of these rural farm families must struggle to produce enough food for their own use.

Clothing. The clothing of most of Malaysia's Chinese and many members of its other ethnic groups is similar to that worn in Western nations. But many Malay men and women, especially in rural areas, wear a skirt called a *sarong* and a jacket. Some rural Malaysians wrap a

David Moore, Black Star

People of Various Ethnic Groups live in Peninsular Malaysia. Malays make up the largest group, followed by Chinese and Indians. Most of the people in the scene above are Malays.

one-piece cloth around their bodies for clothing.

Food and Drink. Rice is the main food of most Malaysians. The people may serve rice with meat, fish or a fish sauce, fruit, or vegetables. *Satay* is a popular Malaysian dish. It consists of small chunks of meat that are grilled and dipped in hot sauce. Beer and soft drinks rank among the most popular beverages.

Religion. Islam, the Muslim faith, is Malaysia's official religion. But the constitution grants freedom of religion. Nearly all Malays are Muslims. Most Chinese follow Buddhism, Confucianism, or Taoism, and most

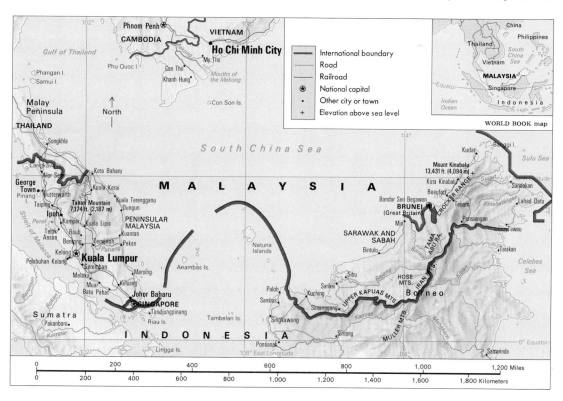

MALAYSIA

Indians practice Hinduism. Many ethnic groups in Sarawak and Sabah follow local traditional religions.

Education. Most Malaysian children complete elementary school. But large numbers of them do not attend high school. They are from poor families and leave school to begin work. About 45 per cent of Malaysia's people can read and write.

Malaysia has 5 universities and 6 colleges. The University Kebangsaan Malaysia is the national university.

The Arts. Traditional arts of Malaysia include folk dances and puppet dramas. The folk dances may represent scenes of adventures, battles, or love. In the puppet dramas, the puppeteer sits behind a screen and moves leather or wood puppets. The puppeteer also tells the story and speaks the part of each puppet.

Land and Climate

Malaysia covers 127,317 square miles (329,749 square kilometers). The country is divided into two regions. The regions and their areas are Peninsular Malaysia, 50,806 square miles (131,588 square kilometers); and Sarawak and Sabah, 76,511 square miles (198,161 square kilometers).

Peninsular Malaysia covers the southern part of the Malay Peninsula. Mountains extend down the center of the peninsula in a north-south direction. Thick tropical rain forests cover much of this mountainous region. Low, swampy plains spread out over parts of the peninsula west and east of the mountains to the coasts. The west coast, which borders the Strait of Malacca, has most of Peninsular Malaysia's cities and major seaports. Much of the land east of the mountains is covered by tropical rain forests. The east coast borders the South China Sea. Major rivers in Peninsular Malaysia include the Kelantan, Perak, and Pahang.

Sarawak and Sabah covers most of the northern part of Borneo. Much of the coastal area, which borders the South China Sea, is low and swampy. Inland areas are mountainous and covered with tropical rain forests.

Mount Kinabalu, the highest peak in Malaysia, rises 13,431 feet (4,094 meters) in the northeast part of Sarawak and Sabah. Major rivers include the Kinabatangan and the Rajang.

Animal Life and Vegetation. Many kinds of wild animals live in Malaysia. They include civets, deer, elephants, monkeys, tapirs, tigers, and wild oxen. Other animals include such reptiles as cobras, crocodiles, lizards, and pythons; more than 500 kinds of birds; and an enormous variety of butterflies.

Mangrove and palm trees cover much of Malaysia's swampy coastal areas. Other plants include camphor, ebony, fig, mahogany, rubber, and sandalwood trees.

Climate. Both Peninsular Malaysia and Sarawak and Sabah have tropical climates. Coastal temperatures usually stay between 70° and 90° F. (21° and 32° C). Mountain temperatures range from 55° to 80° F. (13° to 27° C). About 100 inches (250 centimeters) of rain falls annually in Peninsular Malaysia, and Sarawak and Sabah receives about 150 inches (381 centimeters).

Economy

Malaysia has one of the strongest economies in Southeast Asia. Crop production employs more people than any other economic activity, but the strength of the economy depends largely on rubber, tin, and petroleum production. Manufacturing ranks behind agriculture and mining in importance in Malaysia, but it has been growing at a rapid rate since the 1960's. The economy operates as a free enterprise system, but the government places some regulations on businesses.

Agriculture. Malaysia is the world's leading producer of natural rubber. It is also a leading producer of palm oil. Nearly all of the country's rubber and palm oil are raised for export on large plantations. Farmers grow rice, Malaysia's chief food crop, on small farms throughout the country. The small farms also produce cacao seeds, coconuts, pepper, pineapples, and vegetables. Some farmers raise cattle and goats for meat. About four-fifths of Malaysia's farms cover less than 5 acres (2 hectares) each.

Urban and Rural Areas in Malaysia contrast sharply. A heavily populated Chinese section of Kuala Lumpur, *left*, has narrow streets crowded with motor vehicles. A quiet rural area above, shows a typical house, which is raised on stilts.

Ivan Polunin, Bruce Coleman Inc.

Swampy Lowlands lie along much of Malaysia's coastal areas. Mangrove and palm trees thrive there. The scene above shows people in a swampy area of Peninsular Malaysia.

Jean-Claude Lejeune, Black Star

Tropical Rain Forests cover most mountain areas in Malaysia. This mountain village is in the Sarawak and Sabah region. Mount Kinabalu, the country's peak, rises in the background.

Mining. Malaysia leads the world in the production of tin. Since the 1970's, petroleum production has been important to the economy. Its other minerals include bauxite, copper, gold, ilmenite, and iron ore.

Manufacturing. Malaysia's chief manufactured products include cement, chemicals, rubber goods, and textiles. Food processing is a major industrial activity.

Foreign Trade. Rubber, tin, palm oil, petroleum, and timber rank as Malaysia's chief exports. Imports include chemicals, machinery, and manufactured goods. Malaysia's chief trading partners are Great Britain, Japan, The Netherlands, Singapore, and the United States.

Transportation and Communication. Malaysia has about 18,200 miles (29,290 kilometers) of roads, about 1,400 miles (2,250 kilometers) of railroads, and five international airports. Its chief ports include George Town and Pelabuhan Kelang.

Radio Television Malaysia, a government-owned network, broadcasts radio and television programs in Bahasa Malaysia, Chinese, English, and Tamil. The country has 43 daily newspapers.

History

Early Days. Archaeological evidence indicates that there were human settlements in what is now Peninsular Malaysia in prehistoric times. About 4,000 years ago, ancestors of the Malays moved into the area from southern China. The peninsula became a crossroads for trade between China and India. Chinese and Indian people settled there through the years.

By the A.D. 800's, several small city-states had grown up along the east and west coasts of the peninsula. Indian traders brought Indian culture, including Buddhism and Hinduism, to the area. In the 1400's, Melaka, on the west coast, became a major trading center. Indians and Arabs introduced Islam there, and many Malays on the peninsula soon became Muslims.

European Conquest. Portuguese forces captured Melaka in 1511 and lost it to the Dutch in 1641. During

the 1700's, many Malays from the Dutch-controlled islands of Celebes and Sumatra settled on the peninsula. In the late 1700's, Sumatran immigrants formed nine Malay states on the peninsula.

Also in the late 1700's, people from Great Britain began setting up trading posts on the peninsula and nearby islands and British forces captured Melaka from the Dutch. In 1826, the British formed a colony that included Melaka, the island of Pinang, and the island of Singapore. It was called the Colony of the Straits Settlements. During the 1800's and early 1900's, the British gained control of the nine Malay states on the peninsula and of what is now Sarawak and Sabah.

Under British rule, the peninsula's economy prospered. The rapid growth of the rubber industry and tin mining attracted thousands of workers from India and China. The British delegated much of their authority in the area to local rulers called *sultans*.

Independence. In the early 1940's, during World War II, Japan conquered what is now Malaysia. The area returned to British rule following Japan's defeat in 1945. In 1948, the nine peninsula states, plus Melaka and Pinang, united to form the Federation of Malaya, a partially independent territory under British protection. During the late 1940's and the 1950's, Chinese Communists and other rebels on the peninsula fought against the British. The conflict ended after the Federation of Malaya gained complete independence in 1957.

In 1963, Malaya, Singapore, and what is now Sarawak and Sabah united and formed the new independent nation of Malaysia. Disagreements soon arose between Singapore and the rest of the nation, and Singapore left the nation in 1965. Abdul Rahman became Malaysia's first prime minister.

Malaysia Today. Malaysia has developed one of the strongest economies in Southeast Asia. The continued prosperity of this economy depends on the country's ability to strengthen its export markets. In recent years, Malaysia has greatly increased its manufacturing to less-

Leon V. Kofod

Rubber Processing is one of Malaysia's chief industries. Factory workers make sheets of rubber from a milky fluid called latex, above. The fluid comes from rubber trees.

en its economic reliance on agriculture and mining.

Malays account for a high percentage of Malaysia's poor people, and Chinese make up a high percentage of its wealthy class. But Malays control the country's political system. This situation has helped cause friction between Malay and Chinese people. The friction is one of Malaysia's chief problems.

Abdul Razak succeeded Abdul Rahman as prime minister in 1970. Abdul Razak died in 1976, and Hussein Onn became prime minister. Mahathir bin Mohamed succeeded him in 1981.   DAVID P. CHANDLER

KUALA LUMPUR, *KWAH luh lum PUR* (pop. 1,072,-000), is the capital and largest city of Malaysia. The city lies in the southern part of the Malay Peninsula. For location, see MALAYSIA (map).

Kuala Lumpur spreads out along both banks of the Klang River. Like many Southeast Asian cities, it is extremely crowded. The part of the city east of the river has high-rise buildings, small shops, a busy outdoor market, and *mosques* (Muslim houses of worship). The area west of the river includes modern government buildings, the National Museum, and the National Mosque. Many poor people live near the river. Most of the middle-class and wealthy people live in suburbs north of the city. Kuala Lumpur is the home of the University of Malaya and the Technological University of Malaysia.

Most of Kuala Lumpur's oldest buildings were constructed in the 1880's, after a fire destroyed the city. The design of these buildings is patterned after Moorish architecture. This style of architecture, which developed in northern Africa, features arches, domes, towers, and spiral staircases.

People of Chinese ancestry make up a majority of Kuala Lumpur's population. Most of the rest of the people belong to the Malay ethnic group. The Malay-

sian national government employs many of Kuala Lumpur's people. The city is a center of banking, trade, and other commercial activities. Kuala Lumpur's industries include rubber and tin processing. The government activities are controlled by Malays. The Chinese control most of the city's commerce and industry.

Kuala Lumpur became part of a British colony in the 1870's. It had been a small Malay fishing village for hundreds of years before that time. Kuala Lumpur grew rapidly after rich deposits of tin were discovered in the area. People from southern China and elsewhere moved there to work in the tin mines. Many of the Chinese later established businesses and gained great wealth. In 1957, Kuala Lumpur became part of the independent nation of Malaya. Malaya and nearby states united in 1963 and formed the nation of Malaysia. Since 1970, Kuala Lumpur's population has more than doubled.   DAVID P. CHANDLER

INFLATION is a continual increase in prices throughout a nation's economy. The rate of inflation is determined by changes in the *price level*, an average of all prices. If some prices rise and others fall, the price level may not change. Therefore, inflation occurs only if most major prices go up.

Inflation reduces the value—also called the *purchasing power*—of money. During an inflationary period, a certain amount of money buys less than it previously did. For example, a worker may receive a salary increase of 10 per cent. If prices remain stable, the worker can purchase 10 per cent more goods and services. However, if prices also increase 10 per cent, the worker's purchasing power has not changed. If prices increase more than 10 per cent, the worker cannot buy as much as he or she previously could.

Inflation has many causes. It may result if consumers demand more goods and services than businesses can produce. Inflation may also occur if employers grant wage increases that exceed gains in productivity. The employers pass most or all of the cost of the wage increase along to consumers by charging higher prices. A government can try to control inflation by increasing taxes, decreasing the money supply, reducing government spending, and setting limits on wages and prices. However, the government's task is difficult, chiefly because it may trigger a recession when it tries to reduce inflation.

Measuring Inflation

Economists use measurements called *indexes* to determine changes in the price level. The indexes compare current prices with prices of an earlier period. The earlier period chosen for comparison is called the *base period*.

The most widely used price index in the United States is the *Consumer Price Index* (CPI). The CPI measures monthly changes in the price of a group of goods and services that people buy regularly. Such items include food, clothing, housing, and medical care. The total price of these items is compared with their total price during the base period. During the 1967 base period, for example, consumers paid $100 for a fixed assortment of goods and services. In 1980, those same items cost about $247.

Other price indexes include the *Producer Price Index* and the *Gross National Product Deflator*. The Producer Price Index calculates changes in the prices of regularly used products at various stages of production. The Gross National Product Deflator, also called the *Implicit Price Index* or *Implicit Price Deflator*, measures price changes for everything produced during a certain period.

Kinds of Inflation

Mild Inflation occurs when the price level increases from 2 to 4 per cent each year. If businesses can pass the price increases along to consumers, the economy thrives. Jobs are plentiful and unemployment falls. If wages increase faster than prices, workers have greater purchasing power. However, mild inflation usually lasts only a short time. Employers seek larger profits during periods of economic growth, and unions bargain for higher wages. As a result, prices rise even further.

Moderate Inflation results when the annual rate of inflation ranges from 5 to 9 per cent. During a period of moderate inflation, prices increase more quickly than wages, and so purchasing power declines. Most people purchase more at such times because they would rather have goods and services than money that is declining in value. This increased demand for goods and services causes prices to rise even further.

Severe Inflation occurs when the annual rate of inflation is 10 per cent or higher. This type of inflation is also called *double-digit inflation*. During a period of severe inflation, prices rise much faster than wages, and so purchasing power decreases rapidly.

When inflation is severe, debtors benefit at the expense of lenders. If prices increase during the period of a loan, the debtor repays the debt with dollars less valuable than those that were borrowed. In terms of purchasing power, the lender does not get back as much money as was lent.

Severe inflation also affects a nation's *balance of payments*, the total receipts and expenditures resulting from foreign transactions (see BALANCE OF PAYMENTS). A nation with severe inflation may find that its products become more expensive for other countries to buy. Therefore, the demand for its exports decreases. At the same time, foreign goods become cheaper for the nation's people, and so they import more. The result is a *deficit* in the nation's balance of payments. A deficit is the condition that results when expenditures exceed receipts. The deficit, in turn, causes a decline in the nation's *exchange rate*, the price of its currency compared with the currencies of other countries.

Hyperinflation is rapid, uncontrolled inflation that destroys a nation's economy. Money loses its value, and many people exchange goods and services instead of using currency. Hyperinflation occurs when a government spends much more money than it receives in taxes. The government then borrows or prints additional money to pay for the goods and services it needs. The increased demand for these items causes an overall increase in prices. The government then may have to print even more money to pay its expenses. The vast amount of money in circulation causes its value to drop sharply.

Hyperinflation has ruined the economies of some nations during or after wars. It caused the collapse of the German economy after World War I ended in 1918. The German government printed large amounts of currency to finance itself after the war. As a result, prices in Germany increased more than 1 trillion per cent from August 1922 to November 1923. In 1923, $1 in U.S. currency was worth over 4 trillion marks.

Effects of Severe Inflation

Mild inflation, according to some economists, encourages the growth of a nation's economy. Hyperinflation hurts a nation in many ways, but such uncontrolled inflation rarely occurs. Moderate inflation causes some changes in consumer buying habits, and its economic effects increase if the inflation becomes severe.

Internationale Bilderagentur

Hyperinflation is rapid, uncontrolled inflation. It causes money to drop sharply in value and thus ruins a nation's economy. After hyperinflation struck Germany during the early 1920's, shoppers needed baskets of currency, *left,* to buy groceries.

INFLATION

Effects on Consumer Behavior. Consumer behavior changes during a period of severe inflation. Many people feel discouraged because their income cannot keep up with rising prices. They cannot plan for future expenses because they do not know how much their money will buy at any later time.

Some people buy more than usual during an inflationary period. Many borrow money or use credit for large expenses, rather than buying later when prices will probably have risen even further.

Some consumers fight the effects of inflation by bartering their services, doing their own home repairs, and making their own clothing. Shoppers save money by such means as avoiding luxury items and growing their own vegetables.

Effects on Income. Severe inflation greatly affects people whose incomes do not increase at the same rate as inflation. Most pensions and other retirement benefits are *fixed*—that is, they neither increase nor decrease. Some benefits, such as U.S. Social Security benefits, are adjusted according to changes in price indexes. As the price level rises, money paid to people receiving these benefits also increases. This adjustment is known as *indexing* or *indexation*.

Indexation is also used to adjust interest rates, taxes, and wages and certain other earnings to correspond with the rate of inflation. For example, many union contracts provide automatic wage increases based on the rate of inflation. Inflation has a limited effect on union members with such contracts because their incomes increase as prices rise.

Effects on Investment. Some people try to protect themselves against inflation by investing in items that quickly increase in value. Such items include art objects, diamonds, gold bars, rare stamps, and gold and silver coins. Many people buy real estate during inflationary periods because the value of buildings and land increases rapidly at such times.

Effects on Business. Some businesses prosper during periods of inflation. They include credit-card agencies, discount stores, and agencies that collect overdue debts. Businesses that lease such items as cars and large appliances, which many people cannot afford to buy, also thrive at these times.

Theories About the Causes of Inflation

Economists have various theories that attempt to explain why inflation occurs. Many factors contribute to inflation. One element that is almost always present is an increase in a nation's money supply, which either causes or eases the increase in prices.

Inflation occurs during many wars and periods of reconstruction that follow wars. At such times, a nation's economy operates at full capacity, and the demand for goods and services exceeds the supply. This situation causes prices to increase.

The Quantity Theory states that inflation results when the demand for goods and services exceeds the supply. Such a situation occurs because the money supply increases at a rate faster than that at which goods and services are produced. Increased demand causes prices to increase, resulting in so-called *demand-pull inflation.*

The Keynesian Theory, developed by the British economist John Maynard Keynes, also focuses on excess demand as the cause of inflation. Keynes believed that increased demand for goods and services should be met by expanded production. However, after a nation's economy reaches full capacity, production cannot expand. If the demand for goods and services increases, prices continue to rise and inflation occurs. In such cases, Keynes recommended a tax increase, which would reduce the demand for goods and services and relieve the pressure on prices.

The Cost-Push Theory. When businesses raise their prices in response to cost increases, *cost-push inflation* results. Workers then may demand higher wages to keep up with rising prices, and a *wage-price spiral* occurs. If wages and prices increase but production does not, the supply of goods and services cannot meet the demand for those items.

Cost-push inflation also occurs if a limited number of businesses control the supply of certain products. A *monopoly* exists if one business controls an entire industry. In an *oligopoly*, so few companies provide a product or service that each of the firms can influence the price—with or without an agreement among all of them. In such controlled industries, consumers must buy from a limited number of sellers at prices set by the controlling businesses. But if competition in an industry is intense, each firm tries to offer a better or cheaper product than the others.

In addition, cost-push inflation results if several firms form a *cartel*, a group of businesses that functions as a monopoly. A cartel may limit the supply of a certain product, such as oil or copper, to drive prices up and thus earn higher profits. If that product is used in producing other goods, the cost of those items will also rise.

The Expectations Theory is based on the belief that prices will increase. When prices rise at a certain rate, people expect them to keep going up at that rate or even faster. Many workers attempt to keep ahead of the expected increases by demanding higher wages. Some unions bargain for contracts that include *escalator clauses* or *cost-of-living allowances*. These provisions call for periodic wage increases that keep pace with changes in price indexes. Such increases also contribute to rising prices.

Weapons Against Inflation

Fiscal Policy of a nation is reflected by the government's spending and taxing programs. The government can use these programs to reduce the demand for goods and services. The government can accomplish this goal by reducing its own spending. If the government buys less from businesses, sales go down and people have less money to spend. The government can also reduce the spendable income of consumers by raising taxes. If consumers spend less money, the demand for goods and services decreases—and prices level off.

Many people object to fiscal policy as a means of controlling inflation. They oppose a reduction in government spending because the funds involved help provide education, health care, and other services. No one wants to pay higher taxes, and a sharp reduction in demand often increases unemployment.

Monetary Policy is the program a nation follows to regulate its money supply. The monetary policy of the

United States is controlled by the Federal Reserve System, an independent agency of the government. Most of the nation's large commercial banks belong to the Federal Reserve System. The Federal Reserve determines the amount of money a member bank must have in its vaults or as deposits at its Federal Reserve Bank. This amount is called a *reserve requirement.* Under legislation enacted in 1980, the Federal Reserve's authority to set reserve requirements will be extended to all deposit-taking institutions by 1986.

The Federal Reserve can try to reduce the rate of inflation by decreasing the money supply and thus adopting a *tight money policy.* The Federal Reserve also may increase the money supply by following an *easy money policy.*

The Federal Reserve may decrease the money supply by raising its reserve requirement. This action limits the amount of money that banks can lend. Fewer loans are granted, and so people have less money to spend. As a result, the demand for goods and services decreases, and prices rise more slowly. If the Federal Reserve wants to increase the money supply, it lowers its reserve requirement.

The Federal Reserve also may decrease the money supply by selling government bonds. The purchasers pay for the bonds with checks drawn on their banks. When the banks pay these checks, their reserves are reduced. The banks make fewer loans, and so the money supply shrinks and the rate of inflation decreases.

The Federal Reserve increases the money supply by purchasing government bonds. It pays for the bonds with checks drawn on itself. When these checks are deposited in a member bank, a portion of that money becomes part of the bank's reserve. The bank can lend the remaining amount, and these funds increase the money supply.

The Federal Reserve also influences the money supply through the *discount rate.* This is the rate that banks must pay when they borrow money from Federal Reserve Banks. During inflationary periods, the Federal Reserve increases the discount rate. Banks may pass along this increase by charging customers higher interest rates, thus reducing the demand for loans, and shrinking the money supply. If the Federal Reserve reduces the interest rate, banks may lend more money at lower interest rates. This action increases the money supply.

Wage and Price Controls are established by a government to limit wage and price increases during an inflationary period. When a wage-price spiral occurs, wages and prices increase continually to keep up with each other. Some economists believe that by limiting these increases, wages and prices will eventually level off.

Many economists consider wage and price controls ineffective because such limits are difficult to establish and hard to enforce. Others believe wage and price controls interfere with the natural rise and fall of wages and prices.   RODNEY J. MORRISON

Related Articles in WORLD BOOK include:
Business Cycle   Price
Consumer Price Index   Price Control
Cost of Living   Supply and Demand
Federal Reserve System   Unemployment (Fighting
Money   Unemployment)
Mortgage

MENTAL ILLNESS is any disease of the mind that affects a person's thoughts, feelings, or behavior. Almost everyone has periods of sadness, anger, and fear. However, these periods usually do not last long. Mentally ill people suffer from extreme moods and feelings that may last for years. These disturbances often cause unhappiness and lead to socially unacceptable behavior. Mental illness can make it difficult for a person to carry out everyday tasks or to get along with other people.

People suffering from mental illness react to their condition in various ways. Some explain their behavior by blaming other people. Others withdraw from reality and seem completely unaware of their surroundings. In severe cases, mentally ill people may cause physical harm to themselves or to others.

Mental illness affects people in all nations and at all economic levels. However, behavior considered abnormal in one society may be accepted, or even encouraged, in another. Therefore, the definition of mental illness varies from culture to culture. In the United States, about 9 per cent of the people receive treatment for mental illness at some time during their life.

Mentally ill people can get help from various sources. Some patients receive treatment from psychiatrists and psychologists in private practice. Others obtain help at clinics and community mental health centers. People who suffer from severe mental illnesses may require hospitalization because they cannot take care of themselves properly.

Psychiatrists sometimes refer to mental illnesses as *mental disorders, emotional illnesses,* or *psychiatric illnesses.* The legal term *insanity* is used to describe a mental illness so severe that the person requires hospitalization or a legal guardian. A mental illness that occurs suddenly and requires immediate treatment may be called a *nervous breakdown,* but physicians do not use this term.

Kinds of Mental Illnesses

The major kinds of mental illnesses may be classified into seven groups: (1) organic disorders, (2) schizophrenia, (3) affective disorders, (4) anxiety disorders, (5) dissociative disorders, (6) personality disorders, and (7) childhood mental disorders. Psychiatrists sometimes also use the terms *neurosis* and *psychosis* to describe the severity of various mental illnesses. A neurosis is a mild disorder that causes distress but does not interfere greatly with a person's everyday activities. Most anxiety disorders and personality disorders are considered neuroses. A psychosis is a severe mental disorder that prevents the individual from functioning in a normal manner. Common psychoses include schizophrenia and manic-depressive disorder.

Organic Disorders are mental illnesses known to result from a physical cause, such as a birth defect, a disease, or an injury. Mental illnesses that involve no apparent physical cause are referred to as *functional disorders.* The most common organic disorders are delirium and dementia.

Delirium is a disorder in which a person loses awareness of his or her surroundings. People with delirium are easily distracted and confused, and they act and speak in a disorganized manner. They may have *illusions* (distorted visions) or *hallucinations* (sensations with

Play Therapy enables mentally ill youngsters to act out their emotional problems with dolls and other toys. For example, a child who is angry with his sister may strike a girl doll. A therapist encourages children to relate such actions to feelings about themselves and other people.

University of Illinois at the Medical Center (WORLD BOOK photo)

no real basis). Some delirious people become excited and irritable, but others appear listless and withdrawn. This disorder is most common in children and elderly people. Most cases of delirium begin suddenly and last no longer than a week. Causes of delirium include liver or kidney disease, high blood pressure, head injuries, alcoholism, and drug addiction.

Dementia is characterized by a decrease in mental ability, particularly memory and judgment. People with dementia may forget names, conversations, or recent events. They often neglect personal hygiene, disregard social rules, and experience other changes in personality and behavior. Dementia results from the destruction of brain tissue and occurs mainly in elderly people.

Schizophrenia is a severe mental disorder in which a person suffers unpredictable disturbances in thinking, mood, awareness, and behavior. The word *schizophrenia* means a *splitting of the mind*. It refers to the illogical, confused thoughts and actions that characterize schizophrenic behavior.

In most cases, schizophrenia develops gradually. A schizophrenic patient's conversations become unusual and difficult to understand. The patient may often show inappropriate emotions, such as laughing at a sad story or becoming extremely angry without any obvious cause. Many schizophrenic patients seem neither happy nor sad but have a mood described as blunted or flat.

People with schizophrenia commonly have delusions. For example, patients with *paranoid delusions* imagine that other people are following them or trying to harm them. Some schizophrenic patients also have hallucinations. The most common hallucinations are imaginary voices. A patient may believe that these voices carry messages from important people, or even from God.

Some people with schizophrenia move in unusual ways. When they walk, for example, they may lift their feet too high and hold them up too long. In a condition called *catatonia*, patients become completely still.

Affective Disorders mainly involve disturbances in the patient's mood. The two chief affective disorders are *depression* (sadness) and *mania* (extreme joy and overactivity). Patients with *manic-depressive disorder* suffer alternating periods of depression and mania.

Most people with depression feel hopeless and

Mental Illness Terms

Affective Disorder is a mental illness that mainly affects a person's moods.

Anxiety is a condition of worry, tension, or uneasiness produced by the anticipation of some danger whose source is largely unknown.

Catatonia refers to a condition in which a person remains completely motionless.

Compulsion is an irresistible impulse to perform a certain action.

Delusion is a false belief that a person maintains in spite of evidence that proves it untrue.

Depression is a mental disorder characterized by feelings of deep sadness, hopelessness, and worthlessness.

Functional Disorder refers to a mental illness that has no apparent physical cause.

Hallucination is the sensation of something that does not really exist.

Illusion is a distorted perception of reality.

Mania means a mental disorder that involves extreme optimism and excessive energy, often accompanied by uncontrollable irritability and anger.

Neurosis is a mild mental disorder.

Obsession is a recurring thought that a person considers senseless or terrible but cannot ignore.

Organic Disorder refers to a mental illness that results from a physical cause, such as a birth defect, a disease, or an injury.

Paranoia is a mental condition in which an individual unjustifiably feels threatened by other people.

Phobia means a strong, unreasonable fear of a particular object or situation.

Psychosis is a severe mental disorder.

Schizophrenia is a severe mental disorder characterized by unpredictable thoughts and behavior and a withdrawal from reality.

Unconscious refers to thoughts and feelings that a person is not directly or fully aware of.

worthless. Many suffer from insomnia and loss of appetite. Other symptoms include headaches, backaches, and chest pains. Some people with depression move and think slowly, but others feel restless. In many cases, the patient has difficulty concentrating and may have terrifying and uncontrollable thoughts. Many people with depression attempt suicide because they believe they have no reason to continue living. Others view suicide as an escape from their problems.

A person with mania feels alert, optimistic, and overconfident. However, these feelings may suddenly change to irritability or rage. The mind jumps from one thought to another, and the individual speaks rapidly in a rambling and uncontrollable manner. People with mania move quickly, work energetically, and need little sleep. They move restlessly from project to project but seldom complete any particular task. Most periods of mania begin suddenly, last for a few days or weeks, and then end abruptly.

Anxiety Disorders are mental disturbances in which a person experiences unreasonable fears. The four chief types of anxiety disorders are (1) generalized anxiety, (2) phobias, (3) panic disorder, and (4) obsessive-compulsive disorder.

Generalized Anxiety is a persistent fear without obvious cause that lasts a month or longer. Symptoms of this disorder include muscle tension, nausea, rapid heartbeat, and hot or cold spells. People with generalized anxiety constantly worry that something terrible will happen to them. This worry makes them impatient and irritable, and they often find it difficult to get along with other people.

Phobias are persistent, strong fears of certain objects or situations. Common phobias include *agoraphobia*, the fear of large open spaces; and *claustrophobia*, the fear of small enclosed spaces. A person suffering from a phobia has a strong desire to avoid the dreaded object or situation. If forced into contact with the object of the phobia, the individual may panic or become nauseated.

Panic Disorder is a sudden, intense feeling of fear. Symptoms include shortness of breath, rapid heartbeat, dizziness, numbness, sweating, and trembling. In most cases, a fear of death accompanies these physical disturbances. Most panic attacks last several minutes, but others continue for several hours. A person may have only one attack, or attacks may recur over a period of months or years. This disorder occurs far more commonly in women than in men.

Obsessive-Compulsive Disorder is characterized by illogical and uncontrollable impulses that result in *obsessions* or *compulsions*. Obsessions are persistent thoughts that the patient considers senseless or terrible but cannot ignore. The most common obsessions involve thoughts of committing violent acts or of becoming contaminated. Compulsions are actions performed again and again with little purpose, such as repeated handwashing or counting objects.

People with compulsions believe their actions will produce or prevent some future event. They generally realize the senselessness of their behavior and do not enjoy performing it. However, resisting the compulsion causes increased tension, which immediately disappears after the action is performed. In severe cases, a compulsion becomes a person's major activity and thus prevents the individual from leading a normal life.

Dissociative Disorders involve a loss or change of identity. In one common dissociative disorder, *psychogenic amnesia*, a person forgets his or her past. In a similar disorder, called *psychogenic fugue*, the individual not only forgets the past but also travels to a new location and assumes a new identity. People who suffer from *depersonalization disorder* feel that they are watching themselves from a distance and have no control over their actions. In *multiple personality disorder*, the individual has two or more distinct personalities, each of which dominates at certain times.

Personality Disorders are character traits that create difficulties in personal relationships. For example, *antisocial personality disorder* is characterized by aggressive and harmful behavior that first occurs before the age of 15. Such behavior includes lying, stealing, fighting, and resisting authority. During adulthood, people with this disorder often have difficulty keeping a job or accepting other responsibilities.

Individuals with *paranoid personality disorder* are overly suspicious, cautious, and secretive. They may have delusions that people are watching them or talking about them. They often criticize others but have difficulty accepting criticism.

People who suffer from *compulsive personality disorder* attach great importance to organization. They strive for efficiency and may spend a great deal of time making lists and schedules. But they are also indecisive and seldom accomplish anything they set out to do. They often make unreasonable demands on other people and have difficulty expressing emotions.

Childhood Mental Disorders. Children may suffer from the same mental disorders that affect adults, but sometimes these disorders produce different symptoms in children. For example, a child with depression may demonstrate the depression by getting into trouble in school. In addition, some mental illnesses generally occur only in children. In one such illness, *attention deficit disorder*, the child is disorganized and easily distracted. Most children with this disorder also suffer from *hyperactivity*, a state of almost constant motion. These disturbances often cause youngsters to have learning difficulties in school and behavior problems both in school and at home.

A severe mental disorder called *infantile autism* begins during early childhood. Children with this disorder fail to develop speech and other forms of communication. Autistic children appear detached and unresponsive. They usually stare vacantly and have no facial expression. They may become strongly attached to specific objects and repeatedly perform such rhythmic body movements as handclapping and rocking.

Causes of Mental Illness

Research has shown that mental illnesses have various causes, but the causes are not fully understood. Some mental disorders are due to physical changes in the brain resulting from illness or injury. Chemical imbalances in the brain may cause other mental illnesses. Still other disorders are mainly due to conditions in the environment that affect a person's mental state. These conditions include unpleasant childhood experiences and severe emotional stress. In addition, many cases of

MENTAL ILLNESS

University of Illinois at the Medical Center (WORLD BOOK photo)

A Rorschach Test uses 10 standardized inkblots to help diagnose mental disorders. The patient describes what he or she sees in each inkblot. A trained examiner interprets the descriptions.

mental illness probably result from a combination of two or more of these causes.

Physical Changes in the structure of the brain may cause severe mental disorders, including delirium and dementia. Brain damage may result from such causes as head injuries, infections, or inherited defects. Diseases that damage or destroy brain tissue include encephalitis, meningitis, and brain tumors. A disease called *arteriosclerosis* (hardening of the arteries) may damage the brain by reducing its blood supply. This disease mainly attacks middle-aged and older people.

Chemical Imbalances in the body may affect a person's thoughts, feelings, and behavior. Research suggests that an imbalance of certain brain chemicals may cause such mental illnesses as schizophrenia and manic-depressive disorder. These chemicals, called *neurotransmitters*, enable the nerve cells in the brain to communicate with one another. People with schizophrenia may have a defect that causes brain cells to release excess amounts of *dopamine*, a neurotransmitter. Mania may result from an excess of dopamine and two other neurotransmitters, *norepinephrine* and *serotonin*. A deficiency of these three chemicals may cause depression. See BRAIN (The Chemistry of the Brain).

Both schizophrenia and manic-depressive disorder sometimes run in families. Studies suggest that this happens because children can inherit a tendency to develop the chemical imbalances involved in the disorders. However, environmental conditions generally determine whether a person with such an inherited tendency will actually become mentally ill.

Childhood Experiences that are unpleasant or disturbing may cause unconscious mental conflicts that affect a person throughout life. Most such experiences involve family problems, relationships with other children, or difficulties in school. Many psychiatrists believe

that adults who were overprotected as children are more subject to mental illness because they never learned how to deal with their problems.

Emotional Stress may become so severe that it interferes with a person's ability to deal with everyday problems. Stress may result from overwork, poor health, financial problems, or family responsibilities. If stress becomes overwhelming, a person may reach the "breaking point" and become mentally ill. To a great extent, the ability to deal with emotional stress depends on an individual's physical condition, past experiences, and current problems.

Methods of Treatment

Mentally ill people need specialized treatment from mental health professionals, such as psychiatrists and psychologists. Psychiatrists have an M.D. degree and advanced training in the treatment of mental illness. Most psychologists have a Ph.D. degree and practical training in psychology.

Psychiatrists diagnose and treat most cases of mental illness. First, a psychiatrist thoroughly examines the patient to determine if the mental disorder has a physical cause. The psychiatrist also talks with the patient and, in many cases, with the patient's family. These discussions help the psychiatrist understand the symptoms of the disorder.

A psychologist may help the psychiatrist diagnose mental illnesses. Psychologists give patients special tests that measure a wide variety of personality traits and mental reactions. In a Rorschach test, for example, patients describe what they see in a series of standardized inkblots. These descriptions help the examiner recognize abnormal psychological tendencies.

After diagnosing a patient's disorder, the psychiatrist may treat the illness in a number of ways. The major methods of treatment include (1) drug therapy, (2) psychotherapy, (3) electroconvulsive therapy, (4) psychosurgery, and (5) hospitalization.

Drug Therapy. Since 1950, scientists have developed a number of medications that have proved extremely successful in the treatment of certain mental disorders. Psychiatrists use *tricyclic antidepressants* to treat patients with severe depression. In most cases, these drugs restore the depressed patient to normal. *Lithium carbonate* is the most effective drug for patients who suffer from manic-depressive disorder. It reduces the frequency and severity of both the manic periods and the depressive periods and, in many cases, eliminates them entirely. Medications called *antianxiety drugs* or *tranquilizers* help relieve the tension caused by anxiety disorders. Psychiatrists often use *antipsychotic drugs* to treat schizophrenia. These drugs help relieve hallucinations, delusions, and other symptoms of schizophrenia.

Some drugs used in treating mental illnesses may have serious side effects. Drowsiness and muscle weakness often accompany the use of antianxiety drugs, and antipsychotic drugs may cause restlessness and muscle spasms. In many cases, patients receiving drug therapy become dependent on their medication. If the drugs are discontinued, the symptoms of the disorder often return.

Psychotherapy consists of structured discussions and other activities involving a therapist and one or more patients. In general, the goal of psychotherapy is to help

578

patients discover the cause of their mental disorder and then improve or correct their condition. A psychotherapist has special training in the theories and techniques of psychotherapy. A psychotherapist may be a psychiatrist, a psychologist, or a psychiatric social worker.

Kinds of Psychotherapy include (1) analytic, (2) behavioral, and (3) humanistic. Some psychotherapists use one of these forms for all their patients. Other therapists vary their techniques depending on the patient's individual needs.

Analytic psychotherapy is based on the theory that mental disorders result from conflicts between conscious and unconscious forces in the mind. The best-known form of analytic therapy is called *psychoanalysis*. Psychoanalysts try to make their patients aware of unconscious mental conflicts and help them find ways to resolve these conflicts. Many analysts use a method called *free association*, in which the patient talks about anything that comes to mind. A psychoanalyst may also question patients about their dreams and childhood memories, which can provide insight into unconscious thoughts and feelings.

Behavioral psychotherapy concentrates on relieving current symptoms of the patient's mental disorder rather than on trying to understand unconscious conflicts. According to behavioral theory, mentally ill people never learned how to deal with everyday problems. Behavioral therapists help patients develop appropriate behavior through such methods as rewarding desirable responses and ignoring or punishing undesirable ones.

Humanistic psychotherapy focuses on recent events and personal relationships in the patient's life. The patient and the therapist work as a team to solve the practical problems caused by the mental disorder. Humanistic therapists try to help patients appreciate and accept themselves. The therapist encourages patients to discuss their feelings and then provides reassurance and practical advice.

Psychodrama is a technique used by psychotherapists to help patients view their problems more clearly. In a psychodrama, patients portray themselves and other people in their lives.

Special Techniques may be used in conjunction with any type of psychotherapy. The most widely used techniques include (1) psychodrama, (2) play therapy, and (3) group therapy.

In a psychodrama, a group of patients act out their problems. They may play the roles of themselves and of other people in their lives. Such role-playing encourages the patients to observe their problems from various points of view and thus gain a better understanding of their mental disorder.

Play therapy is used in treating mentally disturbed children. A therapist gives the child dolls and other toys and asks the youngster to tell a story about them. The child generally uses the toys to act out personal conflicts. The therapist then helps the young patient relate these play actions to his or her own situation.

Group therapy is any kind of psychotherapy conducted with a group of six or more people. Many patients learn about their own problems by sharing experiences with people who have similar conflicts. The group members also encourage and support one another during times of personal stress.

Electroconvulsive Therapy (ECT), also called *electroshock treatment*, involves passing an electric current through the patient's brain for a fraction of a second. The patient becomes unconscious and experiences a convulsion that lasts about one minute. Psychiatrists currently use ECT only to treat hospitalized patients who remain depressed and suicidal in spite of drug therapy and psychotherapy. In most cases, ECT shortens the period of depression, but does not prevent future occurrences. ECT also often causes temporary amnesia.

Psychosurgery is used in treating mental disorders that result from an overproduction of chemicals or nerve impulses in a specific area of the brain. Such surgery involves destroying or removing the defective area or cutting the nerve fibers between it and other parts of the brain. The most common type of psychosurgery is a *cingulotomy*. In this operation, the surgeon uses a surgical knife or an electric current to cut through a bundle of nerve fibers called the *cingulum*. The cingulum connects the brain's frontal and temporal lobes and plays a role in controlling emotions.

Psychosurgery is chiefly used in treating patients who suffer from severe depression, compulsions, or anxieties. Psychiatrists generally recommend such surgery only if other methods of treatment have proved ineffective. Many psychiatrists consider psychosurgery unsafe and discourage its use in treating mental illness.

Hospitalization may be necessary for people with severe mental illnesses who require constant medical attention. In many cases, removing patients from the home environment relieves them of any social or personal stress that may have contributed to the development of mental illness. In addition, a hospital has trained personnel who can prevent patients from harming themselves or others.

In most mental hospitals, patients receive specialized treatment for their particular mental disorder. Trained therapists prescribe medications, supervise psychotherapy sessions, and administer electroconvulsive treatments. In many hospitals, patients and staff members work together to plan hospital routines. This feeling of participation helps patients readjust to everyday activities after they leave the hospital.

History

Early Attitudes. Prehistoric peoples believed mental illnesses were caused by evil spirits that possessed the body. Tribal priests performed magical ceremonies, administered potions, and used hypnosis to drive out the evil spirits. Some priests also tried to release the spirits by cutting a hole in the victim's skull.

Many ancient Greeks believed that mental disorders were punishment from their gods, and so they tried to cure these illnesses with prayers and religious ceremonies. About 400 B.C., however, the Greek physician Hippocrates claimed that mental disorders resulted from an imbalance of four body fluids: blood, phlegm, yellow bile, and black bile. For example, depression supposedly resulted from an excess of black bile. The ancient Greek name for this fluid, *melan chole*, is the origin of the English word *melancholy*, which means *sadness*.

During the Middle Ages, a belief in witchcraft spread throughout Europe. Many people with mental illnesses were considered witches and were killed by burning, hanging, or drowning. Mentally ill people who managed to escape charges of witchcraft were generally put in prisons or hospitals.

During the 1500's, many European nations built special institutions for the mentally ill. One of the most famous of these institutions was St. Mary of Bethlehem in London, which became widely known as *Bedlam*. The inmates there suffered from unsanitary conditions, public beatings, and other harsh treatment. Today, the word *bedlam* means *uproar* and *confusion*.

Humane Treatment of mentally ill people began in the late 1700's. During that period, a French physician named Philippe Pinel and William Tuke, a British merchant, worked to improve the conditions of mental institutions in their countries. Through their efforts, many mental hospitals introduced treatments that included fresh air, exercise, and pleasant surroundings.

During the early 1800's, an American physician named Benjamin Rush incorporated the ideas of Pinel and Tuke in his treatment of mentally ill patients at Pennsylvania Hospital in Philadelphia. Dorothea Dix, an American schoolteacher, began visiting mental hospitals throughout the United States in the 1840's. She described the hospitals' miserable conditions to state legislators and persuaded them to pass laws providing state funds for mental institutions.

In 1908, Clifford W. Beers, a former mental patient, wrote a book that described his experiences in three mental hospitals in Connecticut. This book, *A Mind That Found Itself*, stimulated public interest in mental illness. In 1909, Beers helped establish the National Committee for Mental Hygiene (now the National Association for Mental Health). This committee was made up of psychiatrists, psychologists, and private citizens. It worked to promote public understanding of the problems of mental illness. By 1919, the committee had grown into an international organization that provided funds for research in the diagnosis, treatment, and prevention of mental disorders.

Illustration from *The History of Psychiatry* by Franz G. Alexander and Sheldon T. Selesnick, © 1966 Harper & Row, Publishers

A Rotating Chair was used to treat mental disorders during the late 1700's. It supposedly relieved mental illness by increasing the blood supply to the brain.

Medical Approaches to mental illness were first practiced during the late 1800's in Europe. Emil Kraepelin, a German psychiatrist, developed a system of diagnosing and classifying mental disorders in 1883. These classifications were expanded by Eugene Bleuler, a Swiss physician. Bleuler also introduced the practice of examining all areas of a patient's life, not only the symptoms of mental illness. An American psychiatrist named Adolf Meyer taught the ideas of Kraepelin and Bleuler in the United States and encouraged the establishment of psychiatric research centers.

In the early 1900's, the Austrian psychiatrist Sigmund Freud introduced the theory that forces in the unconscious mind strongly influence an individual's personality and behavior. Freud also suggested that conflicts during early childhood affect the development of the unconscious. These theories became the basis for psychoanalysis and a majority of the other forms of psychotherapy.

Recent Developments. In 1956, for the first time, the number of patients discharged from public mental hospitals in the United States exceeded the number admitted. This trend has continued largely because of the effectiveness of drug therapy, which enables many patients to receive treatment while living at home. However, the release of such large numbers of patients has caused serious problems. Many communities lack adequate counseling services to help mentally ill individuals readjust to everyday life. As a result, former patients often find it difficult to obtain housing and employment.

The success of drug therapy has led to increased interest in finding other effective means of treating mental illness. Much of this work involves searching for links between mental disturbances and genetic defects or other physical disorders.   PHILIP A. BERGER

Dictionary Supplement

1976
1977
1978
1979
1980
1981

This section lists important words from the 1982 edition of THE WORLD BOOK DICTIONARY. This dictionary, first published in 1963, keeps abreast of our living language with a program of continuous editorial revision. The following supplement has been prepared under the direction of the editors of THE WORLD BOOK ENCYCLOPEDIA and Clarence L. Barnhart, editor in chief of THE WORLD BOOK DICTIONARY. It is presented as a service to owners of the dictionary and as an informative feature to subscribers to THE WORLD BOOK YEAR BOOK.

A a

act, *n*. **get one's act together**, *U.S. Informal*. to organize oneself, often in order to pursue some objective: *There I was . . . feeling like a miserable, self-indulgent, neurotic, middle-aged woman who couldn't get her act together* (Eleanor Coppola).

ADC[1] **2** advanced developing country: *Foreign aid has contributed to the rise of a series of economically free and prosperous "ADCs," . . . including South Korea, Singapore, Taiwan, Malaysia, and Thailand* (Time).

a|khound|ism (ä kün′diz əm), *n*. government influenced or directed by the priestly class of mullahs: *Iran's Foreign Minister . . . dismissed the charge of too much akhoundism in Iran* (New York Times). [< Persian *ākhūnd* teacher, mullah + English *-ism*]

ALCM (no periods), air-launched cruise missile.

an|ti-choice (an′tē chois′), *adj*. opposed to the right to choose abortion to terminate a pregnancy: *Anti-choice candidates are in lower-case letters . . . Some candidates are anti-choice, but did not accept RTL [right-to-life] endorsement* (New York Times).

an|ti|nuke (an′tē nük′), *adj*. opposed to the use of nuclear energy for military purposes or for the generation of electricity: *Spock, antinuke since 1962, has added the Equal Rights Amendment ratification movement in the U.S. to his list of public concerns* (Maclean's).

A|za|ni|an (ə zā′nē ən), *adj., n.* — *adj.* of or belonging to Azania, a name by which African nationalists call South Africa: *Another newly created group, the Azanian People's Organization . . . was often at loggerheads with the homeland leaders* (Richard Dale). — *n.* a native or inhabitant of Azania. [< *Azania,* originally the name of a southern African culture that flourished from about A.D. 500 to about 1500]

B b

blow[2], *v*. **blow away**, *U.S. Slang*. to kill or destroy: *Like a pack of wolves . . . they are looking for somebody to blow away* (Time).

C c

case[1], *n*. **get off one's case**, *U.S. Slang*. to leave one alone; stop annoying or harassing one: *When pressed about her boyfriends she gets very sarcastic and . . . will say something like "Get off my case"* (New York Post).

course|ware (kôrs′wār′, kōrs′-), *n*. instructional materials designed for or stored in computers: *More than 2,000 users were preparing new courseware to use with or add to the PLATO-course catalogue* (Science News). [< *course* + (soft)*ware*]

D d

de|mand-side (di mand′sīd′, -mänd′-), *adj*. of or having to do with economic policy theoretically designed to stimulate demand in a nation's economy by such methods as increasing government spending to create a demand for goods and services that will be met by increased employment: *The temptation to take up the slack by the old proven Keynesian demand-side measure of doubling and redoubling military spending will be very great indeed* (Wassily Leontief).

down|burst (doun′bėrst′), *n*. a strong downdraft creating a sudden destructive air current near the ground: *T. T. Fujita at the University of Chicago, who coined the word "downburst" . . . showed that they were responsible for a number of commercial airplane accidents* (Louis J. Battan). *Downbursts often accompany tornadoes* (Science News).

dump[1], *v., n*. **dump on**, *U.S. Slang*. to attack verbally; criticize severely: *Black leaders were angrily dumping on President Carter for his scaled-down urban program* (New York Times).

dynamic, *adj*. **6** (of a computer memory) requiring electrical recharging to retain data; not static: *In the "dynamic" version developed by Texas Instruments . . . the method of storage is not permanent, but must be refreshed regularly* (New Scientist).

E e

electronic / church, *U.S*. religious television programs of a church or evangelistic service designed for mass audiences, usually conducted by preachers of great personal appeal: *Some church leaders blamed declining contributions in part on funds sent to the increasingly popular "electronic church"* (James M. Wall).

ex|on[1] (ek′son), *n*. a segment of DNA that specifies the genetic code for a protein, as distinguished from an intervening sequence (intron): *In general the introns of split genes are longer than the exons* (Scientific American). [< *ex-* outer, outside + *-on*]

F f

For|ghan or **For|gan** (fôr′gən), *n*. a Moslem organization in Iran opposing the revolutionary government established in 1979: *As Khomeini pressed through his ideas on the Islamic government of Iran, . . . the ultra-Muslim Forghan terrorist group perpetrated a series of assassinations against the senior clergy* (H. V. Hodson). [< a Persian name for the Koran]

four / modernizations, a program to modernize China's agriculture, industry, national defense, and science and technology: *Peking's ambitious program for turning China into an industrial power by the end of the century is known as the "four modernizations"* (Fox Butterfield). *The topic of the meeting was what Beijing's scientific research institutes . . . should do to coordinate the shifting of the focus of the Party's work to the four modernizations* (Beijing Review).

Frost / Belt or **Frost|-belt** (frôst′ belt′, frost′-), *n. U.S.* **1** the northern region of the United States extending east to west that regularly has frost in colder seasons: *Opponents of the proposed budget cuts contend that, in general, the Frost Belt will suffer more heavily because it is more dependent on Government funds* (New York Times). **2** = Snowbelt (def. 2a). [patterned on *Sunbelt*]

G g

gauge / theory, *Physics*. any theory that attempts to establish relationships between fundamental forces such as gravity, electromagnetism, the weak force, and the like: *The existence of charm has been predicted by a powerful set of theories of the fundamental forces, the gauge theories, and this discovery established those theories* (New Scientist).

gem|el|lol|o|gist (je′mə lol′ə jist), *n*. a scientist who specializes in the study of twins: *Until their reunion took place, and those of other long-separated identical twins which consequently followed, gemellologists . . . had believed there to be fewer than a dozen such pairs of twins alive today* (Science News). [< Latin *gemellus, geminus* twin + English *-ologist*]

glit|ter|a|ti (glit′ə rä′tē, -rā′tī), *n.pl. U.S. Slang*. fashionable people, especially those who conspicuously attend to cultural endeavors and social events: *He must be so transported by the money he's making . . . that $119 (more probably $119.95) for a minuscule jar of something only the glitterati could afford to buy is a bargain for him* (Corinna Marsh). *In New York City, the glitterati got together to help buy vests for the city's police* (Time). [patterned on *literati*]

granny / flat, *British*. an addition to a house, permitting an elderly relative to live independently: *A granny flat is a self-contained, single-story dwelling of about 378 feet; it's designed for easy installation in an average backyard* (Modern Maturity).

H h

HBO (no periods), Home Box Office (a commercial cable television service in the United States): *HBO is available only to cable TV subscribers and people who live in selected apartment buildings* (Time).

helping / profession, *U.S*. any profession, such as vocational guidance or occupational therapy, whose purpose is to help people improve their lives and cope more effectively with everyday problems: *If you are a social worker or a counsellor of some sort, you are a member of the helping professions* (New York Daily News).

I i

intelligent, *adj*. **3a** capable of processing data by a built-in microprocessor: *The computer can be . . . part of the terminal itself (when the terminal is intelligent). Because of the falling costs of hardware, it is becoming economically feasible for students to have their own intelligent terminals* (New Scientist). **b** capable of making fine distinctions or performing certain logical operations: *The gadget . . . is so "intelligent" that it knows immediately if a piece of paper or even a sliver of the same material it is guarding is slid* under the object in an attempt to remove it (New York Times Magazine).

in|ter|ven|ing / se|quence, a segment of DNA that has no specific genetic code; intron: *The genes of higher plants and animals and their viruses contain "inter-vening sequences," segments that are snipped out of the intermediary between DNA and protein synthesis and thus are not represented in any protein product* (Julie Ann Miller).

in|tron (in′tron), *n.* a segment of DNA that has no specific genetic code; intervening sequence: *One possibility is that some of the introns are promoters—regions of DNA where the enzyme RNA polymerase first binds to a gene before transcribing it. Introns may also play a role in control of gene expression* (Thomas H. Maugh II). [< *intro-* inward, inside + *-on*]

J j

jet|foil (jet′foil′), *n.* a jet-propelled hydro-foil: *Three times a day, its jetfoil will "fly" down the river from the heart of London to Belgium and back for less than it costs to go by plane* (Listener).

Ju|no, *n.* **3** an award presented annually in Canada for outstanding achievements in music: *The Junos he has accumulated tell part of the story—three in country categories, two for folk-singer and one for composer of the year* (Maclean's).

K k

kwan|za (kwän′zə), *n., pl.* **-zas.** the unit of money of Angola, equal to 100 lweis: *The Finance Ministry announced the introduction of a new currency, the kwanza (named after the nation's main river), to replace the Portuguese escudo* (Thomas H. Henrikson). [perhaps related to Swahili *kwanza;* see **Kwanza**]

L l

le|gion|el|lo|sis (lē′jə nə lō′sis), *n.* = legionnaires' disease: *Significant also ... was the development of rapid methods for the diagnosis of legionellosis* (Richard C. Tilton). [< New Latin *Legionella (pneumophila),* the bacterium causing it + *-osis*]

lo|ti (lō′tē), *n., pl.* **maloti.** the unit of money of Lesotho, equal in value with the South African rand: *On Jan. 19, 1980, Lesotho issued its new currency, the loti ... backed by South Africa's rand* (Guy Arnold). [< Sesotho *loti*]

lwei (lə wei′), *n., pl.* **lweis.** a unit of money in Angola, equal to 1/100 of a kwanza. [< the native name]

M m

ma|lo|ti (mə lō′tē), *n.* plural of **loti:** *The maloti was ... equal to one South African rand, which would also be legal tender in Lesotho* (Richard Dale).

mo|bile / mis|sile, a missile that can be moved through underground tunnels to any one of several launch sites: *Some respected analysts ... have expressed support for the notion of building a mobile missile, but have counseled against deploying a blockbuster like the MX* (Richard Burt).

mon|go² (mong′gō), *n. U.S. Slang.* objects of salvage, especially as considered of use or value by scavengers: *"Mongo" hunters, usually drug addicts, will set fires and then come back ... for the lead piping, copper fixtures, and other such material that is ... then sold to junk dealers* (Stacey Levere). [origin unknown]

N n

NAAQS (no periods), National Ambient Air Quality Standards: *NAAQS were established for such pollutants as sulfur dioxide, nitrogen dioxide, hydrocarbons, carbon monoxide, photochemical oxidants (smog formers), and particulate matter* (Julian Josephson).

na|cho (nä′chō), *n., pl.* **-chos.** a taco tortilla or chip baked with cheese and Mexican pepper: *A recent meal began with nachos, the appetizer made with cheese and beans and chilies baked on tortillas* (Craig Claiborne). [< Mexican Spanish *nacho*]

neu|ro|met|rics (nur′ō met′riks), *n.* the measurement and analysis of the electrical activity of the brain and nervous system by means of computers: *Neurometrics ... has begun to focus on specific regions of brain tissue in hopes of relating them to specific forms of learning. Perhaps neurometrics will become the diagnostic procedure of the future, pointing to the region of the brain in need of intervention* (Robert O. Pihl).

nu|mer|ol|o|gy, *n.* **2** numerical calculation or assessment: *The verification issue ... seems to be a refuge for senators who do not want to trouble themselves digging into the details of missile numerology* (New Republic). *"I put myself through a crash course in ... the numerology of force levels"* (Time).

O o

O.M.S. 1 orbital maneuvering system: *Using the two 6,000-pound thrust engines ... O.M.S. 1 will be moving Columbia forward and higher on her flight path* (Neil B. Hutchinson).

os|to|mate (os′tə māt, -mit), *n.* a person who has undergone a colostomy, ileostomy, or similar operation: *Once recovery is complete, an ostomate can lead a normal life* (New York Post).

os|to|my (os′tə mē), *n., pl.* **-mies.** a colostomy, ileostomy, or similar operation: *An ostomy may become necessary because part of the intestine or urinary tract is affected with cancer or an inflammatory disease* (Dr. Neil Solomon). [abstracted < *colostomy, cecostomy,* etc.]

P p

par|a³ (par′ə), *n., pl.* **par|as.** *U.S. Informal.* a paraprofessional: *The paras—predominantly black and Hispanic women ... became paras even though the pay they received at the time was less than what they were getting on welfare, because they wanted work rather than welfare* (Albert Shanker).

par|vo (pär′vō), *n.* = parvovirus: *Because the virus is so new ... only two companies were licensed by the U.S. Department of Agriculture to produce a parvo vaccine* (Discover).

par|vo|vi|rus (pär′vō vī′rəs), *n.* any one of a group of small viruses found in various animals, especially a virus transmitted by dog feces and causing a serious and often fatal disease of dogs: *Studies ... suggest that hepatitis A virus is also a parvovirus* (Science). [< Latin *parvus* little + English *virus*]

PAS|CAL (pas kal′, pas′kəl), *n.* a computer language used especially to deal with data in alphabetic form, such as lists and records, and for educational programs: *One of the newest languages to gain popularity is PASCAL, ... favoured by many as the most suitable teaching language* (New Scientist). [< Blaise *Pascal* (see etym. under **Pascal's law**), capitalized by analogy with *ALGOL, COBOL,* etc.]

pass-a|long (pas′ə lông′, -long′), *n. U.S.* any increase in the costs of providing goods or services charged to a customer, especially in the form of increased prices, rent, or fees: *Though the retail price of gasoline has risen 20% in the past few months, almost all of that has represented a simple pass-along of higher wholesale prices* (Time).

pa|tri|ate (pā′trē āt), *v.t.,* **-at|ed, -at|ing.** *Canadian.* to subject to patriation: *The Liberal leader proposed a scheme to immediately patriate the constitution, now lodged in Westminster, with provision for a referendum if the provinces can't agree on a way to amend it* (Maclean's). [< (re)*patriate*]

pho|to|vol|ta|ics (fō′tō vol tā′iks), *n.* the use of photovoltaic cells, especially solar cells for the direct conversion of sunlight into electricity: *As the utility's rates go up, the photovoltaic option will become more attractive to its customers, and more of them will switch to photovoltaics* (New Yorker).

pos|slq (pos′əl kyü′), *n. U.S.* a person of the opposite sex sharing living quarters: *The Census Bureau invented the word "posslq"* (St. Louis Post-Dispatch). *What's more, "Posslq" is so simple to pronounce, so non-judgmental and pleasing to the ear* (Ann Landers). *Love will stay forever new, If you will be my posslq* (Charles Osgood). [< *p*(erson) of *o*(pposite) *s*(ex) *s*(haring) *l*(iving) *q*(uarters)]

pre|quel (prē′kwəl), *n.* a book, motion picture, or play based on another, but dealing with earlier events than those described in the original work: *Old genres were perpetuated in sequels, imitations, and "prequels"* (David Robinson). *This is a daring movie, ... a prequel," as the neologism has it* (Time). [< *pre-* + (se)*quel*]

punt⁴ (pŭnt, punt), *n., pl.* **punt** or **punts.** the unit of money of Ireland. It was known as the Irish pound until 1979, when it was separated from the pound sterling: *Together with other European currencies, the punt fluctuated downward against sterling* (Mavis Arnold). [< Irish Gaelic *púnt* pound]

Q q

QCD (no periods), quantum chromodynamics: *In the QCD theory quarks interact by exchanging a gluon* (New Scientist).

quan|tum / chro|mo|dy|nam|ics, = chromodynamics: *All this is pulled together in a theory called quantum chromodynamics (QCD) analogous to the thoroughly proved quantum electrodynamics* which describes the interaction of particles through electromagnetic forces (Technology Review).

Qube or **QUBE** (kyüb), *n. Trademark.* a cable television service that allows subscribers to send in messages by two-way communication in response to broadcasts on certain channels: *Subscribers to QUBE . . . can vote on contestants on a local amateur show, evaluate newspaper features, order products advertised on the air* (C. P. Gilmore).

R r

rapid / deployment / force, a military unit or group of units that can be sent immediately to effect a military operation in any critical area of the world: *Formation of a rapid deployment force (RDF) had been announced, but it was only a reorganization of existing forces with improved logistic support* (Robin Ranger).

RDF 3 rapid deployment force: *Some questioned whether the units earmarked for the RDF were combat-ready* (Robert M. Lawrence).

re|plan|ta|tion (rē'plan tā'shən), *n.* **1** a second or fresh planting. **2** the attachment of a severed member of the body: *Replantation . . . must be based on the patient's general condition, on the nature of the trauma, and on the time limit for survival of the replanted limb* (Science News).

S s

Sagebrush / Rebellion, *U.S.* a movement to gain state control of federally owned lands in western States: *Arizona, New Mexico, Utah, Washington, and Wyoming formally joined Nevada in the "Sagebrush Rebellion," approving laws calling for state takeover of unreserved land currently controlled by the federal government* (David C. Beckwith).

scape⁴ (skāp), *n. U.S. Aerospace.* a space suit: *This period is referred to officially by NASA as the "Scape-phase," a reference to an acronym used to describe the protective suits* (Robert Lindsey). [< *s*(elf)-*c*(ontained) *a*(tmospheric) *p*(rotective) *e*(nsemble)]

shekel, *n.* **3** a unit of paper money in Israel, introduced in 1980, equal to 10 lirot or Israeli pounds: *The new notes bear the images of key figures in Zionism; on the 10-shekel note, for example, is a likeness of Theodor Herzl* (New York Times).

si|a|bon (sē'ə bən, syä'bən), *n.* the offspring of a siamang (genus *Symphalangus*) and a gibbon (genus *Hylobates*): *The siabon combines the physical features of both parents and has 47 chromosomes—22 from the gibbon father and 25 from the siamang mother. A gibbon ordinarily has 44 chromosomes and a siamang has 50* (Charles F. Merbs). [< *sia*(mang) + (*gib*)*bon*]

SLCM (no periods), submarine-launched cruise missile.

snowbelt, *n.* **2 Snowbelt,** *U.S.* **a** the northern region of the United States extending from east to west that regularly has snowfall in colder seasons. **b** = Frost Belt (def. 1): *Economic issues . . . increasingly are dividing the people and regions of the United States, particularly the Sunbelt and the Snowbelt* (B. Drummond Ayres, Jr.).

sol⁵ (sol), *n.* a Martian day, consisting of 24 hours, 37 minutes, and 22 seconds: *The squat little lander seemed to get through its first sol . . . without any problems* (London Times). [probably < Latin *sōl, sōlis* sun (a Martian day is one rotation of the planet)]

sov|er|eign|ty-as|so|ci|a|tion (sov'rən tē ə sō'- sē ā'shən, suv'-; -shē-), *n.* an economic union between sovereign states based on a common currency and the free movement of people and goods: *Bank of Canada Governor Gerald Bodey . . . reaffirmed earlier dismissals of sovereignty-association with Quebec* (Maclean's).

space / cadet, *U.S. Slang.* a flighty, lightheaded person: *Marie-Carmen arrives—the new one, one of those long, tall Argentine women who wear alpaca all the time but a true space cadet at heart* (New Yorker).

SPF (no periods), sun protection factor (a classification of the U.S. Food and Drug Administration of the degree to which a sun block or sunscreen will protect the skin from sunburn): *If you have a product with an SPF of 8, multiply 10 by 8 and you will know that you can safely stay in the sun 80 minutes without burning* (New York Times Magazine).

split / gene, a gene with one or more intervening sequences that do not have a specific genetic code: *Molecular biologists studying other eucaryotic genes . . . showed that split genes are a common feature of eucaryotes and that introns can occur anywhere in a gene* (Daniel L. Hartl).

sup|ply-side (sə plī'sīd'), *adj.* of or having to do with economic policy theoretically designed to stimulate production of goods and services in a nation's economy by such methods as reducing taxes to increase the amount of money business can invest in new equipment: *Supply-side analysis . . . forecasts dynamic growth as the federal government lessens its tax bite* (New York Post). *Supply-side economists want to reduce the role of government rather than expand it* (New York Times).

T t

tardive / dys|ki|ne|sia (dis'kə nē'zhə), a nervous disorder characterized by uncontrollable twitching of muscles, especially facial muscles, occurring after prolonged therapy using antipsychotic drugs: *Scientists suspect that the cause of tardive dyskinesia is a lack of acetylcholine, which is depleted by years of using antipsychotic drugs* (Prevention). [< New Latin *dyskinesia* < *dys-* abnormal + Greek *kīnēsis* motion]

tho|lin (thō'lən, thol'ən), *n.* a chemical mixture of complex organic compounds found in interstellar space: *The Cornell group proposed that the interstellar solid grains are composed of tholins and that the more complex interstellar gas molecules are their degradation products* (Joseph Ashbrook). [< Greek *tholós* mud + English *-in*]

tim|o|lol (tim'ə lôl, -lol), *n.* a drug that reduces blood pressure and fluid pressure within the eyeball, used in the treatment of glaucoma and experimentally in reducing the incidence of heart attacks. Formula: $C_{13}H_{24}N_4O_3S$ *Timolol is . . . one of a class of drugs known as beta-adrenergic blocking agents, so called because*

they block the action of hormones called catecholamines, which affect heart action, blood pressure, and other body functions (Harold M. Schmeck, Jr.).

toxic / shock / syndrome, an acute and sometimes fatal bacterial infection accompanied by high fever, vomiting, diarrhea, and a sharp drop in blood pressure. It is thought to be especially stimulated by use of vaginal tampons: *Following a bout with toxic shock syndrome, the center advises women to avoid using tampons for several months, and not resume until antibiotic therapy has eliminated Staphylococcus aureus from the vagina* (Jane E. Brody).

trans|pos|on (trans pō'zən), *n. Molecular Biology.* a segment of bacterial DNA capable of transferring its genetic properties from one bacterium to another: *Many plasmid genes which confer resistance to antimicrobial agents—including penicillin, sulfonamide, streptomycin, chloramphenicol, and tetracycline reside upon transposons* (Stanley Falkow).

tuition / tax / credit, an allowance that may be deducted from taxable income for the cost of tuition: *Hit by inflation, many middle-class parents are now asking for "tuition tax credits" to help to send their children to private schools* (Manchester Guardian Weekly).

U u

u|ni|tard (yü'nə tärd), *n.* a leotard covering the torso and legs and, usually, the feet: *In an effective costume by Toer van Schayk—a modified petalled cap à la Nijinsky and a unitard of dark rose red tapering to flame points of greens and grays—he looked slim and handsome* (New Yorker). [< *uni-* + (*leo*)*tard*]

up|time (up'tīm'), *n.* the time in which a machine, department, or the like is working or active: *Fleet uptime has stayed over 96 per cent with operation generally in the region of 98 per cent* (Harper's). [patterned on *downtime*]

V v

vi|car|i|ance (vī kär'ē əns, vi-), *n.* the separation and geographical distribution of a species or similar species of plants and animals by a barrier such as a mountain range or an ocean, usually as a result of massive displacements of the earth's crust: *The debate here is whether a certain pattern of species distribution was caused by dispersal or vicariance* (Niles Eldridge). *Biologists who believe in these newer ideas call themselves vicariance biogeographers; in biology, "vicariance" . . . has come to mean separation by barriers* (New Yorker). [< Latin *vicārius* vicarious + English *-ance*]

W w

wide-out (wīd'out'), *n.* = wide receiver: *Wide-outs tend to be among the best all-around athletes in football* (Phil Patton).

Pronunciation Key: hat, āge, cāre, fär; let, ēqual, tėrm; it, īce; hot, ōpen, ôrder; oil, out; cup, pút, rüle; child; long; thin; ŦHen; zh, measure; ə represents a in about, e in taken, i in pencil, o in lemon, u in circus.

Index

How to Use the Index

This index covers the contents of the 1980, 1981, and 1982 editions of THE WORLD BOOK YEAR BOOK.

Each index entry is followed by the edition year (in *italics*) and the page number, as:

ADVERTISING, *82* - 172, *81* - 172, *80* - 176

This means, for example, that information about Advertising begins on page 172 in the 1982 edition of THE YEAR BOOK.

An index entry that is the title of an article appearing in THE YEAR BOOK is printed in capital letters, as: **AUTOMOBILE.** An entry that is not an article title, but a subject discussed in an article of some other title, is printed: **Pollution.**

The various "See" and "See also" cross references in the index list are to other entries within the index. Clue words or phrases are used when two or more references to the same subject appear in the same edition of THE YEAR BOOK. These make it easy to locate the material on the page, since they refer to an article title or article subsection in which the reference appears, as:

Hepatitis B: health and disease, *82* - 332, *80* - 347; public health, *81* - 458

The indication "*il.*" means that the reference is to an illustration only. An index entry in capital letters followed by "*WBE*" refers to a new or revised WORLD BOOK ENCYCLOPEDIA article in the supplement section, as:

ELEPHANT, *WBE, 82* - 560

A

A Gathering of Days, 81–382
Abbott, Jack Henry: crime, 82–265
Abdul-Jabbar, Kareem, 81–209
Aborigines, 81–196
Abortion: Roman Catholic, 81–470; state government, 82–474, 81–490; Supreme Court, 82–479, 81–493; U.S., Government of the, 82–506
Abscam: Congress, 82–259, 81–262; crime, 81–268; Philadelphia, 81–441
Academy of Motion Picture Arts and Sciences: awards, 82–201, 81–202, 80–207
Academy of the American Book Awards: awards, 82–202, 81–203
Acadia: boating, 82–214
Acadians: New Brunswick, 82–404
Acarbose: dentistry, 81–282
Accidents. See DISASTERS; SAFETY.
Acetaminophen: aspirin, *Special Report,* 81–153
Acetylcholine: psychology, 82–443
Acetylsalicylic acid: aspirin, *Special Report,* 81–141
Acheampong, Ignatius Kutu, 80–338
Acid rain: botany, 81–216; Canada, 82–228, 81–229, 80–235; coal, 80–256; environment, 82–298, 81–305, 80–313; water, *Special Report,* 82–102
Acne: medicine, 80–398
Acoustic microscope, 80–220
Actors' strike: *il.,* 81–367
Acyclovir: drugs, 82–282
Adamek, Donna, 82–216, 81–217, 80–223
Adams, Brock: Cabinet, 80–229; *il.,* 80–459
Adams, Harriet Stratemeyer: personalities, 81–435
Adamson, Joy: deaths, 81–274
Aden. See Yemen (Aden).
Admissions policy: education, 80–302
Adoption Assistance Child Welfare Act: child welfare, 81–243
ADVERTISING, 82–172, 81–172, 80–176; dentistry, 80–287; radio, 82–447, 81–461
Aegyptopithecus zeuxis, 81–184
Aeroflot: aviation, 82–200
Aerospace industry. See AVIATION; SPACE EXPLORATION.
Afars and Issas, Territory of. See Djibouti.
Affirmative action: civil rights, 82–249, 81–252; Supreme Court, 81–493, 80–491
Affirmed, 80–350
AFGHANISTAN, 82–173, 81–173, 80–177, *Close-Up,* 81–174; Asia, 82–192, 81–192, 80–196; Middle East, 82–387, 81–396, 80–400; Pakistan, 82–418, 81–432; President, 81–449; Russia, 81–471; United Nations, 81–513
AFL-CIO: Democratic Party, 82–275; labor, 82–362, 81–371
AFRICA, 82–174, 81–177, 80–178; anthropology, 81–184, *Close-Up,* 80–183; mining, 81–399, 80–404; Roman Catholic, 81–468; United Nations, 82–500; water, *Special Report,* 82–95. See also entries for specific countries.
African Methodist Episcopal Church, 82–452, 81–465, 80–461
African Methodist Episcopal Zion Church, 82–452, 81–465, 80–461
Agca, Mehmet Ali: Italy, 82–353; Roman Catholic, 82–474
Agee, Philip: Supreme Court, 82–479
Agent Orange, 82–253, 81–256, 80–259
Aging: mental health, 82–384; psychology, 82–443
Agriculture. See FARM AND FARMING.
Alluropoda: panda, *Special Report,* 82–80
Air pollution: botany, 80–222; Canada, 82–228, 80–235; chemical industry, 80–242; coal, 80–256; environment, 82–298, 80–313; weather, 80–525
Air traffic controllers: airport, *Special Report,* 82–137; aviation, 82–199; labor, 82–360
Airbag: automobile, 82–198; consumerism, 82–262; transportation, 82–494, 81–508
Airborne Warning and Control System. See AWACS.
Airlines. See AVIATION.
Airport: *Special Report,* 82–123
Akuffo, Frederick William Kwasi: Ghana, 80–338
Alabama, 82–473, 81–488, 80–487
Alaska: conservation, 81–262, 80–267; hunting, 80–355; mining, 81–399, 80–404; state government, 82–473, 81–488, 80–487; taxation, 81–498
Alaska pipeline, 81–230, 440
ALBANIA, 82–179, 81–181, 80–185; Europe, 82–303, 81–310, 80–317; Yugoslavia, 82–517
ALBERTA, 82–179, 81–182, 80–185

Albertson, Jack: deaths, 82–268
Albuquerque, 82–246, 81–248, 80–252
Alcoholic beverages: drugs, 82–283; health, 81–337, 80–347; nutrition, 82–413; psychology, 80–455; science, 81–477
Alekseyeva, Yelizaveta: Russia, 82–459
Alexander, Sadie: 81–529
Algae: botany, 80–222
ALGERIA, 82–180, 81–182, 80–185; Africa, 82–176, 81–178, 80–180; disasters, 81–285
Algren, Nelson: deaths, 82–268
al-Huss, Salim Ahmad: Lebanon, 81–377, 80–383
Ali, Muhammad, 81–217, 80–223
Alien. See IMMIGRATION.
All-American Rose Selections: gardening, 82–320, 81–335, 80–335
All-savers certificates: banks and banking, 82–206; housing, 82–338
Allen, Bryan: personalities, 80–434; science, 80–474
Allen, Hurricane: disasters, 81–285; *il.,* 81–526
Allen, Marcus: *il.,* 82–315
Allen, Richard V.: President, 82–438; Republican Party, 82–454
Allen, Woody: *il.,* 80–66
Alpert, Herb, 80–414
Altered state of consciousness: hypnosis, *Special Report,* 80–70
Aluminum industry: labor, 81–369
Alvarez, Gregorio: Uruguay, 82–506
Alvarez, Luis W.: paleontology, 81–433
Alvin: 81–433
Alzheimer's disease: psychology, 82–443
Amadeus: theater, 82–490
American Association of Museums, 82–398
American Ballet Theatre: dancing, 82–266, 81–271, 80–276
American Baptist Association, 82–452, 81–465, 80–461
American Baptist Churches in the U.S.A., 82–452, 81–465, 80–461
American Bar Association: courts, 81–267, 80–272
American Book Award: poetry, 82–432
American Federation of Teachers, 81–293, 80–301
American Fishing Tackle Manufacturers Association: fishing, 82–310
American Indian. See INDIAN, AMERICAN.
American Institute of Architects: architecture, 82–184, 81–186, 80–189; awards and prizes, 82–201, 81–202, 80–202
American Institute of Physics: awards and prizes, 82–203, 81–204, 80–209
American Kennel Club: dog, 82–281, 81–287, 80–291
AMERICAN LIBRARY ASSOCIATION, 82–180, 81–183, 80–186; awards, 82–202, 81–203, 80–208; literature for children, 82–376, 81–385, 80–391
American Lutheran Church, The: Protestantism, 82–442; religion, 82–452, 81–465, 80–461
American Red Cross: community organizations, 82–253, 81–256
American Telephone and Telegraph Company: communications, 82–252, 81–255
Amin, Hafizullah: Afghanistan, 80–177, *Close-Up,* 81–174; Middle East, 80–400
Amin Dada, Idi: Africa, 80–179; Uganda, 80–512
Amino acids: chemistry, 82–237, 80–243
Amino acid racemization: anthropology, 82–182
Amirthalingam, Appapillai: Sri Lanka, 82–470
Amish: *il.,* 80–455
Amnesty International: courts, 80–271
Amoxapine: drugs, 82–282
Amtrak: railroad, 82–448, 80–459; travel, 80–507
Anchovy: *Special Report,* 80–132
Andean Common Market: Latin America, 82–365, 81–374, 80–381
Anderson, Charles (Chic), 80–279
ANDERSON, JOHN B., 81–183, 80–186; Republican Party, 80–464
Anderson, Maxie, 81–435
Andorra: Europe, 82–303, 81–310, 80–317
Andretti, Mario: automobile racing, 82–198
Androsch, Hannes: Austria, 81–197
Andrus, Cecil Dale: conservation, 80–267
Anesthetics: dentistry, 80–287; hypnosis, *Special Report,* 80–79; zoo medicine, *Special Report,* 80–100
Anglicans: Australia, 82–195; Roman Catholic, 81–470, 80–468
ANGOLA, 82–181, 81–184; Africa, 82–176, 81–178, 80–180; Namibia, 82–403; Zaire, 80–531
Animal. See CAT; CONSERVATION; DOG; FARM AND FARMING; Pet; Wildlife; ZOOLOGY; ZOOS AND AQUARIUMS.

Antarctica: New Zealand, 80–420
Anthony, Earl: bowling, 82–216, 80–222
ANTHROPOLOGY, 82–182, 81–184, 80–187. See also ARCHAEOLOGY.
Antibody: biochemistry, 81–213
Antigua and Barbuda: West Indies, 82–515
Antineutrino: physics, 81–444
Antiochian Orthodox Christian Archdiocese of North America, The: Eastern Orthodox Churches, 82–283; religion, 82–452, 81–465, 80–461
Anti-Semitism: France, 81–322; Jews and Judaism, 82–356, 81–362
Antitrust laws: communications, 82–252; football, 82–314
Apartheid: Africa, 82–175; South Africa, 81–481; Venda, 80–519
Apocalypse Now: *il.* 80–406
Appalachians: geology, 80–336
Aptitude test: careers, *Special Report,* 81–116
Aquariums. See ZOOS AND AQUARIUMS.
Aquifer: water, *Special Report,* 82–95
Aquino, Benigno S., Jr.: Philippines, 81–442, 80–441
Arabia. See MIDDLE EAST; SAUDI ARABIA; Yemen (Aden; Sana).
Arabs: Egypt, 80–363; Israel, 80–364; Jordan, 80–369; Middle East, 82–386, 81–395, 80–400; Russia, 80–470; Saudi Arabia, 80–472; Sudan, 80–490; Tunisia, 80–510; United Nations, 80–513
Arafat, Yasir: Jordan, 80–369; Austria, 80–202; *il.,* 82–507
Archaeological Conservation Act, 80–474
ARCHAEOLOGY, 82–183, 81–185, 80–188; Ireland, 81–357; Jews and Judaism, 82–355; Newfoundland, 81–414; religion, 82–453. See also ANTHROPOLOGY.
Archery: sports, 82–470, 81–485, 80–483
ARCHITECTURE, 82–184, 81–186, 80–189; awards and prizes, 82–201, 81–202, 80–207. See also BUILDING AND CONSTRUCTION.
Arden Court: dancing, 82–268
Ardrey, Robert: deaths, 81–274
Argentavis magnificens: *il.,* 81–433
ARGENTINA, 82–186, 81–187, 80–191; Canada, 80–236; Latin America, 82–366, 81–375, 80–380; Viola, Roberto, 82–508
Ariane: space exploration, 82–467, 81–482, 80–481
Arizona, 82–473, 81–488, 80–487
Arizona State University: football, 80–330
Ark of the Covenant: archaeology, 82–184
Arkansas, 82–473, 81–488, 80–487
ARMED FORCES, 82–187, 81–188, 80–191; Angola, 82–181; Asia, 81–190; Australia, 82–195, 81–196, *Close-Up,* 82–188; drugs, 82–283; economics, 82–284; Europe, 80–318; Germany, West, 82–322; Greece, 82–328; Middle East, 81–396; mining, 81–400; Pakistan, 82–418; President, 82–439, 81–450; U.S., government of the, 81–517. See also entries for specific continents and countries.
Armenian Church of America, Diocese of the, 82–452, 81–465, 80–461
Army, U.S.: armed forces, 82–189, 81–188, 80–193
Arnold, Andre: skiing, 82–463
Arrington, Richard: *il.,* 81–306
Arson: insurance, 80–359
Artificial heart: *il.,* 81–391; medicine, 82–382
Artificial insemination: panda, *Special Report,* 82–90; *Special Report,* 80–113; zoos and aquariums, 82–519, 81–534
Artificial skin: *il.,* 82–382
Artificial sweetener: food, 82–312, 80–327
Arts: awards and prizes, 82–201, 81–202, 80–207; crime, 80–273; Ireland, 82–351; *Perspective,* 80–169. See also ARCHITECTURE; DANCING; LITERATURE; MOTION PICTURES; MUSEUM; MUSIC, CLASSICAL; MUSIC, POPULAR; POETRY; THEATER; VISUAL ARTS.
Asbestos: consumer protection, 80–270; safety, 81–474
ASEAN: Asia, 82–193, 81–190, 80–194, *Close-Up,* 80–198; Cambodia, 82–223; Indonesia, 80–359
Ash, volcanic: weather, 82–513
Ashford, Emmett L.: deaths, 81–274
ASIA, 82–190, 81–190, 80–194; *Close-Up,* 80–198. See also entries for specific countries.
Asia House: museum, 82–398
Asian Americans: census, 82–234
Asimov, Isaac: science fiction, *Special Report,* 80–53
Aspartame: food, 82–312
Aspirin: health, 81–335; *Special Report,* 81–138
Aspirin Myocardial Infarction Study: aspirin, *Special Report,* 81–150
Assad, Hafiz al-: *il.,* 81–379; Syria, 82–481, 81–495, 80–493

Assassinations: Bangladesh, *82–204;* Egypt, *82–291;* Middle East, *82–386*
Assemblies of God, *82–452, 81–465, 80–461*
Association of Southeast Asian Nations. See **ASEAN.**
Astaire, Adele: deaths, *82–268*
Astaire, Fred: personalities, *82–421, 81–435*
Astounding Stories: science fiction, *Special Report, 80–53*
ASTRONOMY, *82–193, 81–194, 80–199;* Jupiter, *Special Report, 80–87*
Ataenius: gardening, *81–325*
Atherosclerosis: nutrition, *81–422*
Athletics. See **OLYMPIC GAMES; SPORTS;** and names of various sports.
Atkins, Humphrey: Northern Ireland, *81–419*
Atlanta: city, *82–246, 81–248, 80–252;* crime, *82–265*
Atlantic City: motion pictures, *82–396*
Atmosphere: ocean, *Special Report, 80–134;* weather, *80–525*
Atwood, Margaret: Canadian literature, *82–230; il., 81–232*
Auchinleck, Field Marshal Sir Claude, *82–268*
Auctions and sales: coin collecting, *82–251, 81–253, 80–257;* hobbies, *82–333, 81–337, 80–348;* publishing, *82–445, 81–459, 80–456;* stamp collecting, *82–471, 81–487, 80–484;* visual arts, *82–510, 81–523, 80–523*
Audubon, John J.: *il., 81–442*
Austin: city, *82–246, 81–248, 80–252*
Austin, Tracy: tennis, *82–486, 81–501, 80–498*
AUSTRALIA, *82–195, 81–195, 80–200;* Asia, *82–192, 81–192, 80–196;* mining, *80–404;* motion pictures, *82–394, 81–401;* Pacific Islands, *82–417, 81–432; Skylab, Close-Up, 80–480*
Australopithecus: anthropology, *81–184*
AUSTRIA, *82–196, 81–197, 80–202;* Czechoslovakia, *82–266;* Europe, *82–303, 81–310, 80–317*
Autographs: hobbies, *82–333, 81–338*
Automated Radar Terminal Service: airport, *Special Report, 82–137*
Automatic transfer account: banks and banking, *82–205, 80–211*
Automation: manufacturing, *82–381;* robot, *Special Report, 82–138*
AUTOMOBILE, *82–196, 81–197, 80–202;* coal, *82–250;* Detroit, *82–277, 81–282;* economics, *81–290, 80–295;* international trade and finance, *81–352;* labor, *81–370, 80–374;* manufacturing, *80–394;* robot, *Special Report, 82–145;* safety, *82–460, 81–474, 80–471;* transportation, *82–494, 81–508, 80–507;* travel, *82–495, 80–507*
AUTOMOBILE RACING, *82–198, 81–199, 80–204*
Automobile tires, *80–270*
Autopsy: zoo medicine, *Special Report, 80–108*
Avant-garde dance: dancing, *82–267*
AVIATION, *82–199, 81–200, 80–205;* advertising, *82–172;* airport, *Special Report, 82–123;* disasters, *82–278, 81–283, 80–288;* labor, *82–360;* Saskatchewan, *82–461;* travel, *82–494, 81–509*
AWACS: armed forces, *82–187;* Congress of the United States, *82–258;* Israel, *82–353;* Middle East, *82–387;* Saudi Arabia, *82–461*
AWARDS AND PRIZES, *82–201, 81–202, 80–207;* American Library Association, *82–180, 81–183, 80–189;* architecture, *82–184, 81–187, 80–189;* Canadian Library Association, *82–229, 81–231, 80–237;* Canadian literature, *82–231, 81–233, 80–238;* gardening, *82–319, 81–325, 80–335;* literature for children, *82–376, 81–385, 80–391;* magazine, *82–378, 81–387;* museum, *80–409;* Nobel Prizes, *82–410, 81–418, 80–423;* poetry, *82–432, 81–446, 80–444;* youth organizations, *82–517, 81–530.* See also entries for specific activities.

B

B-1 bomber: *il., 82–187;* President, *82–439*
B ring of Saturn: *il., 82–194*
Baath Party: Iraq, *81–356, 80–363*
Babar's Anniversary Album: literature for children, *82–373*
Babilonia, Tai: ice skating, *81–345; il., 80–355;* Olympic Games, *81–430*
Babrak Karmal: Afghanistan, *82–173*
Baby dinosaurs: paleontology, *82–419*
Bacteria: biochemistry, *80–218;* biology, *80–219*
Badminton, *82–470, 81–485, 80–483*
Badran, Mudar: Jordan, *81–364*
Baffi, Paolo, *80–366*
Bagnold, Enid: deaths, *82–268*
Bahá'í Faith: religion, *81–465*
Bahamas: Latin America, *82–366, 81–375, 80–380*

Bahrain: Middle East, *82–389, 81–398, 80–402*
Baker, Buddy: auto racing, *81–200*
BAKER, HOWARD HENRY, JR., *80–210;* Congress, *81–257;* Republican Party, *81–466, 80–464*
Baker, Tom: bowling, *82–216*
Baker, Walter: Canada, *80–232*
Bakhtiar, Shahpur: Iran, *80–362*
Bakr, Ahmad Hasan al-, *80–363*
Balanchine, George: dancing, *82–267, 81–272*
BALDRIGE, MALCOLM, *82–204*
Baldwin, Roger: deaths, *82–269*
Ballantrae, Lord: deaths, *81–274*
Ballesteros, Severiano: golf, *81–330*
Ballet: dancing, *82–266, 81–271, 80–276*
Balloon angioplasty: medicine, *82–382*
Ballooning: *ils., 80–268, 482*
Balsemao, Francisco Pinto: Portugal, *82–435, 81–448*
Baltimore: building, *80–227;* city, *82–246, 81–248, 80–252;* zoos and aquariums, *82–520*
Bamboo: panda, *Special Report, 82–84*
Bandaranaike, Sirimavo, *81–486*
BANGLADESH, *82–204, 81–205, 80–210;* Asia, *82–192, 81–192, 80–196;* disasters, *81–285*
Bangui: France, *80–334*
BANI-SADR, ABOL HASSAN, *81–205; il., 81–354;* Iran, *82–349;* Middle East, *82–387*
Bankruptcy: automobile, *80–203;* Belgium, *80–217;* consumer protection, *80–270*
BANKS AND BANKING, *82–205, 81–206, 80–210;* crime, *80–273*
Baptist Missionary Association of America, *82–452, 81–465, 80–461*
Barbados: Latin America, *82–366, 81–375, 80–380;* West Indies, *81–530*
Barber, Samuel, *82–269*
Barbie doll, *80–335*
Barnum!: il., *81–503*
Barragán, Luis: architecture, *81–187*
Barre, Raymond, *80–333*
Barrett, Stan, *80–205*
Barrier islands: conservation, *81–264*
BARRY MARION S., JR., *80–212;* Washington, D.C., *82–510, 81–524*
Barter economy: taxation, *82–482*
Bartlett, Dewey F., *80–279*
Baryshnikov, Mikhail, *82–266, 81–271, 80–276*
Barzani, Mustafa, *80–279, 363*
BASEBALL, *82–206, 81–207, 80–213;* labor, *82–361*
BASKETBALL, *82–208, 81–209, 80–215*
Basques, *82–468, 81–483, 80–481*
Batchelder Award: literature for children, *82–376, 81–385, 80–391*
Baton Rouge, *81–248, 80–252*
Battery: energy, *82–311;* manufacturing, *81–389, 80–395;* photography, *81–443*
Battlestar Galactica: ils., *82–61, 63*
Bazargan, Mehdi: Iran, *80–362*
Beatles: music, popular, *Close-Up, 81–410*
Beaton, Sir Cecil: deaths, *81–274*
BEATRIX, *81–211; il., 81–412*
Beatty, Warren: motion pictures, *82–396*
Bedouins: Israel, *80–365*
Begin, Menachem: *ils., 81–359, 80–401;* Israel, *82–351, 80–364;* Middle East, *82–388*
Behavior: hypnosis, *Special Report, 80–70*
Beheshti, Mohammed: Iran, *82–349*
Béjart, Maurice: *80–276*
BELAUNDE TERRY, FERNANDO, *81–212;* Peru, *82–426, 81–438*
BELGIUM, *82–211, 81–212, 80–217;* Europe, *82–303, 80–317*
BELIZE, *82–211;* Latin America, *82–366, 81–375, 80–380*
Bell, Griffin Boyette: Cabinet, *80–229*
BELL, TERREL HOWARD, *82–212;* education, *82–289*
Belousova, Ludmila, *80–470*
Beltrán, Pedro G., *80–279*
Ben Bella, Ahmed, *80–186*
Benchley, Nathaniel, *82–269*
Bendectin: drugs, *82–283*
BENDJEDID, CHADLI, *80–218;* Algeria, *82–180, 81–182, 80–185*
Bengal. See **BANGLADESH.**
Benin: Africa, *82–176, 81–178, 80–180*
Bennett, Robert R., *82–269*
Bennett, William A. C., *80–279*
Benson, George: recordings, *82–451*
Benzene: chemical industry, *81–239, 80–242*
Benzene rings: chemistry, *80–242*
Berg, Paul: Nobel Prizes, *81–419*
Berlin Wall, *82–321*
Berman, Emile Z., *82–269*
Bernstein, Theodore M., *80–279*
Beta-carboxyaspartic acid: chemistry, *82–237*
Beta decay: physics, *81–444*
Bhave, Acharya Vinoba: religion, *80–463*
Bhutan, *82–192, 81–192, 80–196*

Bhutto, Murtaza, *82–417*
Bhutto, Zulfikar Ali, *80–431*
Biathlon: sports, *82–470, 81–485, 80–483*
Bible: Jews and Judaism, *82–356*
Bicentennial: Australia, *80–201*
Bicycle. See **Cycling.**
Biellmann, Denise: ice skating, *82–340*
Bighorn River: fishing, *82–310*
Bikini Atoll, *82–417*
Bilandic, Michael, *80–244;* elections, *Close-Up, 80–305*
Bilingualism: education, *82–290;* youth organizations, *82–517*
Billiards, *82–470, 81–485, 80–483*
BINAISA, GODFREY L., *80–218;* Uganda, *81–512, 80–512*
BIOCHEMISTRY, *82–212, 81–213, 80–218*
Biography: Canadian literature, *82–230, 81–232, 80–237;* literature, *82–371, 81–380, 80–386.* See also **DEATHS OF NOTABLE PERSONS; PERSONALITIES;** and names of individuals.
BIOLOGY, *82–213, 81–214, 80–219*
BIRD, LARRY, *80–220;* basketball, *81–209; il., 80–215*
Birdsong, Otis: basketball, *82–208*
Birmingham: city, *82–246*
Birth control: Asia, *81–194, 80–197;* health, *82–331;* medicine, *80–396;* public health, *81–459;* Roman Catholic, *81–470*
Birth defects: nutrition, *82–413*
Births: census, *82–232, 81–236, 80–241;* medicine, *80–396;* population, *82–434, 80–446*
Bishop, Jesse W., *80–272*
BISHOP, MAURICE RUPERT, *80–220;* West Indies, *80–528*
Bitterman, Chester A.: Colombia, *82–251*
Black Hills: Indian, American, *81–347*
Blacks: Africa, *80–182;* census, *82–234;* civil rights, *82–249, 81–251, 80–255;* housing, *80–353;* South Africa, *82–466, 81–481, 80–478;* television, *80–496;* United Nations, *80–512;* Zimbabwe Rhodesia, *80–531*
Blake, Eubie: *il., 80–434*
Blakeney, Allan, *80–472*
Blanton, Ray: prison, *80–452*
Blindness: *il., 81–334*
BLOCK, JOHN RUSLING, *82–214;* farm and farming, *82–306*
Block grants: child welfare, *82–239;* United States, Government of the, *82–503*
Bloembergen, Nicolaas, *82–410*
Blood cells: science, *81–477*
Blood clot: aspirin, *Special Report, 81–140*
Blowgun: zoo medicine, *Special Report, 80–101*
"Blue Boy": stamp collecting, *82–471*
Blue Cross and Blue Shield: hospital, *80–351*
Blue-green algae: botany, *80–222*
Blum, Yehuda Z., *80–512*
Blumenthal, W. Michael: Cabinet, *80–229*
Boat people: Asia, *82–191;* Australia, *80–201;* Canada, *80–236; Close-Up, 80–198;* Japan, *80–367;* Malaysia, *80–393;* President, *80–449;* Thailand, *80–500;* United Nations, *80–514;* Vietnam, *80–521*
BOATING, *82–214, 81–215, 80–221*
Bobsledding, *82–470, 81–485, 80–483*
Body language: pet language, *Special Report, 81–122*
Böhm, Karl, *82–269*
Bokassa I: Africa, *80–179*
BOLIVIA, *82–215, 81–216, 80–221;* Latin America, *82–366, 81–375, 80–380*
Bolshoi Ballet, *80–276*
Bolton, Guy, *80–279*
Bombeck, Erma: *il., 80–385*
Bondi, Beulah, *82–269*
Bonds. See **STOCKS AND BONDS.**
Bone plating: zoo medicine, *Special Report, 80–103*
Bone powder: medicine, *82–383*
Bonham, John H.: deaths, *81–274*
Book publishing. See **CANADIAN LITERATURE; LITERATURE; LITERATURE FOR CHILDREN; POETRY; PUBLISHING.**
Boone, Richard, *82–269*
Bophuthatswana: Africa, *82–176, 81–178, 80–180*
Borg, Bjorn: *il., 81–502;* tennis, *82–486, 80–498*
Borge, Victor, *82–421*
Bossert, Patrick, *82–421*
Bossy, Mike: hockey, *82–334*
Boston, *82–246, 81–248, 80–252;* Roman Catholic Church, *81–470*
Boston Pops: Arthur Fiedler, *Close-Up, 80–412; il., 81–408*
BOTANY, *82–215, 81–216, 80–222.* See also **GARDENING.**
Botswana, *82–176, 81–178, 80–180*
Bouabid, Maati: Morocco, *80–405*
Boulin, Robert, *80–333*
Boumediene, Houari, *80–185*

Bourguiba, Habib, *82*–497, *81*–511, *80*–510
Bournonville, August, *80*–276
BOWLING, *82*–216, *81*–217, *80*–222
BOXING, *82*–216, *81*–217, *80*–223; deaths, *Close-Up, 82*–271
Boy Scouts of America, *82*–516, *81*–530, *80*–529
Boycott, Olympic: Olympic Games, *81*–425; President of the U.S., *81*–450; Russia, *81*–472
Boys Clubs of America, *82*–516, *81*–530, *80*–529
Bradley, Omar N.: armed forces, *Close-Up, 82*–188; *il., 82*–273
Bradley, Thomas, *82*–376; *il., 81*–386
Brady, Brian, *82*–426
Brady, James S., *82*–449
Brain: mental health, *82*–384
Brain damage: science, *81*–477
Brain hemispheres: psychology, *81*–458
Brandeis, Louis Dembitz: Supreme Court, *Close-Up, 82*–478
Branotte, Jim: handicapped, *80*–346
Brasher's doubloon: coin collecting, *82*–251; *il., 80*–257
BRAZIL, *82*–217, *81*–218, *80*–224; Latin America, *82*–366, *81*–375, *80*–380; Roman Catholic Church, *81*–468; Uruguay, *80*–519
Breast cancer: medicine, *82*–383
Breckinridge, John B., *80*–279
Breeding: panda, *Special Report, 82*–90; zoos and aquariums, *82*–519, *81*–535, *80*–532, *Special Report, 80*–112
Brethren, The, *80*–491
Breuer, Marcel: deaths, *82*–269
Brewer, Curtis, *81*–335
Brezhnev, Leonid Ilyich: *ils., 81*–329, *80*–192; Russia, *80*–498
BRIDGE, CONTRACT, *82*–218, *81*–220, *80*–225
Bridge and tunnel: building and construction, *82*–220, *81*–222, *80*–226
Brink, Carol Ryrie: deaths, *82*–269
BRITISH COLUMBIA, *82*–218, *81*–220, *80*–225
British North America Act: Canada, *82*–225, *81*–228
British West Indies. See **WEST INDIES.**
Britton, Barbara: deaths, *82*–274
Brixton (England): *il., 82*–328
Brontosaurus: paleontology, *80*–432
Brooke, Edward W., *80*–266
Brooklyn Bridge: *il., 82*–220
Brown, Christy: deaths, *82*–269
BROWN, EDMUND GERALD (JERRY), JR., *80*–225; Democratic Party, *80*–285; farm and farming, *82*–308; *il., 80*–486
Brown, Herbert C., *80*–424
Brown, John Y., Jr., *80*–304
Brown lung disease: safety, *82*–460
BRUNDTLAND, GRO HARLEM, *82*–219; *il., 82*–412
Bruner, Mike: swimming, *81*–495
Brussels: Belgium, *80*–217
Brzezinski, Zbigniew: *il., 80*–473
Bucaram, Asaad, *81*–293, *80*–299
Buchanan, Edgar, *80*–279
Buchanan, John: Nova Scotia, *82*–413, *81*–421
Buckner, Pam: *il., 81*–217
Buddhism, *80*–463
Budget, national: armed forces, *82*–189, *81*–189, *80*–193; child welfare, *82*–239; city, *82*–244; Congress of the United States, *82*–254, *81*–257, *80*–260; Constitution, *81*–264; economics, *82*–284, *81*–292, *80*–298; education, *82*–289; energy, *82*–296; food, *82*–312; labor, *82*–362; Social Security, *82*–465; Stockman, David, *82*–475; taxation, *80*–495; U.S. government, *82*–502, *80*–518; water, *82*–512; welfare, *82*–514
Buffalo: city, *82*–246, *81*–248, *80*–252
BUILDING AND CONSTRUCTION, *82*–219, *81*–221, *80*–226; economics, *81*–290; museum, *80*–409; New York City, *82*–405. See also **ARCHITECTURE.**
BULGARIA, *82*–220, *81*–223, *80*–228; Europe, *82*–303, *81*–310, *80*–317; Yugoslavia, *80*–530
Bullion: *Close-Up, 81*–351
Bundy, Theodore R., *80*–272
Buono, Angelo, Jr., *80*–392
Burger, Warren E.: courts and laws, *82*–263
Burgess Shale Fossil Site: British Columbia, *82*–218
BURMA, *82*–221, *81*–223, *80*–228; Asia, *82*–192, *81*–192, *80*–196
Burnett, Carol: *il., 82*–378
Burpee, David: gardening, *81*–325
Burton, Neil: bowling, *81*–217
Burundi, *82*–176, *81*–178, *80*–180
Bus: disasters, *82*–278, *81*–284, *80*–288; transit, *80*–506; transportation, *81*–508
BUSH, GEORGE H. W., *82*–221, *81*–223, *80*–229; *il., 81*–467; Republican Party, *81*–466, *80*–460

Business. See **ECONOMICS; INTERNATIONAL TRADE; LABOR; MANUFACTURING.**
Busing, school: city, *81*–251, *80*–251; civil rights, *82*–249, *81*–252, *80*–255; education, *81*–294; elections, *80*–307; Los Angeles, *82*–376
Butterfly: botany, *82*–215
Butts, Alfred: personalities, *82*–422
BYRNE, JANE M., *80*–229; Chicago, *82*–238, *81*–242, *80*–244; *Close-Up, 80*–305; *il., 81*–242
Byssinosis: safety, *82*–460

C

CABINET, U.S., *82*–222, *81*–224, *80*–229; education, *80*–300; energy, *82*–296; U.S. government of the, *81*–517. See also names of Cabinet members.
Cable television: advertising, *82*–172, *81*–172; communications, *82*–252; Houston, *82*–338; music, classical, *82*–398; television, *82*–485, *81*–500, *80*–498
Cabrini Green: Chicago, *82*–239
Caddell, Patrick H.: *il., 80*–124
Cadieux, Marcel: deaths, *82*–269
Caetano, Marcello: deaths, *81*–274
Caffeine: nutrition, *82*–413
Caldecott Medal: literature for children, *82*–376, *81*–385, *80*–391
Califano, Joseph Anthony, Jr.: Cabinet, *80*–229; drugs, *80*–292
California: elections, *80*–307; environment, *82*–300; farm and farming, *82*–308; Los Angeles, *82*–376, *81*–385, *80*–391; state government, *82*–473, *81*–488, *80*–487; taxation, *82*–483
Callaghan, James: Europe, *80*–316; Great Britain, *80*–340
Calligraphy: *il., 82*–354
Callisto: astronomy, *80*–199; *ils., 80*–86, 93
CALVO SOTELO Y BUSTELO, LEOPOLDO, *82*–223
CAMBODIA, *82*–223, *81*–224, *80*–230; Asia, *82*–192, *81*–192, *80*–196; *Close-Up, 80*–198; Thailand, *81*–502, *80*–500; United Nations, *82*–500, *81*–516, *80*–514; Vietnam, *80*–520
Camel Dances, The: *il., 82*–374
Camera: photography, *82*–430, *81*–442, *80*–442
Cameroon, *82*–176, *81*–178, *80*–180
Camp David talks: Middle East, *82*–388
Camp Fire: youth organizations, *82*–517, *81*–530, *80*–529
Campbell, John W., Jr.: science fiction, *Special Report, 80*–57
CANADA, *82*–225, *81*–225, *80*–231; Canadian Library Association, *82*–229, *81*–231, *80*–237; Canadian literature, *82*–230, *81*–232, *80*–237; *Close-Up, 81*–227, *80*–233; environment, *81*–305, *80*–313; fishing industry, *82*–311, *81*–317, *80*–325; football, *82*–315, *81*–321, *80*–329; Indian, American, *82*–344; international trade and finance, *82*–347; mining, *80*–404; Schreyer, Edward R., *82*–462, *81*–476; transportation, *82*–494; Trudeau, Pierre E., *82*–496, *81*–511. See also by province.
Canada Cup: hockey, *82*–335
Canadian Football League, *82*–315, *81*–321, *80*–329
CANADIAN LIBRARY ASSOCIATION, *82*–229, *81*–231, *80*–237
CANADIAN LITERATURE, *82*–230, *81*–232, *80*–237
"Canadianization": Canada, *82*–227
Cancer: biochemistry, *80*–218; chemistry, *81*–240; drugs, *82*–282, *80*–292; health and disease, *82*–331, *80*–346; hypnosis, *Special Report, 80*–79; labor, *81*–371; medicine, *82*–383, *81*–391, *80*–396; nutrition, *82*–413, *80*–427; public health, *81*–459
Cancún summit: Canada, *82*–227; international trade and finance, *82*–347
Canetti, Elias: Nobel Prizes, *82*–410
Canine parvovirus: dog, *82*–281, *81*–287
Canker sore: dentistry, *82*–276
Cannes International Film Festival, *82*–201, *81*–202, *80*–207
Canoeing, *82*–470, *81*–485, *80*–483
Cape Verde: Africa, *82*–176, *81*–178, *80*–180
Capital punishment: courts and laws, *82*–272; state government, *81*–490, *80*–487
Capezio Dance Award: awards and prizes, *82*–201, *81*–202, *80*–207
Caponi, Donna: golf, *82*–323, *81*–330
Capote, Truman: *il., 81*–382
Capp, Al, *80*–279
Captive-breeding program: zoos, *81*–535
Capuchin monkey: *il., 80*–345
CARAMANLIS, CONSTANTINE E., *81*–233; Greece, *81*–333, *80*–344
Carbon dioxide: weather, *82*–513, *80*–525

Carbyne: chemistry, *81*–241
Cardiac catheterization: hospital, *82*–337
Careers: *Special Report, 81*–107
Carey, Hugh L.: personalities, *82*–422
Cargo cult: religion, *81*–466
Carl XVI Gustaf: *il., 81*–494
Caroline Islands: Pacific Islands, *82*–416
Carpenter, Phil: United Nations, *Close-Up, 82*–501
CARRINGTON, LORD, *80*–238
Carter, Billy: Congress, *81*–262; *il., 81*–235
CARTER, JAMES EARL, JR., *82*–231, *81*–234, *80*–239; Cabinet, *80*–229; Democratic Party, *81*–280, *80*–285; elections, *81*–297; *ils., 81*–243, 450, 451; U.S. government of the, *81*–517. See also **PRESIDENT OF THE UNITED STATES.**
Carter, Rosalynn: Carter, James Earl, Jr., *80*–239; *ils., 81*–438, *80*–398
Cash, Johnny: *il., 81*–409
Cassidy, Ted, *80*–279
Castillo, Leonel J., *80*–356
Casting: sports, *82*–470, *81*–485, *80*–483
Castro, Fidel: Cuba, *82*–265, *81*–270, *80*–274; *ils., 82*–385, *80*–379
CAT, *82*–232, *81*–235, *80*–240; pet language, *Special Report, 81*–121
Cat scanner: *il., 82*–383; Nobel Prizes, *80*–425
Catastrophe loss: insurance, *82*–345, *81*–350
Categorical grant: child welfare, *82*–239
Catholics. See **ROMAN CATHOLIC CHURCH.**
Caulkins, Tracy: *il., 81*–493; swimming, *82*–480, *80*–240
Cawley, Evonne Goolagong, *81*–502
Cayuga Indians: Indian, American, *81*–347, *80*–357
Ceausescu, Nicolae: Romania, *82*–457, *81*–470, *80*–468
Celler, Emanuel: deaths, *82*–269
Censorship: Canadian Library Association, *81*–231; publishing, *82*–445; Supreme Court of the United States, *82*–479
CENSUS, *82*–232, *81*–236, *80*–240; city, *81*–247; supplement, *82*–521; U.S. government of the, *81*–519. See also **POPULATION.**
Central African Republic: Africa, *82*–176, *81*–178, *80*–180; France, *80*–334
Central Arizona Project: water, *Special Report, 82*–100
Central Intelligence Agency: publishing, *81*–459
Central Kingdom Express: *il., 80*–508
Cereal: advertising, *80*–176
Ceylon. See **SRI LANKA.**
Cha, Chi Chul, *80*–371
CHAD, *82*–235, *81*–239, *80*–241; Africa, *82*–176, *81*–178, *80*–180; Libya, *82*–370, *80*–384
Chain, Sir Ernest B., *80*–279
Chaliapin, Boris, *80*–279
Champion, Gower: deaths, *81*–274
Championship Auto Racing Teams, *81*–200, *80*–204
Chapin, Harry: *il., 82*–272
Chapman, Mark David: courts and laws, *82*–264; crime, *82*–265
Character license: games and toys, *82*–319
Charles, Mary Eugenia: West Indies, *81*–530
CHARLES, PRINCE, *82*–236; Great Britain, *Close-Up, 82*–326; *ils., 82*–324, 326, *80*–280
Charlotte: city, *82*–246, *81*–248, *80*–252
Charter of rights: Canada, *81*–228
Chaves, Aureliano: Brazil, *82*–217
Chayefsky, Paddy: deaths, *82*–269
Checking account, *80*–211
Cheetah: zoos, *81*–535
Chemical bonding: physics, *82*–431
CHEMICAL INDUSTRY, *82*–236, *81*–239, *80*–241; awards and prizes, *82*–203, *81*–204
Chemical warfare: Laos, *82*–363
CHEMISTRY, *82*–237, *81*–240, *80*–242; Nobel Prizes, *82*–410, *81*–419, *80*–424; ocean, *Special Report, 80*–138
Chemotherapy: medicine, *82*–383
Chen Wen-cheng: Taiwan, *82*–481
Chenodeoxycholic acid: health and disease, *82*–332
Chenoweth, Dean: boating, *81*–216
CHESS, *82*–238, *81*–241, *80*–243
Chevron Plaza Building: *80*–189
Chiang Ching: China, *82*–242, *81*–244
Chiang Ching-kuo: Taiwan, *80*–494
Chiburdanidze, Maya: chess, *82*–238
CHICAGO, *82*–238, *81*–242, *80*–244; architecture, *81*–187; census, *82*–233; city, *82*–246, *81*–248, *80*–252; disasters, *80*–288; education, *80*–302; *il., 80*–466; Jane Byrne, *Close-Up, 80*–305; transit, *82*–493
Chicago Sting: *il., 82*–464
Chicken, The: *80*–436
Chicken pox: public health, *82*–444
CHILD WELFARE, *82*–239, *81*–243, *80*–245; advertising, *80*–176; civil rights, *82*–250, *81*–252;

dentistry, *80*–287; medicine, *80*–396; mental health, *82*–384, *80*–398; psychology, *80*–455. See also **WELFARE.**
Children of a Lesser God: *il., 81*–504
Children of God: religious cults, *Special Report, 80*–149
Children's books. See LITERATURE FOR CHILDREN.
CHILE, *82*–240, *81*–244, *80*–246; courts, *80*–272; Latin America, *82*–366, *81*–375, *80*–380
CHINA, PEOPLE'S REPUBLIC OF, *82*–240, *81*–244, *80*–247; *WBE, 80*–544; advertising, *80*–176; Albania, *80*–185; archaeology, *82*–183; Asia, *82*–192, *81*–192, *80*–196; aviation, *81*–200; building and construction, *82*–219, *80*–227; *Close-Up, 80*–248; fashion, *81*–315; gardening, *81*–325; Hu Yaobang, *82*–339; *il., 81*–172; Japan, *80*–368; Laos, *80*–377; Malaysia, *82*–379; medicine, *80*–396; Olympic Games, *80*–429; panda, *Special Report, 82*–75; President, *80*–449; religion, *82*–451, *81*–466; Romania, *80*–468; Russia, *80*–469; ship, *81*–479, *80*–475; travel, *80*–508; Vietnam, *80*–520; weather, *80*–526
Chinese: Asia, *Close-Up, 80*–198; Malaysia, *80*–393
Chinese language: *Close-Up, 80*–248
Chinaglia, Giorgio: soccer, *81*–480
Chlamydia trachomatis: public health, *82*–444
Choi, Kyu Ha, *81*–365, *80*–371
Cholesterol: nutrition, *82*–413, *81*–422
Christian and Missionary Alliance, *82*–452, *81*–465, *80*–461
Christian Church (Disciples of Christ), *82*–452, *81*–465, *80*–461
Christian Churches and Churches of Christ, *82*–452, *81*–465, *80*–461
Christian Methodist Episcopal Church, *82*–452, *81*–465, *80*–461
Christian Reformed Church in North America: Protestantism, *82*–442; religion, *82*–452, *81*–465, *80*–461
Christiansen, Larry: chess, *82*–238
Christopher, Warren: Iran, *Close-Up, 82*–348
Chrysler Corporation: automobile, *82*–197, *81*–198, *80*–203; economics, *80*–295; labor, *80*–374
CHUN DOO HWAN, *81*–247; civil rights, *81*–251; Korea, South, *82*–358, *81*–365
Church. See EASTERN ORTHODOX CHURCHES; JEWS AND JUDAISM; PROTESTANTISM; RELIGION; ROMAN CATHOLIC CHURCH.
Church and state: Roman Catholic, *80*–468
Church of England. See Anglicans.
Church of God (Anderson, Ind.), *82*–452, *81*–465, *80*–461
Church of God (Cleveland, Tenn.), *82*–452, *81*–465, *80*–461
Church of God in Christ, The, *82*–452, *81*–465, *80*–461
Church of God in Christ, International, The, *82*–452, *81*–465, *80*–461
Church of God of Prophecy, *82*–452, *81*–465
Church of Jesus Christ of Latter-day Saints, The, *82*–452, *81*–465, *80*–461; Protestantism, *82*–441, *81*–456, *80*–454
Church of Scientology, *80*–272
Church of the Brethren, *82*–452, *81*–465, *80*–461
Church of the Nazarene, *82*–452, *81*–465, *80*–461
Churches of Christ, *82*–452, *81*–465, *80*–461
Cigarette: advertising, *80*–176; health and disease, *82*–331
Cincinnati: city, *82*–246, *81*–248, *80*–252; music, popular, *80*–415
CISKEI, *82*–243; Africa, *82*–176
Cisneros, Henry: *il., 82*–244
CITY, *82*–244, *81*–247, *80*–250; census, *82*–233, *81*–238; elections, *82*–293, *80*–304; transit, *82*–493, *80*–505. See also entries for specific cities.
City of David: Jews and Judaism, *82*–355
Civil Aeronautics Board: aviation, *82*–199, *81*–200, *80*–205
CIVIL RIGHTS, *82*–248, *81*–251, *80*–254; magazine, *80*–393; U.S., government of the, *80*–518
Civil war: Africa, *82*–174, *81*–177, *80*–182; Burma, *80*–228; Cambodia, *82*–223; El Salvador, *82*–295; Lebanon, *82*–368
CIVILETTI, BENJAMIN RICHARD, *80*–256; Cabinet, *80*–229
Clair, René, *82*–269
CLARK, CHARLES JOSEPH (JOE), *80*–256; Canada, *82*–225, *81*–225, *80*–231
Clark, Edward: personalities, *81*–435
Clavell, James: *il., 82*–370
Clean Air Act: chemical industry, *80*–242; environment, *80*–298; steel industry, *82*–475

Clemency: prison, *80*–452
Cleveland, *82*–246, *81*–248, *80*–252
Cliburn, Van: *il., 82*–399
Climate: ocean, *Special Report, 80*–130. See also **WEATHER.**
Cline, Martin J.: biochemistry, *81*–213
Cloning: biology, *80*–219
Clothing. See FASHION.
Cloud seeding: water, *Special Report, 82*–107
COAL, *82*–251, *81*–253, *80*–256; conservation, *80*–267; environment, *81*–305, *80*–313; labor, *82*–361
Coal-gasification, *82*–297
Coalition for Better Television: Protestantism, *82*–443; television, *82*–484
Coastal Upwelling Ecosystem Analysis: ocean, *Special Report, 80*–132
Cobalt: mining, *80*–404
Coca-Cola: *80*–247
Cochran, Jacqueline: deaths, *81*–274
Cochran, Philip G., *80*–279
Coe, Sebastian: track and field, *82*–491, *81*–506, *80*–503
Coffee: health and disease, *82*–332
Cognitive theory: psychology, *81*–457
COIN COLLECTING, *82*–251, *81*–253, *80*–257
COLA: labor, *82*–360, *81*–367, *80*–373; manufacturing, *80*–395
Collecting: coin collecting, *82*–251, *81*–253, *80*–257; hobbies, *82*–333, *81*–337, *80*–348; photography, *82*–431; stamp collecting, *82*–471, *81*–486, *80*–484
Collective bargaining: labor, *82*–359, *81*–367, *80*–373
College Football Association: football, *82*–315
Collver, Richard, *81*–475, *80*–472
COLOMBIA, *82*–251, *81*–254, *80*–258; drugs, *80*–292; Latin America, *82*–366, *81*–375, *80*–380
Colorado: state government, *82*–473, *81*–488, *80*–487
Columbia: space exploration, *82*–466, *81*–482, *80*–481; space shuttle, *Special Report, 82*–109
Columbus, Ohio, *82*–246, *81*–248, *80*–252
Comaneci, Nadia: *il., 81*–430
Commerce. See ECONOMICS; INTERNATIONAL TRADE AND FINANCE.
Commission for a National Agenda for the Eighties: city, *82*–248
Common Market. See European Community.
Commoner, Barry: personalities, *81*–436
Commonwealth Heads of Government Meeting: Australia, *82*–195
Commonwealth of Nations. See GREAT BRITAIN; articles on various countries of the Commonwealth.
COMMUNICATIONS, *82*–252, *81*–255, *80*–258; psychology, *80*–454. See also **LITERATURE; MOTION PICTURES; POSTAL SERVICE, U.S.; PUBLISHING; RADIO; RECORDINGS; SPACE EXPLORATION; TELEVISION; TRANSPORTATION.**
Communism: economics, *81*–292; Europe, *82*–304. See also articles on individual Communist countries.
Communist Party: Burma, *80*–228; China, *82*–240, *80*–250; Hungary, *82*–340; Poland, *80*–445; Romania, *82*–457; Thailand, *81*–502
Community Churches, National Council of, *82*–452, *81*–465
COMMUNITY ORGANIZATIONS, *82*–253, *81*–256, *80*–259
Comoros, *82*–176, *81*–178, *80*–180
Compensatory aid programs: child welfare, *82*–240
Competency standards, *80*–302
Comprehensive Employment and Training Act: city, *80*–250; welfare, *80*–527
COMPUTER: *WBE, 81*–538; electronics, *82*–294, *81*–300; farm, *80*–322; insurance, *82*–359; manufacturing, *82*–381; newspaper, *81*–415; recordings, *80*–460; robot, *Special Report, 82*–145; zoo medicine, *Special Report, 80*–111
Computerized axial tomograph scan, *80*–425
Condominium: Philadelphia, *80*–440
Condor: zoos, *81*–535
Congo (Brazzaville): Africa, *82*–176, *81*–178, *80*–180
Congo (Kinshasa). See ZAIRE.
CONGRESS OF THE UNITED STATES, *82*–254, *81*–257, *80*–260; automobile, *80*–203; census, *81*–237; communications, *80*–258; consumer protection, *80*–270; Democratic Party, *82*–274, *81*–281; economics, *80*–296; elections, *82*–293, *81*–299; energy, *81*–308; farm and farming, *82*–305, *81*–314; Panama, *80*–433; Republican Party, *82*–453, *81*–467; Saudi Arabia, *82*–461; taxation, *80*–495; U.S., government of the, *82*–505, *81*–519, *80*–516; water, *80*–524; welfare, *80*–527

CONNALLY, JOHN BOWDEN, *80*–266; Republican Party, *81*–466, *80*–464
Connecticut, *82*–473, *81*–488, *80*–487
Conner, Dennis: boating, *81*–215
Connors, Jimmy, *81*–501
Conrail: railroad, *82*–448, *81*–462, *80*–459
Conscription. See DRAFT.
CONSERVATION, *82*–259, *81*–262, *80*–267; architecture, *82*–184; Congress of the United States, *80*–265; environment, *80*–312; farm and farming, *82*–308; forest and forest products, *82*–317, *Special Report, 81*–89; hunting, *80*–355; ocean, *81*–423; panda, *Special Report, 82*–75; visual arts, *82*–510; water, *81*–526, *Special Report, 82*–93; zoos, *81*–534, *80*–532. See also **Endangered species; ENERGY; ENVIRONMENT; Pollution.**
Conservative Baptist Association of America, *82*–452, *81*–465, *80*–461
Consolidated Rail Corporation. See Conrail.
Constantine, King: *82*–329
CONSTITUTION OF THE UNITED STATES, *82*–261, *81*–264, *80*–269; Supreme Court of the United States, *82*–479
Construction. See BUILDING AND CONSTRUCTION.
Consultation on Church Union, *81*–456
Consumer price index: Canada, *80*–234; consumer protection, *81*–265, *80*–269; economics, *80*–294; labor, *81*–367, *80*–372; *Special Report, 81*–73
Consumer Product Safety Commission: consumerism, *82*–262; safety, *82*–461, *80*–472
CONSUMERISM, *82*–261, *81*–265, *80*–269
Conti, Tom: *il., 80*–501
Continental drift: ocean, *80*–427, *Special Report, 80*–140
Contraceptives: medicine, *80*–396
Contreras Sepulveda, Manuel: Chile, *80*–246; courts, *80*–272
Cook, Betty, *80*–221
Cook Islands, *80*–180
Cooke, Hope: literature, *82*–372
Cooke, Terence Cardinal: *il., 80*–463
Copper: Chile, *82*–240; mining, *80*–404; Pacific Islands, *82*–417
Coral reef: biology, *81*–214
Cormack, Allan M., *80*–425
Correctional institution. See PRISON.
Correspondence: literature, *82*–372, *81*–380, *80*–386
Corruption, political: Mexico, *82*–385
Cortisol: mental health, *82*–384
Cosmos: television, *81*–500
Cossiga, Francesco, *81*–267; Italy, *81*–360, *80*–366
Cost of living: labor, *81*–367; travel, *80*–508. See also **ECONOMICS; Inflation; Prices; Recession; Wages;** and articles on various countries and cities.
Cost-of-living adjustment. See COLA.
Costa Rica, *82*–366, *81*–375, *80*–380
Costello, Pat, *81*–217
Coughlin, Charles E., *80*–279
Council for Mutual Economic Assistance: Europe, *82*–304, *81*–311, *80*–319; Germany, East, *82*–321
Council of Energy Resource Tribes, *80*–358
Counsilman, Jim (Doc), *80*–435
Country music, *81*–409, *80*–415
Coup attempts: Africa, *82*–178; Asia, *82*–191; Bangladesh, *82*–204; Spain, *82*–468; Sudan, *82*–476; Thailand, *82*–487; West Indies, *82*–515
Court tennis, *82*–470, *81*–485, *80*–483
COURTS AND LAWS, *82*–263, *81*–267, *80*–271; advertising, *80*–176; census, *82*–235; chemical industry, *80*–242; civil rights, *80*–255; consumer protection, *80*–270; Detroit, *80*–288; drugs, *80*–292; fishing industry, *80*–325; handicapped, *80*–345; Indian, American, *80*–357; labor, *80*–373; mental health, *80*–398; Nixon, Richard M., *80*–423; Philadelphia, *80*–440; prison, *80*–452; safety, *80*–471; science and research, *80*–474; state government, *82*–474. See also **CONGRESS OF THE UNITED STATES; STATE GOVERNMENT; SUPREME COURT OF THE UNITED STATES; UNITED STATES, GOVERNMENT OF THE.**
Cousteau, Philippe, *80*–279
Covenant for Freedom: Philippines, *81*–442
Crafts: hobbies, *82*–333
CRANE, PHILIP MILLER, *80*–272; Republican Party, *80*–464
Creation science: education, *82*–290; Protestantism, *82*–443; state government, *82*–474
Credit: banks, *81*–206, *80*–210; consumer protection, *80*–269
Cretaceous Period: botany, *82*–216
Cricket: sports, *80*–483
CRIME, *82*–264, *81*–268, *80*–273; courts and laws, *82*–263; hypnosis, *Special Report, 80*–79;

Supreme Court, *82*–479, *81*–493. See also **Kidnapping; Terrorism; Violence;** and the articles on various countries and cities.
Crimes of the Heart: theater, *82*–489
Crippen, Robert L.: space shuttle, *Special Report, 82*–109
Criticism: literature, *82*–372, *81*–381, *80*–386
Critics Circle Awards, *81*–202, *80*–208
Croatians: Yugoslavia, *82*–518
Crockett, James U., *80*–279
Crombie, David: Canada, *80*–232
Cronin, A. J., *82*–269
Cronin, James W.: Nobel Prizes, *81*–419
Cronkite, Walter: ils., *82*–425, *80*–124; *Special Report, 81*–55
Croquet, *82*–470, *81*–485, *80*–483
Crosbie, John: Canada, *80*–232
Cross, Christopher: il., *82*–451
Cross country, *82*–470, *81*–485, *80*–483
Cross-district school desegregation, *82*–339, *81*–343
Crow Indian, *82*–343
Crowell, John B.: forest and forest products, *82*–317
Crowther, Bosley, *82*–269
Crude Oil Windfall Profit Tax Act: energy, *81*–302
Cruise missile: armed forces, *82*–187
Crystal Cathedral: il., *81*–456
CUBA, *82*–265, *81*–270, *80*–274; armed forces, *80*–192; Colombia, *82*–251; Ecuador, *82*–288; immigration, *81*–345; Latin America, *82*–366, *81*–375, *80*–380; Namibia, *82*–403; President, *81*–451, *80*–449; Russia, *80*–469; Yugoslavia, *80*–530
Culottes: fashion, *82*–308
Cults: religion, *80*–463; *Special Report, 80*–145
Cultural Revolution: China, *82*–241, *81*–244
Cunningham, Merce, *80*–276
Cured meats, *82*–312
Curling, *82*–470, *81*–485, *80*–483
Curran, Joseph, *82*–269
Currency. See **INTERNATIONAL TRADE AND FINANCE; Money.**
CX system: recordings, *82*–451
Cycling, *82*–470, *81*–485, *80*–483
Cyclosporin A: medicine, *81*–392
Cyprus: Greece, *80*–344; Middle East, *82*–389, *81*–398, *80*–402; United Nations, *80*–513
CZECHOSLOVAKIA, *82*–266, *81*–271, *80*–275; Europe, *82*–303, *81*–310, *80*–317

D

Dacko, David: Africa, *80*–179
Dahl, Steve: music, popular, *80*–414
Dairying. See **FARM AND FARMING.**
Dalai Lama: religion, *80*–463
Dali man: anthropology, *82*–182
Dallas: city, *82*–246, *81*–248, *80*–252; library, *82*–369
"Dallas": television, *81*–498
Dam: building, *82*–219, *81*–222, *80*–226; il., *80*–290
DANCING, *82*–266, *81*–271, *80*–276; awards and prizes, *82*–201, *81*–202, *80*–207
Darts: sports, *82*–470, *81*–485, *80*–483
Darvon: drugs, *80*–292
Data processing. See **Computer.**
Davis, Al: football, *81*–320
Davis, Francis B.: handicapped, *80*–345
Davis, Jim: il., *82*–272
Davis, Patti, *82*–450
Davis, William G., *82*–416
Dayan, Moshe: ils., *82*–270, *80*–364
Days of Remembrance: Jews, *80*–369
DC-10: aviation, *80*–206
Dean, Paul, *82*–270
Death penalty. See **Capital punishment.**
Death rate: population, *81*–447, *80*–446; safety, *81*–474, *80*–472
DEATHS OF NOTABLE PERSONS, *82*–268, *81*–274, *80*–279; Latin America, *82*–368; music, popular, *Close-Up, 81*–410
Declerq, Pierre, *82*–416
Decontrol: petroleum and gas, *82*–427. See also **Deregulation.**
De Cotret, Robert René: Canada, *80*–232
Deep-sea drilling project, *82*–414, *81*–423
Deep Seabed Hard Minerals Resource Act: environment, *81*–305
Defense. See **ARMED FORCES.**
Deficit spending: city, *81*–250
De la Madrid Hurtado, Miguel: Mexico, *82*–385
Delaware, *82*–473, *81*–488, *80*–487
Delbrück, Max, *82*–269
DeLorean, John Z.: il., *82*–197
Delta-9-tetrahydrocannabinol: medicine, *81*–391
Demand management, *82*–287

Demirel, Suleyman: Turkey, *80*–511
DEMOCRATIC PARTY, *82*–274, *81*–280, *80*–285; elections, *82*–292, *81*–299, *80*–304; Jane M. Byrne, *Close-Up, 80*–305
Demography. See **CENSUS; POPULATION.**
de Moraes, Vinicius: Latin America, *81*–376
DE NIRO, ROBERT, *82*–276
Deng Xiaoping. See **Teng Hsiao-p'ing.**
Dengue fever: Cuba, *82*–265
DENMARK, *82*–276, *81*–281, *80*–286; Europe, *82*–303, *81*–310, *80*–317
DENTISTRY, *82*–276, *81*–282, *80*–287; hypnosis, *Special Report, 80*–77
Denver: architecture, *81*–187; city, *82*–246, *81*–248, *80*–252
Deodoros, Patriarch: Eastern Orthodox Churches, *82*–283
Depo-provera: medicine, *80*–396
Depository Institutions Deregulation and Monetary Control Act of 1980: banks, *81*–207
Depression: mental health, *82*–384, *81*–393
Deregulation: aviation, *80*–205; Congress, *81*–258; consumer protection, *81*–265; consumerism, *82*–262; economics, *82*–288; petroleum, *80*–439; radio, *82*–447; railroad, *82*–448, *81*–461, *80*–458; television, *82*–483; transportation, *82*–494, *81*–508, *80*–507; truck, *82*–495, *81*–510, *80*–509
DES: consumer protection, *81*–266; drugs, *81*–288, *80*–292; medicine, *80*–397
Desai, Morarji Ranchhodji: India, *80*–357
Desalination: water, *Special Report, 82*–106
Desegregation: Chicago, *82*–238, *81*–242, *80*–244; city, *81*–251, *80*–251; civil rights, *82*–249; education, *82*–290, *81*–294, *80*–302; housing, *80*–353; Houston, *82*–339, *81*–343; Los Angeles, *82*–376, *81*–385; Namibia, *80*–416. See also **CIVIL RIGHTS.**
Détente: Germany, East, *81*–328; Germany, West, *81*–328
DETROIT, *82*–277, *81*–282, *80*–287; city, *82*–246, *81*–248, *80*–252
Deutsch, Adolph: deaths, *81*–274
Devaluation. See **INTERNATIONAL TRADE AND FINANCE; Money; Recession.**
Developing countries: Canada, *82*–227; energy, *82*–297; food, *82*–312; international trade, *82*–347, *81*–350; shipping, *80*–475
Devolution: Great Britain, *80*–340; Northern Ireland, *81*–419
De Vries, Peter: literature, *82*–372
Dhandy's Favorite Woodchuck: il., *82*–281
DHEA: drugs, *82*–282
Diabetes: dentistry, *82*–277
Diablo Canyon nuclear power plant, *82*–296
DIANA, PRINCESS OF WALES, *82*–278; Great Britain, *Close-Up, 82*–326
Diaz Ordaz, Gustavo, *80*–279
Dickenson, Russell E.: conservation, *81*–264
Dictionary: *World Book Dictionary* supplement, *82*–581, *81*–581, *80*–581
Diefenbaker, John G.: *Close-Up, 80*–233
Diet: anthropology, *80*–188; health, *80*–346; medicine, *81*–392; nutrition, *82*–413, *81*–422, *80*–426
Diethylstilbestrol: consumer protection, *81*–266; drugs, *81*–288, *80*–292; medicine, *80*–397
Different Kind of Gold, A: literature for children, *82*–376
Diggs, Charles C., Jr., *80*–266; il., *81*–257
Digital recording, *80*–460
Digital switching: communications, *80*–258
Dimethyl sulfoxide: drugs, *81*–288
DINOSAUR: *WBE, 80*–536; paleontology, *82*–419, *81*–433, *80*–431
Dionne, Marcel: hockey, *81*–339
Diouf, Abdou: Gambia, *82*–318
Direct-broadcasting satellite: communications, *82*–253
Disability benefits, *80*–478
Disarmament. See **ARMED FORCES.**
DISASTERS, *82*–278, *81*–283, *80*–288; Asia, *82*–190; boating, *80*–221; China, *82*–243; insurance, *82*–345; New Zealand, *80*–420. See also **Violence.**
Discount fare: aviation, *80*–205
Discrimination. See **CIVIL RIGHTS; Desegregation; Racism.**
Disease. See **DRUGS; HEALTH AND DISEASE; MEDICINE; MENTAL HEALTH.**
Disintermediation: banks, *81*–207
Displacement behavior: pet language, *Special Report, 81*–131
Display: pet language, *Special Report, 81*–122.
District of Columbia. See **WASHINGTON, D.C.**
Ditiatin, Alexandr: Olympics, *81*–429
Diving. See **SWIMMING.**
Divorce: census, *80*–241; Roman Catholic Church, *80*–468
Djibouti: Africa, *82*–176, *81*–178, *80*–180

DMSO: drugs, *81*–288
DNA: biochemistry, *80*–218
DOE, SAMUEL KANYON, *81*–286; il., *81*–377; Liberia, *82*–369
DOG, *82*–281; *81*–287, *80*–291; pet language, *Special Report, 81*–121
DOLE, ROBERT J., *80*–291; Republican Party, *80*–464
Doll: games, models, toys, *81*–324
Dolphin: fishing industry, *81*–317; science, *81*–477
Domestic robot: robot, *Special Report, 82*–149
Dominance: pet language, *Special Report, 81*–123
DOMINICA: *WBE, 80*–577; Latin America, *82*–366, *81*–375, *80*–380; West Indies, *82*–515, *81*–530
Dominican Republic: Latin America, *82*–366, *81*–375, *80*–380; West Indies, *82*–515
Dong, Pham Van: il., *82*–507
DONOVAN, RAYMOND JAMES, *82*–282; Cabinet, *82*–222
Doobie Brothers: il., *81*–464
Dornberger, Walter: deaths, *81*–274
Dos Santos, Jose Eduardo: Angola, *82*–181, *81*–184
Douglas, Donald W., Jr.: deaths, *82*–270
Douglas, Helen Gahagan: deaths, *81*–274
Douglas, Melvyn: deaths, *82*–270
Douglas, William O.: deaths, *81*–274
Draft: armed forces, *82*–189, *81*–189; President, *81*–453; Supreme Court, *82*–477
Dragoicheva, Tsola: Yugoslavia, *80*–530
Dragonette, Jessica: deaths, *81*–274
Drama: awards, *81*–202, *80*–207. See also **LITERATURE; THEATER.**
Dresser, The: theater, *82*–490
Drip irrigation: water, *Special Report, 82*–104
Drought: India, *80*–357; water, *81*–525, *Special Report, 82*–94; weather, *82*–512
DRUGS, *82*–282, *81*–287, *80*–292; aspirin, *Special Report, 81*–138; Bolivia, *82*–215; Latin America, *82*–367; medicine, *80*–396; zoo medicine, *Special Report, 80*–100
Duarte, Jose Napoleon: El Salvador, *82*–295
Dubs, Adolph: Afghanistan, *80*–177
Duckbill dinosaur: paleontology, *82*–419
Dudko, Dimitri: Eastern Orthodox, *81*–288
Duke University: Nixon, Richard Milhous, *82*–409
DUNCAN, CHARLES WILLIAM, JR., *80*–292; Cabinet, *80*–229
Duran, Roberto: boxing, *81*–217, *80*–223
Durant, Will and Ariel: il., *82*–272
Durante, Jimmy: il., *81*–275
Dwarfism: medicine, *80*–398
Dylan, Bob, *80*–414
Dymshits, Mark: Russia, *80*–470

E

Eanes, Antonio dos Santos Ramalho: Portugal, *82*–435
Earth Day: environment, *81*–303
Earthquakes: disasters, *82*–279, *81*–285, *80*–289; geology, *80*–336; Los Angeles, *82*–376
Easter, Luscious (Luke), *80*–279
EASTERN ORTHODOX CHURCHES, *82*–283, *81*–288, *80*–293; Roman Catholic, *82*–457
Eaton, Cyrus S., *80*–279
Ebla: archaeology, *82*–184, *80*–189
Ecevit, Bulent, *80*–511
Ecology. See **Endangered species; ENVIRONMENT; Pollution.**
Economic Recovery Act: taxation, *82*–482; United States, government of the, *82*–505
Economic Summit Conference: Canada, *82*–227
ECONOMICS, *82*–284, *81*–289, *80*–294; Asia, *80*–197; Focus, *80*–26; Great Britain, *81*–331; manufacturing, *82*–379, *81*–388; Nobel Prizes, *82*–410, *81*–419, *80*–424; President, *82*–436, *81*–453; stocks and bonds, *80*–489; United States, government of the, *82*–502. See also **BANKS AND BANKING; Budget, national; Cost of living; Inflation; INTERNATIONAL TRADE AND FINANCE; LABOR; MANUFACTURING; Money; Prices; Recession;** and various country, province, and city articles.
ECUADOR, *82*–288, *81*–293, *80*–299; Latin America, *82*–366, *81*–375, *80*–380
Ecumenism: Eastern Orthodox, *81*–288; Roman Catholic, *81*–469, *80*–468
EDUCATION, *82*–289, *81*–293, *80*–300; Chicago, *82*–238, *81*–242, *80*–244; city, *80*–251; *Close-Up, 81*–295; handicapped, *80*–345; Los Angeles, *82*–376; National PTA, *80*–417; Philadelphia, *82*–428; state government, *82*–474, *81*–489; Washington, D.C., *82*–524. See also **Universities and colleges.**

Education, Department of: Cabinet, 80–230; education, 82–289, 81–293, 80–300
Educational Testing Service: education, 81–296
Edward MacDowell Medal, 82–425
EDWARDS, JAMES BURROWS, 82–291
Edwards, Robert G., 80–396
EGYPT, 82–291, 81–297, 80–303; Africa, 82–176, 81–178, 80–180; archaeology, 80–188; civil rights, 82–248; Israel, 80–364; Jordan, 80–369; Middle East, 82–389, 81–398, 80–402, *Close-Up,* 82–390; Mubarak, Mohamed Hosni, 82–397; Saudi Arabia, 80–472
8010 Star Information System: manufacturing, 82–381
Einstein, Albert: *Close-Up,* 80–443
Eisenhower, Dwight D., 82–372
Eisenhower, Mamie Doud, 80–279
ELECTIONS, 82–292, 81–297, 80–304; city, 82–248; *Close-Up,* 80–305; Congress, 81–262; Democratic Party, 82–275, 81–280, 80–285; Europe, 80–315; Houston, 82–338; Los Angeles, 82–376; Pakistan, 82–417; poll, *Special Report,* 80–117; Republican Party, 82–453, 81–466, 80–464; state government, 80–488. See also articles on various countries, provinces, and cities.
Electric power: coal, 80–256; energy, 80–311; Latin America, 81–374; manufacturing, 81–389, 80–395; ocean, 81–423, 80–428; Paraguay, 82–421; weather, 81–527. See also **ENERGY.**
Electronic church: Protestantism, 80–453
Electronic computer-originated mail, 81–449
Electronic news delivery, 82–407, 81–415
ELECTRONICS, 82–294, 81–300, 80–307; communications, 80–258; games, 82–318, 80–334; manufacturing, 80–381; Postal Service, 80–448
Elementary particles: physics, 80–444
ELEPHANT: *WBE,* 80–532
Elias IV: Eastern Orthodox Churches, 80–293
Elizabeth II: *ils.,* 81–466, 80–342
Elizabeth, Queen Mother: *il.,* 81–331
Elliptical galaxy, 82–194
El Niño: ocean, *Special Report,* 80–133
Elon Moreh: Israel, 80–365
El Paso, 82–246, 81–248, 80–252
EL SALVADOR, 82–295, 81–301; Cuba, 82–265; Latin America, 82–366, 81–375, 80–380
Elswick, Bill: boating, 81–216
Elytis, Odysseus, 80–423
Embryo: biology, 80–219
Embryo transplant: zoos, 82–519, 81–534
Emergency Mobilization Board, 80–312
Emigration. See **IMMIGRATION.**
Emmy Awards, 82–202, 81–202, 80–207
Emory University, 80–302
Empire Strikes Back, The: *il.,* 81–403
Employment: civil rights, 80–255; manufacturing, 80–395; UN, *Close-Up,* 82–501. See also **ECONOMICS; LABOR; SOCIAL SECURITY; WELFARE; Unemployment.**
Enayama Tunnel, 80–227
Enceladus: astronomy, 82–193
Endangered species: conservation, 82–261, 80–268; gardening, 82–319; panda, *Special Report,* 82–75; science, 80–474; *Special Report,* 80–112; zoos, 82–519, 81–534, 80–532
Endoperoxide: aspirin, *Special Report,* 81–146
Endorphin: mental health, 80–399
Endrin: environment, 82–300; hunting, 82–340
ENERGY, 82–296, 81–302, 80–308; building, 81–222, 80–226; *Close-Up,* 80–310; coal, 82–250, 81–253, 80–256; Congress, 81–258, 80–265; conservation, 82–260; consumer protection, 80–269; environment, 80–312; Europe, 80–316; farm, 81–314; *Focus,* 80–47; Indian, American, 80–358; manufacturing, 80–395; ocean, *Special Report,* 80–143; President, 81–453, 80–450; Russia, 82–458; science, 80–473; state government, 80–486; transit, 80–505; water, 82–512. See also **CONSERVATION; PETROLEUM AND GAS.**
Energy, Department of: energy, 80–296
Energy Security Act: Congress, 81–258; energy, 81–302
Engineering. See **BUILDING AND CONSTRUCTION.**
England. See **GREAT BRITAIN.**
Enterprise zones: city, 82–245
Entertainment. See **MOTION PICTURES; MUSIC, CLASSICAL; MUSIC, POPULAR; RADIO; RECORDINGS; SPORTS; TELEVISION; THEATER.**
Envelope: Postal Service, 80–448
ENVIRONMENT, 82–298, 81–303, 80–312; botany, 80–222; Canada, 80–235; chemical industry, 82–236, 81–239; *Close-Up,* 81–304; coal, 80–256; fishing industry, 82–311; forest, 82–317, 80–317; mining, 80–404; water, 80–524. See also **CONSERVATION; Pollution.**
Environmental Protection Agency: chemical industry, 82–236; environment, 82–300, 81–305,

80–313; Philadelphia, 80–440; United States, government of the, 82–503
Episcopal Church, The: religion, 82–452, 81–465, 80–461
Equal Employment Opportunity Commission, 82–363
Equal Rights Amendment: Constitution, 82–261, 81–264, 80–269
EQUATORIAL GUINEA, 80–314; Africa, 82–176, 81–178, 80–180
Equestrian events, 82–470, 81–485, 80–483
Erickson, John, 82–423
Eritrea: Africa, 81–177; Ethiopia, 80–314
Erving, Julius, 82–210
Eskimos: census, 82–234
Estrogen: health, 80–346; medicine, 80–397
Estrus: zoology, 81–534
Ethanol: energy, 82–297, 81–303
ETHIOPIA, 82–176, 80–314; Africa, 81–178, 80–180; Somalia, 81–481; Sudan, 81–492
Europa: astronomy, 80–199; *ils.,* 80–86, 95
EUROPE, 82–302, 81–306, 80–315; *Close-Up,* 81–308; motion pictures, 82–393, 81–401; steel industry, 81–490. See also by name of country.
European Community: Africa, 80–184; Europe, 82–302, 81–306, 80–315; farm, 80–322; Great Britain, 80–344; Greece, 82–328; international trade, 82–361; Luxembourg, 82–377; Portugal, 81–448
European Convention on Human Rights, 80–271
European Monetary System: Europe, 80–318; France, 82–317; Germany, West, 82–322; international trade, 80–361
European Space Agency, 82–467, 81–482, 80–481; space shuttle, *Special Report,* 82–121
Eurosystem Hospitalier: Belgium, 80–217
Evangelicals: Protestantism, 81–455
Evans, John Louis, III, 80–488
Evert Lloyd, Chris: *il.,* 81–501; tennis, 82–486, 80–498
Evita: awards, 81–202; Latin America, 81–376
Evolution: anthropolgy, 82–182, 80–187; chemistry, 80–243; education, 82–290; paleontology, 82–418; Protestantism, 82–443; state government, 82–474; zoology, 82–519
Exclusionary rule: courts and laws, 82–263
Exhibitions. See **MUSEUM; VISUAL ARTS.**
Experimental Negotiating Agreement, 81–367
Explosions: disasters, 82–279, 81–285
Exports. See **INTERNATIONAL TRADE AND FINANCE.**
Express Mail Metro, 80–448
Extinction: gardening, 82–319; paleontology, 80–431; panda, *Special Report,* 82–90
Extradition: courts, 80–272
EYSKENS, MARK, 82–305

F

Fagan, Kevin, 80–434
FAIR plan: insurance, 80–359
Faisal: *il.,* 80–473
Falange Party: Lebanon, 82–368, 81–376
Falldin, Thorbjorn, 82–479, 81–494, 80–492
Fallon, George: deaths, 81–275
Falwell, Jerry: *il.,* 81–455
Family: welfare, 82–514, 81–529; zoology, 80–532
Famine: Africa, 82–179, 81–181; Cambodia, 80–230; Uganda, 82–498
FARM AND FARMING, 82–305, 81–311, 80–319; archaeology, 80–188; biochemistry, 82–212; Congress of the United States, 82–258; consumerism, 82–261; economics, 80–296; Ecuador, 82–288; environment, 82–300; Europe, 82–304, 81–307, 80–318; food, 82–312, 81–317, 80–326; insurance, 81–350; international trade and finance, 82–346; water, 82–512, 81–525; water, *Special Report,* 82–97; weather, 81–526
Farrell, James T., 80–279
FASHION, 82–308, 81–315, 80–323
Fast food, 82–172
Fastnet race: boating, 80–221
Federal Aviation Administration: airport, *Special Report,* 82–137; aviation, 81–201, 80–206
Federal Bureau of Investigation: crime, 80–273; U.S., government of the, 80–515
Federal Communications Commission: communications, 80–258; radio, 80–447
Federal Courts Improvements Act, 80–270
Federal Election Commission, 80–239
Federal Reserve Board: banks, 81–206, 80–212; economics, 80–294; stocks, 80–489
Federal Trade Commission: advertising, 80–176; consumer protection, 81–266, 80–270; consumerism, 82–262; dentistry, 80–287
Feld, Eliot, 80–276

Fencing: sports, 82–470, 81–485, 80–482
Fennell, Frederick: *il.,* 80–460
Fetal alcohol syndrome: nutrition, 82–413
Fetal monitor: medicine, 80–396
Fiction. See **CANADIAN LITERATURE; LITERATURE.**
Fiedler, Arthur: *Close-Up,* 80–412
FIELD, SALLY, 81–316
Field hockey, 82–470, 81–485, 80–483
Fields, Dame Gracie, 80–279
Fifth Circuit Court of Appeals: courts and laws, 82–264
Figueiredo, Joao Baptista de Oliveira: Brazil, 82–217, 81–218, 80–224
Figure skating, 82–340, 81–345, 80–356
Fiji, 82–417
Film, 82–430
Final Alice: music, classical, 82–400
Findley, Timothy: Canadian literature, 82–230
Fingers, Rollie, 82–208
FINLAND, 82–310, 81–316, 80–324; Europe, 82–303, 81–310, 80–317
Finnbogadottir, Vigdis, 81–311
Fires: building, 80–226; disasters, 82–279, 81–285; Houston, 80–353; insurance, 80–359
Fischetti, John: deaths, 81–275
Fishery Conservation and Management Act, 80–325
FISHING, 82–310, 81–316, 80–324
FISHING INDUSTRY, 82–310, 81–317, 80–325; Canada, 82–228, 81–229, 80–234; conservation, 80–268; courts, 81–267; Europe, 81–307; France, 81–323; Indian, American, 80–358; Newfoundland, 82–407; ocean, *Special Report,* 80–130
Fitch, Val L.: Nobel Prizes, 81–419
FITZGERALD, GARRET, 82–311
Fitzsimmons, Frank E.: deaths, 82–270
Fixed market basket: inflation, *Special Report,* 81–74
Flags of convenience: ship and shipping, 82–463
Flash Flood Potential Program: weather, 80–526
Flatt, Lester, 80–280
Fleetwood Mac, 82–401
Flood, Daniel, 81–262, 80–266
Floods: disasters, 82–279, 81–285, 80–290; weather, 80–526
Florida: Democratic Party, 80–285; state government, 82–473, 81–488, 80–487; water, *Special Report,* 82–95
Florovsky, Georges, 80–293
Flower. See **GARDENING.**
Flowering Plant Index: gardening, 81–325
Fluidized-bed combustion: coal, 80–256
Fluoride rinse: dentistry, 81–282
Fluorocarbons: chemical industry, 80–242
Flying Dutchman, The: *il.,* 80–411
FONDA, JANE, 80–326
FOOD, 82–311, 81–317, 80–326; advertising, 82–172; Asia, 81–193, 80–197; nutrition, 80–426; Romania, 82–457; Russia, 82–460. See also **FARM AND FARMING.**
Food and Drug Administration: drugs, 82–282, 80–292; food, 80–327; health, 80–347
Food Stamp Program: food, 80–327; welfare, 82–514, 81–528, 80–528
Foot, Michael: Great Britain, 81–333
Foot-and-mouth disease: biochemistry, 82–212; farm and farming, 82–308
FOOTBALL, 82–313, 81–318, 80–327; magazine, 82–378. See also **SOCCER.**
FORD, GERALD RUDOLPH, 82–316, 81–321, 80–331; *il.,* 82–439
Ford, Henry, II: *il.,* 80–394
Ford, Harrison: *il.,* 82–394
Ford Motor Company: automobile, 80–203; courts, 81–268
Forecasting, weather, 80–134
Foreclosure, 82–338
Forensic hypnosis: hypnosis, *Special Report,* 80–76
FOREST AND FOREST PRODUCTS, 82–322, 81–322, 80–332; Alberta, 82–179; energy, 81–303; *Special Report,* 81–89
FORLANI, ARNALDO, 81–322; Italy, 82–353, 81–360
Forsberg, Mark, 80–293
Fort McHenry tunnel: building and construction, 82–220
Fort Worth, 82–246, 81–248, 80–252. See also **Dallas.**
Fossil: anthropology, 82–182, 80–187; botany, 82–216; paleontology, 82–418, 81–433, 80–431; zoology, 82–519
Foster, Andrew, 82–208
Foster care, 80–246
Fouche, Jacobus J.: deaths, 81–275
Four-H Clubs, 82–517, 81–530, 80–529
Four Seasons, The: *il.,* 82–397
Fox, Carol, 82–270

Fox, Terry: British Columbia, 82–218; *il., 81–435*
Fox, Virgil: deaths, 81–275
FRANCE, 82–317, 81–322, 80–333; civil rights, 81–251; Europe, 82–303, 81–310, 80–317; fashion, 82–309; fishing industry, 81–317; Mexico, 80–399; Middle East, 81–396; motion pictures, 82–394; Pacific Islands, 82–416, 80–429; Roman Catholic, 81–468
Frank, Otto: deaths, 81–275
Frankenstein: robot, *Special Report,* 82–142
Fraser, Malcolm: Australia, 82–195, 81–195, 80–200
Fratianne, Linda, 81–345, 80–356
Fredericks, Thomas: Indian, American, 81–348
Frederika, Queen, 82–270
Free agent system: baseball, 82–206; basketball, 82–208
Free-trade zone, 82–206
Free Will Baptists, 82–452, 81–465, 80–461
Freedom: il., 81–215
Freedom of information: Canadian Library Association, 82–229
Freeway murders: crime, 81–269
Freight: *il., 81–462;* transportation, 82–493; truck, 82–495, 81–510, 80–509
Frelich, Phyllis: handicapped, 81–335; *il., 81–504*
French Lieutenant's Woman, The: motion pictures, 82–396
French Polynesia: Pacific islands, 81–431
Frisbee, 82–470, 81–485
Frog, 82–519
Fromm, Erich: deaths, 81–275
Frost protection: gardening, 82–319
Fuel. See **CONSERVATION; ENERGY; PETROLEUM AND GAS.**
Fukuda, Takeo, 80–367
Fukui, Kenichi, 82–410
FUNAFUTI: *WBE,* 80–580
Funding, federal: Detroit, 82–278; food, 82–312; museum, 82–398; nutrition, 82–413; state government, 82–472; transit, 82–493
Furniture: hobbies, 81–337
Future Farmers of America, 82–517, 81–531, 80–529

G

Gabon, 82–176, 81–178, 80–180
Gacy, John Wayne: courts, 81–268; crime, 80–273
Gaines, Ambrose: swimming, 82–480, 81–495
Gairy, Sir Eric M., 80–528
Galactic evolution: astronomy, 82–194
Galante, Carmine (Lilo): crime, 80–273
Galapagos ocean vents: ocean, 82–415
Galapagos Ridge: mining, 82–391
Galento, Two-Ton Tony, 80–280
Galilean satellites: Jupiter, *Special Report,* 80–89
Gallinari, Prospero: Italy, 80–366
Gallipoli: motion pictures, 82–394
Gallstones, 82–332
GAMBIA, 82–318; Africa, 82–176, 81–178, 80–180
Game Fish Association, International, 80–324
GAMES AND TOYS, 82–318, 81–324, 80–334; advertising, 80–176. See also **BRIDGE, CONTRACT; CHESS; SPORTS.**
Gance, Abel: motion pictures, 82–395
GANDHI, INDIRA PRIYADARSHINI, 81–324; *il., 82–342;* India, 81–346, 80–357
Gandhi, Rajiv: India, 82–343
Gandhi, Sanjay: India, 81–347
Gang of Four: China, 82–241, 81–244
Ganymede: astronomy, 80–199; *ils., 80–86, 93*
Garbage-to-energy process, 80–395
Garden Club of America: gardening, 82–319
GARDENING, 82–319, 81–325, 80–335
Gardner, Randy: 81–345; *il., 80–355;* Olympic Games, 81–430
Garrett, Ray D., Jr.: deaths, 81–275
Garrett collection: coin collecting, 82–251, 81–253
Gary, Romain: deaths, 81–275
Gas and gasoline. See **ENERGY; PETROLEUM AND GAS.**
Gasohol: energy, 82–297, 81–302, 80–311; farm, 80–322; state government, 80–486
Gathings, E. C., 80–280
Gehlen, Reinhard, 80–280
Gelinas, John, Jr.: personalities, 81–436
Gene splicing: biochemistry, 81–213, 80–218
General Agreement on Tariffs and Trade: farm, 80–322; international trade, 80–361
General Association of Regular Baptist Churches, 82–452, 81–465, 80–461
General Motors Corporation: automobile, 82–197

Genetic drift: zoos, 80–532
Genetics: biochemistry, 82–212, 81–213, 80–218; biology, 81–214; farm and farming, 82–308; health and disease, 82–332, 80–346; Supreme Court, 81–493; zoology, 82–519
Genuine Risk: *il., 81–340*
GEOLOGY, 82–320, 81–326, 80–336; awards, 82–203, 81–204, 80–209; *Close-Up, 81–327;* ocean, 82–414; paleontology, 80–431
George, Chief Dan: deaths, 82–270
George Polk Memorial Awards, 82–202, 81–203, 80–203
George Washington: Japan, 82–354
Georges Bank: Canada, 82–228; fishing industry, 82–311, 81–317, 80–325; ocean, 82–415
Georgia, 82–473, 81–488, 80–487
Geostationary Operational Environmental Satellite, 81–483, 528
Gerald R. Ford Library: library, 82–369
Gerald R. Ford Museum, 82–316
GERMANY, EAST, 82–321, 81–328, 80–336; armed forces, 80–192; Europe, 82–303, 81–310, 80–317; Russia, 80–469
GERMANY, WEST, 82–322, 81–328, 80–337; Albania, 80–185; coal, 80–257; Europe, 82–303, 81–310, 80–317; Hungary, 80–354; Jews, 80–369; motion pictures, 81–401, 80–406; Russia, 82–458; safety, 80–471
Geweniger, Ute: swimming, 82–480
Gezhouba project: building and construction, 82–219
GHANA, 80–338; Africa, 82–176, 81–178, 80–180
Gheorghiu, Florin: chess, 82–238
GHOTBZADEH, SADEGH, 81–329
Giannini, Margaret J.: handicapped, 81–335
Giannoulas, Ted: *il., 80–436*
Giant panda: 80–114
Gibraltar: Spain, 82–468
Gibson, Bob: baseball, 82–208
Gilbert, Walter: Nobel Prizes, 81–419
Gilbert Islands, 80–429
Ginzburg, Alexander, 80–470
Girl Scouts, 82–517, 81–531, 80–529
Girls Clubs of America, 82–517, 81–531, 80–530
Giscard d'Estaing, Valéry, 80–333
Glashow, Sheldon L., 80–424
Glass, Philip: music, classical, 82–400
Glemp, Jozef: Roman Catholic, 82–456
Global 2000 Report: environment, 81–303
Glomar Challenger: ocean, 82–414, 81–423, 80–427
Gluon: physics, 80–444
Godfrey, Arthur, 80–435
Godunov, Alexander, 80–276
Golan Heights: United Nations, 82–499
Gold: banks, 80–211; coins, 82–251, 81–253, 80–257; international trade, *Close-Up, 81–351,* 80–360; Pacific Islands, 82–417
Golden, Harry: deaths, 82–270
GOLDSCHMIDT, NEIL EDWARD, 80–339; Cabinet, 80–229
GOLF, 82–322, 81–330, 80–339
Gonorrhea: public health, 82–444
Goodwin, Dan: personalities, 82–423
Gospel: popular music, 81–409
Gossamer Albatross: personalities, 80–434; science, 80–474
Gossypol: medicine, 80–396
Gould, Chester: personalities, 82–423
Gouletas, Evangeline, 82–422
Government. See **CITY; STATE GOVERNMENT; U.S., GOVERNMENT OF THE.**
Governor-General's Literary Awards: Canadian literature, 82–231, 81–233, 80–238
Goyan, Jere E., 80–292
Graf Zeppelin: stamps, 81–487
Graham, David: golf, 82–322
Grahame, Gloria: deaths, 82–270
Grain, 81–313, 80–319; Asia, 80–197; China, 81–246; farm and farming, 82–307; food, 80–327; Indonesia, 82–344; Russia, 82–460
Grain embargo: Afghanistan, *Close-Up, 81–174;* Australia, 81–196; farm and farming, 82–307, 81–313; international trade and finance, 82–346
Grammy Awards, 82–201, 81–202, 80–207
Grand Prix: auto racing, 82–199
Grant Bridge: *il., 80–227*
Granville, Joseph: stocks, 82–475
Grasso, Ella T.: deaths, 82–270
Gravity waves: physics, 80–442
GREAT BRITAIN, 82–325, 81–331, 80–340; Africa, 80–182, *Close-Up, 80–183;* Albania, 80–185; *Close-Ups, 82–326, 80–343;* coal, 82–251; Europe, 82–303, 81–310, 80–317; Northern Ireland, 82–411, 81–419, 80–425; Pacific Islands, 80–429
Great Red Spot: *il., 80–88*
GREECE, 82–328, 81–333, 80–344; Europe, 82–303, 81–310, 80–317; Papandreou, Andreas, 82–420

Greek Orthodox Archdiocese of North and South America, 82–452, 81–465, 80–461
Green, Chad, 80–347
Green, Paul E.: deaths, 82–270
Green, William J., III: elections, 80–304; Philadelphia, 81–441, 80–440
Green Revolution: Asia, 81–193
Greenbug: gardening, 81–325
Greenhouse effect: weather, 82–513, 80–525
Greenland, 80–286
Grenada: Bishop, Maurice Rupert, 80–220; Latin America, 82–366, 81–375, 80–380; West Indies, 81–530, 80–528
Gretzky, Wayne: hockey, 82–334, 81–339
Griffin, John H.: deaths, 81–275
Griffith, Darrell: *il., 81–211*
Grigorovich, Uri, 80–276
Gromyko, Andrei A., 80–469
Gross, Sidney, 80–430
Gross national product: Canada, 80–234; economics, 82–284, 81–289, 80–294
Grouse: zoology, 80–532
Growth hormone: biochemistry, 80–218
Guatemala: Latin America, 82–366, 81–375, 80–380
Gueiler Tejada, Lydia, 80–221
Guernica: visual arts, 82–508
Guerrilla warfare: Afghanistan, 82–173; Africa, 82–174; Asia, 82–190; Colombia, 82–251; El Salvador, 82–295; Morocco, 82–393; Philippines, 82–429; Somalia, 82–465, 81–481; Thailand, 82–487
Guevara Arze, Walter, 80–221
Guillaume, Robert: *il., 80–496*
Guinea: Africa, 82–176, 81–178, 80–180
Guinea-Bissau: Africa, 82–176, 81–178, 80–180
Gulf Cooperation Council: Middle East, 82–387
Gum disease: dentistry, 82–277
Gush Emunim: Israel, 80–365
Guyana, 82–366, 81–375, 80–380; Venezuela, 82–507
Gymnastics: sports, 82–470, 81–485, 80–482

H

Habib, Philip C.: United Nations, 82–499
Haddad, Saad: Lebanon, 80–383
Hagler, Marvin: boxing, 82–217
Hagnes, Helen: courts, 82–264
HAIG, ALEXANDER MEIGS, JR., 82–329; Cabinet, 82–222; *il., 82–461;* President, 82–438
Hail: weather, 81–527
Hairdrier: consumer protection, 80–270
Haiti: immigration, 82–342, 81–346; Latin America, 82–366, 81–375, 80–380
Halberstam, Michael J.: courts, 82–264
Haley, Bill: deaths, 82–270
Haley, Jack, 80–280
Halperin, Morton: Nixon, 82–409, 81–417
Hambletonian, 80–351
Hamilton, Scott: ice skating, 82–340
Handball, 82–470, 81–485, 80–483
HANDICAPPED, 82–330, 81–334, 80–345; child welfare, 82–239; robot, *Special Report, 82–152;* transit, 82–493, 80–506; United Nations, *Close-Up, 82–501*
Hang gliding, 82–470, 81–485, 80–483
Hanson, Howard H.: deaths, 82–270
Harding, Ann: deaths, 82–270
Hare Krishna: cults, *Special Report, 80–147*
Harness racing, 82–336, 81–341, 80–351
Harriman, W. Averell: personalities, 82–423
Harris, Jean S.: *il., 82–263*
Harris, John W. K.: *il., 82–182*
Harris, Patricia Roberts: *il., 80–229*
Harris, Roy, 80–280
Hassan II: Africa, 80–182; Morocco, 82–393
Hatch, Orrin G., 80–267
Hatfield, Richard B.: New Brunswick, 82–404, 81–413
HAUGHEY, CHARLES JAMES, 81–335; *il., 81–357;* Ireland, 82–350, 81–357, 80–364
Havel, Vaclav, 80–275
Hawaii, 82–473, 81–488, 80–487
Hawksbill sea turtle: *il., 82–260*
Haymes, Dick: deaths, 81–275
Hazim, Ignatius, 80–293
Head, Edith: deaths, 82–270
Head Start: child welfare, 80–246
Healey, Denis: Great Britain, 82–327
HEALTH AND DISEASE, 82–331, 81–335, 80–346; chemical industry, 80–242; child welfare, 82–240; nutrition, 80–426; zoo medicine, *Special Report, 80–99.* See also **DENTISTRY; DRUGS; HOSPITAL; MEDICINE; MENTAL HEALTH; PUBLIC HEALTH.**
Health and Human Services, Department of: Cabinet, 80–230; child welfare, 81–243; U.S., government of the, 82–503
Hearing impaired: handicapped, 81–335

Hearns, Thomas: boxing, *82*–216
Hearst, Patricia, *80*–435
Heart attack: aspirin, *Special Report*, *81*–138; health, *82*–331; medicine, *82*–382
Heart disease: health, *82*–331, *81*–335, *80*–346; medicine, *82*–382, *81*–392; nutrition, *81*–422
Heart-lung transplant: medicine, *82*–382
Heat wave: disasters, *81*–286; weather, *81*–526
HEIDEN, BETH, *80*–347; ice skating, *81*–344, *80*–355
HEIDEN, ERIC, *80*–347; ice skating, *81*–344, *80*–355; il., *81*–425; sports, *82*–469
Helms, Jesse A.: courts, *82*–264
Henderson, Rickey: baseball, *82*–208
Hendrix, Wanda: deaths, *82*–270
Heng Samrin: Cambodia, *80*–230; United Nations, *80*–514
Henley, Elmer Wayne *80*–353
Henri, Prince: il., *82*–377
Hepatitis B: biochemistry, *82*–212; health and disease, *82*–332, *80*–347; public health, *81*–458
Herbicide, *80*–259
Heredity: dentistry, *82*–277; health and disease, *81*–337
Hernandez, Benjamin, *80*–465
Hernandez Colon, Rafael, *81*–460
Heroin: drugs, *81*–287
Herpes simplex: drugs, *82*–283
HERRERA CAMPINS, LUIS, *80*–347; il., *81*–521; Venezuela, *82*–506, *80*–520
Hershey Foods Corporation: advertising, *82*–173
Hesburgh, Theodore M.: personalities, *82*–424
Hexatrygon bickelli: zoology, *82*–519
Highway. See Roads and highways.
Hijacking: Bulgaria, *82*–221; crime, *82*–264, *81*–268, *80*–273; Indonesia, *82*–344; Pakistan, *82*–417
Hillside Strangler, *80*–392
"Hill Street Blues": il., *82*–484
Hilton, Conrad N., *80*–281
Hinckley, John W.: President, *82*–436
Hindu: religion, *81*–465, *80*–463
Hirshhorn, Joseph H.: deaths, *82*–271
Hispanic Americans: census, *82*–234
History: Canadian literature, *82*–230, *81*–233, *80*–238; literature, *82*–372, *81*–381, *80*–385
HITCHCOCK, ALFRED JOSEPH, *80*–348; il., *81*–276
Hoban, Russell: literature, *82*–371
HOBBIES, *82*–333, *81*–337, *80*–348. See also **COIN COLLECTING; GAMES AND TOYS; PHOTOGRAPHY; SPORTS; STAMP COLLECTING.**
HOCKEY, *82*–334, *81*–338, *80*–349; Olympic Games, *81*–430
Hodic, Josef: Czechoslovakia, *82*–266
Hoffman, Abbie: personalities, *81*–436
HOFFMAN, DUSTIN, *81*–340
Hoffman, Roald: Nobel Prizes, *82*–410
Holden, William: il., *82*–273
Holkeri, Harri: Finland, *80*–324
Holland. See NETHERLANDS.
Holman, Marshall: bowling, *82*–216, *81*–217
Holmes, Larry, *82*–216, *81*–217, *80*–223
Holocaust: Canadian literature, *82*–230; Jews, *82*–355, *80*–369
Holtzman, Linda Joy: il., *80*–368
Holtzman Amendment: insurance, *80*–359
Home rule: Denmark, *80*–286; Great Britain, *80*–340; Spain, *80*–481
Homelands: Ciskei, *82*–243
Hominid: anthropology, *80*–187
Homosexuality: Protestantism, *80*–453
Honduras, *82*–366, *81*–375, *80*–380
Honecker, Erich, *82*–321, *81*–328, *80*–336
Honolulu: city, *82*–246, *81*–248, *80*–252
Hooker Chemical Company: environment, *80*–314
Hooper, Marcus, *80*–435
Hormones: biochemistry, *80*–218
Horne, Lena: il., *82*–422
HORSE RACING, *82*–335, *81*–340, *80*–350
Horseshoe pitching, *82*–470, *81*–485, *80*–483
Horticulture. See BOTANY; GARDENING.
HOSPITAL, *82*–336, *81*–341, *80*–351; zoos, *Special Report*, *80*–99
Hostages: Algeria, *82*–180; armed forces, *81*–188; Colombia, *81*–254; courts, *82*–263; dentistry, *82*–276; elections, *81*–298; il., *82*–405; Iran, *81*–354, *80*–361, *Close-Up*, *82*–348; Middle East, *82*–387; President, *81*–450; United Nations, *81*–513
Hot-Air Henry: literature for children, *82*–374
Hounsfield, Godfrey N., *80*–425
HOUSING, *82*–337, *81*–342, *80*–352; banks, *82*–206; building, *82*–219, *81*–221, *80*–226; economics, *82*–284; forest, *82*–317; prison, *82*–440
HOUSTON, *82*–338, *81*–343, *80*–353; city, *82*–246, *81*–248, *80*–252

Hoveyda, Amir Abbas, *80*–281
Howard, Elston: deaths, *80*–275
Howe, Gordie: hockey, *81*–339
Hsing-Hsing: panda, *Special Report*, *82*–89
HU YAOBANG, *82*–339
Hua Kuo-feng (Hua Guofeng): China, *82*–240, *81*–246, *80*–247
Hubel, David H.: Nobel Prizes, *82*–410
Hübner, Robert: chess, *81*–241
Hulme, Kathryn C.: deaths, *82*–271
Human fossils: anthropology, *82*–182
Human growth hormone: biochemistry, *80*–218; medicine, *80*–398
Human leucocyte antigen: dentistry, *82*–276
Human-powered flight: personalities, *80*–434; science, *80*–474
Human rights: Argentina, *81*–187; Asia, *81*–194; Bolivia, *82*–215; civil rights, *80*–254; courts, *80*–271; Germany, East, *82*–321; Latin America, *82*–367; Malaysia, *80*–393; Paraguay, *82*–421
Humber Bridge: building, *82*–220
Humes, Helen: deaths, *82*–272
HUNGARY, *82*–340, *81*–343, *80*–354; Austria, *80*–202; Europe, *82*–303, *81*–310, *80*–317
Hunger strikes: Northern Ireland, *82*–411
HUNTING, *82*–340, *81*–344, *80*–354; environment, *82*–300
Hurley, Ruby: deaths, *81*–275
Hurricane: disasters, *82*–279, *81*–285, *80*–290; weather, *80*–525
Hurtado Larrea, Oswaldo: Ecuador, *82*–288
Husak, Gustav, *81*–271
Hussain, Ghasi: Austria, *82*–196
HUSSEIN, SADDAM, *80*–355; Iraq, *82*–350, *81*–356, *80*–363
Hussein I: Jordan, *82*–356, *81*–363, *80*–369
Huszár, István: Hungary, *80*–354
Hutchinson, Barbara B.: labor, *82*–363
Hutton, Barbara, *80*–281
Hutton, Jim, *80*–281
Hyaline membrane disease, *80*–397
Hyatt Regency Hotel: building, *82*–219; il., *82*–280; insurance, *82*–345
Hydraulic shovel: il., *82*–391
Hydrogen bomb: science, *80*–474
Hydroplane: boating, *82*–215, *81*–216
Hydroponics: il., *81*–325
Hypertension: food, *82*–312
Hypnosis: *Special Report*, *80*–70

I

Iacocca, Lee A.: automobile, *82*–197; il., *81*–198
Iakovos, Archbishop: il., *80*–293
Iapetus: astronomy, *82*–194
ICBM. See Intercontinental ballistic missile.
Ice hockey. See HOCKEY.
ICE SKATING, *82*–340, *81*–344, *80*–355; Olympic Games, *81*–430
Iceboating: sports, *82*–470, *81*–485
Iceland: Europe, *82*–303, *81*–310, *80*–317
Idaho: forest, *80*–332; Indian, American, *80*–358; state government, *82*–473, *81*–488, *80*–487
Illinois, *82*–473, *81*–488, *80*–487; Chicago, *82*–238, *81*–242, *80*–244
Illiteracy: education, *80*–302
IMMIGRATION, *82*–341, *81*–345, *80*–356; Australia, *81*–197; census, *81*–238; Cuba, *81*–270; Jews, *80*–368; Latin America, *82*–367; Mexico, *80*–399; Puerto Rico, *81*–460
Immunization: public health, *80*–455
Imports. See INTERNATIONAL TRADE AND FINANCE.
Inbreeding depression: zoos, *80*–532
Incest: child welfare, *80*–246
Income, personal: economics, *82*–285
Income tax: taxation, *80*–495; welfare, *80*–527
Independence: Africa, *Close-Up*, *80*–183; Pacific Islands, *80*–429; Puerto Rico, *80*–457; Venda, *80*–519; West Indies, *80*–528
INDIA, *82*–342, *81*–346, *80*–357; Asia, *82*–192, *81*–192, *80*–196; Bangladesh, *82*–204, *80*–210; religion, *82*–453, *81*–465
INDIAN, AMERICAN, *82*–343, *81*–347, *80*–357; census, *82*–234; fishing, *82*–310, *80*–325; Quebec, *81*–461
Indiana, *82*–473, *81*–488, *80*–487
Indianapolis: city, *82*–246, *81*–248, *80*–252
Indianapolis 500: automobile racing, *82*–198, *81*–199, *80*–204
Individualized Education Program: handicapped, *80*–346
Individual retirement account: taxation, *82*–482
Indochinese: Asia, *Close-Up*, *80*–198
INDONESIA, *82*–344, *81*–348, *80*–358; Asia, *82*–192, *81*–192, *80*–196
Industrial robot: robot, *Special Report*, *82*–140
Industry. See MANUFACTURING. See also

ECONOMICS; INTERNATIONAL TRADE; LABOR; entries on specific industries, countries, and provinces.
Infant formula: nutrition, *82*–413
Infant mortality: public health, *82*–444
Infection: hospital, *82*–336
Inflation: *WBE*, *82*–572; banks and banking, *82*–205, *81*–206, *80*–210; city, *80*–250; consumer protection, *81*–265, *80*–269; economics, *82*–284, *81*–290, *80*–294; *Focus*, *80*–26; food, *80*–326; hospital, *80*–351; insurance, *80*–359; international trade and finance, *82*–345, *81*–350, *80*–360; labor, *81*–367, *80*–372; manufacturing, *80*–394; music, classical, *80*–410; *Special Report*, *81*–73; stocks, *80*–489; taxation, *80*–495. See also entries on specific countries and cities.
Insulin: health and disease, *82*–332
INSURANCE, *82*–344, *81*–349, *80*–359; building and construction, *82*–220; hospital, *82*–337, *80*–351; safety, *80*–471. See also **SOCIAL SECURITY.**
Integration. See CIVIL RIGHTS; Desegregation.
Intelligence: psychology, *82*–444
Intelpost, *80*–448
Inter-American Development Bank, *81*–374
Intercontinental ballistic missile: armed forces, *82*–187
Interest rates: automobile, *81*–198; banks and banking, *82*–205, *81*–206, *80*–210; Canada, *80*–234; consumer protection, *80*–270; economics, *82*–284, *81*–290, *80*–294; housing, *80*–352; international trade and finance, *82*–345; stocks, *80*–489
Interferon: biochemistry, *82*–212, *81*–214; health and disease, *82*–332; medicine, *82*–383, *81*–391
Interior, U.S. Department of the: U.S. government of the, *82*–503
Intermarriage: Jews, *80*–368
Internal Revenue Service, *82*–482, *80*–495
International cooperation: space exploration, *80*–481. See also entries on specific countries and cities.
International Court of Justice: courts, *81*–267
International Development and Cooperation Act: farm, *80*–321
International Game Fish Association, *80*–324
International Institute for the Study of Human Origins: anthropology, *82*–182
International Monetary Fund: international trade and finance, *82*–347, *81*–350; Saudi Arabia, *82*–461
International Species Inventory System: il., *80*–113
INTERNATIONAL TRADE AND FINANCE, *82*–345, *81*–350, *80*–360; automobile, *82*–198, *81*–197; Belgium, *82*–211; *Close-Up*, *81*–351; coal, *82*–250; Congress, *80*–264; Denmark, *82*–276; economics, *82*–285; farm, *82*–306, *81*–312, *80*–321; Japan, *82*–354, *81*–362; Latin America, *82*–364; mining, *80*–392, *80*–404; petroleum and gas, *82*–426, *80*–437; ship, *80*–475; steel, *82*–475, *81*–490. See also entries for specific continents and countries.
International Year of the Child: child welfare, *80*–245
International Year of Disabled Persons: handicapped, *82*–330; United Nations, *Close-Up*, *82*–501
Inuit: Northwest Territories, *81*–420; Yukon, *81*–532
Investments: international trade and finance, *82*–347. See also **BANKS AND BANKING; ECONOMICS; STOCKS AND BONDS.**
Io: astronomy, *80*–199; ils., *80*–86, 91, 95, 97; Jupiter, *Special Report*, *80*–89; space exploration, *80*–479
Iowa, *82*–473, *81*–488, *80*–487
IRAN, *82*–347, *81*–353, *80*–361; armed forces, *81*–188; Asia, *82*–192, *81*–192, *80*–196; *Close-Up*, *82*–348, *81*–355; courts, *82*–263, *80*–271; disasters, *82*–278; energy, *80*–309; Europe, *81*–309; immigration, *80*–356; international trade, *80*–360; Iraq, *82*–350; Jews and Judaism, *81*–363; Middle East, *82*–389, *81*–398, *80*–402; petroleum, *81*–438, *80*–437; President, *80*–448; religion, *80*–461; Russia, *80*–470; United Nations, *81*–513, *80*–514
IRAQ, *82*–350, *81*–356, *80*–363; archaeology, *81*–185; Iran, *82*–349; *Close-Up*, *81*–355; Jordan, *82*–356, *81*–363; Middle East, *82*–389, *81*–398, *80*–402; petroleum, *81*–438; Syria, *80*–493; United Nations, *82*–498, *81*–514
IRELAND, *82*–350, *81*–357, *80*–364; crime, *80*–273; Europe, *82*–303, *81*–310, *80*–317; Fitzgerald, Garret, *82*–311. See also **NORTHERN IRELAND.**
Iridium: paleontology, *81*–433
Irish Republican Army: Northern Ireland, *82*–411, *80*–425

Iron and steel. See **STEEL INDUSTRY.**
Irrigation: *il.,* 81–526; water, 80–524, *Special Report,* 82–104; weather, 82–513
Islam: Afghanistan, 82–173; Egypt, 82–291; Iran, 80–361; Middle East, 82–386, 80–400; religion, 80–461; Saudi Arabia, 81–475
Islamabad: Pakistan, 80–430
Islamic Unity of the Mujahedeen: Afghanistan, 82–174
ISRAEL, 82–351, 81–358, 80–364; archaeology, 82–184, 81–185; Egypt, 80–303; Lebanon, 82–368; Middle East, 82–389, 81–398, 80–402, *Close-Up,* 82–390; music, classical, 82–399; President, 82–440, 81–450; religion, 82–453; Syria, 82–481; United Nations, 82–498, 81–515, 80–512; water, *Special Report,* 82–107. See also **JEWS AND JUDAISM.**
Itaipú Dam: Paraguay, 81–434
ITALY, 82–353, 81–360, 80–366; Albania, 80–185; disasters, 81–285; Europe, 82–303, 81–310, 80–317; motion pictures, 82–394; Spadolini, Giovanni, 82–468; visual arts, 82–510
Iturbi, José: deaths, 81–275
Ivory Coast, 82–176, 81–178, 80–180
Ixtoc I oil well: environment, 81–305; *il.,* 80–313; ocean, 81–423, 80–428

J

Jackal: zoology, 80–532
Jacksonville, Fla.: city, 82–246, 81–248, 80–252
Jainism: religion, 82–453
Jamaica: Latin America, 82–366, 81–375, 80–380; West Indies, 82–515, 81–529, 80–528
James, P.D.: *il.,* 81–380
James Bay hydroelectric project, 80–458
Janssen, David: deaths, 81–275
JAPAN, 82–353, 81–361, 80–367; Asia, 82–192, 81–192, 80–196; automobile, 82–198; Germany, East, 82–321; international trade, 80–361; Iran, 82–349; motion pictures, 82–393
Jar of Dreams, A: literature for children, 82–375
JARUZELSKI, WOJCIECH, 82–355
Jawara, Dawda Kairaba, Sir: Gambia, 82–318
Jayewardene, Junius Richard: Sri Lanka, 82–471, 81–486
Jazz: music, popular, 82–402, 81–411, 80–416
Jehovah's Witnesses, 82–452, 81–465, 80–461
Jerry Lewis Telethon: handicapped, 82–331
Jessel, George: deaths, 82–271
Jewish Congregations, 82–452, 81–465, 80–461
JEWS AND JUDAISM, 82–355, 81–362, 80–368; archaeology, 82–184; civil rights, 80–255; Israel, 82–351, 81–358; religion, 82–453; Russia, 82–460; United Nations, 80–512. See also **ISRAEL.**
Joel, Billy: *il.,* 80–460
Joffrey Ballet, 81–271
Johanson, Donald C.: anthropology, 82–182
John, Elton, 80–415
John F. Kennedy Center for the Performing Arts, 82–201, 81–202, 80–207
John F. Kennedy Library: *il.,* 80–190
John Henry: horse racing, 82–335
John Paul II: Eastern Orthodox Churches, 80–293; *ils.,* 81–348, 466, 469; Ireland, 80–364; Latin America, 81–372; Poland, 80–445; religion, *Close-Up,* 80–462; Roman Catholic, 82–454, 81–468, 80–466
Johns, John, 80–223
JOHNSON, EARVIN, 80–369; basketball, 82–209, 81–209
Johnson, Pamela Hansford: deaths, 82–272
Johnson, Philip C., 80–190
Johnson, Sonia, 81–456, 80–454
Jones, Alan: auto racing, 82–199, 81–199
Jones, J. Morris-Bailey K. Howard-WBE-ALA Goals Award, 82–180, 81–183, 80–186
Jones, James H.: literature, 82–373
Jonestown: courts and laws, 82–264
JORDAN, 82–356, 81–363, 80–369; Middle East, 82–389, 81–398, 80–402
Jordan, Hamilton: *il.,* 80–450
Jordan, Vernon E., Jr., 80–255
Jorgensen, Anker Henrik: Denmark, 82–276, 81–281, 80–286
Journalism: awards, 82–202, 81–202, 80–208; civil rights, 81–251, 80–255; courts, 80–272; Roman Catholic, 82–456; Supreme Court, 81–493, 80–491. See also **MAGAZINE; NEWSPAPER.**
Juan Carlos I: Spain, 82–468
Judaism. See **JEWS AND JUDAISM.**
Judiciary. See **COURTS AND LAWS.**
Judo, 82–470, 81–485, 80–483
Judy, Steven T.: prison, 82–441
Junior Achievement, 82–517, 81–531, 80–530
Jupiter: astronomy, 81–195, 80–199; space exploration, 80–479; *Special Report,* 80–87

K

K car: *il.,* 81–198
Kaline, Al: baseball, 81–209
Kaminska, Ida: deaths, 81–275
Kampuchea. See **CAMBODIA.**
KANIA, STANISLAW, 81–364; Poland, 82–434, 81–447
Kansas, 82–473, 81–488, 80–487
Kansas City, Mo., 82–246, 81–248, 80–252
Karate, 82–470, 81–485, 80–483
Karmal, Babrak: Afghanistan, 81–173, *Close-Up,* 81–174; Middle East, 80–440
Karpov, Anatoly, 82–238, 81–241
Kawasaki disease: health, 81–336
Kean, Thomas H.: Democratic Party, 82–275
Kekkonen, Urho: Finland, 82–310, 81–316; *il.,* 80–324
Kelly, Patsy: deaths, 82–272
Kemper Memorial Arena, 80–189
KENNEDY, EDWARD MOORE (TED), 80–370; Democratic Party, 81–280, 80–285
Kennedy Library, John F.: *il.,* 80–190
Kennedy Space Center: space shuttle, *Special Report,* 82–109
Kenny, Finbar B., 80–429
Kenton, Stan, 80–281
Kentucky, 82–473, 81–488, 80–487
KENYA, 82–357; Africa, 82–176, 81–178, 80–180
Keynes, John Maynard, 80–298
Khama, Sir Seretse M.: deaths, 81–275
Khamenei, Ali: Iran, 82–349
Khmer Rouge: Cambodia, 82–223, 81–224; Thailand, 81–502
KHOMEINI, RUHOLLAH, 80–370; *il.,* 81–354; Iran, 82–347, 81–353, 80–361; Middle East, 80–400; religion, 80–461
Kidnapping: Jordan, 82–356. See also **CRIME.**
Kidney dialysis: *il.,* 81–392
Kilian, Victor, 80–281
Kim, Dae Jung: Korea, South, 82–358, 81–366, 80–371
Kim, Jae Kyu, 80–371
Kim, Young Sam, 80–371
Kim Chong-il, 81–365
Kim Il-song: Korea, North, 82–358, 81–365
King, Martin Luther, Jr., 80–265
KINGSTOWN: *WBE,* 81–580
Kirchschlaeger, Rudolf: Austria, 81–197
KIRIBATI, 80–429; Pacific Islands, 82–417; *WBE,* 81–579
KIRKLAND, LANE, 80–370; *ils.,* 81–369, 80–375
KIRKPATRICK, JEANE J., 82–358; *il.,* 82–499
Kissinger v. Halperin: Nixon, 82–409
Kite, Tom: golf, 82–322
Kiwanis International, 82–253, 81–256, 80–259
Klein, Lawrence R.: Nobel Prizes, 81–419
KLUTZNICK, PHILIP MORRIS, 80–371; Cabinet, 80–230
Knight, Bobby, 80–432
Knight, John S.: deaths, 82–272
Koala: *il.,* 80–110; zoos, 82–520
Koch, Edward I.: New York City, 82–404, 81–414, 80–418
Kohout, Pavel, 80–275
Koivisto, Mauno: Finland, 82–310, 80–324
Kondrashin, Kiril: deaths, 82–272
Koop, C. Everett: medicine, 82–383
Korchnoi, Viktor, 82–238, 81–241
KOREA, NORTH, 82–358, 81–365, 80–371; Asia, 82–192, 81–192, 80–196
KOREA, SOUTH, 82–358, 81–365, 80–371; Asia, 82–192, 81–192, 80–196; civil rights, 81–251
Kosovo: Yugoslavia, 82–517
Kostelanetz, Andre: deaths, 81–276
Kovalyonok, Vladimir: space exploration, 82–466
Kozlov, Leonid and Valentina, 80–276
Krajger, Sergej, 80–531
Kreisky, Bruno, 82–196, 81–197, 80–202
Kreps, Juanita Morris: Cabinet, 80–229
Kriangsak Chamanan, 82–487, 81–502, 80–500
Krishnas: cults, *Special Report,* 80–147
Krugerrand, 80–257
KUALA LUMPUR: *WBE,* 82–572
Kucinich, Dennis J.: *il.,* 80–306
Küng, Hans, 81–470, 80–468
Kupchak, Mitch: basketball, 82–208
Kurds: Iran, 81–354, 80–362; Iraq, 80–363
Kush, Frank, 80–330
Kuwait: Middle East, 82–389, 81–398, 80–402; petroleum, 82–428
Kuznetsov, Eduard, 80–470
Kylian, Jiri, 80–276

L

LABOR, 82–359, 81–367, 80–372; automobile, 82–197, 80–203; aviation, 82–200; census, 80–241; *Close-Up,* 81–368; coal, 82–250; Donovan, Raymond J., 82–282; economics, 82–284, 80–294; education, 81–294; farm, 80–231; manufacturing, 82–380, 80–395; postal service, 82–436; President, 82–438; robot, *Special Report,* 82–138; Roman Catholic, 82–456, 80–467; Social Security, 80–478; U.S., government of the, 82–505. See also entries for specific countries, provinces, and cities.
Laboren Exercens: Roman Catholic, 82–456
Lacrosse, 82–470, 81–485, 80–483
Ladies Professional Bowlers Tour, 82–216
Laetoli: anthropology, 81–184
Laetrile: drugs, 82–282, 80–292; health, 80–347; medicine, 81–391
Lake Placid, N.Y., 81–430, 80–428
LaMarsh, Julia V.: deaths, 81–276
Lance, Thomas Bertram: *il.,* 81–268
Lane, Lola: deaths, 82–272
Language: China, *Close-Up,* 80–248; education, 80–302; Montreal, 82–392; psychology, 80–454
LANSBURY, ANGELA, 80–376
LANSING, SHERRY, 81–371
LAOS, 82–363, 81–371, 80–377; Asia, 82–192, 81–192, 80–196, *Close-Up,* 80–198; Vietnam, 80–520
Lapotaire, Jane: theater, 82–489
Large-scale integrated circuit, 81–300
Laser: manufacturing, 81–389
Lasker, Edward: deaths, 82–272
Last Metro, The: motion pictures, 82–395
LATIN AMERICA, 82–364, 81–372, 80–378; population, 81–447; Roman Catholic, 81–468. See also by name of country.
Latin American Integration Association, 82–365, 81–374
Lauti, Toalipi, 80–430
Law of the Sea, UN Conference on: courts, 82–263, 81–267; mining, 82–391; ocean, 82–415, 81–423, 80–428; United Nations, 82–499
Lawn bowling, 82–470, 81–485, 80–483
Lawn mower: safety, 80–472
Laws. See **COURTS AND LAWS; CRIME; SUPREME COURT OF THE U.S.**
Lazar, Gyorgy: Hungary, 81–344
Lead poisoning: hunting, 81–344, 80–354; safety, 82–460
Leadership: *Focus,* 80–38
Leakey, Mary, 81–184
Learning: psychology, 82–443
LEBANON, 82–368, 81–376, 80–383; Middle East, 82–389, 81–398, 80–402; religion, 81–465; United Nations, 82–499, 80–513
Le Duan: Vietnam, 82–507, 81–521
Led Zeppelin, 81–410, 80–414
Lee, James M.: Prince Edward Island, 82–440
Lee's Let the Sunshine In: cat, 82–232
Legal Services Corporation, 82–264
Leger, Jules: deaths, 81–276
Legislation. See **CONGRESS OF THE UNITED STATES; PRESIDENT OF THE UNITED STATES; STATE GOVERNMENT; SUPREME COURT OF THE UNITED STATES; UNITED STATES, GOVERNMENT OF THE.**
Lenarduzzi, Bob: *il.,* 80–477
Lennon, John: *Close-Up,* 81–410
Lenya, Lotte: deaths, 82–272
Leonard, Sugar Ray: boxing, 82–216, 81–217
León, Roberto Eduardo, 80–435
Leonetti, Tommy, 80–281
LESOTHO, 82–176, 81–178, 80–180
Letelier, Orlando: Chile, 80–246; courts, 80–272
Leukemia: medicine, 81–391
Levenson, Sam: deaths, 81–276
Leveridge, Mary Ann: National PTA, 82–403
Lévesque, René: *il.,* 81–460; Quebec, 82–446, 80–457
Levin, Meyer: deaths, 82–272
LEWIS, ANDREW LINDSAY, JR., 82–369; handicapped, 82–330
Libby, Willard F.: deaths, 81–276
Libel: Supreme Court, 80–491
LIBERIA, 82–369, 81–377; Africa, 82–176, 81–178, 80–180
LIBRARY, 82–369, 81–378, 80–383; American Library Association, 82–180, 81–183, 80–186; Canadian Library Association, 82–229, 81–231, 80–237
LIBYA, 82–370, 81–379, 80–384; Africa, 82–176, 81–178, 80–180; armed forces, 82–189; Bulgaria, 81–223; Carter, 81–235; Chad, 82–235; Middle East, 82–387, 81–397; petroleum, 82–428, 80–438; Sudan, 82–476; Syria, 82–481, 81–495
Lichen: botany, 80–222
Lieberman, Nancy, 80–217
Liebman, Max: deaths, 82–272
Liechtenstein, 82–303, 81–310, 80–317
Life expectancy: population, 82–434; public health, 82–444

Lightfoot, Randy: bowling, *82*–216
Limann, Hilla, *80*–338
Lindstrom, Fred: deaths, *82*–272
Linehan, Kim, *80*–492
Ling-Ling: panda, *Special Report, 82*–89
Lions International, *82*–253, *81*–256, *80*–259
Liquid natural gas tanker: *il., 81*–440; ship, *81*–478
Literacy: education, *80*–302
LITERATURE, *82*–370, *81*–379, *80*–384; awards, *82*–202, *81*–203, *80*–208; Canadian literature, *82*–230, *81*–232, *80*–237; Nobel Prizes, *82*–410, *81*–418, *80*–423; poetry, *81*–445, *80*–444; science fiction, *Special Report, 80*–53
LITERATURE FOR CHILDREN, *82*–373, *81*–382, *80*–387
Little Foxes, The: theater, *82*–490
Liu Lin Hai: *il., 80*–475
Liver cancer: medicine, *82*–383
Livestock, *82*–308, *81*–314, *80*–320
Lloyd, Chris Evert, *80*–498; *il., 81*–501
Local network: electronics, *82*–294
Loeb, William: deaths, *82*–272
Logging: forest, *82*–317
Lome II Convention: Africa, *80*–184
Lone Ranger, *80*–435
Long Beach, *82*–246, *81*–248, *80*–252
Longley, James B.: deaths, *81*–276
Longworth, Alice Roosevelt: deaths, *81*–276
Look-alike pills: drugs, *82*–283
Loos, Anita: deaths, *82*–272
Lopez-Melton, Nancy: golf, *81*–330, *80*–339
Lopez Portillo, Jose, *81*–394, *80*–399
LOS ANGELES, *82*–376, *81*–385, *80*–391; architecture, *81*–187; census, *82*–234; city, *82*–246, *81*–248, *80*–252; civil rights, *82*–249; Olympic Games, *82*–410; zoos, *82*–520
Louganis, Greg: swimming, *82*–480, *81*–495
Lougheed, Peter, *80*–185
Louis, Joe: deaths, *Close-Up, 82*–271
Louisiana, *82*–473, *81*–488, *80*–487
Louisiana Crude: boating, *82*–214
Louisiana Offshore Oil Port: petroleum, *82*–428
Louisville, *82*–246, *81*–248, *80*–252
Louisy, Allan, *80*–528
"Love, Sidney": television, *82*–484
Love Canal: environment, *81*–305, *Close-Up, 81*–304
Lowen, Daniel: personalities, *82*–424
Lowery, Joseph E., *80*–255
LP rental: recordings, *82*–450
LRH: medicine, *80*–396
Ludden, Allen E.: deaths, *82*–272
Luescher, Peter, *80*–476
Luge: sports, *82*–470, *81*–485
Lule, Yusufu K., *80*–512
Lumber industry. See FOREST AND FOREST PRODUCTS.
Lung cancer: health, *82*–331
Luteinizing-hormone releasing hormone: medicine, *80*–396
Lutheran Church in America: Protestantism, *82*–442; religion, *82*–452, *81*–465, *80*–461
Lutheran Church-Missouri Synod, The: Protestantism, *82*–442; religion, *82*–452, *81*–465, *80*–461
Lutherans, *81*–470, *80*–468
LUXEMBOURG, *82*–377, *81*–386, *80*–392; Europe, *82*–303, *81*–310, *80*–317
Lyakhov, Vladimir, *80*–479
Lynen, Feodor, *80*–281
Lynn, Carroll M., *80*–353
Lyon, Sterling R.: Manitoba, *81*–388

M

M-X missile: armed forces, *82*–187, *80*–192; conservation, *81*–263, *80*–267; President, *82*–439
M-19 group: Colombia, *81*–254
M1A: bank, *82*–205
M1B: bank, *82*–205
M2: bank, *82*–205
MacCready, Paul B., *82*–424
MacDonald, Flora, *80*–232
MacEachen, Allan J.: Canada, *81*–226
Machel, Samora Moises: Mozambique, *81*–404
Machine. See MANUFACTURING; Technology.
Macias Nguema Biyogo Nague Ndong: Africa, *80*–179; Equatorial Guinea, *80*–314
Mackal, Roy P., *82*–424
Mackey, Bernard: deaths, *81*–276
Madagascar, *82*–177, *81*–178, *80*–180
MAGAZINE, *82*–378, *81*–386, *80*–392; awards, *82*–202, *81*–202, *80*–208; science fiction, *Special Report, 80*–53; Taiwan, *81*–496. See also **PUBLISHING.**
Magnetic Fusion Energy Engineering Act, *81*–476

Magnetic tissue: science, *81*–477; zoology, *80*–532
Magnetic video camera, *82*–430
Mahathir bin Mohamed: Malaysia, *82*–379
Mahre, Phil: skiing, *82*–463
Mailer, Norman: crime, *82*–265
Maine, *82*–473, *81*–488, *80*–487; Indian, American, *81*–347, *80*–357
Malaria, *80*–456
Malathion: environment, *82*–300; farm and farming, *82*–308
Malawi, *82*–177, *81*–179, *80*–180
MALAYSIA: *WBE, 82*–568; *82*–379, *81*–387, *80*–393; Asia, *82*–192, *81*–192, *80*–196, *Close-Up, 80*–198
Maldives, *82*–192, *81*–192, *80*–196
Mali, *82*–177, *81*–179, *80*–180
Malloum Ngakoutou Bey-Ndi, F., *80*–241
Malone, Dumas: *il., 82*–371
Malta, *82*–303, *81*–310, *80*–317
Mammoth: science, *81*–477
Man and the Biosphere Program: forests, *Special Report, 81*–103
Manatt, Charles T.: Democratic Party, *82*–274
Mandlikova, Hana, *82*–486
Mandrell, Barbara: *il., 82*–401
Manganese: mining, *80*–404
Manion, Clarence E., *80*–281
MANITOBA, *82*–379, *81*–388, *80*–393
Manley, Michael Norman, *80*–528
Mann, Marty: deaths, *81*–276
Mantovani, Annunzio P.: deaths, *81*–276
MANUFACTURING, *82*–379, *81*–388, *80*–394; automobile, *82*–196, *81*–197, *80*–202; economics, *82*–284; Hungary, *82*–340; Latin America, *80*–381; robot, *Special Report, 82*–138; safety, *82*–460; steel industry, *82*–475, *81*–490, *80*–488; water, *Special Report, 82*–97. See also **LABOR; Technology.**
Manzur, Mohammed Abul, *82*–204
Mao Tse-tung: China, *82*–241, *81*–244
Marchais, Georges: France, *82*–317, *80*–334
Marcos, Ferdinand: civil rights, *81*–251; Philippines, *82*–429, *81*–442, *80*–441
Marcuse, Herbert, *80*–281
Maree, Sydney: track, *82*–491
Mariana Islands, *82*–416
Marijuana: drugs, *82*–283, *81*–287, *80*–292; medicine, *81*–391, *80*–398; psychology, *82*–444; West Indies, *82*–515
Marine Corps. See ARMED FORCES.
Marley, Bob, *82*–402; *il., 82*–273
Marquard, Rube: deaths, *81*–276
Marriage: Jews, *80*–368; Roman Catholic, *80*–460
Mars: astronomy, *81*–195, *80*–200
Marsh, Othniel Charles, *80*–432
Marshall, Thurgood: Supreme Court, *Close-Up, 82*–478
Marshall Islands, *82*–417, *81*–431
Martens, Wilfried: Belgium, *82*–211, *81*–212, *80*–217
Martial law: Europe, *82*–300; Philippines, *80*–441; Poland, *82*–433
Martin, Billy: baseball, *81*–208; *il., 80*–213
Martin, Ross, *82*–273
Martinez, Maria Povera: deaths, *81*–276
Maryland, *82*–473, *81*–488, *80*–487
Masada: *il., 82*–485
Mass: physics, *81*–444
Massachusetts, *82*–473, *81*–488, *80*–487
Massine, Léonide, *80*–281
Mastectomy: health, *80*–346; medicine, *82*–383
Mastodon, *82*–418
Mauchly, John W.: deaths, *81*–276
Mauritania, *82*–177, *81*–179, *80*–180
Mauritius, *82*–177, *81*–179, *80*–181
Maya: archaeology, *81*–185
Mayor. See CITY.
Mays, Willie, *80*–215
Maytansine: chemistry, *81*–240
McCormack, John W.: deaths, *81*–276
McCready, Robert, *80*–418
McDonald, David J.: deaths, *80*–281; labor, *80*–376
McDonald's Corporation: advertising, *82*–172
McEnroe, John, *82*–486, *81*–501, *80*–498
McGraw-Hill, Incorporated, *80*–456
McHENRY, DONALD F., *80*–396; *il., 80*–514; United Nations, *81*–518
McIntyre, James Francis Cardinal, *80*–281
McKerrow, Amanda: *il., 82*–268
McKinney, Jack: basketball, *81*–209
McKinney, Tamara, *82*–463
McLuhan, Marshall, *81*–276, 436
McQueen, Steve: *il., 81*–279
Meagher, Mary T., *82*–480, *81*–495, *80*–492
Meany, George: labor, *80*–375; ·*Close-Up, 81*–368
Mears, Rich, *80*–204
Measles, *82*–444, *81*–458, *80*–455

Mecca: Saudi Arabia, *80*–472
Medal of Freedom: awards and prizes, *82*–203, *81*–204
Medfly: environment, *82*–300; farm and farming, *82*–308
Medford, Kay: deaths, *81*–277
Media. See Arts; COMMUNICATIONS; MAGAZINE; NEWSPAPER; RADIO; TELEVISION.
MEDICINE, *82*–374, *81*–391, *80*–396; aspirin, *Special Report, 81*–138; dentistry, *81*–282, *80*–287; hospital, *80*–351; hypnosis, *Special Report, 80*–73; Nobel Prizes, *82*–410, *81*–419, *80*–425; zoos, *Special Report, 80*–99. See also **DRUGS; HEALTH AND DISEASE; MENTAL HEALTH.**
Medigap insurance: consumer protection, *81*–266
Medroxyprogesterone acetate: medicine, *80*–396
Memoirs: Canadian literature, *82*–230, *81*–233; literature, *82*–372, *81*–381
Memory: psychology, *82*–443
Memory device: electronics, *81*–301
Memphis, *82*–246, *81*–248, *80*–252
Mendez Manfredini, Aparicio: Uruguay, *80*–518
Mengistu, Haile Mariam: Ethiopia, *80*–314
MENTAL HEALTH, *82*–384, *81*–393, *80*–398
Mental Health Systems Act, *81*–393
MENTAL ILLNESS: *WBE, 82*–575
Mentally retarded: handicapped, *82*–330
Menzogo, Theodore Nguema, *80*–314
Mermelstein, Mel: Jews, *82*–356
Mesmer, Franz: *il. 80*–74
Meteorite: chemistry, *81*–241; paleontology, *81*–433
Meteorology. See WEATHER.
Methane: biology, *80*–220
Metropolitan Opera: music, classical, *81*–406
MEXICO, *82*–385, *81*–394, *80*–399; environment, *80*–313; immigration, *82*–342, *80*–356; Latin America, *82*–366, *81*–375, *80*–380; petroleum, *81*–440, *80*–440
Meza Tejada, Luis Garcia, *81*–216
Miami, *82*–246, *81*–248, *80*–252; courts, *81*–268
Michigan, *82*–473, *81*–488, *80*–487; Detroit, *82*–277, *81*–282, *80*–287
Microenterprise: Latin America, *82*–365
Micronesia, *80*–430
Microprocessor: electronics, *82*–294
Microscope: biology, *82*–213
Microscope, acoustic: biology, *80*–220
Microsurgery, *80*–397
MIDDLE EAST, *82*–386, *81*–395, *80*–400; *Close-Up, 82*–390; Europe, *81*–309; Iran, *Close-Up, 81*–355; Jews, *80*–368; President, *82*–440, *80*–448; religion, *81*–465; United Nations, *82*–498, *81*–515, *80*–513. See also names of countries.
Migration: science, *81*–477; zoology, *80*–532
Mijatovic, Cvijetin: Yugoslavia, *81*–531
Military. See ARMED FORCES.
Milk: biology, *82*–213
Miller, Don, *80*–281
Miller, G. William: Cabinet, *80*–229
Miller, Henry: deaths, *81*–277
Miller, J. Irwin: architecture, *81*–186
Milne-Edwards, Alphonse: panda, *Special Report, 82*–79
Milosz, Czeslaw: *il., 82*–432; Nobel Prizes, *81*–418
Milwaukee, *82*–246, *81*–248, *80*–252
Minchew, Daniel: *82*–260
Mind control: religious cults, *Special Report, 80*–147
Mine scrip: hobbies, *81*–337
Minerals, strategic: mining, *82*–391
Minerals Resource Act: environment, *81*–305
Mingus, Charles, *80*–281
Mini-LP: recordings, *82*–450
Minimum competency: education, *81*–296, *80*–302
MINING, *82*–391, *81*–399, *80*–404; Australia, *80*–200; coal, *80*–256; conservation, *82*–261, *80*–267; disasters, *82*–280, *81*–285, *80*–291; environment, *81*–305; labor, *82*–361; Northwest Territories, *82*–412; ocean, *81*–423, *80*–428; Pacific Islands, *82*–417; Zaire, *80*–531. See also **PETROLEUM AND GAS.**
Mini-OTEC: ocean, *80*–428
Minneapolis, *82*–246, *81*–248, *80*–252
Minnesota, *82*–473, *81*–488, *80*–487
Minorities: census, *82*–234, *81*–236; economics, *82*–284
Miro, Joan: *il., 82*–510
Misery index: economics, *82*–284
Missile, nuclear: armed forces, *82*–187; Europe, *82*–302
Miss Piggy: *il., 80*–407
Mississippi, *82*–473, *81*–488, *80*–487
Missouri, *82*–473, *81*–488, *80*–487
Mitochondrion: biochemistry, *80*–219

MITTERRAND, FRANÇOIS, 82–392; France, 82–317; il., 82–304
Mize, Johnny, 82–208
Mobile missile: armed forces, 80–192; conservation, 80–267
Mobutu Sese Seko, 81–532
Model building. See **GAMES AND TOYS.**
Mohammad Reza Pahlavi, 80–361; Egypt, 81–297; il., 81–275; Middle East, 80–400; Panama, 81–434
Moi, Daniel T. arap: il., 82–357
Molecular physics, 82–431
Molybdenum: mining, 81–400
Mommie Dearest: motion pictures, 82–396
Monaco, 82–303, 81–310, 80–317
MONDALE, WALTER FREDERICK, 81–400, 80–404; ils., 81–280, 417
Monetarism: Great Britain, 82–327
Money: banks, 82–205; economics, 82–284, 80–294; Europe, 82–301, 80–318; international trade, 82–346, 81–350, 80–361
Money market fund, 82–205, 81–207, 80–211
Mongolia, 82–192, 81–192, 80–196
Monitor: ocean, 80–428
Monnet, Jean, 80–281
Monsarrat, Nicholas, 80–281
Montale, Eugenio, 82–273
Montana, 82–473, 81–488, 80–487; Indian, American, 82–343; mining, 80–404
MONTREAL, 82–392
Moon: Jupiter, *Special Report,* 80–89
Moon, Sun Myung, 80–147
Moons of Saturn: astronomy, 82–193
Moore, Clayton, 80–435
Moral Majority: advertising, 82–172; Protestantism, 82–443
Morgenthau, Hans J.: deaths, 81–277
Mormonism: Protestantism, 81–456, 80–454
MOROCCO, 82–393, 81–401, 80–405; Africa, 82–177, 81–179, 80–181; Middle East, 81–397
Moroz, Valentin, 80–470
Morphine: biology, 82–213
Mortgage rates: banks, 82–206, 80–211; consumer protection, 81–265; housing, 82–338, 81–342, 80–352; inflation, *Special Report,* 81–75
Morton, Rogers C.B., 80–281
Moses, Robert, 82–273
Mosque, Great, 80–472
Mota Pinto, Carlos da, 80–447
MOTION PICTURES, 82–393, 81–401, 80–406; awards, 82–201, 81–202, 80–207; music, 81–409, 80–415; science fiction, *Special Report,* 80–66
Motorcycling: safety, 80–471; sports, 82–470, 81–485, 80–483
Mount Rainier: il., 82–330
Mount St. Helens: geology, 82–320, *Close-Up,* 81–327; il., 81–326; insurance, 81–350; museum, 81–405; weather, 82–513, 81–527
Mountbatten of Burma, Earl: Europe, 80–318; Great Britain, 80–344; Ireland, 80–364
Movement of April 19: Colombia, 82–251, 81–254
MOZAMBIQUE, 81–404; Africa, 82–177, 81–179, 80–181
Mozart, Wolfgang Amadeus: music, classical, 82–399; theater, 82–490
MUBARAK, MOHAMED HOSNI, 82–397; Egypt, 82–291
Mueller, Leah Poulos, 80–355
MUGABE, ROBERT GABRIEL, 81–404; Africa, 82–175; il., 81–450; Zimbabwe, 82–518, 81–533, 80–531
Muir, Malcolm, 80–281
Mujahedeen: Afghanistan, 82–173; Iran, 82–349
Mulder, Cornelius P., 80–478
Muldoon, Robert D., 82–406, 81–414, 80–420
Multibridged cyclophanes: chemistry, 80–242
Multiple Mirror Telescope Observatory: il., 80–199
Muncey, Bill, 80–221
Muñoz Marin, Luis: deaths, 81–277
Munson, Thurman, 80–282
Muppets, The: il., 80–407
Murdoch, Rupert: il., 82–445; newspaper, 82–408
Murray, George: UN, *Close-Up,* 82–501
Musavi-Khamenei, Hosein: Iran, 82–349
Muscular dystrophy: handicapped, 82–331; health and disease, 82–332
MUSEUM, 82–398, 81–405, 80–409; visual arts, 82–508, 81–522, 80–521.
Museum of Modern Art: architecture, 80–190; building, 80–226
MUSIC, CLASSICAL, 82–399, 81–406, 80–410; awards, 82–201, 81–202, 80–207; *Close-Up,* 80–412
MUSIC, POPULAR, 82–401, 81–409, 80–414; awards, 82–201, 81–202, 80–207; *Close-Up,* 81–410

Musicals: awards, 82–201, 81–202; theater, 82–490, 80–503
MUSKIE, EDMUND SIXTUS, 81–411
Muslims: Afghanistan, 80–177; Indonesia, 82–344; Iran, 80–361; Middle East, 80–400; Pakistan, 80–430; Philippines, 82–429, 80–441; religion, 82–452, 80–461; Saudi Arabia, 80–472
Mutual fund: banks, 80–211
Muwanga, Paulo: Uganda, 81–512
MUZOREWA, ABEL TENDEKAYI, 80–416; Africa, 80–182, *Close-Up,* 80–183; Protestantism, 80–454; Zimbabwe Rhodesia, 80–531
My Brilliant Career: motion pictures, 81–401
Myers, Michael: il., 81–258

N

NAMIBIA, 82–403, 81–411, 80–416; Africa, 82–177, 81–179, 80–181; Angola, 82–181; United Nations, 82–500
Napoleon: motion pictures, 82–395
Narcotics. See **DRUGS.**
Narragansett Indians, 80–357
Narwhal: zoology, 81–534
Nasal contraceptive: medicine, 80–396
NASCAR: automobile racing, 82–199, 81–200
Nashville: city, 82–246, 81–248, 80–252
Nasser, Gamal Abdel: Middle East, *Close-Up,* 82–390
Natase, Ilie, 80–499
National Academy of Recording Arts and Sciences, 82–201, 81–202, 80–207
National Academy of Television Arts and Sciences, 82–202, 81–202, 80–207
National Aeronautics and Space Administration: *Skylab, Close-Up,* 80–480; space shuttle, *Special Report,* 82–109. See also **SPACE EXPLORATION.**
National Association for the Advancement of Colored People: civil rights, 82–249
National Baptist Convention of America, 82–452, 81–465, 80–461
National Baptist Convention, U.S.A., Inc., 82–452, 81–465, 80–461
National Book Critics Circle Awards: awards and prizes, 82–203
National Coal Association: coal, 82–250
National Collegiate Athletic Association: football, 82–315
National Congress of Parents and Teachers. See **NATIONAL PTA.**
National defense. See **ARMED FORCES** and entries on specific countries.
National Education Association, 81–293, 80–301
National Enquirer: magazine, 82–378
National forests: forest and forest products, 82–317
National Highway Traffic Safety Administration: consumerism, 82–262
National Institutes of Health, 82–212, 80–218
National Library Act, 80–384
National Oceanic Satellite System: ocean, 81–423
National Park Service: conservation, 82–259, 80–267; hunting, 80–355
National Primitive Baptist Convention, Inc., 82–452, 81–465, 80–461
NATIONAL PTA, 82–403, 81–411, 80–417
NATO. See **North Atlantic Treaty Organization.**
Natural gas. See **PETROLEUM AND GAS.**
Natusch Busch, Alberto, 80–221
Nauru: Pacific Islands, 82–417
Navratilova, Martina, 81–502, 80–498
Navy, U.S.: armed forces, 82–189, 81–188, 80–193; Puerto Rico, 80–457
Nazis: Jews, 81–363, 80–269
Ne Win: Burma, 82–221, 81–223, 80–228
Neave, Airey, 80–425
Neblett, Carol: il., 80–411
Nebraska, 82–473, 81–488, 80–487
Negative income tax, 80–527
Negotiable Orders of Withdrawal, 80–211
Neighborhood: city, 80–254
Nenni, Pietro: deaths, 81–277
Nepal, 82–192, 81–192, 80–196
Neptune: astronomy, 82–194
NETHERLANDS, 82–403, 81–412, 80–417; Europe, 82–303, 81–310, 80–317
Neto, Agostinho: deaths, 80–282
Netto, Antonio Delfim, 80–224
Neutrino: physics, 81–444
Neutron bomb: Europe, 82–300
Nevada, 82–473, 81–488, 80–487
Nevelson, Louise: il., 81–459
NEW BRUNSWICK, 82–404, 81–413, 80–418
New Caledonia: Pacific Islands, 82–416
New Christian Right: Protestantism, 82–443, 81–455

New dance: dancing, 82–267
"New federalism": welfare, 82–514
New Hampshire, 82–473, 81–488, 80–487
New Jersey, 82–473, 81–488, 80–487; elections, 82–292; il., 80–374
New Mexico, 82–473, 81–488, 80–487
New Orleans: city, 82–246, 81–248, 80–252
New Residential Community: il., 82–185
New wave rock: music, popular, 80–414
New York (state): drugs, 80–292; education, 80–302; Indian, American, 80–357; state government, 82–473, 81–488, 80–487
NEW YORK CITY, 82–404, 81–413, 80–418; census, 82–233; city, 82–246, 81–248, 80–252; crime, 80–273; water, *Special Report,* 82–94
New York City Ballet, 82–267, 80–276
New York Drama Critics Circle Awards, 82–202, 81–202, 80–208
New York Insurance Exchange: insurance, 81–350
New York Islanders: hockey, 82–335
NEW ZEALAND, 82–406, 81–414, 80–419; Asia, 82–192, 81–192, 80–196; Pacific Islands, 82–417
Newark: city, 82–246, 81–248, 80–252
Newbery Medal, 82–376, 81–385, 80–391
NEWFOUNDLAND, 82–407, 81–414, 80–420
Newhouse, Samuel I., 80–282
NEWSPAPER, 82–407, 81–415, 80–420; advertising, 81–173; awards, 82–202, 81–203, 80–208. See also **PUBLISHING.**
Newton, Judy Kay: music, popular, 82–401
Niatross: horse racing, 81–341
NICARAGUA, 82–408, 81–415, 80–421; Latin America, 82–366, 81–375, 80–380
Nicholas Nickleby: theater, 82–489
NICKLAUS, JACK, 80–422; golf, 81–330
Niehous, William F., 80–520
Nielsen, Arthur C.: deaths, 81–277
Niger, 82–177, 81–179, 80–181
NIGERIA, 82–408, 81–416, 80–422; Africa, 82–177, 81–179, 80–181
Nimeiri, Gaafar Mohamed, 80–490; Sudan, 82–476, 81–492, 80–490
Nimitz: il., 82–279
Nimmo, Robert P.: community organizations, 82–253
Nitrite: food, 82–312, 81–318
Nitrogen fixation: biochemistry, 82–212
NIXON, RICHARD MILHOUS, 82–409, 81–417, 80–423; il., 82–439; Supreme Court, 82–479
Nkomo, Joshua, 82–518, 81–533, 80–531
No-fault insurance, 80–359
NOBEL PRIZES, 82–410, 81–418, 80–423
Nofziger, Lyn: Republican Party, 82–454
Norfolk, Va.: city, 81–248
North American Soccer League: soccer, 82–464, 81–480
North Atlantic Treaty Organization: armed forces, 80–192; Europe, 82–302, 81–309, 80–318; Great Britain, 81–332; Greece, 81–333; Netherlands, 80–418
North Carolina, 82–473, 81–488, 80–487
North Dakota, 82–473, 81–488, 80–487
North Sea: Denmark, 81–282; Norway, 80–426; petroleum, 80–441
North Vietnam. See **VIETNAM.**
NORTHERN IRELAND, 82–411, 81–419, 80–425
Northern Rhodesia. See **Zambia.**
Northern Tier pipeline: Canada, 80–235
Northrop, John K., 82–273
NORTHWEST TERRITORIES, 82–412, 81–420, 80–425
NORWAY, 82–412, 81–421, 80–426; Europe, 82–303, 81–310, 80–317
NOVA SCOTIA, 82–413, 81–421, 80–426
NOW accounts: banks, 82–205, 80–211
Nuclear energy: Asia, 80–193, 80–197; Canada, 80–236; conservation, 81–263; consumer protection, 80–270; Denmark, 81–282; energy, 82–296, *Close-Up,* 80–310; Europe, 80–316; Germany, West, 80–337; President, 80–451; safety, 82–461; Saskatchewan, 81–475; science, 81–476, 80–473; South Africa, 80–478; state government, 81–490, 80–485; Sweden, 80–492; Switzerland, 80–493
Nuclear magnetic resonance spectroscopy: biochemistry, 80–219
Nuclear Regulatory Commission: energy, 82–296; U.S., government of the, 80–515
Nuclear waste disposal: ocean, *Special Report,* 80–139; state government, 80–485
Nuclear weapons: armed forces, 81–188, 80–191; Europe, 82–300; Germany, West, 80–337; Great Britain, 81–332; India, 80–357; Japan, 82–354; Middle East, 81–397; Netherlands, 82–403; Norway, 82–413; Pakistan, 80–430; President, 82–439; Russia, 82–458
Nugent, Elliott: deaths, 81–277
NUTRITION, 82–413, 81–422, 80–426; zoo medicine, *Special Report,* 80–108

Nyad, Diana, *80–436*
Nylon: manufacturing, *80–395*

O

Oakland, *82–246, 81–248, 80–252.* See also **SAN FRANCISCO.**
OAS. See **Organization of American States.**
Oberon, Merle, *80–282*
Obesity: nutrition, *80–427*
Obituaries. See **DEATHS.**
Obote, Milton: *il., 82–357;* Uganda, *82–498, 81–512*
O'Brien, Larry, *80–216*
Occupational Safety and Health Administration: chemical industry, *82–236, 81–239, 80–242;* labor, *81–371;* safety, *82–460;* Supreme Court, *82–477, 81–493*
OCEAN, *82–414, 81–420, 80–423;* environment, *82–299, 81–305;* fishing industry, *80–325;* mining, *82–391; Special Report, 80–128;* weather, *81–527*
Ocean Margin Drilling Program, *81–423*
O'CONNOR, SANDRA DAY, *82–415;* Supreme Court, *82–477, Close-Up, 82–478*
Odinga, Jaramogi Oginga: Kenya, *82–357*
Odlum, George: West Indies, *80–528*
Ogaden: Ethiopia, *80–314;* Somalia, *82–465, 81–481*
Ogallala aquifer: water, *Special Report, 82–97*
Oglala Sioux: Indian, American, *82–343, 81–347*
O'Hare International Airport: airport, *Special Report, 82–123;* disasters, *80–288*
Ohio: state government, *82–473, 81–488, 80–487*
Ohira, Masayoshi: *il., 81–276;* Japan, *81–361, 80–367;* Mexico, *81–394*
Oil. See **PETROLEUM AND GAS.**
Oil-shale: energy, *82–297*
Oklahoma, *82–473, 81–488, 80–487*
Oklahoma City, *82–246, 81–248, 80–252*
Okun, Arthur M.: deaths, *81–277*
Old Age: zoo medicine, *Special Report, 80–108.* See also **SOCIAL SECURITY.**
Old Age and Survivors Insurance: Social Security, *82–465*
Old Testament: archaeology, *82–184*
Oldfield, Sir Maurice, *82–273*
OLYMPIC GAMES, *82–415, 81–424, 80–428;* coin collecting, *82–251;* Russia, *81–472;* Samaranch, Juan, *81–475;* travel, *81–509*
Omaha, *82–246, 81–248, 80–252*
Omaha Indians: Indian, American, *81–348*
Oman: Middle East, *82–389, 81–398, 80–402*
Omnibus Budget Reconciliation Act: city, *82–244;* Social Security, *82–465;* United States, government of the, *82–505;* welfare, *82–514*
O'Neill, Thomas P., Jr.: *il. 81–436*
On Human Work: Roman Catholic, *82–456*
ONTARIO, *82–416, 81–431, 80–429*
Opera: music, classical, *82–400, 81–406, 80–410*
Operation Outreach: community organizations, *82–253*
Opinion Poll: *Special Report, 80–117*
Oral contraceptives: health and disease, *82–331;* medicine, *80–396;* public health, *81–459*
Orang-utan: *il., 80–104*
Orchestra. See **MUSIC, CLASSICAL.**
Order of Canada: Schreyer, Edward, *81–476*
Ordination: Protestantism, *80–452;* Roman Catholic, *80–466*
Oregon, *82–473, 81–488, 80–487;* building, *80–227*
Orfila, Alejandro, *80–381*
Organization for Economic Cooperation and Development: Australia, *82–195;* Europe, *80–316*
Organization of African Unity, *82–178, 81–181, 80–184*
Organization of American States, *80–379;* Uruguay, *80–518*
Organization of Petroleum Exporting Countries: *il., 81–182;* Indonesia, *80–358;* international trade, *82–360;* petroleum, *82–426, 81–438, 80–437*
Organizations. See **COMMUNITY ORGANIZATIONS; YOUTH ORGANIZATIONS;** names of specific organizations.
Ortega Saavedra, Daniel: Nicaragua, *82–408*
Orthodox Church in America, *82–452, 81–465, 80–461*
Oryx: zoos, *81–535*
"Oscar" awards, *82–201, 81–202, 80–207*
Othello: theater, *82–491*
Ottaviani, Alfredo Cardinal, *80–282*
Oueddei, Gounkouni, *80–241*
Outdoor sculpture: visual arts, *82–508, 81–523*
Outpatient surgery: hospital, *82–337*

Overseas Private Investment Corporation Amendments Act: insurance, *82–345*
Overthrust belt: conservation, *82–259;* geology, *82–321*
Ovett, Steve: track, *82–491, 81–506*
Owen, Alison: skiing, *82–463*
Owens, Jesse: deaths, *81–277*

P

PACIFIC ISLANDS, *82–416, 81–431, 80–429;* Australia, *82–195*
Paddle tennis: sports, *82–470, 81–485*
Paddleball: sports, *82–470, 81–485*
Pain: hypnosis, *Special Report, 80–77;* mental health, *80–399*
Painting: visual arts, *82–508, 81–522, 80–521*
PAKISTAN, *82–417, 81–432, 80–430;* Asia, *82–192, 81–192, 80–196;* crime, *82–264;* President, *80–448*
Pal, George: deaths, *81–277*
PALEONTOLOGY, *82–418, 81–433, 80–431.* See also **ANTHROPOLOGY; ARCHAEOLOGY; Fossil; GEOLOGY.**
Palestine. See **ISRAEL; JORDAN; MIDDLE EAST.**
Palestine Liberation Organization: civil rights, *80–255;* Jews, *80–368;* Jordan, *80–369;* Lebanon, *82–368;* Middle East, *82–391, 80–402;* United Nations, *80–512*
Palestinians: civil rights, *80–255;* Israel, *82–352, 81–358, 80–365;* Jordan, *80–369;* Middle East, *82–391, 81–396, 80–401;* Protestantism, *81–456;* Turkey, *80–511;* United Nations, *81–515, 80–512*
PAN AMERICAN GAMES, *80–432*
PANAMA, *82–420, 81–434, 80–433;* Latin America, *82–366, 81–375, 80–380*
Panama Canal: Panama, *82–420*
Panama Canal treaties: Congress, *80–264*
Pancreatic cancer: health and disease, *82–332*
Panda: *il., 80–114; Special Report, 82–75;* zoos, *82–520, 81–535*
PAPANDREOU, ANDREAS, *82–420;* Greece, *82–328*
Paper: manufacturing, *82–382, 81–389, 80–395*
Paperback: literature, *80–387*
Papua New Guinea: Asia, *82–192, 81–192, 80–196;* Pacific Islands, *82–417, 80–429*
Parachute jumping: sports, *82–470, 81–485, 80–483*
PARAGUAY, *82–421, 81–434, 80–433;* Latin America, *82–366, 81–375, 80–380*
Parents and Teachers, National Congress of. See **NATIONAL PTA.**
Parity: physics, *82–431*
Park, Chung Hee, *80–371*
Parks. See **National Park Service; ZOOS AND AQUARIUMS.**
Parliament (Canada), *81–225, 80–232*
Parliament (Great Britain), *81–333, 80–340*
Parliament, European, *81–306, 80–315*
Parole: prison, *82–441*
Parsons, Talcott, *80–282*
Parti Québécois: Quebec, *82–446, 81–460, 80–457*
Passionflower: botany, *82–215*
Passive restraints, *82–198, 81–508, 80–507*
PATCO. See **Professional Air Traffic Controllers Organization.**
Pate, Jerry: *il., 82–323*
Pathology: zoo medicine, *Special Report, 80–108*
Patriotic Catholic Association: Roman Catholic, *82–457*
Pavarotti, Luciano: music, classical, *81–408*
Pay-television: sports, *82–469*
Paz Estenssoro, Victor, *80–221*
PCB: chemical industry, *80–242;* environment, *80–314*
Pea: *il., 80–327*
Peace: Egypt, *80–303;* Middle East, *80–400;* Nobel Prizes, *82–410, 81–418, 80–423*
Peace Form One: *il., 81–515*
Peckford, Brian, *80–420*
Pei, I. M.: architecture, *80–189*
Pennsylvania, *82–473, 81–488, 80–487;* elections, *82–293*
Pension: Supreme Court, *80–491*
Pentathlon, *82–470, 81–485, 80–483*
People's Republic of China: Taiwan, *82–481*
People's Revolutionary Party of Kampuchea: Cambodia, *82–223*
Percy, Walker: *il., 81–381*
Perelman, S. J., *80–282*
Peres, Shimon: Israel, *82–351*
PÉREZ DE CUÉLLAR, JAVIER, *82–421;* United Nations, *82–498*
Pérez Esquivel, Adolfo: Nobel Prizes, *81–418*
Peripheral Canal: water, *Special Report, 82–100*
Perlman, Itzhak: handicapped, *82–330*

Perón, Isabel: Argentina, *82–186*
Perrier water: advertising, *80–176*
Personal computer: electronics, *82–294*
Personal consumption expenditures: inflation, *Special Report, 81–86*
PERSONALITIES, *82–421, 81–435, 80–434.* See also **DEATHS.**
PERU, *82–426, 81–438, 80–437;* civil rights, *81–251;* Ecuador, *82–288;* Latin America, *82–366, 81–375, 80–380;* mining, *80–404*
Pesticide: environment, *82–300;* farm and farming, *82–308*
Pet: pet language, *Special Report, 81–121.* See also **CAT; DOG.**
Peterson, Esther: *il., 81–265*
PETRA: *il., 80–444*
Petraglia, Johnny: bowling, *81–217*
PETROLEUM AND GAS, *82–426, 81–438, 80–437; WBE, 81–558;* aviation, *80–205;* Congress, *81–258, 80–265;* conservation, *82–259, 81–262;* energy, *82–297, 81–302, 80–308;* environment, *82–299;* Europe, *80–316; Focus, 80–47;* geology, *82–320;* international trade, *80–360;* labor, *80–375;* Latin America, *80–382;* manufacturing, *80–394;* mining, *82–391;* ocean, *82–415;* President, *80–450;* state government, *80–486;* travel, *80–507.* See also articles on countries, provinces, and cities.
Petroleum Exporting Countries, Organization of. See **Organization of Petroleum Exporting Countries.**
Petty, Richard, *82–199, 80–204*
PF treatment: medicine, *82–383*
PHILADELPHIA, *82–428, 81–441, 80–440;* city, *82–246, 81–248, 80–252*
Philip, Archbishop: Eastern Orthodox Churches, *82–283*
PHILIPPINES, *82–429, 81–442, 80–441;* Asia, *82–192, 81–192, 80–196;* civil rights, *82–248, 81–251;* Roman Catholic, *82–454*
Phoebe: astronomy, *82–194*
PHOENIX, *82–246, 81–248, 80–252*
Phonograph. See **MUSIC, CLASSICAL; MUSIC, POPULAR; RECORDINGS.**
Phosphate, *80–370*
PHOTOGRAPHY, *82–430, 81–442, 80–442;* awards, *81–208;* visual arts, *80–523*
Photon: physics, *82–431*
Photosynthesis: botany, *81–216*
PHYSICS, *82–431, 81–444, 80–442; Close-Up, 80–443;* Nobel Prizes, *82–410, 81–419, 80–424*
Physiology: Nobel Prizes, *82–410, 81–419*
Piaget, Jean: deaths, *81–277*
Picasso, Pablo: *il., 81–522;* visual arts, *80–522*
Pickford, Mary, *80–282*
PIERCE, SAMUEL RILEY, JR., *82–432*
Pigeon: biology, *80–219;* zoology, *80–532*
PINKOWSKI, JOZEF, *81–445;* Poland, *82–433, 81–447*
Pinochet Ugarte, Augusto, *82–240, 81–244*
Pinta: archaeology, *81–185*
Pintasilgo, Maria de Lurdes, *80–447*
Pinyin: *Close-Up, 80–248*
Pioneer: astronomy, *81–195*
Pious, Minerva, *80–282*
Pipeline: Canada, *80–235;* Northwest Territories, *82–412;* Norway, *80–420;* Russia, *82–458*
Piquet, Nelson: auto racing, *82–199, 81–199*
Pirates of Penzance, The: theater, *82–490*
Pittsburgh: architecture, *81–186;* city, *82–246, 81–248, 80–252*
Pituitary dwarfism: biochemistry, *80–218*
Planet: astronomy, *80–199;* Jupiter, *Special Report, 80–87;* space exploration, *80–479*
Plant: botany, *82–215, 81–216;* gardening, *82–319, 81–325, 80–335*
Plate tectonics: geology, *81–326, 80–336;* ocean, *80–427, Special Report, 80–140*
Platinum: mining, *80–404*
Playing for Time: *il., 81–500*
Pleasant Colony: horse racing, *82–335*
Pluto: astronomy, *81–195*
POETRY, *82–432, 81–445, 80–444;* awards, *82–202, 81–203, 80–208;* Canadian literature, *82–230, 81–238;* Nobel Prizes, *80–423*
Poetzsch, Anett: *il., 81–424*
Pol Pot, *81–224, 80–230;* United Nations, *80–514*
POLAND, *82–433, 81–446, 80–445;* economics, *82–285, 81–292;* Europe, *81–310, 80–317, Close-Up, 81–308;* Germany, East, *82–321;* Roman Catholic Church, *80–466;* Romania, *82–457;* Russia, *82–458, 81–472*
Polar Bear: botany, *80–222; il., 82–520*
Police: Australia, *80–200;* Chicago, *81–242;* city, *81–251, 80–251;* civil rights, *81–252, 80–255;* Detroit, *81–282;* Great Britain, *82–327;* Houston, *80–353;* hypnosis, *Special Report, 80–73; il., 81–490;* Los Angeles, *80–392;* Philadelphia, *80–440;* Supreme Court, *82–479, 80–492;* Taiwan, *82–481*

Polio: public health, *80–456*
Polisario: Africa, *82–178*; Morocco, *82–393*, *81–401*
Polish National Catholic Church of America, *82–452, 81–465, 80–461*
Political parties. See **Communist Party; DEMOCRATIC PARTY; REPUBLICAN PARTY;** and names of other parties.
Political poll: *Special Report, 80–117*
Political prisoners: Algeria, *80–186*; Argentina, *80–191*; Brazil, *80–224*; Burma, *80–228*; civil rights, *80–254*; Cuba, *80–274*; Korea, South, *82–359*; Pakistan, *82–417*; Philippines, *80–441*; Uruguay, *80–518*
Poll: *Special Report, 80–117*
Pollution: botany, *80–222*; Canada, *82–228*, *80–235*; chemical industry, *82–237, 80–242*; environment, *82–298, 80–313, Close-Up, 81–304*; Europe, *81–311*; ocean, *80–428*, *Special Report, 80–130*; Philadelphia, *80–440*; steel industry, *82–475, 80–489*; water, *Special Report, 82–101*; weather, *80–525.* See also **CONSERVATION; ENERGY; ENVIRONMENT.**
Polo, *82–470, 81–485, 80–483*
Polovchak, Walter: child welfare, *81–243*; civil rights, *82–250*; *il., 81–252*
Ponselle, Rosa M., *82–273*
Pope. See **ROMAN CATHOLIC CHURCH;** names of individual popes.
Popov, Leonid I.: space, *81–482*
Popular music. See **MUSIC, POPULAR.**
POPULATION, *82–434, 81–447, 80–446*; Asia, *82–190, 80–197*; census, *82–232, 522, 81–236*; city, *82–248, 81–247, 80–251*; India, *82–342*; Latin America, *82–365, 81–374*; Mexico, *82–385*
Population, U.S. See **CENSUS.**
Porpoises: fishing industry, *81–317*; science, *81–477*
Porter, Katherine Anne: *il., 81–276*
Portillo, Jose Lopez: *il., 82–385*
Portisch, Lajos: chess, *81–241*
Portland, Ore.: city, *82–246, 81–248, 80–252*
PORTUGAL, *82–435, 81–448, 80–447*; Europe, *82–303, 81–310, 80–317*
Positron emission tomography, *82–384, 81–393*
POSTAL SERVICE, U.S., *82–435, 81–449, 80–448*; stamp collecting, *82–471, 80–485*
Potofsky, Jacob: labor, *80–376*
Poverty: Uganda, *82–498*; welfare, *80–527*
Powers, John A.: deaths, *81–277*
Praying hands: il., *82–441*
Pregnancy: drugs, *82–283*; medicine, *82–383, 80–396*; nutrition, *82–413*
Prehistoric site: il., *82–419*; science, *80–474*
PREM TINSULANONDA, *81–449*; Thailand, *82–487, 81–502*
Prenatal treatment: medicine, *82–383*
Presbyterian Church in the U.S., *82–452, 81–465, 80–461*
Preservative, food: health, *81–336*
PRESIDENT OF THE UNITED STATES, *82–436, 81–449, 80–448*; armed forces, *82–187, 81–188*; Cabinet, *82–222, 80–229*; city, *80–250*; coal, *80–256*; Congress, *80–260*; conservation, *82–259*; Democratic Party, *81–280*; elections, *81–297*; energy, *80–308*; environment, *80–312*; *Focus, 80–26*; forest, *80–332*; hospital, *80–351*; immigration, *80–356*; Latin America, *82–367*; mining, *80–404*; Republican Party, *81–466*; Russia, *82–458*; Social Security, *80–478*; U.S., government of the, *80–515*; welfare, *80–527.* See also the names of the Presidents.
Presidential Directive 59: President, *81–453*
Presser, William, *82–273*
Pressler, Larry, *80–465*
Pretrial publicity: Supreme Court, *80–491*
Price, George: Belize, *82–211*
Price fixing: consumer protection, *80–271*
Prices: automobile, *82–196*; aviation, *82–200, 80–205*; Consumer Price Index, *Special Report, 81–72*; consumerism, *82–261, 80–269*; farm, *82–305, 81–312, 80–320*; food, *82–312, 80–326*; housing, *82–338, 80–352*; international trade, *80–360*; manufacturing, *80–394*; petroleum, *80–437*; recordings, *82–450*; Russia, *82–460.* See also **Cost of living; ECONOMICS; Inflation;** and various countries and cities.
Priestley Medal: chemistry, *81–241, 80–243*
Primaries. See **ELECTIONS.**
Primate: anthropology, *80–187*
Prime rate: bank, *82–205*
PRINCE EDWARD ISLAND, *82–440, 81–453, 80–452*
PRISON, *82–440, 81–454, 80–452*; Supreme Court, *82–479*
Prisoners of war: Laos, *82–363*
Pritzker Architecture Prize: awards and prizes, *82–201, 81–202*

Prizes. See **AWARDS AND PRIZES.**
Product Liability Risk Retention Act: insurance, *82–345*
Product Safety Standard: games and toys, *82–319*
Productivity bonus: New York City, *82–405*
Professional Air Traffic Controllers Organization: aviation, *82–199*; labor, *82–360*; travel, *82–494*
Professional Bowlers Association, *82–216, 81–217, 80–222*
Progressive, The: civil rights, *80–255*; magazine, *80–393*; science, *80–474*
Progressive National Baptist Convention, Inc., *82–452, 81–465, 80–461*
Property Insurance Loss Register, *80–359*
Proposition 2½: city, *82–245*
Proposition 13: library, *80–383*
Prostacyclin: aspirin, *Special Report, 81–146*
Prostaglandin: aspirin, *Special Report, 81–146*
Protein: biochemistry, *82–212*
PROTESTANTISM, *82–441, 81–455, 80–452*; religion, *82–451*
Protests: China, *80–247*; France, *80–333*; *il., 82–514*; Jordan, *80–369*; Panama, *81–434*; Switzerland, *82–480, 81–495*; Washington, D.C., *80–524.* See also **Terrorism; Violence.**
Protopopov, Oleg, *80–470*
Prototype Regional Observing and Forecasting Service, *80–526*
Psychiatry. See **MEDICINE; MENTAL HEALTH.**
PSYCHOLOGY, *82–443, 81–454, 80–454*; hypnosis, *Special Report, 80–70*
PTA. See **NATIONAL PTA.**
Public Broadcasting Service, *81–499, 80–498*
PUBLIC HEALTH, *82–444, 81–458, 80–455*; environment, *80–314*
Public opinion poll: *Special Report, 80–117*
Public service: awards, *82–203, 81–203*
Public transportation. See **CITY; TRANSIT; TRANSPORTATION.**
Public welfare. See **CHILD WELFARE; WELFARE.**
PUBLISHING, *82–445, 81–459, 80–456*; civil rights, *80–255*; consumerism, *82–262*; *Perspective, 80–169*; science fiction, *Special Report, 80–53.* See also **LITERATURE; MAGAZINE; NEWSPAPER.**
PUERTO RICO, *82–445, 81–460, 80–457*; Latin America, *82–366, 81–375, 80–380*
Pulitzer Prizes, *82–203, 81–204, 80–209*
Pulsar: astronomy, *82–194*; physics, *80–444*
Punctuated equilibrium theory: anthropology, *82–182*; paleontology, *82–419*

Q

Qadhafi, Muammar Muhammad al-, *81–379, 80–384*; Libya, *82–370*; Middle East, *82–387*
Qatar, *82–389, 81–398, 80–402*
Quaaludes: drugs, *81–287*
Quarantine: farm and farming, *82–308*
Quark, *80–444*
Quarter horse racing, *82–336, 81–341, 80–351*
QUEBEC, *82–446, 81–460, 80–457*; Canada, *Close-Up, 81–227*; Newfoundland, *82–407*
Questionnaire: poll, *Special Report, 80–120*

R

Rabies: health, *82–444, 81–336*
Racing. See **AUTOMOBILE RACING; BOATING; HORSE RACING; ICE SKATING; OLYMPIC GAMES; SKIING; SPORTS; SWIMMING; TRACK AND FIELD.**
Racism: See **Blacks; CIVIL RIGHTS.**
Racquetball, *82–470, 81–485, 80–483*
Racquets, *82–470, 81–485, 80–483*
Radar: airport, *Special Report, 82–137*
Radial keratotomy: medicine, *81–392*
Radiation: energy, *Close-Up, 80–310*; public health, *81–459*
RADIO, *82–447, 81–461, 80–458*; awards, *82–202, 81–203*
Radioactive waste: state government, *80–485*
Radio collar: panda, *Special Report, 82–77*
Raft, George: deaths, *81–277*
Ragtime: motion pictures, *82–396*
Rahman, Ziaur: Bangladesh, *82–204, 80–210*; *il., 81–205*
Raiders of the Lost Ark: archaeology, *82–184*; motion pictures, *82–395, il., 394*
RAILROAD, *82–448, 81–461, 80–458*; Congress, *81–258*; disasters, *82–281, 81–285, 80–291*; transportation, *82–494, 81–508*
RAJAI, MOHAMMED ALI, *81–462*; *il., 81–514*; Iran, *82–350*
RALLIS, GEORGE, *81–463*; Greece, *82–328, 81–334*

Rand, Sally, *80–282*
Randolph, A. Philip, *80–376*
Random access memory, *82–294, 81–301*
Random sampling: poll, *Special Report, 80–125*
Rapid Deployment Strike Force: armed forces, *81–188*; Middle East, *81–396*
RATHER, DAN, *81–463*
Rationing: Congress, *80–265*; state government, *80–486*
Rawlings, Jerry, *80–338*
Reagan, Maureen: Reagan, *82–450*
Reagan, Michael: Reagan, *82–450*
Reagan, Nancy: Reagan, *82–309, 449, 450*
REAGAN, RONALD WILSON, *82–449, 81–463, 80–459; WBE, 81–552*; Cabinet, *81–224*; elections, *81–297*; *ils., 82–222, 309, 482, 81–467*; interview, *82–54*; Republican Party, *81–466, 80–464*; *Special Report, 82–54*; taxation, *81–497.* See also **PRESIDENT OF THE UNITED STATES.**
Real estate: Latin America, *82–365*; Philadelphia, *82–429*
Rebate: automobile, *81–199*
Recession: economics, *82–284, 81–289, 80–294*; international trade and finance, *82–345*; manufacturing, *82–379, 80–394.* See also **Budget, national; Cost of living; Inflation; Prices.**
Reclamation Act, *81–525, 80–524*
Recombinant DNA: biochemistry, *82–212, 81–213, 80–218*; medicine, *80–398*
Recommended dietary allowance: nutrition, *80–426*
Reconstructive surgery: medicine, *82–383*
RECORDINGS, *82–450, 81–463, 80–460*; awards, *82–201, 81–202, 80–207*
Redistricting: Republican Party, *82–453*
Reds: motion pictures, *82–396*
Redundancy: electronics, *82–294*
Reflection seismology: geology, *82–320, 80–336*
Reformed Church in America, *82–452, 81–465, 80–461*
Refugee Act: immigration, *81–346, 80–356*
Refugees: Africa, *81–181*; Asia, *82–191, Close-Up, 80–198*; Australia, *80–201*; Canada, *80–236*; Cuba, *82–265, 81–270*; *ils., 82–190, 81–191, 345, 80–500*; immigration, *81–345*; Indonesia, *80–359*; Japan, *80–367*; Laos, *80–377*; Malaysia, *80–393*; Pakistan, *82–418, 81–432*; President, *81–451, 80–449*; Somalia, *82–465, 81–481*; Sudan, *81–492*; United Nations, *80–514*; Vietnam, *80–521*
REGAN, DONALD THOMAS, *82–451*
Reggae: music, popular, *82–402*
Regional theater, *80–501*
Regulatory Relief, Task Force on: consumerism, *82–262*
Rehabilitation. See **HANDICAPPED.**
Rehabilitation Act: handicapped, *81–334, 80–345*
Relief. See **WELFARE.**
RELIGION, *82–451, 81–465, 80–461*; civil rights, *82–248; Close-Up, 80–462*; cults, *Special Report, 80–145*; Eastern Orthodox, *82–283, 81–288, 80–293*; education, *82–290*; Egypt, *82–291*; Jews, *80–368*; Protestantism, *82–441, 81–455, 80–452*; Roman Catholic, *82–454, 81–468, 80–466*; state government, *81–489*
Rely tampons: advertising, *81–173*; health, *81–336*
Renoir, Jean, *80–282*
Reorganized Church of Jesus Christ of Latter Day Saints: Protestantism, *82–441*; religion, *82–452, 81–465, 80–461*
Representatives, House of. See **CONGRESS.**
Reptiles: biology, *82–213*
REPUBLICAN PARTY, *82–453, 81–466, 80–464*; elections, *82–292, 81–297, 80–304*
Repurchase Agreements: banks, *80–211*
Rescue mission: armed forces, *81–188*; Iran, *Close-Up, 82–348*; personalities, *82–423*
Resolution 242: Israel, *81–358*
Resin: botany, *82–215*
Restoration: architecture, *82–184*; awards and prizes, *82–201*
Retirement: Social Security, *80–478*; taxation, *82–482*
Reverse discrimination: Detroit, *80–288*; Supreme Court, *80–491*
Revolution. See **Civil war; Terrorism; Violence.**
Rhine, Joseph B.: deaths, *81–277*
Rhode Island, *82–473, 81–488, 80–487*; Indian, American, *80–357*
Rhodes, Cecil J.: Africa, *Close-Up, 80–183*
Rhodesia. See **ZIMBABWE.**
Rhoodie, Eschel M., *80–478*
Ribosomes: chemistry, *82–237*
Richards, Ivor A., *80–282*
Richards, Richard: Republican Party, *82–453*

Richie, Lionel: music, popular, *82*-401
Richmond, Julius B.: health, *80*-346; *il., 82*-331
Richter, Karl, *82*-273
Rifkind, Stanley Mark, *80*-272
Right turn on red: safety, *81*-474
Ring system: astronomy, *82*-193, *81*-194
Riots: Albania, *82*-179; Great Britain, *82*-327; India, *81*-347; Morocco, *82*-393; Netherlands, *81*-412; prison, *82*-441, *81*-454; Yugoslavia, *82*-517
Riperton, Minnie: deaths, *80*-282; music, *81*-409
River: weather, *82*-512
Rizzo, Frank L., *80*-440
Roach, Hattie K., *80*-282
Roads and highways: Los Angeles, *82*-377; safety, *80*-471; transportation, *80*-506
Robb, Charles S.: elections, *82*-292
Robb, Inez, *80*-282
Robot: *il., 80*-58; manufacturing, *82*-381, *81*-388; *Special Report, 82*-138
Rockefeller, Nelson A.: deaths, *80*-282; visual arts, *80*-522
Rocky Mountain spotted fever: public health, *82*-444
Rodent: zoology, *81*-534
Rodeo, *82*-470, *81*-485, *80*-483
Rodin, Auguste: museum, *82*-398
Rodnina, Irina: ice skating, *81*-345
Rogers, Adrian P., *80*-453
ROGERS, BERNARD W., *80*-465
Rogers, Bill: golf, *82*-322
Rogers, Kenny: music, *80*-415
ROLDOS AGUILERA, JAIME, *80*-465; Ecuador, *81*-293, *80*-299
Rolf, Ida P., *80*-282
Roller skating: games, *80*-335; sports, *82*-470, *81*-485, *80*-483
Rolling Stones: *il., 82*-402
ROMAN CATHOLIC CHURCH, *82*-454, *81*-468, *80*-466; China, *82*-243; Latin America, *80*-380; Netherlands, *81*-412; Philippines, *80*-441; Poland, *81*-446, *80*-445; religion, *82*-452, *81*-465, *80*-461, *Close-Up, 80*-462
ROMANIA, *82*-457, *81*-470, *80*-468; Europe, *82*-303, *81*-310, *80*-317; Hungary, *80*-354
Romero y Galdamez, Oscar Arnulfo: El Salvador, *81*-301; Roman Catholic Church, *81*-468
Ronstadt, Linda: *il., 81*-410
Roots: television, *80*-496
Roque, *82*-470, *81*-485, *80*-483
Rose, Pete: baseball, *82*-208
ROSEAU: *WBE, 80*-577
Rosenthal, Joe: *il., 82*-430
Rotary International: community organizations, *82*-253, *81*-256, *80*-259
Roth, Lillian: deaths, *81*-277
Roth, Mark, *80*-222
Roth, Philip: literature, *82*-370
Rovere, Richard H., *80*-282
Rowing: sports, *82*-470, *81*-485, *80*-483
Royal Ballet: dancing, *82*-268
Royal Canadian Mounted Police, *82*-225
Royal Weddings: Great Britain, *Close-Up, 82*-326; *ils., 82*-324, 377; stamp collecting, *82*-472
Royalties: Indian, American, *82*-343
Royo, Aristides: Panama, *82*-420
Rozelle, Pete: football, *81*-320
Rubber: labor, *80*-374; manufacturing, *82*-381, *81*-391, *80*-396
Rubik's Cube: *il., 82*-319; personalities, *82*-421
Rubin, Morris H.: deaths, *81*-277
Rugby: Australia, *82*-195; *il., 82*-406; sports, *82*-470, *81*-485, *80*-483
Runcie, Robert A. K.: *ils., 82*-442, *81*-331; Protestantism, *81*-456, *80*-452
Runnels, Harold L.: deaths, *81*-279
Runner's high: mental health, *82*-384
R.U.R.: robot, *Special Report, 82*-142
RUSSIA, *82*-458, *81*-471, *80*-469; Afghanistan, *82*-173, *81*-173, *80*-177, *Close-Up, 81*-174; armed forces, *80*-191; Asia, *82*-192, *81*-192, *80*-196; building, *80*-227; China, *80*-249; conservation, *80*-268; Cuba, *80*-274; dancing, *80*-276; Eastern Orthodox, *82*-283, *81*-288; economics, *81*-292, *80*-296; Europe, *82*-303, *81*-310, *80*-317; farm, *82*-307; Japan, *82*-355, *80*-368; Jews, *82*-355, *81*-363, *80*-368; Latin America, *80*-378; Middle East, *82*-387, *81*-396, *80*-400; music, classical, *80*-410; Nicaragua, *81*-415; Olympic Games, *81*-424, *80*-428; petroleum, *82*-428, *81*-440, *80*-440; Poland, *82*-433, *81*-446; President, *82*-439; Protestantism, *80*-454; Romania, *82*-457, *80*-468; space exploration, *82*-466, *80*-479; Sweden, *82*-479; Vietnam, *82*-507, *81*-521; visual arts, *81*-523
Rutledge, Kevin: football, *80*-330
Rwanda, *82*-177, *81*-179, *80*-181
Ryan, Claude: Canada, *Close-Up, 81*-227

Ryumin, Valery, *81*-482, *80*-479

S

Sa Carneiro, Francisco: Portugal, *81*-448
Saccharin: drugs, *81*-288, *80*-292; food, *80*-327; health, *81*-336
Sadat, Anwar el-: Egypt, *82*-291, *81*-297, *80*-303; *il., 80*-401; Middle East, *Close-Up, 82*-390, *81*-398
SAFETY, *82*-460, *81*-474, *80*-471; aviation, *82*-200, *81*-201, *80*-206; chemical industry, *81*-240; consumer protection, *80*-270; energy, *82*-296, *Close-Up, 80*-310; Germany, West, *80*-337; Skylab, *Close-Up, 80*-480; Supreme Court, *82*-477; transportation, *81*-508. See also **DISASTERS.**
Safety belts: transportation, *82*-494
Sagebrush Rebellion, *82*-299, *81*-263, *80*-267; Watt, James Gaius, *82*-512
Saharan Arab Democratic Republic: Africa, *81*-181, *80*-184; Middle East, *80*-403
Sailing. See BOATING.
St. Gotthard Tunnel: *il., 81*-221
St. Louis: city, *82*-246, *81*-248, *80*-252
SAINT LUCIA: *WBE, 80*-578; Latin America, *82*-366, *81*-375, *80*-380; West Indies, *80*-528
ST. VINCENT AND THE GRENADINES: *WBE, 81*-580; Latin America, *82*-366, *81*-375, *80*-380; West Indies, *80*-529
Sakharov, Andrei D.: civil rights, *81*-251; Russia, *82*-459; science, *81*-476
Salary. See Wages.
Salicylate: aspirin, *Special Report, 81*-141
Salim Ahmad al-Huss: Lebanon, *80*-383
Salmon: fishing industry, *80*-325; Indian, American, *80*-358
Salnikov, Vladimir: *il., 81*-429
Salt: food, *82*-312
SALT: armed forces, *81*-188, *80*-191; Congress, *80*-264; Europe, *80*-318; President, *80*-448; Russia, *81*-471
Salt-tolerant plants: water, *Special Report, 82*-104
Saltonstall, Leverett, *80*-284
Salvation Army: community organizations, *82*-253, *80*-259; *il., 81*-256; Protestantism, *82*-441; religion, *82*-452, *81*-465, *80*-461
Salyut, *82*-466, *81*-482, *80*-479
SAMARANCH, JUAN ANTONIO, *81*-475
Sambo: sports, *81*-485, *80*-483
San Antonio, *82*-246, *81*-248, *80*-252
San Diego: city, *82*-246, *81*-248, *80*-252; elections, *82*-293
San Francisco: city, *82*-246, *81*-248, *80*-252
San Jose, *82*-246, *81*-248, *80*-252
San Marino, *82*-303, *81*-310, *80*-317
Sanders, Colonel Harland, *81*-279
Sands, Bobby: Northern Ireland, *82*-411
Sandinista National Liberation Front: Latin America, *80*-378; Nicaragua, *80*-421
Sanger, Frederick: Nobel Prizes, *81*-419
São Tomé and Príncipe, *82*-177, *81*-179, *80*-181
Sarkis, Elias, *81*-376
Sartre, Jean-Paul: deaths, *81*-279
SASKATCHEWAN, *82*-461, *81*-475, *80*-472
Satellite: energy, *82*-297; space exploration, *82*-467
Satellite, artificial. See SPACE EXPLORATION.
Satellite, communications: communications, *82*-253; farm, *81*-314; radio, *80*-458; space exploration, *82*-467
Sattar, Abdus: Bangladesh, *82*-204
Saturn: astronomy, *82*-193, *81*-194, *80*-199; space, *82*-466, *81*-483, *80*-479
Saud, Prince: *il., 82*-461
SAUDI ARABIA, *82*-461, *81*-475, *80*-472; disasters, *81*-284; Middle East, *82*-389, *81*-398, *80*-402; petroleum, *82*-426, *80*-438
Sauter, Edward: deaths, *82*-273
SAUVE, JEANNE, *81*-476; *il., 81*-229
Savard, Serge: *il., 80*-350
Savings and loan institutions: bank, *82*-206, *80*-211
Savinykh, Victor: space exploration, *82*-466
Scandinavia. See DENMARK; NORWAY; SWEDEN
Scent-marking: pet language, *Special Report, 81*-133
Schary, Dore: deaths, *81*-279
Schawlow, Arthur L.: Nobel Prizes, *82*-410
Schizophrenia: mental health, *80*-398
Schlegel, Ernie: bowling, *81*-217
Schlesinger, James Rodney: Cabinet, *80*-229
Schmidt, Helmut: Germany, West, *82*-322, *81*-328, *80*-337
Schmidt, Mike: baseball, *82*-208; *il., 81*-209
Scholastic Aptitude Tests, *82*-290, *81*-296, *80*-301; personalities, *82*-424

School. See EDUCATION; Universities and colleges.
SCHREYER, EDWARD RICHARD, *82*-462, *81*-476, *80*-473
Schuyler, James: poetry, *82*-432
SCHWEIKER, RICHARD S., *82*-462
SCIENCE AND RESEARCH, *81*-476, *80*-473; awards, *82*-203, *81*-204, *80*-209; electronics, *80*-307; literature, *82*-373; manufacturing, *82*-381; medicine, *82*-382, *81*-391, *80*-396; mental health, *81*-393, *80*-398; ocean, *82*-414, *Special Report, 80*-525; zoo medicine, *Special Report, 80*-99. See also articles on specific sciences.
Science fiction: magazine, *82*-378; *Special Report, 80*-53
Scientific creationism: Protestantism, *82*-443
Scotland, *80*-340
Scott, Steve: track and field, *82*-491
Scott Cowper, David: personalities, *81*-437
Scrabble: personalities, *82*-422
Scribophon system: *il., 81*-255
Sculpture: visual arts, *82*-508, *81*-523, *80*-523
Sea roach: *il., 81*-214
Sea turtle: conservation, *81*-264; *il., 82*-260
Sea worm: *80*-428
Seafloor spreading: ocean, *Special Report, 80*-140
SEAGA, EDWARD, *81*-478; West Indies, *81*-530
Search-and-seizure: Supreme Court, *81*-493
Sears, Roebuck and Company: consumerism, *82*-263
Seat belt: consumerism, *82*-262; safety, *80*-471
Seattle: city, *82*-246, *81*-248, *80*-252
Seismic stratigraphy: geology, *82*-321
Self-incrimination: Supreme Court, *82*-479
Sellers, Peter: *il., 81*-277
Semiconductor technology: electronics, *81*-300
Senate, U.S. See CONGRESS OF THE UNITED STATES.
Senegal, *82*-177, *81*-179, *80*-181; Gambia, *82*-318
Senility: psychology, *82*-443
Separatism: Canada, *Close-Up, 81*-227; Ethiopia, *80*-314; Quebec, *82*-446, *80*-457; Spain, *80*-481; Sri Lanka, *80*-483
Sephardic Jews: Israel, *82*-352
Service organizations, *82*-253, *81*-256, *80*-259
Seuss, Dr.: *il., 81*-183
Seven Days of Creation: literature for children, *82*-373
Seventh-day Adventists: Protestantism, *82*-441; religion, *82*-452, *81*-465, *80*-461
Severance tax: state government, *82*-472
Sex discrimination: anthropology, *81*-185; Supreme Court, *82*-477; United States, government of the, *80*-518
Seychelles, *82*-177, *81*-179, *80*-181
Shaba: Zaire, *80*-531
SHAGARI, SHEHU, *80*-474; Africa, *80*-179; Nigeria, *81*-416, *80*-422
Shaka, Bassam al-: Israel, *80*-365; United Nations, *80*-513
Shanghai Acrobatic Theater, *81*-273
Sharaf, Sharif Abdul Hamid: Jordan, *81*-363
Shaw's Music: literature, *82*-372
Sheen, Fulton J., *80*-284
Shields, Brooke: *il., 82*-172
Shih Huang Ti: archaeology, *82*-183
Shiite Muslims: Iran, *80*-361, *Close-Up, 81*-355; Iraq, *81*-357; religion, *81*-465, *80*-461
Shimada, Mitsuhiro: *80*-367
Shin Aitoku Maru: *il., 81*-478
SHIP AND SHIPPING, *82*-462, *81*-478, *80*-475; coal, *81*-253; disasters, *82*-281, *81*-285, *80*-291; Montreal, *82*-393; Philadelphia, *82*-429
Shock therapy: mental health, *81*-393
Shoemaker, Bill: horse racing, *82*-336
"Shōgun": television, *81*-498
Shooting: sports, *82*-470, *81*-485, *80*-483
Shostakovich, Maxim: *il., 82*-458
Shuffleboard, *82*-470, *81*-485, *80*-483
Siamese twins: medicine, *80*-397
Siegbahn, Kai M.: Nobel Prizes, *82*-410
Sierra Club: conservation, *82*-259
Sierra Leone, *82*-177, *81*-179, *80*-181
Sigma Delta Chi: awards and prizes, *82*-202, *81*-203, *80*-208
Sihanouk, Norodom: Cambodia, *82*-223, *81*-224, *80*-230; United Nations, *80*-514
Siles Zuazo, Hernan, *81*-216, *80*-221
Silfiyyin: Middle East, *82*-388
Silica-fiber tiles: space shuttle, *Special Report, 82*-120
Silkwood, Karen: courts, *80*-272
SILLS, BEVERLY, *80*-476; music, classical, *81*-408, *80*-410

Silver: banks, *80*–211; coins, *82*–251, *81*–253; international trade, *Close-Up*, *81*–351; stocks, *81*–492
Silverheels, Jay: deaths, *81*–279; *il.*, *80*–358; personalities, *80*–436
Sin, Jaime Cardinal, *80*–441
Sinclair, Ian: Australia, *81*–195
Singapore, *82*–192, *81*–192, *80*–196
Singh, Charan, *80*–357
Single-lens-reflex camera, *81*–442, *80*–442
Sinhalese: Sri Lanka, *82*–470
Sinkhole: *il.*, *82*–99
Sioux Nation, *81*–347, *80*–357
Sixth Amendment: civil rights, *81*–252
Skateboard: games, *80*–335; safety, *80*–471; sports, *81*–485
Skating. See **HOCKEY; ICE SKATING; Roller skating.**
SKIING, *82*–463, *81*–479, *80*–476
Skin grafts: *il.*, *82*–382; medicine, *81*–393
Skinner, Cornelia Otis, *80*–284
Skyjacking. See **Hijacking.**
Skylab: Close-Up, *80*–480; *il.*, *80*–201; space exploration, *80*–479
Sled-dog racing: sports, *82*–470, *81*–485, *80*–483
Smith, Bailey: Protestantism, *81*–456
Smith, Charlie, *80*–284
Smith, Ian: Africa, *Close-Up*, *80*–183
Smith, Joseph F.: Democratic Party, *82*–275
Smith, Rex: *il.*, *81*–410
SMITH, WILLIAM FRENCH, *82*–464
Smog: *il.*, *80*–391
Smoking: advertising, *80*–176; health and disease, *82*–331, *81*–337
Snail darter: conservation, *80*–268; science, *80*–474
Snepp, Frank W.: publishing, *81*–459
Snider, Edwin (Duke): baseball, *81*–209
Snow, C. P.: deaths, *81*–279
Snowmobile racing: sports, *82*–470, *81*–485
Snowshoe hare: botany, *82*–215
SOCCER, *82*–464, *81*–480, *80*–477
Social Democratic Party: Great Britain, *82*–325
Social sciences. See **ANTHROPOLOGY; ARCHAEOLOGY; CIVIL RIGHTS; COURTS AND LAWS; CRIME; ECONOMICS; EDUCATION; PSYCHOLOGY.**
SOCIAL SECURITY, *82*–465, *81*–480, *80*–478; Congress of the United States, *82*–258; inflation, *Special Report*, *81*–75; taxation, *82*–482, *81*–496
Sodium nitrite: health, *81*–336
Soft freezing: food, *81*–318
Softball, *82*–470, *81*–485, *80*–483
Solar collector: *il.*, *82*–296
Solar energy: building, *80*–226; chemistry, *80*–242; energy, *82*–297, *80*–311
Solar Molar Module: *il.*, *82*–277
Solidarity: Poland, *82*–433, *81*–447; Roman Catholic Church, *82*–456
SOLOMON ISLANDS, *WBE*, *80*–578; Pacific Islands, *82*–417
SOMALIA, *82*–465, *81*–481; Africa, *82*–177, *81*–179, *80*–181
Somoza Debayle, Anastasio: deaths, *81*–279; *il.*, *80*–381; Latin America, *81*–374; Nicaragua, *80*–421
Soo, Jack, *80*–284
Soong Ching-ling, *82*–273
Sope, Barak: Pacific Islands, *82*–416
Sophisticated Ladies: *il.*, *82*–488
SOUTH AFRICA, *82*–466, *81*–481, *80*–478; Africa, *82*–177, *81*–179, *80*–181; Angola, *82*–181; Australia, *82*–195; coal, *80*–257; Namibia, *82*–403, *81*–411; United Nations, *82*–500, *81*–513; Venda, *80*–519
South America. See **LATIN AMERICA.**
South Carolina, *82*–473, *81*–488, *80*–487
South Dakota, *82*–473, *81*–488, *80*–487; Indian, American, *80*–357
South West Africa. See **NAMIBIA.**
South-West Africa People's Organization: Africa, *82*–174, *80*–182; Namibia, *82*–403, *81*–411, *80*–416
Southern Baptist Convention: Protestantism, *82*–442; religion, *82*–452, *81*–465, *80*–461
Southern Ocean Racing Conference: boating, *82*–214
Southern Yemen, People's Republic of. See **Yemen (Aden).**
Southwestern states: water, *Special Report*, *82*–100
Souvanna Phouma: Laos, *82*–363
Sovan, Pen: Cambodia, *82*–223
Sovereignty: Canada, *82*–225
Soviet Union. See **RUSSIA.**
Soyuz: space exploration, *82*–466, *81*–482
SPACE EXPLORATION, *82*–466, *81*–482, *80*–479; *Close-Up*, *80*–480; Jupiter, *Special Report*, *80*–87

Space shuttle: space exploration, *82*–466, *81*–482; *Special Report*, *82*–109
Space Transportation System: space shuttle, *Special Report*, *82*–110
SPACEK, SISSY, *82*–467
Spacelab: space shuttle, *Special Report*, *82*–121
SPADOLINI, GIOVANNI, *82*–468; Italy, *82*–353
SPAIN, *82*–468, *81*–483, *80*–481; Europe, *82*–303, *81*–310, *80*–317; public health, *82*–444
Spanish Sahara. See **Western Sahara.**
Spectacular Bid, *81*–340, *80*–350
Speed skating: ice skating, *82*–341, *81*–344
Speer, Albert, *82*–273
Spenkelink, John A.: courts, *80*–272; state government, *80*–488
Sperry, Roger W.: Nobel Prizes, *82*–410
Spherand: chemistry, *82*–237
SPORTS, *82*–469, *81*–484, *80*–482; deaths, *Close-Up*, *82*–271; hypnosis, *Special Report*, *80*–81; Pan American Games, *80*–432; television, *82*–485, *81*–499. See also **OLYMPIC GAMES;** entries for specific sports.
Sportswear: fashion, *82*–309
Spousal privilege rule: Supreme Court, *81*–493
Springboks: New Zealand, *82*–406
Springfield, Rick: music, popular, *82*–401
Squash racquets, *82*–470, *81*–485, *80*–483
Squash tennis, *82*–470, *81*–485, *80*–483
Squatters: *il.*, *82*–404; South Africa, *82*–466
SRI LANKA, *82*–470, *81*–486, *80*–483; Asia, *82*–192, *81*–192, *80*–196
STAMP COLLECTING, *82*–471, *81*–486, *80*–484
Standard error: poll, *Special Report*, *80*–126
Stanley Cup, *82*–334, *80*–350; *il.*, *81*–338
Stanwyck, Barbara: personalities, *82*–425
Star Trek: *il.*, *80*–408; science fiction, *Special Report*, *80*–67
Star Wars: games, *80*–334; *il.*, *82*–447; science fiction, *Special Report*, *80*–67
Stargell, Willie, *80*–213
Starr, Ringo: *il.*, *82*–424
STATE GOVERNMENT, *82*–472, *81*–487, *80*–485; census, *81*–237; conservation, *80*–267; Democratic Party, *81*–281; elections, *82*–293, *81*–299, *80*–304; hunting, *80*–354; insurance, *80*–359; library, *80*–383; Republican Party, *81*–468; taxation, *82*–482, *81*–497, *80*–496; water, *80*–525
Statehood: Washington, D.C., *81*–524
Statistics: poll, *Special Report*, *80*–119
Stealth aircraft: armed forces, *82*–187, *81*–188
STEEL INDUSTRY, *82*–475, *81*–490, *80*–488; Europe, *82*–304, *80*–316; France, *80*–333; labor, *81*–367; Luxembourg, *82*–377, *81*–386
Steel shot: hunting, *81*–344, *80*–354
Stenmark, Ingemar: skiing, *82*–463, *81*–479, *80*–476
Stephenson, Jan: golf, *82*–323, *81*–330
Steptoe, Patrick C., *80*–396
Sterilization: health, *80*–347; mental health, *80*–398
Stevens, J. P. and Company: labor, *81*–371
Stevens, Sinclair, *80*–232
Stevie: motion pictures, *82*–395
Stewart, James: personalities, *81*–437
Steyne, M. T., *80*–416
Still, Clyfford: deaths, *81*–279
Sting ray: zoology, *82*–519
Stirling, James: architecture, *82*–185
Stock car, *82*–199, *81*–200, *80*–204
Stock exchange: *il.*, *81*–352
Stockham, Thomas: *il.*, *80*–460
STOCKMAN, DAVID ALAN, *82*–475; *il.*, *82*–285; Republican Party, *82*–454
STOCKS AND BONDS, *82*–475, *81*–491, *80*–489; economics, *81*–292
Stone, Milburn: deaths, *81*–279
Storms: disasters, *82*–279, *81*–285, *80*–290
Strategic Arms Limitation Talks. See **SALT.**
Strategic minerals: mining, *82*–391
Strategic Petroleum Reserve: petroleum and gas, *82*–426
Stratford (Ont.) Shakespearean Festival: theater, *82*–491
"Strawberry Shortcake": games and toys, *82*–318
Strikes: aviation, *82*–199; baseball, *82*–206; Chicago, *81*–242; city, *81*–250, *80*–251; coal, *82*–250; Detroit, *81*–282; Europe, *Close-Up*, *81*–308; labor, *82*–360, *81*–369, *80*–375; Los Angeles, *81*–385; mining, *80*–404; music, popular, *81*–409; newspaper, *81*–415; Philadelphia, *82*–428; Poland, *82*–433, *81*–446; Sweden, *81*–494; television, *82*–484, *81*–498; West Indies, *80*–528. See also articles on specific countries and cities.
Strip mining: conservation, *81*–263, *80*–267; mining, *82*–391
Strip-search: courts, *81*–268
Stroessner, Alfredo, *82*–421, *81*–434, *80*–433
Stroke: aspirin, *Special Report*, *81*–140

Strougal, Lubomir, *82*–266, *80*–275
Suarez Gonzalez, Adolfo, *82*–468, *81*–483, *80*–481
Subscription television service: television, *82*–486
SUDAN, *82*–476, *81*–492, *80*–490; Africa, *82*–177, *81*–179, *80*–181; Middle East, *82*–389, *81*–398, *80*–402
Sugar: dentistry, *80*–287; food, *82*–312
Sugimoto, Katsuko: bowling, *82*–216
Suharto, *82*–344, *81*–348
Suicide: mental health, *80*–399
Sulfinpyrasone: drugs, *81*–287
Sulfur: ocean, *Special Report*, *80*–143
Sulfur dioxide: environment, *80*–313
Sulindac: drugs, *81*–287
Sullivan Award: Caulkins, Tracy, *80*–240
Sun-belt: census, *82*–232
Sunni Muslims: Iran, *Close-Up*, *81*–355
Sunshine Skyway bridge: *il.*, *81*–284
Sunspots: weather, *81*–527
Super 80: aviation, *81*–201
Superfund: chemical industry, *82*–236
Superman II: *il.*, *82*–396
Supply-side economics: economics, *82*–287
SUPREME COURT OF THE U.S., *82*–477, *81*–493, *80*–491; building, *82*–219; chemical industry, *82*–236; city, *81*–251; civil rights, *80*–255; consumer protection, *80*–271; courts, *82*–264, *80*–272; drugs, *80*–292; fishing industry, *82*–440; handicapped, *82*–330, *80*–345; health, *80*–347; Indian, American, *80*–358; mental health, *81*–393, *80*–398; newspaper, *81*–415; O'Connor, Sandra Day, *82*–415; prison, *82*–440, *80*–452; Roman Catholic, *82*–467; safety, *82*–460; Social Security, *80*–478; U.S., government of the, *82*–506, *81*–520, *80*–516
Surface mining: conservation, *80*–267
Surfing: sports, *82*–470, *81*–485
Surgery: health, *80*–346; hospital, *82*–337; hypnosis, *Special Report*, *80*–79; *il.*, *80*–104; medicine, *80*–397
Surinam, *82*–366, *81*–375, *80*–380
Susan B. Anthony dollar, *81*–254, *80*–257
Sutcliffe, Peter: Great Britain, *82*–328
Sutherland, Graham: deaths, *81*–279
SUZUKI, ZENKO, *81*–494; Japan, *82*–353, *81*–361
Swaziland, *82*–177, *81*–179, *80*–181
Swearingen, M. Wesley, *80*–515
SWEDEN, *82*–479, *81*–494, *80*–492; Europe, *82*–303, *81*–310, *80*–317; Russia, *82*–458
SWIMMING, *82*–480, *81*–495, *80*–492
Swing music: music, popular, *82*–402
SWITZERLAND, *82*–480, *81*–495, *80*–493; Europe, *82*–303, *81*–310, *80*–317
Synchronized swimming, *82*–470, *81*–485, *80*–483
Synthetic Fuels Corporation: energy, *82*–297, *81*–302
Synthetic liquid fuel: coal, *80*–256
SYRIA, *82*–481, *81*–495, *80*–493; archaeology, *82*–184, *80*–189; Jordan, *82*–356, *81*–363; Lebanon, *82*–368; Middle East, *82*–389, *81*–398, *80*–402
Szechwan Province: panda, *Special Report*, *82*–76

T

Table tennis, *82*–470, *81*–485, *80*–483
Tae kwon do, *82*–470, *81*–485, *80*–483
TAIWAN, *82*–481, *81*–496, *80*–494; Asia, *82*–192, *81*–192, *80*–196; civil rights, *81*–251; Congress, *80*–264; Olympic Games, *82*–415, *80*–429
Tallchief, Maria: dancing, *81*–271
Talmadge, Herman, *80*–266
Tambay, Patrick: auto racing, *81*–200
Tamils: Sri Lanka, *82*–470, *80*–483
Tamoxifen: medicine, *82*–383
Taney, Roger Brooke: Supreme Court, *Close-Up*, *82*–478
Tang Yiming, Dominic: Roman Catholic Church, *82*–457
Tanner, Roscoe, *80*–498
TANZANIA, *80*–495; Africa, *82*–177, *81*–179, *80*–181; anthropology, *81*–184; Uganda, *80*–512
Tape recording. See **RECORDINGS.**
Taraki, Noor Mohammad: Afghanistan, *80*–177, *Close-Up*, *81*–174; Middle East, *80*–400
TARAWA, *WBE*, *81*–579
Tariffs. See **INTERNATIONAL TRADE.**
Tarnower, Herman: courts and laws, *82*–264; deaths, *81*–279
Task Force on Regulatory Relief: U.S., government of the, *82*–503
Tate, Allen, *80*–284
Tate, John, *81*–218, *80*–223

TAXATION, *82*–482, *81*–496, *80*–495; Chicago, *82*–238; city, *82*–245, *80*–250; Detroit, *82*–277; economics, *82*–287, *81*–290; elections, *82*–393; Great Britain, *80*–340; Houston, *82*–339; Ontario, *82*–416; Philadelphia, *82*–429; state government, *82*–472, *81*–487, *80*–488; transit, *80*–505; Washington, D.C., *82*–510; welfare, *80*–527
Taylor, Elizabeth: *il., 82*–490
Taylor, Kenneth: Canada, *81*–230
Taylor Dance Company, Paul: dancing, *82*–268, *81*–273
Teachers: city, *80*–251; education, *82*–289, *81*–294, *80*–301; National PTA, *80*–417; Philadelphia, *82*–428; Roman Catholic Church, *80*–467
Teamsters Union: labor, *82*–362
Technology: awards, *81*–204, *80*–209; communications, *81*–255, *80*–258; electronics, *81*–300, *80*–307; farm, *80*–322. See also **MANUFACTURING.**
Telecom, *80*–258
Telecommunications Competition and Deregulation Act: communications, *82*–252
Telephone: communications, *81*–255
Teletext system: newspaper, *82*–407
TELEVISION, *82*–483, *81*–498, *80*–496; advertising, *82*–172, *81*–172, *80*–176; Australia, *81*–197; awards, *82*–202, *81*–202, *80*–207; communications, *82*–252, *81*–255; courts, *80*–272; education, *81*–296; electronics, *82*–294, *80*–308; football, *82*–315; games, *80*–334; *il., 80*–264; National PTA, *82*–403, *81*–411, *80*–417; Olympic Games, *80*–429; science fiction, *Special Report, 80*–59; sports, *82*–469, *80*–482
Tellico Dam, *80*–268; science, *80*–474
Temcor Domes: building, *81*–222
Teng Hsiao-p'ing: China, *81*–244, *80*–247; *il., 80*–394
Tennessee, *82*–473, *81*–488, *80*–487; prison, *80*–452
TENNIS, *82*–486, *81*–501, *80*–498; sports, *81*–485, *80*–483
Teresa, Mother, *80*–423
Terrible Secret, The: literature, *82*–372
Terrorism: Austria, *82*–196; Colombia, *82*–251, *81*–254, *80*–258; crime, *82*–264, *81*–268, *80*–273; Cuba, *82*–265; El Salvador, *81*–301; Iran, *80*–363; Ireland, *80*–364; Italy, *82*–353, *81*–360; Latin America, *80*–378; Philippines, *81*–442; Puerto Rico, *82*–445, *80*–457; Spain, *82*–468, *81*–483; Syria, *80*–493. See also **Kidnapping; Protests; Violence.**
Test-tube baby: medicine, *81*–391, *80*–396
Teton Dam: building and construction, *82*–220
Texas, *82*–473, *81*–488, *80*–487
Textiles: manufacturing, *81*–389
THAILAND, *82*–487, *81*–502, *80*–500; Asia, *82*–192, *81*–192, *80*–196; *Close-Up, 80*–198; Cambodia, *80*–230; Laos, *81*–371, *80*–377
Thalidomide: courts, *80*–271
Tharp, Twyla: dancing, *82*–267, *81*–273, *80*–276
THATCHER, MARGARET HILDA, *80*–500; *Close-Up, 80*–343; Europe, *82*–302, *81*–306, *80*–315; Great Britain, *82*–327, *81*–331, *80*–340; *ils., 82*–224, 304, *80*–419
THC: medicine, *81*–391; psychology, *82*–444
THEATER, *82*–489, *81*–503, *80*–501; awards, *82*–201, *81*–202, *80*–207
Theology. See **RELIGION.**
Therapsid: biology, *82*–213
Thomas, Isiah: *il., 82*–210
Thomas, Lowell: deaths, *82*–273
Thoroddsen, Gunnar: Europe, *81*–311
Thorpe, Jeremy, *80*–340
Three Days on a River: literature for children, *82*–374
Three Mile Island: Congress, *80*–265; consumer protection, *80*–270; energy, *82*–297, *Close-Up, 80*–310; environment, *81*–305, *80*–312; President, *80*–451; safety, *81*–474; science, *80*–473
Three-Self Patriotic Movement: religion, *82*–451
Thromboxane: aspirin, *Special Report, 81*–146
Tigre: Ethiopia, *80*–314
TIKHONOV, NIKOLAY A., *81*–505
Timber. See **FOREST AND FOREST PRODUCTS.**
Timerman, Jacobo: Argentina, *82*–186, *80*–191
Tin Drum, The: *il., 81*–401
Tire: consumer protection, *80*–270; manufacturing, *82*–381, *81*–391, *80*–396; safety, *80*–471
Titan: astronomy, *81*–195
Titan missile: armed forces, *81*–189
Titanic: ocean, *81*–423
Title IX: sports, *81*–484
Tito, Josip Broz, *80*–530; deaths, *Close-Up, 81*–278
To Huu: Vietnam, *82*–507
Tobago. See **Trinidad and Tobago.**

Tobin, James: Nobel Prizes, *82*–410
Togo, *82*–177, *81*–179, *80*–181
Tokyo round, *81*–350, *80*–361
Tokyo summit conference: Canada, *80*–236; Japan, *80*–367
Tolbert, William R., Jr.: deaths, *81*–279; Liberia, *81*–377
Toledo: city, *82*–246, *81*–248, *80*–252
Tolstoy, Alexandra L., *80*–284
Tomin, Julius: Czechoslovakia, *81*–271
Tonga: Pacific Islands, *82*–417
Tony Awards, *82*–201, *81*–202, *80*–207
Tools, primitive: anthropology, *82*–182
Topsoil conservation: conservation, *82*–261; farm and farming, *82*–308
Torah: Jews and Judaism, *82*–356
Tornadoes: disasters, *82*–279, *81*–285, *80*–290
Torrelio Villa, Celso: Bolivia, *82*–215
Torrijos Herrera, Omar: *il., 82*–269; Panama, *82*–420
Tourism. See **TRAVEL.**
Tournament Players Association: golf, *82*–323
Townley, Michael V.: Chile, *80*–246; courts, *80*–272
Toxic-shock syndrome: health, *81*–336
Toxic waste: chemical industry, *81*–239; environment, *81*–305, *80*–314; water, *Special Report, 82*–101
Toys. See **GAMES AND TOYS.**
TRACK AND FIELD, *82*–491, *81*–506, *80*–503
Tracy, Dick: personalities, *82*–423
Trade. See **ECONOMICS; Federal Trade Commission; INTERNATIONAL TRADE.**
Trade union. See **Unions.**
Train. See **RAILROAD.**
Tranquilizer: drugs, *81*–287
Trans-Alaska pipeline: Canada, *81*–230
Transatlantic cable: communications, *80*–259
TRANSIT, *82*–493, *81*–507, *80*–505; building, *80*–227; city, *81*–250, *80*–251; handicapped, *82*–330, *81*–334, *80*–345. See also articles on specific cities.
Transkei: Africa, *82*–177, *81*–179, *80*–181
Translations: Canadian literature, *82*–231; literature, *82*–371
Transplant surgery: medicine, *82*–382, *81*–392
TRANSPORTATION, *82*–493, *81*–508, *80*–506; coal, *82*–250; handicapped, *81*–334, *80*–345; Los Angeles, *80*–391; Louis, Drew, *82*–369. See also **AUTOMOBILE; AVIATION; RAILROAD; SHIP; TRANSIT; TRAVEL; TRUCK.**
TRAVEL, *82*–494, *81*–509, *80*–507; advertising, *82*–172; Austria, *80*–202; aviation, *80*–205
Treasury bill: bank, *82*–205
Tredici, David: music, classical, *82*–400
Treen, David C., *80*–304
Triglycerides: nutrition, *81*–422
Trinidad and Tobago: Latin America, *82*–366, *81*–375, *80*–380; West Indies, *82*–515, *81*–530
Trousers: fashion, *82*–308
Troy: horse racing, *80*–351
TRUCK AND TRUCKING, *82*–495, *81*–510, *80*–509; disasters, *82*–278, *81*–284, *80*–288; labor, *82*–374; transportation, *82*–494, *81*–508
TRUDEAU, PIERRE ELLIOTT, *82*–497, *81*–510, *80*–510; Canada, *82*–225, *81*–225, *80*–231; *il., 82*–224
True Confessions: motion pictures, *82*–396
Truffaut, François: motion pictures, *82*–394
Tuberculosis: public health, *80*–455
TUCHMAN, BARBARA, *80*–510
Tucson: city, *82*–246, *81*–248, *80*–252
Tugwell, Rexford Guy, *80*–284
Tulsa: city, *82*–246, *81*–248, *80*–252
Tuna, *80*–325
TUNISIA, *82*–497, *81*–511, *80*–510; Africa, *82*–177, *81*–179, *80*–181
Tunnel: building and construction, *82*–220
Turkana, Lake: paleontology, *82*–419
TURKEY, *82*–497, *81*–512, *80*–511; Eastern Orthodox Church, *80*–293; Europe, *82*–303, *81*–309, *80*–317; Greece, *81*–333; international trade, *81*–352; Middle East, *82*–389, *81*–398, *80*–402
Turkomans: Iran, *80*–362
Turner, Ted: advertising, *81*–172; boating, *81*–215, *80*–217
TUVALU: *WBE, 80*–580; Pacific Islands, *82*–417, *80*–429
Twins: *il., 80*–454
Tynan, Kenneth P.: deaths, *81*–279

U

UGANDA, *82*–498, *81*–512, *80*–512; Africa, *82*–177, *81*–179, *80*–181; Libya, *80*–384; Tanzania, *80*–495
Ullmann, Liv: *il., 82*–502
Ulster. See **NORTHERN IRELAND.**
Unconscious: psychology, *81*–457

Unemployment: automobile, *82*–197; building, *81*–221; China, *81*–246, *80*–249; city, *81*–247; Detroit, *82*–277; economics, *82*–284, *81*–289, *80*–294; housing, *82*–337; labor, *82*–359, *81*–367, *80*–372; manufacturing, *82*–381, *80*–395. See also **Employment; WELFARE.**
Unification Church: cults, *Special Report, 80*–147
Union of Soviet Socialist Republics. See **RUSSIA.**
Unions: automobile, *82*–197; economics, *82*–285; labor, *82*–359; Poland, *82*–433; Williams, Roy, *82*–516
UNITA: Angola, *82*–181
United Arab Emirates: Middle East, *82*–389, *81*–398, *80*–402
United Automobile Workers: automobile, *82*–197; labor, *82*–337
United Church of Christ: religion, *82*–452, *81*–465, *80*–461
United Food and Commercial Workers: labor, *80*–376
United Methodist Church, The: Protestantism, *81*–456; religion, *82*–452, *81*–465, *80*–461
UNITED NATIONS, *82*–498, *81*–513, *80*–512; Burma, *80*–228; Middle East, *81*–399; Namibia, *82*–403, *81*–411; Nobel Prizes, *82*–410; ocean, *81*–423, *80*–428
United Pentecostal Church, International, *82*–452, *81*–465, *80*–461
United Presbyterian Church in the U.S.A., The: Protestantism, *82*–443; religion, *82*–452, *81*–465, *80*–461
UNITED STATES, GOVERNMENT OF THE, *82*–504, *81*–516, *80*–515; Africa, *80*–182; armed forces, *81*–188, *80*–191; banks, *81*–206, *80*–211; Canada, *82*–227, *81*–229, *80*–234; Chile, *80*–246; China, *80*–250; coal, *80*–256; conservation, *80*–267; consumerism, *80*–262; Cuba, *81*–270, *80*–274; drugs, *80*–292; economics, *82*–287, *80*–294; energy, *82*–296, *80*–308; forest, *80*–332; handicapped, *82*–330, *80*–345; immigration, *82*–341, *81*–345, *80*–356; Indian, American, *80*–357; Iran, *81*–353, *80*–361; Korea, South, *80*–371; Latin America, *80*–378; Libya, *80*–384; Mexico, *80*–399; mining, *80*–404; Pacific Islands, *82*–416, *80*–429; Pakistan, *80*–430; Panama, *80*–433; petroleum, *80*–437; Russia, *80*–469; science, *80*–473; Social Security, *80*–478; Taiwan, *80*–494; United Nations, *82*–499, *80*–512; water, *82*–511. See also names of individual government officials and entries on various government agencies.
United States Constitution. See **CONSTITUTION OF THE UNITED STATES.**
United States of America. See entries on specific states, cities, and subjects.
United States Yacht Racing Union: boating, *82*–214
United Steelworkers of America v. Weber: civil rights, *80*–255; Supreme Court, *80*–491
Universities and colleges, *82*–505; education, *82*–289, *Close-Up, 81*–295; handicapped, *80*–345; television, *82*–485
Unser, Bobby: auto racing, *82*–198
Updike, John: literature, *82*–370; personalities, *82*–425
Upper Volta: Africa, *82*–177, *81*–179, *80*–181
Uranium: Australia, *80*–200; mining, *81*–400
Urban Development Action Grant, *80*–250
Urban Education Action Plan: PTA, *81*–411
Urban transportation. See **Roads and highways; TRANSIT; TRANSPORTATION.**
Urey, Harold C.: deaths, *82*–273
URUGUAY, *82*–506, *81*–520, *80*–518; Latin America, *82*–366, *81*–375, *80*–380
Utah, *82*–473, *81*–488, *80*–487
Utilities. See **COMMUNICATIONS;·ENERGY; PETROLEUM AND GAS.**

V

Vaccine: biochemistry, *82*–212; farm, *82*–308; health and disease, *82*–332, *80*–347; public health, *80*–456
Valenzuela, Fernando: baseball, *82*–208
Valium: dentistry, *80*–287; drugs, *81*–287, *80*–292; health and disease, *82*–331; mental health, *80*–399
Van, Bobby: deaths, *81*–279
Van Agt, Andreas A. M.: Netherlands, *82*–403, *81*–412, *80*–417
Vance, Cyrus Roberts: Cabinet, *81*–224; *il., 80*–266
Vance, Vivian, *80*–284
Van DerZee, James, *80*–437
Vang Pao: Laos, *82*–363
Vanity Fair: magazine, *82*–378
Van Slyke, Helen, *80*–284

VANUATU: *WBE,* 82–567; Pacific Islands, 82–417, 81–431
Varicella zoster immune globulin: public health, 82–444
Vasectomy: health and disease, 82–331
VEIL, SIMONE, 80–519
Velasco Ibarra, José M., 80–284
VENDA, 80–519; Africa, 82–177, 81–179, 80–181
Venereal disease: health and disease, 80–347; public health, 82–444, 81–458
VENEZUELA, 82–506, 81–520, 80–520; Latin America, 82–366, 81–375, 80–380
Vent, deep-sea: ocean, 82–415
Venus: astronomy, 81–195, 80–200
Vera-Ellen: deaths, 82–274
Verapamil: drugs, 82–282
Verdy, Violette: dancing, 81–271
Vermont, 82–473, 81–488, 80–487
Very-large-scale integrated circuit: electronics, 82–294, 81–300
Veterans: community organizations, 82–253, 81–256, 80–259
Veterinary medicine: *Special Report,* 80–99
Vice-President of the United States. See names of Vice-Presidents.
Video games, 81–324
Video microscopy: biology, 82–213
Videodisc: *il.,* 82–483
Videotape recorder: advertising, 80–176; photography, 82–430, 81–442
Vieques: Puerto Rico, 80–457
VIETNAM, 82–507, 81–521, 80–520; Asia, 82–192, 81–192, 80–196, *Close-Up,* 80–198; Cambodia, 82–223, 81–224, 80–230; China, 80–249; Laos, 82–363, 80–377; President, 80–449; Russia, 80–469; Thailand, 80–500; United Nations, 80–514
Viewdata: communications, 80–258
Viking project: astronomy, 81–195, 80–200
Vikings: Newfoundland, 81–414
Viljoen, Marais: South Africa, 80–478
Village People: *il.,* 80–414
Villot, Jean Cardinal, 80–284
Vins, Georgi P.: Protestantism, 80–454; Russia, 80–470
VIOLA, ROBERTO EDWARDO, 82–508; Argentina, 82–186
Violence: crime, 82–265, 81–269, 80–273; El Salvador, 82–295, 81–301; India, 82–343, 81–346; Iran, 82–349; Middle East, 82–386; President, 82–436; religion, 81–465; Roman Catholic Church, 82–454; Sri Lanka, 82–470; Uganda, 82–498. See also **Protests; Terrorism.**
Virginia: elections, 82–292; conservation, 80–267; prison, 80–452; state government, 82–473, 81–488, 80–487
VISUAL ARTS, 82–508, 81–522, 80–521
Vital statistics. See **CENSUS; POPULATION.**
Vlasova, Ludmila, 80–276
Vocalization: pet language, *Special Report,* 81–131
Voice synthesis: electronics, 81–300
VOIGHT, JON, 80–523
Voinovich, George V., 80–304
Volcano: geology, 81–326, *Close-Up,* 81–327; Indonesia, 80–359; weather, 82–513, 81–527
VOLCKER, PAUL ADOLPH, 80–523
Volleyball, 82–470, 81–485, 80–483
Von Zell, Harry: deaths, 82–274
Vorster, Balthazar Johannes: South Africa, 80–478
Voting. See **ELECTIONS.**
Voting Rights Act of 1965: civil rights, 82–249; Houston, 80–353; New York City, 82–404
Voyager: astronomy, 82–193, 81–194, 80–199; Jupiter, *Special Report,* 80–87; space exploration, 82–466, 81–483, 80–479

W

Wade-Giles system: China, *Close-Up,* 80–248
Wages: basketball, 80–216; building, 81–221; France, 80–333; Germany, West, 80–337; labor, 82–360; Netherlands, 80–417; New York City, 82–405; postal service, 82–436; sports, 81–485; Tunisia, 80–510. See also **ECONOMICS; LABOR; Unemployment;** and various city articles.
Wailing Wall: *il.,* 82–351
Wajda, Andrzej: motion pictures, 82–395
Waldheim, Kurt, 82–498, 81–513
Wales: Great Britain, 80–340
Walesa, Lech: Poland, 82–433
Wallace, DeWitt: *il.,* 82–273
Wallenberg, Raoul: personalities, 82–425
Ward, Barbara: deaths, 82–274
Ward, Haskell G., 80–418
Warsaw Pact: Europe, *Close-Up,* 81–308; Russia, 81–472

Warwick, Dionne, 80–414
Washakie region: conservation, 82–260
Washington (state), 82–473, 81–488, 80–487; Indian, American, 80–358
WASHINGTON, D.C., 82–510, 81–524, 80–524; city, 82–246, 81–248, 80–252
Washington Star: *il.,* 82–407
Waste disposal: chemical industry, 81–239; consumerism, 82–262; environment, 81–305, 80–314, *Close-Up,* 80–304; manufacturing, 80–395; state government, 80–485
WATER, 82–511, 81–525, 80–524; chemistry, 80–242; *Special Report,* 82–93
Water pollution: Philadelphia, 80–440; water, *Special Report,* 82–101
Water polo, 82–470, 81–485, 80–483
Water skiing, 82–470, 81–485, 80–483
Watergate: Nixon, Richard M., 81–418
Watermelon: *il.,* 80–222
Watson, Tom, 82–323, 81–330, 80–339
WATT, JAMES GAIUS, 82–512; conservation, 82–259; environment, 82–299; mining, 82–391
Wayne, John: *Close-Up,* 80–283; coins, 81–254
Wayne County: Detroit, 80–287
Weapons. See **ARMED FORCES.**
WEATHER, 82–512, 81–526, 80–525; ocean, *Special Report,* 80–130; water, *Special Report,* 82–95
Weaver, Mike: boxing, 82–217, 81–218
Weaver's Gift, The: literature for children, 82–375
Webb, Wayne: bowling, 82–216, 81–217
Weber, Brian: *il.,* 80–254; Supreme Court, 80–491
Wei Ching-chang (Wei Jingsheng), 80–247
Weight lifting, 82–470, 81–485, 80–483
Weinberg, Steven, 80–424
Weinberg-Salam theory: physics, 82–431
WEINBERGER, CASPAR W., 82–513
WELFARE, 82–514, 81–528, 80–527; food, 80–327; Social Security, 82–465; state government, 81–490. See also **CHILD WELFARE.**
Wembley conference: Great Britain, 82–325
Wenzel, Andreas: skiing, 81–479
Wenzel, Hanni: *il.,* 81–479
West, Mae: deaths, 81–279
West Bank: Israel, 81–358, 80–364; Middle East, 80–402
WEST INDIES, 82–515, 81–529, 80–528
West Virginia, 82–473, 81–488, 80–487
Western Five: United Nations, 82–500
Western Sahara: Africa, 82–178, 81–181, 80–182; Middle East, 80–403; Morocco, 82–393, 80–405
Western Samoa: Pacific Islands, 82–417
Westhead, Paul: basketball, 81–210
Westminster Kennel Club: dog, 82–281, 81–287, 80–291
Westway: New York City, 82–405
Weyland, Otto P., 80–284
Whale: conservation, 82–261, 81–264, 80–267
White, Ellen Gould: Protestantism, 82–441
White fly: gardening, 80–335
White House tapes: Nixon, Richard M., 80–423
White-collar crime, 80–273
Whitmire, Kathy: *il.,* 82–339
Whitworth, Kathy: golf, 82–323
Who, The: music, popular, 80–415
Whose Life Is It Anyway?: *il.,* 80–501; motion pictures, 80–396
Wiesel, Torsten N.: Nobel Prizes, 82–410
Wilderness areas: conservation, 82–260; forest and forest products, 82–317, 80–332; mining, 82–391; petroleum, 82–427
Wilding, Michael, 80–284
Wildlife: hunting, 82–340, 81–344, 80–355; panda, *Special Report,* 82–75; zoo medicine, *Special Report,* 80–99
Wilhelmina: deaths, 81–279
Wilkins, Roy: *il.,* 82–269
Williams, Harrison: *il.,* 82–258
Williams, John, 80–410
WILLIAMS, ROY LEE, 82–516; *il.,* 82–360
Williams, Wayne B.: crime, 82–265
Williwaw: boating, 82–214
WILLOCH, KAARE, 82–516; Norway, 82–412
Wilson, Robert: Manitoba, 82–379
Wilmington 10: courts, 81–268
Windfall-profits tax: Congress, 80–265; energy, 81–302; petroleum, 81–440, 80–439; President, 80–450; taxation, 81–497; welfare, 81–529
Winter, William F., 80–304
Wisconsin, 82–473, 81–488, 80–487
Wisconsin Evangelical Lutheran Synod, 82–452, 81–465, 80–461
Wisdom teeth: dentistry, 81–282
Wittig, George, 80–424
Woese, Carl R., 80–220
Wolong Reserve: panda, *Special Report,* 82–85
Wolpoff, Milford H.: anthropology, 81–184

Women: basketball, 82–210, 81–211, 80–217; civil rights, 82–249, 81–252, 80–255; golf, 81–330; Latin America, 82–365; Protestantism, 80–452; Roman Catholic, 82–457, 80–466; sports, 81–484; Supreme Court, *Close-Up,* 82–478; Switzerland, 82–480; tennis, 81–501; theater, 82–489
Wood, Natalie: deaths, 82–274
Woodcock, George, 80–284
Woodhead, Cynthia (Sippy), 80–492
Woodruff, Robert W.: *il.,* 80–302
World Bank: energy, 81–303; United Nations, 82–502
World Book Dictionary: supplement, 82–581, 81–581, 80–581
World Book Encyclopedia: supplement, 82–558, 81–536, 80–536
World Council of Churches: Eastern Orthodox Churches, 82–283; Protestantism, 82–441, 80–454
World Court. See **International Court of Justice.**
World Food Day: nutrition, 82–414
World Health Organization: medicine, 82–382
World Hockey Association: hockey, 80–349
World Series, 82–208, 81–207, 80–213
World War II: armed forces, *Close-Up,* 82–188; Jews and Judaism, 82–355; Newfoundland, 82–407
Wrestling, 82–470, 81–485, 80–483
Wright, James A.: deaths, 81–279
Wright, John J. Cardinal, 80–284
Wyler, William: deaths, 82–274
Wyoming, 82–473, 81–488, 80–487
Wyszynski, Stefan Cardinal: deaths, 82–274

X

Xhosa: Ciskei, 82–243
X rays: *il.,* 82–380; public health, 81–459
Xenon: physics, 80–442

Y

Yachting: boating, 82–214, 81–215, 80–221
Yakunin, Gleb, 81–288, 80–293
Yarborough, Cale, 82–200, 80–204
Yeh Chien-ying (Ye Jianying), 80–247
Yemen (Aden): Middle East, 82–389, 81–398, 80–402; Saudi Arabia, 80–473
Yemen (Sana): Middle East, 82–389, 81–398, 80–402
"Yorkshire Ripper": Great Britain, 82–328
Young, Andrew Jackson, Jr.: civil rights, 80–255; *il.,* 82–293; Jews, 80–368; United Nations, 80–512
Young, Coleman A.: Detroit, 82–277; *il.,* 80–288
Young, John W.: space shuttle, *Special Report,* 82–109
Young Men's Christian Association, 82–253, 81–256, 80–259
Young Women's Christian Association, 82–253, 81–256, 80–259
Youngman, Henny: personalities, 81–437
YOUTH ORGANIZATIONS, 82–516, 81–530, 80–529
YUGOSLAVIA, 82–517, 81–531, 80–530; Albania, 82–179, 81–181; Bulgaria, 82–220, 80–228; deaths, *Close-Up,* 81–278; Europe, 82–303, 81–310, 80–317
YUKON TERRITORY, 82–518, 81–532, 80–531

Z

ZAIRE, 81–532, 80–531; Africa, 82–177, 81–179, 80–181
Zaitsev, Alexander: ice skating, 81–345
Zambia: Africa, 82–177, 81–179, 80–181
Zayak, Elaine: *il.,* 82–341
ZHAO ZIYANG, 81–533; China, 81–245
Zhivkov, Todor: Bulgaria, 82–220, 81–223, 80–228
Zia-ul-Haq: Pakistan, 82–417, 81–432, 80–430
ZIMBABWE, 82–518, 81–533, 80–531; Africa, 82–177, 81–179, 80–181, *Close-Up,* 80–183; Congress, 80–264; President, 80–449; Protestantism, 80–454
Zinc-nickel oxide battery: manufacturing, 80–395
ZIP Code: postal service, 82–436, 81–449
Zomepirac sodium: drugs, 82–282
ZOOLOGY, 82–519, 81–534, 80–532; science, 81–477
Zoom lens: photography, 82–431, 81–443
ZOOS AND AQUARIUMS, 82–519, 81–534, 80–532; medicine, *Special Report,* 80–99
Zuckerman, Yitzhak: deaths, 82–274
Zytel: manufacturing, 80–395

Acknowledgments

The publishers acknowledge the following sources for illustrations. Credits read from top to bottom, left to right, on their respective pages. An asterisk (*) denotes illustrations and photographs that are the exclusive property of THE YEAR BOOK. All maps, charts, and diagrams were prepared by THE YEAR BOOK staff unless otherwise noted.

3	Dan Miller*
9	© Elkoussy, Sygma
10	© Dirck Halstead, Liaison; Lehtikuva, Photoreporters
11	© Alain Dejean, Sygma; © Peter Schaak, *Time* Magazine; Tass from Sovfoto
12	© Jim Pozarik, Liaison; © George Tiedemann, *Time* Magazine
13	NASA; © J. P. Laffont, Sygma; © G. Rancinan, Sygma
14	© Sygma; © 1981 B. Pierce, Contact; © L. Claude Francolon, Gamma/Liaison
15	Bill Smith, *Time* Magazine; Shlomo Arad
16	© Douglas Kirkland, Contact
17	© Yvonne Hemsey, Liaison; © M. Philippot, Sygma; © Tom Zimberoff, Sygma; NASA
18	© Dirck Halstead, Liaison; Michael Evans, The White House; © D. Goldberg, Sygma
19	© Elkoussy, Sygma
20	© Dennis Whitehead, Picture Group; © Giansanti, Sygma; © Sica, Liaison
21	© Sipa Press from Black Star
23-25	Dennis Brack*
27	© Brad Bower, Picture Group
28	© Bryce Flynn, Picture Group; © Martha Tabor, Picture Group
30	© James R. Holland, Black Star
31-32	Dennis Brack*
34	© Bryce Flynn, Picture Group
35	© Owen Franken, Sygma
36	Dennis Brack*
37	© Sepp Seitz, Woodfin Camp, Inc.
38	© J. P. Laffont, Sygma
39	Dennis Brack*
40	© Dennis Brack, Black Star; Dennis Brack*
42	© Peter Morgan, Picture Group
44	© Alain Nogues, Sygma
45	© Benami Neumann and Francois Lochon, Gamma/Liaison
46	Dennis Brack*
48	© M. Philippot, Sygma; © Sipahioglu, Sipa Press from Black Star
50	Dennis Brack*
53	© Nancy Nash
54	Bill Fitz-Patrick, The White House
55-56	Dennis Brack*
57	Michael Evans, The White House; © Michael Evans, Sygma
58	© Dennis Brack, Black Star
59	© Diego Goldberg, Sygma
60	Dennis Brack*
63	© Owen Franken, Sygma; © Bryce Flynn, Picture Group
64-65	© Dennis Brack, Black Star
67	© Dirck Halstead, Liaison; © T. Zimberoff, Sygma; Dennis Brack*
68	© Steve Northup, Black Star
70	© Michael Evans, Sygma
72	Dennis Brack*
74	New China Pictures Company
77	© Nancy Nash
78	Chen Jie, New China Pictures Company
80	© George Schaller, World Wildlife Fund; Chen Jie, New China Pictures Company
81	New China Pictures Company
82	© Nancy Nash; © Timm Rautert, World Wildlife Fund (Bruce Coleman Ltd.); © Timm Rautert, World Wildlife Fund (Bruce Coleman Ltd.)
83	© Timm Rautert, World Wildlife Fund (Bruce Coleman Ltd.); © Kojo Tanaka, World Wildlife Fund (Bruce Coleman Ltd.); © Timm Rautert, World Wildlife Fund (Bruce Coleman Ltd.); © Timm Rautert, World Wildlife Fund (Bruce Coleman Ltd.)
86	© George Schaller, World Wildlife Fund
87	New China Pictures Company
88	© Peter Jackson, Bruce Coleman Ltd.
89	© George Schaller, World Wildlife Fund; Meng Qingbiao, New China Pictures Company
90	© Nancy Nash; New China Pictures Company
92-96	Bill Miller*
98	© Harold Sund, Image Bank; © James Sugar, Woodfin Camp, Inc.; © Jim Tuten, Black Star
99	© Wayne Rowe, After Image
101	© Bryce Flynn, Picture Group
102-103	Bill Miller*
104	USDA; © Ted Spiegel, Black Star
105	Sealed Air Corporation; © Ted Spiegel, Black Star
106	© Chuck O'Rear, West Light; © Shlomo Arad
108	© Jim Tuten, Black Star
109-111	NASA
112-113	NASA; Steve Liska*
114-118	NASA
119	© Perkin-Elmer; NASA; NASA
120	NASA
122-129	Lee Balterman*
130	© Gerald Brimacombe, Image Bank
131	Lee Balterman*
132	© Bohdan Hrynewych, Stock, Boston
133-135	Lee Balterman*
136	Lee Balterman*; © John Blaustein, Woodfin Camp, Inc.; Lee Balterman*
138-139	Cincinnati Milacron; Steve Hale*
140	SCALA from EPA
142	Culver
143	Musée d'Art et d'Histoire, Neuchâtel; Robert H. Glaze, Artstreet; Bettmann Archive
144	From *Magnus Robot Fighter 4000 A. D.* © 1967 Western Publishing Company, Inc. Reprinted by permission; Culver
147	© J. P. Laffont, Sygma; © Dan McCoy, Black Star
148-149	© 1981 Georg Fischer, Visum (Woodfin Camp, Inc.)
150	SCALA from EPA; Fred Ward, *Discover* Magazine © 1981 Time Inc.
151	Bell Laboratories; © 1981 Georg Fischer, Visum (Woodfin Camp, Inc.); Georg Fischer, Visum (Woodfin Camp, Inc.); General Motors Research Laboratories
155-168	The Newberry Library, Chicago
171	United Press Int.
172	United Press Int.
173	Keystone
175-179	Wide World
181	© Stephen Hone, *Time* Magazine
182	Wide World
183	Eric M. Meyers, Duke University
185	© Steve Rosenthal
186	Liaison
187	U.S. Air Force
188	By permission of Bill Mauldin and Wil-Jo Associates, Inc.
190	Wide World
194	Jet Propulsion Laboratory
197	Korody, Sygma
198	Wide World
200	United Press Int.
204	Wide World
205	Steve Hansen, *Time* Magazine
210	United Press Int.
214-224	Wide World
227-231	United Press Int.
236	Goodyear Tire & Rubber Company
239	© Kevin Horan, Picture Group
241	New China Pictures Company
242	Xinhua News Agency from United Press Int.
244	© Herman Kokojan, Black Star
249	*Mobile Press Register*
250	United Press Int.
252	British Telecom
258	© 1981 Andy Levin, Black Star
260	United Press Int.
263-265	Wide World
266	Les Grands Ballets Canadiens (Andrew Oxenham)
268	Alexander Konkov, Tass from Sovfoto

604

A Preview of 1982

January

					1	2
3	4	5	6	7	8	9
10	11	12	13	14	15	16
17	18	19	20	21	22	23
24	25	26	27	28	29	30
31						

1 **New Year's Day.**
St. Basil's Day, Eastern Orthodox feast day.

6 **Epiphany,** 12th day of Christmas, celebrates the visit of the Three Wise Men to the infant Jesus.

15 **Martin Luther King, Jr.'s Birthday,** honoring the slain civil rights leader, celebrated on this day in 10 states and on various days in five other states.

24 **Super Bowl XVI,** the National Football League's championship game, in Pontiac, Mich.

25 **Chinese New Year** begins year 4680, the Year of the Dog, according to the ancient Chinese calendar.

26 **Australia Day** commemorates Captain Arthur Phillip's landing in 1788 where Sydney now stands.

February

	1	2	3	4	5	6
7	8	9	10	11	12	13
14	15	16	17	18	19	20
21	22	23	24	25	26	27
28						

2 **Ground-Hog Day.** Legend says six weeks of winter weather will follow if the ground hog sees its shadow.
Candlemas Day, Roman Catholic and Eastern Orthodox feast day, honors the purification of the Virgin Mary and the presentation of the infant Jesus in the Temple.

8 **Boy Scouts of America Birthday Anniversary** marks the founding of the organization in 1910.

12 **Abraham Lincoln's Birthday,** observed in most states.

14 **Valentine's Day,** festival of romance and affection.

15 **George Washington's Birthday,** according to law, is celebrated on the third Monday in February. The actual anniversary is February 22.
Susan B. Anthony Day commemorates the birth of the suffragist leader.

23 **Mardi Gras,** celebrated in New Orleans and many Roman Catholic countries, is the last merrymaking before Lent.

24 **Ash Wednesday,** first day of Lent for Christians, begins the period of repentance that precedes Easter.

March

	1	2	3	4	5	6
7	8	9	10	11	12	13
14	15	16	17	18	19	20
21	22	23	24	25	26	27
28	29	30	31			

1 **Easter Seal Campaign** through April 11.
Red Cross Month through March 31.

7 **Girl Scout Week,** through March 13, marks the group's 70th birthday.

9 **Purim,** Jewish festival commemorating how Esther saved the Jews from the Persian tyrant Haman.

14 **Camp Fire Birthday Week,** through March 20, marks the 72nd anniversary of the organization.

17 **St. Patrick's Day,** honoring the patron saint of Ireland.

19 **Swallows Return to San Juan Capistrano,** California, from their winter homes.
St. Joseph's Day, Roman Catholic feast day honoring the husband of the Virgin Mary.

20 **First Day of Spring,** 5:56 P.M. E.S.T.

29 **Academy Awards Night,** when the Academy of Motion Picture Arts and Sciences presents the Oscars.

April

				1	2	3
4	5	6	7	8	9	10
11	12	13	14	15	16	17
18	19	20	21	22	23	24
25	26	27	28	29	30	

1 **April Fool's Day,** a traditional day for jokes and tricks.

4 **Palm Sunday** marks Jesus Christ's last entry into Jerusalem, where people covered His path with palm branches.

8 **Passover,** Jewish festival that celebrates the exodus of the Jews from bondage in Egypt.
Maundy Thursday, Christian celebration of Christ's commandment to love others.

9 **Good Friday** marks the death of Jesus on the cross. It is a public holiday in many countries and several states of the United States.

11 **Easter Sunday,** commemorating the Resurrection of Jesus Christ.

15 **Income Tax Day** in the United States.

18 **National Library Week** through April 24.

25 **Daylight-Saving Time** begins at 2 A.M.

30 **Walpurgis Night,** when witches gather in East Germany's Harz Mountains, according to legend.

May

						1
2	3	4	5	6	7	8
9	10	11	12	13	14	15
16	17	18	19	20	21	22
23	24	25	26	27	28	29
30	31					

1 **May Day,** observed as a festival of spring in many countries and as a holiday honoring workers in socialist and Communist countries.
Kentucky Derby, thoroughbred horse race at Churchill Downs in Louisville, Ky.
Law Day U.S.A.

3 **National Music Week** through May 9.

9 **Mother's Day.**

15 **Armed Forces Day** honors men and women in the United States armed forces.

20 **Ascension Day,** or Holy Thursday, 40 days after Easter, celebrates the ascent of Jesus Christ into heaven.

24 **Victoria Day,** in Canada, marks the official birthday of the reigning monarch.

30 **Pentecost,** or Whitsunday, the seventh Sunday after Easter, commemorates the descent of the Holy Spirit upon the 12 disciples.

31 **Memorial Day,** by law, is the last Monday in May.

June

		1	2	3	4	5
6	7	8	9	10	11	12
13	14	15	16	17	18	19
20	21	22	23	24	25	26
27	28	29	30			

6 **D-Day** commemorates the Allied landing in Normandy in 1944, during World War II.
Stratford Festival, drama and music, through October 23 in Stratford, Canada.

14 **Flag Day.**

20 **Father's Day.**

21 **First Day of Summer,** 12:23 P.M. E.S.T.

23 **First Day of Ramadan,** the Islamic holy month, observed by fasting.
Midsummer Day, summer celebration in many European countries.

28 **Shabuot,** Jewish Feast of Weeks, marks the revealing of the Ten Commandments to Moses on Mount Sinai.

July

		1	2	3		
4	5	6	7	8	9	10
11	12	13	14	15	16	17
18	19	20	21	22	23	24
25	26	27	28	29	30	31

1 **Dominion Day,** in Canada, celebrates the confederation of the provinces in 1867.

4 **Independence Day,** in the United States, the anniversary of the day on which the Continental Congress adopted the Declaration of Independence in 1776.

13 **Baseball All-Star Game,** Montreal, Canada.

14 **Bastille Day,** in France, commemorates the uprising of the people of Paris against King Louis XVI in 1789 and their seizure of the Bastille, the hated Paris prison.

15 **St. Swithin's Day.** According to legend, if it rains on this day, it will rain for 40 more.

20 **Partial Eclipse of the Sun** in northwestern North America.

25 **Puerto Rico Constitution Day.**

28 **Terry Fox Day,** in Canada, commemorates the birthday of the young man who ran across Canada to raise funds for cancer research after losing a leg to the disease.

29 **Tishah B'Ab,** Jewish holy day, marks the destruction of the first and second temples in Jerusalem in 587 B.C. and A.D. 70.

August

1	2	3	4	5	6	7
8	9	10	11	12	13	14
15	16	17	18	19	20	21
22	23	24	25	26	27	28
29	30	31				

6 **Hiroshima Day,** memorial observance for victims of the first atomic bombing in Hiroshima, Japan, in 1945.

12 **Perseid Meteor Shower.**

15 **Feast of the Assumption,** Roman Catholic and Eastern Orthodox holy day, celebrates the ascent of the Virgin Mary into heaven.

18 **Canadian National Exhibition** through September 6 in Toronto, Ont.

19 **National Aviation Day** commemorates the birthday of pioneer pilot Orville Wright in 1871.

22 **Edinburgh International Festival,** music, drama, and film, through September 11 in Edinburgh, Scotland.

26 **Women's Equality Day** commemorates the enactment of the 19th Amendment in 1920 giving women the vote.

September

		1	2	3	4
5	6	7	8	9	10	11
12	13	14	15	16	17	18
19	20	21	22	23	24	25
26	27	28	29	30		

6 **Labor Day** in the United States and Canada.

17 **Citizenship Day** celebrates the rights and duties of U.S. citizens.

18 **Rosh Hashanah,** or Jewish New Year, beginning the year 5743, according to the Jewish calendar.
Oktoberfest, fall celebration in Munich, West Germany, through October 3.

23 **First Day of Fall,** 3:46 A.M. E.S.T.

24 **Native American Day** honors American Indians.

27 **Yom Kippur,** or Day of Atonement, the most solemn day in the Jewish calendar.

30 **Commonwealth Games** in Brisbane, Australia, through October 9.

October

					1	2
3	4	5	6	7	8	9
10	11	12	13	14	15	16
17	18	19	20	21	22	23
24	25	26	27	28	29	30
31						

2 **Sukkot,** or Feast of Tabernacles, Jewish festival that originally marked the harvest season.

3 **Fire Prevention Week** through October 9.
National 4-H Week through October 9.

4 **Child Health Day.**

10 **National Handicapped Awareness Week** through October 16.

11 **Columbus Day** commemorates Christopher Columbus' landing in America in 1492. Celebrated in Latin American countries on October 12, the actual anniversary.
Thanksgiving Day in Canada.

12 **Baseball's World Series** begins.

16 **World Food Day,** sponsored by the United Nations (UN) Food and Agriculture Organization to heighten awareness of the world food problem.

24 **United Nations Day** commemorates the founding of the UN in 1945.
National Cleaner Air Week through October 30.

31 **Halloween.**
Standard Time Resumes at 2 A.M.
UN Children's Fund (UNICEF) Day.
Reformation Day, celebrated by Protestants, marks the day in 1517 when Reformation leader Martin Luther posted his Ninety-Five Theses.

November

	1	2	3	4	5	6
7	8	9	10	11	12	13
14	15	16	17	18	19	20
21	22	23	24	25	26	27
28	29	30				

1 **All Saints' Day,** observed by the Roman Catholic Church.

2 **Election Day** in the United States.

5 **Guy Fawkes Day,** in Great Britain, marks the failure of a plot to blow up King James I and Parliament in 1605.

11 **Veterans Day.**

14 **American Education Week** through November 20.

15 **Children's Book Week** through November 21.

25 **Thanksgiving Day** in the United States.

28 **Advent** begins, first of the four Sundays in the season before Christmas.

30 **St. Andrew's Day,** feast day of the patron saint of Scotland.

December

		1	2	3	4
5	6	7	8	9	10	11
12	13	14	15	16	17	18
19	20	21	22	23	24	25
26	27	28	29	30	31	

6 **St. Nicholas Day,** when children in many European countries receive gifts.

10 **Nobel Prize Ceremony** in Stockholm, Sweden.

11 **Hanukkah,** or Feast of Lights, eight-day Jewish festival that celebrates the defeat of the Syrian tyrant King Antiochus IV in 165 B.C.

13 **St. Lucia Day,** in Sweden, celebrates the return of light after the darkest time of the year.

15 **Bill of Rights Day** marks the ratification of that document in 1791.

16 **Beethoven's Birthday,** anniversary of the birth of German composer Ludwig van Beethoven in 1770.

21 **First Day of Winter,** 11:39 P.M. E.S.T.

24 **Christmas Eve.**

25 **Christmas Day.**

26 **Kwanzaa,** black American holiday based on a traditional African harvest festival, through January 1.

27 **Boxing Day** in Canada and Great Britain.

30 **Total Eclipse of the Moon** begins at 3:51 A.M. E.S.T.

31 **New Year's Eve.**

Cyclo-teacher® The easy-to-use learning system

Features hundreds of cycles from seven valuable learning areas

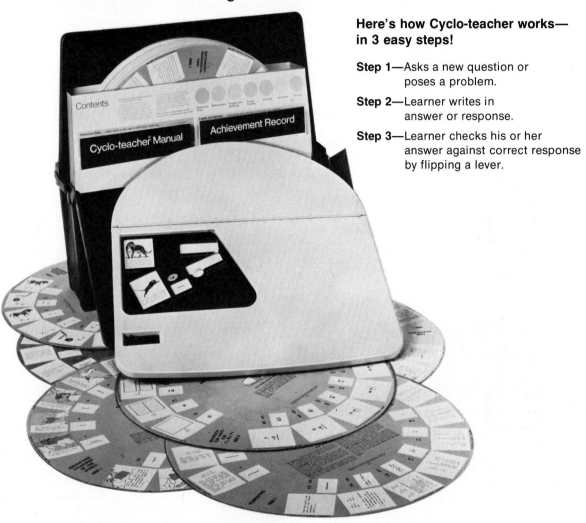

Here's how Cyclo-teacher works— in 3 easy steps!

Step 1—Asks a new question or poses a problem.

Step 2—Learner writes in answer or response.

Step 3—Learner checks his or her answer against correct response by flipping a lever.

Cyclo-teacher —the remarkable learning system based on the techniques of programmed instruction —comes right into your home to help stimulate and accelerate the learning of basic skills, concepts, and information. Housed in a specially designed file box are the Cyclo-teacher machine, Study Wheels, Answer Wheels, a Manual, a Contents and Instruction Card, and Achievement Record sheets.

Your child will find Cyclo-teacher to be a new and fascinating way to learn —much like playing a game. Only, Cyclo-teacher is much more than a game —it teaches new things

... reinforces learning ... and challenges a youngster to go beyond!

Features hundreds of study cycles to meet the individual needs of students —your entire family —just as *Year Book* is a valuable learning aid. And, best of all, lets you track your own progress —advance at your own pace! Cyclo-teacher is available by writing us at the address below:

The World Book Year Book
Post Office Box 3564
Chicago, IL 60654

These beautiful bookstands-

specially designed to hold your entire program, including your editions of *Year Book*.

Height: 26⅜"
with 4" legs.
Width: 28¾"
Depth: 8³/₁₆"

Height: 9"
Width: 28½"
Depth: 8³/₁₆"

Most parents like having a convenient place to house their *Year Book* editions and their *World Book Encyclopedia*. A beautiful floor-model bookstand —constructed of solid hardwood —is available in either walnut or fruitwood finish.

You might prefer the attractive hardwood table racks, also available in either walnut or fruitwood finish. Let us know by writing us at the following address:

The World Book Year Book
Post Office Box 3564
Chicago, IL 60654